THE *Virgin* ENCYCLOPEDIA OF

EIGHTIES MUSIC

Virgin

IN ASSOCIATION WITH MUZE INC.

Dedicated To John Bauldie

First published in Great Britain in 1997 by
VIRGIN BOOKS
an imprint of Virgin Publishing Ltd
332 Ladbroke Grove, London W10 5AH

A catalogue record for this book is available from the British Library

ISBN 0 7535 0159 7

MUSIC
VIDEO
muze BOOKS

Written, edited and produced by
MUZE UK Ltd
to whom all editorial enquiries should be sent
Iron Bridge House, 3 Bridge Approach, Chalk Farm, London NW1 8BD

Editor In Chief: Colin Larkin
Production Editor: Susan Pipe
Editorial and Research Assistant: Nic Oliver
Copy Editor: Sarah Lavelle
Typographic Design Consultant: Roger Kohn
Special thanks to Trev Huxley, Anthony Patterson and Paul Zullo of Muze Inc.,
and to Rob Shreeve of Virgin Publishing.
Typeset by Chicken Fowl Studio
Printed and bound in Great Britain by Butler & Tanner Ltd, Frome and London

INTRODUCTION

Although it was a much-maligned decade the music of the 80s did arrive at an important time in the expansion of popular music. Two major developments were the arrival of the CD and the launching of MTV. The former is without doubt the most important invention since the mass marketing of the LP in 1950. MTV is also vital because it shaped the music video, which is now a prerequisite of most major releases. People have become lazier - viewing is easier than listening - which is something I mourn. For many, the 80s was a dour decade that saw the rise (and fall) of Thatcherism and Reaganism. Much of the music expressed frustration, notably rap and the growth of Grandmaster Flash funk to full-bloodied, obscene anger with NWA. The early period focused on flamboyant New Romantics such as Duran Duran, Spandau Ballet and the static yet infectious Depeche Mode and Gary Numan. House and techno grew out of Chicago and Detroit, soul music became 'urban R&B' and Country suddenly had a prefix, 'new'. The punks of the late 70s went underground and the guitar-based indie /hardcore bands were still learning to tune up, ready to burst out in the 90s. Stadium rock became bigger and bands such as the Police, U2 and Aerosmith exploited this potential. It was a pot-pourri decade, and, as you will see, much better than your memory tells you.

ACKNOWLEDGEMENTS

We lost John Bauldie (*the* Dylanologist), who tragically died in a helicopter crash in 1996. Love and respect to him wherever he is. His contribution to our appreciation of Bob Dylan is immeasurable. To Johnny Rogan, who continues to be a rational ear and sounding board. He was the first person to hear of my proposal for the original Encyclopedia and agree to be involved. His great attention to detail shaped the original editorial stylesheet. John Burton continues to send his never-ending supply of newspaper obituaries.

Our in-house editorial team is even smaller than before, such is our super-efficiency. The Database is now a fully grown child and needs only regular food, attention and love. Thanks to Susan Pipe; reliable and trustworthy as ever. Nic Oliver 'the new boy' is shaping up pretty well, and Sarah Lavelle is our brand new quality controller. Our outside contributors are further reduced in number, as we now write and amend all our existing text. However, we could not function without the continuing

efforts and dedication of Big John Martland, Bruce Crowther and Alex Ogg. Brian Hogg, Hugh T. Wilson, Spencer Leigh and Robert Pruter continue to supply their specialist knowledge. We also received some entries from our newer contributors; Salsri Nyah, Tim Footman, Christen Thomsen, Essi Berilian and Jamie Renton, while Lloyd Peasley sent some important corrections free of charge.

Other past contributors' work may appear in this volume and I acknowledge once again; Simon Adams, David Ades, Mike Atherton, Gavin Badderley, Alan Balfour, Michael Barnett, Steve Barrow, John Bauldie, Lol Bell-Brown, Johnny Black, Chris Blackford, Pamela Boniface, Keith Briggs, Michael Ian Burgess, Paul M. Brown, Tony Burke, John Child, Linton Chiswick, Rick Christian, Alan Clayson, Tom Collier, Paul Cross, Bill Dahl, Norman Darwen, Roy Davenport, Peter Doggett, Kevin Eden, John Eley, Lars Fahlin, John Fordham, Per Gardin, Ian Garlinge, Mike Gavin, Andy Hamilton, Harry Hawk, Mark Hodkinson, Mike Hughes, Arthur Jackson, Mark Jones, Max Jones, Simon Jones, Ian Kenyon, Dave Laing, Steve Lake, Paul Lewis, Graham Lock, John Masouri, Bernd Matheja, Chris May, Dave McAleer, Ian McCann, David McDonald, York Membery, Toru Mitsui, Greg Moffitt, Nick Morgan, Michael Newman, Pete Nickols, Lyndon Noon, Zbigniew Nowara, James Nye, Ken Orton, Ian Peel, Dave Penny, Alan Plater, Barry Ralph, John Reed Emma Rees, Lionel Robinson, Johnny Rogan, Alan Rowett, Jean Scrivener, Roy Sheridan, Dave Sissons, Neil Slaven, Chris Smith, Steve Smith, Mitch Solomons, Christopher Spencer, Jon Staines, Mike Stephenson, Sam Sutherland, Jeff Tamarkin, Ray Templeton, Liz Thompson, Gerard Tierney, John Tobler, Adrian T'Vell, Pete Wadeson, Frank Warren, Ben Watson, Pete Watson, Simon Williams, Val Wilmer, Dave Wilson and Barry Witherden.

Record company press offices are often bombarded with my requests for biogs and review copies. Theirs is a thankless task, but thanks anyway, especially to Alan Robinson of Demon, Sue and Dave Williams at Frontier, Tones Sansom at Creation, Trisha Coogan at Essential, Mal Smith at Delta, Darren Crisp of Science Friction, Julia Honeywell at Ace, Murray Chalmers and Laura at Parlophone, Pat Naylor and Nicola Powell at Ryko/Hannibal, and Dave Bedford at This Way Up.

Press offices in general at: 4AD (Colleen), A&M, All Saints, Alligator, Almo, American Recordings (Louise), Arista, Beggars Banquet, BGO (Andy Gray), Big Cat (Sharon), Blue Note, Che Recordings, Chrysalis (Iona), City Slang (Wyndham Wallace), Coalition, Cooking Vinyl, Deceptive, Dedicated (Paula), Domino, Duophonic, East West, Echo, EMI, Epitaph, Fire, Fontana (Tina Mawjee), Geffen, Grapevine (Jane), Greentrax, Gut, Carol Hayes, Hightone, Hit Label, Hollywood, Dorothy Howe, HTD, Hut, Indigo, Indolent, Infectious, Island (Deborah), Jet, Jive, Junior Boys Own, Koch (Pat), London, MCA (Ted Cummings), Mercury, Mushroom, New Note, No. 9, Nude (Ellie), One Little Indian, Park, Pinnacle, Poole Edwards, Poppy, Qwest, RCA (Sharon), Savage And Best, Silvertone, Sire, Strange Fruit (Jo), Sub Pop, Superior Quality, Telarc, Tommy Boy, Transatlantic, Trauma, Virgin, Warp, all at Richard Wooton's office, and Zoo.

I wish the press offices at Columbia, Epic, Polydor and Warners would take us more seriously; phew, talk about blood out of a stone.

Thanks for the enthusiasm and co-operation of all our new colleagues at Virgin Publishing under the guidance of Rob Shreeve, in particular to Roz Scott who is always reassuringly efficient. To our new owners at Muze Inc., who oil the smooth running of the UK operation and are the business partners I always knew I wanted but never knew where to find them. In particular to the meticulous Tony Patterson, the stunningly dressed Paul Zullo, Steve Figard, Bill Mullar, Marc Miller and the immeasurably controlled Trev Huxley. And lastly to my tin lids; you don't need a weatherman to know which way the wind blows.

ENTRY STYLE

Albums, EPs (extended play 45s), newspapers, magazines, television programmes, films and stage musicals are referred to in italics. All song titles appear in single quotes. We spell rock 'n' roll like this. There are two main reasons for spelling rock 'n' roll with 'n' as opposed to 'n'. First, historical precedent: when the term was first coined in the 50s, the popular spelling was 'n'. Second, the 'n' is not simply an abbreviation of 'and' (in which case 'n' would apply) but as a phonetic representation of n as a sound. The ' ', therefore, serve as inverted commas rather than as apostrophes. The further reading section at the end of each entry has been expanded to give the reader a much wider choice of available books. These are not necessarily recommended titles but we have attempted to leave out any publication that has little or no merit.

We have also started to add videos at the end of the entries. Again, this is an area that is expanding faster than we can easily cope with, but there are many items in the videography and further items in the filmography, which is another new section we have decided to include. Release dates in keeping with albums attempt to show the release date in the country of origin. We have also tried to include both US and UK titles in the case of a title change.

ALBUM RATING

Due to many requests from our readers we have now decided to rate all albums. All new releases are reviewed either by myself or by our team of contributors. We also take into consideration the review ratings of the leading music journals and critics' opinions.

Our system is slightly different to most 5 Star ratings in that we rate according to the artist in question's work. Therefore, a 4 star album from the Beatles may have the overall edge over a 4 star album by Des O'Connor. Sorry Des.

Our ratings are carefully made, and consequently you will find we are very sparing with 5 Star and 1 Star albums.

★★★★★ Outstanding in every way. A classic and therefore strongly recommended. No comprehensive record collection should be without this album.

★★★★ Excellent. A high standard album from this artist and therefore highly recommended.

★★★ Good. By the artist's usual standards and therefore recommended.

★★ Disappointing. Flawed or lacking in some way.

★ Poor. An album to avoid unless you are a completist.

PLAGIARISM

In maintaining the largest text database of popular music in the world we are naturally protective of its content. We license to approved licensees only. It is both flattering and irritating to see our work reproduced without credit. Time and time again over the past few years I have read an obituary, when suddenly: hang on, I wrote that line. Secondly, it has come to our notice that other companies attempting to produce their own rock or pop encyclopedias use our material as a core. Flattering this might also be, but highly illegal. We have therefore dropped a few more textual 'depth charges' in addition to the original ones. Be warned.

Colin Larkin, July 1997

A Certain ratio

No UK act has crystalized independent, punk-influenced funk more than Manchester's A Certain Ratio. The original line-up comprised Jeremy Kerr (bass), Simon Topping (vocals/trumpet), Peter Terel (guitar), Martin Moscrop (guitar/trumpet); Martha Tilson (vocals, ex-Occult Chemistry) joined a little later, although she had left by 1982, and Donald Johnson (drums) who replaced a drum machine. They signed to Factory Records in 1979, for the cassette-only release, *The Graveyard And The Ballroom*. One side was recorded at Graveyard Studios, the other live, supporting Talking Heads at London's Electric Ballroom. After releasing 'All Night Party', in September 1979 there was a pause before 'Flight', a UK independent Top 10 chart hit over a year later. In the meantime, the band had teamed up with Factory's European sister, Benelux, for a cover of Banbarra's mid-70s funk classic, 'Shack Up', in July 1980. This edgy but rhythmic version offered an excellent snapshot of the band's innovative studio technique. *To Each ...*, the band's official debut album, attracted BBC disc jockey John Peel in 1981, a year that also yielded 'Do The Du' (officially intended for release in the USA) and in December 'Waterline' also fared well. 1982 kicked off with a move from the independent to the national charts as *Sextet* further established ACR. Like *To Each ...*, *Sextet* housed an intriguing, mostly instrumental collection hinged around funk rhythms. A 12-inch single for Benelux, 'Guess Who', surfaced in July, followed by the *Knife Slits Water* EP in October, coinciding with the release of *I'd Like To See You Again*. The band also issued an obscure 12-inch single on the Rock Steady label, 'Abracadabra', under the guise Sir Horatio, in September 1982. A year later, 'I Need Someone Tonight' was released, reaching the UK independent Top 10. Topping and Terel had departed, to be replaced by Andy Connell, and 'Brazilia' became the band's first project of 1985, preceding 'Wild Party' in July. Those in anticipation of a new ACR album had to wait until the end of 1986 for *Force*, although a compilation, *The Old And The New*, had provided some consolation earlier in the year.

'Mickey Way' promoted *Force* and continued ACR's run of independent hits. By 1987, the band had outgrown the confines of mere cult status and, looking to branch out, signed with A&M Records. To bridge the gap, the Dojo label issued *Live In America* in February, alongside 'Greetings Four', for the European label Materiali Sonari. It was not until the summer of 1989 that new ACR product arrived; and both 'The Big E' and 'Backs To The Wall' revealed a shift towards a more accessible sound. But neither these, nor 'Your Blue Eyes' in October, the *Four For The Floor* EP in February 1990 nor 'Won't Stop Loving You' in May could provide that elusive hit. As a result September 1989's *Good Together* made little impact and ACR left A&M soon afterwards. The group then switched to New Order manager Rob Gretton's Rob's Records, though Creation Records reissued their back catalogue and also unveiled a sampler album of remixes from their vast discography (including contributions from Electronic and 808 State). Their experimental work and love of collage material has ensured their status as one of the most uncompromisingly original acts working in the post-punk era.

● ALBUMS: *The Graveyard And The Ballroom* cassette only (Factory 1980)★★, *To Each ...* (Factory 1981), *Sextet* (Factory 1982)★★★, *I'd Like To See You Again* (Factory 1982)★★★, *Force* (Factory 1986)★★★, *Live In America* (Dojo 1987)★★, *Good Together* (A&M 1989)★★★, *MCR* (A&M 1990)★★★, *Up In Downsville* (Rob's 1992)★★★, *Looking For A Certain Ratio* (Creation 1994)★★★, *Change That Station* (Robs 1997)★★★.

● COMPILATIONS: *The Old And The New* (Factory 1986)★★★, *Sampler* (Creation 1994)★★★.

A Flock Of Seagulls

This new wave electro-pop group from Liverpool, England, had remarkable success in the USA before finding a large following in Britain. The band comprised Mike Score (b. 5 November 1957; keyboards/vocals), Ali Score (drum machine/vocals), Paul Reynolds (b. 4 August 1962; guitar) and Frank Maudsley (b. 10 November 1959; bass). Following an adventurous EP on Bill Nelson's Cocteau label the band made their album debut with *A Flock Of Seagulls*, a splendid example of futurist pop that contained a number of notable tracks including 'I Ran (So Far Away)', which made the US Top 10 in 1982. Ex-hairdresser Mike Score received numerous press jibes for his 'silly haircut'; he had cultivated his none-too-natural blond locks to hang irritatingly over his keyboards. Although *Listen* was another infectious collection of songs, they were unable to find any lasting popularity in their homeland, other than 'Wishing (I Had A Photograph Of You)' which made the UK Top 10. Paul Reynolds departed after the release of *The Story Of A Young Heart*. That album and *Dream Come True* (made as a trio) were way below par and the band subsequently disintegrated. Score organized a new version of the band in 1989, who toured the USA and issued a single 'Magic', of which commodity this band had little. They, too, broke up.

●ALBUMS: *A Flock Of Seagulls* (Jive 1982)★★★, *Listen* (Jive 1983)★★★, *The Story Of A Young Heart* (Jive 1984)★★, *Dream Come True* (Jive 1986)★★.
●COMPILATIONS: *Best Of* (RCA 1987)★★★.

A WITNESS

Formed in Manchester, England, A Witness shared the distinctive sound adopted by the Ron Johnson label acts; fast, quirky songs with an obvious debt to both Captain Beefheart and Pere Ubu. The band comprised Keith Curtis (vocals), Rick Aitken (b. 18 August 1956, d. October 1989; guitar), Vince Hunt (bass) and Alan Brown (drums). An EP, *Loudhailer Songs*, in 1985, attracted the *New Musical Express*, who included the band on their seminal *C86* sampler tape. An album, *I Am John Pancreas*, followed in 1986, full of manic, awkward guitar riffs and off-beat lyrics. After the release of another EP, *One Foot In The Groove* (1988), the Ron Johnson label folded, prompting a short-lived period at Fundamental Records who issued A Witness's second album, *Sacred Cow Heart*. The Membranes' Vinyl Drip label was responsible for the band's next and possibly finest single, 'I Love You Mr. Disposable Razors' (1990). Since then, Strange Fruit Records have combined A Witness's two 1988 sessions for BBC disc jockey John Peel on a mini-album. The band have also covered the Doors' 'Break On Through' on a tribute album to the music of 1967, *Through The Looking Glass*.

●ALBUMS: *I Am John Pancreas* (Ron Johnson 1985)★★★, *Sacred Cow Heart* (Fundamental 1988)★★★, *Double Peel Sessions* (Strange Fruit 1989)★★★.

A-HA

Formed in early 1982 this Norwegian pop group consisted of Morten Harket (b. 14 September 1959, Konigsberg, Norway; lead vocals), Magne Furuholmen (b. 1 November 1962, Oslo, Norway; vocals/keyboards) and Pal Waaktaar (b. 6 September 1961, Oslo, Norway; vocals/guitar). After five years spent playing in Scandinavian groups such as Spider Empire, Souldier Blue and Bridges, the members finally found the perfect pop combination and set about selling their image to the international market. Warner Brothers Records signed them, but the debut single 'Take On Me', produced by Tony Mansfield, sold poorly. Undeterred, A-Ha's management elected to record the song with Alan Tarney at the consul. With the assistance of a brilliant promotional video, utilizing animated pencil sketches, the single reached number 1 in the USA and climbed to number 2 in the UK. The timing could not have been better and during 1985 the trio neatly assumed the teenage pin-up pop idolatry previously bestowed on Duran Duran and Wham! With their chiselled good looks, soft features and exotic Scandinavian accents, the group could seemingly do no wrong. The expertly enunciated 'The Sun Always Shines On TV' took them to the top of the UK charts and reached the US Top 20. This was followed by a world tour and a further series of hits including 'Train Of Thought', 'Hunting High And Low', 'I've Been Losing You' and 'Cry Wolf'. In 1987, Pal Waaktar was commissioned to compose the theme for the James Bond film *The Living Daylights* with John Barry. After two essentially pop albums, the group attempted a more serious work with 1988's *Stay On These Roads*. Acutely aware of the ephemeral power of the pin-up pop star, A-Ha have been carefully attempting to make the uneasy transition to long-term success. In 1989, Harket starred in the film *Kamilla And The Thief* as well as recording a one-off single with Bjorn Eidsvag. A-Ha's solid musicianship has served them well and their mannered vocal style brought further UK chart success in 1990 with a revival of the Everly Brothers' 'Crying In The Rain' and 'Angel' in 1993. *Memorial Beach*, however, failed to capture the hearts of the critics.

●ALBUMS: *Hunting High And Low* (Warners 1985)★★★, *Scoundrel Days* (Warners 1986)★★, *Stay On These Roads* (Warners 1988)★★★, *East Of The Sun, West Of The Moon* (Warners 1990)★★★, *Memorial Beach* (Warners 1993)★★. Solo: Morten Harket *Wild Seed* (Warners 1995)★★.
●COMPILATIONS: *Headlines And Deadlines - The Hits Of A-Ha* (Warners 1991)★★★.
●VIDEOS: *Headlines And Deadlines* (1991).
●FURTHER READING: *Aha: The Story So Far*, Marcussen.

ABBOTT, GREGORY

b. Harlem, New York City, New York, USA. Abbott exploded on the R&B scene in 1986 with the huge dance hit 'Shake You Down' (number 1 R&B,

number 1 pop). In the UK, the song went to number 6 on the chart. Abbott began pursuing a music career while working for his doctorate at the University of California at Berkeley. He soon moved to Los Angeles and married famed songstress Freda Payne, and she recorded four of his songs. He returned to his home in New York and began working as a researcher in a stock brokerage firm. Associates at the firm took an interest in Abbott's musical career and financed a studio and label, Gramercy Park Records. Abbott recorded a few acts for the label before trying to record himself. In 1986 he signed with Columbia Records, and gained a giant hit with 'Shake You Down'. Abbott continued his success in the R&B field with 'I Got The Feelin' (It's Over)' (number 5 R&B), in 1987, and 'I'll Prove It To You' (number 5 R&B), in 1988.
●ALBUMS: *Shake You Down* (Columbia 1986)★★★, *I'll Prove It To You* (Columbia 1988)★★★.

ABC

Purveyors of 'perfect pop' in the early 80s, ABC were dominated by the stunning vocal range and lyrical songwriting skills of lead singer Martin Fry (b. 9 March 1958, Manchester, England). The band was formed after Fry had interviewed Mark White (b. 1 April 1961, Sheffield, Yorkshire, England; guitar) and Stephen Singleton (b. 17 April 1959, Sheffield, Yorkshire, England; saxophone) as members of a Sheffield-based electronic group, Vice Versa, for his fanzine *Modern Drugs*. Accepting the invitation to join as vocalist, Fry took artistic control of the group, changing the name to ABC, as well as the musical direction, moving them towards a more 'poppy' course. The group was completed by the arrival of bassist Mark Lickley and drummer David Robinson - later replaced by David Palmer (b. 29 May 1961, Chesterfield, Derbyshire, England).

The debut 'Tears Are Not Enough', on their own Neutron label, made the UK Top 20 in late 1981, but it was the following year's intense seven month period when they had three Top 10 hits with 'Poison Arrow', 'The Look Of Love' and 'All Of My Heart' that secured their reputation. Their pristine pop songs were no better displayed than on the superb *Lexicon Of Love*. This Trevor Horn-produced album remains a benchmark of 80s pop, and a formidable collection of melodramatic pop love songs assembled in one neat package. The album reached number 1 and it stayed in the UK charts for a year. The relative failure of the follow-up, *Beauty Stab*, to emulate the debut's success, resulted in a personnel upheaval within the group,

which by 1984 left only Fry and White. They continued as ABC using session musicians as well as a change of image for the promotion of *How To Be Zillionaire*, almost to the extent of becoming caricatures. This image, particularly in videos, gave them some success in the USA with 'Be Near Me' reaching the Top 10 and '(How To Be A) Millionaire' peaking at the Top 20 mark. Fry became seriously ill and was absent for great lengths of time owing to treatment for Hodgkin's Disease. They returned with the memorable UK Top 20/US Top 5 hit 'When Smokey Sings' in 1987, although the success of their debut album has so far not been matched. In the mid-90s only Fry remained from the original band, but his voice was enough, still intact but in desperate need of songs to the standard of *Lexicon Of Love*. *Skyscraping* was a good attempt at recreating their peak but sounded dated in the 90s.
●ALBUMS: *The Lexicon Of Love* (Neutron 1982)★★★★★, *Beauty Stab* (Neutron 1983)★★★, *How To Be A Zillionaire* (Neutron 1985)★★★, *Alphabet City* (Neutron 1987)★★★, *Up* (Neutron 1989)★★★, *Abracadabra* (Parlophone 1991)★★, *ABC 2* (Parlophone 1992)★★, *Skyscraping* (Blatant 1997)★★★.
●COMPILATIONS: *Absolutely* (Neutron 1990)★★★, *The Remix Collection* (1993)★★★.
●VIDEOS: *Mantrap* (1989), *Best Of ABC* (1990), *Absolutely* (1991).

ABERCROMBIE, JOHN

b. 16 December 1944, Portchester, New York, USA. After studying at Berklee College Of Music in Boston, Abercrombie spent four years playing guitar in Johnny 'Hammond' Smith's group. Touring with an established band offered him the kind of practical study which was ideal after the Berklee academic hot-house of the late 60s. Moving back to New York in 1969, his already unusual technical command of the instrument meant he had little difficulty finding opportunities to play with fine musicians. In the ensuing five years he played alongside Randy and Michael Brecker in the group Dreams, and toured with the Chico Hamilton Band, including an appearance at the Montreux Jazz Festival. In demand as a sideman from countless bandleaders, from Gil Evans to Gato Barbieri, it was in Billy Cobham's fusion group Spectrum that Abercrombie's reputation quickly spread. This hard-driving rock-influenced band was the perfect vehicle for his prodigious technique and imagination at this early stage in his career. However, by the mid-70s, Abercrombie was

discovering a new and altogether different voice. Treating fusion in a similar manner to which the MJQ had treated bop, he formed his highly regarded trio Timeless, playing in a softer, more delicate style. This band was replaced in 1975 by his Gateway trio, with Dave Holland and Jack DeJohnette, and then by a quartet three years later. Since 1981, Abercrombie has performed and recorded prolifically. As well as continuing to collaborate with DeJohnette, he has produced some highly regarded duet work with Ralph Towner, led a quartet featuring Michael Brecker and was involved in the all-star big band that recently debuted and recorded Charles Mingus's *Epitaph*. Abercrombie remains one of the most versatile and gifted guitarists of post-war jazz and fortunately appears to be hitting a prolific phase during the 90s with both Gateway and Johnson/Erskine/Surman.
● ALBUMS: *Timeless* (ECM 1974)★★★, with Gateway *Gateway* (ECM 1975)★★★★, *Sargasso Sea* (ECM 1976)★★★★, *Characters* (1977)★★★, with Gateway *Gateway 2* (ECM 1978)★★, *Night* (ECM 1984)★★★, *Current Events* (ECM 1985)★★★★, *Getting There* (ECM 1988)★★★, *John Abercrombie Trio* (ECM 1989)★★★, *Animato* (ECM 1990)★★★, *While We're Young* (ECM 1992)★★★, with Marc Johnson, Peter Erskine, John Surman *November* (ECM 1994)★★★, *Speak Of The Devil* (ECM 1994)★★★, with Gateway *Homecoming* (ECM 1995)★★★, with Dan Wall, Adam Nussbaum *Tactics* (ECM 1997)★★★.
● COMPILATIONS: *Works* (ECM 1989)★★★★.

ABSOLUTE BEGINNERS

British author Colin McInness published *Absolute Beginners* in 1958 as part of a London trilogy. This much-lauded novel foresaw the rise of the Mod movement and much of the iconography of the 60s. Its hero is a photographer in love with music and his scooter. The book has been rightly lauded for its literary and cultural merits, but renewed interest was kindled during the 70s' Mod revival and a 1981 single by the Jam, also titled 'Absolute Beginners'. Julien Temple, once part of the Sex Pistols/Malcolm McLaren entourage, directed this 1986 film adaptation, but rather than focus on the novel's dramatic tension - part of the action revolves around the Notting Hill Race riots - he transformed the narrative into a gaudy musical. The results were not a success. David Bowie joined Ray Davies of the Kinks in an assembled cast, but the empathy both voiced about McInness' work is not apparent in their contributions. A wealth of publicity ensured *Absolute Beginners* an audience - the soundtrack album broached the UK Top 20 - but it remains a flawed, ill-conceived adaptation.

AC/DC

This theatrical Australian hard rock band was formed in 1973 by Malcolm Young (b. 6 January 1953, Glasgow, Scotland; rhythm guitar) after the demise of his previous outfit, the Velvet Underground (no relation to the US group). Young, whose elder brother George had already achieved stardom in Australia as a member of the Easybeats, also enlisted his younger brother Angus Young (b. 31 March 1959, Glasgow, Scotland; guitar). Their sister later suggested that Angus wear his school uniform on stage, a gimmick that rapidly became their trademark. The two brothers made their debut appearance in a bar in Sydney on 31 December 1973, along with Dave Evans (vocals), Larry Van Knedt (bass) and Colin Burgess (drums). In 1974, the Young brothers and Evans moved to Melbourne, where Mark Evans (b. 2 March 1956, Melbourne, Australia; bass) and Phil Rudd (b. 19 May 1954, Melbourne, Australia; drums) joined the band. Another immigrant from the UK, Bon Scott (b. Ronald Scott, 9 July 1946, Kirriemuir, Scotland, d. 19 February 1980; vocals), graduated from being the band's chauffeur to becoming their vocalist when Dave Evans refused to go on stage one night in September 1974. (Evans went on to form Rabbit, releasing two albums for CBS Records in Australia, before joining Hot Cockerel in 1984 and releasing *David Evans And Thunder Down Under* in 1986.) Scott had previously recorded with two Australian outfits, pop group the Valentines (1966-68) and rockers Fraternity (1970-74). Indeed, after he emigrated from Scotland in 1951, he had also spent five consecutive years as drum champion (under-17 section) with the Perth Pipe Band. After such a wholesome start a prison conviction for assault and battery earmarked a more volatile side to his nature, and also resulted in him being refused admission to the army. In 1965 he joined the Spectors, before the aforementioned assignations with the Valentines in 1966, and Fraternity between 1970 and 1974. The AC/DC line-up that welcomed him had already recorded a solitary single, 'Can I Sit Next To You?', but it was his voice that graced their first two albums, *High Voltage* and *TNT*. Both sets were produced by George Young and his writing partner, another former Easybeat, Harry Vanda. Neither of them were issued outside Australia, though Atlantic Records in Britain did offer a selection of material from both records under the title *High Voltage* in 1976. These albums established the group as a major draw in their native territory, and brought them to the attention of Atlantic, who promptly relocated the band to London in January 1976. However, bassist Mark Evans was replaced by Cliff Williams (b. 14 December 1949, Romford, Essex, England; ex-Home) in June 1977 after tiring of touring. He went on to Finch/Contraband, then a variety of bands including Swanee, Heaven, Best and Party Boys. Once AC/DC began to tour outside Australia, the band quickly amassed a cult following, as much for the unashamed gimmickry of its live show as for its furious, frequently *risqué* brand of hard rock. *Let There Be Rock* broke them as a chart act in the UK, with its contents including the perennial crowd-pleaser, 'Whole Lotta Rosie'. However, it was *Highway To Hell* in 1979 that established them as international stars. This, the band's first album with producer Mutt Lange, also proved to be their last with Bon Scott. On 20 February 1980, after a night of heavy drinking, he was left unconscious in a friend's car, and was later found to be dead, having choked on his own vomit. The coroner recorded a verdict of death by misadventure.

Scott's death threatened the band's future, but his replacement, former Geordie lead singer Brian Johnson (b. 5 October 1947, Newcastle, England), proved more than equal to the task. His first album with the band, *Back In Black*, reached number 1 in the UK and Australia, and spawned the hit single 'Rock 'n' Roll Ain't Noise Pollution'. That album was certified as having sold 12 million copies in the USA by March 1996. In 1981 *For Those About To Rock* was released, the band topped the bill at the Castle Donington festival and also achieved two Top 20 UK singles. After *Flick Of The Switch* in 1983, drummer Phil Rudd left the band to become a helicopter pilot in New Zealand, to be replaced by Simon Wright (b. 19 June 1963; ex-A II Z and Tytan) - who in turn departed to join Dio in 1990. His replacement was Chris Slade (b. 30 October 1946; ex-Manfred Mann's Earthband; Firm; and Gary Moore). In keeping with their superstar status, AC/DC maintained an increasingly relaxed schedule through the 80s, touring to support each carefully spaced album release. There were further 'casualties', however. When Malcolm Young was unfit to tour in 1988 his cousin, Stevie Young (ex-Starfighters), temporarily deputized. Paul Greg also stepped in for Cliff Williams on the US leg of their 1991 tour. A year earlier *The Razor's Edge* had been one of the more successful albums of their later career, producing a Top 20 UK hit, 'Thunderstruck'.

In 1992 they issued a live album, while the attendant single, 'Highway To Hell', made the UK Top 20. With Brian Johnson long having buried the ghost of Bon Scott, the band shows no signs of varying its winning musical formula. *Ballbreaker* in 1995 was a near-return to form after a lengthy break.

● ALBUMS: *High Voltage* Australia only (Albert 1974)★★, *TNT* Australia only (Albert 1975)★★, *High Voltage* (Atlantic 1976)★★, *Dirty Deeds Done Dirt Cheap* (Atlantic 1976)★★★, *Let There Be Rock* (Atlantic 1977)★★★★, *Powerage* (Atlantic 1978)★★★, *If You Want Blood You've Got It* (Atlantic 1978)★★★, *Highway To Hell* (Atlantic 1979)★★★★, *Back In Black* (Atlantic 1980)★★★★, *For Those About To Rock We Salute You* (Atlantic 1981)★★★★, *Flick Of The Switch* (Atlantic 1983)★★, *'74 Jailbreak* (Atlantic 1974)★★, *Fly On The Wall* (Atlantic 1985)★★, *Who Made Who* (Atco 1986)★★★, *Blow Up Your Video* (Atlantic 1988)★★, *The Razor's Edge* (Atco 1990)★★★, *Live* (Atco 1992)★★, *Ballbreaker* (Atlantic 1995)★★★.

● COMPILATIONS: *Box Set 1* (EMI 1987)★★★, *Box Set 2* (EMI 1987)★★★.

● VIDEOS: *Let There Be Rock* (1986), *Fly On The Wall* (1986), *High Voltage* (1988), *Who Made Who* (1991), *Live* (1992), *No Bull: Live At The Plaza Del Toros* (Warner Vision 1996).

● FURTHER READING: *The AC/DC Story*, Paul Ezra. *AC/DC*, Malcolm Dome. *AC/DC: Hell Ain't No Bad Place To Be*, Richard Bunton. *AC/DC: An Illustrated Collectors Guide Vols. 1 & 2*, Chris Tesch. *AC/DC Illustrated Biography*, Mark Putterford. *Shock To The System*, Mark Putterford. *HM Photo Book*, no author listed. *The World's Most Electrtifying Rock 'n' Roll Band*, Malcolm Dome (ed.). *Highway To Hell: The Life And Times Of AC/DC Legend Bon Scott*, Clinton Walker. *AC/DC: The World's Heaviest Rock*, Martin Huxley.

ACCELERATORS

Hailing from North Carolina, USA, and unconnected to the New Jersey or Los Angeles bands with the same name (and several others in different territories), these Accelerators were led by singer/guitarist and songwriter Gerald Duncan. It was he who largely orchestrated the band's competent but unenthralling mid-80s career. He had help, however, in the shape of renowned producer and musician Don Dixon, and local star Mitch Easter of Let's Active, who both appeared on the band's appealing debut, *Leave My Heart*. However, only Duncan and drummer Doug Welchel survived the transition to the Accelerators' second line-up, which also featured guitarist Brad Rice. *The Accelerators* featured two songs produced by Dixon, and it was significant that among the strongest tracks was a remake of the debut album's track 'Two Girls In Love'. Another was the cover of the Box Tops' 'The Letter'. Given the four-year interval between recordings, it did not bode well for their future, a suspicion confirmed when the band effectively disappeared from view again, only re-emerging once more in 1991 for the perfunctory *Dream Train*.

●ALBUMS: *Leave My Heart* (Dolphin 1983)★★★, *The Accelerators* (Profile 1987)★★, *Dream Train* (Profile 1991)★★.

ACCEPT

This German heavy rock quintet comprised Udo Dirkschneider on vocals, guitarists Jan Kommet and Wolf Hoffman, drummer Frank Friedrich and bassist Peter Baltes. Formed in 1977, their power metal sound was characterized by Dirkschneider's guttural howl and the speed drumming of Stefan Kaufmann, who replaced Friedrich after the band's debut album. 1981's *Breaker* also featured guitarist Jorg Fischer, who left following a support tour to Judas Priest (although he did return briefly in the late 80s). *Restless And Wild* from 1983 epitomized their blitzing style. This had an undeniable influence on the thrash movement that developed during the late 80s, though *Metal Heart* adopted a more melodic approach. Unhappy with this style, Dirkschneider quit and formed his own outfit, Udo. A series of replacement vocalists came and went, including Rob Armitage (ex-Baby Tuckoo), David Reece and Jim Stacey (Stacey stepping in to complete tracks on *Eat The Heat* after Reese and Baltes had a physical confrontation on tour in the US). Several lacklustre albums were released during these years, which received little critical acclaim or commercial reward. Internal problems persisted, with Kaufmann contracting a muscular disease and being replaced by Ken Mary (House Of Lords). The band eventually disintegrated in 1989. For *Restless And Wild* and *Balls To The Wall* their reputation as a metal act is still high. Reese would form Bangalore Choir while old sparring partner Baltes contributed to Don Dokken. The band reunited in the 90s with a revised line-up (namely Dirkschneider, Hoffman, Baltes and Kaufmann).

●ALBUMS: *Accept* (Brain 1979)★★★, *I'm A Rebel* (Logo 1980)★★★, *Breaker* (Brain 1981), *Restless And Wild* (Heavy Metal 1983)★★★, *Balls To The Wall* (Portrait 1984)★★★, *Metal Heart* (Portrait 1985)★★★, *Kaizoku-Ban* (Portrait 1986)★★,

Russian Roulette (Portrait 1986)★★★, *Eat The Heat* (RCA 1989)★★, *Live In Japan* (1992)★★★, *Objection Overruled* (RCA 1993)★★★.

●COMPILATIONS: *Best Of Accept* (Metronome 1983)★★★, *Accept* (Portrait 1986)★★★, *Hungry Years* (Razor 1991)★★★, *The Collection* (Castle 1991)★★★, *Steel Glove: The Collection* (Castle 1995)★★★.

ACKERMAN, WILLIAM

b. November 1949, Germany. He moved to California at the age of nine when he was adopted by a Stanford professor and his wife. Ackerman started playing the acoustic guitar at 12, shunning the electric guitar and preferring open, modal tunings. He was influenced by John Fahey, Leo Kottke and Robbie Basho. Following a home-made recording, the entrepreneurial Ackerman started the low-key Windham Hill Records in 1976, together with his friend and future wife Anne Robinson. As he built up the label's roster he released several relaxing and sparse new-age albums of guitar music. Tracks like 'The Bricklayer's Beautiful Daughter' from *Passage* and 'Visiting' from *Past Light* are examples of evocative melodic excursions. Occasionally Ackerman's guitar is accompanied by cello, piano or violin, but the music remains hauntingly uncluttered. Alongside his own productions he simultaneously acted as producer to his other artists and led numerous tours as he spread the word about the innovative Windham Hill. His early signings and successes were with George Winston, Michael Hedges and Alex De Grassi. As the label has grown Ackerman's own musical output has slowed down although since he relinquished control of Windham Hill to his former wife Anne Robinson, he planned to concentrate more on his sparse but eclectic playing but in reality he formed a new record label in 1996. Imaginary Road Records is a partnership with Polygram Jazz.

●ALBUMS: *In Search Of The Turtle's Navel* (Windham Hill 1976)★★★, *It Takes A Year* (Windham Hill 1977)★★, *Childhood And Memory* (Windham Hill 1979)★★, *Passage* (Windham Hill 1981)★★★, *Past Light* (Windham Hill 1983)★★★★, *Conferring With The Moon* (Windham Hill 1986)★★★, *Imaginary Roads* (Windham Hill 1988)★★★, *The Opening Of Doors* (Windham Hill 1992)★★★.

●COMPILATIONS: *A Windham Hill Retrospective* (Windham Hill 1993)★★★.

ACOUSTIC ALCHEMY

Formed in the mid-80s, Acoustic Alchemy is essentially Greg Carmichael (b. 1953, London, England; nylon string guitar) and Nick Webb (b. 1954, Manchester, England; steel string guitar). Their blend of instrumental music is neither jazz nor pop, but it has elements of both, together with flamenco, reggae and folk. Similar to Sky in sound, their four albums are refreshing and uplifting. Their debut contains one of their finest compositions, 'Mr Chow', an example of Chinese Reggae! Nick Webb was originally influenced by John Martyn and Pentangle. He recorded one album with Simon James in the early 80s and linked up with Carmichael in 1986 (released as *Early Alchemy*). Carmichael had studied classical guitar at the London College of Music and gained experience playing with jazz groups. Their break came when, frustrated by the apathy for their music in England, they took a Virgin Atlantic Airlines inflight gig, and literally played their way to America. They were signed to MCA as part of their Master Series, and debuted with the excellent *Red Dust And Spanish Lace*. Following *Blue Chip* they joined GRP Records, although their debut there, *Reference Point,* lacked the life and sparkle of their MCA work. They redressed the balance with *Back On The Case* in 1991, although their recent albums have sounded workmanlike.
●ALBUMS: *Red Dust And Spanish Lace* (MCA 1987)★★★★, *Natural Elements* (MCA 1988)★★★, *Blue Chip* (MCA 1989)★★★, *Reference Point* (GRP 1990)★★, *Back On The Case* (GRP 1991)★★★, *Early Alchemy* (1992)★★, *The New Edge* (GRP 1993)★★, *Arcanum* (GRP 1996)★★★.

ADAM AND THE ANTS

Formed in April 1977, the band consisted of Adam Ant (b. Stuart Leslie Goddard, 3 November 1954, London, England; vocals/guitar), backed by Lester Square (guitar), Andy Warren (vocals/bass) and Paul Flanagan (drums). Heavily influenced by the Sex Pistols, they incorporated bondage gear and sado-masochistic imagery into their live act and repertoire. The line-up was relatively *ad hoc* between 1977 and 1979 with Mark Gaumont replacing Lester Square (who joined the Monochrome Set - as Andy Warren later did) and colourful manager Jordan occasionally taking vocals. Ant appeared with Toyah in Derek Jarman's movie *Jubilee* where he seemed more convincing than onstage. Although the first generation Ants released one studio album, *Dirk Wears White Sox*, their critical reputation among new wave writers was poor. At the end of the decade, Ant sought the advice of Pistols manager Malcolm McLaren, who took on the role of image consultant for a £1000 fee. His advice was a radical shift of musical policy and a daring new look combining Native American (Apache) imagery and piratical garb. In January 1980, however, the Ants fell victim to McLaren's charisma and abandoned their leader to form the newsworthy Bow Wow Wow. At this point, most observers assumed that Ant's career was over. In fact, it was just beginning. With an entirely fresh set of Ants consisting of Marco Pirroni (b. 27 April 1959, London, England; vocals/guitar), Kevin Mooney (vocals/bass) and two drummers, Terry Lee Miall (8 November 1958, London, England) and Merrick (b. Chris Hughes, 3 March 1954, London, England), Ant effectively reinvented himself. Out went the punk riffs and bondage to be replaced by a sound heavily influenced by the Burundi Black drummers. With his Red Indian warpaint and colourful costume, the new Ant enjoyed three UK hits in 1980 culminating in the number 2 'Ant Music', in which he boldly dismissed his rivals and proclaimed his sound to be of the moment. His prognosis was correct 1981 was the year of Adam And The Ants whose pop prescience was captured in a series of excellently produced videos. With his striking looks and clever use of costume, Adam Ant was a natural pin-up. His portrayal of a highwayman ('Stand And Deliver') and pantomime hero ('Prince Charming') brought two UK number 1 hits and ushered in an era of 'New Pop', where fancy dressing-up and catchy melodic songs without a message became the norm. In 1981 Mooney was replaced by ex-Roxy Music member Gary Tibbs (b. 25 January 1958, London, England). Having dominated his group since 1977, it came as little surprise when Adam announced that he was dissolving the unit in early 1982 to pursue a solo career as Adam Ant.
●ALBUMS: *Dirk Wears White Sox* (Do It 1979)★★, *Kings Of The Wild Frontier* (Columbia 1980)★★★, *Prince Charming* (Columbia 1981)★★.
●COMPILATIONS: *Antmusic: The Very Best Of* (Arcade 1993)★★★, *B-Side Babies* (Epic/Legacy 1995)★★.
●VIDEOS: *Hits 1980-1986* (1986), *Prince Charming* (1988), *Antmusic: The Very Best Of* (1993).
●FURTHER READING: *Adam And The Ants*, Mike West. *Adam And The Ants*, Chris Welch. *Adam And The Ants*, Fred and Judy Vermorel. *Adam Ant Tribal Rock Special*, Martha Rodriguez (Design). *The Official Adam Ant Story*, James Maw. *Adam And*

The Ants Kings: The Official Adam And The Ants Song Book, Stephen Lavers.

ADAM ANT

b. Stuart Leslie Goddard, 3 November 1954, London, England. After an initially chequered, then immensely successful career leading Adam And The Ants, Goddard went solo in early 1982. For support, he retained an old musical partner Marco Pirroni and relaunched himself with the frantic 'Goody Two Shoes', which hit number 1 in the UK in June. The average 'Friend Or Foe' followed at number 5 but thereafter the spell was broken. Phil Collins was recruited as producer to halt Ant's sudden decline and the pantomime-influenced 'Puss In Boots' duly made the Top 5. The revival was only temporary, however, and by the end of 1983 Ant's chart career was practically non-existent. The original god of the New Pop seemed commercially bankrupt, his place taken by new idols such as Duran Duran, Culture Club and Wham! Even an appearance at Live Aid in 1985 with 'Vive Le Rock' could only produce a number 50 UK chart entry and Ant switched adroitly to acting. A surprise chart comeback in 1990 with 'Room At The Top' appeared a lucky strike which did not seriously distract the singer from his thespian pursuits. A new album in 1995, promoted by concert appearances in West London, provoked further media saturation, good reviews but little in terms of record sales.
●ALBUMS: *Friend Or Foe* (Columbia 1982)★★★, *Strip* (Columbia 1983)★★, *Vive Le Rock* (Columbia 1985)★★, *Manners And Physique* (MCA 1990)★★, *Wonderful* (EMI 1995)★★★.

ADAMS, JOHNNY

b. Lathan John Adams, 5 January 1932, New Orleans, Mississippi, USA. A former member of several gospel groups, Adams' first recordings appeared in 1959 on Ric Records. Three years later he secured a minor R&B success with 'A Losing Battle', a slow ballad co-written by Dr. John. In 1968 he joined Shelby Singleton's SSS International outlet and had a hit the following year with 'Reconsider Me', an inspired piece of country soul. Although subsequent releases failed to match this performance, the strong *Heart And Soul* followed. Johnny signed with Atlantic Records in the early 70s, but his work there was disappointing. A later move to Ariola Records resulted in a remake of Conway Twitty's two-year-old country hit, 'After All The Good Is Gone', giving Adams a 1978 US R&B chart entry. He has since recorded for various labels, including notably, Rounder Records. From 1989 to the present Adams has had something of an artistic revival, recording a number of fine albums including tributes to Percy Mayfield and Doc Pomus, songwriters to whom Adams' excellent voice is particularly suited.
●ALBUMS: *Heart And Soul* (SSS International 1969)★★★, *Stand By Me* (Atlantic 1976)★★, *After All The Good Is Gone* (Ariola 1978)★★, *From The Heart* (Demon 1983)★★★, *After Dark* (Rounder 1986)★★★, *Christmas In New Orleans* (Maison Du Soul 1988)★★, *Walking On A Tightrope: The Songs Of Percy Mayfield* (Zensor 1989)★★★★, *Johnny Adams Sings Doc Pomus: The Real Me* (Zensor 1991)★★★★, *Good Morning Heartache* (Rounder 1993)★★★, *The Verdict* (Rounder 1995)★★★, *One Foot In The Blues* (Rounder 1997)★★★.
●COMPILATIONS: *Heart And Soul '78* (1978)★★, *The Tan Nightingale* (Charly 1984)★★★, *Reconsider Me* (Charly 1987)★★★, *Room With A View Of The Blues* (Rounder 1988)★★★★.

ADC BAND

A funk band from Detroit, Michigan, USA. Members were Artwell Matthews (drums), Audrey Matthews (lead vocals), Mark Patterson (bass), Mike Judkins (keyboards), Curtin Hobson (lead guitar), James Maddox (vocals and percussion), and Sam Burns (trombone). The core of the group were Artwell and Audrey Matthews, son and daughter of the veteran Detroit record entrepreneur Johnnie Mae Matthews. They, along with Mark Patterson, formed a group called Black Nazty, which in 1971 signed with Enterprise, a subsidiary of Stax Records. In their several years with the company the only single that made any kind of noise was 'Talking To The People' (1974). Shortening their name to Nazty they signed with the Mankind label in 1976 and had their first chart single, 'It's Summertime' (number 100 R&B), and recorded an album called *Nazty's Got The Move*. By this time the group consisted of the two Matthews, Patterson, Mike Judkins, Jackie Casper, Larry Thomas, and Alice Myers. In 1977 the group became General Assistance and the ADC Band and recorded an album for Johnnie Mae Matthews' Northern label. Wisely shortening their name, the group signed with Cotillion in 1978 and finally got on the charts with the funk hit 'Long Stroke' (number 6 R&B), which was very much in the George Clinton vein. Subsequent success for ADC was less notable, and of their five subsequent chart records during 1979-82 the most successful of the lot was 'Roll With The Punches' (number 46 R&B),

their last chart record.

●ALBUMS: *Looking For My Roots* (Northern 1978)★★★, *Long Stroke* (Cotillion 1978)★★★, *Talk That Stiff* (Cotillion 1979)★★★, *Renaissance* (Cotillion 1980)★★★, *Brother Luck* (Cotillion 1981)★★★, *Roll With The Punches* (Cotillion 1982)★★★.

ADE, KING SUNNY

b. Sunday Adeniyi, 1 September 1946, Oshogbo, Nigeria. When Ade dropped out of school in 1963 in order to play with semi-professional Lagos juju bands, his parents - from the royal family of Ondo - were horrified. In Nigeria, as in much of Africa, music was regarded by 'respectable' people as a very low-caste occupation. Hopefully, Ade's subsequent national and international success somewhat mollified such parental disapproval - for Ade's star rose fast and high. By 1964, he was lead guitarist in Moses Olaiya's highly regarded band the Rhythm Dandies and by 1966, after a short spell with another major bandleader, Tunde Nightingale, he had formed his own outfit, the Green Spots, playing a speedy but relaxed style of juju characterized by tight vocal harmonies and deliciously melodic guitar work. The band's name was a cheeky riposte to seminal juju stylist I.K. Dairo, whose Blue Spots had ruled the juju roost since the early 50s. Ade's luck continued with his first release, 'Challenge Cup', a song about a local football championship which became a national hit in 1967. The same year, Ade released his first album, *Alanu Loluwa*. The late 60s and early 70s saw Ade and his renamed African Beats go from success to success. By 1975, he felt sufficiently powerful and financially secure to set up his own label, Sunny Alade Records, now a major independent in Nigeria which handles all Ade's domestic releases. The mid-70s also saw him open up his own juju nightclub in Lagos, the Ariya, the African Beats' home venue when not on tour. By the end of the decade he was one of the ruling triumvirate of juju music - alongside Ebenezer Obey and Dele Abiodun - releasing some six albums per year, and selling around 200,000 copies of each release. This achievement was countered by the fact that a substantial proportion of these sales were of bootlegged pressings. By the early 80s, African music was finding a growing audience in the UK, where a number of the more adventurous labels were looking around for African artists to put under contract. In 1982, Island Records signed Ade for Europe and North America (promoting him as 'the African Bob Marley'). His first album under the

arrangement was *Juju Music*, an across-the-board critical success, which charted in the USA. Ade's British breakthrough came with a triumphant concert he and the African Beats gave at London's Lyceum Ballroom in January 1983. Without exception the music press hailed Ade as an emergent international star. He played regularly to a hugely enthusiastic multi-ethnic audience, proving that - in a live context at any rate - juju's use of Yoruba rather than English language lyrics was no barrier to overseas acceptance. (The audience size and composition was in marked contrast to Ade's previous British concerts. In 1975, he had made a three-month tour of the country, playing almost exclusively to expatriate Nigerian audiences at specially organized cultural evenings in municipal halls and community centres.) The critical success of *Juju Music* was matched by the 1983 follow-up, *Synchro System* which also made encouraging UK and further US chart entries. Both albums were produced by the young Frenchman Martin Meissonnier, who must share much of the credit for Ade's, and juju's, international breakthrough. A third Island album, 1984's *Aura*, which included a guest appearance by Stevie Wonder, was also well received, but Island - who were clearly banking on major chart success in the short term rather than career development - declined to renew Ade's contract, dropping him from the label. 1984 was also marred by dissension among the African Beats. Following successful tours of the USA and Japan, they demanded substantial increases in salary. Ade, who was in fact losing money on his international touring due to the large number of musicians he was carrying and the limited audience capacity of the venues he was playing, was unwilling to meet these demands, and the African Beats was dissolved. Returning to Lagos, he formed a new band, Golden Mercury, and now records and performs almost exclusively in Nigeria. While the abatement of his international activities is regretted by juju music fans in the West, Ade continues to record outstanding albums, which are readily obtainable at specialist record stores. Another international release was then cut for Dutch label Provogue Records in 1989 (Rykodisc in the USA). In 1990 Ade's collaboration with Onyeka, Wait For Me, provoked a good deal of intrigue. The album included a song titled 'Choices', and it later emerged that the collection had been funded by the US AID Office of Population as part of a $30 million family planning project. Several African-Americans slammed Onyeka and Ade as 'accomplices to an attack on African cultural traditions and religious beliefs'. This contrasted with Ade's more usual advice about the furtherance of the population (by this time he himself had 12 children). Reports followed of his death in 1991 after an onstage collapse in Lagos, but these were unfounded. He travelled instead to London for recuperation, but Ade's once mighty reputation was clearly in danger of losing its lustre. He returned to form in 1995 with *E Dide* and promoted the album outside Nigeria. In his homeland he retains a huge following, with each release selling at least 200,000 copies. He runs among other things a record label, a film company, a nightclub and a charity foundation.

●ALBUMS: *Alana Loluwa* (Nigeria-Africa Song 1967)★★★, *Vintage King Sunny Ade* (Nigeria-Africa Song 1970)★★★, *E K'ilo Fomo Ode* (Sunny Alade 1974)★★, *The Late General Murtala Muhammed* (Sunny Alade 1975)★★★, *Sunny Ade Live Play* (Sunny Alade 1976)★★★, *In London* (Sunny Alade 1976)★★, *Sound Vibration* (Sunny Alade 1976)★★, *The Royal Sound* (Sunny Alade 1976)★★★, *Private Line* (Sunny Alade 1978)★★★, *Festac 77* (Sunny Alade 1978)★★★, *The Royal Sound* (Sunny Alade 1979)★★★, *Searching For My Love* (Sunny Alade 1979)★★★, *Orimi Ja Fun Mi* (Sunny Alade 1980)★★★, *The Message* (Sunny Alade 1981)★★, *Ariya Special* (Sunny Alade 1982)★★★, *Conscience* (Sunny Alade 1982)★★★, *Juju Music* (Mango 1982)★★★★, *Synchro System* (Mango 1983)★★★★, *Live At Montreaux* (Sunny Alade 1983)★★★, *Aura* (Mango 1984)★★★, *Otito* (Sunny Alade 1985)★★★, *Sweet Banana* (Sunny Alade 1986)★★★, *My Dear: New Direction* (Sunny Alade 1986)★★★, *Let Them Say* (Sunny Alade 1986)★★★, *Saviour* (Sunny Alade 1986)★★★, *Jealousy* (Sunny Alade 1987)★★★, *Merciful* (Sunny Alade 1987)★★★, *The Child* (Sunny Alade 1988)★★★, *Live Juju Live* (Provogue/Rykodisc 1988)★★★, *Destiny* (Sunny Alade 1988)★★★, *The Good Shepherd* (Sunny Alade 1988)★★★, with Onyeka *Wait For Me* (Sunny Alade 1989)★★, *Funmilayo* (Sunny Alade 1989)★★★, *Authority* (Sunny Alade 1990)★★, *Get Up* (Sunny Alade 1990)★★★, *E Dide* (Atlantic 1995)★★★.

●VIDEOS: *Live At Montreaux 1983* (1988), *Ju Ju* (1988).

ADICTS

The Adicts can be singled out from the host of other UK punk hopefuls of the early 80s largely due to their image. The adoption of black bowler hats and face make-up shared more than a passing resemblance to those rather unruly characters in Stanley Kubrick's controversial film, *A Clockwork*

Orange, and reflected the Adicts' brand of bootboy new wave music. The group were originally based in Ipswich, Suffolk, England, and comprised lead singer Monkey (b. Keith Warren), who had grotesquely perfected droog Alex's grin, plus Kid Dee (b. Michael Davison; drums), Pete Davidson (guitar) and Mel Ellis (bass). Their debut EP, *Lunch With The Adicts*, was the first release for the Dining Out label in 1981. This was followed by *Songs Of Praise* for DWED in October, which has subsequently become something of a cult classic in punk record collecting circles. The band then moved to the Fall Out label for 'Viva La Revolution', before they again changed labels, settling at the appropriately named Razor Records. There they achieved two UK Independent Top 10 singles, 'Chinese Takeaway' (1982) and 'Bad Boy' (1983). The ensuing album, *Sound Of Music*, even managed to scrape into the lower reaches of the UK chart for one week, which was only 380 weeks less than Julie Andrews' collection of the same title. All was then quiet for two years, until the Adicts popped up in 1985, back at Fall Out, with a new EP, *Bar Room Bop*. The compilation *This Is Your Life* covered the band's earliest recordings from 1978-80. Since then there has been a trickle of albums to little interest outside of hardened punk audiences in Europe and the US.

●ALBUMS: *Songs Of Praise* (DWED 1981)★★★, *Sound Of Music* (Razor 1982)★★★, *Fifth Overture* (Fall Out 1987)★★, *Live And Loud!* (Dojo 1987)★★, *Rockers In Rags (Live In Alabama)* (Fall Out 1990)★★.

●COMPILATIONS: *This Is Your Life (1978-80)* (Fall Out 1985)★★★, *The Best Of ...* (Dojo 1997)★★★.

●VIDEOS: *Live At The Manhattan Club* (1983), *Let's Go* (Visionary 1994).

ADOLESCENTS

The first line-up of the early-80s hardcore band the Adolescents, from Fullerton, Orange County, California, USA, comprised Frank Agnew (rhythm guitar), Rikk Agnew (lead guitar), Casey Royer (drums/vocals), Tony 'Montana' Brandenburg (vocals) and Steve 'Soto' Rodgers (bass/vocals). Montana formed the band with the other three, who were all formerly members of Social Distortion. Rikk Agnew, in addition, had formerly played with several Los Angeles bands including the Detours, while Rodgers had been part of Agent Orange. Following a flirtation with Posh Boy Records (the 'Amoeba' single, of which only 15 copies were pressed), the band's debut emerged on Frontier Records in 1981. Straight afterwards the

band collapsed. Rikk Agnew went on to release a solo album for Frontier the following year, which largely consisted of songs written for the intended second Adolescents album. Afterwards he played with both Christian Death and TSOL. The Adolescents reformed for reunion gigs in 1986 and effectively became an active unit once more. *Brats In Battalions*, released on the group's own label, included guitarist Alfie Agnew deputizing for brother Frank on a powerful punk/metal hybrid. The line-up switched for *Balboa Fun Zone*, but the songwriting of the remaining original members Rikk Agnew and Steve Soto was seen to its best advantage. It was followed by a live album taken from concerts recorded five years apart. Agnew's second solo effort, credited to Rikk Agnew's Yard Sale, featured his returning two brothers, Alfie and Frank. The Adolescents finally called it a day in 1989, though further reunions are probably not out of the question given the band's record.
●ALBUMS: *Adolescents* (Frontier 1981)★★★, *Brats In Battalions* (SOS 1987)★★★, *Balboa Fun Zone* (Triple X 1988)★★★, *Live 1981* and *1986* (Triple X 1989)★★★. Solo: Rikk Agnew *All By Myself* (Frontier 1982)★★★. Rikk Agnew's Yard Sale *Emotional Vomit* (Triple X 1990)★★★.

ADRENALIN OD
Formed in October 1981 in New Jersey, USA, the hardcore band Adrenalin OD consists of Paul Richard (vocals), Jack Steeples (bass), Dave Scott (drums) and Jim Foster (guitar). Following their 1983 debut (the six-track *Let's Barbeque With Adrenalin OD* EP, for their own Buy Our Records label), Foster was replaced by Bruce Wingate on guitar. *The Wacky Hi-Jinks Of ...* delighted in song titles such as 'A.O.D. Vs Godzilla' and 'Middle Aged Whore' and featured rousing three-minute punk pop songs. The logical progression was to tackle 'A.O.D. Vs Son Of Godzilla' on the follow-up collection, 1986's *Humungousfungusamongus*, and that is just what the band did, this time with the aid of hugely improved studio technique. The Ramones' producer Daniel Rey joined the band in time for *Cruisin' With Elvis In Bigfoot's UFO*, which continued the group's preoccupation with monster movies and other offbeat subjects, notably 'Bulemic Food Fight' and 'Something About ... Amy Carter'. By this point the band had slowed down their sound, now relying on a more conventional, yet still energized, rock 'n' roll platform. Produced by Andy Shernoff (Dictators/Wild Kingdom), *Ishtar* did not advance on previous gains, despite the band tackling Queen's 'Sheer Heart Attack' (they

had previously covered the same band's 'We Will Rock You' on a 1985 split EP with Bedlam).
●ALBUMS: *The Wacky Hi-Jinks Of* (Buy Our Records 1984)★★, *Humungousfungusamongus* (Buy Our Records 1986)★★★, *Cruising With Elvis In Bigfoot's UFO* (Buy Our Records 1988)★★★, *Ishtar* (Restless 1991)★★.

ADVENTURES
Formed in early 1984, the Adventures' story can be traced back six years to the Belfast, Northern Ireland powerpop/punk group the Starjets, which featured vocalist Terry Sharpe and guitarist Pat Gribben. The duo eventually sought their fortune on the London pub circuit and put together the Adventures with Pat Gribben's wife Eileen on vocals, aided by Gerard 'Spud' Murphy (guitar), Tony Ayre (bass) and Paul Crowder (drums). A deal with Chrysalis Records brought minimal chart success during 1984 and 1985, prompting the group to take a sabbatical in order to rethink their approach. A new deal with Elektra Records saw them achieve modest acclaim for *The Sea Of Love*, while the single, 'Broken Land', entered the UK Top 20. Although they attempted to consolidate their position, 'Down In The Sea Of Love' failed to reach the Top 40 and their subsequent career proved less than eventful.
●ALBUMS: *Theodore And Friends* US title *The Adventures* (Chrysalis 1985)★★, *The Sea Of Love* (Elektra 1988)★★★, *Trading Secrets With The Moon* (Elektra 1989)★★★, *Lions & Tigers & Bears* (Elektra 1993)★★★.

AFRAID OF MICE
Previously known variously as Beano, the Press and the Jones, Liverpool's Afraid Of Mice were formed in early 1979 by ex-Next member Philip Franz Jones (guitar/vocals), who for six years struggled with continuously fluctuating personnel to find a suitable, permanent line-up. With the emergence of bands like Echo And The Bunnymen, Teardrop Explodes and OMD, there was a great deal of interest in the second 'Liverpool Scene'. Consequently their appearance on a local compilation, *A Trip To The Dentist*, initiated a deal with Charisma Records. Following two well-received singles, 'I'm On Fire' and 'Intercontinental', 1982 saw the release of *Afraid Of Mice*, with one-time David Bowie producer Tony Visconti at the controls. Described as 'power-pop with an edge', its mixture of punchy guitars, angry lyrics and simple classic pop achieved considerable critical acclaim. Even so, commercial success was

to prove much more elusive. After one last single, 'At The Club', and a give-away flexi-disc, 'Transparents', they parted company with Charisma. Although they continued to play live under various names, including the Lumberjack Ballet, Afraid Of Mice's final vinyl appearances were the live *Official Bootleg* in 1983 and a solitary track, 'Don't Take Your Love Away', on the *Jobs For The Boys* compilation in 1985. The Mice were finally laid to rest in 1986 when Phil Jones teamed up with Alex McKechnie (ex-Passage; Modern Eon) in Two's A Crowd, who eventually became Up And Running.

●ALBUMS: *Afraid Of Mice* (Charisma 1982)★★★, *Afraid Of Mice - The Official Bootleg* (Own Label 1983)★★.

AFRIKA BAMBAATAA

b. Afrika Bambaataa Aasim, 4 October 1960, New York, USA. His name taken from that of a nineteenth-century Zulu chief, translating as 'Chief Affection', Bambaataa was the founding father of New York's Zulu Nation. The name was inspired by the film *Zulu*, starring Michael Caine, and the code of honour and bravery of its black participants. A loose community of mainly black street kids, Zulu Nation and its head, more than any other element, helped transform the gangs of the late 70s into the hip hop crews of the early 80s. Bambaataa himself had been a member of the notorious Black Spades, among other sects, and from 1977-85 he had a social importance to match his towering MC and DJ profiles, organising breakdance competitions and musical events promoting the ethos of peace and racial tolerance. By 1980 he was the pre-eminent hip hop DJ in New York, commanding massive followings and eclipsing even Grandmaster Flash in popularity. He made his recording debut the same year, producing two versions of 'Zulu Nation Throwdown' for two rap groups associated with the Zulu Nation - Cosmic Force and Soul Sonic Force. Signing to the independent label Tommy Boy Records, he made his first own-name release in 1982, as Afrika Bambaataa And The Jazzy Five, with 'Jazzy Sensation' (based on Gwen Guthrie's 'Funky Sensation'). It was followed by his seminal 'Planet Rock', a wholly synthesized record, this time based on Kraftwerk's 'Trans-Europe Express'. In one leap it took hip hop music far beyond its existing street rhyme and percussion break format. The contribution of Arthur Baker and John Robie in programming its beats is also highly significant, for in turn they gave birth to the 'electro' rap movement that dominated the mid-80s. 'Planet Rock'

also gave its name to the record label Bambaataa established in the Bronx. 'Looking For The Perfect Beat' continued the marriage of raw lyrics and synthesized electro-boogie, and was another major milestone for the genre. The follow-up album, *Beware (The Funk Is Everywhere)*, even included a take on the MC5's 'Kick Out The Jams' (produced by Bill Laswell). Bambaataa also recorded an album as part of Shango, backed by Material members Laswell and Michael Beinhorn, in a party dance vein which accommodated a cover of Sly Stone's 'Thank You'. Never one to stay in one place for long, he went on to record two vastly different and unexpected singles - 'World Destruction' with ex-Sex Pistols vocalist John Lydon, and 'Unity' with the funk godfather, James Brown. He fell out of the limelight in the latter half of the 80s, as new generations of disc jockeys and rappers stepped forward with their own innovations and fresh beats. However, *The Light* included an enterprising cast (UB40, Nona Hendryx, Boy George, Bootsy Collins, Yellowman and George Clinton - the latter a huge early musical and visual influence on Bambaataa). *The Decade Of Darkness (1990-2000)* also went some way towards redressing the balance, including an update of James Brown's 'Say It Loud (I'm Black And I'm Proud)'. Bambaataa's influence on rap's development is pivotal, and is felt in many more subtle ways than, say, the direct sampling of his work on 90s crossover hits like 95 South's 'Whoot, There It Is' or Duice's 'Dazey Duks'.

●ALBUMS: with Zulu Nation *Zulu Nation* (1983)★★★, with Shango *Funk Theology* (Celluloid 1984)★★★, *Planet Rock - The Album* (Tommy Boy 1986)★★★★, *Beware (The Funk Is Everywhere)* (Tommy Boy 1986)★★ *The Light* (Capitol 1988)★★★, *The Decade Of Darkness (1990-2000)* (EMI 1991)★★★, *Hip Hop Funk Dance 2* (1992)★★.

AGENT STEEL

This heavy metal unit was formed in Los Angeles, California, USA, and had been around in various guises since the early 80s. The most popular line-up consisted of John Cyriis (vocals, ex-Abbatoir), Juan Garcia (guitar), Bernie Versye (guitar), Michael Zaputil (bass) and Chuck Profus (drums). Signing to Combat Records the band released their debut, *Operation Redeye*, in 1985, but it was the same year's *Skeptics Apocalypse* which was well-received by both music press and the public. However, the group ran into difficulty with both their record label and internal wrangles owing to Cyriis' reputed eccentricity. With label problems resolved, the band released an EP entitled *Mad*

Locust Rising and quickly followed this with their finest recording, the trash-fixated *Unstoppable Force*. However, they experienced further disruption when Cyriis decided he wanted to relocate the band to Florida. The rest of the group were less than delighted with the provisional change in locale and left (or rather stayed). Cyriis carried on with various musicians in the new location but could never quite match previous standards. Disillusioned, he dissolved the group in 1988 and, after a brief tenure alongside Profus in Pontius Prophet, has since quit the music business.

●ALBUMS: *Operation Redeye* (Combat 1985)★★, *Skeptic's Apocalypse* (Combat 1985)★★★, *Unstoppable Force* (Music For Nations 1987)★★★.
●VIDEOS: *Mad Locust Rising* (1989).

AIR SUPPLY

Formed around the partnership of Russell Hitchcock (b. 15 June 1949, Melbourne, Australia; vocals) and Graham Russell (b. 1 June 1950, Sherwood, Nottingham, England; guitar/vocals), soft-rockers Air Supply turned out a solid string of seven US Top 5 singles between 1980-82. The duo first came together in Sydney, Australia, during 1976 while performing in a production of the Tim Rice and Andrew Lloyd Webber musical *Jesus Christ Superstar*. Forming a sextet with Frank Esler-Smith (b. 5 June 1948, London, England; keyboards), Ralph Cooper (b. 6 April 1951, Coffs Harbour, Australia; drums), David Green (b. 30 October 1949, Melbourne, Australia; bass) and David Moyse (b. 5 November 1957, Adelaide, Australia; lead guitar), they were only successful locally, notably with the hit single 'Love And Other Bruises', until 1977 when they left for a North American tour supporting Rod Stewart. By this time the group was augmented by an additional guitarist, Rex Goh (b. 5 May 1951, Singapore). Signing with Arista Records in 1980, the group's first album included the hit title track 'Lost In Love' and successful singles 'All Out Of Love' (their only substantial UK success) and 'Every Woman In The World'. The Top 10 *The One That You Love* yielded three more major hit singles including the number 1 title track. In 1983 they achieved their second US number 2 with 'Making Love Out Of Nothing At All'. Towards the end of the decade the popularity of Air Supply declined, although they continued to tour regularly. They disbanded in 1988 but reformed again in 1991.

●ALBUMS: *Lost In Love* (Arista 1980)★★, *The One That You Love* (Arista 1981)★★★, *Now And Forever* (Arista 1982)★★, *Air Supply* (Arista 1985)★★, *Hearts In Motion* (Arista 1986)★★, *The Christmas Album* (1987)★★, *The Earth Is ...* (1991)★★, *The Vanishing Race* (1993)★★.
●COMPILATIONS: *Making Love ... The Best Of Air Supply* (Arista 1983)★★★, *Greatest Hits* (Arista 1983)★★★.

AKKERMAN, JAN

b. 24 December 1946, Amsterdam, The Netherlands. When Akkerman surfaced in 1973 as Best Guitarist in a *Melody Maker* poll, it was the public zenith of a professional career that started in Amsterdam in 1958 as one of Johnny And The Cellar Rockers Their drummer, Pierre Van Der Linden, later played with Akkerman in the Hunters - who owed much to the Shadows artistically - during the guitarist's five years of study at the city's Music Lyceum, from which he graduated with a catholic taste that embraced mainstream pop, Latin, medieval and the music of Frank Zappa among leading preferences. With Van Der Linden, Bert Ruiter (bass) and Kaz Lux (vocals) Akkerman formed Brainbox, a hard rock outfit whose only album (featuring the single 'Down Man') was issued on Parlophone Records in 1969. For Akkerman's keen participation in rehearsals with the nascent Focus, Brainbox dismissed him. Then in 1971, after the release of the Focus album *In And Out Of Focus*, Akkerman asked Van Der Linden to join him in a new group for which it made sense to retain the name Focus, having recruited Thijs Van Leer and Cyril Havermans from that band. Among the major factors in the band's success over the next few years were Akkerman's powers of improvisation on his trademark Les Paul guitar and his skill as an arranger. On top of this his solo albums were widely acclaimed, although the first, *Profile*, was simply an accumulation of tracks taped during the interval between Brainbox and Focus. Orchestrated by Columbia University professor of music, George Flynn, *Tabernakel* was a more ambitious affair, containing Akkerman's developing dexterity on the lute, and guest appearances by Tim Bogert and Carmine Appice.

Suddenly unhappy with their overall musical drift and tired of the treadmill of the road, Akkerman left Focus in March 1976 to begin sessions with Lux for what became *Eli*. Several more jazz fusion collections followed including the lushly orchestrated *Arunjuez* and a 1979 live set. During the 80s, many Akkerman albums reached only Dutch shops until re-released by Charly Records for the UK market. Although his periodic reunions with Focus have attracted most attention, he also recorded the albums *The Talisman* (1988) and *To Oz And Back* (1989) on President Records as part of Forcefield with Ray Fenwick (ex-Spencer Davis Group) and Cozy Powell, before retracing a solo path with *The Noise Of Art* for Miles Copeland's IRS label.

●ALBUMS: *Talent For Sale* (Imperial 1968)★★★, *Guitar For Sale* reissue of debut (EMI International 1972)★★★, *Profile* (Harvest 1973)★★★, *Tabernakel* (Atlantic 1974)★★★★, with Kaz Lux *Eli* (Atlantic 1977)★★★, *Jan Akkerman* (Atlantic 1978)★★★, *Arunjuez* (Columbia 1978)★★★, *Live* (Atlantic 1979)★★★, *3* (Atlantic 1980)★★★, *It Could Happen To You* (Charly 1985)★★★, *Can't Stand Noise* (Charly 1986)★★★, *The Noise Of Art* (IRS 1990)★★★.

●COMPILATIONS: *A Phenomenon* (Bovena Negram 1979)★★★, *Best Of* (1980)★★★, *Complete Guitarist* (Charly 1985)★★★, *Pleasure Point* (Charly 1987)★★★.

ALABAMA

One of the biggest US country rock acts of the 80s, the band's origins can be traced back to Fort Payne, Alabama. They were originally formed in 1969 as Wild Country by cousins Jeff Cook (b. 27 August 1949, Fort Payne, Alabama, USA; vocals/guitar), Randy Owen (b. 13 December 1949, Fort Payne, Alabama, USA; vocals/guitar), and Teddy Gentry (b. 22 January 1952, Fort Payne, Alabama, USA; bass/vocals). Their original drummer was the only non-relation and was soon rejected. After several misfires at the start of their career their big break-through came with a residency at a club in Myrtle Beach, South Carolina, in 1973. Soon afterwards they turned professional. They recorded for several small labels in the 70s before they changed their name to Alabama in 1977. Their career blossomed with a sequence of hits in the country charts which followed the success of 'I Want To Be With You'. At this point they sought out a full-time drummer to complete their sound and recruited Mark Herndon (b. 11 May 1955, Springfield, Massachusetts, USA). After 'My Home's In Alabama' reached the US Top 20 they signed to RCA Records in 1980 and found immediate success. A rich vein of country hits followed with 'Tennessee River' and 'Feels So Right'. Later singles like 'Love In The First Degree' also acquired crossover pop success. Of their five platinum albums during the 80s, the most successful was *40 Hour Week* which reached US number 10. In 1986 they worked with Lionel Richie, but their recent work has seen them return to the C&W charts almost exclusively. Despite an increasingly formu-

laic sound, they remain a major live attraction, although their commercial profile has suffered from the rival attractions of younger bands. However, their environmental anthem 'Pass It On Down' in 1990 confirmed that they are still capable of surprising their audience. In 1995 the group celebrated its 15th anniversary, in which time it could lay claim to many outstanding achievements including sales of over 50 million albums, and the Academy Of Country Music's Artist Of The Decade Award for their work in the 80s. Singer Randy Owen described their enduring appeal thus: 'What you see is what you get with Alabama. We're basically a blue-collar working band. We work really hard at what we do, and we work for our fans and listen to them.' By 1995 they had amassed 40 number 1s, equalling Conway Twitty's remarkable feat.

●ALBUMS: *Wild Country* (LSI 1977)★★★, *Deuces Wild* (LSI 1978)★★★, *My Home's In Alabama* (RCA 1980)★★★, *Feels So Right* (RCA 1981)★★★, *Mountain Music* (RCA 1982)★★★, *The Closer You Get* (RCA 1983)★★★, *Roll On* (RCA 1984)★★★, *Alabama Christmas* (RCA 1985)★★, *40 Hour Week* (RCA 1985)★★★, *The Touch* (RCA 1986)★★★, *Just Us* (RCA 1987)★★★, *Alabama Live* (RCA 1988)★★, *Southern Star* (RCA 1989)★★★, *Pass It On Down* (RCA 1990)★★★, *American Pride* (RCA 1992)★★★, *Cheap Seats* (1993)★★★, *In Pictures* (RCA 1995)★★★, *Christmas Volume II* (RCA 1996)★★.

●COMPILATIONS: *Wild Country* (LSI 1981)★★★, *Greatest Hits* (RCA 1986)★★★★, *Greatest Hits Volume 2* (RCA 1991)★★★, *Super Hits* (RCA 1996)★★★.

ALARM

Formed in Rhyl, Wales, during 1981, this energetic pop group comprised Mike Peters (b. 25 February 1959; vocals/guitar), David Sharp (b. 28 January 1959; vocals/guitar), Eddie MacDonald (b. 1 November 1959; bass) and Nigel Twist (b. 18 July 1958; drums). Originally known as Seventeen, they changed their name after recording a self-penned song titled 'Alarm Alarm'. Peters was anxious to steer the group in the direction of U2, whose commitment and dedication appealed to his sense of rock as an expression of passion. However, by the time of the Alarm's first UK hit, '68 Guns', their style and imagery most closely recalled punk rockers the Clash. The declamatory verve continued on 'Where Were You Hiding When The Storm Broke' and the traditional rock influence was emphasized in their long spiked hair, skin tight leather trousers and ostentatious belts. Behind the high energy, however, there was a lighter touch which was eloquently evinced on their reading of Pete Seeger's 'The Bells Of Rhymney', which they performed in aid of the coal miners' strike in 1984. The original U2 comparisons began to make more sense on the fourth album, *Electric Folklore Live*, which displayed the power of their in-concert performance. *Change* (produced by Tony Visconti) saw them investigating their Celtic origins with the assistance of members from the Welsh Symphony Orchestra. It was also issued in a Welsh language version. The much-maligned Mike Peters embarked on a solo career in the 90s following the dissolution of the band.

●ALBUMS: *Declaration* (IRS 1984)★★★, *Strength* (IRS 1985)★★★, *Eye Of The Hurricane* (IRS 1987)★★★, *Electric Folklore Live* mini-album (IRS 1988)★★★, *Change* (IRS 1989)★★, *Raw* (IRS 1991)★★.
●COMPILATIONS: *Standards* (IRS 1990)★★★.
●VIDEOS: *Spirit Of '86* (1986), *Change* (1990).
●FURTHER READING: *The Alarm*, Rick Taylor.

ALIEN SEX FIEND

Essentially an alias for the eccentric Nick Wade, Alien Sex Fiend emerged as part of the early 80s gothic punk movement from the UK, centred around London's Batcave venue. Wade previously served time with obscure acts such as the Earwigs and Mr. And Mrs. Demeanour before releasing two singles as Demon Preacher. This was shortened to the Demons for a third single, but like its predecessors it vanished without trace. After various short-lived projects, Wade eventually stumbled upon his long-term guise, Alien Sex Fiend, in 1982, aided by David James (guitar), partner Christine Wade (synthesizer) and Johnny 'Ha Ha' Freshwater (drums). On the strength of a nine-track demo tape, the band played the Batcave at the end of the year. Live tracks were added to the tape and released as the cassette-only release, *The Lewd, The Mad, The Ugly And Old Nik*, before signing with Cherry Red Records subsidary, Anagram. Wade, whose stage image of ghoulish thick white pancake make-up revealed his strongest influence, Alice Cooper, further essayed that debt with 'Ignore The Machine' (1983). *Who's Been Sleeping In My Brain*, was followed by 'Lips Can't Go' and in 1984 by 'R.I.P.'/'New Christian Music', 'Dead And Buried' and 'E.S.T. (Trip To The Moon)', to coincide with *Acid Bath*. Such was the album's reception in Japan that the group embarked on a tour there. *Liquid Head In Tokyo* celebrated the event, but was the last output for Johnny Ha Ha. As a three-piece, the band came up with 'I'm Doin' Time In A Maximum Security Twilight Home' (1985), accompanied by *Maximum Security*. *IT - The Album*, in time for a tour supporting Alice Cooper. A cover of Red Crayola's late 60s classic, 'Hurricane Fighter Plane', surfaced in early 1987, followed by 'The Impossible Mission'. A retrospective, *All Our Yesterdays*, coincided with Yaxi Highriser's departure. Under the guise of the Dynamic Duo, Wade then issued 'Where Are Batman And Robin?' (on the Riddler label!). 'Bun Ho' was the next Alien Sex Fiend single, continuing a more open-minded musical policy. *Another Planet* confirmed this, while 'Haunted House' saw the adoption of out-and-out dance techniques. After a tour (with Rat Fink Junior and Doc Milton) was captured on the double album *Too Much Acid?*, the band returned with 'Now I'm Being Zombified' in September 1990. That same month, Alien Sex Fiend released the experimental *Curse* and bounced back three years later with *The Altered States Of America*.

●ALBUMS: *Who's Been Sleeping In My Brain* (Anagram 1983)★★, *Acid Bath* (Anagram 1984)★★★, *Liquid Head In Tokyo - Live* (Anagram 1985)★★★, *Maximum Security* (Anagram 1985)★★★, *IT - The Album* (Anagram 1986)★★★, *Here Cum Germs* (Anagram 1987)★★★, *Too Much Acid?* (Anagram 1989)★★, *Curse* (Anagram 1990)★★★, *The Altered States Of America* (Anagram 1993)★★★, *Inferno* (Anagram 1995)★★★.
●COMPILATIONS: *All Our Yesterdays* (Anagram 1988)★★★.
●VIDEOS: *A Purple Glistener* (1984), *Edit* (1987), *Overdose* (1988), *Liquid Head In Tokyo* (1991), *Re-Animated - The Promo Collection* (Visionary 1994).

ALL ABOUT EVE

Originally called the Swarm, All About Eve emerged on the late 80s UK 'Gothic' scene. The group's nucleus of erstwhile rock journalist and Gene Loves Jezebel bass player Julianne Regan (b. 1964, England; vocals), along with Tim Bricheno (guitar; ex-Aemotti Crii), provided much of the band's song material. After various early personnel changes, the rhythm section was stabilized with Andy Cousin (bass; also ex-Aemotti Crii) and Mark Price (drums). Given encouragement by rising stars the Mission (for whom Regan had in the past sung backing vocals), All About Eve developed a solid following and with a backdrop of hippy mysticism and imagery, along with Regan's predilection for white-witchcraft and Tarot cards, provided a taste of the exotic with a mixture of goth-rock and 70s folk. Early singles 'Our Summer' and 'Flowers In Our Hair' achieved great success in the UK independent charts and after signing to Mercury Records, their modest showings in the national charts finally gave them a Top 10 hit in July 1988 with 'Martha's Harbour'. Both albums reached the UK Top 10, confirming their aspirations to be among the frontrunners in British rock in the late 80s. However, this ambition was dealt a blow in 1990 when a rift between the group and guitarist Bricheno resulted in his departure to join the Sisters Of Mercy. The recruitment of Church guitarist Marty Willson-Piper on a part-time basis revitalized the group's drive, although the subsequent album, *Touched By Jesus*, only managed a brief visit to the UK Top 20, and indications that the group had undergone a born-again transformation have yet to be vindicated. A stormy dispute with their distributor, Phonogram Records, over the company's alleged priority for chart single success saw All About Eve leave the label in late 1991 and shortly afterwards sign to MCA Records.

●ALBUMS: *All About Eve* (Mercury 1987)★★★, *Scarlet And Other Stories* (Mercury 1989)★★★, *Touched By Jesus* (Vertigo 1991)★★, *Ultraviolet* (MCA 1992)★★.

●COMPILATIONS: *Winter Words, Hits And Rarities* (MCA 1992)★★★.

●VIDEOS: *Martha's Harbour* (1988), *What Kind Of Fool* (1989), *Evergreen* (1989).

ALLEN, GERI

b. 12 June 1957, Pontiac, Michigan, USA. Pianist Allen grew up in Detroit, steeped in the city's strong bebop and black pop traditions (and one early gig was playing with Mary Wilson and the Supremes) though Eric Dolphy, Herbie Nichols and Thelonious Monk were also major influences. She studied music at Washington's Howard University and at the University of Pittsburgh (with Nathan Davis) and later with Roscoe Mitchell. Moving to New York in the early 80s she played with numerous contemporary jazz musicians, including James Newton and Lester Bowie, and recorded her debut *The Printmakers* in 1984 with a trio that featured Andrew Cyrille. She also became involved with the M-BASE and Black Rock Coalition organizations and the former's Steve Coleman and Robin Eubanks played on her *Open On All Sides In The Middle*. Later in the 80s she was a regular member of Oliver Lake's groups (*Plug It, Gallery, Impala, Otherside*) and toured and recorded with several leaders, including Dewey Redman

(*Living On The Edge*), Frank Lowe (*Decision In Paradise*), Greg Osby (*Mindgames*) and Charlie Haden's Liberation Music Orchestra. With Haden and Paul Motian she formed an acoustic trio that has become celebrated for its intimate versions of modern mainstream jazz; and she also guested on Motian's own *Monk In Motian* and Betty Carter's *Droppin' Things*. An acutely sensitive player with a lovely touch, in the early 90s Allen signed to Blue Note Records.

●ALBUMS: *The Printmakers* (Minor Music 1984)★★★, *Homegrown* (Minor Music 1985)★★★★, *Open On All Sides In The Middle* (Impetus 1987)★★★, with Charlie Haden, Paul Motian *Etudes* (Soul Notes 1988)★★★, with Haden, Motian *In The Year Of The Dragon* (JMT 1989)★★★, with Haden, Motian *Segments* (DIW 1989)★★★, *Twylight* (Impetus 1989)★★★, with Haden, Motian *Live At The Village Vanguard* (DIW 1991)★★★, *The Nurturer* (Blue Note 1991)★★★, *Maroons* (Blue Note 1993)★★★.

ALLISON, LUTHER

b. 17 August 1939, Mayflower, Arkansas, USA. In his youth guitarist Allison sang with a family gospel group and moved to Chicago in 1951. Around 1957 he formed his own band to work on the west side. After a year the group disbanded and Allison went on to work with Jimmy Dawkins, Magic Sam, Freddie King and others until the mid-60s. In March 1967 he recorded a session for Bill Lindemann, later issued by the collector label Delmark. He toured California, recording there as accompanist to Sunnyland Slim and Shakey Jake Harris. He made his first album under his own name in 1969 and was one of the major successes of the Ann Arbor festivals of 1969 and 1970. In the early 70s he recorded for Motown Records' subsidiary label Gordy and since the late 70s he has spent much of his time in France, where he has a large and faithful following. He has since recorded for many labels, usually adequate live albums or studio sessions comprising funk or Jimi Hendrix and Rolling Stones-influenced rock. However, when Allison remembers his roots, he is still an incredibly exciting blues guitarist.

●ALBUMS: *Love Me Mama* (Delmark 1969)★★★, *Bad News Is Coming* (Motown 1973)★★★, *Luther's Blues* (Motown 1974)★★★, *Night Life* (Motown 1976)★★★, *Love Me Papa* (Black & Blue 1977)★★★, *Live In Paris* (Free Bird 1979)★★★, *Live* (Blue Silver 1979)★★★, *Gonna Be A Live One In Here Tonight* (Rumble 1979)★★★, *Time* (Paris Album 1980)★★★, *South Side Safari* (1982)★★★,

Lets Have A Natural Ball (1984)★★★, Serious (Blind Pig 1984)★★★, Here I Come (Encore 1985)★★★, Powerwire Blues (1986)★★★, Rich Man (Entente 1987)★★★, Life Is A Bitch (Encore 1988)★★, Love Me Mama (1988)★★★, Let's Try It Again - Live '89 (Teldec 1989)★★, More From Berlin (Melodie 1991)★★, Hand Me Down My Moonshine (In-Akustik 1992)★★, Sweet Home Chicago (1993)★★★, Soul Fixin' Man (Alligator 1994)★★★, Bad Love (Ruf 1994)★★★, Blue Streak (Ruf 1995)★★★, Reckless (Ruf 1997)★★★, Live In Montreux 1976-1994 (Ruf 1997)★★★★.

ALMOND, MARC

b. Peter Marc Almond, 9 July 1956, Southport, Lancashire, England. Following the demise of the hit group Soft Cell and their adventurous offshoots Marc And The Mambas and Marc And The Willing Sinners, Almond embarked on a solo career. His first such venture was Vermin In Ermine which barely consolidated his reputation and proved his last album for Phonogram Records. Stories Of Johnny, released on Some Bizzare Records through Virgin Records, was superior and displayed Almond's undoubted power as a torch singer. Prior to the album's release, he had charted in a camp disco-inspired duet with Bronski Beat titled 'I Feel Love (Medley)'. The single combined two Donna Summer hits ('I Feel Love' and 'Love To Love You Baby') with snatches of John Leyton's 'Johnny Remember Me', all sung in high register by fellow vocalist Jimmy Somerville. The controversial Mother Fist And Her Five Daughters did little to enhance his career which seemed commercially in the descendent by the time of the Singles compilation. Another change of licensed label, this time to Parlophone Records, saw the release of 'Tears Run Rings' and Almond's old commercial sense was emphasized by the opportune revival of 'Something's Gotten Hold Of My Heart' with Gene Pitney. This melodramatic single was sufficient to provide both artists with their first number 1 hits as soloists. Almond returned in 1990 with a cover album of Jacques Brel songs and Enchanted which featured the singer's usual flamboyant style complemented by flourishes of flamenco guitar and violin and a solid production. In 1992 Almond revived the David McWilliams song 'The Days Of Pearly Spencer'. He returned to the cold electronic sounds of the 80s with Fantastic Star in early 1996. That year he ended a fifteen year contract with 'Stevo' as his manager.
●ALBUMS: Vermin In Ermine (Some Bizzare 1984)★★, Stories Of Johnny (Some Bizzare 1985)★★★, A Woman's Story: A Compilation (Some Bizzare 1986)★★, Mother Fist And Her Five Daughters (Some Bizzare 1987)★★, The Stars We Are (Parlophone 1988)★★★, Marc Sings Jacques (Some Bizzare 1989)★★★, Enchanted (Parlophone 1990)★★★, Tenement Sympony (Warners 1991)★★, Twelve Years Of Tears (Some Bizzare 1993)★★★, Absinthe: The French Album (Some Bizzare 1994)★★★, Fantastic Star (Mercury 1995)★★★.
●COMPILATIONS: Singles 1984-1987 (Virgin 1987)★★★, Best Of (1991)★★★, A Virgin's Tale Vols. 1 & 2 (Virgin 1992)★★★.
●VIDEOS: Video's: 1984 - 1987 (1987), Marc Almond (1988), Live In Concert (Windsong 1993).
●FURTHER READING: The Last Star: A Biography Of Marc Almond, Jeremy Reed.

ALTAN

This Irish traditional group, in the mould of De Danann, has achieved popularity on its own merits. Their name was taken from Loch Altan (near Gweedore). The line-up of Frankie Kennedy (b. 30 September 1955, Belfast, Northern Ireland, d. 19 September 1994, Belfast, Northern Ireland; flute), Mairéad Ni Mhaonaigh (b. 26 July 1959, Donegal, Eire; vocals/fiddle), Ciarán Curran (b. 14 June 1955, Enniskillen, Co. Fermanagh, Northern Ireland; bouzouki), Dáithí Sproule (b. 23 May 1950, Co. Derry, Northern Ireland; guitar/vocals), and Ciarán Tourish (b. 27 May 1967, Buncrana, Co. Donegal, Eire; fiddle) has built a strong following both in Britain, and in the USA, where they first toured in 1983. The group was formed in 1987, after the release of Altan. At that point the group was ostensibly Frankie and Mairéad, who were married in 1981, but the others were playing on the recording and a more permanent arrangement was made. Their repertoire comes largely from Co. Donegal, and due to the area's historical links with Scotland, the music has absorbed influences from both Irish and Scottish sources. Two other members of the group, who appear occasionally, are Paul O'Shaughnessy (b. 9 June 1961, Dublin, Eire; fiddle) and Mark Kelly (b. 15 March 1961, Dublin, Eire; guitar). Altan now regularly tour the USA and Europe, and have made frequent festival appearances. In 1996 the band signed with Virgin and issued an excellent album, Blackwater, even without the participation of Frankie Kennedy.
●ALBUMS: Ceol Aduaidh (Gael Oinn 1983)★★★, Altan (Green Linnet 1987)★★★, Horse With A Heart (Green Linnet 1989)★★★, The Red Crow (Green Linnet 1990)★★★, Harvest Storm (Green Linnet 1992)★★★, Island Angel (Green Linnet

1993)★★★, *Blackwater* (Virgin 1996)★★★.
●COMPILATIONS: *The First Ten Years: 1986-1995* (Green Linnet 1995)★★★.

ALTERED IMAGES

Formed in 1979, this Glasgow pop ensemble featured Clare Grogan (vocals), Johnny McElhone (guitar), Tony McDaid (bass) and Michael 'Tich' Anderson (drums). Even before their recorded debut, Grogan found herself cast in a film, *Gregory's Girl,* by director Bill Forsyth. In 1980 Altered Images toured with Siouxsie And The Banshees and subsequently employed the services of their bassist, Steve Severin, as producer. Another champion of their work was the influential UK disc jockey, John Peel. Their BBC radio sessions resulted in the offer of a major recording contract by Epic Records, and two unsuccessful singles followed; the early 80s indie classic 'Dead Pop Stars' and 'A Day's Wait'. With the addition of guitarist Jim McInven, the group completed their debut, *Happy Birthday*, in 1981. The infectious title track, produced by Martin Rushent, soared to number 2 in the UK charts, establishing the elfin Grogan as a punkish Shirley Temple. 'I Could Be Happy' and 'See Those Eyes' were also hits, but the group's second album, *Pinky Blue*, was not well received by the critics. With 1983's *Bite*, Grogan took on a more sophisticated, adult image, lost Tich and McInven, gained Stephen Lironi (guitar/drums) and found new producers, Tony Visconti and Mike Chapman. The experiment brought another Top 10 hit, 'Don't Talk To Me About Love'. Following a brief tour with the addition of David Wilde (drums) and Jim Prime (keyboards) the group disbanded. Grogan pursued an acting career (notably in television sitcom *Red Dwarf*), recorded a solo album, *Love Bomb*, and later reappeared fronting a new group, Universal Love School. Meanwhile, Altered Images' guitarist Johnny McElhone moved on to Hipsway and Texas.
●ALBUMS: *Happy Birthday* (Epic 1981)★★★, *Pinky Blue* (Epic 1982)★★, *Bite* (Epic 1983)★★.
●COMPILATIONS: *Collected Images* (Epic 1984)★★★, *The Best Of Altered Images* (Receiver 1992)★★★, *Reflected Images: The Best Of ...* (Epic 1996)★★★.

AMAZULU

This predominantly female ska band earned themselves a string of UK hit singles in the mid-80s. They comprised Annie Ruddock (b. Ann-Marie Teresa Antoinette Ruddock, 2 July 1961; lead vocals), Claire Kenny (bass), Lesley Beach (b. 30 September 1954; saxophone), Sharon Bailey (b. 22 November 1957; percussion) and Margo Sagov (guitar), plus the lone male of the group, Nardo Bailey (drums). They made their initial impact on the lower regions of the UK single charts with 'Cairo', but achieved greater success in July 1985 with 'Excitable', which reached the UK Top 20. This success was followed by other hits, including 'Don't You Just Know It', 'Too Good To Be Forgotten' and 'Montego Bay'. Their album was released on Island Records in 1988. Claire Kenny later joined the initial line-up of Coming Up Roses and subsequently joined Shakespears Sister.
●ALBUMS: *Amazulu* (Island 1988)★★★, *Only Love* (1993)★★.

AMERICAN MUSIC CLUB

One of their country's most undervalued groups, San Francisco's American Music Club have taken a similar path to Australia's Go-Betweens in reaping rich harvests of critical acclaim not yet reflected in their sales figures. The group's mastermind and musical springboard is Mark Eitzel (b. 30 January 1959, Walnut Creek, San Francisco, California, USA; vocals/guitar), a lyricist of rare scope. The name of his publishing company, I Failed In Life Music, is a good indicator as to Eitzel's world view: 'I see humanity, including myself, as basically a bunch of sheep or ants. We're machines that occasionally do something better than machines.' The rest of American Music Club is Danny Pearson (b. 31 May 1959, Walnut Creek, San Francisco, California, USA; bass), Tim Mooney (b. 6 October 1958, Las Vegas, Nevada, USA; drums), Vudi (b. Mark Pankler, 22 September 1952, Chicago, Illinois, USA; guitar) and occasionally Bruce Kaphan (b. 7 Janaury 1955, San Francisco, California, USA; steel guitar). When he was seven Eitzel's family moved to Okinawa, Taiwan, before settling in Southampton, England. He wrote his first songs aged 14, and was 17 when he saw the new punk bands. Two years later he moved to Ohio with his family. There he put together Naked Skinnies, who emigrated to San Francisco in 1981. It was during their show at the San Francisco punk venue, the Mabuhay Gardens, that Vudi walked in and saw them. From his earliest appearances Eitzel's on-stage demeanour rivalled the extravagances of Iggy Pop's. In the early days he was also a fractious heavy drinker, until the day AMC signed to a major label after several acclaimed independent albums. Before this he had quit the band twice, once after the tour to support *Engine*, and once after *Everclear*. He also temporarily fronted Toiling Midgets. Following *Everclear*, in 1991, *Rolling Stone* magazine elected Eitzel their Songwriter Of The Year, but as he conceded: 'Yes, I'm songwriter of the year for 1991; a month later I'm still songwriter of the year, and still no-one comes to see us play!' *Mercury* was the band's debut for a major record label, although song titles such as 'What Godzilla Said To God When His Name Wasn't Found In The Book Of Life' illustrated that Eitzel's peculiar lyrical scenarios were still intact. The album was primarily written while Eitzel was living in the decidedly down-at-heel Mission District of San Francisco. The critical acclaim customarily heaped on the group could be heard for 1994's *San Francisco*, and *Melody Maker* journalist Andrew Mueller grew exasperated when reviewing one of the singles drawn from it, 'Can You Help Me?' - 'We're obviously not explaining ourselves tremendously well . . . Every album they have ever made we have reviewed with prose in the most opulent hues of purple . . . We have, in short, shouted ourselves hoarse from the very rooftops in this band's name, and still nobody who doesn't work here owns any of their records'. Eitzel left the band for a solo career in 1995.

●ALBUMS: *The Restless Stranger* (Grifter 1986)★★★, *Engine* (Grifter/Frontier 1986)★★★, *California* (Grifter/Frontier 1988)★★★, *United Kingdom* (Demon 1990)★★★, *Everclear* (Alias 1991)★★★, *Mercury* (Warners/Reprise 1993)★★★★, *San Francisco* (Warners/Reprise 1994)★★★.

ANASTASIA SCREAMED

Anastasia Screamed were formed in 1987 by Christopher Burdett (b. 8 March 1968, Boston, Massachusetts, USA; drums), Christopher Cugini (b. 23 November 1966, Malden, Massachusetts, USA; guitar), Andy Jagolinzer (b. 11 June 1969, Framingham, Massachusetts, USA; vocals) and Scott Lerner (b. 3 March 1966, Boston, Massachusetts, USA), the last being the first of a number of short-term bass players the band had. Chick Graning (b. 28 October 1966, Vancouver, Canada) replaced Jagolinzer before the end of the year, and added an extra touch of hysteria to a flowing, sub-hardcore guitar sound which hardly needed to be destabilized any further. Following two independent singles which were often played on US college radio, in 1989 the band solved their bass playing problems by bringing in Charlie Bock (b. 26 January 1965, Nashville, Tennessee, USA). That year they also relocated from Boston to Nashville. A year later Anastasia Screamed signed

to the UK's Fire Records and started to earn applause from Europe, broadening their horizons with a topsy-turvy brand of rock 'n' roll, touring extensively with Throwing Muses. Graning became romantically attached to the Throwing Muses' Tanya Donelly. However, soon afterwards his band collapsed, which many commentators lamented as an awful waste of talent. Graning emerged from the wreckage with his capacity to write vivid, often disturbing lyrics intact. By the mid-90s he had formed a new band, Scarce, based in Rhode Island New York, also featuring Joyce Raskin. However, their momentum too was disrupted when after a support tour with Hole, Graning suffered a near-fatal brain aneurysm in 1995.

●ALBUMS: *Laughing Down The Limehouse* (Fire 1990)★★★, *Moontime* (Fire 1991)★★★.

ANDERSON, LAURIE

b. Laura Phillips Anderson, 5 June 1950, Chicago, Illinois, USA. A product of New York's *avant garde* art scene, Laurie Anderson eschewed her initial work as a sculptor in favour of performing. *The Life And Times Of Josef Stalin*, premiered at Brooklyn's Academy of Music in 1973, was a 12-hour epic containing many of the audio-visual elements the artist brought to her subsequent canon. Anderson's debut, *Big Science*, included the eight-minute vocoder-laden 'O Superman', which had become a cult hit in Europe in 1981 on the 1/10 label and subsequently hit number 2 in the UK chart after Warner Brothers Records picked it up. The song's looped, repeated pattern combined with the singer's part-spoken intonation created a hypnotic charm. *Mr. Heartbreak*, arguably Anderson's most accessible release, featured contributions from Peter Gabriel and writer William Burroughs, while her next release, a sprawling five-album set, *United States*, chronicled an ambitious, seven-hour show. *Home Of The Brave* resumed the less radical path of her second album and was co-produced by former Chic guitarist Nile Rodgers. The guests on her 1994 album, *Bright Red*, meanwhile, included Lou Reed, Adrian Belew and ex-Fixx guitarist Jamie West-Oram, with production expertise leant by Gabriel. Although operating at rock's outer, experimental fringes, Laurie Anderson nonetheless remains an influential and respected figure.

●ALBUMS: *Big Science* (Warners 1982)★★★★, *Mr. Heartbreak* (Warners 1984)★★★, *United States* (Warners 1985)★★, *Home Of The Brave* (Warners 1986)★★★, *Strange Angels* (Warners 1989)★★★, *Bright Red* (Warners 1994)★★★, *The Ugly One With*

The Jewels And Other Stories (Warners 1995)★★★.
●VIDEOS: *Home Of The Brave* (Warners 1991).

ANDY, HORACE
b. Horace Hinds, 1951, Kingston, Jamaica, West Indies. This artist was affectionately renamed Andy as a tribute to Bob Andy, in respect of their mutual songwriting abilities, by Coxsone Dodd. Andy, also known as Sleepy, has always been a favoured vocalist among reggae fans and his eerie, haunting style has been imitated endlessly by scores of lesser talents over the years. It was his work with Dodd that would make his reputation. His career at Studio One began with the single 'Something On My Mind', and eventually resulted in the classic 'Skylarking', one of reggae's most popular songs. From the mid-70s onwards, after leaving Studio One, Andy has worked with many important reggae producers in Jamaica, America and England. In the process he has recorded literally hundreds of records, most of which are now only available on impossible-to-find 45s, although some of the highpoints of his work with Coxsone, Bunny Lee and Wackies are still available on the listed albums. In the late 70s Andy moved to his new home in Hartford, Connecticut. His influence on reggae music in general, and reggae singers in particular is incalculable, yet he remains a diffident figure amongst much brasher yet less talented reggae 'stars'.
●ALBUMS: *Skylarking* (Studio One 1972)★★★★, *You Are My Angel* (Trojan 1973)★★★, *In The Light* (Hungry Town 1977)★★★, *Dance Hall Style* (Wackies 1982)★★★, released in the UK as *Exclusively* (Solid Groove 1982)★★★, *Showcase* (Vista Sounds 1983)★★★, *Sings For You And I* (Striker Lee 1985)★★★, *Confusion* (Music Hawk 1985)★★★, with Patrick Andy *Clash Of The Andys* (Thunderbolt 1985)★★★, *Elementary* (Rough Trade 1985)★★★, *Big Bad Man* (Rockers Forever 1987)★★★, *Haul And Jack Up* (Live & Love 1987)★★★, *Fresh* (Island In The Sun 1988)★★★, *Shame And Scandal* (1988)★★★, *Everyday People* (Wackies 1988)★★★.
●COMPILATIONS: *Best Of Horace Andy* (Coxsone 1974)★★★, *Best Of Horace Andy* (Culture Press 1985)★★★, *Skylarking: The Best Of Horace Andy* (Melankolic 1996)★★★★.

ANGELIC UPSTARTS
This politically motivated hard-line punk quartet formed in 1977, in South Shields, England. They were the brainchild of Mensi (vocals), and strongly influenced by the Clash, Damned and Sex Pistols.

With Cowie, Warrington and Taylor completing the line-up, they signed to the independent Small Wonder label and released the underground classic 'Murder Of Liddle Towers' in 1979. The song condemned police brutality and identified strongly with the youth culture of the day. It led to a contract with Warner Brothers Records, which produced *Teenage Warning* and *We Gotta Get Out Of This Place* in 1979 and 1980, respectively. Both these albums are regarded by some within the punk community as classics, featuring provocative lyrics which ridiculed the politics of the British government of Margaret Thatcher. Characterized by Mensi's nasal snarl, the band suffered from regular outbreaks of violence at their live shows from National Front fascist supporters, who sought to counter the group's left-wing politics after initially misinterpreting their patriotic stance. As the 80s progressed, the band gradually saw their fan-base disappear. They had become entrenched in a musical style that was rapidly becoming outdated. The Angelic Upstarts continued to release material, but with declining success. The band ground to a halt in 1986, but re-formed for a brief period in 1988 and then once again in 1992, releasing *Bombed Out* on the Roadrunner label. In the 90s, Mensi has become a leading member of the Anti Fascist Action group.
●ALBUMS: *Teenage Warning* (Warners 1979)★★★, *We Gotta Get Out Of This Place* (Warners 1980)★★★, *2 Million Voices* (EMI 1981)★★, *Live* (EMI 1981)★★, *Still From The Heart* (EMI 1982)★★, *Reason Why?* (Anagram 1983)★★, *Last Tango In Moscow* (Picasso 1984)★★, *Live In Yugoslavia* (Picasso 1985)★★, *Power Of The Press* (Gas 1986)★★, *Bombed Out* (Roadrunner 1992)★★.
●COMPILATIONS: *Angel Dust (The Collected Highs 1978-1983)* (Anagram 1983)★★★, *Bootlegs And Rarities* (Dojo 1986)★★, *Blood On The Terraces* (Link 1987)★★, *Live And Loud* (Link 1988)★★, *Greatest Hits Live* (Streetlink 1992)★★.

ANGRY SAMOANS
Formed in August 1978, in Van Nuys, California, USA, the Angry Samoans were one of the original Los Angeles punk bands, along with Fear, Black Flag, Circle Jerks and X. The fact that they never achieved quite what those other bands did can be put down to a disappointingly curt discography. After numerous personnel changes, the most solid line-up consisted of core duo Mike Saunders (guitar/vocals) and Gregg Turner (guitar/vocals), plus Todd Homer (bass/vocals), Steve Drojensky (guitar) and Bill Vockeroth (drums). Leaning

toward the humorous side of punk, in the same way as the Ramones and Dickies, some of the Samoans' songs featured titles such as 'I'm A Pig', 'My Old Man's A Fatso', 'Attack Of The Mushroom People' and 'They Saved Hitler's Cock'. Following two EPs and one album for Bad Trip, they laid low for some time, before re-emerging in the late 80s via the auspices of Triple X Records.

●ALBUMS: *Back From Somoa* (Bad Trip 1982)★★, *STP Not LSD* (PVC 1988)★★, *Live At Rhino Records* (XXX 1990)★★.

●COMPILATIONS: *Return To Somoa* (Shakin' Street 1990)★★, *The Unboxed Set* (XXX 1995)★★★.

ANIMAL NIGHTLIFE

This early 80s UK pop/jazz group featured Andy Polaris (vocals), Steve 'Flid' Brown (guitar), Steve Shanley (bass), Billy Chapman (saxophone), Declan John Barclay (trumpet) and Mae (bongos). Their first single 'Nature Boy (Uptown)' reached the lower regions of the UK pop charts in 1983, but the following year's 'Mr. Solitaire' hit the Top 30, as did 1985's 'Love Is Just The Great Pretender'. Animal Nightlife's sparse output over a comparatively long period is probably due to their failure to capitilize on early media interest.

●ALBUMS: *Shangri-la* (Island 1985)★★★, *Lush Life* (Ten 1988)★★★.

ANTHRAX

This New York-based thrash metal outfit came to the fore in 1982 with a line-up comprising Scott 'Not' Ian (b. Scott Rosenfeld, 31 December 1963; rhythm guitar), Neil Turbin (vocals), Dan Spitz (lead guitar), Dan Lilker (bass; replaced by Frank Bello in 1983) and Charlie Benante (drums). Managed by Johnny Z, head of the independent Megaforce Records, the quintet released *Fistful Of Metal* in 1984. Despite its tasteless sleeve, the album garnered fair reviews and was a small but steady seller. For a time Ian, Lilker and Benante were also part of Stormtroopers Of Death (SOD, who were revived briefly in 1991), a hardcore band with a satirical outlook, and Lilker subsequently left Anthrax to pursue just such a direction with Nuclear Assault. Turbin also departed, with his initial replacement, Matt Fallon, being quickly succeeded by Joey Belladonna (b. 30 October 1960, Oswego, New York, USA). This line-up released the *Armed And Dangerous* EP in 1985, and their rising popularity led to a contract with Island Records. *Spreading The Disease* was deservedly well received, and the band's European profile was raised considerably by their support slot on Metallica's Damage Inc tour. *Among The Living*, co-produced by the band with Eddie Kramer, established Anthrax as a major force in the speed metal scene, producing UK hits in 'I Am The Law' and 'Indians', and their riotously entertaining live shows made them many friends among press and public alike. A humorous rap song, 'I'm The Man', became both a hit and a favourite encore. However, *State Of Euphoria* was a disappointing, patchy affair, with the group suffering an undeserved media backlash over their image, until sterling live work restored their reputation, with Anthrax's commitment to expanding their audiences' musical tastes demonstrated by their choice of UK support acts, Living Colour and Kings X. *Persistence Of Time* showed a return to form, a dark and relentless work which produced another hit in the shape of a cover of Joe Jackson's 'Got The Time'. Classed by the band as an EP, *Attack Of The Killer B's* was essentially a collection of b-sides for the curious fan, but became one of Anthrax's most popular albums, with the hit collaboration with Public Enemy, 'Bring The Noise', leading to the two bands touring together in a co-headlining package. Shortly after the band signed a new contract with Elektra Records Belladonna was fired, with ex-Armored Saint frontman John Bush stepping in. *Sound Of White Noise* was hailed as the band's finest hour, a post-thrash *tour de force* of power metal with bursts of hardcore speed. Bush's creative input helped Ian and Benante to write some of their best work, while Dave Jerden's production updated and re-energized the Anthrax sound. In 1994 Bush started his own R&B offshoot, Ho Cake, which includes former Armored Saint personnel Joey Vera (bass) and Jeff Duncan (guitar), as well as Shawn Duncan (drums), Tony Silbert (keyboards) and Bruce Fernandez. In 1995 Anthrax began work on *Stomp 442*, an unremittingly brutal collection of hardcore and metal produced by the Butcher Brothers (best known for their work with Urge Overkill). However, Spitz was ejected from the band just prior to recording and his guitar parts were played instead by his former guitar technician, Paul Cook. Pantera's Dimebag Darrell, and the group's drummer, Charlie Benante. Auditions for a full-time lead guitarist were held prior to a national tour at the end of 1995.

●ALBUMS: *Fistful Of Metal* (Megaforce 1984)★★, *Spreading The Disease* (Island/Megaforce 1986)★★★, *Among The Living* (Island/Megaforce 1987)★★★, *State Of Euphoria* (Island/Megaforce 1988)★★, *Persistence Of Time* (Island/Megaforce 1990)★★★★, *Attack Of The Killer B's*

(Island/Megaforce 1991)★★★, *Sound Of White Noise* (Elektra 1993)★★★★, *Live - The Island Years* (Island 1994)★★★, *Stomp 442* (Island 1995)★★★. ●VIDEOS: *Oidivnikufesin N.F.V.* (1988), *Videos P.O.V.* (1990), *Persistence Through Time* (1990), *Through Time* (1991), *N.F.V.* (1991).

ANTI-NOWHERE LEAGUE

Leading lights in the early 80s UK punk scene, along with contemporaries GBH and the Exploited, this quartet from Tunbridge Wells, Kent, England, betrayed their talent in biker leather, chains and hardcore obscenity. Led by Animal (b. Nick Karmer; vocals) and Magoo (guitar), their catalogue of sexual outrage veered from the satirical to the genuinely offensive, with a string of four-letter words, rabid misogyny and the glorification of bestiality. Their most memorable moment was a thrashy re-run of Ralph McTell's 'Streets Of London' which replaced the song's folksy sentiments with the barbed, snarling rhetoric of the gutter. Thousands of copies of the single were seized and destroyed by the police as the b-side, 'So What', was deemed obscene. This incident, however, did nothing to prevent the group reaching number 1 in the UK Independent single charts, a feat accomplished a further three times in 1982 with 'I Hate People', 'Woman' and 'For You'. As their punkish appeal receded, the group abbreviated their name to the League and turned to a punk/metal hyrbrid in keeping with their biker image. Surprisingly, the results were not as appalling as might have been imagined, with *The Perfect Crime* boasting several fine songs, not least the very nearly subtle '(I Don't Believe) This Is My England'. The group disbanded in 1988 but there have been several revivals, including the one-off 1989 reunion recorded for release as *Live And Loud*.
●ALBUMS: *We Are ... The League* (WXYZ 1982)★★, *Live In Yugoslavia* (ID 1983)★★, *The Perfect Crime* (GWR 1987)★★★, *Live And Loud* (Link 1990)★★.
●COMPILATIONS: *Long Live The League* (Dojo 1986)★★★.

ANY TROUBLE

In 1980, *Melody Maker* labelled Any Trouble: 'the most exciting new rock 'n' roll group since the Pretenders'. Formed in Stoke, England, by songwriter Clive Gregson (b. 4 January 1955, Ashton-Under-Lyne, Manchester, England), they were part of a 'pub-rock' scene that also included Dr. Feelgood and Elvis Costello's Flip City. The line-up was completed with Chris Parks (lead guitar), Mel Harley (drums) and Phil Barnes (bass). Stiff Records signed them and backed the single 'Yesterday's Love' with full-page adverts in the music press. *Where Are All The Nice Girls* was an assured debut but the promotional-only live album (just 500 were pressed) was a better example of their tough, bluesy music.

They toured Europe and the USA as part of 'The Stiff Tour' but the label began concentrating on the US market because in the UK, Gregson, with his black-rimmed glasses and cynical lyrics, was often dismissed as an Elvis Costello imitator. *Wheels In Motion* lacked brightness, and Mike Howlett was an odd choice as producer, having just worked with OMD. Stiff lost faith and after releasing Any Trouble from their contract, drummer Martin Hughes (who had replaced Mel Harley) and Chris Parks both quit. Any Trouble made a comeback in 1982, supporting John Martyn on a British tour and signing to EMI America. Only Gregson and Barnes remained from the first line-up with new members Steve Gurl on keyboards and Andy Ebsworth on drums. *Any Trouble* was over-produced and Gregson himself later referred to it as 'dull'. *Wrong End Of The Race*, a double album, was the band's swansong but it was not backed by EMI America and soon afterwards the group split. Their final performance was at London's Dingwalls venue at Christmas 1984. Gregson went on to work with Richard Thompson and record with the accomplished vocalist, Christine Collister, as Gregson And Collister.
●ALBUMS: *Where Are All The Nice Girls* (Stiff 1980)★★★, *Wheels In Motion* (Stiff 1981)★★★, *Any Trouble* (EMI America 1983)★★, *Wrong End Of The Race* (EMI America 1984)★★★, *Home And Away* (1986)★★, *Mischief* (1987)★★, *A Change In The Weather* (1989)★★, *Love Is A Strange Hotel* (1990)★★, *The Last Word* (1992)★★.

ARGENT, ROD

b. 14 June 1945, St. Albans, Hertfordshire, England. At this ancient town's fee-paying Abbey School, he studied clarinet, violin and, crucially, keyboards to scholarship level. Although his preferences lay in jazz and the classics, he was broadminded enough to consider a career in pop. In 1962, he was a founder-member of the Zombies, and became the quintet's principal composer - notably of the 1964 million-seller 'She's Not There'. Argent himself invested in a Worcester musical equipment shop and conducted session work for the Who, the Hollies, John Williams, Andrew Lloyd Webber and Cleo Laine and John Dankworth, before releasing

Moving Home and its attendant single, 'Light Fantastic'. This was his first essay as a soloist (albeit with aid from famous friends). After collaborating with Lloyd Webber and Don Black on singer Marti Webb's *Tell Me On A Sunday* concept album in 1980, Argent penned *Masquerade*, an ambitious musical based on the Kit Williams book, which opened at the Young Vic in 1982. That same year, he was also seen on the boards in person with John Hiseman and Barbara Thompson with whom he recorded the jazzy *Siren Songs*. Argent's portfolio since has embraced incidental music for films and new age ventures epitomized by 1988's *Red House* (named after his Chiswick studio) - which hedged its bets with vocal items. More lucrative, however, was his production (with drummer Peter Van Hooke) of Tanita Tikaram's first two albums - and the use of sturdy old 'She's Not There' (sung by former Zombie Colin Blunstone) in a 1990 British Telecom television advertisement.

●ALBUMS: *Moving Home* (1979)★★★, *Masquerade* (1982)★★, *Siren Songs* (1983)★★★, *Red House* (1988)★★.
●COMPILATIONS: *The Best Of Argent* (Epic 1976)★★★.

ARMOURY SHOW

Formed in 1984 by Richard Jobson (b. 6 October 1960, Dunfermline, Fife, Scotland; vocals/guitar) and Russell Webb (bass/vocals), longstanding members of the Skids. The group was initially completed by John McGeoch (b. 28 May 1955, Greenock, Strathclyde, Scotland; guitar), formerly of Magazine and Siouxsie And The Banshees, and John Doyle (drums). Although the quartet enjoyed two minor hit singles with 'Castles In Spain' (1984) and 'We Can Be Brave Again' (1985), the two latter musicians proved incompatible and left following the completion of the group's sole album. *Waiting For The Floods* was an uncomfortable mix of different styles, but a 1987 single, 'New York City', which featured Jobson, Webb and sundry session musicians, showed a greater sense of purpose. Although redolent of early Simple Minds, the release suggested a newfound confidence, but the group broke up in the wake of Jobson's burgeoning modelling and media-based career.

●ALBUMS: *Waiting For The Floods* (Parlophone 1985)★★.

ARROWS (CANADA)

A Canadian 80s pop rock outfit, the Arrows enjoyed some commercial success in their home country and mainland Europe during the lifetime of their two-album career. Making their debut with a four-track EP *Misunderstood* on Spontaneous Records, they went on to release two albums on A&M Records. Produced by Canadian songwriter David Tyson, who co-wrote most of the material with vocalist Dean McTaggart, they displayed a groundbreaking sophisticated AOR sound and a flair for poppy choruses, setting standards at which the likes of A=440 and Tim Feehan would aim. *Stand Back* was released in 1984 and featured McTaggart, Rob Gusevs (keyboards), Earl Seymour (saxophone) and Doug Macaskill (guitars). With the addition of Bobby Economou (drums) and Glenn Olive (bass) the follow-up *The Lines Are Open* was released the following year. This included 'Talk Talk', which was their most successful single, later covered by Gregg Rolie (ex-Santana; Journey) on his *Gringo* album, and taken as the name of the compilation released on Long Island Records in 1995.

●ALBUMS: *Stand Back* (A&M 1984)★★★, *The Lines Are Open* (A&M 1985)★★★.
●COMPILATIONS: *Talk Talk* (Long Island 1995)★★★.

ART OF NOISE

Formed in 1983, the UK-based Art Of Noise were the first artists to be signed to Trevor Horn's ZTT Records. The nucleus of the group was Anne Dudley (keyboard/arrangements), J.J. Jeczalik (keyboards/production) and Gary Langan (various instruments/production). Dudley had already achieved considerable experience arranging for a number of artists, including ABC, Frankie Goes To Hollywood and Paul McCartney. At the end of 1984, the ensemble registered a Top 10 UK hit with the cleverly produced 'Close (To The Edit)'. The following year the group fell out with ZTT over their marketing strategies and switched labels to the independent label China Records. Thereafter, their career consisted chiefly of working with other artists. A revival of 'Peter Gunn' with Duane Eddy hit the UK Top 10 and this was followed by a collaboration with the television cartoon-animated character Max Headroom on 'Paranoimia'. Their finest and most bizarre backing role, however, was reserved for Tom Jones who made a Top 10 comeback courtesy of an amusing bump and grind version of Prince's 'Kiss'. Having enjoyed several years of quirky chart success, Art Of Noise split in 1990, with Dudley going on to work with Phil Collins and Killing Joke's Jaz Coleman.

●ALBUMS: *Who's Afraid Of The Art Of Noise* (ZTT 1984)★★★, *Into Battle With* (ZTT 1984)★★★, *Daft*

(China 1987)★★, *In No Sense? Nonsense* (China 1987)★★, *In Visible Silence* (Chrysalis 1987)★★★, *Below The Waste* (China 1989)★★★, *The Ambient Collection* (China 1990)★★★, *Drum And Bass Collection* (China 1996)★★★.
●COMPILATIONS: *The Best Of The Art Of Noise* (China 1988)★★★★.
●VIDEOS: *In Visible Silence* (1988).
●FILMS: *Breakdance - The Movie* (1984).

ARTICLES OF FAITH

From Chicago, Illinois, USA, the highly politicized mid-80s punk band Articles Of Faith (previously known as Direct Drive) originally comprised Vic Bondi (vocals/guitar), Dave Shield (bass), Bill aka Virus X (drums) and Joe Scuderi (guitar). Dorian Tijbakash was added as second guitarist in 1983, and the line-up also included musicians such as Pat Grueber, Steve Ross and Jon Smith at various times. Bondi, however, was very much the focal point, an articulate presence who also wrote columns for the fanzine *Maximum Rock 'n' Roll*, and, by the time of the band's demise, he had become a history lecturer at the University of Massachusetts. Following two EPs, Articles Of Faith's debut album was produced by Hüsker Dü's Bob Mould, and remains one of the most thoughtful and incisive documents in the development of hardcore, with Bondi's astute lyrics matching the group's instrumental skill. Live, he was also an extremely engaging figure. Mould also produced *Is This Life* in 1985 (not released until 1987). This showed progress from their debut, with melody replacing the grit of before. It proved to be the final Articles Of Faith release, however, although the posthumous *Core* LP collected their first two singles and unreleased material. While continuing to teach history, Bondi went on to lead Jones Very, and also recorded a solo album.
●ALBUMS: *Give Thanks* (Reflex 1984)★★★, *Is This Life* (Lone Wolf 1987)★★★. Solo: Vic Bondi *The Ghost Dance* (Wishing Well 1988)★★★.
●COMPILATIONS: *Core* (Bitzcore 1991)★★★.

ASIA

A supergroup consisting of well-known musicians from British art-rock bands, Asia formed in early 1981 and included John Wetton (b. 12 July 1949, Derby, England; vocals), keyboardist Geoff Downes, Steve Howe (b. 8 April 1947, London, England; guitar) and Carl Palmer (b. 20 March 1947, Birmingham, England; drums/percussion). At the time, Wetton had recently left the English progressive band UK, Howe and Downes had just

vacated Yes and Palmer had left Emerson, Lake And Palmer. The group's self-titled debut album was released a year later and, although dismissed by critics as unadventurous and overly commercial, it topped the US album charts for nine weeks, becoming one of the year's bestsellers. A single, 'Heat Of The Moment', also reached the US Top 5. Neither fared as well in the group's homeland. A follow-up single, 'Only Time Will Tell', was a moderate US success.

The group released its second album, *Alpha*, in 1983 and although it was a Top 10 hit in the USA, as was the single 'Don't Cry', its sales failed to match those of the debut. Wetton then left the group, to be replaced by Greg Lake (b. 10 November 1948, Bournemouth, England), another Emerson, Lake And Palmer alumnus. As testament to the residual affection for the band a live television concert from Japan drew over 20 million US viewers in late 1983. In late 1985 Wetton rejoined the band and a third album, *Astra*, was released. However, its comparatively low chart position precipitated the band's dissolution. By early 1990 Howe had left to join a regenerated Yes, with Pat Thrall, an ex-Pat Travers Band member, moving in to take his place. *Then And Now*, released the same year, was a mixture of six earlier recordings and four new songs. The group then moved from European label Musidisc to a new home on Music For Nations' subsidiary Bullet Proof.
●ALBUMS: *Asia* (Geffen 1982)★★★, *Alpha* (Geffen 1983)★★, *Astra* (Geffen 1985)★★, *Then And Now* (Warners 1990)★★, *Live In Moscow* (Rhine 1992)★★, *Aqua* (Musidisc 1992)★★, *Aria* (Bullet Proof 1994)★★.
●VIDEOS: *Asia In Asia* (1984), *Asia (Live)* (1991).

ASSEMBLY

This was a one-off project consisting of former Depeche Mode and Yazoo synthesizers/keyboard player Vince Clarke (b. 3 July 1961, Basildon, Essex, England) and ex-Undertones singer Feargal Sharkey (b. 13 August 1958, Londonderry, Northern Ireland). Their resulting single, 'Never Never', reached the UK number 4 spot in November 1983. No album was ever recorded by the duo. After many similar liaisons with Neil Arthur of Blancmange, The The's Matt Johnson and Paul Quinn of Orange Juice, Clarke found a stable rapport with Andy Bell in Erasure, while Sharkey departed for the USA and a solo career.

ASSOCIATES

Vocalist Billy MacKenzie (b. 27 March 1957,

Dundee, Scotland, d. 23 January 1997) and Alan Rankine had performed in a variety of local groups before finally forming the Associates in 1979. After a minor label recording of David Bowie's 'Boys Keep Swinging', they were signed to Fiction Records where they released the critically acclaimed *The Affectionate Punch*. After a spell on the Beggars Banquet Records subsidiary, Situation 2, they formed their own Associates label distributed by Sire/WEA Records. The extra push provided a Top 10 chart breakthrough courtesy of 'Party Fears Two', which boasted an engaging and distinctive keyboard arrangement. Two further Top 30 hits followed with 'Club Country' and '18 Carat Love Affair'/'Love Hangover'. Meanwhile MacKenzie became involved in other projects, most notably a cameo appearance on BEF's extravagant *Songs Of Quality And Distinction*. It was not until 1984 that the Associates reconvened and this was followed by several very low chart entries and a relatively poor selling album, *Perhaps*. Not surprisingly, Rankine and MacKenzie reverted to solo work, leaving the Associates as something of an occasional group. It was not until 1990 that the group returned with a new album, *Wild And Lonely*, which was stylistically similar to their earlier work. Following a bout of depression after his mother's death, MacKenzie was found dead at his parent's home in January 1997.

●ALBUMS: *The Affectionate Punch* (Fiction 1980)★★★, *Sulk* (Sire 1982)★★★, *Perhaps* (Associates/Warners 1985)★★, *Wild And Lonely* (Circa/Charisma 1990)★★★.

●COMPILATIONS: *Fourth Drawer Down* (Situation 2 1981)★★★, *The Radio 1 Sessions* (Nighttracks 1995)★★★.

ASTLEY, RICK

b. 6 February 1966, Warrington, England. Astley was the drummer in a local band called Give Way, before joining the soul group FBI in 1984 as lead vocalist. He was discovered by the successful producer/writer Pete Waterman in 1985 and worked at Waterman's PWL studios while waiting for a recording break. In 1987 he recorded a duet 'Learning To Live' with Ochi Brown and was also part of Rick And Lisa whose single 'When You Gonna' was released on RCA Records. He also sang on the UK number 1 hit 'Let It Be' by Ferry Aid before gaining his first solo success with 'Never Gonna Give You Up'. This single topped the UK chart, became the biggest UK single of 1987 (winning the BRITS award) and helped make him the top singles act of the year. His debut album,

Whenever You Need Somebody, also reached the top in the UK and sold over a million copies. When Astley was launched in the USA in 1988 he was an instant success. When 'Together Forever' followed 'Never Gonna Give You Up' into the top spot, he became the first artist in the 80s to top the US charts with his first two singles. In 1988 he was the most played US club act and also had the top selling 12-inch record. Under the wing of Stock, Aitken And Waterman, Astley achieved seven UK and four US Top 10 singles. Despite the fact that he possessed one of the most excellent voices in pop music he became a target for the UK media who saw him as a puppet of his producers. Astley wanted to have more involvement in his recordings and he left the winning production and writing team. After a lengthy break, he resurfaced in 1991 with the successful album *Free* which included guest appearances from Elton John and Mark King (of Level 42). This album also included the single 'Cry For Help', which he had co-written and produced, and this put him back into the Top 10 on both sides of the Atlantic. Since that time very little has been heard of him.

●ALBUMS: *Whenever You Need Somebody* (RCA 1987)★★★, *Hold Me In Your Arms* (RCA 1988)★★, *Free* (RCA 1991)★★★.

●VIDEOS: *Video Hits* (1989).

ASTLEY, VIRGINIA

b. 1960, Watford, Hertfordshire, England. Astley was a former member of the Ravishing Beauties along with Nicola Holland and Kate St. John. As classically trained musicians they attempted, with some degree of success, to cross over into the pop field, working with, amongst others, Echo And The Bunnymen and the Teardrop Explodes. Astley broke away to pursue a solo career in 1982. Her first single, 'Love's A Lonely Place To Be' was a melancholy paeon to the feeling of isolation when a love affair breaks down and the song's choral, almost boy soprano feel, gave it an ephemeral quality. It reached number 7 in the UK Independent chart and fitted in well with the then-current fashion for 'quiet pop'. Her debut album in 1983 confirmed her love of all things English and pastoral. Largely an instrumental album, this dreamy atmospheric piece incorporated the sounds of the countryside on a summer's day. Complete with authentic bird songs and farm sounds, it gave the feel of a modern-day piece by Delius. It took three years for her second album to be released and the Ryuichi Sakamoto-produced *Hope In Darkened Heart* concentrated on Astley's preoccupation with the loss of childhood's innocence and adulthood's uncertainty. This accomplished musician remains for the time being, on the periphery of the music scene and can occasionally be found guesting for other artists.

●ALBUMS: *From Gardens Where We Feel Secure* (Rough Trade 1983)★★★, *Hope In Darkened Heart* (Warners 1986)★★★.

●FURTHER READING: *The World Of Virginia Astley*, Robert Brown and Deke Rivers.

ATLANTIC STARR

Soul/dance act comprising Sharon Bryant (vocals), David Lewis (vocals, keyboards, guitar), Jonathan Lewis (keyboards, trombone), Wayne Lewis (vocals, keyboards), Koran Daniels (saxophone), William Suddeeth III (trumpet), Clifford Archer (bass), Joseph Phillips (percussion) and Porter Caroll Jnr. (drums). The Lewis component of the group are three brothers who had previously led their own bands, Newban, Exact Change and Unchained Youth, on the east coast of America. Atlantic Starr were formed in 1976 when they moved to Los Angeles. Later in the 70s they picked up the services of New York-born Daniels as lead singer, and signed to A&M Records. Under the auspices of Philadelphia producer Bobby Eli (whose other work includes Major Harris, Brenda and the Tabulations, Booker Newbury III and Ronnie Dyson) they recorded their first two albums. 'Gimme Your Lovin' from the first of these became a hit in the UK charts, before they switched to the production tutelage of James Anthony Carmichael (Commodores, Lionel Ritchie) for a series of three albums. Bryant departed after *Yours Forever* to marry Rick Gallway from Change. She then worked as a session singer before re-emerging in 1989 with the solo *Here I Am* and single 'Foolish Heart'. Her replacement in Atlantic Starr was Barbara Weathers, although Daniels, Suddeeth, Archer and Carroll also parted company around the same time. The nucleus of the brothers Lewis and Weathers continued, and took to producing themselves, starting with *The Band Turns* which spawned hits in 'Silver Shadow', 'One Love', 'Secret Lovers', and 'If Your Heart Isn't In It' during 1985 and 1986 - their first singles chart success since 1978. In 1987 they signed to Warner Brothers Records, an association which produced a US number 1 (UK number 3) in the ballad 'Always'. Weathers left in 1989 for a solo career (aided by Wayne Lewis, and Maurice White from Earth, Wind And Fire), to be replaced by Porscha Martin.

●ALBUMS: *Atlantic Starr* (A&M 1978)★★★, *Straight To The Point* (A&M 1979)★★★, *Radiant* (A&M 1980)★★★, *Brilliance* (A&M 1982)★★★, *Yours Forever* (A&M 1983)★★★, *The Band Turns* (A&M 1985)★★★, *All In The Name Of Love* (Warners 1987)★★★, *We're Movin' Up* (Warners 1989)★★★.

ATTILA THE STOCKBROKER

After graduating from the University of Kent with a degree in French, this performance poet (b. John Baine, 21 October 1957, England) really was a stockbroker, or on the way to becoming one, before he set out on the live music circuit. Accompanied on occasion by his own mandolin backing, he regaled his audience with good-humoured invective on the state of the world. Viewed as one of the new 'Ranting Poets', a term he disliked, his influences were poets Roger McCoughlan and Brian Patton, alongside Monty Python and the energy of punk. After playing in forgotten punk bands English Disease and Brighton Riot Squad, he joined Brussels-based new wave band, Contingent. His usual early environment, indeed, was supporting punk bands. He played frequently enough to earn himself a session for BBC disc jockey John Peel, which in turn led to a deal with Cherry Red Records and his debut, *Ranting At The Nation*, was a highly colourful selection of verse and spoken word highlighting the absurdity of British life. Nightmare visions of Soviets running the social security system and his affection for obscure European soccer clubs were among the targets: 'So go to your Job Centre - I'll bet you'll see, Albanian students get handouts for free, and drug-crazed punk rockers cavort and caress, in the interview booths of the D.H.S.S.' Critics were not convinced, however, one citing the contents as 'an inarticulate mish-mash of bad humour and popular clichés'. The *Cocktails* EP, from October 1982, boasted some of his finest pieces to date, from the serious ('Contributory Negligence') to the absurd ('The Night I Slept With Seething Wells'). 1984's *Sawdust And Empire* saw a greater emphasis on music. Increasingly Attila was seeing himself as a folk artist, and between releases was becoming a near permanent fixture at various festivals, working alongside John Otway and TV Smith (ex-Adverts). He has also managed The Tender Trap. He was involved in the staging of *Cheryl The Rock Opera*, alongside Otway and Blyth Power, for whom he occasionally plucks a fiddle, and has contributed to the pages of the *Guardian* with his essays on social change in eastern Europe while on tour in the region. In 1994 he emerged with a new venture,

Barnstormer, which conceptualized his long-standing interest in medieval/early music.

●ALBUMS: *Ranting At The Nation* (Cherry Red 1983)★★★, *Sawdust And Empire* (Cherry Red 1984)★★★, *Libyan Students From Hell* (Cherry Red 1987)★★★, *Scornflakes* (Probe 1988)★★★, *Live At The Rivioli* (Musidisc 1990)★★, *Donkey's Years* (Musidisc 1991)★★★.

ATTRACTIONS

Formed in May 1977 to back Elvis Costello, the Attractions provided sympathetic support to the singer's contrasting, and often demanding, compositions. Steve Nieve (b. Steven Nason; keyboards), Bruce Thomas (b. Stockton-on-Tees, Cleveland, England; bass) and Pete Thomas (b. 9 August 1954, Sheffield, Yorkshire, England; drums) were already experienced musicians - Bruce Thomas with the Sutherland Brothers and Quiver, Pete Thomas with Chilli Willi And The Red Hot Peppers and John Stewart - while Nieve's dexterity on keyboards added colour to many of the unit's exemplary releases. In 1980 the Attractions completed a low-key album, *Mad About The Wrong Boy*, but their position as Costello's natural backing group became increasingly unsure as their leader embarked on a plethora of guises. Nieve recorded a solo collection, *Playboy* (1987) and later led the house band, along with Pete Thomas as Steve Nieve And The Playboys, on UK television's *Jonathan Ross Show*, while Bruce Thomas began a literary career with *The Big Wheel* (1990), an impressionistic autobiography.

●ALBUMS: *Mad About The Wrong Boy* (F-Beat 1980)★★.

AU PAIRS

Arguably the Midlands' key contribution to the early 80s post-punk scene, Birmingham band the Au Pairs consisted of Lesley Woods (lead vocals/guitar), Paul Foad (lead guitar), Jane Munro (bass), and Pete Hammond (drums). They began their career in 1980 with the *You* EP on their own Human label, which also housed their long-playing debut. Critically acclaimed for their social insight and thoughtful, agit-prop music, they continued with singles such as 'It's Obvious' and 'Inconvenience', which brought them closest to a hit. Covering a variety of subjects from the controversial ('Armagh') to the frankly personal ('Sex Without Stress'), they signed to Kamera Records and released a live album on a.k.a. Records in 1983 before vanishing when Woods failed to show for a concert in Belgium. The latter artefact, recorded at the Berlin Women's Festival, is probably the best introduction to the band - missing as it does some of the duff tracks that marred their previous studio efforts. Woods later blamed the split on 'lack of money, nervous breakdowns and drugs . . . the usual rock 'n' roll story'. She settled in Europe for a few years before returning to London to undertake a law degree and form all-female band the Darlings. Foad formed End Of Chat with Hammond and trumpeter Graham Hamilton (who deputized for Woods on that aborted Belgium date). Munro, who left six months prior to the band's eventual dissolution, spent the early 90s training as an aromatherapist.

●ALBUMS: *Playing With A Different Sex* (Human 1981)★★★, *Sense And Sensuality* (Kamera 1982)★★, *Live In Berlin* (a.k.a. 1983)★★★.

AUSTIN, PATTI

b. 10 August 1948, California, USA. Austin first sang on stage at the age of three at the famous Apollo Theatre in New York City during Dinah Washington's set. As a child performer, she appeared on television, including Sammy Davis Jnr's programme, and in the theatre. Her stage work included *Lost In The Stars* and *Finian's Rainbow*. At the age of nine she travelled to Europe with the bandleader/arranger Quincy Jones. As a 16-year-old, she toured with Harry Belafonte and began recording at the age of 17. Austin's first recordings were for Coral in 1965, and in 1969, 'Family Tree' (United Artists) was an R&B hit. Austin's immaculate vocals brought work on television jingles and during the 70s she was one of the busiest session singers in New York. Her session work includes credits for Paul Simon, Billy Joel, Frankie Valli, Joe Cocker, George Benson and Roberta Flack. Her solo albums included material she had written herself, and showed some jazz influences. Further session work during 1980 saw Austin working with Marshall Tucker, Steely Dan and the Blues Brothers. Her long-standing association with father-figure Quincy Jones continued, and his compositio, 'The Dude' featured her lead vocal and won a Grammy in 1982. Austin had another hit with the title track of *Every Home Should Have One* on Jones' Qwest label. Although it only just made the UK Top 100, 'Razzamatazz' (with Quincy Jones) was a UK Top 20 hit in 1981. Her duet with James Ingram, 'Baby Come To Me', became the theme music for the television soap opera *General Hospital* and was a US number 1 and a UK number 11 in 1983. Another Austin/Ingram duet, 'How Do You Keep The Music Playing?', from the film *Best Friends,* was nominated for an Oscar. She also sang themes for the films *Two Of A Kind* (1984) and *Shirley Valentine* (1988) and had R&B hits with 'Gimme Gimme'. *The Real Me* was a collection of standards ranging from Duke Ellington's 'Mood Indigo' to 'How Long' by the UK group Ace. Her 1990 album was produced by Dave Grusin for GRP Records while Austin was a guest vocalist on an album of George Gershwin songs released in 1992 by the Hollywood Bowl Orchestra. Already successful, Austin has yet to receive the critical acclaim her achievements merit.

●ALBUMS: *End Of A Rainbow* (CTI 1976)★★★, *Havana Candy* (CTI 1977)★★★, *Live At The Bottom Line* (CTI 1979)★★★, *Body Language* (CTI 1980)★★★, *Every Home Should Have One* (Qwest 1981)★★★★, *Patti Austin* (Qwest 1984)★★★, *Gettin' Away With Murder* (Qwest 1985)★★, *The Real Me* (Qwest 1988)★★★, *Love's Gonna Get You* (GRP 1990)★★, *Carry On* (GRP 1991)★★★, *Live* (1992)★★★.

AZTEC CAMERA

This acclaimed UK pop outfit was formed in 1980 by Roddy Frame (b. 29 January 1964, East Kilbride, Scotland), as a vehicle for his songwriting talent. The other members, Campbell Owens (bass), and Dave Mulholland (drums), soon passed through, and a regular turnover in band members ensued while Frame put together the songs that made up the exceptionally strong debut *High Land, Hard Rain*. Their three hits in the UK independent charts on the influential Postcard label had already made the band a critics' favourite, but this sparkling album of light acoustic songs with a mature influence of jazz and Latin rhythms was a memorable work. 'Oblivious' reached number 18 in the UK singles chart, while excellent songs like the uplifting 'Walk Out To Winter' and the expertly crafted 'We Could Send Letters' indicated a major talent in the ascendant. The Mark Knopfler-produced *Knife* broke no new ground, but now signed to the massive WEA Records, the band was pushed into a world tour to promote the album. Frame was happier writing songs on his acoustic guitar back home in Scotland and retreated there following the tour, until *Love* in 1987. This introverted yet over-produced album showed Frame's continuing development with Elvis Costello-influenced song structures. The comparative failure of this collection was rectified the following year with two further hit singles, 'How Men Are' and the catchy 'Somewhere In My Heart'. This stimulated interest in *Love* and the album became a substantial suc-

cess. After a further fallow period, allowing Frame to create more gems, the band returned in 1990 with the highly acclaimed *Stray*, leaving no doubt that their brand of intelligent, gentle pop has a considerable following. In the summer of 1993 Roddy Frame finally delivered the album that fans and critics had waited for. *Dreamland* and *Frestonia* were both good collections of emotionally direct, honest songs which rivalled Aztec Camera's sparkling debut a decade earlier. The band disintegrated in 1996 as Frame became embroiled in his own writing for a solo project.

●ALBUMS: *High Land, Hard Rain* (Rough Trade 1983)★★★★, *Knife* (Warners 1984)★★★, *Aztec Camera* 10-inch album (Warners 1985)★★★, *Love* (Warners 1987)★★★, *Stray* (Warners 1990)★★★★, *Dreamland* (Warners 1993)★★★, *Live On The Test* rec. 1983 (Windsong 1995)★★★, *Frestonia* (Warners 1995)★★★.

●VIDEOS: *Aztec Camera* (1989).

B-52's

The quirky appearance, stage antics and lyrical content of the B-52's belie a formidable musical ability, as the band's rhythmically perfect pop songs show many influences, including 50s rock 'n' roll, punk and commercial dance music. However, it was the late 70s' new wave music fans that took them to their hearts. The group were formed in Athens, Georgia, USA, in 1976, and took their name from the bouffant hairstyle worn by Kate Pierson (b. 27 April 1948, Weehawken, New Jersey, USA; organ/vocals) and Cindy Wilson (b. 28 February 1957, Athens, Georgia, USA; guitar/vocals). The line-up was completed by Cindy's brother Ricky (b. 19 March 1953, Athens, Georgia, USA, d. 12 October 1985; guitar), Fred Schneider (b. 1 July 1951, Newark, Georgia, USA; keyboards/vocals) and Keith Strickland (b. 26 October 1953, Athens, Georgia, USA; drums). The lyrically bizarre but musically thunderous 'Rock Lobster' was originally a private pressing of 2000 copies and came to the notice of the perceptive Chris Blackwell, who signed them to Island Records in the UK. Their debut, *B-52's*, became a strong seller and established the band as a highly regarded unit with a particularly strong following on the American campus circuit during the early 80s. Their anthem, 'Rock Lobster', became a belated US hit in 1980 and they received John Lennon's seal of approval that year as his favourite band. Subsequent albums continued to defy categorization, their love of melodrama and pop culture running side by side with outright experimentalism (witness 50s sci-fi parody 'Planet Claire'). Ricky Wilson died of AIDS in 1985 (although it was initially claimed that cancer was the cause, to save his family from intrusion). Nevertheless the band reached a commercial peak in 1989, winning a new generation of fans with the powerful hit single 'Love Shack', and its enticing accompanying video. *Cosmic Thing* showed that the band had not lost their touch and blended several musical styles with aplomb. In 1992 the group parted company with Cindy Wilson and recorded *Good Stuff* under the eyes of previous producer

Don Was (Was (Not Was)) and Nile Rodgers (Chic). During a Democratic party fund-raising concert in April of that year, actress Kim Basinger stood in for Wilson, as did Julee Cruise the following year. 1994 brought huge commercial success with the theme song to *The Flintstones*, yet despite the 'cheese' factor, it remained hard not to warm to the full-blooded performances from Schneider and Pierson.

●ALBUMS: *B-52's* (Warners 1979)★★★★, *Wild Planet* (Warners 1980)★★★, *Party Mix!* remix of the first two albums (Warners 1981)★★★, *Mesopotamia* mini-album (Warners 1982)★★, *Whammy!* (Warners 1983)★★, *Bouncing Off The Satellites* (Warners 1986)★★, *Cosmic Thing* (Reprise 1989)★★★, *Good Stuff* (Warners 1992)★★★. Solo: Fred Schneider *Just Fred* (Reprise 1996)★★★.

●COMPILATIONS: *Best Of The B-52's: Dance This Mess Around* (Island 1990)★★★★, *Party Mix-Mesopotamia* (Warners 1991)★★★, *Planet Claire* (Spectrum 1995)★★★.

B., DEREK

b. Derek Bowland, 1966, Bow, East London, England. Derek grew up a fan of the Who as well as the more conventional black sounds of Aretha Franklin, Al Green and Bob Marley. He started out as a DJ when he was 15 as part of a mobile unit touring London clubs. He then moved into radio, working for pirate stations such as Kiss FM and LWR before beginning his own WBLS station. In 1987 he became bored with the disc jockey role and took a job at the Music Of Life label as an A&R man. Alongside Simon Harris (world yo-yo champion, it has been alleged) he signed several of the most notable early UK hip hop groups, including Overlord X, MC Duke, Hijack, the She Rockers and Demon Boyz. He subsequently started to record his own material for the label. While in New York (visiting his family who had moved there), Derek met the DJ Mr Magic, who played his record to Profile Records, granting him a licensing deal in the USA. His debut single, 'Rock The Beat', and its follow up, 'Get Down' (which featured the rapping of EZQ - Derek B under another pseudonym), both made an early impact. His hip hop sounded a little hamfisted in comparison to New York's more natural feel, which made the self-congratulatory raps sound increasingly hysterical: 'We kept on goin' for hours and hours/Straight after to the bathroom for a shower/Just before leaving she held me close and said/I think you're the greatest thing in bed' ('Get Down'). He hit the UK charts in 1988 with 'Goodgroove' and was the only rapper on the Free

Mandela bill at Wembley Stadium. Further minor hits came with 'Bad Young Brother' and 'We've Got The Juice', after he set up his own Tuff Audio label through Phonogram. However, that relationship declined when he attempted to push for a harder sound. Further one-off deals with a variety of labels failed to offer anything of significance, though while at SBK he ghost-wrote tracks for Vanilla Ice. He is currently a member of PoW.

●ALBUMS: *Bullet From A Gun* (Tuff Audio 1988)★★★.

B.A.L.L.

Formed in New York, USA, in 1987, B.A.L.L. comprised of Mark Kramer (bass/vocals/production) and David Licht (drums) - both formerly of Shockabilly - and two ex-members of the Velvet Monkeys: Don Fleming (guitar/vocals) and Jay Speigel (drums). The quartet's debut, *Period (Another American Lie)*, established their sound wherein grunge-styled pop songs were driven by loud, distorted guitar work and the two drummers' solid, uncompromising beat. Humour was an equally integral part of the group's *raison d'être*, a facet that came to fruition on *Bird*. Its sleeve parodied the infamous Beatles 'butcher cover' and the second side was devoted to a pastiche of the *Concert For Bangla Desh*. Several sacred cows of rock were mercilessly savaged in a suite which married Ringo Starr's 'It Don't Come Easy', George Harrison's 'Wah Wah' and Marc Bolan's 'Buick Mackane'. However, the concept was arguably stronger than the aural results and the group's own material lacked sparkle. Billed on the reverse as 'the disappointing third album', *Trouble Doll* was indeed inferior, comprising one studio side and another recorded live at CBGB's, some of which was reprised from *Bird*. *Four (Hardball)* captures the quartet at their best, despite the fact that they fell apart during its recording. The first side is devoted to powerful pop songs; its counterpart consists of ravaged instrumentals. Fleming left the group before completing vocals. The friction was latterly resolved - a similarly charged album, *Special Kiss* appeared in 1991 under a new name, Gumball - but the four achieved a greater profile elsewhere. Speigel and Fleming re-formed the Velvet Monkeys; the latter became a producer of note (Teenage Fanclub; Free Kitten) while Kramer continued to administer his Shimmy-Disc label, which issued B.A.L.L.'s albums, and recorded with Bongwater and as a solo artist.

●ALBUMS: *Period (Another American Lie)* (Shimmy-Disc 1987)★★★, *Bird* (Shimmy-Disc 1988)★★, *Trouble Doll* (Shimmy-Disc 1989)★★, *Four ... Hardball* (Shimmy-Disc 1990)★★★.

BAD BOY

The origins of this Milwaukee, USA, rock band date back to the mid-70s, when Steve Grimm (guitar/vocals) teamed up with John Marcelli (bass). The first incarnation of Bad Boy had included Lars Hanson (drums) and Joe Luchessie (guitar/keyboards/vocals). The band chemistry was wrong, however, and their debut album was a disappointing, half-hearted affair. Things improved with their second release, as the band moved in a heavier direction and made greater use of an up-front guitar sound, including Earl Slick (ex-David Bowie). Following a period of inactivity between 1978 and 1982, the band hit back with a revamped line-up that saw Xeno (keyboards) and Billy Johnson (drums) alongside Grimm and Marcelli. Unfortunately, they switched back to a melodic pop-rock style once more. Both albums sold poorly and the band split up as a result.

●ALBUMS: *The Band That Made Milwaukee Famous* (United Artists 1977)★★, *Back To Back* (United Artists 1978)★★★, *Private Party* (Indie 1982)★★, *Electric Eyes* (Indie 1984)★★.

BAD BRAINS

This black American hardcore punk and dub reggae outfit originated in 1978. The band were all playing together earlier in a fusion group, 'doing Chick Corea and Stanley Clarke type stuff. They moved from Washington, DC, to New York where they established a reputation as prime exponents, alongside the Dead Kennedys and Black Flag, of the new 'hardcore' hybrid of punk, based on a barely credible speed of musicianship. The line-up consisted of H.R. (b. Paul Hudson; vocals) and brother Earl Hudson (drums), Dr. Know (guitar) and Darryl Jennifer (bass). They broke up their sets with dub and reggae outings and attracted a mixed audience, which was certainly one of their objectives: 'We're a gospel group, preaching the word of unity.' It is frustrating that so little studio material remains to document this early period, though the singles 'Pay To Cum' and 'Big Takeover' are regarded as punk classics. They were due to support the Damned in the UK in October 1979, having sold most of their equipment to buy aeroplane tickets. On arrival, however, they were denied work permits. They continued through the 80s, although H.R. went on to a solo career. In May 1988 he was temporarily replaced by ex-Faith No More vocalist Chuck Moseley, while Mackie (ex-

Cro-Mags) took over on drums. The move, which allowed the remaining founding members to gig, was singularly unsuccessful. More recently bands such as Living Colour have sung their praises as one of the forerunners of articulate black rock music, while in 1994 even Madonna took notice, offering them a place on her Maverick label, with H.R. returning to the fold. *God Of Love*, produced by ex-leader of the Cars, Ric Ocasek, concentrated more on dub and rasta messages than hardcore, but proved again there was still fire in the belly of this group. In 1995 H.R. left the band after assaulting various Bad Brains members before a show on their promotional tour to support *God Of Love*. He was subsequently arrested at the Canadian border and charged with a drugs offence.

●ALBUMS: *Bad Brains* (ROIR 1982)★★, *Rock For Light* (PVC 1983)★★★, *I Against I* (SST 1985)★★★, *Live* (SST 1988)★★, *Attitude: The ROIR Sessions* (In-Effect 1989)★★★, *Quickness* (Caroline 1989)★★★, *The Youth Are Getting Restless* (Caroline 1990)★★★, *Rise* (1993)★★★, *God Of Love* (Maverick 1995)★★★, *Black Dots* (Caroline 1996)★★★.

BAD MANNERS

Formed in 1979 when the UK 2-Tone ska revival was at its peak, the group comprised Buster Bloodvessel (b. Douglas Trendle, 6 September 1958; lead vocals), Gus 'Hot Lips' Herman (trumpet), Chris Kane (saxophone), Andrew 'Marcus Absent' Marson (saxophone), Winston Bazoomies (harmonica), Brian 'Chew-it' Tuitti (drums), David Farren (bass), Martin Stewart (keyboards) and Louis 'Alphonzo' Cook (guitar). Fronted by the exuberant Bloodvessel, whose shaven head, rotund build, protruding tongue and often outrageous costume provided a strong comic appeal, the group enjoyed a brief run of UK hits in the early 80s. Released on the Magnet label, their string of UK hits commenced with the catchy 'Ne-Ne Na-Na Na-Na Nu-Nu', followed by 11 UK chart entries, including four Top 10 hits, 'Special Brew', 'Can Can', 'Walking In The Sunshine' and a remake of Millie's hit retitled 'My Girl Lollipop'. Although this musically tight unit is still very popular on the live circuit, the group's mass novelty appeal had worn thin by the middle of 1983 when the hits ceased. In 1990 Bloodvessel formed Buster's Allstars to motivate the other members of Bad Manners into doing something. In recent years he has toured occasionally with the band but now works as an hotelier in Brighton.

●ALBUMS: *Ska 'N' B* (Magnet 1980)★★★, *Loonee Tunes* (Magnet 1981)★★★, *Gosh, It's Bad Manners* (Magnet 1981)★★★★, *Forging Ahead* (Magnet 1982)★★, *Return Of The Ugly* (Dojo 1989)★★.
●COMPILATIONS: *The Height Of Bad Manners* (Telstar 1983)★★★.

BAD NEWS

Originally written by Adrian Edmondson as a part of UK television's *The Comic Strip Presents* series in 1982, the *Bad News Tour* told the story of an ambitious (but inept) London heavy metal band played by Edmondson as vocalist/guitarist Vim Fuego, Rik Mayall as bassist Colin Grigson, Nigel Planer as the dim rhythm guitarist Den Dennis and finally Comic Strip co-writer/founder member Peter Richardson as drummer Spider Webb - on tour and en-route to Grantham with a television documentary crew. The music and lyrics for the show were put together by Edmondson and composer Simon Brint as a clever parody on the clichés of the UK heavy metal scene. After the success of the *American National Lampoon*-based *Spinal Tap* movie and its resulting move into legend, Edmondson decided to bring Bad News back for another Comic Strip episode, writing a basic storyline that would mean they would really have to play live. In 1986, armed with a recording contract with EMI Records, a producer in Queen's Brian May, clever management and photo sessions by Gered Mankowitz, they set about recording an album of songs and sketches. The full promotional machinery of interviews, television appearances and a slot at the Donington festival in August, all required for the film, were set in motion. Four months later they had a short tour set up which included a couple of charity concerts with Iron Maiden. In 1987 *More Bad News* was shown in the cinemas as support to another comic strip film, *Eat The Rich*, which incidentally starred Lemmy from Motörhead. This was backed up with a cover version of Queen's 'Bohemian Rhapsody' on single, and a self-titled debut album. The music was badly received but in retrospect was actually both well constructed and executed. Following the album they set out on a two month tour and released a second single, 'Cashing In On Xmas'. However, by this time the joke had worn too thin for both press and public and the actors returned to their day jobs. The name briefly appeared the next year when EMI Records released the bootleg album which contained the Edmondson-produced outtakes of music and comedy and a Brian May remix of the 'Christmas' single.

●ALBUMS: *Bad News* (EMI 1987)★★, *Bootleg* (EMI 1938)★★.

●COMPILATIONS: *Collection* (Castle 1994)★★.
●VIDEOS: *Bad News Tour And A Fistful Of Traveller's Cheques* (1986), *More Bad News* (1987), *Bohemian Rhapsody* (1987).

BAD RELIGION

This American hardcore band were formed in 1980 in the suburbs of north Los Angeles, California. Their first incarnation comprised Greg Graffin (vocals), Brett Gurewitz (guitar), Jay Lishrout (drums) and Jay Bentley (bass), with the name originating from their mutual distaste for organized religion. Their debut release was the poorly produced EP, *Bad Religion*, on Epitaph records, formed by founder-member Gurewitz. Following several appearances on local compilation albums, Pete Finestone took over as drummer in 1982. The milestone album *How Could Hell Be Any Worse* was recorded in Hollywood, creating a fair degree of local and national interest. The subsequent *Into The Unknown* proved a minor disaster, disillusioning hardcore fans with the emphasis shifted to slick keyboard textures, though the record itself stands up well. In 1984 there were more changes and Graffin was soon the only surviving member from the previous year, with Greg Hetson and Tim Gallegos taking over guitar and bass, and Pete Finestone returning on drums, while Gurewitz took time out to conquer his drink and drug problems. A comeback EP, *Back To The Known*, revealed a much more purposeful outfit. A long period of inactivity was ended in 1987 when Gurewitz rejoined for a show which Hetson (working with former band Circle Jerks once more) could not attend. New material was written, and *Suffer* was released in 1988 to wide critical acclaim. The band's albums since then have featured intelligent lyrics set against their compelling punk sound. Despite this, Gurewitz retired in 1994 to spend more time looking after the Epitaph label, which was enjoying success with Offspring and others. The line-up of the band in 1996 was Graffin, Hetson, Brian Baker (guitar), Bentley and Bobby Schayer (drums). *The Gray Race* was their major label debut and spread their fan-base wider with an assured release that addressed famine, world disorder and politics without losing their grip on the fact that they are out and out metal/punks of the finest degree.

●ALBUMS: *How Could Hell Be Any Worse?* (Epitaph 1982)★★★★, *Into The Unknown* (Epitaph 1983)★★★, *Suffer* (Epitaph 1988)★★★★, *No Control* (Epitaph 1989)★★★, *Against The Grain* (Epitaph 1990)★★★, *Generator* (Epitaph 1992)★★★, *Recipe For Hate* (Epitaph 1993)★★★, *Stranger Than Fiction* (Atlantic 1994)★★★, *The Gray Race* (Columbia 1996)★★★★, *Tested* (Epic 1997)★★★.

●COMPILATIONS: *80-85* (Epitaph 1991)★★★, *All Ages* (Epitaph 1995)★★★.

BADOWSKI, HENRY

After serving his apprenticeship in UK bands Norman And The Baskervilles, Lick It Dry and the New Rockets, Badowski joined punk band Chelsea on bass, but in early 1978, after only a few months, he left to enlist as drummer for Stiff Records artist Wreckless Eric. During the summer of that year, he sang and played keyboards with the short-lived King, a punk/psychedelic group that included Dave Berk (drums; also Johnny Moped), Kim Bradshaw (bass) and ex-Damned, Captain Sensible (guitar). Consequently, when King folded, Badowski took up the bass with the re-formed the Damned off-shoot, the Doomed. With the new year came the new position of drummer with the Good Missionaries, an experimental band created by Mark Perry from Alternative TV. This association led to the start of his solo career in the summer of 1979, with the release of 'Making Love With My Wife' on Perry's Deptford Fun City label. Recorded at Pathway Studios, the track was performed completely by Badowski and displayed a strong 60s influence, with echoes of Syd Barrett and Kevin Ayers. The b-side, 'Baby Sign Here With Me', was originally part of the King live set and utilized the talents of James Stevenson (bass/guitar) from Chelsea, and Alex Kolkowski (violin) and Dave Berk (drums), both from the Johnny Moped Band. The single attracted favourable reviews and within a month he had signed a contract with A&M Records, releasing a further two singles, 'My Face' and 'Henry's In Love', closely followed by the album *Life Is A Grand*, a classic slice of psychedelia that signalled the end of Badowski's solo career.

●ALBUMS: *Life Is A Grand* (A&M 1981)★★★.

BAILEY, PHILIP

b. 8 May 1951, Denver, Colorado, USA. Bailey is a talented soul singer who originally joined Earth, Wind And Fire in 1972 as a co-vocalist and percussionist. By 1983 he had released his first solo effort, *Continuation*, produced by George Duke. However, more influential was Phil Collins' production of his second album. Collins provided percussion throughout, and also co-wrote the sparkling duet 'Easy Lover', which topped the UK charts in March 1985 and reached number 2 in the US.

Unfortunately his only other UK hit to date has been the follow-up, 'Walking On The Chinese Wall', while the album of the same name made number 11 in the USA. Bailey also released several pop-gospel albums during the 80s.

●ALBUMS: *Continuation* (Columbia 1983)★★, *The Chinese Wall* (Columbia 1984)★★★, *The Wonders Of His Love* (Myrrh 1984)★★★, *Inside Out* (Columbia 1986)★★★★, *Triumph* (Myrrh 1986)★★★, *Family Affair* (Myrrh 1989)★★★, *Philip Bailey* (Zoo Entertainment 1995)★★★.

●COMPILATIONS: *The Best Of Philip Bailey: A Gospel Collection* (Word 1991)★★★★.

BAKER, ANITA

b. 20 December 1957, Detroit, Michigan, USA. Soul singer Anita Baker was being hailed as the voice of the 90s after working her way up the ladder during the late 70s and early 80s. The grand-daughter of a minister, she had a religious upbringing which included church music and gospel singing. After vocal duties with local bands she joined the semi-professional Chapter 8 in 1979 and was the vocalist on their minor US hit 'I Just Wanna Be Your Girl' the following year. Several years later she left the band and was working in an office when she persuaded the Beverly Glen label to record and release her debut album in 1983. *The Songstress* got her noticed and after disagreements with Beverly Glen she chose to sign with Elektra Records. Her second album was partly funded by Baker herself who also acted as executive producer, with former Chapter 8 colleague Michael Powell helping with writing and production. *Rapture*, a wonderfully mature and emotional album, saw Baker hailed as 'a female Luther Vandross' and she began to win R&B awards with 'Sweet Love', 'Caught Up In The Rapture' and 'Giving You The Best That I Got'. In 1987 she appeared on the Winans' 'Ain't No Need To Worry' and in 1990 duetted with former Shalamar singer Howard Hewlett. *Compositions* was self-penned bar two and featured former Wonderlove musician Greg Phillinganes on keyboards, ex-Average White Band Steve Ferrone on drums along with top Los Angeles session drummer Ricky Lawson, and Nathan East on bass. The album was recorded live in the studio with few overdubs.

●ALBUMS: *The Songstress* (Beverly Glen 1983)★★★, *Rapture* (Elektra 1986)★★★★, *Giving You The Best That I've Got* (Elektra 1988)★★★, *Compositions* (Elektra 1990)★★★, *Rhythm Of Love* (Elektra 1994)★★.

●VIDEOS: *Sweet Love* (1989), *One Night Of Rapture* (1989).

BAKER, ARTHUR

b. Boston, Massachusetts, USA. Arthur Baker began in music as a club DJ in Boston, Massachusetts, playing soul and R&B for the club-goers. He moved into production for Emergency Records shortly thereafter, including work on Northend and Michelle Wallace's 'Happy Days' (his first record, only released in Canada, was Hearts Of Stone's 'Losing You'). This preceded a move to New York where he became intrigued by the rap scene of 1979. He entered the studios once more, this time in tandem with Joe Bataan, to record a pseudo rap record, 'Rap-O-Clap-O', but the projected record company, London, went under before its release. The proceeds of the session did emerge later, though Baker went uncredited, after he returned to Boston. His next project was 'Can You Guess What Groove This Is?', by Glory, a medley that hoped to find a novelty market. From there, back in New York, he joined Tom Silverman's Tommy Boy Records operation to record 'Jazzy Sensation' with Afrika Bambaataa and Shep Pettibone. Afterwards he partnered Bambaataa on 'Planet Rock', before starting Streetwise Records. Though interwoven with the development of hip hop, Baker's later releases were inspired by the club scene (Wally Jump Jnr's 'Tighten Up', Jack E Makossa's 'The Opera House' and Criminal Orchestra Element's 'Put The Needle On The Record'). He went on to become an internationally renowned producer, working with legends like Bob Dylan and Bruce Springsteen. In 1989 he collaborated with the Force MD's, ABC and CMD among others on a showcase album that saw Baker working through various dance styles under his own auspices. A year was spent working on a biography of Quincy Jones' life before returning in 1991 with rapper and former MTV security guard Wendell Williams for club-oriented material such as 'Everybody'.

●ALBUMS: with the Backbeat Disciples *Merge* (A&M 1989)★★★, *Give In To The Rhythm* (Arista 1991)★★★.

BALAAM AND THE ANGEL

This UK rock band included both post-punk gothic and 60s elements in their output. They were originally made up of the three Morris brothers, Jim (b. 25 November 1960, Motherwell, Scotland; guitar/occasional recorder/keyboards), Mark (b. 15 January 1963 Motherwell, Scotland; lead vocals/bass) and Des (b. 27 June 1964, Motherwell, Scotland; drums) They began their career playing working men's clubs as a children's cabaret act in their native Motherwell, encouraged by their father who had insisted they all watch television's *Top Of The Pops* as children. They eventually moved down to Cannock in Staffordshire, where they are still based. An early gig at the ICA in London in 1985 saw a completely different approach to that with which Balaam would later become identified. Playing in bare feet and pyjamas, they played numerous covers of 60s love paeans, and also a recorder solo. Somewhat falsely categorized as a gothic group after supporting the Cult on three successive tours, they were, in fact, self-consciously colourful in both appearance and approach.

Early in their career they founded Chapter 22 Records, along with manager Craig Jennings. Their debut on the label came when 'World Of Light' appeared in 1984, although 'Day And Night' was their most impressive release from this period. Their debut set, *The Greatest Story Ever Told*, was named after the headline under which their first interview in *Melody Maker* appeared, and saw them rehoused on Virgin Records. Apparently intended to be reminiscent of the Doors, while there were stylistic similarities, it fell some way short of the visionary qualities associated with the west coast phenomenon. In September 1988 the band's second album was released after they had returned from support slots with Kiss and Iggy Pop in the USA. A new guitarist, Ian McKean, entered because of the need for two guitar parts on *Live Free Or Die*. They were dropped by Virgin, however, and their first tour for over four years took place in 1990. Press speculation that Mark would join the Cult as replacement bass player for Jamie Stewart collapsed as Ian Astbury decided that he was too much of a 'front man'. In 1991, they truncated their name to Balaam, marking the switch with the release of a mini-album, *No More Innocence*. By the advent of *Prime Time* any residual press interest in their career had dried up completely.

●ALBUMS: *The Greatest Story Ever Told* (Virgin 1986)★★★, *Live Free Or Die* (Virgin 1988)★★, *No More Innocence* (Intense 1991)★★, *Prime Time* (Bleeding Hearts 1993)★★.

BALL, MICHAEL

b. 27 July 1962, Stratford-Upon-Avon, England. After spending his early life in Plymouth, this popular singer studied at the Guildford School of Drama in Surrey before embarking on what has been, even by modern standards, a meteoric rise to fame. His first professional job was in the chorus of *Godspell* on a tour of Wales, after which he auditioned for a Manchester production of *The Pirates Of Penzance* - again for the chorus. Much to his surprise, he was given a leading role alongside Paul Nicholas and Bonnie Langford. In 1985, Ball created the role of Marius in the smash-hit musical *Les Misérables* at the Palace Theatre in London, and introduced one of the show's oustanding numbers, 'Empty Chairs At Empty Tables'. He subsequently took over the role of Raoul, opposite Sarah Brightman, in *The Phantom Of The Opera*, and then toured with her in the concert presentation of *The Music Of Andrew Lloyd Webber*. In 1989 his career really took off when he played Alex, a role that called for him to age from 17 to 40, in the same composer's *Aspects Of Love*. He was also in the 1990 Broadway production. Ball took the show's hit ballad, 'Love Changes Everything', to number 2 in the UK chart, and had modest success with one of the others, the poignant 'The First Man You Remember'. Further national recognition came his way when he was contracted (for a reported £100,000) to sing all six of Britain's entries for the 1992 Eurovision Song Contest on the top-rated *Wogan* television show. He came second with the chosen song, 'One Step Out Of Time', which just entered the UK Top 20. In the same year he embarked on an extensive tour of the UK, playing many top venues such as the London Palladium and the Apollo, Hammersmith. He surprised many people with his lively stage presence and a well-planned programme that catered for most tastes, and included rock 'n' roll, Motown, standards such as 'Stormy Weather', 'You Made Me Love You', and 'New York, New York', and the inevitable show songs. 1993 saw more concerts, the release of his version of the title song from *Sunset Boulevard* (he was tipped for the lead at one time), and his participation in a new studio recording of *West Side Story*, with Barbara Bonney, La Verne Williams, and the Royal Philharmonic Orchestra. The highlight of the year was his own six-part television series which gave him the opportunity to sing with some of the most illustrious names in music, including Cliff Richard, Dionne Warwick, Ray Charles, Monserrat Caballe, and Tammy Wynette.

●ALBUMS: *Michael Ball* (Polydor 1992)★★★, *Always* (Polydor 1993)★★★, *West Side Story* (1993)★★★, *One Careful Owner* (Columbia 1994)★★★, *The Musicals* (Polygram 1996)★★★.

BAMBI SLAM

An ambitious UK rock dance outfit, the Bambi Slam were formed in the mid-80s around would-be eccentric Roy Feldon (b. Lancashire, England). After a fairly inconsequential upbringing in the rosy suburbs of Pickering, Toronto, Canada, the expatriate Feldon moved to California for a spell. Coming to Britain to seek fame and fortune, he recruited Nick Maynard (drums) and Linda Mellor (cello) through an advert in the Royal Academy. Under the name Bambi Slam they toured the country, sending demos to dozens of record companies. The music contained on these cassettes resembled a rockier Public Image Limited. Product Inc., a subsidiary of Mute Records, picked up on them and released three singles, 'Bamp Bamp' through to the stirring 'Happy Birthday'. A tour supporting the Cult and a debut album were well under way and things were seemingly going to plan. However, Feldon suddenly underwent a period of artistic introspection resulting in the band going way over budget. This led to a split with Product Inc. and an unfinished album on which they owed a considerable amount of money. However, Rough Trade Records supremo Geoff Travis thought they had promise and signed them to Blanco y Negro. There they released a flawed debut, after which Feldon jettisoned the rest of the band.

●ALBUMS: *The Bambi Slam* (Blanco y Negro 1987)★★★.

BANANARAMA

Formed in London in 1980, this all-female pop trio comprised Keren Woodward (b. 2 April 1961, Bristol, Avon, England), Sarah Dallin (b. 17 December 1961, Bristol, Avon, England) and Siobhan Fahey (b. Siobhan Marie Deidre Fahey, 10 September 1958, Dublin, Eire). After singing impromptu at various parties and pubs in London, the group were recorded by former Sex Pistols drummer Paul Cook on the Swahili Black Blood cover 'Ai A Mwana'. The single caught the attention of Fun Boy Three vocalist Terry Hall, who invited the girls to back his trio on their revival of 'It Ain't What You Do, It's The Way That You Do It'. In return, the Fun Boy Three backed Bananarama on their Velvelettes cover 'Really Saying Something', which reached the UK Top 10 in 1982. From the outset, Bananarama had a strong visual image and an unselfconsciously amateur approach to choreography which was refreshing and appealing. Although they initially played down their talents, they retained considerable control over their careers, eschewing the usual overt sexism associated with the marketing of female troupes in pop. A tie-up with producers Tony Swain and Steve

Jolley brought them Top 10 hits with 'Shy Boy', the Steam cover 'Na Na, Hey Hey, Kiss Him Goodbye' and 'Cruel Summer'. Their high point during this phase was the clever and appealing 'Robert De Niro's Waiting', which justly reached the Top 3 in the UK. In an attempt to tackle more serious subject matter, they next released 'Rough Justice', a protest song on the political situation in Northern Ireland. The title prophetically summed up the disc's chart fate. A lean period followed before the girls teamed up with the Stock, Aitken And Waterman production team for a remake of Shocking Blue's 'Venus', which brought them a number 1 in the USA. 'I Heard A Rumour' maintained the quality of their recent output, with some excellent harmonies and a strong arrangement. Their biggest UK hit followed with the exceptional 'Love In The First Degree', an intriguing lyric dramatizing a Kafkaesque nightmare in which Love itself is placed on trial. It proved to be their finest pop moment. In December 1987 Siobhan Fahey left the group, married the Eurythmics' David A. Stewart and subsequently formed Shakespears Sister. Her replacement was Jacqui Sullivan, an old friend whose image fitted in reasonably well. During the early 90s, the hits continued, making Bananarama the most consistent and successful British female group in pop history. This effective formula underwent yet another change in 1991 when Sullivan departed for a solo career resulting in Dallin and Woodward continuing for the first time as a duo. The last chart entry before the band dissolved in 1993 was 'Last Thing On My Mind' in November 1992.

●ALBUMS: *Deep Sea Skiving* (London 1983)★★★, *Bananarama* (London 1984)★★★, *True Confessions* (London 1986)★★★, *Wow!* (London 1987)★★★, *Pop Life* (London 1991)★★, *Please Yourself* (London 1993)★★.

●COMPILATIONS: *The Greatest Hits Collection* (London 1988)★★★★, *Bunch Of Hits* (London 1993)★★★.

●VIDEOS: *Bananarama* (1984), *Bananarama: Video Singles* (1987), *Love In The First Degree* (1988), *Greatest Hits: Bananarama* (1988), *And That's Not All* (1988), *Greatest Hits Collection* (1991).

BAND AID/LIVE AID

Millions saw the 1984 BBC Television news report narrated by Michael Buerk, showing the famine in Ethiopia. Bob Geldof was so moved that he organized, promoted and produced a fund-raising enterprise like the world had never seen before. Geldof's likeable bullying and eloquently cheeky

publicity endeared him to millions. The song 'Do They Know It's Christmas?', co-written with Midge Ure, assembled a cavalcade of rock and pop stars under the name Band Aid. It included members from; Status Quo, Culture Club, Bananarama, Style Council, Duran Duran, Spandau Ballet, Heaven 17 and U2. Solo stars included Phil Collins, Sting, George Michael and Paul Young. Geldof brilliantly bludgeoned artists, record companies, pressing plants, distributors and record shops to forgo their profit. The record scaled the UK charts and stayed on top for 5 weeks, eventually selling millions of copies. Geldof topped this masterstroke in July 1985 by organizing Live Aid. This spectacular rock and pop concert was televised worldwide, live from London and Philadelphia. Among the stellar cast were; Sade, Queen, Bob Dylan, Neil Young, the Cars, Beach Boys, Pat Metheny, Santana, Madonna, Kenny Loggins, Bryan Adams, Crosby, Stills And Nash, Eric Clapton, Phil Collins (who via Concorde appeared at both venues), Judas Priest, REO Speedwagon, Jimmy Page, Robert Plant, Status Quo, Bryan Ferry, Sting, Paul Young, Simple Minds, U2, the Who, Paul McCartney, Mick Jagger, Adam Ant, Elvis Costello, Tina Turner, Elton John, Spandau Ballet and David Bowie. The largest television audience of all time raised over £50 million through pledged donations. Geldof carried through his sincere wish to help starving children with integrity, passion and a sense of humour. The Live Aid concert remains one of the greatest musical events of all time. Geldof received an honorary knighthood in 1986 for his humanitarian activities.
●VIDEOS: *Do They Know It's Christmas?* (1986).
●FURTHER READING: *Live Aid: The Greatest Show On Earth*, Peter Hillmore

BAND OF SUSANS

The membership of this articulate US guitar-based assembly was fluid but evolved around the songwriting partnership of Robert Poss (b. 20 November 1956, Buffalo, New York, USA; guitar/vocals) and Susan Stenger (b. 11 May 1955, Buffalo, New York, USA; bass/guitar/vocals). Poss had once been offered the guitarist's role in Public Image Limited when Keith Levene left. Both he and Stenger formerly worked with guitar composers Rhys Chatham, and eventually formed their own group. Their title was lifted from the fact that the original line-up contained three Susans. Other members of the group have included Ron Spitzer (drums, replaced by Joey Kaye), Page Hamilton (guitar/vocals, who later formed Helmet in 1992) and Anne Husick, who took over from Karen

Haglof as third guitarist. Bruce Gilbert from Wire also temporarily filled in for Haglof because of her aversion to touring. However, personnel changes have had little effect on the internal dynamics of the band because when they audition new people, 'we're not looking for an influx of new ideas, we like the way the band is . . . '. Two independent albums won them supporters on both sides of the Atlantic, after which they moved to Restless Records for 1991's *The Word And The Flesh*. The massed barrage of guitars on stage remains a unique visual and aural experience which the *New Musical Express* described as 'nothing less than pure, demonic euphoria'. 1995's *Here Comes Success*, an ironic title given that the band was apparently on the verge of dissolution, opened with the charming 'Elizabeth Stride (1843-1888)', the tale of a Jack The Ripper victim who had lived on the same street as Stenger.
●ALBUMS: *Hope Against Hope* (Further/Blast First 1988)★★★, *Love Agenda* (Restless/Blast First 1989)★★★, *The Word And The Flesh* (Restless/Blast First 1991)★★★, *Veil* (Restless/Blast First 1993)★★, *Here Comes Success* (Blast First 1995)★★★.
●COMPILATIONS: *Wired For Sound: 1986-1993* (Blast First 1995)★★★.

BANGLES

Formerly known as the Colours, the Bangs and finally the Bangles, this all-female Los Angeles quartet mastered the art of melodic west coast guitar-based pop and, like the Go-Go's immediately before them, led the way for all-female groups in the latter half of the 80s. The band was formed in 1981 and originally comprised Susanna Hoffs (b. 17 January 1962, Newport Beach, California, USA; guitar/vocals), Debbi Peterson (b. 22 August 1961, Los Angeles, California, USA; drums/vocals), Vicki Peterson (b. 11 January 1958, Los Angeles, California, USA; guitar/vocals) and Annette Zilinkas (bass/vocals). They emerged from the 'paisley underground' scene which spawned bands like Rain Parade and Dream Syndicate. The Bangles' first recordings were made on their own Downkiddie label and then for Miles Copeland's Faulty Products set-up which resulted in a flawed self-titled mini-album. On signing to the major CBS label in 1983, the line-up had undergone a crucial change. Zilinkas departed (later to join Blood On The Saddle) and was replaced by former Runaways member Michael Steele (b. 2 June 1954; bass/vocals). Their superb debut, 'Hero Takes A Fall', failed to chart, as did their interpretation of

Kimberley Rew's Soft Boys/Katrina And The Waves song 'Going Down To Liverpool'. The idea of four glamorous middle-class American girls singing about trotting down to a labour exchange in Liverpool with their UB40 cards, was both bizarre and quaint. The Bangles' energetic and harmonious style showed both a grasp and great affection for 60s pop with their Beatles and Byrds-like sound. Again, they failed to chart, although their sparkling debut *All Over The Place* scraped into the US chart. Following regular live work they built up a strong following, although it was not until the US/UK number 2 hit single 'Manic Monday', written by Prince, and the huge success of *Different Light* that they won a wider audience. The media, meanwhile, were picking out Hoffs as the leader of the group. This sowed the seeds of dissatisfaction within the line-up that would later come to a head. Both album and single narrowly missed the top of both US and UK charts, and throughout 1986 the Bangles could do no wrong. Their interpretation of Jules Shear's 'If She Knew What She Wants' showed touches of mid-60s Mamas And The Papas, while 'Walk Like An Egyptian' (composed by former Rachel Sweet svengali Liam Sternberg) was pure 80s quirkiness and gave the group a US number 1/UK number 3 hit. The unusual choice of a cover version of the Simon And Garfunkel song 'Hazy Shade Of Winter', which was featured in the film *Less Than Zero*, gave them a US number 2 hit/UK number 11 hit in 1988. The third album, *Everything*, continued to offer a collection of classy pop which generated the hit singles 'In Your Room' (US number 5, 1988) and the controversial 'Eternal Flame' in the spring of 1989, which gave the group a UK/US number 1 hit. Both these songs featured lead vocals from Hoffs, but 'Eternal Flame' was viewed by the other group members as an unnecessary departure from the Bangles' *modus operandi* with its use of string backing and barely any instrumental contribution from the rest of the group. Rather than harking back to the 60s the song was reminiscent of the pop ballads of the early to mid-70s of Michael Jackson and Donny Osmond. It also once again compounded the illusion in the public's eye that the Bangles was Hoffs' group. The year that had started so well for the group was now disintegrating into internal conflict. 'Be With You' and 'I'll Set You Free' failed to emulate their predecessors' success and by the end of the year the decision was made to dissolve the group. Susanna Hoffs embarked on a solo career while the remaining members have yet to make any impact with their respective plans.

● ALBUMS: *All Over The Place* (Columbia 1985)★★★, *Different Light* (Columbia 1986)★★★★, *Everything* (Columbia 1988)★★.
● COMPILATIONS: *The Bangles Greatest Hits* (Columbia 1990)★★★★, *Twelve Inch Mixes* (Columbia 1993)★★.
● VIDEOS: *Bangles Greatest Hits* (SMV 1990).

BANGS

The Bangs were formed in Los Angeles, California, USA, in 1981 from the ashes of the Colours. The line-up was Susanna Hoffs (vocals/guitar), Vickie Peterson (vocals/guitar) and Debbie Peterson (drums), later joined by Annette Zilinskas (bass) after the release of their debut single. Early comparisons with the Go-Go's became an albatross round their necks from which, in this form at least, they never really escaped. They made their debut in 1981 with 'Getting Out Of Hand', issued on Down Kiddies Records. This was followed by an EP for East West Records. Despite their obvious 'pop' appeal, they nevertheless performed regularly with local punk and hardcore bands such as the Descendents and Channel 3. They found much greater success as the Bangles, though Zilinskas departed before their breakthrough to join Blood On The Saddle.

BANTON, PATO

b. Patrick Murray Birmingham, England. Banton first came to the public's attention in 1982 on the Beat's *Special Beat Service* album, duelling with Ranking Roger on 'Pato And Roger A Go Talk', before releases on the Fashion Records and Don Christie labels. His debut single, 'Hello Tosh', was a novelty take on the Toshiba advertising campaign of 1985. His first long-playing effort saw him paired with the wizardry of the Mad Professor, a combination that he returned to four years later for the *Recaptured* set. On his solo debut Banton was backed by the Birmingham-based Studio 2 house band. Throughout, he coloured his Rasta toasting/dub with comic impersonations of those characters populating his songs. Since then his records have leaned progressively towards pop and soul, blurring the dividing lines between Jamaican toasting and American rap. For *Wize Up!*, which contained an unlikely alternative radio hit in his cover of the Police's 'Spirits In The Material World', Banton was joined by David Hinds of Steel Pulse. In the 90s Banton began to attract a large US following, where he was signed to IRS Records. However, his tremendous live popularity never transferred to his records, and in 1994 IRS persuaded him to release a pop cover version. Backed by Robin and Ali Campbell of UB40 and written by Eddy Grant, 'Baby Come Back' became a world-wide success, selling one-and-a-half million copies in Europe and Australasia. In its wake Sting invited Banton to chat over his 'Cowboy Song' single, which became another major chart success.

●ALBUMS: *Mad Professor Captures Pato Banton* (Ariwa 1985)★★★, *Never Give In* (Greensleeves 1987)★★★, *Visions Of The World* (IRS 1989)★★★, *Recaptured* (Ariwa 1989)★★★, *Wize Up! (No Compromize)* (IRS 1990)★★★, *Collections* (IRS 1995)★★★.

BARELY WORKS

This eclectic folk group was assembled in 1988 by former Boothill Foot-Tappers singer and banjoist Chris Thompson (b. 19 March 1957, Ashford, Middlesex, England), together with Richard Avison (b. 9 July 1958, Rothbury, Northumberland, England; trombone/vocals, ex-Happy End; Dead Can Dance), Sarah Allen (b. 22 July 1964, Tiverton, Devon, England; accordion/tin whistle/flutes, ex-Happy End; Di's New Outfit), Alison Jones (b. 6 April 1965, Sketty, Swansea, West Glamorgan, Wales; violin/vocals, ex-Di's New Outfit), Keith Moore (tuba, also a member of poet John Hegley's Popticians), Mat Fox (b. 8 November 1956; hammer dulcimer/percussion/vocals) and former Redskins drummer Paul Hookham, later replaced in 1990 by Tim Walmsley (b. 29 March 1956, Paddington, London, England; ex-Happy End). This strange mixture of personalities signed to the radical world music label, Cooking Vinyl, and emerged from the UK folk club circuit in the late 80s and early 90s. Their performances boasted a broad range of tradi-tional ('Byker Hill') and original material, mostly from Thompson and Allen as well as tackling the works of such artists as Captain Beefheart ('Tropical Hot Dog Nite'). The Barely Works have managed to break away from the constrictive pigeon hole of an 'English Folk Group' and crossed over to the rock club circuit where their virtuosity proved them more than capable of moving a rock audience. Mat Fox left the group in early 1992 and Keith Moore was replaced by Alice Kinloch. In 1993 the group disbanded.

●ALBUMS: *The Beat Beat* (Cooking Vinyl 1990)★★★, *Don't Mind Walking* (Cooking Vinyl 1991)★★★, *Shimmer* (Cooking Vinyl 1992)★★★, *Glow* (Cooking Vinyl 1992)★★★.

●COMPILATIONS: *The Best Of ...* (Cooking Vinyl 1995)★★★★.

BARRACUDAS

Formed in 1979 as a neo-surfing band - their lone UK Top 40 entry in 1980 was the derivative 'Summer Fun' - Jeremy Gluck (vocals), Robin Wills (guitar/vocals), David Buckley (bass/vocals) and Nicky Turner (drums/vocals) eschewed this direc-tion during the recording of their debut album, *Drop Out With The Barracudas*. Newer tracks, including 'I Saw My Death In A Dream Last Night', bore a debt to US-styled psychedelia and garage bands, and the group became one of the genre's leading proponents during its revival in the early 80s. The original rhythm section was then replaced by Jim Dickson and Terry Smith. However, the group only asserted an individual style with the arrival of Chris Wilson, formerly of the Flamin' Groovies. His influence was felt on the Barracudas' next two studio albums, *Mean Time* and *Endeavour To Persevere*, but these excellent releases were only issued in France. Failure to generate a British con-tract inevitably hampered the group's progress and they broke up in December 1984. Wilson and Wills were later reunited in a new venture, the Fortunate Sons, while Gluck, a former columnist on the music paper *Sounds*, resumed his journalistic career, principally with Q Magazine (as Jeremy Clarke) and also released two solo albums. Bentley ran his own vegetarian catering company before forming High Noon and, later, East West. Nick Turner joined Lords Of The New Church before taking a job at IRS Records. Gluck and Wills reformed the Barracudas in the 90s to record *Wait For Everything*, but were hampered by lack of money.

●ALBUMS: *Drop Out With The Barracudas* (Voxx 1981)★★★, *Mean Time* (Closer 1983)★★★, *Live 1983* (Coyote 1983)★★★, *Endeavour To Persevere* (Closer 1984)★★★, *Live In Madrid* (Impossible 1986)★★, *Wait For Everything* (1993)★★★.

●COMPILATIONS: *The Big Gap* (Coyote 1984)★★★, *I Wish It Could Be 1965 Again* (GMG 1987)★★★, *The Garbage Dump Tapes* remixes and re-recordings (Shakin' Street 1989)★★, *The Complete EMI Recordings* (EMI 1991)★★★, *Two Sides Of A Coin 1979-84* (Anagram 1993)★★★.

BARRY, JOHN

b. Jonathan Barry Prendergast, 3 November 1933, York, Yorkshire, England. Renowned as one of the leading composers of film soundtrack music, Barry began his career leading the John Barry Seven. This rousing instrumental unit enjoyed several notable UK hits between 1960 and 1962, the best-known of which were 'Hit And Miss' and a version of the Ventures' Walk Don't Run' (both 1960). The former, which reached number 11 in the UK charts, was the theme to *Juke Box Jury*, BBC Television's long-running record release show. Barry made regular appearances on several early pop programmes, including *Oh Boy* and *Drumbeat* and also enjoyed concurrent fame as a writer and arranger, scoring the distinctive pizzicato strings on numerous Adam Faith hits including the number 1 'What Do You Want' (1959). He also composed the soundtrack to *Beat Girl*, the singer's film debut, and later took up a senior A&R post with the independent Ember label. In 1962 Barry had a UK Top 20 hit with the 'James Bond Theme' which was part of Monty Norman's score for the film *Dr. No*, the first in a highly successful series. He produced music for several subsequent Bond films, including *From Russia With Love*, *Goldfinger* and *You Only Live Twice*, the title songs from which provided hit singles for Matt Monro (1963), Shirley Bassey (1964) and Nancy Sinatra (1967). Such success led to a series of stylish soundtracks that encompassed contrasting moods and music, including *The Ipcress File*, *The Knack* (both 1965), *Born Free* (which won an Oscar in 1966), *Midnight Cowboy* (1969), and *Mary, Queen Of Scots* (1971). Although his theme songs have enjoyed a high commercial profile, it is Barry's imaginative incidental music that has assured his peerless reputation. By contrast he pursued another lucrative direction, composing television commercials for disparate household items.

His consistency remained intact throughout the 70s and 80s, although several attendant films, including *King Kong* (1976) and *Howard The Duck* (1986), were highly criticized. 'Down Deep Inside', the theme from *The Deep* (1977), was a UK Top 5 hit for Donna Summer, and this disco-influenced composition emphasized the writer's versatility. *Out Of Africa* (1985) and *The Living Daylights* and *Hearts Of Fire* (both 1987) demonstrated his accustomed flair, while his music to *Dances With Wolves* (1990) earned him another Oscar. In the early 90s his scores included *Ruby Cairo*, *Indecent Proposal*, and Richard Attenborough's *Chaplin* (Oscar nomination), *My Life* (1993), and *The Specialist* (1994). His orchestrations combine elements of classical, jazz and popular themes and command the respect of enthusiastic aficionados.

●ALBUMS: *Beat Girl* soundtrack (Columbia 1959)★★★, *Stringbeat* (Columbia 1961)★★★, *Man In The Middle* soundtrack (Stateside 1962)★★★, *Dr. No* (United Artists 1962)★★★★, *It's All Happening* (1963)★★★, *A Handful Of Songs* (Ember 1963)★★★, *Zulu* soundtrack (Ember 1963)★★★, *Elizabeth Taylor In London* television soundtrack (Colpix 1963)★★★, *From Russia With Love* (United Artists 1963)★★★, *Goldfinger* (United Artists 1964)★★★, *The Ipcress File* (Decca 1965)★★★, *Sophia Loren In Rome* (1965)★★★, *King Rat* (1965)★★★, *The Knack ... & How To Get It* (MCA 1965)★★★, *Four In The Morning* (1965)★★★, *Thunderball* (United Artists 1965)★★★, *Passion Flower Hotel* (1965)★★★, *The Wrong Box* (1966)★★★, *The Chase* (1966)★★★, *Born Free* (MGM 1966)★★★, *The Quiller Memorandum* (1966)★★★, *You Only Live Twice* (United Artists 1967)★★★, *Dutchman* (1967)★★★, *The Whisperers* (1967)★★★, *Deadfall* (1968)★★★, *Petulia* (1968)★★★, *Boom* (1968)★★★, *The Lion In Winter* (Columbia 1968)★★★★, *On Her Majesty's Secret Service* (United Artists 1969)★★★, *Midnight Cowboy* (United Artists 1969)★★★★, *The Last Valley* (Probe 1970)★★★, *Diamonds Are Forever* (United Artists 1971)★★★, *Follow Me* (1971)★★★, *Lolita My Love* (1971)★★★, *The Persuaders* (Columbia 1971)★★★, *Mary Queen Of Scots* (MCA 1971)★★★, *Alice's Adventures In Wonderland* (Warners 1972)★★★, *The John Barry Concert* (1972)★★★, *A Doll's House* (1973)★★★, *Billy* (1974)★★★, *The Dove* (1974)★★★, *The Man With The Golden Gun* (United Artists 1974)★★★, *The Day Of The Locust* (1974)★★★, *Americans* (1975)★★★, *Robin And Marian* (1976)★★★, *King Kong* (Reprise 1976)★★★, *The Deep* (Casablanca 1977)★★★, *The Game Of Death* (1978)★★★, *Starcrash* (1978)★★★, *The Black Hole* (1979)★★★, *Moonraker* (United Artists 1979)★★★, *Inside Moves* (Warners 1980)★★★, *The Legend Of The Lone Ranger* (1981)★★★, *Frances* (1982)★★★, *High Road To China* (1983)★★★, *The Golden Seal* (1983)★★★, *Body Heat* (1983)★★★, *Until September* (1984)★★★, *Jagged Edge* (1985)★★★, *Out Of Africa* (MCA 1985)★★★, *A View To A Kill* (Capitol 1985)★★★, *Peggy Sue Got Married* (TER 1986)★★★, *Howard The Duck* (MCA 1986)★★★, *Golden Child* (Capitol 1986)★★★, *Somewhere In Time* (MCA 1986)★★★, *Living Daylights* (Warners 1987)★★★, *Dances With Wolves* (Epic 1990)★★★, *My Life* (Epic 1994)★★★, *Moviola II - Action And Adventure* (Epic 1995)★★★.

●COMPILATIONS: *Six-Five Special* (Parlophone 1957)★★★, *Oh Boy* (Parlophone 1958)★★★, *Drumbeat* (Parlophone 1959)★★★, *Saturday Club* (Parlophone 1960)★★★, *Blackpool Nights* (Columbia 1960)★★★, *The Great Movie Sounds Of John Barry* (1966)★★★, *John Barry Conducts His*

Great Movie Hits (1967)★★★, *Ready When You Are, John Barry* (1970)★★★, *John Barry Revisited* (1971)★★★, *Play It Again* (1974)★★★, *The Music Of John Barry* (1976)★★★, *The Very Best Of John Barry* (1977)★★★, *The John Barry Seven And Orchestra* (1979)★★★, *The Best Of John Barry* (Polydor 1981)★★★, *The Big Screen Hits Of John Barry* (Columbia 1981)★★★, *James Bond's Greatest Hits* (1982)★★★, *Music From The Big Screen* (Pickwick 1986)★★★, *Hit Or Miss* (1988)★★★, *The Film Music Of John Barry* (1989)★★★, *John Barry Themes* (1989)★★★, *The Ember Years Vol. 1* (Play It Again 1992)★★★, *The Ember Years Vol. 2* (Play It Again 1992)★★★, *Moviola* (1992)★★★, *The Best Of EMI Years Vol. 2* (1993)★★★, *The Ember Years Vol. 3* (Play It Again 1996)★★★.
●FILMS: *It's All Happening* (1963).

BASIL, TONI

b. 1950. American singer/dancer Basil was responsible for the choreography on the legendary US 60s pop shows, *Hullabaloo* and *Shindig*. She was also actively involved in the Monkees' 1968 cult movie *Head* and the highly successful *American Graffiti* in 1974. David Bowie employed Basil's choreographical services for his elaborately staged *Diamond Dogs* tour and other rock artists followed his lead. By the early 80s, Basil had moved into the video field, co-directing Talking Heads among others. Backed by her own dance troupe, the Lockers, she recorded the hit album *Word Of Mouth* in 1981, which featured musical backing by two former members of Seatrain. The Chinn And Chapman composition 'Mickey' brought her a surprise UK number 2 in 1982 and several months later it reached number 1 in her homeland. With her related interests in different fields of the music business, Basil seemed unlikely to pursue an exclusively vocal career and failed to register any further major hits.
●ALBUMS: *Word Of Mouth* (Radialchoice 1981)★★★, *Toni Basil* (Virgin 1983)★★.

BATES, DJANGO

b. Leon Bates, 2 October 1960, Beckenham, Kent, England. A self-taught pianist, Bates formally studied the instrument, together with trumpet and violin, at London's Centre for Young Musicians in the 70s and later attended the young musicians' course at Morley College. In 1978, he dropped out of the Royal College of Music (after two weeks). Bates began a series of important associations with many of the leading young musicians who graced the burgeoning British jazz scene of the 80s and several of the concurrently popular African jazz musicians. In 1983, by which time he had already experienced stints with Tim Whitehead, Steve Argüelles (with whom he formed the trio Human Chain), Bill Bruford, Harry Beckett and Dudu Pukwana's Zila, he became a founder member of Loose Tubes. In 1986, Bates guested with the George Russell Orchestra on their UK tour, and by this time was also playing in the quartet First House, with alto saxophonist Ken Stubbs, and in Bruford's jazz rock group, Earthworks. Bates's eclectic musical tastes are evidenced by his playing and composing, neither of which can be readily pigeon holed. Whether on keyboards or on tenor horn (an unusual instrument in jazz circles and one on which Bates is particularly effective) he is a distinctive and adventurous musician and one who seems incapable of a bad or uninteresting performance. In 1990, Bates' suite *Music For The Third Policeman* (based on the novel by Flann O'Brien), was recorded by his specially-formed Powder Room Collapse Orchestra, and in the summer of 1991 he assembled another big band, Delightful Precipice (named after a Loose Tubes' album), for a show that also featured a circus! Earlier that year he toured the UK in a group led by Norwegian singer Sidsel Endresen.
●ALBUMS: *First House* (1985)★★★★, with Human Chain *Cashin' In* (1988)★★★, with First House *Cantilena* (1989)★★★, *Music For The Third Policeman* (Ah-Um 1990)★★, *Summer Fruits (And Unrest)* (PolyGram 1993)★★★, as Doran, Studer, Minton, Bates, Ali *Play The Music Of Jimi Hendrix* (Call It Anything 1994)★★, *Winter Truce (And Homes Ablaze)* (JMT 1995)★★★, *Good Evening ... Here Is The News* (Argo 1996)★★★.

BAUHAUS

Originally known as Bauhaus 1919, this Northamptonshire quartet comprised Peter Murphy (vocals), Daniel Ash (vocals/guitar), David Jay aka David J. (vocals/bass) and Kevin Haskins (drums). Within months of their formation they made their recording debut in 1979 with the classic, brooding, nine-minute gothic anthem, 'Bela Lugosi's Dead'. Their career saw them move to various independent labels (Small Wonder, Axix, 4AD and Beggars Banquet) and along the way cut some interesting singles, including 'Dark Entries', 'Terror Couple Kill Colonel' and a reworking of T. Rex's 'Telegram Sam'. Often insistent on spontaneity in the studio, they recorded four albums in as many years, of which *Mask* (1981) proved the most accessible. A cameo appearance in the movie *The Hunger*, starring David Bowie, showed them playing their memorable Bela Lugosi tribute. They later took advantage of the Bowie connection to record a carbon copy of 'Ziggy Stardust', which gave them their only UK Top 20 hit. Although there was further belated success with 'Lagartija Nick' and 'She's In Parties', the group disbanded in 1983. Vocalist Peter Murphy briefly joined Japan's Mick Karn in Dali's Car and the remaining three members soldiered on under the name Love And Rockets.

●ALBUMS: *In The Flat Field* (4AD 1980)★★, *Mask* (Beggars Banquet 1981)★★★, *The Sky's Gone Out* (Beggars Banquet 1982)★★★, *Press The Eject And Give Me The Tape* (Beggars Banquet 1982)★★, *Burning From The Inside* (Beggars Banquet 1983)★★.
●COMPILATIONS: *1979-1983* (Beggars Banquet 1985)★★★.
●VIDEOS: *Shadow Of Light* (1984), *Archive* (1988).
●FURTHER READING: *Dark Entries: Bauhaus And Beyond*, Ian Shirley.

BEASTIE BOYS

Former hardcore trio who went on to find international fame as the first crossover white rap act of the 80s. After forming at New York University, original members John Berry and Kate Shellenbach departed after the release of 'Pollywog Stew', leaving Adam 'MCA' Yauch (b. 15 August 1967, Brooklyn, New York, USA), Mike 'D' Diamond (b. 20 November 1965, New York, USA) and the recently recruited guitarist Adam 'Ad Rock' Horovitz (b. 31 October 1966, New York City, New York, USA) to hold the banner. The group was originally convened to play at MCA's 15th birthday party, adding Horovitz to their ranks from The Young And The Useless (one single, 'Real Men Don't Use Floss'). Horovitz, it transpired, was the son of dramatist Israel Horwitz, indicating that, far from being the spawn of inner-city dystopia, the Beasties all came from privileged middle-class backgrounds. They continued in similar vein to their debut with the *Cookie Puss* EP, which offerred the first evidence of them picking up on the underground rap phenomenon. The record, later sampled for a British Airways commercial, earned them $40,000 in royalties. Friend and sometime band member Rick Rubin quickly signed them to his fledgling Def Jam label. They did not prove difficult to market. Their debut album revealed a collision of bad attitudes, spearheaded by the raucous single, 'Fight For Your Right To Party', and samples of everything from Led Zeppelin to the theme to

Mister Ed. There was nothing self-conscious or sophisticated about the lyrics, Mike D and MCA reeling off complaints about their parents confiscating their pornography or telling them to turn the stereo down. Somehow, however, it became an anthem for pseudo rebellious youth everywhere, achieving a number 11 hit in the UK. In the wake of its success, *Licensed To Ill* became the first rap album to top the US charts. By the time follow-up singles 'No Sleep Till Brooklyn' and 'She's On It' charted, the band had become a media *cause célèbre*. Their stage shows regularly featured caged, half-naked females, while their Volkswagen pendants resulted in a crimewave with fans stealing said items from vehicles throughout the UK. A reflective Horovitz recalled how that never happened in the USA, where they merely stole the car itself. More disturbing, it was alleged that the band derided terminally ill children on a foreign jaunt. This false accusation was roundly denied, but other stories of excess leaked out of the Beastie Boys camp with grim regularity. There was also friction between the group and Def Jam, the former accusing the latter of withholding royalties, the latter accusing the former of withholding a follow-up album. By the time the band reassembled after a number of solo projects in 1989, the public, for the most part, had forgotten about them. Rap's ante had been significantly raised by the arrival of Public Enemy and NWA, yet *Paul's Boutique* remains one of the genre's most overlooked pieces, a complex reflection of pop culture that is infinitely subtler than their debut. Leaving their adolescent fixations behind, the rhymes plundered cult fiction (*Clockwork Orange*) through to *The Old Testament*. It was co-produced by the Dust Brothers, who would subsequently become a hot production item. Moving to California, *Check Your Head* saw them returning, partially, to their thrash roots, reverting to a guitar, bass and drums format. In the meantime the Beasties had invested wisely, setting up their own magazine, studio and label, Grand Royal. This has boasted releases by Luscious Jackson, plus The Young And The Useless (Adam Horwitz's first band) and DFL (his hardcore punk project). Other signings included DJ Hurricane (also of the Afros), Noise Addict and Moistboyz. There has been a downside too. Horovitz pleaded guilty to a charge of battery on a television cameraman during a memorial service for River Phoenix in 1993. He was put on two years probation, ordered to undertake 200 hours community service and pay restitution costs. His connections with the Phoenix family came through his actress wife Lone Sky. He himself had undertaken film roles in *The Santa Anna Project*, *Roadside Prophets* and *Lost Angels*, also appearing in a television cameo for *The Equalizer*. By this time both he and Diamond had become Californian citizens, while Yauch had become a Buddhist, speaking out in the press against US trade links with China, because of that country's annexation of Tibet. *Ill Communication* was another succesful voyage into inspired Beastie thuggism, featuring A Tribe Called Quest's Q Tip, and a second appearance from Biz Markie, following his debut on *Check Your Head*. *The In Sound From Way Out* was merely a space-filler of b-sides and instrumental takes.

● ALBUMS: *Licensed To Ill* (Def Jam 1986)★★★, *Paul's Boutique* (Capitol 1989)★★★★, *Check Your Head* (Capitol 1992)★★★★, *Ill Communication* (Capitol 1994)★★★★, *The Root Down EP* (Capitol 1995)★★, *Aglio E Olio* (Grand Royal 1996)★★★, *In Sound From Way Out* (Capitol 1996)★★.

● COMPILATIONS: *Some Old Bullshit* (Capitol 1994)★★★.

● VIDEOS: *Sabotage* (1994), *The Skills To Pay The Bills* (1994).

BEAT (UK)

Founded in Birmingham, England, in 1978, the original Beat comprised Dave Wakeling (b. 19 February 1956, Birmingham, England; vocals/guitar), Andy Cox (b. 25 January 1956, Birmingham, England; guitar), David Steele (b. 8 September 1960, Isle Of Wight, England; bass) and Everett Morton (b. 5 April 1951, St Kitts; drums). Local success on the pub circuit brought them to the attention of Jerry Dammers who duly signed them to his Coventry-based Two-Tone label. In the meantime, the Beat had expanded their ranks to include black punk rapper Ranking Roger (b. Roger Charlery, 21 February 1961, Birmingham, England) and a saxophonist simply named Saxa (b. Jamaica), who had the distinction of having played alongside that premier exponent of bluebeat Prince Buster. The new line-up proved perfect for the ska/pop fusion that exemplified the Beat at their best. Their debut single, a cover of Smokey Robinson's 'Tears Of A Clown', was a surprise Top 10 hit, but the best was yet to come. After forming their own label, Go Feet, they registered several hits during 1980 which ably displayed their talents as sharp-witted lyricists with the necessary strong danceability quotient. The uplifting yet acerbic 'Mirror In The Bathroom' and 'Best Friend' worked particularly well both as observations on personal relationships and more generalized putdowns of the 'Me' gener-

ation. This political awareness was more explicitly exposed on 'Stand Down Margaret', one of several anti-Thatcherite songs that appeared during the British Prime Minister's reign. Donations to CND and benefit gigs for the unemployed linked the Beat with other radical Two-Tone outfits, such as the Specials.

On record, the Beat sustained their verve and their debut album, *I Just Can't Stop It*, proved a solid collection, boosted by the inclusion of several hit singles. Within a year, however, their essentially pop-based style was replaced by a stronger reggae influence. *Wha'ppen* and *Special Beat Service* were generally well received, but the previously effortless run of chart hits had temporarily evaporated. By April 1982, Saxa had retired to be replaced by Wesley Magoogan. Although the Beat continued to tour extensively, their dissolution was imminent. Ironically, they ended their career as it had begun with an opportune cover of a 60s song, this time Andy Williams' 'Can't Get Used To Losing You', which gave the group their biggest UK hit. After the split, Ranking Roger and Dave Wakeling formed General Public while Andy Cox and David Steele recruited Roland Gift to launch the Fine Young Cannibals.

● ALBUMS: *I Just Can't Stop It* (Go-Feet 1980)★★★★, *Wha'ppen* (Go-Feet 1981)★★★, *Special Beat Service* (Go-Feet 1982)★★★.

● COMPILATIONS: *What Is Beat* (Go-Feet 1983)★★★, *BPM - The Very Best Of ...* (Arista 1995)★★★.

● FURTHER READING: *The Beat: Twist And Crawl*, Malu Halasha.

BEAT (USA)

Formed in San Francisco in 1979, the new wave/pop band the Beat were led by Paul Collins, who had previously played in the power pop band, the Nerves, with Peter Case, who later joined the Plimsouls, and songwriter Jack Lee (whose 'Hanging On The Telephone' was a hit for Blondie). The Beat signed with Bill Graham's management company and secured a recording contract with Columbia Records. Their debut, *The Beat*, was popular on college radio but never broke nationally. Their second album and a 1983 EP for Passport Records, recorded with a new line-up, failed to garner much interest and the group broke up.

● ALBUMS: *The Beat* (Columbia 1979)★★★, *The Kids Are The Same* (Passport 1982)★★★, *To Beat Or Not To Beat* mini-album (Passport 1983)★★.

BEAT HAPPENING

Formed in Olympia, Washington, USA, the guitar band Beat Happening are led by Calvin Johnson. Two five-song tapes, *Beat Happening* and *Three Tea Breakfast* introduced their primitive art which echoed the jejune style of Jonathan Richman. The group's charming amateurism flourished on their debut album, *Beat Happening*, issued on their own K label and produced by Wipers guitarist, Greg Sage. Their work drew parallels with Scottish act the Pastels, and a 12-inch EP, *Crashing Through*, was released in Britain on 53rd & 3rd, a label co-founded by Stephen Pastel. Scottish acts Teenage Fanclub and Melody Dog reciprocally recorded for K. *Jamboree* revealed a more electric sound although the group's overall innocence remained intact. A collaborative EP with the Screaming Trees ensued, notable for the Cream-inspired 'Tales Of Brave Aphrodite', before the disappointing *Black Candy* appeared in 1989. Its inconsistent short-comings were ironed out for *Dreamy*, which shows the group ageing without sacrificing their charm.

●ALBUMS: *Beat Happening* (K 1985)★★★, *Jamboree* (K 1988)★★★, *Black Candy* (K 1989)★★, *Dreamy* (K 1991)★★★, *You Turn Me On* (K 1992)★★★.

●COMPILATIONS: *1983-85* (K 1990)★★★

BEAUSOLEIL

Widely considered to be the pre-eminent Cajun band of the 80s and 90s, BeauSoleil (the initialized 'S' having been added in the 90s) have amassed a huge discography during that time which features some of the most exciting music extant within the traditional music realm. Rather than contemplate retirement, if anything, their output seems to have increased and intensified during recent years. They were almost entirely responsible for the Cajun music boom of the late 80s when their music was featured extensively in *The Big Easy*. Formed in 1975 by fiddler, vocalist and songwriter Michael Doucet (who had formerly piloted a Cajun group entitled Coteau which he revived in the mid-90s), the regular group additionally comprises brother David Doucet (guitar/vocals), Tommy Alesi (drums), Al Tharp (bass), Billy Ware (percussion) and Jimmy Breaux (accordion). Other prominent members over the years include guitarist Bessyl Duhon (of Riff Raffs fame), while guest collaborators have included artists of the calibre of Richard Thompson, Keith Richards, the Grateful Dead and Augie Meyers. Despite their already vast recorded legacy, BeauSoleil remain predominantly a live attraction, the group having rarely left the road for any extended period during their 25 years together. 1989's *Bayou Cadillac* and *Cajun Conja*, a collaboration with Thompson, which was nominated for a Grammy, are but two standouts in a distinguished recording career. Despite their genre-popularity, they have too often had to rely on the recommendations or lip-service of others to gain media prominence. For example, they received a major boost in 1991 when Mary-Chapin Carpenter mentioned the group in the lyrics to her hit, 'Down At The Twist And Shout'. The video she shot of the award-winning song featured BeauSoleil prominently. In 1997 the group joined Carpenter for a reprisal of the song at the Super Bowl in New Orleans.

●ALBUMS: *The Spirit Of Cajun Music* (Swallow 1977)★★★, *Zydeco Gris Gris* (Rounder 1980)★★★, *Parlez-Nous A Boire* (Arhoolie 1981)★★★, *Bayou Boogie* (Rounder 1986)★★★, *Allons A Lafayette* (Arhoolie 1986)★★★, *Hot Chili Mama* (Arhoolie 1988)★★★★, *Live From The Left Coast* (Rounder 1989)★★★, *Bayou Cadillac* (Rounder 1989)★★★★, *Déja Vu* (Swallow 1990)★★★, *Cajun Conja* (Rhino 1991)★★★★, *L'Echo* (Rhino 1995)★★★, *L'Amour Ou La Folie* (Rhino 1997)★★★.

●COMPILATIONS: *Their Swallow Recordings* (Ace 1992)★★★★, *Vintage Beausoleil* (Music Of The World 1995)★★★★.

BEAUTIFUL SOUTH

This highly literate adult pop group were built from the ashes of the Housemartins. The line-up features vocalists Paul Heaton (b. 9 May 1962, Birkenhead, Merseyside, England) and David Hemmingway (b. 20 September 1960, England) from Hull's self-proclaimed 'Fourth Best Band'. In reference to their previous dour Northern image, Heaton sarcastically named his new band Beautiful South, recruiting Sean Welch (bass), Briana Corrigan (vocals, ex-Anthill Runaways), former Housemartins roadie David Stead (drums) and Heaton's new co-writer, David Rotheray (guitar). Continuing an association with Go! Discs, their first single was the ballad 'Song For Whoever' which gave them instant UK chart success (number 2 in June 1989). After the rejection of the original sleeve concept for their debut album (a suicidal girl with gun in her mouth), *Welcome To The Beautiful South* emerged in October 1989 to a good critical reception. 'A Little Time' became their first number 1 the following year. A bitter duet between Corrigan and Hemmingway, it was supported by a memorable video which won The

Best Music Video award at the 1991 BRIT Awards. Lyrically, Heaton had honed his songwriting to a style which allowed the twists and ironies to develop more fully: 'I find it difficult to write straightforward optimistic love songs . . . I throw in a row, a fight, get a few knives out . . .'. Though giving the band their least successful chart position to date (number 43), 'My Book' provided one of Heaton's most cutting lyrics (including a hilarious reference to the football player Peter Beardsley) and also saw Jazzie B. of Soul II Soul sue for the slight use of the 'Back To Reality' refrain. Always a writer able to deal with emotive subjects in an intelligent and forthright manner, Heaton's next topic was lonely alcoholism in 'Old Red Eyes Is Back', the first fruits of a protracted writing stint in Gran Canaria. However, Corrigan became a little unsettled at some of the subject matter now expressed in Heaton's lyrics (notably '36D', a song about *The Sun* newspaper's 'Page 3' topless models, which was open to a variety of interpretations) and left the band after *0898*, although press statements suggested she may return in the future. Her replacement, Jacqui Abbot, was introduced on 'Everybody's Talkin'', and more fully on the band's fourth studio album, *Miaow*. However, its success was dwarfed by the singles collection, *Carry On Up The Charts*, which dominated the listings in late 1994 and early 1995. 'Rotterdam' preceded the album *Blue Is The Colour* at the end of 1996.

●ALBUMS: *Welcome To The Beautiful South* (Go! Discs 1989)★★★, *Choke* (Go! Discs 1990)★★★, *0898* (Go! Discs 1992)★★★, *Miaow* (Go! Discs 1994)★★★, *Blue Is The Colour* (Go! Discs 1996)★★★.

●COMPILATIONS: *Carry On Up The Charts* (Go! Discs 1994)★★★★.

●VIDEOS: *The Pumpkin* (1992), *Carry On Up The Charts* (1995).

BEF

The BEF (or British Electric Foundation) was a UK duo formed by ex-Human League members Martyn Ware (b. 19 May 1956) and Ian Craig Marsh (b. 11 November 1956). The first in the *Music Of Quality And Distinction* series arrived in 1982, featuring a series of guest artists covering songs of their own selection. Among them were Gary Glitter, Tina Turner, Billy McKenzie (ex-Associates) and Sandie Shaw. The concept was innovative and achieved minor commercial success, but the project was abandoned when Ware and Marsh reunited with vocalist Glenn Gregory in their other incarnation, Heaven 17. When that group ended, a lucrative career in production ensued, notably with Terence Trent D'Arby and Tina Turner. It was only in 1991 that they managed to burrow through the legal contracts binding the second volume's artists and repeat the formula. This time the album was more cohesive, consisting entirely of soul covers. It saw the return of Tina Turner, alongside Terence Trent D'Arby (his version of Bob Dylan's 'Its Alright Ma, I'm Only Bleeding' was approached as Otis Redding might have sung it), Chaka Khan, Billy Preston, and Mavis Staples, among others. Most surprising of all was the appearance of Billy McKenzie's version of Deniece Williams' 'Free'. Another unexpected facet of the recordings was the duo's use of traditional instruments and a backing band.

●ALBUMS: *Music Of Quality And Distinction Volume 1* (1982)★★★, *Music Of Quality And Distinction Volume 2* (1991)★★★.

BELEW, ADRIAN

b. Kentucky, USA. Guitarist Adrian Belew has enjoyed a rich and varied career, with a number of left-field stars having used his skills. His chameleon-like style, which ranges from overwrought progressive rock to impish and self-deprecating pop, has helped make his contributions more anonymous than otherwise might have been the case. Having cut his teeth with Frank Zappa, Belew contributed admirably to Talking Heads' tensely orchestrated early 80s output (*Remain In Light*, *The Name Of This Band*, *Stop Making Sense*, etc.). His other clients included the Talking Heads spin-off group the Tom Tom Club. He also joined the reformed King Crimson before Robert Fripp decided to resurrect his solo career, and spurred Belew to do the same. The funk-influenced style with which he had spiced *Remain In Light* resurfaced on his debut, on which he reunited with friends from the Midwest. Ill-focused and without a prevailing musical ethos to guide it (the album lurches from funk to rock), it failed to illustrate his proven skills to their best advantage. *Twang Bar King* concentrated on technique and, although occasionally draining, would have appealed to committed King Crimson fans. *Desire Caught By The Tail*, its title taken from Picasso's play, was a one-man home studio exercise, which prefaced his sojourn with the Bears. Recruiting former friends the Raisins, a Midwest rock band, Belew embarked on creating a set of originals that could accommodate his musical effects and guitar improvisations within an offbeat pop framework. The Bears' debut invoked comparisons with Squeeze and XTC, and for good reason. Far more accessible than previous offerings, Belew clearly had a knack for pop composition and performance which had previously been buried under layers of musicianship. Even the lyrics, though not yet quite in the stately Difford/Tilbrook or Moulding/Partridge sphere, were coming along well. The same was true of the second and final Bears album, which repeated this successful formula. However, despite their obvious qualities and rave reviews in the more discerning musical papers, sales were not great and the three remaining Bears formed the Psychodots. Belew carried over some of his new-found accessibility and pop instinct to his second attempt at a solo career, this time on Atlantic Records. It became clear that Belew was now composing songs on the piano, which altered the feel of subsequent recordings, even if they retained the occasional outbreak of fretboard abandon. *Young Lions* featured two songs written and sung by David Bowie, with whom Belew was about to tour as guitarist and musical director. Bowie's 'Pretty Pink Rose' was certainly a highlight but so were some of Belew's own songs. 'Men In Helicopters' was a particularly affecting one, depicting rogue hunters gunning down rhinos. The cover versions of Buddy Holly's 'Heartbeat' and the Traveling Wilburys' 'Not Alone Anymore' filled out the set. *Inner Revolution*, meanwhile, saw a full-scale Beatles pastiche, with superbly observed singing and playing, before Belew regrouped with Fripp for a new King Crimson album, *Thrak*, in 1995.

●ALBUMS: *Lone Rhino* (Island 1982)★★★★, *Twang Bar King* (Island 1983)★★★, *Desire Caught By The Tail* (Island 1986)★★★, *Mr. Music Head* (Atlantic 1989)★★★, *Young Lions* (Atlantic 1990)★★, *Inner Revolution* (Atlantic 1992)★★★★, with the Bears *The Bears* (Primitive Man 1987)★★★, with the Bears *Rise And Shine* (Primitive Man 1988)★★★, *Here* (Caroline 1994)★★★, *The Acoustic Adrian Belew* (Discipline 1995)★★★, *The Experimental Guitar Series Volume 1: The Guitar As Orchestra* (Adrian Belew Presents 1996)★★★, *Op Zop Too Wah* (Passenger 1996)★★★.

BELLE STARS

A splinter group from the Two-Tone influenced Bodysnatchers, this all-female septet from the UK comprised Sarah-Jane Owen (guitar), Miranda Joyce (saxophone), Judy Parsons (drums) and Jennie McKeown (bass). Signed by the independent Stiff Records in 1981, they charted the following year with remakes of the Dixie Cups' 'Iko Iko' and Shirley Ellis's 'The Clapping Song'. Unable to sustain a long term commercial appeal and subject to changing personnel, they nevertheless produced one memorable smash hit with 'Sign Of The Times', a catchy pop tune with a spoken word section reminiscent of the great girl group sound of the mid-60s.

●ALBUMS: *The Belle Stars* (Stiff 1983)★★★.
●COMPILATIONS: *The Very Best Of ...* (Repertoire 1993)★★★.
●VIDEOS: *Live Signs, Live Times* (1989).

BELOVED

Initially known in 1983 as the Journey Through and comprising Jon Marsh (b. *c.*1964), Guy Gousden and Tim Havard, UK band the Beloved fell into place a year later when Cambridge University student and ex-postman Steve Waddington (b. *c.*1959) joined on guitar. It was no straightforward initiation ceremony either. Marsh had placed an advert in the music press which ran thus: 'I am Jon Marsh, founder member of the Beloved. Should you too wish to do something gorgeous, meet me in exactly three year's time at exactly 11am in Diana's Diner, or site thereof, Covent Garden, London, WC2'. Tentative stabs at heavy psychedelia evolved into a more pop orientated formula by the mid-80s, with the Beloved's dark, danceable sounds often being compared to New Order and garnering attention throughout Europe. Marsh became a contestant on television quiz show *Countdown* in 1987, featuring on nine programmes before being knocked out in the semi-finals. It was not until 1988, however, that the Beloved started living up to their name: Waddington and Marsh, heavily influenced by the nascent 'rave' scene in London at that time, split from Gousden and Harvard and started forging their own path. Unshackled from the confines of a four-cornered set-up, the revitalised duo dived into the deep end of the exploding dance movement, subsequently breaking into commercial waters with the ambient textures of 'Sun Rising'. The *Happiness* album, backed by Marsh and Waddington's enthusiastic chatter concerning the virtues of floatation tanks and hallucinogenic substances, perfectly embodied the tripped-out vibe of the times and sealed the Beloved's fashionable success in worldwide territories. By 1993's *Conscience*, Marsh had left his former partner Waddington, using his wife Helena as his new creative foil. The resultant album was more whimsical and understated than previous affairs, with a pop rather than club feel. Their third album relied too heavily on electronic gimmickry detracting attention from individual songs.

●ALBUMS: *Happiness* (Atlantic 1990)★★★, *Blissed Out* remix of *Happiness* (East West 1990)★★★, *Conscience* (East West 1993)★★★, *X* (East West 1996)★★.

BENATAR, PAT

b. Pat Andrzejewski, 10 January 1953, Brooklyn, New York, USA. Pat Benatar, after training as an opera singer, became a major hitmaker in the early 80s, adept at both mainstream rock and powerful ballads, often focusing on personal relationships and sexual politics. She married Dennis Benatar after graduating from high school and relocated to Virginia. By the 70s she had returned to New York, where she was discovered by Rick Newman in 1979 at the latter's Catch A Rising Star club. With Newman as manager, she signed to Chrysalis Records that year and released her debut album *In The Heat Of The Night*, produced by Mike Chapman, which became a substantial hit and spawned three US chart singles. Benatar (who retained the name after divorcing) released her second album, *Crimes Of Passion*, in 1980. This collection, which later won a Grammy for Best Female Rock Vocal Performance, rose to number 2 in the US charts, while the hard-rocking 'Hit Me With Your Best Shot', became her first *Billboard* Top 10 single. *Precious Time* was released in 1981 and this time reached number 1 in the USA. Although no Top 10 singles resulted, Benatar won another Grammy for 'Fire And Ice'. In 1982 Benatar married producer Neil Geraldo, who played guitar in her band and wrote most of her material, and released *Get Nervous*, which reached US number 4. The following year, a live album, also including two new studio tracks, was released. One of those tracks, 'Love Is A Battlefield', reached number 5 in the USA, the same position attained in 1984 by 'We Belong', from the next album, *Tropico*. The former single eventually became a UK Top 20 hit in 1985 after initially stalling a year earlier at 49 and was reissued in the wake of the British success of 'We Belong'. That same year, 'Invincible', from the film *Legend Of Billie Jean*, was Benatar's last US Top 10 single of the decade. An album, *Seven The Hard Way*, followed later that year but indicated a decline in Benatar's popularity. Inactivity marked the next couple of years as Benatar devoted her attentions to motherhood. A compilation album, *Best Shots*, was released in 1987. Although moderately successful in her homeland, it became a major hit in Europe, putting her into the UK Top 10

album charts for the first time. Since 1988 Benatar has also, reportedly, pursued an acting career.

●ALBUMS: *In The Heat Of The Night* (Chrysalis 1979)★★★, *Crimes Of Passion* (Chrysalis 1980)★★★, *Precious Time* (Chrysalis 1981)★★, *Get Nervous* (Chrysalis 1982)★★, *Live From Earth* (Chrysalis 1983)★★, *Tropico* (Chrysalis 1984)★★, *Seven The Hard Way* (Chrysalis 1985)★★★, *Wide Awake In Dreamland* (Chrysalis 1988)★★, *True Love* (Chrysalis 1991)★★, *Gravity's Rainbow* (Chrysalis 1993)★★.

●COMPILATIONS: *Best Shots* (Chrysalis 1987)★★★.

●VIDEOS: *Hit Videos* (1988), *Best Shots* (1988), *Benatar* (1988).

●FURTHER READING: *Benatar*, Doug Magee.

●FILMS: *American Pop* (1981).

BENOIT, DAVID

b. 1953, Bakersfield, California, USA. Benoit gained an early appreciation of music from his parents who played guitar and piano. He began piano lessons at the age of 14 by which time he was steeped in the influences of both Ramsey Lewis and Henry Mancini. Following his musical studies at El Camino College he met with composer Richard Baskin and played piano on the movie soundtrack *Nashville* in 1975. He gained valuable experience playing in clubs and bars and became Gloria Lynne's pianist. He toured with the Duke Ellington Orchestra in 1976 as Lainie Kazan's arranger and accompanist. His debut recording was with drummer Alphonse Mouzon and it was during these sessions he met with Dave Grusin, who became an important figure in his future career. He recorded a number of albums on a small label that demonstrated his fluid and skilful playing, although these recordings suffered from an overall blandness which resulted in their disappointing sales. *This Side Up* in 1985 changed everything. It contained the stunning 'Beach Trails', put Benoit in the US jazz bestsellers and led to a call from Larry Rosen, Dave Grusin's partner at GRP Records. Benoit has now become one of their leading artists with a series of best-selling albums of easy yet beautifully constructed music, forging a similar path to that of Grusin and bridging the gap between jazz and pop. Each album contains a balanced mixture but it is Benoit's delicate rippling style on some of the quieter numbers that best demonstrates his dexterity. 'Kei's Song' from *Freedom At Midnight* and 'The Key To You' from *Every Step Of the Way* are fine compositions. His pure acoustic style was highlighted on *Waiting For*

Spring, a concept album featuring Emily Remler and Peter Erskine. Imaginative readings of 'Cast Your Fate To the Wind', 'Secret Love' and 'My Romance' were mixed with Benoit originals. He maintained this high standard with *Inner Motion* in 1990, which opened with the Grusin-styled 'M.W.A' and peaked with the sublime tribute to the late Remler, 'Six String Poet'. His *Letter To Evan* was another acoustic excursion enlisting the talent of Larry Carlton. The collaboration with guitarist Russ Freeman in 1994 was a wholehearted success and stayed in the *Billboard* jazz chart for many weeks. That same year Benoit attempted another theme album, this time echoing his remembrances of the 60s, but as good as *Shaken Not Stirred* was, it sounded just like another David Benoit album clean, accessible and easy. Benoit is now an established artist, having refined his brand of music to perfection. His collaboration with Russ Freeman in 1994 was particularly inspiring. In his own words, 'I didn't want instant stardom like those artists whose fall is as quick as their rise'. Jazz purists may throw their arms up in horror but until another genre is invented, jazz remains the closest category for his music.

●ALBUMS: *Can You Imagine* (1980)★★, *Stages* (Bluemoon 1981)★★, *Waves Of Raves* (1982)★★, *Digits* (Bluemoon 1983)★★, *Heavier Than Yesterday* (1983)★★, *Christmastime* (1984)★★, *This Side Up* (GRP 1985)★★★★, *Freedom At Midnight* (GRP 1987)★★★, *Every Step Of The Way* (GRP 1988)★★★★, *Urban Daydreams* (GRP 1989)★★★, *Waiting For Spring* (GRP 1989)★★★★, *Inner Motion* (GRP 1990)★★★, *Shadows* (GRP 1991)★★★, *Letter To Evan* (GRP 1993)★★★, with Russ Freeman *The Benoit/Freeman Project* (GRP 1994)★★★, *Shaken Not Stirred* (GRP 1994)★★★, *Remembering Christmas* (GRP 1996)★★.

●COMPILATIONS: *The Best Of David Benoit 1987-1995* (GRP 1995)★★★.

BENSON, GEORGE

b. 22 March 1943, Pittsburgh, Pennsylvania, USA. This guitarist and singer successfully planted his feet in both the modern jazz and easy listening pop camps in the mid-70s when jazz-pop as well as jazz-rock became a most lucrative proposition. Before a move to New York in 1963, he had played in various R&B outfits local to Pittsburgh, and recorded a single, 'It Should Have Been Me', in 1954. By 1965, Benson was an established jazz guitarist, having worked with Brother Jack McDuff, Herbie Hancock - and, crucially, Wes Montgomery, whose repertoire was drawn largely from pop, light clas-

sical and other non-jazz sources. When Montgomery died in 1969, critics predicted that Benson - contracted to Columbia Records in 1966 - would be his stylistic successor. Further testament to Benson's prestige was the presence of Hancock, Earl Klugh, Miles Davis, Joe Farrell and other jazz musicians on his early albums. Four of these were produced by Montgomery's Creed Taylor who signed Benson to his own CTI label in 1971. Benson was impressing audiences in concert with extrapolations of songs such as 'California Dreamin'', 'Come Together' and, digging deeper into mainstream pop, Cry Me A River' and 'Unchained Melody'. From *Beyond The Blue Horizon*, an arrangement of Jefferson Airplane's 'White Rabbit' was a turntable hit, and chart success seemed inevitable - especially as he was now recording a majority of vocal items. After *Bad Benson* reached the US album lists and, via disco floors, the title song of *Supership* cracked European charts, he was well placed to negotiate a favourable agreement with Warner Brothers Records who reaped an immediate Grammy-winning harvest with 1976's *Breezin'* (and its memorable 'This Masquerade'). Then companies with rights to the prolific Benson's earlier product cashed in, with reissues such as *The Other Side Of Abbey Road*, a track-for-track interpretation of an entire Beatles album. Profit from film themes like 'The Greatest Love Of All' (from the Muhammed Ali bio-pic *The Greatest*), million-selling *Give Me The Night* and the television-advertised *The Love Songs* have allowed him to indulge artistic whims such as a nod to jazz roots via 1987's excellent *Collaboration* with Earl Klugh, and a more commercial merger with Aretha Franklin on 'Love All The Hurt Away'. Moreover, a fondness for pop standards has proved marketable too, epitomized by revivals of 'On Broadway' - a US Top 10 single from 1978's *Weekend In LA* - and Bobby Darin's 'Beyond The Sea (La Mer)'. Like Darin, Benson also found success with Nat 'King' Cole's 'Nature Boy' (a single from *In Flight*) - and a lesser hit with Cole's 'Tenderly' in 1989, another balance of sophistication, hard-bought professionalism and intelligent response to chart climate. 1990 brought a full-length collaboration with the Count Basie Orchestra, accompanied by a sell-out UK tour. Benson is one of a handful of artists who have achieved major critical and commercial success in different genres - soul, jazz and pop; this pedigree makes him one of the most respected performers of the past 30 years even though recent output has been lacking.

●ALBUMS: with the Brother Jack McDuff Quartet

The New Boss Guitar Of George Benson(Prestige 1964)★★★★, *It's Uptown* (Columbia 1966)★★★★, *Most Exciting* (Columbia 1966)★★★, *Benson Burner* (Columbia 1966)★★★★, *Giblet Gravy* (Verve 1967)★★★, *The George Benson Cook Book* (Columbia 1967)★★★, *Goodies* (Verve 1969)★★★, *Shape Of Things To Come* (A&M 1969)★★, *Tell It Like It Is* (A&M 1969)★★, *The Other Side Of Abbey Road* (A&M 1970)★★★, *Beyond The Blue Horizon* (CTI 1970)★★★, *White Rabbit* (CTI 1973)★★, *Body Talk* (CTI 1974)★★★, *Bad Benson* (CTI 1974)★★, *Supership* (CTI 1975)★★★, with Joe Farrell *Benson And Farrell* (CTI 1976)★★★, *Good King Bad* (CTI 1976)★★★, *Breezin'* (WEA 1976)★★★★, *In Concert At Carnegie Hall* (CTI 1977)★★, *In Flight* (WEA 1977)★★★★, with Jack McDuff *George Benson And Jack McDuff* (Prestige 1977)★★★, *Weekend In LA* (WEA 1978)★★, *Living Inside Your Love* (WEA 1979)★★, *Give Me The Night* (WEA 1980)★★★★, *Blue Benson* (Polydor 1983)★★★, *In Your Eyes* (WEA 1983)★★★, *Stormy Weather* (Columbia 1984)★★, *20/20* (WEA 1985)★★, *The Electrifying George Benson* (Affinity 1985)★★★, *In Concert* (Premier 1985)★★, *Love Walked In* (Platinum 1985)★★, *While The City Sleeps* (WEA 1986)★★, with Earl Klugh *Collaboration* (1987)★★★★, *Love For Sale* (Masters 1988)★★★, *Twice The Love* (WEA 1988)★★, *Detroit's George Benson* (Parkwood 1988)★★★, *Tenderly* (WEA 1989)★★, with the Count Basie Orchestra *Big Boss Band* (WEA 1990)★★★, *Lil' Darlin'* (Thunderbolt 1990)★★★, *Live At The Casa Caribe Vols. 1-3* (Jazz View 1992)★★★, *Love Remembers* (Warners 1993)★★, *That's Right* (MCA 1996)★★★.

●COMPILATIONS: *The George Benson Collection* (Warners 1981)★★★★, *Early Years* (CTI 1982)★★★, *Best Of George Benson* (A&M 1982)★★★, *The Wonderful Years* (Proton 1984)★★★, *The Love Songs* (K-Tel 1985)★★★★, *The Silver Collection* (Verve 1985)★★★, *Compact Jazz* (Verve 1988)★★★, *Best Of* (Epic 1992)★★, *Guitar Giants* (Pickwick 1992)★★★, *The Best Of George Benson* (Warners 1995)★★★.

BERLIN

This US band from Los Angeles was formed in the summer of 1979 as a new wave/electro pop group. The founding members were John Crawford (bass/synthesizer, ex-Videos) with Terri Nunn (b. 26 June 1961; vocals), Virginia McCalino (vocals), Jo Julian (synthesizer), Chris Velasco (guitar) and Dan Van Patten (drums, ex-Barbies). They signed to IRS in the USA, but managed only one single before they broke up in 1981. However, Crawford

and Nunn formed a new band almost immediately with David Diamond (guitars), Rick Olsen (guitar), Matt Reid (keyboards) and Rod Learned (drums). Their first recording was the 1983 mini-album *Pleasure Victim* (not released in the UK), followed by the full long-player *Love Life* the following year. They gained a US Top 30 hit in April 1984 with 'No More Words', before dropping down to a three piece of Crawford, Nunn and Rob Brill on drums the following year. By 1986 they had a number 1 hit on both sides of the Atlantic with a song with which they would become almost exclusively associated, 'Take My Breath Away'. It was the theme song to the highly lucrative film *Top Gun*, and had been produced and co-written by veteran producer Giorgio Moroder. Although follow-up singles fared less well, 'Breath...' has proved to be a perennial favourite, re-entering the charts in 1988 and entering the UK Top 3 on reissue in 1990 as a result of its use in television car commercials.

●ALBUMS: *Pleasure Victim* (Geffen 1983)★★, *Love Life* (Geffen 1984)★★, *Count Three And Pray* (Mercury 1987)★★.

●COMPILATIONS: *Best Of Berlin 1979-1988* (Geffen 1988)★★★.

BERLINE, BYRON

b. 6 July 1944, Caldwell, Kansas, USA. The masterful newgrass fiddle player has been a much sought after sessionman in addition to his spells with a number of prestigious country/rock groups, notably the Dillards, Dillard And Clark Expedition, the Flying Burrito Brothers and his own highly respected Country Gazette. His father Luke was also a bluegrass fiddler and Byron started playing at the age of five. Later he studied music at the University Of Oklahoma and it was there that he formed his first band. He joined the Dillards in 1967 after a spell with Bill Monroe and followed Doug Dillard when he teamed up with Gene Clark in 1968. Over the years he has appeared on albums by the Rolling Stones ('Honky Tonk Woman', and 'Country Honk' from *Let It Bleed*), Dan Baird and Vince Gill, in addition to his ongoing work with Dan Crary and John Hickman.

●ALBUMS: with Dan Crary, John Hickman *Progressive Bluegrass* (1975)★★★, *Four* (Sugar Hill 1989)★★★, *Fiddle And A Song* (Sugar Hill 1995)★★★, with Hickman *Double Trouble* (Sugar Hill 1995)★★★.

BERRY, NICK

b. 1961, Woodford, Essex, England. Berry attended the Sylvia Young Theatre School in north London.

Minor appearances in films, television and West End plays led to a leading role in the BBC1 soap opera *EastEnders* as 'Wicksy', a youth with aspirations to become a musical entertainer. Fiction became truth when 'Every Loser Wins', a song Simon Wicks sang in one episode was issued as a single. Co-written by Simon May and produced by Mike Batt, it reached the top of the UK charts in 1986, necessitating a hastily recorded Berry album and a round of personal appearances in discos and nightclubs. Nevertheless, his duty as a pop star done, he returned to full-time acting. His voice was heard on the Buddy Holly title theme of the 1992 television series, *Heartbeat*, in which he played a police constable, and once again Berry returned to the UK charts.

●ALBUMS: *Nick Berry* i (BBC 1986)★★, *Nick Berry* ii (Columbia 1992)★★.

BEVIS FROND

Often mistakenly believed to be a group, the Bevis Frond is actually just one person: Nick Saloman. Influenced by Jimi Hendrix and Cream Saloman formed the Bevis Frond Museum while still at school. The group disbanded and after a period playing acoustic sets in the Walthamstow area of London he formed the Von Trap Family, later known as Room 13. In 1982 Saloman was seriously hurt in a motorcycle accident. He used the money he received in compensation to record *Miasma* in his bedroom and it quickly became a collector's item. *Pulsebeat* magazine referred to the tracks as 'like fireworks for inside your head'. Saloman then released *Inner Marshland* and *Triptych* on his own Woronzow Records and his long psychedelic guitar workouts mapped out a style that was shamelessly archaic but nevertheless appealing. London's Reckless Records re-released his first three albums and in 1988 provided *Bevis Through The Looking Glass* and, a year later, *The Auntie Winnie Album*. Saloman's brand of raw, imaginative blues guitar drew many converts and *Any Gas Faster* recorded in better-equipped studios, was widely lauded. *Rolling Stone* magazine said of it: 'With so much modern psychedelia cheapened by cliché or nostalgia, the Bevis Frond is the actual out-there item.' In 1991 Saloman released a double set, *New River Head*, on his own Woronzow Records, distributed in the USA by Reckless. He followed it up with 1992's *Just Is*, again a double, and *Beatroots*, recorded under the pseudonym Fred Bison Five. As a tireless believer in the need for communication, he set up an underground magazine, *Ptolemaic Terrascope*, in the late 80s, and like Saloman's music, it is a loyal correspondent of the UK psychedelic scene.

●ALBUMS: *Miasma* (Woronzow 1987)★★★, *Inner Marshland* (Woronzow 1987)★★★, *Triptych* (Woronzow 1987)★★★, *Bevis Through The Looking Glass* (Reckless 1988)★★★, *Acid Jam* (Woronzow 1988)★★★, *The Aunty Winnie Album* (Reckless 1989)★★★, *Any Gas Faster* (Woronzow 1990)★★★★, *New River Head* (Woronzow 1991)★★★★, *London Stone* (Woronzow 1992)★★★, *It Just Is* (Woronzow 1993)★★★, *Sprawl* (Woronzow 1994)★★★, *Superseeder* (Woronzow 1995)★★★.
●COMPILATIONS: *A Gathering Of Fronds* (Woronzow 1992)★★★.

BHUNDU BOYS

The Bhundu Boys were formed in Harare, Zimbabwe, in 1980 by Biggie Tembo (b. Rodwell Marasha, 30 September 1958, Chinhoye, Mashonaland, d. 30 July 1995, London, England; guitar/vocals/leader), Rise Kagona (guitar), David Mankaba (d. 1991; bass guitar), Shakie Kangwena (b. 16 August 1956, Salisbury, Rhodesia, d. 5 December 1993, Harare, Zimbabwe; keyboards) and Kenny Chitsvatsa (drums), most of whom had previously played together in another Harare outfit, the Wild Dragons. Although the Bhundu Boys achieved prominence both at home in Zimbabwe and overseas in Britain with their own idiosyncratic jit style of dance music, their rise in both territories owed much to the work of bandleader and vocalist Thomas Mapfumo. He was the first modern Zimbabwean performer to make traditionally rooted music acceptable and stylish in a social climate where previously all things European had been deemed preferable to anything African (the result of a national cultural inferiority complex engendered by decades of white colonial rule). The band itself was a product of Zimbabwe's late 70s war of liberation, the name Bhundu ('bush') being chosen to commemorate the freedom fighters who fought against the white settlers in rural areas. As the Wild Dragons, a back-up group for vocalist Son Takura, the quintet had already forged a reputation as respectful modernizers of traditional Zimbabwean folk music, and after 1980 - in the cultural renaissance which followed independence - they replaced any lingering vestiges of rock and soul for a wholly Zimbabwean approach. However, while Mapfumo's style was based on traditional, rural Shona mbira ('thumb piano') music, the Bhundu's, which did from time to time embrace the mbira, was altogether more eclectic and urban, drawing on the traditions of all the tribal peoples in Zimbabwe. Their early style also drew freely on the mbaqanga township music of neighbouring South Africa. Jit found almost immediate acceptance among the youth of post-independence Zimbabwe, and between 1981 and 1984 the band had four number 1 hits - 'Baba Munini Francis', 'Wenhamo Haaneti', 'Hatisitose' and 'Ndimboze'. Three albums, *The Bhundu Boys, Hupenyu Hwenasi* and *Shabini*, proved equally popular. In 1986, the band decided to make a sustained onslaught on the British music scene, and moved to the country in readiness for a long stay. Basing themselves first in Scotland and then in London, they spent most of the following two years on a near-permanent tour of the country, establishing a reputation as one of the most exciting bands in the country (BBC Radio 1 disc jockey John Peel described them as playing 'the most perfect music I've ever heard'). The incessant touring boosted British sales of *Shabini* (released in the UK in 1986 on the independent label Discafrique), which sold some 10,000 copies in the first six months of its release and reached number 1 in the *Melody Maker* independent charts. Early in 1987, the band were signed to major label WEA Records, released a second Discafrique album, *Tsvimbodzemoto*, and supported Madonna at London's Wembley Stadium. However, while the sales of *Shabini* had made the Bhundus stars of the independent scene, sales of 10,000 copies were insignificant to a major international label, and as WEA were unable to lift the group beyond this plateau they lost interest in the group, dropping them from the roster early in 1990. A few months later, Biggie Tembo was asked to leave the group, before several members succumbed to AIDS. The Bhundu Boys re-emerged in 1991 with the excellent live set, *Absolute Jit*, recorded in Zimbabwe, which saw them return to the Discafrique label. But their crushing late 80s run-in with the record industry had shrunk the band's fan base, and when Tembo was discovered hanged by his own hand in 1995, it served as a chilling epitaph to a once pioneering group.

●ALBUMS: *The Bhundu Boys* (1981)★★★, *Hupenyu Hwenasi* (1984)★★★, *Shabini* (Discafrique 1985)★★★★, *Tsvimbodzemoto* (Discafrique 1987)★★★★, *True Jit* (WEA 1988)★★★★, *Pamberi* (WEA 1989)★★★, *Absolute Jit* (Discafrique 1991)★★★, *Friends Of The Road* (Discafrique 1992)★★★, *Muchiyedza* (Cooking Vinyl 1997)★★★.

BIBLE

The Bible were formed in Cambridge, England, and their debut single 'Gracelands' (1986) was a classy pop song, as was its follow-up, 'Mahalia' (a tribute to the gospel singer Mahalia Jackson). The band consisted of Boo Hewerdine (vocals/guitar), Tony Shepherd (keyboards/percussion), Dave Larcombe (drums) and Leroy Lendor (bass), and by the time Chrysalis Records had signed them, they already had an album's worth of well-crafted songs in *Walking The Ghost Back Home*. Chrysalis duly reissued 'Gracelands' in early 1987, but it eluded the charts, and the band spent the year recording a second album. Released in January 1988, *Eureka* shared the melodic quality of the Bible's debut, but neither of the singles, 'Crystal Palace' in April and 'Honey Be Good' in September, made much impression. Desperate for success, they tried revamping 'Gracelands' and when that failed, reissued 'Honey Be Good'. A compilation release in late 1989, *The Best Of The Bible*, signalled the end of the band's association with their label. Hewerdine, who had previously played in short-lived bands such as the Great Divide, subsequently embarked on a fruitful solo career.

●ALBUMS: *Walking The Ghost Back Home* (Backs 1986)★★★★, *Eureka* (Ensign/Chrysalis 1988)★★★.

●COMPILATIONS: *The Best Of The Bible* (Ensign/Chrysalis 1989)★★★★.

BIFF BANG POW!

Biff Bang Pow! - a name derived from a song by 60s cult group the Creation - is an outlet for the musical aspirations of Glaswegian Alan McGee, the motivating force behind Creation Records, one of the UK's most inventive independent outlets. The group also featured business partner Dick Green (guitar) and despite its part-time nature, has completed several excellent releases, including the neo-psychedelic singles, '50 Years Of Fun' (1984) and 'Love's Going Out Of Fashion' (1986). *Pass The Paintbrush Honey* and *The Girl Who Runs The Beat Hotel* offered idiosyncratic, and often contrasting, views of pop, while *Love Is Forever* showed the influence of Neil Young, notably on 'Ice Cream Machine'. In the 90s, however, with his record label achieving major success with Oasis and the Boo Radleys, McGee has found less time for his own band.

●ALBUMS: *Pass The Paintbrush Honey* (Creation 1985)★★★, *The Girl Who Lives At The Beat Hotel* (Creation 1987)★★★, *Oblivion* (Creation 1987)★★★, *Love Is Forever* (Creation 1988)★★★, *Songs For The Sad Eyed Girl* (Creation 1990)★★★, *Me* (Creation 1991)★★★.

●COMPILATIONS: *The Acid House Album*

(Creation 1989)★★★, *L'amour, Demure, Stenhousemuir: A Compilation 1984-1991* (Creation 1991)★★★★.

BIG AUDIO DYNAMITE

After Clash guitarist Mick Jones (b. 26 June 1955, Brixton, London, England) was fired from that group in 1984, he formed an ill-fated outfit with former Clash drummer Topper Headon, before linking up with DJ and film-maker Don Letts to form Big Audio Dynamite (or B.A.D., as they were commonly known). With Jones (guitar), Letts (keyboards and effects), they completed the line-up with Dan Donovan (keyboards), son of famed photographer Terence Donovan, Leo Williams (bass) and Greg Roberts (drums). *This Is Big Audio Dynamite* was a natural progression from tracks such as 'Inoculated City' on *Combat Rock*, the last Clash album that featured Jones, with cut-up funk spiced with sampled sounds (the first time this technique had been used). The follow-up album included writing contributions from the former Clash vocalist Joe Strummer, who happened across the band while they were recording in Soho, London. The group continued to record but hit their first crisis in 1988 when Jones came close to death from pneumonia, which caused a delay in the release of *Megatop Phoenix*. This in turn led to the break-up of the band and by 1990 and *Kool-Aid*, Jones had assembled a completely new line-up (B.A.D. II) featuring Nick Hawkins (guitar), Gary Stonedage (bass) and Chris Kavanagh (drums, ex-Sigue Sigue Sputnik). DJ Zonka was drafted in to provide live 'scratching' and mixing. Jones also contributed to the *Flashback* soundtrack and 'Good Morning Britain' single from Aztec Camera. Meanwhile he attracted disdain, not least from former colleagues, by insisting on putting a B.A.D. track on the b-side to the posthumous Clash number 1, 'Should I Stay Or Should I Go'. Donovan proved to be no stranger to controversy either, having married and separated from the actress and Eighth Wonder vocalist Patsy Kensit. He went on to join the reformed Sigue Sigue Sputnik, while his former employers were being hailed as a great influence on the new wave of 90s British dance-pop (EMF, Jesus Jones). Jones regrouped in 1995 for the accomplished *P-Funk*, which mixed imported west coast hip hop beats with jungle textures and rock 'n' roll. Although the commercial fortunes of Big Audio Dynamite (as they were now, again, named) were in freefall following Columbia Records' decision to drop his band, *P-Funk* reaffirmed Jones' status as an intelligent artist working on the periphery of the 90s rock scene.

●ALBUMS: *This Is Big Audio Dynamite* (Columbia 1985)★★★★, *No. 10 Upping Street* (Columbia 1986)★★★★, *Tighten Up, Vol 88* (Columbia 1988)★★★, *Megatop Phoenix* (Columbia 1989)★★★, *P-Funk* (Radioactive 1995)★★★. As B.A.D.: *Kool-Aid* (Columbia 1990)★★. As B.A.D. II: *The Globe* (Columbia 1991)★★. As Big Audio: *Higher Power* (Columbia 1994)★★, *Looking For A Song* (Columbia 1994)★★.

●COMPILATIONS: *Planet B.A.D.: Greatest Hits* (Columbia 1995)★★★.

BIG BLACK

Initially based in Evanstown, Illinois, USA, Big Black made its recording debut in 1983 with the six-track EP *Lungs*. Fronted by guitarist/vocalist Steve Albini, the group underwent several changes before completing *Bulldozer* the following year. A more settled line-up was formed around Albini, Santiago Durango (guitar) and Dave Riley aka Dave Lovering (bass) as Big Black began fusing an arresting, distinctive sound and *Atomizer* (1986) established the trio as one of America's leading independent acts. This powerful, compulsive set included 'Kerosene', a lyrically nihilistic piece equating pyromania with teenage sex as a means of escaping small-town boredom. The combined guitar assault of Albini and Durango was underpinned by Riley's emphatic bass work, which propelled this metallic composition to its violent conclusion. Melvin Belli (guitar) replaced Durango, who left to study law, for *Songs About Fucking*, Big Black's best-known and most popular album. Once again their blend of post-hardcore and post-industrial styles proved exciting, but Albini had now tired of his creation: 'Big Black are dumb, ugly and persistent, just like a wart' - and announced the break-up of the group prior to the record's release. He later became a respected but idiosyncratic producer, working with the Pixies (*Surfer Rosa*), the Breeders (*Pod*) and Tad (*Salt Lick*), before forming a new venture, the controversially named and short-lived Rapeman. When that group shuddered under the weight of criticism at its name (though Albini insisted this was merely a UK phenomenon), he returned to production duties. Undoubtedly the highest profile of these were PJ Harvey's *Rid Of Me* and Nirvana's *In Utero*. Afterwards he returned to a group format with Shellac.

●ALBUMS: *Atomizer* (Homestead/Blast First 1986)★★★, *Sound Of Impact* live album (Walls Have Ears 1987)★★, *Songs About Fucking* (Touch And Go/Blast First 1987)★★★.

●COMPILATIONS: *The Hammer Party* (Homestead/Blast First 1986)★★★, *Rich Man's 8-Track* (Homestead/Blast First 1987)★★★, *Pigpile* (Blast First 1992)★★★.

BIG COUNTRY

Stuart Adamson (b. 11 April 1958, Manchester, England; guitar/vocals) formed Big Country in 1982 upon his departure from Scottish new wave group the Skids. His first recruit was childhood friend Bruce Watson (b. 11 March 1961, Timmins, Ontario, Canada; guitar), but early plans to work solely as a studio ensemble were quickly abandoned. An initial rhythm section proved incompatible and was replaced by Mark Brzezicki (b. 21 June 1957, Slough, Buckinghamshire, England; drums) and Tony Butler (b. 2 February 1957, London, England; bass), two former members of On The Air, a group that had supported the Skids on a earlier tour. Despite several overtures, Adamson preferred to remain close to his adopted hometown of Dunfermline, emphasizing a prevalent Scottish influence in his music. Both guitarists wove a ringing, 'bagpipe' sound from their instruments and the group's debut album, which included the hit singles, 'Fields Of Fire (400 Miles)' and 'In A Big Country', established their rousing, anthem-like approach. Further releases, 'Chance', 'Wonderland' and 'Look Away' all reached the UK Top 10, while a second collection, *Steeltown*, produced by Steve Lillywhite, was also a commercial success. However, the group seemed unable to tackle fresh directions and despite a two-year hiatus, their fourth album offered little that was new, although its leading single, 'King Of Emotion', broached the UK Top 20. The band continued into the 90s regularly reaching the lower end of the singles charts. *Live - Without The Aid Of A Safety Net* was a lacklustre album, not highlighting the band's strength of excitement and volume. Quite different, however, was the energetic single 'I'm Not Ashamed' which preceded their 1995 album. The band sounded fresh and had taken some 90s influences to embellish their own sound. *Eclectic*, in 1996, was their attempt at an unplugged album, and although not wholly satisfying on CD, the accompanying tour was a revelation. A much-revitalized band playing their back catalogue was highly refreshing. It also allowed, possibly for the first time, the essence of their folk roots to show through - without the chiming guitars masking the quality of some of their songs. Additionally, an acoustic Adamson belting out songs by Springsteen, Dylan and Neil Young (notably 'Rockin' In The Free World') was a rare treat.

●ALBUMS: *The Crossing* (Mercury 1983)★★★★, *Steeltown* (Mercury 1984)★★★, *The Seer* (Mercury 1986)★★, *Peace In Our Time* (Mercury 1988)★★★, *No Place Like Home* (Vertigo 1991)★★, *The Buffalo Skinners* (Compulsion 1993)★★, *Live - Without The Aid Of A Safety Net* (Compulsion 1994)★★, *BBC Live In Concert* (Windsong 1995)★★, *Why The Long Face* (Castle 1995)★★★, *Eclectic* (TRA 1996)★★★.

●COMPILATIONS: *Through A Big Country: Greatest Hits* (Mercury 1990)★★★, *The Collection* (Castle 1993)★★★.

●VIDEOS: *Big Country Live* (1986), *King Of Emotion* (1988), *In A Big Country* (1988), *Peace In Our Time: Moscow 1988* (1989), *Greatest Hits: Big Country* (1990), *Through A Big Country* (1991), *The Seer: Live* (1991), *Without The Aid Of A Safety Net - Live* (PMI 1994).

●FURTHER READING: *Big Country: A Certain Chemistry*, John May.

BIG DISH

Formed in Airdrie, Lanarkshire, Scotland, in 1983, the Big Dish, comprising Steven Lindsay (vocals/guitar/keyboards), Brian McFie (guitar), Raymond Docherty (bass) and Ian Ritchie (saxophone/programming) rose to prominence in 1986 with the release of their debut album, *Swimmer*, which garnered a succession of positive reviews. Commentators compared their crafted pop with Prefab Sprout, Aztec Camera and Danny Wilson, but a series of excellent singles, including 'Prospect Street' and 'Big New Beginning', failed to chart. The trio of Lindsay, McFie and Docherty then completed *Creeping Up On Jesus*. This second effort betrayed a greater debt to American music, yet, despite a more commercial sound, also proved unsuccessful, and the group was dropped from its record label when Lindsay refused to countenance recording a 'cover' version. In 1991 the Big Dish re-emerged with a new contract, an official line-up of Lindsay and McFie and a minor hit single in 'Miss America'. The attendant release, *Satellites*, maintained the unit's quest for excellence, yet lacked the depth and purpose of their initial work.

●ALBUMS: *Swimmer* (Virgin 1986)★★★, *Creeping Up On Jesus* (Virgin 1988)★★★, *Satellites* (East West 1991)★★.

●COMPILATIONS: *Rich Man's Wardrobe - A Concise History Of …* (Virgin 1993)★★★.

BIG FUN

This UK group comprised Philip Creswick (b. 12 October 1965, Charlwood, Surrey, England;

vocals), Mark Gillespie (b. 28 November 1966, Elgin, Scotland; vocals) and Jason John (b. 18 March 1967, Coventry, Warwickshire, England; vocals). Encouraged by their friends they started singing and dancing together, and then recorded with the house specialist, Marshall Jefferson. These sessions were enough to interest Stock, Aitken And Waterman, whose production work contributed significantly towards their UK number 4 in 1989 with a revival of the Jacksons' 'Blame It On The Boogie'. The fresh-faced youths' next single also went into the UK Top 10. Stock, Aitken And Waterman then teamed them with Sonia and achieved success on 'You've Got A Friend'. Their biggest claim to fame was having three simultaneous Top 15 hits in Spain.

●ALBUMS: *Pocketful Of Dreams* (Jive 1990)★★.
●VIDEOS: *Pocketful Of Dreams* (1990).

BIG IN JAPAN

For a band that issued very few recordings, Big In Japan received strong critical acclaim. The main reason for this interest was their line-up: Jayne Casey (vocals, later with Pink Industry/Military), Bill Drummond (guitar, later formed Lori And The Chameleons, ran the Zoo Records label, released a solo album and comprised half of the KLF), Dave Balfe (bass, worked with Drummond in Lori And The Chameleons, was later enrolled as keyboard player in the Teardrop Explodes and then founded the Food Records label), Budgie (drums, later briefly with the Slits then, more permanently, Siouxsie And The Banshees), Ian Broudie (guitar, who subsequently joined the Original Mirrors before carving out a successful career as producer, and later enjoyed success under the guise of the Lightning Seeds) and finally Holly on bass. After two country-styled singles, Holly joined Frankie Goes To Hollywood and is now the solo artist Holly Johnson. On the b-side of their 1977 self-titled debut single was a track from the Chuddy Nuddies, who turned out to be the Yachts. After Big In Japan split, Drummond used four of their tracks for the first Zoo single, *From Y To Z And Never Again*, which stands as a delightfully quirky period piece. The remaining members of Big In Japan (vocalist Ken Ward and drummer Phil Allen) failed to emulate the success of their fellow travellers.

BIG SOUND AUTHORITY

This promising UK group was formed in 1983 by two vocalists Tony Burke (who handled the rock material) and Julie Hadwin (who sang the blues parts), and the band were complemented by a fine brass section. On the small Source label they released the 60s-influenced 'This House (Is Where Your Love Stands)', which was a minor UK hit early in 1985. The follow-up, 'A Bad Town', did even less well, and despite moving to Source's distributing label and being produced by Tony Visconti, subsequent singles 'Moving Heaven And Earth' and 'Don't Let Our Love Start A War' also failed.

●ALBUMS: *An Inward Revolution* (Source 1985)★★★.

BIRTHDAY PARTY

One of the most creative and inspiring 'alternative' acts of the 80s, this Australian group had its roots in the new wave band Boys Next Door. After one album, the band relocated to London and switched names. In addition to featuring the embryonic genius of Nick Cave (b. 22 September 1957, Warracknabeal Australia; vocals), their ranks were swelled by Roland S. Howard (guitar, ex-Obsessions; Young Charlatans), Mick Harvey (b. 29 September 1958, Rochester, Australia; guitar, drums, organ, piano), Tracy Pew (d. 5 July 1986; bass) and Phil Calvert (drums). They chose the newly launched 4AD Records offshoot of Beggars Banquet Records as their new home, and made their debut with the impressive 'Fiend Catcher'. Music critics and BBC disc jockey John Peel became early and long-serving converts to the band's intense post-punk surges. Back in Australia, they recorded their first album, a transitional piece which nevertheless captured some enduring aggressive rock statements. Their finest recording, however, was the single 'Release The Bats'. It was John Peel's favourite record of 1981, though its subject matter unwittingly tied in the band with the emerging 'Gothic' subculture populated by Bauhaus and Sex Gang Children. As Pew was imprisoned for three months for drink-driving offences, Barry Adamson (ex-Magazine), Roland Howard's brother Harry and Chris Walsh helped out on the recording of the follow-up, and the band's increasingly torrid live shows. After collaborating with the Go-Betweens on the one-off single, 'After The Fireworks', as the Tuf Monks, they shifted to Berlin to escape the constant exposure and expectations of them in the UK. Calvert was dropped (moving on to Psychedelic Furs), while the four remaining members moved on to collaborative projects with Lydia Lunch and Einsturzende Neubaten amongst others. They had already recorded a joint 12-inch, 'Drunk On The Pope's Blood', with Lunch, and Howard featured on much of her future output. When Harvey left in the summer of 1983, the band seemed set to fulfil their solo careers, even though he was temporarily replaced on drums by Des Heffner. However, after a final gig in Melbourne, Australia, in June the band called it a day. Howard went on to join Crime And The City Solution alongside his brother and Harvey, who also continued in Cave's solo band the Bad Seeds.

●ALBUMS: *The Birthday Party* (Missing Link 1980)★★★, *Prayers On Fire* (Thermidor 1981)★★★, *Drunk On The Pope's Blood* mini-album (4AD 1982)★★★, *Junkyard* (4AD 1982)★★★, *It's Still Living* live recording (Missing Link 1985)★★★.
●COMPILATIONS: *A Collection* (Missing Link 1985)★★★, *Hee Haw* (4AD 1989)★★★, *The Peel Sessions Album* (Strange Fruit 1991)★★★, *Definitive Missing Link Recordings 1979-1982* (Missing Link 1994)★★★★.
●VIDEOS: *Pleasure Heads Must Burn* (IKON 1988).

BLACK

Originally a three-piece pop outfit from Roby, near Liverpool, England, the group featured Colin Vearncombe (vocals), Dave Dickie (keyboards) and Jimmy Sangster (bass). Vearncombe was previously in the Epileptic Tits at the age of 16, playing punk covers. He then moved on to producing his own tapes until Dickie (ex-Last Chant), then Sangster, formed a unit together. A previous incarnation had released 'Human Features' on a local label. Black's next base was the Liverpool independent record label Eternal, sponsored by Pete Wylie and Wah. However, Vearncombe's distinctive voice soon attracted the attention of WEA Records. Unfortunately, after the failure of two singles, 'Hey Presto' (written about existential novel *The Dice Man*) and 'More Than The Sun', they dropped the band. Despite this setback, Black soon found themselves with an unexpected hit on their hands. Vearncombe was approached by two brothers after a gig who wanted to put one of the band's singles out on their Ugly Man label. That single was the seductive, bittersweet ballad, 'Wonderful Life', and after using a record plugger it was played regularly on the radio and took off in the independent charts. Its success attracted the attention of A&M Records, and the second single for the label, 'Sweetest Smile', gave them a Top 10 UK hit. Their debut album followed, though 1988's *Comedy* was the more impressive long player, highlighting Vearncombe's natural romanticism. A hiatus followed which allowed Vearncombe time for marriage and new material, before a third album, titled simply *Black*. Produced by Robin Millar, guest vocalists included Robert Palmer and Sam Brown. A single featuring the latter, 'Fly To The Moon', also boasted an ironic cover of Janet Jackson's 'Control'. *Are We Having Fun Yet?* continued in a similar vein but received little commercial reward.
●ALBUMS: *Wonderful Life* (A&M 1987)★★★, *Comedy* (A&M 1988)★★★★, *Black* (A&M 1991)★★★, *Are We Having Fun Yet?* (A&M 1993)★★★.

BLACK FLAG

Formed in 1977 in Los Angeles, California, Black Flag rose to become one of America's leading hardcore groups. The initial line-up - Keith Morris (vocals), Greg Ginn (guitar), Chuck Dukowski (bass) and Brian Migdol (drums) - completed the *Nervous Breakdown* EP in 1978, but the following year Morris left to form the Circle Jerks. Several members joined and left before Henry Rollins (b. 13 February 1961; vocals), Dez Cadenza (guitar) and Robo (drums) joined Ginn and Dukowski for *Damaged*, the group's first full-length album. Originally scheduled for release by MCA Records, the company withdrew support, citing outrageous content, and the set appeared on the quintet's own label, SST Records. This prolific outlet has not only issued every subsequent Black Flag recording, but also has a catalogue including Hüsker Dü, Sonic Youth, the Minutemen, the Meat Puppets and Dinosaur Jr. Administered by Ginn and Dukowski, the latter of whom left the group to concentrate his efforts more fully, the company has become one of America's leading, and most influential, independents. Ginn continued to lead Black Flag in tandem with Rollins, and although its rhythm section was still subject to change, the music's power remained undiminished. Pivotal albums included *My War* and *In My Head* while their diversity was showcased on *Family Man*, which contrasted a side of Rollins' spoken word performances with four excellent instrumentals. However, the group split up in 1986 following the release of a compulsive live set, *Who's Got The 10 1/2?*, following which Ginn switched his attentions to labelmates Gone. Rollins went on to a successful solo career. The glory days of Black Flag are warmly recalled in one of Rollins' numerous books for his 2.13.61. publishing empire, *Get In The Van*.
●ALBUMS: *Damaged* (SST 1981)★★★★, *My War* (SST 1984)★★★, *Family Man* (SST 1984)★★, *Slip It In* (SST 1984)★★★, *Live '84* (SST 1984)★★, *Loose Nut* (SST 1985)★★, *The Process Of Weeding Out* mini-album (SST 1985)★★★, *In My Head* (SST 1985)★★★, *Who's Got The 10 1/2?* (SST 1986)★★★.

●COMPILATIONS: *Everything Went Black* (SST 1982)★★★, *The First Four Years* (SST 1983)★★★★, *Wasted ... Again* (SST 1988)★★★★.
●VIDEOS: *Black Flag Live* (1984).
●FURTHER READING: *Get In The Van*, Henry Rollins.

BLACK LACE

This duo consisting of Colin Routh and Alan Barton (b. 16 September 1953, Barnsley, Yorkshire, England, d. 23 March 1995, Cologne, Germany) were responsible for a string of hits in the mid-80s which enjoyed enormous popularity in discos and parties across the UK. However, those in pursuit of music with a marginally more cerebral nature made Black Lace a target for their relentless scorn. After failing to represent Great Britain in the 1979 Eurovision Song Contest with 'Mary Ann', Black Lace carried on regardless, unleashing upon the nation (via Spanish holiday discos), a series of party songs initiated by 'Superman (Gioca Jouer)' which reached the UK Top 10 and was succeeded in 1984 by 'Agadoo' which reached the UK number 2 slot and remained in the charts for 30 weeks. This was followed by 'Do The Conga' (UK number 10), 'El Vino Collapso', 'I Speaka Da Lingo' and 'Hokey Cokey'. Their last UK chart entry came in the summer of 1989 with 'I Am The Music Man' which reached number 52.
●ALBUMS: *Party Party - 16 Great Party Icebreakers* (Telstar 1984)★★, *Party Party 2* (Telstar 1985)★, *Party Crazy* (Telstar 1986)★.
●VIDEOS: *The Ultimate Party Video* (Prism 1995).

BLACK UHURU

Formed in Jamaica by Garth Dennis, Derrick 'Ducky' Simpson and Don McCarlos in the early 70s, Black Uhuru first recorded a version of Curtis Mayfield's 'Romancing To The Folk Song' for Dynamic's Top Cat label as Uhuru (the Swahili word for 'Freedom'), which met with limited success. Garth Dennis then joined the Wailing Souls and McCarlos (as Don Carlos) went on to a solo career. 'Ducky' then enlisted Michael Rose as lead singer, who himself had previously recorded as a solo artist for Yabby You (on the excellent 'Born Free') and for Winston 'Niney' Holness, including the first recording of 'Guess Who's Coming To Dinner', inspired by the Sidney Poitier film. Errol Nelson, from the Jayes, was used for harmonies. This line-up sang on an album for Prince Jammy in 1977 entitled *Love Crisis*, later reissued and retitled *Black Sounds Of Freedom*, after the group had found success. Nelson returned to the Jayes soon

afterwards and Puma Jones (b. Sandra Jones, 5 October 1953, Columbia, South Carolina, USA, d. 28 January 1990, New York) took over. Formerly a social worker, she had worked with Ras Michael And The Sons Of Negus as a dancer in a bid to retrace her African ancestry via Jamaica. This combination began work for Sly Dunbar and Robbie Shakespeare's Taxi label in 1980, and Black Uhuru mania gripped the Jamaican reggae audience. The solid bedrock of Sly And Robbie's rhythms with Puma and Duckie's eerie harmonies provided a perfect counterpoint to Rose's tortured vocals as his songs wove tales of the hardships of Jamaican life which managed to convey a far wider relevance. Their first album for Taxi, *Showcase*, later reissued as *Vital Selection*, gave equal prominence to the vocal and instrumental versions of songs such as 'General Penitentiary', 'Shine Eye Gal' and 'Abortion', and was a massive reggae seller.
Island Records signed the group and they became a hot property throughout the musical world over the next few years. Their albums for Mango/Island continued in the same militant vein, and *Anthem* was remixed for the American market and earned a Grammy for the band. They toured all over the globe with the powerhouse rhythm section of Sly And Robbie in addition to a full complement of top Jamaican session musicians. For a time they were widely touted as the only reggae band with the potential to achieve international superstar status, but, although their popularity never waned after their initial breakthrough, it sadly never seemed to grow either. Michael Rose left the band in the mid-80s for a solo career that has always promised more than it has delivered, although his 1990 album *Proud* was very strong. Junior Reid took over on lead vocals but, in retrospect, his approach was too deeply rooted in the Jamaican dancehalls at the time for Black Uhuru's international approach, and after a couple of moderately well-received albums he too left for a solo career, which to date has been remarkably successful. For *Now* Don Carlos returned to his former position as lead singer, reuniting the original triumvirate of Carlos, Duckie Simpson and Garth Dennis, and the group still tour and release records, which are particularly popular in America. Tragically, Puma Jones died of cancer in 1990. She had left the band after *Brutal*, and been replaced by soundalike Olafunke. Black Uhuru will always remain one of *the* great reggae acts despite the fact that the international status that they deserved proved elusive.
●ALBUMS: *Love Crisis* (Prince Jammys/Third

World 1977)★★★, *Showcase* (Taxi/Heartbeat 1979)★★★, *Sinsemilla* (Mango/Island 1980)★★★, *Black Sounds Of Freedom* (Greensleeves 1981)★★★, *Red* (Mango/Island 1981)★★★★, *Black Uhuru* (Virgin 1981)★★★, *Chill Out* (Mango/Island 1982)★★★, *Tear It Up - Live* (Mango/Island 1982)★★★, *Guess Who's Coming To Dinner* (Heartbeat 1983)★★★, *The Dub Factor* (Mango/Island 1983)★★★, *Anthem* (Mango/Island 1984)★★★, *Uhuru In Dub* (CSA 1985)★★★, *Brutal* (RAS 1986)★★★★, *Brutal Dub* (RAS 1986)★★★, *Positive* (RAS 1987)★★★, *Positive Dub* (RAS 1987)★★★, *Live In New York City* (Rohit 1988)★★★, *Now* (Mesa 1990)★★★, *Now Dub* (Mesa 1990)★★★, *Iron Storm* (Mesa 1991)★★★, *Mystical Touch* (Mesa 1993)★★★.

●COMPILATIONS: *Reggae Greats* (Mango/Island 1985)★★★★, *Liberation: The Island Anthology* 2-CD box set (Mango/Island 1993)★★★★.

●VIDEOS: *Tear It Up* (1989), *Black Uhuru Live* (1991).

BLACK, MARY

b. 22 May 1955, Eire. Mary is a member of the Black Family, who all have musical backgrounds, and with whom she has recorded and performed. Her father was a fiddle player and her mother a singer. Black's early days were spent singing in the folk clubs of Dublin, but with *Mary Black* reaching number 4 in the Irish charts in 1983, it was obvious that she was destined for bigger things. In addition, she was awarded the Irish Independent Arts Award for Music for the album. Shortly after this, Black joined De Dannan, recording two albums with them, *Song For Ireland* and *Anthem*, before leaving the group in 1986. Although not credited, Mary did provide some backing vocals and production work for *The Black's Family Favourites* in 1984. Mary still maintained her solo career while with De Dannan, and teamed up with producer Declan Sinnott for *Without The Fanfare*, featuring mostly contemporary songs, which subsequently went gold. In 1987 and 1988, Mary was voted Best Female Artist in the Irish Rock Music Awards Poll. *No Frontiers*, apart from being one of Ireland's best-selling albums in 1989, also reached the Top 20 of the New Adult Contemporary charts in the USA, in 1990. The album also had a great deal of success in Japan, resulting in Black's first Japanese tour in December 1990. Although in the eyes of some critics, more recent works have seen Mary tagged as 'middle of the road' she defies straight categorization, still retaining an honest feel for her traditional background. Nevertheless, she also remains a fine interpreter of more contemporary works. With the Black Family, she has only made two albums, owing to many of them living in different parts of the world. Apart from backing Nanci Griffith in concert, Black also sang with Emmylou Harris and Dolores Keane in Nashville, in the television series *Bringing It All Back Home*. In April 1991, Black returned from an American tour in order to finish *Babes In The Wood*, released in July the same year. The album went straight to number 1 in the Irish charts, staying there for five weeks. 1991 saw a concerted effort to capitalize on her success and reach a wider audience, with tours of England and another of Japan. Until *Babes In The Wood*, her albums, all on Dara, had not previously had a full distribution in Britain.

●ALBUMS: *Mary Black* (Dara 1983)★★★, *Collected* (Dara 1984)★★★, *Without The Fanfare* (Dara 1985)★★★, with the Black Family *The Black Family* (Dara 1986)★★★, *By The Time It Gets Dark* (Dara 1987)★★★, with the Black Family *Time For Touching Home* (Dara 1989)★★★, *No Frontiers* (Dara 1989)★★★, *Babes In The Wood* (Grapevine 1991)★★★★, *Circus* (Grapevine 1995)★★★, *Shine* (Grapevine 1997)★★★.

●COMPILATIONS: *The Best Of Mary Black* (Dara 1991)★★★★, *The Collection* (Dara 1992)★★★.

BLACKFOOT

Southern US rock practitioners Blackfoot initially comprised Rick Medlocke (guitar/vocals), Charlie Hargrett (guitar), Greg Walker (bass) and Jakson Spires (drums/vocals). The quartet shared common origins with Lynyrd Skynyrd (Medlocke co-writing four songs and singing lead on two tracks on the latter's platinum *First And Last*) and in turn offered a similar blues/rock-based sound, centred on their leader's confident playing. Medlocke himself was the grandson of Shorty Medlocke, a popular Jacksonville, Florida, bluegrass musician of the 50s, whose 'Train, Train' was successfully covered by both Blackfoot and, in the 90s, Warrant. Rick took the name Blackfoot from his own native Indian tradition. Session pianist Jimmy Johnson produced Blackfoot's early work at the revered Muscle Shoals studio, but despite this impressive pedigree, the group was unable to translate an in-concert popularity, especially in the UK, into record sales. *Strikes*, the unit's first release for Atlantic/Atco Records, offered a heavier perspective, while the cream of their early work was captured live on *Highway Song*. After this, the group bowed to record company pressure and pursued a more commercial approach that did not always convince. Ken Hensley, formerly of Uriah Heep, joined the line-up for *Siogo* and *Vertical Smiles*, and was eventually replaced by Bobby Barth of Axe, but Blackfoot was disbanded following the latter's release. The name was revived at the end of the decade with a revised line-up, with Medlocke now backed by Neal Casal (guitar), Rikki Mayer (bass; ex-Lizzy Borden) and Gunner Ross (drums). However, none of these survived for Blackfoot's 1994 album with new label Bullet Proof/Music For Nations, with Mark Woerpel (guitar/vocals, ex-Wardrive), Benny Rappa (drums/vocals) and Tim Stunson (bass) stepping in to support the venerable Medlocke. Rappa was replaced by ex-W.A.S.P. drummer Stet Howland for touring.

●ALBUMS: *No Reservations* (Island 1976)★★★, *Flyin' High* (Epic 1977)★★★, *Blackfoot Strikes* (Atco 1978)★★★, *Tomcattin'* (Atco 1980)★★★, *Maurauder* (Atco 1981)★★★, *Highway Song* (Atco 1982)★★★, *Siogo* (Atco 1983)★★★, *Vertical Smiles* (Atco 1984)★★★, *Medicine Man* (Loop 1990)★★, *After The Reign* (Bullet Proof 1994)★★.

●COMPILATIONS: *Rattlesnake Rock 'N' Roll: The Best Of ...* (Rhino 1995)★★★.

BLACKMORE, RITCHIE

b. 14 April 1945, Weston-Super-Mare, Avon, England. Guitarist Blackmore spent his early career in Mike Dee And The Jaywalkers before joining Screaming Lord Sutch And His Savages in May 1962. Within months he had switched to the Outlaws, a popular, principally instrumental, group which also served as the studio house band for producer Joe Meek. Blackmore's exciting style was already apparent on the group's releases, notably 'Keep A Knockin''/'Shake With Me', and on sessions for Heinz and Mike Berry. The guitarist briefly joined the former singer's group, the Wild Boys, in 1964, and completed a suitably idiosyncratic solo single, 'Little Brown Jug'/'Getaway', before forging an erratic path as a member of Neil Christian's Crusaders, the Savages (again) and the Roman Empire. When a short-lived act, Mandrake Root, broke up in October 1967, Ritchie opted to live in Hamburg, but the following year was invited back to London to join organist Jon Lord in the embryonic Deep Purple. Although initially envisaged as an 'English Vanilla Fudge' the group quickly became a leading heavy metal act, with Blackmore's powerful, urgent runs an integral part of their attraction. He left the group in 1975, unhappy with their increasingly funk-based sound, and joined forces with the USA-based Elf to form

Ritchie Blackmore's Rainbow. This powerful band became a highly popular hard rock attraction, but was blighted by its leader's autocratic demands. Multiple firings ensued as the guitarist searched for the ideal combination, but such behaviour simply enhanced a temperamental reputation. He was nonetheless involved in the Deep Purple reunion, undertaken in 1984, although animosity between the guitarist and vocalist Ian Gillan resulted in the latter's departure. Blackmore's prowess as a guitar 'hero' is undisputed, while his outstanding technique has influenced everyone from the New Wave Of British Heavy Metal bands to conventional modern rock outfits.

●COMPILATIONS: *Ritchie Blackmore Volume 1: Early Sessions To Rainbow* (1990)★★★, *Ritchie Blackmore Volume 2* (1991)★★, *Session Man* (RPM 1993)★★★, *Take It! - Sessions 63/68* (RPM 1995)★★★.

BLADE RUNNER

Of the few rock bands of any note to emerge from the Humberside region in England (in the two decades the same area was not designated as part of Lincolnshire), most seemed to draw their principal influence from Status Quo. Blade Runner were no exception, despite the fact that they took their name from a science fiction film set in the distant future. Comprising Steve Mackay (vocals), Gary Jones (guitar), Mark Wilde (guitar), Mick Cooper (bass) and Gregg Ellis (drums), they made their debut in 1984 with *Hunted* for Ebony Records. It was followed two years later by *Warriors Of Rock*, but with neither record selling substantially the members of Blade Runner settled back into semi-retirement, with some members remaining active on the local club rock scene.

●ALBUMS: *Hunted* (Ebony 1984)★★, *Warriors Of Rock* (Ebony 1986)★★.

BLADES, RUBÉN

b. 16 July 1948 Panama City. Both of Rubén's parents were musicians, his mother Anoland a pianist and singer, his father Rubén Snr. a bongo player. While he was at school in 1966, he became a vocalist with the band Conjunto Latino and then belonged to the group Los Salvajes del Ritmo until 1969. In 1970, he journeyed to New York to record *De Panama a Nuevo York* with the band of ex-boogaloo star Pete Rodríguez. After graduating from the University of Panama he worked as a lawyer with the National Bank of Panama. In 1974, while visiting his family in Miami (they had relocated there in 1973), Blades made a side trip to

New York and secured a job in the mail-room of Fania Records. When Tito Allen left Ray Barretto's band in 1974, Blades was recommended to. Barretto, who auditioned him in the mail-room and hired him, and in July of that year, Blades appeared at Madison Square Garden with the band. Blades performed on *Barretto* (1975) and when Barretto left to form a fusion concert band, Blades stayed with his former band (renamed Guarare) for a time. Blades also appeared on the debut double *Barretto Live: Tomorrow* (1976) by Barretto's new band. Meanwhile, he composed and sang lead vocals on the hit track 'El Cazangero' from *The Good, The Bad, The Ugly* (1975) by Willie Colón, whom he had initially met back in Panama. The tune won him the 'Composer of the Year' award in the 1976 *Latin NY* magazine poll. Blades supplied songs to a number of bands and artists during the 70s, including: Ricardo Ray and Bobby Cruz, Ismael Miranda, Bobby Rodríguez y La Compañia, Cheo Feliciano, Conjunto Candela, Tito Rodríguez II, Tito Puente, Roberto Roena, Tito Gómez, Héctor Lavoe, Pete 'El Conde' Rodríguez; 12 original recordings of his compositions by other artists were collected on the album *Interpretan A Rubén Blades* (1981). In 1976 he joined the Fania All Stars and made his debut with them on *Tribute To Tito Rodríguez*; he continued as a member until 1980. Three years earlier, Blades sang lead and chorus on Larry Harlow's salsa suite *La Raza Latina*. Blades' and Colón's partnership began in earnest with *Metiendo Mano!* (1977 - released in the UK on the Caliente label in 1988). They collaborated on four more albums: *Siembra* (1978) went gold and was regarded as 'The Renaissance of Salsa'; the controversial two album set *Maestra Vida* (*Life The Teacher*, 1980) incorporated theatrical elements and also received a gold record; *Canciones del Solar de los Aburridos* (*Songs From The Place Of Bored People*, 1981) was nominated for a Grammy Award in 1983 and *The Last Fight* (1982) was released in tandem with the film of the same name, in which they both starred.

The Last Fight was Fania Records' boss Jerry Masucci's attempt to break into the film industry and it fared badly. At the same time, Blades was playing a leading role over the issue of alleged non-payment of royalties by the label and there was speculation that he tried to form a union of Fania's artists in 1979. The result was that Masucci sold Fania for a million dollars to an Argentinian business group called Valsyn and retained a consultancy affiliation with the label. Blades switched to Elektra Records in 1984 and debuted on *Buscando America*, with a sextet, Seis del Solar, which substituted synthesizer for horns.

He starred in the low budget film *Crossover Dreams* (1985) and contributed songs to the soundtrack album. Film of Blades at his Harvard Law School graduation ceremony was included in the UK television documentary *The Return of Rubén Blades* (1986), in which he also expressed his views about a possible future political career in Panama. He made his UK concert debut with Seis del Solar in 1986. Blades' plunge into crossover territory with the rock orientated English language *Nothing But The Truth* (1988), flopped. He made a U-turn with the Spanish language Grammy Award-winning album, *Antecedente* (1988), on which his backing band (renamed Son del Solar) was augmented by a trombone section and some arrangements (by keyboardist Oscar Hernández and bassist Mike Viñas) were reminiscent of his work with Colon. Blades' most significant contribution to salsa has been in terms of quality of lyrical content. He has described his body of composed work as 'musical journalism' and an 'urban chronicle'. Blades has developed a successful movie-acting career and his films include: *Critical Condition* (with Richard Prior, 1987), *The Milagro Beanfield War* (with Robert Redford, 1988), *The Lemon Sisters* (with Diane Keaton) and *The Two Jakes* (with Jack Nicholson); he was the first Latino to win an ACE (American Cable Excellence) award for his portrayal of a death-row prisoner in *Dead Man Out* (1989); he composed the music for Sidney Lumet's *Q And A*. He provoked controversy in Panama and his mother's wrath when he criticized the 1990 US invasion of Panama.

●ALBUMS: with Pete Rodríguez *De Panama a Nuevo York* (1970)★★★, with Ray Barretto *Barretto* (1975)★★★, with Willie Colón *The Good, The Bad, The Ugly* (1975)★★★, with Barretto *Barretto Live: Tomorrow* (1976)★★★, with Colón *Metiendo Mano!* (1977)★★★, with Larry Harlow *La Raza Latina* (1977)★★★, with Louie Ramírez *Louie Ramírez Y Sus Amigos* (1978)★★★, with Colón *Siembra* (1978)★★★, *Bohemio Y Poeta* (Fania 1979)★★★, with Colón *Maestra Vida, Primera Parte* (Fania 1980)★★★, with Colon *Maestra Vida, Segunda Parte* (Fania 1980)★★★, with Colón *Canciones Del Solar De Los Arburridos* (1981)★★★, with Colón *The Last Fight* (1982)★★★, *el que la hace la paga* (Fania 1983)★★★, *Buscando America* (Warners 1984)★★★★, *Mucho Mejor* (Fania 1984)★★★, *Crossover Dreams* soundtrack (Elektra 1985)★★★★, *Escenas* (Elektra 1985)★★★★, *Agua De Luna* (Elektra 1987)★★★★, *Doble Filo* (Fania

1987)★★★, *Nothing But The Truth* (Elektra 1988)★★★, *Antecedente* (Warners 1988)★★★★, *Rubén Blades Y Son Del Solar ... Live!* (Elektra 1990)★★★★, *Caminando* (Sony Discos 1991)★★★, *La Rosa De Los Vientos* (Sony 1996)★★★.
●VIDEOS: *The Return Of Ruben Blades* (Rhapsody 1995).

BLAKE BABIES

This trio from Boston, Massachusetts, USA, comprised Julianna Hatfield, John Strohm (guitar/vocals) and Freda Love (drums). As part of a succession of groups that emerged from a healthy rock scene in the Boston area in the late 80s/early 90s, Blake Babies were able to mature slowly, showing signs of a major breakthrough in early 1992. Their debut, *Nicely Nicely*, was released on the group's own Chewbud label and the follow-up, the mini-album *Slow Learner*, on Billy Bragg's re-activated Utility label. Signed to the North Carolina Mammoth label, *Earwig* and *Sunburn* consolidated the praise garnered from the music press, often drawing comparisons with fellow Bostonians, the Lemonheads. Hatfield would enjoy a celebrated romance with Evan Dando of the Lemonheads, while Strohm had also briefly been a member during their *Creator* sessions. The release of the EP *Rosy Jack World*, coupled with sell-out dates on a UK visit early in 1992 promised a bright future for the group. However, Hatfield turned solo, just as *Sunburn* began to attract rave reviews. On her departure Hatfield concluded: 'When Blake Babies was happening it was really romantic to sleep on floors and not have any money. But when I look back on it, I can't believe some of the stuff we did.' Strohm and Love, meanwhile, went on to form Antenna.
●ALBUMS: *Nicely Nicely* (Chewbud 1988)★★★, *Slow Learner* (Utility 1989)★★★, *Earwig* (Mammoth 1989)★★★, *Sunburn* (Mammoth 1990)★★★.

BLANCMANGE

This UK electro-pop duo featured Neil Arthur (b. 15 June 1958, Lancashire, England; vocals/guitar) and Steven Luscombe (b. 29 October 1954; keyboards). After debuting with an EP, *Irene And Mavis*, they were invited by disc jockey/entrepreneur Stevo to appear on his influential 1981 Some Bizzare compilation. This led to a contract with London Records and a synthesizer-based album, *Happy Families*, which spawned two Top 10 singles, 'Living On The Ceiling' and 'Blind Vision'. Ambitiously eclectic at times, Blancmange

employed orchestration and raga influences on their second album *Mange Tout* and enjoyed an unlikely hit with a cover of Abba's 'The Day Before You Came'. By 1985, the Blancmange experiment had effectively run its course and after a final album, *Believe You Me*, Luscombe and Arthur went their separate ways.
●ALBUMS: *Happy Families* (London 1982)★★★, *Mange Tout* (London 1984)★★★, *Believe You Me* (London 1985)★★.
●COMPILATIONS: *Heaven Knows* (1992)★★, *Best Of ...* (Connoisseur Collection 1997)★★★.
●VIDEOS: *Live At The Hacienda* (1994).

BLASTERS

Formed in Los Angeles, California, USA, in 1979, the Blasters were one of the leading proponents of the so-called US 'roots-rock' revival of the 80s. Originally comprising Phil Alvin (vocals), his songwriter brother Dave (guitar), John Bazz (bass) and Bill Bateman (drums), the group's first album in 1980 was *American Music* on the small Rollin' Rock label. Incorporating rockabilly, R&B, country and blues, the album was critically applauded for both Dave Alvin's songwriting and the band's ability to update the age-old styles without slavishly recreating them. With a switch to the higher-profile Slash label in 1981, the group released a self-titled album that was also well received. Pianist Gene Taylor was added to the line-up and 50s saxophonist Lee Allen guested (and later toured with the group). With Slash picking up distribution from Warner Brothers Records the album reached the Top 40, due largely to good reviews. (Three later albums charted at lower positions.) A live EP recorded in London followed in 1982 but it was the following year's *Non Fiction*, a thematic study of the working class which critics likened to Bruce Springsteen and Tom T. Hall, that earned the band its greatest acclaim so far. By this time saxophonist Steve Berlin had also joined the fold. Berlin then joined Los Lobos when *Hard Line* was issued in 1985. The album included a song by John Mellencamp and guest backing vocals by the Jordanaires. Dave Alvin departed the group upon its completion to join X and was replaced by Hollywood Fats, who died of a heart attack at the age of 32 while a member of the band. Phil Alvin and Steve Berlin kept a version of the group together until 1987, at which point it folded. Both Alvin brothers have recorded solo albums and worked on other projects.
●ALBUMS: *American Music* (Rollin' Rock 1980)★★★, *The Blasters* (Slash 1981)★★★, *Non*

Fiction (Slash 1983)★★★, *Hard Line* (Slash 1985)★★★.
●COMPILATIONS: *The Blasters Collection* (Slash 1991)★★★★.
●FURTHER READING: *Any Rough Times Are Now Behind You*, Dave Alvin.

BLEY, CARLA

b. Carla Borg, 11 May 1938, Oakland, California, USA. Bley began to learn piano from her father, who was a piano teacher and church organist, at an early age, but discontinued the formal lessons when she was five years old. Her main musical experience was in church choirs and as a church organist until she became interested in jazz at the age of 17. On moving to New York City she had to work as a waitress, unable to earn a living either as a pianist or composer. In 1957 she married Paul Bley and from 1959 began writing many fine compositions, still using her maiden name initially: thus, the composer credit was to 'Borg' when George Russell first recorded one of her pieces ('Dance Class') in 1960. Russell used several of her tunes, as did husband Paul. As her reputation grew, her compositions were sought by the likes of Jimmy Giuffre, Art Farmer, Gary Burton and Charlie Haden (with whom she would work on his various Liberation Music Orchestra projects). In 1964 Bill Dixon invited her to be a charter member of the Jazz Composers' Guild, and at the end of the year she and Michael Mantler, who later became her second husband, led the Jazz Composers' Guild Orchestra in a series of concerts at Judson Hall. Her critical standing really began to blossom after she joined the Jazz Composers' Orchestra Association, founded by Mantler in 1966 on the model of the defunct Guild. The Association and its associated Orchestra (JCO) gave writers the opportunity to write works of an epic scale for large forces, and Bley grasped the opportunity. Two works, *A Genuine Tong Funeral* (Dark Opera Without Words) (recorded by a band centred on the Gary Burton Quartet) and the massive *Escalator Over The Hill* (taking up six album sides) were conceived as a kind of music theatre, and were widely acclaimed: *Escalator* in particular remains a genre in itself. Many of her small-scale pieces have also achieved standard status, including 'Mother Of The Dead Man' (originally part of *Tong Funeral*), 'Closer', 'Ida Lupino' and 'Sing Me Softly Of The Blues'. She became a full-time musician in 1964, working with Pharoah Sanders and Charles Moffett at the start of that year. From December she co-led the JCO with Mantler. Her first orchestral piece, 'Roast', dates from this time, but she was also heavily committed to free jazz at this point. After the JCO appeared at the 1965 Newport Jazz Festival, Bley organized the Jazz Realities Quintet, which also included Mantler and Steve Lacy, to tour Europe. During another tour of Europe, this time with Peter Brötzmann and Peter Kowald in 1966, she became disillusioned with free jazz, a change of heart that led ultimately to the production of *Funeral*. For some years she concentrated on writing, though there was a spell with Jack Bruce's band in 1974, but from 1976 she again began leading a band on a regular basis. Throughout the 80s she continued to play keyboards and to lead medium to small-sized bands. As she pointed out herself on a visit to London in 1990, although she is not among the great pianists she is a unique writer. Her association with composer and former Gary Burton bassist Steve Swallow contributed to the flavour of her successful and accessible Sextet, which toured regularly in the late 80s. While the critics (though not the jazz public) began to grow cool towards the Sextet, her tour with the Very Big Carla Bley Band at the end of 1990 confirmed that she had not lost her individual writing voice, nor her ability to deal convincingly with orchestral forces. Bley's contribution on the 'administrative' side of music deserves recognition too. She is part of the movement to give musicians a degree of control, self-determination and independence from the industry's establishment. With Paul Bley she was a member of the Jazz Composers' Guild, a co-operative formed in autumn 1964, and subsequently helped establish the JCOA. She and Mantler also set up two record labels, Watt for their own recordings and JCOA Records to promote the work of others. Her compositions have been recorded by a number of musicians.
●ALBUMS: with others *Jazz Realities* (1966)★★, *A Genuine Tong Funeral* (1968)★★★, with Charlie Haden *Liberation Music* (1969)★★★, *Escalator Over The Hill* (ECM 1971)★★★★, *Tropic Appetites* (1974)★★★, with Michael Mantler *The Hapless Child* (1976)★★★, *Dinner Music* (Watt 1977)★★★, *Carla Bley Band European Tour 1977* (Watt 1978)★★★, *Musique Mecanique* (Watt 1979)★★★, with Steve Swallow *Afterglow* (80s)★★★, *Social Studies* (Watt 1981)★★★, *Carla Bley Live!* (Watt 1982)★★, *Ballad Of The Fallen* (1983)★★★, *Mortelle Randonnee* (IMS 1983)★★★, *I Hate To Sing* (ECM 1984)★★★, *Heavy Heart* (Watt 1984)★★★, *Night-Glo* (Watt 1985)★★★, *Sextet* (Watt 1987)★★★, *European Tour 1977* (ECM 1987)★★★, with

Swallow *Duets* (Watt 1988)★★★, *Fleur Carnivore* (Watt 1990)★★★, *The Very Little Big Carla Bley Band* (Watt 1991)★★★★, with Swallow *Go Together* (Watt 1992)★★★, *Big Band Theory* (ECM 1993)★★★, with Swallow, Andy Sheppard *Songs With Legs* (Watt 1994)★★★.

BLOCK, RORY

b. 6 November 1949, Greenwich Village, New York, USA. American blues singer and guitarist, raised in New York. Her father played classical violin, but at the age of 10, Block started learning to play folk music on the guitar. She later became involved in the burgeoning Greenwich Village Folk scene. It was as a teenager that she first heard the blues, and it was during this time that she played with such names as Rev. Gary Davis, and Mississippi John Hurt. From then on she was hooked. Meeting up with Stefan Grossman, when she was 13, further encouraged her interest in the music. It was to be some 10 years before she resumed playing, having bowed out to bring up a family. In 1975, she recorded tracks for the small Blue Goose label, for an album entitled *Rory Block (I'm In Love)*. This album was re-released in 1989, and remixed minus two tracks from the original recordings, but including an extra song, 'Blues Again', discovered on the original master tapes. Her first release for Rounder records, *High Heeled Blues*, was co-produced with John Sebastian. She continued in the same vein of recording, and performing, traditional blues and country blues material alongside her own compositions. The recording of *I've Got A Rock In My Sock* included such luminaries as Taj Mahal, and David Bromberg. In 1986, her 19-year-old son, Thiele, was killed in a car accident. The subsequent tribute album from Block, *House Of Hearts*, contained 10 tracks, and all but one were Block originals. *Turning Point*, despite having a bigger production sound overall, did not detract from her earlier blues influences. *Tornado* in 1996 was her most commercial offering to date and was bolstered with some guest 'heavy friends', including Mary-Chapin Carpenter and guitarist David Lindley. Her track record speaks for itself, with her earlier apprehension that a white girl from New York might not sound authentic singing the blues, remaining quite unfounded.

●ALBUMS: *Rory Block* (Blue Goose 1975)★★, *High Heeled Blues* (Rounder 1981)★★★, *Blue Horizon* (Rounder 1983)★★★, *Rhinestones And Steel Strings* (Rounder 1983)★★★, *I've Got A Rock In My Sock* (Rounder 1986)★★★, *House Of Hearts* (Rounder 1987)★★★, *Turning Point* (Munich 1989)★★★, *Mama's Blues* (Rounder 1991)★★★, *Ain't I A Woman* (Rounder 1992)★★★, *Angel Of Mercy* (Rounder 1994)★★★, *When A Woman Gets The Blues* (Rounder 1995)★★, *Women In (E)Motion Festival* (Indigo/Tradition & Moderne 1995)★★★, *Tornado* (Rounder 1996)★★★.
●COMPILATIONS: *Best Blues And Originals* (1987)★★★★.

BLOOD BROTHERS

Opening at the Lyric Theatre in London on 11 April 1983, the stage musical *Blood Brothers* was distinctly contemporary. Its tough and realistic setting, Liverpool in the depths of that city's despairing inner-urban collapse, mirrored the harshly unsentimental tale of brothers, separated as children, who grow up in very different and opposed social conditions. Despite being worlds apart in their social lives, they are drawn together and one eventually murders the other. At the end, a further tradition of the musical theatre was broken with both brothers lying dead. Written by Willy Russell, one of a handful of brilliant chroniclers of Liverpool's contemporary traumas and dramas, the show starred Barbara Dickson and what Sheridan Morley referred to as a 'hit-squad cast capable of slamming Russell's score out across the footlights'. Despite its grim atmosphere, the pungent reality of *Blood Brothers* helped make it a popular and critical success. Clive Hirschhorn, writing in the *Sunday Express*, called it 'a significant milestone in British musicals'. It was certainly that and remains a hard act to follow. Among Russell's songs were 'Marilyn Monroe', 'My Child', 'I'm Not Saying A Word', 'Light Romance' and 'Tell Me It's Not True'. The show earned a Laurence Olivier Award for best musical, and Dickson won for best actress. She was succeeded in the leading role of Mrs. Johnstone by Kiki Dee and later, Stephanie Lawrence. At first, for all its virtues, *Blood Brothers* proved difficult to export. Perhaps its greatest strength its grittily uncompromising portrayal of the survival instinct that has helped make Liverpool such a unique city, is not only what makes it so good but also renders it difficult to transfer to stages in other countries. However, following a successful 1989 London revival, the show opened on Broadway in April 1993. Initial reaction was extremely cool until some members of the original cast were succeeded by more mature artists from the world of popular music, such as Petula Clark, David Cassidy and his brother Shaun. Business then picked up considerably. Subsequent stars included Carole King and Helen Reddy.

BLOW MONKEYS

Led by the politically opinioned Dr. Robert (b. Bruce Robert Howard, 2 May 1961, Norfolk, England; guitar), the Blow Monkeys took their name from Australian slang for Aboriginal didgeriedoo players, something Robert picked up while living in Australia as a teenager. The nickname Doctor was pinned on him at boarding school because he was seen as a sympathetic listener. Before the Blow Monkeys began in the early 80s, he also had a spell at Norwich City Football Club, and dabbled in pop journalism. The other members of the band were Tony Kiley (b. 16 February 1962; drums), Neville Henry (saxophone) and Mick Anker (b. 2 July 1957; bass). They started recording for RCA Records in 1984 but singles 'Man From Russia', 'Atomic Lullaby' and 'Forbidden Fruit' made no headway in the charts. They finally broke through in 1986 with the jazz tinged 'Digging Your Scene', one of the earliest songs about AIDS. The following January they had their biggest hit with 'It Doesn't Have To Be This Way'. Come May, this strongly socialist and vehemently anti-Thatcher band found their latest single, '(Celebrate) The Day After You', banned from the airwaves by the BBC until the General Election was over. The record also featured the voice of Curtis Mayfield. Although reasonably successful, the band were sent a financial lifeline by contributing the track 'You Don't Own Me' to the hugely successful *Dirty Dancing* soundtrack. A series of minor hits followed, and Dr. Robert recorded a duet (under his own name) with soul singer Kym Mazelle. 'Wait' went into the UK Top 10, and the year ended with 'Slaves No More' back with the Monkeys, also featuring the vocal prowess of Sylvia Tella. Their last minor hit was 'Springtime For The World'. Following the break-up of the band Dr. Robert worked with Paul Weller and started a solo career. A debut album was released in 1996.

●ALBUMS: *Limping For A Generation* (RCA 1984)★★★, *Animal Magic* (RCA 1986)★★★, *She Was Only A Grocer's Daughter* (RCA 1987)★★★, *Whoops! There Goes The Neighbourhood* (RCA 1989)★★, *Choices* (RCA 1989)★★.
●COMPILATIONS: *The Best Of* (RCA 1993)★★★, *For The Record* (BMG 1996)★★★.
●VIDEOS: *Video Magic* (1988), *Digging Your Scene* (1988), *Choices* (1989).

BLOW, KURTIS

b. Kurt Walker, 9 August 1959, Harlem, New York, USA. A producer and rap pioneer who had one of the genre's earliest hits with 'Christmas Rappin' in 1979, written for him by J.B. Ford and *Billboard* journalist Robert Ford Jnr. Blow had previously studied vocal performance at the High School Of Music and Art at the City College of New York. Afterwards he began working as a DJ in Harlem where he added his first tentative raps to liven up proceedings. By this time he had made the acquaintance of fellow City College student Russel Simmons (see Run DMC), who convinced him to change his name from Kool DJ Kurt to Kurtis Blow. Playing in small clubs alongside other early innovators like Grandmaster Flash, he signed to Mercury Records just as the Sugarhill Gang had the first rap chart success with 'Rapper's Delight'. Blow in turn became the first rap artist to cut albums for a major label. His 1979 hit, 'The Breaks', for which his partner Davy D (b. David Reeves Jnr.), originally titled Davey DMX, and best known for recording 'One For The Table (Fresh)', provided the first of his backing tracks, was a massive influence on the whole hip hop movement. The early 80s were quiet in terms of chart success, before he re-emerged in 1983 with the *Party Time* EP and an appearance in the movie, *Krush Groove*. *Ego Trip* was an impressive selection bolstered by the presence of Run DMC on the minor hit '8 Million Stories'. He rapped on Rene And Angela's hit 'Save Your Love (For Number One)', doubtless an experience of which he would not wish to be reminded. He has also produced for the Fearless Four, Dr. Jeckyll And Mr Hyde, among others. His yearly album cycle continued with the patriotic *America*, whose earnest, sensitive moments (particularly 'If I Ruled The World', which appeared on the soundtack to *Krush Groove* and as a single) were rather undermined by the presence of 'Super Sperm'. The following year he organized the all-star King Dream Chorus and Holiday Crew who recorded the Martin Luther King tribute, 'King Holiday', which argued for MLK's birthday to be enshrined as a national holiday. *Kingdom Blow* featured guest appearances from the likes of Bob Dylan, and George Clinton on an amazing interpretation of 'Zip-A-Dee-Doo-Dah'. However, Blow was largely overtaken by the young guns of the genre (notably Run DMC, ironically) he helped to create, a fact underlined by the miserable reception offered the misnomered *Back By Popular Demand*, and he has not had a chart hit since 'I'm Chillin'' in 1986.

●ALBUMS: *Kurtis Blow* (Mercury 1980)★★★, *Deuce* (Mercury 1981)★★, *Tough* (Mercury 1982)★★, *Ego Trip* (Mercury 1984)★★★, *America* (Mercury 1985)★★★, *Kingdom Blow* (Mercury

1986)★★, *Back By Popular Demand* (Mercury 1988)★★.
●COMPILATIONS: *Best Of* (Mercury 1994)★★★.

BLOWZABELLA

Essentially a UK folk dance band, formed in 1978, which achieved a deal of success both on the live music circuit and on record. The group were almost as well-known for the frequent changes of personnel as their music. In 1987, sole remaining founder member John Swayne (b. Jonathan Rock Phipps Swayne, 26 June 1940, Hereford, England; alto and soprano saxophones, bagpipes) left, and Jo Fraser (b. Jo-Anne Rachel Newmarch Fraser, 4 December 1960, St. Albans, Hertfordshire, England; saxophone, vocals, whistles) joined. In 1989, Jo changed her name to Freya, as there was an Equity member of the same name. The rest of the group were Paul James (b. 4 April 1957, Southampton, Hampshire, England; bagpipes, soprano saxophone, percussion), Nigel Eaton (b. 3 January 1966, Lyndhurst, Hampshire, England; hurdy gurdy), Ian Luff (b. 4 January 1956, Brighton, Sussex, England; cittern, bass guitar), Dave Roberts (d. 23 February 1996; melodeon, darabuka) and Dave Shepherd (fiddle). Shepherd had joined the group in 1982, having previously played with folk rock band Dr. Cosgill's Delight, alongside James. Luff joined in 1985. Blowzabella toured Brazil for the British Council in 1987, playing a large number of concerts, and *Pingha Frenzy* emerged from over 50 hours of taped sessions. *A Richer Dust* came from the music the band had written for the 500th Anniversary of the Battle of Stoke Field. A concert featuring the piece was performed on 18 June 1987. Fraser, by 1989, was also pursuing a career outside Blowzabella, notably touring with Kathryn Locke (b. 30 May 1961, Upminster, Essex, England; 'cello). Shepherd left to get married and moved to live in Germany, and Andy Cutting (b. 18 March 1969, West Harrow, Middlesex, England; melodeon) joined in 1989. Cutting had previously filled in on occasional dates when Shepherd was unavailable, so was no stranger to the music. Later that same year, Swayne rejoined the band. The group's repertoire included a wealth of dance material from northern Europe and France. Although considered a dance band, Blowzabella gave many concerts in such places as Ghana, Nigeria, Sierra Leone, Europe and Brazil. They played a 'farewell tour' in 1990 as it had become uneconomical to stay together and tour. The various members have become involved in their own projects and continue to perform.

●ALBUMS: *Blowzabella* (Plant Life 1982)★★★, *Blowzabella In Colour* (Plant Life 1983)★★, *Bobbityshooty* (Plant Life 1984)★★★, *Tam Lin* (Plant Life 1984)★★★, *The Blowzabella Wall Of Sound* (Plant Life 1986)★★★, *The B To A Of Blowzabella* (1987)★★★, *Pingha Frenzy* (Some Bizzare 1988)★★★, *Vanilla* (Topic 1990)★★.
●COMPILATIONS: *** (Osmosys 1995)★★★.

BLUE AEROPLANES

Since forming in Bristol, England, in the early 80s, the Blue Aeroplanes have had endless line-up changes, but maintained their original aim, a desire to mix rock and beat poetry and to involve a large number of musicians in an almost communal manner. The nucleus of the band has always revolved around deadpan vocalist Gerard Langley, his brother John (drums/percussion), Nick Jacobs (guitar), Dave Chapman (multi-instrumentalist) and dancer Wojtek Dmochowski. Along the way, individuals such as Angelo Bruschini (guitar/bass/organ), John Stapleton (tapes), Ruth Coltrane (bass/mandolin), Ian Kearey (guitar/banjimer/harmonium), Rodney Allen (guitar), Simon Heathfield (bass) and Caroline Halcrow (guitar - who later left to pursue a solo career as Caroline Trettine) have all contributed to the Aeroplanes' melting pot. After a debut album for the Abstract label, *Bop Art*, in April 1984, the band signed with the fledgling Fire Records. Several well-received EPs followed - *Action Painting And Other Original Works* (1985), *Lover And Confidante And Other Stories Of Travel* and *Religion And Heartbreak* (March, 1986) - succeeded by their second album, *Tolerance* (October 1986). The Aeroplanes' third set, *Spitting Out Miracles*, surfaced in 1987. All were characterized by Langley's monotone verse and a deluge of instruments and sounds hinged around the guitar. 'Veils Of Colour' (1988) coincided with the release of *Night Tracks*, their February 1987 session for BBC Radio disc jockey, Janice Long. A double album, *Friendloverplane*, neatly concluded their time with Fire, compiling the Aeroplanes' progress to date. It was not until the start of the new decade that, following a stint supporting R.E.M. in the UK, the band re-emerged on the Ensign label with 'Jacket Hangs' in January 1990 and a new album, *Swagger*, the following month. Both suggested a more direct, straightforward approach, and this was confirmed on the EP *And Stones*. In 1991, an eight-strong line-up now comprising; Langley, Bruschini, Dmochowski, Allen, Paul Mulreany (drums - a former member of the Jazz Butcher), Andy McCreeth, Hazel Winter and

Robin Key, released the roundly acclaimed *Beatsongs*, co-produced by Elvis Costello and Larry Hirsch. Further activity in 1994 indicated a major push forward with that year's album for new home Beggars Banquet Records. *Life Model* sounded as fresh as the band ever has and engendered further press acclaim, and featured new recruits Marcus Williams (bass, ex-Mighty Lemon Drops), Susie Hugg (vocals, ex-Katydids).

●ALBUMS: *Bop Art* (Abstract 1984)★★★, *Tolerance* (Fire 1986)★★★, *Spitting Out Miracles* (Fire 1987)★★★, *Swagger* (Ensign 1990)★★★, *Beatsongs* (Ensign 1991)★★★, *Life Model* (Beggars Banquet 1994)★★★, *Rough Music* (Beggars Banquet 1995)★★★, *Fruit* (Fire 1996)★★★.

●COMPILATIONS: *Friendloverplane* (Fire 1988)★★★★, *Friendloverplane 2* (Ensign 1992)★★★, *Huh! Best Of: 1987-1992* (Chrysalis 1997)★★★.

BLUE NILE

The Blue Nile formed in Glasgow, Scotland, in 1981 and consist of Paul Buchanan (b. Glasgow, Scotland; vocals/guitar/synthesizers), Robert Bell (b. Glasgow, Scotland; synthesizers) and Paul Joseph Moore (b. Glasgow, Scotland; piano/synthesizers). Their debut single, 'I Love This Life', was recorded independently and subsequently picked up on by RSO Records, which promptly folded. Eventually, their demo tapes found their way to hi-fi specialists Linn Products, so the company could test various types of music at their new cutting plant. In spite of their lack of experience in the record retail market, Linn immediately signed the band to make *A Walk Across The Rooftops*, which came out in 1984 to considerable praise. Suddenly, thanks to some gently emotive synthetics and an overall mood that seemed to revel in nocturnal atmospherics, the unsuspecting trio were thrust into the limelight. Blue Nile pondered over the reasons for their success and, as a consequence, found themselves incapable of repeating the feats of the first album. Indeed, it was to be five years before the follow up, *Hats*, finally continued the shimmering legacy of its predecessor, whereupon the studio-bound collective took their first tentative steps into the live arena with enthusiastically received shows in the USA and Britain before returning to the studio for another anticipated lengthy recording period. Another hold-up was caused by contractual difficulties with Linn and Virgin Records ('It's amazing how you can be generating fantastically small amounts of money and still have fantastically complicated scenarios'). In the 90s the band journeyed to California to record backing vocals for Julian Lennon, eventually working with Robbie Robertson and several others. They also signed a new contract with Warner Brothers Records in 1993, and by 1995 stated they had a large stockpile of songs written in the interim on which to draw. The greatly anticipated *Peace At Last* was highly praised (*Q Magazine* bestowed five stars); however, once the dust had settled its modest success was soon forgotten.

●ALBUMS: *A Walk Across The Rooftops* (Linn/Virgin 1984)★★★★, *Hats* (Linn/Virgin 1989)★★★, *Peace At Last* (Warners 1996)★★★.

BLUE RODEO

This folk rock band from Toronto, Canada, have often found themselves fielding comparisons with the Band, although in truth their sound owes as much to Buffalo Springfield and the Beatles. Two distinctive singer-songwriters and guitarists, Jim Cuddy and Greg Keelor (ex-Crash Vegas), helped retain the group's individual edge. After a strong debut in *Outskirts*, which dealt almost exclusively in broken hearts, loss and yearning, *Diamond Mine* encompassed a wider lyrical scope with targets that included Colonel Oliver North and others who used 'God And Country' to justify their self-interest (in the song of the same title). The recording took place in an empty hall in Toronto which dulled the songs' potential impact, but production aside, it confirmed the arrival of a strong writing team, embellished with skilful musical interplay. *Casino* saw the arrival of Michelle Shocked and Dwight Yoakam producer Pete Anderson, who returned the band to a more considered, intricate sound. With the Beatles-esque harmonies now in the foreground, critics greeted the new model Blue Rodeo with open arms. A year previously keyboard player Bob Wiseman had made his solo debut with an album of upbeat and quirky self-written compositions. The collection, with guests that included k.d. lang associate Ben Mink and Mary Margaret O'Hara, was an odd but amusing release.

●ALBUMS: *Outskirts* (Risqué Disque/Atlantic 1987)★★★, *Diamond Mine* (Risqué Disque/Atlantic 1989)★★★, *Casino* (Atlantic 1991)★★★, *Nowhere To Here* (Warners 1996)★★★. Solo: Bob Wiseman *Bob Wiseman Sings Wrench Turtle: In Her Dream* (Risqué Disque/Atlantic 1990)★★★.

BLUE RONDO A LA TURK

Named after a Dave Brubeck tune, this UK-based group comprised: Moses Mount Bassie (saxophone), Mick 'Lloyd' Bynoe (drums/percussion), Art Collins (saxophone), Geraldo d'Arbilly (b. Brazil; percussion), Kito Poncioni (b. Rio de Janeiro, Brazil; bass), Mark Reilly (b. 20 February 1960, High Wycombe, Buckinghamshire, England; guitar), Chris Sullivan (vocals), Christos Tolera (vocals), Tholo Peter Tsegona (trumpet) and Daniel White (b. 26 August 1959, Letchwood, Hertfordshire, England; keyboards). Founder member and chief lyricist, Sullivan formed the core of the band in early 1981. The group were heavily promoted in the fashion and style magazines of the period, but were received less enthusiastically by the music press. Their debut, *Chewing The Fat*, produced by Clive Langer and Alan Winstanley, nevertheless showed promise. 'Me And Mr Sanchez' peaked at number 40 and 'Klactoveesedstein' just made the Top 50, and a parting of the ways had occurred even before the second album. Reilly and White went on to form Matt Bianco.

●ALBUMS: *Chewing The Fat* (Diable Noir 1982)★★, *Bees Knees And Chicken Elbows* (Virgin 1984)★★.

BLUEBELLS

This Scottish quintet were formed in 1982, and originally comprised brothers David McCluskey (b. 13 January 1964; drums) and Ken McCluskey (b. 8 February 1962; vocals/harmonica), plus Robert 'Bobby Bluebell' Hodgens (b. 6 June 1959; vocals/guitar), Russell Irvine (guitar) and Lawrence Donegan (bass). The latter two were later replaced, respectively, by Craig Gannon (b. 30 July 1966) and Neal Baldwin. The group were fine exponents of the 'jangly pop' produced by Scottish bands such as Orange Juice and Aztec Camera. Despite strong airplay on British radio, the inexplicable failure of 'Cath' to rise any further than number 62 in the UK chart in 1983 perplexed critics and fans, as did the similar fate that befell 'Sugar Bridge' in the same year. The Bluebells did at last gain their deserved success in 1984 with the number 11 hit, 'I'm Falling', and 'Young At Heart' (co-written by Siobhan Fahey of Bananarama and Shakespears Sister) which reached the UK Top 10, while their solitary album for London Records achieved Top 30 status. Riding on the wave of this success, a reissued 'Cath'/'She Will Always Be Waiting' belatedly hit the Top 40. After splitting, siblings Ken and David formed the McCluskey Brothers, releasing an album, *Aware Of All*, while Bobby formed Up and later worked with Paul Quinn (ex-Bourgie Bourgie). Craig Gannon stood in, briefly, for the Smiths' bassist Andy Rourke, who was having drug problems, then on Rourke's return, Gannon continued with the Smiths as second guitarist, subsequently joining the Adult Net. In 1993 Volkswagen used 'Young At Heart' in one of their television advertisements. The song re-entered the UK charts in April, reaching number 1 and staying there for a month. However, the group promised 'not to outstay their welcome', with the McCluskey brothers returning to folk singing (releasing a new album, *Favourite Colours*). Bobby Bluebell was to be found in Bob's, his Glasgow house/hip hop club, while Russel Irvine had become a chef, but returned for their appearances on *Top Of The Pops*, replacing Donegan. The Bluebells' former bass player was ejected after a previous apearance on the programme, when he used the opportunity to write an exposé of the show for the *Guardian* newspaper.

●ALBUMS: *Sisters* (London 1984)★★★, *Bloomin' Live* (London 1993)★★.

●COMPILATIONS: *Second* (London 1992)★★★, *The Singles Collection* (London 1993)★★★.

●VIDEOS: *The Bluebells* (1989).

BLUES BAND

This vastly experienced British blues-rock outfit was put together - initially 'just for fun' - in 1979 by former Manfred Mann band colleagues Paul Jones (b. Paul Pond, 24 February 1942, Portsmouth, England; vocals/harmonica) and Tom McGuinness (b. 2 December 1941, London, England; guitar). They brought in slide guitarist and singer Dave Kelly (b. 1948, London, England; ex-John Dummer Blues Band and Rocksalt), who suggested the bass player from his then current band Wildcats, Gary Fletcher (b. London, England). On drums was McGuinness's hit-making partner from the early 70s, Hughie Flint (b. 15 March 1942, Manchester, England). Such a confluence of name players brought immediate success on the pub/club/college circuit and, despite the group's humble intentions, recordings followed. *The Official Blues Band Bootleg Album* was literally just that; inability to pay studio bills had forced them to press copies privately from a second copy tape. It sold extremely well, however, and Arista Records soon stepped in, releasing the master recording and putting out four further albums by 1983. The band had split in 1982, but reformed three years later after a one-off charity performance. Recent releases have placed far more emphasis on original material and augur well for the future. Ex-Family drummer Rob Townsend (b. 7 July 1947, Leicester, England) replaced Flint in 1981. In the 90s the band were still regularly performing even though Jones and Kelly had substantial careers of their own. Jones has become one of the UK's leading Blues/R&B broadcasters and Kelly has released a number of solo albums. The latest Blues Band venture is their version of the 'Unplugged' phenomenon, recorded not for MTV, but at the famous Snape Maltings in Aldeburgh, Suffolk.

●ALBUMS: *The Official Blues Band Bootleg Album* (Blues Band 1980)★★★★, *Ready* (Arista 1980)★★★, *Itchy Feet* (Arista 1981)★★★, *Brand Loyalty* (Arista 1982)★★★, *Bye-Bye Blues* (Arista 1983)★★★, *These Kind Of Blues* (Date 1986)★★★, *Back For More* (Arista 1989)★★★, *Fat City* (RCA 1991)★★★, *Live* (1993)★★★, *Homage* (Essential 1993)★★★, *Wire Less* (Cobalt 1995)★★★.

●FURTHER READING: *Talk To Me Baby: The Story Of The Blues Band*, Roy Bainton.

BLUES BROTHERS, THE

John Landis, director of *An American Werewolf In London* and Michael Jackson's *Thriller*, was responsible for this 1980 feature. John Belushi (b. 24 January 1949, Wheaton, Illinois, USA, d. 5 March 1982), star of a previous Landis project, *Animal House*, shared top billing with Dan Aykroyd (b. 1 July 1952, Ottawa, Ontario, Canada) as Jake and Elwood Blues who reform their R&B band following the former's prison release. 'We're on a mission from God', the pair proclaim when, after a vision, they attempt to raise funds for the orphanage in which they were raised. A highly popular slapstick comedy, *The Blues Brothers* contains some priceless scenes, notably when the band attempt to play soul at a redneck venue. However, it is equally prone to cliché, in particular the car chase and wrecking sequences, and it is reported that the shot in which one vehicle is dropped from a crane cost more than the rest of the film put together. Despite the presence of former Booker T. And The MGs members Steve Cropper and Duck Dunn, many critics sensed a patronising, almost pantomime, view to R&B in its content. Cameo roles for James Brown, Ray Charles, Aretha Franklin and John Lee Hooker, however memorable, seemed to marginalize performers actually at the forefront of the genre. However, there is little doubt many of the musicians and singers featured found their careers galvanised by their appearances therein. A successful soundtrack album ensued, while Belushi and Aykroyd, aided by Cropper and Dunn, recorded further albums under the Blues Brothers banner.

Belushi's sudden death brought that pastime to a premature end. The film that inspired that career has retained its appeal and it remains one of the most popular rock features of its era.

●FILMS: *The Blues Brothers* (1980).

BLYTH POWER

The driving force behind this collection of post-punk train spotters (their name derives from the name of a steam engine) is drummer, lead singer and songwriter Josef Porta (b. Joseph Porter, 21 February 1962, Templecombe, Somerset, England). He had previously worked with a variety of bands; Valley Forge - while in Somerset in 1978, and on moving to London in 1979, Attitudes and the Entire Cosmos - which primarily comprised the road crew of Here And Now. After brief stints joining and recording with Zounds, Null And Void and the Mob, Porta formed Blyth Power in 1983 with Curtis Youé. Porta's eloquent lyrics, coupled with a punk-influenced mixture of folk and rock, drew analogies from England's history, such as Watt Tyler and Oliver Cromwell's army, to the state of present day politics, in particular a resistance to the 1979-onwards Conservative government. His attacks on the ruination of the common man's right to English heritage have endeared him to an audience of kindred spirits, though this has been no exercise in austerity - Porta being just as likely to document the rise and fall of a cricket match as a government's fortunes. Though many of Blyth Power's albums have been blighted by inadequate production, each has achieved a consistent quality, with the highlight Porta's mocking social analysis. The group's debut cassette, for example, included songs such as their debut single, 'Chevy Chase' - 'And from Yorkshire to Somerset I was king of the field/With my barn-door defence of my lofty ideals/They tell me that anarchy and peace became real/And it lives in a field outside Reading'. Vivid characters, historical, rural and cricketing, have continued to populate Porta's songs ever since. They certainly have their supporters, among them *Folk Roots'* editor Ian A. Anderson: '(they) are among the rare outfits who have sufficient roots in our culture to bring that unmistakable feeling of swelling, thrilling pride; whose lyrical literacy and grasp of a great, powerful melody line lift them way above just about any multi-millionaire household-name pop icons you can name.' Their sixth studio album was released in 1995, this time without the services of long-serving member 'Wob', who had departed for a solo career. Nevertheless, *Paradise Razed*, completed in 10 days with Whisky

Priests collaborator Fred Purser, was as accessible an introduction to the band as any, Porta (now calling himself Porter) offering further entertaining insights into British history in songs such as 'Ghilbert De Haace' and 'Rowan's Riding'.

●ALBUMS: *A Little Touch Of Harry In The Middle Of The Night* cassette only (96 Tapes 1984)★★★, *Wicked Women, Wicked Men And Wicket Keepers* (Midnight 1986)★★★, *The Barman And Other Stories* (Midnight 1988)★★★, *Alnwick And Tyne* (Midnight 1990)★★★, *The Guns Of Castle Cary* (Downward Spiral 1991)★★★, *Pastor Skull* (Downward Spiral 1993)★★★, *Paradise Razed* (Downward Spiral 1995)★★★.

●COMPILATIONS: *Pont Au-Dessus De La Brue* (Midnight 1988)★★★.

BODINES

This UK rock/pop group achieved a degree of critical success in the mid to late 80s, principally, and unjustly, through their connections with the fashionable Creation Records label. The band's line-up featured: lyricist Mike Ryan (vocals), Paul Brotherton (guitar), Tim Burtonwood (bass) and John Rowland (drums). Ryan and Rowland were schoolfriends from Glossop, while Brotherton grew up in Salford. The band was put together while its members were unemployed. Their first demo tape included raw versions of songs that would surface later, and Alan McGee at Creation decided he was interested. They became the youngest band to play the Factory Funhouse (at the Hacienda in Manchester), and two singles on Creation, 'God Bless' and 'Therese', produced by Ian Broudie (Lightning Seeds), were impressive. However, they soon moved on when record sales failed to follow their good press. Subsequent singles 'Skankin' Queen' and 'Slip Slide' were undeservedly ignored, though their debut album was critically revered: 'Mick Ryan . . . is not going suddenly to sing songs about being happy; he's still stuck with betrayal, guilt and worry, but these feelings aren't smothered in some wet blanket, they're distilled into a crystal glass.' By this time they employed a brass section (Graham Lambyekski and Nelson Pandela), but when new label Magnet disappeared, so did the Bodines.

●ALBUMS: *Played* (Magnet 1987)★★★.

BOLTON, MICHAEL

b. Michael Bolotin, 1953, New Haven, Connecticut, USA, Bolton became one of the most successful rock balladeers of the late 80s. He grew up listening to soul artists such as Stevie Wonder, Ray Charles and Marvin Gaye, before recording his first single for Epic in 1968. Among the backing musicians on Bolton's first solo album for RCA Records were Bernard 'Pretty' Purdie, David Sanborn and Muscle Shoals sessionman Wayne Perkins. Critics made frequent comparisons between Bolton and Joe Cocker. In the late 70s, Michael became lead singer with hard rock band Blackjack. However, despite the presence of top producers Tom Dowd (Allman Brothers and Eric Clapton) and Eddy Offord (Yes), their two albums for Polydor sold poorly. After the band split, guitarist Bruck Kulick played with Billy Squier, while drummer Sandy Gennaro joined the Pat Travers Band and bassist Jim Haslip became a session musician. Bolton himself turned to songwriting and to a new solo recording deal with Columbia.

Initially, he had greater success as a composer, providing Laura Branigan with the 1983 hit 'How Am I Supposed To Live Without You', which was co-written with Doug James. He started using the more accessible name of Bolton in 1983. As a solo performer he persevered with a heavy rock approach and it was not until he shifted to a soul ballad style on *The Hunger* that he had his own first Top 20 single, 'That's What Love Is All About' in 1987. From that point Bolton had a series of blue-eyed soul hits which included a new chart-topping version of 'How Am I Supposed To Live Without You' in 1990, as well as 'How Can We Be Lovers' and the 1991 successes 'Love Is A Wonderful Thing' and Time, Love And Tenderness'. He also enjoyed a brief, and unexpected, songwriting collaboration with Bob Dylan, but by the middle of the 90s his career had peaked. In 1995 he resurfaced with a hit single, 'Can I Touch You ... There?', and a greatest hits package.

●ALBUMS: *Michael Bolotin* (RCA 1975)★★, *Every Day Of My Life* (RCA 1976)★★, *Michael! Bolton* (Columbia 1983)★★, *Everybody's Crazy* (Columbia 1985)★★, *The Hunger* (Columbia 1987)★★★, *Soul Provider* (Columbia 1989)★★★, *Time, Love And Tenderness* (Columbia 1991)★★, *The One Thing* (Columbia 1993)★★, *This Is The Time - The Christmas Album* (Columbia 1996)★.

●COMPILATIONS: with Blackjack *Blackjack* (Polydor 1979)★★, *Worlds Apart* (Polydor 1980)★★, *Timeless (The Classics)* (Columbia 1992)★★★, *Greatest Hits 1985-1995* (Sony 1995)★★★, *The Early Years* (RCA 1997)★★.

●VIDEOS: *Soul Provider: The Videos* (1990), *This Is Michael Bolton* (1992), *Decade: Greatest Hits 1985-1995 The Videos* (SMV 1995).

BON JOVI

This commercial hard rock band was formed in New Jersey, USA, and fronted by Jon Bon Jovi (b. John Francis Bongiovi Jnr., 2 March 1962, Perth Amboy, New Jersey, USA; vocals). His four co-members were: Richie Sambora (b. 11 July 1959; guitar, ex-Message), David Bryan (b. David Rashbaum, 7 February 1962, Edison, New Jersey, USA; keyboards), Tico Torres (b. 7 October 1953; drums, ex-Franke And The Knockouts) and Alec John Such (b. 14 November 1956; bass, ex-Message). Bongiovi, of Italian descent, met Rashbaum (ex-Phantom's Opera) at Sayreville High School, where they shared a mutual interest in rock music. They soon joined eight other musicians in the R&B cover band Atlantic City Expressway. When Rashbaum moved to New York to study at the Juilliard School of Music, Bongiovi followed. Charming his way into the Power Station recording studios, he performed menial tasks for two years before Billy Squier agreed to produce his demo tape. One track, 'Runaway', was played on local radio and appeared on a local artist compilation album (his work also graced oddities like the novelty track, 'R2D2 I Wish You A Merry Christmas'). Reunited with Rashbaum, he acquired the services of Sambora, an established session musician, Such and Torres. By July 1983, they had a recording contract with Polygram and support slots with Eddie Money and ZZ Top, the latter at Madison Square Garden. Jon Bon Jovi's looks attracted immediate attention for the band, and he turned down the lucrative lead role in the dance film *Footloose* in order to concentrate on his music. Their debut album preceded a headline tour and supports with the Scorpions, Whitesnake and Kiss. *7800 Degrees Fahrenheit* was greeted with cynicism by the media, which was already reticent at the prospect of the band's manicured image and formularized heavy rock. A mediocre album only fuelled their scorn. The band responded with style. *Slippery When Wet* was the biggest-selling rock album of 1987, although it originally appeared in August 1986. Three of its tracks; 'Wanted Dead Or Alive', 'You Give Love A Bad Name' and 'Livin' On A Prayer', were US hits. Headlining the Monsters Of Rock shows in Europe, they were joined on stage by Gene Simmons and Paul Stanley (Kiss), Dee Snider (Twisted Sister) and Bruce Dickinson (Iron Maiden) for an encore of 'We're An American Band'. It merely served to emphasize the velocity with which Bon Jovi had reached the top of the rock league. The tour finally closed after 18 months in Australia, while the album sold millions of copies. When *New Jersey* followed, it contained 'Living In Sin', a Jon Bon Jovi composition which pointed to his solo future, although the song owed a great debt to his hero Bruce Springsteen. The rest of 1989 was spent on more extensive touring, before the band temporarily retired. As Jon Bon Jovi commented, it was time to 'Ride my bike into the hills, learn how to garden, *anything* except do another Bon Jovi record.' He subsequently concentrated on his solo career, married karate champion Dorothea Hurley and appeared in his first movie, *Young Guns II* and released a quasi-soundtrack of songs inspired by it as his debut solo album in 1990. However, the commercial incentive to return to Bon Jovi would be hard to resist. *Keep The Faith*, with their sound stripped down, was an impressive album, satisfying critics and anxious fans alike who had patiently waited almost four years for new material. If any had considered the group a spent commercial force then the success of the slick ballad, 'Always', a chart fixture in 1994, revealed no such decline. On the back of its success Bon Jovi would occupy the UK number 1 spot with the compilation set, *Crossroads*, amid rumours that bass player Alec John Such was about to be replaced by Huey McDonald. Bryan, meanwhile, released his first solo album, through Phonogram in Japan. Sambora, meanwhile, had married Hollywood actress Heather Locklear (ex-*Dynasty*). *These Days* was a typically slick collection of ballads and party rock, and included the hit single 'This Ain't A Love Song'. With their position already secure as one of the world's most popular rock bands, the album lacked ambition and the band seemed content to provide fans with more of the old formula. Their popularity had never been greater than in 1995 when in the annual readers' poll of the leading metal magazine *Kerrang* the band won seven categories, including best band and best album (for *These Days*) and astonishingly worst band and worst album (for *These Days*)! *These Days Tour Edition* was a live mini-album released in Australia only. Jon Bon Jovi began to nurture an acting career in the 90s with roles in *Moonlight And Valentino* and *The Leading Man*.

● ALBUMS: *Bon Jovi* (Vertigo 1984)★★, *7800 Degrees Fahrenheit* (Vertigo 1985)★★, *Slippery When Wet* (Vertigo 1986)★★★★, *New Jersey* (Vertigo 1988)★★★, *Keep The Faith* (Phonogram 1992)★★★★, *These Days* (Jambco/Mercury 1995)★★★, *These Days Tour Edition* mini-album (Mercury 1996)★★. Solo: David Bryan *On A Full Moon* (Phonogram 1994)★★. Jon Bon Jovi *Blaze Of*

Glory (Vertigo 1990)★★. Richie Sambora *Stranger In This Town* (Mercury 1991)★★.
●COMPILATIONS: *Crossroads - The Best Of* (Phonogram 1994)★★★★.
●VIDEOS: *Breakout* (1986), *Slippery When Wet* (1988), *New Jersey* (1989), *Dead Or Alive* (1989), *Access All Areas* (1991), *Keep The Faith: An Evening With Bon Jovi* (1993), *Crossroads The Best of* (PolyGram 1994), *Live From London* (Polygram 1995).
●FURTHER READING: *Bon Jovi: An Illustrated Biography*, Eddy McSquare. *Faith And Glory*, Malcolm Dome. *Bon Jovi: Runaway*, Dave Bowler and Bryan Dray. *The Illustrated Biography*, Mick Wall. *The Complete Guide To The Music Of ...* , Mick Wall and Malcolm Dome. *Bon Jovi*, Neil Jeffries.

BORBETOMAGUS

An incredibly prolific, powerful and adventurous *avant garde* jazz group, the core element of Borbetomagus comprises Don Dietrich (wind instruments), Jim Sauter (wind instruments) and Donald Miller (guitar). They formed in Hudson Valley, New York, USA, in 1978, both Dietrich and Sauter having been friends since kindergarten. They continued their musical collaborations through high school, eventually linking with Miller (ex-Slick Dick And The Volkswagens) after meeting him on an experimental radio show. Their self-titled 1980 debut album, which also featured keyboard player Brian Doherty, provided an abrasive, almost overwhelming sonic introduction, with Miller's layered feedback counterpointing the unfettered dual saxophone playing of his partners. The additional musician for *Work On What Has Been Spoiled* was English producer Hugh Davies, while *Sauter, Dietrich, Miller* was recorded at live shows between 1979 and 1981 to clearly bemused audiences. Beginning with 1983's *Industrial Strength* set, Borbetomagus embarked on a series of collaborations with obscure and well-known musicians. Many of these recordings are taken from free improvisation sessions, making them less concisely vital as the band's unaccompanied albums. There have also been several further live collections, including the double album *Zurich* (live at the Rote Fabik), *New York Performances* and *Live At Inroads*. Further collaborations with Swiss duo Voice Crack, bass player Adam Nodelman and Shaking Ray Levis were all artistically successful, though more attention was focused on their comparatively accessible 1990 album, *Barefoot In The Head*, named after a Bryan Aldiss science fiction novel, recorded with Thurston Moore of Sonic

Youth. Uncompromisingly innovative, even within the free-form jazz world, Borbetomagus have produced a rich discography which combines the eloquent expressionism of the best jazz music with the attack and vigour of rock.
●ALBUMS: *Borbetomagus* (Agaric 1980)★★★, *Work On What Has Been Spoiled* (Agaric 1981)★★★, *Sauter, Dietrich, Miller* (Agaric 1982)★★, *Barbed Wire Maggots* (Agaric 1983)★★★, *Life At Inroads* (Agaric 1983)★★★, with Toshinori Kondo, Tristan Honsinger, Peter Kowald, Milo Fine *Industrial Strength* (Leo 1983)★★, *Zurich* (Agaric 1984)★★, with Kondo, Honsinger, Kowald, Fine *Borbeto Jam* (Cadence 1985)★★★, with Jim Sauter, Don Dietrich *Bells Together* (Agaric 1985)★★★, *New York Performances* (Agaric 1986)★★★, *Seven Reasons For Tears* (Purge 1988)★★★, with Voice Crack *Fish That Sparkling Bubble* (Agaric 1988)★★★, *Snuff Jazz* (Agaric 1990)★★★, Sauter, Dietrich, Thurston Moore *Barefoot In The Head* (Forced Exposure 1990)★★★, with Voice Crack *Asbestos Shake* (Agaric 1992)★★★, *Buncha Hair That Long* (Agaric 1993)★★★, with Shaking Ray Levis *Coelacanth* (Agaric/Lyndhurst Society 1994)★★★.

Bow Wow

The name translates literally into 'Barking Dog'; a fitting title for Japan's finest exponents of melodic heavy metal. Formed in 1976, the band comprised Kyoji Yamamoto (vocals/guitar), Mitsuhiro Saito (vocals/guitar), Kenji Sano (bass) and Toshiri Niimi (drums). Intriguingly, they incorporated classical Japanese musical structures within a framework of westernized hard rock. Influenced by Kiss, Led Zeppelin and Aerosmith, they released a sequence of impressive albums during the late 70s. Characterized by explosive guitar work and breathtaking arrangements, the only disappointment to western ears was the Japanese vocals, which doubtless restricted their international appeal. On *Asian Volcano* their eleventh album released in 1982, the vocals were sung in English for the first time, but the band sounded uncomfortable with the transition. They played the Reading Festival the same year and were afforded an encouraging reception. Two subsequent shows at London's Marquee Club were recorded for the live album, *Holy Expedition*, which followed in 1983. At the end of that year the band changed their name to Vow Wow, adding an extra vocalist and keyboard player to pursue a more melodic direction. Lead guitarist Yamamoto has released two solo albums, representing an instrumental fusion of classical, rock and jazz styles; *Horizons* and *Electric Cinema* in 1980 and 1982, respectively. Outside the Far East success has continued to elude this first-class rock outfit, despite Whitesnake's Neil Murray joining for a short time in 1987.

●ALBUMS: *Bow Wow* (Invitation 1976)★★★, *Signal Fire* (Invitation 1977)★★★, *Charge* (Invitation 1977)★★★, *Super Live* (Invitation 1978)★★★, *Guarantee* (Invitation 1978)★★★, *The Bow Wow* (Invitation 1979)★★★, *Glorious Road* (SMS 1979)★★★, *Telephone* (SMS 1980)★★★, *X Bomber* (SMS 1980)★★★, *Hard Dog* (SMS 1981)★★★, *Asian Volcano* (VAP 1982)★★, *Warning From Stardust* (VAP 1982)★★, *Holy Expedition* (Heavy Metal 1983)★★. As Vow Wow: *Beat Of Metal Motion* (VAP 1984)★★★, *Cyclone* (Eastworld 1985)★★★, *III* (Eastworld 1986)★★★, *Live* (Passport 1987)★★, *V* (Arista 1987)★★★, *VIB* (EMI 1989)★★★, *Helter Skelter* (Arista 1989)★★★.

Bow Wow Wow

Formed in London in 1980 by former Sex Pistols manager Malcolm McLaren, Bow Wow Wow consisted of three former members of Adam And The Ants: David Barbe (b. David Barbarossa, 1961, Mauritius; drums), Matthew Ashman (b. 1962, London, England, d. 21 November 1995) and Leigh Gorman (b. 1961; bass). This trio was called upon to back McLaren's latest protégée, a 14-year-old Burmese girl whom he had discovered singing in a dry cleaners in Kilburn, London. Annabella Lu Win (b. Myant Myant Aye, 1966, Rangoon, Burma) was McLaren's female equivalent of Frankie Lymon, a teenager with no previous musical experience who could be moulded to perfection. Bow Wow Wow debuted with 'C30, C60, C90, Go' a driving, Burundi Black-influenced paean to home taping composed by McLaren. Its follow-up, the cassette-only *Your Cassette Pet*, featured eight tracks in an EP format (including the bizarre 'Sexy Eiffel Towers'). In addition to the African Burundi-influence, the group combined a 50s sounding Gretsch guitar complete with echo and tremelo. Although innovative and exciting, the group received only limited chart rewards during their stay with EMI Records and like the Pistols before them soon sought a new record company. After signing with RCA Records, McLaren enlivened his promotion of the group with a series of publicity stunts, amid outrageous talk of paedophiliac pop. The jailbait Annabella had her head shaven into a Mohican style and began appearing in tribal clothes. Further controversy ensued when she was photographed semi-nude on an album sleeve pas-

tiche of Manet's *Déjeuner sur l'Herbe*. A deserved UK Top 10 hit followed with 'Go Wild In The Country', a frenzied, almost animalistic display of sensuous exuberance. An average cover of the Strangeloves/Brian Poole And The Tremeloes' hit 'I Want Candy' also clipped the Top 10, but by then McLaren was losing control of his concept. A second lead singer was briefly recruited in the form of Lieutenant Lush, who threatened to steal the limelight from McLaren's *ingenue* and was subsequently ousted, only to reappear in Culture Club as Boy George. By 1983, amid uncertainty and disillusionment Bow Wow Wow folded. The backing group briefly soldiered on as the Chiefs Of Relief, while Annabella took a sabbatical, reappearing in 1985 for an unsuccessful solo career. Matthew Ashman died in 1995 following complications after suffering from diabetes. At the time of his death he was working with Agent Provocateur.

●ALBUMS: *Your Cassette Pet* mini-album (EMI 1980)★★★★, *See Jungle! See Jungle! Go Join Your Gang, Yeah, City All Over! Go Ape Crazy!* (RCA 1981)★★★, *I Want Candy* (RCA 1982)★★, *When The Going Gets Tough, The Tough Get Going* (RCA 1983)★★.

●COMPILATIONS: *The Best Of Bow Wow Wow* (Receiver 1989)★★★, *Girl Bites Dog - Your Compact Disc Pet* (EMI 1993)★★★.

Box Of Frogs

Box Of Frogs were welcomed with widespread excitement in the UK press on their arrival in the early 80s by dint of their collective heritage. Jim McCarty (b. 25 July 1943, Liverpool, Lancashire, England; drums), Paul Samwell-Smith (b. 8 May 1943, Richmond, Surrey, England; bass) and Chris Dreja (b. 11 November 1945, Surbiton, Surrey, England; guitar) had all previously been founding members of the Yardbirds. The fourth member, vocalist John Fiddler, had been recruited from Medicine Head. Box Of Frogs released its debut album for Epic Records in 1984. *Box Of Frogs* saw them reprise the spirit of energized R&B for which the Yardbirds had been renowned, though the quality of the songwriting barely hinted at a 'For Your Love' or 'Heart Full Of Soul'. Although it was not a commercial success, pockets of nostalgic fans throughout the world and particularly in the USA purchased it. It included a cameo appearance from Jeff Beck, while both Rory Gallagher and Jimmy Page contributed to the follow-up collection, *Strange Land*. However, deterred by the lack of commercial activity their reunion had created, Box Of Frogs dispersed shortly after its release.

McCarty subsequently joined the British Invasion All-Stars.

●ALBUMS: *Box Of Frogs* (Epic 1984)★★★, *Strange Land* (Epic 1986)★★★.

BOY GEORGE

b. George O'Dowd, 14 June 1961, Eltham, Kent, England. During the early 80s O'Dowd became a regular on the London 'New Romantic' club scene. His appearances at clubs such as Billy's, Blitz, Heaven and Hell were regularly featured in the pages of magazines such as *Blitz* and *The Face*. Flaunting a series of flamboyant cross-dressing styles he caught the attention of pop svengali Malcolm McLaren who enrolled him to appear alongside Bow Wow Wow's Annabella Lu Win, as Lieutenant Lush, at a concert at London's Rainbow Theatre. This partnership proved short-lived but useful as George's name was pushed further into the spotlight. A meeting with former disc jockey Mikey Craig (b. 15 February 1960, Hammersmith, London, England; bass) resulted in the forming of a band, In Praise Of Lemmings. After the addition of former Adam And The Ants drummer Jon Moss (b. 11 September 1957, Wandsworth, London, England; drums) plus Roy Hay (b. 12 August 1961, Southend-on-Sea, Essex, England; guitar/keyboards), the group was renamed Culture Club. To the public, however, Culture Club was, to all intents and purposes, Boy George, and his appetite for publicity and clever manipulation of the media seemed effortless. His barely concealed homosexuality, though no problem to his many fans, caused considerable comment in the tabloid press, as did his comment about sex that he'd 'much rather have a cup of tea'. Ultimately, however, it was not his sexuality but his involvement with drugs that brought his downfall. A week after he teased journalists with the proclamation that he was 'your favourite junkie' at an anti-apartheid concert in London, the British national press revealed that he was indeed addicted to heroin. No sooner had this episode hit the headlines than another scandal broke. A visiting New York keyboard player, Michael Rudetski, died of a heroin overdose while staying at George's London home. Soon after, George was arrested on a charge of possession of cannabis resulting in successful treatment for his drug dependence. His public renouncement of drugs coincided with the dissolution of Culture Club and the launch of a solo career. His debut effort, a cover version of the Bread/Ken Boothe hit, 'Everything I Own', in the spring of 1987, gave him his first UK number 1 since 'Karma Chameleon' in

1983. George's outspoken opposition to the Conservative government's anti-homosexual bill, Clause 28, triggered a series of releases damning the bill. He formed his own record label, More Protein, in 1989, and fronted a band, Jesus Loves You, which reflected his new-found spiritual awareness and continuing love of white reggae and soul. *Cheapness And Beauty* was a blend of punky glam pop, at odds with his perceived 90s image of fading superstar. The songs, co-written with guitarist John Themis, were the result of a more confident Boy George, altogether more comfortable with his publicly gay persona and completely free of heroin addiction. The album was preceded by an unlikely cover of Iggy Pop's 'Funtime', whilst its release date in 1995 coincided with the publication of the artist's self-deprecating autobiography.

●ALBUMS: *Sold* (Virgin 1987)★★★, *Tense Nervous Headache* (Virgin 1988)★★; as Jesus Loves You *The Martyr Mantras* (More Protein/Virgin 1991)★★, *Cheapness And Beauty* (Virgin 1995)★★★.

●COMPILATIONS: *At Worst . . . The Best Of Boy George And Culture Club* (Virgin 1993)★★★★.

●FURTHER READING: *Take It Like A Man*, Boy George.

BOYS DON'T CRY

The members of Boys Don't Cry had all variously played with Sad Café, Andy Brown, Jackson Heights, Byzantium and Mike Oldfield. Nick Richards, Brian Chatton, Nico Ramsden, Mark Smith and Jeff Seopardi had first played together in an earlier incarnation of the group known as the Jazz Sluts. With unlimited studio time due to Richards' ownership of the Maison Rouge studio, their recording career began in 1983 with 'Heart's Bin Broken'. They signed to US label Profile Records in the mid-80s and secured an immediate hit single with 'I Wanna Be A Cowboy'. With a video featuring Motörhead's Lemmy, it reached number 12 in the US charts in 1986. Its follow-up, 'The Cities On Time', failed to repeat its success. Following one charting album the group then switched labels to Atlantic Records. Subsequent efforts such as 'Who The Am Dam Do You Think I Am?' failed to revive their career. The members eventually returned to session work.

●ALBUMS: *Boys Don't Cry* (Legacy/Profile 1986)★★.

BRADY, PAUL

b. 19 May 1947, Strabane, Co. Tyrone, Northern Ireland. A member of an R&B group, the Kult, while a student in Dublin, Brady later embraced folk music with the Johnstons. Renowned as a commercial attraction, the group enjoyed a minor success with a version of Joni Mitchell's 'Both Sides Now'. Brady subsequently joined Planxty, a much-respected traditional unit, where the multi-instrumentalist forged an empathy with fellow member Andy Irvine. *Andy Irvine/Paul Brady* prefaced Brady's solo career which began with the much-lauded *Welcome Here Kind Stranger* in 1978. The singer abandoned folk in 1981 with *Hard Station*, which included the Irish chart-topping single, 'Crazy Dreams' (covered by Roger Chapman and Dave Edmunds), while a further inclusion, 'Night Hunting Time', was later recorded by Santana. *True For You* followed a prolific period where Brady toured supporting Dire Straits and Eric Clapton, winning the approbation of their audiences. Bob Dylan and U2's Bono also professed admiration for the artist's talents while Tina Turner's versions of 'Steel Claw' and 'Paradise Is Here' cemented Brady's reputation as a songwriter. He collaborated with Mark Knopfler on the soundtrack to *Cal*, before completing a strong live album, *Full Moon*. Subsequent releases show the flowering of a mature talent, reminiscent of Van Morrison. *Trick Or Treat* was recorded under the aegis of former Steely Dan producer, Gary Katz. Bonnie Raitt, an admirer of Brady's work, gave his career a significant boost by including two of his songs on her outstanding 1991 album, including the title track 'Luck Of The Draw'. It is hoped that Brady's work will receive major recognition in the future as he is clearly an important songwriter, although the signs are, that as with talented artists such as Richard Thompson and John Martyn his work will not get the exposure it certainly deserves.

●ALBUMS: *Andy Irvine/Paul Brady* (Mulligan 1976)★★★, with Tommy Peoples *The High Part Of The Road* (Shanachie 1976)★★★, *Welcome Here Kind Stranger* (Mulligan 1978)★★★, *Hard Station* (Polydor 1981)★★★, *True For You* (Polydor 1983)★★★, *Full Moon* (Demon 1984)★★★★, *Back To The Centre* (Mercury 1986)★★★, with Peoples, Matt Molloy *Molloy, Brady, Peoples* (Mulligan 1986)★★★, *Primitive Dance* (Mercury 1987)★★★★, *Trick Or Treat* (Fontana 1991)★★★, *Songs And Crazy Deams* (Fontana 1992)★★★, *Spirits Colliding* (Fontana 1995)★★★★.

●VIDEOS: *Echoes And Extracts* (1991).

BRAGG, BILLY

b. Steven William Bragg, 20 December 1957, Barking, Essex, England. Popularly known as 'The Bard Of Barking' (or variations of), Bragg is generally regarded as one of the most committed left-wing political performers working in popular music. After forming the ill-fated punk group Riff Raff, Bragg briefly joined the British Army (Tank Corp), before buying his way out with what he later described as the most wisely spent £175 of his life. Between time working in a record store and absorbing his new found love of the blues and protest genre, he launched himself on a solo musical career. Armed with guitar, amplifier and voice, Bragg undertook a maverick tour of the concert halls of Britain, ready at a moment's notice to fill in as support for almost any act. He confounded the local youth with what would usually be a stark contrast to the music billed for that evening. Seeing himself as a 'one man Clash', his lyrics, full of passion, anger and wit, made him a truly original character on the UK music scene. During this time, managed by ex-Pink Floyd supremo Peter Jenner, his album *Life's A Riot With Spy Vs Spy*, formerly on Charisma, but now with the emergent independent label, Go! Discs/Utility, had begun to take a very firm hold on the UK independent charts, eventually peaking in the UK national charts at number 30. His follow-up, *Brewing Up With Billy Bragg* reached number 16 in the UK charts. As always, at Billy's insistence, and helped by the low production costs, the albums were kept at a below-average selling price. His credentials as a songwriter were given a boost in 1985 when Kirsty MacColl reached number 7 in the UK charts with his song 'New England'. Bragg became a fixture at political rallies, and benefits, particularly during the 1984 Miners Strike with his powerful pro-Union songs 'Which Side Are You On', 'There Is Power In The Union' and the EP title-track, 'Between The Wars'. He was instrumental in creating the socialist musicians' collective 'Red Wedge', which included such pop luminaries as Paul Weller, Junior Giscombe and Jimmy Somerville. Despite the politicizing, Bragg was still able to pen classic love songs such as the much-acclaimed 'Levi Stubbs' Tears', which appeared on the UK Top 10 album *Talking To The Taxman About Poetry*. Bragg's political attentions soon spread to Russia and Central/South America. He often returned the host musician's hospitality by offering them places as support acts on his future UK tours. In 1988 he reached the UK number 1 slot with a cover of the Beatles song, 'She's Leaving Home', on which he was accompanied by Cara Tivey on piano - this was part of a children's charity project of contemporary artists performing various John Lennon and Paul McCartney songs. Bragg shared this double a-side single release with Wet Wet Wet's version of 'With A Little Help From My Friends', which received the majority of radio play, effectively relegating Bragg's contribution to that of a b-side. In 1989 he reactivated the label Utility, for the purposes of encouraging young talent who had found difficulty in persuading the increasingly reticent major companies to take a gamble. These artists included Coming Up Roses, Weddings Parties Anything, Clea And McLeod, Caroline Trettine, Blake Babies, Jungr And Parker and Dead Famous People. In 1991, Bragg issued the critically acclaimed *Don't Try This At Home*, arguably his most commercial work to date. The album featured a shift towards personal politics, most noticeably on the liberating hit single, 'Sexuality'. *William Bloke* was less angry and more ironic than Bragg had ever sounded but coated with almost graceful confidence and maturity. The powerful 'Nothern Industrial Town' for example, could not have been written by Bragg ten years ago. On this album Bragg ceases to be the 'bard from Barking' or the 'quirky left-wing troubadour'; instead he becomes a major 'English' songwriter.

●ALBUMS: *Life's A Riot With Spy Vs Spy* (Utility 1983)★★★, *Brewing Up With Billy Bragg* (Go! Discs 1984)★★★★, *Talking With The Taxman About Poetry* (Go! Discs 1986)★★★★, *Workers Playtime* (Go! Discs 1988)★★★, *Help Save The Youth Of America - Live And Dubious* US/Canada release (Go! Discs 1988)★★★, *The Internationale* (Utility 1990)★★★, *Don't Try This At Home* (Go! Discs 1991)★★★★, *The Peel Sessions Album* recordings from 1983-88 (Strange Fruit 1992)★★★, *William Bloke* (Cooking Vinyl 1996)★★★★.
●COMPILATIONS: *Back To Basics* a repackage of the first two albums (Go! Discs 1987)★★★.
●VIDEOS: *Billy Bragg Goes To Moscow And Norton, Virginia Too* (1990).
●FURTHER READING: *Midnight In Moscow*, Chris Salewicz.

BRANIGAN, LAURA

b. 3 July 1957, Brewster, New York, USA. Pop vocalist Branigan's breakthrough came in 1982 when her energetic voice was demonstrated to its fullest effect with her belting rendition of the continental hit 'Gloria'. It reached number 2 in the US charts and stayed in the charts for eight months. It also reached the UK Top 10. Her debut album *Branigan*, featuring 'Gloria', sold a million, as did her follow-up *Branigan 2* which included 'Solitaire', another slice of power pop and another US Top 10 smash in 1983. She was first choice to sing 'All

Time High', the title tune to the James Bond film *Octopussy* but lost out to Rita Coolidge. Branigan's chart success continued with the original version of Michael Bolton's self-penned early 1990 US chart-topper, the emotional 'How Am I Supposed To Live Without You', which made the US Top 20 and the catchy medium-paced 'Self Control', a US and UK Top 5 hit in 1984. After several minor hits she returned to the US Top 30 in late 1987 with her rousing interpretation of Jennifer Rush's 1985 UK chart-topper 'The Power Of Love'.
●ALBUMS: *Branigan* (Atlantic 1982)★★★, *Branigan 2* (Atlantic 1983)★★, *Self Control* (Atlantic 1984)★★★, *Hold Me* (Atlantic 1985)★★.
●VIDEOS: *Laura Branigan* (1987).
●FILMS: *Body Rock* (1984).

BRANSON, RICHARD

b. 18 July 1950. Branson's achievements while at the liberal Stowe public school hinted at an entrepreneurial flair that later extended to a multi-national empire by the mid-80s. It began in 1968 with his establishment of a student journal and advisory service. Profits were then ploughed back into Virgin, a mail-order record business centred in London, and then Britain's first cut-price record store - which eventually had branches in 25 other countries. By 1973, Branson also founded an independent label, Virgin Records, which produced a million-seller with its first album, Mike Oldfield's *Tubular Bells*. If considered bold in embracing punk and new wave acts such as Sex Pistols and Culture Club, the company also remained reputable enough to attract veterans such as Scott Walker and Steve Winwood. After launching Virgin Records in the USA, Branson - 'the nice guy nobody in the business trusts' - hit the jackpot in 1991 in his signing of the Rolling Stones. By then, records were but one division of a business that included recording studios, book and sheet music publishing, board games, discotheques, condoms, video, cable television franchises, Virgin Atlantic Airlines and the rich man's folly of a loss-making holiday villa in the Virgin Islands.
No shrinking violet, Branson cut an urbane public figure with his clipped beard, gold-rimmed spectacles and perpetual Aran sweater as he appeared in television commercials for Virgin products and services, and lent his name to government anti-litter campaigns and charities such as 1987's Healthcare Foundation. After relaxing on golf course and tennis court, he became better known as a hot-air balloonist, breaking the sport's speed record and managing a daredevil Atlantic crossing with Per

Lindstrand. In 1992, Branson sold his interests in Virgin Records to Thorn-EMI in order to concentrate on his airline. Since then he has become a favourite of the media, who, try as they might cannot seem to find any dirt to blemish his character.

●FURTHER READING: *Branson: The Inside Story*, Mick Brown.

BRASS MONKEY

This short-lived group, formed in 1981, comprised John Kirkpatrick (anglo-concertina, melodeon, accordion, vocals), Roger Williams (b. 30 July 1954, Cottingham, Yorkshire, England; trombone), Howard Evans (b. 29 February 1944, Chard, Somerset, England; trumpet, flugelhorn), Martin Brinsford (b. 17 August 1944, Gloucester, England; saxophone, mouth organ, percussion) and Martin Carthy (guitar, mandolin, vocals). Brinsford had earlier been a member of the Old Swan Band. Meanwhile, another band, Home Service, still included Evans and Williams as members. Williams was replaced in 1984 by Richard Cheetham (b. 29 January 1957, Ashton-under-Lyne, Manchester, England; trombone). The group provided something of an eyebrow-raiser when their combination of traditional folk instruments were played alongside brass instruments. The combination of folk stalwarts Carthy and Kirkpatrick and classically trained brass musicians produced the highly acclaimed *Brass Monkey*. The group appeared on the Loudon Wainwright III release *More Love Songs* in 1986, but with the various members of the band having so many other commitments, they went their separate ways the following year.

●ALBUMS: *Brass Monkey* (Topic 1983)★★★, *See How It Runs* (Topic 1986)★★★.

●COMPILATIONS: *The Complete Brass Monkey* (1993)★★★.

BRAVE COMBO

Formed in Denton, Texas, USA, the Brave Combo ensemble has pioneered a wholly refreshing sound which matches musical discipline with learned eclecticism and good humour. The seeds for the band were sewn in 1974 when Carl Finch became bored with contemporary music and began to delve deeper into the obscurities of folk and ethnic sounds. As a result he fell in love with polka records. By 1979 he had decided to put a band together in an attempt to revitalise the tradition. Having previously played in rock bands as a guitarist and keyboard player, he now switched to the accordion. However, this early formation of the Brave Combo was greeted with confusion by onlookers, who imagined them to be a satirical group. Nothing could be further from the truth, and Finch eventually found a more sympathetic audience at punk and new wave gigs, where viewers proved more open-minded. Their most successful early performance came at a Czech polka festival in the town of West (near Waco). By this time they had already begun releasing material on their own Four Dots record label. They made their debut in 1980 with the *Polkamania* double EP. Numerous line-up changes (including the addition of wind player Jeffrey Barnes in 1983) followed before the release of their debut album, *World Dance Music*. By now the group had established its sound. Although polkas remained the central component, there were flashes of Latin, Middle Eastern and Cajun music. They were also becoming renowned for their sense of humour (for example, segueing a version of 'Tubular Bells' into 'Little Brown Jug'). Following the release of a cassette album, *Polkatharsis*, released to sell at live performances, the group was picked up by Rounder Records who re-released the album with four extra songs. Subsequent albums for Rounder, particularly *Humansville* and *A Night On Earth*, have seen the group develop a strong bond with both roots music and purist polka fans. Tours of Japan have also extended their international audience, particularly through the group's efforts to record material such as 'Eejhanaika' in the Japanese language. The Brave Combo have recorded with Japanese ondo star Kikusuimaru as well as US singer-songwriter Lauren Agnelli (ex-Washington Squares), Tish Hinjosha and Tiny Tim. The group's 1995 album, *Polkas For A Gloomy World*, was nominated for a Grammy as Best Polka Album. Other activities included the issue of a 1991 Christmas album (*It's Christmas, Man!*) which included a samba recording of 'O, Christmas Tree' and a ska version of 'The Christmas Song', and the establishment of a new label, Dentone Records.

●ALBUMS: *World Dance Music* (Four Dots 1984)★★★, *No Sad Faces* (Four Dots 1985)★★, *Polkatharsis* cassette (Four Dots 1986)★★, *Polkatharsis* re-recorded version of latter album with new tracks (Rounder 1986)★★, *Humansville* (Rounder 1989)★★★, *It's Christmas, Man!* (Rounder 1991)★★, *A Night On Earth* (Rounder 1992)★★★, *Polkas For A Gloomy World* (Rounder 1995)★★★.

●COMPILATIONS: *Musical Varieties* (Rounder 1987)★★★, *Early Brave Combo* (Japan 1994)★★.

BRECKER BROTHERS

Randy and Michael Brecker are two of the most in-demand musicians around, having supplied the horn licks to untold major records over the last twenty five years. Randy originally attended Indiana University to study under David Baker, and did a lengthy State Department tour with the university's band directed by Jerry Coker. He relocated to New York in 1966 and joined Blood, Sweat And Tears, staying for a year before joining up with Horace Silver's quintet. Michael, another Indiana University student, turned professional at the age of 19 with Edwin Birdsong's band before teaming up with his older brother, Billy Cobham, Chuck Rainey and Will Lee in the pop-jazz co-operative, Dreams. Both became in demand for session work (notably on Cobham's three Atlantic albums of the mid-70s) but, by 1974, were ready to branch out on their own. They signed with Arista early the following year, releasing their debut, 'Sneakin' Up Behind You', in a style reminiscent of the Average White Band. It received heavy club rotation, although it was 'East River' from their second album that broke onto the singles charts in 1978. The group split in 1982, with both brothers recording solo albums in addition to session work (Michael with Ashford And Simpson and Spyro Gyra, Randy with Breakwater, among others). The success of the *Collection* issues brought the brothers back together in 1992.

●ALBUMS: *The Brecker Brothers* (Arista 1975)★★★, *Back To Back* (Arista 1976)★★★, *Don't Stop The Music* (Arista 1977) *Heavy Metal Be-Bop* (Arista 1978)★★★, *Detente* (Arista 1980)★★★, *Straphangin'* (Arista 1981)★★, *Return Of The Brecker Brothers* (GRP 1992)★★★, *Out Of The Loop* (GRP 1994)★★.

●COMPILATIONS: *The Brecker Bros. Collection Volume One* (RCA 1989)★★★, *The Brecker Bros. Collection Volume Two* (RCA 1992)★★.

●VIDEOS: *Return Of The Brecker Brothers: Live In Barcelona* (1993).

BRECKER, MICHAEL

b. 29 March 1949, Philadelphia, Pennsylvania, USA. Like many musicians of his generation, saxophonist Brecker was attracted in equal measure to R&B and the music of John Coltrane. In 1970 he left home for New York and joined a band led by drummer Billy Cobham. Subsequent gigs included work with the jazz rock group Dreams, Horace Silver, James Taylor and Yoko Ono. With his brother, Randy Brecker, he formed the Brecker Brothers, which became one of the pre-eminent fusion units. In the early 80s he toured and recorded with David Sancious and recorded as Steps Ahead, for many the definitive jazz rock group. A very in-demand player, Brecker also freelanced with a wide variety of jazz and pop artists, including Charles Mingus, John Lennon, Pat Metheny, Eric Clapton, Herbie Hancock and John Abercrombie. In 1987, at the prompting of Impulse! Records, he started recording as a leader. Brecker's smooth, strong version of Coltrane's middle-period playing has been much imitated by mainstream and session players. In 1991 he was a featured soloist on Paul Simon's Rhythm Of The Saints tour. *Tales From The Hudson* became a major success for him in 1996.

●ALBUMS: *Michael Brecker* (MCA 1987)★★★, *Don't Try This At Home* (MCA 1989)★★★, *Now You See It ... Now You Don't* (GRP 1990)★★, *Tales From The Hudson* (Impulse 1996)★★★.

BRECKER, RANDY

b. 27 November 1945, Philadelphia, Pennsylvania, USA. Brecker studied classical trumpet at school, meanwhile playing in local R&B bands. He turned to jazz when at Indiana University and was a member of a student band that visited Europe. He quit the band and the university, remaining in Europe for a while before returning to the USA to take up a career in music. In 1967 he was with Blood, Sweat And Tears and thereafter played with various jazz groups including those led by Horace Silver, Art Blakey and Clark Terry. He also accompanied performers from the worlds of rock and pop, including Janis Joplin, Stevie Wonder and James Brown. In 1969 he became co-leader with his brother, Michael Brecker, of the band, Dreams. In the early 70s he worked in the studios, playing jazz gigs with Larry Coryell, Billy Cobham, Hal Galper and others. He also formed another band with his brother, this time simply named the Brecker Brothers, which made some enormously successful albums and became one of the most popular and musically skilled and influential jazz-rock bands. In the late 70s he played with Charles Mingus and in the early 80s Brecker led his own groups and also worked with his wife, Eliane Elias, and with various jazzmen including Lew Tabackin. An exceptionally talented musician with great technical facility and flair, Brecker has become one of the major figures in jazz-rock.

●ALBUMS: with Dreams *Imagine My Surprise* (70s)★★, with Billy Cobham *Crosswinds* (1974)★★, with Charles Mingus *Me, Myself An Eye*

(1978)★★★, with Lew Tabackin *Lew Tabackin Quartet* (1983)★★★, *Amanda* (Sonet 1986)★★★, *In The Idiom* (Denon 1987)★★, *Live At Sweet Basil* (Sonet 1988)★★★, *Toe To Toe* (MCA 1989)★★, *Mr Max!* (Nable 1990)★★, *Score* (Blue Note 1993)★★★.

BRICKELL, EDIE, AND THE NEW BOHEMIANS

The US group, the New Bohemians - Kenny Withrow (guitar), John Bush (percussion), Brad Houser (bass), and Brando Aly (drums) already existed as a unit in their own right before Edie Brickell (guitar/vocals) jumped up on stage to sing with them. Following their contribution to the Island Records compilation *Deep Ellum*, Aly left and was replaced by Matt Chamberlain, with Wes Martin joining as additional guitarist. The new line-up signed to Geffen Records and recorded their debut *Shooting Rubberbands At The Stars* from whence came the UK hit single 'What I Am'. The work immediately established Brickell as one of the most interesting new songwriters of her era with a distinctive vocal style. The group subsequently toured with Bob Dylan. Their follow-up single 'Circle' also charted but only reached number 74 in the UK. *Ghost Of A Dog* included guest vocals by John Lydon on 'Strings Of Love' and displayed Brickell's characteristically oblique lyrics. In June 1992, Brickell married Paul Simon.
●ALBUMS: *Shooting Rubberbands At The Stars* (Geffen 1988)★★★, *Ghost Of A Dog* (Geffen 1991)★★★. Solo: Edie Brickell *Picture Perfect Morning* (Geffen 1994)★★.

BRIGHTMAN, SARAH

b. 14 August 1961, England. An actress and singer who first came to notice in 1978 when, with the dance group Hot Gossip, she made the UK Top 10 with the disco-pop single 'I Lost My Heart To a Starship Trouper'. It was all a far cry from her childhood ambition to become a ballet dancer. Three years after her chart success, she won a part in Andrew Lloyd Webber's musical *Cats*, and was noticed again - this time by the composer himself - and they were married in 1984. The marriage lasted for six years, and, during that time, Brightman became established as one of the premier leading ladies of the musical theatre. After *Cats*, she appeared for a season at the Old Vic in Frank Dunlop's 1982 adaptation of *Masquerade*, and later in the year she was in Charles Strouse's short-lived musical *Nightingale*. All the while she was taking singing lessons, training her superb soprano voice so that she could undertake more demanding roles than those in conventional musical comedy. In 1984 she appeared in the television version of Lloyd Webber's *Song And Dance*, and also sang on the Top 30 album. A year later, she made her operatic debut in the role of Valencienne in *The Merry Widow* at Sadlers Wells, and gave several concerts of Lloyd Webber's *Requiem* in England and America, which resulted in another best-selling album. It also produced a Top 5 single, 'Pie Jesu', on which Brightman duetted with the 12-year-old Paul Miles-Kingston. In 1986 she had a great personal triumph when she co-starred with Michael Crawford in *The Phantom Of The Opera*, and recreated her role two years later on Broadway. She had UK Top 10 hits with three songs from the show, 'The Phantom Of The Opera' (with Steve Harley), 'All I Ask Of You' (with Cliff Richard), and 'Wishing You Were Somehow Here Again'. In the late 80s and early 90s, she toured many parts of the world, including Japan and the UK, in a concert production of *The Music Of Andrew Lloyd Webber*. In December 1991, at the end of American leg of the tour, she took over the leading role of Rose in *Aspects Of Love* for the last few weeks of the Broadway run. She also joined the West End production for a time, but, while her presence was welcomed and her performance critically acclaimed, she was unable to prevent its closure in June 1992. In the same year Brightman was high in the UK chart again, this time duetting with opera singer José Carreras on the Olympic Anthem, 'Amigos Para Siempre (Friends For Life)', which was written, inevitably, by Andrew Lloyd Webber, with lyric by Don Black. In 1993 she made her debut in the straight theatre with appearances in *Trelawny Of The Wells* and *Relative Values*. For some years it had been forecast that Lloyd Webber would write a stage musical or film for her based on the life of Jessie Matthews, the graceful star of many 20s and 30s musicals, and to whom she bears an uncanny facial resemblance. However, in 1994 the composer dropped his option on Michael Thornton's biography of Matthews, and announced that there 'no further plans to develop the project'. In 1997 she had a surprise UK hit single when 'Timeless' went near the top of the charts.
●ALBUMS: *Britten Folk Songs* (Angel 1988)★★★, with Peter Ustinov *Howard Blake: Granpa* (Columbia 1988)★★, *The Songs That Got Away* (Really Useful 1989)★★, *As I Came Of Age* (Polydor 1990)★★★, with José Carreras *Amigos Para Siempre* (East West 1992)★★★, *Dive* (1993)★★★, and Original Cast recordings.

BRILLIANT CORNERS

Purveyors of intelligent and undervalued pop music, the Brilliant Corners originated from Bristol, England, and took their name from a Thelonious Monk jazz passage. Davey Woodward (b. *c.*1966, Avonmouth, Bristol, England; vocals/guitar), Chris (bass), Winston (percussion/backing vocals), Bob (drums) and Dan (occasional keyboards) comprised the line-up. Early material was absorbed into the *New Musical Express'* C86 phenomenon, and comparisons to other 'shambling' bands became a near permanent albatross around the group's necks. Their own SS20 label was home to their first three singles and mini-album *Growing Up Absurd*. However, their latter day career was characterized by an absence of press coverage, bearing no relation to the quality of the band's output. Thus far they had sustained only a single line-up change, losing a trumpeter, though a substitute guitarist called Phil was drafted in when Woodward broke his arm. In March 1988 the band set up their own label McQueen.

●ALBUMS: *Growing Up Absurd* mini-album (SS20 1985)★★★, *Somebody Up There Likes Me* (McQueen 1988)★★★, *A History Of White Trash* (1993)★★★.
●VIDEOS: *Creamy Stuff* (1991).

BRONSKI BEAT

Formed in 1983, this Anglo-Scottish group comprised Jimmy Somerville (b. 22 June 1961, Glasgow, Scotland; vocals), Steve Bronski/Forrest (keyboards) and Larry Steinbachek (keyboards). After establishing themselves in London's gay community, the trio were awarded a support slot for a Tina Turner show, and were subsequently signed to London Records. Their memorable debut single, 'Smalltown Boy', immediately drew attention to Somerville's arresting falsetto vocal, which became the hallmark of their sound. The single climbed to number 3 in the UK charts and also fared well in Europe and in the US dance charts. The follow-up, 'Why?', another Top 10 single, emphasized their debut to producer Giorgio Moroder whose Euro disco sound they so admired. The song was inspired by a paedophile friend of theirs, whose illegal sexual activities had forced him to flee the country. By the end of 1984, Somerville was already well-known as a tireless homosexual rights campaigner. The group's debut album, *The Age Of Consent*, emphasized their homosexual politics and met a mixed reaction in the music press. The summer of 1984 saw them supporting Elton John at Wembley, London, and a major UK tour followed that winter. Meanwhile, a third single, a sprightly cover of George Gershwin's 'It Ain't Necessarily So', scaled the charts. Early the following year, the Bronskis teamed up with Marc Almond for an extraordinary version of Donna Summer's 'I Feel Love' interwoven with the refrains of 'Love To Love You Baby' and 'Johnny Remember Me'. The single climbed into the UK Top 3 during April 1985, but at the end of that same month, Somerville left the group, citing disillusionment as a major factor. He later resurfaced in the Communards, before relocating to San Francisco. Bronski Beat found a replacement in John Foster and initially enjoyed some success. The catchy 'Hit That Perfect Beat' returned them to the Top 3 and two further albums followed. The impetus was gradually lost, however, and Foster was replaced in 1988 by Jonathan Hellyer.

●ALBUMS: *The Age Of Consent* (Forbidden Fruit 1984)★★★, *Hundreds And Thousands* (Forbidden Fruit 1985)★★★, *TruthDareDoubleDare* (Forbidden Fruit 1986)★★.
●VIDEOS: *The First Chapter* (1986).

BROWN, DENNIS

b. Dennis Emanuel Brown, 1957, Kingston, Jamaica, West Indies. Now regularly billed as 'The Crown Prince Of Reggae', it is only Brown's self-effacing nature that has denied him advancement to the office of king. He is loved in reggae music like no other singer and has been regularly courted by the major record labels, and even enjoyed a couple of token chart hits in Britain. More to the point, he has produced more reggae classics than just about anyone else. He began his career at the age of 11 as one of the Studio One label's many child stars. His first hit, 'No Man Is An Island' (1969), found him singing in much the same style he now uses, only with a far less croaky voice. 'If I Follow My Heart', his other chief hit at Studio One, was every bit as good. He spent the early 70s freelancing between studios, recording for Lloyd Daley, Impact, Joe Gibbs and Aquarius, before recording his third collection, *Super Reggae And Soul Hits*, a mature, classic record, full of Derrick Harriott's soulful arrangements and Brown's rich tones. A move to Winston 'Niney' Holness' label was no less profitable, with the two albums he made there, *Just Dennis* and *Wolf & Leopards*, recorded with a three year gap between them, yet with a seamless rootsy artistry making them clearly part of one body of work. Many regard the latter album as his best. A long, fruitful liaison with Joe Gibbs and Errol Thompson resulted in a further series of classic albums, among them *Visions, Joseph's Coat Of Many Colours, Spellbound*, and *Yesterday, Today & Tomorrow*.

While the rock critics were latching onto dub in the mid-70s, it was Brown who was drawing a mass audience almost unnoticed outside reggae's heartlands. His combination of serious, 'message' songs and soul-wailing love melodies was irresistible. His stage shows too were genuine 'events', and always packed a punch. 'Money In My Pocket' (1979) was the first of three incursions into chart territory, with Brown eventually signing with A&M Records in the early 80s. Simultaneously, he became co-owner of the DEB label, successfully producing Junior Delgado and female lovers rock trio 15-16-17. Brown gradually spent more time in London as a consequence, eventually settling there for much of the 80s. His Joe Gibbs connection was terminated in 1982, marking the *de facto* end of Gibbs's prominence as a producer. Brown's series of reggae hits, including 'To The Foundation' for Gussie Clarke, 'Revolution' for Taxi or cuts on his own Yvonne's Special label (named after his wife), saw him become one of the few established singers to ride the early dancehall boom unscathed. However, when digital music exploded onto reggae in 1985-86, Brown faltered for the first time in his career, seemingly unsure of his next move. Eventually he settled into the new style, recording *The Exit* for King Jammys in the digital mode. A move to Gussie Clarke's Music Works Studio in 1989 gave him more kudos with the youth market, particularly on the duet with Gregory Isaacs, 'Big All Around'. Once again Dennis Brown was in-demand in Jamaica, back at the roots of the music, and rolling once again, recording everywhere and anywhere for a few months. It remains to be seen what his next move will be: clearly he has the ability and energy to do whatever he wants.

●ALBUMS: *No Man Is An Island* (Studio One 1970)★★, *If I Follow My Heart* (Studio One 1971)★★, *Super Reggae & Soul Hits* (Trojan 1972)★★★★, *Just Dennis* (Trojan 1975)★★★★, *West Bound Train* (Third World 1977)★★★, *Visions* (Joe Gibbs 1977)★★★★, *Wolf & Leopards* (DEB-EMI 1978)★★★★, *Words Of Wisdom* (Laser 1979)★★★★, *So Long Rastafari* (Harry J 1979)★★★, *Joseph's Coat Of Many Colours* (Laser 1979)★★★★, *20th Century Dubwise* (DEB 1979)★★★, *Yesterday, Today & Tomorrow* (JGM 1982)★★★★, *Satisfaction Feeling* (Tads 1983)★★★, *The Prophet Rides Again* (A&M 1983)★★★, *Love's Gotta Hold On Me* (JGM 1984)★★★, *Dennis* (Vista Sounds 1984)★★★, *Time And Place* (Clock Tower 1984)★★★, with Gregory Isaacs *Two Bad Superstars* (Burning Sounds 1984)★★★, with Isaacs *Judge Not* (Greensleeves 1984)★★★, *Live At Montreaux* (Blue Moon 1984)★★★, *Slow Down* (Greensleeves 1985)★★★, *Revolution* (Yvonne's Special 1985)★★★, *Spellbound* (Blue Moon 1985)★★★, *Wake Up* (Natty Congo 1985)★★★, *The Exit* aka *History* (Jammys/Trojan 1986)★★★, *Money In My Pocket* (Trojan 1986)★★★, *Hold Tight* (Live & Love 1986)★★★, with Enos McLeod *Baalgad* (Goodies 1986)★★★, *Brown Sugar* (Taxi 1986)★★★, *Smile Like An Angel* (Blue Moon 1986)★★★, with Horace Andy *Reggae Superstars Meet* (Striker Lee 1986)★★★, with John Holt *Wild Fire* (Natty Congo 1986)★★★, *In Concert* (Ayeola 1987)★★★, *Love Has Found Its Way* (A&M 1988)★★★, *Inseparable* (J&W 1988)★★★, *More* (Black Scorpio 1988)★★★, *My Time* (Rohit 1989)★★★, with Isaacs *No Contest* (Greensleeves 1989)★★★, with Isaacs *Big All Around* (Greensleeves 1989)★★★, *Unchallenged* (Greensleeves 1990)★★★, *Overproof* (Greensleeves 1990)★★★, *Good Tonight* (Greensleeves 1990)★★★, *Go Now* (Rohit 1991)★★★, *Victory Is Mine* (Blue Moon 1991)★★★, *Friends For Life* (1992)★★★, *Some Like It Hot* (1992)★★★, *Limited Edition* (1992)★★★, *Blazing* (Greensleeves 1992)★★★, *Beautiful Morning* (1992)★★★, *Cosmic Force* (1993)★★★, *Unforgettable* (Charm 1993)★★★, with Janet Kay *So Amazing* (1993)★★★, *Light My Fire* (Heartbeat 1994)★★★, *Temperature Rising* (Trojan 1995)★★★.

●COMPILATIONS: *Best Of* (Joe Gibbs 1975)★★★, *Best Of Vol. 2* (Joe Gibbs 1982)★★★, *Super Hits* (Trojan 1983)★★★, *Collection* (Dennis Ting 1985)★★★, *20 Classic Reggae Tracks* (Meteor 1985)★★★, *Good Vibrations* (Charthits 1989)★★★, *Classic Hits* (Sonic Sounds 1992)★★★, *20 Magnificent Hits* (1993)★★★, *Musical Heatwave* (Trojan 1993)★★★, *The Prime Of Dennis Brown* (Music Club 1993)★★★.

●VIDEOS: *Dennis Brown Live At Montreux* (1987), *The Living Legend* (1992).

BROWN, SAM

b. Samantha Brown, 7 October 1964, Stratford, London, England. The daughter of Joe Brown, Sam made her recording debut aged 12, on the Small Faces' *In The Shade*. Three years later she toured singing with the National Youth Jazz Orchestra, and started writing songs. She continued to gain experience providing backing vocals on records for Adam And The Ants and Dexys Midnight Runners, and toured with Spandau Ballet when she was 19. After demo-ing her songs with some help from her brother, Sam signed to A&M Records in 1986. The debut single and album had a distinctive white soul sound, and both went into the UK Top 5 in 1988. Her powerful version of 'Can I Get A Witness' charted the following year. The band with which she toured the first album also recorded the second. In August 1990 she produced an album for her mother Vikki Brown, shortly before the latter's death. In 1991 she released a single with Jools Holland, 'Together Again', the proceeds of which went to AIDS research. *Box* suffered from weak material, especially theclumsy lyrical links, although undeniably she has a magnificent voice.

●ALBUMS: *Stop* (A&M 1988)★★★★, *April Moon* (A&M 1990)★★, *43 Minutes* (A&M 1993)★★, *Box* (Demon 1997)★★.

●VIDEOS: *The Videos* (1990).

BROWN, T. GRAHAM

b. Anthony Graham Brown, c.1954, Arabi, Georgia, USA. As much a southern R&B singer as a country singer-songwriter, Brown was at school in Athens, Georgia, with members of the B-52's. He earned extra money singing cover versions in lounge bars, until he saw a television documentary on David Allen Coe, after which he formed Rio Diamond, an 'outlaw' band in 1976. By 1979, he was fronting T. Graham Brown's Rack Of Spam, a white soul band, singing Otis Redding material. In 1982, he moved to Nashville, where he worked as a demo singer, recording songs for publishers who wanted famous artists to record their copyrighted material. A song he demoed as '1962' was later recorded by Randy Travis as '1982', but more lucrative was the use of his voice on jingles for products like Budweiser beer and McDonald hamburgers. Signed to a major label in 1985, he was known as T. Graham Brown to avoid confusion with the noted Nashville producer Tony Brown. His first album *I Tell It Like It Used To Be*, included two US country number 1 singles, 'Hell Or High Water' and 'Don't Go To Strangers', and he returned to the top again in 1988 with 'Darlene'. His albums were never huge hits, and an attempt to penetrate the European market in the late 80s was unsuccessful.

●ALBUMS: *I Tell It Like It Used To Be* (Capitol 1986)★★★, *Brilliant Conversationalist* (Capitol 1987)★★★, *Come As You Were* (1988)★★★, *Bumper To Bumper* (Capitol 1990)★★★, *You Can't Take It With You* (1991)★★★.

BRUFORD, BILL

b. 17 May 1949, Sevenoaks, Kent, England. A founder member of Yes in 1968, Bruford left the group four years later at the height of its popularity. An accomplished drummer, he opted to join King Crimson, where his skills were put to even greater test, and remained there until leader Robert Fripp dissolved the line-up in 1974. Bruford subsequently worked with Pavlov's Dog, before forming the jazz-rock ensemble, UK. The initial line-up also featured guitarist Allan Holdsworth, who joined the drummer for his solo debut *Feels Good To Me*. The two musicians then broke away to found Bruford, which was completed by Dave Stewart (keyboards) and Jeff Berlin (bass). However, the artist's independent career was sidelined in 1981 when Fripp invited him to join the reconstituted King Crimson. Following the second collapse of King Crimson, Bruford toured with Al DiMeola and David Torn. Bruford subsequently formed his own jazz-based group, Bill Bruford's Earthworks, which included keyboardist Django Bates and saxophonist Iain Ballamy. He became involved with the reunion of Yes in the late 80s, touring and recording under the banner of Anderson, Bruford, Wakeman And Howe until such legal matters as to the ownership of the Yes name had been resolved, becoming once more the Yes drummer in 1990 and was part of the reformed King Crimson for their album *Thrak* in 1995. One of the finest drummers in British rock, Bruford continues his desire to progress, rather than rest on his laurels.

●ALBUMS: *Feels Good To Me* (Polydor 1978)★★, *One Of A Kind* (Polydor 1979)★★, *The Bruford Tapes* (Editions EG 1980)★★★★, *Gradually Going Tornado* (Editions EG 1980)★★★, *Earthworks* (Editions EG 1987)★★★★, *Dig* (Editions EG 1989)★★★, *All Heaven Broke Loose* (1991)★★★, *Earthworks Live* (Virgin 1994)★★.

●COMPILATIONS: *Master Strokes 1978-1985* (Editions EG 1986)★★★.

BRYSON, PEABO

b. Robert Peabo Bryson, 13 April 1951, Greenville, South Carolina, USA. This talented soul singer and producer is a former member of Moses Dillard and the Tex-Town Display and Michael Zager's Moon Band. Between 1976 and 1978, Bryson scored hits with this latter group, with 'Reaching For The Sky' and 'I'm So Into You'. His numerous appearances in *Billboard*'s R&B chart include 'Underground Music', 'Feel The Fire', 'Crosswinds', 'She's A Woman' and 'Minute By Minute'. 'Gimme Some Time', a 1979 duet with Natalie Cole, was the first of several successful partnerships. However, despite hits with Melissa Manchester and Regina Belle, the singer is best known for his work with Roberta Flack and in particular the dewy-eyed ballad, 'Tonight, I Celebrate My Love', which reached number 5 on the US R&B chart and number 2 in the UK pop chart in 1983. Such releases have obscured Bryson's own career with notably the US Top 10 hit 'If Ever You're In My Arms Again' from 1984, but he remains an able and confident performer blessed with an effortless voice.

●ALBUMS: *Reaching For The Sky* (Capitol 1978)★★★, *Crosswinds* (Capitol 1978)★★★, with Natalie Cole *We're The Best Of Friends* (Capitol 1979)★★★, with Roberta Flack *Live And More* (Atlantic 1980)★★, *Paradise* (Capitol 1980)★★★, *I Am Love* (Capitol 1981)★★★, *Turn The Hands Of Time* (Capitol 1981)★★★, *Don't Play With Fire* (Capitol 1982)★★★, with Flack *Born To Love* (Capitol 1983)★★★, *Straight From The Heart* (Elektra 1984)★★★, *Quiet Storm* (1986)★★★, *Take No Prisoners* (Elektra 1987)★★★, *Positive* (Elektra 1988)★★★, *Can't You Stop The Rain* (Capitol 1991)★★★.

●COMPILATIONS: *The Peabo Bryson Collection* (Capitol 1984)★★★★.

BUCKINGHAM, LINDSEY

b. 3 October 1947, Palo Alto, California, USA. The pop mastermind behind Fleetwood Mac's golden era, Buckingham began his career as a folk singer before joining Fritz, an aspiring Bay Area rock band which also featured vocalist Stevie Nicks. When Fritz folded in 1971, the couple, now linked professionally and romantically, formed a new unit, Buckingham Nicks. The group's 1973 self-titled album offered glimpses of the harmonized style the duo later forged, but it made little commercial impression and Buckingham undertook session work. However, the album was later used to demonstrate technical facilities when Mick Fleetwood was researching likely studio locations for Fleetwood Mac's next album. By chance, both Buckingham and Nicks were in an adjacent room and the seeds of a fruitful partnership were sown. When Bob Welch left Fleetwood Mac in December 1974, Fleetwood invited the pair to join as replacements. Their arrival signalled a renaissance in the group's fortunes when *Fleetwood Mac* and the multi-million selling *Rumours* established them as one of the world's top-selling acts. Buckingham's skills as a singer, composer, guitarist and producer were crucial to this success, but following the release of the ambitious *Tusk*, both he and Nicks, who had, by now, severed their romantic attachment, embarked on solo careers. Buckingham's

debut album, *Law And Order*, continued the craftsmanship displayed on earlier work, but although one of the tracks, 'Trouble', reached the US Top 10, it failed to match the profile Nicks had achieved with her first release. Both artists resumed their roles with Fleetwood Mac for the 1982 album, *Mirage*, but subsequently pursued individual paths. The title song from a second collection, *Go Insane*, provided another hit single, and although he returned to the parent group's fold for the excellent *Tango In The Night* (1987), Buckingham officially parted from the unit the following year rather than embark on a promotional tour. A decade later, having found little in the way of solo success he returned to work with the 1973 *Rumours* line-up of Fleetwood Mac.

●ALBUMS: *Law And Order* (Asylum 1981)★★★, *Go Insane* (Elektra 1984)★★, *Out Of The Cradle* (Reprise 1992)★★.

BUCKS FIZZ

'Britain's answer to Abba', Bucks Fizz was originally conceived as a vehicle for singer/producer/manager Nichola Martin to appear in the Eurovision Song Contest. With her partner, and later, husband Andy Hill producing and composing material, Martin auditioned hundreds of applicants before deciding on Mike Nolan (b. 7 December 1954), Bobby G (b. Robert Gubby, 23 August 1957, Epsom, Surrey, England), Jay Aston (b. 4 May 1961, London, England) and Cheryl Baker (b. Rita Crudgington, 8 March 1954, Bethnal Green, London, England). Of the four, Baker had the most experience having previously appeared as a Eurovision entrant with Coco. So impressed was Martin with her discoveries that she suppressed her singing ambitions and reverted to a wholly managerial role. Having signed the group for publishing, she soon abandoned the management reins which were passed over to Jill Shirley of the Razzmatazz agency. Armed with the catchy 'Making Your Mind Up', the manufactured Bucks Fizz duly won the 1981 Eurovision Song Contest and had a UK number 1 in the process. During the next 12 months they had two further UK number 1 hits, 'The Land Of Make Believe' and 'My Camera Never Lies'. For the next two years all was well but after 'When We Were Young', their chart performance declined significantly. In 1984 the group was involved in a much-publicized coach crash and Nolan was incapacitated for a considerable period. Matters worsened when Aston became involved in an affair with Hill, thereby straining the relationship with the awesome Martin. Feeling ostracized, guilty and emotionally confused, Aston attempted suicide, sold her dramatic story to the press and sought legal redress against Martin's Big Note Music after departing from the group. Martin and Shirley subsequently conducted another mass audition to find a replacement before choosing the totally unknown 21-year-old Shelley Preston (b. 16 May 1964, Salisbury, Wiltshire, England). Although the new line-up could not hope to match the success of its predecessor, the aptly titled 'New Beginning' returned them to the Top 10. Chart success was relatively sparse thereafter and America remained unconquered, yet Bucks Fizz remained a strong live draw thanks mainly to their middle of the road appeal and backlog of eminently hummable hits. Cheryl Baker, meanwhile, has increasingly found work as a television presenter.

●ALBUMS: *Bucks Fizz* (RCA 1981)★★, *Are You Ready?* (RCA 1982)★★, *Hand Cut* (RCA 1983)★★, *I Hear Talk* (RCA 1984)★★, *The Writing On The Wall* (Polydor 1986)★★.

●COMPILATIONS: *Greatest Hits* (RCA 1983)★★★, *The Story So Far* (Stylus 1988)★★, *Golden Days* (RCA 1992)★★★, *The Best And The Rest* (1993)★★, *Greatest Hits Of ...* (RCA/Camden 1996)★★★.

●VIDEOS: *Greatest Hits: Bucks Fizz* (1986).

BUCKWHEAT ZYDECO

Founded by Stanley Dural (b. 1947, Lafayette, Louisiana, USA). Dural started his musical career playing piano and organ in local bands around southeast Louisiana. In the late 80s and early 90s, Buckwheat Zydeco emerged as one of the leaders of zydeco music, the accordion-led dance music of southern Louisiana's French-speaking Creoles. Dural, taking the nickname 'Buckwheat' worked with R&B singers Joe Tex, Barbara Lynn and Clarence 'Gatemouth' Brown during the 60s. Following a period playing keyboards in Clifton Chenier's band, he took up accordion and moved to the indigenous sound of zydeco. He formed his own funk band, the Hitchhikers, in the 70s, followed by the Ils Sont Partis Band in 1979. That outfit recorded eight albums for Blues Unlimited, Black Top and Rounder Records before accordionist Dural formed Buckwheat Zydeco. Signed to Island Records in 1987, the group had recorded three albums for the label by 1990, the latter produced by David Hidalgo of Los Lobos. Newcomers to this music should start with the excellent compilation *Menagerie*.

●ALBUMS: *One For The Road* (1979)★★ *Take It Easy Baby* (Blues Unlimited 1980)★★★, *100% Fortified Zydeco* (Rounder 1983)★★★, *Turning Point*

(Rounder 1984)★★★, *Waitin' For My Ya Ya* (Rounder 1985)★★★, *Buckwheat Zydeco* (Rounder 1986)★★★, *Zydeco Party* (Rounder 1987)★★★, *On A Night Like This* (Island 1987)★★★★, *Taking It Home* (Island 1988)★★★, *Buckwheat Zydeco And The Ils Sont Partis Band* (Island 1988)★★★, *Where There's Smoke There's Fire* (Island 1990)★★★★, *On Track* (Charisma 1992)★★★.

●COMPILATIONS: *Menagerie: The Essential Zydeco Collection* (Mango 1994)★★★★.

●VIDEOS: *Taking It Home* (1989), *Buckwheat Zydeco Live* (1991).

BUGGLES

Trevor Horn and Geoff Downes first met as session musicians in 1977 and after appearing in a backing group for Tina Charles they pooled their resources under the name Buggles. Their debut single, 'Video Killed The Radio Star' became Island Records' first number 1 single at the end of 1979 and its innovative video was later used to launch the MTV music channel in the USA. The duo enjoyed three further chart entries with 'The Plastic Age', 'Clean Clean' and 'Elstree', but remained essentially a studio group, having never toured. Astonishingly, they were invited to join Yes in the summer of 1980, replacing Jon Anderson and Rick Wakeman. The unlikely liaison lasted until the end of the year when Downes departed to form Asia and Horn went on to become a record producer and founder of ZTT Records.

●ALBUMS: *The Age Of Plastic* (Island 1980)★★.

BURNEL, JEAN JACQUES

Out of the four original members of the Stranglers, bassist Jean Jacques Burnel (b. 1952, London, England) was probably the most forthright. Born of French parents he was staunchly pro-European. A keen biker, former skinhead, a black belt in karate and an Economics graduate from Bradford University he was employed as a van driver in Guildford, Surrey when he first met Hugh Cornwell through the American lead singer of the band Bobbysox, with whom Cornwell was playing guitar in the early 70s. Original plans to become a karate instructor were shelved (although he would return to this profession part-time), so he could play bass and sing in a band with Cornwell. As the Stranglers soared to success Burnel waged a personal battle with the press who dismissed the band as either being of higher intellect than their punk cohorts, or alternatively abject and brutal chauvinists. Several well-documented episodes led to violent resolution at Burnel's hands. Burnel was the first Strangler to work on a solo project, *Euroman Cometh*. As the title implied, this was a plea for the cause of European federalism This was released early in 1979 with guests Brian James (guitar, ex-Damned), Lew Lewis (harmonica, ex-Eddie And The Hot Rods) with Carey Fortune (ex-Chelsea) and Pete Howells (ex-Drones) both playing the drums. A short tour to promote the album was something of a disaster. The Euroband put together for the tour featured John Ellis (ex-Vibrators - who was also playing for the support band Rapid Eye Movement), Lewis, Howells, and Penny Tobin on keyboards. In 1980 'Girl From The Snow Country' was scheduled as a solo release but was withdrawn. Despite a later bootleg, the copies that slipped out are among the most collectable of new wave releases. The next musical project outside of the Stranglers was a collaboration with Dave Greenfield on a soundtrack for the Vincent Coudanne film *Ecoutez Vos Murs*. Ensuing years saw Burnel getting involved with a number of bands as either producer, guest musician or both. Typically the groups were largely non-English, including Taxi Girl (France), Ping Pong (Norway), the Revenge (Belgium) and ARB (Japan). The next major project was the formation in 1986 of a 60s cover outfit called the Purple Helmets. Consisting of Burnel, Ellis, Alex Gifford, and Laurent Sinclair the group was put together for a one-off gig at the *Trans Musicale Avant Festival* in France. So successful was the concert that the Helmets became an ongoing concern with Greenfield replacing Sinclair and Tears For Fears drummer Manny Elias joining. Burnel has since made one further solo album, *C'est Un Jour Parfait*, which was recorded almost entirely in French and released just about everywhere in Europe except Britain.

● ALBUMS: *Euroman Cometh* (United Artists 1979)★★★, with Dave Greenfield *Fire And Water* (Epic 1983)★★, *C'est Un Jour Parfait* (Columbia 1989)★★.

BUSH, KATE

b. Catherine Bush, 30 July 1958, Bexleyheath, Kent, England. While still at school, the precocious Bush was discovered by Pink Floyd's Dave Gilmour, who was so impressed by the imaginative quality of her songwriting that he financed some demo recordings. EMI Records were equally taken with the product and in an unusual act of faith decided not to record her immediately. Instead, she was encouraged to develop her writing, dancing and singing in preparation for a long-term career. The apprenticeship ended in 1978 with the

release of the extraordinary 'Wuthering Heights'. Inspired by Emily Bronte's novel, Bush had created a hauntingly original piece, complete with an ethereal, almost demented, vocal that brilliantly captured the obsessive love of the novel's heroine, and her namesake, Cathy. It was no surprise when the single rapidly reached number 1 in the UK and established Bush in Europe. An attendant album, *The Kick Inside*, recorded over the previous three years, was a further example of her diversity and charm as a songwriter. A follow-up single, 'The Man With The Child In His Eyes' was typical of her romantic, sensual style of writing, and provided her with another Top 10 success. Bush consolidated her position with a new album, *Lionheart* and during 1979 undertook her first major tour. The live shows were most notable for her characteristically extravagant mime work and elaborate stage sets. An EP from the show, *Kate Bush On Stage* gave her another Top 10 hit. After guesting on Peter Gabriel's 'Games Without Frontiers', Bush was back in the charts with 'Breathing' and 'Babooshka'. The latter was her most accomplished work since 'Wuthering Heights' with a clever story line and strong vocal. Her next album, *Never For Ever* entered the UK album charts at number 1 and further hits followed with 'Army Dreamers' and 'December Will Be Magic'. At this point, Bush was still regarded as a mainstream pop artist whose charm and popularity was likely to prove ephemeral. Her 1982 album *The Dreaming* suggested a new direction, however, even though its less melodic approach alienated some critics. A two-year hiatus followed during which Bush perfected a work that would elevate her to new heights in the pop pantheon. The pilot single, 'Running Up That Hill' was arguably her greatest work to date, a dense and intriguing composition with a sound uniquely her own. The album *Hounds Of Love* soon followed and was greeted with an acclaim that dwarfed all her previous accolades and efforts. By any standards, it was an exceptional work and revealed Bush at the zenith of her powers. Songs such as the eerily moving 'Mother Stands For Comfort' and the dramatic 'Cloudbusting' underlined her strengths, not only as a writer and singer, but most crucially as a producer. The outstanding video accompanying the latter featured Donald Sutherland. An entire side of the album, titled 'The Ninth Wave', fused Arthurian legend and Jungian psychology in a musical framework, part orchestral and part folk. After this, Bush could never again be regarded as a quaint pop artist. Following another brief tie-up with Peter Gabriel on the hit 'Don't Give Up', Bush took an extended sabbatical to plot a follow-up album. In 1989 she returned with *The Sensual World*, a startling musical cornucopia, in which she experimented with various musical forms, even using a Bulgarian folk troupe. The arrangements were as evocative and unusual as her choice of instrumentation, which included uiliean pipes, whips, valiha, celtic harp, tupan and viola. There was even a literary adaptation *a là* 'Wuthering Heights', with Bush adapting Molly Bloom's soliloquy from James Joyce's *Ulysses* for the enticing 'The Sensual World'. The album attracted the keen attention of the high-brow rock press and Bush found herself celebrated as one of the most adventurous and distinctively original artists of her era. A variety of artists contributed on *The Red Shoes* including Eric Clapton, Prince, Jeff Beck, Trio Bulgarka and Gary Brooker.

●ALBUMS: *The Kick Inside* (EMI 1978)★★★, *Lionheart* (EMI 1978)★★, *Never For Ever* (EMI 1980)★★★, *The Dreaming* (EMI 1982)★★★, *Hounds Of Love* (EMI 1985)★★★, *The Sensual World* (EMI 1989)★★★★, *The Red Shoes* (EMI 1993)★★★.

●COMPILATIONS: *The Whole Story* (EMI 1986)★★★, *This Woman's Work* (EMI 1990)★★★★.

●VIDEOS: *Live At Hammersmith Odeon* (1984), *The Whole Story* (1986), *Hair Of The Hound* (1986), *Sensual World* (1990), *The Single File* (1992), *The Line, The Cross & The Curve* (1994).

●FURTHER READING: *Kate Bush: An Illustrated Biography*, Paul Kerton. *Leaving My Tracks*, Kate Bush. *The Secret History Of Kate Bush (& The Strange Art Of Pop)*, Fred Vermorel. *Kate Bush: The Whole Story*, Kerry Juby. *Kate Bush: A Visual Documentary*, Kevin Cann and Sean Mayes.

BUTTHOLE SURFERS

Formerly known as the Ashtray Baby Heads, this maverick quartet from Austin, Texas, USA, made its recording debut in 1983 with a self-titled mini-album (the name Butthole Surfers comes from an early song about beach transvestites). Gibson 'Gibby' Haynes (vocals) Paul Leary Walthall aka Paul Sneef (guitar) and King Koffey (drums) were initially indebted to the punk/hardcore scene, as shown by the startling 'The Shah Sleeps In Lee Harvey's Grave', but other selections were inspired by a variety of sources. Loping melodies, screaming guitar and heavy-metal riffs abound in a catalogue as zany as it is unclassifiable. Lyrically explicit, the group has polarized opinion between those who appreciate their boisterous humour and

those deeming them prurient. Having endured a succession of bass players, including Kramer from Shockabilly and Bongwater, the Buttholes secured the permanent services of Jeff Pinker, alias Tooter, alias Pinkus, in 1985. The Surfers' strongest work appears on *Locust Abortion Technician* and *Hairway To Steven*, the former memorably including 'Sweet Loaf', a thinly disguised version of Black Sabbath's 'Sweet Leaf. On the latter set, tracks are denoted by various simple drawings, including a defecating deer, rather than song titles. In 1991 the release of *Digital Dump*, a house-music project undertaken by Haynes and Tooter under the Jack Officers epithet, was followed closely by the Buttholes' ninth album, *pioughd*, which showed that their ability to enrage, bewilder and excite remained as sure as ever. It was marked by a curiously reverential version of Donovan's 'Hurdy Gurdy Man'. This set was closely followed by Paul Leary's excellent solo debut, *The History Of Dogs*. The delay of *Electriclarryland* was as a result of objections received from the estate of Rodgers And Hammerstein when the band wanted to call the album *Oklahoma!* It is difficult to be indifferent about this band, it's a simple love or loathe. Tagged as the sickest band in the world, they thrive on their own antics which include simulated sex, urinating and masturbation on stage. This tends to mask their musical ability and commercial potential which *Electriclarryland* clearly demonstrated.

●ALBUMS: *Butthole Surfers* (Alternative Tentacles 1983)★★★, *PCP PEP* (Alternative Tentacles 1984)★★★, *Another Man's Sac* (Touch And Go 1985)★★★, *Rembrandt Pussyhorse* (Touch And Go 1986)★★★, *Locust Abortion Technician* (Touch And Go 1987)★★★, *Hairway To Steven* (Touch And Go 1988)★★★, *pioughd* (Rough Trade 1991)★★, *Independent Worm Saloon* (Capitol 1993)★★, *Electriclarryland* (Capitol 1996)★★★★.

●COMPILATIONS: *Double Live* (Latino Bugger 1989)★★★, *The Hole Truth ... And Nothing But* (Trance Syndicate 1995)★★★.

●VIDEOS: *Blind Eye Sees All*.

BYRNE, DAVID

b. 14 May 1952, Dumbarton, Scotland, but raised in Baltimore, Ohio, USA. A graduate of the Rhode Island School of Design, Byrne abandoned his training in visual and conceptual arts in favour of rock. He formed Talking Heads with two fellow students and this highly respected unit evolved from its origins in the New York punk milieu into one of America's leading attractions. Much of its appeal was derived from Byrne's quirky, almost paranoid, diction and imaginative compositions, but the group rapidly proved too limiting for his widening artistic palate. *My Life In The Bush Of Ghosts*, a collaboration with Brian Eno, was widely praised by critics for its adventurous blend of sound collages, ethnic influences and vibrant percussion, which contrasted with Byrne's ensuing solo debut, *The Catherine Wheel*. The soundtrack to Twyla Tharp's modern ballet, this fascinating set was the prelude to an intensive period in the parent group's career, following which the artist began composing and scripting a feature film. Released in 1985, *True Stories*, which Byrne also directed and starred in, was the subject of an attendant Talking Heads' album. *The Knee Plays*, on which Byrne worked with playwright Robert Wilson, confirmed interests emphasized in 1987 by his collaboration with Ryuichi Sakamoto and Cong Su on the soundtrack for Bertolucci's *The Last Emperor*. This highly acclaimed film won nine Oscars, including one for Best Original Score. Byrne, meanwhile, continued recording commitments to his group, but by the end of the 80s intimated a reluctance to appear live with them. He instead assembled a 14-strong Latin-American ensemble which toured the USA, Canada, Europe and Japan to promote *Rei Momo*, while a 1991 statement established that Talking Heads were on 'indefinite furlough'. *The Forest* confirmed the artist's prodigious talent by invoking European orchestral music while his Luaka Bop label served as an outlet for a series of world music albums, including several devoted to Brazilian recordings.

●ALBUMS: with Brian Eno *My Life In The Bush Of Ghosts* (Polydor 1981)★★★, *The Complete Score From The Broadway Production Of The Catherine Wheel* soundtrack (Sire 1981)★★★★, *Music For The Knee Plays* (ECM 1985)★★★, with Ryuichi Sakamoto, Cong Su *The Last Emperor* film soundtrack (Virgin 1987)★★★, *Rei Momo* (Warners 1989)★★★, *The Forest* film soundtrack (Warners 1991)★★★, *Uh-Oh* (Luaka Bop 1992)★★★, *David Byrne* (Luaka Bop/Warners 1994)★★, *Feelings* (Warners 1997)★★★.

●VIDEOS: *Catherine Wheel* (Sire 1989), *David Byrne: Between The Teeth* (1993).

●FURTHER READING: *American Originals: David Byrne*, John Howell. *Strange Ritual: Pictures And Words*, David Byrne.

CABARET VOLTAIRE

Formed in Sheffield, Yorkshire, England, in 1974, and named after the Dadaist collective, this experimental, innovative electronic-dance group consisted of Stephen Mallinder (bass/lead vocals), Richard H. Kirk (guitar/wind instruments) and Chris Watson (electronics and tapes). Influenced by Can and Brian Eno, the group strived to avoid the confines of traditional pop music and the trio's early appearances veered towards performance art. This attitude initially attracted the attention of Factory Records and the group contributed two tracks to the Manchester label's 1978 double EP, *A Factory Sample*. They eventually signed to Rough Trade Records that same year, producing the *Extended Play* EP which confirmed the band's experimental stance, although 'Nag, Nag, Nag' (1979) was a head-on rush of distorted guitar with a driving beat. The trio continued to break new ground, using sampled 'noise', cut-up techniques and tape loops. Often viewed as inaccessible, in the ensuing years Cabaret Voltaire released the UK Independent Top 10 singles 'Silent Command' (1979), 'Three Mantras' and 'Seconds Too Late' (both 1980). Their 1979 debut album, *Mix Up*, was followed by a more conventional offering, *The Voice Of America*. After *Live At The YMCA 27.10.79*, the group widened their horizons, with video and collaborative work, including outings on the Belgian label, Les Disques du Crépuscule and two Industrial label cassettes, *Cabaret Voltaire 1974-76* (their early recordings) and Kirk's solo *Disposable Half Truths*. In 1981, the group's prolific output was increased by the morbid but successful *Red Mecca* and by another cassette, *Live At The Lyceum*. Watson left in October 1981 to work in television and later resurfaced in the Hafler Trio. In 1982 Eric Random was recruited on guitar for a Solidarity benefit concert, performing under the name Pressure Company. The resulting album, *Live In Sheffield 19 January 1982* , was released on Paradox Product. The year also saw the release of *2 x 45*, 'Temperature Drop', plus the Japanese live album *Hai!* and a solo set from Mallinder, *Pow Wow*.

Departing from Rough Trade in 1983, while also releasing 'Fools Game' on Les Disques du Crépuscule and 'Yashar' on Factory, the group signed a joint deal with Some Bizzare/Virgin Records. The first fruits of this move, 'Just Fascination' and 'The Crackdown' confirmed Cabaret Voltaire's new approach and signalled a drastic shift towards rhythmic dance sounds (assisted by Soft Cell, later Grid keyboard player, Dave Ball's presence). Yet another label entered the frame when Doublevision released the film soundtrack *Johnny YesNo*. Kirk's double set, *Time High Fiction*, came at the end of this productive year. Aside from a compilation video, *TV Wipeout*, 1984 was a quiet year, until 'Sensoria' (Some Bizzare) ripped the dance charts apart, setting the tone for much of Cabaret Voltaire's subsequent work, including 'James Brown', both featuring on *Micro-phonies*, and 'I Want You' (1985). In between, the pair concentrated on the video *Gasoline In Your Eye*, paralleled by the similarly titled, double 12-inch 'Drinking Gasoline'. The critically acclaimed *The Covenant, The Sword And The Arm Of The Lord*, echoed the group's earlier phase. Kirk's solo work continued apace in 1986 with *Black Jesus Voice*, and a mini-album, *Ugly Spirit*, plus a project with the Box's Peter Hope resulting in *Hoodoo Talk* on Native Records in 1987. By July 1987 the duo had transferred to EMI/Parlophone Records, debuting with 'Don't Argue'. As with the follow-up releases, 'Here To Go' and 'Code', its sound introduced a more commercial dance slant, lacking the pair's earlier, experimental approach. In 1988, Mallinder collaborated with Dave Ball and Mark Brydon, collectively known as Love Street, releasing 'Galaxy'. A new Cabaret Voltaire single, 'Hypnotised' (1989), reflected their visit to the house music capital, Chicago. Kirk's 'Test One' (1990), issued under the guise of Sweet Exorcist, was pure acid house. The group continued this style with 'Keep On' and *Groovy, Laid Back And Nasty* and *Clonk's Coming* in 1991. In the meantime, Mute Records methodically reissued the band's early back catalogue on CD. Leaving EMI, Cabaret Voltaire returned to Les Disques du Crépuscule for 'What Is Real' (1991), followed by the well-received *Body And Soul*. This only consolidated Cabaret Voltaire's pivotal role in hi-tech dance music, which they have helped develop over a decade and a half.

●ALBUMS: *Mix Up* (Rough Trade 1979)★★, *Live At The YMCA 27.10.79.* (Rough Trade 1979)★★, *Three Mantras* (Rough Trade 1980)★★, *The Voice Of America* (Rough Trade 1980)★★, *Red Mecca* (Rough Trade 1981)★★★, *Johnny YesNo* film soundtrack (Doublevision 1981)★★, *Live At The Lyceum* (Rough Trade 1981)★★★, *2 x 45* (Rough Trade 1982)★★★, *Hai!* (Rough Trade 1982)★★★, *The Crackdown* (Some Bizzare 1983)★★★, *Micro-Phonies* (Some Bizzare 1984)★★★, *Drinking Gasoline* (Some Bizzare 1985)★★★, *The Covenant, The Sword And The Arm Of The Lord* (Some Bizzare 1985)★★★, *Code* (Parlophone 1987)★★★★, *Groovy, Laid Back And Nasty* (Parlophone 1990)★★★, *Body And Soul* (Crépuscule 1991)★★★, *Percussion Force* (Crépuscule 1991)★★★, *International Language* (1993)★★★. Solo: Richard H. Kirk *Disposable Half Truths* (Rough Trade 1981)★★★, *Time High Fiction* (Rough Trade 1983)★★★, *Black Jesus Voice* (Rough Trade 1986)★★★, *Ugly Spirit* (Rough Trade 1986)★★★. Stephen Mallinder *Pow Wow* (1982)★★.

●COMPILATIONS: *Cabaret Voltaire 1974-76* (Industrial 1981)★★, *The Golden Moments Of Cabaret Voltaire* (Rough Trade 1987)★★★, *8 Crépuscule Tracks* (Interior Music 1988)★★★, *Listen Up With Cabaret Voltaire* (Mute 1990)★★★, *The Living Legends* (Mute 1990)★★, *Technology* (Virgin 1992)★★★.

●VIDEOS: *TV Wipeout* (1984), *Gasoline In Your Eye* (1985), *Cabaret Voltaire* (1990).

CALVERT, ROBERT

b. c.1945, Pretoria, South Africa, d. 14 August 1988. Domiciled in London's bohemian Ladbroke Grove/Portobello Road area, Calvert became acquainted with Hawkwind, one of the area's atypical 'underground' attractions. His poetry readings became part of the group's act during the early 70s and in 1972 he joined the line-up as an official member. Calvert wrote, and originally sang, 'Silver Machine', their Top 3 hit, although by that point his vocal had been overdubbed. He left Hawkwind the following year but three of the group - Dave Brock (guitar), Lemmy (bass) and Simon King (drums) - joined ex-Pink Fairies Twink (drums) and Paul Rudolph (guitar) on *Captain Lockheed And The Starfighters*, the artist's highly praised solo debut. His second set, *Lucky Leif And The Longships*, which featured science fiction writer Michael Moorcock, was produced by Brian Eno, but it proved less popular than its predecessor. Calvert returned to the Hawkwind fold in 1977, but left again at the end of the decade. Two more solo albums, blending science fiction with rock ensued, before this respected performer succumbed to a heart attack in 1988.

●ALBUMS: *Captain Lockheed And The Starfighters* (United Artists 1974)★★★, *Lucky Leif And The*

Longships (United Artists 1975)★★, *Hype* (A-Side 1980)★★★, *Freq* (Flicknife 1984)★★★, *Test Tube Conceived* (Demi-Monde 1986)★★★, *Blueprints From The Cellar* (Beat Goes On 1992)★★★, *Live At The Queen Elizabeth Hall* (Clear 1993)★★.

CAMEO

This US soul/funk group, originally called the New York City Players, was formed in 1974 by the core members Larry 'Mr. B' Blackmon (b. New York City, New York, USA; drums/vocals) and vocalists Thomas Jenkins and Nathan Leftenant. Building up a strong following by undergoing rigorous touring schedules, with their backing group at times numbering almost a dozen members, they signed with the Casablanca subsidiary label, Chocolate City, where they recorded their debut, *Cardiac Arrest*, produced by Blackmon. Touring alongside Parliament and Funkadelic enhanced their reputation and subsequent album releases gained modest positions in the US pop chart. In Britain, they enjoyed a loyal cult following, but it was not until Cameo's seventh release, *Knights Of The Sound Table*, that they were afforded a UK release. However, in 1984, the single 'She's Strange' crossed over from soul/funk into the pop market and Cameo found themselves with their first UK Top 40 single. After the success of the following year's 'Single Life' (UK Top 20), 'She's Strange' was remixed and peaked at number 22. Three sell-out shows at London's Hammersmith Odeon followed. Having won over the UK pop market, it was not until 1986 that they finally broke into the US Top 40 chart. 'Word Up', having already reached number 3 in the UK, reached number 1 in the US R&B chart and number 6 in the *Billboard* pop chart. Having now trimmed down the group to the trio of Blackmon, Jenkins and Leftenant and only using additional session players when necessary, Blackmon attracted most of the media attention. His image was helped in no small degree by the expansive, bright red cod-piece worn on stage. Blackmon's own studio Atlanta Artists allowed him almost total control over Cameo's sound and enabled him to promote and nurture local musical talent.

●ALBUMS: *Cardiac Arrest* (Chocolate City 1977)★★, *We All Know Who We Are* (Chocolate City 1978)★★, *Ugly Ego* (Chocolate City 1978)★★, *Secret Omen* (Chocolate City 1979)★★, *Cameosis* (Chocolate City 1980)★★★, *Feel Me* (Chocolate City 1980)★★★, *Knights Of The Sound Table* (Chocolate City 1981)★★★, *Alligator Woman* (Chocolate City 1982)★★, *Style* (Atlanta Artists 1983)★★★, *She's Strange* (Atlanta Artists 1984)★★★, *Single Life* (Atlanta Artists 1985)★★★★, *Word Up!* (Atlanta Artists 1986)★★★★, *Machismo* (Atlanta Artists 1988)★★★, *Real Men Wear Black* (Atlanta Artists 1990)★★★, *Emotional Violence* (Reprise 1992)★★★.

●COMPILATIONS: *Best Of Cameo* (1993)★★★★.

●VIDEOS: *Cameo: The Video Singles* (1987), *Back And Forth* (1987).

CAMPBELL, JOHN

b. 1952, Shreveport, Louisiana, USA, d. 13 June 1993, New York. Campbell, a white man, became an authentic sounding blues singer/guitarist after a serious drag racing accident in 1967, which left him without one of his eyes and a mass of stitches in his face, which became permanently scarred. Prior to this crash, he had been curious about music - his grandmother played lap steel guitar - but he was more interested in becoming a tearaway. During his lengthy period of recuperation, much of it spent in solitude, he taught himself to play guitar and became devoted to the work of the black bluesmen who had recorded for the local Jewel label in Shreveport; in particular John Lee Hooker and Lightnin' Hopkins, who became his major influence. Leaving school in the late 60s, he became a travelling troubadour, working as the opening act for 'Gatemouth' Brown and Hubert Smith, ultimately relocating to New York where he played local clubs for many years. His recording debut came in 1988, when guitarist Ronnie Earl sent a tape of Campbell to the specialist Crosscut label in Germany. Earl produced his first album *A Man And His Blues*, but it was hardly distributed in the USA, and he remained an obscure cult figure until he began working with guitarist Alexander Kennedy. He and Kennedy were opening for Albert King in New York when he was signed by Elektra Records, and in 1991 released *One Believer*, produced by Dennis Walker (also Robert Gray's producer) backed by members of both Gray's band and Joe Ely's group. Campbell played solely amplified acoustic guitar, and his songwriting partnership with Walker and Kennedy produced several modern blues classics like 'Devil In My Closet', 'Tiny Coffin' and 'Take Me Down'. *Howlin' Mercy* consolidated his standing as an important (although cult) figure in the recent blues boom. He died in 1993 prior to undertaking a European tour.

●ALBUMS: *A Man And His Blues* (Crosscut 1988)★★★, *One Believer* (Elektra 1991)★★★★, *Howlin' Mercy* (Elektra 1993)★★★.

CAMPER VAN BEETHOVEN

A band for whom the term 'alternative' might first have been coined. In fact, principal songwriter David Lowery suggests that is exactly the case: '(We) were arguably the prototypical alternative band. I remember first seeing that word applied to us. The nearest I could figure is that we seemed like a punk band, but we were playing pop music, so they made up the word 'alternative' for those of us who do that'. Camper Van Beethoven were a witty, often sarcastic garage rock band formed in Redlands, California, USA, in 1983 by school friends, transferring to Santa Cruz when members attended college there. They were named by early member David McDaniels, though initial line-ups were frequently unstable. By 1987 the band solidified as David Lowery (b. 10 October 1960, San Antonio, USA; vocals/guitar), Greg Lisher (guitar), Chris Pederson (drums), Jonathan Segal (violin) and Victor Krummenacher (bass). Krummenacher was formerly a member of jazz ensemble Wrestling Worms. Their debut, *Telephone Free Landslide Victory*, contained the classic single cut 'Take The Skinheads Bowling', as well as the surreal ethnic instrumentation of 'Balalaika Gap' and 'Border Ska', and a strange Black Flag cover ('Wasted'). It was typical of an armoury of songs that included titles like 'The Day Lassie Went To The Moon', 'Joe Stalin's Cadillac', and 'ZZ Top Goes To Egypt'. They played their UK debut in March 1987, where 'Skinheads' had become something of a cult hit, but neither there nor in the USA did their critical popularity transfer into sales. The anagramatical *Vampire Can Mating Oven* wrapped up the last of their Rough Trade distributed fare before a move to Virgin Records. *Our Beloved Revolutionary Sweetheart* found them in fine form with a bigger budget and a sympathetic producer, Dennis Herring. However, the tone of *Key Lime Pie* proved infinitely more sombre than previous outings and prophesied their split. In retrospect it is hard to listen to a track like 'When I Win The Lottery' without reading it as allegory for the band's unsuccessful transition from indie to major label chart prospect. A bizarre cover version of Status Quo's 'Pictures Of Matchstick Men', released as a single, served as a reminder of their former discordant eclecticism. Four members of Camper Van Beethoven, Lisher Krummenacher, Pederson and former Ophelias guitarist David Immerglück (who joined the band over their final recordings) put together Monks Of Doom. Jonathon Segal released a solo album, and main songwriter David Lowery, after waiting fruitlessly for his former colleagues to return from their 'stupidity', finally made the deserved transition to that of major band with Cracker.

●ALBUMS: *Telephone Free Landslide Victory* (Independent Project 1985)★★★, *Take The Skinheads Bowling* mini-album (Pitch-A-Tent 1986)★★★, *Camper Van Beethoven II/III* (Pitch-A-Tent 1986)★★★★, *Camper Van Beethoven* (Pitch-A-Tent 1986)★★★, *Vampire Can Mating Oven* mini-album (Pitch-A-Tent 1987)★★★, *Our Beloved Revolutionary Sweetheart* (Virgin 1988)★★★★, *Key Lime Pie* (Virgin 1989)★★★.

CAPERCAILLIE

The line-up of this traditional Scottish group consists of Karen Matheson (b. 11 February 1963, Oban, Argyll, Scotland; vocals), Marc Duff (b. 8 September 1963, Ontario, Canada; bodhran/whistles), Manus Lunny (b. 8 February 1962, Dublin, Eire; bouzouki/vocals), Charlie McKerron (b. 14 June 1960, London, England; fiddle), John Saich (b. 22 May 1960, Irvine, Scotland; bass/vocals/guitar), and Donald Shaw (b. 6 May 1967, Ketton, Leicestershire, England; keyboards/accordion/ vocals). Formed in 1984 at Oban High School in Scotland, initially to play for local dances, the band have now built a strong reputation for their treatment of traditional and Gaelic music from the West Highlands of Scotland. Strong musicianship, featuring Manus Lunny, who is equally well known for his work with Andy M. Stewart, and the haunting vocals of Karen Matheson, have established the group wherever they have performed. Having toured the Middle East, South America, and the USA between 1984 and 1990, the band's appeal would seem to be widening, moving beyond the restrictions of the folk music market. In 1988, the group were commissioned to compose and record the music for *The Blood Is Strong*, the television series about the history of the Gaelic Scots. The resultant success of both series and music led to the soundtrack being released, and within six months it had been awarded a platinum disc for sales in Scotland. In 1990, Capercaillie signed to Survival Records and, as evidence of their widening appeal, the single from *Delirium*, 'Coisich a Ruin' (Walk My Beloved), a traditional Gaelic work song, achieved daytime airplay on BBC's Radio 1. Touring and promoting *Delirium*, Capercaillie were on the bill at Loch Lomond, Scotland, in the summer of 1991, the venue for a 40,000 strong concert by Runrig. *To The Moon* moved the band further from traditional folk into a stronger rock-based sound using African rhythm, it also introduced the band to a much wider audience, one the band has deserved for some time.

●ALBUMS: *Cascade* (SRT 1984)★★★, *Crosswinds* (Green Linnet 1987)★★★, *The Blood Is Strong* (Celtic Music 1988)★★★, *Sidewaulk* (Green Linnet 1989)★★★, *Delirium* (RCA 1991)★★★, *Secret People* (Survival 1993)★★★, *To The Moon* (Survival 1995)★★★.

●COMPILATIONS: *Get Out* (1992)★★★.

CAPTAIN SENSIBLE

b. Raymond Burns, 24 April 1954, Balham, London, England. Having drifted from job to job after leaving school, Burns fell in with fellow reprobate Chris Miller, while working at the Croydon Fairfield Halls. Sharing common interests in drink, chaos and music, they eventually found themselves part of the burgeoning punk scene in west London in 1976. Together with Dave Vanian and Brian James, Miller (Rat Scabies) and Burns (Captain Sensible) formed what was to be one of the major punk bands of the period; the Damned. Initially enrolled as their bass player, he moved on to guitar following James's departure from the group. A riotous character with an unnerving sense of charm, Sensible frequently performed at gigs dressed in various guises, often in a tu-tu, a nurse's uniform or even nothing at all. Behind the comic-strip facade lurked a keen fan of 60s and 70s psychedelia; he was often quoted in later interviews as being influenced by Jimi Hendrix, Syd Barrett-era Pink Floyd and the Soft Machine. This went against the punk ethos of the time. He was able to indulge in his esoteric taste in music by carving out a solo career by accident rather than design, owing to the frequent bouts of forced inactivity by the Damned. With ex-Chelsea bassist Henry Badowski, Sensible formed King, an outfit that lasted barely three months. That same year, he recorded 'Jet Boy Jet Girl', a lyrically improbable translation of Plastic Bertrand's 'Ca Plane Pour Moi' with the Softies and also performed on Johnny Moped's *Cycledelic*. A fervent campaigner for animal rights, and a CND supporter, he confirmed his anti-establishment credentials by recording an EP on the Crass label, *This Is Your Captain Speaking*, in 1981.

With fellow Damned member Paul Gray, he produced the Dolly Mixture singles 'Been Teen' and 'Everything And More'. Signed by A&M Records as a solo act, he recorded a cover version of Richard Rodgers/Oscar Hammerstein II's 'Happy Talk' which included Dolly Mixture on backing vocals. The single shot to the UK number 1 position in the summer of 1982. With his distinctive red beret and round shades, he become an instant media and family favourite, revealing an endearing fondness for rabbits, cricket and trains. He subsequently released two albums in close collaboration with lyricist Robyn Hitchcock, and had further hit singles with 'Wot' and the glorious anti-Falklands war song 'Glad It's All Over'. Although he was keen not to let his solo success interfere with the Damned's activities, Sensible found himself gradually becoming isolated from the group due to internal politics and managerial disputes, resulting in his leaving the band in 1984, although he occasionally dropped in to guest on live performances.

One single in 1985 in partnership with girlfriend Rachel Bor of Dolly Mixture, billed as Captain Sensible And The Missus, 'Wot, No Meat?', emphasized his commitment to vegetarianism. He undertook one national tour in 1985, as well as studio work which culminated in the formation of his own Deltic label. His 1991 album *Revolution Now* received less favourable reviews. The double set did, however, show that his talent for catchy pop had not deserted him. He reunited with Paul Gray for some live performances in 1991, and in 1994 augmented by Gray, Malcolm Dixon (organ) and Garrie Dreadful (drums) he released *Live At The Milky Way*. This was the album the Captain should have made years ago, as it captures both his humour and considerable songwriting talent. The band perform as if it is their last day on the planet, and rewarding versions of 'Neat Neat Neat', 'New Rose' and an energetic version of his number 1 hit 'Happy Talk' are but three gems from an excellent album. At the same time Sensible was playing bass in the psychedelically inclined The Space Toad Experience, who released *Time Machine* (Blueprint) in 1996. In 1995 Sensible put together Captain Sensible's Punk Floyd with Dreadful and Monty The Moron (keyboards) and, following live work with Dave Vanian, reformed The Damned in 1996. Sensible is enigmatic, hugely talented and highly underrated.

●ALBUMS: *Women And Captains First* (A&M 1982)★★★, *The Power Of Love* (A&M 1983)★★, *Revolution Now* (Deltic 1991)★★, *Universe Of Geoffrey Brown* (1993)★★, *Live At The Milky Way* (Humbug 1994)★★★★, *Meathead* (Humbug 1995)★★★, *Mad Cows And Englishmen* (Scratch 1996)★★★.

●COMPILATIONS: *Sensible Singles* (1984)★★★.

CARA, IRENE

b. 18 March 1959, New York City, New York, USA. Having spent most of her childhood as a successful actor, singer and dancer, Cara's role as Coco Hernandez in the 1980 Alan Parker film *Fame*, was tailor-made. Based around the lives, loves and ambitions of students at the New York School of Performing Arts, Cara's rendition of the jubilant title song was an Oscar-winning international hit reaching the number 1 spot, belatedly, in the UK. This sparked off an entire 'Fame' industry and a worldwide boost to sales of leg warmers and a new generation of 'Mrs Worthingtons'. Another movie song, 'Flashdance ... What A Feeling' from *Flashdance*, earned Cara a US number 1, a UK number 2 and and yet another Oscar for Best Song. Signing to Geffen Records, Cara scored further US hits with 'Why Me' (1983), a further movie hit with 'The Dream (Hold On To Your Dream)' from *DC Cab*, and the Top 10 hit 'Breakdance' (both 1984). Contractual disputes delayed her recording career in the mid-80s and Irene re-emerged with a new album in 1987 on Elektra Records.
●ALBUMS: *Anyone Can See* (Network 1982)★★, *What A Feelin'* (Geffen 1983)★★, *Carasmatic* (Elektra 1987)★★.
●FILMS: *Fame* (1980).

CARDIACS

Formed in 1978 by Tim Smith (b. 3 July 1961, Carshalton, Surrey, England; guitar/vocals), brother Jim (b. 14 April 1958, Carshalton, Surrey, England), Peter Tagg (b. London, England; drums) and Mick Pugh (b. 21 September 1958, Kingston, Surrey, England; vocals), they started life known as Philip Pilf And The Filth which, although bizarre, was to be no less strange than the rest of a career riddled with personnel changes and eccentric activities. The name was soon changed to Cardiac Arrest, whereupon Colvin Myers (b. London, England; keyboards) joined for the first single, 'A Bus For A Bus On The Bus', in 1979. In the same year, Mark Cawthra replaced Tagg, who went on to form the Trudy. His departure was followed by Mick Pugh and Colvin Myers, who joined the Sound. The Cardiacs resolutely strived to avoid the traditional machinations of the record business by releasing a series of independent label cassette-only albums. Saxophonist Sara Smith (b. 30 November 1960, Coleford, Gloucestershire, England) and drummer Dominic Luckman (b. 29 November 1961, Brighton, East Sussex, England) both merged with the ranks, as had William D.

Drake (b. 7 February 1962, Essex, England; keyboards) and Tim Quy (b. 14 August 1961, Brixton, London, England; percussion) toward the end of 1983.
Fortunately, this line-up was to remain stable for the next six years, allowing the Cardiacs to build a devoted live following with oddball performances involving flour, ill-fitting suits and several other crazy theatrical elements. Long overdue vinyl album releases followed, revealing how the band were perfecting a thoroughly unique musical sound that flummoxed the critics, although one offered the opinion that 'Genesis on a frantic amphetamine overdose' fitted the bill adequately.
By 1988, the Cardiacs started to infringe upon the hitherto alien mainstream, reaching number 80 in the UK singles chart with the epic 'This Is The Life', but changes were on the way again as Sarah Smith, Tim Quy and William D. Drake all left and guitarist Christian Hayes (b. 10 June 1964, London, England) joined briefly before departing for the equally indefinable Levitation in 1991, paving the way for more chapters in the Cardiacs' fairy story. In 1995 the entire Cardiacs back catalogue was reissued, together with a specially priced sampler CD. This comprised one track from each of their previous albums and one each from projected new releases from Tim Smith, W.D. Drake and Sarah Smith (*The Sea Nymphs*), Tim Smith's solo album (*Oceanland World*) and a new, as yet untitled, Cardiacs studio album. The band then joined with Sidi Bou Said for a widespread UK tour and supported long-standing fans, Blur, at the Mile End Stadium in London.
●ALBUMS: *The Obvious Identity* cassette only (Alphabet 1980)★★★, *Toy World* cassette only (Alphabet 1981)★★★, *Archive Cardiacs* cassette only (Alphabet 1983)★★★, *The Seaside* cassette only (Alphabet 1983)★★★, *Mr & Mrs Smith And Mr Drake* cassette only (Alphabet 1984)★★★, *Big Ship* (Alphabet 1985)★★★, *Rude Bootleg (Live At The Reading Festival, 1986)* (Alphabet 1986)★★★, *A Little Man And A House And The Whole World Window* (Alphabet 1988)★★★, *Cardiacs Live At The Paradiso, Amsterdam* (Alphabet 1988)★★★, *On Land And In The Sea* (Alphabet 1989)★★★, *Songs For Ships And Irons* (Alphabet 1990)★★★, *Heaven Born And Ever Bright* (Alphabet 1992)★★★, *All That Glitters Is A Mare's Nest* (Alphabet 1993)★★★.
●COMPILATIONS: *Cardiacs Sampler* (Aphabet 1995)★★★.
●VIDEOS: *Cardiacs Live* (1990).

CARLISLE, BELINDA

b. 17 August 1958, Hollywood, California, USA. When the Go-Go's broke up in 1985, Carlisle remained with the IRS label and pursued a solo career. After the excesses of her former group, Belinda underwent a period of physical recuperation and image remodelling - emerging as the quintessential modern young Californian female. With artistic assistance from former fellow Go-Go Charlotte Caffey, Carlisle hit the US Top 3 with her debut single 'Mad About You' in 1986 and her first album peaked at number 13 in the *Billboard* chart. It was not until a move to the MCA label in the States and on signing to Virgin Records in the UK that she achieved international acclaim with the release of 'Heaven Is A Place On Earth'. This infectious piece of perfect pop reached number 1 in the USA and UK and gave her a whole new generation of fans who had previously never heard of the Go-Go's. This winning formula was subsequently used for a string of albums and other chart singles such as 'I Get Weak' (US number 2/UK Top 10, 1988), 'Circle In The Sand' (US number 7/UK number 4, 1988), 'Leave A Light On' (UK number 4, 1989) and 'We Want The Same Thing' (UK number 6). Using her new-found position as a respected pop star, Carlisle, along with another ex-Go-Go, Jane Wiedlin, put her name to various environmental and humanitarian/animal rights causes. *A Woman And A Man* featured an eclectic mix of bedfellows, notably ex-Kajagoogoo bassist Nick Beggs, ex-Bangle Susannah Hoffs and ex-Beach Boy Brian Wilson.

● ALBUMS: *Belinda* (IRS 1986)★★★, *Heaven On Earth* (Virgin 1987)★★★, *Runaway Horses* (Virgin 1989)★★, *Live Your Live Be Free* (Virgin 1991)★★, *Real* (Virgin 1993)★★, *A Woman And A Man* (Chrysalis 1996)★★.

● VIDEOS: *Belinda Live* (1988), *Runaway - Live* (1990), *Runaway Videos* (1991), *The Best Of ... Vol. 1* (Virgin 1992).

CARLTON AND HIS SHOES

Carlton, Donald and Lynford Manning (and sometimes Alexander Henry of 'Please Be True' fame) made up the harmony group known as Carlton And His Shoes. Carlton Manning, probably the purest singer of love songs to ever come out of Jamaica, originally named the group Carlton And His Shades, but a printer's misspelling on their debut release for Sonia Pottinger stuck with them for their entire career. Their debut single vanished but their subsequent work for Coxsone Dodd at Studio One established them as a seminal force in Jamaican music. 'Love Me Forever', for Dodd's Supreme label, was a massive rocksteady hit in the late 60s and has been re-released and interpreted countless times since its original recording. The b-side, 'Happy Land', formed the basis for 'Satta Amassa Ganna' - one of the most covered tunes in the history of reggae and its most enduring anthem, first performed by the Abyssinians: Donald and Lynford with the addition of Bernard Collins. Carlton, who had by now trademarked the double and treble tracking of his own sweet, aching lead vocals, continued to make fine records at Studio One. (He was also working at their Brentford Road Studios as a session guitarist.) The last, 'Let Me Love You', was released on 12-inch in Jamaica in 1979 and showcased one of his finest-ever performances. He has also occasionally worked for other producers and released some excellent self-produced tracks since the halcyon days of the late 60s. Unfortunately, he has never been able to repeat his original success but remains a legendary figure in the development of Jamaican music.

● ALBUMS: *Love Me Forever* (Studio One 1978)★★★, *This Heart Of Mine* (1980)★★★.

CARLTON, LARRY

b. 2 March 1948, Torrance, California, USA. Often cited as the guitarist's guitarist, Carlton has courted rock, jazz and acoustic 'new age' with considerable success. The former member of the Crusaders carved a career during the 70s as a sought after session musician. His profile improved following some outstanding fluid playing over a number of years with Steely Dan. His distinctive 'creamy' Gibson 335 guitar sound was heard on countless records and his work on numerous Joni Mitchell albums arguably contributed to their success. Two notable examples are *Court And Spark* and *Hejira*. His solo debut appeared in 1978. It was not until *Sleepwalk*, including its title track (formerly a hit for Santo And Johnny), that Carlton was fully accepted as a solo artist in his own right. *Alone But Never Alone* found Larry playing acoustic guitar and the record proved a critical and commercial success. Both that album and *Discovery* broadened Carlton's following. The live *Last Night*, however, saw a return to his jazz roots, and contains flashes of breathtaking virtuosity. His version of Miles Davis's 'So What' is one of the finest ever interpretations. With *On Solid Ground* Carlton demonstrated a stronger rock influence and produced a credible cover of Eric Clapton's 'Layla' and Steely

Dan's 'Josie'. He was awarded a Grammy in 1981 and again in 1987 for his version of 'Minute By Minute'. In 1988 Carlton was shot in the neck by an intruder at his studio. After an emergency operation and many months of physiotherapy he made a full recovery. Carlton joined the GRP stable in 1991 and found a home that perfectly suited his music. His duet with label mate Lee Ritenour in 1995 was wholly satisfying, and bodes well for future collaborations. Carlton remains a master musician with an almost flawless catalogue of accesible and warming music.

●ALBUMS: *Larry Carlton* (Warners 1978)★★★, *Live In Japan* (Flyover 1979)★★★, *Mr 335* (1979)★★★, *Strikes Twice* (1980)★★★, *Sleepwalk* (Warners 1982)★★★, *Friends* (Warners 1983)★★★, *Alone But Never Alone* (MCA 1986)★★★★, *Discovery* (MCA 1987)★★★★, *Last Night* (MCA 1987)★★★★, *One Night Of Sin* (1989)★★★, *Christmas At My House* (1989)★★, *On Solid Ground* (MCA 1989)★★★, *Kid Gloves* (GRP 1992)★★★, *Renegade Gentleman* (GRP 1993)★★★, with Lee Ritenour *Larry And Lee* (GRP 1995)★★★★, *The Gift* (GRP 1996)★★★.

●COMPILATIONS: *The Collection* (GRP 1990)★★★★.

CARMEL

This UK group was formed in Manchester in 1981 by Carmel McCourt (b. 24 November 1958, Scunthorpe, Lincolnshire, England; vocals) and former members of Bee Vamp, Jim Paris (b. 13 January 1957, Finchley, London, England; double bass) and Gerry Darby (b. 13 October 1959, Finchley, London, England; drums/percussion). On the release of the single 'Storm' and a mini-album in 1982 on the independent Red Flame label, Carmel drew praise for the fiery passion of all three members. Paris and Darby remarkably conjured the effect of a full ensemble backing to McCourt's powerful vocals, and were able to alternate between soulful ballads, gospel, blues and stomping jazz. The stand-out 'Tracks Of My Tears' was performed with confidence, as though the song had been a group original rather than a new arrangement of the Smokey Robinson classic. An appearance at the 1983 ICA Rock Week led to the group signing to London Records, while a sell-out date at the prestigious Ronnie Scott's jazz club confirmed Carmel's status amongst the British 'new jazz/pop' scene. In accentuating the 'jazz' motif, the music and 'style' press unfortunately saddled the group with an unwanted Billie Holiday image, which was eventually passed on to future 'rival',

Sade. Carmel tasted success first time that year in the UK Top 20 singles chart with the glorious gospel-tinged 'Bad Day', featuring the Attractions' Steve Nieve and the swooping backing vocals of Helen Watson and Rush Winters. Carmel's '50s jazz club' image was evocatively captured on the single's cover by Serge Clerc who supplied the artwork to the subsequent releases, 'Willow Weep For Me', the Top 30 hit 'More More More', and the album, *The Drum Is Everything*. Despite attaining UK Top 20 status, the album failed to capture the vitality of the singles or of the earlier Red Flame issues. While the jazz fashion faded in the UK, Carmel found a much more attentive and appreciative audience in Europe, particularly France. A more satisfying release in *The Falling* saw the trio achieve their most successful studio performance up to that time, aided by several producers including Brian Eno and Hugh Johns. Subsequent albums displayed an increasing maturity that manifested itself in original compositions such as 'Easy For You', 'Nothing Good', 'Napoli' and 'I'm Over You'. The group's earlier talent for producing imaginative cover versions has seen them tackling Randy Newman's 'Mama Told Me Not To Come', Charles Dawes and Carl Sigman's Tommy Edwards hit 'It's All In The Game' and Duke Ellington's 'Azure'. Despite the disappointing lack of mass appeal in the home market, Carmel continue to command respect from critics and fans alike and the group are able to work equally well within the confines of an intimate jazz club (selling out a season of dates at Ronnie Scott's in 1991) or in the larger auditoriums. After a long association with London Records, Carmel split from the label in 1991, signing with Warner Brothers Records/East West in 1992 but moved to Musidisc in 1996.

●ALBUMS: *Carmel* (Red Flame 1982)★★★, *The Drum Is Everything* (London 1984)★★, *The Falling* (London 1986)★★★, *Everybody's Got A Little ... Soul* (London 1987)★★★, *Set Me Free* (London 1989)★★★, *Good News* (East West 1992)★★★, *World's Gone Crazy* (East West 1995)★★★, *Live In Paris* (Musidisc 1997)★★★.

●COMPILATIONS: *Collected* (London 1990)★★★.

●VIDEOS: *Collected: A Collection Of Work 1983-1990* (1990).

CARNES, KIM

b. 20 July 1945, Los Angeles, California, USA. The gravelly voiced Carnes is best known for her 1981 pop classic 'Bette Davis Eyes' which won a Grammy award. Her career started as a member of the influential New Christy Minstrels in the 60s.

The solo *Kim Carnes* in 1975 brought her critical favour, although she was reaping greater success as a songwriter with her husband Dave Ellington. Renowned artists such as Frank Sinatra and Barbra Streisand recorded her songs, as did Kenny Rogers who duetted with her on their hit 'Don't Fall In Love With A Dreamer' in 1980. The previous year Carnes/Ellington had written all the material for Rogers' best-selling *Gideon*. In 1981 the Jackie DeShannon/Carnes composition 'Bette Davis Eyes' topped the US charts for an astonishing nine weeks. This lyrically strong number featured Carnes' husky vocal over a chiming guitar, utilizing one of the best examples of 'flanging guitar effect' ever recorded. The follow-up 'Draw Of The Cards' gave prominence to a contagious, swirling organ-dominated sound but stalled inside the US Top 30. *Mistaken Identity* included both these tracks and topped the US chart for a month during its year-long stay. Subsequent albums have made a respectable showing in the best sellers and Carnes enjoys regular visits to the US singles chart. During 1984 she had two major duetted hits, the first 'What About Me' with Kenny Rogers and James Ingram and three months later with Barbra Streisand and 'Make No Mistake, He's Mine'. Carnes was one of the select few stars to appear on the USA For Africa single 'We Are The World'. Her country roots returned with the 1988 *View From the House*, featuring the country hit 'Speed Of The Sound Of Loneliness' with Lyle Lovett on backing vocals. Carnes has now completed a full circle, having proved herself as a successful songwriter in rock, pop and country and going in the record books as one of the longest stays at the coveted number 1 position.

●ALBUMS: *Rest On Me* (Amos 1972)★★, *Kim Carnes* (A&M 1975)★★★, *Sailin'* (A&M 1976)★★★, *St Vincent's Court* (EMI America 1979)★★, *Romance Dance* (EMI America 1980)★★★, *Mistaken Identity* (EMI America 1981)★★★★, *Voyeur* (EMI America 1982)★★★, *Cafe Racers* (EMI America 1983)★★, *Barking At Airplanes* (EMI America 1985)★★, *Lighthouse* (EMI America 1986)★★★, *View From the House* (MCA 1988)★★★★.

●COMPILATIONS: *Gypsy Honeymoon - The Best Of* (EMI America 1993)★★★.

CARRACK, PAUL

b. 22 April 1951, Sheffield, Yorkshire, England. Justified success finally arrived for keyboard/vocalist Paul Carrack during the late 80s. As an unassuming personality it seemed that he would only be remembered as the man who sang 'How Long'. This memorable pop song from pub-rock band Ace took Carrack's voice into the UK Top 20 in 1974, and to number 3 in the US charts in 1975. When investigated, Carrack's career reveals first-class credentials. Following the demise of Ace in 1977 he joined Frankie Miller's band and the following year moved on to Roxy Music, appearing on *Manifesto* and *Flesh And Blood*. After recording a solo album, *Nightbird*, Carrack was invited to join Squeeze as Jools Holland's replacement. He sang lead vocal on the sublime 'Tempted' (1981), and made a considerable contribution to their *East Side Story*. Paul then teamed up with Nick Lowe under various guises, during which time he released his second solo album, *Suburban Voodoo*, and achieved a US Top 40 hit with 'I Need You'. Carrack was seen as a regular member of Eric Clapton's band in the mid-80s. He was enlisted as lead singer of Mike And The Mechanics in 1985 and his distinctive voice was heard on two major hits in 1986, 'Silent Running (On Dangerous Ground)' and 'All I Need Is A Miracle'. During 1987, again as a solo artist, he had a minor UK hit with 'When You Walk In The Room', still suffering from anonymity with the mass British record-buying public. His standing in the USA, however, was much more respected, endorsed that same year with the Top 10 hit, 'Don't Shed A Tear'. In 1989 *Groove Approved* was highly successful in America and did much to place his name in the foreground of male vocalists. As a session musician, his pedigree has always secured him positions alongside many of the top acts of the day and his smooth and effortless delivery gives him one of the most distinctive voices in pop music, albeit one which it is difficult to put a face. In the 90s his career was mostly taken up with Mike And The Mechanics. He stepped outside in 1995 with an excellent solo album that spawned two hit singles, notably a beautiful reworking of his Albatross 'How Long' and the equally fine 'Eyes Of Blue'. *Blue Views* at last gave him the solo recognition he has long deserved.

●ALBUMS: *Nightbird* (Vertigo 1980)★★, *Suburban Voodoo* (Epic 1982)★★, *One Good Reason* (Chrysalis 1987)★★★, *Groove Approved* (Chrysalis 1989)★★★, *Blue Views* (IRS 1995)★★★★.

●COMPILATIONS: *Ace Mechanic* (1987)★★★, *Carrackter Reference* (1991)★★★.

CARROLL, CATH

b. 25 August 1960, Chipping Sodbury, Avon, England. Carroll had previously made a name for herself on the Manchester club and music scene, founding with friend Liz Naylor the magazine *City*

Fun; forming the short-lived Gay Animals; and developing a penchant for cross-dressing. On moving south to London, she pursued a parallel career as a journalist and gossip columnist for the rock weekly, *New Musical Express* and listings magazine, *City Limits*. An often used pseudonym, Myrna Minkoff (influenced by the character in John Kennedy Toole's novel, *A Confederacy Of Dunces*) was a direct contradiction of Carroll's true quiet nature. Leading the mid-80s 'indie' band, Miaow, which also comprised Chris Fenner (drums), Ron Caine (bass/guitar) and Steve MacGuire (guitar), she found herself linked with the *NME*'s seminal C86 project, contributing 'Sport Most Royal' for the album and appearing at London's ICA rock week celebration. Her smooth vocals coupled with the jangling rhythm section won critical acclaim, particularly with the anti-Thatcher song, 'Grocer's Devil Daughter', on the Venus label, and the triumphant 'yodelling' high point, 'When It All Comes Down', on Factory Records, which reached the UK independent Top 20. Their final single, 'Break The Code', gave some clue as to the musical direction Carroll was later to pursue. She subsequently became involved in low-key collaborations with Julian Henry in the Hit Parade, then married Big Black's guitarist Santiago Durango (who had left the group to study law), and continued her own solo career, spending recording time in San Paulo, Brazil, as well as London and Sheffield, England. Remaining with Factory as a solo artist (and becoming the label's first artist actually to sign a contract), Carroll recorded her debut album, assisted by Mark Brydon (guitar), Sim Lister (sax/drums/keyboards), Oswaldinho da Cuica (congas), Antenor Soares Gandra Neto (guitar), Dirceu Simoes de Medeiros (drums), Vincente da Paula Silva (piano), Valerie A. James (backing vocals), Steve Albini (guitar) and Santiago Durango (guitar). The result was the critically acclaimed *England Made Me*, released in the summer of 1991. The set confirmed the complete departure from Carroll's past English 'indie' workings, revealing a set of smooth, steamy Latin-samba, mixed with electro-dance rhythms. She currently resides in Chicago, USA, and released the lyrically strong *True Crime Motel* in 1995.

●ALBUMS: *England Made Me* (Factory 1991)★★★, *True Crime Motel* (Matador 1995)★★★.

CARROLL, JIM

b. 1951, New York City, USA. Jim Carroll was a poet and author who became a rock singer in the late 70s. He had a difficult childhood on New York's rough streets, but became a proficient basketball player before his teens. He then became exposed to the seedy aspects of city life. He began writing down his experiences at the age of 12, describing his initiation to heroin at 13 as well as his encounters with sex and crime. (Those notes were later published as a critically acclaimed book, *The Basketball Diaries*, in 1980.) Carroll became interested in poetry through reading the works of modern poets such as Jack Kerouac and Allen Ginsberg and had his own first book of poetry, *Living At The Movies*, published when he was 16. He spent three months in jail for heroin possession in 1966, and continued his obsessions with drugs, literature and basketball upon his release. Having already befriended the writer William Burroughs and the rock group the Velvet Underground, Carroll was introduced to poet Patti Smith in the early 70s. Smith was in the process of setting her poetry to music and after Carroll moved to Marin County, north of San Francisco, in 1974 to rid himself of his heroin habit, he maintained contact with Smith. When Smith and her group went to California in the late 70s, Carroll, having also taken an interest in setting his poetry to music, and having been inspired by the punk movement, performed as her opening act. He produced a demo tape of his music in 1979 and was signed to Atco Records. Carroll recorded his debut album *Catholic Boy* that year and formed the Jim Carroll Band with Brian Linsley (guitar), Steve Linsley (bass), Terrell Winn (guitar) and Wayne Woods (drums). The album reached only number 73 but was a critical success, particularly the song 'People Who Died', a graphic description of individuals known to the singer who met horrible deaths. Carroll made two further albums, *Dry Dreams* and *I Write Your Name*, with several personnel changes in the band for each album. He performed music infrequently after the mid-80s, and has concentrated instead on poetry readings. Carroll published his second book *Forced Entries* in 1987. In 1991, Carroll signed with Giant Records and released a spoken-word album, *Praying Mantis*, recorded live at St. Mark's Church in New York City.

●ALBUMS: *Catholic Boy* (Atco 1980)★★★, *Dry Dreams* (Atco 1982)★★★, *I Write Your Name* (Atco 1983)★★★, *Praying Mantis* (Giant 1991)★★★.

CARS

In a recording career that started in 1977 the Cars' output has been a meagre 6 albums. Each one, however, has sold over a million copies and all have reached high chart positions in the USA.

Formerly known as Cap'n Swing the stable line-up comprised; Ric Ocasek (b. Richard Otcasek, 23 March 1949, Baltimore, Maryland, USA; guitar/vocals), Benjamin Orr (b. Benjamin Orzechowski, Cleveland, Ohio, USA; bass/vocals), Greg Hawkes (keyboards), Elliot Easton (b. Elliot Shapiro, 18 December 1953, Brooklyn, New York City, New York, USA; guitar) and David Robinson (drums). Their catchy pop/rock songs have been hard to categorize and when they arrived with 'Just What I Needed' they were embraced by the new wave art-rock fraternity in the USA. They were an instant success in Britain, notching up a number of hits, debuting with a top 3 single, the irresistible 'My Best Friend's Girl'. The Cars have never deviated from writing catchy well-crafted songs, each containing at least one memorable and instantly hummable riff. Today they are accepted by the AOR market, which no doubt contributes to their massive record sales.

In 1984 they enjoyed world-wide success with 'Drive,' and a year later the same song was opportunistically but tastefully used to pull at people's consciences during the Live Aid concert. A film accompanying the song showing the appalling famine in Ethiopia will forever be in people's minds. As the lyric 'Who's gonna plug their ears when you scream' was played, it was replaced by a heart-rending scream from a small child. This memorable yet tragic segment left few dry eyes in the world. Predictably the song became a hit once more. The band broke up at the end of the 80s in favour of solo work, with Ocasek also becoming busy as a record producer, notably with Weezer in 1994.

● ALBUMS: *The Cars* (Elektra 1978)★★★★, *Candy-O* (Elektra 1979)★★★, *Panorama* (Elektra 1980)★★, *Shake It Up* (Elektra 1981)★★★, *Heartbeat City* (Elektra 1984)★★★★, *Door To Door* (Elektra 1987)★. Solo: Rick Ocasek *Beautitude* (Geffen 1983)★★, *The Side Of Paradise* (Geffen 1986)★★, *Fireball Zone* (Warners 1991)★★, *Quick Change World* (Reprise 1993)★★, *Troublizing* (Columbia 1997). Elliot Easton *Change No Change* (Elektra 1985)★★. Benjamin Orr *The Lace* (Elektra 1986)★★, Greg Hawkes *Niagara Falls* (Passport 1983)★★.

● COMPILATIONS: *The Cars Greatest Hits* (Elektra 1985)★★★, *Just What I Needed: The Cars Anthology* (Elektra/Rhino 1995)★★★★.

● VIDEOS: *Heartbeat City* (1984), *Cars Live* (1988).

● FURTHER READING: *The Cars*, Philip Kamin.

CARTER, BETTY

b. Lillie Mae Jones, 16 May 1930, Flint, Michigan, USA. Growing up in Detroit, Carter sang with touring jazzmen, including Charlie Parker and Dizzy Gillespie. In her late teens, she joined Lionel Hampton, using the stage name Lorraine Carter. With Hampton she enjoyed a love-hate relationship; he regularly fired her only to have his wife and business manager, Gladys Hampton, re-hire her immediately. Carter's predilection for bop earned from Hampton the mildly disparaging nickname of 'Bebop Betty', by which name she became known thereafter. In the early 50s she worked on the edge of the R&B scene, sharing stages with blues artists of the calibre of Muddy Waters. Throughout the remainder of the 50s and into the 60s she worked mostly in and around New York City, establishing a reputation as a fiercely independent and dedicated jazz singer. She took time out for tours with packages headlined by Ray Charles (with whom she recorded a highly regarded album of duets), but preferred to concentrate on her own shows and club performances. She also found time for marriage and a family. Her insistence upon certain standards in her recording sessions led eventually to the formation of her own record company, Bet-Car. During the 80s, Carter continued to perform in clubs in New York and London, occasionally working with large orchestras but customarily with a regular trio of piano, bass and drums, the ideal setting for her spectacular improvisations. Taking her inspiration from instrumentalists such as Parker and Sonny Rollins rather than from other singers, Carter's technique draws little from the vocal tradition in jazz. Her kinship with the blues is never far from the surface, however complex and contemporary that surface might be. In performance, Carter tends to employ the lower register of her wide range. Always aurally witty and frequently displaying scant regard for the lyrics of the songs she sings, Carter's inventiveness is ably displayed on such performances as 'Sounds', a vocalese excursion which, in one recorded form, lasts for more than 25 minutes. Despite such extraordinary performances and the breakneck tempos she employs on 'The Trolley Song' and 'My Favourite Things', she can sing ballads with uncloying tenderness. In concert, Carter dominates the stage, pacing like a tigress from side to side and delivering her material with devastating attack. The authority with which she stamps her performances, especially in vocalese and the boppish side of her repertoire, helps make unchallengable her position as the major jazz singer of the 80s and early 90s. It also helps support her assertion that she sees no one waiting in the wings to challenge her superiority.

●ALBUMS: *Meet Betty Carter And Ray Bryant* (1955)★★★, *The Bebop Girl* (1955-56)★★★, *Social Call* (1956)★★★, *Out There* (1958)★★★, *Finally* i (1959)★★★, *The Modern Sound Of Betty Carter* (1960)★★★, *I Can't Help It* (Impulse 1961)★★★, with Ray Charles *Ray Charles And Betty Carter* (ABC 1961)★★★★, *'Round Midnight* (1963)★★★, *Inside Betty Carter* (1963)★★★, *Finally* ii (Roulette 1969)★★★, *Live At The Village Vanguard* (Verve 1970)★★★, *The Betty Carter Album* (1972)★★★, *Now It's My Turn* (1976)★★★, *What A Little Moonlight Can Do* (1977)★★★, *I Didn't Know What Time It Was* (Verve 1979)★★★, *The Audience With Betty Carter* (Verve 1979)★★★★, *Whatever Happened To Love?* (Bet-Car 1982)★★★, *Look What I Got* (Verve 1988)★★★, *Droppin' Things* (Verve 1990)★★★, *It's Not About The Melody* (Verve 1992)★★★, *Feed The Fire* (Verve 1993)★★★, *I'm Yours, You're Mine* (Verve 1996)★★★.

●COMPILATIONS: *Compact Jazz* (Philips 1990)★★★.

CARTER, CARLENE

b. Rebecca Carlene Smith, 26 September 1955, Nashville, Tennessee, USA. Carter is the daughter of country singers Carl Smith and June Carter and the grand-daughter of Maybelle Carter of the Carter Family. She learnt piano at six years old and guitar at 10, having lessons from Carl Perkins. Her parents divorced and, when she was 12, her mother married Johnny Cash. Carlene Carter herself first married when 16, and had a daughter Tiffany, but she and Joe Simpkins were divorced within two years. After college she joined her mother and stepfather on the road and was featured on Johnny Cash's family album, *The Junkie And The Juicehead Minus Me* in 1974. Carter met Jack Routh, a writer for Cash's publishing company, and within three months they were married. They had a son, John Jackson Routh, but they separated in 1977. Carter brought her new boyfriend, Rodney Crowell, to the UK where she made an appealing, upbeat rock album with Graham Parker And The Rumour. Crowell's song, 'Never Together But Close Sometimes', was almost a UK hit and her song, 'Easy From Now On', was recorded by Emmylou Harris. Carter had an assertive personality but she struggled with the dance tracks on her second album, *Two Sides To Every Woman*, which was made in New York. *Musical Shapes* was pro-

duced by her new husband Nick Lowe; the songs included her 'Appalachian Eyes' and a duet with Dave Edmunds, 'Baby Ride Easy'. Her 1981 album, *Blue Nun*, was also produced by Lowe and featured members of Rockpile and Squeeze. The album, with such titles as 'Do Me Lover' and 'Think Dirty', was an explicit celebration of sex, but just as she seemed to be rejecting her country roots, she joined her family on stage at the Wembley Country Music Festival for 'Will The Circle Be Unbroken?'. Carter, whose marriage to Lowe broke up, was prevented from calling her next album *Gold Miner's Daughter*, and settled for *C'est Bon*. She was featured in *Too Drunk To Remember*, a short film shown at the London Film Festival, based on one of her songs. In 1985 she won acclaim for her role as one of the waitresses in the London cast of the country musical *Pump Boys And Dinettes*, which starred Paul Jones and Kiki Dee. In 1990 Carter, by making an album, *I Fell In Love*, aimed to please rather than alienate country fans. Produced by Howie Epstein, the musicians included Dave Edmunds, Kiki Dee, Albert Lee, Jim Keltner, and such songs as 'Me And Wildwood Rose' celebrated her country music heritage. Carter has the potential of a fine country songwriter and the song 'Guardian Angel' shows she has enough experiences to draw on. Unfortunately Carter may have discarded much of her personality in order to become a mainstream country artist. *Little Acts Of Treason* was comparatively bland, a word not previously associated with her.

●ALBUMS: *Carlene Carter* (Warners 1978)★★★, *Two Sides To Every Woman* (Warners 1979)★★, *Musical Shapes* (Warners 1980)★★★, *Blue Nun* (1981)★★★, *C'est Bon* (Epic 1983)★★★, *I Fell In Love* (Reprise 1990)★★★, *Musical Shapes & Blue Nun* reissue (Demon 1992)★★★, *Little Love Letters* (Giant 1993)★★★, *Little Acts Of Treason* (Giant 1995)★★★.

●COMPILATIONS: *Hindsight 20/20* (Giant 1996)★★★.

CASH, ROSANNE

b. 24 May 1955, Memphis, Tennessee, USA. The daughter of Johnny Cash from his first marriage to Vivian Liberto, Cash lived with her mother in California after her parents divorced in 1966. Perhaps inevitably, she returned to Nashville, where she studied drama at Vanderbilt University, before relocating to Los Angeles to study 'method' acting at Lee Strasberg's Institute, after which she worked for three years in her father's roadshow. In the late 70s, she spent a year in London working for CBS Records, the same label as her father, and signed a record contract in Germany with Ariola, resulting in her debut album, which has become a collector's item. Mainly recorded and produced in Germany with German-based musicians, it also included three tracks recorded in Nashville and was produced by Rodney Crowell. At the time, Cash was influenced by punk which she had experienced in Britain, but on her return to Nashville, she worked on demos with Crowell that gained her a contract with CBS as a neo-country act. She married Crowell in 1979, the same year her first CBS album, *Right Or Wrong*, was released. While not a huge success, the album, again produced by Crowell, included three US country hits: 'No Memories Hangin' Round' (a duet with Bobby Bare), 'Couldn't Do Nothin' Right, and 'Take Me, Take Me', while many of the backing musicians were also members of Emmylou Harris's Hot Band. 1981 brought the *Seven Year Ache*, again produced by Crowell, which went gold and reached the Top 30 of the US pop chart. It included three US country chart number 1 singles: the title track, her own composition, which reached the Top 30 of the US pop chart, 'My Baby Thinks He's A Train' (written by Leroy Preston, then of Asleep At The Wheel), and another of her own songs 'Blue Moon With Heartache'.

Somewhere In The Stars also made the Top 100 of the US pop album charts, and included three US country chart singles, 'Ain't No Money', 'I Wonder' and 'It Hasn't Happened Yet', but overall the album was considerably less successful than its predecessor. Her next album, *Rhythm And Romance*, included four US country hit singles, two of which were overseen by Crowell: 'Never Be You', another number 1 which was written by Tom Petty and Benmont Tench, and 'Hold On'. David Malloy produced most of the album, including another country number 1 single, 'I Don't Know Why You Don't Want Me' (which Cash co-wrote with Crowell) and 'Second To No-One'. After another two years' hiatus came *King's Record Shop*, titled after, and with a sleeve picture of the store of that name in Louisville, Kentucky. This album included four US country number 1 singles: John Hiatt's 'The Way We Make A Broken Heart', her revival of her father's 1962 country hit, 'Tennessee Flat Top Box', 'If You Change Your Mind', which she co-wrote with pedal steel ace Hank DeVito, and 'Rainway Train', written by John Stewart. This album was again produced by Crowell, with whom she duetted on a fifth US country number 1 within 13 months, 'It's A Small World'. This song was included on Crowell's *Diamond And Dirt*.

Cash won a Grammy award in 1985 for Best Country Vocal Performance Female, and in 1988 won *Billboard*'s Top Single Artist Award. A wife and mother, Cash has rarely had time to work live, but this has clearly had little effect on her recording career. In 1989 came a compilation album, *Hits 1979-1989* (retitled *Retrospective 1979-1989* for UK release), and in late 1990, *Interiors*, a hauntingly introspective album which was criticized for its apparently pessimistic outlook. The video for *Interors* shows her berating Crowell in song after song, only then to have him come on for a guest appearance. Its release was later followed by the news that her marriage to Crowell had broken down. Cash was one of the pioneers of the 'new country' movement of the late 80s, but her relative unavailability - she places her family firmly before her career - may ultimately result in others taking the glory for this forward thinking. Nevertheless, her achievements to date have ensured that the Cash family heritage in country music is far from disgraced.

●ALBUMS: *Rosanne Cash* (Ariola 1978)★★, *Right Or Wrong* (Columbia 1980)★★★, *Seven Year Ache* (Columbia 1981)★★★, *Somewhere In The Stars* (Columbia 1982)★★★, *Rhythm And Romance* (Columbia 1985)★★★, *King's Record Shop* (Columbia 1988)★★★, *Interiors* (Columbia 1990)★★★★, *The Wheel* (1993)★★★, *10 Song Demo* (Capitol 1996)★★★★.
●COMPILATIONS: *Hits 1979-1989* (Columbia 1989)★★★★, *Retrospective* (Columbia 1995)★★★★.
●VIDEOS: *Live - The Interiors Tour* (1994).
●FURTHER READING: *Bodies Of Water*, Rosanne Cash.

CAVE, NICK

After the Birthday Party disbanded, the enigmatic Australian vocalist Nick Cave (b. 22 September 1957, Warracknabeal, Australia) retained his association with Berlin by teaming up with ex-Einsturzende Neubauten member Blixa Bargeld (b. 12 Janaury 1959, Berlin, Germany; guitar), together with ex-Magazine personnel Barry Adamson (bass and other instruments) and multi-instrumentalist Mick Harvey (b. 29 September 1958, Rochester, Australia); they became the Bad Seeds. The debut album, *From Here To Eternity*, was accompanied by a startling rendition of the Elvis Presley classic, 'In the Ghetto', showing Cave had lost none of his passion or the ability to inject dramatic tension in his music. *The First Born Is Dead* followed a year later, promoted by the excellent 'Tupelo', but the Bad Seeds made their mark with *Kicking Against The Pricks* in the summer of 1986, bolstered by the UK Independent number 1, 'The Singer'. Cave had always drawn from a variety of sources, from Captain Beefheart to delta blues, and the Bad Seeds' material betrayed a claustrophobic, swamp-like aura. Although purely cover versions, *Kicking Against The Pricks* (which included drummer Thomas Wylder) fully displayed his abilities as an original interpreter of other artist's material. The subsequent *Your Funeral, My Trial* emphasized the power of his self-penned compositions, with improved production giving his vocals added clarity. After a brief hiatus from recording, it was two years before Cave returned, but it was worth the wait. 'The Mercy Seat' was a taut, brooding example of Cave's ability to build a story, followed by the milder 'Oh Deanna', which still contained considerable menace in its lyric. Both elements were present on October 1988's *Tender Prey*, as well as a more melodious approach to both his song constructions and singing voice. 'The Ship Song', released in February 1990, continued Cave's exploration of the more traditional ballad, and was followed by another strong album, *The Good Son*, in April. This accentuated several themes previously explored; notably spirituality and mortality, aided by the introduction of strings. Cave's literary aspirations had already been given an outlet by Black Spring Press in 1989, who published his first novel, *And The Ass Saw The Angel*. His film appearances include Wim Wenders' *Wings Of Desire* (1987) and a powerful performance as a prison inmate in the Australian production, *Ghosts Of The Civil Dead* (1989). An unlikely musical coupling with Kylie Minogue on 'Where The Wild Roses Grow' proved to be a commercial success; this in turn spawned *Murder Ballads* a brilliantly dark concept album. In 1997 Cave released another excellent album, arguably his best work, *The Boatman's Call*. Sounding deeply introspective yet never mundane on this offering he sounded like a cross between Tom Waits and a depressed Leonard Cohen.

●ALBUMS: *From Here To Eternity* (Mute 1984)★★★, *The First Born Is Dead* (Mute 1985)★★★, *Kicking Against The Pricks* (Mute 1986)★★★, *Your Funeral, My Trial* (Mute 1986)★★★, *Tender Prey* (Mute 1988)★★★, with Mick Harvey, Blixa Bargeld *Ghosts Of The Civil Dead* soundtrack (Mute 1989)★★★, *The Good Son* (Mute 1990)★★★★, *Henry's Dream* (Mute 1992)★★★, *Live Seeds* (Mute 1993)★★★, *Let Love In* (Mute 1994)★★★★, *Murder Ballads* (Mute/Reprise 1996)★★★★, with Harvey Bargeld *To Have And To Hold* soundtrack (Mute 1996)★★★, *The Boatman's Call* (Mute 1997)★★★★.

●VIDEOS: *Road To God Knows Where* (1990), *Live At The Paradiso* (Mute 1993).

●FURTHER READING: *And The Ass Saw The Angel*, Nick Cave. *Fish In A Barrel: Nick Cave & The Bad Seeds On Tour*, Peter Milne. *Hellfire: Life According To Nick Cave*, Jeremy Dean. *Bad Seed: The Biography Of Nick Cave*, Ian Johnston. *Nick Cave: The Birthday Party And Other Epic Adventures*, Robert Brokenmouth.

CBGB's

CBGB's is practically as intrinsic to the development of American alternative rock music as the guitar. A downtown, 300-capacity New York nightclub/venue, its legendary status grew quickly among aficionados of the city's 'No Wave' scene, and the subsequent punk movement. Established in December 1963, the venue was founded by owner Hilly Kristal (b. c.1931), giving it the name Country, Bluegrass, Blues and Other Music for Uplifting Gourmandizers, though the last sections of these initials were soon dropped. Previously it had been a low-rent drinking establishment. The club came into its own in the mid-70s, when Television manager Terry Ork brought in new groups. A who's who of New York music quickly followed, including Patti Smith, Blondie, Richard Hell, Ramones, Dead Boys, Talking Heads and the Cramps. A second generation also saw the light of day through CBGB's, including Sonic Youth and the Swans. In 1993 20th Anniversary Celebrations were held, with some of the venue's favourite artists taking part in the celebrations, including Joan Jett, the Damned, David Byrne and more recent graduates, Jesus Lizard and J. Mascis (Dinosaur Jr). The Dictators, Tuff Darts and the Shirts all reunited for the occasion. Other notable attractions over the years have included Guns N'Roses, AC/DC, Pearl Jam, and the Spin Doctors. Though many like Joey Ramone retain fond memories of its illustrious past as a 'birthplace', the venue remains popular to this day because of its booking policy, whereby bands receive 80% of the door minus expenses.

●ALBUMS: *Live At CBGBs* (1976)★★★.

●FURTHER READING: *This Ain't No Disco*, Roman Kozak.

CHAMELEONS

Formed in 1981 in Middleton, Manchester, this highly promising but ill-fated group comprised

Mark Burgess (vocals/bass), Reg Smithies (guitar), Dave Fielding (guitar) and Brian Schofield (drums). After some successful BBC Radio sessions, the unit were signed to the CBS Records subsidiary Epic and released 'In Shreds'. Its lack of success saw the group switch to the independent label Statik where they issued 'As High As You Can Go' and 'A Person Isn't Safe Anywhere These Days'. Their *Script Of The Bridge* and *What Does Anything Mean Basically?* revealed them as a promising guitar-based group with a strong melodic sense. Regular touring won them a contract with Geffen Records and their third album *Strange Times* was very well received by the critics. Just as a breakthrough beckoned, however, their manager Tony Fletcher died and amid the ensuing chaos the group folded. Two spin-off groups, the Sun And The Moon and the Reegs lacked the charm of their powerful but unrealized mother group.
●ALBUMS: *Script Of The Bridge* (Statik 1983)★★★, *What Does Anything Mean Basically?* (Statik 1985)★★★★, *Fan And The Bellows* (Statik 1986)★★★, *Strange Times* (Geffen 1987)★★★★, *Tripping Dogs* early recordings (1990)★★, *Peel Sessions* early recordings (Strange Fruit 1990)★★, *The Free Trade Hall Rehearsal* (1992)★★, *The Radio 1 Evening Show Sessions* (1993)★★★.
●VIDEOS: *Live At Camden Palace* (1986), *Live At The Hacienda* (1994), *Arsenal* (Visionary 1995), *Live At The Gallery* (Visionary 1996).

CHAPMAN, TRACY

b. 30 March 1964, Cleveland, Ohio, USA. During Nelson Mandela's satellite-linked 70th birthday concert at Wembley Stadium, London in 1988, this guitar-playing singer-songwriter got her big break when, owing to headliner Stevie Wonder's enforced walk-out, her spot was extended. She won the hearts of enough viewers world-wide for her debut album, *Tracy Chapman* to climb to number 1 in the British album chart within days, and become an international success. Following the Mandela show, album sales shot past the 3 million mark. 'Fast Car' became a UK Top 5 hit and the track 'Talkin' 'Bout A Revolution' became a concert favourite. She was, however, neither a second Joan Armatrading nor the overnight sensation many thought her to be. The daughter of estranged but well-heeled parents, she had attended a Connecticut school before attending the University of Massachusetts, where she became the toast of the campus folk club. Contracted by SBK Publishing, her first album had the advantage of the sympathetic production of David Kershenbaum who had worked previously with Joan Baez and Richie Havens. Next, she acquired a most suitable manager in Elliot Roberts - who also had Neil Young on his books - and a deal with the similarly apposite Elektra Records. She appeared with Peter Gabriel, Sting and other artists for a world-wide tour in aid of Amnesty International. Afterwords, she lost momentum. Although the impact of her second album, *Crossroads* was not insubstantial, its title track single was only a minor hit. *New Beginning* found a much wider audience in the USA.
●ALBUMS: *Tracy Chapman* (Elektra 1988)★★★★, *Crossroads* (Elektra 1989)★★, *Matters Of The Heart* (Elektra 1992)★★, *New Beginning* (Elektra 1995)★★★.

CHASE, TOMMY

b. 22 March 1947, Manchester, England. Largely self-taught at the drums, Chase had to wait for a jazz revival pioneered by the next generation to bring his chosen genre - steaming soul jazz - into favour. Professional since the mid-60s he began playing pure jazz in London from the early 70s, with tenor saxophonist Art Themen and trumpeter Harry Beckett. The jazz dancers of the mid-80s responded to a band of young-bloods (including tenor saxophonist Alan Barnes, 1983-86), bringing out the lindy-hop basis of breakdancing to tunes like 'Night In Tunisia'. Later on, his use of a Hammond organ, featuring the excellent Gary Baldwin, confirmed what many people had suspected: boasting that he was the Art Blakey of British jazz, in actual fact he is its Dr Feelgood - playing unpretentious, driving music with a great feel for stage dynamics. His quartet in 1992 is arguably his finest, featuring the inspired driving string bass of Australian Les Miller, Chris Watson (guitar) and Dave Lewis (tenor saxophone/saxello). Chase is in complete control of his drumkit, he can change pace in breathtaking fashion, willing on his musicians to follow his extraordinary timing.
●ALBUMS: with Ray Warleigh *One Way* (Spotlite 1983)★★★, *Hard* (Boplicity 1984)★★★, *Drive!* (Paladin 1985)★★★, *Groove Merchant* (Stiff 1987)★★★★, *Rebel Fire* (Mole 1990)★★.

CHEFS

The Chefs, from Brighton, East Sussex, England, only survived three singles before splitting, and one of those was a reissue. Along with other aspiring local talent in the late 70s, the Chefs - Helen McCookerybook (b. Helen McCallum;

vocals/bass), James McCallum (guitar), Russell Greenwood (drums), Carl Evans (guitar) - were signed to the town's resident label, Attrix Records. The E, *Sweetie*, issued in September 1980, was far from being sweet, dealing frankly with sex, personal hygiene and other matters. But '24 Hours' (1981) was nothing short of a great pop song and was strong enough to warrant a reissue on the Midlands label, Graduate Records. The band changed their name to Skat for a guitar-based cover of the Velvet Underground's 'Femme Fatale'. Helen McCookerybook then left to form Helen And The Horns, a bold brass dominated group with influences taken from the American west. 'Pioneer Town' and a remake of Doris Day's 'Secret Love' were both interesting excursions, although the band eventually floundered due to Helen's increasing stage fright.

CHER

b. Cherilyn Sarkarsian La Pier, 20 May 1946, El Centro, California, USA. Cher began working as a session singer in an attempt to finance an acting career. While recording with Phil Spector as a backing vocalist, she met and later married Sonny Bono. After releasing two singles under the name Caeser And Cleo, the duo then achieved international acclaim as Sonny And Cher. Throughout this period Cher also sustained a solo career, initially singing a paeon to Ringo Starr ('Ringo I Love You') under the pseudonym Bonnie Jo Mason. Thereafter, she secured several hits, including an opportunistic cover of the Byrds' 'All I Really Want To Do'. The sultry 'Bang Bang', with its gypsy beat and maudlin violins was a worldwide smash in 1966, leading Cher to tackle more controversial themes in 'I Feel Something In The Air' and 'You Better Sit Down Kids'. Although her acting aspirations seemed long-forgotten, she did appear in two minor 60s films, one with Sonny, *Good Times* (1967), and her solo debut *Chastity* (1969).

In 1971, the zestful, chart-topping 'Gypsies, Tramps And Thieves' and its attendant album saw her back in the ascendant. Two further US number 1 hits ('Half Breed' and 'Dark Lady') preceded her divorce from Sonny, though for a time the duo continued to appear together on stage and television. In 1975, she switched to Warner Brothers Records for the Jimmy Webb-produced *Stars*, while her on-off relationship with Gregg Allman (whom she divorced in 1979) resulted in one album, the punningly titled, *Allman And Woman: Two The Hard Way*. By the late 70s, she became a regular fixture in gossip columns and fashion magazines which lauded over her sartorial outrageousness and much-publicized musical and personal relationships with Allman, Gene Simmons (of Kiss) and Les Dudek.

In 1981, Cher appeared on Meat Loaf's 'Dead Ringer For Love' but recording interests increasingly took a back seat to her first love: acting. A leading role in *Come Back To The Five And Dime, Jimmy Dean, Jimmy Dean* (1982) was followed by a lucrative part in *Silkwood* (1983), and an Oscar nomination. Appearances in *Mask* (1985), *The Witches Of Eastwick* (1987) and *Suspect* (1987) emphasized that her thespian aspirations were no mere sideline. For *Moonstruck* (1987), she won an Oscar for Best Actress and celebrated that honour with another musical comeback courtesy of *Cher* and its concomitant Top 10 single, 'I Found Someone'. Her 1991 number 1 hit, a cover of the Betty Everett song, 'The Shoop Shoop Song (It's In His Kiss)' was the theme song to another screen appearance, *Mermaids*. In 1995 she did a credible cover of Marc Cohn's 'Walking In Memphis' which preceded *It's A Man's World*. In addition to the James Brown title track her voice admirably suited a reworking of the Walker Brothers classic 'The Sun Ain't Gonna Shine Anymore'. With her professional life as a singer and actress now scrutinised by the mass media, as well as the added attraction of her love-life and public fascination for her penchant for cosmetic surgery, Cher has become one of the great American icons of the 90s. Her powerful voice is often overlooked amidst the AOR glitz.

●ALBUMS: *All I Really Want To Do* (Liberty 1965)★★, *The Sonny Side Of Cher* (Liberty 1966)★★, *Cher* i (Imperial 1966)★★★, *With Love, Cher* (Imperial 1968)★★, *Backstage* (1968)★★, *3614 Jackson Highway* (Atco 1969)★★, *Gypsies, Tramps And Thieves* (Kapp 1971)★★★, *Foxy Lady* (Kapp 1972)★★, *Half Breed* (MCA 1973)★★, *Dark Lady* (MCA 1974)★★, *Bittersweet White Light* (MCA 1974)★★, *Stars* (Warners 1975)★★, *I'd Rather Believe In You* (1976)★★, *Allman And Woman: Two The Hard Way* (Warners 1977)★★, *Take Me Home* (Casablanca 1979)★★, *Prisoner* (Casablanca 1980)★★, *Black Rose* (1980)★★, *I Paralyze* (Columbia 1982)★★, *Cher* ii (Geffen 1987)★★, *Heart Of Stone* (Geffen 1989)★★, *Love Hurts* (Geffen 1991)★★★, *It's A Man's World* (Warners 1995)★★★.

●COMPILATIONS: *Cher's Golden Greats* (Imperial 1968)★★, *The Best Of Cher* 60s recordings (EMI America 1991)★★★, *Sonny And Cher Collection: An Anthology Of Their Hits Alone And Together* (1991)★★★, *Greatest Hits* (Geffen 1992)★★★.

●VIDEOS: *Extravaganza - Live At The Mirage* (1992).

●FURTHER READING: *Cher*, J. Randy Taraborrelli. *Totally Uninhibited: The Life & Times Of Cher*, Lawrence J. Quirk. *Cher: In Her Own Words*, Nigel Goodall. *Cher: The Visual Documentary*, Mick St. Michael.

CHERRY, DON (TRUMPET)

b. 18 November 1936, Oklahoma City, Oklahoma, USA, d. 19 October 1995. Cherry began playing trumpet while still attending high school in Los Angeles, where he was raised. He also played piano and some of his first public performances were on this instrument when he worked in R&B bands. An early musical associate was Billy Higgins and in the mid-50s the two men, by then playing bebop, joined Ornette Coleman and began to adapt their musical thought to the new concept of free jazz. Cherry and Higgins played on Coleman's 1958 quintet album, *Something Else!!!!*, an album that represents an early and important flowering of the freedom principle. Coleman's group became a quartet, the fourth member being Charlie Haden. The quartet's success was recognized by an extended engagement at New York's Five Spot Cafe which began in November 1959 and continued into the following spring when Higgins was replaced by Ed Blackwell. Later, Haden too was succeeded by Scott La Faro and then Jimmy Garrison. The group made several important albums, which established the concept of free jazz as a major 60s movement in jazz and also demonstrated the qualities of the individual musicians. During this same period, Cherry recorded with John Coltrane and with Archie Shepp, in whose group he played alongside John Tchicai and Bill Dixon. In 1964 Cherry and Tchicai joined Albert Ayler's group for a recording session which was later used as soundtrack for the film, *New York Eye And Ear Control*. Later that year Cherry visited Europe with Ayler and also recorded *Vibrations* with him. Cherry's next association was with Gato Barbieri, with whom he led a small band which toured and recorded in Europe and the USA. While in Europe, he also worked with George Russell. Towards the end of the decade, Cherry began touring Europe, Africa and Asia, absorbing ethnic musical concepts and learning to play a variety of instruments including wooden flutes from northern Europe and the doussn'gouni (a kind of guitar). He was also using a Pakistani pocket trumpet with a distorted mouthpiece, an instrument which he favoured in much of his subsequent work. He began to adapt Asian ideas and sounds into his own music, becoming one of the few jazz musicians to do so successfully. By the early 70s, Cherry, who was then living in Sweden with his wife, Moki, was the most authoritative voice in the development of a musical style that was eventually established as 'world music'. Together with his wife, he created performances that depended almost as much upon visual and other senses as upon sounds. In the mid-70s Cherry again teamed up with Haden and Blackwell and, with Dewey Redman, formed a quartet that created new concepts of Coleman's music alongside original material. This group, which took its name, Old And New Dreams, from the title of its first album, was only one of Cherry's musical ventures of the late 70s and early 80s. He also played with rock bands, guested with Abdullah Ibrahim and formed a trio, Codona, with Collin Walcott and Nana Vasconcelos. His continued association with Blackwell, himself a gatherer of musical concepts and instruments, added to Cherry's status as a major figure in world music in the late 80s and early 90s. In his trumpet playing, especially on the pocket trumpet, Cherry might not have dazzled in the manner of many of his contemporaries who remained more closely linked to bop, but he nevertheless achieved a bright, incisive sound. As a composer, both in the formal sense of that term and in the manner in which he created musical happenings, Cherry was one of the most distinctive contributors to stretching the boundaries of contemporary music.

●ALBUMS: *Complete Communion* (Blue Note 1965)★★★, *Where Is Brooklyn?* (Blue Note 1966)★★★, *Live At The Montmartre Vols 1* and *2* (Magnetic 1966)★★★, *Eternal Rhythm* (1968)★★★, with Charlie Haden *Liberation Music Orchestra* (1969)★★★, *Human Music* (1969-70)★★★, *Mu* (Affinity 1970)★★★★, *Orient* (Affinity 1973)★★★, *Eternal Now* (Sonet 1973)★★, *Hear And Now* (Atlantic 1976)★★, *Brown Rice* (1976)★★★, *Live In Ankara* rec. 1969 (Sonet 1978)★★★, as Codona *Codona i* (ECM 1980)★★★, with Ed Blackwell *El Corazón* (ECM 1982)★★★, *Codona ii* (ECM 1982)★★★, *Codona iii* (ECM 1983)★★★, *Home Boy* (Decca 1985)★★, *A Tribute To Blackwell* (1987)★★★, *Art Deco* (A&M 1988)★★★, *Multikulti* (A&M 1990)★★★★, *Dona Nostra* (ECM 1994)★★★.

CHIEFTAINS

The original Chieftains line-up - Paddy Moloney (b. 1938, Donnycarney, Dublin, Eire; uilleann pipes/tin whistle), Sean Potts (b. 1930; tin whistle/bodhran), Michael Tubridy (b. 1935; flute/concertina/whistle) and Martin Fay (b. 1936; fiddle) - met in the late 50s as members of Ceolteoiri Chaulann, a folk orchestra led by by Sean O'Raida. The quartet's first album on the Claddagh label, *Chieftains 1*, released in 1964, introduced their skilled interpretations of traditional Celtic tunes. However the group chose to remain semi-professional, and further recordings were sporadic. Despite their low-key approach, the Chieftains became established as leading exponents of Irish music. Newcomers Sean Keane (b. 1946; fiddle/whistle), Peadar Mercier (b. 1914; bodhran/bones) and Derek Bell (b. 1935; harp/dulcimer/oboe) augmented the line-up which, by *Chieftains 4*, had become a popular attraction in Britain. The group then became a full-time venture and began an association with folk entrepreneur Jo Lustig. *Chieftains 5* marked their debut with a major outlet, Island Records, and the unit was feted by rock aristocrats Mick Jagger, Eric Clapton and Emmylou Harris. They were featured on Mike Oldfield's *Ommadawn* album and contributed to the soundtrack of Stanley Kubrick's film, *Barry Lyndon* (1975). In 1976 Mercier was replaced by Kevin Conneff (b. Dublin, Eire) and later in 1979, former Bothy Band and Planxty member Matt Molloy (b. Ballaghaderreen, Co. Roscommon, Eire; flute) joined the ranks. Moloney's skilled arrangements allowed the group to retain its freshness despite the many changes in personnel. During the 80s the group continued their enchanting direction and provided two further film soundtracks plus collaborations with the popular classical flute player, James Galway. However this period is better marked by *Irish Heartbeat*, their superb 1988 collaboration with singer Van Morrison. In the 90s the band found favour in the USA and both the *New York Post* and *LA Times* made *The Long Black Veil* albums of the year (1995). *The Bells Of Dublin* featured participation from Rickie Lee Jones, Elvis Costello, Nanci Griffith, Jackson Browne and Marianne Faithfull.

● ALBUMS: *Chieftains 1* (Claddagh 1964)★★★, *Chieftains 2* (Claddagh 1969)★★★, *Chieftains 3* (Claddagh 1971)★★★, *Chieftains 4* (Claddagh 1973)★★★★, *Chieftains 5* (Island 1975)★★★, *Women Of Ireland* (Island 1976)★★★, *Bonaparte's Retreat* (Columbia 1976)★★★, *Chieftains Live* (Columbia 1977)★★★, *Chieftains 7* (Claddagh 1977)★★★, *Chieftains 8* (Columbia 1978)★★★, *Vol. 9* (Claddagh 1979)★★★, *Boil The Breakfast Early* (Columbia 1980)★★★★, *Chieftains 10* (Claddagh 1981)★★★, *Year Of The French* original soundtrack (Claddagh 1983)★★★, *The Chieftains In China* (Shanachie 1984)★★★, *Ballad Of The Irish Horse* soundtrack (Shanachie 1985)★★★, *Celtic Wedding* (RCA 1987)★★★, with James Galway *The Chieftains In Ireland* (RCA 1987)★★★, with Van Morrison *Irish Heartbeat* (Mercury 1988)★★★, *A Chieftains Celebration* (RCA 1989)★★★★, *The Celtic Connection - James Galway And The Chieftains* (1990)★★★, *Bells Of Dublin* (RCA 1991)★★★★, *An Irish Evening: Live At The Grand Opera House, Belfast* (RCA 1992)★★★, *Another Country* (1992)★★★, with the Belfast Harp Orchestra *The Celtic Harp* (1993)★★★, *The Long Black Veil* (RCA 1995)★★★★, *The Bells Of Dublin* (RCA Victor 1995)★★★★, *Film Cuts* (RCA Victor 1996)★★★, *Santiago* (RCA Victor 1996)★★★.

● COMPILATIONS: *Chieftains Collection* (1989)★★★★, *The Best Of The Chieftains* (Columbia 1992)★★★, Sean Keane, Matt Molloy And Liam O'Flynn *The Fire Aflame* (1993)★★★.

● VIDEOS: *Live In China* (1991), *An Irish Evening* (1992).

CHINA CRISIS

This UK, Liverpool-based group was formed in 1979 around the core of Gary Daly (b. 5 May 1962, Kirkby, Merseyside, England; vocals) and Eddie Lundon (b. 9 June 1962, Kirkby, Merseyside, England; guitar). In 1982, their first single, 'African And White', initially on the independent Inevitable label, was picked up for distribution by Virgin Records and made a critical impact, despite only just breaking into the UK Top 50. The single's b-side was 'Red Sails', a perfect early example of China Crisis's pastoral electro-pop. Having now signed to the Virgin label, the duo formed a more permanent line-up with the recruitment of Gazza Johnson (bass) and Kevin Wilkinson (drums). The following single, 'Christian', taken from the debut album *Difficult Shapes And Passive Rhythms* was a UK number 12 hit. With the follow-up to their second album, they had two further Top 50 hits with 'Tragedy And Mystery' and 'Working With Fire And Steel', the former featuring the trademark on the forthcoming album - the ethereal oboe accompaniment. 'Wishful Thinking' in 1984 gave the group a Top 10 hit, while the following year gave them two further Top 20 hits with 'Black Man Ray' and 'King In A Catholic Style (Wake Up)'. While *Flaunt The Imperfection*, produced by Walter Becker, reached the UK Top 10, the follow-up, the uneven *What Price Paradise?* (produced by Clive Langer and Alan Winstanley), saw a drop in China Crisis's fortunes, when the album peaked at number 63. A two-year hiatus saw a reunion with Becker which resulted in the critically acclaimed *Diary Of A Hollow Horse*, although this success was not reflected in sales. Since their split with Virgin and the release of a deserved reappraisal of the group's career with a compilation in 1990, activities within the China Crisis camp have been low-key.

●ALBUMS: *Difficult Shapes And Passive Rhythms* (Virgin 1983)★★★, *Working With Fire And Steel - Possible Pop Songs Volume Two* (Virgin 1983)★★★, *Flaunt The Imperfection* (Virgin 1985)★★★, *What Price Paradise?* (Virgin 1986)★★, *Diary Of A Hollow Horse* (Virgin 1989)★★★, *Warped By Success* (Stardumb 1994)★★★, *Acoustically Yours* (Telegraph 1995)★★.

●COMPILATIONS: *The China Crisis Collection* (Virgin 1990)★★★, *China Crisis Diary* (1992)★★★.

●VIDEOS: *Showbiz Absurd* (90s).

CHRIS AND COSEY

Chris Carter and Cosey Fanni Tutti (b. Christine Newby) became partners while with late 70s 'industrial' sound pioneers, Throbbing Gristle. When the latter split in 1981, the couple decided to operate both as Chris And Cosey and as CTI (Creative Technology Institute). Their debut album, *Heartbeat*, credited to CTI, drew from Throbbing Gristle's rhythmic undercurrents, but the pair's next collection, *Trance*, was soured by a disagreement with Rough Trade Records over its selling price. 1983 yielded two singles, the Japanese-only 'Nikki' (a collaboration with John Duncan) and the relatively mainstream 'October (Love Song)'. These were followed in 1984 by *Songs Of Love And Lust*. That year the duo also issued *Elemental 7* in collaboration with John Lacey on Cabaret Voltaire's Doublevision label and further projects, as CTI, with Lustmord's Brian Williams and Glenn Wallis of Konstructivitis. These projects were also accompanied by *European Rendezvous*. CTI's *Mondo Beat*, released in 1985, was originally conceived by Chris as a 12-inch single, but expanded beyond that format. By this time, the pair's relationship with Rough Trade had become strained and they left after *Techno Primitiv* and 'Sweet Surprise', a project with the Eurythmics. They then joined Vancouver label Nettwerk Productions, while in Europe they were handled by renowned Brussels label, Play It Again Sam (who have also reissued much of their product). Since then, Chris And Cosey have gradually steered towards the 'New Beat' dance sound, with singles such as 'Obsession', 'Exotica' (both 1987)

and 'Rise' (1989). Early 90s albums *Reflection* and *Pagan Tango*, confirmed their adoption of hi-tech dance music.

●ALBUMS: *Heartbeat* (Rough Trade 1981)★★, *Trance* (Rough Trade 1982)★★, *Songs Of Love And Lust* (Rough Trade 1984)★★★, *Elemental 7* (Rough Trade 1984)★★★, *European Rendezvous* (Doublevision 1984)★★★, *Techno Primitiv* (Rough Trade 1985)★★, *Action* (Licensed 1987)★★★, *Exotica* (Nettwerk 1987)★★★, *Trust* (Play It Again Sam 1989)★★★, *Reflection* (Play It Again Sam 1990)★★★, *Pagan Tango* (Play It Again Sam 1991)★★★, *Muzik Fantastique* (Play It Again Sam 1992)★★★.

●COMPILATIONS: *Best Of Chris And Cosey* (Play It Again Sam 1989)★★★, *Collectiv 1, 2, 3, & 4* (Play It Again Sam 1990)★★★.

CHRISTIAN DEATH

This incredibly prolific art-rock group were formed in Los Angeles, California, USA, in 1979 by singer Rozz Williams. The original line-up additionally comprised Rikk Agnew (guitar, ex-Adolescents), James McGearly (bass) and George Belanger (drums), but afterwards the group's composition would fluctuate rapidly. In finding success in their homeland elusive, the group relocated to Europe in 1983, where they fitted in perfectly with the gothic rock fashion. Shunning the easy route to success, the band have since remained on the periphery of rock, and Christian Death's independence from prevailing trends has secured themselves a strong cult following, if little commercial or critical recognition. In 1986 the group fell under the control of songwriter and singer Valor Kand (b. Australia), who made radical changes to the line-up. Principal members now included Gitane Demone (vocals/keyboards) and David Glass (drums). Their often provocative material made as its principal target grand passion and organised religion, particularly that of Catholicism, citing corruption in the church and links with politicians. Album cover artwork, such as that which bedecked *Sex, Drugs And Jesus Christ*, depicting a Christ-like figure injecting heroin, caused a suitable furore of publicity and controversy; similarly with *All The Hate*'s 'poignant' use of swastika imagery. Despite the attention-seeking nature of some of their product, their vast discography has rarely risen above such crude devices. It is complicated, too, by the fact that during the 90s there have been at least two bands operating under the same banner, resulting in all manner of litigation and dubious album issues.

●ALBUMS: *Only Theatre Of Pain* (Frontier 1982)★★★, *Catastrophe Ballet* (L'Invitation Au Suicide 1984)★★, *Ashes* (Nostradamus 1985)★★★, *The Decomposition Of Violets* cassette only (ROIR 1986)★★, *Anthology Of Live Bootlegs* (Nostradamus 1986)★★, *Atrocities* (Normal 1986)★★, *Scriptures* (Jungle 1987)★★★, *Sex, Drugs And Jesus Christ* (Jungle 1988)★★★, *The Heretics Alive* (Jungle 1989)★★, *All The Love* (Jungle 1989)★★★, *All The Hate* (Jungle 1989)★★★, *Insanus, Ultio, Proditio Misericordiaque* (Supporti Fonografici 1990)★★, *Love And Hate* (Jungle 1992)★★, *Iconolgia: Apparitions, Dreams And Nightmares* live recording (Triple X 1993)★★, *Sleepless Nights* live recording (Cleopatra 1993)★★, *Invocations: 1981-1989* live recording (Cleopatra 1993)★, *The Doll's Theatre* live recording (Cleopatra 1994)★, *Sexy Death God* (Bullet Proof 1994)★★★, *The Rage Of Angels* (Cleopatra 1994)★★★, *Death In Detroit* (Cleopatra 1995)★★.

●COMPILATIONS: *The Wind Kissed Pictures (Past And Present)* (Supporti Fonografici 1988)★★, *The Wind Kissed Pictures (Past, Present And Future)* (Supporti Fonografici 1990)★★, *Jesus Points The Bone At You* singles collection from 1986-90 (Jungle 1992)★★★, *Tales Of Innocence: A Continued Anthology* (Cleopatra 1994)★★★.

CHRISTIANS

This UK group was formed in Liverpool in 1984 and comprised former Yachts and It's Immaterial keyboard player Henry Priestman (b. 21 June 1955, Hull, Humberside, England) and the Christian brothers Roger (b. 13 February 1950, Merseyside, England), Garry (b. Garrison Christian, 27 February 1955, Merseyside, England) and Russell (b. 8 July 1956, Merseyside, England). Up until then, the brothers, who came from a family of 11, with a Jamaican immigrant father and Liverpudlian mother, had performed as a soul a cappella trio and had previously worked under a variety of names, most notably as Natural High when they made an appearance on UK Television's *Opportunity Knocks* talent show in 1974. The Christian brothers met Priestman, who became the group's main songwriter, at Pete Wylie's Liverpool studios, where Priestman convinced the trio to try recording his compositions. The resulting demo session tapes eventually led to the Christians signing to Island Records. The group's combination of pop and soul earned the group a string of UK hits including, in 1987, 'Forgotten Town', 'Hooverville (They Promised Us The World)', 'When The Fingers Point' and 'Ideal World'. The

media usually focused their attention on the striking appearance of the tall, shaven-headed Garry. This, and a reluctance to tour, led to Roger quitting the group in 1987. The Christians' self-titled album meanwhile, would become Island's best-selling debut. With the exception of the Top 30 hit 'Born Again' in the spring, 1988 was much quieter with the group touring and recording. The year was brought to a climax, however, with the Top 10 cover of the Isley Brothers hit, 'Harvest For The World'. The Hillsborough football crowd disaster in April 1989, resulted in them being given joint credit on the charity single 'Ferry Across The Mersey' with Paul McCartney, Gerry Marsden, Holly Johnson and Stock, Aitken And Waterman. In 1989, Roger Christian released a solo single 'Take It From Me' achieving a minor UK hit (number 63), plus a well-received album, *Roger Christian*, which did not chart. The Christians' only hit that year came with the the the Top 20 'Words'. The labours over recording the second album, *Colours*, paid off when it hit the UK number 1 spot on its first week in the chart. Despite subsequent singles failing to break into the Top 50, the group have established a mature fan-base.

●ALBUMS: *The Christians* (Island 1987)★★★★, *Colours* (Island 1990)★★★, *Happy In Hell* (Island 1992)★★★.

●VIDEOS: *The Best Of ...* (Island 1993)★★★★.

CHRON GEN

The name an abbreviation of 'chronic generation', this early 80s, third generation UK punk band, ranked only below the Exploited, Vice Squad and Discharge in popularity. More melodic than the vast majority of their peers, Chron Gen earned early comparisons to the Buzzcocks, though they never really justified such heady praise. The band was originally formed as the Condemned in 1977 in Hitchin, Hertfordshire, England. At this time Glynn Baxter (guitar/vocals) and John Johnson (drums) were still at school, and they were joined by bass player Adam in the formative line-up. The early repertoire consisted of ramshackle versions of old Sex Pistols and Ramones' standards, and Adam was soon replaced by Pete Dimmock, before Jon Thurlow was drafted in on rhythm guitar to complete the band's enduring line-up. While frontman Baxter's lyrics were fuelled by a life on the dole, his fellow guitarist, Thurlow, actually admitted to a job as a civil servant. The group made their debut with the *Puppets Of War* EP, a spirited four-tracker where the production partially deprived the band of their live punch. Released initially on the group's own Gargoyle label, the record sold out of its 1000 pressing and was picked up for wider distribution by Fresh Records. Following national exposure on the infamous Apocalypse Now tour (with the Exploited, Anti-Pasti, etc.), it rose into the Top 5 of *Sounds* music paper's Alternative Chart. *Sounds*, with its coverage of both the Oi! and new punk movements, remained the band's only real advocates within the mainstream. Chron Gen then lost many of their new-found supporters with a debut album that was an unfocused, patchy affair. The promise of songs such as 'Hound Of The Night' was tempered by the lack of power and studio skill employed elsewhere, and Chron Gen never really recovered from the blow. They soldiered on for a couple of years, but to diminishing rewards.

●ALBUMS: *Chronic Generation* (Secret 1982)★★, *Nowhere To Run* (Picasso 1985)★★.
●COMPILATIONS: *The Best Of ...* (Captain Oi! 1994)★★★.

CHURCH

Formed in Canberra, Australia, in 1980, the Church, led by Steven Kilbey (b. *c*.1960, England; bass/vocals), who emigrated with his family at an early age, comprised Peter Koppes (b. Australia; guitar/vocals), Marty Willson-Piper (b. England; guitar/vocals) and Nick Ward (drums). Richard Ploog (b. Australia; drums) would replace the latter after the completion of the group's debut album. That release came in 1981, when *Of Skins And Heart* gained some radio and television exposure. The European release, *The Church*, which included stand-out cut 'The Unguarded Moment' (with its accompanying early pixelated image effect video) gave indications of great promise. The Church's 60s/Byrds revivalist stance, coupled with a distinctive 12-stringed 'jangly' guitar approach was exemplified on *The Blurred Crusade* by such songs as 'Almost With You', 'When You Were Mine' and 'Fields Of Mars'. *Starfish* saw the band gain college radio airplay in the USA, earning them a US Top 30 hit with 'Under The Milky Way', and strengthened their audiences in parts of Europe - although generally the group found themselves restricted to a loyal cult following. Much of the group's activities have been interrupted periodically due to internal problems and for solo projects and collaborations. Ploog's departure in 1991 saw the addition of former Patti Smith and Television drummer, Jay Dee Daugherty. Willson-Piper released two solo albums and took on a part-time role as guitarist for All About Eve in 1991. Kilbey has recorded several

albums as well as publishing a book of poems. In 1991 he teamed up with Go-Betweens guitarist Grant McLennan under the name of Jack Frost and they recorded a self-titled album for Arista Records in 1991. Peter Koppes completed an EP, *When Reason Forbids*, in 1987, before embarking on his own sequence of album releases. Kilbey and McLennan made a second Jack Frost album, *Snow Job*, released by Beggars Banquet Records in 1996.

●ALBUMS: *Of Skins & Heart* (Parlophone 1981)★★, *The Church* (Carrere 1982)★★★, *Blurred Crusade* (Carrere 1982)★★★, *Seance* (Carrere 1983)★★★, *Remote Luxury* (Warners 1984)★★★★, *Heyday* (Warners 1986)★★★, *Starfish* (Arista 1988)★★★, *Gold Afternoon Fix* (Arista 1990)★★★★, *Priest = Aura* (Arista 1992)★★★, *Sometime Anywhere* (Arista 1994)★★★, *Magician Among The Spirits* (Deep Karma 1996)★★★. Solo: Marty Willson-Piper *In Reflection* (Chase 1987)★★★, *Art Attack Survival* (Rykodisc 1988)★★★, *Rhyme* (Rykodisc 1989)★★★. Peter Koppes *Manchild & Myth* (Rykodisc 1988)★★★, *From The Well* (TVT 1989)★★★. Steve Kilbey *Unearthed* (Enigma 1987)★★★, *Earthed* (Rykodisc 1988)★★★, *The Slow Crack* (Red Eye 1988)★★★, *Remindlessness* (Red Eye 1990)★★★.
●COMPILATIONS: *Conception* (Carrerre 1988)★★★, *Hindsight* (EMI 1988)★★★, *A Quick Smoke At Spots (Archives 1986-1990)* (Arista 1991)★★★, *Almost Yesterday 1981-1990* (Raven 1995)★★★★.
●VIDEOS: *Goldfish (Jokes, Magic and Souvenirs)* (1990).

CLANNAD

This group, from Gweedore in Co. Donegal, Eire, have successfully crossed the bridge between folk and rock. The line-up consists of Maire Brennan (b. Marie Ni Bhroanain, 4 August 1952, Dublin, Eire; harp/vocals), Pol Brennan (guitar/vocals/percussion/flute), Ciaran Brennan (guitar/ bass/vocals/keyboards), Padraig Duggan (guitar/vocals/mandolin) and Noel Duggan (guitar/vocals). They formed in 1970, playing at Leo's Tavern, run by Leo Brennan, a former showband musician, and father of the Brennan group members of Clannad. The word Clannad means 'family' in Gaelic, and the group formed initially to play folk festivals in Ireland. At the time, the line-up consisted of three of the Brennan children, and two of their uncles. The group's first successes came in Germany where they toured in 1975. Clannad initially caught the attention of the wider public in the UK when they recorded the theme tune for television's

Harry's Game in 1982. The single reached number 5 in the UK charts, and received an Ivor Novello Award. In 1984 they recorded the soundtrack to television's *Robin Of Sherwood* and reached the Top 50 in May the same year. The following year the song received a British Academy Award for best soundtrack. Further chart success followed with the 1986 UK Top 20 hit 'In A Lifetime', on which Maire duetted with Bono from U2. From their early days, despite establishing themselves into the rock mainstream, Clannad have always retained the Celtic quality in the music. Maire's sister, Enya (b. 17 May 1961, Eire), left the group in 1982 having joined in 1979, and pursued a successful solo career. Clannad, meanwhile, have not lost contact with their folk audience and continue to perform, although there can be little progression with such a distinctive, and therefore, hampered sound.

●ALBUMS: *Clannad* (Philips 1973)★★★, *Clannad 2* (Gael Linn 1974)★★★, *Dulaman* (Gael Linn 1974)★★★, *Clannad In Concert* (Ogham 1979)★★★, *Crann Ull* (Philips 1981)★★, *Fuaim* (Tara 1982)★★★★, *Magical Ring* (RCA 1983)★★★, *Legend* (RCA 1984)★★★, *Macalla* (RCA 1985)★★★, *Ring Of Gold* (Celtic Music 1986)★★★, *Sirius* (RCA 1987)★★, *Clannad In Concert* (Shanachie 1988)★★★, *Atlantic Realm* soundtrack (BBC 1989)★★★, with narration by Tom Conti *The Angel And The Soldier Boy* (RCA 1989)★★★, *Anam* (RCA 1990)★★★, *Banba* (RCA 1993)★★★, *Lore* (RCA 1996)★★★, *Lore/Themes* (RCA 1996)★★★.

●COMPILATIONS: *Clannad: The Collection* (K-Tel 1988)★★★, *Pastpresent* (RCA 1989)★★★, *Themes* (K-Tel 1993)★★★, *Back2Back* (RCA 1995)★★★.

●VIDEOS: *Past Present* (1989).

CLAPTON, ERIC

b. Eric Patrick Clapp, 30 March 1945, Ripley, Surrey, England. The world's premier living rock guitarist will be forever grateful to his grandparents, for it was they who bought him his first guitar. The young Eric was raised by his grandparents Rose and Jack Clapp after his natural mother could not face bringing up an illegitimate child at the age of 16. Eric received the £14 acoustic guitar for his 14th birthday, then proceeded to copy the great blues guitarists, note for note. His first band was the Roosters, a local R&B group whose members included Tom McGuinness, a future member of Manfred Mann, and latterly part of the Blues Band. Clapton stayed for eight months until he and McGuinness left to join Casey Jones And The Engineers. This brief sojourn ended in 1963 when Clapton was sought out by the Yardbirds, an aspiring R&B band, who needed a replacement for their guitarist Tony Topham. The reputation the Yardbirds swiftly built was largely centred on Clapton, who had already attained his nickname 'Slowhand' by the partisan crowd at Richmond's Crawdaddy club. Clapton stayed for 18 months until musical differences interfered. The Yardbirds were taking a more pop-orientated direction and Clapton just wanted to play the blues. He departed shortly after the recording of 'For Your Love'. The perfect vehicle for his frustrations was John Mayall's Bluesbreakers, one of Britain's top blues bands. It was with Mayall that Clapton earned a second nickname; 'God'! Rarely had there been such a meteoric rise to such an exalted position. Clapton only made one album with Mayall but the record is now a classic. *Bluesbreakers* shows Clapton on the now famous cover behind a copy of the *Beano* comic.

Between Mayall and his next band Clapton made numerous session appearances and an interesting recording session with a conglomeration called the Powerhouse. They recorded three tracks, 'Crossroads, 'I Want To Know' and 'Steppin' Out'. The line-up comprised; Paul Jones, Steve Winwood, Jack Bruce, Pete York and Clapton. He was elevated to superstar status with the formation of Cream in 1966 and together with ex-Graham Bond Organisation members, Jack Bruce and Ginger Baker, he created one of the most influential rock bands of our time. Additionally, as L'Angelo Mysterioso he played the beautiful lead solo on George Harrison's 'While My Guitar Gently Weeps' for the Beatles *The Beatles* ('The White Album'). Cream lasted just over two years, and shortly after their demise he was back again with Ginger Baker, this time as Blind Faith. The line-up was completed by Steve Winwood and Rick Grech. This 'supergroup' was unable to stay together for more than one self-titled album, although their financially lucrative American tour made the impending break-up easier to bear. During the tour Clapton befriended Delaney And Bonnie and decided he wanted to be their guitarist. He joined them before the sweat had dried, following his last Blind Faith gig in January 1970. He played on one album, *Delaney And Bonnie On Tour*, and three months later he had absconded with three of the former band to make the disappointing *Eric Clapton*. The band then metamorphized into Derek And The Dominos. This memorable unit, together with Duane Allman, recorded one of his most famous compositions: the perennial 'Layla'. This clandestine love song was directed at George

Harrison's wife Pattie, with whom Clapton had become besotted. George, unaware of this, invited Eric to play at his historic Bangla Desh Concert in August 1971. Clapton then struggled to overcome a heroin habit that had grown out of control, since being introduced to the drug during the recording of *Layla And Other Assorted Love Songs*. During the worst moments of his addiction he began to pawn some of his precious guitars and spent up to £1500 a week to feed his habit.

Pete Townshend of the Who was appalled to discover that Clapton was selling his guitars and proceeded to try to rescue Clapton and his girlfriend Alice Ormsby-Gore from certain death. Townshend organized the famous Eric Clapton At The Rainbow concert as part of his rehabilitation crusade, along with Steve Winwood, Rick Grech, Ron Wood and Jim Capaldi. His appearance broke two years of silence, and wearing the same suit he had worn at the Bangla Desh concert he played a majestic and emotional set. Although still addicted, this was to be the turning point in his life and following pleas from his girlfriend's father, Lord Harlech, he entered the famous Harley Street clinic home of Dr Meg Patterson for the initial treatment.

A rejuvenated Clapton began to record again and released the buoyant *461 Ocean Boulevard* in August 1974. The future pattern was set on this album; gone were the long guitar solos, replaced instead by relaxed vocals over shorter, more compact songs. The record was an incredible success, a number 1 hit in the US and number 3 in the UK. The singles drawn from it were also hits, notably his number 1 US hit with Bob Marley's 'I Shot The Sheriff'. Also included was the autobiographical message to himself, 'Give Me Strength' and the beautifully mantric 'Let It Flow'. Clapton ended 1974 on a high note, not only had he returned from the grave, but he had finally succeeded in winning the heart of Pattie Harrison.

During 1975 he maintained his drug-free existence, although he became dependent on alcohol. That same year he had further hits with *There's One In Every Crowd* and the live *E.C. Was Here*. Both maintained his reputation. Since then Clapton has continued to grow in stature. During 1977 and 1978 he released two further big-selling albums, *Slowhand* and *Backless*. Further single success came with the gentle 'Lay Down Sally' (co-written with Marcella Detroit, later of Shakespears Sister) and 'Promises', while other notable tracks were 'Wonderful Tonight', J.J. Cale's 'Cocaine', and John Martyn's 'May You Never'. Clapton had completely shrugged off his guitar hero persona and had now become an assured vocalist/songwriter, who, by chance, played guitar. A whole new audience, many of whom had never heard of the Yardbirds or Cream, saw Clapton as a clean, healthy individual with few vices, and no cobwebs in his attic. Clapton found additional time to play at the Band's historic *Last Waltz* concert.

The 80s have been even kinder to Clapton with every album selling vast quantities and being critically well-received. *Another Ticket* and *Money And Cigarettes*, which featured Ry Cooder, were particularly successful during the beginning of the 80s. *Behind The Sun* benefited from the firm production hand of Clapton's close friend Phil Collins. Collins played drums on his next album, *August*, which showed no signs of tiredness or lack of ideas. This particularly strong album contained the excellent hit 'Behind The Mask' and an exciting duet with Tina Turner on 'Tearing Us Apart'. Throughout the record Clapton's voice was in particularly fine form. *Journeyman* in 1989 went one better; not only were his voice and songs creditable but 'Slowhand' had discovered the guitar again. The album contains some of his finest playing. Not surprisingly it was a major success. Clapton has contributed to numerous artists' albums over many years, including; John Martyn, Phil Collins, Duane Allman, Marc Benno, Gary Brooker, Joe Cocker, Roger Daltrey, Jesse Davis, Dr. John (Mac Rebannack), Bob Dylan, Aretha Franklin, Rick Danko, Champion Jack Dupree, Howlin' Wolf, Sonny Boy Williamson, Freddie King, Alexis Korner, Ronnie Laine, Jackie Lomax, Christine McVie, the Mothers Of Invention, the Plastic Ono Band, Otis Spann, Vivian Stanshall, Stephen Stills, Ringo Starr, Leon Russell, Doris Troy, Roger Waters and many, many more. He also appeared as the Preacher in Ken Russell's film of Pete Townshend's rock-opera *Tommy*.

Clapton has enjoyed a high profile during the past few years with his touring, the Live Aid appearance, television documentaries, two biographies, and the now annual season of concerts at London's Royal Albert Hall. His 24 nights there in 1991 was a record. Such is his popularity that he could fill the Albert Hall every night for a year. As a final bonus to his many fans he plays three kinds of concerts, dividing the season with a series of blues nights, orchestral nights and regular nights. In the 90s Clapton's career went from strength to strength, although the tragic death of his son Conor in 1991 halted his career for some months. During December 1991 he toured Japan with George Harrison, giving Harrison the moral support that he had received more than a decade earlier. *Unplugged* in 1992 became one of his most successful albums (USA sales alone, by 1996 were 10 million copies). On this he demonstrated his blues roots, playing acoustically in relaxed circumstances with his band (including sterling support from Andy Fairweather-Low), Clapton oozed supreme confidence. The poignant 'Tears In Heaven', about the death of his son, was a major hit worldwide. *From The Cradle* was a worthy release, bringing him full circle in producing an electric blues album. Those guitar buffs who mourned his departure from Mayall and despaired when Cream called it a day could rejoice once again. God had returned. Clapton has already earned the title of the greatest white blues guitarist of our time, but he is now on the way to becoming one of the greatest rock artists of the era too. An encouraging thought for a man whose life had all but ended in 1973.

●ALBUMS: three tracks as the Powerhouse with Steve Winwood, Jack Bruce, Pete York, Paul Jones *What's Shakin'?* (Elektra 1966)★★★, *Eric Clapton* (Polydor 1970)★★★, *Eric Clapton's Rainbow Concert* (RSO 1973)★★★, *461 Ocean Boulevard* (RSO 1974)★★★★, *There's One In Every Crowd* (RSO 1975)★★★, *E.C. Was Here* (RSO 1975)★★, *No Reason To Cry* (RSO 1976)★★★, *Slowhand* (RSO 1977)★★★★, *Backless* (RSO 1978)★★★, *Just One Night* (RSO 1980)★★★, *Another Ticket* (RSO 1981)★★★, *Money And Cigarettes* (Duck 1983)★★★, *Behind The Sun* (Duck 1985)★★★, *August* (Duck 1986)★★★, with Michael Kamen *Homeboy* television soundtrack (Virgin 1989)★★, *Journeyman* (Duck 1989)★★★★, *24 Nights* (Duck 1991)★★, *Rush* film soundtrack (Reprise 1992)★★, *MTV Unplugged* (1992)★★★★, *From The Cradle* (Duck 1994)★★★.

●COMPILATIONS: *Time Pieces - The Best Of Eric Clapton* (RSO 1982)★★★, *Time Pieces Volume II: Live In The Seventies* (RSO 1983)★★★, *Backtrackin'* (Starblend 1984)★★★★, *Crossroads* 4-CD box set (Polydor 1988)★★★★★, *The Cream Of Eric Clapton* (Polydor 1989)★★★★, *The Magic Of ...* (1993)★★★, *Crossroads 2: Live In The 70s* (Polydor 1996)★★★★.

●VIDEOS: *Eric Clapton On Whistle Test* (1984), *Live At The NEC Birmingham* (1987), *Live 85* (1987), *Cream Of Eric Clapton* (1989), *Man And His Music* (1990), *Eric Clapton In Concert* (1991), *24 Nights* (1991).

●FURTHER READING: *Conversations With Eric Clapton*, Steve Turner. *Eric Clapton: A Biography*, John Pidgeon. *Survivor: The Authorized Biography*

Of Eric Clapton, Ray Coleman. *Clapton: The Complete Chronicle*, Marc Roberty. *Eric Clapton: The New Visual Documentary*, Marc Roberty. *Eric Clapton: Lost In The Blues*, Harry Shapiro. *Eric Clapton: The Complete Recording Sessions*, Marc Roberty. *The Man, The Music, The Memorabilia*, Marc Roberty. *Edge Of Darkness*, Christopher Sandford. *The Authorised Biography*, Ray Coleman. *The New Visual Documentary*, Marc Roberty. *Complete Guide To The Music Of*, Marc Roberty.

CLÁSICO, CONJUNTO

For over a decade, the New York salsa band, Conjunto Clásico, have managed to keep the traditional Cuban conjunto format of trumpets (three in their case), conga, bongo, maracas, güiro (scraper), bass, piano, tres (six or nine-string Cuban guitar) and voices, sounding modern and fresh. The nucleus of the band has been executive producer/chorus singer/percussionist Raymond Castro and composer/producer/chorus singer/percussionist Ramón Rodríguez. Between 1979 and 1990, Clásico released 11 albums on their own Lo Mejor Records label. After the bands' 1986 album, lead singer and founder-member Tito Nieves left to pursue a solo career. He was replaced by ex-Grupo Fascinación lead vocalist, Johnny Rivera, on Clásico's 1988 and 1989 albums. He too departed and made his solo debut in 1990 with *Y Ahora De Verdad*.

Prior to Conjunto Clásico's formation, Ramón Rodríguez had produced the 1979 debut album by Julio Castro and his Orquesta La Masacre, with Tito Nieves on lead vocals. Additionally he composed the hit track 'El Pregonero'. In 1988 and 1990 Rodríguez produced and wrote all the songs for *Nuevas Ideas* and *El Bautizo* by his own trombone-led band. 1990 saw the marriage of Clásico with the fine voice of Rafael de Jesús (see Luis 'Perico' Ortiz) on *Ray Castro Presenta Conjunto Clásico Con Rafael De Jesús - Sensaciones*, one of their best albums to date. José Febles replaced Rodríguez as producer and wrote all the charts. However, Ramón performed on the album and penned five tracks. Febles contributed arrangements to all Clásico's previous releases and was musical director on their 1979 and 1980 albums. Castro and Rodríguez also produced albums by other artists on their Lo Mejor label: *Lo Mejor Presenta: José Bello Y Su Orquesta* (1981), *Jose Bello Y Su Orquesta* (1983) and *Expresa E Interpreta Sus Sentimientos* (1984) by the young talented Dominican bandleader/singer/composer José Bello; *Cantar* (1981) by Tito Allen; *Daniel Santos con el Conjunto Clásico* (1981) by the veteran former heart-throb Daniel Santos (b. 6 June 1916, Tras Talleres, San Juan, Puerto Rico); *Con La Misma Piedra* (1983) by Cesar Nicolas y su Orquesta 'Show'; *El Encuentro* (1983) by Johnny 'Dandy' Rodríguez, former co-leader of Típica 73. Ramón Rodríguez, Ray Castro and Tito Nieves performed on all these Lo Mejor productions and Ramón contributed compositions to the majority of them. Bello returned in 1989 as co-label boss with *B&B Records presenta A José Bello*; Castro and Rodríguez sang in the chorus.

● ALBUMS: with Tito Nieves *Los Rodríguez* (1979)★★★, with Nieves *Felicitaciones* (1980)★★★, with Nieves *Si No Bailan Con Ellos, No Bailan Con Nadie* (1981)★★★, with Nieves *Clásicas de Clásico* (1982)★★★, with Nieves *Las Puertas Abiertas* (1983)★★★, with Nieves *El Panadero* (1985)★★★, with Nieves *Llego La Ley* (1985)★★★, with Nieves *Asi Es Mi Pueblo* (1986)★★★, with Johnny Rivera *Clásico '88* (1988)★★★, with Rivera *Mas Clásico Que Nunca* (1989)★★★, with Rafael de Jesús *Ray Castro Presenta Conjunto Clásico Con Rafael De Jesús - Sensaciones* (1990)★★★.

● COMPILATIONS: *Ray Castro Presenta ... Lo Mejor De Conjunto Clásico Con Tito Nieves* (1990)★★★.

CLASSIX NOUVEAUX

This 80s UK experimental quartet was fronted by the shaven-headed Sal Solo (b. 5 September 1954, Hatfield, Hertfordshire, England), whose uncompromising vocal style jelled uneasily with his musicians' synthesizer dance beat. Originally appearing on Stevo's Some Bizzare Records sample album, the group signed to Liberty Records in 1981 and recorded a series of albums, ranging from the gargantuan to the quirkily unmelodic. Four of their singles reached the UK Top 75 during 1981 and the following year they scored their biggest success with 'Is It A Dream' which climbed to number 11. Perpetually on the periphery, the group's limited chart success and affiliation with a major label did little to offset their determinedly *avant garde* approach. By the mid-80s, the unit folded with Sal going solo releasing *Heart And Soul* in 1985.

● ALBUMS: *Night People* (Liberty 1981)★★★, *La Verité* (Liberty 1982)★★★, *Secret* (Liberty 1983)★★★.

CLAYDERMAN, RICHARD

b. Philippe Pages, 1954, Paris, France. This highly popular pianist specializes in light classical compositions, with a romantic, yet low profile image. His father was a piano teacher, and at the age of 12, Clayderman enrolled at the Conservatoire in Paris,

and won the first prize four years later. He was encouraged to study classical piano, but his ambition was to be in a rock band. The dream was never realized, although in the 70s he did play with French pop stars such as Johnny Halliday and Michel Sardou. After working as a bank clerk, Clayderman was signed to the Delphine label, and had a hit in several European countries with 'Ballade Pour Adeline', which sold several million copies. He followed up with albums that contained show tunes, film themes and familiar classical pieces, with his relaxed, low-key piano playing cushioned by a large string orchestra.

In the early 80s he was reputed to be the top album seller in France, and in other countries such as South Africa and Japan. In 1982 he broke into the UK market with the number 2 hit album *Richard Clayderman* and, the following year, with the television-promoted *The Music Of Richard Clayderman*. In the same year he played his first sell-out UK concerts and appeared several times on television. By the early 90s his publicity machine was claiming album sales totalling 60 million worldwide, and plans to play to audiences of 120,000 in Japan, Brazil and Australia, but some of his 1990 UK concerts were less well attended. One of his 1991 albums, *Together At Last*, in collaboration with James Last, contained recent hits by Bryan Adams and Elton John.

● ALBUMS: many albums contain a mixture of new recordings and previously released tracks *Ballade Pour Adeline (The Love Song)* (Decca 1981)★★★, *Dreaming (Traumereien)* (IMS 1981)★★★, *Dreaming (Traumereien) 2* (Teldec 1981)★★★, *Dreaming (Traumereien) 3* (Teldec 1981)★★★, *Richard Clayderman* (Decca 1982)★★★, *A Comme Amour* (Teldec 1982)★★★, *Lettre A Ma Mere* (Teldec 1982)★★★, *Musiques De L'Amour* (Decca 1982)★★★, *The Music Of Richard Clayderman* (Decca 1983)★★★, *A Pleyel* (Delphine 1983)★★★, *Marriage Of Love* (Delphine 1984)★★★, *The Music Of Love* (Delphine 1984)★★★, *Christmas* (Decca 1984)★★, with the Royal Philharmonic *The Classic Touch* (Decca 1985)★★, *Hollywood And Broadway* (Delphine 1986)★★★, *Songs Of Love* (Decca 1987)★★★, *A Little Night Music* (Delphine 1988)★★★, *Eleana* (Delphine 1988)★★★, *The Love Songs Of Andrew Lloyd Webber* (Delphine 1989)★★, *My Classic Collection* (Delphine 1990)★★★, *Together At Last* (Delphine/Polydor 1991)★★★, *The Carpenters Collection* (Polygram 1995)★★★, *Mexico Con Amor* (Polygram 1996)★★.

● COMPILATIONS: *The Very Best Of ...* (Delphine 1992)★★★, *A Special Collection* CD set (Pickwick

1992)★★★.

●VIDEOS: *Richard Clayderman In Concert* (1988), *Richard Clayderman* (1989), *Richard Clayderman - Live In Concert* (1990).

CLINT EASTWOOD AND GENERAL SAINT

Jamaican born Eastwood (Trinity's younger brother) came to prominence with British reggae fans in the late 70s with a series of big-selling singles recorded in his home country, and albums such as *African Youth, Death In The Arena* and *Sex Education*. In the early 80s he teamed up with General Saint, who had already established a serious following working in London's Front Line International sound system, and the pair formed a talented pop reggae duo. Their first release, a tribute to the late General Echo, topped the reggae charts and the follow-up, 'Another One Bites The Dust', repeated the feat in 1981, reaching as far as the lower rungs of the national chart. Their subsequent records and live appearances enhanced their reputation further and they were instrumental in the Jamaican DJ style crossing over to the early 80s pop audience.

●ALBUMS: as Clint Eastwood *African Youth* (Third World 1978)★★★, *Death In The Arena* (Cha Cha 1978)★★★, *Love & Happiness* (Burning Sounds 1979)★★★, *Sex Education* (Greensleeves 1980)★★★, *Jah Lights Shining* (Vista Sounds 1984)★★★.

●COMPILATIONS: as Clint Eastwood *Best Of Clint Eastwood* (Culture Press 1984)★★★★, *Two Bad DJ* (Greensleeves 1981)★★★, *Stop That Train* (Greensleeves 1983)★★★.

CLINTON, GEORGE

b. 22 July 1941, Kannapolis, North Carolina, USA. The mastermind behind the highly successful Parliament(s) and Funkadelic, George 'Dr Funkenstein' Clinton's seemingly impregnable empire crumbled at the beginning of the 80s. Restrained from recording by a damaging breach-of-contract lawsuit and unable to meet the running expenses of his considerable organization, he found himself personally and professionally destitute. Clinton, nonetheless, tackled his problems. He settled most of his outstanding debts, overcame an addiction to freebase cocaine and resumed recording. An *ad hoc* group, the P. Funk All Stars, secured two minor hits with 'Hydrolic Pump' and 'One Of Those Summers' (both 1982), before the singer introduced a solo career with the magnificent 'Loopzilla', a rhythmic *tour de force* abounding

with references to black music past (the Supremes and the Four Tops), and present (Afrika Baambaataa's 'Planet Rock'). The ensuing album, *Computer Games*, featured several ex-Funkadelic/Parliament cohorts, including Bernie Worrell and Bootsy Collins, while a further track, 'Atomic Dog', was a US R&B number 1 single in 1983. Clinton then continued to work both as a soloist and with the P. Funk All Stars, pursuing his eclectic, eccentric vision on such innovatory albums as *Some Of My Best Jokes Are Friends* and *Cinderella Theory*. The latter was the first of a succession of recordings released on Prince's Paisley Park label. His *Hey Man ... Smell My Finger* set featured a cameo by ex-NWA artist Dr. Dre, who in turn invited Clinton to guest rap on 'You Don't Wanna See Me' from Dre's collaboration with Ice Cube, *Helter Skelter*. As Dre and many other recent American rappers confess, they owe a great debt to Clinton, not least for their liberal use of his music. Clinton was not one to complain, however, as the young guns' heavy use of Parliament and Funkadelic samples had helped him overcome a crippling tax debt in the early 80s. Ironically enough, Clinton too makes use of samples in his recent recordings, returning to his past ventures for beats, breaks and riffs as so many of his legion of admirers had done before him.

●ALBUMS: *Computer Games* (Capitol 1982)★★★, *You Shouldn't-Nuf Bit Fish* (Capitol 1984)★★★★, with the P. Funk All Stars *Urban Dance Floor Guerillas* (1984)★★★, *Some Of My Best Jokes Are Friends* (Capitol 1985)★★★★, *R&B Skeletons In The Closet* (Capitol 1986)★★★, *Cinderella Theory* (Paisley Park 1989)★★★, *Sample A Bit Of Disc And A Bit Of Dat* (AEM 1993)★★★, *Hey Man ... Smell My Finger* (Paisley Park 1993)★★★, *A Fifth Of Funk* (Castle Communications 1995)★★★, *The Music Of Red Shoe Diaries* (Wenerworld 1995)★★★, *Mortal Kombat* (London 1996)★★★, with the P. Funk All Stars *Tapoaform* (Epic 1996)★★★, *The Awesome Power Of A Fully Operational Mothership* (Epic 1996)★★★.

●COMPILATIONS: *The Best Of George Clinton* (Capitol 1986)★★★★, *Greatest Funkin' Hits* (Capitol 1996)★★★★.

●VIDEOS: *Mothership Connection* (1987).

CLOCK DVA

One of a batch of groups forming the so-called 'industrial' scene of Sheffield in the early 80s, Clock DVA's first release was, appropriately, on Throbbing Gristle's Industrial label. The cassette-only (until its re-release in 1990) *White Souls In*

Black Suits featured Adi Newton (vocals, ex-the Studs; the Future; Veer), Steven James Taylor (bass/vocals/guitar, ex-Block Opposite), Paul Widger (guitar, ex-They Must Be Russians), Roger Quail (drums) and Charlie Collins (saxophone). However, there had already been three previous line-ups, including guitarist Dave Hammond, and synthesizer players Joseph Hurst and Simon Elliot-Kemp. In 1981 the band offered *Thirst*, available through independent label Fetish. With the ground for such 'difficult music' having been prepared by Throbbing Gristle, the press reaction was remarkably favourable. Nevertheless, the band disintegrated at the end of the year. Newton kept the name while the other three joined the Box. By 1983, replacements were found in John Valentine Carruthers (guitar), Paul Browse (saxophone), Dean Dennis (bass) and Nick Sanderson (drums). A brace of singles prefaced *Advantage*, their first album for Polydor Records. The following year Carruthers and Sanderson departed and Clock DVA continued as a trio. Though it would be five years before a follow-up, Newton was kept busy with his visual project the Anti Group (TAGC), and several singles. *Buried Dreams* finally arrived in 1989. By the time of 1991's *Transitional Voices*, Browse had been replaced by Robert Baker, a veteran of TAGC. Newton has long since described the process of making music as his research: 'We feel music is something that should change and not remain too rigid, evolve with ourselves as we grow, change our perception' Although their recorded history is sparse, it represents a more thoughtful and reflective body of work than that which dominates their peer group. In particular, Newton's grasp of the philosophical connotations of technology have placed him apart from the majority of its practitioners.

●ALBUMS: *White Souls In Black Suits* cassette only (Industrial 1980)★★, *Thirst* (Fetish 1981)★★★, *Advantage* (Polydor 1983)★★★, *Buried Dreams* (Interfish 1989)★★★, *Transitional Voices* (Amphetamine Reptile 1991)★★★, *Man-Amplified* (Contempo 1992)★★★, *Digital Soundtrack* (Contempo 1993)★★★.

●VIDEOS: *Kinetic Engineering* (1994).

CLUB NOUVEAU

This disco act from Sacramento, California, USA, was formed by producer Jay King and comprised Valerie Watson, Denzil Foster, Thomas McElroy and Samuelle Prater. All bar Prater had previously been members of the Timex Social Club, a local vocal group. With Watson singing lead, a 1987 revival of Bill Withers' 'Lean On Me' - issued on King's own King Jay Records - climbed to number 1 in the USA and reached the Top 10 in most European countries. However, the follow-up, 'Why You Treat Me So Bad', was only a modest domestic hit. Some later singles made ripples regionally, but the replacement in 1988 of McElroy and Prater with David Agent and Kevin Irving failed to rekindle chartbusting enthusiasm for the the the group.

●ALBUMS: *Life, Love And Pain* (Warners 1986)★★★, *Listen To The Message* (Warners 1988)★★, *Under A Nouveau Groove* (Warners 1989)★★.

COCKNEY REJECTS

Discovered by Jimmy Pursey of Sham 69, this skinhead group came to the fore in London, England, in 1980 with an irreverent brand of proletarian-focused punk. The group comprised Jefferson Turner (vocals), Vince Riordan (bass/vocals), Micky Geggus (guitar/vocals) and Keith Warrington (drums). Daring and anti-everything, they were virtually a parody of the 'kick over the traces' punk attitude, while also betraying a stubborn parochialism in keeping with their group title. The 'anarchic' contents of their albums were reflected in their garishly tasteless record sleeves. Yet they had a certain subversive humour, titling their first two albums *Greatest Hits* when the sum of their UK Top 40 achievements rested with 'The Greatest Cockney Ripoff' at number 21 and the West Ham United football anthem, 'I'm Forever Blowing Bubbles', at number 35. On their second album they included the 'Oi! Oi! Oi!' song/chant, thereby giving birth to a musical genre which came to define the brash inarticulacy of skinhead politics. Their gigs during this time also became an interface for working-class culture and the extreme right, though just like Sham 69, the Rejects were judged guilty by default. By the time of 1982's *The Wild Ones* the group were veering away from their original punk influences towards heavy metal. Significantly, their new producer was UFO bassist Pete Way. Equally significantly, their career was well on the decline by this point. The group disbanded in 1985 but reformed to public apathy at the turn of the decade, *Lethal* hardly living up to its title.

●ALBUMS: *Greatest Hits Volume 1* (Zonophone 1980)★★★, *Greatest Hits Volume 2* (Zonophone 1980)★★★, *The Power And The Glory* (Zonophone 1981)★★, *The Wild Ones* (AKA 1982)★★★, *Rock The Wild Side* (Heavy Metal 1984)★★, *Lethal* (Neat

1990)★★.

●COMPILATIONS: *Unheard Rejects* early unreleased recordings (Wonderful World 1985)★, *We Are The Firm* (Dojo 1986)★★, *Greatest Hits Volume 3 (Live And Loud)* (Link 1987)★★.

COCTEAU TWINS

Formed in 1982 in Grangemouth, Scotland, the Cocteau Twins originally consisted of Elizabeth Fraser (b. 29 August 1958), Robin Guthrie and bass player Will Heggie. Able to convey an astonishing variety of moods and emotions, using words more for their sound than their meaning, Fraser's voice has become one of the most recognizable and imitated of the last two decades. The accompanying musical backdrop is assembled by Guthrie, using guitar, tape loops, echo boxes and drum machines, who formed the group with Heggie after seeing Fraser dancing at a disco. Demo tapes were passed to Ivo Watts-Russell, the owner of 4AD Records and his enthusiasm for the Cocteaus' music prompted the band's move to London to record for the label. The first album generated enormous interest and airplay from BBC Radio 1 disc jockey John Peel. *Garlands* was initially rather lazily compared to Siouxsie And The Banshees, but the Cocteau Twins soon began to carve out their own niche. By spring 1983, Heggie had departed (later to join Lowlife). *Head Over Heels* smoothed over the rougher edges of its predecessor with Guthrie adding layers of echo and phased drum effects that allowed Fraser's voice full rein. During this period the group were also involved in the 4AD label project, This Mortal Coil, for which Fraser and Guthrie's version of the Tim Buckley song, 'Song To the Siren', has since been acknowledged as one of the finest independent label recordings of the 80s. Simon Raymonde had by now been enrolled as bass player, eventually becoming a valuable asset in composing, arranging and production. The release of two superb EP collections, *Sunburst And Snowblind* and *Pearly-Dewdrops' Drops*, dominated the independent charts, with the latter broaching the UK Top 30. The Cocteaus' reluctance to reveal anything of their private lives or play the music business game won them respect from many quarters and annoyance from others. This did leave them, however, less able to counter the image imposed upon them by fans as fey, mystical creatures - in the interviews to which the band did acquiesce, the principals transpired as earthy, occasionally cantankerous and most definitely of this world. One benefit of their refusal to have their photographs taken for record sleeves was the superb cover art produced by the 23 Envelope studio, a presentational aspect utterly synonymous with their early career. The arrival of *Treasure* in 1984 saw the group scaling new heights, and over the next couple of years they released several EPs, *Aikea-Guinea*, *Tiny Dynamine* and *Echoes In A Shallow Bay*, each displaying rich, complex textures without ever repeating themselves. *Victorialand*, recorded without Raymonde, had a lighter, acoustic sound and featured Richard Thomas (saxophone/tablas) of 4AD stablemates Dif Juz. Raymonde returned for the *Love's Easy Tears* EP and the collaboration with Harold Budd in late 1986. *Blue Bell Knoll* seemed to confirm that the Cocteau Twins had lost their touch, but the emotional impact of the birth of Fraser and Guthrie's child revived their career on the stunning *Heaven Or Las Vegas*. The single 'Iceblink Luck' reached the UK Top 40 and the band started to tour again. In 1991 Guthrie continued with studio production work, notably with the 4AD group, Lush. The Cocteau Twins signed a new deal with Fontana Records in March 1992 and following work with a speech therapist, Fraser returned to recording and completed *Four-Calendar Café*. There were some surprises in store for the band's long-term fans - for the first time Fraser's lyrics were audible, and the band then released a Christmas single, 'Frosty The Snowman'. *Milk And Kisses* was recorded in Brittany and the group's own September Sound Studios in Twickenham, and was preceded by two EP releases, the 'ambient' *Otherness* (recorded with Mark Clifford of Seefeel) and the 'acoustic' *Twinlights*. The latter was accompanied by the group's first film short.

●ALBUMS: *Garlands* (4AD 1982)★★★, *Head Over Heels* (4AD 1983)★★★, *Treasure* (4AD 1984)★★★, *Victorialand* (4AD 1986)★★★, with Harold Budd, Elizabeth Fraser, Robin Guthrie, Simon Raymonde *The Moon And The Melodies* (4AD 1986)★★★, *Blue Bell Knoll* (4AD 1988)★★, *Heaven Or Las Vegas* (4AD 1990)★★★★, *Four-Calendar Café* (Fontana 1993)★★★, *Milk And Kisses* (Fontana 1996)★★★.

●COMPILATIONS: *The Pink Opaque* (4AD 1986)★★★, *The Singles Collection* (Capitol 1991)★★★.

COLE, LLOYD

b. 31 January 1961, Buxton, Derbyshire, England. Despite his birthplace, this literate singer-songwriter emerged from Glasgow's post-punk renaissance. The Commotions, Neil Clark (b. 3 July 1955; guitar), Blair Cowan (keyboards), Lawrence Donegan (b. 13 July 1961; bass) and Stephen Irvine (b. 16 December 1959; drums) completed the line-up responsible for *Rattlesnakes*, a critically lauded set which merged Byrds-like guitar figures to Cole's languid, Lou Reed-inspired intonation. A representative selection from the album, 'Perfect Skin', reached the UK Top 30 when issued as a single, while a follow-up album, *Easy Pieces*, spawned two Top 20 entries in 'Brand New Friend' and 'Lost Weekend'. However, the style that came so easily on these early outings seemed laboured on *Mainstream*, after which Cole disbanded his group. Retaining Cowan, he switched bases to New York, and emphasized the infatuation with Lou Reed's music by recruiting sidemen Robert Quine (guitar) and Fred Maher (drums), the latter of whom also acted as producer. *Lloyd Cole* showed signs of an artistic rejuvenation, but Cole was yet to stamp a wholly original persona and capitalize on his undoubted talent. Both *Don't Get Weird On Me, Babe* and *Bad Vibes* failed to lift the atmosphere of bookish lyrics rendered without the requisite soul, but neither were these collections without merit. Instead the listener was once again left to reminisce about the power of writing and performance that coalesced on tracks like 'Down On Mission Street' and 'Forest Fire' from the artist's debut.

●ALBUMS: with the Commotions *Rattlesnakes* (Polydor 1984)★★★★, with the Commotions *Easy Pieces* (Polydor 1985)★★★, with the Commotions *Mainstream* (Polydor 1987)★★★, *Lloyd Cole* (Polydor 1989)★★★, *Don't Get Weird On Me, Babe* (Polydor 1991)★★★, *Bad Vibes* (Fontana 1993)★★, *Love Story* (Fontana 1995)★★★.

●COMPILATIONS: *1984 - 1989* (Polydor 1989)★★★★.

●VIDEOS: *Lloyd Cole & The Commotions* (1986), *From The Hip* (1988), *1984 - 1989 (Lloyd Cole & The Commotions)* (1989).

COLE, NATALIE

b. 6 February 1950, Los Angeles, California, USA. The daughter of celebrated singer/pianist Nat 'King' Cole, Natalie survived early pressures to emulate her father's laid-back style. Signed to Capitol Records in 1975, her debut release, 'This Will Be', was an US Top 10 hit and the first of three consecutive number 1 soul singles. This early success was continued with 'I've Got Love On My Mind' and 'Our Love' (both 1977), which continued the astute, sculpted R&B style forged by producers Chuck Jackson and Marvin Yancey, who like herself, attended Jerry Butler's Writers Workshop. Yancey and Cole later married. Cole's work continued to enjoy plaudits, and although it lacked the intensity of several contemporaries, there was no denying its quality and craft. She maintained her popularity into the 80s but an increasing drug dependency took a professional and personal toll. Her marriage ended in divorce, but in May 1984, the singer emerged from a rehabilitation centre. Now cured, Cole picked up the pieces of her career, and a 1987 album, *Everlasting*, provided three hit singles, 'Jump Start', 'I Live For Your Love' and 'Pink Cadillac', the latter reaching number 5 in the UK and US pop charts. This Bruce Springsteen song was uncovered from the b-side of 'Dancing In The Dark'. In 1991, she recorded a unique tribute to her late father - a 'duet' with him on his original recording of the song 'Unforgettable'. The song took on a moving significance with the daughter perfectly accompanying her deceased father's voice. The single's promotional video featured vintage black-and-white footage of Nat 'King' Cole at his peak on his US television show, interspersed with colour clips of Natalie. The accompanying album on Elektra Records later won seven Grammy Awards, including best album and song the following year.

●ALBUMS: *Inseparable* (Capitol 1975)★★★★, *Natalie* (Capitol 1976)★★★, *Unpredictable* (Capitol 1977)★★★, *Thankful* (Capitol 1977)★★★, *Natalie ... Live!* (Capitol 1978)★★★★, *I Love You So* (Capitol 1979)★★★, with Peabo Bryson *We're The Best Of Friends* (Capitol 1979)★★★, *Don't Look Back* (Capitol 1980)★★, *Happy Love* (Capitol 1981)★★, with Johnny Mathis *Unforgettable: A Musical Tribute To Nat 'King' Cole* (Columbia 1983)★★★, *I'm Ready* (Epic 1983)★★, *Everlasting* (Manhattan 1987)★★, *Good To Be Back* (EMI/USA1989)★★, *Unforgettable ... With Love* (Elektra 1991)★★★★, *Take A Look* (Elektra 1993)★★★, *Star Dust* (Elektra 1996)★★★.

●COMPILATIONS: *Natalie Cole Collection* (Capitol 1988)★★★, *The Soul Of Natalie Cole (1974-80)* (Capitol 1991)★★★★.

●VIDEOS: *Video Hits* (1989), *Holly & Ivy* (Warner Music Vision 1995).

COLLINS, PHIL

b. 30 January 1951, Chiswick, London, England. The former child actor has, in a comparatively short time, established himself as the world's premier singing drummer. The appearance of the self-confessional *Face Value* in 1981, immediately confirmed him as a songwriter of note, outside of his existence as vocalist/drummer with the highly successful rock band Genesis. The record focused on Collins' distinctive voice, something that had previously been underrated and under-used. Collins, who had spent a number of years as their drummer, had also recorded with Brand X. He came out from behind the drum-stool in 1975 and took over the vocals previously handled by the departed Peter Gabriel. Collins' vocal delivery owed much to Gabriel. *Face Value* was recorded during the collapse of his first marriage and he conveyed all the intense emotional feelings of that crumbled relationship into most of the compositions. *Face Value* contained such stand-outs as the melancholic 'If Leaving Me Is Easy', the stark, yet beautiful piano accompanied 'You Know What I Mean' and the soulful 'It Must Be Love'. The album's main axis was the hauntingly powerful 'In The Air Tonight'. a song that slowly builds until it reaches a climax that explodes with such a clamour of drums that the listener cannot fail to be moved. The single narrowly failed to make the top spot in the UK singles chart, while the album became a worldwide success. In the UK it became a number 1, and spent over five years in the charts. Following its extraordinary success and media interest, Collins went to great lengths to insist that he would not be leaving Genesis. Over the past decade he has made a further five albums with them, in addition to his own additional solo work. *Hello, I Must Be Going* was similarly successful although the angst had disappeared now that Phil was happily ensconced in a secure relationship with his future wife. The excellent cover of the Supremes 'You Can't Hurry Love' was another worldwide hit in 1982, reaching the top spot in the UK. Collins continued with a gruelling schedule of work, which he managed to complete with enthusiasm and King Midas-like success. He became a highly successful record producer and session drummer, working with such artists as John Martyn, Robert Plant, Adam And The Ants, Frida, Eric Clapton, Brand X and Howard Jones. Additionally, his specially commissioned film soundtrack song for *Against All Odds* reached the top of the US charts and narrowly missed the top spot in the UK. A few weeks later he appeared on television giving a confident performance as an actor in one episode of *Miami Vice*, resulting in a glut of film scripts being sent to him. He played drums on the famous Band Aid single, 'Do They Know Its Christmas', which spent the early weeks of 1985 at the top of the charts. A few weeks later he was again near the top of the US charts duetting with Philip Bailey on the infectious 'Easy Lover', and, barely pausing for breath, released *No Jacket Required* which topped the charts in most countries in the world for many weeks.

Collins made history on 13 July 1985 by appearing at the Live Aid concert twice, both at Wembley, and, following a dash to catch Concorde, in Philadelphia. Incredibly he found further energy a few hours later to play drums with Jimmy Page and Robert Plant and Eric Clapton. A second duet and film soundtrack, this time with Marilyn Martin for the film *White Nights* made 'Separate Lives' his fourth chart-topper in the US at the end of a phenomenal year. Collins had a comparatively quiet time during 1986, spending part of it touring the world as drummer with Eric Clapton's band. The following year was spent filming for his starring role as a great train robber, Buster Edwards, in *Buster*, which was released to mainly good reviews. His fourth solo album was released in 1989 and immediately topped the charts, spawning further hit singles.

For over 10 years Collins has pursued, at a punishing pace, one of the most successful careers since Elvis Presley and the Beatles. In the 90s in addition to continuing with Genesis he contributed to David Crosby's album *Thousand Roads*, co-writing the hit 'Hero', and starred in the film *Frauds*. *Both Sides* in 1993 was a return to the stark emotion of *Face Value*. Collins, although stating in interviews that he was a happily married man, opened old relationship wounds with powerful lyrics. He was rewarded by the album debuting at number 1 in the UK chart and finding similar success in the USA and most countries in the world. His broad public appeal was not unlike that bestowed upon the Beatles in their heyday. Collins is respected by his fellow musicians as a technically brilliant drummer, in addition to being a major songwriter. There would seem little else for the teenager who played the Artful Dodger in *Oliver* onstage in 1964, to achieve. Collins' untarnished image suffered a major setback when it was revealed that his highly publicized second marriage was over, following his defection to a much younger woman. Collins relocated to Switzerland leaving his wife alone but with the almost unanimous support of the UK public and press. The lyrical intensity of *Both Sides* can now be viewed in a different light. When the underwhelming *Dance A Little Light* was released, Collins went to great lengths during interviews to regain credibility with his public.

●ALBUMS: *Face Value* (Virgin 1981)★★★★, *Hello, I Must Be Going* (Virgin 1982)★★★★, *No Jacket Required* (Virgin 1985)★★★, ... *But Seriously* (Virgin 1989)★★★, *Serious Hits ... Live!* (Virgin 1990)★★, *Both Sides* (Virgin 1993)★★★, *Dance A Little Light*

(Face Value 1996)★.

●VIDEOS: *Live: Phil Collins* (1984), *Video EP: Phil Collins* (1986), *No Ticket Required* (1986), *Live At Perkin's Palace* (1986), *You Can't Hurry Love* (1987), *No Jacket Required* (1988), *The Singles Collection* (1989), *Seriously Live* (1990), *But Seriously, The Videos* (1992).

●FURTHER READING: *Phil Collins* Johnny Waller.

COLOUR FIELD

After appearing with the Specials and the Fun Boy Three, Terry Hall (b. 19 March 1959, Coventry, West Midlands, England; guitar/vocals) formed the Colour Field with Karl Sharle (bass) and Toby Lyons (guitar/keyboards) in 1983. Having been involved in a band that was responsible for the ska/mod revival, (then a vocal based trio), Hall's third band of the 80s was a basic group of three musicians. He was aided by friends, and produced strong pop songs featuring his rather flat vocals. After the instant success of his two previous bands, Colour Field found the going hard. Although they had positive reviews from the music press, it took nearly 18 months for the band to break into the UK Top 20 with 'Thinking Of You' in 1985. Their debut album reached number 12 in the UK, but the failure of subsequent singles soon reduced them down to a duo of Hall and Lyons. They reappeared in 1987 with a weak cover version of Sly And The Family Stone's 'Running Away' and a second album which gave a poor showing on the UK chart, which resulted in the group dissolving. In 1989 Hall released a solo album with assistance from Blair Booth (keyboards/vocals) and Anouchka Grooe (guitar).

●ALBUMS: *Virgins And Philistines* (Chrysalis 1985)★★★, *Deception* (Chrysalis 1987)★★★. Solo: Terry Hall *Ultra Modern Nursery Rhymes* (Chrysalis 1989)★★★, *Home* (AnXious 1994)★★★★.

COMING UP ROSES

This unit was formed in 1986 by the songwriting partnership of ex-Dolly Mixture members, Debsey Wykes (b. 21 December 1960, Hammersmith, London, England; guitar/vocals) and Hester Smith (b. 28 October 1960, West Africa; drums) along with Nicky Brodie (vocals/percussion), Patricia O'Flynn (saxophone, ex-Shillelagh Sisters), Leigh Luscious (guitar) and Claire Kenny (bass, ex-Amazulu), later replaced by bassist Sophie Cherry. Their melodic pop dance style, described by the group as 'ballroom soul', mixed witty and caustic lyrics - in 'I Could Have Been Your Girlfriend (If You'd Asked Me To)' Wykes sang; 'She's so dumb, she's so sweet/I didn't think she'd last a week . . . She's so pretty she's so fine, she is such a waste of time/Well so she's cute, well I don't care, she's got stinking underwear!' They signed to Billy Bragg's Utility Records label releasing, one album in 1989. The group had already toured the UK as part of the pop-socialist collective Red Wedge troupe in 1987. After various personnel changes, but still retaining the nucleus of Wykes and Smith along with Brodie, the group settled on a more stable line-up in 1990 with Tony Watts (lead guitar), Midus (bass) and Jane Keay (saxophone). However, disillusion with the music business's preoccupation with current trends prompted the group's demise in March 1991, leaving behind a legacy of timeless pop songs.

●ALBUMS: *I Said Ballroom* (Utility 1989)★★★.

COMMUNARDS

After leaving Bronski Beat in the spring of 1985, vocalist Jimmy Somerville (b. 22 June 1961, Glasgow, Scotland) teamed up with the classically trained pianist Richard Coles (b. 23 June 1962, Northampton, England) to form the Committee. When a rival group laid claim to that name, they became the Communards, a title borrowed from a 19th century group of French Republicans. Their debut single, the disco-styled 'You Are My World', reached the UK Top 30. The follow-up, 'Disenchanted', was another minor hit, after which the duo decided to augment the line-up with various backing musicians. Meanwhile, their self-titled debut album climbed to number 2 in the UK. In September 1986, the group unexpectedly reached number 1 with a revival of Harold Melvin's 'Don't Leave Me This Way'. The song was most memorable for the vocal interplay between the falsetto of Somerville and the husky tones of guest singer Sarah Jane Morris. Her statuesque presence added much to the group's live appeal, especially when dancing alongside the diminutive Somerville. A further UK Top 10 hit followed with 'So Cold The Night'. After touring extensively, the group issued a second album, *Red*, produced by Stephen Hague. A series of singles were culled from the album, including 'Tomorrow', their comment on wife-beating, which reached number 23. The group returned to the Top 5 with a stirring revival of Gloria Gaynor's 'Never Can Say Goodbye'. During 1988, they registered two more minor UK hits with 'For A Friend' and 'There's More To Love'. With their fusion of disco-revival and falsetto pop, the Communards proved one of the more accomplished new acts of the mid-to late

80s and seemed likely to enjoy further success in the new decade. As with Bronski Beat, however, Somerville showed a restlessness with the British music scene and wound down the group's activities, after which he went solo and enjoyed hits with a cover of Sylvester's 'You Make Me Feel (Mighty Real)' and 'Read My Lips' before relocating to San Francisco.

● ALBUMS: *Communards* (London 1986)★★★, *Red* (London 1987)★★★. Solo: Jimmy Somerville *Read My Lips* (London 1989)★★★, *Dare To Love* (London 1995)★★.

● COMPILATIONS: *The Singles Collection, 1984-1990* includes recordings from Bronski Beat, Communards, Jimmy Somerville (London 1990)★★★★.

● VIDEOS: *Communards: The Video Singles* (1987).

COMSAT ANGELS

Three major record contracts, no hit singles, legal complications - and yet the Comsat Angels have survived to make thoughtful, expressive guitar music for more than 15 years. Formed in Sheffield, England, at the end of the 70s as Radio Earth, they initially merged the zest of punk with a mature songwriting approach, using a strong keyboard element on their promising debut, *Waiting For A Miracle*. The line-up of Stephen Fellows (guitar/vocals), Mik Glaisher (drums), Kevin Bacon (bass) and Andy Peake (keyboards) was to remain constant throughout their early career. In the USA they were forced to shorten their name to CS Angels after the communications giant Comsat, threatened legal action. *Sleep No More* was their highest UK chart placing at number 51 but after *Fiction* only skimmed the lower reaches of the Top 100, Polydor Records lost patience and the band moved to the CBS Records subsidiary, Jive. *Land* spawned a near-hit single with the catchy 'Independence Day', which had previously appeared on their first album. It was released in various formats, including a double-single set, but did not provide the success the band or their label envisioned. Other groups with a similar driving guitar sound fared better and they were surpassed commercially by the likes of Simple Minds and U2. The band invested heavily in their own recording studio in Sheffield and it has subsequently become a focus for the city's musical creativity. Another attempt to regenerate their career was made by Island Records in the late 80s but early in 1990 the Comsat Angels announced they were changing their name to Headhunters in the hope that it would bring about a change of fortune. However,

they reverted to their original name again shortly afterwards, signing to RPM Records for the release of a new album, *My Mind's Eye*, in addition to two compilations of radio sessions. 1995's *The Glamour* saw the Comsat Angels story continue in familiar fashion: with their superbly crafted, wry rock pop heard only by their existing clutch of die-hard European and American fans.

● ALBUMS: *Waiting For A Miracle* (Polydor 1980)★★, *Sleep No More* (Polydor 1981)★★★, *Fiction* (Polydor 1982)★★★, *Land* (Jive 1983)★★★, *Seven Day Weekend* (Jive 1985)★★★, *Chasing Shadows* (Island 1987)★★★, *My Mind's Eye* (RPM 1992)★★★, *The Glamour* (Thunderbird 1995)★★★.

● COMPILATIONS: *Enz* Dutch release (Polydor 1984)★★, *Time Considered* (RPM 1992)★★★, *Unravelled* (RPM 1994)★★★.

CONFLICT

This anarchist punk band were formed in southeast London, England, in 1979, previously existing under a variety of names such as Splattered Rock Stars. Having followed Crass around the country they were essentially motivated by similar concerns: pacifism, animal welfare and anarchism. 'We call ourselves anarchists. That doesn't mean we believe in chaos - our ideal society would be one of small self-governing communities, with people being able to run their own lives. But above all we're trying to say that we don't want to be used by the political left or right.' They played their first gig in their native Eltham in April 1981. The basic line-up featured Colin Jerwood (b. 6 May, 1962, London, England; vocals) Graham (guitar) Ken (drums) and John Clifford (bass), although their early line-ups were very fluid, with newcomers Steve and Paco taking over on guitar and drums soon after. Paul Fryday, meanwhile, became technician, visuals supervisor and general motivator. Their debut EP, *The House That Man Built*, came out on the Crass label, with Pauline Beck adding vocals. 'To A Nation Of Animal Lovers', on which Crass's Steve Ignorant guested, saw the band faced with incitement charges over the cover. Their policy of direct action in protest to many causes, in particular the Orkney seal hunters, led to many live appearances being broken up by police action. After this there were numerous line-up changes, the most significant of which was the two-year tenure of Ignorant as joint vocalist between 1987 and 1989. Jerwood, meanwhile, had been assaulted at a pub in Eltham, nearly losing the use of his eye in the process. Conflict set up their own

Mortarhate label, going on to release albums throughout the 80s for a loyal audience of social miscreants. The best of their efforts were the studio side of *Increase The Pressure* and *The Ungovernable Force*, in 1984 and 1985, respectively. The widescale rioting that occurred after the band's 1987 Brixton Academy gig was documented by *Turning Rebellion Into Money*. In 1993 the group recorded their first 7-inch single since 1985, followed in December by an album, *Conclusion*.

●ALBUMS: *It's Time To See Who's Who* (Corpus Christi 1983)★★, *Increase The Pressure* (Mortarhate 1984)★★★, *The Ungovernable Force* (Mortarhate 1985)★★★, *Only Stupid Bastards Help EMI* (New Army 1986)★★, *Turning Rebellion Into Money* (Mortarhate 1987)★★, *The Final Conflict* (Mortarhate 1989)★★, *Against All Odds* (Mortarhate 1989)★★, *Conclusion* (Mortarhate 1993)★★.

●COMPILATIONS: *Standard Issue* (Mortarhate 1989)★★★.

CONNICK, HARRY, JNR.

b. 11 September 1967, New Orleans, Louisiana, USA. As a pianist and singer, Connick is a young man with a sound that has been around for some time, often being favourably compared to Frank Sinatra. Connick's studied influences take in many from the late 40s and 50s, encompassing bebop, 'cocktail' jazz and swing. Despite the critical acclaim afforded to his first two albums, it was not until he sang a group of standard songs on the soundtrack of the 1989 film, *When Harry Met Sally*, that he came to national prominence. His work on the film earned him the Grammy Award for Male Jazz Vocal, and his clean cut, chisel-jawed good looks, plus a penchant for sharp suits, also made him a favourite with the ladies. He won another Grammy in 1990 for *We Are In Love*. Supported by Shannon Powell (drums) and Ben Wolfe (bass), Connick's Trio has earned sufficient plaudits from their jazz peers, endorsed by *Blue Light, Red Light* elevation to number 1 on the *Billboard* jazz chart. In 1990, he extended himself further when he played the role of a crew member of a US B17 bomber aircraft in the World War II film, *Memphis Belle*, and a year later co-starred with Jodie Foster in *Little Man Tate*. In 1992 he was arrested, and charged with having a 9mm pistol in his possession while passing through Kennedy Airport, New York. He spent a night in jail before agreeing to make a public service television commercial warning against breaking gun laws, in exchange for a promise to drop the charges if he stayed out of trouble for six months. After giving a splendid, 'old fashioned' rendering of the Oscar-nominated 'A Wink And A Smile' in the 1993 movie *Sleepless In Seattle*, Connick's 1994 album *She*, and his *Funk Tour* of the UK in the same year, came as somewhat of a surprise. It signalled a departure from the 'smooth crooning' and a move to down-home New Orleans funk - or as one of the many disillusioned fans who left before the end of each performance put it: 'We expected Frank Sinatra but we got Motorhead instead.'

●ALBUMS: *Harry Connick Jnr.* (Columbia 1987)★★★, *20* (Columbia 1989)★★★, *When Harry Met Sally* film soundtrack (Columbia 1989)★★★★, *We Are In Love* (Columbia 1990)★★★, *Blue Light, Red Light* (Columbia 1991)★★★, as the Harry Connick Jnr. Trio *Lofty's Roach Souffle* (Columbia 1991)★★, *25* (Columbia 1992)★★★, *11* (1993)★★★, *Forever For Now* (Columbia 1993)★★, *She* (Columbia 1994)★★, *Star Turtle* (Columbia 1996)★★★.

●VIDEOS: *Singin' And Swingin'* (1990), *Swinging Out Live* (1992), *The New York Big Band Concert* (1993).

●FURTHER READING: *Wild About Harry: The Illustrated Biography*, Antonia Felix.

COPE, JULIAN

b. 21 October 1957, Deri, Glamorgan, Wales. Cope first attracted attention as an integral part of Liverpool's post-punk renaissance, most notably as a member of the short-lived but seminal group, the Crucial Three, which also included Ian McCulloch and Pete Wylie. In 1978 Cope began writing songs with Ian McCulloch in A Shallow Madness, but the pair quickly fell out over the direction of the group. While McCulloch formed Echo And The Bunnymen, Cope founded the Teardrop Explodes whose early releases enjoyed critical acclaim. The band had several hit singles but an introspective second album, *Wilder*, was heavily criticized before dissent within the ranks led to their demise.

In 1984 Cope embarked on a solo career with *World Shut Your Mouth*, but misfortune dogged his progress. The singer intentionally gashed his stomach with a broken microphone stand during an appearance at London's Hammersmith Palais and his pronouncements on the benefits of mind-expanding substances exacerbated an already wayward, unconventional image. The sleeve of his second album, *Fried*, featured a naked Cope cowering under a turtle shell and commentators drew parallels with rock casualties Roky Erickson and Syd Barrett, both of whom Cope admired. Another of his heroes, Scott Walker, enjoyed a upsurge in interest in his recordings when Cope constantly gave the reclusive 60s singer name-checks in interviews. A third album, *Skellington*, was rejected by his label, which resulted in Cope switching to Island Records. Paradoxically he then enjoyed a UK Top 20 single with 'World Shut Your Mouth'. *Saint Julian* became the artist's best-selling album to date, but a tour to promote Cope's next collection, *My Nation Underground*, was abandoned when he became too ill to continue. Over subsequent months Cope maintained a low profile, but re-emerged in 1990 at London's anti-Poll Tax demonstration dressed in the costume of a space alien, Mr Sqwubbsy. However, this unconventional behaviour was tempered by a new realism and in 1991 he had another major hit with 'Beautiful Love'. Commentators also noted a new-found maturity on the attendant double album, *Peggy Suicide*, which garnered considerable praise. Two albums for his own mail order record companies followed. However, none of this was enough to discourage Island from dropping the artist following the release of *Jehovakill*, though the move caused considerable surprise within critical circles (in retrospect it may have had more to do with Cope's legendary contrariness and recessionary times than any comment on his ability).

He announced a new US contract with American Records in June 1993 and outlined his plans to publish a book on ley lines. *Autogeddon* provided no clear-cut evidence as to whether or not his powers were on the wane, but kept the faithful happy for another year. *20 Mothers* was conceived as a double album of 'devotional songs ranging from pagan rock 'n' roll through sci-fi pop to bubblegum trance-music.' Although his book on ley lines was yet to be completed, he did publish another tome, dedicated to German Krautrock bands such as Can and Tangerine Dream who had such a great musical influence on him. In reviewing *Interpreter Q Magazine* succinctly called him 'the Andrew Lloyd Webber of garage rock'.

●ALBUMS: *World Shut Your Mouth* (Mercury 1984)★★★, *Fried* (Mercury 1984)★★★, *Saint Julian* (Island 1987)★★★★, *My Nation Underground* (Island 1988)★★★, *Skellington* limited edition release (Capeco-Zippo 1990)★★★, *Droolian* limited edition release (Mofoco-Zippo 1990)★★, *Peggy Suicide* (Island 1991)★★★★, *Jehovahkill* (Island 1993)★★, *Autogeddon* (Echo 1994)★★, *Rite* (Echo 1994)★★, *Queen Elizabeth* (Echo 1994)★★, *Julian Cope Presents 20 Mothers* (Echo 1995)★★★, *Interpreter* (Echo 1996)★★★★.

●COMPILATIONS: *Floored Genius - The Best Of Julian Cope And The Teardrop Explodes 1981-91* (Island 1992)★★★★, *Floored Genius 2 - Best Of The BBC Sessions 1983-91* (Nighttracks 1993)★★★.
●VIDEOS: *Copeulation* (1989).
●FURTHER READING: *Head-On*, Julian Cope, *Krautrocksampler: One Head's Guide To Great Kosmische Music*, Julian Cope.

COPELAND, STEWART

b. 16 July 1952, Alexandria, Egypt. Following the dissolution of the hugely successful Police, whom he originally formed in the late 70s, Copeland has kept his career going without ever overworking chart compilers. Copeland began his career in the progressive group Curved Air (his long-time girlfriend Sonja Kristina was the singer), and then took up the mantle of 'Welsh' artist Klark Kent, under whose guise he issued a 10-inch album, shaped as a 'K', and pressed on green vinyl. He was also widely rumoured to have been involved as the drummer in the UK's notorious Moors Murderers. After the Police disbanded, Copeland immersed himself in television and film recording projects. He wrote, produced and played most of the music for Francis Ford Coppola's film *Rumble Fish*. Without an obvious reliance on percussion, Copeland's score was hugely effective, though like so many soundtracks it failed to transfer to vinyl successfully. However, 'Don't Box Me In', co-written and sung by ex-Wall Of Voodoo vocalist Stan Ridgway, is perfectly listenable. A second album, *The Rhythmatist*, offered a Paul Simon-like cultural survey of the sounds of Africa within a rock idiom. Fusing rhythms from Zaire, Burundi, Kenya, Tanzania and the Congo, Copeland found a rich seam of ethnic music to mine. It also introduced solo artist Ray Lema to the west, and it is his vocals that are the record's high point. Copeland's next soundtrack work became his most famous as he penned the theme tune to morally asinine and gratuitously violent US television serial *The Equalizer*. Despite the subject matter, Copeland's compositions were never less than interesting and, in the case of the synthesizer-driven title track, they could be genuinely tuneful. After this and other oddments from the series were cobbled together for a patchy album released in 1988, Copeland moved on to work with Stanley Clarke and Deborah Holland in Animal Logic.

●ALBUMS: as Klark Kent *Music Madness From The Kinetic Kid* (Kryptone/IRS 1980)★★, *Rumble Fish* film soundtrack (A&M 1983)★★, *The Rhythmatist* (A&M 1985)★★★, *The Equalizer & Other Cliff*

Hangers soundtrack (IRS 1988)★★, *The Leopard Son* (Ark 21 1996)★★★.
●VIDEOS: *The Rhythmatist* (1988).

CORNWELL, HUGH

b. 28 August 1949, London, England. Cornwell had long since launched his solo career before his defection in August 1990 from the Stranglers, with whom he was lead vocalist and guitarist. His extra-curricular activities began in 1979, when he recorded an album, *Nosferatu*, with Captain Beefheart drummer Robert Williams, which also featured contributions from members of Devo. It is of considerable interest to Stranglers fans as it pre-figures some of the lyrical and musical aspects of the band in the next decade. Cornwell returned to the Stranglers for much of the 80s, enduring several adventures, not least a jail term for heroin possession which he would later recall in a privately published indictment of the justice system - *Who Guards The Guards?* He also appeared alongside Bob Hoskins in a London stage play. Cornwell's next album, *Wolf*, was a hugely disappointing affair, a limp attempt to craft himself a pop niche. Rightly considered a potent songwriter for his work with the Stranglers, this attempt to convert himself into a gruff Ray Davies fell flat, despite the presence of old pals Jools Holland and Manny Elias (Tears For Fears). The album had been prefaced by one notable single, 1987's 'Facts And Figures', which featured on the soundtrack of the animated film *When The Wind Blows*. Following his departure from the Stranglers after 16 years, Cornwell started to develop songs he had already half-written while still with the band. Before unveiling these he collaborated with Robert Cook and Andy West for the largely ignored *CCW* album. Afterwards he recruited former collaborator Williams (drums), Alex Gifford (bass), Ted Mason and Chris Goulstone (guitars) and Art Of Noise producer Gary Langan to shape *Wired*. Far superior to its predecessor, this collection of songs revealed a grasp of vibrant pop. *Guilty* continued his move towards the mainstream.
●ALBUMS: with Robert Williams *Nosferatu* (Liberty 1979★★★, *Wolf* (Virgin 1988)★★, with CCW *CCW* (UFO 1992)★★, *Wired* (Transmission 1993)★★★, *Guilty* (Snapper 1997)★★.

CORROSION OF CONFORMITY

This mid-80s American hardcore crossover band, originally known as No Labels, was formed in Raleigh, North Carolina, USA, by Reed Mullin (drums), Woody Weatherman (guitar) and Mike Dean (bass/vocals) in 1982, and rose to become one of the biggest draws in the American underground with their stunning live shows. *Eye For An Eye*, with vocals supplied by Eric Eyke, separated them from the pack by mixing hardcore speed with Black Sabbath and Deep Purple-influenced power riffing. A more metallic crossover style became evident with *Animosity*, although the group lost neither their aggression nor their hardcore ideals. Following the blistering *Technocracy*, with Simon Bob (ex-Ugly Americans) on vocals, the size of the band's audience expanded with the rise of thrash, but record company problems and the loss of Simon Bob and Dean led to Corrosion Of Conformity's collapse. However, just as it seemed that *Six Songs With Mike Singing* was to be their epitaph, Corrosion Of Conformity returned, with Mullin and Weatherman joined by Karl Agell (vocals, ex-School Of Violence), Pepper Keenan (guitar/vocals) and Phil Swisher (bass). Impressive tours with DRI and Danzig helped gain a new contract, and the acclaimed *Blind* saw the band adopt a slower, more melodic, but still fiercely heavy style. It also continued the hardcore lyrical stance of an increasingly politically active band, challenging social, political and ecological issues. Success with 'Vote With A Bullet' and electrifying live shows, including a UK tour supporting Soundgarden, re-established Corrosion Of Conformity as a force, but the departure of Agell and Swisher slowed the momentum once more. *Deliverance*, with Keenan taking lead vocals and Dean back in place, saw the band incorporate ever more diverse influences into their weighty sound, adding southern rock grooves and, perhaps most surprisingly, Thin Lizzy-style guitar harmonies for a varied album that was a considerable departure from their hardcore musical roots. The hardcore image continued to fade as *Wiseblood* demonstrated an excellent grasp of 70s heavy rock.
●ALBUMS: *Eye For An Eye* (No Core 1984)★★★, *Animosity* (Death/Metal Blade 1985)★★★, *Technocracy* mini-album (Metal Blade 1987)★★★, *Six Songs With Mike Singing* rec. 1985, mini-album (Caroline 1988)★★★, *Blind* (Relativity 1991)★★★, *Deliverance* (Columbia 1994)★★★, *Wiseblood* (Columbia 1996)★★★.

COSTELLO, ELVIS

b. Declan McManus, 25 August 1954, Paddington, London, England, but brought up in Liverpool. The son of singer and bandleader Ross McManus first came to prominence during the UK punk era of 1977. The former computer programmer toured

A&R offices giving impromptu performances. While appealing to the new wave market, the sensitive issues he wrote about, combined with the structures he composed them in, indicated a major talent that would survive and outgrow this musical generation. Following a brief tenure in Flip City he was signed to Dave Robinson's pioneering Stiff Records. Costello failed to chart with his early releases, which included the anti-fascist 'Less Than Zero' and the sublime ballad 'Alison'. His Nick Lowe-produced debut, *My Aim Is True*, featured members of the west coast cult band Clover, who in turn had Huey Lewis as their vocalist. The album introduced a new pinnacle in late 70s songwriting. Costello spat, shouted and crooned through a cornucopia of radical issues, producing a set that was instantly hailed by the critics. His first hit single, 'Watching The Detectives', contained scathing verses about wife-beating over a beautifully simple reggae beat. His new band, the Attractions, gave Costello a solid base: the combination of Bruce Thomas (b. Stockton-on-Tees, Cleveland, England; bass), ex-Chilli Willi And The Red Hot Peppers' Pete Thomas (b. 9 August 1954, Sheffield, Yorkshire, England; drums) and Steve Nieve (b. Steven Nason; keyboards), became an integral part of the Costello sound. The Attractions provided the backing on the strong follow-up, *This Year's Model*, and further magnificent singles ensued prior to the release of another landmark album, *Armed Forces*. This vitriolic collection narrowly missed the coveted number 1 position in the UK and reached the Top 10 in the USA. Costello's standing across the Atlantic was seriously dented by his regrettably flippant dismissal of Ray Charles as 'an ignorant, blind nigger', an opinion that he later recanted. 'Oliver's Army', a major hit taken from the album, was a bitter attack on the mercenary soldier, sung over a contrastingly upbeat tune. By the end of the 70s Costello was firmly established as both performer and songwriter with Linda Ronstadt and Dave Edmunds having success with his compositions. During 1981 he spent time in Nashville recording a country album, *Almost Blue*, with the producer Billy Sherrill. George Jones's 'Good Year For The Roses' became the album's major hit, although a superb reading of Patsy Cline's 'Sweet Dreams' was a comparative failure. The following year, with seven albums already behind him, the prolific Costello released another outstanding collection, *Imperial Bedroom*. Many of the songs herein were romantic excursions into mistrust and deceit, including 'Man Out Of Time' and 'I'm Your Toy'. The fast paced 'Beyond Belief' was a perfect example of vintage Costello lyricism: 'History repeats the old conceits/the glib replies the same defeats/keep your finger on important issues with crocodile tears and a pocketful of tissues'. That year Robert Wyatt recorded arguably the best-ever interpretation of a Costello song. The superlative 'Shipbuilding' offered an imposingly subtle indictment of the Falklands War, with Wyatt's strained voice giving extra depth to Costello's seamless lyric. The next year Costello as the Imposter released 'Pills And Soap', a similar theme cleverly masking a bellicose attack on Thatcherism. Both *Punch The Clock* and *Goodbye Cruel World* maintained the high standards that Costello had already set and he also found the time to produce albums by the Specials, Squeeze, the Bluebells and the Pogues (where he met future wife, Cait O'Riordan). During 1984 he played a retarded brother on BBC television in Alan Bleasdale's *Scully*, which would not be the last time he would attempt a low-key acting career. The following year he took to a different stage at Live Aid, and in front of millions sang John Lennon's 'All You Need Is Love'. His version of the Animals' 'Don't Let Me Be Misunderstood' was a minor hit in 1986 and during another punishing year he released two albums: the rock 'n' roll-influenced *King Of America*, with notable production from T-Bone Burnett and guitar contributions from the legendary James Burton and, reunited with the Attractions and producer Nick Lowe, Costello stalled with the less successful *Blood And Chocolate*. Towards the end of the 80s he collaborated with Paul McCartney and co-wrote a number of songs for *Flowers In The Dirt*, and returned after a brief hiatus (by Costello standards) with the excellent *Spike* in 1989. During 1990 he wrote and sang with Roger McGuinn for his 1991 comeback album, *Back To Rio*. During that year a heavily bearded and hirsute Costello also co-wrote the soundtrack to the controversial television series, *GBH* (written by Alan Bleasdale), and delivered another artistic success, *Mighty Like A Rose*. With lyrics as sharp as any of his previous work, this introspective and reflective album had Costello denying he was ever cynical - merely realistic. His perplexing collaboration with the Brodsky Quartet in 1993 was a brave yet commercially ignored outing. *Brutal Youth* brought him back to critical approbation. *Kojak Variety*, was a second album of cover versions recorded in 1991 but released four years later, with selections from major artists such as Screaming Jay Hawkins, Supremes, Bob Dylan, Willie Dixon, Ray Davies and Bacharach And David. *All This Useless Beauty* (with the Attractions), although containing songs offered or recorded to other artists, was as lyrically sharp as ever. Although he no longer tops the charts he remains a critic's favourite. Costello is without doubt one of the finest songwriter/lyricists the UK has ever produced. His contribution was acknowledged in 1996 when he collected the Q Magazine songwriter award. His left-of-centre political views have not clouded his horizon and he is now able to envelope all his musical influences and to some degree, rightly indulge himself.

●ALBUMS: *My Aim Is True* (Stiff 1977)★★★★, *This Year's Model* (Radar 1978)★★★★★, *Armed Forces* (Radar 1979)★★★, *Get Happy* (F-Beat 1980)★★★, *Trust* (F-Beat 1981)★★★★, *Almost Blue* (F-Beat 1981)★★★, *Imperial Bedroom* (F-Beat 1982)★★★★★, *Punch The Clock* (F-Beat 1983)★★★, *Goodbye Cruel World* (F-Beat 1984)★★, *King Of America* (Demon 1986)★★★★, *Blood And Chocolate* (Demon 1986)★★★, *Spike* (Warners 1989)★★★, *Mighty Like A Rose* (Warners 1991)★★★, with the Brodsky Quartet *The Juliet Letters* (Warners 1993)★★★, *Brutal Youth* (Warners 1994)★★★, *Kojak Variety* (Warners 1995)★★, with Bill Frisell *Deep Dead Blue, Live At Meltdown* (Nonesuch 1995)★★★, with Richard Harvey *Original Music From Jake's Progress* (Demon Soundtracks 1996)★★, *All This Useless Beauty* (Warners 1996)★★★, with Steve Nieve *Costello & Nieve* (Warners 1996)★★★.

●COMPILATIONS: *Ten Bloody Marys And Ten Hows Your Fathers* (Demon 1980)★★★★, *The Best Of Elvis Costello - The Man* (Telstar 1985)★★★★, *Out Of Our Idiot* (Demon 1987)★★★, *Girls Girls Girls Girls* (Demon 1989)★★★★★, *The Very Best Of ... 1977-1986* (Demon 1994)★★★★.

●VIDEOS: *Best Of Elvis Costello* (1986), with Brodsky Quartet *The Juliet Letters* (1993), *The Very Best Of* (1994), *Live: A Case For Song* (Warner Vision 1996).

●FURTHER READING: *Elvis Costello: Completely False Biography Based On Rumour, Innuendo And Lies*, Krista Reese. *Elvis Costello*, Mick St. Michael. *Elvis Costello: A Man Out Of Time*, David Gouldstone. *The Big Wheel*, Bruce Thomas. *Going Through The Motions (Elvis Costello 1982-1985)* Richard Groothuizen and Kees Den Heyer.

●FILMS: *Americation* (1979).

COUGHLAN, MARY

b. 1956, Co. Galway, Eire. Coughlan had a variety of jobs including modelling and street-sweeping before beginning her singing career in 1984. The following year she made her first album. Produced by Dutch guitarist Erik Visser in Headford, Co. Galway, it showcased her powerful and bluesy jazz stylings and its unexpected success led to a recording contract with WEA Records. On *Under The Influence*, Coughlan revived the 1948 Peggy Lee hit 'Don't Smoke In Bed' and the Billie Holiday ballad 'Good Morning Heartache', as well as Christy Moore's 'Ride On'. Coughlan's fourth album, *Uncertain Pleasures*, was recorded in England with producer Peter Glenister, former musical director for Terence Trent D'Arby. It included new compositions by Mark Nevin (Fairground Attraction) and Bob Geldof as well as versions of the Rolling Stones' 'Mother's Little Helper' and the Elvis Presley hit 'Heartbreak Hotel'. She made her acting debut in the film *High Spirits*, directed by Neil Jordan.

●ALBUMS: *Tired And Emotional* (WEA 1985)★★★, *Under The Influence* (WEA 1987)★★★★, *Ancient Rain* (WEA 1988)★★★, *Uncertain Pleasures* (East West 1990)★★★★, *Sentimental Killer* (1992)★★★, *Love For Sale* (1993)★★★, *After The Fall* (Big Cat 1997)★★★.

COULTER, PHIL

b. February 1942, Derry, Northern Ireland. One of the most eclectic and accomplished arranger/musicians to emerge from Ireland during the 60s, Coulter first began as songwriter, composing the hit 'Foolin' Time' for the Capitol Showband. At the time, Coulter was studying at Queen's University, Dublin, but his talents were swiftly captured by leading entrepreneur Philip Solomon. Initially working with such showbands as the Cadets and Pacific, he continued to compose for the Capitol and even penned their 1965 Eurovision Song Contest entry, 'Walking The Streets In The Rain'. In the meantime, he worked on Solomon's other acts, including Twinkle, who enjoyed a major hit with the Coulter-arranged 'Terry'. Coulter also contributed to Them's song catalogue, with the driving 'I Can Only Give You Everything'. After leaving the Solomon stable in 1967, Coulter formed a partnership with Bill Martin, which became one of the most successful of its era. The duo were particularly known for their ability to produce instantly memorable pop hits, and achieved international fame after penning Sandie Shaw's Eurovision winner, 'Puppet On A String'. They barely missed repeating that feat the following year with Cliff Richard's stomping 'Congratulations'. Coulter subsequently led his own country to victory in the contest by arranging Dana's 1970 winner, 'All Kinds Of Everything'. That

same year, Coulter/Martin were commissioned to write 'Back Home', the official song for the England World Cup Squad, which proved a lengthy UK number 1. As well as his pop outings, Coulter maintained his connection with the Irish folk scene, via his work with another of Solomon's acts, the Dubliners. Later he produced Planxty. During the mid-70s, Coulter/Martin were called in to assist the Bay City Rollers, and subsequently composed a string of hits for the Scottish teenyboppers, including 'Remember (Sha La La)', 'Shang-A-Lang', 'Summerlove Sensation' and 'All Of Me Loves All Of You'. During the same period, they enjoyed hits with Kenny and reached the top again thanks to Slik's 'Forever And Ever'. Coulter also produced several records by comedian Billy Connolly, including the UK number 1 'D.I.V.O.R.C.E.' After his partnership with Martin ended in the late 70s, Coulter specialized in orchestral recordings, which proved particularly successful in Irish communities. Despite his successes, Coulter has suffered several family tragedies. His son was born with Down's Syndrome and died at the age of three; the song 'Scorn Not His Simplicity' was written in his memory. Coulter's sister also died tragically in a drowning incident in Ireland, which briefly caused him to retreat from the music business. His lengthy career, as producer, arranger, songwriter and performer, is all the more remarkable for encompassing such contrasting musical areas, from folk and orchestral to straightforward Tin Pan Alley pop.
●ALBUMS: *Classic Tranquility* (K-Tel 1983)★★★, *Sea Of Tranquility* (K-Tel 1984)★★★, *Phil Coulter's Ireland* (K-Tel 1985)★★★, *Peace And Tranquility* (Harmac 1989)★★, *Serenity* (Harmac 1989)★★, *Forgotten Dreams* (Harmac 1989)★★★, *Phil Coulter's Christmas* (Harmac 1989)★★, *The Live Experience* (Shanachie 1996)★★★, with James Galway *Legends* (RCA 1997)★★★.
●VIDEOS: *The Live Experience* (Shanachie Entertainment 1996).

COUNTY, JAYNE/WAYNE

b. Georgia, USA. One of the most intriguing artists thrown up by the 'no rules' exchanges of late 70s punk was transsexual vocalist/songwriter Wayne County. The artist had grown up on stages in seedy New York clubs playing alongside the New York Dolls, revelling in an act that approximated the Doll's sleaze rock combined with various acts of vulgarity. She soon found kindred spirits in Andy Warhol's enclave and the Max's Kansas City crowd. County then migrated to London, England, just as the punk scene in that metropolis was taking hold. Consequently none of County's albums were ever released in his/her own country. Together with a rudimentary but competent backing band, titled the Electric Chairs, the group made its debut with a self-titled album for Safari Records in 1978. The Electric Chairs' most popular live numbers at this stage were the enduring low-rent punk favourites, 'Fuck Off' and 'Cream In My Jeans'. 'Eddie And Sheena', meanwhile, became a minor hit in the genre, with its depiction of a crushed love affair between a Ted (rock 'n' roll revivalist) and punk - two warring factions during the late 70s. However, two subsequent albums, with a new line-up of Electric Chairs, proved less inspiring, with the shock value of County's performances provoking a diminishing reaction. *Rock 'n' Roll Resurrection*, a live show in Toronto, Canada, was the first to be credited to Jayne County, and it was subsequently reported that the artist had undergone a sex change (this was not true - the assumption was largely based on speculation caused by the change of name). After a career lull (and allegedly, a nervous breakdown) the artist returned in 1986 with the self-produced *Private Oyster*, though there had been little other artistic development. A second return came in 1994, at which time she unveiled her new band, Queen Elizabeth, and proposals for an autobiography.
●ALBUMS: As Wayne County And The Electric Chairs *The Electric Chairs* (Safari 1978)★★★, *Storm The Gates Of Heaven* (Safari 1979)★★★, *Things Your Mother Never Told You* (Safari 1979)★★. As Jayne County *Rock 'N' Roll Resurrection* (Safari 1981)★★★, *Private Oyster* aka *Amerikan Cleopatra* (Revolver 1986)★★, *Deviation* (SPV 1994)★★, *Let Your Backbone Slip* (RPM 1995)★★.
●COMPILATIONS: *The Best Of Jayne/Wayne County And The Electric Chairs* (Safari 1982)★★★, *Rock 'N' Roll Cleopatra* (RPM 1993)★★★, *Goddess Of Wet Dreams* (1994)★★.
●FURTHER READING: *Man Enough To Be A Woman: The Trials And Tribulations Of An Underground Cult Figure.*

COWBOY JUNKIES

Toronto-based musicians, Michael Timmins (b. 21 April 1959, Montreal, Canada; guitar) and Alan Anton (b. Alan Alizojvodic, 22 June 1959, Montreal, Canada; bass), formed a group called Hunger Project in 1979. It was not successful and, basing themselves in the UK, they formed an experimental instrumental group, Germinal. Returning to Toronto, they joined forces with

Timmins' sister Margo (b. 27 June 1961, Montreal, Canada; vocal) and brother Peter (b. 29 October 1965, Montreal, Canada; drums). As the Cowboy Junkies (which was simply an attention-grabbing name), they recorded their first album, *Whites Off Earth Now!!*, in a private house. Their second album, *The Trinity Session*, was made with one microphone in the Church of Holy Trinity, Toronto for $250. The band's spartan, less-is-more sound captivated listeners and, with little publicity, the second album sold 250,000 copies in North America. The tracks included a curious reinterpretation of 'Blue Moon' called 'Blue Moon Revisited (Song For Elvis)' and the country standards, 'I'm So Lonesome I Could Cry' and 'Walking After Midnight'. Lou Reed praised their version of his song, 'Sweet Jane', and, in 1991, they contributed 'To Lay Me Down' in a tribute to the Grateful Dead, *Deadicated*. Their 1990 album, *The Caution Horses*, included several vintage country songs which, true to form, were performed in their whispered, five miles-per-hour style. The extent of the Cowboy Junkies' fast growing reputation was sufficient for them to promote the 1992 album *Black-Eyed Man* at London's Royal Albert Hall. By the release of *Lay It Down* in 1996 the band had firmly settled into such a distinctive style that it was hard to see how they could expand their appeal to make them reach a wider audience. Critically acclaimed and cultishly adored, their debut for Geffen in 1996 was recorded to the highest standards; Timmons' understated guitar was very much the lead instrument, with barely a hint of a solo, while Margo Timmons' eerie vocals have found favour with a rock audience. The Junkies are highly original and deserve to be heard.

●ALBUMS: *Whites Off Earth Now!!* (RCA 1986)★★★, *The Trinity Session* (RCA 1988)★★★★, *The Caution Horses* (RCA 1990)★★★, *Black-Eyed Man* (RCA 1992)★★★, *Pale Sun, Crescent Moon* (RCA 1993)★★★, *200 More Miles: Live Performances 1985-1994* (RCA 1995)★★★★, *Lay It Down* (Geffen 1996)★★★, *Whorn* (Amphetamine Reptile 1996)★★★.

CRAMPS

Formed in Ohio, USA, in 1976, the original Cramps, Lux Interior (b. Erick Lee Purkhiser; vocals), 'Poison' Ivy Rorschach (b. Kirsty Marlana Wallace; guitar), Bryan Gregory (guitar) and his sister, Pam Balam (drums), later moved to New York, where they were embroiled in the emergent punk scene centred on the CBGB's rock venue. Miriam Linna briefly replaced Balam, before Nick Knox (b. Nick

Stephanoff) became the group's permanent drummer. The Cramps' early work was recorded at the famed Sun Records studio under the aegis of producer Alex Chilton. Their early singles and debut album blended the frantic rush of rockabilly with a dose of 60s garage band panache and an obvious love of ghoulish b-movies. Bryan Gregory's sudden departure followed the release of the compulsive 'Drug Train' single. Former Gun Club acolyte, Kid Congo (Powers) (b. Brian Tristan), appeared on *Psychedelic Jungle*, but he later rejoined his erstwhile colleagues and the Cramps have since employed several, often female, replacements, including Fur and Candy Del Mar. Despite the group's momentum being rudely interrupted by a protracted legal wrangle with the IRS Records label during the early 80s, the Cramps' horror-cum-trash style, supplemented with a healthy dose of humour and sex, has nonetheless remained intact throughout their career. However, the best examples of their work can still be found on their early albums (and compilations), with songs such as 'You've Got Good Taste', 'Human Fly' and 'I'm Cramped' perfectly capturing a moment in time in the evolution of alternative rock music. Next best is probably 1986's *A Date With Elvis*, which appealed because the formula was still relatively fresh. Wary of outside manipulation, the Cramps continue to steer their own course to good effect by touring and recording, proving themselves the masters of their particular genre. Their live shows, especially, are rarely found wanting in terms of entertainment value. In 1991 Interior and Rorschach re-emerged fronting a rejuvenated line-up with Slim Chance (bass) and Jim Sclavunos (drums).

●ALBUMS: *Songs The Lord Taught Us* (Illegal/IRS 1980)★★★, *Psychedelic Jungle* (IRS 1981)★★★, *Smell Of Female* live recording (Enigma 1983)★★★, *A Date With Elvis* (Big Beat 1986)★★★, *Rockinnreelininaucklandnewzelandxxx* live recording (Vengeance 1987)★★★, *Stay Sick* (Enigma 1990)★★★, *Look Mom No Head!* (Big Beat 1991)★★, *Flamejob* (Medicine 1994)★★★.

●COMPILATIONS: *Off The Bone* (IRS 1983)★★★, *Bad Music For Bad People* (IRS 1984)★★★.

●FURTHER READING: *The Wild, Wild World Of The Cramps*, Ian Johnston.

CRANES

Based in Portsmouth, England, the Cranes are clearly influenced by the Cocteau Twins and My Bloody Valentine. They were formed by sister/brother team Alison (b. c.1964; vocals/bass)

and Jim Shaw (drums), who comprise the principal songwriting unit. As children they listened to New Order, Nick Cave and the Young Gods, which became an approximation of their later sound (although they ferociously objected to the 'Gothic' tag they earned in their early days). The line-up is completed by Mark Francombe (guitar) and Matt Cope (bass/guitar). After five years of introspection, writing and perfecting songs for themselves, and contributions to a plethora of various artist compilations, the band picked up support from BBC disc jockey John Peel with 1990's mini-album, Self-Non-Self. They signed to BMG/RCA Records subsidiary Dedicated in July 1990, attracting further plaudits for Wings Of Joy, described variously as 'foetal, minimalist, metallic and funereal'. Forever saw the band pick up world tour support slots with an admiring Cure, while Loved, a more accessible offering with Shaw's vocals noticeably more prominent in the mix, suggested they might break through in the wake of the Cranberries' commercialization of 'dream pop', an American term that still fits this UK band admirably.

●ALBUMS: Fuel cassette only (Bite Back 1987)★★, Self-Non-Self (Dedicated 1990)★★, Wings Of Joy (Dedicated 1991)★★★, Forever (Dedicated 1993)★★★, Loved (Dedicated 1994)★★★, La Tragédie D'Oreste Et Électre (Dedicated 1996)★★, Population Four (Dedicated 1997)★★★.

CRAWFORD, RANDY

b. Veronica Crawford, 18 February 1952, Macon, Georgia, USA. Raised in Cincinnati, from the age of 15 onwards, Randy Crawford was a regular performer at the city's nightclubs. She later moved to New York and began singing with several jazz musicians including George Benson and Cannonball Adderley. Crawford was subsequently signed to Warner Brothers Records as a solo act, but achieved fame as the (uncredited) voice on 'Street Life', a major hit single for the Crusaders. Crawford toured extensively with the group whose pianist, Joe Sample, provided her with 'Now We May Begin', a beautiful ballad that established the singer's independent career. Crawford enjoyed further successes with 'One Day I'll Fly Away', (UK number 2), 'You Might Need Somebody', 'Rainy Night in Georgia' (both UK Top 20 hits), and her 1981 album Secret Combination, considered by many to be her finest, reached number 2 in the UK. After a five-year respite, she made a return to the top flight of the chart in 1986 with 'Almaz' which reached the Top 5. Curiously, this soulful, passionate singer has found greater success in the

UK than in her homeland and her recent album, Rich And Poor was recorded in London.

●ALBUMS: Miss Randy Crawford (Warners 1977)★★★, Raw Silk (Warners 1979)★★★, Now We May Begin (Warners 1980)★★★, Everything Must Change (1980)★★★, Secret Combination (Warners 1981)★★★★, Windsong (Warners 1982)★★★, Nightline (Warners 1983)★★★, Abstract Emotions (Warners 1986)★★★, The Rich And Poor (Warners 1989)★★★, Naked And True (Bluemoon 1995)★★★.

●COMPILATIONS: Miss Randy Crawford - Greatest Hits (K-Tel 1984)★★★, Love Songs (Telstar 1987)★★★, The Very Best Of (Dino 1992)★★★, The Best Of (Warners 1996)★★★★.

CRAY, ROBERT

b. 1 August 1953, Columbus, Georgia, USA. The popularity of guitar-based blues during the 80s had much to do with the unassuming brilliance of Cray. Although he formed his first band in 1974, it was not until Bad Influence in 1983 that his name became widely known. His debut, Who's Been Talking, failed because the record label folded (it has since been reissued on Charly). Cray's music is a mixture of pure blues, soul and rock and his fluid, clean style owes much to Albert Collins and Peter Green, while on faster numbers a distinct Jimi Hendrix influence is heard. The Robert Cray Band features long-time bassist Richard Cousins, Dave Olson (drums) and Peter Boe (keyboards). Strong Persuader in 1987 became the most successful blues album for over two decades and Cray has taken this popularity with calm modesty. He is highly regarded by experienced stars like Eric Clapton, who in addition to recording Cray's 'Bad Influence', invited him to play at his 1989 marathon series of concerts at London's Royal Albert Hall and record with him. In 1988 Cray consolidated his reputation with the superb Don't Be Afraid Of The Dark, which featured some raucous saxophone playing from David Sanborn. Midnight Stroll featured a new line-up which gave Cray a tougher sounding unit and moved him out of mainstream blues towards R&B and soul. Some Rainy Morning was Cray's vocal album, no blinding solos to be found, but a mature and sweet voice that moved Cray to be viewed as a soul singer rather than a blues guitarist. Cray's quartet in the mid-90s featured Kevin Hayes (drums), Karl Sevareid (bass) and Jim Pugh (keyboards). Sweet Potato Pie featured the Memphis Horns on a cover of Isaac Hayes and David Porter's 'Trick Or Treat'

●ALBUMS: Who's Been Talkin' (1979)★★★, Bad

Influence (High Tone 1983)★★★★, *False Accusations* (Demon 1985)★★★, with Albert Collins, Johnny Copeland *Showtime* (Alligator 1985)★★★★, *Strong Persuader* (Mercury 1986)★★★, *Don't Be Afraid Of The Dark* (Mercury 1988)★★★★, *Midnight Stroll* (Mercury 1990)★★★★, *Too Many Cooks* (Tomato 1991)★★★, *I Was Warned* (Mercury 1992)★★★, *The Score* (1992)★★, *Shame And A Sin* (Mercury 1993)★★★, *Some Rainy Morning* (Mercury 1995)★★★, *Sweet Potato Pie* (Mercury 1997)★★★★.
●VIDEOS: *Collection: Robert Cray* (1991).

CRENSHAW, MARSHALL

b. 1954, Detroit, Michigan, USA. After portraying John Lennon in the stage show *Beatlemania*, Crenshaw forged a solo career as a solid and dependable performer of the classic urban American pop song. His rock 'n' roll songs were sprinkled with lyrics discoursing on the perennial problems of the love-lorn and that of being in love. With a echo-laden guitar sound that harked back to the 60s with a little Buddy Holly and Eddie Cochran thrown in for effect, Crenshaw's future looked bright with the release of his first album for Warner Brothers Records in 1982. Performing alongside his brother Robert (drums/vocals) and Chris Donato (bass/vocals), this debut album contained Crenshaw's only US single hit to date, 'Someday, Someway'. His album of modern pop also contained such classics as 'Cynical Girl' and 'Mary Ann', but only reached number 50 on the US chart. His follow-up was dealt a similar fate. Although the album was packed with what seemed to be 'radio-friendly' hits, songs like 'Whenever You're On My Mind', 'What Time Is It?' and 'For Her Love' found only cult-status appreciation. The lean period of commercial success was relieved by the success of Owen Paul's cover of his 'My Favourite Waste Of Time', which reached the UK Top 3 in 1986. Crenshaw made film appearances in *Peggy Sue Got Married* and portrayed Buddy Holly in *La Bamba*. Further acclaimed album releases have seen the guitarist cover other artists' songs including sterling performances of Richard Thompson's 'Valerie' and John Haitt's 'Someplace Where Love Can't Find Me' on *Good Evening*. A split with Warners in 1990 saw Crenshaw sign to MCA and the release of *Life's Too Short*. In the mid-90s Crenshaw guested on various tribute albums for Nilsson, Arthur Alexander and Merle Haggard in addition to finding a new audience with his contribution for the Gin Blossoms' 'Til I Hear It From You'. He broke a five-year silence with a new album in 1996, although his lengthy cult-status is unlikely to break new ground for this criminally underrated talent.
●ALBUMS: *Marshall Crenshaw* (Warners 1982)★★★★, *Field Day* (Warners 1983)★★★, *Downtown* (Warners 1985)★★★, *Sings Mary Jean & Nine Others* (Warners 1987)★★★, *Good Evening* (Warners 1989)★★★, *Life's Too Short* (MCA 1991)★★★, *My Truck Is My Home* (Razor And Tie 1994)★★★, *Miracle Of Science* (Razor And Tie 1996)★★★.

CRISWELL, KIM

b. Hampton, Virginia, USA. An actress and singer who came to prominence in stage musicals during the 80s, with a style and voice reminiscent of the much-missed Ethel Merman. Criswell grew up in Chattanooga, Tennessee, where, so she says, the 'live' theare used to arrive in a bus and stay for just two nights. Her early influences were Julie Andrews, Barbra Streisand, and Judy Garland, and, like them, she started performing from an early age. After graduating from high school, she studied musical theatre at the University of Cincinnatti's College Conservatory of Music before moving to New York where she gained a featured part in a revival of *Annie Get Your Gun*. She made her Broadway musical debut in *The First* (1981), and then appeared in *Nine*, which was staged by Tommy Tune and had a cast of 21 women and only one male adult. Her other Broadway credits during the 80s included revivals of the *Three Musketeers* and *The Threepenny Opera* (retitled as *3 Penny Opera*). In the latter show Criswell played Lucy, one of the leading roles in a production that was headed by the popular rock singer Sting. She has appeared as the featured soloist with several of America's leading symphony orchestras, and took part in concert stagings of Jerome Kern's *Sitting Pretty* at Carnegie Hall, and George and Ira Gershwin's *Girl Crazy* at the Lincoln Centre. She won the Helen Hayes award for her performance in *Side By Side By Sondheim*, and played the role of Grizabella (the feline who sings 'Memory') for six months in the Los Angeles production of Andrew Lloyd Webber's *Cats*. Between 1989 and 1991 Criswell starred in three London studio recordings of famous Broadway shows, *Anything Goes, Kiss Me, Kate*, and *Annie Get Your Gun*, accompanied by a large orchestra directed by John McGlinn. He also conducted the London Sinfonietta when Criswell joined Brent Barrett in *Cole Porter And The American Musical* at the Royal Festival Hall. In September 1991 she presented her one-woman show, *Doin' What Comes Naturally*, at the Shaw Theatre in London, and, just over a year later, co-starred with John Diedrich in a West End revival of *Annie Get Your Gun*. The show was acclaimed by the critics ('Criswell is the best Annie we have seen since Dolores Gray') but it folded after less than two months. In 1993 she appeared in two very different kind of shows in the UK. The first, *Elegies For Angels, Punks And Raging Queens*, was a musical play that purported to tell the real-life stories of 33 individuals who have met their death through AIDS; while the other, a touring nostalgia show, *Hollywood And Broadway II*, with Bonnie Langford and Wayne Sleep, found her on more familiar ground. Her 1993 record releases were dissimilar, too: *The Lorelei* contained a mixture of well-known and neglected show tunes, while *Human Cry* turned out to be a pop album in a contemporary, and sometimes funky style and the power of the single 'Moment Of Weakness' demonstrated her ability to cross over to be a major pop vocalist should she decide to abandon the stage.

●ALBUMS: *Songs Of New York* (1984)★★★, *Fifty Million Frenchmen* (1986)★★★, *Anything Goes* (Studio Cast 1989)★★★★, *Kiss Me, Kate* (Studio Cast 1990)★★★, *Annie Get Your Gun* (Studio Cast 1991)★★★, *The Lorelei* (1993)★★★, *Human Cry* (1993)★★, and Original Cast recordings.

CROKER, BRENDAN

b. 15 August 1953, Bradford, Yorkshire, England. Croker had studied sculpture at art school before becoming a British Rail guard, a refuse collector, and a theatre set designer. It was during the last job that he met fellow guitarist Steve Phillips, with whom he formed the duo Nev And Norris. During the early 80s, when Phillips temporarily retired from music to concentrate on his own art career, Croker set about assembling his own band - the 5 O'Clock Shadows. As well as Croker, the Shadows consisted of Marcus Cliffe (bass), and Mark Cresswell (guitar). Cresswell also played alongside Tanita Tikaram. The 5 O'Clock Shadow's debut, *Close Shave*, emerged on the Leeds independent label Unamerican Activities, and was promoted with the single 'That's The Way All My Money Goes' in 1986. They moved to Red Rhino but released just one single before that company ceased trading. Croker gained a high profile for his work with Mark Knopfler, Guy Fletcher and Steve Phillips as the Notting Hillbillies and was signed to Andrew Lauder's Silvertone label. In 1989 they released a self-titled album, with guest appearances by Tikaram, Eric Clapton, Steve Goulding

and Katie Kissoon (of Mac And Katie Kissoon) amongst others. Croker and Cresswell also guested on Tikaram's *Ancient Heart*.

●ALBUMS: *Close Shave* (Unamerican Activities 1986)★★★, *Brendan Croker And The 5 O'Clock Shadows* (1989)★★★, *The Great Indoors* (Silvertone 1991)★★★, *The Acoustic Sessions* (Windsong 1995)★★★, *The Kershaw Sessions* (Strange Fruit 1996)★★★.

CROSS, CHRISTOPHER

b. Christopher Geppert, 3 May 1951, San Antonio, Texas, USA. Formerly a member of Texas heavy-rock band Flash, Cross was signed to Warner Brothers Records on the strength of his songwriting talents. His debut album, full of smooth AOR songs ideal for radio-play, spawned hits in 'Ride Like The Wind' (US number 2 - featuring Michael McDonald), 'Sailing (US number 1)', 'Never Be The Same' and 'Say You'll Be Mine'. Christopher Cross was awarded 5 Grammy awards in 1981, including Best Album of the Year. Cross also sang and co-wrote, along with Carole Bayer Sager, Burt Bacharach and Peter Allen, the theme song, 'Best That You Can Do' for the top-grossing Dudley Moore film *Arthur* in 1981. The song gave Cross another US number 1 hit and his only UK Top 10 single. Despite having a UK number 14 album, Cross's singles sales propelled him no further than number 48 ('Sailing'). His second album, *Another Page* (US number 11/UK number 4), supplied him with a further US Top 10 hit with 'Think Of Laura' in 1983, which was featured on US ABC television's *General Hospital* series. Later years have seen a decline in Cross's sales, indicating either a loss of touch in songwriting or in popularity, or both. A revamped dance version of 'Ride Like The Wind' was used by East Side Beat in late 1991 and reached the UK Top 10.

●ALBUMS: *Christopher Cross* (Warners 1980)★★★, *Another Page* (Warners 1983)★★★, *Every Turn Of The World* (Warners 1985)★★, *Back Of My Mind* (1988)★★.

CROWD (USA)

The Crowd were a brief component of the 'beach punk' scene of Huntington Beach, California, USA, in the early 80s. Featuring Jim 'Trash' Decker (vocals), Jay Decker (bass), James Kaa (guitar), Tracy (guitar) and Barry Cuda (drums), they were almost completely divorced from the prevailing hardcore punk ethos. Dressed in dayglo beach wear and with their own version of communal dancing (it is often suggested that Decker invented the 'slam dance'), the Crowd specialized in trashy surf punk, akin to a less skilled Agent Orange. Their debut album, *A World Apart*, failed to build on their early impact, however, and the Crowd were quickly overtaken by many of the bands they had helped influence. When Cuda and Decker departed, Dennis Walsh (aka Dennis Racket) joined from the Flyboys. The group broke up shortly afterwards, leaving Decker and Tracy's ambition to be 'the Frankie and Annette of the 80s' unrealized. Various ex-members went on to join Sextet.

●ALBUMS: *A World Apart* (Posh Boy 1980)★★.

CROWELL, RODNEY

b. 7 August, 1950, Houston, Texas, USA. Combining careers as country songwriter, producer and artist, Crowell has become an influential figure in Nashville's new breed, along with Emmylou Harris (in whose Hot Band he worked for three years), Rosanne Cash, and fellow songwriters such as Guy Clark. Crowell's introduction to playing music came before he was a teenager, when he played drums in his Kentucky-born father's bar band in Houston. He dropped out of college in the early 70s to move to Nashville, where he was briefly signed as a songwriter to Jerry Reed's publishing company, and in 1973 was appearing on local 'writer's night' with contemporaries like Clark, John Hiatt and Richard Dobson.

In 1974, a demo tape of his songs was heard by Brian Ahern, who was about to produce *Pieces Of The Sky* for Emmylou Harris, and that album eventually began with Crowell's 'Bluebird Wine'. Harris's 1975 *Elite Hotel* included Crowell's 'Till I Gain Control Again', and her 1979 *Quarter Moon In A Ten Cent Town* featured his 'I Ain't Living Long Like This' and 'Leaving Louisiana In The Broad Daylight'. During this period, Crowell also worked as a permanent member of Harris's Hot Band, playing rhythm guitar and singing harmony and duet vocals. In 1978, he also recorded his own debut album for Warner Brothers Records, *Ain't Living Long Like This*, using Ahern as producer and an all-star line-up of musicians including the entire Hot Band plus Ry Cooder, Jim Keltner, and Willie Nelson. Although it included two minor US country hit singles, the album was not a commercial success.

In 1979, Crowell married Rosanne Cash, and has subsequently produced most of her albums. In 1980, he tried again on his own account with *But What Will The Neighbors Think*, which he co-produced with Craig Leon. It remained in the US album charts for 10 weeks, and included a US Top 40 single, 'Ashes By Now', and in 1981, he released the self-produced *Rodney Crowell*, which just failed to reach the Top 100 of the US album chart. These albums were later the basis for *The Rodney Crowell Collection*, a 1989 compilation which was virtually a 'Best Of' of his early career.

In 1984, he delivered *Street Language* to Warner Brothers, who rejected it, whereupon Crowell changed four tracks and signed it to Columbia Records, for whom he continues to record. The album, released in 1986, included three US country chart singles, and established him as a country artist (although many feel that he could easily cross over to rock). *Diamond And Dirt*, co-produced by Crowell and his erstwhile Hot Band colleague, Tony Brown, was much more successful, spawning five US country number 1 singles, 'It's Such A Small World' (a duet with Rosanne Cash), 'I Couldn't Leave You If I Tried' and 'She's Crazy For Leavin''. The success of this album provoked the release of the previously mentioned compilation. In 1989, Crowell and Brown co-produced *Keys To The Highway*, which was largely recorded with his fine band, the Dixie Pearls, whose personnel includes Stewart Smith (lead guitar), Jim Hanson (bass), Vince Santoro (drums) and another erstwhile Hot Band colleague, Hank DeVito (pedal steel). Crowell's songs have been covered by Bob Seger, Waylon Jennings, George Jones and others, while he has also produced albums for Sissy Spacek, Clark and Bobby Bare. His 1992 album, *Life Is Messy*, followed soon after the revelation that his marriage to Rosanne Cash had broken down. Taken by most observers as a reply to Cash's stunning *Interiors*, the album attempted - with some success - to marry melancholy themes to up-tempo songs. Subsequent albums such as *Let The Picture Paint Itself* and *Jewel Of The South* have also chronicled his personal problems. As long as life is messy it appears he will be able to write great songs.

●ALBUMS: *Ain't Living Long Like This* (Warners 1978)★★★★, *But What Will The Neighbors Think* (Warners 1980)★★★, *Rodney Crowell* (Warners 1981)★★★, *Street Language* (Columbia 1986)★★★★, *Diamonds And Dirt* (Columbia 1988)★★★★, *Keys To The Highway* (Columbia 1989)★★★★, *Life Is Messy* (Columbia 1992)★★★, *Let The Picture Paint Itself* (MCA 1994)★★★, *Jewel Of The South* (MCA 1995)★★★.

●COMPILATIONS: *The Rodney Crowell Collection* (Warners 1989)★★★★, *Greatest Hits* (Columbia 1993)★★★★.

CUDDLY TOYS

Emerging from the ashes of glam-punk outfit Raped, the Ireland-based Cuddly Toys consisted of Sean Purcell (vocals), Tony Baggett (bass), Faebhean Kwest (guitar), Billy Surgeoner (guitar) and Paddy Phield (drums). Both their 1980 offerings, *Guillotine Theatre* and a cover of Marc Bolan and David Bowie's 'Madmen', were co-releases for Raped's old label Parole and Fresh Records. 'Astral Joe' came later that year, followed by 'Someone's Crying' in 1981, but the band seemed derivative in comparison to more exciting members of their peer group and soon endured line-up changes. Terry Noakes joined on guitar and Robert Parker on drums. After 'It's A Shame' and a second album, *Trials And Crosses*, in 1982, the group disappeared from view.

●ALBUMS: *Guillotine Theatre* (Fresh 1981)★★★, *Trials And Crosses* (Fresh 1982)★★★.

CULT

Originally known as first Southern Death Cult then Death Cult, the band were formed by lead singer Ian Astbury (b. 14 May 1962, Heswell, Merseyside, England) in 1981. After a youth spent in Scotland and Canada (where he gained early exposure to the culture of native Indians on the Six Nations Reservation, informing the early stages of the band's career), Astbury moved into a Bradford, Yorkshire, house and discovered a group in rehearsal in the basement. The group's personnel included Haq Quereshi (drums), David 'Buzz' Burrows (guitar) and Barry Jepson (bass). As their vocalist, Astbury oversaw a rapid rise in fortunes, their fifth gig and London debut at the Heaven club attracting a near 2000-strong audience. Southern Death Cult made their recording debut in December 1982 with the double a-side, 'Moya'/'Fatman', and released a self-titled album on Beggars Banquet Records. They supported Bauhaus on tour in early 1983. However, by March the group had folded, Astbury reeling from his perceived image of 'positive punk' spokesman, and the fact that his native Indian concept was being diluted by the group's format. His new band, operating under the truncated name Death Cult, would, he vowed, not become a victim of hype in the same way again (Quereshi, Jepson and Burrows would go on to join Getting The Fear, subsequently becoming Into A Circle before Quereshi re-emerged as the centrepiece of Fun-Da-Mental's 'world dance' ethos under the name Propa-Ghandi). A combination of the single, demo and live tracks was posthumously issued as the sole SDC album. Death Cult comprised the rhythm section of recently deceased gothic band Ritual, namely Ray 'The Reverend' Mondo (drums) and Jamie Stewart (bass), plus guitarist Billy Duffy (b. 12 May 1959, Manchester, England; ex-Ed Banger And The Nosebleeds and Theatre Of Hate). They made their debut in July 1983 with an eponymous four-track 12-inch, at which time Astbury also changed his own name (he had previously been using Ian Lindsay, which, it later transpired, was his mother's maiden name). After an appearance at the Futurama festival Mondo swapped drumming positions with Sex Gang Children's Nigel Preston (d. 7 May 1992), a former colleague of Duffy's in Theatre Of Hate. However, 1984 brought about a second and final name change - with the band feeling that the Death prefix typecast them as a 'Gothic' act, they became simply the Cult. They recorded their first album together, *Dreamtime*, for release in September 1984, its sales boosted by a number 1 single in the indepedent charts with the typcially anthemic 'Spiritwalker'. Another strong effort followed early the next year, 'She Sells Sanctuary', but this was to prove Preston's swansong. Mark Brzezicki of Big Country helped out on sessions for the forthcoming album until the permanent arrival of Les Warner (b. 13 February 1961), who had previously worked with Johnny Thunders, Julian Lennon and Randy California. The band's major commercial break came with *Love* in 1985, which comprised fully-fledged hard rock song structures and pushed Duffy's guitar lines to the fore. It spawned two UK Top 20 hit singles in the aforementioned 'She Sells Sanctuary' and 'Rain'. *Electric* saw the band's transition to heavy rock completed. There was no disguising the group's source of inspiration, with Led Zeppelin being mentioned in nearly every review. Part-produced by Rick Rubin, *Electric* was a bold and brash statement of intent, if not quite the finished item. It became a success on both sides of the Atlantic, peaking at number 4 and 38 in the UK and US charts respectively. The gigs to promote it saw the band add bass player Kid 'Haggis' Chaos (b. Mark Manning; ex-Zodiac Mindwarp And The Love Reaction), with Stewart switching to rhythm guitar. Both he and Warner were dispensed with in March 1988, the former joining 4 Horsemen. Reduced to a three-piece of Astbury, Stewart and Duffy, the sessions for *Sonic Temple* saw them temporarily recruit the services of drummer Mickey Curry. It was an album which combined the atmospheric passion of *Love* with the unbridled energy of

Electric. A 1989 world tour saw the band augmented by Matt Sorum (drums) and Mark Taylor (keyboards; ex-Alarm and Armoury Show). Stewart quit in 1990, while Sorum went on to a tenure with Guns N'Roses. *Ceremony* was released in 1991, with the help of Charley Drayton (bass) and the returning Mickey Curry. This was a retrogressive collection of songs, that had more in common with *Love* than their previous two albums. Nevertheless, having already established an enormous fan base, success was virtually guaranteed. 1994's *The Cult* saw them reunited with producer Bob Rock once more, on a set which included the rather clumsy Kurt Cobain tribute, 'Sacred Life'. By this time, however, Astbury had departed and later resurfaced with a new band the Holy Barbarians.

●ALBUMS: *Dreamtime* (Beggars Banquet 1984)★★, *Love* (Beggars Banquet 1985)★★, *Electric* (Beggars Banquet 1987)★★★, *Sonic Temple* (Beggars Banquet 1989)★★★, *Ceremony* (Beggars Banquet 1991)★★, *The Cult* (Beggars Banquet 1994)★★.

●COMPILATIONS: as Southern Death Cult *Complete Recordings* (Situation Two 1991)★★; as the Cult *Pure Cult* (Beggars Banquet 1993)★★★.

●VIDEOS: *Dreamtime At The Lyceum* (1984), *Electric Love* (1987), *Cult: Video Single* (1987), *Sonic Ceremony* (Beggar's Banquet 1992), *Pure Cult* (1993), *Dreamtime Live At The Lyceum* (Beggars Banquet 1996).

CULTURE CLUB

Harbingers of the so-called 'new pop' that swept through the UK charts in the early 80s, Culture Club comprised: Boy George (b. George O'Dowd, 14 June 1961, Eltham, Kent, England; vocals), Roy Hay (b. 12 August 1961, Southend-on-Sea, Essex, England; guitar/keyboards), Mikey Craig (b. 15 February 1960, Hammersmith, London, England; bass) and Jon Moss (b. 11 September 1957, Wandsworth, London, England; drums). The group came together in 1981 after George, a nightclub *habitué*, had briefly appeared with Bow Wow Wow (under the name Lieutenant Lush) and played alongside Craig in the Sex Gang Children. The elder drummer Moss had the most band experience having already appeared with London, the Damned and Adam Ant. After failing an audition with EMI, Culture Club were signed to Virgin Records in the spring of 1982, and released a couple of non-chart singles, 'White Boy' and 'I'm Afraid Of Me'. By autumn of that year, however, the group were firmly established as one of the most popular new acts in the country. The melodic and subtly arranged 'Do You Really Want To Hurt Me?'

took them to number 1 in the UK and they deserved another chart-topper with the Top 3 follow-up, 'Time (Clock Of The Heart)'. Although their first album *Kissing To Be Clever* lacked the consistent excellence of their singles, it was still a fine pop record. By this time, George was already one of pop's major talking points with his dreadlocks, make-up and androgynous persona. Never short of a quote for the press, he would later stress such virtues as celibacy with the anti-sex quip, 'I'd rather have a cup of tea'. The launching of MTV in the USA ensured that many UK acts were infiltrating the American charts and the colourful persona of George, coupled with the irresistible charm of Culture Club's melodies, effectively broke them Stateside early in 1983. *Kissing To Be Clever* climbed into the Top 20 of the US album charts, while their two UK singles hits both reached number 2. Suddenly, Culture Club were one of the most popular groups in the world. Back at home, the passionate 'Church Of The Poison Mind', with Helen Terry on counter vocals with George, gave them another number 2 hit. The group reached their commercial peak later that year with the release of the infectious 'Karma Chameleon', which topped the charts on both sides of the Atlantic and sold in excess of a million copies. The second album, *Colour By Numbers* was another UK number 1 and was only kept off the top in the US by Michael Jackson's mega-selling *Thriller*. The momentum was maintained through 1983-84 with strong singles such as 'Victims', 'It's A Miracle' and 'Miss You Blind', which charted in either the US or UK Top 10. Ironically, it was one of their biggest UK hits which presaged Culture Club's fall from critical grace. In October 1984, 'The War Song' hit number 2 but was widely criticized for its simplistic politicizing. Thereafter, chart performances took an increasing backseat to the tabloid newspaper adventures of George. Indeed, 1986's 'Move Away' was to be their only other Top 10 hit. The media-conscious singer had signed a Faustian pact with Fleet Street which led to his downfall in 1986. Having confessed that he was a heroin addict, he found himself persecuted by the press and was eventually arrested for possession of cannabis. Early in 1987, he appeared on the high-rating UK television show Wogan and declared that he was cured. The announcement coincided with the news that Culture Club no longer existed. However, George continued to enjoy chart-topping success as a soloist.

●ALBUMS: *Kissing To Be Clever* (Virgin 1982)★★★, *Colour By Numbers* (Virgin 1983)★★★★, *Waking*

Up To The House On Fire (Virgin 1984)★★, *From Luxury To Heartache* (Virgin 1986)★★, *This Time* (Virgin 1987)★★★.
●COMPILATIONS: *At Worst . . . The Best Of Boy George And Culture Club* (Virgin 1993)★★★★.
●VIDEOS: *Kiss Across The Ocean* (1984), *This Time (The First Four Years)* (1987).
●FURTHER READING: *Culture Club: When Cameras Go Crazy*, Kasper de Graaf and Malcolm Garrett. *Mad About The Boy: The Life And Times Of Boy George & Culture Club*, Anton Gill. *Boy George And Culture Club*, Jo Dietrich. *Like Punk Never Happened: Culture Club and the New Pop*, Dave Rimmer.

CURE

Formed in 1976 as the Easy Cure, this UK group was based around the musicianship of Robert Smith (b. 21 April 1959, Crawley, Sussex, England; guitar/vocals), Michael Dempsey (bass) and Laurence 'Lol' Tolhurst (b. 3 February 1959; drums). After struggling to find a niche during the first flashes of punk, the group issued the Albert Camus-inspired 'Killing An Arab' on the independent Small Wonder Records in mid-1978. It proved sufficient to draw them to the attention of producer and Fiction Records label manager Chris Parry, who reissued the single the following year. By May 1979, the group were attracting glowing reviews, particularly in the wake of 'Boys Don't Cry', whose style recalled mid-60s British beat, with the added attraction of Smith's deadpan vocal. The attendant album, *Three Imaginary Boys*, was also well-received, and was followed by a support spot with Siouxsie And The Banshees, on which Smith joined the headliners onstage. Another strong single, 'Jumping Someone Else's Train', performed predictably well in the independent charts but, in common with previous releases, narrowly missed the national chart. A pseudonymous single, 'I'm A Cult Hero', under the name the Cult Heroes, passed unnoticed and, soon after its release, Dempsey was replaced on bass by Simon Gallup. Amid the shake-up keyboards player Mathieu Hartley was added to the line-up. By the spring of 1980, the Cure were developing less as a pop group than a guitar-laden rock group. The atmospheric 12-inch single, 'A Forest', gave them their first UK Top 40 hit, while a stronger second album, *17 Seconds*, reached the Top 20. Thereafter the Cure's cult following ensured that their work regularly appeared in the lower regions of the charts. After consolidating their position during 1981 with 'Primary', 'Charlotte Sometimes' and 'Faith', the

group looked to the new year for a new direction. A major breakthrough with *Pornography* threatened to place them in the major league of new UK acts, but there were internal problems to overcome. The keyboards player, Hartley, had lasted only a few months and, early in 1982, the other 'new boy', Gallup, was fired and replaced by Steve Goulding. Meanwhile, Smith briefly joined Siouxsie And The Banshees as a temporary replacement for John McGeoch. As well as contributing the excellent psychedelic-tinged guitar work to their hit, 'Dear Prudence', Smith subsequently teamed up with Banshee Steve Severin and Jeanette Landray in the Glove. The Cure, meanwhile, continued to record and during the summer enjoyed their first UK Top 20 single appearance with the electronics-based 'The Walk'. Four months later they were in the Top 10 with the radically contrasting pop single, 'The Love Cats' (Smith subsequently attempted to distance himself from this song which was initially intended more as a parody). Further success followed with 'The Caterpillar', another unusual single, highlighted by Smith's eccentric violin playing. This chart success confirmed the Cure as not only one of the most eclectic and eccentric ensembles working in British pop - but one of the very few to make such innovations accessible to a wider audience. Smith's heavy eye make-up, smudged crimson lipstick and shock-spiked hair was equally as striking, while the group's videos, directed by Tim Pope, became increasingly wondrous. In 1985 the group released their most commercially successful album yet, *The Head On The Door*. The following year, they re-recorded their second single, 'Boys Don't Cry', which this time became a minor UK hit. By now, the group was effectively Smith and Tolhurst, with members such as Gallup and others flitting through the line-up from year to year. With the retrospective *Staring On A Beach* singles collection the Cure underlined their longevity during an otherwise quiet year. During 1987 they undertook a tour of South America and enjoyed several more minor UK hits with 'Why Can't I Be You?', 'Catch' and 'Just Like Heaven'. The latter also reached the US Top 40, as did their double album, *Kiss Me, Kiss Me Kiss Me*.
A two-year hiatus followed before the release of the follow-up, *Disintegration*. A fiendishly downbeat affair, with some of Smith's most moribund lyrics, it nevertheless climbed into the UK Top 3. During the same period the group continued to register regular hits with such singles as 'Lullaby', 'Lovesong', 'Pictures Of You' and the fiery 'Never

Enough'. Along the way, they continued their run of line-up changes, which culminated in the departure of Tolhurst (to form Presence), leaving Smith as the sole original member. Although it was assumed that the Cure would attempt to consolidate their promising sales in the USA, Smith announced that he would not be undertaking any further tours of America. 1990 ended with the release of *Mixed Up*, a double album collecting re-recordings and remixes of their singles.

By 1992 the Cure line-up comprised Smith, a reinstated Gallup, Perry Bamonte (keyboards/guitar), Porl Thompson (guitar) and Boris Williams (drums), and with the critically acclaimed *Wish*, the band consolidated their position as one of the world's most consistently successful groups. Thompson would leave the unit in June 1993, at which time former member Tolhurst sued Smith, the band and its record label, for alleged unpaid royalties. The ensuing court transcripts made for colourful reading, and confirmed the Cure's reputation for drinking excess (Tolhurst was summarily defeated in the action and left with a huge legal debt). Following a successful bill-topping gig at the 1995 Glastonbury Festival the band started work on what was to become *Wild Mood Swings*, issued in May 1996. The line-up on this album was Smith, Bamonte, Gallup, Jason Cooper (drums) and Roger O'Donnell (keyboards). The revealing lyrics hinted that all was not well with Smith's family life.

●ALBUMS: *Three Imaginary Boys* (Fiction 1979)★★★, *Boys Don't Cry* (Fiction 1979)★★, *Seventeen Seconds* (Fiction 1980)★★★, *Faith* (Fiction 1981)★★★★, *Pornography* (Fiction 1982)★★★★, *The Top* (Fiction 1984)★★★, *Concert - The Cure Live* (Fiction 1984)★★, *Concert And Curiosity - Cure Anomalies 1977-1984* (Fiction 1984)★★, *Head On The Door* (Fiction 1985)★★★, *Kiss Me, Kiss Me, Kiss Me* (Fiction 1987)★★★, *Disintegration* (Fiction 1990)★★★★, *Entreat* (Fiction 1991)★★★, *Wish* (Fiction 1992)★★★★, *Show* (Fiction 1993)★★★, *Paris* (Fiction 1993)★★★, *Wild Mood Swings* (Fiction 1996)★★★★.

●COMPILATIONS: *Japanese Whispers - The Cure Singles Nov 1982-Nov 1983* (Fiction 1983)★★★, *Standing On The Beach - The Singles* titled *Staring At The Sea* on CD (Fiction 1986)★★★★, *Mixed Up* (Fiction 1990)★★★.

●VIDEOS: *Staring At the Sea: The Images* (1986), *Close To Me* (1989), *The Cure In Orange* (1989), *The Cure Play Out* (1991), *Cure Picture Show* (1991), *The Cure Show* (1993).

●FURTHER READING: *The Cure: A Visual Documentary*, Dave Thompson and Jo-Anne Greene. *Ten Imaginary Years*, Lydia Barbarian, Steve Sutherland and Robert Smith. *The Cure Songwords 1978 - 1989*, Robert Smith (ed.). *The Cure: Success Corruption & Lies*, Ross Clarke. *The Cure On Record*, Daren Butler. *The Cure: Faith*, Dave Bowler and Bryan Dray. *The Making Of: The Cure's Disintegration*, Mary Elizabeth Hargrove.

CURIOSITY KILLED THE CAT

This late 80s UK pop group graced the covers of all the teen-pop magazines. The various group members all had showbusiness/theatrical backgrounds. The line-up comprised: Ben Volpeliere-Pierrot (b. 19 May 1964, London, England), Julian Godfrey Brookhouse (b. 13 May 1963, London, England), Nicholas Bernard Throp (b. 25 October 1964, London, England) and Migi/Michael Drummond (b. Miguel John Drummond, 27 January 1964, Middlesex, England). Volpeliere-Pierrot's father was a celebrity photographer and his mother a model - Ben's surname was a double-barrelled convolution of their surnames. His childhood was dotted with visits from various Beatles, Rolling Stones and other faces of the 60s who held court at his parents' home. A pretty child, he was in a Kodak commercial in 1970 and by his teens was a regular model in teenage girls' magazines. He also appeared in videos for XTC and the Thompson Twins in the early 80s. Volpeliere-Pierrot first played alongside the other members in the punk-influenced Twilight Children. Drummond was the son of a film and video maker and also brushed with the stars when his father's company made videos for bands such as the Police. After discovering punk he took up drumming, and met Throp at art school before an invitation to join the Twilight Children. In mid-1984 Volpeliere-Pierrot was dating Drummond's sister and the boys invited him to sing in their band, kicking out the old vocalist in the process. Later that same year Toby Anderson also joined the group as keyboardist and songwriter. A demo of a song called 'Curiosity Killed the Cat' was heard by businessman Peter Rosengard who became their manager and they changed their name to that of the song. A debut gig was held at the Embassy Club in December 1984 at which point there were still numerous extra musicians and singers on stage. They shed the excess baggage although Anderson remained the 'fifth' Cat until late 1986. Signed to Phonogram in 1985, they started recording towards the end of the year. Their album was held up for almost a year after original producers Sly Dunbar and Robbie

Shakespeare were dropped in favour of Stewart Levine. 'Misfit' followed in July but flopped. Another face from the 60s, Andy Warhol, met the band at a London art exhibition and he championed them, even appearing in a video for 'Misfit'. His involvement, though useful, was cut short when he died in 1987. Several television appearances helped to push the second single, 'Down To Earth', which entered the charts in December 1986 reaching the Top 10 in the New Year. A series of further hits followed, including a reissued 'Misfit'. However, after 'Free' in September 1987 they underwent a quiet period but returned in 1989 with 'Name And Number' - now simply credited to Curiosity.
●ALBUMS: *Keep Your Distance* (Mercury 1987)★★★, *Getahead* (Mercury 1989)★★.
●VIDEOS: *Running The Distance* (1988).

CURRY, TIM
b. 19 April 1946, Cheshire, England. A versatile actor and singer, with much flair and a dashing style, Curry studied drama and English at Birmingham University. In the 60s, he was a member of the Royal Shakespeare company, and joined the cast of *Hair* early on in its run. After appearing in a supporting role in the 1970 flop musical, *Lie Down, I Think I Love You*, three years later he created the role of the outrageous Frank N. Furter in Richard O'Brien's phenomenally successful *The Rocky Horror Show*. In 1975 he reprised the part in the short-lived New York production, and also starred in the film adaptation which was entitled *The Rocky Horror Picture Show*. In 1981 Curry was nominated for a Tony Award for his performance in the title role of the Broadway production of *Amadeus*, and in the following year received a Variety Club Award when he played the role of the Pirate King, with George Cole and Bonnie Langford, in a West End revival of *The Pirates Of Penzance*. In 1986 he was 'bold, muscular and in fine ample baritone voice' as Macheath in the UK National Theatre's *The Threepenny Opera*, and two years later played Bill Sibson in the US tour of *Me And My Girl*. In 1993, Curry received another Tony nomination for his performance as the ageing and alcoholic swashbuckler Alan Swann in *My Favorite Year*. The musical, which had a book by Joseph Dougherty and a score by Stephen Flaherty and Lynn Ahrens, was based on the 1982 Peter O'Toole movie of the same name. Negative revues forced its closure after 37 performances.
Curry's own film career has flourished since the mid-70s, and has included several critically acclaimed performances among movies such as *The Shout, Times Square, Annie, The Ploughman's Lunch, Blue Money, Clue, Legend, Pass The Ammo, Stephen King's It, The Hunt For Red October, Home Alone 2: Lost In New York, Passed Away, National Lampoon's Loaded Weapon, The Three Musketeers* and *The Shadow* (1994). He also provided the voice of the evil spirit Hexxus, and sang Thomas Dolby's 'Toxic Love' in *Ferngully: The Last Rainforest* (1992). Three years later he was the voice of the 'macho, strutting Drake' in MGM's animated *The Pebble And The Penguin*. Curry has appeared extensively on television, especially in the USA, in productions such as *Wiseguy, Oliver Twist* (as Bill Sikes) and *The Worst Witch*.
●ALBUMS: *Fearless* (A&M 1979)★★★, *Simplicity* (A&M 1981)★★★.

CUTTING CREW
Fronted by vocalist/guitarist Nick Van Eede (b. Nicholas Van Eede, 14 June 1958, East Grinstead, West Sussex, England), Cutting Crew were formed when he began working with Canadian guitarist Kevin Scott MacMichael (b. Halifax, Nova Scotia, Canada). The duo came together when MacMichael's group Fast Forward were supporting Eede's unit the Drivers on a Canadian tour. The two subsequently recorded some demos in Toronto and during 1986 added Colin Farley (b. 24 February 1959; bass) and Martin Beadle (b. 18 September 1961, Hull, North Humberside, England; drums) to form Cutting Crew. The title of their debut single '(I Just) Died In Your Arms' was a phrase Van Eede coined after making love to his girlfriend. This memorable song reached number 4 in the UK but surpassed expectations by climbing to number 1 in the USA in the spring of 1987. A further US Top 40 hit followed with the frantic 'One For The Mockingbird' backed with the anti-cocaine 'Mirror And A Blade'. The plaintive 'I've Been In Love Before' returned them to the US Top 10 later that year, yet the single struggled to reach the UK Top 30 the following year after its third chart entry.
●ALBUMS: *Broadcast* (Siren 1986)★★, *The Scattering* (Virgin 1989)★★, *Compus Mentus* (1992)★★.
●COMPILATIONS: *The Best Of* (1993)★★★.

D

D-MOB

D-Mob is essentially the creative vehicle of 'Dancin'' Danny D (b. Daniel Kojo Poku), an ex-McDonald's employee. He found solace by Djing for three or four years in the evenings, at one point working with journalist James Hamilton at Gullivers in Park Lane, London. He subsequently started club promotions for Loose Ends (for whom he contributed his first remix), Total Contrast and Full Force, before taking up an A&R post at Chrysalis Records. This brought a number of further remixing opportunities, including Nitro Deluxe, Kid 'N Play, Adeva and Eric B And Rakim's 'I Know You Got Soul' in tandem with Norman Cook. By the time he had started using the name D-Mob he had already released two records, as the Taurus Boys, which were minor hits in the USA. Then came 'Warrior Groove', about the tribe his Ghanese parents came from, the Ashantis. The first D-Mob release was 1989's crossover hit 'We Call It Acieed' which featured Gary Haisman on vocals. It was a stirring acid house tune, bringing the underground scene a good deal of notoriety when politicians and papers determined its subject matter was drugs-related. The BBC, in its wisdom, banned it from Top Of The Pops. However, as Poku confirmed to the press: 'I don't take any form of drugs. I don't even go the doctor to get something for my cold.' Follow-up hits included 'It Is Time To Get Funky' (with London Rhyme Syndicate), 'C'mon And Get My Love' and 'That's The Way Of The World' (with Cathy Dennis) and 'Put Your Hands Together' (with Nuff Juice). He also produced/remixed records for Adeva, Juliet Roberts ('Another Place, Another Day, Another Time'), Monie Love, Diana Ross ('Working Overtime'), Chaka Khan ('I'm Every Woman') and the Cookie Crew ('Love Will Bring Us Together'). In 1993 he brought back Dennis (who had enjoyed huge subsequent solo success) for vocals on 'Why', his 'comeback' single as D-Mob. As an in-demand producer/remixer he had never been away.

●ALBUMS: A Little Bit Of This, A Little Bit Of That (ffrr 1989)★★★.

D.A.F.

This German band, based in Dusseldorf, specialized in minimalist electro-dance music. The initials stood for Deutsch Amerikanische Freundschaft, a term first invoked on local posters to symbolise post-war American-German friendship, and the line-up comprised Robert Gorl (drums/synthesizer), W. Spelmans (guitar), Chrislo Hass (saxophone/synthesizer/bass) and Gabi Delgado-Lopez (vocals). Die Kleinen Und Die Bosen was their first album available in the UK because Produkt had only been available in Germany. Die Kleinen was released on the Mute Records label in 1980; the title translates as The Small And The Evil. Recorded in London, the album was uneven and is generally considered as unrepresentative, dominated by 'songs' whose heritage combined Pink Flag era Wire and Can influences. Afterwards Gorl and Delgado-Lopez continued as a duo (Haas would later join Crime And The City Solution), recording three albums for Virgin Records in an 18-month period. These comprised a mixture of Teutonic fantasy, love songs, and social statements. Delgado-Lopez's refusal to sing in English condemned them to a minority international market. Contrary to their dour image, there was much to admire in the exemplary pop of singles such as 'Verlieb Dich In Mich'. Indeed in 1981 they guested on the Eurythmics first album, In The Garden. Later Annie Lennox would return the compliment by adding vocals to Gorl's solo 'Darling Don't Leave Me' single and several tracks from the accompanying album.

●ALBUMS: Ein Produkt Der D.A.F. (Warning/Atatack 1979)★★★, Die Kleinen Und Die Bosen (Mute 1980)★★, Alles Ist Gut (Virgin 1981)★★★, Gold Und Liebe (Virgin 1981)★★★, Für Immer (Virgin 1982)★★★, Live In London (Music For Midgets 1984)★★. Solo: Robert Gorl Night Full Of Tension (Mute 1984)★★. Gabi Delgado Mistress (Virgin 1983)★★★.

●COMPILATIONS: DAF (Virgin 1988)★★★.

DADA (90s)

Named after the art movement (which also inspired the Bonzo Dog Doo Dah Band), this three-piece college-rock band from Los Angeles, California, USA, features old schoolfriends Joie Calio (vocals/bass) and Michael Gurley (guitar/keyboards). Calio and Gurley had originally been part of Louis & Clark, with Louis Guitierrez, who recorded for Chameleon Records between 1986 and 1988. When Guitierrez left to

form Mary's Danish the remaining duo joined up with Phil Leavitt (drums) to produce Dada. Chastened by their experiences with their previous band, Dada hid themselves away in rehearsal rooms for two years to perfect their craft, constructing a set of college-rock material, built on improvisation and rich vocal harmonies (comparisons to Crowded House were never far away). Their debut, *Puzzle*, was produced by Ken Scott (David Bowie, Supertramp). A collection of cool, contemporary rock songs (though there were definite shades of late 70s US new wave bands like the Beat), the record was at its strongest on the more biting cuts such as 'Dizz Knee Land'. This was released as a single, but although they had supported Sting on tour throughout the USA earlier in the year and had been pushed heavily by their record company, many reviewers were still not impressed.
●ALBUMS: *Puzzle* (IRS 1993)★★★, *American Highway Flower* (EMI 1994)★★★.

DALEK I LOVE YOU
From the ashes of Liverpool punk band Radio Blank, Alan Gill (guitar/vocals) and David Balfe (bass/vocals/synthesizer), formed Dalek I Love You in November 1977. Disagreement over the band's name - David wanted the Daleks, whereas Alan preferred Darling I Love You - resulted in the compromised title, and with the addition of Dave Hughes (keyboards), Chris 'Teepee' Shaw (synthesizer), plus a drum machine, the first of many loose line-ups was complete. In July 1978 Balfe left to join Big In Japan. After a string of critically acclaimed synthesizer-pop singles, 1980 saw the release of *Compass Kum'pass*, which came in the wake of groups like OMD and Tubeway Army bringing electronics into the mainstream charts. A worldwide contract with Korova Records produced the singles 'Holiday In Disneyland', 'Ambition', and the album, *Dalek I Love You*, which meshed layered synth and psychedelic fragments with starry-eyed vocals, augmented by excellent harmonies. Again, none achieved any real commercial success and Phil Jones decided to put the band 'on ice'. During this period he was busy writing and recording the soundtrack for the film *Letter To Brezhnev* (1985), and formed the Bopadub label in Birkenhead, which put out a series of cassettes culminating in 1985 with *Naive*, recorded by the reformed Dalek I. In 1986, after eight years of tentative existence, Phil Jones was still optimistic about future releases and subsequently, *Compass Kum'pass* was re-released by Fontana in 1989,

acknowledging the importance of this seminal electronic band.
●ALBUMS: *Compass Kum'pass* (Backdoor 1980)★★★, *Dalek I Love You* (Korova 1983)★★★, as Dalek I *Naive* (Bopadub 1985)★★.

DALTON, LACY J.
b. Jill Byrem, 13 October 1948, Bloomsburg, Pennsylvania, USA. Her father played guitar and mandolin, but she was originally determined to be an artist. At the age of 18 she moved to Los Angeles and then settled in Santa Cruz, where she played the clubs for 12 years. She worked as a protest singer and then became the lead singer with a psychedelic band Office under the name of Jill Croston. A demo tape impressed record producer, Billy Sherrill, who signed her to Columbia Records in Nashville in 1979. Her gravelly, bluesy voice was unusual for country singers and thus made her work distinctive. Her first album, *Lacy J. Dalton*, is regarded by many as a classic, and she is often described by the title of one of its songs, 'Hillbilly Girl With The Blues'. Her US country hits include 'Crazy Blue Eyes', 'Tennessee Waltz', 'Hard Times' and '16th Avenue'. Her *Highway Diner* album moved her into Bruce Springsteen country and she had a pop hit with 'Working Class Man'. By way of contrast, she was featured alongside Bobby Bare, George Jones and Earl Scruggs on her album, *Blue Eyed Blues*.
●ALBUMS: *Jill Croston* (1978)★★, *Lacy J. Dalton* (Columbia 1979)★★★★, *Hard Times* (Columbia 1980)★★★, *Takin' It Easy* (Columbia 1981)★★★, *16th Avenue* (1982)★★★, *Dream Baby* (1983)★★★, *Can't Run Away From Your Heart* (1985)★★, *Highway Diner* (1986)★★, *Blue Eyed Blues* (Columbia 1987)★★, *Survivor* (1989)★★★, *Lacy J.* (1990)★★★, *Crazy Love* (Capitol 1991)★★★, *Chains On The Wind* (Liberty 1992)★★.
●COMPILATIONS: *Greatest Hits* (1983)★★★.

DANCEHALL
Dancehall, a particularly spare, uncluttered form of reggae, first emerged at the start of the 80s and was so named because it literally began in the dances that have always been the lifeblood of Jamaican music. Essentially, a sound system would play a song, usually specially recorded on a dub plate, and a singer or DJ would extemporise over the top of it live. Drawing its lead from the empty, slow rhythms of Roots Radics, and, to a lesser extent, Sly And Robbie, dancehall was the least fanciful genre of reggae to date, offering the rhythm, a voice, the dancers' energy and little else.

By 1982 various acts had emerged who had recorded predominantly dancehall music, among them Yellowman, an albino MC with a witty, if rude, way about a lyric, Barrington Levy, a ferocious singer who never knew how to give less than 100 per cent, and General Echo, another rudely talented chatter. Sound systems such as Jammy's, Volcano and Black Scorpio kept the public thirsting for more material, which they then began to supply on their own labels, with the sound bosses Prince Jammy, Henry 'Junjo' Lawes and Scorpio creating new stars like Junior Reid, Michael Palmer and Josey Wales. A similar process went on in the UK, with the sounds of Saxon Studio, Wassifa Hi-Fi and Unity all offering something different to their Jamaican counterparts. Dancehall never 'finished' as such. Instead, Jammy released a record in 1985 featuring singer Wayne Smith, 'Under Me Sleng Teng', which single-handedly created the 'digital' style of dancehall, and subsequently, raggamuffin.
●ALBUMS: Various *Best Of Reggae Dance Hall Vol. 1* (Rohit 1984)★★★, *Best Of Reggae Dance Hall Vol. 2* (Rohit 1985)★★★, *Dance Hall Session* (RAS 1986)★★★. Yellowman *Nobody Move, Nobody Get Hurt*. (Greensleeves 1984)★★★. Barrington Levy *Here I Come* (Time 1985)★★★. Josey Wales *The Outlaw Josey Wales* (Greensleeves 1983)★★★.

DANIELS, PHIL, AND THE CROSS

Daniels, a graduate of London's Anna Scher Theatre School and a member of the Royal Shakespeare Company, had flirted with pop as part of Renoir. Following his involvement in the Mod blockbuster, *Quadrophenia*, the persona of Jimmy the Mod was launched into the rock world with the aid of Peter Hugo-Daly (keyboards), Barry Neil (bass) and John McWilliams (drums), Daniels himself handling both vocal and guitar duties. A solitary album on RCA Records was offered, but sales were minimal, this despite full-page advertisements in the music press, a charitable reaction from some critics and a concert itinerary centred on the metropolis. Daniels returned to stage, television and film work, notably satirizing the music industry in Hazel O'Connor's *Breaking Glass*. In 1994 he was to be found singing in a new West End production of *Carousel*, while also being celebrated as a cult icon of the 70s and 80s (being featured on the cover of the hip dance compilation, *The Junior Boy's Own Collection*). His vocals on Blur's *Parklife* title track gave him further exposure.
●ALBUMS: *Phil Daniels And The Cross* (RCA 1980)★★.

DANNY WILSON

This pop act from Dundee, Scotland, whose clean-cut image was enshrined by their reputation for tidying up hotel rooms after 'trashing' them, had their first hit in 1985 with a blend of Steely Dan and soul harmonics on a promising debut album. *Meet Danny Wilson* boasted the hit singles 'Mary's Prayer', an extended Catholic metaphor, and 'Davy'. The subsequent album was too derivative in its focus on 60s beat, although it did provide another hit in 'Second Summer Of Love'. *Sweet Danny Wilson* is a retrospective compiling the best of the two aforementioned albums. After the group split up, vocalist Gary Clark released his debut solo album in 1993, *Ten Short Songs About Love*.
●ALBUMS: *Meet Danny Wilson* (Virgin 1987)★★★, *Be Bop Mop Top* (Virgin 1989)★★★.
●COMPILATIONS: *Sweet Danny Wilson* (Virgin 1991)★★★.

DANSE SOCIETY

These UK gothic rock innovators evolved from Sheffield bands Y? and Lips-X. The two groups merged as Danse Crazy, establishing the line-up as Steve Rawlings (vocals) Paul Gilmartin (drums) Lyndon Scarfe (keyboards) and Paul Nash (guitar), as additional guitar and keyboard players were jettisoned. These included Paul Hampshire (aka Bee and Paul Hertz). They came to prominence first at the Futurama Festival 2 in Leeds which was filmed by BBC Television. After a slight change of name to Danse Society, and the filling of the bass position with Tim Wright, they performed their first gig at the Marples venue in Sheffield. The self-produced 'Clock' single provided the band with some acclaim, despite its short run of 1000 copies. Management duties were taken over by Marcus Featherby, who released their EP, *No Shame In Death*, on his own Pax Records label. However, they soon returned to their own Society Records. The mini-album, *Seduction*, garnered strong support in the media and the band embarked on a series of interviews and live dates. Following one more independent single they signed to Arista Records: 'We'd done the Society Records thing and taken it as far as we could independently, we were totally out of money.' The dramatic 'Wake Up' was their debut, its sense of mystery and dark charm pre-dating the 'gothic' scene by at least a year. *Heaven Is Waiting* provided their first full album's worth of material, and further airplay from BBC disc jockeys John Peel and Janice Long kept them in the ascendent.

However, internal rifts saw the replacement of Scarfe with former Music For Pleasure member David Whitaker. Relations with their record company also deteriorated when Arista failed to back a US tour. Litigation delayed further activities until a compromise was reached in March 1985. When they returned with 'Say It Again' (produced by Stock, Aitken And Waterman), it was to a bemused audience who had not anticipated such a sudden shift in style. The more commercial nature of their subsequent work failed to impress, and Arista rejected their proposed second album, *Heaven Again*. When they split in April 1986, Rawlings attempted to persevere with the funk-orientated Society, while the rest of the band continued briefly as Johnny In The Clouds. Since then Rawlings has only dabbled with music, Wright and Scarfe both work in the computer industry.

●ALBUMS: *Seduction* mini-album (Arista 1982)★★★, *Heaven Is Waiting* (Arista 1984)★★★.

DARLING BUDS

Formed in Wales in 1987 by Andrea Lewis (b. 25 March 1967, Newport, Wales; vocals), Harley Farr (b. 4 July 1964, Singapore; guitar), Bloss (drums) and Chris McDonagh (b. 6 March 1962, Newport, Wales; bass), the early part of the Darling Buds' career was as much a pure adrenalin rush as was their poppy/punk music. Following in the tradition of classic pop records by Blondie and the Waitresses, the Buds produced a series of sparkling sub-three minute singles on the independent Native Records label ('Shame On You', etc.), becoming embroiled in the superfluous 'Blond' scene of that time alongside the Primitives. With the added incentive of increasingly celebrational live performances, Epic Records swiftly signed the band in 1988 and earned moderate chart success for subsequent singles 'Burst' and 'Hit The Ground'. Unfortunately, in the true spirit of bubblegum pop, the Darling Buds' balloon soon began to deflate. Drummer Bloss was replaced by Jimmy Hughes (b. Liverpool, England) and the band's second album, *Crawdaddy*, witnessed a new sophisticated approach to recording that was at odds with their early material, creating few ripples in the musical pond. *Erotica* then emerged just one month before Madonna's opus of the same title, though doubtless it would have been ignored by a now disinterested music media no matter under what flag it sailed.

●ALBUMS: *Pop Said* (Epic 1989)★★★, *Crawdaddy* (Epic 1990)★★★, *Erotica* (Epic 1992)★★★

DAVIS, MAC

b. Mac Scott Davis, 21 January 1942, Lubbock, Texas, USA. Davis grew up with a love of country music but turned to rock 'n' roll in 1955 when he saw Elvis Presley and Buddy Holly on the same show, an event referred to in his 1980 song, 'Texas In My Rear View Mirror'. Davis, who was already writing songs, learned the guitar and moved to Atlanta, Georgia, where he 'majored in beer and rock 'n' roll'. Davis married when he was 20 and his son, Scotty, became the subject of several songs including 'Watching Scotty Grow', recorded by Bobby Goldsboro and Anthony Newley. In the early 60s Davis took administrative jobs with Vee Jay and Liberty Records and made several unsuccessful records including a revival of the Drifters' 'Honey Love': much of this early work was collected in a 1984 compilation, inaccurately called *20 Golden Songs*. A parody of Bob Dylan, 'I Protest', was produced by Joe South. Davis wrote 'The Phantom Strikes Again', which was recorded by Sam The Sham And The Pharaohs, and, in 1967, he had his first chart success when Lou Rawls recorded 'You're Good For Me'. 'Friend, Lover, Woman, Wife' and 'Daddy's Little Man' were both recorded by O.C. Smith. Davis wrote 'Memories' and 'Nothingsville' for Elvis Presley's 1968 comeback television special, and Presley's renaissance continued with Davis's social commentary, 'In The Ghetto'. Presley also recorded 'Don't Cry, Daddy', inspired by Scotty telling Davis not to be upset by television footage of the Vietnam war, 'Clean Up Your Own Back Yard', 'Charro' and 'A Little Less Conversation'. 'Something's Burning' was a hit for Kenny Rogers And The First Edition, while Gallery made the US charts with the much-recorded 'I Believe In Music'. Davis wrote the songs for the Glen Campbell film, *Norwood*, including 'Everything A Man Could Ever Need'. Davis's second marriage was to 18-year-old Sarah Barg in 1971. His first album, named from Glen Campbell's description of him, *Song Painter*, was full of good material but his voice was limited and the album was bathed in strings. Davis topped the US charts in 1972 with the pleasant but inconsequential 'Baby, Don't Get Hooked On Me', its success ironically being due to the publicity from angry feminists. Davis says, 'The record sounded arrogant but I was really saying, 'don't get involved with me because I don't deserve it.' Davis also had US success with 'One Hell Of A Woman', 'Stop And Smell The Roses', 'Rock 'n' Roll (I Gave You The Best Years Of My Life)' and 'Forever Lovers'. *Rolling*

Stone, disliking his pop-country hits, claimed that Davis had 'done more to set back the cause of popular music in the 70s than any other figure'. The curly-haired golfer often wrote of his love for his wife but in 1975 she left him for a short marriage to Glen Campbell. Davis's own career has included playing Las Vegas showrooms and the films *North Dallas 40*, *Cheaper To Keep Her* and *The Sting II*. 'You're My Bestest Friend', an obvious nod to Don Williams' success, was a US country hit in 1981 and 'I Never Made Love (Till I Made Love To You)' was on the US country charts for six months in 1985. His witty 'It's Hard To Be Humble' has become Max Bygraves' closing number. Davis's UK success has been limited but even if he has no further hits, he is assured of work in Las Vegas showrooms. He chose to retire in 1989 but after intensive treatment for alcoholism he eventually resumed his career with a new album in 1994.

●ALBUMS: *Song Painter* (Columbia 1971)★★, *I Believe In Music* (Columbia 1972)★★, *Baby, Don't Get Hooked On Me* (Columbia 1972)★★, *Mac Davis* (Columbia 1973)★★, *Stop And Smell The Roses* (Columbia 1974)★★, *All The Love In The World* (Columbia 1974)★★, *Burning Thing* (Columbia 1975)★★, *Forever Lovers* (Columbia 1976)★★, *Thunder In The Afternoon* (Columbia 1977)★★, *Fantasy* (1978)★★, *It's Hard To Be Humble* (Casablanca 1980)★★, *Texas In My Rear View Mirror* (Casablanca 1980)★★, *Midnight Crazy* (Casablanca 1981)★★, *Forty '82* (1982)★★, *Soft Talk* (Casablanca 1984)★★, *Who's Loving You?* (1984)★★, *Till I Made It With You* (MCA 1985)★★, *Will Write Songs For Food* (Columbia 1994)★★.

●COMPILATIONS: *20 Golden Songs* (Astan 1984)★★★.

DAX, DANIELLE

b. Southend, Essex, England. Dax first came to prominence in 1980 with Karl Blake in the engaging Lemon Kittens. After *We Buy A Hammer For Daddy* and *The Big Dentist*, the group broke up in 1982. Dax next pursued a more straightforward pop route, mixed with forays into ethnic music and the *avant garde*. Her first solo album, *Pop-Eyes*, featured her playing 15 instruments, as well as composing and producing. She also displayed talents as a sleeve designer, contributing to Robert Fripp's *League Of Gentlemen* among others. After a brief detour into acting, during which she appeared in the film, *A Company Of Wolves*, she returned to the recording scene in 1984. *Jesus Egg That Wept* was a mini-album which preceded an extensive UK tour during which she was backed by Dave Knight,

Steve Reeves, Ian Sturgess and Martin Watts. Former artistic partner Blake also made a comeback on that album's 'Ostrich'. Her 1985 single, 'Yummer Yummer Man', was well received and revealed her love of 60s psychedelia. *Inky Bloaters* was an exceptionally eclectic work which maintained that reputation, and saw reviewers recall a myriad of influences in an attempt to get a handle on its contents. After appearing at the new music seminar in Boston, she was signed more permanently by Seymour Stein to Sire Records. He launched her on the US market with *Dark Adapted Eye*, which added five new picks to selections from *Inky Bloaters*. Her fourth album, *Blast The Human Flower*, produced by Stephen Street, included a revival of the Beatles' 'Tomorrow Never Knows', but was an unhappy mainstream compromise which sacrificed Dax's earlier esotericism for accessibility.

●ALBUMS: *Pop-Eyes* (Initially 1983)★★★, *Jesus Egg That Wept* mini-album (Awesome 1984)★★★, *Inky Bloaters* (Awesome 1987)★★★, *Dark Adapted Eye* (Sire 1988)★★★, *Blast The Human Flower* (Sire 1990)★★.

●COMPILATIONS: *Comatose-Non-Reaction: The Thwarted Pop Career Of ...* (Biter Of Thorpe 1995)★★★.

●VIDEOS: *Danielle Dax* (1987).

DAZZ BAND

Bobby Harris masterminded the formation of the Dazz Band in the late 70s when he combined two Cleveland funk outfits, Bell Telefunk and the Kinsman Grill house band. The result was an eight-piece line-up, with Harris, Pierre DeMudd and Skip Martin III handling horns and vocals, and Eric Fearman (guitar), Kevin Frederick (keyboards), Kenny Pettus (percussion), Michael Wiley (bass) and Isaac Wiley (drums) providing the instrumental support.

Coining the word 'Dazz' as a contraction of 'danceable jazz', Harris initially named the band Kinsman Dazz, under which moniker they registered two minor US hits in 1978 and 1979. The following year, they signed to Motown Records, where their irresistible blend of dance rhythms and commercial melodies established them as one of the label's hottest acts of the 80s. Their early albums were firmly in the jazz-funk style pioneered by Earth, Wind And Fire and George Benson. They graduated towards a harder, less melodic funk sound, enjoying a US Top 10 hit with 'Let It Whip' in 1982, which won them a Grammy award for the best performance by an R&B Vocal

Duo or Group. Notable British success followed with the tougher, sparse rhythm of 'Let It All Blow'. *Jukebox* marked a transition towards a more rock-orientated sound which brought them continued success in the specialist black music charts, though crossover recognition among pop fans proved more elusive. The band suffered two personnel changes in 1985, when Marlon McClain and Keith Harrison replaced Eric Fearman and Kevin Frederick. A switch to Geffen Records in 1986 proved unfulfilling, and the group quickly moved on to RCA Records, where they have yet to re-establish their hit-making form.

●ALBUMS: *Invitation To Love* (Motown 1980)★★★, *Let The Music Play* (Motown 1981)★★★, *Keep It Live* (Motown 1982)★★★, *On The One* (Motown 1983)★★★, *Joystick* (Motown 1983)★★★, *Jukebox* (Motown 1984)★★★, *Hot Spot* (Motown 1985)★★, *Wild And Free* (Geffen 1986)★★, *Rock The Room* (RCA 1988)★★, *Under The Streetlights* (Lucky 1996)★★★.

DB'S

Founder-members of the US pop unit the dB's, Chris Stamey (guitars/vocals), Gene Holder (bass) and Will Rigby (drums) had made their name around North Carolina, USA, with the Sneakers, alongside Mitch Easter (guitar/vocals). After two EPs (in 1976 and 1978) on Alan Betrock's Car label, Easter departed (later surfacing with Let's Active); the remaining three teamed up with keyboardist Peter Holsapple (ex-H-Bombs), to create the dB's. Stamey and Holsapple had previously worked together in Rittenhouse Square as early as 1972, while Stamey had indulged in a solo effort, 'Summer Sun' on Ork, in 1977. The dB's' debut single, 'I Thought (You Wanted To Know)', on the Car label, was issued towards the end of 1978, by which time the band had relocated to New York City. Signing with Shake, they then came up with 'Black And White', attracting attention in the UK, and sealing a contract with Albion. The dB's delivered two albums in as many years for Albion, both capturing an evocative blend of melodic, occasionally Beatles-styled songs and new wave sensibilities. 'Dynamite', 'Big Brown Eyes' and 'Judy' were drawn from *Stands For Decibels* (1981) while the following year's *Repercussions* spawned 'Amplifier', 'Neverland' and 'Living A Lie'. However, the dB's failed to make any significant commercial impact. Stamey was the first to leave and release a solo work, *In The Winter Of Love*, in 1984. An apathetic British reception meant that his second album, *It's Alright* on A&M Records, failed to secure a UK

release. In the meantime, the dB's replaced Stamey with Jeff Beninato and reunited for *The Sound Of Music* on IRS, joined by guests Van Dyke Parks and Syd Straw. Since then, Peter Holsapple has been busy working in the wings with R.E.M..

●ALBUMS: *Stands For Decibels* (Albion 1981)★★★★, *Repercussions* (Albion 1982)★★★, *Like This* (Bearsville 1985)★★★★, *The Sound Of Music* (IRS 1987)★★★.

●COMPILATIONS: *Amplifier* (1986)★★★, *The dB's Ride The Wild Tom Tom* (Rhino 1993)★★★★.

DE BURGH, CHRIS

b. Christopher Davidson, 15 October 1948, Argentina. The son of a UK diplomat, DeBurgh began writing pop songs while studying at Trinity College in Dublin. After being signed to A&M Records he was pushed out as support act for Supertramp, when they were enjoying massive success in 1975. His debut, *Far Beyond These Castle Walls*, had strong shades of the cosmic period Moody Blues, although his light-rock tales of historical fantasy were deemed a little fey by the critics. A single 'Flying' taken from the album failed to sell in the UK, but became a number 1 hit in Brazil. His follow-up *Spanish Train And Other Stories* also failed to sell, but one track, the hauntingly catchy 'A Spaceman Came Travelling', was picked up by British disc jockeys and became a perennial Christmas radio hit. Whilst DeBurgh could not break through in Britain and the USA, he was highly successful in Canada, South Africa, Europe and South America. His fifth album *Eastern Wind* outsold the Beatles' *Let It Be* in Norway, as it topped their charts. After an interminable wait he finally had a UK hit in 1982 with the Rupert Hine-produced *The Getaway*, containing the infectious minor hit 'Don't Pay The Ferryman'. His best-received album to date, *Man On The Line*, came in 1984, with another minor hit, 'High On Emotion', but it was the following year that the compilation *The Very Best Of* made him a big name in the UK. After 11 years of touring and two dozen singles, DeBurgh finally made the UK number 1 in 1986 with the irresistibly romantic 'Lady In Red'. The record became a worldwide hit and established him as a major artist. All his back catalogue began to sell to a new generation of fans and the re-released 'A Spaceman Came Travelling' finally made the UK charts in 1987. DeBurgh maintained his ability to write a perfect pop song with the infectious 'Missing You' in 1988, which narrowly missed the top spot in the UK, while *Into The Light* continued his now easier march into the best sellers. *Flying Colours* became his biggest-selling album to date when it topped the UK album lists in 1988. In 1991, following the Gulf War, DeBurgh donated all proceeds from his song 'The Simple Truth' to the Kurdish refugees. His 1992 release *Power Of Ten* maintained his standards. DeBurgh is to be congratulated for the way he has stuck to his guns by not changing his musical direction for the sake of commercial gain, and in his own words from his letter to the A&M Records chairman: 'There is life after the Sex Pistols'. Much controversy surrounded the singer in 1995 when he had a brief affair with his children's nanny. The press took glee in the fact that this could be the lady in red. A few months later De Burgh was again hitting the headlines when he confessed that the aforementioned song was not about his wife after all. At the end of a turbulent year he released *Beautiful Dreams*, a live album with an orchestra. On this collection he revisited his past by covering tracks by Elvis, the Beatles and Roy Orbison.

●ALBUMS: *Far Beyond These Walls* (A&M 1975)★★, *Spanish Train And Other Stories* (A&M 1976)★★, *At The End Of A Perfect Day* (A&M 1977)★★, *Crusader* (A&M 1979)★★, *Eastern Wind* (A&M 1980)★★, *Best Moves* (A&M 1981)★★★, *The Getaway* (A&M 1982)★★★, *Man On The Line* (A&M 1984)★★★, *Into The Light* (A&M 1986)★★★, *Flying Colours* (A&M 1988)★★★, *High On Emotion - Live From Dublin* (A&M 1990)★★, *Power Of Ten* (A&M 1992)★★, *This Way Up* (A&M 1994)★★, *Beautiful Dreams* (A&M 1995)★★.

●COMPILATIONS: *The Very Best Of Chris DeBurgh* (Telstar 1984)★★★, *From A Spark To A Flame: The Very Best Of Chris DeBurgh* (A&M 1989)★★★.

DE DANNAN

Formed in Eire during the 70s, this group have amalgamated contemporary and traditional folk music. With a line-up of Alec Finn (guitar/bouzouki), Frankie Gavin (fiddle/flute/whistle), Dolores Keane (b. Caherlistrane, Co. Galway, Eire; vocals), Johnny 'Ringo' McDonagh (bodhran/percussion), and Jackie Daly (melodeon), they produced a highly original sound. Original singer Maura McConnell, left to pursue a solo career, with her replacement, Mary Black, doing likewise in 1986. Keane, who took over, has since gone on to record and perform in a solo capacity. At one time, invited by Gavin, they were joined by cellist Caroline Lavelle. The current line-up - Gavin, Finn, Aiden Coffey (accordion), Colm Murphy (bodhran), and Eleanor Shanley (vocals) - still retain the distinctive sound for which

the group is known. Even after 15 years, with the various changes in personnel, De Dannan have still retained the quality that distinguishes them from a number of other groups that have inevitably followed in their wake. Even when Charlie Piggot, Maura O'Connell and Jackie Daly left, at one point leaving just Finn, McDonagh and Gavin, many would have given up; instead they took on Mary Black and Martin O'Connor and produced *Song For Ireland*. The group is still popular in concert, and tour regularly, both at home and overseas.

●ALBUMS: *De Dannan* (1975)★★★, *Selected Jigs Reels And Songs* (1977)★★★, *The Mist Covered Mountain* (Gael-Linn1980)★★★, *Star Spangled Molly* (Ogham 1981)★★★, *Song For Ireland* (Cara 1983)★★★★, *Anthem* (Cara 1985)★★★, *Ballroom* (Warners 1987)★★★, *A Jacket Of Batteries* (Harmac 1989)★★★, *1/2 Set In Harlem* (Celtic Music 1991)★★★. Solo: Frankie Gavin *Frankie Goes To Town* (Bees Knees 1991)★★★.

●COMPILATIONS: *Best Of De Dannan* (Shanachie 1985)★★★.

DE GRASSI, ALEX

b. 13 February 1952, Yokosuka, Japan. The acoustic guitar sound of De Grassi had much to do with the growth and success of the Windham Hill label during the 80s. His clean, open-tuned new-age music was similar, although more complex, to that of founder William Ackerman. Together with another Windham Hill artist Michael Hedges they pioneered much of the solo acoustic guitar terrain to which the new-age market was receptive. Although he started his musical education on trumpet, he took up the guitar at 13. Like Ackerman he was drawn to the music of John Fahey and Leo Kottke but also cites John Renbourn as a major influence. De Grassi's music is both sombre and uplifting, good examples are 'Western' from *Southern Exposure* and 'Clockwork' from *Clockwork*. The arrangements include minimal accompaniment from a small ensemble. De Grassi moved away from the label in the mid-80s, wanting to expand his musical horizon and feeling constricted by the stigma attached to Windham Hill. On *Altiplano* he used piano and guitar synthesizer and with an expanded line-up including bassist Mark Egan he demonstrated a strong South American and Middle-Eastern influence. By 1992 De Grassi had returned to the Windham Hill fold and remains an outstanding acoustic guitarist.

●ALBUMS: *Turning: Turning Back* (Windham Hill 1978)★★★, *Slow Circle* (Windham Hill 1979)★★, *Clockwork* (Windham Hill 1980)★★★, *Southern*

Exposure (Windham Hill 1983)★★★★, *Altiplano* (1987)★★★, *Deep At Night* (1991)★★.
●FURTHER READING: *Guitar Collection*, Alex De Grassi.

DEAD KENNEDYS

The undoubted kings of US punk, the Dead Kennedys, formed in San Francisco, California, USA, arrived on the 80s music scene with the most vitriolic and ultimately persuasive music ever to marshal the US underground (at least until the arrival of Nirvana). Even today the sight of their name can send the uninitiated into a fit of apoplexy. Originally a quintet with a second guitarist called 6025, he left before recordings for the debut album took place, leaving a core group of Jello Biafra (b. Eric Boucher, 17 June 1958, Denver, Colorado, USA; vocals), Klaus Flouride (bass), East Bay Ray Glasser (guitar) and Ted (b. Bruce Slesinger; drums). As soon as they hit a studio the results were extraordinary. Biafra, weaned partially on 70s Brit Punk as well as local San Francisco bands like Crime and the Nuns, was the consummate frontman, his performances never far away from personal endangerment, including stage-diving and verbally lambasting his audience. He was certainly never destined to be an industry conformist - some of his more celebrated stunts included getting married in a graveyard, running for Mayor of San Francisco (he finished fourth) and allowing the crowd to disrobe him on stage. Lyrically, the Dead Kennedys always went for the jugular but twisted expectations; writing an anti-neutron bomb song called 'Kill The Poor' is a good example of their satire. The band's debut single, 'California Uber Alles', attacked the 'new age' fascism of Californian governor Jerry Brown, a theme developed over a full blown musical rollercoaster ride. Just as enduring is its follow-up, 'Holiday In Cambodia', which mercilessly parodied college student chic and the indifference to the suffering caused to others by America's foreign policy: 'Playing ethnicky jazz to parade your snazz on your five grand stereo/Bragging that you know how the niggers feel cold and the slum's got so much soul'. 'Too Drunk To Fuck', naturally despite a complete absence of airplay, made the UK Top 40 (there were a number of prosecutions linked to those wearing the accompanying T-shirt). Biafra established his own Alternative Tentacles Records after a brief flirtation with Miles Copeland's IRS Records label (Cherry Red Records in the UK), and this has gone to on be a staple of the US alternative record scene, releasing music by both peers and progeny:

Hüsker Dü, TSOL, DOA, No Means No, Beatnigs and Alice Donut. Slesinger broke away to form the Wolverines at this point, having never been quite in tune with the Kennedys' musical dynamic. His eventual replacement was Darren H. Peligro (ex-Nub; Speedboys; Hellations; SSI; who had also played guitar with the Jungle Studs and was the drummer for an early incarnation of Red Hot Chili Peppers). If the band's debut album, *Fresh Fruit For Rotting Vegetables*, had followed a broadly traditional musical format, *In God We Trust Inc.* indulged in full blown thrash. Undoubtedly the long-term inspiration behind literally hundreds of US noise merchants, it certainly took many by surprise with its minimalist adrenaline ('Dog Bite/On My Leg/S'Not Right, S'posed to Beg' practically encompassed the entire lyrics to one song). *Plastic Surgery Disasters* saw the band branch out again. Though it did not share *Fresh Fruit*'s immediacy, there were several stunning songs on offer once more ('Trust Your Mechanic' with Biafra's typically apocalyptic delivery, attacked the values of the service industry and 'Well Paid Scientist', which mocked the career ladder). *Frankenchrist* was more considered, allowing songs like 'Soup Is Good Food' to bite hard. The cornerstone of the recording was 'Stars And Stripes Of Corruption', which predicted some of Biafra's later solo excursions by relentlessly pursuing a single theme. *Bedtime For Democracy* was the band's final studio recording, and a return to the aggressive speed of the previous mini-album, though without the shock value. Meanwhile Biafra was on trial for the artwork given away with *Frankenchrist*, a pastiche of American consumerism by H.R. Giger (*Landscape #20* - often referred to as 'Penis Landscape'), which made its point with a depiction of row upon row of male genitalia entering anuses (i.e. everybody fucking everybody else). Long an irritant to the US moral 'guardians', the PMRC now had Biafra in their sights. In truth the band had elected to call it a day anyhow, but there was a long hibernation while Biafra weathered the storm (he was eventually cleared on all counts and the case thrown out of court) before embarking on his next creative phase - an episodic solo career marked by collaborations with DOA and No Means No. Flouride released two albums for Alternative Tentacles, while East Bay Ray formed Scrapyard. The Dead Kennedys' contribution meanwhile, is best measured not by the number of copy bands who sprung up around the world, but by the enduring quality of their best records and Biafra's admirable and unyielding stance on artistic censorship.

●ALBUMS: *Fresh Fruit For Rotting Vegetables* (IRS/Cherry Red 1980)★★★, *In God We Trust Inc.* mini-album (Alternative Tentacles/Faulty 1981)★★★, *Plastic Surgery Disasters* (Alternative Tentacles 1982)★★★, *Frankenchrist* (Alternative Tentacles 1985)★★★, *Bedtime For Democracy* (Alternative Tentacles 1986)★★★.
●COMPILATIONS: *Give Me Convenience Or Give Me Death* (Alternative Tentacles 1987)★★★★.
●VIDEOS: *Live In San Francisco* (1987).

DEAD MILKMEN

US crypto punk band the Dead Milkmen came from the active Philadelphian underground scene of the mid-80s and drew members who rejoiced in the unlikely names Joe Jack Talcum (guitar/vocals), Rodney Anonymous Melloncamp (vocals), Dave Blood (bass) and Dean Clean (drums). With each of their album titles punning a more famous rock release and songs such as 'Takin' Retards To The Zoo', 'Beach Party Vietnam', and 'The Thing That Only Eats Hippies', the Dead Milkmen were always destined for college favouritism. Utilizing an uncomplicated adolescent punk rock foundation, the group's debut album set out its stall by loading up on youthful satire and demanding to know the answer to the eternal questions - like why does anybody like the Doors. As basic but slightly more astute was *Eat Your Paisley!*, its b-movie song titles suggesting there was no immediate end in sight for the Milkmen's hyperactive juvenilia. *Bucky Fellini* saw a more fully fledged musical format, aided by guest musicians and improved songwriting - though with lyrical targets including '(Theme From) Blood Orgy Of The Atomic Fern' and 'Nitro Burning Funny Cars' it was obvious that the band had not yet turned into a 'proper' rock group. *Beelzebubba* boasted the minor hit single 'Punk Rock Girl', but was undistinguished elsewhere. The best song title yet arrived in 'If You Love Somebody, Set Them On Fire', drawn from the improved *Metaphysical Graffiti*. Guests included Butthole Surfers' Gilby Clarke on the near-hysterical prog rock bluff, 'Anderson, Walkman, Buttholes and How!'
●ALBUMS: *Big Lizard In My Back Yard* (Fever/Enigma 1985)★★, *Eat Your Paisley!* (Fever/Restless 1986)★★, *Bucky Fellini* (Fever/Enigma 1987)★★★, *Instant Club Hit (You'll Dance To Anything)* mini-album (Fever/Enigma 1987)★★, *Beelzebubba* (Fever/Enigma 1988)★★, *Metaphysical Graffiti* (Enigma 1990)★★, *Soul Rotation* (Hollywood 1992)★★★, *Not Richard, But Dick* (Hollywood 1993)★★★, *Chaos Rules: Live At* *The Trocadero* (Restless 1994)★★, *Stoney's Extra Stout (Pig)* (Restless 1996)★★.

DEAD OR ALIVE

One of this group's principal assets was the androgynous persona of Pete Burns (b. 5 August 1959; vocals) who had fronted Liverpool's Mystery Girls in 1977, then Nightmares In Wax, in which he was accompanied by Mick Reid (guitar), Martin Healy (keyboards), Walter Ogden (bass) and ex-Mystery Girl Phil Hurst (drums). The group recorded an EP for a local label and a track for a 1980 compilation *Hicks From The Sticks*, before Burns and Healy formed Dead Or Alive with Sue James (bass), Joe Musker (drums) and a flux of guitarists. The line-up stabilized when the act was signed to Inevitable for some flop singles before soliciting the attentions of Epic, which saw their singer as an 'answer' to Boy George. With Burns dressed in a feminine fashion, the band's television plugs sent a revival of KC And The Sunshine Band's 'That's The Way I Like It' into the UK Top 30 in 1984. Slowly but surely, 'You Spin Me Round (Like A Record)', from *Youthquake*, arrived at number 1 in the New Year and was the first UK chart topper for Stock, Aitken And Waterman. Soundalike follow-ups fared less well but, after the UK chart-topper entered the US Top 20, the band enjoyed further major record success in the late 80s with *Youthquake* moderately high in *Billboard*'s album list, and its title track returning them to the UK Top 10. By this time, Burns' backing musicians comprised Timothy Lever (keyboards), Mike Percy (bass) and Steve McCoy (drums), augmented in concert by former Gary Numan sidemen Russ Bell (guitar) and Chris Page (keyboards). In the 90s they found greater success abroad, especially in Japan where *Nukleopatra* was a major hit. Epic Records failed to renew their contract in the UK and the band have had to work hard at building a following overseas.
●ALBUMS: *Sophisticated Boom Boom* (Epic 1984)★★, *Youthquake* (Epic 1985)★★★, *Mad, Bad And Dangerous To Know* (Epic 1987)★★, *Nude* (Epic 1989)★★, *Nukleopatra* (Sony 1995)★★.
●VIDEOS: *Youthquake* (1988).

DEBARGE

One sister, Bunny DeBarge, and four brothers, Mark, James, Randy and El DeBarge, combined to form this family group in Grand Rapids, Michigan in 1978. Signed to Motown Records in 1979, they were viewed and marketed as successors to the young Jackson Five, a ploy helped by the physical similarity between El DeBarge and Michael

Jackson. After several years of grooming from Motown's A&R department, the group (then known as the DeBarges) were launched with the album *The DeBarges* in March 1981, and achieved their initial soul hit 18 months later. 'I Like It' repeated this success and crossed over into the pop charts, while two 1983 hits, 'All This Love' and 'Time Will Reveal', established DeBarge as one of America's most popular acts in the teenage market.

A support slot on Luther Vandross's 1984 USA tour brought them to a wider audience, and in 1985 they scored their biggest hit with the seductive 'Rhythm Of The Night', taken from the soundtrack to Motown's film *The Last Dragon*, in which the group also appeared. This single reached number 3 in the US charts, a success which the follow-up release, 'Who's Holding Donna Now?', came close to repeating. Lead vocalist Eldra DeBarge had become synonymous with the group's name, and his decision to go solo in February 1986 effectively sabotaged the group's career. In 1987, Bunny also departed when the rest of the group signed to Striped Horse Records. In the event, only Mark and James (who had briefly been married to Janet Jackson in the mid-80s) appeared on the resulting *Bad Boys*, by which time their commercial impetus had been lost. The group's wholesome image was seriously damaged by the arrest and conviction of their other brothers Bobby and Chico DeBarge in 1988 on cocaine trafficking charges.

●ALBUMS: *The DeBarges* (Motown 1981)★★★, *All This Love* (Motown 1982)★★★, *In A Special Way* (Motown 1983)★★, *Rhythm Of The Night* (Motown 1985)★★, *Bad Boys* (Striped Horse 1988)★★.
●COMPILATIONS: *Greatest Hits* (Motown 1986)★★★.

DeBarge, Bunny

b. Grand Rapids, Michigan, USA. Bunny DeBarge was a vocalist in the family group DeBarge from their inception in 1978 until 1987. She was the first member of the group to be married, and missed several national tours during her three pregnancies, although she appeared regularly on their Motown Records releases. In 1987, she chose to remain as a solo artist with the label rather than follow the rest of the group to Striped Horse Records. Her loyalty was rewarded when *In Love*, a light pop/soul concoction, was a minor US hit album, and 'Save The Best For Me' became a US Top 20 black music hit.

●ALBUMS: *In Love* (Motown 1987)★★.

DeBarge, Chico

b. Jonathan 'Chico' DeBarge, 1966, Grand Rapids, Michigan, USA. Chico DeBarge was too young to join the family group DeBarge in 1978, but he was signed to a solo deal with Motown Records in 1986, issuing a self-titled album in a harder, funk-rooted style than his brothers and sisters. His debut single, 'Talk To Me', was a major US hit, and he achieved four more black music chart entries up to 1988. His career was effectively ended when he and his brother Bobby DeBarge (a former member of the Motown group Switch) were arrested and then convicted on charges of trafficking cocaine in October 1988.

●ALBUMS: *Chico DeBarge* (Motown 1986)★★★.

DeBarge, El

b. 4 June 1961, Grand Rapids, Michigan, USA. Eldra DeBarge became the lead singer of the family vocal group DeBarge from their formation in 1978. He was featured on all the group's hits between 1982 and 1985, when he elected to pursue a solo career, leaving DeBarge the following year. His eponymous debut album was an attractive mixture of pop and soul, fashioned in the style of Michael Jackson, on whom DeBarge has modelled his career. He scored a US number 1 black music hit in 1986 with 'Who's Johnny?', the theme song of the film *Short Circuit*, and re-emerged after a two-year pause in his career with the single 'Real Love' in 1989.

●ALBUMS: *El DeBarge* (Gordy 1986)★★★, *Heart, Mind & Soul* (Warners/Reprise 1994)★★★.

Def Leppard

This supremely popular hard rock band was formed in Sheffield by Pete Willis (b. 16 February 1960, Sheffield, England; guitar), Rick Savage (b. 2 December 1960, Sheffield, England; bass) and Tony Kenning (drums), as Atomic Mass. They assumed their current name when Joe Elliott (b. 1 August 1959, Sheffield, England; vocals) joined the band. The quartet initially hired a tiny room in a spoon factory, which served as a rehearsal area, for £5 per week. Early in 1978, Willis met another young guitarist Steve Clark (b. 23 April 1960, Sheffield, England, d. 8 January 1991, London, England), and invited him to join. Clark agreed only on condition that they would play some 'proper' shows, and in July that year Def Leppard debuted at Westfield School before an audience of 150 children. After several gigs, the band voted to dismiss their drummer, replacing him with Frank Noon, who was working with another Sheffield group, the Next Band. In 1979 they recorded a debut EP for Bludgeon Riffola Records, which included 'Ride Into The Sun', 'Getcha Rocks Off' and 'The Overture'. Shortly after its release, Noon returned to the Next Band, and Rick Allen (b. 1 November 1963, Sheffield, England) became Def Leppard's permanent drummer. Later that year the band supported Sammy Hagar and AC/DC on short UK tours. This generated considerable interest and they were then offered a deal by Vertigo Records. Their Tom Allom-produced debut, *On Through The Night*, was issued in 1980. The band subsequently staged their first headlining tour of Britain and also visited America for the first time - something which prompted fans to accuse them of 'selling out', making their displeasure known by throwing cans at the band during their appearance at the Reading Festival that summer. *Pyromania* in 1983 saw the first change in the band's line-up since 1979. After missing many pre-production meetings and turning up drunk for a recording session, Pete Willis was sacked and replaced by ex-Girl guitarist Phil Collen (b. 8 December 1957, Hackney, London, England). The album was Def Leppard's most successful to date, but they were unable to build on that momentum. On New Year's Eve 1984, tragedy struck when drummer Rick Allen was involved in a car crash in which he lost his left arm. The band maintained faith with their percussionist, and did not resume work until Allen had perfected a specially designed kit which made it possible for him to play most of the drums with his feet. His recovery severely delayed the recording of *Hysteria*, which was finally released in 1987 and eventually sold a staggering 15 million copies worldwide. It topped both the British and American charts, and produced two Top 5 US singles, 'Armageddon It' and the anthemic 'Pour Some Sugar On Me'. To promote the album, the band embarked on a 14-month world tour, which ended at the Memorial Arena, Seattle, in October 1988. This was destined to be Steve Clark's last show with the band. As they began work on their belated follow-up to *Hysteria*, Clark was found dead in his London flat after consuming a mixture of drugs and alcohol. The rest of the band subsequently revealed that they had spent years trying to dissuade Clark from his self-abusive lifestyle. Faced once again by tragedy, Def Leppard soldiered manfully through the recording sessions for their fifth album, *Adrenalize*, which was released in March 1992 and immediately scaled the charts, topping the US list almost on release. Greeted with the usual mixture of critical disdain and public delight (the group's fans had chosen the title), Def Leppard celebrated by performing at the Freddy Mercury tribute concert at Wembley Stadium. This event also sought to introduce replacement guitarist Vivian Campbell (b. 25 August 1962, Belfast, Northern Ireland; ex-Dio, Trinity, Whitesnake and Shadow King), who had made his debut at a low-key Dublin gig. In 1995 Rick Allen faced the possibility of two years in jail after he was arrested for assaulting his wife in America. In the meantime, a greatest hits package was released, and a new studio collection *Slang* was released. In 1996 Joe Elliott appeared in the film of Nick Hornby's novel *When Saturday Comes*.

●ALBUMS: *On Through The Night* (Mercury 1980)★★★, *High 'N' Dry* (Mercury 1981)★★★, *Pyromania* (Mercury 1983)★★★★, *Hysteria* (Mercury 1987)★★★★, *Adrenalize* (Mercury 1992)★★★, *Slang* (Mercury 1996)★★★.
●COMPILATIONS: *CD Box Set* (Mercury 1989)★★★, *Retro Active* (Mercury 1993)★★★, *Vault - Def Leppard Greatest Hits 1980-1995* (Mercury 1995)★★★★.
●VIDEOS: *Love Bites* (1988), *Historia* (1988), *Rocket* (1989), *Rock Of Ages* (1989), *In The Round - In Your Face* (1989), *Animal* (1989), *Visualise* (1993), *Unlock The Rock: Video Archive 1993-1995* (Polygram 1995).
●FURTHER READING: *Def Leppard: Animal Instinct*, David Fricke. *Def Leppard*, Jason Rich. *Biographize: The Def Leppard Story*, Dave Dickson.

DEFUNKT

This hard-funk act from the USA centred on trombonist Joseph Bowie who rose to prominence as a member of the Black Artists Group, an *avant garde* collective, based in St. Louis, and patterned after the Art Ensemble Of Chicago. Defunkt drew on this 'new wave' tradition but fused such radical jazz with the dancefloor punch of Parliament and Funkadelic to create an thrilling, invigorating style. Bowie, the brother of trumpeter Lester Bowie, was an inspired frontman and several propulsive albums, notably *Thermonuclear Sweat*, captured their exciting style. Defunkt undertook an enforced four-year sabbatical while its leader battled heroin addiction but emerged anew with *In America*. Bill Bickford, Ronnie Drayton (guitars), John Mulkerik (trumpet), Kim Annette Clarke (bass) and Kenny Martin (drums) joined Bowie for this compulsive set which, if shorn of melody, compensated with sheer excitement.

●ALBUMS: *Defunkt* (Hannibal 1980)★★★, *Thermonuclear Sweat* (Hannibal 1984)★★★, *In*

America (Antilles/New Direction 1988)★★★, Cum Funky (1993)★★★.
●COMPILATIONS: Avoid The Funk (Hannibal 1988)★★★.

DEL FUEGOS

Roots rock 'n' roll revivalists from Boston, Massachusetts, USA, whose early 80s recordings stand as a fine testament to their influences, even if some of their later output was dulled by commercial considerations. The band, led by vocalist Dan Zanes and guitarist brother Warren, with Tom Lloyd (bass) and B. Woody Giessmann (drums), was formally introduced to its public on a 1984 debut album for Slash Records. A winning collection of rounded songs drawing principally from the 60s beat boom, it explored a full complement of moods with energy and belief. 1985's Boston, Mass, a eulogy to their working-class origins, was a more commercially orientated affair, though it lacked something of the sparkle of their debut. If this set had mapped out the possibility of future indulgence, that fear was confirmed with the arrival of Stand Up. With numerous guest appearances (including Tom Petty and James Burton), neither the songwriting nor performances possessed the same spirit or character of old. It was universally panned by reviewers. Presumably as a result, drummer Giessmann (who had formerly worked with the underrated Embarrassment) departed. Smoking In The Fields marked a welcome return to form. With the addition of harp player Magic Dick (ex-J. Geils Band), the band's sound had now soothed to a classy R&B/soul timbre. Producer Dave Thoerner gave the new dynamic a sympathetic treatment and restored the Del Fuegos to critical favour.
●ALBUMS: The Longest Day (Slash 1984)★★★, Boston, Mass (Slash/Warners 1985)★★★, Stand Up (Slash/Warners 1987)★★, Smoking In The Fields (RCA 1989)★★★.

DELTA 5

Leeds, England-originated post-punk band who had much in common with the Au Pairs - though the inspired amateurism that fuelled their early releases proved more reminiscent of the Slits. They released several singles on Rough Trade Records which highlighted insipid but endearing hook lines, the John Peel favourite 'Mind Your Own Business' being a good example (they also recorded two 1980 radio sessions for the programme). The line-up featured Julz Sale (vocals), Alan Riggs (guitar), Ros Allen (bass), Bethan Peters

(bass/vocals) and Kelvin Knight (drums). Sale and Peters were the only two remaining following a major transformation in personnel as they moved to Pre Records. They split up shortly afterwards, though history would prove them to be a great influence on mid-80s indie pop bands like the Shop Assistants and Tallulah Gosh.
●ALBUMS: See The Whirl (Pre 1981)★★★.

DEMON RECORDS

Demon Records was founded in 1980 by Andrew Lauder, fresh from his employment as A&R executive for United Artists Records, and Jake Riviera, manager of Elvis Costello, Nick Lowe and the Damned. Previously, both had worked together in establishing Radar Records in 1978, which they formed to provide an outlet for Costello and Lowe after both had broken from Stiff Records in 1977. After Radar they established F-Beat Records, for whom Elvis Costello And The Attractions recorded 'I Can't Stand Up For Falling Down'. Initially, the Demon label geared itself up for one-off single releases. Among the featured artists were the Subterraneans (who featured New Musical Express journalist Nick Kent), the Spectres (formed by former Sex Pistols' bass player Glen Matlock), TV21 and Department S. The latter band gave Demon its first chart success with 'Is Vic There?', in 1981. Further chart success followed when Bananarama's debut single, 'Aie-A-Mwana', was released (though it was later picked up for distribution by Phonogram Records). Soon the singles-only policy was abandoned with the hope of launching long-term artists. Lauder left the label to join Island Records in 1981. At the same time Demon launched its own subsidiary label, Edsel Records, as a reissue/archive label. Edsel's early releases included a single by mod pioneers the Action (with a sleevenote by Paul Weller), the Escorts and Screamin' Jay Hawkins. It boldly reissued Moby Grape, the Byrds and Gene Clark when they were out of fashion (they continue this policy in the 90s with Spooky Tooth and Ronnie Lane). The parent label, Demon, also moved into reissues as the market for deleted records boomed in the mid-80s. By 1982 Lauder had rejoined the label, which had now expanded to incorporate further labels such as the soul specialist label Hi (Ann Peebles, Willie Mitchell, Al Green) and the psychedelic rock-orientated Drop Out label. Through the 80s Demon became closely identified with imported American roots rock, and, in particular, what became known as the Paisley Underground scene (Green On Red, Long Ryders, Giant Sand,

Beat Farmers and Replacements). Among the UK album acts featured on the roster at this time were The Men They Couldn't Hang, Shamen, Paul Brady, That Petrol Emotion and Christy Moore. All these acts used Demon as a stepping stone to major recording contracts. Lauder left the label for a final time in 1988 (to establish Silvertone and then the This Way Up labels), with Demon concentrating increasingly on the reissue market. Current artists include Lowe, Martin Stephenson, Clive Gregson and Kate Campbell. Much of the respect the company currently enjoys is due to the genuine and tireless enthusiasm of their director of press, Alan Robinson. Demon remain one of the 'dream indies', who clearly love and nurture their product.

DEPECHE MODE

During the UK post-punk backlash at the turn of the 80s, when bands dispensed with guitars and drums in favour of synthesizers and drum machines, Depeche Mode were formed, taking their name from a phrase in a French style magazine. More than a decade later they are recognized as the most successful 'electro-synth' group ever. Ironically enough, given their reputation as the kings of synth-pop, they had made their debut as a trio playing only guitars at Scamps in Southend. The band originally came together in the neighbouring borough of Basildon, Essex, England, in 1980, and comprised: Vince Clarke (b. 3 July 1960, Basildon, Essex, England; synthesizer, ex-No Romance In China), Andy Fletcher (b. 8 July 1960, Basildon, Essex, England; synthesizer) and Martin Gore (b. 23 July 1961, Basildon, Essex, England; synthesizer, ex-The French Look; Norman & The Worms). Following a series of concerts that attracted packed houses at the Bridge House Tavern in London's Canning Town, they were spotted by Daniel Miller. Shortly afterwards they were signed to his independent Mute Records, where they remain. They had already tasted vinyl exposure by issuing one track on Stevo's Some Bizzare compilation in 1981. This had been recorded by the original trio, with Clarke on vocals, before they elected to recruit Dave Gahan (b. 9 May 1962, Epping, Essex, England) as their permanent lead vocalist.

'Dreaming Of Me' in 1981 started a remarkable run of hit singles which by the turn of the decade had totalled 23 chart entries. Principal songwriter Vince Clarke left shortly after Speak And Spell to form Yazoo with Alison Moyet, and the writing reins were taken over by Martin Gore, as Alan Wilder (b. 1 June 1959, England; synthesizer, vocals, ex-Dragons; Hitmen) settled into Clarke's place. The gentle, hypnotic ambience of 'See You' was an early demonstration of Gore's sense of melody.

Only briefly have Depeche Mode found their craft compatible with the tastes of the music press, yet their success reamins a testament to the power of their music, which is arresting yet generally easy on the ear, and often compulsively danceable. Lyrically Gore has tended to tackle subjects a shade darker than the musical content might suggest, including sado-masochism ('Master And Servant'), capitalism ('Everything Counts') and religious fetishism ('Personal Jesus'). As the 90s dawned their albums continued to make the UK Top 10, and they also began to make inroads on the European and American markets, which were late in discovering them. The Violator tour would make them huge concert stars in the USA, selling several million copies worldwide. The album presented a harder sound, informed by Gahan's patronage of the American rock scene, which was continued on Songs Of Faith & Devotion. As their standing throughout the world continued to be enhanced by ambitious stage shows, the latter album debuted in both the US and UK charts at number 1 on its week of release. This despite the fact that thinly veiled acrimony seemed to surround the Depeche Mode camp as it entered the 90s. Wilder departed in 1996. That year, following a catalogue of events surrounding Gahan, he was once again in hospital for a suspected overdose. The change in Gahan over the past few years has seen him relocate from Essex to Los Angeles, divorce his wife, remarry his tattooed American girlfriend, divorce her and then attempt suicide. Additionally Gahan's serious drug dependency seems to have reached a peak when he came close to death in 1996. In a revealing interview with the New Musical Express he spoke about his drug problems to such an extent that the reader is convinced of his determination to stay clean and see a future with his longest love affair, his band. Ultra was a surprisingly good album, considering the fragmentation that had been occurring within the ranks.

●ALBUMS: Speak And Spell (Mute 1981)★★, A Broken Frame (Mute 1982)★★, Construction Time Again (Mute 1983)★★★, Some Great Reward (Mute 1984)★★★, Black Celebration (Mute 1986)★★★, Music For The Masses (Mute 1987)★★★, 101 (Mute 1989)★★, Violator (Mute 1991)★★★★, Songs Of Faith & Devotion (Mute 1993)★★★★, Ultra (Mute 1997)★★★.

●COMPILATIONS: *The Singles 81-85* (Mute 1985)★★★★.
●VIDEOS: *Some Great Videos* (1986), *Strange* (1988), *101* (1989), *Strange Too - Another Violation* (1990), *Devotional* (1993), *Live In Hamburg* (1993).
●FURTHER READING: *Depeche Mode: Strangers - The Photographs*, Anton Corbijn. *Depeche Mode: Some Great Reward*, Dave Thompson.

DESCENDENTS

Los Angeles, California, USA punk band, whose first stage of development was as a three-piece; Frank Navetta (vocals/guitar), Tony Lombardo (vocals/bass) and Bill Stevenson (drums), playing power pop along the lines of the Buzzcocks. It was this formation who were intact for the debut 'Ride The Wild' single. They joined with singer Cecilia for some six months before the near-legendary Milo Auckerman became the first regular vocalist. The resulting period was characterized by songs about fishing and food. Titles like 'Weinerschnitzel' and the self-parodying 'Fat' hail from these merry times. There was also a predilection for loading up on caffeine and measuring the results in song velocity on tour. Shortly afterwards things became more serious, as they recorded their debut album for posterity. Again, the title was self explanatory, with Auckerman indeed being college-bound. There was something of a hiatus in the band's fortunes following this traumatic experience, with Ray Cooper replacing Navetta on guitar in 1985 (he originally tried out as vocalist). Doug Carrion (bass, ex-Anti; Incest Cattle) came in around 1986. He later served in Dag Nasty. Stevenson joined up with Black Flag. Auckerman remembers his choice of career as being a question of priorities: 'I went to El Camino College for my first year, then I went to UC San Diego. I have a problem. I like to immerse myself in things. I'm obsessed with music and I'm obsesssed with biology - so what can I do?'. When the band reconvened three years later, *I Don't Want To Grow Up* followed swiftly on the heels of the reunion. This time the production values were more polished: 'On 'Grow Up' I was more melancholy. We're singing about the same things, just approaching it in a different way. To bring out the feeling behind it rather than just punking it out'. The Descendents were hugely popular in the US because they addressed the burning issues facing their audience; relationships and the hassles of being young. Auckerman's eventual replacement in the band was Dave Smalley (ex-DYS; Dag Nasty). Stevenson also played guitar in the unspeakable Nig Heist. After the Descendents finished the members formed All, who continued in much the same vein, but without Lombardo or Carrion. Their influence on UK pop punk outfits like Mega City Four and particularly the Senseless Things (who covered 'Marriage') should not be underestimated.
●ALBUMS: *Milo Goes To College* (New Alliance 1982)★★, *I Don't Want To Grow Up* (New Alliance 1985)★★★, *Enjoy* (New Alliance 1986)★★★, *All* (SST 1987)★★★, *Liveage* live (SST 1987)★★, *Hellraker* live (SST 1989)★★, *Everything Sucks* (Epitaph 1996)★★★.
●COMPILATIONS: *Bonus Fat* (New Alliance 1985)★★, *Two Things At Once* combines *Milo Goes To College* and *Bonus Fat* (SST 1988)★★, *Somery* (SST 1995)★★★.

DEXYS MIDNIGHT RUNNERS

Conceived by the uncompromising Kevin Rowland (b. 17 August 1953, Wolverhampton, England), Dexys proved one of the most original, eclectic and fascinating UK groups to achieve success in the early 80s. Vocalist Rowland and rhythm guitarist Al Archer were previously members of punk group the Killjoys, before rehearsing the soul-inspired Dexys in July 1978. A further six members were added to the first line-up: Pete Williams (piano/organ), J.B. (tenor saxophone), Steve Spooner (alto saxophone), Pete Saunders (piano/organ), Big Jim Patterson (trombone) and Bobby Junior (drums). The unit took their name from the amphetamine dexedrine, a stimulant favoured by northern soul dancers. Their name notwithstanding, Dexys gained an almost puritanical reputation for their aversion to drink and drugs. Rowland brilliantly fashioned the group's image, using Robert De Niro's film *Mean Streets* as an inspiration for their New York Italian docker chic. The group's debut 'Dance Stance' was an extraordinary single, its simple title belying what was a lyrically devastating attack on racism directed at the Irish community, with a superb background litany extolling the virtues of Ireland's finest literary figures. The single crept into the UK Top 40, but the follow-up, 'Geno' (a tribute to 60's soul singer Geno Washington), climbed confidently to number 1 in May 1980. Two months later, *Searching For The Young Soul Rebels* was released to critical acclaim and commercial success. Many polls, perhaps rightly, suggested that it was one of the finest debut albums ever issued; it showed Rowland's mastery of the pop-soul genre to spectacular effect. The epistolary 'There There My Dear', taken from the album, brought the group another UK Top 10 hit. The flip was a revival of Cliff Noble's instrumental 'The Horse', in keeping with the Dexys' soul revivalism. The first signs of Rowland's artistic waywardness occurred with the release of the blatantly uncommercial 'Keep It Part Two (Inferiority Part One)', much against the group's wishes. Unquestionably his most intensely passionate work from the first Dexys phase, the song's almost unbearably agonized vocal line was double-tracked to create a bizarre but rivetting effect. The song precipitated the fragmentation of the original Dexys line-up. With JB, Steve Spooner and Pete Williams defecting to the Bureau, Rowland and Patterson found a fresh line-up: former Secret Affair drummer Seb Shelton, Micky Billingham (keyboards), Paul Speare (tenor saxophone), Brian Maurice (alto saxophone), Steve Wynne (bass) and Billy Adams (guitar). After one more single for EMI Records, the excellent 'Plan B', Dexys switched to Phonogram. By 1981 they had abandoned soul revivalism in order to investigate different music and a new look. Out went the balaclavas to be replaced by a new uniform of red anoraks, boxing boots, tracksuit bottoms, hoods and pony tails. Their 'ascetic athlete' phase saw the release of the more commercial 'Show Me' produced by Tony Visconti. This was followed by the idiosyncratic 'Liars A To E'. A highly acclaimed live show, 'The Projected Passion Review', followed, including a performance at London's Old Vic. Early 1982 saw Dexys augmented by a fiddle section, the Emerald Express, featuring Helen O'Hara, Steve Brennan and Roger McDuff. Rowland's latest experiment was to fuse Northern soul with Irish traditional music. As before, the shift in musical style was reflected in the image as Rowland created his own brand of hoedown gypsy chic - neckerchiefs, earrings, stubble and leather jerkins. The first release from the new group, 'The Celtic Soul Brothers', was a vital work that failed to chart, but its successor, 'Come On Eileen', restored them to number 1 in the summer of 1982. The second album, Too-Rye-Ay, was another startling work and a best seller, reaching number 2 in the UK album charts. The group subsequently undertook an extensive tour, which revealed Rowland's love of theatre in its self-conscious grandeur. Further line-up changes followed, with the departure of Kevin's right-hand man Jim Patterson and two other brass players. Continuing under the autocratic title 'Kevin Rowland And Dexys Midnight Runners', the group went on to reap considerable success in the USA where 'Come On Eileen' reached number 1 in 1983. Further hits followed with a snappy cover of

Van Morrison's 'Jackie Wilson Said' and 'Let's Get This Straight From The Start' before Dexys underwent a long hibernation. They returned as a quartet comprising Rowland, Adams, O'Hara and Nicky Gatefield, and boasting a radically new image 'College Preppie' - chic shirts and ties and neatly-cut hair. Don't Stand Me Down received very favourable reviews but sold poorly in spite of its qualities. An edited version of the brilliant 'This Is What She's Like' was issued as a single, but received little airplay. Although Dexys charted again with 'Because Of You' (later used as the theme for BBC Television's Brush Strokes), the commercial failure of the latest experiment forced Rowland to think again, and he finally dissolved the group in 1987. He returned the following year as a soloist with the light pop album, The Wanderer, which failed to produce a hit single. In 1990, Rowland, amid not unusual record company trouble, announced that he was resurrecting Dexys and bringing back his old colleague Jim Patterson. A similar announcement came in 1993. The group's career has been a series of broken contracts, group upheavals, total changes of image, diverse musical forays and an often bitter association with the music press. Creation Records signed Rowland for an album in 1996. For all this, Rowland remains a fascinating renegade; original, temperamental and brutally uncompromising at times, yet still capable of producing number 1 hits on both sides of the Atlantic.

●ALBUMS: Searching For The Young Soul Rebels (EMI 1980)★★★★, Too-Rye-Ay (Mercury 1982)★★★★, Don't Stand Me Down (Mercury 1985)★★★, BBC Radio One Live In Concert rec. 1982 (Windsong 1994)★★★.
●COMPILATIONS: Geno (EMI 1983)★★★, The Very Best Of (Mercury 1991)★★★★, 1980-1982: The Radio One Sessions (Nighttracks 1995)★★★, It Was Like This (EMI 1996)★★★★.

DIAMOND HEAD

Formed in Stourbridge, England, in 1979, the original line-up of Diamond Head comprised Sean Harris (vocals), Brian Tatler (guitar), Colin Kimberley (bass) and Duncan Scott (drums). The band were one of the pioneers of the New Wave Of British Heavy Metal and their debut single, 'Sweet And Innocent', showcased the band's blues influences and Harris's impressive vocal talents. After gigging extensively, the band recorded a session for the Friday night rock show on BBC Radio 1. 'Play It Loud' and 'Shoot Out The Lights' were both released in 1981 to minor critical acclaim. The press even went as far as to hail the band as the new Led Zeppelin. With interest growing they decided to self-finance their debut, which they sold through the pages of *Sounds* magazine under the title *Lightning To The Nation*. This was quickly snapped up by the German-based Woolfe Records in the same year, and released on import. The album was full of hard rock, soaring vocals and tasteful guitar work, and attracted the attention of several major record companies. As a stop-gap, the band released a 12-inch EP, *Diamond Lights*, again on DHM Records in 1981, before signing to MCA. Their first release for the label was an EP, *Four Cuts*, which was quickly followed up by their most popular album to date, *Borrowed Time*. Again the material was Led Zeppelin-style hard rock, and the band also included a couple of re-recorded tracks that had originally appeared on their first album. During sessions for the follow-up, *Canterbury*, both Kimberley and Scott exited. They were quickly replaced by ex-Streetfighter bassist Merv Goldsworthy (later a member of FM) and drummer Robbie France. The album was a brave change of direction for the band, still melodic but much more inventive and unconventional. Unfortunately, this change in style was not well received and despite a very successful appearance at the Monsters Of Rock Festival it flopped, and the group split up in 1985. Tatler then remixed their debut album, dropped two of the original tracks and added four previously released single tracks. This was then released under the new title of *Behold The Beginning* (1986). Tatler went on to form Radio Moscow while Sean Harris teamed up with guitarist Robin George in the ill-fated Notorious album project. Even though Diamond Head were no longer in existence, they retained a healthy press profile owing to the acclaim heaped on them by Metallica drummer Lars Ulrich, who made no secret of the fact that the band were one of his main influences and inspired him to begin his musical career. Metallica subsequently recorded a cover version of Diamond Head's old stage favourite, 'Am I Evil'. Early in 1991 Harris and Tatler re-formed Diamond Head with newcomers Eddie Nooham (bass) and Karl Wilcox (drums). The band undertook a short, low-key UK club tour using the name Dead Reckoning, then declared officially that they had reformed. The first release from this new incarnation was a limited edition 12-inch single, 'Wild On The Streets'. Housed on the newly relaunched Bronze label in 1991 it showed the band had returned in fine form and rediscovered the spirit lost in 1985. By the time they had

pieced together a new collection (after shelving a projected mini-album the year before) many of the rock world's biggest names were only to pleased to help out (including Tony Iommi of Black Sabbath, Dave Mustaine of Megadeth, and still-fervent supporter Lars Ulrich). The band finally broke up after the tour to support the release of their final album in 1993.

● ALBUMS: *The White Label Album* (Happy Face 1980)★★, *Lightning To The Nations* (Woolfe 1981)★★★, *Borrowed Time* (MCA 1982)★★★, *Canterbury* (MCA 1983)★★, *Behold The Beginning* (Heavy Metal 1986)★★, *Am I Evil* (FM/Revolver 1987)★★★, *Death & Progress* (Bronze 1993)★★★.
● VIDEOS: *Diamond Head* (1981).

DIAMOND, JIM

b. 28 September 1951, Glasgow, Scotland. Diamond is a veteran of several Glasgow-based groups. He sang with the Jade, which featured bassist Chris Glen, later of the Sensational Alex Harvey Band, but did not achieve prominence until the mid-70s when he joined Bandit. This traditionally styled rock band struggled in the face of punk, but Diamond's persistence paid dividends in 1982 when, as a member of PhD, he was the featured voice on their UK number 3 hit, 'I Won't Let You Down'. The singer then embarked on a solo career, and in 1984 he enjoyed an unexpected UK chart-topper with the emotional ballad, 'I Should Have Known Better'. Diamond next scored two minor hits, before achieving another major success with 'Hi Ho Silver', the theme song to the popular British television series, *Boon*. A UK television advertised compilation album released in 1993 put Diamond back in the UK Top 20.
● ALBUMS: *Double Crossed* (A&M 1985)★★, *Desire For Freedom* (A&M 1986)★★.
● COMPILATIONS: *Jim Diamond* (PolyGram 1993)★★★.

DIE KRUPPS

German group Die Krupps have been a pioneering force in experimental music ever since they were formed in 1981 by Jurgen Engler (vocals, keyboards, guitars and group spokesman, ex-famed German punk band Male) and Ralf Dorper (ex-Propaganda). Together with Front 242 they formulated the Body Music sub-genre of Euro rock, a sound lush in electronics but harsh in execution. Several albums of synthesized material emerged, venerated by a loyal fan base. However, Engler spent the mid-80s, which were largely quiet for the band, absorbing the new sounds, pioneered by

Metallica, pushing back the frontiers of metal. When Die Krupps eventually returned in 1992 they added layers of metal guitar. The most famous of two excellent sets in that year was a tribute album to the band who had revolutionised Engler's thinking: 'Metallica were coming to Germany for some dates and I wanted to present something to them because I really admired what they did. So we put together this tape, and that's all it was intended for, but our label heard of it and wanted to put it out . . .' On *The Final Option* Lee Altus (guitar, ex-Heathen) and Darren Minter (drums) were brought in, Die Krupps stuck to their bleak lyrical thematic, notably on 'Crossfire', a reaction to the Yugoslavian conflict. A remix album, with contributions from Gunshot, Jim Martin (ex-Faith No More), Andrew Eldritch (Sisters Of Mercy) and Julian Beeston (Nitzer Ebb, who in 1989 had remodelled the group's classic 'Wahre Arbeit, Wahrer Lohn') was also unveiled. On *III: Odyssey Of The Mind* the band moved to a new record company and embraced further still the metallic guitar sound, which now subsumed their distinctive hard dance electronics. It was produced by Tony Platt (a veteran of work with Motörhead and the Cult). Engler said of it: 'The guitars are definitely louder on this one. We still get put into different sections in record stores all over the world. In Germany we're in the independent section. In France the techno, and in England in the metal. It's all right, but it's all wrong too. We should be in every section!'

●ALBUMS: *Stahlwerksinfonie* (Zick Zack 1981)★★, *Volle Kraft Voraus* (Warners 1982)★★, *Entering The Arena* (Statik 1984)★★, *Metalle Maschinen Musik 91-81 Past Forward* (Rough Trade 1991)★★★, *One* (Rough Trade 1992)★★★, *Metal For The Masses Part II - A Tribute To Metallica* (Rough Trade 1992)★★★, *The Final Option* (Rough Trade 1993)★★★, *The Final Mixes* (Rough Trade 1994)★★★, *III: Odyssey Of The Mind* (Music For Nations 1995)★★★, *Paradise Now* (Music For Nations 1997)★★★.

●COMPILATIONS: *Die Krupps Box* 3-CD box set (Rough Trade 1993)★★★.

DIFFORD AND TILBROOK

The two principal songwriters of Squeeze met after Chris Difford (b. 4 November 1954, London, England) had placed an advert in a Blackheath, south London shop window in search of a guitarist to join a (non-existent) band with a (non-existent) record contract. In answering the advert, Glenn Tilbrook (b. 31 August 1957, London, England) found a compatible songwriting partner and

together they led one of the most popular British groups of the late 70s/early 80s. After suffering from the strain of holding Squeeze together, the duo decided to reassess their situation in 1982. Prior to recording an album, the duo had worked on the fringe theatre production of *Labelled With Love* at the Albany Theatre in their home area of Deptford. The album received a mixed reception and the only single to make any impact upon the UK charts was 'Love's Crashing Waves', narrowly missing out on the Top 50. Assisted by Andy Duncan (drums), Keith Wilkinson (bass), Guy Fletcher (keyboards), with a production credit by Tony Visconti, the album was an improvement on the last Squeeze offering, *Sweets From A Stranger*. Tracks like 'You Can't Hurt The Girl', 'Hope Fell Down' and 'On My Mind Tonight' particularly stood out. Having given themselves a sufficient rest from the group set-up, the duo resurrected Squeeze in 1985 after a successful charity reunion pub-date which led to the recording the excellent *Cosi Fan Tutti Frutti* that same year.

●ALBUMS: *Difford And Tilbrook* (A&M 1984)★★★.

DIGANCE, RICHARD

b. 24 February 1949, West Ham, London, England. Digance was formerly with a trio entitled Pisces, alongside John O'Connor and Tim Greenwood. Digance subsequently re-formed Pisces in 1972, but this time as a duo, with guitarist Frank McConnell. Digance is best known for his humorous style of presentation, and he has long performed numbers by many of the music-hall greats, including Harry Champion, alongside comic monologues. After many years playing the folk club circuit, Digance has, more recently, become broadly accepted by both television and radio. One time presenter of *Richard Digance And Friends* on Capital Radio, as well as a late night show on the same station, he also fronted a series of television programmes called *A Dabble With Digance*. He has more recently entered into the cabaret and concert circuit.

Having founded Dambuster Records, based in Essex, Digance sold the company after a relatively short time, as the pressures were conflicting with his own career which was by then taking off in a big way. *How The West Was Lost* featured musicians such as Alex Atterson, Nigel Pegrum (formerly with Steeleye Span, but now the drummer with the Barron Knights), Dik Cadbury (formerly with Decameron) and Michael Chapman. The album also included two tracks for which Digance became especially well-known. 'Working Class

Millionaire' and 'Drag Queen Blues'. A long-time friend of Jim Davidson, Digance continues to work in television, bringing his unique, unpretentious, and down-to-earth humour to a far wider audience than the folk club circuit could stimulate.

●ALBUMS: with Pisces *Pisces* (1971)★★★, *In Concert 74* (1976)★★★, *England's Green And Pleasant Land* (1974)★★★, *How The West Was Lost* (Transatlantic 1975)★★★, *Treading The Boards* (1975)★★★, *In Concert* (1975)★★★, *Richard Digance* (1975)★★★, *Live At The Queen Elizabeth Hall* (Chrysalis 1978)★★★, *Commercial Road* (Chrysalis 1979)★★★, *Backwater-Songs From The Boo* (Coast 1983)★★★, *Homework* (Coast 1984)★★★, *A Digance Indulgence* (Dambuster 1985)★★★, *Live At Fairfield Halls* (Dambuster 1985)★★★, *Drag Queen Blues* (Conifer 1986)★★★.

DINOSAUR JR

This uncompromising alternative rock band from the university town of Amherst, Massachusetts, USA, were originally called simply Dinosaur. Their musical onslaught eventually dragged them, along-side the Pixies, into the rock mainstream of the late 80s. Both J. Mascis (b. 10 December 1965, Amherst, Massachusetts, USA; vocals/guitar) and Lou Barlow (bass) were formerly in the hardcore band Deep Wound, along with a singer called Charlie. He recruited his best friend Murphy (b. Patrick Murphy; ex-All White Jury) from Connecticut, and was rewarded by the first line-up of Dinosaur ejecting him and thus becoming a trio. Mascis had by this time switched from drums to guitar, to accommodate the new arrival. Mascis, apparently a huge fan of Sham 69 and the UK Oi! movement, had actually known Murphy at high school but they had never got on. He formed Deep Wound as a response to seeing 999 play live when he was 14 years old. During Dinosaur Jr's career internal rifts never seemed far from the surface, while their leader's monosyllabic press interviews and general disinterest in rock 'n' roll machinations gave the impression of 'genius anchored by lethargy'. Two albums for Homestead were issued then SST Records saw them establish their name as a credible underground rock act. The best of the pair was *You're Living All Over Me*, which featured backing vocals from Sonic Youth's Lee Renaldo. However, their debut album had brought them to the attention of ageing hippie group Dinosaur, who insisted the band change their name. Mascis elected to add the suffix Junior. Real recognition came with the release of the huge underground anthem 'Freak Scene', which more than one journalist called the

perfect pop single. Its sound was constructed on swathes of guitar and Mascis's laconic vocals, which were reminiscent of Neil Young. However, the parent album (*Bug*) and tour saw Barlow depart (to Sebadoh) and Donna became a temporary replacement. This line-up recorded the version of the Cure's 'Just Like Heaven' which impressed Robert Smith and led to joint touring engagements. Soon after they signed to Warner Brothers Records subsidiary Blanco Y Negro, remixing their Sub Pop Records cut, 'The Wagon', as their debut major label release. Subsequent members included Don Fleming (Gumball, etc.) Jay Spiegel and Van Connor (Screaming Trees), while Mascis himself flirted with other bands, principally as a drummer, such as Gobblehoof, Velvet Monkeys and satanic metal band, Upside Down Cross. By *Green Mind* Dinosaur Jr. had effectively become the J. Mascis show, with him playing almost all the instruments. Murphy departed because of misgivings about the band's finances. However, although critically acclaimed, *Where You Been* did not manage to build on the commercial inroads originally made by *Green Mind*. *Without A Sound* included several strong compositions such as 'Feel The Pain' and 'On The Brink', with the bass now played by Mike Johnson (b. 27 August 1965, Oregon, USA). Mascis has also produced other artists including the Breeders, and wrote the soundtrack for and appeared in Allison Anders' film, *Gas, Food, Lodging*. Mascis appeared solo in 1995 and it appeared for a while that the future of the band was in the balance. This was quashed by the release of *Hand It Over* in March 1997, a full bodied Dinosaur Jr. album that sounded like the band were committed. While the lyrics were often muddied, Mascis's melodic grunge was very much intact.

●ALBUMS: as Dinosaur *Dinosaur* (Homestead 1985)★★★, as Dinosaur Jr *You're Living All Over Me* (SST 1987)★★★, *Bug* (SST 1988)★★★★, *Green Mind* (Blanco y Negro 1991)★★★, *Where You Been* (Blanco y Negro 1993)★★★★, *Without A Sound* (Blanco y Negro 1994)★★★, *Hand It Over* (Blanco Y Negro 1997)★★★. Solo: Mike Johnson *Year Of Mondays* (Atlantic 1996)★★. J Mascis *Martin And Me* (Reprise 1996)★★★.

DINOSAURS

Formed in 1982 in San Francisco, California, USA, the Dinosaurs consisted of former members of the popular San Francisco rock bands of the 60s. The initial line-up comprised guitarist Barry Melton (ex-Country Joe And The Fish), guitarist John

Cipollina (ex-Quicksilver Messenger Service), bassist Peter Albin (formerly of Big Brother And The Holding Company), drummer Spencer Dryden (Jefferson Airplane) and songwriter/vocalist Robert Hunter (Grateful Dead). The band came together with the intent of recreating the sound and ambience of the era from which the members sprang. Long, winding improvisations were the norm whether the group performed new, original material or songs associated with the 60s. They played locally in the San Francisco area. In 1985, Hunter left and was replaced by keyboardist Merl Saunders, who worked with the Grateful Dead's Jerry Garcia in a number of extra-curricular bands during the 70s. They recorded their only album in 1988. After Cipollina's death in 1989 the group went on a hiatus, but by the mid-90s had replaced him with violinist Papa John Creach, formerly of Jefferson Airplane/Starship and Hot Tuna.

●ALBUMS: *Dinosaurs* (Big Beat 1988)★★★.

DIRE STRAITS

Few groups can claim to be synonymous with a lifestyle, but Dire Straits are an exception, whether they like it or not. *Brothers In Arms*, released in 1985, established them as the first real darlings of the compact disc 20-something generation that initially grew out of the boom years of the UK Thatcher government of the 80s. Their accessible, traditional blues-based music made them perfect for the massive, mature, relatively wealthy strata of the public which likes its music tightly performed and readily digestible. The album was number 1 in the US charts for nine weeks and spent three years in the UK chart. Surprisingly, Dire Straits first surfaced during a period that was the antipathy of what they later became - the London punk scene of 1976/7. Mark Knopfler (b. 12 August 1949, Glasgow, Scotland) and his brother David Knopfler (b. 27 December 1951, Glasgow, Scotland) are the sons of an architect who moved to Newcastle-upon-Tyne, England, when the boys were young. Mark Knopfler studied English literature at Leeds University, and for a short time worked as a junior reporter with the *Yorkshire Evening Post* and with a local Essex newspaper. After university he formed a part-time pub band called Brewer's Droop but his main income was drawn from teaching.

The Knopflers moved to London during the early 70s and Mark met bassist John Illsley (b. 24 June 1949, Leicester, England) and drummer Pick Withers. Illsley, a sociology graduate, was working in a record shop and Withers had been a session drummer for many years. The climate was not right for the group as punk took a grip on music and almost every UK record label passed on the offer to press up Dire Straits' polished music. One song began to stand out from their repertoire, a basic blues progression with dry, affectionate lyrics, called 'Sultans Of Swing'. It was picked up by Radio London DJ and Oval Records proprietor, Charlie Gillett, and by the end of 1977 the group were recording their debut, *Dire Straits*, for Vertigo Records with producer Muff Winwood. 'Sultans Of Swing' was a hit first in Holland and later made the UK Top 10. The powerful Warner Brothers Records took over distribution in the USA and massively backed the album until in March 1979 it had reached number 2 in the *Billboard* chart. Their second single, 'Lady Writer', was a relative failure but it did not impair their attraction as an 'albums band'. *Communique*, produced by Jerry Wexler and Barry Beckett, sold three million copies worldwide. It missed the commercial edge of the debut but developed Mark Knopfler's trademark of incisive, cynical lyricism. Before the recording of *Making Movies*, David Knopfler opted out to begin a solo career and has since released several records with various small independent labels. David was replaced by Hal Lindes, formerly a member of Darling, and Alan Clark joined on keyboards. Knopfler was heavily criticized for not varying his songwriting formula but the album still spawned a UK Top 10 single with the poignant love ballad, 'Romeo And Juliet'. *Love Over Gold* fared better than its predecessor in the USA and the single from it, 'Private Investigations', became their biggest hit, reaching number 2 in the UK during September 1982.

Knopfler spent some time away from the group and produced Bob Dylan's *Infidels* in 1983 and wrote 'Private Dancer', which became a hit for Tina Turner in 1984. Now respected as both a songwriter and exceptionally gifted guitarist, it looked for a while as if Dire Straits might not record again because of Knopfler's other production commitments with artists as diverse as Aztec Camera, Randy Newman and Willy de Ville. They reassembled, however, in 1983 with ex-Man drummer Terry Williams replacing Withers, and completed an arduous world tour. A live double record *Alchemy Live* filled the gap before the band's next studio album release, *Brothers In Arms* in 1985. Like many others, Dire Straits' appearance at the Live Aid concert boosted sales and their own 200-date tour helped it become one of the decade's biggest selling albums. Knopfler used it to make several wry observations on his own position as a rock star, laughing at the folly of videos and MTV on 'Money For Nothing' - a number 1 in the USA. Three other songs from the record, 'Walk Of Life', 'So Far Away' and the title track, also charted on both sides of the Atlantic, with 'Walk Of Life' reaching number 2 in the UK. Knopfler turned once again to other projects. Having already written two film scores in 1983 and 1984 for *Local Hero* and *Cal,* respectively, he wrote the music for the fantasy comedy film, *The Prince's Bride* in 1987. In 1990 Knopfler formed an *ad hoc* group fronted by Leeds singer, Brendan Croker, called the Notting Hillbillies. Their self-titled debut album was a disappointing, soporific release and the group disbanded after one UK tour. As a solo artist, John Illsley has released two albums, *Never Told A Soul* in 1984 and *Glass* in 1988, neither of which sold in significant quantities. During the summer of 1991 Dire Straits announced a massive 'comeback' tour and the release of a new album, *On Every Street.* Their world tour, taking two years to complete, represented their first concerts since their 1988 appearance as part of the Nelson Mandela Birthday concert at London's Wembley Stadium. While Knopfler has strived to find new challenges in various music-related spheres, his group can leave a six-year gap between album releases and still maintain their incredible popularity. This is owing, in no small measure, to masterful global marketing and the unflinching mainstream appeal of their music.

●ALBUMS: *Dire Straits* (Vertigo 1978)★★★★, *Communique* (Vertigo 1979)★★, *Making Movies* (Vertigo 1980)★★★★, *Love Over Gold* (Vertigo 1982)★★★, *Alchemy - Live* (Vertigo 1984)★★, *Brothers In Arms* (Vertigo 1985)★★★, *On Every Street* (Vertigo 1991)★★★, *On The Night* (Vertigo 1993)★★, *Live At The BBC* (Windsong 1995)★★★.
●COMPILATIONS: *Money For Nothing* (Vertigo 1988)★★★★.
●VIDEOS: *Brothers In Arms* (1988), *Alchemy Live* (1988), *The Videos* (1992).
●FURTHER READING: *Dire Straits,* Michael Oldfield. *Mark Knopfler: The Unauthorised Biography,* Myles Palmer.

DIRTY DANCING

If films that adhered to a conventional musical formula could be counted on the fingers of one hand in the 80s, the excitement of dance never ceased to attract enthusiastic audiences. Following in the dance steps of the success of *Footloose* and *Flashdance, Dirty Dancing,* released in 1987, caught the imagination of many with its combination of raunchy dancing, romance and upbeat soundtrack. Directed by Emile Ardolino, with a screenplay by Eleanor Bergstein, it tells the story of Baby (Jennifer Grey), her father's favourite daughter, who suffers the ups-and-downs of growing up while on a family holiday at a Catskills resort in the summer of 1963. Baby is an idealistic girl, soon to begin at college, who thinks she can right any problem, and help anyone, whatever the situation. These are all characteristics that one of the resort's leading dancers, Johnny (Patrick Swayze), finds refreshing and attractive. When someone is desperately needed to fill the shoes of Johnny's dancing partner, Penny (Cynthia Rhodes), it's hardly surprising that Baby is chosen to substitute, learning all the steps from scratch - almost a mild modern variation of the chorus girl becomes star routine. It is at this point that Baby and Johnny begin to fall in love, and despite the protestations of most of the adults around them - particularly Baby's father (Jerry Orbach) - the young lovers are isolated for a time before the inevitable happy ending. The uplifting finale features the film's biggest song hit, '(I've) Had The Time Of My Life', sung by Bill Medley and Jennifer Warnes, which won an Oscar and a Grammy, and topped the US chart. Many of the other tracks reflect the film's theme of 60s nostalgia with contributions from Frankie Valli, the Four Seasons, Otis Redding, the Shirelles and Mickey And Sylvia. There is even one song on the soundtrack, 'She's Like The Wind', performed and written by Swayze (with Stacy Widelitz). *Dirty Dancing* was the first feature release for the home video company Vestron Pictures. While its plot is simplistic, it is a sensitive and original portrayal of a young girl's coming of age, helped along by fine performances and some great frenetic and exciting dancing.

DIVINYLS

Led by the provocative Chrissie Amphlett, whose songwriting with guitarist Mark McEntee is the basis of the band, the Divinyls have recorded some excellent work. Amphlett's sexy image complemented the mesmerizing urgency of the music, and the band was guaranteed the audience's undivided attention. They formed in Sydney in 1981, and their first mini-album was written for the 1982 film *Monkey Grip,* and produced the Australian Top 10 single 'Boys In Town' as well as the excellent ballad, 'Only The Lonely'. Signing with the UK label Chrysalis Records, their first album *Desperate* was a hit in Australia. Several hit singles and extensive touring bridged the gap to *What A Life* (1985), which was greeted enthusiastically; but the sales did not match the reviews. Later material, with the exception of the next single 'Pleasure And Pain', did not compare well with their earliest work. The band now is basically a duo, with musicians added whenever a tour is undertaken. It has undergone a revival with its controversial single, 'I Touch Myself', a deliberately blatant reference to masturbation, released in 1991 and reaching the UK Top 10.

●ALBUMS: *Desperate* (Chrysalis 1983)★★★, *What A Life* (Chrysalis 1985)★★★, *Temperamental* (Chrysalis 1988)★★★, *Divinyls* (Virgin America 1991)★★★.

DJ JAZZY JEFF AND THE FRESH PRINCE

The Fresh Prince (b. Will Smith, 25 September 1968, Philadelphia, Pennsylvania, USA) is just as famous for being the star of television series *The Fresh Prince of Bel Air*, wherein he plays a streetwise tough who suffers culture shock when transplanted into an affluent Beverley Hills household. However, this is very much a second career for Smith. Together with DJ Jazzy Jeff (b. Jeffrey Townes, 22 January 1965, Philadelphia, Pennsylvania, USA), this young duo had already recorded a highly successful debut album. Smith was offered the show because of the airing of his raps on MTV. Musically the duo operate in familiar territory, working a variety of inoffensive, borrowed styles to quite good effect. Jazzy Jeff started Djing in the mid-70s when he was a mere 10 years old, (though he is not to be confused with the similarly-titled Jazzy Jeff who cut an album, also for Jive, in 1985). He was frequently referred to in those early days as the 'bathroom' DJ, because, hanging out with better-known elders, he would only be allowed to spin the decks when they took a toilet break. He met the Fresh Prince at a party, the two securing a recording deal after entering the 1986 New Music Seminar, where Jeff won the coveted Battle Of The Deejays. Embarking on a recording career, the obligatory James Brown lifts were placed next to steals from cartoon characters like Bugs Bunny, which gave some indication of their debut album's scope. In the late 80s they cemented their reputation with million-selling teen anthems like 'Girls Ain't Nothing But Trouble', which sampled the *I Dream Of Jeannie* theme, and was released three weeks before Smith graduated from high school. They became the first rap act to receive a Grammy Award for their second long

player's 'Parents Just Don't Understand', even though the ceremony was boycotted by most of the prominent hip hop crews because it wasn't slated to be 'screened' as part of the television transmission. In its wake the duo launched the world's first pop star 900 number (the pay-phone equivalent of the UK's 0898 system). By January 1989 3 million calls had been logged. *He's The DJ, I'm The Rapper* contained more accessible pop fare, the sample of *Nightmare On Elm Street* being the closest they come to street-level hip hop. The raps were made interesting, however, by the Prince's appropriation of a variety of personas. This is doubtless what encouraged the television bosses to make him an offer he couldn't refuse, and *The Fresh Prince Of Bel Air*'s enormous success has certainly augmented his profile (he also moved on to various film roles including *Six Degrees Of Separation* and *Independence Day*). Jeff, meanwhile, has formed A Touch Of Jazz Inc, a stable of producers working on rap/R&B projects. The duo picked up a second Grammy for 'Summertime' in 1991, before scoring a shock UK number 1 in 1993 with 'Boom! Shake The Room', the first rap record (Vanilla Ice and MC Hammer aside) to top the British singles chart.

●ALBUMS: *Rock The House* (Word Up 1987)★★, *He's The DJ, I'm The Rapper* (Jive 1988)★★★, *And In This Corner* (Jive 1990)★★★, *Homebase* (Jive 1991)★★, *Code Red* (Jive 1993)★★.

DNA (USA)

This US band was a short-lived collaboration between guitarist Rick Derringer and drummer Carmine Appice. With the assistance of Duane Hitchings (keyboards) and Jimmy Johnson (bass), they released *Party Tested* in 1983. This featured a wide range of styles which included jazz, rock, funk, blues and pop. The playing was beyond criticism, but the songs were devoid of soul, and the album as a whole lacked unity and cohesion. Failing to win support in the media, DNA disintegrated when Carmine Appice accepted the offer to join Ozzy Osbourne's band. He subsequently formed King Kobra.

●ALBUMS: *Party Tested* (Polydor 1983)★★.

DOCTOR AND THE MEDICS

This psychedelic UK pop-rock outfit came to prominence in 1986 with a cover of Norman Greenbaum's 'Spirit In The Sky'. The single hit number 1 in the UK, but they found it difficult to consolidate their success, with the subsequent 'Burn' and 'Waterloo' only achieving UK chart placings of 29 and 46, respectively. *Laughing At The*

Pieces peaked at number 25 in the charts, primarily on the back of major single success. Since then, every release has sunk without trace and the band were dropped by their label.

●ALBUMS: *Laughing At The Pieces* (MCA 1986)★★★, *Keep Thinking It's Thursday* (MCA 1987)★★, *The Adventures Of Boadicea And The Beetle* (1993)★★.

DOGS D'AMOUR

This rock outfit was originally formed in Birmingham, England, during 1983, with a line-up comprising Tyla (guitar), Ned Christie (vocals), Nick Halls (guitar), Carl (bass) and Bam Bam (drums). After making their London debut in April 1983 and recording a track for the Flicknife compilation, *Trash On Delivery*, they underwent a rapid series of personnel changes. Halls, Bam Bam and Christie departed prompting Tyla to assume lead vocal responsibilities. He and Carl recruited replacements, Dave Kusworth (guitar) and Paul Hornby (drums). They relocated to Finland where their hard rock style won them an underground following. After returning to the UK in 1985, further changes in the line-up were underway, with Bam Bam replacing Hornby, while Kusworth departed in favour of the elegantly named Jo-Dog. Later that year, the procession of changes continued with the departure of Carl in favour of Doll By Doll bassist Mark Duncan, who lasted until 1987 when Steve James arrived. The group finally broke through with the minor hit, 'How Come It Never Rains', and the mini-album, *A Graveyard Of Empty Bottles*. The follow-up, 'Satellite Kid', also reached the UK Top 30, as did their album, *Errol Flynn*. The latter met some resistance in the USA where it was forcibly retitled *The King Of The Thieves*. Having at last stabilized their line-up, Dogs D'Amour failed to establish themselves in the top league of hard rock acts but continued to tour extensively. During a lull in the early 90s James formed the Last Bandits while Bam Bam joined the Wildhearts. The group reformed in 1993 with Darrell Barth (ex-Crybabys) replacing Jo-Dog. However, by 1994 the group had ground to a halt, with Tyla considering a solo career while Steve James and Bam Bam formed Mary Jane.

●ALBUMS: *The State We're In* (Kumibeat 1984)★★, *The (Un)Authorized Bootleg* (China 1988)★★, *In The Dynamite Jet Saloon* (China 1988)★★★, *A Graveyard Of Empty Bottles* (China 1989)★★★, *Errol Flynn* (China 1990)★★★, *More Uncharted Heights Of Disgrace* (China 1993)★★.

DOLBY, THOMAS

b. Thomas Morgan Robertson, 14 October 1958, Cairo, Egypt. Dolby is a self-taught musician/vocalist/songwriter, and computer programmer. After studying meteorology and projectionism at college, he started building his own synthesizers at the age of 18. With his own hand-built PA system he acted as sound engineer on tours by the Members, Fall and the Passions. Afterwards, he co-founded Camera Cub with Bruce Wooley in January 1979 before joining the Lene Lovich backing group in September 1980, for whom he wrote 'New Toy'. His first solo output was the single 'Urges' on the Armageddon label in 1981, before he enjoyed hits the following year with 'Europa' and 'The Pirate Twins'. For a series of 1982 concerts at the Marquee he recruited ex-Soft Boy Matthew Seligman and Kevin Armstrong of the Thompson Twins, while finding time to contribute to albums by M, Joan Armatrading and Foreigner. Other collaborations included Stevie Wonder, Herbie Hancock, Dusty Springfield, Howard Jones and Grace Jones. The most visual of such appearances came when he backed David Bowie at Live Aid. A strong 'mad scientist' image proliferated in his videos, which also featured famous British eccentric Magnus Pike. These earned him a strong media profile, but, surprisingly, his best-known singles 'She Blinded Me With Science' and 'Hyperactive' only peaked at numbers 31 and 17, respectively. The latter did, however, reach the Top 5 in the USA, and charted in the UK again when re-released in 1996. As well as production for Prefab Sprout and Joni Mitchell, he has scored music for several films including *Howard: A New Breed Of Hero*. He is married to actress Kathleen Beller (Kirby Colby from *Dynasty*). Dolby commands high respect in the music business, as his backroom contributions have already been considerable.

●ALBUMS: *The Golden Age Of Wireless* (Venice In Peril 1982)★★★★, *The Flat Earth* (Parlophone 1984)★★★, *Aliens Ate My Buick* (Manhattan 1988)★★, *Astronauts And Heretics* (Virgin 1992)★★.

●VIDEOS: *The Gate To The Mind's Eye* (Miramar Images 1994).

DOLLY MIXTURE

This female UK pop trio comprised Debsey Wykes (b. 21 December 1960, Hammersmith, London, England; bass/piano/vocals), Rachel Bor (b. 16 May 1963, Wales; guitar/cello/vocals) and Hester

Smith (b. 28 October 1960, West Africa; drums). The group was formed by the three school friends in Cambridge, with a musical style that echoed the Shangri-Las and the 70s Undertones. Championed by influential UK disc jockey, John Peel, the group released a cover of the Shirelles hit, 'Baby It's You' on Chrysalis Records in 1980 - which at the time of issue the group disowned, protesting at the label's attempted manipulation of their image. They were one of the first bands to record for Paul Weller's Respond label, releasing, 'Been Teen' (1981) and 'Everything And More' (1982), both of which were produced by Captain Sensible and Paul Gray of the Damned. The UK record-buying public found difficulty coming to terms with the trio's idiosyncratic mode of dress and independent attitude; something with which some of the music press also had problems. They proved their worth, however, in their exhilarating live performances. In 1982 they released a double album, on their own Dead Good Dolly Platters label, featuring demo tapes collected over the previous four years. The album has since achieved cult status among later 80s independent groups. Dolly Mixture eventually found national fame by acting as Sensible's backing vocalists on his UK number 1 single, 'Happy Talk', in 1982. They also guested on his subsequent singles and albums, while Rachel and the Captain formed a romantic partnership. Meanwhile, their own career floundered, despite the critical plaudits. The trio dissolved as a working band in 1984, leaving as their swan song *The Fireside EP*, released on Cordelia Records, a set consisting mainly of 'pop/chamber' music, featuring their often ignored talents on piano and cello. In 1986 Debsey and Hester resurfaced with Coming Up Roses.

●ALBUMS: *The Demonstration Tapes* double album (Dead Good Dolly 1982)★★★.

DOMINGO, PLACIDO

b. 21 March 1941, Madrid, Spain. One of the world's leading tenors who, along with Luciano Pavarotti, has attempted to give opera in recent years a widespread, classless appeal. Domingo's family emigrated to Mexico in 1950, where he studied piano, conducting and singing. He debuted as a baritone in 1957, and his first major tenor role came in 1960 performing in Giuseppe Verdi's *La Traviata*. Domingo became a member of the Israel National Opera from 1962-65 and latter made acclaimed performances at the New York City Opera and Metropolitan, and at La Scala (Milan) and Covent Garden (London) - singing alongside sopranos such as Katria Ricciarelli, Rosalind Plowright and

Montserrat Caballe. His first flirtation with the pop world came in 1981, when he recorded a duet with John Denver, 'Perhaps Love'. This Denver-penned song reached the UK Top 50 and US Top 20, consequently opening up a parallel career for Domingo in light entertainment and simultaneously introducing to the mass-market the delights of the operatic aria as well as Spanish love songs. In 1985 he joined forces with Sarah Brightman and Lorin Maazel for Andrew Lloyd Webber's *Requiem*, which became a UK Top 10 album. 'Till I Loved You', a duet with Jennifer Rush, reached the UK Top 30 in 1989. Domingo's efforts, plus those of similar promotions from Luciano Pavarotti, Nigel Kennedy and José Carreras, signalled the beginnings of the early 90s boom in sales of populist classical and operatic music.

●ALBUMS: with John Denver *Perhaps Love* (Columbia 1981)★★, *Domingo-Con Amore* (RCA 1982)★★★, *My Life For A Song* (Columbia 1983)★★★, *Be My Love* (DGS 1984)★★★, *Christmas With Placido Domingo* (Columbia 1984)★★, *Placido Domingo Sings Zarzuelas* (HMV 1988)★★★, *Goya ... A Life In A Song* (1989)★★★, with Luciano Pavarotti, José Carreras *In Concert* (1990)★★★, *Be My Love ... An Album Of Love* (EMI 1990)★★★, *The Broadway I Love* (1991)★★★.

●COMPILATIONS: *Placido Domingo Collection* (Stylus 1986)★★★, *Greatest Love Songs* (Columbia 1988)★★★, *The Essential Domingo* (Polygram 1989)★★★★.

DONINGTON FESTIVAL

Held annually during August at the Castle Donington race-track in north Leicestershire, England, the Donington Festival has come to represent the highlight of UK heavy metal's calendar. First staged in 1980, Donington was conceived as an alternative to the Reading Festival as that event moved away from its hard-rock roots to encompass new wave and indie acts. Donington's one-day event, billed 'Monsters Of Rock', generally features at least six top-flight rock bands, with the opening slot reserved for 'talented newcomers'. This has resulted in commercially successful acts such as Mötley Crüe (1984), Cinderella (1987), Thunder (1990) and the Black Crowes (1991) all using the spot as a platform to launch international careers. Among the headliners, AC/DC have returned three times (1982, 1984, 1991), and Iron Maiden (1988, 1992) and Whitesnake (1983, 1990) twice. Though the festival has encountered fewer public disorder problems than most, in 1988 two attendees were killed during a Guns N'Roses performance when a video screen and supporting scaffolding collapsed at the side of the stage. Two years earlier heavy metal satirists Bad News were 'bottled off' as their caricatures of heavy metal lifestyle wore thin. In 1992 Radio 1 presented its first live broadcast of the festival in its entirety - with the provision of a 15 second delay before 9 pm so engineers could delete any expletives. Though that year's audience fell 10,000 below the 72,500 maximum capacity imposed by safety regulators, Donington continues to be the one annual festival for heavy metal and hard rock fans which remains uncontaminated by the presence of other forms of music.

DORE, CHARLIE

Dore is a respected UK songwriter who originally trained as an actress, and is best known for her 1979 hit 'Pilot Of The Airwaves', which reached number 11 in the US. Her 1977 country influenced band Prairie Oyster included Pick Withers on drums, who was also playing with the early Dire Straits, at that time doing the same UK pub circuit. The band evolved through various personnel changes into Charlie Dore's Back Pocket (guitarist Julian Littman having since become a long-time songwriting collaborator). When the band broke up, Dore started a solo career. *Where To Now* was recorded partly in Nashville, and produced by the Shadows' Bruce Welch and songwriter Alan Tarney, with session musicians such as Sonny Curtis. The first single, 'Fear Of Flying', failed to make a commercial impact, although it was a major 'turntable hit', but 'Pilot' charted on both sides of the Atlantic and received extensive airplay. She signed to Chrysalis Records in 1981 and released *Listen*, but, unable to capitalize on her early success, focused her varied talents on songwriting and acting.

As well as repertory work with Michael Bogdanov, she co-starred with Jonathan Pryce in Richard Eyre's award-winning film *The Ploughman's Lunch*, and appeared in several television series, including *Hard Cases* (playing in a band with former Cockney Rebel drummer Stuart Elliot) and *South Of The Border*. She was also a founder-member of the London-based comedy improvisation team Dogs On Holiday, who have been resident at their own Hurricane Club since 1990. Her songwriting credits include many album tracks and a number of highly successful singles. 'Strut' was a worldwide hit for Sheena Easton, reaching number 4 in the US, where it also won an ASCAP award. She wrote a range of material for Barbara Dickson, and in 1992 enjoyed a UK number 1 with Jimmy Nail's

'Ain't No Doubt', which she co-wrote. 'Refuse To Dance', taken from Celine Dion's hugely successful *The Colour Of My Love*, was released as a single in 1995. Following a return to the recording studio, working with Julian Littman, Danny Schogger (co-writer of 'Ain't No Doubt' and 'Refuse To Dance'), Ricky Fataar and Paul Carrack on a collection of new material, Dore released *Things Change* in 1995, an album co-produced by Littman. Dore's ability, enthusiasm and commitment have helped many others to commercial success while she remains something of a hidden talent.

● ALBUMS: *Where To Now* (Island 1979)★★★, *Listen* (Chrysalis 1981)★★★, *Things Change* (Grapevine 1995)★★★.

DORO

b. Dorothee Pesch, 3 June 1964, Dusseldorf, Germany. Pesch, the leading light and vocalist of the German heavy metal band Warlock, dissolved the unit after the release of 1987's *Triumph And Agony*. Retaining only bassist Tommy Henriksen, she embarked on a solo career under the name of Doro. To complete the new line-up she recruited guitarist John Devin and drummer Bobby Rondinelli (ex-Rainbow). Using Joey Balin as a writing partner, *Force Majeure* offered a departure from her previous heavy style, moving towards a more mainstream AOR approach in a bid for commercial success. It featured an embarrassing cover version of Procol Harum's 'A Whiter Shade Of Pale' as the opening track and fared poorly. Ditching the entire band in favour of hired hands, she recorded *Doro* with Gene Simmons (of Kiss) as producer. Musically, this was even further away from her roots, an attempt to achieve chart success that verged on desperation.

Rare Diamonds was a compilation of older material, giving Doro time for a re-think about her next career move. When she did re-emerge in 1993 with *Angels Never Die*, however, the interest was minimal. *Machine II Machine* featured the producer and songwriter Jack Ponti and managed to avoid the overt commercial overtones of its forerunners. Despite this improvement, tracks such as 'Tie Me Up' still offered little evidence of songwriting maturity.

● ALBUMS: *Force Majeure* (Vertigo 1989)★★, *Doro* (Vertigo 1990)★★, *Angels Never Die* (Vertigo 1993)★★ *Machine II Machine* (Mercury 1995)★★.
● COMPILATIONS: *Rare Diamonds* (Vertigo 1991)★★.

DOUG E. FRESH

b. Douglas E. Davis, St. Thomas, Virgin Islands, though he grew up in the Bronx and Harlem districts of New York, USA. Self-proclaimed as The Original Human Beatbox, i.e. being able to imitate the sound of a rhythm machine, Fresh broke through in 1985 with the release of one of rap's classic cuts, 'The Show'. Joined by partner MC Ricky D (aka Slick Rick), the single matched rhymes with a bizarre array of human sound effects, courtesy of Fresh. It marked a notable departure in rap's development, and was so distinctive it began a small flurry of similarly inclined rappers, as well as Salt 'N' Pepa's answer record, 'Showstopper'. Despite its impact, it was a song that was hardly representative of Fresh fare: far too much of his recorded material is workmanlike and soundalike. A debut album included live contributions from Bernard Wright (synthesiser) and Jimmy Owens (trumpet), as well as a dubious anti-abortion cut. The follow-up saw him allied to Public Enemy's Bomb Squad production team. To give him his due Fresh was very nearly rap's first superstar, but rather than capitalize on 'The Show', he would end up in court trying to sue Reality Records for non-payment of royalties on the song. He was also the first genuine rapper to appear at Jamaica's Reggae Sunsplash festival, stopping in the West Indies long enough to record alongside Papa San and Cocoa Tea. He made something of a comeback at the end of 1993 with the release of party record 'I-Right (Alright)', after he was reunited with Slick Rick (recently returned from a period of incarceration), and signed with Gee Street Records. Fresh has also enjoyed the distinction of seeing a 'Doug E. Fresh' switch added to the Oberheim Emulator, in order to provide samples of his human beat box talents. On *Play* Fresh employed Luther Campbell of 2 Live Crew to add a gangsta edge.

●ALBUMS: *Oh, My God!* (Reality 1985)★★★, *The World's Greatest Entertainer* (Reality 1988)★★, *Doin' What I Gotta Do* (Bust It 1992)★★, *Play* (Gee Street 1995)★★.

DOWNING, WILL

b. New York, USA. Downing was an in-demand session singer during the late 70s, appearing on recordings by artists including Rose Royce, Billy Ocean, Jennifer Holliday and Nona Hendryx. The soul singer's career was really launched when he met producer/performer Arthur Baker in the mid-80s. This led to him joining Baker's group Wally Jump Jnr. And The Criminal Element, whose other members included Brooklyn-bred Wally Jump, Craig Derry (ex-Moments; Sugarhill Gang), Donny Calvin and Dwight Hawkes (both ex-Rockers Revenge), Rick Sher (ex-Warp 9), Jeff Smith, and the toasting pair Michigan And Smiley. After a spell with Wally Jump Jnr. recording for Baker's Criminal Records label, Downing secured a solo deal with Island Records and recorded his debut album in 1988 with Baker producing. The first release under Downing's own name was 'A Love Supreme' (4th & Broadway 1987) which set lyrics to one of John Coltrane's most famous compositions. The single reached number 1 in the UK, while his first album, produced by Baker, was a Top 20 hit. He had further hits with 'In My Dreams' and a remake of the Roberta Flack and Donny Hathaway duet 'Where Is The Love', on which he partnered Mica Paris. Downing himself produced the second album, co-writing tracks with Brian Jackson, Gil Scott-Heron's collaborator. Neither this nor *A Dream Fulfilled*, on which Barry J. Eastmond and Wayne Braithwaite co-produced, was able to approach the popularity of his debut. *Moods* put Downing firmly in the smooth late-night music category, and although his exquisite vocals are suited to the melancholy, the fear of merely sounding lethargic is only one step away.

●ALBUMS: *Will Downing* (4th & Broadway 1988)★★★★, *Come Together As One* (4th & Broadway 1989)★★, *A Dream Fulfilled* (4th & Broadway 1991)★★, *Love's The Place To Be* (4th & Broadway 1993)★★, *Moods* (4th & Broadway 1995)★★★.

DREAD, MIKEY

b. Michael Campbell, Port Antonio, Jamaica, West Indies. Dread achieved prominence in Jamaica in the late 70s as a DJ on the JBC station with his four hour Saturday night *Dread At The Controls* show. Campbell's show played strictly reggae (bizarrely, until the rise of IRIE FM, most official Jamaican radio consisted of anything but). His selections - many of them hot off the cutting lathe, dub plate specials - were punctuated by wild sound effects and suitably manic utterances. This made him a hero to the grass roots audience, but put him at odds with fellow broadcasters, jealous of his success, and the conservative, reggae-loathing JBC directorship, leading to his resignation in 1979. He had already entered the recording business with DJ sides such as 'Dread At The Controls' and 'Homeguard' for Lee Perry, and 'Rootsman Revival' for Sonia Pottinger's High Note label. After a brief spell as engineer for Treasure Isle studio, he formed a working relationship with producer Carlton Patterson, for whom he cut 'Barber Saloon', and helped produce Ray I's popular 'Weatherman Skank'. He inaugurated his own DATC label in 1979 and began releasing records by Earl Sixteen, Rod Taylor, Edi Fitzroy, Sugar Minott and others, as well as his own popular DJ titles like 'Love The Dread', 'African Map' and 'Proper Education'. These were sought after as much for the entertaining 'version' sides, mixed by Campbell and King Tubby, as for his own sides. Perhaps his most enduring contributions are the two albums, *Dread At The Controls* and *African Anthem*, replete with many of the effects and jingles featured on his radio show. In 1982 he narrated Channel 4's six-part *Deep Roots* programme, and presented *The Rockers Road Show* for the same company the following year. He has also worked with UB40 and the Clash, toasting on the latter's 'Bank Robber'. He now resides in America where he continues to record, make stage appearances and host a music programme for television.

●ALBUMS: *Dread At The Controls* (DATC/Trojan 1979)★★★, *African Anthem* (DATC 1979)★★★★, *At The Control Dubwise* (DATC 1979)★★★★, *World War III* (DATC 1981)★★, *S.W.A.L.K.* (DATC 1982)★★, *Dub Merchant* (DATC 1982)★★★, *Pave The Way* (Heartbeat 1984)★★★, *Pave The Way Parts I & II* (DEP 1985)★★★, *Beyond World War III* (DATC 1986)★★, *Happy Family* (RAS 1989)★★★, *African Anthem Revisited* (RAS 1991)★★★, *Dub Party* (ROIR 1995)★★★.

DREAM ACADEMY

This 80s UK group comprised Nick Laird-Clowes (guitar/vocals, ex-the Act), Gilbert Gabriel (keyboards) and Kate St. John (vocals/oboe/saxophone, ex-Ravishing Beauties). Laird-Clowes, who as a child experienced the last days of the London underground movement at first hand, revived memories of that earlier era with the polished folky-pop 'Life In A Northern Town', dedicated to the memory of singer songwriter Nick Drake. The single, released on the Blanco y Negro label, reached UK number 15 in 1985 (and US number 7 the following year). Hailed, or conversely, derided as one the leading lights of the new breed of English psychedelic revivalists, the group's momentum was halted by the relative failure of 'The Love Parade'. Since then the group has periodically released albums which have shown the trio sticking gamely to their formula. David Gilmour contributed guitar and production work to

their third album. Kate St. John has during this time regularly composed theme music for British television programmes.

●ALBUMS: *The Dream Academy* (Blanco y Negro 1985)★★★, *Remembrance Days* (Blanco y Negro 1987)★★, *A Different Kind Of Weather* (Blanco y Negro 1990)★★.

DREAM SYNDICATE

The early 80s were an exciting time for those with a taste for American west coast rock. Several aspiring new acts appeared in the space of a few months that were obviously indebted to the late 60s, but managed to offer something refreshingly vital in the process. The Dream Syndicate's debut, *The Days Of Wine And Roses* (recorded in September 1982), more than justified the attention that the 'paisley underground' bands were attracting. Consisting of songwriter Steve Wynn (guitar/vocals) Karl Precoda (guitar), Kendra Smith (bass) and Dennis Duck (drums), the band chose their finest song 'Tell Me When It's Over', for their first UK single, issued on Rough Trade Records in late 1983. A contract with A&M Records followed, and *Medicine Show* appeared in 1984. Like their debut, there was a definite acknowledgement of the influence of both Lou Reed and Neil Young. By this time, though, Kendra Smith had joined partner David Roback in Opal. *This Is Not The New Dream Syndicate Album*, released the following year recycled their early recordings live, but it was to be their last engagement with A&M. Another move, this time to Chrysalis Records' offshoot Big Time, resulted in *Out Of The Grey* a year later, but the band's approach was gradually shifting to the mainstream. After a 12-inch single, '50 In A 25 Zone', the Dream Syndicate moved to the Enigma Records label, distributed in the UK by Virgin Records. 1988's *Ghost Stories* was followed by 'I Have Faith', and then came a live swansong offering, *Live At Raji's*, in 1989. However, the band never surpassed the dizzy heights of their first album, leaving Wynn to go on to a similarly acclaimed but commercially unsuccessful solo career.

●ALBUMS: *The Days Of Wine And Roses* (Ruby 1982)★★★★, *Medicine Show* (A&M 1984)★★★, *This Is Not The New Dream Syndicate Album* (A&M 1984)★★, *Out Of The Grey* (Big Time 1986)★★★, *Ghost Stories* (Enigma 1988)★★★, *Live At Raji's* (Restless 1989)★★★.

●COMPILATIONS: *It's Too Late To Stop Now* (Fan Club 1989)★★★.

DUDLEY, ANNE

One of five children in a London household appreciative of classical music (her parents turned the television off rather than see their children exposed to pop music), Dudley nevertheless saw the connection between the two forms when the Beatles' and Smokey Robinson's expanded orchestrations played on her transistor radio. By this time she was well on her way to a classical music career, but after leaving college in 1981 she started work as Trevor Horn's musical arranger and keyboardist. This involved working on some of 80s pop's most successful and innovative recordings, including music by Frankie Goes To Hollywood, Wham! and ABC. She then became the key member behind the adventurous Art Of Noise, who stealthily offered the public *avant garde* compositions packaged as dance music. The influence of tracks like 'Beat Box' and, in particular, 'Moments In Love', continue to reverberate around the 90s music scene. After the group disbanded at the end of the 80s, Dudley enjoyed a successful career scoring soundtracks for film and television (including *The Crying Game*, *Jeeves And Wooster* and *Kavanagh QC*). An album of Egyptian-derived recordings made jointly with Killing Joke's Jaz Coleman followed, before she returned to her roots in 1995 for an album of mainly classical compositions. Titled *Ancient And Modern*, this was scored for a full orchestra and 18 singers, with the material drawn largely from historical sources. 'I'm not a pop musician who is attempting something in a style with which they're not familiar. I've always come from a classical orientation. Even the pop music I do has its classical side; the way I score it, voice it, colour it.'
●ALBUMS: with Jaz Coleman *Songs From The Victorious City* (China 1990)★★★, *Ancient And Modern* (Echo 1995)★★★.

DUFFY

b. 30 May 1960, Birmingham, Worcestershire, England. Stephen Duffy first came to prominence in the UK under the moniker of Stephen 'Tin Tin' Duffy, with the release of his second single, 'Kiss Me', in early 1985. The track confirmed Duffy's power as a weaver of engaging pop melodies. His debut *The Ups And Downs* divided the critics, but his formula pop was most suitable for daytime radio play. 'Icing On The Cake' restored him to the UK Top 20, but his subsequent solo work proved less enticing. He later formed the Lilac Time. Following their demise he signed with Indolent Records and relaunched himself as the much more

name-friendly Duffy. Having been around for more than a decade his self-deprecating quote 'it's an accident of birth, that had me a born loser' can cover him against any lack of future success. His debut album, however, is a sparkling collection of guitar pop with some occasionally glorious harmonies. Duffy has now matured into a witty, perceptive songwriter and even though there is more than a glance over his shoulder to the Kinks, Beatles and quality 60s pop, these songs stand up well. Duffy was produced by Mitch Easter and features wistful harmony vocals from Velvet Crush. For once the press release is accurate, it is a bejewelled guitar album.
●ALBUMS: as Stephen 'Tin Tin' Duffy *The Ups And Downs* (Ten 1985)★★★, *Because We Love You* (Ten 1986)★★, *Music In Colours* (1993)★★; as Duffy *Duffy* (Indolent 1995)★★★.

DUKES OF STRATOSPHEAR

An alter ego of XTC, this group was a vehicle for Andy Partridge's psychedelic frustrations of being born a decade or two out of time. Both albums released so far contain brilliant pastiches of virtually every pop band during the mid-to late 60s. In many cases the Dukes' tongue-in-cheek parables are far superior to the songs to which they are gently alluding. It was suggested that their albums actually outsold the XTC product available at the same time.
●ALBUMS: *25 O'Clock* (Virgin 1985)★★★★, *Psonic Psunspot* (Virgin 1987)★★★★.
●COMPILATIONS: *Chips From The Chocolate Fireball* (Virgin 1987)★★★★.

DUNBAR, SLY

b. Lowell Dunbar, 10 May 1952, Kingston, Jamaica, West Indies. In 1969 Dunbar commenced his recording career with Lee Perry, playing drums on 'Night Doctor' by the Upsetters, which appears on both *The Upsetter* and *Return of Django*. The following year, he played on Dave Barker and Ansell Collins' massive hit 'Double Barrel'. Around this time he also joined the Youth Professionals who had a residency at the Tit For Tat Club on Red Hills Road, Kingston. He paid frequent visits to another club further up the same road, Evil People, where he struck up a friendship with bass player Robbie Shakespeare (b. 27 September 1953, Kingston, Jamaica, West Indies). Deciding to work together, their professional relationship as Sly And Robbie began. In 1972/3, Sly joined Skin Flesh And Bones, backing Al Brown on his best-selling cover of Al Green's 'Here I Am Baby'. The same year, Sly and

Robbie became founder members of the Revolutionaries, Channel One studio's house band. They recorded hit after hit, and the studio soon became the most in-demand on the island. Dunbar's technical proficiency and relentless inventiveness drove him constantly to develop original drum patterns, and while most of the island's other drummers were copying his latest innovations, he would move on and create something new. In this way, he had an enormous influence on the direction that reggae took from the mid-70s onwards. Dunbar's inventive and entertaining playing can be heard on dub and instrumental albums such as *Vital Dub, Satta Dub* and *Revolutionary Sounds*, as well as supporting the Mighty Diamonds on their classic *Right Time*. He also recorded extensively with the Professionals, Joe Gibbs' house band, playing on classics such as *Visions* by Dennis Brown, *Two Sevens Clash* by Culture and *African Dub Chapter 3*. Derrick Harriott went one step further and put him on the cover of *Go Deh Wid Riddim* (1977), which was credited to Sly And The Revolutionaries. He was then signed to Virgin Records, who released two disappointing solo albums, *Simple Sly Man* (1978) and *Sly Wicked And Slick* (1979). Around this time, Dunbar was the first drummer to integrate successfully synthesized drums into his playing, and later became the first reggae drummer to use a Simmons electronic drum kit.

In 1979 Sly And Robbie moved into record production with their own Taxi label, finding success with Black Uhuru's best-selling *Showcase*. Further recordings included Gregory Isaacs' *Showcase* and the various artists compilation, *Presenting Taxi* (1981). They had their greatest commercial success with Black Uhuru, with whom they recorded four further albums. In 1984, they became official members of the group, but left later that year after the departure of Michael Rose. At the same time, they established Ini Kamoze as a major new reggae artist, released Dennis Brown's *Brown Sugar* and Sugar Minott's *Sugar And Spice*, plus three groundbreaking albums with Grace Jones which were hugely successful and introduced their talents to the world outside of reggae. They have since recorded widely with artists such as Mick Jagger, Carly Simon, Gwen Guthrie, Bob Dylan, Robert Palmer, James Brown, Manu Dibango and Herbie Hancock. They also teamed up with Bill Laswell for a series of innovative soul/funk/crossover albums including *Language Barrier, Rhythm Killers, Silent Assassin* and Material's *The Third Power*. They have continued to develop their own reggae sound with recordings from their new discoveries 54-46 and Kotch, some of which are included on the compilations *Sound Of The 90s* and *Carib Soul*. They have already changed the musical world, and their restless creativity ensures that they will continue to do so.

●ALBUMS: *Go Deh Wid Riddim* (Crystal 1977)★★★, *Simple Sly Man* (Virgin 1978)★★, *Sly Wicked And Slick* (Virgin 1979)★★, *Sly-Go-Ville* (Mango/Island 1982)★★★.

DUNN, HOLLY

b. Holly Suzette Dunn, 22 August 1957, San Antonio, Texas, USA. Dunn's father was a preacher and her mother a professional artist, but they encouraged their children to sing and entertain. Dunn learned guitar and became a lead vocalist with the Freedom Folk Singers, representing Texas in the White House bicentennial celebrations. After university, she joined her brother, Chris Waters (Chris Waters Dunn), who had moved to Nashville as a songwriter. (He wrote 'Sexy Eyes' for Dr. Hook.) Together they wrote 'Out Of Sight, Not Out Of Mind' for Cristy Lane. Among her other songs are 'An Old Friend' (Terri Gibbs), 'Love Someone Like Me' (New Grass Revival), 'Mixed Emotions' (Bruce Murray, brother of Anne Murray) and 'That Old Devil Moon' (Marie Osmond). Dunn sang on numerous demos in Nashville. Her self-named album for the MTM label in 1986, and her own composition 'Daddy's Hands', drew considerable attention. *Across The Rio Grande* was a traditional yet contemporary country album featuring Vince Gill and Sam Bush and it won much acclaim. However, MTM went into liquidation and Dunn moved to Warner Brothers Records. Her up-tempo 'You Really Had Me Going' was a country number 1 and other country hits include 'Only When I Love', 'Strangers Again' and 'That's What Your Love Does To Me'. Her 'greatest hits' set, *Milestones*, aroused some controversy when she issued one of its tracks, the newly recorded 'Maybe I Mean Yes', as a single. The song was accused of downplaying the trauma of date-rape, and Dunn was sufficently upset to ask radio stations not to play the record. Her career was restored to equilibrium with the low-key, but impressive, *Getting It Dunn* in 1992. *Getting It Dunn* was her last album for Warner, and she is now signed to the independent label River North. Her debut for that label, *Life And Love And All The Stages*, was undistinguished, and she may find it hard getting back into the mainstream.

●ALBUMS: *Holly Dunn* (MTM 1986)★★★,

Cornerstone (MTM 1987)★★★, *Across The Rio Grande* (MTM 1988)★★★, *The Blue Rose Of Texas* (Warners 1989)★★★, *Heart Full Of Love* (Warners 1990)★★★, *Getting It Dunn* (Warners 1992)★★★, *Life And Love And All The Stages* (River North 1995)★★.

●COMPILATIONS: *Milestones* (Warners 1991)★★★.

●VIDEOS: *Cowboys Are My Weekness* (1995).

DURAN DURAN

Borrowing their name from a character in the movie *Barbarella*, this 80s new romantic UK pop group featured vocalist Simon Le Bon (b. 27 October 1958, Hertfordshire, England), pianist Nick Rhodes (b. Nicholas Bates, 8 June 1962), guitarist Andy Taylor (b. 16 February 1961, Wolverhampton, England), bassist John Taylor (b. 20 June 1960, Birmingham, England) and drummer Roger Taylor (b. 26 April 1960, Birmingham, England). Prior to this stable line-up, the group had included among its personnel, Simon Calley (bass/clarinet), Stephen Duffy (vocals), Andy Wickett (vocals) and John Curtis (guitar). The group came to prominence in late 1980 when they toured with Hazel O'Connor and won a contract with EMI Records. Firmly in the new romantic bracket, they enjoyed early publicity and charted with their debut single, 'Planet Earth'. The follow-up 'Careless Memories' barely scraped into the UK Top 40, but this proved merely a minor setback. 'Girls On Film', which was accompanied by a risqué Godley And Creme video featuring nude models, brought them their first UK Top 10 hit. Two albums quickly followed and hits such as 'Hungry Like A Wolf' and 'Say A Prayer' revealed that there was considerable songwriting substance behind the hype. By March 1983, they were in the ascendant, having twice broken into the US Top 10. 'Is There Something I Should Know?', a gloriously catchy pop song, entered the UK charts at number 1, thereby underlining the strength of their fan base. They were now, unquestionably, the most popular teen-idols in the country. An impressive run of UK Top 10 hits followed over the next three years, including 'Union Of The Snake', 'New Moon On Monday', 'The Reflex' (a UK/US number 1), 'Wild Boys', 'A View To A Kill' (a James Bond movie theme) and 'Notorious'. At the peak of their success, they decided to wind down and venture into other projects, such as the Power Station and Arcadia. Le Bon caused many a teenage heart to flutter when he was almost killed in a yachting accident in 1986. By the late 80s, they had lost

many of their original following, and even such interesting songs as 'The Skin Trade' could only reach the Top 20. The trio of Le Bon, Rhodes and John Taylor continued recording, knowing that they had already secured a place in pop history. Warren Cuccurullo and Sterling Campbell became permanent members of the band in June 1989, the former having worked extensively with Frank Zappa and Missing Persons. Campbell left in 1991 and go on to play with Cyndi Lauper and David Bowie, among others. Renewed interest came in 1993 when 'Ordinary World' became a major transatlantic hit. It was followed by 'Come Undone', both taken from *Duran Duran*. Critics who had written them off were having to amend their opinions, especially in light of the highly praised covers album *Thank You*, which showed a metallic edge. The cogniscenti decided: it's ok to like Duran Duran again.

●ALBUMS: *Duran Duran* (EMI 1981)★★★, *Rio* (EMI 1982)★★★, *Seven And The Ragged Tiger* (EMI 1983)★★, *Arena* (Parlophone 1984)★★, *Notorious* (EMI 1986)★★★, *Big Thing* (EMI 1988)★★, *Liberty* (Parlophone 1990)★, *Duran Duran (The Wedding Album)* (Parlophone 1993)★★, *Thank You* (Capitol 1995)★★★.

●COMPILATIONS: *Decade* (EMI 1989)★★★★.

●VIDEOS: *Sing Blue Silver* (1984), *Duran Duran Video Album* (1984), *Arena* (1985), *The Making Of Arena* (1986), *Duran Duran: Video Single* (1987), *Dancing On The Valentine* (1987), *Working For The Skin Trade* (1988), *Decade* (1989), *6ix By 3Hree* (1989), *Three To Get Ready* (1990), *Extraordinary World* (1994).

●FURTHER READING: *Duran Duran: Their Story*, Kasper De Graff and Malcolm Garrett.

DURUTTI COLUMN

One of the more eclectic bands to emerge from Manchester's punk scene, Vini Reilly (b. Vincent Gerard Reilly, August 1953, Manchester, England) and his Durutti Column combined elements of jazz, electronic and even folk in their multitude of releases. However, Vini's musical beginnings were as guitarist in more standard 1977 hopefuls Ed Banger And The Nosebleeds. Two other groups from 1977 - Fastbreeder and Flashback - had since merged into a new group, who were being managed by Manchester television presenter and Factory Records founder, Anthony Wilson. Wilson invited Reilly to join guitarist Dave Rowbotham and drummer Chris Joyce in January 1978, and together they became the Durutti Column (after a political cartoon strip used by the SI in Strasbourg during the 60s). They were joined by vocalist Phil Rainford and bass player Tony Bowers and recorded for the famous 'A Factory Sampler EP' with the late Martin Hannett producing. These were the only recordings made by this line-up and the band broke up. Reilly carried on with the Durutti Column alone, while the others (except Rainford) formed the Moth Men. The debut *The Return Of The Durutti Column* appeared on Factory in 1980 and was largely recorded by Reilly, although Hannett, Pete Crooks (bass), and Toby (drums) also contributed. Durutti Column soon established a solid cult following, particularly abroad, where Reilly's moving instrumental work was widely appreciated. Live appearances had been sporadic, however, as Reilly suffered from an eating disorder and was frequently too ill to play. The album was notable for its sandpaper sleeve, inspired by the anarchist movement Situationist Internatiside. Reilly and producer Hannett helped out on Pauline Murray's first solo album later in 1980. The Durutti Column's own recordings over the next few years were a mixed batch recorded by Reilly with assistance from drummers Donald Johnson, then Bruce Mitchell (ex-Alberto Y Lost Trios Paranoias), Maunagh Flemin and Simon Topping on horns, and much later further brass players Richard Henry, Tim Kellett, and Mervyn Fletcher plus violinist Blaine Reininger and celloist Caroline Lavelle. Dozens of other musicians have joined the nucleus of Reilly and Mitchell over the years and the band are still active today. A striking example of late period Durutti Column was captured on *Vini Reilly*, released in 1989. The guitarist cleverly incorporated the sampled voices of Joan Sutherland, Tracy Chapman, Otis Redding and Annie Lennox into a moving world of acoustic/electric ballads. Reilly has also lent some mesmerizing guitar to a host of recordings by artists such as Anne Clarke and Richard Jobson, and fellow Mancunian and friend Morrissey. On 8 November 1991, former Durutti guitarist Dave Rowbotham was discovered axed to death at his Manchester home. A murder hunt followed.

●ALBUMS: *The Return Of The Durutti Column* (Factory 1980)★★★, *Another Setting* (Factory 1983)★★★, *Live At The Venue London* (VU 1983)★★★, *Amigos En Portugal* live album (Fundacio Atlantica 1984)★★, *Without Mercy* (Factory 1984)★★★, *Domo Arigato* (Factory 1985)★★★, *Circuses And Bread* (Factory 1986)★★★, *The Guitar And Other Machines* (Factory 1987)★★★, *Live At The Bottom Line New York* cassette only (ROIR 1987)★★★, *Vini Reilly* (Factory 1989)★★★, *Obey The Time* (Factory 1990)★★★, *Lips That Would Kiss Form Prayers To Broken Stone* (Factory 1991)★★★, *Dry* (Materiali Sonori 1991)★★★, *Sex & Death* (Factory 1994)★★★, *Fidelity* (Crepescule 1996)★★★. Solo: Vini Reilly *The Sporadic Recordings* (Sporadic 1989)★★★.

●COMPILATIONS: *Valuable Passages* (Factory 1986)★★★, *The Durutti Column - The First Four Albums* (Factory 1988)★★★.

E

EARLE, STEVE

b. 17 January 1955, Fort Monroe, Virginia, USA. Earle's father was an air traffic controller and the family was raised in San Antonio, Texas. Earle played an acoustic guitar from the age of ll, but he also terrorized his schoolfriends with a sawn-off shotgun. He left home many times and sang 'Help Me Make It Through The Night' and 'all that shit' in bars and coffee houses. He befriended Townes Van Zandt, whom he describes as a 'a real bad role model'. Earle married at the age of 19 but when his wife went with her parents to Mexico, he moved to Nashville, playing for tips and deciding to stay. He took several jobs to pay his way but they often ended in arguments and violence. Johnny Lee recorded one of Earle's songs, and Elvis Presley almost recorded 'Mustang Wine'. His second marriage was based, he says, 'on a mutual interest in drug abuse'. Earle formed a back-up band in Texas, the Dukes, and was signed to CBS Records, who subsequently released *Early Tracks*. Recognition came when he and the Dukes signed to MCA and made a famed 'New Country' album, *Guitar Town*, the term being the CB handle for Nashville. The title track, with its Duane Eddy-styled guitar riff, was a potent blend of country and rock 'n' roll. 'Good Ol' Boy (Gettin' Tough)' was Earle's response to President Reagan's firing of the striking air-traffic controllers, including Earle's brother. Like Bruce Springsteen, his songs often told of the restlessness of blue collar workers. 'Someday' is a cheerless example - 'There ain't a lot you can do in this town/You drive down to the lake and then you turn back around.' Earle wrote 'The Rain Came Down' for the Farm Aid II benefit, and 'Nothing But A Child' was for an organization to provide for homeless children. Waylon Jennings recorded 'The Devil's Right Hand' and Janie Fricke, 'My Old Friend The Blues'. Earle saw in the 1988 New Year in a Dallas jail for punching a policeman and during that year, he married his fifth wife and released an album with a heavy metal look, *Copperhead Road*, which included the Vietnam saga, 'Johnny Come Lately', which he recorded with the Pogues. His answering machine says, 'This is Steve. I'm out shooting heroin, chasing 13 year old girls and beating up cops. But I'm old and I tire easily so leave a message and I'll get back to you.' After a lengthy break, allegedly because Earle had to detox, he returned with a fine album in 1995. *Train A Comin'* was mellow, acoustic and emotional, and featured some exceptional playing from Peter Rowan and harmony vocals from Emmylou Harris. Some of Earle's compositions are regarded as redneck anthems, but the views are not necessarily his own: he writes from the perspective of his creation, Bubba, the archetypal redneck. Another is The Beast - 'It's that unexplainable force that causes you to be depressed. As long as The Beast is there, I know I'll always write!' In the mid-90s, fired by the acclaim for *Train A Comin'*, a cleaned-up Earle started his own label E-Squared and contributed to the film soundtrack of *Dead Man Walking*. Earle is determined never to return to drugs. He stated in January 1996, 'I am real, real active and that is how I stay clean. It's a matter of survival to me. My life's pretty together right now. I got my family back.'

●ALBUMS: *Guitar Town* (MCA 1986)★★★★, *Early Tracks* (Epic 1987)★★★, *Exit O* (MCA 1987)★★★, *Copperhead Road* (MCA 1988)★★★★, *The Hard Way* (MCA 1990)★★★, *Shut Up And Die Like An Aviator* (MCA 1991)★★★★, *BBC Radio 1 Live In Concert* (Windsong 1992)★★★, *Train A Comin'* (Transatlantic 1995)★★★★, *I Feel Alright* (Transatlantic 1996)★★★.

EASTON, SHEENA

b. Sheena Shirley Orr, 27 April 1959, Bellshill, Scotland. Easton began performing while studying drama in Glasgow and was signed to EMI Records in 1979. A television film about the creation of her chic image helped 'Modern Girl' into the UK charts. This was followed by the chirpy 'Nine To Five' which sold over a million copies in the USA known as 'Morning Train'. Extraordinary success followed in America where she spent most of her time. Now established as an easy listening rock singer, Easton was given the theme to the 1981 James Bond film, *For Your Eyes Only*. Further hits followed from her second album, including 'When He Shines' and the title track, 'You Could Have Been With Me'. In 1983, Easton, who had now emigrated to California, joined the trend towards celebrity duets, recording 'We've Got Tonight' with Kenny Rogers. 'Telephone' was in a funkier dance mode and her career took a controversial turn in 1984 with attacks by moralists on the sexual implications of 'Sugar Walls', a Prince song which became one of her biggest hits. Easton also sang on Prince's 1987 single, 'U Got The Look'. Easton's later albums for EMI included *Do You*, produced by Nile Rodgers. In 1988 she switched labels to MCA, releasing *The Lover In Me*. The album's list of producers read like a Who's Who of contemporary soul music, with L.A. And Babyface, Prince, Jellybean and Angela Winbush among the credits. Her album, *What Comes Naturally*, is a hard and fast dance record produced to the highest technical standards but lacks the charm of her earlier work. In 1996 she was appearing in the Broadway production of *Grease*.

●ALBUMS: *Take My Time* (EMI 1981)★★, *You Could Have Been With Me* (EMI 1982)★★, *Madness, Money And Music* (EMI 1982)★★, *The Best Kept Secret* (EMI 1983)★★, *A Private Heaven* (EMI 1984)★★★★, *Do You* (EMI 1985)★★, *No Sound But A Heart* (EMI 1987)★★★, *The Lover In Me* (MCA 1988)★★★, *What Comes Naturally* (MCA 1991)★★★, *The World Of Sheena Easton* (1993)★★.
●COMPILATIONS: *The Gold Collection* (EMI 1996)★★★.

EAVIS, MICHAEL

b. 17 October 1935, England. Dairy farmer Michael Eavis will forever be synonymous with rock 'n' roll via the use of his land at Worthy Farm, in the Vale of Avalon, for the UK's premier rock event, the Glastonbury Festival. The idea originally came to him while watching the two-day Bath Blues Festival with Led Zeppelin and Frank Zappa in a field in Shepton Mallet in the summer of 1970. 'I fell in love with the idea of organising my own festival. It seemed romantic and a great way to spend mid-summer.' The first Glastonbury Festival took place weeks later, with T. Rex headlining. 1500 fans attended. From the start Eavis remained committed to the 60s ideals that he had developed in his youth, and to this day continues to contribute 10% of Glastonbury's gross receipts to charity. He has also limited music to 50% of activities on offer, which generally also include comedy, cabaret, theatre and environmental activism. The festival only became an annual event in 1982, with an eight year gap between June 1971's Glastonbury Fayre with David Bowie and Fairport Convention and 1979's Year Of The Child benefit. It has continued to grow in prestige in the 80s and 90s, with many stellar artists agreeing to appear at a fraction of their usual fees in sympathy with the broadly philanthropic ethos of the festival. In keeping with this, and contrary to rumours, Eavis has profited little from the exercise, running the entire event from his farmhouse, and, in the early 90s, a small office space in Glastonbury. In 1995 the Festival sold out its 80,000 ticket allocation within a week of going on sale, a tribute to both a unique event in the British music calendar and to Eavis's continued enthusiasm and professionalism in organizing it. In 1996 Eavis announced that there would be no festival that year. He cited that needing a rest and being able to spend more time on his farm as the main reasons. He was back in the foreground in 1997 with what turned out to be the wettest and muddiest festival since Woodstock in 1969. Eavis managed to pursuade the local authorities not to cancel the three-day event; instead many name bands were unable to perform.

ECHO AND THE BUNNYMEN

The origins of this renowned 80s Liverpool, England group can be traced back to the spring of 1977 when vocalist Ian McCulloch (b. 5 May 1959, Liverpool, England) was a member of the Crucial Three with Julian Cope and Pete Wylie. While the last two later emerged in the Teardrop Explodes and Wah!, respectively, McCulloch put together his major group at the end of 1978. Initially a trio the group featured McCulloch, Will Sergeant (b. 12 April 1958, Liverpool, England; guitar); Les Patterson (b. 18 April 1958, Ormskirk, Merseyside, England; bass) and a drum machine which they christened 'Echo'. After making their first appearance at the famous Liverpool club, Eric's, they made their vinyl debut in March 1979 with 'Read It In Books', produced by whizz kid entrepreneurs Bill Drummond and Dave Balfe. The production was sparse but intriguing and helped the group to establish a sizeable cult following. McCulloch's brooding live performance and vocal inflections were already drawing comparisons with the Doors' Jim Morrison. After signing to Korova Records (distributed by Warner Brothers Records) they replaced 'Echo' with a human being: Pete De Freitas (b. 2 August 1961, Port Of Spain, Trinidad, West Indies, d. 14 June 1989). The second single, 'Rescue', was a considerable improvement on its predecessor, with a confident, driving sound that augured well for their forthcoming album. *Crocodiles* proved impressive with a wealth of strong arrangements and compulsive guitar work. After the less melodic single, 'The Puppet', the group toured extensively and issued an EP, *Shine So Hard*, which crept into the UK Top 40. The next album, *Heaven Up Here*, saw them regaled by the music press. Although a less accessible and melodic work than its predecessor, it sold well and topped numerous polls. *Porcupine* reinforced the group's appeal, while 'The Cutter' gave them their biggest hit so far. In 1984 they charted again with 'The Killing Moon', an excellent example of McCulloch's ability to summon lazy melodrama out of primary lyrical colours. The epic quality of his writing remained perfectly in keeping with the group's grandiloquent musical character. The accompanying 1984 album, *Ocean Rain*, broadened their appeal further and brought them into the US Top 100 album charts. In February 1986 De Freitas left the group to be replaced by former Haircut 100 drummer, Mark Fox, but he returned the following September. However, it now seemed the band's best days were behind them. The uninspiringly titled *Echo And The Bunnymen* drew matching lacklustre performances, while a version of the Doors' 'People Are Strange' left both fans and critics perplexed. This new recording was produced by Ray Manzarek, who also played on the track, and it was used as the haunting theme for the cult film, *The Lost Boys* (1989). Yet, as many noted, there were simply dozens of better Bunnymen compositions which could have benefitted from that type of exposure. In 1988 McCulloch made the announcement that he was henceforth pursuing a solo career. While he completed the well-received *Candleland*, the Bunnymen made the unexpected decision to carry on. Large numbers of audition tapes were listened to before they chose McCulloch's successor, Noel Burke, a Belfast boy who had previously recorded with St Vitus Dance. Just as they were beginning rehearsals, De Freitas was tragically killed in a road accident. The group struggled on, recruiting new drummer Damon Reece and adding road manager Jake Brockman on guitar/synthesizer. In 1992 they introduced the next phase of Bunnymen history with *Reverberation*, but public expectations were not high and the critics unkind, and it was to be a final instalment. The Bunnymen Mark II broke up in the summer of the same year, with Pattinson going on to work with Terry Hall while Sergeant conducted work on his ambient side project, B*O*M, and formed Glide for one single. McCulloch, whose solo career had stalled after a bright start, and Sergeant worked together again from 1993 as Electrafixion, also pulling in Reece from the second Bunnymen incarnation. In 1996 an annoucement was made that three original members would go out as Echo And The Bunnymen once again. Pattinson McCulloch and Sergeant then released a new album, *Evergreen*, in 1997.

●ALBUMS: *Crocodiles* (Korova 1980)★★★★, *Heaven Up Here* (Korova 1981)★★★, *Porcupine* (Korova 1983)★★★★, *Ocean Rain* (Korova 1984)★★★, *Echo And The Bunnymen* (Warners 1987)★★, *Reverberation* (Korova 1990)★★, *Evergreen* (London 1997)★★★. Solo: Will Sergeant *Themes For Grind* (92 Happy Customers 1983)★★. Ian McCulloch *Candleland* (Warners 1988)★★★, *Mysterio* (Warners 1992)★★, *Evergreen* (London 1997)★★★.

●COMPILATIONS: *Songs To Learn And Sing* (Korova 1985)★★★★, *Live In Concert* (Windsong 1991)★★★, *The Cutter* (Warners 1993)★★★, *The Peel Sessions* (Strange Fruit 1995)★★★, *Ballyhoo* (Warners 1997)★★★★.

●FURTHER READING: *Liverpool Explodes: The Teardrop Explodes, Echo And The Bunnymen*, Mark Cooper. *Never Stop: The Echo & The Bunnymen Story*, Tony Fletcher.

EDELMAN, RANDY

This US vocalist won his audience by writing and performing some classic love songs. He made his debut in 1972, with a self-titled album that went largely unnoticed. During the 70s, however, he slowly built up his reputation and finally reached the big time with the worldwide smash 'Uptown Uptempo Woman'. His highest chart entry in the UK came with a revival of Unit Four Plus Two's 1965 hit 'Concrete And Clay'. By 1978 his singles career had ground to a halt. During this period one of his songs 'Weekend In New England' was covered and made into a million selling record by Barry Manilow. An attempted comeback in 1982 failed, but a new career was found when he was invited to provide the music for a new animated feature *The Care Bears*. He went on to write and perform the soundtrack for a number of movies and by 1988 was in the big league writing scores for movies including *Parenthood* and *Kindergarten Cop*. His other credits in the late 80s and early 90s included *Twins* (with George Delarue), *Troop Beverly Hills*, *Ghostbusters II*, *Come See The Paradise*, *Quick Change*, *Drop Dead Fred*, *V.I. Warshawski*, *Beethoven*, *The Last Of The Mohicans*, *The Distinguished Gentlemen*, *Dragon: The Bruce Lee Story*, *Beethoven's Second*, *Gettysburg*, and *The Mask* (1994).

●ALBUMS: *Randy Edelman* (1972)★★★, *Laughter And Tears* (1973)★★★, *Prime Cuts* (20th Century 1975)★★, *Fairwell Fairbanks* (1976)★★, *If Love Is Real* (Arista 1977)★★, *You're The One* (20th Century 1979)★★, *On Time* (Rocket 1982)★★, ... *And His Piano* (Elecstar 1984)★★, *The*

Distinguished Gentlemen (1993)★★.
●COMPILATIONS: *Uptown, Uptempo: The Best Of ...* (20th Century 1979)★★★.

EEK A MOUSE

b. Ripton Joseph Hilton, 1957, Kingston, Jamaica, West Indies. One of the most individual talents to emerge from Jamaica, Eek A Mouse's unique phrasing and singing style were to become as instantly recognizable as his 6 feet 6 inches frame. (Eek A Mouse was the name of a racehorse on which Hilton frequently lost money at the races; the one time he refused to back it, the horse, of course, won.) His first two releases, 'My Father's Land' and 'Creation', he made under his real name in the mid-70s. After spells with the Papa Roots, Black Ark, Gemini, Jah Life, Black Scorpio and Virgo sound systems he began recording with Joe Gibbs in 1980. 'Once A Virgin', 'Modelling Queen' and 'Virgin Girl' became sizeable hits the following year, by which time he had joined forces with producer and Volcano sound owner, Henry 'Junjo' Lawes. Utilizing the Roots Radics at Channel One with Scientist invariably mixing the final results. Junjo and Linval Thompson coaxed a series of best-selling albums and numerous hit singles from the idiosyncratic DJ throughout the years 1980 to 1984.
In 1981 following his debut album *Wa Do Dem*, he became the unscheduled star of that year's Reggae Sunsplash. In 1982 singles like 'Ganja Smuggling', 'For Hire And Removal' and 'Do You Remember' maintained his rocketing profile, as did the album *Skidip*. 'Terrorists In The City', 'Anarexol' and 'Operation Eradication' - voiced in response to the death of his friend Errol Scorcher - all sold well, and *The Mouse And The Man* and *Assassinator* albums (not to mention several appearances on live dancehall albums) quickly followed in 1983, but already there were signs that his distinctive trademark 'biddy biddy bengs' were becoming all too familiar. After *Mouseketeer* - last of his albums with Junjo - his popularity began to wane despite the occasional good record and a steady reputation as a performing artist. *U-Neek* heralded a comeback in 1991 with tracks produced by Gussie Clarke, Daddy O and Matt Robinson. That year he enjoyed a walk-on part in the movie *New Jack City*, and recorded for both Wild Apache and former Channel One engineer, Soljie.
●ALBUMS: *Wa Do Dem* (Greensleeves 1981)★★★, *Skidip* (Greensleeves 1982)★★★, *The Mouse And The Man* (Greensleeves 1983)★★★, *Assassinator* (RAS 1984)★★★, *Mousekateer* (Greensleeves 1984)★★, *King And I* (RAS 1987)★★, *U-Neek* (Mango/Island 1991)★★★.
●COMPILATIONS: *The Very Best Of Eek A Mouse* (Greensleeves 1987)★★★.

808 STATE

Manchester's finest dance group of the late 80s/early 90s, comprising Martin Price (b. 26 March 1955), owner of the influential Eastern Bloc record shop, Graham Massey (b. 4 August 1960, Manchester, Lancashire, England; ex-Beach Surgeon; Danny And The Dressmakers; Biting Tongues), Darren Partington (b. 1 November 1969, Manchester, Lancashire, England) and Andy Barker (b. 2 November 1969, Manchester, Lancashire, England). The final two had already worked together as DJ double act the Spin Masters. Massey had previously worked in a cafe opposite the Eastern Bloc shop, while Partington and Barker had been regular visitors to the premises, proffering a variety of tapes in the hope of gaining a contract with Price's Creed label. Together with Gerald Simpson, they began recording together as a loose electro house collective, and rose to prominence at the end of 1989 when their singl, 'Pacific State' became a massive underground hit. It proved to be a mixed blessing for the band, however, as they were lumped in with the pervading Manchester indie dance boom (a term they despised). *Newbuild* and *Quadrastate* helped to establish them as premier exponents of UK techno dance, leading to a lucrative contract with ZTT Records. However, Simpson had left to form his own A Guy Called Gerald vehicle, and launched a series of attacks on the band concerning unpaid royalties in the press. *Ex:El* featured the vocals of New Order's Bernard Sumner on 'Spanish Heart', and then-Sugarcube Björk Gudmundsdottir on 'Oops' (also a single) and 'Qmart'. They also worked with Mancunian rapper MC Tunes on the LP *North At Its Heights* and several singles. In October 1991 Price declined to tour the US with the band electing to work on solo projects instead, including managing Rochdale rappers the Kaliphz, and his own musical project, Switzerland. 808 State persevered with another fine album in 1993, which again saw a new rash of collaborations. Featured this time were Ian McCulloch (Echo And The Bunnymen) adding vocals to 'Moses', and samples from the Jam's 'Start', UB40's 'One In Ten' and even *Star Wars*' Darth Vader. Massey occupied himself with co-writing Björk's 'Army Of Me' single and other material on *Post*. Martin Price departed after being much sought after as a remixer (David

Bowie; Shamen; Primal Scream; Soundgarden; and many more). *Don Solaris* finally arrived after a gap of four years.

●ALBUMS: *Newbuild* (Creed 1988)★★★, *Quadrastate* (Creed 1989)★★★, *808:90* (Creed 1989)★★★★, with MC Tunes *North At Its Heights* (ZTT 1990)★★★, *Ex:El* (ZTT 1991)★★★, *Gorgeous* (Warners 1992)★★★, *Don Solaris* (ZTT 1996)★★★.

EIGHTH WONDER

A vehicle for 'sex-kitten' singer Patsy Kensit (b. 4 March 1968, Waterloo, London, England), a former child actress at one time known for her role in a UK television advertisement. She pursued a parallel career as an actress, including a role in the Royal Shakespeare Company production of *Silas Marner* in 1984, and as a pop singer in Eighth Wonder, which comprised Geoff Beauchamp (guitar), Alex Godson (keyboards) and Jamie Kensit (guitar). The group gained a minor UK hit with 'Stay With Me' in 1985. Kensit later landed the role of Crêpe Suzette in Julien Temple's 1986 film of Colin McInnes's novel, *Absolute Beginners*. Surrounded by an intense media hype, the film, which also featured David Bowie, Sade Adu and Ray Davies of the Kinks, was a critical and commercial flop. Kensit and Eighth Wonder found greater success in 1988 with the UK Top 10 single, 'I'm Not Scared'. Two more chart singles followed that same year including the Top 20 hit, 'Cross My Heart' and a Top 50 album, *Fearless*. Kensit later restored her credibility as an actress in the 1991 Don Boyd film, *Twenty-One*, although the subsequent *Blame It On The Bellboy* drew less favourable reviews. Her marriage in January 1992 to Simple Minds singer Jim Kerr caused considerable interest in the UK tabloid press. Since then she has been a favourite of the paparazzi lens, which reached a peak during 1996/7 when she started a relationship with Liam Gallagher of Oasis. She married him in the spring of 1997.

●ALBUMS: *Fearless* (Columbia 1988)★★.

EINSTURZENDE NEUBATEN

Formed out of the Berlin Arts Conglomerate Geniale Dilletanten, Einsturzende Neubaten made their live debut in April 1980. The line-up comprised Blixa Bargeld (b. 12 January 1959, Berlin, Germany), N.U. Unruh, Beate Bartel and Gudrun Gut. Alexander Van Borsig, an occasional contributor, joined in time for the band's first single, 'Für Den Untergang'. When Bartel and Gut departed to form Mania D and Matador they were replaced by F.M. (Mufti) and Einheit (ex-Abwarts). Einheit and

Unruh formed the band's rhythmic backbone, experimenting with a variety of percussive effects, while Bargeld provided vocals and guitar. Their first official album (there were previously many tapes available) was *Kollaps*, a collage of sounds created by unusual rhythmic instruments ranging from steel girders to pipes and canisters. Their 1982 12-inch single, 'Durstiges Tier', involved contributions from the Birthday Party's Rowland S. Howard and Lydia Lunch, at which point Van Borsig had joined the band permanently as sound technician alongside new bass player Marc Chung (also ex-Abwarts). A British tour with the Birthday Party introduced them to Some Bizzare Records which released *Die Zeichnungen Das Patienten O.T.* 1984's *Strategien Gegen Architekturen* was compiled with Jim Thirlwell (Foetus), while the band performed live at the ICA in London. Joined by Genesis P. Orridge (Psychic TV), Frank Tovey (Fad Gadget) and Stevo (Some Bizzare), the gig ended violently and attracted heated debate in the press. Bargeld spent the rest of the year touring as bass player for Nick Cave, going on to record several studio albums as a Bad Seed. In 1987 Einsturzende Neubaten performed the soundtrack for *Andi*, a play at the Hamburg Schauspielhaus, and also released *Funf Auf Der Nach Oben Offenen Richterskala*. This was intended as a farewell album, but they continued after its release. Bargeld's part-time career with the Bad Seeds continued, and in 1988 he featured alongside them in Wim Wenders' film *Angels Über Berlin*. Von Borsig, ironically, was now contributing to the work of Crime And The City Solution, featuring Cave's old Birthday Party colleagues. The band reunited, however, in time for 1989's *Haus Der Luge*.

●ALBUMS: *Kollaps* (Zick Zack 1981)★★★, *Die Zeichnungen Des Patienten O.T.* (Some Bizzare 1983)★★★, *2x4* (ROIR 1984)★★, *Half Mensch* (Some Bizzare/Rough Trade 1985)★★★, *Funf Auf Nach Oben Offenen Richterskala* (Some Bizzare 1987)★★★, *Haus Der Luge* (Some Bizzare 1989)★★★, *Die Hamletmaschine* soundtrack (Ego 1991)★★, *Tabula Rasa* (Mute 1993)★★★, *Malediction* (Mute 1993)★★★, *Faustmusik* soundtrack (Ego 1996)★★, *Ende Neu* (Mute 1996)★★★.

●COMPILATIONS: *Strategien Gegen Architekturen* (Mute 1984)★★★, *Strategies Against Architecture II* (Mute 1991)★★★.

●VIDEOS: *Liebeslieder* (Stud!o 1993).

ELECTRO HIPPIES

This eccentric 'grindcore' outfit formed in Liverpool, England, in 1988. Specializing in low-technology studio techniques, they went on to issue a sequence of albums for Peaceville, and, later, Necrosis. In each case, a distorted, bass-laden barrage was overridden by stomach-churning vocals that lacked both finesse and cohesion (though that was hardly the intention anyway). The group's initial line-up included the surname-less Simon (drums), Dom (bass/vocals) and Andy (guitar/vocals). Chaotic and extreme, Electro Hippies used their platform to chastise the whole recording industry. Their mantle was upheld in the first case by Radio 1 disc jockey John Peel, for whom the group recorded a July 1987 session consisting of some nine tracks. Titles such as 'Starve The City (To Feed The Poor)' and 'Mega-Armageddon Death Part 3' summed up both their appeal and limitations.

● ALBUMS: *Peel Sessions* (Strange Fruit 1987)★★★, *The Only Good Punk Is A Dead One* (Peaceville 1988)★★, *Electro Hippies Live* (Peaceville 1989)★★, *Play Loud Or Die* (Necrosis 1989)★★.

● COMPILATIONS: *The Peaceville Recordings* (Peaceville 1989)★★.

ELY, JOE

b. 9 February 1948, Amarillo Texas. Singer, song-writer, guitarist Ely, latterly regarded as the link between country rock and so-called new country, moved with his parents in 1958 to Lubbock, the major city of the flatlands of Texas from which such luminaries as Buddy Holly, Roy Orbison and Waylon Jennings had previously emerged. Ely formed his first band at the age of 13, playing a fusion of country and R&B, before dropping out of high school and following in the footsteps of Woody Guthrie and Jack Kerouac, hopping freight trains and working at a variety of non-musical jobs (including a spell with a circus) before finding himself stranded in New York with nothing but his guitar. He joined a theatrical company from Austin, Texas (where he now lives) and first had the chance to travel to Europe with his theatrical employers in the early 70s before returning to Lubbock, where he teamed up with fellow singer-songwriters Jimmie Gilmore and George 'Butch' Hancock and a couple of other local musicians (including a musical saw player!) in an informal group known as the Flatlanders. Although they were never immensely successful, the group did some recording in Nashville for Shelby Singleton's Plantation label, but only a couple of singles were released at the time. Later, when Ely was signed to MCA Records in the late 70s, the recordings by the Flatlanders, which had achieved legendary status,

were anthologized on *One Road More*, an album which was first released by European label Charly Records in 1980, but did not appear in the USA until the mid-80s. (This album is also available with the title *More A Legend Than A Band*.) In 1976 Ely formed his own band, whose members included Jesse Taylor (guitar), Lloyd Maines (steel drum), Gregg Wright (bass) and Steve Keeton (drums) plus auxiliary picker Ponty Bone (accordion). This basic line-up recorded three albums *Joe Ely*, *Honky Tonk Masquerade*, and *Down On The Drag*, before Keeton was replaced by Robert Marquam and Wright by Michael Robertson for *Musta Notta Gotta Lotta*, which also featured Reese Wyhans (keyboards), among others. Although these albums were artistic successes, featuring great songs mainly written by Ely, Hancock (especially) and Gilmore, the musical tide of the times was inclined far more towards punk/new wave music than to Texan singer-songwriters. In 1980, the Ely Band had toured extensively as opening act for the Clash, with whom Ely became very friendly, and *Live Shots* was released that year. The album featured Taylor, Marquam, Wright, Bone and Maines and was recorded on dates with the Clash, but was no more successful than the three studio albums which preceded it. In 1984 he recorded *Hi-Res*, which featured a completely new band of little-known musicians, but was no more successful than the previous albums in commercial terms.

By 1987, Ely had assembled a new band which has largely remained with him to date: David Grissom (lead guitar), Jimmy Pettit (bass) and Davis McLarty (drums). This line-up recorded two artistically stunning albums for the US independent label Hightone, *Lord Of The Highway* and *Dig All Night*, the latter featuring for the first time a repertoire totally composed of Ely's own songs. Both albums were licensed in the UK to Demon Records, and in the wake of this renewed interest, a tiny London label, Sunstorm Records launched by Pete O'Brien the editor of *Omaha Rainbow* fanzine, licensed two albums' worth of Ely's early material. *Milkshakes And Malts*, a compilation of Ely's recordings of songs by Butch Hancock, appeared in 1988, and *Whatever Happened To Maria?*, which similarly compiled Ely's own self-penned songs, in 1989.

At this point, the band had been together for three years and had achieved an incredible onstage empathy, especially between Ely and Grissom, whose R&B guitar work had moved the band's music away from country. In 1990, they recorded a powerhouse live album in Austin, *Live At Liberty*

Lunch, which was sufficiently impressive for Ely's old label, MCA, to re-sign him.

Among Ely's extra-curricular activities are contributions to the soundtrack of *Roadie*, a movie starring Meat Loaf, in which he can be heard playing 'Brainlock' and 'I Had My Hopes Up High', and his participation as a member of the *ad hoc* group, Buzzin Cousins, in which his colleagues are John Mellencamp, John Prine, Dwight Yoakam and James McMurtry, on the soundtrack to the Mellencamp movie *Falling From Grace*. Ely, Terry Allen and Butch Hancock have together written a stage musical about a prostitute, *Chippy*. His 1995 album *Letter To Laredo* was a return to the sound of his first MCA albums and included an update of Butch Hancock's 'She Never Spoke Spanish To Me' as 'She Finally Spoke Spanish To Me'. The key track is a fine version of Tom Russell's song about cockfighting, 'Gallao Del Cielo'. Joe Ely is one of the most completely realized artists in country music of the 90s, especially in the live situation where he excels.

●ALBUMS: *Joe Ely* (MCA 1977)★★★★, *Honky Tonk Masquerade* (MCA 1978)★★★★, *Down On The Drag* (MCA 1979)★★★★, *Live Shots* (SouthCoast 1980)★★★, *One Road More* (Charly 1980)★★★, *Musta Notta Gotta Lotta* (SouthCoast 1981)★★★, *Hi-Res* (MCA 1984)★★★, *Lord Of The Highway* (Demon 1987)★★★★, *Dig All Night* (Demon 1988)★★★★, *Milkshakes And Malts* (Sunstorm 1988)★★★, *Whatever Happened To Maria* (Sunstorm 1989)★★★, *Live At Liberty Lunch* (MCA 1990)★★★, *Love And Danger* (1992)★★★, *Highways And Heartaches* (1993)★★★, *Letters To Laredo* (Transatlantic 1995)★★★★.

●COMPILATIONS: *No Bad Talk Or Loud Talk '77 - '81* (Edsel 1995)★★★★, *The Time For Travellin': The Best Of ... Vol. 2* (Edsel 1996)★★★★.

ENYA

b. Eithne Ni Bhraonain, 17 May 1961, Gweedore, Co. Donegal, Eire. Enya, a classically trained pianist, was formerly a member of Clannad before embarking on a solo career that blossomed unexpectedly with her UK chart-topper 'Orinoco Flow'. Daughter of noted Irish Showband leader Leo Brennan (Brennan is the non-Gaelic form of Bhraonain) who led the Slieve Foy Band, Enya was born into a highly musical family. Her mother was also a musician, and in 1976 some of her brothers, sisters and uncles formed the band Clannad (Gaelic for family). Enya joined the band on keyboards in 1979 and shared in some of their success as they recorded haunting themes for a variety of

television programmes, giving them their first chart success. However, Enya, who has professed she has little time for conventional pop music, never quite fitted into the band and left amicably in 1982. A few years later she was asked to record the music for the BBC television series *The Celts* which was subsequently released as her debut album in 1987. An endearing blend of ethereal singing (in Gaelic and English), the album was largely ignored, as was the accompanying single 'I Want Tomorrow'. However, the following year, Enya released *Watermark* in much the same vein and had a surprise UK number 1 with the single 'Orinoco Flow'. Working with her long-time collaborators, Roma Ryan (her lyric writer) and Nicky Ryan (her producer), Enya followed the chart-topper with two smaller hits - 'Evening Falls' and 'Storms In Africa Part II'. She adopted a lower profile for the next couple of years except for an appearance with Sinead O'Connor. She returned in the early 90s with *Shepherd Moons*, which was still selling strongly in the mid-90s having reached world sales of 10 million copies. *The Memory Of Trees* was more of the same. At present her reluctance to change is holding firm, but at some stage her warm ambient music will begin to pale as listeners will begin to realize it is the same cake with a different topping.

●ALBUMS: *Enya* (BBC 1987)★★, *Watermark* (Warners 1988)★★★★, *Shepherd Moons* (Warners 1991)★★★, *The Memory Of Trees* (Warners 1995)★★★.

ERASURE

Keyboard player and arranger Vince Clarke (b. 3 July 1961) had already enjoyed success as a member of Depeche Mode, Yazoo, and the Assembly when he decided to undertake a new project in 1985. The plan was to record an album with 10 different singers, but after auditioning vocalist Andy Bell, the duo Erasure was formed. Erasure broke into the UK chart in 1986 with 'Sometimes' which reached number 2, and was followed by 'It Doesn't Have To Be Me' in 1987. The following month their second album, *Circus*, reached the UK Top 10 and since then their popularity has rapidly grown. Memorable and infectious hits such as 'Sometimes', 'Victim Of Love', 'The Circus', 'Ship Of Fools', 'A Little Respect', *Crackers International* EP, 'Drama!', 'Blue Savannah', 'Chorus', 'Love To Hate You' and 'Breath Of Life' have established them as serious rivals to the Pet Shop Boys as the world's leading vocal/synthesizer duo. Erasure's appeal lies in the unlikely pairing of the flamboyant Bell and the low-profile keyboards wizard and songwriter Clarke. Their stage show is a spectacular event, while the overtly gay Bell's taste in clothes is brilliantly outrageous. Their singles and album sales continue to increase with successive releases and *The Innocents*, *Wild!* and *Chorus* have all reached number 1 in the UK. An excellent pastiche of Abba in 1992, resulted in the *Abba-Esque* EP reaching number 1 in the UK. It is also worth stressing that they have achieved their extraordinary success working through an independent label, Mute Records.

●ALBUMS: *Wonderland* (Mute 1986)★★★, *The Circus* (Mute 1987)★★★, *The Two Ring Circus* (Mute 1987)★★, *The Innocents* (Mute 1988)★★★, *Wild!* (Mute 1989)★★★, *Chorus* (Mute 1991)★★★, *I Say, I Say, I Say* (Mute 1994)★★★, *Erasure* (Mute 1995)★★★, *Cowboy* (Mute 1997)★★.
●COMPILATIONS: *Pop - The First Twenty Hits* (Mute 1992)★★★★.
●VIDEOS: *Pop - 20 Hits* (1993).

ERIC B AND RAKIM

A Queens, New York rap duo consisting of Eric Barrier (b. Elmhurst, New York, USA) and William 'Rakim' Griffin (b. William Griffin Jnr., Long Island, New York, USA) who use additional musicians such as Sefton the Terminator and Chad Jackson as required; Rakim is the lyricist, Eric B the DJ. Or, as Rakim himself put it in 'I Ain't No Joke': 'I hold the microphone like a grudge, Eric B hold the record so the needle don't budge'. They met in 1985 when Eric was working for the New York radio station WBLS and was looking for NY's top MC. They started working together before emerging with the demo, 'Eric B Is President'. Released as a 45 on an obscure Harlem independent, Zakia Records, in the summer of 1986, it eventually led to a contract with 4th and Broadway. Their long-playing debut was preceded by a stand-out single of the same name, 'Paid In Full', which inspired over 30 remixes. When the album arrived it caused immediate waves. Representatives of James Brown and Bobby Byrd took legal action over the sampling of those artists' works. Conversely, they helped to galvanize Brown's career as a legion of rap imitators cut in on his back catalogue in search of samples. They also originated the similarly coveted 'Pump Up The Volume' sample. As well as Eric B putting the funk back into rap music, Rakim was responsible for introducing a more relaxed, intuitive delivery which was distinctly separate from the machismo of Run DMC and LL Cool J. That influence can still be detected in present day records by big name West Coast stars. The duo hit the UK charts in 1987 with 'Paid In Full (The Coldcut Remix)', though the duo themselves hated the version. Later hits included 'Move The Crowd', 'I Know You Got Soul', 'Follow The Leader' and 'The Microphone'. Label moves may have diminished their probable impact, though the band themselves have never gone out of their way to cross over into the mainstream. Instead, each of their albums to date have offered a significant musical development on the last, Rakim's raps growing in maturity without sacrificing impact. The split came in the early 90s, with Rakim staying with MCA to deliver solo material like 'Heat It Up', produced by new co-conspirator Madness 4 Real, included on the soundtrack to Mario van Peebles vehicle, *Gunmen*.

●ALBUMS: *Paid In Full* (4th & Broadway 1987)★★★, *Follow The Leader* (MCA-Uni 1988)★★★, *Let The Rhythm Hit 'Em* (MCA 1990)★★★★, *Don't Sweat The Technique* (MCA 1992)★★★.

ESTEFAN, GLORIA, AND MIAMI SOUND MACHINE

Formed in Miami, Florida, USA, in 1973, this Latin/funk/pop group was originally a trio called the Miami Latin Boys, comprising Emilio Estefan (keyboards), Juan Avila (bass) and Enrique 'Kiki' Garcia (drums) each of whom was born in Cuba and raised in Miami. The following year the group played at a friend's wedding where they were joined onstage by singer Gloria Fajardo (b. 1 September 1957). She at first refused to join the group, then agreed to sing with them part-time as she pursued her studies. In Miami, Fajardo had attended a Catholic high school and learned to play guitar and sing during her leisure hours. In 1975 the quartet changed its name to Miami Sound Machine. They recorded their first single, 'Renecer', for a local Hispanic company that year. Emilio and Gloria married in 1978. In 1979 the group recorded its first album, sung entirely in Spanish; it was picked up for distribution by CBS Records International. The group recorded seven Spanish-language records during the next six years, becoming successful in predominantly US Hispanic areas, Central and South America, as well as in Europe. Meanwhile, the group's membership grew to nine musicians. Their first English-language single, 'Dr. Beat', was released in 1984 and became a club Top 10 hit in the UK, where the group then flew to appear on the BBC television programme *Top Of The Pops*, resulting in the song becoming a Top 10 hit. The following year the group toured Japan successfully, and were honoured by their hometown Miami which renamed a local street Miami Sound Machine Boulevard. Signed to Epic Records, their first US chart single was 'Conga' in 1985, reaching number 10 by early 1986. That same year saw two other US Top 10 singles, 'Bad Boy' and the ballad 'Words Get In The Way'. *Billboard* named them the top singles act of 1986. Their first English-language album, *Primitive Love*, reached number 23 that same year. The group officially changed its name to Gloria Estefan And Miami Sound Machine in 1987, a year that brought one Top 10 single, 'Rhythm Is Gonna Get You', and *Let it Loose*, which reached number 6 by the spring of 1988. Another Top 10 single, 'Can't Stay Away From You', and the number 1 ballad, 'Anything For You', were highlights of early 1988. The year closed with another US/UK Top 10 single, '1-2-3'.

Gloria Estefan released a solo album, *Cuts Both Ways*, which also made the Top 10, in the summer of 1989. Three singles from that album found their way to the US Top 10: the number 1 'Don't Wanna Lose You', 'Get On Your Feet' and 'Here We Are'. However, in early 1990 they were in the news for another reason when on 20 March their tour bus was involved in a serious accident in Syracuse, New York. The incident occurred following a meeting with President George Bush to discuss their participation in an anti-drugs campaign. The group was heading north when its bus was struck from behind by a truck. Estefan suffered from a broken vertebra and underwent surgery which kept her and the group off the road for most of the year. Husband Emilio and the couple's son Nayib received minor injuries, but thankfully recovered. In 1991, Estefan returned after her long absence with new material, an extensive tour and she was reportedly awarded £5 million compensation for loss of earnings caused by the bus accident. *Abriendo Puertas* marked a return to her roots.

●ALBUMS: as Miami Sound Machine *Miami Sound Machine* (Columbia 1976)★★★, *Rio* (Columbia 1978)★★★, *Eyes Of Innocence* (Columbia 1984)★★★, *Primitive Love* (Epic 1986)★★★. As Gloria Estefan And Miami Sound Machine *Let it Loose* (USA) *Anything For You* (UK) (Epic 1988)★★★★, *Goya* (Epic 1989)★★★, *Cuts Both Ways* (Epic 1989)★★★, *Exitos De Gloria Estefan* (Epic 1990)★★★, *Into The Light* (Epic 1991)★★, *Mi Terra* (Epic 1993)★★★, *Hold Me, Thrill Me, Kiss Me* (Epic 1994)★★★, *Abriendo Puertas* (Epic 1995)★★★.

●COMPILATIONS: *Greatest Hits* (Epic 1992)★★★.
●VIDEOS: *Everlasting Gloria* (SMV Epic 1995).
●FURTHER READING: *Gloria Estefan*, Grace Catalano.

EURYTHMICS

David A. Stewart (b. 9 September 1952, Sunderland, Tyne and Wear, England) and Annie Lennox (b. 25 December 1954, Aberdeen, Scotland). The worldwide popularity and critical acclaim of one of pop music's leading duos came about by fastidious determination and Stewart's remarkably good ear in being able to write the perfect song for his musical partner Lennox. Both artists rely heavily on each other's considerable talent and, as former lovers, they know better than most their strengths and weaknesses. Stewart met Lennox in London while he was still a member of the folk rock band Longdancer. She was supplementing her income by waitressing while a student at the Royal College of Music. Together they formed the Tourists, a fondly remembered band that were able to fuse new wave energy with well-crafted pop songs. Following the Tourists' split, with Lennox and Stewart now embroiled in their much-publicized doomed love affair, they formed the Eurythmics in 1980. The debut *In The Garden* was a rigidly electronic sounding album, very Germanic, haunting and cold. The record failed to sell. During one of the low points in their lives, having ended their four-year relationship, the duo persevered professionally and glanced the charts with the synthesizer-based 'Love Is A Stranger'. This gave them the confidence they needed, and the material on the subsequent *Sweet Dreams* was superb and bringing deserved success. The album spawned a number of hits, all accompanied by an imaginative series of self-produced videos with the stunning Lennox in countless guises, showing incredible natural confidence in front of a camera. The spooky 'Sweet Dreams' narrowly missed the top of the UK chart, but made the top spot in the USA and was followed in quick succession by a reissued 'Love Is A Stranger', 'Who's That Girl' (featuring Stewart's future wife Siobhan Fahey from Bananarama in the video), and the celebratory 'Right By Your Side'. *Touch* in 1984 became a huge success, containing a varied mixture of brilliantly accessible pop music. A remixed mini-LP of four tracks from *Touch* followed before they embarked upon scoring the music for the film *1984*, starring John Hurt. The soundtrack was not up to standard and they immediately remedied this by delivering the excellent *Be Yourself Tonight*. The album contained less synthesized pop and more rock music, with Stewart using guitar-based songs including a glorious soul duet with Aretha Franklin on 'Sisters (Are Doin' It For Themselves)' and the earthy 'Ball And Chain'. During 1985 Lennox experienced serious throat problems, which forced the band to cancel their appearance at Live Aid. That same month, however, the group enjoyed their sole UK chart topper, the exuberant 'There Must Be An Angel'. Lennox made her big-screen debut in *Revolution* with Donald Sutherland and Al Pacino. Stewart, meanwhile, became one of the most sought-after record producers, working with Bob Dylan, Tom Petty, Feargal Sharkey, Daryl Hall (of Hall And Oates), Bob Geldof and Mick Jagger. The following year another gem, *Revenge*, was released, which included 'Missionary Man', 'Thorn In My Side' and the comparatively lightweight 'The Miracle Of Love'. *Savage* in 1987 maintained the standard and featured one of Lennox's finest vocal accomplishments with the R&B rocker 'I Need A Man'. In 1988 their performance at the televised Nelson Mandela Concert from Wembley was one of its highlights, and the acoustic 'You Have Placed A Chill In My Heart' was a triumph. Later that year Lennox duetted with Al Green for a rousing and soulful version of Jackie DeShannon's 'Put A Little Love In Your Heart'. *We Too Are One* at the end of 1989 became their most successful album to date, staying at number 1 into 1990. The Eurythmics have gained a mass following by the sheer quality of their songs and have managed to stay favourites with the media. Lennox is one of the most visually striking female performers, with a voice of rare quality. Stewart stays in the background, using his talent as a producer and songwriter. During their hiatus of the early 90s when they both needed to be away from each other, Stewart in addition to his production work made his own solo albums. In 1992, Lennox issued her debut solo *Diva* and consolidated her reputation with *Medusa* in 1995.

● ALBUMS: *In The Garden* (RCA 1981)★★, *Sweet Dreams (Are Made Of This)* (RCA 1983)★★★★, *Touch* (RCA 1983)★★★★, *Touch Dance* (RCA 1984)★★, *1984 (For The Love Of Big Brother)* (Virgin 1984)★★, *Be Yourself Tonight* (RCA 1985)★★★★, *Revenge* (RCA 1986)★★★★, *Savage* (RCA 1987)★★★, *We Too Are One* (RCA 1989)★★★, *Eurythmics Live 1983-89* (RCA 1993)★★★.

● COMPILATIONS: *Greatest Hits* (RCA 1991)★★★★.

● FURTHER READING: *Eurythmics: Sweet Dreams: The Definitive Biography*, Johnny Waller.

EVERYTHING BUT THE GIRL

The duo of Tracey Thorn (b. 26 September 1962, Hertfordshire, England) and Ben Watt (b. 6 December 1962, Barnes, London, England), first came together when they were students at Hull University, their name coming from a local furniture shop. Thorn was also a member of the Marine Girls who issued two albums. They performed together in 1982 and released a gentle and simply produced version of Cole Porter's 'Night And Day'. Thorn made a solo acoustic mini-album in 1982, *A Distant Shore*, which was a strong seller in the UK independent charts, and Watt released the critically acclaimed *North Marine Drive* the following year. They subsequently left Cherry Red Records and signed to the major-distributed Blanco y Negro label. In 1984 they made the national chart with 'Each And Everyone', which preceded their superb *Eden*. This jazz-flavoured pop collection hallmarked the duo's understated but beautific compositional skills, displaying a great leap from the comparative naïvéte of their previous offerings. Their biggest single breakthrough, meanwhile, came with a version of Danny Whitten's 'I Don't Want To Talk About It', which reached the UK Top 3 in 1988. Their subsequent albums have revealed a much more gradual growth in songwriting, though many contend they have never surpassed that debut. *The Language Of Life*, a collection more firmly fixated with jazz stylings, found further critical acclaim, and stands as their best effort post-*Eden*. One track, 'The Road', featured Stan Getz on saxophone. However, a more pop-orientated follow-up, *World-wide*, was released to mediocre reviews in 1991. *Amplified Heart* repaired the damage somewhat, with contributions from Danny Thompson, Dave Mattacks, Richard Thompson and arranger Harry Robinson. Following Thorn's vocal contributions to trip-hop pioneers Massive Attack's *Protection*, a drum and bass remix of 'Missing' from 1996's *Walking Wounded* became a big club hit and responsible for putting Everything But The Girl back in the charts.

● ALBUMS: *Eden* (Blanco y Negro 1984)★★★★, *Love Not Money* (Blanco y Negro 1985)★★, *Baby The Stars Shine Bright* (Blanco y Negro 1986)★★, *Idlewild* (Blanco y Negro 1988)★★★, *The Language Of Life* (Blanco y Negro 1990)★★★★, *World-wide* (Blanco y Negro 1991)★★, *Amplified Heart* (Banco y Negro 1994)★★★, *Walking Wounded* (Atlantic 1996)★★★★. Solo: Tracey Thorn *A Distant Shore* (Cherry Red 1982)★★★. Ben Watt *North Marine Drive* (Cherry Red 1983)★★★.

●COMPILATIONS: *Home Movies: The Best Of* (Blanco y Negro 1993)★★★, *The Best Of ...* (Blanco y Negro 1997)★★★★.
●FURTHER READING: *Patient: The History Of A Rare Illness*, Ben Watt.

EXPLOITED

This abrasive and unruly Scottish punk quartet was formed in East Kilbride in 1980 by vocalist Wattie Buchan and guitarist 'Big John' Duncan. Recruiting drummer Dru Stix (b. Drew Campbell) and bassist Gary McCormack, they signed to the Secret Records label the following year. Specializing in two-minute blasts of high-speed blue vitriol, they released their first album, *Punk's Not Dead*, in 1981. Lyrically they sketched out themes such as war, corruption, unemployment and police brutality, amid a chaotic blur of crashing drums and flailing guitar chords. The band quickly become entrenched in their own limited musical and philosophical ideology, and earned themselves a certain low-life notoriety. Songs such as 'Fuck A Mod', for example, set youth tribe again youth tribe without any true rationale. 'Sid Vicious Was Innocent', meanwhile, deserves no comment whatsoever. Yet they were the only member of the third generation punk set to make it on to *Top Of The Pops*, with 1981's 'Dead Cities'. Continuing to release material on a regular basis, they have retained a small, but ever-declining, cult following. The line-ups have fluctuated wildly, with Duncan going on to join Goodbye Mr Mackenzie and, very nearly, Nirvana, while Buchan has stayed in place to marshall the troops. The diminutive but thoroughly obnoxious lead singer, with a multi-coloured mohican haircut, strikes an oddly anachronistic figure today as he presides over his talentless musical curio.
●ALBUMS: *Punk's Not Dead* (Secret 1981)★★★, *On Stage* (Superville 1981)★★★, *Troops Of Tomorrow* (Secret 1982)★★★, *Let's Start A War* (Pax 1983)★★★, *Horror Epics* (Konnexion 1985)★★★, *Death Before Dishonour* (Rough Justice 1989)★★, *The Massacre* (Rough Justice 1991)★★, *Beat The Bastrads* (Rough Justice 1996)★★.
●COMPILATIONS: *Totally Exploited* (Dojo 1984)★★, *Live On The Apocalypse Now Tour '81* (Chaos 1985)★★, *Live And Loud* (Link 1987)★★, *Inner City Decay* (Snow 1987)★★★, *The Exploited On Stage 91/Live At The Whitehouse 1985* (Dojo 1991)★★.
●VIDEOS: *Live In Japan* (Visionary 1993), *Rock & Roll Outlaws* (Visionary 1995).

EXQUISITES

Vocal group the Exquisites were formed in 1981 in Long Island, New York, USA, by former Gino And The Dells' baritone Pete Chacona and tenor Bernie Festo, after Chacona had attended an audition for Festo's then group. Through local newspaper advertising John O'Keefe (first tenor) and Bob Thomas (lead, ex-Fascinations) were recruited, while familial ties brought in bass singer George Chacona, Pete's brother. Rehearsing material from the Moonglows, Flamingos and Harptones, they set about performing at local shows and nostalgia rallies. When O'Keefe left to join the Teenchords in 1983, he was replaced on first tenor by Mike Paccione. Their first recording came in early 1985 when their version of the Shirelles' 'Dedicated To The One I Love' was released on Avenue D Records, followed by an update of the El Dorados' 'At My Front Door'. After sending a tape to local R&B revival disc jockey Don K. Reed's *Doo-Wop Shop* show in 1985 they found their version of the Solitaires' 'Walking Along' earn a regular slot as opening theme to the highly influential oldies programme. When Paccione departed in 1987 George Santiago (ex-Eternals) came on board, with the line-up also expanded by the arrival of Al Pretea (ex-Dolphins). Later Zeke Suarez replaced Festo. The group embarked on sessions for a debut album in 1990 with Crystal Ball Records, with versions of songs by the Drifters, Jive Five and El Dorados, as well as doo-wop standard 'Over The Rainbow'.
●ALBUMS: *The Exquisites* (Crystal Ball 1991)★★★.

EXTREME NOISE TERROR

A band whose name truly encapsulates their sound, Extreme Noise Terror formed in January 1985 and were signed by Manic Ears Records after their first ever gig. Their debut release was a split album with Chaos UK, and although there were musical similarities, ENT, along with Napalm Death, were already in the process of twisting traditional punk influences into altogether different shapes. Along with the latter, they became the subject of disc jockey John Peel's interest in 1987, recording a session (one of three) which would eventually see release on Strange Fruit Records. Afterwards drummer Mick Harris, who had left Napalm Death to replace the group's original drummer, in turn departed, joining Scorn. His replacement was Stick (Tony Dickens), who joined existing members Dean Jones (vocals), Phil Vane (vocals) and Pete Hurley (guitar). Mark Bailey had by now replaced Mark Gardiner, who himself had replaced Jerry Clay, on bass. Touring in Japan preceded the release of *Phonophobia*, while continued Peel sessions brought the group to the attention of the KLF's Bill Drummond. He asked them to record a version of the KLF's '3am Eternal', with the intention of the band appearing on *Top Of The Pops* live at Christmas to perform the tune (the BBC decided this was not in the best interests of their audience). Eventually released as a limited edition single, the two band's paths crossed again in 1992 when the KLF were invited to perform live at the 1992 Brit Awards. This crazed event, which included the firing of blanks into the audience, has already passed into music industry legend. Back on their own, 1993 saw Extreme Noise Terror touring widely, and the group signed to Earache Records the following year. By this time the line-up had swelled to include Lee Barrett (bass; also Disgust) replacing Bailey, and Ali Firouzbakht (lead guitar), with a returning Pig Killer on drums. Together they released *Retro-bution*, ostensibly a compilation, but nevertheless featuring the new line-up on re-recorded versions of familiar material.

●ALBUMS: split with Chaos UK *Radioactive* (Manic Ears 1985)★★, *A Holocaust In Your Head* (Hurt 1987)★★, *The Peel Sessions* (Strange Fruit 1990)★★★, *Phonophobia* (Vinyl Japan 1992)★★, *Retro-bution* (Earache 1995)★★★.
●VIDEOS: *From One Extreme To The Other* (1989).

EYELESS IN GAZA

Taking their name from Aldous Huxley's famous novel, this UK group was the brainchild of vocalists/musicians Martyn Bates and Peter Becker. Known for their tortured vocals and impressive arranging skills, the group established a reasonable following on the independent circuit with their 1981 debut, *Photographs As Memories*. Several more albums for Cherry Red Records saw them alternate between a melodramatic and meandering style which increasingly veered towards improvisation. Bates subsequently teamed up with former Primitives bassist Steve Gullaghan in Hungry I, also working solo. Eyeless In Gaza re-formed in 1992, releasing an album titled *Fabulous Library* the following year as a trio comprising Bates, Becker and chanteuse Elizabeth S. Reverting to the original two-piece line-up later in 1993, the two recorded and toured Europe and the USA extensively with self-styled 'performance poet' Anne Clark, also collaborating with Derek Jarman film soundtrack composer Simon Turner. In 1994 Eyeless In Gaza signed to the Belgian based dance/experimental label Antler Subway.

●ALBUMS: *Photographs As Memories* (Cherry Red 1981)★★★, *Caught In Flux* (Cherry Red 1981)★★★, *Pale Hands I Loved So Well* (Uniton 1982)★★★, *Drumming The Beating Heart* (Cherry Red 1983)★★★, *Rust Red September* (Cherry Red 1983)★★★, *Back From The Rains* (Cherry Red 1986)★★★, *Kodak Ghosts Run Amok* (Cherry Red 1987)★★★, *Transience Blues* (Integrity/Antler 1989)★★★, *Fabulous Library* (Orchid 1993)★★★, *Bitter Apples* (A-Scale 1995)★★★.
●COMPILATIONS: *Orange Ice And Wax Crayons* (Cherry Red 1992)★★★.

F

FABULOUS THUNDERBIRDS

Formed in Texas, USA, in 1977, the Thunderbirds comprised Jimmie Vaughan (b. 20 March 1951, Dallas, Texas, USA; guitar), Kim Wilson (b. 6 January 1951, Detroit, Michigan, USA; vocals/harmonica), Keith Ferguson (b. 23 July 1946, Houston, Texas, USA; bass) and Mike Buck (b. 17 June 1952; drums). They emerged from the post-punk vacuum with a solid, unpretentious brand of R&B. Their debut album, *The Fabulous Thunderbirds* aka *Girls Go Wild,* offered a series of powerful original songs as well as sympathetic cover versions, including a vibrant reading of Slim Harpo's 'Scratch My Back'. This mixture has sustained the group throughout its career, although it took a move from Chrysalis Records to the Epic label to provide the success that their exciting music deserved. The Thunderbirds' line-up has undergone some changes, with former Roomful Of Blues drummer Fran Christiana (b. 1 February 1951, Westerly, Rhode Island, USA) replacing Mike Buck in 1980, and Preston Hubbard (b. 15 March 1953, Providence, Rhode Island, USA) joining after Ferguson departed. Throughout these changes, Wilson and Vaughan, the brother of the late blues guitarist Stevie Ray Vaughan, have remained at the helm until Vaughan jumped ship in 1995. Drummer Buck formed the Leroi Brothers in 1980, while Ferguson went on to forge a new career with the Tail Gators. Although both of these groups offer a similar bar band fare, the Thunderbirds remain, unquestionably, the masters. The Danny Korchmar-produced *Roll Of the Dice* was the first album with Kim Wilson leading the band in the wake of Jimmy Vaughan departing and the new new lead guitarist Kid Ramos having a hard job to fill.

●ALBUMS: *The Fabulous Thunderbirds* aka *Girls Go Wild* (Chrysalis 1979)★★★★, *What's The Word* (Chrysalis 1980)★★★, *Butt Rockin'* (Chrysalis 1981)★★★, *T-Bird Rhythm* (Chrysalis 1982)★★★, *Tuff Enuff* (Columbia 1986)★★★, *Hot Number* (Columbia 1987)★★★, *Powerful Stuff* (Columbia 1989)★★★, *Walk That Walk, Talk That Talk* (Columbia 1991)★★★, *Roll Of The Dice* (Private Music 1995)★★.

●COMPILATIONS: *Portfolio* (Chrysalis 1987) ★★★★.

FACTORY RECORDS

Cambridge graduate Tony Wilson (b. 1950, Salford, Lancashire, England) was a regional television reporter working in Manchester when he started the Factory label in 1978. He was also responsible for the *So It Goes* and *What's On* television programmes, which in themselves had acted as an invaluable platform for the emerging new wave scene. Previously he had edited his university's *Shilling Paper*. From there he joined television news company ITN as a trainee reporter, writing bulletins for current events programmes. It was on regional news programmes based in Manchester that he first encountered his future collaborators in the Factory operation; Alan Erasmus, Peter Saville, Rob Gretton (manager of Joy Division) and producer Martin Hannett. Erasmus and Wilson began their operation by jointly managing the fledgling Durutti Column, opening the Factory Club venue soon after. The label's first catalogue number, FAC 1, was allocated to the poster promoting its opening event. This typified Wilson's approach to the whole Factory operation, the most famous assignation of which was FAC 51, the Hacienda nightclub. However, it was their records, and the impersonal, nondescriptive packaging that accompanied them, that saw the label make its mark. Among the first releases were OMD's 'Electricity' (later a hit on Dindisc), and A Certain Ratio's 'All Night Party'. But it was Joy Division, harnessing the anxieties of Manchester youth to a discordant, sombre musical landscape, that established the label in terms of public perception and financial security. With Curtis gone, New Order continued as the backbone of the Factory operation throughout the 80s, establishing themselves in the mainstream with the biggest-selling 12-inch up until that time, 'Blue Monday'. Other mainstays included Section 25 and Stockholm Monsters, who steered a path too close to that of New Order, and the resourceful Durutti Column. It took the brief arrival of James to restore a pop sensibility (their subsequent departure would be a huge body blow), while New Order, somewhat astonishingly, took the England Football Squad to number 1 in the UK Charts with 'World In Motion'. The latter-day success of Electronic, the most successful of various New Order offshoots, and the Happy Mondays, a shambolic post-punk dance conglomerate, has dif-

fused accusations of Factory being too reliant on a single band. Reported cashflow problems in 1991, although vehemently denied by Wilson, were eased by a bumper crop of albums that followed, including new material by New Order and the Happy Mondays. Additionally the four-album compilation, *Palatine*, showcased the label's achievements, of which Wilson had never been reticent: 'In my opinion (popular art is as valid as any other art form . . . a lot of the tracks on *Palatine* are phenomenal art. We're 35 years into pop now, and great records do not lose their power. The deference with which we treat this stuff is deserved.'
●ALBUMS: *Palatine* (Factory 1991)★★★.
●FURTHER READING: *From Joy Division To New Order*, Mick Middles.

FAD GADGET

Effectively a moniker for UK-born vocalist and synthesizer player Frank Tovey, Fad Gadget enjoyed cult success with a series of bizarre releases on the Mute Records label during the early 80s. Tovey's background lay in his study of performance art at Leeds Art College. After moving to London, he transferred this interest into an unpredictable, often self-mutilating stage show. The first artist to sign with Daniel Miller's Mute label, Fad Gadget's 'Back To Nature' was released in 1979. 'Ricky's Hand' further combined Tovey's lyrical skill (observing the darker aspects of life) with an innovative use of electronics. Both these traits were evident on 'Fireside Favourites', a single and also the title of Fad Gadget's debut album. For the latter, Tovey was joined by Eric Radcliffe (guitar/bass), Nick Cash (drums), John Fryer (noises), Daniel Miller (drum machine/synthesizer) and Phil Wauquaire (bass synthesizer/guitar). After 'Make Room' in 1981 came *Incontinent*, which was more violent, unnerving and disturbing than before. Tovey had also recruited new staff, working with Peter Balmer (bass/rhythm guitar), David Simmons (piano/synthesizer), singers B.J. Frost and Anne Clift, John Fryer (percussion), plus drummer Robert Gotobed of Wire. In 1982 'Saturday Night Special' and 'King Of Flies' preceded a third album, *Under The Flag*. Dealing with the twin themes of the Falklands conflict and Tovey's new-born child, the album featured Alison Moyet on saxophone and backing vocals. The following year saw new extremes as Tovey returned from a European tour with his legs in plaster, having broken them during a show. On the recording front, the year was fairly quiet, apart from 'For Whom The Bell Tolls' and 'I Discover

Love'. 'Collapsing New People' continued an impressive run of singles at the start of 1984, and was followed by Fad Gadget's final album, *Gag*. By this time, the band had swelled and supported Siouxsie And The Banshees at London's Royal Albert Hall. Tovey opted to use his real identity from this point on. In November, he teamed up with American Boyd Rice for *Easy Listening For The Hard Of Hearing*. Since then, Tovey has issued four solo works, each of them as highly distinct and uncompromising as Fad Gadget's material.
●ALBUMS: *Fireside Favourites* (Mute 1980)★★★, *Incontinent* (Mute 1981)★★★, *Under The Flag* (Mute 1982)★★★, *Gag* (Mute 1984)★★★. As Frank Tovey: with Boyd Rice *Easy Listening For The Hard Of Hearing* (Mute 1984)★★★, *Snakes And Ladders* (Mute 1985)★★★, *Civilian* (Mute 1988)★★★, *Tyranny And The Hired Hand* (Mute 1989)★★★, Frank Tovey with the Pyros *Grand Union* (Mute 1991)★★★.
●COMPILATIONS: *The Fad Gadget Singles* (Mute 1986)★★★.

FAIRGROUND ATTRACTION

This jazz-tinged Anglo/Scottish pop band comprised Eddi Reader (b 28 August 1959, Glasgow, Scotland; vocals), Mark Nevin (guitar), Simon Edwards (guitaron, a Mexican acoustic guitar shaped bass) and Roy Dodds (drums). After art school Reader made her first musical forays as backing singer for the Gang Of Four. She moved to London in 1983 where session and live work with the Eurythmics and Alison Moyet kept her gainfully employed. She first hooked up with Nevin for the Compact Organisation sampler album *The Compact Composers*, singing on two of his songs. Nevin and Reader began their first collaborations in 1985, after Nevin had graduated by playing in one of the numerous line-ups of Jane Aire And The Belvederes. He was also closely involved with Sandie Shaw's mid-80s comeback. Around his songs they built Fairground Attraction, adding Edwards and Dodds, a jazz drummer of over 20 years' standing who had spent time with Working Week and Terence Trent D'Arby. They signed to RCA Records and quickly set about recording a debut album, as the gentle skiffle of 'Perfect' topped the UK singles charts in May 1988. They subsequently won both Best Single and Best Album categories at the Brit awards. A slight hiatus in their career followed when Reader became pregnant. They followed their natural inclinations by filming the video for their 1989 single 'Clare' in Nashville, and were supplemented on tour by

Graham Henderson (accordion) and Roger Beaujolais (vibes). The group's promise was then cut short when the band split, and Reader went on to acting (appearing in a BBC drama *Your Cheatin' Heart*, about the Scottish country and western scene) and a solo career releasing her debut, *Mir Mama*, in 1992.

●ALBUMS: *First Of A Million Kisses* (RCA 1988)★★★, *Ay Fond Kiss* (RCA 1990)★★★.

FALL

Formed in Manchester, England, in 1977, the Fall was the brainchild of the mercurial Mark E. Smith (b. Mark Edward Smith, 5 March 1957, Salford, Manchester, England). Over the years, Smith ruthlessly went through a battalion of musicians while taking the group through a personal odyssey of his wayward musical and lyrical excursions. His truculent press proclamations, by turns hysterically funny or sinister, also illuminated their career. Just as importantly, BBC disc jockey John Peel became their most consistent and fervent advocate, with the group recording a record number of sessions for his Radio 1 programme. The first Fall line-up, featuring Una Baines (electric piano), Martin Bramah (guitar), Karl Burns (drums) and Tony Friel (bass), made their debut on 'Bingo Master's Breakout', a good example of Smith's surreal vision, coloured by his relentlessly northern working class vigil. Initially signed to the small independent label Step Forward the group recorded three singles, including the savage 'Fiery Jack', plus *Live At The Witch Trials*. In 1980 the unit signed to Rough Trade Records and went on to release the critically acclaimed but still wilful singles 'How I Wrote Elastic Man' and 'Totally Wired'. Meanwhile, a whole series of line-up changes saw the arrival and subsequent departures of Marc Riley, Mike Leigh, Martin Bramah, Yvonne Pawlett and Craig Scanlon. The Fall's convoluted career continued to produce a series of discordant, yet frequently fascinating albums from the early menace of *Dragnet* to the chaotic *Hex Enduction Hour*. At every turn Smith worked hard to stand aloof from any prevailing trend, his suspicious mind refusing to make concessions to the mainstream. An apparent change in the group's image and philosophy occurred during 1983 with the arrival of future wife Brix (Laura Elise Smith). As well as appearing with the Fall as singer/guitarist, Brix later recorded with her own group, the pop-orientated Adult Net. She first appeared on the Fall's *Perverted By Language*, and her presence was felt more keenly when the group unexpectedly emerged as a potential chart act, suc-cessfully covering R. Dean Taylor's 'There's A Ghost In My House' and later the Kinks' 'Victoria'. Despite this, Mark E. Smith's deadpan voice and distinctive, accentuated vocals still dominated the band's sound. That and his backing band's ceaseless exploration of the basic rock riff. On later albums such as the almost flawless *This Nation's Saving Grace* and *The Frenz Experiment*, they lost none of their baffling wordplay or nagging, insistent rhythms, but the work seemed more focused and accessible. The line-up changes had slowed, although more changes were afoot with the arrival of drummer Simon Wolstenscroft and Marcia Schofield. Proof of Smith's growing stature among the popular art cognescenti was the staging of his papal play *Hey! Luciani* and the involvement of dancer Michael Clark in the production of *I Am Kurious Oranj*. Any suggestions that the Fall might be slowly heading for a degree of commercial acceptance underestimated Smith's restless spirit. By the turn of the decade Brix had left the singer and the group (he maintains he 'kicked her out'), and Schofield followed soon after. A succession of labels did little to impair the band's 90s output, with the Fall's leader unable to do wrong in the eyes of the band's hugely commited following, which now had outposts throughout America. Brix returned in time to guest on 1995's *Cerebral Caustic*, although Smith had persevered in her absence, recording four consistently strong albums. Unpredictable and unique, the Fall under Smith's guidance remain one of the most uncompromising groups.

●ALBUMS: *Live At The Witch Trials* (Step Forward 1979)★★★★, *Dragnet* (Step Forward 1979)★★★, *Totale's Turns (It's Now Or Never) (Live)* (Rough Trade 1980)★★, *Grotesque (After The Gramme)* (Rough Trade 1980)★★, *Slates* mini-album (Rough Trade 1981)★★★, *Hex Enduction Hour* (Kamera 1982)★★★, *Room To Live* (Kamera 1982)★★★, *Perverted By Language* (Rough Trade 1983)★★★, *The Wonderful And Frightening World Of ...* (Beggars Banquet 1984)★★★★, *This Nation's Saving Grace* (Beggars Banquet 1985)★★★★, *Bend Sinister* (Beggars Banquet 1986)★★★★, *The Frenz Experiment* (Beggars Banquet 1988)★★★★, *I Am Kurious Oranj* (Beggars Banquet 1988)★★★, *Seminal Live* (Beggars Banquet 1989)★★★, *Extricate* (Cog Sinister/Fontana 1990)★★★, *Shiftwork* (Cog Sinister/Fontana 1991)★★★★, *Code Selfish* (Cog Sinister/Fontana 1992)★★★, *The Infotainment Scan* (Cog Sinister/Permanent 1993)★★★, *BBC Live In Concert* rec. 1987 (Windsong 1993)★★★, *Middle Class Revolt*

(Permanent 1994)★★★, *Cerebral Caustic* (Permanent 1995)★★★★, *27 Points* (Permanent 1995)★★★, *Sinister Waltz* archive recordings (Receiver 1996)★★, *Fiend With A Violin* archive recordings (Receiver 1996)★★, *Oswald Defence Lawyer* archive recordings (Receiver 1996)★★, *The Light User Synrome* (Jet 1996)★★★, *In The City* (Artful 1997)★★★.
●COMPILATIONS: *77 - Early Years - 79* (Step Forward 1981)★★★, *Live At Acklam Hall, London, 1980* cassette only (Chaos 1982)★★★, *Hip Priests And Kamerads* (Situaton 2 1985)★★★, *In Palace Of Swords Reversed (80-83)* (Cog Sinister 1987)★★★★, *458489 A Sides* (Beggars Banquet 1990)★★★★, *458489-B Sides* (Beggars Banquet 1990)★★★, *The Collection* (Castle 1993)★★★,
●VIDEOS: *VHS8489* (Beggars Banquet 1991), *Perverted By Language Bis* (IKON 1992).
●FURTHER READING: *Paintwork: A Portrait Of The Fall*, Brian Edge.

FALTSKOG, AGNETHA

b. 5 April 1950, Jonkoping, Sweden. Faltskog started her musical career in 1965 at the age of 15, when she sang for a Swedish dance band. In 1968 she released her debut single - 'Jag Var Sa Kar' ('I Was So In Love'). It was a smash in Sweden and the rest of Scandinavia, and she successfully followed it up with further hits. In 1969 she appeared on a television show where she met Bjorn Ulvaeus, a former member of the Hootenanny Singers, and a songwriting partner of Hep Star Benny Anderson. Agnetha (who was normally known as Anna) and Ulvaeus married on 7 July 1971. By this time Ulvaeus and Anderson were recording together and Anna and Anderson's girlfriend Anni Fred Lyngstad were singing backing vocals for the boys. Eventually a permanent group was formed and in 1974 they became Abba, who first conquered Sweden then took the UK by storm when they won the Eurovision Song Contest. Faltskog's relationship with Ulvaeus ended with divorce in 1979 and by 1982 the group had worked together for the last time. Neither Lyngstad nor Faltskog wasted anytime in launching their solo careers. Faltskog opened with an album - *Wrap Your Arms Around Me* - produced by famed pop producer Mike Chapman and hit the singles chart three times in 1983 with 'The Heat Is On', 'Wrap Your Arms Around Me' and 'Can't Shake Loose'; the latter written by Russ Ballard. In 1988, Faltskog moved to WEA Records with ex-Chicago vocalist Peter Cetera as producer. However, the album and the single 'The Last Time' made little impact and latterly Faltskog seems to have retired from the music business.
●ALBUMS: *Wrap Your Arms Around Me* (Epic 1983)★★★, *Eyes Of A Woman* (Epic 1987)★★, *I Stand Alone* (Warners 1988)★★.
●COMPILATIONS: *My Love My Life* (Columbia 1996)★★.

FANIA ALL STARS

The house band of Fania Records, comprised of the label's bandleaders, top sidemen and vocalists; and whose history represents the rise and promulgation of salsa as a marketing tag for Latin music. Italian-American lawyer Jerry Masucci, who co-founded Fania in 1964 with Dominican Republic-born bandleader Johnny Pacheco, explained the genesis and early development of the band in 1973: 'In December 1967 . . . I was vacationing in Acapulco. I was out fishing and when I got back I received a phone call from New York from two promoters Jack Hooke and Ralph Mercado of Cheetah fame (a club on the southwest corner of 52nd Street and 8th Avenue, which Mercado co-managed in the 60s, promoting R&B acts like James Brown and Aretha Franklin). At that time they were holding concerts at the Red Garter (in Greenwich Village) Monday nights and were interested in getting the Fania All Stars together to do a jam session with invited guests Tito Puente of Tico Records and Eddie Palmieri and Ricardo Ray and Bobby Cruz of Alegre Records. It sounded like a good idea to me, so I flew back and got in touch with Johnny Pacheco. We put some material together and packed the place with 800 people. We also made the first two recordings of the Fania All Stars: *Live At The Red Garter* volumes 1 and 2 (1968). Although the albums were not too spectacular regarding sales.'
'At that concert . . . I got the idea to make a movie. In 1971 I was ready to begin production of the second Fania All Stars concert, which would be recorded and filmed live. My first idea was to hold it at the Fillmore East . . . for exposure to both rock and black audiences. However, we were unable to get the Fillmore . . . we contacted different promoters about various places . . . but they turned us down, saying that a concert by the Fania All Stars was a bad idea and that it wouldn't draw. I called Ralph Mercado who thought it might work, but would make no deals. I was to give him the act free, make a record, film the concert and he would promote and take the door. Since no one else wanted it I made the deal according to his terms. We held the concert on (26 August 1971) a

Thursday night (Ralph wouldn't give us Friday or Saturday). The Cheetah held 2000 people and no one thought we would sell-out. But the night of the concert 4000 people squeezed into the Cheetah and the lines outside stretched around the block. Volumes 1 and 2 of the Fania All Stars *Live At The Cheetah* which were recorded that night became the biggest selling Latin albums ever produced by one group from one concert.' The Cheetah concert was filmed and featured in the documentary *Our Latin Thing (Nuestra Cosa)* produced by Masucci and directed by Leon Gast, which premiered in New York on 19 July 1972.

After sell-out concerts in Puerto Rico, Chicago and Panama, the Fania All Stars made their first appearance at New York's 63,000 capacity Yankee Stadium on 24 August 1973, with Fania's leading lights Ray Barretto, Willie Colón, Larry Harlow, Johnny Pacheco, Roberto Roena, Bobby Valentín and others, jamming with Manu Dibango, Mongo Santamaría and Jorge Santana (younger brother of Carlos Santana and guitarist with Malo, the Latin rock group he founded in 1971). Before the event, Masucci ambitiously predicted: 'this concert will revolutionize the music business like the Beatles in the early 60s and Woodstock in 1969.' Material from their August 1973 Yankee Stadium concert and a concert at the Roberto Clemente Coliseum in San Juan, Puerto Rico, made up one side of *Latin-Soul-Rock* (1974). In 1974, the All Stars performances at the 80,000 seat Stadu du Hai in Kinshasa, Zaire, were also filmed by Gast and released as the movie *Live In Africa* (1974, issued on video in the UK under the title *Salsa Madness* in 1991). This Zairean appearance occurred alongside Stevie Wonder and others at a music festival held in conjunction with the Mohammed Ali/George Foreman heavyweight title fight.

The Fania All Stars' return to the Yankee Stadium in 1975 resulted in two volumes of *Live At Yankee Stadium* (1975), which highlighted Fania's and stalemate Vaya's top vocalists Celia Cruz, Héctor Lavoe, Cheo Feliciano, Ismael Miranda, Justo Betancourt, Ismael Quintana, Pete 'Conde' Rodríguez, Bobby Cruz and Santos Colón. Clips from their August 1973 and 1975 Yankee Stadium concerts, as well as from the Roberto Clemente Coliseum, were included in Masucci's movie production *Salsa* (1976), co-directed by Masucci and Gast. The film was picked up by Columbia Pictures for distribution, which was regarded as a major coup in marketing salsa for the general audience. Venezuelan salsa authority César Miguel Rondón commented on the marked stylistic contrast

between the movie *Our Latin Thing (Nuestra Cosa)* and its successor *Salsa* in his 1980 book *El Libro De La Salsa*: 'The producers' intention was evident: so that the salsa industry could really become a million-dollar business, it had to go beyond an exclusively Latin market; it had to penetrate the North American public majority market, and from here become an authentic fashion for the masses and succeed in coming to affect even the European audiences. In order to succeed in this, Fania's impresarios felt an obligation to radically change salsa's image. The first film, *Our Latin Thing (Nuestra Cosa),* was totally harmful in this sense; it spoke about the ghetto, about how salsa came up and developed in the haunts of the marginal barrios, in environments of poverty and misery in direct contrast to all the display and gaudiness of the North American enslaving pop culture. It therefore had to make a film that would radically say the contrary: that salsa was, in reality, a fundamental part of that pop culture, that it was susceptible to being enjoyed by the majority publics and that it, absolutely, had nothing to do with minority groups and their always repugnant misery. And this, without further ado, would be the fundamental characteristic under which the so-called salsa boom would be animated; a boom that, in effect, would increase the markets and sales, but equally weaken the true meaning of the *raison d'être* of salsa music.' This extract was translated by the sociologist Vernon W. Boggs for his article 'Salsa's Origins: Voices From Abroad', a survey of various texts on the source of the word salsa, published in *Latin Beat* magazine, December/January 1992. He found that various authors seemed to agree that: 'The popularity of the term (salsa), as a generic term for several musical modalities, was consciously universalized and successfully popularized by the Fania All Stars, Jerry Masucci, Leon Gast and the 'Fania Machine''.

In Masucci's pursuit of a wider market for salsa, he made an agreement with Columbia in the USA for a series of crossover-orientated albums by the Fania All Stars. The first project was a coupling of Steve Winwood with the All Stars reduced to a rhythm section (Pacheco, Valentín, Barretto, Roena, Nicky Marrero and Papo Lucca) for the instantly forgettable *Delicate & Jumpy* (1976), released on Columbia Records in the USA and Island Records in the UK. Around that time, Island issued the Fania collection *Salsa!* (1975), compiled and annotated by Richard Williams, and *Live* (1976) by the Fania All Stars; the latter moved *NME* reviewer Miles to comment: 'Lock up your Rock 'n'

Roll chauvinism and take a listen to what's coming up from the Third World.' In 1976 the Fania All Stars made their one and only UK appearance with a memorable sell-out concert at London's Lyceum Ballroom, with Steve Winwood guesting (his first time on a British stage since May 1974).

Prior to *Delicate & Jumpy*, the last 'regular' Fania All Stars album on Fania for a couple of years was the solid *Tribute to Tito Rodríguez* (1976), introducing Rubén Blades to the band. The Columbia series continued in lightweight vein with *Rhythm Machine* (1977), again with the slimmed down Fania All Stars and keyboardist Bob James (executive producer) and guitarist Eric Gale guesting; and *Spanish Fever* (1978), with guests Maynard Ferguson, Hubert Laws, David Sanborn, Gale and others. 1978 also saw the release of *Live*, a 'regular' Fania All Stars album on Fania with a full-blown version of the band recorded in concert at New York's Madison Square Garden in September 1978. The last in the Columbia series, *Crossover*, appeared the following year, as did *Habana Jam* (1979) on Fania, which came from a historic concert recorded on 3 March 1979 in Havana, Cuba. One track by the Fania All Stars was included on the various artists double album *Havana Jam* (1979) on Columbia, containing performance highlights from a trio of concerts at Havana's Karl Marx Theatre (2, 3 and 4 March 1979) with Billy Joel, Rita Coolidge, Kris Kristofferson, Stephen Stills and Weather Report, together with Cuba's Irakere and Orquesta Aragón.

From 1980, Fania went into a downturn (attributed to the flop of Masucci's major movie *The Last Fight*; agitation by artists for unpaid royalties; the distribution deals with Columbia and Atlantic Records not catapulting salsa into the mainstream US market as expected; and Masucci claiming he had tired of 'the same old thing' after 15 years); and the New York salsa scene, to which the label was inextricably linked, became eclipsed by the Dominican merengue craze in the first half of the decade and by the Puerto Rico-driven salsa romántica trend in the latter 80s and early 90s. Reflecting the company's decline, Fania All Stars releases slowed to a trickle as the 80s drew to a close. Their albums between 1980 and 1989 included the Latin jazz outings *California Jam* (1980) and the particularly feeble *Guasasa* (1989); the crossover effort *Social Change* (1981) with guests Steel Pulse and Gato Barbieri; *Bamboleo* (1988) with four salsa-fied versions of Gypsy Kings hits; along with the sturdier *Commitment* (1980), *Latin Connection* (1981), *Lo Que Pide La Gente* (1984) and *Viva La Charanga*

(1986). To mark the 20th anniversary of the band, *Live In Africa*, recorded in Zaire in 1974, and *Live In Japan 1976* were issued in 1986. Thirty years of Fania Records was commemorated in 1994 by a three city tour (San Juan, Miami and New York) by the reconvened All Stars.

●ALBUMS: *Live At The Red Garter, Vols. 1 & 2* (1968), *Live At The Cheetah, Vols. 1 & 2* (1971)★★★, *Our Latin Thing (Nuestra Cosa)* soundtrack recording (1972)★★, *Latin-Soul-Rock* (1974)★★★, *Live At Yankee Stadium, Vols. 1 & 2* reissued 1994 on one CD in UK by Charly Records (1975)★★★, *Salsa* soundtrack recording (1976)★★, *Tribute To Tito Rodríguez* (1976)★★★, *Delicate And Jumpy* (1976)★★★, *Rhythm Machine* (1977)★★★, *Spanish Fever* (1978)★★★, *Crossover* (1979)★★★, *Habana Jam* (1979)★★★, *Commitment* (1980)★★★, *California Jam* (1980)★★★, *Social Change* (1981)★★★, *Latin Connection* (1981)★★★, *The Last Fight* soundtrack recording (1982)★★, *Lo Que Pide La Gente* (1984)★★★, *Viva La Charanga* (1986)★★★, *Live In Africa* (1986)★★★, *Live In Japan 1976* (1986)★★★, *Bamboleo* (1988)★★★, *Guasasa* (1989)★★★.

●COMPILATIONS: *Greatest Hits* (1977)★★★, *Featuring Jan Hammer* (1986)★★★, *Perfect Blend* (1987)★★★.

FARLEY JACKMASTER FUNK

The resident DJ at Chicago's Playground between 1981 and 1987 (often combining live drum machine with his selection of Philly soul and R&B), Farley was also one of the earliest house producers, with 'Yellow House' being the first record on Dance Mania Records. He was also a key component of the Hot Mix 5, the DJ group that provided Chicago's WBMX radio station with its groundbreaking mix shows. As Chicago backroom boy Mike 'Hitman' Wilson once stated: 'To me Farley started house. Because while Frankie [Knuckles] had an audience of 600, Farley reached 150,000 listeners.' He had a hit in 1986 with a cover version of 'Love Can't Turn Around', with a vocal from Greater Tabernacle Baptist Choir's Daryl Pandy (although this actually hijacked a Steve 'Silk' Hurley song). Other notable releases include 'Aw Shucks', 'As Always' (with Ricky Dillard) and 'Free At Last' (with the Hip House Syndicate). When WBMX went off air his career ground to a halt, an intermission he occupied by exploring rap and R&B. He returned to Djing in England in the 1990s, where his reputation had not diminished, and started a new Chill-London label.

FAT BOYS

From the Bronx, New York, the Fat Boys were originally known as the Disco 3, before deciding to trade in the appellation in exchange for something more gimmicky. The bulk of their material dealt with just that, emphasizing their size, and did little to avert the widely held perception of them as a novelty act. The trio consisted of Darren 'The Human Beatbox/Buff Love' Robinson (b. 1968, New York, USA, d. 10 December 1995), Mark 'Prince Markie Dee' Morales, and Damon 'Kool Rockski' Wimbley. They were discovered by Charlie Stetler (later manager of MTV's Dr. Dre and Ed Lover), whose interest was aroused by Robinson's amazing talent for rhythmic improvisation, effectively using his face as an instrument. It was Stetler that suggested they take the name-change, after winning a nationwide talent contest at Radio City Music Hall in 1983. Legend has it that this was prompted during an early European tour when Stetler was presented with a bill of $350 for 'extra breakfasts'. Their initial run of records were produced by Kurtis Blow, and largely discussed the size of the group's appetites. All their LPs for Sutra offered a consistent diet (a phrase not otherwise within the Fat Boy lexicon) of rock, reggae and hip hop textures, with able if uninspiring raps. Their fortunes improved significantly once they signed up with Polydor Records, however. Crushin' is probably their best album, crammed with party anecdotes that stand up to repeated listening better than most of their material. It yielded a major hit with the Beach Boys on 'Wipe Out' in 1987. One year and one album later they scored with another collaboration, this time with Chubby Checker on 'The Twist (Yo' Twist)'. It peaked at number 2 in the UK chart, the highest position at the time for a rap record. In truth the Fat Boys had become more pop than hip hop, though the process of revamping rock 'n' roll chestnuts had begun as far back as 1984 with 'Jailhouse Rock'. Also contained on Coming Back Hard Again was a strange version of 'Louie Louie' and 'Are You Ready For Freddy', used as the theme song for one of the Nightmare On Elm Street films. They also starred in another movie, Disorderlies, after appearing with Checker as part of Nelson Mandela's 70th Birthday Party at Wembley Stadium in June 1988 (they had previously been the only rap participants at Live Aid). The decade closed with the release of On And On. It proved a hugely disappointing set, overshadowed by its 'concept' of being a 'rappera', and offering a lukewarm adaptation of gangsta concerns. News broke in the 90s of a $6 million law suit filed against their former record company, while Robinson was put on trial in Pennsylvania for 'sexual abuse of a minor'. Prince Markie Dee went on to a solo career, recording an album as Prince Markie Dee And The Soul Convention. He also produced and wrote for Mary J. Blige, Christopher Williams, Father, El DeBarge, Trey Lorenz and others. Their career never recovered from the bad press after Robinson was found guilty and the Fat Boys' true legacy remains firmly in the era of rap party records, Swatch television ads and cameo appearances on television's Miami Vice. Robinson died in 1995 after a cardiac arrest following a bout of respiratory flu.
●ALBUMS: Fat Boys (Sutra 1984)★★★, The Fat Boys Are Back! (Sutra 1985)★★★, Big & Beautiful (Sutra 1986)★★★, Cruisin' (Tin Pan Apple/Polydor 1987)★★★★, Coming Back Hard Again (Tin Pan Apple/Polydor 1988)★★★, On And On (Tin Pan Apple/Mercury 1989)★★. Solo: Prince Markie Dee Free (Columbia 1992)★★.
●COMPILATIONS: The Best Part Of The Fat Boys (Sutra 1987)★★★, Krush On You (Blatant 1988)★★.

FAT LARRY'S BAND

'Fat' Larry James (b. 2 August 1949, Philadelphia, Pennsylvania, USA, d. 5 December 1987; drums) formed this funk/disco outfit in Philadelphia following his spell as a back-up musician for the Delfonics and Blue Magic. The group comprised Art Capehart (trumpet/flute), Jimmy Lee (trombone/saxophone), Doug Jones (saxophone), Erskine Williams (keyboards), Ted Cohen (guitar), Larry LaBes (bass), Darryl Grant (percussion). James found success easier in the UK than in his homeland, having a UK Top 40 hit with 'Center City' in 1977, and in 1979 achieved a Top 50 with 'Boogie Town' under the title of FLB. That same year, one of James' other projects, the studio group Slick, had two UK hit singles with 'Space Bass', and 'Sexy Cream'. These two releases established them with the disco market. However, it was not until 1982 that the group enjoyed a major national hit, with a recording of the Commodores' song 'Zoom' taking them to number 2 in the UK charts, although it only managed to scrape into the US soul chart at 89. It proved however to be the band's last success of any note and hope of a regeneration was cut short on their founder's death in 1987.
●ALBUMS: Feel It (Atlantic 1977)★★, Off The Wall (1978)★★, Stand Up (Fantasy 1980)★★, Breakin' Out (Virgin 1982)★★, Straight From The Heart (1983)★★, Nice (1986)★★.

●COMPILATIONS: *Bright City Lights* (Fantasy 1980)★★, *Close Encounters Of A Funky Kind* (Southbound/Ace 1995)★★★.

FELT

Cultivated, experimental English pop group formed in 1980 whose guru is the enigmatic Lawrence Hayward (b. Birmingham, West Midlands, England; vocals/guitar). Early collaborators included Maurice Deebank (guitar) and Nick Gilbert (bass), who practised together in a small village called Water Orton just outside Birmingham. By the time of their first album, released on Cherry Red Records, drummer Tony Race was replaced by Gary Ainge, and Gilbert departed to be replaced on bass by Mick Lloyd. Martin Duffy joined on organ for *Ignite The Seven Cannons*. Cult status had already arrived with the archtypal Felt cut, 'Penelope Tree'. The critical respect they were afforded continued, though they enjoyed little in the way of commercial recognition. The nearest they came was the 1985 single 'Primitive Painters', where they were joined by Elizabeth Fraser of the Cocteau Twins in a stirring, pristine pop song produced by fellow Cocteau Robin Guthrie. They signed to Creation Records in 1985. However, as Felt's contract with Cherry Red expired, so did the tenure of Lawrence's fellow guitarist and co-writer, Deebank. The latter, classically trained, had been an important component of the Felt sound, and was chiefly responsible for the delicate but intoxicating drama of early releases. Their stay at Creation saw high points in *Forever Breathes The Lonely Word* (1986) and *Poem Of The River* (1987). On the latter they were joined by Marco Thomas, Tony Willé and Neil Scott to add to the melodic guitar broadside. Felt bowed out with *Me And A Monkey On The Moon*, after moving to Él Records, by which time guitar duties had switched to John Mohan. By the end of the 80s the band were no more, having achieved their stated task of surviving 10 years, 10 singles, and 10 albums (*Bubblegum Perfume* is an archive release of their Creation material, *The Felt Box Set* compiles their Cherry Red recordings). Lawrence chose to concentrate on his new project; 70s revivalists Denim.
●ALBUMS: *Crumbling The Antiseptic Beauty* mini-album (Cherry Red 1982)★★★, *The Splendour Of Fear* mini-album (Cherry Red 1983)★★★, *The Strange Idols Pattern And Other Short Stories* (Cherry Red 1984)★★★, *Ignite The Sevon Cannons* (Cherry Red 1985)★★★, *Let The Snakes Crinkle Their Heads To Death* (Creation 1986)★★★, *Forever Breathes The Lonely Word* (Creation 1986)★★★★, *Poem Of The River* (Creation 1987)★★★, *The Pictorial Jackson Review* (Creation 1988)★★★, *Train Above The City* (Creation 1988)★★★, *Me And A Monkey On The Moon* (Él 1989)★★.
●COMPILATIONS: *Gold Mine Trash* (Cherry Red 1987)★★★, *Bubblegum Perfume* (Creation 1990)★★★★, *Absolute Classic Masterpieces Vol.2* (Creation 1993)★★★, *The Felt Box Set* 4-CD (Cherry Red 1993)★★★★.

FIELDS OF THE NEPHILIM

This UK rock group were formed in Stevenage, Hertfordshire, in 1983. The line-up comprised Carl McCoy (vocals), Tony Pettitt (bass), Peter Yates (guitar) and the Wright brothers, Nod (b. Alexander; drums) and Paul (guitar). Their image, that of neo-western desperados, was borrowed from films such as *Once Upon A Time In America* and *The Long Ryders*. They also had the bizarre habit of smothering their predominantly black clothes in flour and/or talcum powder for some of the most hysterically inept videos ever recorded. Their version of Goth-rock, tempered with transatlantic overtones, found favour with those already immersed in the sounds of the Sisters Of Mercy and the Mission. Signed to the Situation Two label, Fields Of The Nephilim scored two major UK Independent hit singles with 'Preacher Man' and 'Blue Water', while their first album, *Dawn Razor*, made a modest showing on the UK album chart. The second set, *The Nephilim*, reached number 14, announcing the group's arrival as one of the principal rock acts of the day. Their devoted following also ensured a showing on the national singles chart, giving them minor hits with 'Moonchild' (1988 - also an independent chart number 1), 'Psychonaut' (1989) and 'Summerland (Dreamed)' (1990). In October 1991 McCoy left the group taking the 'Fields Of The Nephilim' name with him. The remaining members have since vowed to carry on. With the recruitment a new vocalist, Alan Delaney, they began gigging under the name Rubicon in the summer of 1992, leaving McCoy yet to unveil his version of the Nephilim. Nod Wright departed to form Swallowed Soul.
●ALBUMS: *Dawn Razor* (Situation 2 1987)★★, *The Nephilim* (Situation 2 1988)★★★, *Elyzium* (Beggars Banquet 1990)★★, *Earth Inferno* (Beggars Banquet 1991)★★, *BBC Radio 1 In Concert* (Windsong 1992)★★, *Revelations* (Beggars Banquet 1993)★★.
●VIDEOS: *Forever Remain* (1988), *Morphic Fields* (1989), *Earth Inferno* (1991), *Revelations* (1993).

FINE YOUNG CANNIBALS

This sophisticated English pop trio from the Midlands appeared after the demise of the Beat in 1983. Former members Andy Cox (b. 25 January 1960, Birmingham, England; guitar) and David Steele (b. 8 September 1960, Isle of Wight, England; bass/keyboards) invited Roland Gift (b. 28 April 1961, Birmingham, England; vocals, ex-Acrylic Victims and actor for the Hull Community Theatre) to relinquish his tenure in a London blues group to join them. Taking their name from the Robert Wagner movie of similar name (relinquishing the 'All The' prefix), the group were quickly picked up by London Records after a video screening on the UK music television show *The Tube*. 'Johnny Come Home' was soon released on single, with the band joined on percussion by Martin Parry and on trumpet by Graeme Hamilton. Dominated by Gift's sparse and yearning vocal, it reached the UK Top 10 and defined the band's sound for years to come. The follow-up 'Blue' set out an early political agenda for the band, attacking Conservative Government policy and its effects. After the band's debut album rose to UK number 11, the first of a series of distinctive cover versions emerged with 'Suspicious Minds'. Backing vocals were handled by Jimmy Somerville. It was followed by a surprise, and radical, rendition of 'Ever Fallen In Love', which the Buzzcocks' Steve Diggle claimed he preferred to his band's original. Meanwhile, Gift's parallel acting career got underway with the parochial *Sammy And Rosie Get Laid*, after all three members of the band had appeared in the previous year's *Tin Men*. While Gift's commitments continued Cox and Steele became involved in the release of an opportunistic house cut, 'I'm Tired Of Being Pushed Around', under the title Two Men, A Drum Machine And A Trumpet. On the back of regular club airings it became a surprise Top 20 hit in February 1988. More importantly, it attracted the interest of several dance acts who would seek out the duo for remixes, including Wee Papa Girl Rappers and Pop Will Eat Itself. Before the unveiling of Gift's latest film, *Scandal*, the band enjoyed their biggest hit to date with the rock/dance fusion of 'She Drives Me Crazy'. The second album duly followed, featuring cultivated soul ballads to complement further material of a politically direct nature. It would top the charts on both sides of the Atlantic. Of the five singles taken from the album 'Good Thing' was the most successful, claiming a second US number 1. In 1990 they won both Best British Group and Best Album categories at the BRIT Awards, but felt compelled to return them because: '. . . it is wrong and inappropriate for us to be associated with what amounts to a photo opportunity for Margaret Thatcher and the Conservative Party'. It led to a predictable backlash in the right wing tabloid press. In 1990 Gift's appeared in Hull Truck's *Romeo And Juliet* stage performance, and left Cox and Steele to work on a remixed version of *The Raw And The Cooked*. Still with the ability to bounce back after long pauses, the band's 1996 compilation reminded us of their sparse but sound string of hits

● ALBUMS: *Fine Young Cannibals* (London 1985)★★★, *The Raw And The Cooked* (London 1989)★★★★, *The Raw And The Remix* (London 1990)★★★.

● COMPILATIONS: *The Finest* (London 1996)★★★★.

● VIDEOS: *The Finest* (London 1996).

● FURTHER READING: *The Sweet And The Sour: The Fine Young Cannibals' Story*, Brian Edge.

FIREHOSE

This propulsive US hardcore trio (usually titled fIREHOSE) was formed by two ex-members of the Minutemen, Mike Watt (vocals/bass) and George Hurley (drums), following the death of the latter group's founding guitarist, David Boon, in 1985. Ed Crawford, aka eD fROMOHIO, completed the new venture's line-up, which made its debut in 1987 with the impressive *Ragin', Full-On*. Although undeniably powerful, the material Firehose offered was less explicit than that of its predecessor, and showed a greater emphasis on melody rather than bluster. Successive releases, *If'n* and *fROMOHIO*, revealed a group which, although bedevilled by inconsistency, was nonetheless capable of inventive, exciting music. At their best these songs merged knowing sarcasm (see 'For The Singer Of REM') with an unreconstructed approach to music making (as on drum solo, 'Let The Drummer Have Some'). This variety argued against commercial fortune, but the band were still picked up by a major, Columbia Records, in 1991, who released the slightly more disciplined *Flyin' The Flannel* that year. Later Mike Watt would also unveil a solo album for the same record company, completed with an all-star cast of US hardcore and punk legends.

● ALBUMS: *Ragin', Full-On* (SST 1987)★★★, *If'n* (SST 1988)★★, *fROMOHIO* (SST 1989)★★★, *Flyin' The Flannel* (Columbia 1991)★★★, *Mr Machinery Operator* (Columbia 1993)★★.

FIRM

It seemed to be a marriage made in heaven when ex-Led Zeppelin guitarist Jimmy Page and former Free/Bad Company vocalist Paul Rodgers began working together as the Firm in 1984. Enlisting ex-Uriah Heep/Manfred Mann drummer Chris Slade (the Damned's Rat Scabies also auditioned) and virtual unknown Tony Franklin on bass, an acquaintance of Page's from work with Roy Harper, the partnership never quite jelled in a manner to match either protagonist's earlier achievements. However, the band was not without musical merit, with Slade's precise backbeat providing a solid base for Page and the stylish Franklin to create a distinctive sound on *The Firm*, with Rodgers in fine voice on varied material from the lengthy and Zeppelinesque 'Midnight Moonlight' to the more commercial strains of 'Radioactive', which was a minor hit, plus a cover of 'You've Lost That Loving Feeling'. Live dates proved successful, with Page producing his customary show-stopping solo spot replete with laser effects, although neither Page nor Rodgers were willing to reprise their previous work. *Mean Business* continued in the warm, understated and bluesy style of the debut, but failed to raise the band to new heights, and the Firm split after the subsequent world tour. Page and Rodgers returned to their respective solo careers, while Slade joined AC/DC and Franklin teamed up with John Sykes in Blue Murder.
●ALBUMS: *The Firm* (Atlantic 1985)★★★, *Mean Business* (Atlantic 1986)★★★.

FISHER, MORGAN

Beginning his apprenticeship with the Love Affair and then Mott The Hoople as a pianist in 1973, initially only for live appearances, Fisher went on to form the abbreviated Mott in May 1975 with Dale Griffin and Overend Watts. They were completed by new members Ray Major and Nigel Benjamin, becoming the British Lions in May 1977 with John Fidler (ex-Medicine Head) replacing Benjamin. After two albums they split in the late 70s, and Fisher produced two albums for Cherry Red Records as Hybrid Kids (*A Collection Of Classic Mutants* and *Claws*). The first of these was supposedly filled by unknown new wave acts doing cover versions, but was actually Fisher and a few cronies. The tracks included Jah Wurzel's (Jah Wobble meets the Wurzels) 'Wuthering Heights', British Standard Unit's 'Do Ya Think I'm Sexy', the Burton's 'MacArthur Park', and a new version of 'All The Young Dudes'. Another 'concept' album,

Miniatures, came out on Fisher's own Pipe label, and featured various artists doing songs less than a minute long. Included among the 51 tracks are Dave Vanian (Damned), John Otway, Andy Partridge (XTC), Robert Wyatt, George Melly, the Residents and David Cunningham. The album was later reissued on micro-cassette, presumably suitable solely for playing on dictaphones. Fisher continued to record for Cherry Red throughout the 80s, later relocating to Japan where he changed his name to Veetdharm.
●ALBUMS: *A Collection Of Classic Mutants* (Cherry Red 1980)★★★ *Miniatures* (Pipe 1980)★★★, *Claws* (Cherry Red 1982)★★★, *Seasons* (Cherry Red 1983)★★★, *Look At Life* (Cherry Red 1984)★★★, *Ivories* (Cherry Red 1987)★★★.

FIVE STAR

This commercial pop act was formed by the five siblings of the Pearson family, all of whom shared vocal duties and were born in Romford, Essex, England; Deniece (b. 13 June 1968), Doris (b. 8 June 1966), Lorraine (b. 10 August 1967), Stedman (b. 29 June 1964) and Delroy (b. 11 April 1970). Their father, Buster, had been a professional guitarist with a variety of groups including Wilson Pickett, Desmond Dekker and Jimmy Cliff. After his retirement from the live circuit he formed, first, reggae label K&B, then the more commercially disposed Tent Records. His daughters persuaded him to let them record a version of his recently written composition 'Problematic'. It showed promise and he decided to throw his weight behind their career as manager, while the brothers elected to fill out the group to a five-piece. Although 'Problematic' failed to chart, Buster secured a licensing deal for Tent with RCA Records, but follow-ups 'Hide And Seek' and 'Crazy' also missed out. However, when Nick Martinelli took over production duties 1985's 'All Fall Down' reached the charts. Heavy promotion, and the group's choreographed dance routines, ensured that the follow-up 'Let Me Be The One' followed it into the Top 20. By the time the band's debut album was released they had worked through six different producers and countless studios. Despite the relative disappointment of chart placings for subsequent singles 'Love Take Over' and 'R.S.V.P.', the band departed for a major US promotional tour. The Walt Disney organization immediately stepped in to offer the band their own show, but Buster declined. Back in the UK 'System Addict', the seventh single milked from *Luxury Of Life*, became the first to break the Top 10. Both 'Can't

Wait Another Minute' and 'Find The Time' repeated the feat, before the band acquired the sponsorship of Crunchie Chocolate Bars for their UK tour. Their next outings would attract the sponsorship of Ultrabite toothpaste, much to the derision of critics who were less than enamoured by their 'squeaky clean' image. Meanwhile *Silk And Steel*, the second album, climbed slowly to the top of the UK charts. It would eventually receive triple platinum status, unleashing another steady stream of singles. The most successful of these, 'Rain And Shine', achieved their best placing in the singles chart, at number 2. Continued success allowed the family to move from Romford, Essex, to a mansion in Sunningdale, Berkshire, where they installed a massive studio complex. Ever a favourite home for media attacks, Buster was variously accused of keeping his offspring in a 'palatial prison', and of spending wanton sums of money on trivia. However, as their records proved increasingly unsuccessful, the family were the subject of several media stories concerning their financial instability. These hit a peak when the band were forced to move from their home in 1990. Attempts to resurrect their career in America on Epic have so far failed, with their fortunes hitting an all-time low in October 1991 when Stedman Pearson was fined for public indecency.
●ALBUMS: *Luxury Of Life* (Tent 1985)★★, *Silk And Steel* (Tent 1986)★★★, *Between The Lines* (Tent 1987)★★, *Rock The World* (Tent 1988)★★, *Five Star* (Tent 1990)★★.
●COMPILATIONS: *Greatest Hits* (Tent 1989)★★★.

Fixx

The members of this UK band include Cy Curnin (13 December 1957; vocals/guitar), Adam Woods (b. 8 April 1953; drums), Rupert Greenall (keyboards), Jamie West-Oram (guitar) and Charlie Barret (bass). The group formed at the turn of the 80s when college friends Curnin and Woods made the decision to pursue music as a full-time vocation. After advertising in the music press for new members, the band released a 'one off' single for Ariola Records, 'Hazards In The Home', credited as 'The Portraits'. A year later with a more complete line-up, they changed their name to the Fixx, and recorded the quirky 'Lost Planes' which led to the band's signing with MCA. Their debut album *Shuttered Room* remained on the US album chart for over a year, but UK reaction was less than enthusiastic and the album and subsequent releases have all suffered the same fate. *Reach The Beach* was released in 1983 and earned platinum status in the

USA, and marked the recording debut of Dan K. Brown, replacing Charlie Barret. Further success followed with a string of single and album hits in the America and Europe. In 1984 their contribution to the soundtrack of the film *Streets Of Fire* was arguably the most interesting. They have proved themselves to be a group of musicians who have been able to maintain credibility and longevity through a willingness to change with the times without compromising their creative vision.
●ALBUMS: *Shuttered Room* (MCA 1982)★★★, *Reach The Beach* (MCA 1983)★★★, *Phantoms* (MCA 1984)★★★, *Walkabout* (MCA 1986)★★★, *React* (MCA 1987)★★, *Calm Animals* (MCA 1988)★★, *Ink* (MCA 1991)★★.
●COMPILATIONS: *Greatest Hits: One Thing Leads To Another* (MCA 1989)★★★.

Flaming Lips

Formed in Oklahoma City, Oklahoma, USA, the Flaming Lips have won a deserved reputation in the late 80s and early 90s for their discordant, psychedelia-tinged garage rock. They are led by lyricist, vocalist and guitarist Wayne Coyne (b. Wayne Ruby Coyne, 17 March 1965, Pittsburgh, Pennsylvania, USA), who started playing music during his high school days. The Flaming Lips have recorded a fine body of off-kilter and unpredictable work. Coyne was joined in the group by his brother, Mark Coyne, who is best remembered for his vocals on the debut album's 'My Own Planet'. Taking up the microphone following his brother's departure, Wayne Coyne now fronts a line-up which is completed by Steven Drozd (b. Steven Gregory Drozd, 6 December 1969, Houston, Texas, USA; drums/vocals, replacing Richard English and Nathan Roberts), Ron Jones (b. Ronald Lee Jones, 26 November 1970, Angeles, Philippines; guitars/vocals) and Michael Ivins (b. Michael Lee Ivins, 17 March 1965, Omaha, Nebraska, USA; bass/vocals). John 'Dingus' Donahue, of Mercury Rev fame, was also a member during the sessions for *In A Priest Driven Ambulance*. In 1993 they played at the Reading Festival and toured with Porno For Pyros, Butthole Surfers and Stone Temple Pilots. They returned to Reading in 1994 to support the release of 'She Don't Use Jelly' which finally took off on MTV over the following year. This, combined with a storming appearance on the second stage at Lollapalooza, at last helped to build a substantial popular as well as critical following. A two-year break preceded the release of *Clouds Taste Metallic*, their seventh album, a typically confusing but arresting exercise in wide-eyed, skewed pop rock, akin to a restrained Pavement. Song titles such as 'Guy Who Got A Headache And Accidentally Saved The World' and 'Psychiatric Explorations Of The Fetus With Needles' continued the penchant for adolescent shock value.

●ALBUMS: *Hear It Is* (Pink Dust 1986)★★★, *Oh My Gawd!!! . . .The Flaming Lips* (Restless 1987)★★★, *Telepathic Surgery* (Restless 1989)★★, *In A Priest Driven Ambulance* (Restless 1990)★★★, *Hit To Death In The Future Head* (Warners 1992)★★★, *Transmissions From The Satellite Heart* (Warners 1993)★★★, *Providing Needles For Your Balloons* (Warners 1995)★★, *Clouds Taste Metallic* (Warners 1995)★★★.

FLESH FOR LULU

This UK rock band were the creation of singer/guitarist Nick Marsh and drummer James Mitchell and took their name from an American cult movie. They were joined by Rocco Barker (ex-Wasted Youth) on guitar and Glen Bishop, replaced by Kevin Mills (ex-Specimen) on bass after the single 'Restless'. Derek Greening (keyboards/guitar) became the fifth member shortly afterwards. Previously, their debut single had been 'Roman Candle' prefacing a first album that they would 'rather forget about'. *Blue Sisters Swing*, on the tiny Hybrid label, followed as a stop gap. The sleeve illustration of two nuns kissing resulted in bans in the USA and Europe. The release of *Big Fun City* was the first to do the band justice, even though it was hampered by artwork problems at Polydor Records, and featured everything from country ballads to basic rock 'n' roll.

The group's succession of labels grew longer as they moved on to Beggars Banquet Records in 1986. *Long Live The New Flesh* followed a year later, recorded at Abbey Road Studios and produced by Mike Hedges. Their approach to the sophistication of their new surroundings was typical: 'Forget the cerebral approach - just turn up them guitars!' Their most pop orientated album to date, *Plastic Fantastic*, was recorded in Australia by Mark Opitz, several titles from which were used for film soundtracks (*Uncle Buck* and *Flashback*). By this time, original members Marsh, Barking and Greening had been joined by Hans Perrson (drums) and Mike Steed (bass). Despite stronger songwriting than had been evident on previous recordings, the album failed and Beggars did not renew their option.

●ALBUMS: *Flesh For Lulu* (Polydor 1984)★★, *Blue Sisters Swing* mini-album (Hybrid 1985)★★, *Big*

Fun City (Caroline 1985)★★★, *Long Live The New Flesh* (Beggars Banquet 1987)★★★, *Plastic Fantastic* (Beggars Banquet 1990)★★★.

FLESHEATERS

Innovative rock group built around cult hero Chris 'D' Desjardins (vocals), who had been active on the Los Angeles, California scene from the 70s, making films and acting as well as co-ordinating the Flesheaters. Their first established line-up added Robyn Jameson (bass), Don Kirk (guitar), and Chris Wahl (drums), but the nature of the band can be surmised by the frequency of its personnel shifts. Those passing through the ranks include; Bill Bateman (drums), Steve Berlin (saxophone), Gene Taylor (keyboards), John Bazz (bass), Dave Alvin (guitar), all ex-Blasters; Pat Garrett (guitar/bass), Joe Ramirez (bass), Joe Nanini (drums), all ex-Black Randy; John Doe (bass), Don Bonebrake (drums), Excene Doe (vocals), all ex-X. Stan Ridgway (Wall Of Voodoo; guitar) and Tito Larriva (Plugz; guitar) were also present in an early incarnation. These represent only a fraction of former members in a band which effectively operated in a 'pick up and play' mode. This did not diminish their appeal, however: 'The one thing that we do that mystifies our audience is we don't play in one category. The music that we play is real loud. Its real metallic. It could be described as heavy metal, or what was in 1977 punk.' Chris D split the band at the end of the 80s after the years of cut and paste line-ups finally took their toll. However, they were back on the circuit in the 90s. *Dragstrip Riot*, with which Desjardins reinstated the band after years of inactivity, was a sprawling double album set that saw the band crashing out riotous swamp rock of a virulent, Cramps-type character. The intervening years had seen him operate with his own band, Chris D And The Divine Horsemen, while Jameson played with Alex Gibson and Passionel.

●ALBUMS: *No Questions Asked* (Upsetter 1979)★★★, *A Minute To Pray, A Second To Die* (Ruby 1981)★★★, *Forever Came Today* (Ruby 1982)★★★, *A Hard Road To Follow* (Upsetter 1983)★★★, *Dragstrip Riot* (SST 1991)★★, *Sex Diary Of Mr Vampire* (SST 1991)★★★.

●COMPILATIONS: *Greatest Hits - Destroyed By Fire* (SST 1986)★★★, *Prehistoric Fits* (SST 1990)★★★.

FLYING LIZARDS

The brainchild of pianist David Cunningham, the Flying Lizards were a novelty group with a difference, taking and subverting classic pop songs in a

unique and striking fashion. In the summer of 1979, they reached the UK Top 5 with an spoken, arrogant upper-middle class, English accent-version of the Berry Gordy classic, 'Money'. The changing line-up, which included Patti Paladin, Peter Gordan and Steve Beresford on *Fourth Wall*, enabled Cunningham to pursue his love of electronic pop. *The Times* newspaper writer and ambient experimentalist David Toop was part of the line-up at one point. After an extended retirement, the Lizards re-emerged in 1984 with *Top Ten*, which included eccentric versions of the work of Jimi Hendrix, Leonard Cohen and Little Richard.
●ALBUMS: *The Flying Lizards* (Virgin 1979)★★★, *Fourth Wall* (Virgin 1981)★★★, *Top Ten* (Statik 1984)★★★. Solo: David Cunningham *Grey Scale* (1980)★★★.

FLYING PICKETS

This a cappella UK sextet were formed in 1980 with a line-up comprising Rick Lloyd, Gareth Williams, David Brett, Ken Gregson and Red Stripe (b. 4 March 1946, Manchester, England). Originally they came together informally and were warmly received at the 1982 Edinburgh Festival. In keeping with their unusual group title, they played at benefit concerts for the National Union of Mineworkers and performed in pubs and clubs. Their novel cover of Yazoo's hit 'Only You' proved spectacularly successful, reaching the coveted UK Christmas number 1 spot in 1983. Although their appeal seemed ephemeral, they enjoyed a second Top 10 hit with Van McCoy's 'When You're Young And In Love' and their albums included spirited reworkings of familiar vocal classics from different eras, ranging from the Teddy Bears' 'To Know Him Is To Love Him' to Bob Dylan's 'Masters Of War' and even Talking Heads' 'Psycho Killer'. Their last appearance on the UK charts was a lowly 71 with a rendition of the Eurythmics' 'Who's That Girl'.
●ALBUMS: *Live At The Albany Empire* (AVM 1982)★★, *Lost Boys* (Ten 1984)★★, *Live* (Ten 1985)★★.

FM

FM Radio was pioneered in San Francisco by DJ Tom Donahue at stations KMPX and, later, KSAN. They were a conscious attempt to throw out a Top 40-based playlist and instead offer album-orientated acts. By the early 70s this formula had become common and many such concerns offered as restrictive a programme as their AM counterparts. Released in 1978, *FM* tells the fictional tale of a Los Angeles station, staffed by mavericks, who

attempt to remain on air by hijacking a Linda Ronstadt concert, scheduled for their main rival. The film completely fails to question why the founding ethos of FM radio had been subverted, preferring the tiresome 'good versus bad' scenario which has plagued rock films from their inception. Jimmy Buffett, REO Speedwagon and Tom Petty And The Heartbreakers join Ronstadt in contributing musical interludes, while the soundtrack also features material by Steely Dan (who provided the title song), Fleetwood Mac, Boz Scaggs, Joe Walsh, Steve Miller, the Eagles, Foreigner and Foghat. Despite its plot, *FM* enshrines the complacency of AOR music and gives good reason for the rise of punk.

FOETUS

You've Got Foetus On Your Breath, Scraping Foetus Off The Wheel, Foetus Uber Alles, Foetus Inc - all these titles are actually the pseudonym of one person: Australian emigré, Jim Thirlwell, alias Jim Foetus and Clint Ruin. After founding his own record company, Self Immolation in 1980, he set about 'recording works of aggression, insight and inspiration'. Backed with evocatively descriptive musical slogans such as 'positive negativism' and 'bleed now pay later', Foetus released a series of albums, several of which appeared through Stevo's Some Bizzare Records. With stark one-word titles such as *Deaf*, *Ache*, *Hole* and *Nail*, Thirlwell presented a harrowing aural netherworld of death, lust, disease and spiritual decay. In November 1983, Foetus undertook a rare tour, performing with Marc Almond, Nick Cave and Lydia Lunch in the short-lived Immaculate Consumptive. Apart from these soul-mates, Foetus has also played live with the Swans' Rolli Mossiman in Wiseblood, Lydia Lunch in Stinkfist, and appeared on albums by several artists including The The, Einsturzende Neubauten, Nurse With Wound and Anne Hogan. In 1995 Thirlwell announced plans to release his first studio album in seven years. The result was *Gash*, an album that led to the reappraisal of his work as one of the key figures in the development of the 'Industrial' music movement
●ALBUMS: *Deaf* (Self Immolation 1981)★★★, *Ache* (Self Immolation 1982)★★★, *Hole* (Self Immolation 1984)★★★, *Nail* (Self Immolation 1985)★★★, *Thaw* (Self Immolation 1988)★★★, *Male* (Big Cat 1993)★★★, *Gash* (Big Cat 1995)★★★, *Boil* (Big Cat 1996)★★★.
●COMPILATIONS: *Sink* (Self Immolation 1989)★★★.
●VIDEOS: *!Male!* (Visionary 1994).

FORBERT, STEVE

b. 1955, Meridien, Mississippi, USA. Forbert played guitar and harmonica in local rock bands before moving to New York in 1976. There he busked at Grand Central Station before making his first recordings in 1977 for Nemperor and was briefly heralded as 'the new [Bob] Dylan' because of the tough poetry of his lyrics. Forbert's biggest commercial success came when he had a Top 20 hit with 'Romeo's Tune' (1979). After four albums his contract was terminated. For most of the 80s, Forbert was based in Nashville, songwriting and playing concerts around the South with a touring group including Danny Counts (bass), Paul Errico (keyboards) and Bobby Lloyd Hicks (drums). His 1988 album for Geffen Records had Garry Tallent from Bruce Springsteen's E Street Band as producer. Nils Lofgren was a guest musician. After a four-year gap, Forbert returned with the highly praised *The American In Me*, produced by Pete Anderson.

●ALBUMS: *Alive On Arrival* (Epic 1979)★★★, *Jackrabbit Slim* (Epic 1979)★★★, *Little Stevie Orbit* (Epic 1980)★★, *Steve Forbert* (Epic 1982)★★, *Streets Of This Town* (Geffen 1988)★★★, *The American In Me* (Geffen 1992)★★★, *Mission Of The Crossroad Palms* (Giant 1995)★★★, *Rocking Horse Head* (Revoloution 1996)★★★.

FORD, LITA

b. 23 September 1959, London, England. Ford was one of the original members of the Kim Fowley-conceived Runaways, first joining the band at age 15. A disagreement within the ranks in 1979 over musical direction led to the Runaways' break-up, leaving Ford to explore a solo career on the US glam metal circuit (initially subsidized by her day job as a beautician). Her debut album was recorded for Mercury Records with the assistance of Neil Merryweather on bass, though it was Ford's guitar playing which took centre stage. *Dancin' On The Edge* made a minor impact on the US album charts reaching number 66, though this was a less seamless collection. Almost four years later in 1988 came *Lita*. Housed on RCA Records (a third album for MCA, *The Bride Wore Black*, had been abandoned) it reached the Top 30 and spawned the US number 12 hit, 'Kiss Me Deadly', plus a Top 10 hit on the duet with Ozzy Osbourne, 'Close My Eyes Forever'. Later that year she married W.A.S.P. guitarist Chris Holmes, though this would be an ill-starred union. *Stiletto* continued to display Ford's commitment to the formula rock format prevalent in the USA, but she left RCA following disappointing sales for 1991's *Dangerous Curves*.

●ALBUMS: *Out For Blood* (Mercury 1983)★★★, *Dancin' On The Edge* (Mercury 1984)★★, *Lita* (RCA 1988)★★★, *Stiletto* (RCA 1990)★★★, *Dangerous Curves* (RCA 1991)★★, *Black* (ZYX 1995)★★.

●COMPILATIONS: *Best Of* (BMG 1992)★★★.

●VIDEOS: *Lita Live* (1988), *A Midnight Snack* (1990).

FORD, ROBBEN

b. Robben Lee Ford, 16 December 1951, Woodlake, California, USA. A jazz, blues and rock guitarist, Robben is the most celebrated member of the musical Ford family. His father Charles was a country musician, his brothers Patrick and Mark are bluesmen playing drums and harmonica, respectively. Inspired initially by Mike Bloomfield and Eric Clapton, Ford's first professional engagement was with Charlie Musslewhite in 1970. He formed the Charles Ford Band with his brothers in 1971, then backed Jimmy Witherspoon from 1972-74. He toured and recorded with both Joni Mitchell (as part of L.A. Express) and George Harrison in 1974, the resulting exposure bringing him a considerable amount of session work. In 1978, he formed the Yellowjackets with keyboards player Russell Ferrante and also found time to record a patchy solo debut *Inside Story*. The early 80s saw him performing with Michael McDonald and saxophonist Sadao Watanabe; in 1986 he joined the Miles Davis band on its tour of the USA and Europe. *Talk To Your Daughter* was a triumphant return to his blues roots, and picked up a Grammy nomination in the 'Contemporary Blues' category. In 1993 he recorded with a new unit, the Blue Line featuring Roscoe Beck (bass), Bill Boublitz (keyboards) and Tom Brechtlein (drums). Ford plays cleanly in an uncluttered style (like Mike Bloomfield), but occasionally with the frantic energy of Larry Carlton.

●ALBUMS: with the Charles Ford Band *The Charles Ford Band* (1972)★★★, *Inside Story* (1978)★★★, with the Charles Ford Band *Reunion* (1982)★★★, *Talk To Your Daughter* (Warners 1988)★★★, *Mark Ford With The Robben Ford Band* (1991)★★★, *Robben Ford And The Blue Line* (1992)★★★★, with Jimmy Witherspoon *Live At The Notodden Blues Festival* (1993)★★★, with the Blue Line *Mystic Mile* (Stretch/GRP 1993)★★★, *Handful Of Blues* (Blue Thumb 1995)★★★★.

●VIDEOS: *Highlights* (Warner Music 1995).

FORDHAM, JULIA

b. 10 August 1962, Portsmouth, Hampshire, England. Formerly one of Mari Wilson's backing vocalists, the Wilsations, Fordham embarked on a solo career in 1986 as the archetypal angst-woman of the 80s. She achieved an initial UK chart hit with the Top 30 'Happy Ever After' (which also reached number 1 in Japan) in 1988, and a self-titled debut album and the follow-up both reached the UK Top 20. However her biggest success came with the non-original '(Love Moves In) Mysterious Ways', which reached number 19 in February 1992. These releases, and the subsequent *Swept*, all on the Circa label, have established the singer with a 'thirtysomething' audience, enabling her to perform headlining dates at venues such as London's Royal Albert Hall.

● ALBUMS: *Julia Fordham* (Circa 1988)★★★, *Porcelain* (Circa 1989)★★★, *Swept* (Circa 1991)★★★, *Falling Forward* (Circa 1994)★★★.

● VIDEOS: *Porcelain* (Virgin 1990).

FOREIGNER

A band which took its name from the fact that original members were drawn from both sides of the Atlantic, this mixture of influences is much in evidence in its music. Mick Jones (b. 27 December 1944, London, England; guitar, vocals) formed the band in 1976, having spent time in Nero & The Gladiators (one hit, 'Entry Of The Gladiators', in 1961). The rest of the 60s were taken up with sessions, while the early 70s saw him working with musicians such as Johnny Halliday as well as his second major band, Wonderwheel. Later he recorded one album with Spooky Tooth, then worked with Leslie West and Ian Lloyd, before taking a job as an A&R man who never signed anyone. Prepared to give the music scene one last try, Jones auditioned musicians, eventually forging a line-up that consisted of Ian McDonald (b. 25 June 1946, London, England; guitar, keyboards, horns, vocals), formerly of King Crimson, Lou Gramm (b. Lou Grammatico, 2 May 1950, Rochester, New York, USA; vocals), who had played with Black Sheep in the early 70s, Dennis Elliott (b. 18 August 1950, London, England; drums), Al Greenwood (b. New York, USA; keyboards) and Edward Gagliardi (b. 13 February 1952, New York, USA; bass). In 1977 the band released *Foreigner*, and in a poll conducted by *Rolling Stone* magazine, came out as top new artists. Jones and Gramm wrote most of the band's material, including classic tracks such as 'Feels Like The First Time' and 'Cold As Ice'. Despite playing at the Reading Rock Festival in England twice in the 70s, Foreigner had more consistent success in the USA. In 1979 Rick Wills (b. England; bass) replaced Gagliardi, having served a musical apprenticeship with King Crimson and Peter Frampton. Gagliardi reportedly 'fell on the floor and passed out' on being told the news. *Head Games*, meanwhile, proved most notable for its 'exploitative' sleeve design, which contrasted with the subtle brand of rock it housed. 1980 saw the departure of McDonald and Greenwood which led to the guest appearances of Thomas Dolby and Junior Walker on *4*, produced by Mutt Lange. 'Waiting For A Girl Like You' was the hit single lifted from the album. Though it demonstrated the band's highly musical approach, taking the form of a wistful yet melodious ballad, it pigeonholed the group as purveyors of the epic AOR song, a reputation which was hardly infringed by the release of 'I Want To Know What Love Is', which proved to be Foreigner's greatest commercial success. It topped the charts on both sides of the Atlantic and featured the New Jersey Mass Choir backing Gramm's plaintive vocal. In the mid-80s the members of Foreigner were engaged in solo projects, and the success of Gramm's *Ready Or Not* in 1987 led to widespread speculation that Foreigner were about to disband. This was not the case, as *Inside Information* proved, though in other respects it was a poor record and a portent of things to come. In 1989 Gramm enjoyed success with another solo project, *Long Hard Look*, before leaving the band officially in 1990 to form Shadow King. Jones refused to face the inevitable, and, amid much press back-biting, recruited Johnny Edwards (ex-King Kobra) to provide vocals for *Unusual Heat*. By 1994 both Jones and Gramm grasped the nettle and got back in touch, launching a reunited Foreigner, though both Wills and Elliott (the latter going on to a career as a master ornamental wood lather) were deemed surplus to requirements. The 1994 model boasted a line-up of Bruce Turgon (bass; a former colleague of Gramm in Black Sheep), Jeff Jacobs (keyboards, ex-Billy Joel circa *Storm Front*) and Mark Schulman (drums, ex-Billy Idol; Simple Minds), in adition to Jones and Gramm. The band were back on the road during the early part of 1995 to promote *Mr Moonlight*. The album was only a moderate success, even though it was a typical Foreigner record. At their well-attended gigs, however, it was still 'Cold As Ice', 'Urgent' and 'I Wan't To Know What Love Is' that received the biggest cheers. Whether or not their legacy grows further, Foreigner will continue to epitomize the classic sound of 'adult orientated rock' better than anybody. Gagliardi and Greenwood had gone on to form Spys.

●ALBUMS: *Foreigner* (Atlantic 1977)★★★, *Double Vision* (Atlantic 1978)★★★, *Head Games* (Atlantic 1979)★★★, *4* (Atlantic 1981)★★★★, *Agent Provocateur* (Atlantic 1985)★★★, *Inside Information* (Atlantic 1987)★★★, *Unusual Heat* (Atlantic 1991)★★★, *Mr Moonlight* (BMG 1994)★★★. Solo: Mick Jones *Everything That Comes Around* (Atlantic 1989)★★.

●COMPILATIONS: *Records* (Atlantic 1982)★★★★, *Greatest Hits* (Atlantic 1992)★★★★, *The Very Best Of And Beyond* (Atlantic 1992)★★★★.

●FILMS: *Footloose - (Soundtrack Song)* (1984).

4 SKINS

As their name suggests, this London, England band comprised four skinheads, who specialized in vitriolic three-chord 'yob-rock'. Their membership was fluid, including no less than four lead singers, with only Hoxton Tom (bass) still resident between their first and second albums. Taking their musical brief from outfits such as Sham 69, the Angelic Upstarts and the Cockney Rejects, they were a third generation punk band heavily associated with the Oi! movement alongside fellow travellers the Business. With a blatantly patriotic image, the band attracted National Front supporters to their live shows, which occasionally erupted into full-scale riots. Lyrically they expounded on racism, police brutality and corrupt governments. However, musically they were not so adventurous, being rigidly formularized and unable to develop from their simplistic origins (basic punk spiced by the odd foray into skinhead's 'other' music, ska). From a creative standpoint, the band had ground to a halt by 1983. Their fan base continued to contract and they soon faded into oblivion, though re-releases and compilations have reminded many of their enduring street popularity.

●ALBUMS: *The Good, The Bad And The 4 Skins* (Secret 1982)★★, *A Fistful Of 4 Skins* (Syndicate 1983)★★, *From Chaos To 1984* (Syndicate 1984)★★.

●COMPILATIONS: *Wonderful World Of The 4 Skins* (Link 1987)★★, *A Few 4 Skins More Vol. 1* (Link 1987)★★, *A Few 4 Skins More Vol. 2* (Link 1987)★★, *Live And Loud* (Link 1989)★★.

FOX, SAMANTHA

b. 15 April 1966, London, England. While studying for her O-level examinations, 16-year-old Fox was 'discovered' by the *Sun* newspaper and promoted as a topless model. Before long she became some-

thing of a British institution and a recording career beckoned. Her debut single in 1986, 'Touch Me', elicited almost universally favourable reviews with critics registering surprise at her strong vocal performance. After the disc charted at number 3, she followed up with the sultry 'Do Ya, Do Ya (Wanna Please Me)', which also hit the UK Top 10. Further major British hits followed with 'Hold On Tight', 'Nothing's Gonna Stop Me Now' and 'I Surrender'. Having proven that former newspaper models can be hit artists, Fox defied all expectations by exporting her talents to the USA, where she enjoyed even greater chart success with three Top 10 hits including 'Naughty Girls', recorded with Full Force. Her two albums were uneven but displayed her range to some effect, most notably on the acid house-inspired 'Love House', which was also a UK hit. Over-exposure and increasing media prejudice finally persuaded her to relocate to America, but despite her strong visual appeal, particularly to the MTV audience, further hits have not so far been forthcoming. In 1991, Fox completed work on her first film, tentatively titled, *The Final Embrace*. In January 1996 she was banned from singing at a charity concert in Calcutta, India, owing to police fears she might cause a riot.

●ALBUMS: *Touch Me* (Jive 1986)★★, *Samantha Fox* (Jive 1987)★★. *I Wanna Have Some Fun* (Jive 1989)★★.

FOXTON, BRUCE

b. 1 September 1955, Woking, Surrey, England. Following the break-up of the Jam, guitarist Foxton set out on a predictably difficult solo career. During the summer of 1983, he enjoyed UK Top 30 success with 'Freak'. His strong, straightforward pop, with often distinct Jam overtones, was generally well-produced, with Steve Littlewhite's 'This Is The Way', proving particularly effective. In 1984, Foxton released *Touch Sensitive*, which featured all-original compositions and another solid production. While deserving chart success, Foxton's work has, not surprisingly, been compared unfavourably with that of the Jam and, consequently, his solo career has suffered.

●ALBUMS: *Touch Sensitive* (Arista 1984)★★.

●FURTHER READING: *Our Story*, Bruce Foxton and Rick Buckler with Alex Ogg.

FOXX, JOHN

b. Dennis Leigh Chorley, Lancashire, England. Foxx moved to London in 1974 and was a key instigator of 70s electro-pop. He was the founder-member of Ultravox with whom he wrote, sang and dabbled in synthetic noises, before handing over to Midge Ure. Gary Numan cited him as his main influence, which was some consolation for the fact that Numan was having hits when Ultravox were dropped by Island Records. Foxx went solo in 1979 and formed his own label MetalBeat, distributed by Virgin Records. The infectious 'Underpass' began a short string of minor Top 40 UK hits which included 'No-One Driving', 'Burning Car' and 'Europe After The Rain'. Foxx's appearances on the singles and album charts ended in the mid-80s.

●ALBUMS: *Metamatic* (MetalBeat 1980)★★★, *The Garden* (Virgin 1981)★★★, *The Golden Section* (Virgin 1983)★★, *In Mysterious Ways* (Virgin 1985)★★.

FRANKIE GOES TO HOLLYWOOD

Formed in the summer of 1980, this Liverpool group comprised former Big In Japan vocalist Holly Johnson (b. William Johnson, 19 February 1960, Khartoum, Sudan) backed by Paul Rutherford (b. 8 December 1959, Liverpool, England; vocals), Nasher Nash (b. Brian Nash, 20 May 1963; guitar), Mark O'Toole (b. 6 January 1964, Liverpool, England; bass) and Peter Gill (b. 8 March 1964, Liverpool, England; drums). It was a further two years before the group started to make any real headway with television appearances and a record deal with Trevor Horn's ZTT Records. Their debut single, 'Relax', produced by Horn, was a pyrotechnic production and superb dance track with a suitably suggestive lyric that led to a BBC radio and television ban in Britain. Paradoxically, the censorship produced even greater public interest in the single which topped the UK charts for five weeks, selling close to two million copies in the process. The promotion behind Frankie, engineered by former music journalist Paul Morley, was both clever and inventive, utilizing marketing techniques such as single word slogans and the production of best-selling T-shirts that offered the enigmatic message 'Frankie Says...' The group's peculiar image of Liverpool laddishness coupled with the unashamed homosexuality of vocalists Johnson and Rutherford merely added to their curiosity value and sensationalism, while also providing them with a distinctive identity that their detractors seriously underestimated.

The follow up to 'Relax' was the even more astonishing 'Two Tribes'. An awesome production built round a throbbing, infectiously original riff, it showed off Johnson's distinctive vocal style to striking effect. Like all Frankie's singles, the record was available in various 7-inch and 12-inch remixed formats with superb packaging and artwork. The power of the single lay not merely in its appropriately epic production but the topicality of its lyric which dealt with the escalation of nuclear arms and the prospect of global annihilation. In order to reinforce the harrowing theme, the group included a chilling voiceover from actor Patrick Allen taken from government papers on the dissemination of information to the public in the event of nuclear war. Allen's Orwellian instructions on how to avoid fallout while disposing of dogs, grandparents and other loved ones gave the disc a frightening authenticity that perfectly captured the mood of the time. Johnson's closing lines of the song, borrowed from an unnamed literary source, provided a neat rhetorical conclusion: 'Are we living in a land where sex and horror are the new gods?' The six-minute plus version of 'Two Tribes' was played in its entirety on UK lunchtime radio shows and duly entered the chart at number 1, remaining in the premier position for an incredible nine weeks while the revitalized 'Relax' nestled alongside its successor at number 2. A Godley And Creme promotional film of 'Two Tribes' which featured caricatures of US President Reagan and Soviet leader Mr. Chernenko wrestling was rightly acclaimed as one of the best videos of the period and contributed strongly to the Frankie package.

Having dominated the upper echelons of the chart like no other artist since the Beatles, the pressure to produce an album for the Christmas market was immense. *Welcome To The Pleasure Dome* finally emerged as a double with a number of cover versions including interesting readings of Bruce Springsteen's 'Born To Run', Dionne Warwick's 'Do You Know The Way To San Jose?' and Gerry And The Pacemakers' 'Ferry Across The Mersey'. Like all Frankie recordings, the sound was epic and glorious and the reviews proclaimed the album an undoubted hit, though some commentators felt its irresistible charm might prove ephemeral. 1984 ended with a necessary change of style as Frankie enjoyed their third number 1 hit with the moving festive ballad 'The Power Of Love'. Thus they joined Gerry And The Pacemakers as only the second act in UK pop history to see their first three singles reach the top. History repeated itself the following year when, like Gerry, Frankie saw their fourth single ('Welcome To The Pleasure Dome') stall at number 2. Thereafter, they were never again to attain the ascendancy that they had enjoyed during the golden year of 1984.

A sabbatical spent in Eire for tax purposes meant that their comeback in 1986 had to be emphatic.

Having failed to conquer America during the same period, merely increased the pressure. Critics had long been claiming that the group were little more than puppets in the hands of a talented producer despite the fact that they sang, played and even wrote their own material. The grand return with 'Rage Hard' (the title borrowed from Dylan Thomas) won them a number 4 UK hit, but that seemed decidedly anti-climactic. The second album, *Liverpool*, cost a small fortune but lacked the charm and vibrancy of its predecessor. Within a year Frankie broke up, having crammed a decade of sales, creativity and controversy into less than 24 months. In many ways their fate was the perfect pop parable of the 80s. For a group that was so symptomatic of their age, it was appropriate that the Frankie saga should end not in the recording studio, but in the High Court. In a battle royal between Johnson and his former record company ZTT in early 1988, the artist not only won his artistic freedom but substantial damages which were to have vast implications for the UK music business as a whole.

● ALBUMS: *Welcome To The Pleasure Dome* (ZTT 1984)★★★, *Liverpool* (ZTT 1986)★★.

● COMPILATIONS: *Bang! - The Greatest Hits Of Frankie Goes To Hollywood* (ZTT 1993)★★★★.

● VIDEOS: *Shoot!: The Greatest Hits* (1993).

● FURTHER READING: *Give It Loads: The Story Of Frankie Goes To Hollywood*, Bruno Hizer. *Frankie Say: The Rise Of Frankie Goes To Hollywood*, Danny Jackson. *A Bone In My Flute*, Holly Johnson.

FRAZIER CHORUS

Originally a four-piece band from Brighton, Sussex, England, this mid-80s pop group, originally under the name Plop!, set out with the grand ambition of being the antithesis of Wham!. Singer and keyboard player Tim Freeman's songs were circulated on a demo tape and he and the rest of the band; Michele Allardyce, percussion; Kate Holmes, flute; and Chris Taplin, clarinet, were signed to 4AD Records under the name Frazier Chorus, a name taken from the back of a 50s US baseball jacket. With their unusual instrumental line-up, which lent an almost synth-pop/pastoral feel, their 4AD debut, 'Sloppy Heart' (1987), did not fit easily with the harder edge towards which the label was moving. As a consequence, the band soon switched to Virgin Records. In 1989 they released their debut album, *Sue*, which featured orchestral arrangements from David Bedford and contributions from Tim Sanders (tenor saxophone), Roddy Lorimer (trumpet/flugelhorn) and Simon Clarke (piccolo/saxophones). Freeman's whispered lyrics eloquently chronicled a mundane existence with keen, ironic observations of 'everyday' life and sexual relations. Minor UK hits with 'Dream Kitchen' and 'Typical' promised much, but none reached the Top 50. A reissue of 'Sloppy Heart' featured a laconic version of the Sex Pistols' 'Anarchy In The UK' on its b-side. Allardyce left acrimoniously during the recording of the second album (with the Lightning Seeds' Ian Broudie on production) leaving the band as a trio. Allardyce, whose orientation was geared more to dance music, would continue to work as a journalist for disc jockey magazine *Jocks*. Freeman had previously collaborated on the 4AD house project, This Mortal Coil. Further minor Frazier Chorus hits included the Paul Oakenfold remixes of 'Cloud 8' and 'Nothing'. The disappointing performance of 1991's 'Walking On Air' confirmed that Frazier Chorus's cult appeal had apparently peaked, but the group pressed on regardless. Freeman's muse had not deserted him, and 1995's *Wide Awake* included further strong songwriting in songs such as 'If The Weather Was Up To Me'.

● ALBUMS: *Sue* (Virgin 1989)★★★, *Ray* (Virgin 1991)★★, *Wide Awake* (Pinkerton 1995)★★★.

FREEEZ

This British-funk group was led by John Rocca (b. 23 September 1960, London, England), included Peter Maas (bass), Andy Stennet (keyboards) and Paul Morgan (drums). Rocca, a former van salesman for the dance music specialist shop Disc Empire, formed the group in 1978. They released their first single 'Keep In Touch' on their own Pink Rythm (sic) label (one of the first British acts to form their own label) and it narrowly missed the UK Top 40 in 1980 when picked up by Calibre. After moving to Beggars Banquet Records in 1981 they hit the UK Top 10 with 'Southern Freeze', which included vocals by Ingrid Mansfield-Allman (b. London, England). The album of the same name reached the Top 20. The group expanded to a seven piece with the addition of Gordon Sullivan, George Whitmore and new vocalist Alison Gordon. Later reduced to the basic duo of Rocca and Maas, they had their biggest success in 1983 with 'I.O.U.', written and produced in the USA by Arthur Baker with mixing help from Jellybean. In 1985 Rocca and Stennet recorded as Pink Rhythm whilst Freeez continued with Maas, Morgan, Billy Crichton and Louis Smith and recorded on Siren in 1986. As a solo artist Rocca had a US dance number 1 with 'I Want To Be Real' in 1987, the same year a remix of Freeez's 'I.O.U.' on Citybeat made the UK Top 30. Rocca later recorded on Who'd She Coo and Cobra (where he re-recorded 'Southern Freeze') and re-appeared in 1991 as Midi Rain on Vinyl Solution.

●ALBUMS: *Southern Freeze* (Beggars Banquet 1981)★★★, *Gonna Get You* (Beggars Banquet 1983)★★★.

FREHLEY, ACE

b. Paul Frehley, 22 April 1951, Bronx, New York, USA. Ace Frehley rose to fame as the lead guitarist for premier US hard rock band Kiss during its prime years. Often nicknamed 'Space Ace' by fans, Frehley released his first, self-titled solo album in September 1978, with albums by the other three members of Kiss also cut simultaneously. Released on Casablanca Records, the album, which found the guitarist attempting more diverse musical styles than he was allowed to follow within the context of Kiss, reached the Top 30 and spawned a number 13 single, the Russ Ballard-penned 'New York Groove'. Frehley left Kiss in 1983, following a near-fatal car accident, and attempted to free himself of a drug habit over the next four years. He formed his own band, Frehley's Comet, in 1987, with whom he recorded three studio albums.

●ALBUMS: *Ace Frehley* (Casablanca 1978)★★★.

FREY, GLENN

b. 6 November 1948, Detroit, Michigan, USA. Frey's early career was forged as singer and guitarist in a number of local attractions, including the Mushrooms and Subterraneans. He appeared on several sessions by the Bob Seger System, singing back-up on 'Ramblin' Gamblin' Man', a 1968 hit, before moving to Los Angeles. Here Frey formed Longbranch Pennywhistle with J.D. Souther, but this harmony duo floundered on record label intransigence and in 1972 the now disengaged musician opted for singer Linda Ronstadt's backing group. Frey then joined fellow band members Bernie Leadon, Don Henley and Randy Meisner in the Eagles which grew from humble country-rock origins into one of America's most successful attractions. Glenn co-wrote many of the unit's best-known songs, including 'Take It Easy', 'Lyin' Eyes', 'Take It To The Limit' and 'Hotel California', while his distinctive vocal formed the ideal counterpoint to that of Henley. The Eagles broke up in 1980 amid rancorous professional and personal circumstances. A new-found partnership with songwriter Jack Tempchin formed the basis of Frey's solo debut, *No Fun Aloud*, which achieved gold status

and spawned US hits in 'I Found Somebody' and 'The One You Love'. In 1984 he wrote and performed 'The Heat Is On', the theme to the highly-successful film, *Beverly Hills Cop*, before resuming his association with Tempchin for *The Allnighter*. The following year Frey reached number 2 in the US charts with 'You Belong To The City', a song culled from the soundtrack of *Miami Vice*. He subsequently took an acting role in this popular television crime series and in 1988 completed *Soul Searchin'*, the third in a series of slick, professional AOR-styled albums. Frey was a key member of the highly successful Eagles reunion in 1994 During the financially lucrative tour in 1995 he was taken seriously ill and received surgery for a stomach complaint.

●ALBUMS: *No Fun Aloud* (Asylum 1982)★★, *The Allnighter* (MCA 1985)★★, *Soul Searchin'* (MCA 1988)★★, *Strange Weather* (1992)★★, *Live* (1993)★★.

●COMPILATIONS: *Solo Collection* (MCA 1995)★★★.

FRIDA

b. Anni-Frid Synni-Lyngstad, 15 November 1945, Narvik, Norway. Frida attempted a career as a solo singer after the break-up of Abba in 1981. She was the first of the group to make a solo album, which was produced by Phil Collins. Somewhat downbeat in tone (many thought it reflected the recent breakdown of the separate marriages of both Frida and Collins), it included songs by Per Gessle, later of Roxette. The most successful track, 'I Know There's Something Going On' reached the US Top 20 and was written by Russ Ballard who also composed the first solo hit for another ex-Abba soloist Agnetha Faltskog. 'To Turn To Stone' was also successful in Europe. The following year, Frida's duet with B.A. Robertson, 'Time', was a minor British hit but her second solo album made little impact on either side of the Atlantic, although the title track was a hit across Europe.

●ALBUMS: *Something's Going On* (Epic 1982)★★★, *Shine* (Epic 1984)★★, *Djupa Andetag* (Anderson 1996)★★.

FUN BOY THREE

When the Specials topped the UK charts in June 1981 with 'Ghost Town' few would have guessed that three of their members would depart immediately to form an offshoot group. By October, Terry Hall (vocals), Neville Staples (vocals, drums) and Lynval Golding (guitar) had launched the Fun Boy Three. Their UK Top 20 debut single was the extraordinary 'The Lunatics Have Taken Over The Asylum', a haunting protest against political conservatism, made all the more effective by Hall's deadpan, languid vocal. The single effectively established the trio as both original and innovative commentators, whose work compared favourably with that of their mother group, the Specials. For their follow-up, the Fun Boy Three teamed up with the then unknown Bananarama for a hit revival of bandleader Jimmie Lunceford's 'It Ain't What You Do It's The Way That You Do It'. The Bananarama connection continued when the Fun Boy Three appeared on their hit 'Really Saying Something'. The girl trio also sang on several tracks of their mentors' self-titled debut album. By 1982, the Fun Boy Three were proving themselves adept at writing political songs and reviving classic songs which they moulded into their own distinctive style. Hall's lazy vocal on George Gershwin's 'Summertime' was a typical example of this and provided another Top 20 hit. A wonderfully cynical comment on teenage love and pregnancy, 'Tunnel Of Love' proved the trio's last major statement. Following a second album, they split during 1983, with Hall going on to form the Colour Field.

●ALBUMS: *Fun Boy Three* (Chrysalis 1982)★★★, *Waiting* (Chrysalis 1983)★★★.

●COMPILATIONS: *Really Saying Something: The Best Of ...* (Chrysalis 1997)★★★★.

FUREYS

This musical family group from Ballyfermont, Dublin, Eire, featured George Furey (b. 11 June 1951, Dublin, Eire; vocals, guitar, accordion, mandola, autoharp, whistles), Finbar Furey (b. 28 September 1946, Dublin, Eire; vocals, uillean pipes, banjo, whistles, flute), Eddie Furey (b. 23 December 1944, Dublin, Eire; guitar, mandola, mandolin, harmonica, fiddle, bodhran, vocals) and Paul Furey (b. 6 May 1948, Dublin, Eire; accordion, melodeon, concertina, whistles, bones, spoons, vocals). During the 60s Finbar and Eddie Furey had performed as a duo, playing clubs and doing radio work. Despite the offer of a recording contract, they turned it down, and went to Scotland to play. Having established a reputation for themselves, they later signed to Transatlantic, and joined the Clancy Brothers on the latter group's American tour in 1969. In 1972, the duo toured most of Europe, but while they were away, Paul and George had formed a group called the Buskers, with Davey Arthur (b. 24 September 1954, Edinburgh, Scotland; multi-instrumentalist, vocals). This group were involved in a road crash,

bringing Finbar and Eddie back home, where they formed Tam Linn with Davey and Paul, and played the Cambridge Folk Festival. George later joined the line-up, and they became the Fureys And Davey Arthur. The following year, 1981, the group, credited as the Fureys And Davey Arthur, reached the UK Top 20 with 'When You Were Sweet Sixteen'. By contrast, the album, having the same title, only just made the Top 100 in the UK during 1982. A follow-up single, 'I Will Love You (Every Time When We Are Gone)' failed to make the Top 50. *Golden Days*, released on K-Tel, made the UK Top 20 in 1984, selling in excess of 250,000 copies, while *At The End Of A Perfect Day*, also on K-Tel, made the UK Top 40 in 1985. Numerous compilations abound, but *The Sound Of The Fureys And Davey Arthur*, on PolyGram, was released only in Ireland. *Golden Days* and *At The End Of A Perfect Day* were re-packaged, in 1991, as *The Very Best Of The Fureys And Davey Arthur*. The group have successfully followed the middle-of-the-road folk musical path, by producing melodic and popular music. Folk purists argue that this detracts from 'real' folk music, whilst others say that the group have encouraged people, to listen to folk music. Either way, their concerts are popular worldwide, and while not a hugely successful chart act domestically, their records still sell extremely well. Towards the end of 1993 Davey Arthur left the group and formed Davey Arthur And Co.

●ALBUMS: *The Cisco Special* (1960)★★★, *Songs Of Woody Guthrie* (1961)★★★, *I Ain't Got No Home* (1962)★★★, *When You Were Sweet Sixteen* (Castle Classics 1982)★★★, *Steal Away* (Ritz 1983)★★★, *In Concert* (Ritz 1984)★★★, *Golden Days* (K-Tel 1984)★★★★, *At The End Of A Perfect Day* (K-Tel 1985)★★★, *The First Leaves Of Autumn* (Ritz 1986)★★★, *The Scattering* (BMG/Ariola 1989). Solo: Finbar And Eddie Furey *The Dawning Of The Day* (1972)★★★. Finbar Furey *Love Letters* (BMG/Ariola 1990)★★★.

●COMPILATIONS: *The Sound Of The Fureys And Davey Arthur* (Polygram Ireland 1981)★★★, *The Fureys Finest* (Telstar 1987)★★★★, *The Fureys Collection* (Castle Communications 1989)★★★★, *The Very Best Of The Fureys And Davey Arthur* (Music Club 1991)★★★★, *The Winds Of Change* (Ritz 1992)★★★.

FURNITURE

Led by James Irvin (b. 20 July 1959, Chiswick, London, England; vocals), UK guitar band Furniture originally formed in 1981 with the intention of marrying the influences of 'the Undertones

and Chic'. With their line-up completed by Tim Whelan (b. 15 September 1958, London, England; guitar) and Hamilton Lee (b. 7 September 1958, London, England; drums), they released their debut single 'Shaking Story' on their own The Guy From Paraguay label. Afterwards they were joined by Sally Still (b. 5 February 1964, London, England; bass) and Maya Gilder (b. 25 April 1964, Poonak, India; keyboards), and recorded a debut mini-album for independent label Survival Records in September 1983. Reaction was almost non-existent, and the group considered an early exit before Stiff Records heard one of the new songs they had written, 'Brilliant Mind', and signed them. Released as a single, this evocative, understated song reached number 21 in the UK charts in May 1986. Stiff, however, collapsed after the release of only one further single, 'Love Your Shoes' (itself a new version of a 1985 Premonition single). ZTT Records acquired the Stiff catalogue, and Furniture spent the next two years attempting to free themselves of contract. They finally achieved this in 1989 via a new contract with Arista Records, but their chart stature had long since declined. Arista released an album, *Food Sex And Paranoia*, but sacked almost half of its A&R department (including the team which had signed Furniture) immediately afterwards. Underexposed and overlooked, the album which should have resurrected their career managed only 5,000 sales. Irvin broke up the group after a farewell performance at the 1990 Reading Festival, before recording his debut solo album (attributed to Because) in 1991. He then became Reviews Editor at *Melody Maker* magazine, then Features Editor at *Mojo* magazine and rose to the lofty heights of 'filter editor' in 1997. His former colleagues, Lee and Whelan, enjoyed notable success as members of Transglobal Underground. Gilder joined the BBC.

●ALBUMS: *When The Boom Was On* (Premonition 1983)★★★, *The Wrong People* (Stiff 1986)★★★, *Food Sex And Paranoia* (Arista 1990)★★★. Jim Irvin as Because: *Mad, Scared, Dumb And Gorgeous* (Haven 1991)★★★.

●COMPILATIONS: *The Lovemongers* (Survival 1986)★★★, *She Gets Out The Scrapbook* (Survival 1991)★★★.

GABRIEL, PETER

b. 13 February 1950, London, England. After seven years fronting Genesis, Gabriel tired of the extensive touring and group format and went solo in 1975. Until *Plays Live*, released in 1983, his four solo albums were all called *Peter Gabriel*. The first included the track 'Solsbury Hill', a metaphorical account of his split from Genesis which made the Top 20 in the UK. The album charted in the UK and the USA and Gabriel began his solo touring career in the USA, expressing a nervousness of facing his home country audiences. Unlike his earlier extravagant, theatrical presentations, he favoured minimalism and often played shows in a plain boiler suit. Robert Fripp was brought in as producer for the second album which made the UK Top 10 and just missed out on a Top 20 place in the *Billboard* chart. The album contained chiefly introspective, experimental music, but healthy sales figures were encouraging. However, Atlantic Records refused to distribute his third album in the USA, claiming its maudlin nature would mean 'commercial suicide'. Mercury Records stepped in and with Steve Lillywhite's disciplined production the striking collection was far from the flop Atlantic feared. 'Games Without Frontiers' was a Top 5 hit in the UK and the track 'Biko', about the murdered South African activist Stephen Biko, became an anti-racist anthem. Continuing his deliberated approach, his fourth album, given the full title of *Peter Gabriel (Security)*, was not released until 1982 and appeared to be hinting at a more accessible approach. A German-language edition of the album was also released. *Peter Gabriel Plays Live*, was released by Charisma/Geffen in 1983. Two years later Gabriel composed the haunting soundtrack to the Alan Parker film, *Birdy*. The journey to complete commercial acceptance was finished in 1986 with *So*, containing the US number 1 single 'Sledgehammer' which was supported by a pioneering, award-winning video featuring puppetry and animation. He was celebrated as an artist whose work was popular without being compromised. A duet with Kate Bush, 'Don't Give Up', also lifted from *So*, became a UK Top 10 hit in November 1986. Throughout the 80s, Gabriel dedicated much of his time to absorbing world music and in 1982 sponsored the WOMAD (World Of Music And Dance) Festival. He also became heavily involved in Amnesty International and recorded with Senegalese star Youssou N'Dour. The pair toured the USA under the banner of 'Conspiracy Of Hope' and raised money for Amnesty. He invited musicians from all over the world to record at his luxurious self-built studios in Bath and incorporated many non-Western ideas into his own music. In 1989 he wrote the score for the film *The Last Temptation Of Christ*, released on a label backed by WOMAD. Virgin Records, the owners of the Charisma back-catalogue, released a greatest hits collection in 1990, *Shaking The Tree*. The title track was written by Gabriel with N'Dour and was included originally on N'Dour's album, *The Lion*. Although *Us* fell short of the high standard set by *So*, it put Gabriel back in the public eye with a series of outstandingly creative videos to accompany the release.

●ALBUMS: *Peter Gabriel* (Charisma 1977)★★★, *Peter Gabriel* (Charisma 1978)★★★, *Peter Gabriel* (Charisma 1980)★★★, *Peter Gabriel (Security)* (Charisma 1982)★★★★, *Peter Gabriel Plays Live* (Charisma 1983)★★, *Birdy* (Charisma 1985)★★, *So* (Virgin 1986)★★★★, *Passion* (Real World 1989)★★, *Us* (Real World 1993)★★★, *Secret World - Live* (Real World 1994)★★★.

●COMPILATIONS: *Shaking The Tree* (Virgin 1990)★★★★.

●VIDEOS: *Point Of View (Live In Athens)* (1989), *The Desert And Her Daughters* (1990), *CV* (1991), *All About Us* (1993), *Secret World Live* (1994), *Computer Animation: Vol. 2.*(1994).

●FURTHER READING: *Peter Gabriel: An Authorized Biography*, Spenser Bright. *In His Own Words*, Mick St. Michael.

GALAXIE 500

Ex-Harvard College alumni Dean Wareham (b. New Zealand; guitar/vocals), Naomi Yang (bass/vocals) and Damon Krukowski (drums) formed this group in Boston, Massachusetts, USA. Having released one track, 'Obvious', on a flexidisc given away with the magazine *Chemical Imbalance*, they moved to New York. Maverick producer Kramer allowed the trio's brittle amateurism to flourish on *Today*, wherein Wareham's plaintive voice and scratchy guitarwork inspired comparisons with the Velvet Underground and Jonathan Richman. A version of the latter's 'Don't Let Our Youth Go To Waste' was featured on this engaging set which inspired Rough Trade Records to sign the group. *On Fire* continued their established métier and a growing self-confidence imbued the songs with resonance and atmosphere. *This Is Our Music* provided a greater emphasis on light and shade, sacrificing some of Yang's silky bass lines for traditional dynamism. A cover version of Yoko Ono's 'Listen, The Snow Is Falling' proved captivating, but the set lacked the warmth of its predecessors. Rumours of internal disaffection proved true when Wareham left the group in 1991. He subsequently formed the enthralling Luna 2, later known simply as Luna, while his former Galaxie 500 partners continued as Pierre Etoile, then simply Damon And Naomi. After releasing a 1992 album (*More Sad Hits*) as such, the duo joined Magic Hour.

●ALBUMS: *Today* (Aurora 1987)★★, *On Fire* (Rough Trade 1989)★★★, *This Is Our Music* (Rough Trade 1990)★★★.

●COMPILATIONS: *1987-1991* 4-CD box set (Rykodisc 1996)★★★.

GALWAY, JAMES

b. 8 December 1939, Belfast, Northern Ireland. The future president of the British Flute Society inherited his woodwind skills from his paternal grandfather. Progressing from mouth-organ and penny whistle, Galway's victories in all three classes of the Irish Flute Championships at the age of 10 led to a place in the Belfast Youth Orchestra and his first BBC broadcasts. A brief spell as a trainee piano tuner preceded scholarships at London's Guildhall School of Music and then the Paris Conservatoire - where he supplemented his grant by busking on city subways. From the rank-and-file at Sadlers Wells, he rose to become principal flautist with the Berlin Philharmonic in 1969. Six years later, manager Michael Emerson suggested he go solo. While averaging 120 concerts per annum, his award-winning recordings of Mozart and Vivaldi paralleled a more financially rewarding venture into pop in the late 70s which culminated with three hit albums and, also in 1978, an international smash with an arrangement of John Denver's 'Annie's Song'. As well as two more best-selling albums, Galway has written his autobiography, an album (*Sometimes We Touch*) with Cleo Laine and world tours with full houses. Currently, he lives in Switzerland with his wife and four children.

●ALBUMS: *The Magic Flute Of James Galway* (RCA 1978)★★★, *The Man With The Golden Flute* (RCA 1978)★★, *James Galway Plays The Songs For Annie* (RCA 1978)★★, *Songs Of The Seashore* (Solar

1979)★★, *Songs Of The Southern Cross* (RCA 1981)★★, *Sometimes When We Touch* (RCA 1982)★★, with Henry Mancini *In The Pink* (RCA 1984)★★, *The Wayward Wind* (1984)★★, *Christmas Carol* (1986)★★, *. . . And The Chieftains In Ireland* (RCA 1987)★★★, *The Celtic Connection - James Galway And The Chieftains* (1990)★★★, with Phil Coulter *Legends* (RCA 1997)★★★.
●COMPILATIONS: *The James Galway Collection* (Telstar 1982)★★★, *The James Galway Collection Vol 2* (Telstar 1986)★★★, *Masterpieces - The Essential Flute Of ...* (RCA 1993)★★★.
●FURTHER READING: *James Galway*, James Galway.

GANG OF FOUR

Formed in Leeds, Yorkshire, England in 1977, Gang Of Four: Jon King (vocals/melodica), Andy Gill (guitar), Dave Allen (drums) and Hugo Burnham (drums) - made their debut the following year with *Damaged Goods*. This uncompromising three-track EP introduced the group's strident approach, wherein Burnham's pounding, compulsive drumming and Gill's staccato, stuttering guitar work, reminiscent of Wilko Johnson from Dr. Feelgood, framed their overtly political lyrics. The quartet maintained this direction on *Entertainment*, while introducing the interest in dance music which marked future recordings. Its most impressive track, 'At Home He's A Tourist', was issued as a single, but encountered censorship problems over its pre-AIDS reference to prophylactics ('rubbers'). Internal strife resulted in Allen's departure, later to join Shriekback, in July 1981. He was replaced by Sara Lee, formerly of Jane Aire And The Belvederes, as the group pursued a fuller, more expansive sound. *Songs Of The Free* featured the tongue-in-cheek single, 'I Love A Man In Uniform', which seemed destined for chart success until disappearing from radio play lists in the wake of the Falklands conflict. Burnham was fired in 1983 and a three-piece line-up completed *Hard* with sundry session musicians. This disappointing release made little difference to a group unable to satisfy now divergent audiences and they split up the following year. However, following several rather inconclusive projects, King and Gill exhumed the Gang Of Four name in 1990. The reunion was marked by *Mall* for Polydor Records, which justified the decision to resume their career with a set of typically bracing, still politically motivated songs. However, it did little to revive their commercial fortunes, and was never released in the UK. *Shrinkwrapped* was better still, with the band

joined by former Curve drummer Steve Monti. The furious rhythms and dark musical scenarios of earlier years also made a welcome return, while the group's lyrics continued to paint the agents of capitalism as the enemy (notably on 'Lord Of The Anthill').
●ALBUMS: *Entertainment* (Warners 1979),★★★★ *Solid Gold* (Warners 1981)★★★, *Songs Of The Free* (Warners 1982)★★★, *Hard* (Warners 1983)★★, *At The Palace* (Phonogram 1984)★★, *Mall* (Polydor 1991)★★★, *Shrinkwrapped* (Castle 1995)★★★.
●COMPILATIONS: *The Peel Sessions* (Strange Fruit 1990)★★★, *A Brief History Of The Twentieth Century* (Warners 1990)★★★★.

GARBAREK, JAN

b. 4 March 1947, Norway. Inspired by hearing John Coltrane on the radio in 1961, Garbarek taught himself to play tenor saxophone (subsequently adding soprano and bass saxophone). In 1962 he won an amateur competition, which resulted in his first professional work, and he was soon leading a group with Jon Christensen, Terje Rypdal and Arild Andersen. In 1968 he was the Norwegian representative at the European Broadcasting Union festival, and the recordings of this (notably an impressive version of Coltrane's 'Naima') brought him to wider notice when they were transmitted throughout Europe. Subsequently his style has become more severe, sometimes almost bleak, although there is a restrained warmth to his sound. Garbarek's playing is representative of the kind of music associated with Manfred Eicher's ECM Records and of a characteristically Scandinavian strand of jazz, melodic and atmospheric, which has little overt emotionalism but does not lack intensity. His writing and playing display considerable concern with tone and texture and appear to have exerted some influence on Tommy Smith and post-sabbatical Charles Lloyd (with whom he has shared colleagues Christensen, Keith Jarrett and Palle Danielsson) as well as a variety of European players such as Joakim Milder and Alberto Nacci. In the mid-70s he worked in Jarrett's 'Belonging' band with Christensen and Danielsson, recording the much-praised *Belonging* and *My Song*, and also played with Ralph Towner on *Solstice* and *Sounds And Shadows*. In the 80s his own groups have featured Eberhard Weber, Bill Frisell and John Abercrombie among others. His tours in the late 80s with a band including the remarkable percussionist Nana Vasconcelos were highly acclaimed and inspired many other musicians and bands to essay the juxtaposition of glacially imposing saxophone lines with exotic, tropical rhythm. Garbarek has also worked with Don Cherry, Chick Corea, David Torn and with George Russell during Russell's residency in Scandinavia in the late 60s - an association which resulted in a fine series of recordings that featured the young Garbarek, notably *Othello Ballet Suite, Trip To Prillarguri* and *Electronic Sonata For Souls Loved By Nature* (though none was released until the 80s). Garbarek has also shown an increasing interest in folk and ethnic musics that has not only coloured his own playing but led to him recording with Ravi Shankar on the 1984 *Song For Everyone* and producing an ECM album for the Norwegian folk singer Agnes Buen Gårnas, 1991's *Rosensfole*. For *Ragas & Sagas* (1993), Garbarek collaborated with the Pakistani classical singer, Usted Fateh Ali Khan and trio of musicians playing tabla and sarangi, a 39-string violin. Garbarek's melodic solos effectively complemented the traditional Pakistani instrumental sounds. In the same year, Garbarek's *Twelve Moons* concentrated once again on the Scandinavian folk melodies he is continually exploring. The album's emphatic rhythmic 'feel' was due in no small part to the presence of drummer Manu Katche and bassist Eberhard Weber. Rather surprisingly, given his avoidance of gallery-pleasing pyrotechnics, Garbarek has steadily acquired a public following equal to his huge critical reputation. Observers of the UK Top 75 album chart in the spring of 1996 would not have been as shocked as would a jazz fan, but horror upon horror, Garbarek's *Visible World* became a hit. The highly accessible nature of the opening tracks such as 'Red Wind', 'The Creek' and the folk-inspired 'The Survivor' aided its wider appeal. World music followers would also have found a great rapport with the 12-minute mantra 'Evening Land', featuring some wonderful vocals from Mari Boine.

●ALBUMS: *Esoteric Circle* (1969)★★★, *Afric Pepperbird* (ECM 1971)★★★, *Sart* (ECM 1972)★★★, *Triptykon* (ECM 1973)★★★, with Art Lande *Red Lanta* (ECM 1974)★★★, with Babo Stenson *Witchi-Tai-To* (ECM 1974)★★★, with Stenson *Dansere* (ECM 1976)★★★, *Dis* (ECM 1977)★★★★, *Places* (ECM 1978)★★★★, *Photo With Blue Sky* (ECM 1979)★★★, with Charlie Haden, Egberto Gismonti *Magico* (1980)★★★, with Kjell Johnsen *Aftenland* (ECM 1980)★★★, with Haden, Gismonti *Folksongs* (ECM 1981)★★★★, *Eventyr* (ECM 1981)★★★, *Paths, Prints* (ECM 1982)★★★, *Wayfarer* (1983)★★★, *It's OK To Listen To The Gray Voice* (ECM 1985)★★★★, *All Those Born With Wings* (ECM 1986)★★★, *Legend Of The Seven Dreams* (ECM 1988)★★★, *I Took Up The Runes* (ECM 1990)★★★★, *Star* (ECM 1991)★★★, with Agnes Buen Gårnas *Rosensfole* (ECM 1991)★★★, with Usted Fateh Ali Khan and Musicians From Pakistan *Ragas & Sagas* (ECM 1992)★★★, *Twelve Moons* (ECM 1993)★★★★, with Miroslav Vitous *Atmos* (1993)★★★, *Madar* (ECM 1993)★★★, with the Hilliard Ensemble *Officium* (ECM New Series 1994)★★★, *Visible World* (ECM 1996)★★★★.

●COMPILATIONS: *Works* (ECM 1984)★★★.

GAUGHAN, DICK

b. Leith, Scotland. A veteran of Scotland's thriving folk circuit, Gaughan rose to national prominence in the 70s as a member of the Boys Of The Lough. From there he became a founder member of Five Hand Reel, an electric folk group that enjoyed considerable critical acclaim. Gaughan left them in 1978 following the release of their third album, *Bonnie Earl Of Moray*, having already embarked on a concurrent solo career. His early releases, *No More Forever* and *Kist O' Gold*, concentrated on traditional material, while *Coppers And Brass* showcased guitar interpretations of Scottish and Irish dance music. However, it was the release of *Handful Of Earth* that established Gaughan as a major force in contemporary folk. This politically charged album included the beautifully vitriolic 'Workers' Song' and 'World Turned Upside Down' while at the same time scotched notions of nationalism with the reconciliatory 'Both Sides Of The Tweed'. This exceptional set is rightly regarded as a landmark in British traditional music, but its ever-restless creator surprised many commentators with *A Different Kind Of Love Song*, which included a version of Joe South's 60s protest song, 'Games People Play'. Gaughan has since enjoyed a fervent popularity both at home and abroad while continuing to pursue his uncompromising, idiosyncratic musical path. Gaughan calls himself a 'hard-nosed Communist' and is a passionate lover and supporter of Scotland, while not tolerating any anti-English feeling. Both his playing and singing come from the heart and in the 90s he is arguably Scotland's greatest living troubadour.

●ALBUMS: *No More Forever* (Trailer 1972)★★, *Coppers And Brass* (Topic 1977)★★, *Kist O' Gold* (Transatlantic 1977)★★★, *Gaughan* (Topic 1978)★★★, with Tony Capstick, Dave Burland *Songs Of Ewan MacColl* (RCA 1978)★★★, *Handful Of Earth* (Topic 1981)★★★★, with Andy Irvine *Parallel Lines* (1982)★★★, *A Different Kind Of Love Song* (1983)★★★, *Fanfare For Tomorrow* (1985)★★★, *Live In Edinburgh* (Sliced Bread

1985)★★★, *True And Bold* (1986)★★★, *Songs For Peace* (Folk Freak 1988)★★★, *Woody Lives* (Black Crow 1988)★★, *Call It Freedom* (Celtic 1989)★★★, *Sail On* (Greentrax 1996)★★★.

GAYE BYKERS ON ACID

This UK rock group employed an image which combined traditional biker attire with elements of psychedelia and hippie camp. They were led by the colourful figure of Mary Millington, aka Mary Mary (b. Ian Garfield Hoxley; vocals), alongside Kevin Hyde (drums), Robber (b. Ian Michael Reynolds; bass) and Tony (b. Richard Anthony Horsfall; guitar). They were later complemented by disc jockey William Samuel Ronald Monroe ('Rocket Ronnie'). Mary Mary, who had once come second in Leicester's Alternative Miss Universe competition, was often to be seen in platform shoes and dresses, which fuelled the critics' confusion with regard to the band's name and gender orientation. Their debut album, *Drill Your Own Hole*, required purchasers to do just that, as the record was initially issued without a hole in its centre. After leaving Virgin Records they set up their own label, Naked Brain, quite conceivably because nobody else would have them. Subsequent to the band's demise, which may or may not prove permanent, Kevin instigated a new band, GROWTH, with Jeff (ex-Janitors). Tony teamed up with Brad Bradbury in Camp Collision, while Mary Mary joined ex-members of Killing Joke, Ministry and Public Image Limited in the multi-member outfit, Pigface. The 90s would bring a more permanent home for his talents in the shape of Hyperhead, formed with Karl Leiker (ex-Luxuria; Bugblot).

●ALBUMS: *Drill Your Own Hole* (Virgin 1987)★★★, *Stewed To The Gills* (Virgin 1989)★★★, *GrooveDiveSoapDish* (Bleed 1989)★★★, *Cancer Planet Mission* (Naked Brain 1990)★★, *From The Tomb Of The Near Legendary* (1993)★★.
●VIDEOS: *Drill Your Own Brain* (1987).

GEFFEN, DAVID

b. 1941, New York, USA. Geffen has become one of the richest individuals in rock through his activities as manager, label owner and film producer. Geffen got his start in show business in the mailroom of the William Morris Agency. He became the manager of Laura Nyro in 1968, signing her to Columbia Records. Next Geffen formed a company with Elliott Roberts, to manage Crosby, Stills And Nash, Joni Mitchell, Jackson Browne, Linda Ronstadt and others. He started his first label,

Asylum Records in 1970. A year later it was sold to WEA Records for $7,000,000 and Geffen stayed on as chairperson. He was promoted to chief of Elektra/Asylum in 1973, briefly signing Bob Dylan. He became vice-chairman of Warner Brothers Pictures two years later. Ill health forced Geffen to leave the music business for four years but he returned in 1980 with Geffen Records, whose roster included John Lennon. During this period, David also started Geffen Films, with distribution by Warner Brothers. Among his movie productions were *Risky Business* and *Little Shop Of Horrors*, while on Broadway he produced *Cats* and *Dreamgirls*. In 1989, Geffen sold his label to MCA for over 500 million dollars in stock and when MCA itself was bought by Japanese company Matsushita he took further profits. At MCA, he remained chairman of Geffen Records and introduced a new label, DGC. He recently founded Dreamworks, who financed the buy out of George Michael from Sony.

●FURTHER READING: *The Hit Men*, Frederick Dannen.

GENE LOVES JEZEBEL

Identical twins Jay (John) and Mike Aston, ostensibly Gene Loves Jezebel, enjoyed cult appeal, largely within the UK gothic rock community, but achieved greater success in America. The pair grew up in the South Wales town of Porthcawl, together with guitarist Ian Hudson. After moving to London, they made their debut in late 1981 supporting the Higsons. A recording deal with Situation 2 resulted in 'Shavin' My Neck' (a collection of demos) the following May. The dense, experimental sound was matched by live performances, featuring bassist Julianne Regan and drummer Dick Hawkins, where they mixed almost tribal rhythms with furious guitar work. Hawkins was replaced by a succession of drummers, including John Murphy (ex-Associates; SPK) and Steve Goulding, while Regan left to front All About Eve. Her space was filled by Hudson, allowing Albio De Luca (later of Furyo) to operate as guitarist in time for 'Screaming (For Emmalene)' in 1983. Following Luca and Goulding's departure, Hudson reverted to guitar and Hawkins/Murphy offered a two-pronged drum attack. Murphy then left before a third single, the strong, commercial sound of 'Bruises' (1983). Hot on its heels came the Jezebels' powerful debut album, *Promise*, promoted by a John Peel BBC radio session. A trip to the USA in 1984 to work with John Cale ensued, before returning for two quick-fire singles 'Influenza

(Relapse)' and 'Shame (Whole Heart Howl)'. Marshall then left, Mike Aston briefly switching from rhythm guitar to play bass, before Peter Rizzo was recruited. Ex-Spear Of Destiny drummer Chris Bell arrived in place of Hawkins, but it was a year before 'The Cow' hit the UK independent charts, preceding *Immigrant* in June 1985. After 'Desire' in November, the band left for a further north American tour, a traumatic time that led to Hudson's departure, ex-Generation X guitarist James Stevenson taking his place. The group skirted the Top 75 with 'Sweetest Thing' and *Discover* (which included a free live album) while 'Heartache' hinted at a passing interest in dance music. They subsequently concentrated their efforts on the US market. However, all was not well in the Jezebels camp, and Mike Aston left the group in mid-1989. In 1993 Gene Loves Jezebel, now comprising Jay Aston, Rizzo, Stevenson and Robert Adam, released *Heavenly Bodies*.

●ALBUMS: *Promise* (Situation 2 1983)★★★, *Immigrant* (Beggars Banquet 1985)★★★, *Discover* (Beggars Banquet 1986)★★★, *The House Of Dolls* (Beggars Banquet 1987)★★, *Kiss Of Life* (Beggars Banquet 1990)★★, *Heavenly Bodies* (Savage/Arista 1993)★★★.

●COMPILATIONS: *Some Of The Best Of Gene Loves Jezebel: From The Mouths Of Babes* (Avalanche 1995)★★★.

GENERAL PUBLIC

When the Birmingham ska-influenced Beat disbanded, the band's two vocalists Dave Wakeling and Ranking Roger formed General Public with ex-Specials bassist Horace Panter (bass) Stoker (drums), Micky Billingham (keyboards) and Kevin White (guitar), plus veteran saxophonist Saxa. A self-titled debut single on Virgin Records combined a strong pop sound with an underlying dance feel and brushed the UK charts. 'Tenderness', in October, fared better in the USA (on IRS), coinciding with a fine debut album, *All The Rage*. Without a British hit, its blend of musical influences, characterized by Roger's all-round skills, were largely ignored. General Public tried again in 1986 with *Hand To Mouth* but despite a stab at the singles market with 'Faults And All', the world seemed oblivious and the band disappeared. Ranking Roger more recently surfaced in a revitalized International Beat. A new album finally appeared in 1995 with the line-up now consisting of Wakeling, Ranking Roger, Michael Railton (vocals/keyboards), Norman Jones (vocals/percussion), Wayne Lothian (bass) and Dan Chase

(drums). Produced by Jerry Harrison the album sounded fresh and energetic. In addition to invigorating originals such as 'It Must Be Tough' and 'Rainy Days' there was an interesting ska/reggae version of Van Morrison's 'Warm Love'.

●ALBUMS: . . . *All The Rage* (Virgin 1984)★★★, *Hand To Mouth* (Virgin 1986)★★★, *Rub It Better* (Epic 1995)★★★.

GENESIS

This leading UK band first came together at the public school Charterhouse. Peter Gabriel (b. 13 May 1950, London, England; vocals), Tony Banks (b. 27 March 1951, East Heathly, Sussex, England; keyboards) and Chris Stewart (drums) were in an ensemble named the Garden Wall, and joined forces with Anthony Philips (guitar/vocals) and Mike Rutherford (b. 2 October 1950; bass/guitar/vocals), who were in a rival group, the Anon. In January 1967, the student musicians sent a demonstration tape to another Charterhouse alumnus, Jonathan King, then at Decca Records. King financed further recordings and also christened the band Genesis. They recorded one single, 'The Silent Sun' in 1968, but it was not until the following year that their debut album *From Genesis To Revelation* was issued. Its lack of success left them without a label until the enterprising Tony Stratton-Smith signed them to his recently formed Charisma Records in 1970. The group had already lost three drummers from their line-up before finding the perfect candidate that August. Phil Collins (b. 31 January 1951, London, England) had already worked with a professional group, Flaming Youth, and his involvement would later prove crucial in helping Genesis achieve international success.

The already recorded *Trespass* was issued in October 1970, but sold poorly. Further line-up changes ensued with the arrival of new guitarist Steve Hackett (b. 12 February 1950, London, England). The group were already known for their highly theatrical stage act and costumes, but this did not help record sales. When the 1971 album *Nursery Cryme* also failed commercially, the group were again in danger of being dropped from their label. Success on the continent brought renewed faith, which was vindicated with the release of *Foxtrot*. The album reached the UK Top 20 and included the epic live favourite 'Supper's Ready'. Over the next two-and-a-half years, Genesis increased their profile with the bestselling albums *Selling England By The Pound* and *The Lamb Lies Down On Broadway*. Having reached a new peak, however, their prospects were completely undermined by the shock departure of singer Gabriel in May 1975.

Many commentators understandably wrote off Genesis at this point, particularly when it was announced that the new singer was to be their drummer Collins. The streamlined quartet proved remarkably resilient, however, and the succeeding albums *A Trick Of The Tail* and *Wind And Wuthering* were well received. In the summer of 1977, Hackett left to pursue a solo career, after which Genesis carried on as a trio, backed by various short-term employees. Amazingly, the group appeared to grow in popularity with the successive departure of each key member. During 1978, they received their first gold disc for the appropriately titled *And Then There Were Three* and two years later enjoyed a chart-topping album with *Duke*. With various solo excursions underway, Genesis still managed to sustain its identity as a working group and reached new levels of popularity with hits in the USA. By late 1981, they were in the US Top 10 with *Abacab* and could rightly claim to be one of the most popular groups in the world. Helped by Collins' high profile as a soloist, they enjoyed their biggest UK singles hit with 'Mama' and followed with 'Thats All' and 'Illegal Alien'. Both *Genesis* and *Invisible Touch* topped the UK charts, while the latter also reached number 1 in the USA. By the mid-80s, the group format was not sufficient to contain all their various projects and Collins pursued a parallel solo career, while Rutherford formed the hit group Mike And The Mechanics. Meanwhile, Genesis soldiered on, reuniting at various intervals for tours and albums. There was no sign of decline in their popularity and in America they had a number 1 single in 1986 with 'Invisible Touch', while the following four singles all made the US Top 5. Although their working partnership is less prolific these days, the concept of Genesis continues, amid a myriad of offshoot projects. In 1991, the group reconvened to record and issue *We Can't Dance*. Although this was their first album in over five years it immediately topped the charts throughout the world confirming their status as one of the world's leading bands.

●ALBUMS: *From Genesis To Revelation* (Decca 1969)★, *Trespass* (Charisma 1970)★★, *Nursery Cryme* (Charisma 1971)★★★, *Foxtrot* (Charisma 1972)★★★, *Genesis Live* (Charisma 1973)★★, *Selling England By The Pound* (Charisma 1973)★★★, *The Lamb Lies Down On Broadway* (Charisma 1974)★★★★, *A Trick Of The Tail* (Charisma 1976)★★★, *Wind And Wuthering* (Charisma 1977)★★★, *Seconds Out* (Charisma 1977)★★, *And Then There Were Three* (Charisma 1978)★★★, *Duke* (Charisma 1980)★★★★, *Abacab* (Charisma 1981)★★★, *3 Sides Live* (Charisma 1982)★★, *Genesis* (Charisma 1983)★★★, *Invisible Touch* (Charisma 1986)★★★, *We Can't Dance* (Virgin 1991)★★★, *The Way We Walk - Vol. 1: The Shorts* (Virgin 1992)★★, *Live The Way We Walk - Vol. 2: The Longs* (Virgin 1993)★★.

●VIDEOS: *Three Sides Live* (1986), *Live: The Mama Tour* (1986), *Visible Touch* (1987), *Genesis 2* (1988), *Genesis 1* (1988), *Invisible Touch Tour* (1989), *Genesis, A History 1967-1991* (1991), *A History* (1992), *Live: The Way We Walk* (1993).

●FURTHER READING: *Genesis: The Evolution Of A Rock Band*, Armando Gallo. *Genesis Lyrics*, Kim Poor. *Genesis: Turn It On Again*, Steve Clarke. *Genesis: A Biography*, Dave Bowler and Brian Dray.

GEORGIA SATELLITES

This rock quartet was formed in 1980 in Atlanta, USA, when Dan Baird (vocals) and Rick Richards (guitar) started jamming together inspired by the Rolling Stones, Kinks and Pretty Things. Rick Price (bass) and Mauro Magellan (drums) completed the band. Magellan was the only one of the four not to originate from the Deep South, hailing from Miami. After a small-budget independent label album they forged their debut UK and US hit in 1987 with the original song 'Keep Your Hands To Yourself' from a self-titled album. They followed up with two cover versions; the Woods' 'Battleship Chains' and Chan Romero's 'Hippy Hippy Shake'. Signed to Elektra Records, their debut album rose to number 5 in the US charts. One of their heroes, Ian McLagen (Small Faces), later joined them for *In The Land Of Salvation And Sin*. The group has now disbanded.

●ALBUMS: *Keep The Faith* (Making Waves 1985)★★★, *The Georgia Satellites* (Elektra 1986)★★★, *Open All Night* (Elektra 1988)★★★, *In The Land Of Salvation And Sin* (Elektra 1989)★★★, *Shaken Not Stirred* (3NM 1997)★★★.

●COMPILATIONS: *Let It Rock: Best Of* (Elektra 1993)★★★★.

GILL, JOHNNY

b. 1965, Washington, DC, USA. Gill's expertly delivered soul vocal chords have been working since an early age. At the age of seven he was singing with his three brothers in the gospel quartet the Wings Of Faith. Following his meeting and subsequent recording with Stacey Lattishaw (*Perfect Combination*) she proffered his rough demo to

Ahmet Ertegun at Atlantic Records. His debut came the following year in 1983 with *Johnny Gill*; although this and the follow up failed to dent the charts he had built a considerable reputaion with his voice. In 1986 he replaced Bobby Brown in New Edition towards the end of their heyday and sang on their comeback hit and swansong 'If It Isn't Love' in 1988. He reinvented himself once again forming a similar pattern; working with Lattishaw followed by another self-titled solo album, this time on Motown Records. The mix was favourable having been produced by Jimmy Jam And Terry Lewis and LA And Babyface. The album was a major success and established him a potential modern R&B giant spawning a number of US hits including 'Rub You The Right Way', 'My My My' and 'Fairweather Friend'. Futher success came as a featured vocalist with Shanice ('Silent Prayer') and Shabba Ranks ('Slow And Sexy'). 'This Floor' kept his profile alive in 1993, together with Provocative, but is was not until 1996 that a new solo album was announced, three years after his last.

●ALBUMS: *Johnny Gill* (Cotillion 1983)★★, with Stacey Lattishaw *Perfect Combination* (Cotillion 1984)★★, *Chemistry* (Cotillion 1985)★★★, *Johnny Gill* (Motown 1990)★★★★, *Provocative* (Motown 1993)★★★, *Let's Get The Mood Right* (Motown 1996)★★★.

GILL, VINCE

b. Vincent Grant Gill, 5 April 1957, Norman, Oklahoma, USA. Gill's father, a lawyer who played in a part-time country band, encouraged his son to have a career in country music. While still at school, Gill joined the bluegrass group Mountain Smoke. He moved to Louisville in 1975 and joined Bluegrass Alliance with Sam Bush and Dan Crary. In 1979, he was able to demonstrate his vocal, guitar, banjo and fiddle talents with Pure Prairie League and he is present on their albums, *Can't Hold Back*, *Firin' Up* and *Something In The Night*. Gill then became part of Rodney Crowell's backing group, the Cherry Bombs. He began his solo recording career with a six-track mini-album for RCA Records, *Turn Me Loose*. His duet with Rosanne Cash, 'If It Weren't For Him', was withdrawn due to contractual difficulties. He was among the musicians on Patty Loveless's albums, and she repaid the compliment by duetting with him on 'When I Call Your Name', which was named Single Of The Year by the Country Music Association. Gill married Janis Oliver from Sweethearts Of The Rodeo and he wrote 'Never Knew Lonely' while he was homesick in Europe.

He added vocal harmonies to Dire Straits' best-selling album, *On Every Street*, and Mark Knopfler in turn appears on his album, *Pocket Full Of Gold*. In 1991, he had Top 10 US country chart hits with 'Pocket Full Of Gold', 'Liza Jane' and 'Look At Us' and was voted the Male Vocalist Of The Year at the 1991 Country Music Association's Annual Awards Show. In 1992, he went one better when he not only picked up the Male Vocalist Of The Year award but also the award for Song Of The Year with 'Look At Us', a song he co-wrote with Max D. Barnes. In 1992 additions to his chart successes included 'I Still Believe In You' (number 1) and 'Take Your Memory With You' (number 2). Gill later revealed he had turned down the offer to join Dire Straits for their 1992 world tour, preferring to concentrate on his own career. Among performers and public alike, Gill is now established as one of the most successful figures in country music. The excellent *When Love Finds You* included a tribute to Conway Twitty, 'Go Rest High On That Mountain', with harmonies from Patty Loveless and Ricky Skaggs. Gill has mainly concentrated on romantic ballads although he proved he could turn his hand to soul music when he duetted with Gladys Knight on 'Ain't Nothing Like The Real Thing', (although at the time, Knight was not quite sure who he was). His duet with Dolly Parton on her incredibly successful 'I Will Always Love You' was a US country hit in 1995, after they performed it on the CMA awards. Gill also proved he has a long future in the limelight by being an excellent host at the awards ceremony.

●ALBUMS: *Turn Me Loose* mini-album (RCA 1983)★★, *The Things That Matter* (RCA 1984)★★★, *Vince Gill* (RCA 1985)★★★, *The Way Back Home* (1987)★★★, *When I Call Your Name* (MCA 1989)★★★, *Pocket Full Of Gold* (MCA 1991)★★★, *I Never Knew Lonely* (MCA 1992)★★★, *I Still Believe In You* (MCA 1992)★★★★, *Let There Be Peace On Earth* (MCA 1993)★★, *When Love Finds You* (MCA 1994)★★★★, *High Lonesome Sound* (MCA 1996)★★★.

●COMPILATIONS: *Souvenirs* (MCA 1995)★★★★, *The Essential Vince Gill* (RCA 1996)★★★★.

●VIDEOS: *I Still Believe In You* (1993).

GIPSY KINGS

These popular flamenco artists initially formed as an offshoot of the family group Los Reyes (the Kings), who in the 70s and 80s were led by father José Reyes. Together with sons Nicolas and Andre Reyes, they enjoyed significant domestic success in Spain, though contrary to popular belief their origins lay on the other side of the French border. In 1982 Nicolas and Andre Reyes teamed up with Chico Bouchikhi when he married into the family. The Gipsy Kings were formed when they joined with three cousins from the Baliardo family (Diego, Tonino and Paci), each member singing and playing guitar with Nicolas Reyes as their lead vocalist. As the Gipsy Kings they attempted to reach a worldwide market for the first time, initially earning their reputation by playing to film stars and royalty at France's St. Tropez holiday resort. They made their worldwide debut with a self-titled album for Elektra Records in 1988, by which time several collections had already been released in Spain and mainland Europe. As before, the music blended elements of the Nueva Andalucia flamenco style, with the inclusion of percussive foot stamps, handclaps and vocals drawn from Arabic music. As well as their trademark multi-guitar sound, they also added other components, including drums, bass, percussion and synthesizers. This effort to broaden their appeal resulted in a massive international breakthrough, including number 1 status in the Canadian and Australian charts, with *Gipsy Kings* peaking at number 16 in the UK. The ensuing *Mosaique*, though marginally less successful, saw the group incorporate elements of jazz (collaborating with jazz/salsa artist Ruben Blades) and 50s/60s pop. In the early 90s the personnel shuffled, and the group lost much of the momentum they had built up in the previous decade, despite the release of a live album in 1993.

●ALBUMS: *Luna De Fuego* (Phillips 1983)★★★, *Alegria* (Elektra 1986)★★★, *Gipsy Kings* (Elektra 1988)★★★, *Mosaique* (Elektra 1989)★★★, *Love & Liberty* (Elektra 1993)★★, *Tierra Gitana* (Atlantic 1996)★★.

GIRLSCHOOL

The all-female heavy metal band had its origins in Painted Lady, founded by teenagers Enid Williams (bass/vocals) and Kim McAuliffe (b. 13 April 1959; guitar/vocals). The remaining members of Painted Lady formed Tour De Force. After Kelly Johnson (guitar/vocals), and Denise Dufort (drums) had joined in 1978, the name became Girlschool and the independently produced single, 'Take It All Away', for City Records, led to a tour with Motörhead. As a direct result of Lemmy's sponsorship of the band they signed to the Bronze label in 1980, for whom Vic Maile produced the first two albums. There was a minor hit with a revival of Adrian Gurvitz's 'Race With The Devil', a 1968 suc-

cess for Gun, before the group combined with Motörhead to reach the UK Top 10 as Headgirl with an EP entitled *St Valentine's Day Massacre*. The lead track was a frenetic version of Johnny Kidd's 'Please Don't Touch'. Girlschool had smaller hits later in 1981 with 'Hit And Run' and 'C'mon Let's Go', but soon afterwards a bored Williams was replaced by former Killjoys bass player Gill Weston (introduced to the band by Lemmy). Williams would subsequently form melodic rockers Framed, record two singles with Sham 69's Dave Parsons, and work on sessions with disco producer Biddu, before joining Moho Pack. Later she sang, variously, country and opera (appearing in Fay Weldon's *The Small Green Space* and her own opera, *The Waterfall*) and taught performance and vocal skills. Girlschool persevered, meanwhile, with Slade's Noddy Holder and Jim Lea producing the glam-influenced *Play Dirty*, which found the group opting for a more mainstream rock sound.

In 1984 Johnson left the band for an unsuccessful solo career (later abandoning music and taking up sign language to work with the deaf) and Girlschool added guitarist Chris Bonacci and lead singer Jacqui Bodimead from Canis Major. The group also switched visual style towards a more glam rock look as they recorded 'I'm The Leader Of The Gang' with Gary Glitter in 1986. After the departure of Weston in 1987 ex-Rock Goddess bass player Tracey Lamb was brought in, while McAuliffe left to work with punk singer Beki Bondage and present the cable show *Raw Power*. She also wrote an unpublished script for a rock show with Philthy Taylor of Motörhead. Later she formed Strange Girls with Toyah, Dufort and Williams. Girlschool persevered until splitting following a Russian tour supporting Black Sabbath. In the 90s McAuliffe brought the group back together with the addition of ex-Flatmates bass player Jackie Carrera.

●ALBUMS: *Demolition* (Bronze 1980)★★, *Hit 'N' Run* (Bronze 1981)★★★, *Screaming Blue Murder* (Bronze 1982)★★★, *Play Dirty* (Bronze 1983)★★★, *Running Wild* (Mercury 1985)★★, *Nightmare At Maple Cross* (GWR 1986)★★, *Take A Bite* (GWR 1988)★★, *Live* (Communiqué 1995)★★.

●COMPILATIONS: *Race With The Devil* (Raw Power 1986)★★★, *Cheers You Lot* (Razor 1989)★★, *Collection* (Castle 1991)★★★, *From The Vaults* (Sequel 1994)★★.

●VIDEOS: *Play Dirty Live* (1984), *Bronze Rocks* (1985).

GLASS, PHILIP

b. 31 January 1937, Chicago, Illinois, USA. Glass was educated at the University of Chicago and the Juilliard School before going to Paris to study with Nadia Boulanger between 1963 and 1965. By this time he knew that 'playing second fiddle to Stockhausen didn't seem like a lot of fun. . . . There didn't seem to be any need to write any more of that kind of music. The only thing to do was to start somewhere else . . .' He did not know where that point was until he was hired to work on an Ornette Coleman film score. He did not want to change the music so Ravi Shankar was asked to write additional material which Glass orchestrated. As he struggled with the problem of writing down this music, Glass came to see that there was another way that music could be organized. It could be structured by rhythm. Instead of dividing the music up as he had been trying to do to write it down, the Indian musicians added to rhythmic phrases and let the music expand. With Ravi Shankar he had now also worked with a composer who was a performer. Glass travelled to North Africa and Asia before returning to New York in 1967 where he studied with the tabla player Alla Rakha. In 1968 he formed the ensemble he needed to perform the music he was now writing. This was the period of the purest minimalism with extending and contracting rhythmic figures in a stable diatonic framework performed at the kind of volume more often associated with rock music. Glass later described it as music which 'must be listened to as a pure sound event, an act without any dramatic structure.' It did not stay in that abstract world of pure sound for very long. In 1975 he had no record contract and began work with Robert Wilson on Einstein On The Beach which turned out to be the first of three operas on 'historical figures who changed the course of world events through the wisdom and strength of their inner vision'. Einstein On The Beach was premiered in Europe and reached the Metropolitan on 21 November 1976. He was signed by CBS Records in 1982 and produced the successful Glassworks. In 1970 he had been joined by Kurt Munkacsi, sound designer, mixer and engineer and the two explored all the potential studios and new technology on offer. The operas were produced in the studio first so that others could work with them and their final recordings were enhanced by the capabilities of the studio: 'We don't hang a mike in front of an orchestra. . . . Almost every section is extended electronically.' Although Glass's music has stayed close to the method he established in the early 70s, from Einstein On The Beach onwards the harmony has been richer and he has been willing to explore orchestral colour because 'the most important thing is that the music provides an emotional framework or context. It literally tells you what to feel about what you're seeing.' Much of his work since has been either for the stage or for film. This includes the two operas Satyagraha (1980) and Akhnaten (1984) and the films with Godfrey Reggio - Koyanisqatsi (1983) and Powaqqatsi (1988). In the late 80s and early 90s Glass also wrote film scores for The Thin Blue Line, Hamburger Hill, Candyman, Compassion In Exile: The Life Of The 14th Dalai Lama (1992). Glass's plans include a second opera with author Doris Lessing; a theatre work based on Cocteau's Orphee; a film based on Stephen Hawking's A Brief History Of Time, more work with Wilson and Hydrogen Jukebox; and an opera with Allen Ginsberg. Most recently, he co-operated with Brian Eno on an reappraisal of the latter's Low project for David Bowie and repeated the formula with Heroes in 1997.

● ALBUMS: Two Pages (Folkways 1974)★★★, Music In 12 Parts 1&2 (Cardine 1976)★★★, Solo Music (Shandar 1978)★★★★, Einstein On The Beach (CBS 1979)★★★, Glassworks (Columbia 1982)★★★★, Akhnaten (1984)★★★, Mishima (Nonesuch 1985), Satyagraha (1985)★★★, Songs From Liquid Days (Columbia 1986)★★★, Powaqqatsi soundtrack (Nonesuch 1988)★★, North Star (Virgin 1988)★★★, The Photographer (CBS 1988)★★, 1000 Airplanes On The Roof (Venture 1989)★★★, Solo Piano (1989)★★★★, with Ravi Shankar Passages (Private Music 1990)★★★, Low (Philips 1993)★★★, Hydrogen Jukebox (1994)★★★, Heroes (Point 1997)★★★.

GLASTONBURY FESTIVAL

The Glastonbury Festival, one of the most prestigious and distinctive occasions on the UK's music calendar, was started by the dairy farmer Michael Eavis (b. 17 October 1935, England) on his own land at Worthy Farm, in the Vale of Avalon, in 1970. Inspired by watching Led Zeppelin and Frank Zappa at the Bath Blues Festival of that year, the first Glastonbury Festival (or Fayre) took place a few weeks later. T. Rex were the headline act before an audience of 1500. After 1971's follow-up event with David Bowie and Fairport Convention the festival was not held again until 1979's Year Of The Child Benefit Concert. In the 80s and 90s it has grown in size and prestige, often signing major artists who share the festival's idealism and com-

mitment to good causes at a fraction of their normal fees. The event (usually running over three days from Friday to Sunday) was inspired by the 60s idealism of Eavis's youth, and 10 per cent of Glastonbury's gross receipts are always passed on to charity. Each year there are displays of cabaret, film, theatre and environmental activism (notably the Campaign For Nuclear Disarmament), as well as a musical doctrine which encompasses folk, jazz, classical and world music as well as the headline rock bands. However, not all the artists concerned have necessarily advocated the same radicalism, as Eavis recalled in his introduction to the 1986 festival programme: 'There are still some old hands that winge on about it being too political. Some of them even covered the CND symbol over the stage with a sun one year.' Continuing to grow in popularity, in 1995 Glastonbury sold its entire 80,000 allocation within one week of tickets going on sale. That year's festival celebrated 25 years since the first Glastonbury, and accordingly a live compilation of artists recorded at the show accompanied it (sadly few selections were in any way representative of the festival's past, with current headline bands such as Oasis, Blur and Radiohead dominating the track-listing). In recent years parts of the festival have also been filmed for broadcast on Channel 4, furthering the importance of the event as an outlet for left-field bands and as a melting pot for alternative lifestyles. Eavis took the decision not to hold a 1996 festival as he needed a rest and more time to devote to his farming activities. The 1997 event came close to being a disaster as artists and organizers struggled to keep the audience amused amidst a deluge of mud and rain. A number of acts had to be cancelled due to safety restrictions. Kula Shaker were one of the highlights, appearing twice in place of the cancelled Steve Winwood.
●ALBUMS: Various *Glastonbury 25th Anniversary - A Celebration* (Chrysalis 1995)★★★.

GO WEST

Peter Cox (b. 17 November 1955; vocals) and Richard Drummie (guitar/keyboard/vocals) were a songwriting partnership before forming Go West in 1982. The publishers, ATV Music, had teamed them up to write with artists such as Peter Frampton and David Grant. Chrysalis Records signed the duo and the result was a string of quality pop-rock hits in 1985, with 'We Close Our Eyes', 'Call Me', 'Don't Look Down' and a successful debut album. Sylvester Stallone heard the latter and liked it, and they wrote 'One Way Street'

for the *Rocky IV* soundtrack. The songs were well-crafted, well-arranged and produced and they used a regular session crew of talented and innovative players. Cox's voice was strong and distinctive and the Godley And Creme video for 'We Close Our Eyes' was extremely inventive. *Indian Summer* came after a lengthy gap and they demonstrated that they had developed and matured since they were first viewed as pop pin-ups.
●ALBUMS: *Go West* (Chrysalis 1985)★★★, *Bangs And Crashes* (Chrysalis 1985)★★, *Dancing On The Couch* (Chrysalis 1987)★★, *Indian Summer* (Chrysalis 1992)★★★.
●VIDEOS: *Aces And Kings: The Best Of The Videos* (Chrysalis 1993).

GO! DISCS

Small but perfectly formed record label founded by managing director Andy McDonald in 1983 with a loan of £1500. By the following year the label had found additional finance with a worldwide licensing agreement through Chrysalis Records. The highest profile early name attached to the label would be Billy Bragg, but it was the Housemartins who made the commercial breakthrough. Their 'Happy Hour' made the number 3 slot in 1986 and was followed by the Christmas number 1, 'Caravan Of Love'. Polygram took out a minority stake in the company in the following year, by which point their most successful act were on the verge of transmuting into the Beautiful South. *Welcome To The Beautiful South* duly emerged in 1989 as the label's first million-selling release. By the turn of the decade the same band's 'A Little Time' had gone to number 1, as had Beats International with 'Dub Be Good To Me' - a strong Housemartins connection maintained, as that group were headed by former drummer Norman Cook. A rare talent was unearthed with the discovery of the La's, while Go! Discs envisioned future trends by launching a dance subsidiary, Go! Beat (headed by Ferdy Hamilton). However, 1991 brought the first major setbacks. With bands like Father Father, Southernaires and Sound Systemme failing to recoup the label's promotion of them, and the recession biting, by the following year McDonald had been forced to lay off five staff. This was merely a temporary blip, and one straightened by the arrival of a revitalized Paul Weller. The Frank And Walters failed to sell in nearly the quantities envisaged, but this was compensated for by a number 1 single from Gabrielle. Weller's second album for the label, *Wild Wood*, was nominated for the Mercury Music Prize in 1994, before the multi-platinum Beautiful South compilation *Carry On Up The Charts* became Go! Discs' first number 1 album. Arguably just as significant was the arrival of the critically drooled-over Portishead. New arrivals for 1995 include Drugstore, Brit hip hop act the Muddie Funksters, while Go! Beat's roster boasts Gabrielle and Gloworm. John Martyn was signed in 1996. During a flurry of activity in the summer of 1996 founder McDonald walked out and then resigned following Polygram's purchase of his 51% equity. In a statement McDonald attacked Polygram and insisted he had been forced out.

GO-BETWEENS

Critics' favourites the Go-Betweens were formed in Brisbane, Australia, by Robert Forster (b. 29 June 1957, Brisbane, Queensland, Australia; guitar/vocals) and Grant McLennan (b. 12 February 1958, Rockhampton, Queensland, Australia; bass/guitar/vocals). These two song-writers were influenced by Bob Dylan, the Velvet Underground, the Monkees and the then-burgeoning New York no wave scene involving Television, Talking Heads and Patti Smith. Although sharing the same subject matter in trouble torn love songs, melancholy and desolation, Forster and McLennan's very different compositional styles fully complemented each other. The Go-Betweens first recorded as a trio on the Able label with drummer Dennis Cantwell. McLennan took on bass playing duties for 'Lee Remick'/'Karen' (1978) and 'People Say'/'Don't Let Him Come Back' (1979). By the time of the latter release the line-up had expanded to include Tim Mustafa (drums), Malcolm Kelly (organ), and Candice and Jacqueline on tambourine and vocals. The duo later reverted to the trio format on recruiting ex-Zero drummer, Lindy Morrison (b. 2 November 1951, Australia). At the invitation of Postcard Records boss Alan Horne, the band came to Britain to record a single, 'I Need Two Heads'. After this brief visit the group returned to Australia and recorded *Send Me A Lullaby* for the independent label, Missing Link. This roughly hewn but still charming set was heard by Geoff Travis at Rough Trade Records in London, who picked it up for distribution in the UK. Travis proposed that the Go-Betweens return to the UK, sign a recording deal and settle in London, which the group accepted. *Before Hollywood* garnered favourable reviews prompting many to predict a rosy future for the group. The highlight of this set was McLennan's evocative 'Cattle And Cane', one of the Go-Betweens' most enduring tracks (later covered by the Wedding Present). The problem of finding a permanent bass player was solved with the enrolment of Brisbane associate Robert Vickers (b. 25 November 1959; Australia) to the post, thus enabling McLennan to concentrate on guitar and giving the group a fuller sound. The move to a major label, Sire Records, brought expectations of a 'big breakthrough' in terms of sales, but for all the critical acclaim heaped upon *Springhill Fair*, success still eluded them. The break with Sire left the group almost on the brink of returning to Australia. The intervention of Beggars Banquet Records led them to a relationship which allowed the group to develop at their own pace. *Liberty Belle And The Black Diamond Express* presented what was by far their best album to date. The successful use of violins and oboes led to the introduction of a fifth member, Amanda Brown (b. 17 November 1965, Australia; violin/oboe/guitar/keyboards), adding an extra dimension and smoother texture to the band's sound. With *Tallulah* in 1987, the Go-Betweens made their best showing so far in the UK album chart, peaking at number 91. That same year, Robert Vickers left the group to reside in New York and was replaced by John Willsteed (b. 13 February 1957, Australia). Prior to the release of *16 Lovers Lane* in 1988 the single, 'Streets Of Your Town', an upbeat pop song with a dark lyric tackling the subject of wife-battering, was given generous airplay. However, once again, the single failed to make any impact on the charts despite being lavished with praise from the UK music press. The album only managed to peak at number 81, a hugely disappointing finale. After touring with the set, Forster and McLennan dissolved the group in December 1989. Remaining with Beggars Banquet, they both released solo albums. Forster's collection, *Danger In The Past*, was recorded with substantial assistance from Bad Seeds member, Mick Harvey. McLennan released an album with fellow Antipodean, Steve Kilbey from the Church, under the title Jack Frost (for Arista Records), before crediting himself as G.W. McLennan. His full solo set, *Watershed*, proved that neither artist was lost without the other. Lindy Morrison and Amanda Brown meanwhile, had formed a group, Cleopatra Wong. Since McLennan joined Forster onstage in 1991, continued rumours of a Go-Betweens reformation were strengthened by a Forster/McLennan support slot with Lloyd Cole in Toronto that same year. However, both artists continued to release solo records at regular intervals throughout the 90s, although critical acclaim was not matched by commercial success. In 1997, the group reformed for special live dates.

●ALBUMS: *Send Me A Lullaby* (Missing Link/Rough Trade 1981)★★, *Before Hollywood* (Rough Trade 1983)★★★, *Springhill Fair* (Sire 1984)★★★★, *Liberty Belle And The Black Diamond Express* (Beggars Banquet 1986)★★★★, *Tallulah* (Beggars Banquet 1987)★★★, *16 Lover's Lane* (Beggars Banquet 1988)★★★★. Solo: Robert Forster *Danger In The Past* (Beggars Banquet 1990)★★★★, *Calling From A Country Phone* (Beggars Banquet 1993)★★★, *I Had A New York Girlfriend* (Beggars Banquet 1994)★★★, *Warm Nights* (Beggars Banquet 1996)★★★. As Jack Frost *Jack Frost* (Arista 1990)★★★, *Snow Job* (Beggars Banquet 1996)★★★. Grant McLennan *Watershed* (Beggars Banquet 1991)★★★★, *Fireboy* (Beggars Banquet 1993)★★★, *Horsebreaker Star* (Beggars Banquet 1995)★★★, *In Your Bright Ray* (Beggars Banquet 1997).

●COMPILATIONS: *Very Quick On The Eye* (Man Made 1982)★★★, *Metals And Shells* (PVC 1985)★★★, *Go-Betweens 1978-1990* (Beggars Banquet 1990)★★★★.

●VIDEOS: *That Way* (1993).

Go-Go's

This all-female group, originally called the Misfits, were formed in California, USA, in 1978 by Belinda Carlisle (b. 17 August 1958, Hollywood, California, USA; lead vocals) and Jane Wiedlin (b. 20 May 1958, Oconomowoc, Wisconsin, USA; rhythm guitar/vocals). They were joined by Charlotte Caffey (b. 21 October 1953, Santa Monica, California, USA; lead guitar/keyboards), Elissa Bello (drums) and Margot Olaverra (bass). Inspired by the new wave scene, the Go-Go's performed bright, infectious harmony pop songs and were initially signed to the UK independent label Stiff Records and to Miles Copeland's IRS Records in the US, where they would enjoy practically all their success. By the time of the release of debut album *Beauty And The Beat*, Olaverra was replaced by ex-Textone Kathy Valentine and Bello by Gina Schock. Produced by Richard Gottehrer, who had earlier worked with a long line of female singers in the 60s, the sprightly pop qualities of *Beauty And The Beat* drew comparisons with Blondie, with whom Gottehrer had also worked. The album, which stayed at the US number 1 spot for 6 weeks in 1981, included 'Our Lips Are Sealed' (US Top 20), which was co-written by Wiedlin with Terry Hall of the Fun Boy Three, and 'We Got The Beat', which gave the group a US number 2 hit the following year.

The second album provided a further US Top 10 hit with the title track, but the group were by now showing signs of burn-out. Despite their 'safe' image, it later transpired that the Go-Go's were more than able to give the average all-male group a run for their money when it came to on-road excesses, which eventually took their toll. *Talk Show* reached the US Top 20, as did the most successful single culled from the set, 'Head Over Heels' (1984). With the break-up of the group in 1985, Belinda Carlisle subsequently pursued a successful solo career with assistance from Charlotte Caffey, who, for a time, appeared in her backing group. Caffey later formed the Graces with Meredith Brooks and Gia Campbell and recorded for A&M Records, releasing *Perfect View* in 1990, before moving into soundtrack work (*Clueless*). As well as recording as a solo artist, Wiedlin attempted to break into acting with a few minor film roles. Galvanized by her, the Go-Go's reformed briefly in 1990 for a benefit for the anti-fur trade organization, PETA (People for the Ethical Treatment of Animals). A fuller reunion took place in 1994 for well-paid shows in Las Vegas, prompted by which, IRS issued *Return To The Valley Of The Go-Go's*, a compilation of the band's best known moments with the addition of two new tracks. Carlisle then resumed her solo career, whilst Valentine and Schock formed The Delphines.

●ALBUMS: *Beauty And The Beat* (IRS 1981)★★★, *Vacation* (IRS 1982)★★★, *Talk Show* (IRS 1984)★★.

●COMPILATIONS: *Go-Go's Greatest* (IRS 1990)★★★, *Return To The Valley Of The Go-Go's* (IRS 1995)★★★.

GODARD, VIC, AND THE SUBWAY SECT

Godard, of Mortlake, London, England, put the band together during 1976, centring it on the friends with whom he used to attend Sex Pistols gigs. Subway Sect made their live debut on 20 September 1976 at the 100 Club, featuring Godard (vocals), Paul Myers (bass), Robert Miller (guitar), and Paul Smith (drums). They rehearsed in the Clash's studio. Their name came from brief flirtations with busking upon their inauguration. A series of short sets followed around the capital, featuring embryonic songwriting prowess to add to the abrasiveness they learnt at the hands of the Pistols. They opened for the Clash at Harlesdon and subsequently joined them for their *White Riot* tour. Mark Laff had replaced Smith, but he too was lured away (to Generation X) before they set out on their first European trek. Bob Ward was their new drummer when they released their April 1978 debut 'Nobody's Scared'. However, a major split followed leaving Ward and Godard to recruit John Britain (guitar), Colin Scott (bass) and Steve Atkinson (keyboards) in the summer of 1978. 'Ambition' was a trailblazing single, but afterwards the band fell into inactivity before reviving in 1980 with another new line-up with definite New Romantic leanings. This time the group featured Rob March (b. 13 October 1962, Bristol, England; guitar), Dave Collard (b. 17 January 1961, Bristol, England; keyboards), Chris Bostock (b. 23 November 1962, Bristol, England; bass) and Sean McLusky (b. 5 May 1961, Bristol, England; drums). *Songs For Sale* presented a collection of slick, swing-style songs with Godard adopting a cocktail-lounge, crooner image. Supports with the Clash and Buzzcocks had transformed into guest spots on the Altered Images tour, and Godard's new backing band would depart to find commercial success with JoBoxers. Disillusioned, Godard retired from the music scene, until in 1992 he beagn to show some interest in music again and tampered with his home recording studio. The results were found on his 1993 album.

●ALBUMS: *What's The Matter Boy* (Oddball 1980)★★, *Songs For Sale* (London 1982)★★★, as Vic Godard *T.R.O.U.B.L.E.* (Upside 1986)★★, as Vic Godard *The End Of The Surrey People* (Overground 1993)★★.

●COMPILATIONS: *A Retrospective (1977-81)* (Rough Trade 1984)★★★.

GOLDEN PALOMINOS

This unorthodox rock group's profile has been much enhanced by the glittering array of celebrities who have contributed to their work. They are led by drummer Anton Fier, who gave birth to the group in 1981. Prior to this he had spent time in the ranks of experimental bands Lounge Lizards and Pere Ubu. The band's albums have seen guest appearances by John Lydon (Sex Pistols, PiL), Michael Stipe (R.E.M.), Daniel Ponce, T-Bone Burnett, Jack Bruce and Syd Straw amongst others. The other core members of the band have been Bill Laswell (bass), Nicky Skopelitis (guitar) and Amanda Kramer (vocals). *Drunk With Passion* featured Stipe on 'Alive And Living Now', while Bob Mould provided the vocal on the excellent 'Dying From The Inside Out'. Richard Thompson also put in an appearance. Both Thompson and Stipe had already made their bow with the Palominos on *Visions Of Excess*, along with Henry Kaiser and Lydon. The maverick talents employed on *Blast Of Silence* included Peter Blegvad and Don Dixon, though it failed to match the impact of the debut - an obvious example of the sum not being as great as the parts. For *This Is How It Feels* in 1993, Frier avoided the super-session framework, recruiting instead singer Lori Carson who added both warmth and sexuality to that and the subsequent *Pure*. Mainstays Skopelitis and Laswell were additionally joined by the guitar of Bootsy Collins. His more recent work has also seen Frier adopted by the techno cognoscenti of Britain, where he believes the most innovative modern music is being made. This has led to remixes of Golden Palominos' work from Bandulu and Psychick Warriors Of Gaia appearing in UK clubs.

●ALBUMS: *The Golden Palominos* (OAO/Celluloid 1983)★★★★, *Visions Of Excess* (Celluloid 1985)★★★★, *Blast Of Silence* (Celluloid 1986)★★★, *A Dead Horse* (Celluloid 1989)★★★, *Drunk With Passion* (Restless 1991)★★★★, *This Is How It Feels* (Restless 1993)★★★, *Pure* (Restless 1995)★★★, *Dead Inside* (Restless 1996)★★★.

GORKA, JOHN

b. New Jersey, USA. Singer/songwriter Gorka, who possesses a rich and emotive baritone, honed his craft in America's north eastern folk scene of the early 80s before cutting a succession of acclaimed albums. Influenced by Tom Paxton, Richard Thompson and Tom Waits, among others, his musical career began in 1986 when he was attending Moravian College in Bethlehem, with the intention of studying history and philosophy. A small coffee-house folk scene had sprung up at a venue entitled Godfrey Daniels nearby, and Gorka graduated from open-mic spots to leading a group, the Razzy Dazzy Spasm Band. However, he then packed his guitar and took his songs out to the wider world, playing throughout north east America, then travelling to Texas where he won the Kerrville Folk Festival's New Folk Award in 1984. His debut album, *I Know*, was released on Red House Records in 1987, and featured the best of his early songwriting, including 'Blues Palace', 'Downtown Tonight' and 'Down In The Milltown'. Afterwards he would enjoy a more stable relationship with High Street/Windham Hill Records. The ensuing albums explored a multi-faceted talent, with earnest vocals bedecking Gorka's dry wit and sharp observations and character sketches. By the advent of *Temporary Road* in 1993 the artist found increased exposure, touring with Mary-Chapin Carpenter and Nanci Griffith. Meanwhile, a single drawn from the album, 'When She Kisses Me', was voted the CMT Best Independent Video Of The Year. For *Out Of The Valley* Gorka relocated from Bethlehem to Nashville, teaming up with producer/guitarist John Jennings. Together they recruited an all-star cast to accompany the singer, including Mary-Chapin Carpenter, Kathy Mattea, Leo Kottke and Dave Mattacks (Fairport Convention). Gorka also drew on the rich musical environment that surrounded him in the studio, using a guitar once owned by Buddy Holly, the piano with which Carole King had recorded *Tapestry* and a mixing board that had been used for sessions with Elvis Presley and Roy Orbison. This time the songs were less personally defined, using a third person mechanism to allow the artist to explore his characters, giving them individual motivation and colour.

●ALBUMS: *I Know* (Red House 1987)★★★★, *Land Of The Bottom Line* (Windham Hill 1990)★★★, *Jack's Crows* (High Street 1992)★★★, *Temporary Road* (High Street 1993)★★★, *Out Of The Valley* (High Street 1994)★★★★, *Between Five And Seven* (High Street 1996)★★★.

●VIDEOS: *Good Noise* (1994).

GRANT, AMY

b. 25 November 1960, Augusta, Georgia, USA. A huge influence on the development of modern gospel music, Grant's perennially youthful but always convincing vocal has imbued her many recordings with a purity of spirit and performance which can be awe-inspiring. Songs such as 'Angels', 'Raining On The Inside' and 'Find A Way', scattered through a consistently high quality recording career, have endeared her to both her massive contemporary and gospel audience as well as critics. Though originally primarily a religious performer, her material also blends in rhythms derived from modern R&B and soul while her lyrics contemplate subjects outside of the average gospel singer's repertoire. However, when secular subjects are tackled, there is an abiding spirituality to Grant's treatment of them that ensures her positioning as a gospel singer despite her 90s R&B success. 'The point of my songs is never singer-focused. It's experience-focused. When I go in the studio, I'm taking my experience as a wife and a mother with me.' Married to country singer-songwriter Gary Chapman, her audience is now as varied as her songwriting. 'When I was in high school, I listened to Aretha Franklin and the Jackson Five. I remember discovering R&B music then and Joni Mitchell too.' Though earlier albums had flirted with pop, rock, soul and country, her first truly secular release arrived in 1991 with *Heart In Motion*. With a major hit in 'Baby Baby', this move into the contemporary pop world was rewarded with platinum sales, and 52 consecutive weeks on the US Album Chart. Long-term collaborators Keith Thomas and Michael Omartian were again in place for the follow-up, *House Of Love*. Boosted by a strong duet with Vince Gill on the title-track and the presence of another hit single, 'Lucky One', this collection also included a cover version of the Joni Mitchell standard, 'Big Yellow Taxi'. By this time Grant was estimated to have sold in excess of 15 million albums, and, artistically and commercially, there is little to suggest that she is nearer the end than the beginning of that career.

●ALBUMS: *My Father's Eyes* (Myrrh/Reunion 1979)★★★, *Never Alone* (Myrrh/Reunion 1980)★★★, *In Concert Volumes One And Two* (Myrrh/Reunion 1981)★★★★, *Age To Age* (Myrrh/Reunion 1982)★★★★, *Straight Ahead* (A&M 1984)★★★★, *Unguarded* (A&M 1985)★★★, *A Christmas Album* (Myrrh/Reunion 1988)★★★, *Lead Me On* (A&M 1988)★★★, *Heart In Motion* (A&M 1991)★★★, *House Of Love* (A&M 1994)★★★.

●COMPILATIONS: *The Collection* (Myrrh/Reunion 1986)★★★★.

GRANT, DAVID

b. 8 August 1956, Kingston, Jamaica, West Indies. By the time everyone realized that Linx was not the spearhead of a new UK soul movement, singer David Grant had swapped his glasses and moustache for a sweatband and aerobics gear and went solo. Suddenly he was Britain's answer to Michael Jackson. He could dance, he was pretty and his voice was high, and 'Stop And Go', 'Watching You Watching Me', and 'Love Will Find A Way' all made the UK Top 30 in 1983. His songwriting partnership with Derek Bramble developed, resulting in the Steve Levine-produced, self-titled album. More memorable were his duets with Jaki Graham on the Spinners 'Could It Be I'm Falling In Love' and Todd Rundgren's 'Mated'. 'Hopes And Dreams' was an altogether weightier offering, with contributions from Aswad and Go West, but it just made the Top 100. Grant penned further hits for Gavin Christopher, Cheryl Lynn and Hot Chocolate. He has since maintained a loyal club following where his energetic 'soul' music is highly popular.

●ALBUMS: *David Grant* (Chrysalis 1983)★★★, *Hopes And Dreams* (Chrysalis 1985)★★, *Change* (Polydor 1987)★★, *Anxious Edge* (4th & Broadway 1990)★★.

GREEN ON RED

Formed as the Serfers in Tucson, Arizona, USA in 1981, the group featured Dan Stuart (guitar/vocals), Jack Waterson (bass) and Van Christian (drums). Christian was replaced by Alex MacNicol, and Chris Cacavas added on keyboards for the first EP, *Two Bibles*, released under their new group name. The band attracted attention as part of the 60s-influenced 'paisley underground' alongside the Rain Parade and the Dream Syndicate. However, Green On Red's sound owed more to Neil Young and country/blues traditions, an influence that became more apparent when Chuck Prophet IV joined on lead guitar in 1984. Sophisticated arrangements on 1987's *The Killer Inside Me* saw the group pushing for mainstream recognition, but shortly afterwards Waterson and Cacavas left to pursue solo careers. The remaining duo, Prophet and Stuart, forged ahead, using session musicians for the excellent *Here Come The Snakes*. Both members have operated outside the confines of the group, most notably Stuart's involvement on *Danny And Dusty* featuring Steve Wynn and members of the Long Ryders. In 1991 Green On Red re-emerged with *Scapegoats* recorded in Nashville with the help of Al Kooper on keyboards. Prophet's solo career took off in 1993 with the well-received *Balinese Dancer*.

● ALBUMS: *Green On Red* (Down There 1982)★★★, *Gravity Talks* (Slash 1984)★★★, *Gas Food Lodging* (Demon 1985)★★★, *No Free Lunch* (Mercury 1985)★★★, *The Killer Inside Me* (Mercury 1987)★★★★, *Here Come The Snakes* (Red Rhino 1989)★★★★, *Live At The Town And Country Club* limited edition mini-album (Polydor 1989)★★, *This Time Around* (Polydor 1990)★★★, *Scapegoats* (China 1991)★★★, *Too Much Fun* (Off Beat 1992)★★★. Solo: Chuck Prophet *Brother Aldo* (Fire 1990)★★★, *Balinese Dancer* (China 1993)★★★, *Feast Of Hearts* (China 1995)★★★. Dan Stuart *Danny And Dusty - The Lost Weekend* (1985)★★★. Chris Cacavas *Junkyard Love* (Normal 1989)★★★. Jack Waterson *Whose Dog* (World Service 1988)★★★.

GREGSON AND COLLISTER

This UK duo comprised Clive Gregson (b. 4 January 1955, Ashton-Under-Lyne, Manchester, England; guitar/keyboards/vocals), and Christine Collister (b. 28 December 1961, Douglas, Isle Of Man; guitar/percussion/vocals), and were one of the most notable duos working in folk music. Gregson was already known as the writer and prominent front man of the group Any Trouble, with whom he recorded five albums before turning solo. He released *Strange Persuasions* in 1985, and then became a member of the Richard Thompson Band. In addition, he acquired the role of producer on albums by such artists as the Oyster Band, Stephen Fearing and Keith Hancock. Another solo album was released in 1990, *Welcome To The Workhouse*, comprising material that had hitherto been unreleased. Collister had made a living singing and playing guitar in Italian bars, and as a session singer for Piccadilly Radio in Manchester. She was discovered performing in a local club by Gregson and this led to her place in the Richard Thompson Band, and subsequent position in the duo with Gregson himself. Collister has also provided backing vocals for Loudon Wainwright III and Mark Germino. Her warm sensuous vocals were instantly recognizable as the soundtrack to the BBC television series *The Life And Loves Of A She Devil*. Gregson's lyrical ability and harmonies, together with Collister's unmistakable vocal style produced a number of critically acclaimed albums of note. The duo toured extensively throughout the UK, USA and Canada, and also played in Japan and Europe. In 1990 the duo completed their first tour of Australia. In March 1992 they announced the start of a farewell tour. Later that year following the tour, Collister worked with Barb Jungr (of Jungr And Parker) and Heather Joyce in a part-time unit, the Jailbirds. Both Gregson and Collister continue to work and perform but no longer together. Collister was touring with Richard Thompson in the mid-90s, and Gregson started to work with Boo Hewerdine in addition to releasing his own solo records.

● ALBUMS: *Home And Away* (Eleventh Hour 1986)★★★, *Mischief* (Special Delivery 1987)★★★, *A Change In The Weather* (Special Delivery 1989)★★★★, *Love Is A Strange Hotel* (Special Delivery 1990)★★★, *The Last Word* (Special Delivery 1992)★★★★. Solo: Clive Gregson *Strange Persuasions* (Demon 1985)★★★, *Welcome To The Workhouse* (Special Delivery 1990)★★★, *Carousel Of Noise* (Flypaper 1994)★★★, *People And Places* (Demon 1995)★★★, *I Love This Town* (Compass 1996)★★★.

GRIFFIN

US rock band Griffin were originally formed in 1981 around a trio of William Rodrick McCay (vocals), Rick Cooper (guitar) and Rick Wagner (drums). However, it was only with the expanded line-up of Yaz (guitar) and Thomas Sprayberry (bass) that the group began to make progress. Signed to Shrapnel/SPV Records in 1985, they made their debut with *Flight Of The Griffin*, a solid hard rock collection with the material consistently accentuating McCay's vocal delivery. Yaz and Sprayberry then left the group, leaving Cooper to double up on bass for Griffin's second album, 1987's *Protectors Of The Lair*. Once again this failed to expand their audience and the original trio parted soon after its release.

●ALBUMS: *Flight Of The Griffin* (Shrapnel/SPV 1985)★★★, *Protectors Of The Lair* (SPV 1987)★★★.

GRIFFITH, NANCI

b. 6 July 1953, Seguin, Texas, USA. Singer/songwriter Griffith brilliantly straddles the boundary between folk and country music, with occasional nods to the mainstream rock audience. Her mother was an amateur actress and her father a member of a barbershop quartet. They passed on their interest in performance to Nanci, and although she majored in education at the University of Texas, she eventually chose a career in music in 1977, by which time she had been performing in public for 10 years. In 1978 her first album, *There's A Light Beyond These Woods*, was released by a local company, BF Deal Records. Recorded live in a studio in Austin, it included mainly her own compositions, along with 'Dollar Matinee', written by her erstwhile husband, Eric Taylor. The major song on the album was the title track, which Griffiths later re-recorded, concerning the dreams she shared with her childhood friend, Mary Margaret Graham, of the bigger world outside Texas. As a souvenir of her folk act of the time, this album was adequate, but it was not until 1982 that *Poet In My Window* was released by another local label, Featherbed Records. Like its predecessor, this album was re-released in 1986 by the nationally distributed Philo/Rounder label. It displayed a pleasing maturity in composition, the only song included which she had not written herself being 'Tonight I Think I'm Gonna Go Downtown' penned by Jimmie Gilmore and John Reed (once again, Eric Taylor was involved as associated producer/bass player), while the barbershop quartet in which her father, Marlin Griffith, sang provided harmony vocals on 'Wheels'.

By 1984 she had met Jim Rooney, who produced her third album, *Once In A Very Blue Moon*, released in 1985 by Philo/Rounder. This album featured such notable backing musicians as lead guitarist Phillip Donnelly, banjo wizard Bela Fleck, Lloyd Green and Mark O'Connor. It was recorded at Jack Clement's Nashville studio. As well as more of her own songs, the album included her version of Lyle Lovett's 'If I Was The Woman You Wanted', Richard Dobson's 'Ballad Of Robin Wintersmith' and the superb title track written by Pat Alger - Griffiths named the backing band she formed in 1986 the Blue Moon Orchestra. Following on the heels of this artistic triumph came 1986's *Last Of The True Believers*. Released by Philo/Rounder with a similar recipe to that which set its predecessor apart from run of the mill albums by singer/songwriters, it included two songs which would later achieve US country chart celebrity as covered by Kathy Mattea, Griffith's own 'Love At The Five And Dime' and Pat Alger's 'Goin' Gone', as well as several other songs which would become Griffith classics, including the title track, 'The Wing And The Wheel' (after which Griffiths formed her music publishing company), 'More Than A Whisper' and 'Lookin' For The Time (Working Girl)', plus the fine Tom Russell song 'St. Olav's Gate'. This album became Griffith's first to be released in the UK when it was licensed by Demon Records around the time that Griffith was signed by MCA Records. Her debut album for her new label, *Lone Star State Of Mind*, was released in 1987, and was produced by MCA's golden-fingered Tony Brown, who had been the most active A&R person in Nashville in signing new talent, including Steve Earle and Lyle Lovett as well as Griffith herself, who co-produced it. The stunning title track again involved Alger as writer, while other notable tracks included the remake of 'There's A Light Beyond These Woods' from the first album, Robert Earl Keen Jnr.'s 'Sing One For Sister' and Griffith's own 'Ford Econoline' (about the independence of 60s folk singer Rosalie Sorrels). However, attracting most attention was Julie Gold's 'From A Distance', a song which had become a standard by the 90s as covered by Bette Midler, Cliff Richard and many others. Griffith herself published the song, and her version was the first major exposure given to the song. *Little Love Affairs*, released in 1988, was supposedly a concept album but major songs included 'Outbound Plane', which she co-wrote with Tom Russell, veteran hit writer Harlan Howard's '(My Best Pal's In Nashville) Never Mind' and John Stewart's 'Sweet Dreams Will Come', as well as a couple of collaborations with James Hooker (ex-Amazing Rhythm Aces), and keyboard player of the Blue Moon Orchestra. Later that year Griffith recorded and released a live album, *One Fair Summer Evening*, recorded at Houston's Anderson Fair Retail Restaurant. Although it only included a handful of songs which she had not previously recorded, it was at least as good as *Little Love Affairs*, and was accompanied by a live video. However, it seemed that Griffiths' talent was falling between the rock and country audiences, the latter apparently finding her voice insufficiently radio-friendly, while Kathy Mattea, who recorded many of the same song some time after Griffith, became a major star.

In 1989 came *Storms*, produced by the legendary Glyn Johns, who had worked with the Beatles, the Rolling Stones, the Eagles, Steve Miller, the Who, Joan Armatrading and many more. Johns made an album with a bias towards American radio, which became Griffith's biggest seller at that point. The album featured, as well as Hooker, Irish drummer Bran Breen (ex-Moving Hearts), Bernie Leadon (ex-Eagles), guitarist Albert Lee and Phil Everly of the Everly Brothers providing harmony vocals on 'You Made This Love A Teardrop'. Although it was a sales breakthrough for Griffith, it failed to attract country audiences, although it reached the Top album chart in the UK, where she had regularly toured since 1987. However her major European market was Ireland, where she was regarded as virtually a superstar.

Late Night Grande Hotel was produced by the British team of Rod Argent and Peter Van Hook, and again included a duet with Phil Everly on 'It's Just Another Morning Here', while English singer Tanita Tikaram provided a guest vocal on 'It's Too Late'. In 1991, singing 'The Wexford Carol', she was one of a number of artists who contributed tracks to the Chieftains' *The Bells Of Dublin*. *Other Voices Other Rooms* was a wholehearted success artistically and commercially. Griffith interpreted some outstanding songs by artists such as Bob Dylan ('Boots Of Spanish Leather'), John Prine ('Speed Of The Sound Of Loneliness') and Ralph McTell ('From Clare To Here'). *Flyer*, another exquisite record, maintained her popularity with some excellent new material, which indicated a strengthening and hardening of her vocals, with greater power and a hint of treble. She continues to fail to put a foot wrong.

●ALBUMS: *There's A Light Beyond These Woods* (BF Deal 1978)★★, *Poet In My Window* (Philo 1982)★★, *Once In A Very Blue Moon* (Philo 1984)★★★, *Last Of The True Believers* (Philo 1986)★★★★, *Lone Star State Of Mind* (MCA 1987)★★★★, *Little Love Affairs* (MCA 1988)★★★★, *One Fair Summer Evening* (MCA 1988)★★★★, *Storms* (MCA 1989)★★★★, *Late Night Grande Hotel* (MCA 1991)★★★★, *Other Voices Other Rooms* (MCA 1993)★★★★, *Flyer* (MCA

1994)★★★★, *Blue Roses From The Moon* (East West 1997)★★★★.
●COMPILATIONS: *The Best Of* (MCA 1993)★★★★.

GRP RECORDS

One of the most recent success stories in the recording industry has been the growth of the New York 'niche' market label, GRP Records. With a clearly defined path of MOR Jazz, the company has grown from a small production unit to a major turnover organization. The founders were Larry Rosen and Dave Grusin, who in 1976 started ancillary production work for Patti Austin and Earl Klugh. By 1982 they had created such a reputation that they were able to start GRP. Much of their success has been due to a refusal to compromise on quality. Both were early converts to new digital technology and pioneered compact disc recordings. With a strategy aimed at the 25-50 age group their 'all digital recordings' have been extraordinarily successful. In addition to Dave Grusin's considerable output their roster of artists is formidable and includes: Lee Ritenour, David Benoit, Diane Schuur, Special EFX, Eddie Daniels, Dave Valentin, Kevin Eubanks and the Rippingtons. Additionally they have released works by older established artists from the world of jazz like Gerry Mulligan, the Count Basie Orchestra, the Glenn Miller Orchestra, Dizzy Gillespie and Stéphane Grappelli. Still viewed as an independent company, the organization is now mainly handled by the original visionaries, Grusin and Rosen.
●VIDEOS: *GRP All-Star Big Band Live!* (GPR 1993).

GRUSIN, DAVE

b. 26 June 1934, Littleton, Colorado, USA. He played piano semi-professionally while studying at the University of Colorado, and almost abandoned music to become a veterinary surgeon. Grusin stated: 'I'm still not sure I made the right decision, a lot of dead cows might still be alive today if I hadn't gone to music school.' His musical associates at the time included Art Pepper, Terry Gibbs and Spike Robinson, with whom he worked extensively in the early 50s. In 1959 Grusin was hired as musical director by singer Andy Williams, a role he maintained into the mid-60s. An eclectic musician, Grusin worked with mainstream artists such as Benny Goodman and Thad Jones and also worked with hard bop players. He made many recording dates, including several in the early 70s, accompanying singers, among whom were Sarah Vaughan and Carmen McRae. Around this same time Grusin began to concentrate more and more on electric piano and keyboards, recording with Gerry Mulligan, Lee Ritenour in the jazz world and with Paul Simon and Billy Joel in pop. He has arranged and produced for the Byrds, Peggy Lee, Grover Washington Jnr., Donna Summer, Barbra Streisand, Al Jarreau, Phoebe Snow and Patti Austin. He is also co-founder and owner, with Larry Rosen, of GRP Records, a label that they founded in 1976 and has an impressive catalogue of singers, jazz and jazz-rock artists including Diane Schuur, Lee Ritenour, David Benoit, his brother Don Grusin, Michael Brecker, Chick Corea, Steve Gadd, Dave Valentin, Special EFX and Gary Burton. The success of GRP has much to do with Grusin's refusal to compromise on quality. With Rosen he pioneered an all digital recording policy, and using 'state of the art' technology their productions reach a pinnacle of recorded quality.

In addition to his activities as a player and producer, Grusin has written extensively for films and television. His portfolio is most impressive; in addition to winning a Grammy in 1984 his film scores have received several Academy Award nominations, and include *Divorce Italian Style*, *The Graduate*, *The Heart Is A Lonely Hunter*, *Three Days Of The Condor*, *Heaven Can Wait*, *Reds*, *On Golden Pond*, *The Champ*, *Tootsie*, *Racing With The Moon*, *The Milagro Beanfield War*, *Clara's Heart*, *Tequila Sunrise*, *A Dry White Season*, *The Fabulous Baker Boys*, *Bonfire Of The Vanities*, *Havana*, *For The Boys*, and *The Firm* (1993). Additionally, one of his most evocative songs, 'Mountain Dance', was the title song to *Falling In Love*. His American television credits include *St. Elsewhere*, *Maude*, *Roots*, *It Takes A Thief* and *Baretta*. Grusin is a master musical chemist - able to blend many elements of pop and jazz into uplifting, intelligent and accessible music. In 1993 he appeared as a performer on the international jazz circuit.

●ALBUMS: *Candy* soundtrack (1961)★★, *The Many Moods Of Dave Grusin* (1962)★★, *Kaleidoscope* (1964)★★, *Don't Touch* (1964)★★★, *Discovered Again* (1976)★★, *One Of A Kind* (GRP 1977)★★★, *Dave Grusin And The GRP All Stars Live In Japan Featuring Sadao Watanabe* (GRP 1980)★★★, *Out Of The Shadows* (GRP 1982)★★★, *Mountain Dance* (GRP 1983)★★★★, *Night Lines* (GRP 1984)★★★, with Lee Ritenour *Harlequin* (GRP 1984)★★, *The NYLA Dream Band* (GRP 1988)★★★, with Don Grusin *Sticks And Stones* (GRP 1988)★★★, *Migration* (GRP 1989)★★, *The Fabulous Baker Boys* film soundtrack (GRP 1989)★★★, *Havana* (GRP 1990)★★★, *The Gershwin Collection* (GRP 1992)★★★★, *Homage To Duke* (GRP 1993)★★★.

●COMPILATIONS: *Cinemagic* (1987)★★★★, *Dave Grusin Collection* (GRP 1991)★★★★.

GUN CLUB

Briefly known as Creeping Ritual, the Gun Club were formed in Los Angeles, California, USA, in 1980. Led by vocalist Jeffrey Lee Pierce (b. 27 June 1958, El Monte, California, USA, d. 31 March 1996, Salt Lake City, Utah, USA), the group was initially completed by Kid Congo Powers (b. Brian Tristan; guitar), Rob Ritter (bass) and Terry Graham (drums). *Fire Of Love* established the unit's uncompromising style which drew from delta blues and the psychobilly tradition of the Cramps. The set included anarchic versions of Robert Johnson's 'Preaching The Blues' and Tommy Johnson's 'Cool Drink Of Water'. Pierce's own compositions followed a similar pattern. There would be some clumsy 'deep southisms' in his early lyrics: 'Searching for niggers down in the dark', being one example, but generally most of Pierce's lyrics were non-specific in their hate-mongering (example: 'I'm gonna buy me a gun just as long as my arm, And kill everyone who ever done me harm'). However, the Gun Club's progress was undermined by Congo's defection to the Cramps. *Miami* was the first Gun Club recording for Animal Records, owned by ex-Blondie guitarist Chris Stein (Pierce had previously been president of the Blondie fan club). Although lacking the passion of its predecessor, it established the group as one of America's leading 'alternative' acts, but further changes in personnel, including the return of the prodigal Congo, ultimately blunted Pierce's confidence (which itself was hardly aided by a self-destructive alcohol problem). He disbanded the group for a solo career in 1985; *Two Sides Of The Beast* was then issued in commemoration, but the group reformed in 1987 to record *Mother Juno* (produced by Robin Guthrie of the Cocteau Twins). Subsequent albums were disappointing and the singer, frequently based in London, continued to battle with his personal demons while the Gun Club's ranks fluctuated. Former members of the Gun Club, including Patricia Morrison who joined Sisters Of Mercy, looked elsewhere for employment. In the 90s he reconstituted the Gun Club with a returning Kid Congo, Nick Sanderson (drums) and his Japanese wife Romi Mori on bass. The occasional inspired live performance was all that remained, however, in continuation of the benchmark for impulsive, powerful music he had established in the early 80s. By the mid-90s Pierce's self-destructive lifestyle had begun to catch up with him, and he died in March 1996 from a brain haemorrhage although years of alcoholism and drug problems had probably been a contributing factor.

●ALBUMS: *Fire Of Love* (Ruby 1981)★★, *Miami* (Animal 1982)★★, *Sex Beat 81* (Lolita 1984)★★, *Las Vegas Story* (Animal 1984)★★★, *Danse Kalinda Boom* (Dojo 1985)★★, *Mother Juno* (Fundamental 1987)★★★, *Pastoral Hide And Seek* (Fire 1990)★★★, *Divinity* (New Rose 1991)★★★, *The Gun Club Live In Europe* (Triple X 1992)★★, *Lucky Jim* (New Rose 1993)★★★. Solo: Jeffrey Lee Pierce *Wildweed* (Statik 1985)★★, *Ramblin' Jeffrey Lee And Cypress Grove With Willie Love* (Triple X 1992)★★★, *Ahmed's Wild Dream* (Solid 1993)★★.

●COMPILATIONS: *The Birth, The Death, The Ghost* (ABC 1984)★★, *Two Sides Of The Beast* (Dojo 1985)★★★, *In Exile* (Triple X 1992)★★★.

●VIDEOS: *Live At The Hacienda, 1983* (1994), *Preaching The Blues* (Visionary 1995).

GUNS N'ROSES

The founder-members of the most controversial heavy rock band of the late 80s included Axl Rose (an anagram of Oral Sex) (b. William Bailey, 6 February 1962, Lafayette, Indiana, USA) and Izzy Stradlin (b. Jeffrey Isbell, 8 April 1962, Lafayette, Indiana, USA). Vocalist Rose, who had first sung at the age of five in a church choir, met guitarist Stradlin in Los Angeles in 1984. He changed his name to Rose at age 17 when he discovered who his real father was, the Axl prefix coming from a band with whom he had rehearsed in Indiana. With Tracii Guns (guitar) and Rob Gardner (drums), they formed a rock band called, in turn, Rose, Hollywood Rose and L.A. Guns. Soon afterwards, Guns and Gardner left, to be replaced by two members of local band Road Crew, drummer Steven Adler (b. 22 January 1965, Cleveland, Ohio, USA) and guitarist Slash (b. Saul Hudson, 23 July 1965, Stoke-on-Trent, Staffordshire, England), the son of a clothes designer and an album cover artist. With bass player Duff McKagan (b. Michael McKagan, 5 February 1964, Seattle, Washington, USA; ex-Fartz; Fastbacks; Ten Minute Warning; and approximately 30 other north-west outfits), the band was renamed Guns N'Roses. Following a disastrous US Hell Tour '85, Guns N'Roses released an EP, *Live?!*@ Like A Suicide* on the independent Uzi/Suicide label. This brought intense interest from critics and record companies and in 1986 the group signed to Geffen Records who reissued the EP the following year. During 1987 they toured extensively, though the group's appetite for self-

destruction became readily apparent when Fred Coury of Cinderella was recruited to temporarily replace Adler after the latter had broken his hand in a brawl. February 1988 also saw the first internal rift when Rose was kicked out, then reinstated, within three days. Their debut album, *Appetite For Destruction*, produced by Mike Clink, went on to sell 20 million copies worldwide and reached number 1 in America a year after its release date. 'Welcome To The Jungle' was used on the soundtrack of the Clint Eastwood film, *Dead Pool*, and reached the Top 30 in the UK. The group's regular live shows in the USA and Europe brought frequent controversy, notably when two fans died during crowd disturbances at the Monsters Of Rock show in England in 1988. In 1989 the eight-song album *G N' R Lies* was issued, becoming a big hit on both sides of the Atlantic, as were the singles 'Sweet Child O' Mine' (written about Axl's girlfriend and later wife Erin Everly, daughter of Don Everly), 'Paradise City' and 'Patience'. However, Rose's lyrics for 'One In A Million' were widely criticized for their homophobic sentiments. Although Guns N'Roses appeared at the *Farm Aid IV* charity concert, their career was littered with incidents involving drugs, drunkenness and public disturbance offences in 1989/90. At times their excesses made the band seem like a caricature of a 60s supergroup, with headlines screaming of Stradlin urinating in public on an aeroplane, Slash and McKagan swearing live on television while collecting trophies for Favorite Heavy Metal/Hard Rock Artists and Album at the American Music Awards, and Rose's on-off relationship with Everly. In September 1990 Adler was replaced by Matt Sorum (b. 19 November 1960, Mission Viejo, California, USA) from the Cult. Apparently more restrained in their private life, Guns N'Roses added Dizzy Reed (b. Darren Reed; keyboards) for a 1991 world tour where their exciting and unpredictable performances brought favourable comparisons with the heyday of the Rolling Stones. In September the group released the highly publicized pair of albums, *Use Your Illusion I* and *II*, preceded by a version of Bob Dylan's 'Knockin' On Heaven's Door' from the soundtrack of *Days Of Thunder*. Further hit singles, 'You Could Be Mine' (featured in the film *Terminator II*) and 'Don't Cry', followed. The *Illusion* brace immediately sat astride the top two album positions in the *Billboard* chart, the first occasion on which they had been thus dominated since Jim Croce enjoyed both number 1 and 2 spots in 1974. Izzy Stradlin found the pressure too much and left late in 1991, going on to form the Ju Ju Hounds. He was replaced by Gilby Clarke (ex-Kill For Thrills). Meanwhile, Slash's growing reputation brought guest appearances on recordings by Dylan and Michael Jackson. He also contributed to tribute albums to Muddy Waters and Les Paul. Guns N'Roses' appearance at the 1992 Freddie Mercury AIDS Benefit concert prompted the reissue of 'Knockin' On Heaven's Door', and while Dylan fans groaned with disbelief the band's vast following were happy to see their heroes scale the charts shortly after its release. While both of their previous albums remained on the US chart, having sold more than 4 million copies each, it was not until the end of 1993 that any new material emerged. When it arrived it came in the form of *The Spaghetti Incident*, a much vaunted collection of covers with a punk foundation. A perfunctory affair, it was mainly notable for lining the pockets of several long-forgotten musicians (UK Subs, Nazareth, Misfits, Fear, etc.), and including a song written by mass murderer Charles Manson. The main inspiration behind the project, Duff McKagan, had his debut solo album released at the same time. However, reports of an unhappy camp continued to filter through in 1994, leading to the dismissal of Gilby Clarke towards the end of the year, following his own, highly public, outbursts about Rose. His replacement was Paul Huge, a former flatmate of Rose from his Indiana days. Huge's first recording with the band was a cover of the Rolling Stones' 'Sympathy For The Devil' for the soundtrack to Anne Rice's *Interview With A Vampire*. However, Paul Huge stayed only briefly with the band, as did his replacement, Zakk Wylde (ex-Ozzy Osbourne), who did not record a single note with the band before falling out irreconcilably with Rose. In May 1995 Izzy Stradlin was reinstated as second guitarist but by the end of the year Rose and Slash were again at loggerheads and no new album was imminent. Sorum and McKagen meanwhile teamed up with guitarist Steve Jones for the spin-off band the Neurotic Outsiders. Slash confirmed Rose's departure in November 1996, although this was reversed in February 1997 when Rose allegedly purchased the rights to the Guns N'Roses name.

●ALBUMS: *Appetite For Destruction* (Geffen 1987)★★★★, *G N' R Lies* (Geffen 1989)★★★, *Use Your Illusion I* (Geffen 1991)★★★, *Use Your Illusion II* (Geffen 1991)★★★, *The Spaghetti Incident* (Geffen 1993)★★.

●VIDEOS: *Use Your Illusion I* (1992), *Making Fuckin' Videos Vol. 1* (1993), *Making Fuckin' Videos Vol. 2* (1993), *The Making Of Estranged - Part IV Of The Trilogy* (1994).

●FURTHER READING: *In Their Own Words*, Mark Putterford. *Appetite For Destruction: The Days Of Guns N'Roses*, Danny Sugerman. *Guns N'Roses: The World's Most Outrageous Hard Rock Band*, Paul Elliot. *The Most Dangerous Band In The World*, Mick Wall. *The Pictures*, George Chin. *Over The Top: The True Story Of ...* , Mark Putterford. *Lowlife In The Fast Lane*, Eddy McSquare. *Live!*, Mick St. Michael.

H

HAGAR, SAMMY

b. 13 October 1947, Monterey, California, USA.
Hagar is a singer, guitarist and songwriter whose
father was a professional boxer. Legend has it that
Elvis Presley persuaded him not to follow in his
father's footsteps, and instead he started out in 60s
San Bernardino bands the Fabulous Castillas,
Skinny, Justice Brothers and rock band, Dust
Cloud. He joined Montrose in 1973 (formed by ex-
Edgar Winter guitarist Ronnie Montrose) and
became a minor rock hero in the Bay Area of San
Francisco, in particular acquiring a reputation as a
potent live performer. After two albums with
Montrose he left to go solo, providing a string of
semi-successful albums and singles. He took with
him Bill Church (bass), and added Alan Fitzgerald
(keyboards), and later Denny Carmassi (drums,
also ex-Montrose). The band picked up good press
on support tours with Kiss, Boston and Kansas, but
by 1979 Hagar had a radically altered line-up with
Gary Pihl (guitar), Chuck Ruff (drums) and Geoff
Workman (keyboards) joining Hagar and Church.
1983's *Three Lock Box* became their first Top 20
entry, including 'Your Love Is Driving Me Crazy',
which made number 13 in the singles chart. Hagar
then took time out to tour with Journey guitarist
Neal Schon, Kenny Aaronson (bass) and Mike
Shrieve (drums, ex-Santana), recording a live
album under the band's initials HSAS. Under this
title they also cut a studio version of Procol
Harum's 'Whiter Shade Of Pale'. Returning to solo
work Hagar scored his biggest hit to date with the
Voice Of America out-take, 'I Can't Drive 55'. In 1985
he surprised many by joining Van Halen, from
whom Dave Lee Roth had recently departed.
However, he has continued to pursue a parallel, if
intermittent solo career. His solo work continues to
be characterized by a refreshing lack of bombast in
a genre not noted for its subtlety.
●ALBUMS: *Nine On A Ten Scale* (Capitol 1976)★★,
Red (Capitol 1977)★★★, *Musical Chairs* (Capitol
1978)★★★, *All Night Long - Live* (Capitol 1978)★★,
Street Machine (Capitol 1979)★★★, *Danger Zone*
(Capitol 1979)★★★, *Live, Loud And Clear* (Capitol
1980)★★, *Standing Hampton* (Geffen 1982)★★★,
Three Lock Box (Geffen 1983)★★, *Live From London
To Long Beach* (Capitol 1983)★★, *VOA* (Geffen
1983)★★★, as Hagar, Schon, Aaronson And
Shrieve *Through The Fire* (Geffen 1984)★★, *Sammy
Hagar* (Geffen 1987)★★, *Red* (Geffen 1993)★★,
Unboxed (Geffen 1994)★★, *Marching To Mars* (MCA
1997)★★.
●COMPILATIONS: *Rematch* (Capitol 1983)★★★,
The Best Of (Geffen 1993)★★★.
●FILMS: *Footloose* (1984).

HAGEN, NINA

b. 11 March 1955, Berlin, Germany. After her parents divorced in 1957, she was raised in a suburb in
the eastern bloc by her actress mother and her
stepfather, dissident poet and songwriter Wold
Biermann. In 1964, she joined the Thalmann-
Pioneers, a Communist youth organization and,
four years later, the Freie Deutsche Jugend - from
which she was excluded for her hand in a demonstration (instigated by Biermann) against the participation of East German militia in the Soviet invasion of Czechoslovakia. On failing a 1972 entrance
test for a Berlin-Schönweide drama college, she
sang a mixture of blues and soul with a Polish
outfit for several months prior to enrolment at the
Studio Für Unterhaltungsmusik (Studio For
Popular Music) where she was an outstanding student. She toured East Germany as featured vocalist
with the Alfons Wonneberg Orchestra before
fronting Automobil and then Fritzens
Dampferband (Fred's Steamboat Band) but when
Biermann was expelled from Soviet territory in
1976, she followed him to West Germany where
her worth as an entertainer was sufficiently known
for a recording contract to be offered. Her imagination captured by punk, she flew to London
where she and Ari Up of the Slits collaborated on a
number of songs. Back in Germany, she formed
the Nina Hagen Band with former members of Lok
Kreuzberg - Bernhard Potschka (guitar) and
Manfred Praeker (bass) - plus Herwig Mitteregger
(drums). From the group's debut album, 'African
Reggae' was enough of a 'turntable hit' to bring
Hagen a cult following - particularly in Australia -
which grew steadily during the 80s. Nevertheless,
the saga of her rise to qualified fame remains more
intriguing than her subsequent career.
●ALBUMS: *The Nina Hagen Band* (1978)★★★,
Unbehagen (Columbia 1979)★★, *Nunsexmockrock*
(Columbia 1982)★★, *Angstios* (Columbia 1983)★★,
Fearless (Columbia 1984)★★, *Revolution Ballroom*
(Activ 1995)★★.

HAIRCUT 100

Formed in Beckenham, Kent, England in 1980, the group began on a part-time basis with a line-up comprising Nick Heyward (b. 20 May 1961, Beckenham, Kent, England; vocals), Les Nemes (b. 5 December 1960, Croydon, Surrey, England; bass) and Graham Jones (b. 8 July 1961, Bridlington, North Yorkshire; guitar). Early the following year they were augmented by Memphis Blair Cunningham (b. 11 October 1957, Harlem, New York, USA; drums) , Phil Smith (b. 1 May 1959, Redbridge, Ilford, Essex; saxophone), and Mark Fox (b. 13 February 1958; percussion). Engineer/manager Karl Adams secured them a contract with Arista Records where they were placed in the hands of producer Bob Sargeant. Their teen appeal and smooth punk-pop sound was perfect for the time and it came as no surprise when their debut single 'Favourite Shirts (Boy Meets Girl)' climbed to number 4 in the UK charts. The follow-up, 'Love Plus One' did even better, firmly establishing the group as premier pop idols in 1982. Their career received a serious setback, however, when the engaging frontman Nick Heyward split for a solo career. In January 1983 Haircut 100 were relaunched with replacement vocalist Mark Fox. Although the group hoped to succeed with a new audience, their singles sold poorly, and following the release of their 1984 album *Paint On Paint*, they disbanded. Drummer Cunningham later reappeared in one of the many line-ups of the Pretenders.

●ALBUMS: *Pelican West* (Arista 1982)★★★★, *Paint On Paint* (Arista 1984)★★.
●COMPILATIONS: *Best Of Nick Heyward And Haircut 100* (Ariola 1989)★★★★, *The Greatest Hits Of Nick Heyward & Haircut 100* (RCA Camden 1996)★★★★.
●FURTHER READING: *The Haircut 100 Catalogue*, Sally Payne. *Haircut 100: Not A Trace Of Brylcreem*, no editor listed.

HAIRSPRAY

A 1988 film set in America in 1962, *Hairspray* featured rock and pop luminaries Deborah Harry (as Velma Von Tussle), Sonny Bono (as Franklin Von Tussle) and Divine (as Edna Turnblad). It is among writer/director John Waters most famous 'schlock classics'. The plot introduced later mainstream chat show host Ricki Lake's character, Tracy Turnblad. By entering the Baltimore *Corny Colins* television show and winning their talent contest, she proves that 'fat girls can dance'. However,

jealous schoolfriends and anxious teachers make her life a misery after Tracy becomes the regular star of the show. She and friend Penny travel to Baltimore's black quarter and find boyfriends - Tracy's being an Elvis impersonator/lookalike. However, when their new boyfriends are brought back to the studio their colour causes problems. Eventually it is decided that a live *Corny Colins* show is to be broadcast from Mr and Mrs Von Tussle's amusement arcade. A riot follows and Tracy is arrested. This means she is unable to compete at the car show pageant and Amber Von Tussle (Colleen Fitzpatrick) usurps her place. Predictably, Tracy is returned to her rightful position as queen of the pageant after the students protest. As a nostalgia spoof the film included some nice touches - not least cameos by Ric Ocasek of the Cars as 'the beatnik cat' and an excellent period soundtrack - but failed to convince cinema reviewers. Divine died just two weeks after the film's premiere.

HALF MAN HALF BISCUIT

Five piece 'scally' outfit whose penchant for seeing the funny side of British society's underbelly won them many friends in the mid-80s. From Birkenhead, Merseyside, England, their line-up comprised Nigel Crossley (vocals/bass), S. Blackwell (guitar), N. Blackwell (vocals/guitar), D. Lloyd (keyboards) and P. Wright (drums). Their original demo tape for Skeleton Records was heard by Probe Plus boss Geoff Davies; who signed the band to his label in 1985. Test pressings of their first release were dispatched to disc jockey John Peel who immediately arranged a session. *The Trumpton Riots* 12-inch EP, released in February 1986, became a resident in the indie charts for weeks, propelled by the Biscuits' endearing view of the idiosyncracies of British life. Their songwriting vernacular included cult television programmes and celebrities (snooker referee Len Ganley; sports presenter Dickie Davies) in unforgettable song titles; '99% Of Gargoyles Look Like Bob Todd', 'I Love You Because (You Like Jim Reeves)', 'Rod Hull Is Alive - Why?' Throughout their work they displayed an admirable lack of careerism; turning down key television appearances due to favoured football club Tranmere playing at home that night. They also decided to split up at the peak of their success, though they did reform in mid-1990 to release a remarkable version of 'No Regrets'; featuring another cult television personality, Margi Clarke, on vocals. The subsequent *McIntyre, Treadmore And Davitt* and *This Leaden Pall* continued to mine the band's parochial good humour and downbeat view of life, including songs of the calibre of 'Outbreak Of Vitas Geralitis', 'Everything's AOR' and '13 Eurogoths Floating In The Dead Sea'.

●ALBUMS: *Back In The DHSS* (Probe Plus 1986)★★★, *McIntyre, Treadmore & Dewitt* (Probe Plus 1991)★★★, *This Leaden Pall* (Probe Plus 1993)★★★, *Some Call It Godcore* (Probe Plus 1995)★★★.

●COMPILATIONS: *Back Again In The DHSS* (Probe Plus 1987)★★★, *ACD* same album as *Back Again* on CD with extra tracks (Proble Plus 1989)★★★.

●VIDEOS: *Live* (Alternative Image 1993).

HAMMER, M.C.

b. Stanley Kirk Burrell, 30 March 1962, Oakland, California, USA. Immensely popular rap artist, originally working under the MC Hammer prefix, who synthesized the street sounds of black cultural alienation, or his interpretation thereof, to great commercial gain. After failing in professional baseball and attending a college course in communications, Hammer (named after his likeness to Oakland A's big hitter Henry 'Hammerin' Hank' Aaron) joined the US Navy for three years. Indeed, his first forays into music were financed by baseball players Mike Davis and Dwayne Murphy, allowing him to form Bustin' records and release the solo single, 'Ring 'Em'.

He had previously been part of religious rap group The Holy Ghost Boys. Together with a backing band consisting of two DJs and singers Tabatha King, Djuana Johnican and Phyllis Charles, he cut a 1987 debut set, *Feel My Power*. A minor hit, it did enough to bring Hammer to the attention of Capitol Records. After contracts were completed, including a reported advance of $750,000 (unheard of for a rap artist), the album was reissued under the title *Let's Get It Started*. Such success was overshadowed, however, by that of the follow-up, *Please Hammer Don't Hurt 'Em*. Following massive exposure due to sponsorship deals with British Knights footwear and Pepsi Cola, the album began a residency at the top of the US charts for a record-breaking 21 week run. The single, 'U Can't Touch This', embodied his appeal, with near constant rotation on pop channel MTV, and dance routines which were the equal of Michael Jackson. The single sampled Rick James' 'Super Freak', creating a precedent for follow-ups 'Have You Seen Her' (the Chi-Lites) and 'Pray' (Prince; 'When Doves Cry'). While an on-going duel with white rapper Vanilla Ice raged, critics pointed out the plagiarism

that underpinned both artists' most successful work. Unperturbed, Hammer was being praised as a suitable role model for black youth (not least by himself), and was honoured by 'MC Hammer Days' in Los Angeles and Fremont. His first single to be free of sampling, 'Here Comes The Hammer', became an unexpected failure by stalling at number 51 in the US charts, despite its appearance on the soundtrack to *Rocky V*. A multitude of awards, including Grammys, Bammys and International Album Of The Year at the Juno awards in Canada, reflected the worldwide success of the album.

Its long awaited successor, *Too Legit To Quit*, featured a direct challenge this time: 'I'm taking on Michael Jackson from a spirit of competition . . . t's an opportunity to put on the world's greatest musical event . . . You've had Ali and Frazier . . . so why not Hammer versus Jackson?' The sleevenotes to the album expanded on his desire for black youth to rid themselves of drugs and resurrect their Christian morality through self education. His exposure to US audiences already included the TV adventures of cartoon hero 'Hammerman', and a Mattel Hammer doll and attached ghetto blaster. However, his ability to sustain a challenge to the Jackson crown would inevitably be limited by his own admission that: 'I'm not a singer. I'm a rapper'. Despite a soundtrack hit with 'The Addams Family', heavily promoted in the film of the same title, Hammer's fortunes declined. In 1992 *The San Francisco Examiner* reported that Hammer faced financial ruin after poor attendances for his *Too Legit To Quit* tour, promoting an album that had seen him tracing a more R&B-based groove. Though Hammer denied there was any truth in such stories, it was obvious a rethink was needed.

By 1994 there had been a huge image switch, from harem pants and leather catsuits to dark glasses and a goatee beard. The resultant album pulled in producers G-Bomb from Grand Jury Records, the Hines brothers from Detroit, Teddy Riley and members of the Dogg Pound, and specifically went after the Oakland G-Funk sound of artists like Too Short. Hammer as a gangsta rapper? As Simon Price of the *Melody Maker* bluntly pointed out: 'Please Hammer, don't hurt me. My sides are killing me'. Hammer reverted to using the M.C. for his 1995 album *Inside Out*.

●ALBUMS: As M.C. Hammer *Feel My Power* (Bustin' 1987)★★★, *Let's Get It Started* (Capitol 1988)★★★, *Please Hammer Don't Hurt 'Em* (Capitol 1990)★★★, *Inside Out* (Giant 1995)★★.

As Hammer *Too Legit To Quit* (Capitol 1991)★★, *The Funky Headhunter* (RCA 1994)★★.
●FURTHER READING: *M.C. Hammer: U Can't Touch This*, Bruce Dessau.

HANOI ROCKS

This Finnish heavy rock band were distinguished by their leaning towards 70s glam rock, which they carried off with more style and conviction than any of their peers. Initially the brainchild of Andy McCoy (b. Antti Hulkko) and Michael Monroe (b. Matti Fagerholm) back in 1976, they were not formed until 1980 when singer Monroe gathered up Nasty Suicide (b. Jan Stenfors; guitar), Stefan Piesmack (guitar), Pasi Sti (bass) and Peki Senola (drums). By September, when they recorded their debut album, *Bangkok Shocks, Saigon Shakes, Hanoi Rocks* (initially only released in Scandinavia), the line-up was Monroe, Suicide, McCoy (guitar), Sam Yaffa (b. Sami Takamaki; bass) and Gyp Casino (b. Jesper Sporre; drums). McCoy had previously played with two Finnish punk bands, Briard and Pelle Miljoona Oy. In addition Suicide had played in Briard, while Yaffa had also been a member of Pelle Miljoona Oy at various times. Hanoi Rocks' debut single - 'I Want You', was released on the Finnish Johanna label in 1980 and preceded the album. The band then travelled to London where they began recording *Oriental Beat*. Soon after it was finished Casino was sacked (and joined the Road Rats) and replaced by Razzle (b. Nicholas Dingley, 2 December 1963, Isle Of Wight, England), who had previously played with Demon Preacher and the Dark. In 1983 they were signed to CBS Records and started to attract attention in the British music press. They hit the UK charts for the first and only time in 1984 with a cover version of Creedence Clearwater Revival's 'Up Around The Bend', but the year ended in tragedy. The band were in the USA when Razzle was killed in a car crash on 7 December. The car driver - Vince Neil of Mötley Crüe - was later found guilty of Vehicular Manslaughter. Former Clash drummer Terry Chimes was brought in as a replacement and when Yaffa left (to form Chain Gang then join Jetboy), Rene Berg (ex-Idle Flowers) also joined the group. However, Monroe never really accepted the loss of Razzle and in early 1985 he told the band he intended to quit. Hanoi Rocks played their final gig in May 1985. Monroe has since embarked on a solo career. Piesmack joined Pelle Miljoona Oy, then quit music, Sti and Senola also left the music scene, and McCoy (who had already formed a side project in 1983 - the Urban Dogs with Charlie Harper, Alvin Gibbs (UK Subs) and Knox (Vibrators) - went on to form the Cherry Bombz with Suicide, Chimes and ex-Toto Coelo vocalist Anita Chellemah. The Cherry Bombz barely lasted a year and the members went on to play in various short-lived outfits, most notably Suicide (with Gibbs once more) in Cheap 'N' Nasty. A near reunion of Hanoi Rocks, featuring Monroe with Suicide and Sam Yaffa, emerged as Demolition 23 in 1994.
●ALBUMS: *Bangkok Shocks, Saigon Shakes, Hanoi Rocks* (Johanna 1981)★★★, *Oriental Beat* (Johanna 1982)★★★, *Self Destruction Blues* (Johanna 1982)★★★, *Back To Mystery City* (Lick 1983)★★★, *Two Steps From The Move* (Columbia 1984)★★★.
●COMPILATIONS: *All Those Wasted Years* (Johanna 1985)★★, *Rock 'N' Roll Divorce* (Lick 1985)★★, *Best Of Hanoi Rocks* (Lick 1985)★★★, *Dead By Christmas* (Raw Power 1986)★★, *Tracks From A Broken Dream* (Lick 1990)★★★.
●VIDEOS: *All Those Wasted Years* (1988), *The Nottingham Tapes* (1988).

HAPPY MONDAYS

Few debut records could lay claim to have had the impact (or length of title) of Happy Mondays' *Squirrel And G-Man Twenty Four Hour Party People Plastic Face Carnt Smile (White Out)*. The sextet's raw brand of urban folk with Shaun Ryder's accented, drawled vocals was almost universally acclaimed. John Cale, formerly of the Velvet Underground, produced and gave the record a fresh, live feel. The original line-up remained unchanged (apart from the addition of backing singer, Rowetta) since the group formed in Manchester, England, early in the 80s. Joining singer Ryder (b. 23 August 1962) was his brother, Paul Ryder (b. 24 April 1964; bass), Mark Day (b. 29 December 1961; guitar), Gary Whelan (b. 12 February 1966; drums), Paul Davis (b. 7 March 1966; keyboards) and Mark Berry (percussion). Nicknamed 'Bez', the latter was widely noted for his manic onstage antics, especially his gaunt, skeleton dance appearance. Martin Hannett, famous for his work with a number of Manchester bands including Joy Division, produced *Bummed*, and layered their music with diverse but strong dance rhythms. In 1990 they covered John Kongos' 'He's Gonna Step On You Again' (retitled 'Step On') and reached the Top 10 in the UK. *Pills 'N' Thrills And Bellyaches* went to number 1 in the UK and established the band as a major pop force. The album also coincided with support and re-promotion of 60s singer Donovan, who appeared alongside them on the front covers of the music press. They even recorded a tribute song, 'Donovan', which paraphrased the lyrics of the singer's 60s hit, 'Sunshine Superman'. Strong support from Factory Records and an unusually consistent output meant Happy Mondays quickly rose to the status of favourite sons, alongside the Stone Roses, of the readership of the *New Musical Express* and *Melody Maker*, and they were achieving sales to match. However, the band's successes were tempered with a fair share of unpleasant publicity which came to a head when Sean Ryder announced he was a heroin addict and was undergoing detoxification treatment. A highly publicized strife-torn recording session in the Caribbean, with producers Tina Weymouth and Chris Frantz (of Talking Heads), resulted in ... *Yes Please!* However, its impact was dulled by a fall off in press interest, at least outside of Ryder's drug habits. Fittingly, the Happy Mondays eventual collapse could not be tied to a specific date, with various members breaking off at various points throughout 1993. The band's focal points, Ryder and Bez, eventually re-emerged in 1995 as part of a new coalition, Black Grape, after Ryder had contributed vocals to 'Can You Fly Like You Mean It' by fellow Mancunians, Intastella.

●ALBUMS: *Squirrel And G-Man Twenty Four Hour Party People Plastic Face Carnt Smile* (*White Out*) (Factory 1986)★★★, *Bummed* (Factory 1988)★★★, *Pills 'N' Thrills And Bellyaches* (Factory 1990)★★★★, *Live* (Factory 1991)★★, *Yes Please!* (Factory 1992)★★, *The Peel Sessions* (Strange Fruit 1996)★★.

●COMPILATIONS: *Loads - The Best Of* (London 1995)★★★, *Loads More* limited edition (London 1995)★★.

HARDCASTLE, PAUL

b. 10 December 1957, London, England. Hardcastle is a producer, mixer, composer and keyboard wizard specializing in dance orientated product. He first worked in a hi-fi shop and developed an interest in electronics in his teens. His first group was First Light, alongside Derek Green, whose output included a deplorable 'Horse With No Name'. After four solo minor hits in 1984, '19', a record about the Vietnam conflict utilizing spoken news reports, went straight to number 1 in the UK in 1985. The follow up, 'Just For The Money', was based on the Great Train Robbery and boasted the voices of Bob Hoskins and Sir Laurence Olivier. Further singles were progressively less successful before he scored with 'Papa's Got A Brand New Pigbag' under the pseudonym Silent Underdog. He also wrote the *Top Of The Pops* theme, 'The Wizard', in 1986, before switching to production for young funk band LW5, providing remixes for anyone from Third World to Ian Dury. Another production credit was the last ever Phil Lynott single, coincidentally called 'Nineteen'. Other engagements came with Carol Kenyon (previously vocalist on Heaven 17's 'Temptation'), most notably on her 1986 Top 10 hit 'Don't Waste My Time'. Recently Hardcastle has 'retired' to his Essex home studio and releases records under pseudonyms such as the Def Boys, Beeps International, Jazzmasters and Kiss The Sky (the last of which is Hardcastle and Jaki Graham). He is also founder of his own label, Fast Forward, and has recently written the theme music to two BBC nature series, *Supersense* and its sequel, *Lifesense.*

●ALBUMS: *Zero One* (Blue Bird 1985)★★, *Paul Hardcastle* (Chrysalis 1985)★★★, *No Winners* (Chrysalis 1988)★★.

●COMPILATIONS: *Soul Syndicate* (K-Tel 1988)★★.

HARLEQUIN

An under-achieving melodic rock act formed in the USA in the late 70s, Harlequin attracted a modicum of interest over a four album-long career without ever threatening to break into the mainstream. Comprising George Belanger (vocals), Glen Willows (guitar) Gary Golden (keyboards), Ralph James (bass) and David Budzak (drums), they made their debut for Epic Records in 1978 with *Victim Of A Song*. The follow-up, 1980's *Love Crimes*, is widely considered to be their strongest set, with Willows' guitar and Golden's keyboards having moulded a distinctive AOR sound. Subsequent albums failed to produce any showing in the US charts however, and the group had disbanded by the mid-80s.

●ALBUMS: *Victim Of A Song* (Epic 1978)★★, *Love Crimes* (Epic 1980)★★★, *One False Move* (Epic 1982)★★, *Harlequin* (Epic 1984)★★.

HARMAN, JAMES

b. 8 June 1946, Anniston, Alabama, USA. One of the leading white harmonica players on America's west coast, Harman's love of the instrument was instilled in him by his father. As a youngster in Alabama, James played with a local blues musician called Radio Johnson, and bought R&B discs. By the age of 16 he led his own band. In 1970 he moved to California and had to abandon music for some years due to health problems. However, he was unable to stop playing music for very long. In the 80s he made acclaimed recordings for the

Rivera and Rhino labels. Harman is a fine singer and harmonica player whose approach to the blues is one of having fun.

●ALBUMS: *Those Dangerous Gentlemens* (Rhino 1987)★★★, *Extra Napkins* (Rivera 1988)★★★, *Strictly Live ... In '85 Volume One* (Rivera 1990)★★★, *Two Sides To Every Story* (Black Top 1993)★★★, *Cards On The Table* (Black Top 1994)★★★, *Black And White* (Black Top 1995)★★★.

HARRIS, EMMYLOU

b. 12 April 1947, Birmingham, Alabama, USA. Starting as a folk singer, Harris tried her luck in the late 60s in New York's Greenwich Village folk clubs, making an album for the independent Jubilee label in 1970, *Gliding Bird*, which was largely unrepresentative of her subsequent often stunning work. It included covers of songs by Bob Dylan, Fred Neil and Hank Williams, as well as somewhat ordinary originals and a title track written by her first husband, Tom Slocum. Harris then moved to Washington, DC, where latter-day Flying Burrito Brother Rick Roberts heard her sing in a club, and recommended her to Gram Parsons, who was looking for a female partner. Parsons hired Harris after discovering that their voices dovetailed perfectly, and she appeared on his two studio albums, *GP* (1973) and *Grievous Angel* (1974). The latter was released after Parsons died, as was a live album recorded for a US radio station which was released some years later.

Eddie Tickner, who had been involved with managing the Byrds, and who was also managing Parsons at the time of his drug-related demise, encouraged Harris to make a solo album using the same musicians who had worked with Parsons. The cream of Los Angeles session musicians, they were collectively known as the Hot Band, and among the 'pickers' who worked in the band during its 15-year life span backing Harris were guitarist James Burton (originally lead guitarist on 'Suzy Q' by Dale Hawkins, and simultaneously during his time with Harris, lead player with Elvis Presley's Las Vegas band), pianist Glen D. Hardin (a member of the Crickets post-Buddy Holly and also working simultaneously with both Harris and Presley), steel guitarist Hank DeVito, bass player Emory Gordy Jnr (now a highly successful Nashville-based producer), John Ware (ex-Michael Nesmith's First National Band, and a member of Linda Ronstadt's early 70s backing group), and the virtually unknown Rodney Crowell. Backed by musicians of this calibre (subsequent Hot Band

members included legendary British lead guitarist Albert Lee and Ricky Skaggs, later a country star in his own right), Harris released a series of artistically excellent and often commercially successful albums starting with 1975's *Pieces Of The Sky*, and also including *Elite Hotel* (1976), *Luxury Liner* (1977) and *Quarter Moon In A Ten Cent Town* (whose title was a line in the song 'Easy From Now On', co-written by Carlene Carter and Susanna Clark, wife of singer songwriter Guy Clark). *Blue Kentucky Girl* was closer to pure country music than the country rock that had become her trademark and speciality, and 1980's *Roses In The Snow* was her fourth album to make the Top 40 of the US pop chart. *Light Of The Stable*, a 1980 Christmas album also featuring Linda Ronstadt, Dolly Parton, Willie Nelson and Neil Young, was surprisingly far less successful. Two more albums in 1981 (*Evangeline* and *Cimmaron* - the latter featuring a cover of the Poco classic, 'Rose Of Cimmaron') were better sellers, but a 1982 live album, *Last Date*, was largely ignored. The following year's *White Shoes* was Harris's final album produced by Canadian Brian Ahern, her second husband, who had established a reputation for his successful work with Anne Murray, prior to producing all Emmylou's classic albums up to this point. Harris and Ahern separated both personally and professionally, marking the end of an era which had also seen her appearing on Bob Dylan's *Desire* in 1976 and *The Last Waltz*, the farewell concert/triple album/feature film by the Band from 1978.

Around this time, Harris was invited by producer Glyn Johns and British singer/songwriter Paul Kennerley to participate in a concept album written by the latter, *The Legend Of Jesse James* (Kennerley's follow-up to the similarly conceptual *White Mansions*). Harris and Kennerley later married, and together wrote and produced *The Ballad Of Sally Rose* (a concept album which by her own belated admission reflected her relationship with Gram Parsons) and the similarly excellent *13*, but never marked a return to previous chart heights. 1987 brought two albums involving Harris: *Trio*, a multi-million selling triumph which won a Grammy Award, was a collaboration between Harris, Linda Ronstadt and Dolly Parton, but Harris's own *Angel Band*, a low key acoustic collection, became the first of Harris's not to be released in the UK, where it was felt to be too uncommercial. This fall from commercial grace occurred simultaneously (although perhaps coincidentally) with the virtual retirement of manager Eddie Tickner, who had guided and protected Harris through 15 years of mainly classic albums.

1989's *Bluebird* was a definite return to form with production by Richard Bennett and featuring a title track written by Butch Hancock, but a commercial renaissance did not occur. 1990's *Duets*, a compilation album featuring Harris singing with artists including Gram Parsons, Roy Orbison, George Jones, the Desert Rose Band, Don Williams, Neil Young and John Denver, was artistically delightful, but appeared to be an attempt on the part of the marketing department of WEA (to whom she had been signed since *Pieces Of The Sky*) to reawaken interest in a star whom they feared might be past her commercial peak. The same year's *Brand New Dance* was not a success compared with much of her past catalogue, and in that year, the much changed Hot Band was dropped in favour of the Nash Ramblers, a bluegrass-based acoustic quintet composed of Sam Bush (mandolin/fiddle/duet vocals, ex-New Grass Revival), Al Perkins (dobro/banjo, ex-Manassas, Flying Burrito Brothers, Souther Hillman Furay), *Grand Ole Opry* double bass player Roy Huskey Jnr., drummer Larry Atamanuik and 22 year old new boy John Randall Stewart (acoustic guitar/harmony vocal - the Rodney Crowell replacement). In 1991, Harris and the Nash Ramblers were permitted to record a live album at the former home of the *Grand Ole Opry*, the Ryman Auditorium in Nashville. The record was poorly received in some quarters, however, and at the end of 1992, it was reported that she had been dropped by Warner Brothers Records, ending a 20-year association. Harris remained in the incongruous position of being a legendary figure in country music who is always in demand as a guest performer in the studio, but who cannot match the record sales of those younger artists who regard her as a heroine. Her 1995 album was the severing of the cord; she boldly stepped away from country-sounding arrangements and recorded the stunning Daniel Lanois-produced *Wrecking Ball*. The title track is a Neil Young composition and other songs featured were written by Steve Earle, Lanois and Anna McGarrigle. Harris described this album as her 'weird' record, but i's wandering and mantric feel creeps into the psyche and is one of the most rewarding releases of her underrated and lengthy career. She picked up a Grammy for it in 1996 as the Best Contemporary Folk Album.

●ALBUMS: *Gliding Bird* (Jubilee 1970),★★ *Pieces Of The Sky* (Reprise 1975)★★★★, *Elite Hotel* (Reprise 1976)★★★, *Luxury Liner* (Warners 1977)★★★★, *Quarter Moon In A 10 Cent Town* (Warners 1978)★★★, *Blue Kentucky Girl* (Warners 1979)★★★, *Roses In The Snow* (Warners 1980)★★★★, *Light Of The Stable* (Warners 1980)★★★, *Evangeline* (Warners 1981)★★★, *Cimarron* (Warners 1981)★★★, *Last Date* (Warners 1982)★★★, *White Shoes* (Warners 1983)★★★, *The Ballad Of Sally Rose* (Warners 1985)★★★, *13* (Warners 1986)★★★, with Dolly Parton, Linda Ronstadt *Trio* (Warners 1987)★★★, *Angel Band* (Warners 1987)★★★, *Bluebird* (Reprise 1989)★★★, *Duets* (Warners 1990)★★★★, *Brand New Dance* (Reprise 1990)★★★, *At The Ryman* (Reprise 1992)★★★, with Carl Jackson *Nashville Country Duets* (1993)★★★, *Cowgirl's Prayer* (Grapevine 1993)★★★, *Songs Of The West* (Warners 1994)★★★, *Wrecking Ball* (Grapevine 1995)★★★★.
●COMPILATIONS: *Her Best Songs* (K-Tel 1980)★★★, *Portraits* (Reprise Archives 1996)★★★★.
●VIDEOS: *Thanks To You* (1990), *At The Ryman* (1992).

HARRIS, LARNELLE

b. Louisville, Kentucky, USA. After graduating from Kentucky University with a degree in music education, Harris has gone on to become one the most prominent talents in contemporary Christian music. He has been well served by his early apprenticeship as a member of the Spurrlows, a gospel group who toured extensively during the early 70s. He has also worked with the Gaither Vocal Band and First Gear, usually as a vocalist, though he is also a competent saxophone player and percussionist. From a more conventional gospel base for his early albums in the 70s he has successively grafted elements of secular pop and MOR onto his Christian-themed songs, the best of which include 'Friends In High Places' and the title-track from his well-received 1989 album, *I Can Begin Again*. However, arguably his best album of the 80s was *Larnelle Live - Psalms, Hymns & Spiritual Song*, where a full orchestra and the Brooklyn Tabernacle Choir provided the perfect backing for Harris's supple tenor voice.

●ALBUMS: *Tell It To Jesus* (Word 1974)★★★, *Larnelle ... More* (Word 1976)★★★, *Free* (Word 1978)★★★, *Larnelle Live - Psalms, Hymns & Spiritual Songs* (Benson 1985)★★★, *From A Servant's Heart* (Heartwarming 1987)★★★, *The Father Hath Provided* (Heartwarming 1988)★★★, *I Can Begin Again* (Heartwarming 1989)★★★.
●COMPILATIONS: *The Best Of 10 Years Vol. 1* and *2* (Benson 1991)★★★.

HARRISON, JERRY

b. Jeremiah Harrison, 21 February 1949, Milwaukee, Wisconsin, USA. He built his reputation as guitarist and keyboard player for Talking Heads. Previously he had played in a similar capacity for Jonathan Richman And The Modern Lovers, between 1970 and 1974, before going on to study at Harvard and work with computers in Boston. Like other core members of the Talking Heads, he has enjoyed several fruitful extra-curricular pursuits. These began with a debut solo album in 1981, titled *The Red And The Black*. Recorded while the parent group were enjoying a sabbatical, many of those who had contributed to recent Talking Heads fare such as *Remain In Light* - including Adrian Belew, Bernie Worrell and Nona Hendryx - were on hand to aid Harrison. However, apart from scant critical interest there was little public support for this exploration of international rhythms and ethnic music.

Harrison then returned to his role in Talking Heads before 1984 brought a solitary 12-inch release for rap label, Sleeping Bag Records. Titled '5 Minutes' and credited to Bonzo Goes To Washington, this combined a Bootsy Collins bass riff with a sample of President Reagan declaring 'We begin bombing . . .' Although a footnote to Harrison's own career, this document pre-empted much of the politically motivated sampling that spread through the remainder of the 80s. The artist retained a political agenda for his second album, released in 1987. Joined by a core of accomplished musicians (the 13-piece Casual Gods), the music was once again primarily a rhythmic experience, moving from funk to urban hip hop. Three years later, and with the Talking Heads' career seemingly on permanent hold, Harrison returned to the Casual Gods. The resultant album, *Walk On Water*, credited to Jerry Harrison's Casual Gods, revealed a more pop/rock-orientated sound. The additional personnel this time included former Modern Lover colleague Ernie Brooks, Dan Hartman, Bernie Worrell and the Thompson Twins. Although the musicianship remained exemplary, critics were still dissuaded against the overall merits of the project by Harrison's somewhat untutored vocal delivery. Perhaps this has given impetus to his position in the 90s as overseer of a steady influx of production work (notably Crash Test Dummies). He also worked with some of his previous musical collaborators, notably on Bernie Worrell's *Funk Of Ages* album.

●ALBUMS: *The Red And The Black* (Sire 1981)★★, *Casual Gods* (Sire 1987)★★★, as Jerry Harrison's Casual Gods *Walk On Water* (Fly/Sire 1990)★★★.

HARRY, DEBORAH

b. 1 July 1945, Miami, Florida, USA. Raised in New Jersey, Harry was drawn to the alternative music emanating from New York's Greenwich Village in the mid-60s. Spells in a succession of *avant garde* groups, including the First National Unaphrenic Church And Bank, preceded her tenure in the Wind In The Willows, a baroque folk rock act which completed an album for Capitol Records in 1968. For five years Harry abandoned music altogether, but resumed singing in 1973 as a member of the Stilettos, an exaggerated version of girl-group the Shangri-Las. The following year she formed Blondie with Fred Smith (bass), Billy O'Connor (drums) and long-time boyfriend Chris Stein (guitar). Having made its debut at the New York punk haven CBGBs, the group rose to become one of the leading pop attractions of the late 70s, scoring a succession of hits in the US and UK. Meanwhile, Harry established herself as the leading female rock sex symbol of the time. However, as the dividing line between the group and its photogenic lead singer became blurred, so inner tensions proved irreconcilable. In 1981 Harry released her solo debut *Koo Koo*, produced by Chic mainstays Nile Rodgers and Bernard Edwards. Despite the presence of Stein, the set failed to capture Blondie's sense of simple pop and the singer resumed her commitment to the parent act. Stein's recurrent ill heath brought the group to an end and a further period of retirement ensued. Harry did pursue an acting career, including roles in *Union City Blue*, *Videodrome* and a memorable comic role in the 1987 John Waters film, *Hairspray*. In 1986 she released *Rockbird* which featured the UK Top 10 hit 'French Kissing In The USA'. It was not until three years later that Harry made a return to the UK Top 20, this time with the Tom Bailey and Alannah Currie (aka the Thompson Twins) composition, 'I Want That Man'. The accompanying album, *Def, Dumb And Blonde*, credited to Deborah Harry, achieved a similar chart position, since when the singer has completed several tours, performing material drawn from Blondie and her subsequent work. *Once More Into The Bleach* is credited to, and includes, tracks from Debbie Harry's solo career and with Blondie.

●ALBUMS: *Koo Koo* (Chrysalis 1981)★★, *Rockbird* (Chrysalis 1986)★★, *Def, Dumb And Blonde* (Chrysalis 1989)★★★, *Debravation* (Chrysalis 1993)★★, with the Jazz Passengers *Individually*

Twisted (32 Records 1997)★★★.
●COMPILATIONS: *Once More Into The Bleach* (Chrysalis 1988)★★★, *The Complete Picture - The Very Best Of Deborah Harry And Blondie* (Chrysalis 1990)★★★★.

HART, COREY

b. *c.*1962, Canada. Corey Hart was one of the biggest-selling Canadian acts of the 80s before his career entered what seemed to be terminal decline at the end of that decade. He had always intended to become a singer from childhood, an ambition hardly qualified by exposure to other musical traditions when his father moved the family to Malaga, Spain, when he was four, then Mexico City when he was nine. While living in Key Biscayne, Florida, his sister introduced him to Tom Jones, who recommended his abilities to Canadian superstar Paul Anka. Anka personally financed the recording of two Hart songs in Las Vegas when the young artist was just 13 years old. Hart eventually made his recording debut with a version of Anka's 'Ooh Baby' for United Artists Records in 1974, but it failed to chart and his contract was not renewed. After an abortive attempt to launch a songwriting career in Los Angeles, he returned to Montreal. There he struck a deal with the EMI Records-distributed Aquarius label, making his long-playing debut in 1983 with *First Offense*. This became a major success both in Canada and the USA when the singles, 'Sunglasses At Night' and 'It Ain't Enough', both reached the Top 20 of the *Billboard* charts. After only six warm-up performances, he made his professional performing debut supporting Culture Club in Toronto in 1984. His second album, *Boy In The Box*, also featured another major hit single, 'Never Surrender', a number 1 hit in Canada that peaked at number 3 in the US charts. The single won a Juno Award and Hart was also nominated for a Grammy. However, his commercial bubble burst in 1987 when *Fields Of Fire* stalled at US number 55. Hart was also exhausted from excessive touring, leading to the cancellation of dates in Canada. His commercial decline continued over the course of two further albums until, in 1991, he made the move to Sire Records. However, *Attitude And Virtue* failed to resurrect his career, and Hart retired from the music industry. He finally returned in 1996 with a suite of songs written about, among other things, the break-up of his marriage to graphic designer Erika Gagnon, and his relationship with Quebec singer Julie Masse and the birth of their child, India.
●ALBUMS: *First Offense* (Aquarius 1983)★★★, *Boy*

In The Box (Aquarius 1985)★★★, *Fields Of Fire* (Aquarius 1986)★★★, *Young Man Running* (Aquarius 1988)★★★, *Bang* (Aquarius 1990)★★★, *Attitude And Virtue* (Sire 1991)★★★, *Corey Hart* (Columbia 1996)★★★.

HARVEY, RICHARD

b. 25 September 1953, Enfield, Middlesex, England; keyboards, woodwinds, mandolin. The ex-Gryphon keyboard genius recorded classical recorder music while still in the band. He then moved into the advertising world to compose jingles and television scores. His credits include the soundtrack to Channel 4's award-winning *GBH*. His album, *A New Way Of Seeing*, is the result of a commission from ICL. Despite working in a new area, it seems a logical extension of Gryphon's work. His writing partnership with Elvis Costello has been particularly rewarding
●ALBUMS: *A New Way Of Seeing* (1984)★★★, *Evening Falls* (Telstar 1989)★★★, *Shroud For A Nightingale* (Silva Screen 1996)★★★.

HAWKES, CHESNEY

b. 22 September 1971. He is the son of former Tremeloes writer and vocalist Chip Hawkes. Chesney shot to prominence with UK chart topper 'The One And Only', his first single, written for him by Nik Kershaw. The follow-up 'I'm A Man Not A Boy' invited an obvious retort from incredulous critics. Chrysalis Records attempted to cash in on the success of 'The One And Only' by re-releasing *Buddy's Song* and crediting it solely to Hawkes. The film co-starred Roger Daltray as Hawkes' father, obsessed with the legend of Buddy Holly.
●ALBUMS: *Buddy's Song* soundtrack (Chrysalis 1991)★★, *Get The Picture* (Chrysalis 1993)★.

HAWKINS, TED

b. Theodore Hawkins Jnr., 28 October 1937, Biloxi, Mississippi, USA, d. 1 January 1995, Los Angeles, California, USA. Hawkins was more of a modern-day 'songster' than a bluesman, his repertoire encompassing pop hits, country and folk standards, soul numbers and originals. He grew up with gospel music, and learned to play guitar at the age of 12, taught in the bluesy 'Vestapol' (or Open C) style by local musicians. He played with such force that he protected his left hand with a glove. As a boy, he was sent to a reformatory, and spent several terms behind bars. He left home in the 50s, hoboing first to Chicago, Illinois, then to New York, Pennsylvania and New Jersey, ending up in California. He recorded 'Baby'/'Whole Lot Of

Women' for the Hollywood-based Money label in 1966; in 1971 he was spotted busking by producer Bruce Bromberg with whom he made an album in 1972. He continued to perform on street corners and California's Ocean Front Walk; this aspect of Hawkins' career was documented on the *Venice Beach Tapes* recorded, ironically, in Tennessee in 1985. *Happy Hour* consolidated his reputation, particularly in Britain where he had a sizeable following. Despite retaining an undoubtedly 'rural' feel in performance, Hawkins owed much vocally to his hero Sam Cooke and to the great soul stylists of the 60s. Above all, he was one of the finest contemporary interpreters of melancholic material.

●ALBUMS: *Watch Your Step* (Rounder 1982)★★★, *Happy Hour* (Rounder 1986)★★★, *On The Boardwalk: The Venice Beach Tapes* (no label 1986)★★★, *Dock Of The Bay: The Venice Beach Tapes II* (Unamerican Activities 1987)★★, *I Love You Too* (P.T. Music 1989)★★, *The Next Hundred Years* (Geffen 1994)★★★, *Songs From Venice Beach* (Evidence 1995)★★★.

●COMPILATIONS: *The Best Of Venice Beach Tapes* (Unamerican Activities 1989)★★★, *The Kershaw Sessions* (Strange Fruit 1995)★★★.

●VIDEOS: *Ted Hawkins: Amazing Grace* (Geffen Home Video 1995).

HAWKINS, WALTER

b. 18 May 1949, Oakland, California, USA. The brother of Edwin Hawkins, who enjoyed huge success with his hit single 'Oh Happy Day', Walter Hawkins is a gospel singer with strong family connections to the gospel tradition. In addition to Edwin, his wife Tramaine is a singer, as are his sisters Carole, Freddie and Lynette. He is the cousin of Shirley Miller, while his younger brother Daniel and nephew Joe Smith also play with the family group under his stewardship. After graduating from Berklee College Of Music with a Master of Divinity degree, Edwin founded the Love Center church in 1975 and became an ordained minister and pastor of the Church of God in Christ. These activities eventually led to him proposing the idea of releasing an album. In what he later claimed to be an impulsive decision, he contacted friend Andrae Crouch and Light Records president Bill Cole. *Love Alive* followed as his debut release, the most distinctive feature being the excellent vocal interplay between Hawkins and his wife. Subsequent albums, including *Jesus Christ Is The Way* and *Love Alive II*, saw him garlanded with numerous awards from *Cash Box* magazine as well as a 1979 Grammy nomination for Best Soul Gospel

Performance, Contemporary.

●ALBUMS: *Love Alive* (Light 1975)★★★, *Jesus Christ Is The Way* (Light 1977)★★★, *Love Alive II* (Light 1979)★★★.

HAZA, OFRA

b. 1959, Israel. Haza was the daughter of Yemenite parents who had fled from the Muslim regime in Yemen. At the age of 12 she joined the theatre group Hatvika, run by Bezalel Azoni. In her seven years with the group, Haza recorded with them and won a Grammy award for an outstanding performance. After serving two years' national service in the Israeli army she recorded her first solo album and quickly rose to become one of Israel's top singers. She was voted second in the 1983 Eurovision Song Contest with 'Hi!' (translated: 'stay alive'). Haza's introduction to international music came when her singing was sampled for the Eric B And Rakim Top 20 hit, 'Paid In Full' (1987). Her unlikely success, in her own right, in the US dance charts in 1988 with 'Im Nin'alu' spread to the UK where it reached number 15. Her visual image with her colourful national dress and the exotic mixture of middle-eastern ballads and rhythms blended with western styles, helped to make her Israel's best-known female solo singer in the UK. This success has seen Haza fêted by artists in various fields of music; from world music and traditional folk, to disco and house styles. In an unlikely alliance in 1992, Haza linked with the Sisters Of Mercy for the remix of their single, 'Temple Of Love'. That same year also saw the release of *Kirya*, which involved both Was (Not Was) and Iggy Pop.

●ALBUMS: *50 Gates Of Wisdom* (Shanachie 1984)★★★★, *Shaday* (Sire 1988)★★★, *Desert Wind* (Sire 1990)★★★, *Kirya* (Shanachie 1992)★★★.

HEAVEN 17

An offshoot project from the UK production company BEF, this featured the synthesizer duo Ian Craig Marsh (b. 11 November 1956, Sheffield, England) and Martyn Ware (b. 19 May 1956, Sheffield, England) and vocalist Glenn Gregory (b. 16 May 1958, Sheffield, England). Heaven 17's first UK hit was the dance-orientated '(We Don't Need This) Fascist Groove Thang', which reached number 45. In late 1981, they released the best-selling album *Penthouse And Pavement*, which reflected the hedonistic themes of the period. Alternating with BEF projects and various guest appearances, Heaven 17 recorded intermittently. In May 1983, they achieved their finest moment with the electrifying UK Top 10 hit, 'Temptation', which featured guest vocalist Carol Kenyon. A series of albums followed, but Heaven 17 always appeared a predominantly studio group, whose group name was used irregularly as a brand name to experiment with various new ideas. Meanwhile, the group's services as producers were still in demand and Ware co-produced Terence Trent D'Arby's best-selling *The Hardline According To Terence Trent D'Arby*. In 1991, Marsh and Ware completed another ambitious BEF album of star cover versions and in 1996 surprised the market with a new Heaven 17 album.

●ALBUMS: *Penthouse And Pavement* (Virgin 1981)★★★, *Heaven 17* (Virgin 1983)★★★, *The Luxury Gap* (Virgin 1983)★★★, *How Men Are* (BEF 1984)★★, *Endless* (Virgin 1986)★★, *Pleasure One* (Virgin 1987)★★★, *Teddy Bear, Duke & Psycho* (Virgin 1988)★★★, *That's How Love Is* (1989)★★, *Bigger Than America* (Warners 1996)★★.

●COMPILATIONS: *Higher & Higher (The Very Best Of...)* (Virgin 1993)★★★.

HEDGES, MICHAEL

b. 31 December, California, USA. This American guitarist, singer and composer has moved from being known to possess a highly individual instrumental style to a growing acclaim as a singer and composer. Hedges grew up in Enid, Oklahoma, and began playing the piano at the age of four. At high school he played cello and clarinet, then flute and guitar. He underwent a formal musical education, studying flute and composition at Philips University in Oklahoma then classical guitar and electronic music at the Peabody Conservatory in Baltimore. Hedges has cited as his early influences, the Beatles, guitarist Leo Kottke and the twentieth-century composers Morton Feldman, Bela Bartok and Anton Webern. In 1980, he moved to California to study computer music at Stanford University and was signed by the Windham Hill Records label. The company's image, as purveyors of ethereal 'New Age' music was, in part, forged by Hedges' early recordings with them, in particular *Breakfast In The Field* and *The Shape Of The Land*. However, while mysticism has been a force behind his songwriting and he admits being deeply influenced by the ideas of the anthropologist Joseph Campell, Hedges has built a solid and grittier reputation as a musical innovator. Freewheeling experiments with tuning, two-handed fretwork tapping and harmonics pre-figured his more recent work in both recordings and concerts which have also seen the use of the harp guitar (an obscure instrument augmenting the standard six-strings with a tangential set of five bass strings) and synthesizers. The experiments are not merely embellishments to the music, but structural - Hedges' route to a distinctive musical voice. He is not, he says, a instrumentalist, but a composer. That is clearly disputed by his standing with the specialist music press who see him as one of the great guitarists of the past two decades.

●ALBUMS: *Breakfast In The Field* (Windham Hill 80s)★★★, *Aerial Boundaries* (Windham Hill 1985)★★★★, *Watching My Life Go By* (Windham Hill 1987)★★, *The Shape Of The Land* (Windham Hill 80s)★★, *Live On The Double Planet* (Windham Hill 1987)★★★, *Taproot* (Windham Hill 80s)★★★, *Strings Of Steel* (Windham Hill 1988)★★★, *The Road To Return* (Windham Hill 1994)★★, *Oracle* (Windham Hill 1996)★★★.

HELLOWEEN

Formed in 1984 in Hamburg, Germany, from the ashes of local bands Second Hell and Iron Fist, their original line-up comprised Kai Hansen (guitar/vocals), Michael Weikath (guitar), Markus Grosskopf (bass) and Ingo Schwichenburg (drums). After having two tracks included on the *Death Metal* compilation album released by Noise Records in 1984, the label issued their self-titled debut mini-album in 1985. This was soon followed by *Walls Of Jericho* and an EP, *Judas*. The band gained a strong following with their unique blend of high-speed power metal. Soon after its release, Helloween decided to add a vocalist/frontman, namely Michael Kiske, a charismatic 18-year-old. *Keeper Of The Seven Keys Part I*, released in 1987, showed the band to be taking a much more melodic approach and Kiske proved himself a worthy addition. Helloween then toured Europe relentlessly, building a sizeable following in the process. *Keeper Of The Seven Keys Part II* was released in 1988, together with a successful appearance at the Donington Monsters Of Rock Festival that year. After which came an EP, *Dr. Stein*, but behind the scenes all was not well. The band had become increasingly unhappy with their record company and started to negotiate with several major labels who had previously shown an interest. As a stop-gap the band released *Live In The UK*, recorded at the Hammersmith Odeon in 1989. Kai Hansen then left to form his own outfit, Gamma Ray. His replacement was Roland Grapow. A protracted legal battle with their record company ensured that it was not until 1990 that the band was back in action. They finally signed to EMI Records and gained major management in the form of the Smallwood/Taylor organization. The band's debut for their new label, *Pink Bubbles Go Ape*, released in 1990, depicted Helloween as a shadow of their former selves, sadly missing Kai Hansen and his songwriting skills. Shortly after the dismissal of Kiske, Ingo Schwichenberg was also given his marching orders due to personal health problems and a clash with Weikath, who was now the main force behind the band. Their replacements were Andi Deris (vocals, ex-Pink Cream 69) and Ulli Kusch (drums), who were in place in time for their Castle/Raw Power debut, *Master Of The Rings*. This became Helloween's most successful album for several years, topping the Japanese charts. 1996's *The Time Of The Oath* featured writing contributions from Weikath, Deris and Kusch, while the group composition 'Mission Motherland' saw the band tackle one of the social problems effecting Germany since the fall of the Berlin wall - refugees. Kiske went solo and released a solo album *Instant Charity* in 1996.

●ALBUMS: *Helloween* mini-album (Noise 1985)★★, *Walls Of Jericho* (Noise 1986)★★, *Keeper Of The Seven Keys Part I* (Noise 1987)★★★, *Keeper Of The Seven Keys Part II* (Noise 1988)★★★, *Live In The UK* (Noise 1989)★★, *Pink Bubbles Go Ape* (EMI 1990)★★, *Chameleon* (EMI 1993)★★, *Master Of The Rings* (Raw Power 1994)★★★, *The Time Of The Oath* (Raw Power 1996)★★★, *Tore Down House* (Mesa 1996)★★.

HEYWARD, NICK

b. 20 May 1961, Beckenham, Kent, England. The original lead vocalist in UK chart group Haircut 100, Heyward left for a solo career in late 1982. Early the following year he returned with a couple of chart hits, 'Whistle Down The Wind' and 'Take That Situation', both close to the 'boy next door blue-eyed soul' style developed by his former group. His debut solo album, *North Of A Miracle*, which included the up-tempo 'Blue Hat For A Blueday', was a solid effort which won critical approval and sold well. It featured Beatles engineer Geff Emerick as co-producer. An uneasy move away from his teenage audience was completed with the funk-influenced 'Warning Sign' but like many former teenage pin-ups the transition brought only limited commercial success. In 1988 he moved to Warner Brothers Records, but both the single, 'You're My World', and accompanying album, *I Love You Avenue*, failed to re-establish him in the mainstream. For the next four years Heyward concentrated on his second career as a graphic artist, until returning in 1992 with a new

album for Epic Records and tour dates alongside Squeeze. Over the next two years he toured regularly, particularly in the USA, where he supported such alternative luminaries as Belly, Lemonheads, Mazzy Star and Therapy? (arguably the most unlikely coupling given Heyward's reputation for gentle, pastoral songs). Much effort was put into *Tangled*, the result was an outstanding album of great melody and fascinating lyrics. Released at the height of renewed interest in the Beatles in 1995, Heyward's album identifies him with the fab four and much of the late 60s quality pop song era. Neither the album nor the singles taken from it found much commercial favour. It is difficult to imagine what he has to do in the future as on this showing Heyward had reached a creative peak. He signed to Creation Records in 1997 and worked with Edward Ball on his 1996 solo album.

●ALBUMS: *North Of A Miracle* (Arista 1983)★★★, *Postcards From Home* (Arista 1986)★★, *I Love You Avenue* (Warners 1988)★★, *From Monday To Sunday* (Epic 1992)★★, *Tangled* (Epic 1995)★★★★.

●COMPILATIONS: *Best Of Nick Heyward And Haircut 100* (Ariola 1989)★★★★, *The Greatest Hits Of Nick Heyward & Haircut 100* (RCA Camden 1996)★★★★.

●FURTHER READING: *The Haircut 100 Catalogue*, Sally Payne. *Haircut 100: Not A Trace Of Brylcreem*, no editor listed.

HIATT, JOHN

b. 1952, Indianapolis, Indiana, USA. The archetypal musicians' musician, John Hiatt is a powerful singer, guitarist and talented songwriter whose material has been recorded by various acts including Dr. Feelgood, Searchers, Iggy Pop, Three Dog Night, Desert Rose Band, Bonnie Raitt, Bob Dylan, Nick Lowe, Rick Nelson and the Neville Brothers. Hiatt started out in local R&B bands in the late 60s, most notably the White Ducks. Moving to Nashville in 1970 he signed to Epic and recorded two highly acclaimed albums. After the second album he left the label and toured for a spell as a solo performer before being offered a new contract by MCA at the end of the decade. This resulted in two further albums. In 1980, guitarist Ry Cooder was looking for some new songs and was recommended Hiatt's material. Cooder received a tape of demos from Hiatt's publisher and though he was not sure the material was right for him, he decided he could use the talented guitarist in his own band. Hiatt duly accepted Cooder's offer and started playing with him on *Borderline* and on several albums and tours since. His first solo album after his engagements with Cooder was 1982's *All Of A Sudden* and it was followed by almost one new album every year produced by Tony Visconti and Nick Lowe. Lowe regularly forms part of Hiatt's band both in the studio and on tour. Lowe and Hiatt later became half of a new 'supergroup' when they teamed up with Cooder and Jim Keltner (veteran journeyman drummer) to form Little Village, who released their first disappointing self-titled album in 1992. Since then Hiatt's reputation as a songwriter has grown and his own recent recorded output has recently produced two of his best albums, the title tracks to both *Perfectly Good Guitar* and *Walk On* are two of his most infectious songs.

●ALBUMS: *Hanging Around The Observatory* (Epic 1974)★★★, *Overcoats* (Epic 1975)★★★, *Slug Line* (Epic 1979)★★★, *Two Bit Monsters* (MCA 1980)★★★, *All Of A Sudden* (MCA 1982)★★, *Riding With The King* (Geffen 1983)★★★★, *Warming Up To The Ice Age* (Geffen 1985)★★★, *Bring The Family* (A&M 1987)★★★★, *Slow Turning* (A&M 1988)★★★, *Stolen Moments* (A&M 1990)★★★, *Perfectly Good Guitar* (A&M 1993)★★★★, with The Guilty Dogs *Hiatt Comes Alive At Budokan?* (A&M 1994)★★★, *Walk On* (Capitol 1995)★★★, *Little Head* (Capitol 1997)★★★.

●COMPILATIONS: *Y'All Caught - The Ones That Got Away* (Geffen 1991)★★★.

HIGHWAY 101

Like the Monkees, Highway 101 is a manufactured US group. Chuck Morris, the manager of the Nitty Gritty Dirt Band and Lyle Lovett, wanted to form a group which would play 'traditional country with a rock 'n' roll backbeat'. He recruited session man, Scott 'Cactus' Moser, to help him. He worked with bassist Curtis Stone, the son of Cliffie Stone, in the film, *Back To School*, and then he added session guitarist, Jack Daniels. Morris then heard some demos by Paulette Carlson. She had had songs recorded by Gail Davies and Tammy Wynette and had a cameo role as a nightclub singer in the film *Twins*. Their first single, 'Some Find Love', was not successful but, in 1987, they had their first US country hits with 'The Bed You Made For Me' (number 4), which Carlson wrote, and 'Whiskey, If You Were A Woman' (number 2). They topped the US country charts with 'Somewhere Tonight' with its songwriting credit of 'old' and 'new' country, Harlan Howard and Rodney Crowell. In 1988 they had a further chart-toppers with 'Cry, Cry, Cry' (which was a new song and not a revival of the Johnny Cash hit), 'If You Love Me, Just Say Yes' (being based on the slogan of Nancy Reagan's anti-drugs

campaign, 'Just say no') and 'Who's Lonely Now' in 1989. Paulette Carlson took a turn off the Highway in 1990, and Nikki Nelson was recruited for *Bing Bang Boom*. The title track was an infectious and successful single, but the album failed to sell in the same quantities as before. Daniels quit in 1992 and the group made a final album *The New Frontier*, before disbanding in 1995. In 1995 Carlson initiated a reunion, missing only 'Cactus' from the line up, and they released a new album.

●ALBUMS: *Highway 101* (Warners 1987)★★★, *101 2* (Curb 1988)★★★, *Paint The Town* (Atlantic 1989)★★★, *Bing Bang Boom* (1991)★★★, *The New Frontier* (Liberty 1993)★★★, *Reunited* (Willow Tree 1996)★★★.

HIPSWAY

Hipsway emerged in the mid-80s onto a Scottish pop scene that had enjoyed a high profile, both commercially and critically, with acts like Orange Juice, the Associates, Simple Minds and Altered Images. It was ex-Altered Images bassist Jon McElhone who teamed up with guitarist Pim Jones, drummer Harry Travers and vocalist Graham Skinner (previously in the White Savages) around 1984. As Hipsway, the band secured a deal with Mercury Records who were impressed enough to strongly promote both 'Broken Years' in June and the catchy 'Ask The Lord' later in 1985, though neither made much impact. However, the momentum led to a chart hit with their third single, 'Honey Thief', early in 1986, and in its wake came both Hipsway's self-titled album and a reissue of 'Ask The Lord' in April. Unfortunately, Graham Skinner's dramatic vocal style was the only distinctive feature aside from the previous promising singles. Drawn from the album came 'Long White Car' in August, but both fell quickly by the wayside after a modest chart run. It was three years before Hipsway would return but unfortunately they failed to manage what their second album, *Scratch The Surface*, suggested. 'Young Love' disappeared without trace, the album followed suit, and Hipsway broke up soon afterwards. Skinner and Jones moved on to Witness.

●ALBUMS: *Hipsway* (Mercury 1986)★★★, *Scratch The Surface* (Mercury 1989)★★.

HITCHCOCK, ROBYN

The possessor of a lyrical vision of a latter-day Syd Barrett, UK born Hitchcock made his early reputation with the post-punk psychedelic group, the Soft Boys, having previously appeared in various groups including the Beetles and Maureen And

The Meat Packers. After the Soft Boys split in 1981 he spent some time writing for Captain Sensible, then formed his own group, the Egyptians, around erstwhile colleagues Andy Metcalfe (bass), Morris Windsor (drums) and Roger Jackson (keyboards). Hitchcock's live performances were punctuated by epic, surreal monologues of comic invention capable of baffling the uninitiated and delighting the converted. His sharp mind and predilection for the bizarre has revealed itself in many titles, such as 'Man With The Light Bulb Head' ('. . . I turn myself on in the dark'), 'My Wife And My Dead Wife', a tragi-comedy of a man coming to accept the intrusion into his life of a deceased spouse, 'Trash' a well aimed diatribe against hopeless rock star hangers-on, 'Trams Of Old London', a love and remembrance saga of an era long gone, and a guide to bringing up children in the a cappella, 'Uncorrected Personality Traits'. A move to A&M Records saw the release of *Globe Of Frogs*, which included the 'Ballroom Man', a favourite on US college radio which went some way to breaking new ground and earning Hitchcock a fresh audience. As a result, and despite his devoted cult following in the UK, the artist has in the early 90s concentrated more on recording and performing in the United States (occasionally guesting with R.E.M.). He has also re-formed the Soft Boys and seen his back-catalogue re-packaged with loving commitment by Sequel Records. It remains to be seen whether the oddball workings of this endearing eccentric's mind will find a way into anything other than the US collegiate consciousness. Warner Brothers Records were prepared to take the risk in 1996 when a revitalized Hitchcock released *Moss Elixir*.
●ALBUMS: *Black Snake Diamond Role* includes material recorded with the Soft Boys (Armageddon 1981)★★★, *Groovy Decay* (Albion 1982)★★, *I Often Dream Of Trains* (Midnight Music 1984)★★★, *Groovy Decoy* original demos of *Groovy Decay* (Glass Fish)★★★, with the Egyptians *Fegmania!* (Slash 1985)★★★★, with the Egyptians *Gotta Let This Hen Out!* (Relativity 1985)★★★★, with the Egyptians *Exploding In Silence* mini-album (Relativity 1986)★★★, *Invisible Hitchcock* (Glass Fish 1986)★★★, with the Egyptians *Element Of Light* (Glass Fish 1986)★★★★, with the Egyptians *Globe Of Frogs* (A&M 1988)★★★, with the Egyptians *Queen Elvis* (A&M 1989)★★, *Eye* (Twin/Tone 1990)★★★, *Perspex Island* (A&M 1991)★★★, with the Egyptians *Respect* (A&M 1993)★★★, *Gravy Deco* (Rhino 1995)★★★, *You And Oblivion* (Rhino 1995)★★★, *Mossy Liquor (Outtakes And Prototypes)* limited vinyl-only edition

(Warners 1996)★★★, *Moss Elixir* (Warners 1996)★★★.
●COMPILATIONS: *The Kershaw Sessions* (ROOT 1994)★★★.

HOLLIDAY, JENNIFER

b. 19 October 1960, Houston, Texas, USA. This powerful vocalist first attracted attention as lead in the Broadway show *Your Arm's Too Short To Box With God*. She is, however, better known for her Tony-winning role in the movie *Dreamgirls*, a thinly disguised adaptation of the Supremes' story, which former member Mary Wilson took as the title of her autobiography. The show's undoubted highlight was Holliday's heart-stopping rendition of 'And I Am Telling You I'm Not Going', one of soul's most emotional, passionate performances. The single's success in 1982 prompted Holliday's solo career, but subsequent work was overshadowed by that first hit. She returned to the stage in 1985 in *Sing, Mahalia Sing* and has also acted in the television series *The Love Boat*, which was shown in the UK and the USA. Holliday was also part of the backing choir on Foreigner's 1984 UK number 1 hit single, 'I Wanna Know What Love Is'. *Say You Love Me* won her a second Grammy award in 1985. She appeared in the musical *Grease* in the 90s and has recorded only sporadically. Holliday possesses an outstandingly powerful and emotional voice that has seen it compared to the range of Aretha Franklin.
●ALBUMS: with Loretta Devine, Cleavant Derricks *Dreamgirls* Original Broadway Cast (Geffen 1982)★★★, *Feel My Soul* (Geffen 1983)★★★, *Say You Love Me* (Geffen 1985)★★★, *Get Close To My Love* (Geffen 1987)★★★, *I'm On Your Side* (Arista 1991)★★★, *On And On* (Inter Sound 1994)★★★.
●COMPILATIONS: *The Best Of Jennifer Holliday* (Geffen 1996)★★★★.

HOME SERVICE

Formed in 1980 as the First Eleven, this UK group evolved from the ever-changing Albion Band, which at the time included John Kirkpatrick in the line-up. Led by John Tams (vocals), the group featured Bill Caddick (b. June 1944, Wolverhampton, England; vocals/guitar/dobro), Graeme Taylor (b. 2 February 1954, Stockwell, London, England; vocals/guitar), Michael Gregory (b. 16 November 1949, Gower, South Wales; drums/percussion), Roger Williams (b. 30 July 1954, Cottingham, Yorkshire, England; trombone), Howard Evans (b. 29 February 1944, Chard, Somerset, England; trumpet) and Jonathan Davie (b. 6 September

1954, Twickenham, Middlesex, England; bass). Both Evans and Williams were concurrently members of Brass Monkey, and Caddick had already released a number of solo albums. The group was involved with work for the National Theatre, for which they provided the music for the York Mystery Plays. The resultant album appeared in 1985. This release included Linda Thompson, and covered both traditional and contemporary material. By 1985, Caddick had left the group, unhappy with the lack of live concert work. This situation was caused by the many commitments the group had to theatre, television and film work. The following year, 1986, Andy Findon (saxophone) and Steve King (keyboards) were added to the line-up. It was 1991 before the line-up played together again, on the Hokey Pokey charity compilation *All Through The Year*.

●ALBUMS: *The Home Service* (Jigsaw 1984)★★★, *The Mysteries* (Coda 1985)★★★, *Alright Jack* (Celtic Music 1986)★★★, *Wild Life* live rec. 1992 (Fledg'ling 1995)★★★.

●COMPILATIONS: *All Through The Year* (Hokey Pokey 1991)★★★.

HONEYMAN-SCOTT, JAMES

b. 1956, Hereford, England, d. 16 June 1982, London, England. This flaxen-headed guitarist who doubled on keyboards was a founder-member of the Pretenders in 1978. If less prominent onstage than Chrissie Hynde, he was solidly at the music's heart: loud enough for vocal harmonies, but quietly ministering to overall effect instrumentally. Remembered principally as a guitarist, his riffs and solos were constructed to integrate with melodic and lyrical intent, rather than a flashier reaction to underlying chord sequences. This style was commensurate with a personality that permitted Hynde to take increasing control of the band's destiny after Pretenders II in 1981 - the year he married Peggy Sue Fender. Weakened by a detoxification course for drug addiction, his death in June 1982 occurred shortly after snorting cocaine at a London party. The group found a replacement in Robert McIntosh, a Honeyman-Scott soundalike.

HOODOO GURUS

An Australian rock band whose belief in the power of the bar chord has never diminished, Sydney's Hoodoo Gurus share links with that city's other major alternative rock attraction of the 80s, the Scientists (after both relocated from Perth). That connection was instigated by singer/songwriter Dave Faulkner, who had previously played in a band titled the Gurus, before joining Scientists guitarist Rod Radalj (guitar) in an untitled band. Bolstered by the arrival of another ex-Scientist member, drummer Jim Baker, the trio named their new band Le Hoodoo Gurus. That group would eventually evolve into the tight, hypnotic garage rock machine which, under a slightly abbreviated title, became widely venerated in underground circles through their releases for a variety of American labels. Indeed, much of their popularity stemmed from the USA, where tours of the west coast made them as popular as the musically aligned Fleshtones.

Led by the power-pop playing of Brad Sheperd (guitar/harmonica), with the rhythm section of Baker (drums) and Clyde Bramley (bass), their ceaseless exploration of the riff has seen them compared to everyone from the Cramps to the Fall, beginning with their influential *Stoneage Romeos* debut of 1983. Dedicated to US television sitcom legends Arnold Ziffel and Larry Storch, it included the stage favourite '(Let's All) Turn On' and the nonsensical 'I Was A Kamikaze Pilot'. *Mars Needs Guitars!*, with Mark Kingsmill taking over on drums, was slightly hampered by inferior production, but the tunes were still memorable and even adventurous given their limited musical range, which veered from country punk to booming, bass-driven sleaze rock. A rarer outbreak of melodicism was introduced on *Blow Your Cool!*, with the band joined by the Bangles on several selections, although elsewhere they retreated to pounding rhythms and tough rock 'n' roll. The gap between albums in 1988 saw Bramley replaced by Rick Grossman on bass. More feedback and heightened songwriting tension, together with improved production, produced the band's finest album to date in 1989s *Magnum Cum Louder*. *Kinky* mined a similar furrow, drawing lyrical targets from US and Australian pop culture, though there was little stylistic variation to the band's themes. It seems unlikely that the Hoodoo Gurus will now rise above their current cult status.

●ALBUMS: *Stoneage Romeos* (Big Time/A&M 1983)★★★, *Mars Need Guitars!* (Big Time/Elektra 1985)★★★, *Blow Your Cool!* (Big Time/Elektra 1987)★★★, *Magnum Cum Louder* (RCA 1989)★★★★, *Kinky* (RCA 1991)★★★, *Crank* (RCA 1995)★★, *Blue Cave* (Zoo 1996★★.

●COMPILATIONS: *Electric Soup* Australian release (RCA 1992)★★★★, *Gorilla Bisquit* Australian release (RCA 1992)★★★.

HOOTERS

The long-running Philadelphia band the Hooters have become well versed in the fickle nature of fame since their formation in 1978. Originally a quintet fusing folk, rock and ska, they spent the early 80s building a formidable live reputation throughout surrounding states. Led by Rob Hyman and Eric Brazilian, the Hooters took their name from the distinctive keyboard and harmonica sound that dominated their early recordings. They had several US hits in the mid-80s as MTV exposure took 'All You Zombies' (number 58), 'And We Danced' (number 21), 'Day By Day' (number 18) and 'Where Do The Children Go' (number 38) into the *Billboard* charts. All four were included on their debut album, which received universally strong reviews. Two more singles, 'Johnny B' and 'Satellite', failed to break the Top 50, although the latter did become a strong international seller, topping several European lists. On *Zig Zag* they pursued a more sober direction, with songs such as 'Give The Music Back' and 'Don't Knock It 'Til You Try It' adding darker shades to their repertoire. However, when the sales of the album were only moderate, a dramatic self-appraisal was undertaken. 'We did talk about ending the band, but we came to the conclusion that we still have too much energy.' *Out Of Body* revealed plenty of the Hooters' customary catchy rock verve, but with a new focus on folk rock (including the use of a mandolin, violin and accordion). They had also moved to a new label, following Columbia Records' purchase by Sony (which had upset the promotion of their previous album). They also changed producers (Richard Chertoff departing in favour of Steve Earle collaborator Joe Hardy). Multi-instrumentalist Mindy Jostyn (formerly part of Donald Fagen's New Rock 'N' Soul Revue) was also added as a sixth member. Despite a revitalized sound, the Hooters failed to regain the commercial ground lost in the early 90s, and the band returned to session playing. Most in-demand was Hyman who had already worked with Sophie B. Hawkins, Willie Nelson and Johnny Clegg. He also continued to write for Cyndi Lauper.
●ALBUMS: *Nervous Night* (Columbia 1985)★★★, *One Way Home* (Columbia 1987)★★★, *Zig Zag* (Columbia 1989)★★★, *Out Of Body* (1993)★★★.

HORN, SHIRLEY

b. 1 May 1934, Washington, DC, USA. After studying piano formally, Horn continued her musical education at university. She began leading her own group in the mid-50s and made several records, often in company with front-rank bop musicians. For some years Horn spent much of her time in Europe where her cabaret-oriented performances went down especially well. Nevertheless, this absence from the USA tended to conceal her talent, something her return to the recording studios in the 80s has begun to correct. Although her piano playing is of a high order most attention is centred upon her attractive singing. Interpreting the best of the Great American Song Book in a breathily personal manner, Horn continues to perform and record. She is strikingly adept at the especially difficult task of accompanying herself on the piano. Her 1996 album *The Main Ingredient* was an interesting concept of creating a relaxed jam session atmosphere by having the musicians drop by her home. Recorded over 5 days in-between Horn preparing the food for her house guests, it featured Charles Ables; bass/guitar), Joe Henderson (tenor saxophone), Elvin Jones (drums), Buck Hill (tenor saxophone), Steve Williams (drums), Roy Hargrove (trumpet) and Billy Hart (drums).
●ALBUMS: *Embers And Ashes* (1961)★★★, *Live At The Village Vanguard* (1961)★★★, *Loads Of Love* (Mercury 1963)★★★, *Shirley Horn With Horns* (Mercury 1963)★★★, *Shirley Horn* (1965)★★★, *Trav'lin Light* (Impulse 1965)★★★, *A Lazy Afternoon* (Steeplechase 1978)★★★, *All Night Long* (Syeeplechase 1981)★★★, *Violets For Your Furs* (Steeplechase 1981)★★★, *The Garden Of The Blues* (Steeplechase 1984)★★★, *Softly* (Audiophile 1987)★★★, *I Thought About You* (Verve 1987)★★★, *Close Enough For Love* (Verve 1988)★★★, *You Won't Forget Me* (Verve 1990)★★★, *Here's To Life* (Verve 1991)★★★, *Light Out Of Darkness (A Tribute To Ray Charles)* (1993)★★★, *I Love You Paris* (Verve 1994)★★★, *The Main Ingredient* (Verve 1996)★★★, *Loving You* (Verve 1997)★★★.

HORNETS ATTACK VICTOR MATURE

Until the mid-80s, this American band was one of the most influential groups that never existed. During the late 70s, against the backdrop of new wave, legions of young rockers with thin ties and excess safety pins were congregating under increasingly strange names that eschewed the rakishness and romance of earlier eras (the Searchers, the Telstars, the Temptations, the Kinks), using everything from body parts (the Brains) to *realpolitik* (Gang Of Four) to establish mystique.
One afternoon two rock journalists, both neighbours and columnists for competing music week-

lies, saw a perfect new name for a band in a headline in the *Los Angeles Times*. 'Hornets Attack Victor Mature'. The actor had been whisked off to the Encino burn centre. It is unknown whether he was still under observation several days later when both scribes faced Wednesday deadlines for their rather similar columns, both devoted to reporting the latest news in Hollywood music circles. What is known is that both reporters encountered a not uncommon problem, a surfeit of committed editorial space against a shortfall of compelling fact, and that both reporters arrived at the same solution. As many journalistic professionals know, a misstatement of fact is a gross miscarriage of the truth. A misstatement with a question mark at the end is entirely legal. Thus, these resourceful members of the Fourth Estate wondered aloud: 'Will Hornets Attack Victor Mature be the next L.A. power pop band to snare big bucks in a record deal?' The following week, two respected industry journals both queried a heretofore disinterested collective readership about the fate of this group. A week thereafter, a rock radio newsletter not known for its exhaustive fact-checking protocols reprinted the informations, *sans* question mark. Thus was the long and largely fruitless career of Hornets Attack Victor Mature launched, accumulating momentum and new copy lines without benefit of single, album, video, tour or lawsuit. In 1980, *Musician* magazine named the band winner in both the Best Name For A New Band and Worst Name For A New Band categories. At the beginning of the 80s a buxom centrefold in *Oui* magazine was quoted as loving new wave and punk, naming Hornets Attack Victor Mature alongside the Clash as among her favourites (possibly the bio was ghosted by one of our former columnists).

This virtual career might have gone on indefinitely, but in the mid-80s the members of R.E.M. actually booked themselves into an Athens club under this very name, an event documented in the pages of *Q Magazine*.
●ALBUMS: *The Underground Car Park Tapes* (Redmond West 1997)★★.

HOTHOUSE FLOWERS

This folk-inspired Irish rock group, who took their name from the title of a Wynton Marsalis album, are based around the nucleus of Liam O'Maonlai and Fiachna O'Broanain. O'Maonlai was formerly in a punk band called Congress which later evolved into My Bloody Valentine. They started performing together as the Incomparable Benzini Brothers and busked in their native Dublin. In 1985

they won the Street Entertainers Of The Year Award. Recruiting Maria Doyle they became the Hothouse Flowers and landed a regular gig at the Magic Carpet Club just outside Dublin. Their notoriety spreading, they were highly praised in *Rolling Stone* magazine before they had even concluded a recording contract. An appearance on RTE's Saturday night chat programme - *The Late Show* - led to the issue of a single on U2's Mother label. 'Love Don't Work That Way' came out in 1987 and though it was not a great success it brought them to the attention of PolyGram Records who signed them up. Their debut single for the major - 'Don't Go' - was a number 11 UK hit. Further hits followed, including a cover of Johnny Nash's 'I Can See Clearly Now', 'Give It Up', and 'Movies'. Their debut, *People*, reached number 2 in the UK charts. The band exist as part of a larger, looser 'Raggle Taggle' musical community, and members can be heard on material by the Indigo Girls, Adventures, Michelle Shocked and Maria McKee. In the early 90s they made their 'acting' debut in an episode of the UK television series *Lovejoy*.
●ALBUMS: *People* (London 1988)★★★, *Home* (London 1990)★★, *Songs From The Rain* (London 1993)★★★.

HOUSE OF LOVE

After a short spell with the ill-fated glam-rock inspired Kingdoms, UK-born vocalist/guitarist Guy Chadwick teamed up with drummer Pete Evans, guitarist Terry Bickers, bassist Chris Groothuizen and vocalist/guitarist Andrea Heukamp to form UK group, the House Of Love. Throughout 1986, the quintet played at small pubs and despatched a demo tape to Creation Records which, after constant play in the office, attracted the attention of label head, Alan McGee. He financed the recording of their debut single, the sparkling 'Shine On', which was released in May 1987. A follow-up, 'Real Animal', was also issued, but sold relatively poorly. After touring extensively under tough conditions, Andrea Heukamp decided to leave the group. Continuing as a quartet, the House Of Love spent the spring of 1988 recording their debut album, which cost an astonishingly meagre £8000 to complete. A pilot single, 'Christine', was rightly acclaimed as one of the best UK independent singles of the year. Its shimmering guitar work was exemplary and indicated the enormous potential of the ensemble. The debut album did not disappoint and was included in many critics' nominations for the best record of 1988. Already, the House Of Love were being tipped as the group most likely to succeed in 1989 and the release of the excellent 'Destroy The Heart' reinforced that view. Speculation was rife that they would sign to a major label and eventually PhonoGram secured their signatures. In keeping with their 60s/guitar-based image the group's releases were subsequently issued on the newly revived Fontana Records label. A torturous period followed. The first two singles for the label, 'Never' and 'I Don't Know Why I Love You', both stalled at number 41, while the album suffered interminable delays. By Christmas 1989, guitarist Terry Bickers had quit over what was euphemistically termed a personality clash. He was immediately replaced by Simon Walker, and early the following year the group's long-awaited £400,000 second album, *Fontana*, appeared to mixed reviews. As Chadwick later acknowledged: 'We'd stated everything on the first album'. Extensive touring followed, ending with the departure of Walker, tentatively replaced by original member Andrea Heukamp, who returned from Germany. Thereafter, Chadwick suffered a long period of writer's block while the departing Bickers enjoyed acclaim in Levitation. Although the House Of Love lost ground to newly revered guitar groups such as the Stone Roses, they re-emeged in October 1991 with an acclaimed EP featuring the excellent 'The Girl With The Loneliest Eyes'. In 1992, the group's long-awaited new album, *Babe Rainbow*, was released to a degree of critical acclaim, but the impression of under-achievement was hard to avoid. Following 1993's *Audience Of The Mind* the band collapsed, Chadwick re-emerging a year later with the Madonnas.

● ALBUMS: *House Of Love* (Creation 1988)★★★, *Fontana* (Fontana 1989)★★, *Babe Rainbow* (Fontana 1992)★★★, *Audience Of The Mind* (Fontana 1993)★★★.
● COMPILATIONS: *A Spy In The House Of Love* (Fontana 1990)★★★.

HOUSEMARTINS

Formed in 1984, this UK pop group comprised Paul Heaton (b. 9 May 1962, Hull, Humberside, England; vocals/guitar), Stan Collimore (b. 6 April 1962, Hull, Humberside, England; bass), Ted Key (guitar) and Hugh Whitaker (drums). After signing to Go! Discs the group humorously promoted themselves as 'the fourth best band from Hull'. Their modesty and distinctly plain image disguised a genuine songwriting talent, which soon emerged. During late 1985, Key departed and was replaced by Norman Cook (b. 31 July 1963, Brighton, Sussex,

England). By 1986, the group achieved their first UK hit with their third release, the infectious 'Happy Hour', which climbed to number 3. Their UK Top 10 debut album *London 0 Hull 4* displayed a wit, freshness and verve that rapidly established them as one of Britain's most promising groups. In December 1986, their excellent a cappella version of 'Caravan Of Love' gave them a deserved UK number 1 hit. Early in 1987 the Housemartins received a coveted BPI award as the Best Newcomers of the year. In the summer, they underwent a line-up change, with Dave Hemmingway replacing drummer Hugh Whitaker. Another acclaimed release 'Five Get Over Excited' followed, after which the group displayed their left-wing political preferences by performing at the 'Red Wedge' concerts. After securing another Top 20 hit with the catchy 'Me And The Farmer', the group issued their final studio album, the self-mocking *The People Who Grinned Themselves To Death*. Although still at the peak of their powers, the group split in June 1988, annoucing that they had only intended the Housemartins to last for three years. The power of the original line-up was indicated by the subsequent successes of offshoot groups such as the Beautiful South and Beats International. In 1993 Hugh Whitaker was charged and sentenced to six years imprisonment for wounding with intent and three arson attacks on a business acquaintance.

● ALBUMS: *London 0 Hull 4* (Go! Discs 1986)★★★★, *The People Who Grinned Themselves To Death* (Go! Discs 1987)★★.
● COMPILATIONS: *Now That's What I Call Quite Good!* (Go! Discs 1988)★★★★.
● FURTHER READING: *The Housemartins, Tales From Humberside*, Nick Swift.

HUE AND CRY

Based in Coatbridge, Scotland, brothers Patrick (b. 10 March 1964, Coatbridge, Strathclyde, Scotland) and Gregory Kane (b. 11 September 1966, Coatbridge, Strathclyde, Scotland) started as a band in 1986. Patrick handles the lyrics and singing duties while his brother concentrates on writing music, and plays piano and keyboards. Although they use session players both on stage and in the studio, some of their most powerful work has been just voice and piano - including the 1989 *Bitter Suite*. Their first single, 'I Refuse', was released in 1986 and flopped, but the following year the soul-fired 'Labour Of Love' gave them a UK hit. They received much attention for the memorable single 'Looking For Linda' (the true story of a woman who left home to buy a packet of cigarettes and ended up on a southbound train heading away from her old life). Since then, only their work as a bare duo has attracted any attention. The *Violently* EP in 1989 contained a cover of Kate Bush's 'The Man With The Child In His Eyes', and in 1991 they parted company with their long-term label Circa. In early 1992 they sought a new contract, while Patrick remained prominent outside of music. Always one of the more articulate of personalities within the pop world, he has served as both an outspoken television presenter and music journalist. He is also the Rector of Glasgow University (narrowly edging out Tony Benn). A firm socialist, he has recently turned his back on the Labour Party and given very vocal support to the Scottish Nationalist Party. Certainly he refuses to accept the boundaries between music and politics, as the lyrics to the single 'Peaceful Face' demonstrate: 'The future I see, The century comes and it goes, And my child will be there to bear all its woes'. He has been instrumental in forming the Artists For An Independent Scotland organization which is supported by other Scottish 'celebrities' and rock stars such as Fish. *Stars Crash Down*, their most recent album, features contributions from fellow Scots Eddi Reader and Vernal and Prime from Deacon Blue. *Piano & Vocal* was a bold project that worked because of the strength of Pat Kane's voice, even when tackling syrupy standards such as 'Send In The Clowns'.

●ALBUMS: *Seduced And Abandoned* (Circa 1987)★★★, *Remote/The Bitter Suite* (Circa 1989)★★★, *Stars Crash Down* (Circa 1991)★★, *Truth And Love* (Fidelity 1992)★★, *Showtime!* (Permanent 1994)★★, *Piano & Voice* (Permanent 1995)★★★.

●COMPILATIONS: *Labours Of Love - The Very Best Of* (Circa 1993)★★★.

HUGHES, GLENN

b. 21 August 1952, Cannock, Staffordshire, England. He left school at the age of 15 to follow his dream of becoming a musician. He began playing lead guitar with the News in 1967, where he also sang, emulating his heroes Otis Redding and Wilson Pickett. Later he switched to bass guitar inspired by James Jamerson from the Tamla/Motown Records 'house band'. These influences, added to a love of rock 'n' roll, led him to form Trapeze with Dave Holland (drums) and Mei Galley (guitar). Trapeze signed to the Moody Blues' record label, Threshold, and released four albums up to 1973, when Hughes was offered a job with a new Birmingham band

Electric Light Orchestra. He declined and in June joined Deep Purple instead. It is with Purple that Hughes made his mark in the UK with his superb singing on *Burn*, where he joined with, and some believe outclassed, their new vocalist David Coverdale. Hughes' influence over Purple became a contributing factor in Ritchie Blackmore deciding to quit, and his association with the band continued until 1976 when he re-formed Trapeze with the original line-up, though this venture failed to tour or record. When they did finally begin a US tour Hughes walked out halfway through. The band continued without him while their leader disappeared from public view. Two years later he surfaced with a solo album before again dropping out of sight. 1982 saw him join with Pat Thrall (guitar, ex-Pat Travers Band) and Quiet Riot drummer Frankie Banali to form Hughes/Thrall, who released one album to a poor reception (though this set would posthumously achieve 'legendary' status and become one of the most sought after rock albums of the 80s). After the project fell apart Hughes worked for a while with Gary Moore but nothing came of it. Then in 1985 he reunited with Mel Galley and a host of stars to record the concept album, *Phenomena*. Though considered obsolete by rock critics it did serve to put Hughes back on the map and Tony Iommi, looking for a replacement for Ian Gillan in Black Sabbath, contacted him. Hughes spent less than a year with the band but did record some fine vocals for *Seventh Star*. He then sank back into obscurity and personal problems but help from an unusual quarter was at hand. Bill Drummond of the KLF had always enjoyed the idea of blending rock with dance music (he had already obtained infamy in such matters with Extreme Noise Terror) so he coaxed Hughes back into the limelight in 1991 for the hit single, 'America - What Time Is Love?' This success reanimated the vocalist's efforts and he set about forming a new band which has since enjoyed a small degree of concert success, and he has also renewed his partnership with Pat Thrall for a projected second album. A new band, World, was put together in 1993 although his solo career continues. On *Feel* he edged closer to AOR balladry. Follow-up *Addiction* was a stronger set.

●ALBUMS: *Play Me Out* (Safari 1978)★★★, as Hughes/Thrall *Hughes/Thrall* (Epic 1982)★★★, with Phenomena *Phenomena* (Bronze 1985)★★, *From Now On* (Roadrunner 1994)★★★, *Feel* (SPV 1995)★★, *Addiction* (Steamhammer 1996)★★★.

HUGHES, JOE 'GUITAR'

b. 29 September 1937, Houston, Texas, USA. A product of Houston's third ward, Joe 'Guitar' Hughes turned to music at an early age under the influence of the work of T-Bone Walker. He claims to have used money earned washing dishes to buy his first electric guitar at the age of 14 and to have been appearing professionally by the time he was 16. His first band was the Dukes Of Rhythm which included in its line-up Hughes' neighbour and friend Johnny Copeland. When this group disbanded in 1964 Hughes joined Grady Gaines working for Little Richard's old group the Upsetters. His next job was working as a member of Bobby Bland's band which he left in the wake of Bland's supporting star Al 'TNT' Braggs. After three years with Braggs, Hughes moved on to playing lead with Julius Jones and the Rivieras and from there to various groups operating around the Houston area. An upsurge of interest in the post-war Texas blues brought Joe to some prominence during the early 80s, since which he has toured in Europe and recorded for Double Trouble Records of Holland. Texas Guitar Slinger was co-produced by Jerry Jenkins.

●ALBUMS: *Craftsman* (Double Trouble 1988)★★★, *Down & Depressed: Dangerous* (Munich 1993)★★★, *Live At Vrendenburg* (Double Trouble 1993)★★★, *Texas Guitar Slinger* (Me And My Records 1996)★★★.

HUMAN LEAGUE

The history of the Human League is essentially that of two radically different UK groups, one experimental and arcane, the other melodic and commercial. The first incarnation of the group formed in the summer of 1978 with a line-up comprising Ian Craig Marsh (b 11 November 1956, Sheffield, England; synthesizer), Martyn Ware (b. 19 May 1956, Sheffield, England; synthesizer), Phil Oakey (b. 2 October 1955, Sheffield, England; vocals) and Addy Newton. The latter left soon after the group was named Human League and was replaced by Adrian Wright (b. 30 June 1956, Sheffield, England), who was credited as 'visual director'. Early in 1978, the group was signed to Robert Last's Edinburgh-based independent label Fast Product. Their first single was the unusual 'Being Boiled', which sold 16,000 copies and resulted in them securing a tie-in deal with Virgin Records. Their debut, *Reproduction*, sold steadily, while the EP *Holiday, '80*, won them an appearance on the prestigious television show *Top Of The Pops*.

By this point, Philip Oakey's pierced nipples and geometric haircut had made him the focal point of the group. This led to some friction within the Human League, which was not overcome by the chart success of their second album, *Travelogue*. Matters culminated at the end of 1980 with the shock departure of Marsh and Ware, who went on to found BEF and its offshoot group Heaven 17. In return for a percentage of royalties on future releases, Marsh and Ware allowed Oakey to retain the name Human League. Instead of recruiting experienced musicians as replacements Oakey, somewhat bizarrely, chose two teenage girls, whom he discovered at a Sheffield discotheque. Susanne Sulley (b. 22 March 1963, Sheffield, England) and Joanne Catherall (b. 16 September 1962, Sheffield, England) had absolutely no knowledge of the music business, had never sung professionally and were busy at school studying for A-levels when Oakey made his offer. The new line-up was completed by bassist Ian Burden (b. 24 December 1957, Sheffield, England) and former Rezillos guitarist Jo Callis (b. 2 May 1955, Glasgow, Scotland) The new group contrasted radically with the cold, remote image of the original Human League and pursued a pure pop Holy Grail, which delivered a series of UK hits during 1981. 'Boys And Girls', 'The Sound Of The Crowd', 'Love Action' and 'Open Your Heart' paved the way for the group's celebrated pop album, *Dare*, which sold over five million copies. An extraordinary year ended with the awesome Christmas chart-topper, 'Don't You Want Me', the biggest-selling UK single of 1981. The song was particularly notable for its use of a double point of view, which was brilliantly captured in the accompanying video with Oakey and Catherall trading perspectives on a fragmenting relationship. The track went on to become a number 1 in the USA, spearheading a British invasion of 'new pop' artists. The Human League then took a long sabbatical, interrupted only by a couple of further hits with 'Mirror Man' and '(Keep Feeling) Fascination' and a mini-album of dance remixes. The 1984 comeback album, *Hysteria*, met a mixed response, while the attendant singles, 'The Lebanon', 'Life On Your Own' and 'Louise', all reached the UK Top 20. Oakey ended 1984 by teaming up with disco producer Giorgio Moroder for a surprisingly successful single and album. A further two years passed before the next Human League album, *Crash*, and, along the way, Wright and Callis departed. Several of the tracks on the new album were composed by producers Jam and Lewis, among them a US number 1 'Human'. In 1990, the group returned with a new album, which met a cool response. Following a lengthy break from the public eye, and just when the world had seemingly buried them they returned five years later with *Octopus* and a series of sparkling hit singles. Much of the freshness and simplicity of *Dare* was present in the new collection. Singles such as 'Tell Me When' indicated a strong grasp of how repeated hooklines in pop songs can creep into the subconcious - and cannot be resisted. Despite their erratic career, the Human League have shown a remarkable ability to triumph commercially and aesthetically, and usually at the least predictable moments.

●ALBUMS: *Reproduction* (Virgin 1979)★★, *Travelogue* (Virgin 1980)★★, *Dare* (Virgin 1981)★★★★, *Love And Dancing* (Virgin 1982)★★★, *Hysteria* (Virgin 1984)★★, *Crash* (Virgin 1986)★★, *Romantic* (Virgin 1990)★★, *Octopus* (East West 1995)★★★.

●COMPILATIONS: *Human League's Greatest Hits* (Virgin 1988)★★★★, *Greatest Hits* (Virgin 1995)★★★★.

●VIDEOS: *Greatest Video Hits* (Warners 1995).

●FURTHER READING: *The Story Of A Band Called The Human League*, Alaska Ross and Jill Furmanovsky. *The Human League: Perfect Pop*, Peter Nash.

HUNNIGALE, PETER

UK reggae star Peter Hunnigale, aka Mr Honey Vibes, has built his name in the lovers rock idiom, and is clearly one of the stars of the genre. His career began in Vibes Corner, a loose collective, which also featured Barrington Levine, Jimmy Simpson, Ray Simpson and Fitzroy Blake. This eventually led to Hunnigale's debut single, 'Slippin' Away'/'Swing And Dine', which sold respectably on LGR Records. 'Got To Know You'/'Money Money' then found a home on his own Street Vibes imprint which he co-founded with long-term collaborator Blake (it is now run in association with Tippa Irie and Crucial Robbie). A further string of singles emerged, notably 'Be My Lady' in 1987, which won him the Topline Entertainments Celebrity Award for Best Newcomer. The debut album that followed also garnered favourable reviews, while his single profile increased with 'Falling' and the formidable 'Raggamuffin Girl'. A duet with Tippa Irie released in 1989, this went straight to number 1 in the UK reggae charts, and was voted Best British Reggae Record by *Echoes* newspaper at the close of the year. With this success behind them they embarked on two album

collaborations: *The New Decade* for Island Records and *Done Cook And Currie* for Rebel MC's Tribal Base label. The former collection was produced by Hunnigale himself and featured two songs popular on the UK sound system circuit, 'Shocking Out' and 'Dibi Dibi'. He also produced and played all the instruments on *Done Cook And Currie*, which produced another major domestic reggae hit with 'Inner City'. His second solo album, *Mr Vibes*, followed in the same year. His next collaboration with Irie came in 1993, this time a single, 'Shouting For The Gunners', to celebrate their mutual fondness for the London football club Arsenal. 1994's *Mr Government* was a more roots-flavoured offering, released on the Mad Professor's Ariwa Sounds label, after which Hunnigale worked with Crucial Robbie once more on a version of Desmond Dekker's '007'. *Nah Give Up*, which saw him return to the sweet sounds of lovers' rock for which he has a natural vocal affinity, was released in 1995, featuring a string of reggae chart hits such as 'Trust Me' and 'Sorry'. His already distinguished career has seen him work with artists such as the Original Pioneers, Maxi Priest (writing the title track to his *Best Of Me* hit album), Chosen Few, Trevor Hartley, Double Trouble, Tinga Stewart and B.B. Seaton as well as many others, either as musician, producer or writer.

●ALBUMS: *In This Time* (Street Vibes 1987)★★★, with Tippa Irie *The New Decade* (Mango/Island 1991)★★★, *Mr Vibes* (Street Vibes 1992)★★★, with Tippa Irie *Done Cook And Currie* (Tribal Base 1992)★★★, *Mr Government* (Ariwa Sounds 1994)★★★, *Nah Give Up* (Kalymazoo 1995)★★★.

HÜSKER DÜ

Formed in Minneapolis, Minnesota, USA, in 1979, Hüsker Dü were a punk trio consisting of guitarist/vocalist Bob Mould, bassist Greg Norton and drummer Grant Hart, whose melding of pop and punk influences inspired thousands of UK, US and European bands. Indeed, it is hard to think of a single other band who have had such a profound impact on modern alternative music than this trio. Taking their name, which means 'Do you remember?', from a Norwegian board game, they started out as an aggressive hardcore thrash band before challenging that genre's restrictions and expanding to other musical formats. Their primary strength, like so many other truly great groups, was in having two songwriting partners (Mould and Hart) that for the entirety of their career fully complemented each other. Their first single, 'Statues', was released on the small Reflex label in

1981. The following year, a debut album, *Land Speed Record*, arrived on New Alliance Records, followed by an EP, *In A Free Land*. *Everything Falls Apart* in 1983 saw them back on Reflex. By the advent of their second EP, *Metal Circus* (now on SST Records), Hüsker Dü had become a critics' favourite in the USA - a rapport which was soon to be exported to their UK brethren. *Zen Arcade* in 1984 brought about a stylistic turning point - a two-record set, it followed a single storyline about a young boy leaving home and finding life even more difficult on his own. A 14-minute closing song, 'Reoccurring Dreams', in which it was revealed the boy's entire ordeal was a dream, broke all the rules of punk. A non-album cover of the Byrds' 'Eight Miles High' followed, and a 1985 album, *New Day Rising*, maintained the trio's reputation as a favourite of critics and college radio stations, with its irresistible quicksilver pop songs. After *Flip Your Wig* the band signed with Warner Brothers Records (there were several other interested parties), with whom they issued *Candy Apple Grey* in 1986 and *Warehouse: Songs And Stories,* another double set, the following year. In 1988 Hart was dismissed from the group (though there are many conflicting versions of events leading up to this juncture), who summarily disbanded. Mould and Hart continued as solo artists, before Mould formed the equally rumbustious Sugar in 1991.

●ALBUMS: *Land Speed Record* (New Alliance 1982)★★, *Everything Falls Apart* (Reflex 1982)★★, *Zen Arcade* (SST 1984)★★★★, *New Day Rising* (SST 1985)★★★, *Flip Your Wig* (SST 1985)★★★★, *Candy Apple Grey* (Warners 1986)★★★★, *Warehouse: Songs And Stories* (Warners 1987)★★★★, *The Living End* rec. 1987 (Warners 1994)★★★.

●COMPILATIONS: *Everything Falls Apart And More* (Warners 1993)★★★★.

I, LUDICROUS

Offbeat indie band I, Ludicrous comprise Will Hung (b. David Rippingale, London, England, 4 November 1956; vocals) and John Procter (b. Epsom, England, 9 May 1957; instruments). The duo first met in 1981 while working for Finsbury Data Services in London. Their mutual passion for the Fall and Crystal Palace Football Club cemented the partnership. They had additionally been involved in various failed punk bands over the years, but only formed a group together in February 1985. After witnessing a performance by John Cooper Clarke and Nico at the Cricketers in Kensington, London, the duo decided they could do much better than the third support, a talentless comedian. Their debut gig was dreamed up as support to performance artist friend Max Couper, with Procter providing a musical soundtrack to Hung's off the cuff observations on the day he had endured. This intention soon metamorphosized into a songwriting partnership, which after just three gigs secured them a contract with Kaleidoscope Records. Armed only with a Cassio keyboard and Littlewoods mail-order guitar, their central appeal lay in the monotone delivery of unlikely narratives about 'Lunch With The Geldofs' or 'Preposterous Tales In The Life Of John Mackenzie'. The latter was their first release, on a flexi disc which accompanied *Blah Blah Blah* fanzine in April 1987. It was received warmly by disc jockey John Peel, who offered them a Radio 1 session, while his favourite band, the Fall, invited them to support at London's Astoria venue. Their debut album, *It's Like Everything Else*, duly emerged in September 1987 to glowing and/or confused reviews. 'Quite Extraordinary' followed in 1988 as their first single, but then the band were hamstrung by a series of business problems. The collapse of Red Rhino distribution led to a deal with the tiny Rodney, Rodney! label, but this failed to give the requisite push to either *A Warning To The Curious* or *Light And Bitter*, their next two albums. Forced to finance their own output, the duo offered a new album in 1992, *Idiots Savants*, while the attendant single, 'We Stand Around', was Single Of The Week in the *New Musical Express* in September 1992. None of this was enough to allow the participants to give up their many and various day jobs, however, though the release of 'Hats Off To Eldorado' in 1994 confirmed their continued wry presence in the UK music industry's under-belly.

●ALBUMS: *It's Like Everything Else* (Kaleidoscope 1987)★★★, *A Warning To The Curious* (Rodney, Rodney! 1989)★★★, *Light And Bitter* (Rodney, Rodney! 1990)★★★, *Idiots Savants* (I, Ludicrous 1992)★★★.

ICE-T

One of the most outspoken rappers on the west coast, Ice-T (b. Tracy Marrow, *c.*1958, Newark, New Jersey, USA) boasts (sometimes literally) a violent past in which he was shot twice - once while involved in an armed robbery. His name, fittingly, is taken from black exploitation author Iceberg Slim, and he is backed on record by Afrika Islam and DJ Aladdin's hardcore hip hop. His first record was actually 'The Coldest Rapper' in 1983, which was improvised over a Jimmy Jam And Terry Lewis rhythm, and made him the first Los Angeles hip hop artist. Unfortunately, he was subsequently held under contract by mogul Willie Strong for several years. Disillusioned, he made his money from petty and not so petty crime, and also appeared in the breakdance film *Breakin'*, which included his 'Reckless' cut on the soundtrack. He followed it with the faddish 'Killers' 45, wherein he dressed himself up as a full-blown medieval warrior. The breakthrough, however, came with 'Ya Don't Know', which was widely credited with being the first west coast hip hop artefact (although the honour was undoubtedly Ice-T's, the real beneficiary should have been the obscure 'The Coldest Rapper' cut). Four LPs in just three years created something of a stir in the USA, based as they were largely on his experiences as a gang member in Los Angeles. In 1989 he reached the lower end of the UK charts with 'High Rollers', but did better the following year teaming up with Curtis Mayfield on a remake of 'Superfly'. He is married to Darlene who normally appears semi-clad on his record sleeves, and owns a pit pull terrier affectionately titled Felony. For a time, too, he delighted in inviting journalists to his luxury Beverly Hills home to show them his personal armoury of semi-auto-matic weapons. Success has also enabled him to start his own record company, Rhyme Syndicate. His vision of the black man as sophisticated and

articulate (being hard as nails is, of course, *de rigeur*) ranks him among the most potent forces in contemporary black culture. His refusal to engage in a white liberal agenda (he was the first rap artist to have warning stickers placed on his album sleeves) has irritated many, but helped establish him as an authentic spokesperson for dispossessed black youth. His debut album *Rhyme Pays*, with an Uzi emblazoned on the cover, served as a mission statement: hardcore raps on street violence and survival being the order of the day. By the time of its follow-up, there was demonstrably greater imagination displayed in terms of backing music. Like many of his west coast brethren, Ice-T had rediscovered funk. Notable tracks included 'Girls L.G.B.N.A.F.', which the PMRC later discovered stood for 'Let's Get Butt Naked And Fuck'. Their reaction to this (arguably among the least offensive statements on Ice-T's records) was so overheated that the debate heavily informed his follow-up set. However, his crowning glory so far was *OG* (an acronym for Original Gangster which has passed into rap's lexicon) which ranks alongside the best work of Ice Cube, Public Enemy or NWA in terms of sustained intensity, yet managed to maintain a little more finesse than his previous work. In 1991, with appealing irony, he starred as a cop in the movie *New Jack City*. He had earlier contributed the title track to the LA gangster movie, *Colors*, rapping the title song. He also appeared with former NWA and solo artist Ice Cube in the Walter Hill film *Looters* (renamed *Trespassers* due to its release at the same time as the LA riots), as well as *Surviving The Game* and the cult comic hero movie, *Tank Girl*. His other soundtrack credits include *Dick Tracy*. Ice-T's hobbies include his own thrash metal outfit, Body Count, who released an album in 1992 and stirred up immeasurable controversy via one of its cuts, 'Cop Killer' (detailed under Body Count entry). Little wonder that he was targeted on right wing assassination lists discovered by the police in 1993. His album from that year, *Home Invasion*, saw him take on the mantle of agent provocateur in the young white male's home, a theme reinforced in its cover and title - Ice-T was a threat in your neighbourhood, with another manifesto of spiteful intent ('I'm takin' your kids' brains, You ain't getting them back, I'm gonna fill 'em with hard drugs, big guns, bitches, hoes and death'). Then he went and spoiled all the good work by writing a book, the *Ice-T Opinion*, which was so full of dumb ideas that it largely discredited such achievements. On 22 March 1994 he introduced Channel 4's *Without Walls*, a documentary on the rise of the blaxploitation movie. His own life would make an excellent documentary subject. He continues to fascinate those on both sides of the rap lobby, and, as he notes in *Home Invasion*'s 'Ice Muthafuckin' T': 'Every fucking thing I write, Is going to be analysed by somebody white'.

●ALBUMS: *Rhyme Pays* (Sire 1987)★★★, *Power* (Sire 1988)★★, *The Iceberg/Freedom Of Speech . . . Just Watch What You Say* (Sire 1989)★★★, *OG: Original Gangster* (Syndicate/Sire 1991)★★★★, *Home Invasion* (Priority 1993)★★★, *Born Dead* (Priority 1994)★★★.

●VIDEOS: *O.G. - The Original Gangster Video* (1991).

●FURTHER READING: *The Ice Opinion*, Ice-T and Heidi Seigmund.

ICEHOUSE

This Australian rock band was formed as Flowers in the late 70s by songwriter and multi-instrumentalist Iva Davies (b. Ivor Davies, 22 May 1955). Influenced by Roxy Music and David Bowie, Flowers' other members included Keith Welsh (bass), John Lloyd (drums) and Michael Hoste (keyboards). The first single, 'Can't Help Myself' was a Top 10 hit in 1980. The following year the group signed to Chrysalis Records, touring the UK and North America. Its name was changed to Icehouse (the title of the debut album) to avoid confusion with a US group called Flowers. Despite further Australian success with 'Love In Motion' and 'Great Southern Land', Davies disbanded the group in 1982 to concentrate on the solo *Primitive Man*. However, he was persuaded to re-form Icehouse the next year with British musicians Andy Qunta (keyboards) and ex-Killing Joke member Guy Pratt (guitar). The new line-up also included Lloyd, Hoste and leading Australian guitarist Bob Kretshmer. Almost immediately, Icehouse had a British hit with 'Hey Little Girl', which was accompanied by a striking video directed by Russell Mulcahy. After touring Europe in support of David Bowie, Davies took the band off the road for a further two years. During this time he composed scores for Mulcahy's feature film *Razorback* and (with Kretshmer) for a ballet for the Sydney Dance Company. The group returned in 1986 with the tougher 'No Promises' and the glam-rock flavoured 'Baby You're So Strange' from *Measure For Measure*. In 1987 there were more Australian hits with 'Crazy' and 'Electric Blue', both of which reached the US Top 20 the following year.

●ALBUMS: *Icehouse* (Chrysalis 1980)★★★, *Love In Motion* (Chrysalis 1992)★★, *Primitive Man* (Chrysalis 1983)★★, *Sidewalk* (Chrysalis 1984)★★, *Measure For Measure* (Chrysalis 1986)★★★, *Man Of Colours* (Chrysalis 1987)★★.

●COMPILATIONS: *Great Southern Land* (Diva 1990)★★★, *Masterfile* (Diva 1992)★★★.

Solo: Iva Davies *Code Blue* (Diva 1990)★★★, *Big Wheel* (Diva 1993)★★★, *Full Circle* (Diva 1994)★★★, *The Berlin Tapes* (Diva 1995)★★★.

ICICLE WORKS

Emerging from the profligate network of Liverpudlian bands that existed during the punk rock and new wave era, the Icicle Works were formed by Ian McNabb (b. 3 November 1962; vocals/guitar), Chris Layhe (bass) and Chris Sharrock (drums). McNabb was formerly in City Limits with the near legendary Edie Shit (Howie Mimms), and Sharrock played with the Cherry Boys (who also included Mimms at one point). Taking their name from a science fiction novel - *The Day The Icicle Works Closed Down* - they made their recording debut with a six-track cassette entitled *Ascending*, released on the local Probe Plus emporium in 1981. The band then founded their own Troll Kitchen label on which they prepared 'Nirvana', their first single. Gaining much support from BBC disc jockey John Peel they came to the attention of Beggars Banquet Records, initially through their Situation 2 offshoot. Their second single, 'Birds Fly (Whisper To A Scream)', was an 'indie' hit but they had to wait for the next effort, 'Love Is A Wonderful Colour', to breach the UK Top 20. The subject matter was typically subverted by McNabb's irony and cynicism ('When love calls me, I shall be running swiftly, To find out, just what all the fuss is all about'). Teaming up with producer Ian Broudie (ex-Big In Japan; Care; Lightning Seeds) he helped them to a string of single successes over the ensuing years including 'Hollow Horse' and 'Understanding Jane', with their sound gradually shifting from subtle pop to harder rock territory. In 1986 they recruited Dave Green on keyboards, but the following year the group was turned upside down when both Sharrock and Layhe left within a short space of time. Sharrock joined the La's and later drummed for World Party. Layhe's role was taken by former Black bassist Roy Corkhill, whilst the drummer's stool was claimed by Zak Starkey whose father Ringo Starr formerly drummed for another Liverpool band. This line-up prospered for a short time but in 1989 McNabb assembled a new band. Retaining only Corkhill he added Mark Revell on guitar, Dave Baldwin on keyboards, and Paul Burgess on drums. The band signed a new contract with Epic Records and released an album before McNabb left to go solo. One of England's most underrated, natural lyricists, his cult status looks set to continue, while his time with the Icicle Works has left behind a rich legacy of songwriting.

●ALBUMS: *The Icicle Works* (Beggars Banquet 1984)★★★, *The Small Price Of A Bicycle* (Beggars Banquet 1985)★★★, *If You Want To Defeat Your Enemy Sing His Song* (Beggars Banquet 1987)★★★, *Blind* (Beggars Banquet 1988)★★★, *Permanent Damage* (Epic 1990)★★★, *BBC Radio One Live In Concert* rec. 1987 (Windsong 1994)★★.

●COMPILATIONS: *Seven Singles Deep* (Beggars Banquet 1986)★★, *The Best Of* (Beggars Banquet 1992)★★★.

IGLESIAS, JULIO

b. 23 September 1943, Madrid, Spain. Iglesias trained as a lawyer and played football (goalkeeper) for Real Madrid before suffering severe injuries in a car accident. While recuperating, he learned guitar and began to write songs. After completing his studies at Cambridge University, he entered the 1968 Spanish Song Festival at Benidorm. Performing his own composition 'La Vida Sigue Igual' ('Life Continues All The Same'), he won first prize and soon afterwards signed a recording contract with the independent Discos Columbia where Ramon Arcusa became his producer. In 1970, Iglesias represented Spain in the Eurovision Song Contest, subsequently recording the song 'Gwendolyne' in French, Italian and English. During the next few years he toured widely in Europe and Latin America, scoring international hits with 'Manuela' (1975) and 'Hey' (1979). His global reach was increased in 1978 when he signed to CBS International and soon had hits in French and Italian. The first big English-language success came in 1981 when his version of 'Begin The Beguine' topped the UK charts. This was followed by the multi-language compilation album *Julio* which sold a million in America. Co-produced by Arcusa and Richard Perry, *1100 Bel Air Place* was aimed directly at American audiences and included duets with Willie Nelson ('To All The Girls I've Loved Before') and Diana Ross ('All Of You'). A later duet (and international hit) was 'My Love' with Stevie Wonder in 1988. By the end of the 80s Iglesias had sold in excess of 100 million albums in seven languages. He won the Billboard Latin album of the year award in 1996 for *La Carreterra*.

●ALBUMS: *Yo Canto* (Columbia 1968)★★★, *Todos Los Dias Un Dia* (Columbia 1969)★★★, *Soy* (Columbia 1970)★★, *Gwendolyne* (Columbia 1970)★★, *Como el Alamo al Camino* (Columbia 1971)★★, *Rio Rebelde* (Columbia 1972)★★, *Asi Nacemos* (Columbia 1973)★★, *A Flor de Piel* (Columbia 1974)★★, *El Amor* (Columbia 1975)★★, *A Mexico* (Columbia 1975)★★, *America* (Columbia 1976)★★, *En El Olympia* (Columbia 1976)★★, *A Mis 33 Anos* (Columbia 1977)★★, *Mi Vida en Canciones* (Columbia 1978)★★, *Emociones* (Columbia 1979)★★, *Hey* (Columbia 1980)★★, *De Nina A Mujer* (Columbia 1981)★★, *Begin The Beguine* (Columbia 1981)★★★, *Momentos* (Columbia 1981)★★, *En Concierto* (Columbia 1982)★★, *Amor* (Columbia 1982)★★, *Julio* (Columbia 1983)★★, *1100 Bel Air Place* (Columbia 1984)★★, *Libra* (Columbia 1985)★★, *Un Hombre Solo* (Columbia 1987)★★, *Non Stop* (Columbia 1988)★★, *Sentimental* (Columbia 1988)★★, *Raices* (Columbia 1989)★★, *Starry Night* (Columbia 1990)★★★, *Calor* (Columbia 1992)★★, *La Carreterra* (Columbia 1995)★★★, *Tango* (Columbia 1996)★★.

●FURTHER READING: *Julio!*, Jeff Rovin.

IMAGINATION

One of the most successful British funk bands of the early 80s, Imagination were formed by the idiosyncratically named Lee John (b. John Lesley McGregor, 23 June 1957, Hackney, London, England; vocals), Ashley Ingram (b. 27 November 1960, Northampton, England; guitar) and Errol Kennedy (b. Montego Bay, West Indies). John (of St. Lucian descent) was educated in New York where he also became a backing vocalist for the Delfonics and Chairmen Of The Board. He met Ingram who played bass for both bands, and they formed a duo called Fizzz. Back in England, John, who had already appeared on *Junior Showtime* as a child, enrolled at the Anna Scher Theatre School where he studied drama. Kennedy was an experienced singer with Jamaican bands and learnt the drums through the Boys Brigade and later the Air Training Corps band. He had also spent some time in the soul group Midnight Express. Kennedy met John and Ingram in early 1981 after which they put together Imagination as a pop/soul three piece. They made an immediate impact with their debut 'Body Talk', and further Tony Swain-produced hits followed including UK Top 5 entries with 'Just An Illusion' and 'Music And Lights'. However, the run of hits dried up by 1984, when John returned to acting. He had already appeared in the *Dr Who* story *Enlightenment* in 1983. Having switched to RCA Records in 1986, Imagination made a minor comeback in 1988 with the small hit 'Instinctual'.

●ALBUMS: *Body Talk* (R&B 1981)★★★, *In The Heat Of The Night* (R&B 1982)★★, *Night Dubbing* (R&B 1983)★★, *Scandalous* (R&B 1983)★★, *Imagination* (RCA 1989)★★.

●COMPILATIONS: *Imagination Gold* (Stylus 1984)★★★.

IMMACULATE FOOLS

UK pop band consisting of two sets of brothers from Kent, Kevin Weatherall (vocals), Paul Weatherall, Andy Ross and Peter Ross. They made their debut with 'Nothing Means Nothing' in September 1984, before hitting with 'Immaculate Fools' in January 1985. Afterwards they spent much time touring the continent where they enjoyed more popularity, especially in Spain. Further singles included 'Hearts Of Fortune' and 'Save It' in 1985. Their second album, *Dumb Poet*, was well-received by critics (including a five star review in *Sounds* magazine), though it did not replicate earlier chart success. It spawned the singles 'Tragic Comedy' and 'Never Give Less Than Anything'. Barry Wickens (fiddle) joined in time for *Another Man's World*, but by then impetus had been lost, and the media proved less sympathetic to the group's summery, fey pop songs.

●ALBUMS: *Hearts Of Fortune* (A&M 1985)★★★, *Dumb Poet* (A&M 1987)★★★, *Another Man's World* (A&M 1990)★★.

●VIDEOS: *Searching For Sparks* (1987).

IN TUA NUA

This septet from Dublin, Eire combined traditional Irish instrumentation (pipes and whistles) with commercial instruments. Unlike the Pogues or the Saw Doctors, however, they used this musical platform to play more in the style of a rock act. Led by vocalist Leslie Dowdall other members included Brian O'Briaian, Martin Colncy, Vinnie Kilduf and Steve Wickham. 'Discovered' by Bono (U2) they were originally signed to Island Records but later moved to Virgin Records. Their singles included 'Comin' Thru', 'Take My Hand' (their Island debut in 1984), a version of Jefferson Airplane's 'Somebody To Love' (1985), 'Seven Into The Sea' (1986), 'Heaven Can Wait' (1987) and 'The Long Acre' (1988). Only 'All I Wanted' (1989) gave them a hit, and then it proved to be only a minor breakthrough. They gigged with Bob Dylan at the Irish Self Aid show, before Wickham left in 1986 to join the Waterboys. He was replaced on violin by Angela De Burca. *The Long Acre* was produced by Don Dixon of R.E.M. fame.

●ALBUMS: *Vaudeville* (Virgin 1987)★★★, *The Long Acre* (Virgin 1988)★★★.

INGRAM, JAMES

b. Akron, Ohio, USA. A singer, composer, and multi-instrumentalist, Ingram moved to Los Angeles in the early 70s where he played keyboards for Leon Haywood, and formed his own group, Revelation Funk. He also served as demo singer for various publishing companies, an occupation that led to his meeting and working with Quincy Jones. Ingram's vocals were featured on 'Just Once' and 'One Hundred Ways', from *The Dude* (1981), one of Jones's last albums for A&M Records. Both tracks made the US Top 20. Signed to Jones's own Quest label, Ingram had a US number 1 in 1982, duetting with Patti Austin on 'Baby, Come To Me', which became the theme for the popular television soap, *General Hospital*. In the same year, he released *It's Your Night*, an album that eventually spawned the hit single, 'Ya Mo B There' (1984), on which he was joined by singer/songwriter, Michael McDonald, and made the US Top 20 again, when he collaborated with Kenny Rogers and Kim Carnes for 'What About Me?'. Ingram's subsequent albums, *Never Felt So Good* (1986), produced by Keith Diamond, and *It's Real* (1989), on which he worked with Michael Powell and Gene Griffin, failed to live up to the promise of his earlier work, although he continued to feature in the singles chart with 'Somewhere Out There', a duet with Linda Ronstadt from Steven Spielberg's animated movie, *An American Tail*, and 'I Don't Have The Heart', which topped the US chart in 1990. Also in that year, Ingram was featured, along with Al B. Sure!, El DeBarge and Barry White, on 'The Secret Garden (Sweet Seduction Suite)', from Quincy Jones's album *Back On The Block*. Ingram has also served as a backing singer for several other big-name artists such as Luther Vandross and the Brothers Johnson. His compositions include 'P.Y.T. (Pretty Young Thing)', which he wrote incollaboration with Quincy Jones for Michael Jackson's 1982 smash hit album, *Thriller*.

●ALBUMS: *It's Your Night* (Qwest 1983)★★, *Never Felt So Good* (Qwest 1986)★★, *It's Real* (Qwest 1989)★★, *Always You* (Qwest 1993)★★.

●COMPILATIONS: *The Power Of Great Music* (Qwest 1991)★★★.

INMATES

The Inmates - Bill Hurley (vocals), Peter Gunn (b. Peter Staines; guitar), Tony Oliver (guitar) Ben Donnelly (bass) and Jim Russell (drums) - emerged in the late 70s as a UK R&B group in the style of Dr. Feelgood. Their adaptation of 'Dirty Water', a garage band classic originally recorded by the Standells, led to the Inmates' debut album. In common with several similarly styled groups, the quintet was unable to transfer their live excitement on to record and despite other promising collections, the Inmates were restricted to a narrow, pub rock-influenced ghetto. Singer Bill Hurley recorded the solo *Double Agent* in 1985, but its gritty mixture of soul and R&B classics fared no better than those of the parent group. *Meet The Beatles, Live In Paris* is a set of Beatles songs performed in a hard R&B and Chicago blues vein.

●ALBUMS: *First Offence* (Polydor 1979)★★★, *Shot In The Dark* (Radar 1980)★★★, *Heatwave In Alaska* (1982)★★★, *True Live Stories* (1984)★★★, *Five* (Lolita 1984)★★★, *Meet The Beatles, Live In Paris* (1988)★★★, *Fast Forward* (Sonet 1989)★★★, *Inside Out* (New Rose 1991)★★★, *Wanted* (1993)★★★.

INSPIRAL CARPETS

During the late 80s UK music scene, the city of Manchester and its surrounds spawned a host of exciting new groups, and the Inspiral Carpets were at the head of the pack alongside the Happy Mondays, James, the Stone Roses and 808 State. The group was formed in Oldham by schoolfriends Graham Lambert (guitar) and Stephen Holt (vocals). They were joined by drummer Craig Gill and performed in their hometown of Oldham with various other members until they were joined by organist Clint Boon and bassist David Swift. Boon met the group when they began rehearsing at his studio in Ashton-under-Lyne. His Doors-influenced playing later became the group's trademark. Their debut EP, *Planecrash*, was released by the independent label, Playtime, and the group were consequently asked to record a John Peel session for BBC Radio 1. In 1988 there was an acrimonious split between the band and label and also between the group members. Holt and Swift were replaced by Tom Hingley and Martin Walsh, formerly with local bands Too Much Texas and the Next Step, respectively. The band formed their own label, Cow Records, and after a string of well-received singles they signed a worldwide contract with Mute Records. 'This Is How It Feels' was a hit and *Life* was critically acclaimed for its mixture of

sparkling pop and occasional experimental flashes. Further singles had less impact and *The Beast Inside* received a mixed response, some critics claiming the band were becoming better known for their merchandise, like T-shirts and promotional milk bottles. The T-shirts, bearing the immortal words 'Cool as Fuck!', inevitably aroused considerable controversy, particularly when a fan was arrested for causing offence by wearing such a garment. Afterwards the group journeyed onwards without ever arousing the same level of interest, though both *Revenge Of The Goldfish* and *Devil Hopping* had their moments. 'Bitch's Brew', from the former, stronger album, was a classy stab at Rolling Stones-styled sweeping pop revival, though elsewhere too many songs continued to be dominated by Boon's organ, which, once a powerful novelty, now tended to limit the band's songwriting range. The band were released from Mute Records in 1995 with their former company issuing an epitaph in the shape of *The Singles*.

●ALBUMS: *Life* (Mute 1990)★★★, *The Beast Inside* (Mute 1991)★★, *Revenge Of The Goldfish* (Mute 1992)★★★, *Devil Hopping* (Mute 1994)★★★.

●COMPILATIONS: *The Singles* (Mute 1995)★★★.

INXS

Formed in 1977 as the Farriss Brothers in Sydney, Australia, INXS comprised the three Farriss brothers Tim (b. 16 August 1957; guitar), Jon (b. 18 August 1961; drums) and Andrew (b. 27 March 1959; keyboards); Michael Hutchence (b. 22 January 1960, Lain Cove, Sydney, Australia; lead vocals), Kirk Pengilly (b. 4 July 1958; guitar/saxophone/vocals) and Garry Beers (b. 22 June 1957; bass/vocals). The group moved to Perth, Western Australia to develop their own distinctive rock sound which incorporated both black dance music and white soul influences. The band began its recording career in 1980 with a single, 'Simple Simon'/'We Are The Vegetables' on the independent Deluxe label. Over the next three years, half a dozen singles reached the lower Top 40 in Australia, but the second album, *Underneath The Colours*, sold well, and the next, *Shabooh Shoobah* reached the Top 5. It was with the 'Original Sin' single of early 1985 and its accompanying album, *The Swing*, that the band finally hit the top of the charts in Australia. The album and single generated interest in the band from the USA, Europe and South America, and the follow-up album, *Listen Like Thieves*, consolidated their worldwide success, except in the UK where critics savaged the band, but it was not long before sales finally took off there as well. In 1986 Hutchence made his acting debut in the film *Dogs In Space*. One song from the film, 'Rooms For The Memory' earned him a solo Australian Top 10 single. The band toured the USA and Europe constantly, and MTV aired their videos, providing success with *Kick* receiving over 1 million sales on advance orders in the USA alone and finally a number one US hit with 'Need You Tonight' in January 1988. The band's success can be attributed to many factors including an unchanged line-up from the beginning, the sultry good looks of vocalist Michael Hutchence, unstinting touring schedules, a variety of song-writers in the band and consistently good and fresh production with the help of a new producer for each album. After *Kick* and before the release of *X*, all members had a 12-month break and became involved with other projects - Hutchence with Max Q; Andrew Farriss in production work with Jenny Morris; and Garry Beers joined the loose collection of friends for a tour and to record with Absent Friends. *Live Baby Live* is a document of the INXS Wembley Stadium concert in July 1991. Hutchence's much-publicized, fleeting romance with Kylie Minogue brought the group's name to the attention of a whole new generation of potential fans. Their 1993 set, *Full Moon, Dirty Hearts*, included a Hutchence/Chrissie Hynde (Pretenders) duet on 'Kill The Pain' and the single 'The Gift'. The video of the latter was banned by MTV, formerly INXS' greatest ally, due to its use of Holocaust and Gulf War footage.

●ALBUMS: *INXS* (Deluxe 1980)★★, *Underneath The Colours* (RCA 1981)★★, *Shabooh Shoobah* (Mercury 1982)★★, *The Swing* (Mercury 1984)★★★, *Listen Like Thieves* (Mercury 1985)★★★, *Kick* (Mercury 1987)★★★, *X* (Mercury 1990)★★, *Live Baby Live* (Mercury 1991)★★, *Welcome To Wherever You Are* (Mercury 1992)★★★, *Full Moon, Dirty Hearts* (Mercury 1993)★★★, *Elegantly Wasted* (Mercury 1997)★★. Solo: Max Q *Max Q* (Mercury 1989)★★. Absent Friends *Here's Looking Up Your Address* (Roo Art 1990).

●COMPILATIONS: *Greatest Hits* (Mercury 1994)★★★★.

●VIDEOS: *Truism* (PMI 1991), *The Best Of INXS* (1994).

●FURTHER READING: *INXS: The Official Story Of A Band On The Road*, St John Yann Gamblin (ed.).

IOVINE, JIMMY

b. 11 March 1953, Brooklyn, New York, USA. One of the leading record producers of the 80s, Iovine found his first studio job through songwriter Ellie Greenwich in 1977, and by 1973 he was an engineer at the Record Plant in New York City. There he worked on tracks by John Lennon, Southside Johnny and Bruce Springsteen. His first assignment as producer was for New Jersey band Flame in 1977, but his first hit album was *Easter* by Patti Smith, which included the Top 40 single 'Because The Night'. Iovine was now established as a top-grade producer and during the 80s he worked with numerous major rock acts. In 1979 he began his association with Tom Petty for whom he produced three albums. There was later work with Dire Straits (*Making Movies*) and with Stevie Nicks on her first two solo albums. In 1983 he was called in for the U2 live recording *Under A Blood Red Sky*, followed by the group's double album *Rattle & Hum*. Often co-producing with the artist, Iovine's other credits include work with Simple Minds (*Once Upon A Time*), Alison Moyet (*Raindancing*), Shakespears Sister, the Eurythmics (*We Two Are One*) and Gene Loves Jezebel. He renewed his partnership with Patti Smith in 1988, co-producing her *Dream Of Life* with Fred Smith. In 1990, Iovine began a new career in A&R, setting up the Interscope label with Ted Fields. During its first year the company had hits from Marky Mark And The Funky Bunch, Primus and Gerardo.

IRON MAIDEN

Formed in London, England, in 1976, Iron Maiden was from the start the brainchild of Steve Harris (b. 12 March 1957, Leytonstone, London, England; bass), formerly a member of pub rockers Smiler. Named after a medieval torture device, the music was suitably heavy and hard on the senses. The heavy metal scene of the late 70s was widely regarded as stagnant, with only a handful of bands proving their ability to survive and produce music of quality. It was just at this time that a new breed of young British bands began to emerge. This movement, which began to break cover in 1979 and 1980, was known as the New Wave Of British Heavy Metal, or NWOBHM. Iron Maiden were one of the foremost bands in the genre, and many would say its definitive example. Younger and meaner, the NWOBHM bands dealt in faster, more energetic heavy metal than any of their forefathers (punk being an obvious influence). There were several line-up changes in the Iron Maiden ranks in the very early days, and come the release of their debut EP, the group featured Harris, Dave Murray (b. 23 December 1958, London, England; guitar), Paul Di'anno (b. 17 May 1959, Chingford, London, England; vocals) and Doug Sampson (drums). The group made its live debut at the Cart & Horses Pub in Stratford, east London, in 1977, before honing its sound on the local pub circuit over the ensuing two years. Unable to solicit a response from record companies, the group sent a three-track tape, featuring 'Iron Maiden', 'Prowler' and 'Strange World', to Neal Kay, DJ at North London's hard rock disco, the Kingsbury Bandwagon Soundhouse. Kay's patronage of Iron Maiden won them an instant welcome, which translated itself finally into the release of *The Soundhouse Tapes* on the band's own label. November 1979 saw the group add second guitarist Tony Parsons to the line-up for two tracks on the *Metal For Muthas* compilation, but by the time the group embarked on sessions for their debut album, he had been replaced by Dennis Stratton (b. 9 November 1954, London, England), and Sampson by Clive Burr (b. 8 March 1957; drums). A promotional single, 'Running Free', reached number 34 on the UK charts and brought an appearance on BBC programme *Top Of The Pops*. Refusing to mime, they became the first band since the Who in 1973 to play live on the show. *Iron Maiden* was a roughly produced album, but reached number 4 in the UK album listings on the back of touring stints with Judas Priest and enduringly popular material such as 'Phantom Of The Opera'. *Killers* boasted production superior to that of the first album, and saw Dennis Stratton replaced by guitarist Adrian Smith (b. 27 February 1957). In its wake Iron Maiden became immensely popular among heavy metal fans, inspiring fanatical devotion, aided by blustering manager Rod Smallwood and apocalyptic mascot Eddie (the latter had been depicted on the cover of 'Sanctuary' standing over PM Margaret Thatcher's decapitated body).

The release of *Number Of The Beast* was crucial to the development of the band. Without it, Iron Maiden might never have gone on to be such a force in the heavy metal arena. The album was a spectacular success, the sound of a band on the crest of a wave. It was also the debut of former infantryman and new vocalist Bruce Dickinson (b. Paul Bruce Dickinson, 7 August 1958, Worksop, Nottinghamshire, England) replacing Paul Di'anno (who went on to front Lone Wolf, Battlezone and Killers). Formerly of Samson, history graduate Dickinson made his live debut with Maiden on 15 November 1981. Singles such as 'Run To The Hills' and 'The Number Of The Beast' were big UK chart hits, Iron Maiden leaving behind their NWOBHM counterparts in terms of success, just as the movement itself was beginning to peter out. *Piece Of Mind* continued their success and was a major hit in the USA (number 14). Clive Burr was replaced by Nicko McBrain on the sessions, formerly drummer with French metal band Trust, who had supported Maiden on their 1981 UK tour (he had also played in Streetwalkers). *Piece Of Mind* was not dissimilar to the previous album, showcasing the strong twin guitar bite of Murray and Smith, coupled with memorable vocal lines and a sound that fitted their air-punching dynamic perfectly. Single offerings, 'Flight of Icarus' and 'The Trooper', were instant hits, as the group undertook two massive tours, the four-month *World Piece* jaunt in 1983, and a *World Slavery* retinue which included four sell-out dates at London's Hammersmith Odeon a year later. With the arrival of *Powerslave* in November some critics accused Iron Maiden of conforming to a self-imposed writing formula, and playing safe with tried and tested ideas. Certainly, there was no significant departure from the two previous albums, but it was nonetheless happily consumed by the band's core supporters, who also purchased in sufficient quantities to ensure UK chart hits for 'Aces High' and 'Two Minutes To Midnight'. *Live After Death* was a double album package of all their best-loved material recorded live on their gargantuan 11 month world tour. By this time Iron Maiden had secured themselves an unassailable position within the metal hierachy, their vast popularity spanning all continents. *Somewhere In Time* was a slight departure. It featured more melody than before, and heralded the use of guitar synthesizers. Their songwriting still shone through and the now obligatory hit singles were easily attained in the shape of 'Wasted Years' and 'Stranger In A Strange Land'. Reaching number 11 in the USA, this was another million-plus seller. Since the mid-80s Maiden had been staging increasingly spectacular live shows, with elaborate lighting effects and stage sets. The *Somewhere In Time* tour (seven months) was no exception, ensuring their continued status as a live band, which had been the basis for much of their success. A period of comparative inactivity preceded the release of *Seventh Son Of A Seventh Son*, which was very much in the same vein as its predecessor. A concept album, it still retained its commercial edge and yielded hit singles in 'Can I Play With Madness', the surprisingly sensitive 'Evil That Men Do' and 'The Clairvoyant'.

After another exhausting mammoth world trek, the band announced their intention to take a well-earned break of at least a year. Speculation abounded that this meant the dissolution of the band, exacerbated by Dickinson's solo project, *Tattooed Millionaire*, his book, *The Adventures Of Lord Iffy Boatrace*, and EMI Records' policy of re-releasing Maiden's single catalogue in its entirety (on 12-inch). After a considerable hiatus, news of the band surfaced again. Steve Harris felt that the direction pursued with the last two albums had been taken as far as was possible, and a return to the style of old was planned. Not wishing to pursue this game plan, Adrian Smith left to be replaced by Janick Gers (b. Hartlepool, Lancashire, England), once guitarist with White Spirit and Gillan (he had also contributed to Dickinson's solo release). The live show was also to be scaled down in a return to much smaller venues. *No Prayer For The Dying* was indeed much more like mid-period Iron Maiden, and was predictably well-received, bringing enormous UK hit singles with 'Holy Smoke' and 'Bring Your Daughter To The Slaughter'. The latter, previously released in 1989 on the soundtrack to *A Nightmare On Elm Street 5*, had already been granted the Golden Raspberry Award for Worst Song in that year. Yet it gave Iron Maiden their first ever UK number 1. The obligatory world tour followed. Despite being denounced as 'satanists' in Chile in 1992 the band gained their first number 1 in the UK album charts with *Fear Of The Dark*, which housed another major single success in 'Be Quick Or Be Dead' (number 2). However, it was Dickinson's swansong with the band, who invited demo tapes to be sent to them following his announcement that he would permanently depart following current touring engagements. His eventual replacement was Blaze Bayley (b. 1963, Birmingham, West Midlands, England) from Wolfsbane. His debut album was *X-Factor*, and on this and at live gigs (which they only resumed in November 1995) he easily proved his worth. This was a daunting task, having to learn Maiden's whole catalogue and win over patriotic Dickinson followers. Smith resurfaced in a new band, Psycho Motel, in 1996.

●ALBUMS: *Iron Maiden* (EMI 1980)★★★, *Killers* (EMI 1981)★★, *Number Of The Beast* (EMI 1982)★★★★, *Piece Of Mind* (EMI 1983)★★, *Powerslave* (EMI 1984)★★, *Live After Death* (EMI 1985)★★★, *Somewhere In Time* (EMI 1986)★★★, *Seventh Son Of A Seventh Son* (EMI 1988)★★★★, *No Prayer For The Dying* (EMI 1990)★★★, *Fear Of The Dark* (EMI 1992)★★★, *A Real Live One (Volume One)* (EMI 1993)★★★, *A Real Dead One* (EMI 1993)★★, *Live At Donington '92* (EMI 1993)★★, *The X Factor* (EMI 1995)★★★.

●COMPILATIONS: *Best Of The Beast* (EMI 1996)★★★.

●VIDEOS: *Live At The Rainbow* (1984), *Behind The Iron Curtain Video EP* (1986), *Live After Death* (1986), *Run To The Hills* (1987), *Twelve Wasted Years* (1987), *Maiden England* (1989), *First Ten Years (The Videos)* (1990), *Raising Hell* (1993), *Donington Live 1992* (1994).

●FURTHER READING: *Running Free: The Official Story Of Iron Maiden*, Garry Bushell and Ross Halfin. *A Photographic History*, Ross Halfin.

ISAACS, GREGORY

b. 1951, Kingston, Jamaica, West Indies. Reggae superstar Gregory Isaacs has seldom looked back during a three decade career which has gone from strength to strength, and while many rock stars like to play with an 'outlaw' image, Isaacs is the real thing - the ultimate rude boy reggae star - who shows no signs of letting up in the 90s. Like so many other others before him he began by doing the rounds of Kingston's producers and entering various talent competitions, before scoring with Rupie Edwards' Success Records in the early 70s. He set up his own African Museum shop and label in 1973 with Errol Dunkley in order to gain artistic and financial control of his own destiny. He continued to record for many other producers during the rest of the decade to finance his own label, notably Winston 'Niney' Holness, Gussie Clarke, Lloyd F. Campbell, Glen Brown, Alvin Ranglin and Phil Pratt. His early recordings were romantic ballads crooned in the inimitable Isaacs style, cool, leisurely, and always sounding vulnerable or pained by his adventures in love. But these translated effortlessly into social protest or 'reality' songs as the decade progressed and the preoccupations of reggae music shifted towards songs with a more cultural emphasis. By 1980 Isaacs was the number one star in the reggae world, touring the UK and the USA extensively, and his live appearances resulted in frenzied crowd scenes, with audiences eating out of the palm of his hand. He had by now signed with Virgin Records' Front Line label and was gaining a considerable name for himself outside of the confines of the traditional reggae music audience and, even though he had recorded many classic sides for outside producers, he still managed to put out his best 45s on African Museum (and subsequently Front Line). His pre-eminence during this period was confirmed in the mantle of 'Cool Ruler', chosen for him by critics and fans after the title of the album.

A new contract with Charisma Records' Pre label set up the UK release of two further classic albums, though he was never less than prodigious even by Jamaican standards. He was, however, beset by personal and legal problems in the mid-80s and was even jailed in Kingston's notorious General Penitentiary. His release was celebrated with *Out Deh*. His spell inside left him short of ready money and he proceeded to record for anyone and everyone who was prepared to pay him the necessary cash to get back on his feet. Because of his name he was inundated with offers of work and the market was soon flooded with Gregory Isaacs releases on any number of different labels. Incredibly his standards did not drop, and he generally stuck to original material which was still head and shoulders above the competition. Most weeks in the latter half of the decade would see the release of yet more Isaacs material, voiced with current hot producers such as Jammys, Red Man, Bobby Digital and Steely And Clevie among others; by so doing he took on the youth of Jamaica at its own game, and won. Rumours abound about Isaacs' rude boy lifestyle - but he would claim he has to be tough to maintain his position within Kingston's notorious musical industry. Certainly the reasons for his lofty seat in the reggae hierarchy are purely musical; a combination of his boundless talent and his uncompromising attitude. Alone - out of all reggae's star performers - Isaacs has actually improved over the years and to look forward to more quality releases from him is not mere wishful thinking, but a justifiable expectancy cultivated by his high standards. It is very difficult to see how anyone will now be able to take away his crown - his legendary status and reputation in the reggae business are truly second to none.

●ALBUMS: *Gregory Isaacs Meets Ronnie Davis* (Plant 1970)★★★, *In Person* (Trojan 1975)★★★, *All I Have Is Love* (Trojan 1976)★★★, *Extra Classic* (Conflict 1977, Shanachie 1981)★★★, *Mr Isaacs* (Earthquake 1977)★★★, *Slum Dub* (Burning Sounds 1978)★★★★, *Best Of Vol. 1 & 2* not compilations (GG's 1976, 1981)★★★, *Cool Ruler* (Front Line 1978)★★★★, *Soon Forward* (Front Line 1979)★★★★, *Showcase* (Taxi 1980)★★★, *The Lonely Lover* (Pre 1980)★★★, *For Everyone* (Success 1980)★★★, *More Gregory* (Pre 1981)★★★, *Night Nurse* (Mango/Island 1982)★★★, *The Sensational Gregory Isaacs* (Vista 1982)★★★, *Out Deh!* (Mango/Island 1983)★★★★, *Reggae Greats (Live)* (Mango/Island 1984)★★★, *Live At The Academy Brixton* (Rough Trade 1984)★★★, with Dennis Brown *Two Bad Superstars Meet* (Burning Sounds 1984)★★★, *Judge Not* (Greensleeves 1984)★★★, with Jah Mel *Double Explosive* (Andys 1984)★★★, *Private Beach Party* (RAS 1985)★★★, *Easy* (Tad's 1985)★★★, *All I Have Is Love, Love Love* (Tad's 1986)★★★, with Sugar Minott *Double Dose* (Blue Mountain 1987)★★★, *Victim* (C&E 1987)★★★, *Watchman Of The City* (Rohit 1988)★★★, *Sly And Robbie Presents Gregory Isaacs* (RAS 1988)★★★, *Talk Don't Bother Me* (Skengdon 1988)★★★, *Come Along* (Live & Love 1988)★★★, *Encore* (Kingdom 1988)★★★, *Red Rose For Gregory* (Greensleeves 1988)★★★, *I.O.U.* (RAS 1989)★★★, *No Contest* (Music Works 1989)★★★, *Call Me Collect* (RAS 1990)★★★, *Dancing Floor* (Heartbeat 1990)★★★, *Come Again Dub* (ROIR 1991)★★★, *Can't Stay Away* (1992)★★★, *Pardon Me* (1992)★★★, *No Luck* (1993)★★★, *Absent* (Greensleeves 1993)★★★, *Over The Bridge* (Musidisc/I&I Sound 1994)★★★, *Reggae Greats - Live* rec. 1982 (1994)★★★, *Midnight Confidential* (Greensleeves 1994)★★★, *Mr Love* (Virgin Front Line 1995)★★★, *Memories* (Musidisc 1995)★★★, *Dem Talk Too Much* (Trojan 1995)★★★.

●COMPILATIONS: *The Early Years* (Trojan 1981)★★★, *Lover's Rock* double album comprising *The Lonely Lover* and *More Gregory* (Pre 1982)★★★, *Crucial Cuts* (Virgin 1983)★★★, *My Number One* (Heartbeat 1990)★★★, *Love Is Overdue* (Network 1991)★★★, *The Cool Ruler Rides Again - 22 Classics From 1978-81* (Music Club 1993)★★★.

ISHAM, MARK

b. *c*.50s, New York City, New York, USA. Born into a musical family that encouraged him to learn the piano, violin and trumpet at an early age, Mark Isham began studying the jazz trumpet while at high school and then explored electronic music while in his early 20s. For a time he pursued parallel careers as a classical, jazz and rock musician, performing, for instance, with the San Francisco Opera, the Beach Boys and Pharoah Sanders, but by the early 70s, he concentrated his efforts on jazz. As co-leader of pianist Art Lande's Rubisa Patrol, he recorded two albums on ECM Records in the late 70s, continuing his partnership with Lande through to the late 80s. Together with guitarist Peter Mannu, Synthesizer player Patrick O'Hearn and drummer Terry Bozzio, he set up the Group 87 ensemble in 1979, releasing a self-titled debut album in 1981. At the same time, Isham continued his links with rock music, recording and touring as part of Van Morrison's band, where his trumpet and flugelhorn set off the saxophone of Pee Wee Ellis to good effect. During the 80s, Isham developed his compositional skills, using a synthesis of brass, electronics and his own plaintive trumpet to

produce a very visual, narrative form of music. He recalls that 'my mother once told me that, as a kid, even before I really played music, I tried to tell stories with music. So, whether it's in the vocabulary of heavy metal or Stravinsky, the thread has to do with images.' Isham has taken that thread into film music, scoring the Academy award-winning documentary *The Life and Times Of Harvey Milk*, the film *Mrs Soffel* (both recorded on *Film Music*), and writing music to accompany children's fairy tales. His feature credits include *Trouble In Mind*, *Everybody Wins*, *Reversal Of Fortune*, *Billy Bathgate*, *Little Man Tate*, *Cool World*, *Of Mice And Men*, *Sketch Artist*, *The Public Eye*, *A River Runs Through It*, *Nowhere To Run*, *Fire In The Sky*, *A Midnight Clear*, *Made In America*, *Romeo Is Bleeding*, *Short Cuts*, *The Getaway*, *The Moderns*, *The Browning Version*, *Timecop*, *Mrs. Parker And The Vicious Circle*, *Nell*, *Quiz Show* (1994) and *Gotti* (1996). Throughout his career, Isham has remained a prolific session man, whose work encompasses recordings with artists as varied as saxophonist David Liebman, guitarist David Torn, and singers Suzanne Vega, Tanita Tikaram and Marianne Faithfull. Isham is blessed with an instantly memorable trumpet sound, one that is burnished, resonant, in places lush but which can, at times, be bleakly powerful, relying on minimalist fragments to achieve its subdued effect.
●ALBUMS: with Art Lande *Rubisia Patrol* (ECM 1976)★★, with Lande *Desert Marauders* (ECM 1978)★★★, *Group 87* (1981)★★, *Vapour Drawings* (Windham Hill 1983)★★★★, *A Career In Dada Processing* (1984)★★★, with Lande *We Begin* (1987)★★★, *Film Music* (Windham Hill 1987)★★★★, *Fire In The Sky* (1993)★★★, *Blue Sun* (Columbia 1995)★★★.

IT BITES

Formed in Egremont, Cumbria, England, in 1982, the members of this rock/pop band had all previously played together in various guises, usually in cover bands. Dunnery spent time with a punk band called Waving At Trains, having previously worked as an engineer. The rest of the band's *curriculum vitae* ranged from bricklayer to factory worker. The band's stable line-up has remained: Francis Dunnery (vocals and guitars), John Beck (keyboards), Dick Nolan (bass), Bob Dalton (drums). Their first release was the strictly amateur 'All In Red', but under the wing of Virgin Records they hit in 1986 with 'Calling All The Heroes'. Unjustly assumed to be strictly for teenagers, they were continually marketed as such

by their record company. They demonstrated considerable talent with 'Whole New World' which surprisingly stalled outside the UK Top 50. It Bites, however, wanted to be a rock band. This fact was born out by some of their influences (10cc to Led Zeppelin to Can) and a tour with Robert Plant. Later albums were more blues-based, and included 'green' material like 'Murder Of The Planet Earth'.
●ALBUMS: *Big Lad In The Windmill* (Virgin 1986)★★, *Once Around The World* (Virgin 1988)★★, *Eat Me In St Louis* (Virgin 1989)★★, *Thank You And Goodnight* (Virgin 1991)★★.

JACKSON, JERMAINE

b. Jermaine Lajuan Jackson, 11 December 1954, Gary, Indiana, USA. Jermaine was one of five brothers who made up the Jackson Five in 1962. Besides playing bass, he acted as vocal counterpoint to his younger brother Michael Jackson, a musical relationship that continued after the group were signed to Motown Records in 1968. Jermaine contributed occasional lead vocals to their albums in the early 70s, and his performance of 'I Found That Girl' on *Third Album* was one of their most affecting ballads. Like his brothers Michael and Jackie, Jermaine was singled out by Motown for a solo career, and he enjoyed an immediate US Top 10 hit with a revival of Shep And The Limeliters' doo-wop classic 'Daddy's Home' in 1972. Later releases were less favourably received, but he consolidated his position within the company in 1973 with his marriage to Hazel, the daughter of Motown boss Berry Gordy. His new family connections entailed a stark conflict of interest when the other members of the Jackson Five decided to leave the label in 1975. Given the choice of deserting either his brothers or his father-in-law, he elected to remain with Motown, where his solo releases were subsequently given a higher priority than before. Despite heavy promotion, Jermaine's late 70s recordings failed to establish him as a distinctive soul voice, and he faced constant critical comparisons with the Jacksons' work on Epic. His career was revitalized by the intervention of Stevie Wonder, who wrote and produced the 1979 hit 'Let's Get Serious' in 1979, which successfully echoed the joyous funk of Wonder's own recordings. The gentle soul of 'You Like Me Don't You' brought him another hit in 1981, while the US Top 20 single 'Let Me Tickle Your Fancy' the following year featured an unlikely collaboration with new wave band Devo.

Jermaine's increased public profile won him a more generous deal with Motown in the early 80s. He formed his own production company, launching Michael Lovesmith as a recording artist and overseeing the career development of Syreeta.

But this increased freedom was not enough to keep him at Motown, and in 1983 he signed with Arista Records. The following year, he was reconciled with his brothers: he joined the Jacksons on the *Victory* album and tour, and his own *Jermaine Jackson* featured a sparkling duet with Michael Jackson on 'Tell Me We're Not Dreaming'. He subsequently collaborated with Pia Zadora on the theme from the film *Voyage Of The Rock Aliens*, and with Whitney Houston on his 1986 project *Precious Memories*. In that same year, he formed his own label, WORK Records, and accepted the offer to portray the late Marvin Gaye in a bio-pic which was never completed. He has continued to work with the Jacksons and as a soloist since then, although his recent projects have been overshadowed by the media circus surrounding his brother Michael, a subject touched upon in Jermaine's 'Word To The Badd'.

●ALBUMS: *Jermaine* (Motown 1972)★★, *Come Into My Life* (Motown 1973)★★, *My Name Is Jermaine* (Motown 1976)★★, *Feel The Fire* (Motown 1977)★★, *Frontier* (Motown 1978)★★, *Let's Get Serious* (Motown 1980)★★★, *Jermaine* (Motown 1980)★★, *I Like Your Style* (Motown 1981)★★, *Let Me Tickle Your Fancy* (Motown 1982)★★, *Jermaine Jackson* (USA) *Dynamite* (UK) (Arista 1984)★★★, *Precious Moments* (Arista 1986)★★, *Don't Take It Personal* (Arista 1989)★★, *You Said* (La Face 1991)★★.

JACKSON, JOE

b. 11 August 1955, Burton-upon-Trent, Staffordshire, England. Having learned violin and piano as a teenager, Jackson gained entrance to study piano at London's Royal College of Music. After two years of finding his way in the music business, first through being in Arms And Legs and then as musical director to Coffee And Cream, he was signed up by A&M Records in the summer of 1978. His accomplished debut 'Is She Really Going Out With Him?' was not an immediate hit; however, by the time *Look Sharp* was released that song had become one of his live shows' stand-out numbers and reached the UK charts, albeit some months after nudging the US Top 20. Jackson's first two albums demonstrated a confident writer of thoughtful lyrics, coupled with exciting new wave energy. 'Is She Really Going Out With Him?' has a classic opening line containing humour, irony and jealousy; 'Pretty women out walking with gorillas down my street'. While *Look Sharp* and *I'm The Man* were power pop, the following *Beat Crazy* (containing some reggae) started a trend of changing musical direction that Jackson began to relish. *Jumpin' Jive*, although superb, was a throwback to the music of the 40s; on this he covered classic songs by Cab Calloway and Louis Jordan. One of his most satisfying works came in 1982 with *Night And Day*. The album was recorded in New York, where Joe departed following his marriage break-up. The songs are introspective but positive. The hauntingly hummable 'Steppin' Out' with its mantric bass line and crisp piano is a superbly crafted pop song that won him many new admirers. The subsequent *Body And Soul* came close to repeating the success, and Jackson was critically acclaimed. *Big World*, minus the long-standing bass of Graham Maby, was a three-sided direct to two-track disc. The songs had less of an appeal and Jackson's commercial fortunes began to decline. The instrumental *Will Power*, although faultlessly recorded with a high standard of musicianship, put Jackson in a musical nether world. He had come so far musically, in such a short time, that his followers found it hard to keep up with him. The live album and the film soundtrack to *Tucker* both arrived in 1988 and despite the critical plaudits, following the commercial failure of *Blaze Of Glory* in 1989, his contract with A&M was not renewed. It was inconceivable that a talent as great as Jackson would be without a contract for long; by early 1991 he was signed to Virgin Records and released *Laughter And Lust* to little commercial success.

Jackson finds himself in the difficult position of being part of the new wave pop movement yet having developed way beyond those realms. He is a serious musician and should be allowed to be one without the constraints of commercial considerations. Film scores and orchestral works are well within his boundries.
●ALBUMS: *Look Sharp!* (A&M 1979)★★★★, *I'm The Man* (A&M 1979)★★★★, *Beat Crazy* (A&M 1980)★★, *Joe Jackson's Jumpin' Jive* (A&M 1981)★★★★, *Night And Day* (A&M 1982)★★★★, *Mike's Murder* soundtrack (A&M 1983)★★, *Body And Soul* (A&M 1984)★★★★, *Big World* (A&M 1986)★★, *Will Power* (A&M 1987)★★★, *Joe Jackson - Live* (A&M 1988)★★★, *Tucker; Original Soundtrack* (A&M 1988)★★, *Blaze Of Glory* (A&M 1989)★★, *Laughter And Lust* (Virgin 1991)★★, *Night Music* (Virgin 1994)★★★.
●COMPILATIONS: *Steppin' Out - The Very Best Of ...* (A&M 1990)★★★, *This Is It - The A&M Years* (A&M 1997)★★★★.

JACKSON, LATOYA

b. 29 May 1956, Gary, Indiana, USA. As a member of the singing Jackson family, LaToya served her apprenticeship as a backing vocalist to the Jacksons group along with her sisters, Rebbie and Janet Jackson. LaToya embarked on a solo career in 1980, signing to the Polydor label. Despite the family connection, LaToya's solo career found difficulty in emulating the success of her younger sister Janet; her highest single chart position was with the US number 56, 'Hearts Don't Lie' (1984) on her new label, Private I/Epic. A later label change to RCA Records did not alter her fortunes. She later exacerbated family relations with a somewhat scurrilous autobiography in 1991.
●ALBUMS: *LaToya Jackson* (Polydor 1980)★★, *My Special Love* (1981)★★, *Heart Don't Lie* (Private Stock 1984)★★, *Imagination* (Private Stock 1985)★★, *You're Gonna Get Rocked* (RCA 1988)★★.
●FURTHER READING: *LaToya Jackson*, LaToya Jackson with Patricia Romanowski.

JACKSON, MICHAEL

b. Michael Joseph Jackson, 29 August 1958, Gary, Indiana, USA. Jackson has spent almost his entire life as a public performer. He was a founder member of the Jackson Five at the age of four, soon becoming the group's lead vocalist and frontman. Onstage, he modelled his dance moves and vocal styling on James Brown, and portrayed an absolute self-confidence that belied his shy, private personality. The Jackson Five were signed to Motown Records at the end of 1968; their early releases, including chart-toppers 'I Want You Back' and 'I'll Be There', illustrated his remarkable maturity. Although Michael was too young to have experienced the romantic situations that were the subject of his songs, he performed with total sincerity, showing all the hallmarks of a great soul artist. Ironically, his pre-adolescent vocal work carried a conviction that he often failed to recapture later in his career. When MGM Records launched the Osmonds as rivals to the Jackson Five in 1970, and singled out their lead singer, 13-year-old Donny Osmond, for a solo career, Motown felt duty bound to reply in kind. Michael Jackson's first release as a solo performer was the aching ballad, 'Got To Be There', a major US and UK hit. A revival of Bobby Day's rock 'n' roll novelty 'Rockin' Robin' reached the top of the US charts in 1972, while the sentimental film theme, 'Ben', repeated that achievement later in the year. Motown capitalized on Jackson's popularity with a series of hurried albums, which mixed material angled towards the teenage market with a selection of the label's standards. They also stockpiled scores of unissued tracks, which were released in the 80s to cash in on the success of Jackson's Epic recordings.

As the Jackson Five's sales slipped in the mid-70s, Michael's solo career was put on hold, and he continued to reserve his talents for the group after they were reborn as the Jacksons in 1976. He regained the public eye with a starring role in the film musical *The Wiz*, collaborating on the soundtrack album with Quincy Jones. Their partnership was renewed in 1979 when Jones produced *Off The Wall*, a startlingly successful collection of contemporary soul material which introduced the world to the adult Michael Jackson. In his new incarnation, Jackson retained the vocal flexibility of old, and added a sophistication and sensuality which celebrated his entry into manhood. The album topped the charts in the UK and USA, and contained two number 1 singles, 'Don't Stop Till You Get Enough' (for which Jackson won a Grammy Award) and 'Rock With You'. Meanwhile, Motown capitalized on his commercial status by reissuing a recording from the mid-70s, 'One Day In Your Life', which duly topped the UK charts. Michael continued to tour and record with the Jacksons after this solo success, while media speculation grew about his private life. He was increasingly portrayed as a figure trapped in an eternal childhood, surrounded by toys and pet animals, and insulated from the traumas of the real world. This image was consolidated when he was chosen to narrate an album based on the 1982 fantasy film *ET - The Extra Terrestrial*. The record was quickly withdrawn because of legal complications, but still won Jackson another Grammy Award. In 1982 *Thriller*, Jackson's second album with Quincy Jones, was released. In purely commercial terms, no other album has ever made such an impact on the record industry; it remains the most successful album of all time, having sold more than 42 million copies by the early 90s. It produced a run of enormous hit singles, each accompanied by a promotional video that widened the scope of the genre. 'The Girl Is Mine', a duet with Paul McCartney, began the sequence in relatively subdued style; it reached number 1 in the US and UK, but merely set the scene for 'Billie Jean', an effortless mix of disco and pop which spawned a series of answer records from other artists. The record's promo video was equally spectacular, portraying Jackson as a master of dance, a magician who could transform lives, a shadowy figure who lived outside the everyday world. Its successor, 'Beat It', established another precedent, with its determinedly rock-flavoured guitar solo by Eddie Van Halen making it the first black record to receive rotation airplay on the MTV video station. Its promo film involved Jackson at the centre of a choreographed street battle, a conscious throwback to the set pieces of *West Side Story*. But even this was a modest effort compared to 'Thriller', a rather mannered piece of disco-funk accompanied by a stunning long-form video, which placed Jackson in a parade of Halloween horrors. This promo clip spawned a follow-up, *The Making Of 'Thriller'*, which in turn sold more copies than any other home video to date.

The *Thriller* album and singles won Jackson a further seven Grammies; amid this run of hits, Jackson slotted in 'Say Say Say', a second chart-topping duet with Paul McCartney. He accepted the largest individual sponsorship deal in history from Pepsi Cola in 1983; the following year, his involvement in the Jacksons' 'Victory Tour' sparked the greatest demand for concert tickets in the history of popular music. Jackson had by now become an almost mythical figure, and like most myths he attracted hyperbole. A group of Jehovah's Witnesses announced that he was the Messiah, he was said to be taking drugs to change his skin colour to white; it was claimed that he had undergone extensive plastic surgery to alter his appearance, and photographs were published which suggested that he slept in a special chamber to prevent himself ageing. More prosaically, Jackson began 1985 by co-writing and performing on the USA For Africa benefit single 'We Are The World', another international number 1. He then spent $47.5 million in purchasing the ATV Music company which controlled the songs of John Lennon and Paul McCartney, effectively sabotaging his musical relationship with his erstwhile partner. Later that year he took part in *Captain Eo*, a short film laden with special effects which was only shown at the Disneyworld amusement park; he also announced plans to write his autobiography. The book was delayed while he recorded *Bad*, another collaboration with Quincy Jones which finally appeared in 1987. It produced seven Top 10 singles, among them the title track, which again set fresh standards with its promotional video. The album suffered by comparison with his previous work, however, and its multi-million sales were deemed disappointing after the phenomenal success of *Thriller*. In musical terms, *Bad* certainly broke no fresh ground; appealing though its soft funk confections were, they lacked substance, and represented only a cosmetic advance over his two earlier albums with Jones.

Unabashed, Jackson continued to work in large scale. He undertook a lengthy world concert tour to promote *Bad*, utilizing stunning visual effects to capture the atmosphere of his videos. At the same time, he published his autobiography, *Moonwalker*, which offered little personal or artistic insight; neither did the alarmingly expensive feature film that accompanied it, and that buttressed his otherworldly image.

The long-awaited new release *Dangerous* came in 1992 and it justifiably scaled the charts. This lengthy album (76 minutes) is a tour-de-force of gutsy techno pop with Teddy Riley contributing to a number of tracks. The sweet pop is sharpened to a hard point, yet it still has the unmistakable Jackson sound. By maintaining a leisurely working schedule, Jackson has guaranteed that each new project is accompanied by frenzied public anticipation. Up until 1992 his refusal to undergo in-depth interviews has allowed the media to portray him as a fantasy figure, a hypochondriac who lives a twilight existence cut off from the rest of humanity, and who is terrified both by the outside world and by the prospect of growing old. He attempted, and succeeded to a degree, with a carefully rehearsed interview with Oprah Winfrey in 1992. The televised programme was shown all over world, during which viewers saw his personal funfair, in the back garden, and watched as Jackson spoke of his domineering father. The unthinkable happened in 1993, just as Jackson's clean image was at its peak. Allegations of sexual abuse were made by one of Jackson's young friends and the media had a riotous time. Jackson's home was raided by police while he was on tour in the Far East and the artist, clearly disturbed, cancelled a number of performances due to dehydration. No charges were made, and things began to quieten down until November 1993, when Jackson left the USA and went into hiding. Additionally, he confessed to being addicted to painkillers and was seeking treatment. After this admission, Jackson's long-time sponsors Pepsi Cola decided to pull out of their agreement with the now damaged career of the world's most popular superstar. The media were handed more bait when he married Lisa Marie Presley, perhaps in an attempt to rebuild his image. The marriage soon collapsed, giving further rise to allegations that it was merely a put up job to enhance his damaged image. He did, however, enhance his reputation with *HIStory Past, Present And Future, Book 1*. One half of the double set chronicled his past hits, but there was the eqivalent of a new album on the second half. Lyrically the new material was strong, and Jackson very cleverly gave himself a forum to speak back to his critics. Musically, although it did not break down any barriers, the sound was interestingly varied and, as ever, highly polished. The downside was a sickening display of self-grandeur at the 1995 Brits Awards. Controversy surrounded Jarvis Cocker (of Pulp) who invaded the stage in protest while Jackson, dressed in Messiah-white, was surrounded by, among others, worshipping children and a rabbi.

● ALBUMS: *Got To Be There* (Tamla Motown 1971)★★★, *Ben* (Tamla Motown 1972)★★★, *Music And Me* (Tamla Motown 1973)★★★, *Forever, Michael* (Tamla Motown 1975)★★★, *Off The Wall* (Epic 1979)★★★★, *One Day In Your Life* (Motown 1981)★★★, *Thriller* (Epic 1982)★★★★★, *ET - The Extra Terrestrial* (MCA 1983)★★, *Farewell My Summer Love* (Motown 1984)★★★, *Looking Back To Yesterday* (Motown 1986)★★★, *Bad* (Epic 1987)★★★★, *Dangerous* (Epic 1992)★★★, *HIStory Past, Present & Future, Book 1* (Epic 1995)★★★★, *Blood On The Dance Floor* (Epic 1997)★★★.

● COMPILATIONS: *Best Of* (Motown 1981)★★★, *Michael Jackson 9 Single Pack* (Epic 1983)★★★, *The Michael Jackson Mix* (Stylus 1987)★★★, *Souvenir Singles Pack* (1988)★★★, *Anthology* (Motown 1993)★★★★.

● VIDEOS: *The Making Of Thriller* (1986), *The Legend Continues* (1988), *Moonwalker* (1992), *Dangerous - The Short Films* (1994), *HIStory Past, Present & Future, Book 1* (1995).

● FURTHER READING: *Michael Jackson*, Stewart Regan. *The Magic Of Michael Jackson*, No editor listed. *Michael Jackson*, Doug Magee. *The Michael Jackson Story*, Nelson George. *Michael In Concert*, Phyl Garland. *Michael Jackson: Body And Soul: An Illustrated Biography*, Geoff Brown. *Michael!: The Michael Jackson Story*, Mark Bego. *On The Road With Michael Jackson*, Mark Bego. *Sequins & Shades: The Michael Jackson Reference Guide*, Carol D. Terry. *Michael Jackson: Electrifying*, Greg Quill. *Moonwalk*, Michael Jackson, *Michael Jackson: The Magic And The Madness*, J. Randy Taraborrelli. *Michael Jackson: The Man In The Mirror*, Todd Gold. *Sequins And Shades*, Carol D. Terry. *Michael Jackson: The King Of Pop*, Lisa D. Campbell. *Michael Jackson: In His Own Words*, Michael Jackson. *The Visual Documentary*, Adrian Grant. *Michael Jackson Unauthorized*, Christopher Andersen.

JACKSON, MILLIE

b. 15 July 1944, Thompson, Georgia, USA. A former model, Millie Jackson's controversial singing career began professionally in 1964 at a club in Hoboken, New Jersey, USA. Her first recordings followed in 1970; over the next three years she made several excellent, if traditional, soul singles, which included two US R&B Top 10 entries, with 'Ask Me What You Want' and 'My Man A Sweet Man'. 'Hurts So Good', a song from a pseudo-feminist 'blaxploitation' film, *Cleopatra Jones*, was Jackson's biggest hit to date, but her subsequent direction was more fully shaped in 1974 with the release of *Caught Up*. Tracks, with backing from the Muscle Shoals rhythm section, included a fiery interpretation of '(If Lovin' You Is Wrong) I Don't Wanna Be Right'. The accompaniment intensified the sexual element in her work as Millie embraced either the pose of adultress or of wronged wife. A further collection, *Still Caught Up*, continued the saga, but Jackson's style later verged on self-parody as she progressed down an increasingly blind alley. The raps became longer and more explicit, and two later albums, *Feelin' Bitchy* and *Live And Uncensored*, required warning stickers for public broadcast. Despite excursions into C&W and a collaboration with Isaac Hayes, Jackson seemed unable to abandon her 'bad mouth' role, exemplified in 80s titles such as 'Sexercise Pts 1 & 2' and 'Slow Tongue (Working Your Way Down)'. Despite her strong cult following, the only occasion on which Jackson has made any significant impact on the UK singles market was in 1985 when duetting with Elton John on 'Act Of War', which reached the Top 40. She possesses one of soul's outstanding voices, yet sadly chooses to limit its obvious potential. Nearly all of Jackson's Spring albums saw CD release in the 90s on UK Ace's Southbound label.

●ALBUMS: *Millie Jackson* (Spring 1972)★★★, *It Hurts So Good* (Spring 1973)★★★, *Caught Up* (Spring 1974)★★★★, *Soul Believer* (Spring 1974), *Still Caught Up* (Spring 1975)★★★, *Free And In Love* (Spring 1976), *Lovingly Yours* (Spring 1977)★★★, *Get It Out 'Cha System* (Spring 1978)★★★, *A Moment's Pleasure* (Spring 1979)★★★, with Isaac Hayes *Royal Rappings* (Polydor 1979)★★, *Live And Uncensored* (Spring 1980)★★★, *For Men Only* (Spring 1980)★★★, *Just A Lil' Bit Country* (1981)★★, *Live And Outrageous* (Spring 1982)★★, *Hard Times* (Spring 1982)★★, *E.S.P. (Extra Sexual Persuasion)* (Sire 1984)★★, *An Imitation Of Love* (Jive 1986)★★★, *The Tide Is Turning* (Jive 1988)★★★, *Back To The Sh*t* (Jive 1989)★★★.

●COMPILATIONS: *Best Of Millie Jackson* (Spring 1976)★★★★, *21 Of The Best* (Southbound/Ace 1994)★★★.

JAGGER, MICK

b. Michael Philip Jagger, 26 July 1943, Dartford, Kent, England. The celebrated singer of the Rolling Stones, Jagger has become less a pop star than a media icon. Initially a shy, middle-class student at the London School of Economics, his love of blues, distinctive vocal style and charismatic stage persona marked him out as an original. The image of Jagger is arguably as crucial to the ultimate long-term success of the Stones as the quality of their songwriting and musicianship. The antithesis of the pretty-boy lead vocalists of the era, Jagger's surly demeanour, rubber lips and scarecrow body were initially greeted with bemusement by the pin-up pop magazines of the time. What Jagger did was to reinforce those apparent pop star deficiencies and, with remarkable effect, transform them into commodities. The lascivious stage presence was emphasized to such a degree that Jagger became both an appealing and strikingly odd-looking pop star. His self-reconstruction even extended as far as completely altering his accent. In mid-60s television interviews Jagger came across as an urbane, well-spoken university student, but as the decade progressed pseudo-cockney inflexions infiltrated his speech, ultimately creating the multi-mouthed media monster of the present - a figure equally at home talking yobbish platitudes to the gutter press and high-brow after-dinner conversation to the quality monthlies. Jagger's capacity to outrage the elder members of the community in the 60s was perfected in his highly energetic dervish stage persona, anti-authoritarian stance and unromantic songwriting. In songs such as '(I Can't Get No) Satisfaction', 'Get Off Of My Cloud', '19th Nervous Breakdown' and 'Have You Seen Your Mother Baby, Standing In The Shadow?', Jagger gave short shrift to sex, women, religion and even life itself. He was, undoubtedly, one of rock's most underrated and nihilistic lyricists. The force of his negative catechism was, of course, complemented by the musical contribution of Keith Richards, the architect behind the Rolling Stones' most memorable melodies. Jagger was also assisted by the quality of his players, especially Bill Wyman, Charlie Watts, Brian Jones and later, Mick Taylor.

From the mid-60s onwards the rebellion implicit in Jagger's lyrics was reflected in increasingly bizarre real life situations. From urinating against an East London garage wall to saturnalian drug sessions and short-term imprisonment, Jagger came to embody the changing social values and bohemian recklessness that characterized the rock culture of the 60s. It must also be said that he performed a similar role in the 70s when his broken marriage, jet-set romances, café society fraternization and millionaire seclusion in exotic climes typified the bloated complacency of the musical élite of the period. The barometer of his time, Jagger yet resisted the temptation to branch out from the Stones into too many uncharted areas. A desultory appearance in the film *Ned Kelly* revealed that his powers of mimicry did not extend as far as a convincing Australian/Irish accent. By contrast, the extraordinary *Performance* captured the combined innocence and malevolence of Jagger's pop persona to striking effect in the guise of a decadent rock star The experiment was not repeated.

Jagger was even less concerned about expressing himself in a literary form, unlike John Lennon, Pete Townshend and others of his generation. The most articulate of the Stones frankly admitted that he could not even remember sufficient details of his life to pen a ghosted biography. That peculiar combination of indolence and disinterest may have kept the Rolling Stones together as a performing unit, for Jagger studiously avoided customary rock star solo outings for virtually 25 years. When he finally succumbed to the temptation in the late 80s, the results were insubstantial. Apart from a small handful of tracks, most notably the driving 'Just Another Night', the albums *She's The Boss* and *Primitive Cool* proved disappointing and no doubt contributed to his decision to take the Rolling Stones back on the road at the end of the decade. He has since teamed up with Tina Turner for a Live Aid performance and with David Bowie for a charity cover of Martha And The Vandella's 'Dancin' In The Street'. Jagger once stated that he would retire before middle-age for fear that the Rolling Stones might become an anachronistic parody of themselves. These days such fears appear to have been banished as the Stones are still recording and, in 1990/1, embarked upon a massive US and European stadium tour. Six years passed before Jagger made his third solo album; the critics were once again unmoved. The addition of Courtney Pine and Billy Preston could not produce a significant hit album.

●ALBUMS: *She's The Boss* (Columbia 1985)★★, *Primitive Cool* (Columbia 1987)★★, *Wandering Spirit* (Atlantic 1993)★★.

●FURTHER READING: *Mick Jagger: The Singer Not The Song*, J. Marks. *Mick Jagger*, Tony Scaduto. *Up And Down With The Rolling Stones*, Tony Sanchez. *The Stones*, Philip Norman. *The True Adventures Of The Rolling Stones*, Stanley Booth. *Jagger Unauthorised*, Christopher Andersen. *Mick Jagger: Primitive Cool*, Christopher Sandford.

JAH WOBBLE

b. John Wardle, London, England. An innovative bass player, Wobble began his career with Public Image Limited. Previously he had been known as one of the 'four Johns' who hung around Malcolm McLaren's 'Sex' boutique. Heavily influenced by the experimental rhythms of bands like Can, his input to PiL's *Metal Box* collection inspired, in turn, many novice post-punk bass players. By August 1980 he had become one of the many instrumentalists to fall foul of Lydon in PiL's turbulent career, and set about going solo. In 1983 he collaborated with his hero Holger Czukay and U2's The Edge for *Snake Charmer*, before he put together the Human Condition, a group specializing in free-form jazz and dub improvisation. However, when they disbanded, the mid-80s quickly became wilderness years for Wobble: 'The biggest kickback I have had was from sweeping the platform at Tower Hill station. It was a scream. You felt like getting on the intercom and saying "The next train is the Upminster train, calling at all stations to Upminster and by the way, I USED TO BE SOMEONE!"'. However, when he began listening to North African, Arabic and Romany music, he was inspired to pick up his bass once more. It was 1987 when he met guitarist Justin Adams, who had spent much of his early life in Arab countries. Their bonding resulted in Wobble putting together Invaders Of The Heart, with producer Mark Ferda on keyboards. After tentative live shows they released *Without Judgement* in the Netherlands, where Wobble had maintained cult popularity. As the late 80s saw a surge in the fortunes of dance and rhythmic expression, Invaders Of The Heart and Wobble suddenly achieved a surprise return to the mainstream. This was spearheaded by 1990's 'Bomba', remixed by Andy Weatherall on the fashionable Boy's Own Records. Wobble was in demand again, notably as collaborator on Sinead O'Connor's *I Do Not Want What I Haven't Got* and Primal Scream's 'Higher Than The Sun'. This was quickly followed by Invaders Of The Heart's *Rising Above Bedlam*, in turn featuring contributions from O'Connor (the dance hit, 'Visions Of You') and Natacha Atlas. Wobble's creative renaissance has

continued into the 90s, with Invaders Of The Heart slowly building a formidable live repuation and releasing a series of infectious, upbeat albums for Island Records.
●ALBUMS: *The Legend Lives On ... Jah Wobble In 'Betrayal'* (Virgin 1980)★★, with Holger Czukay and The Edge *Snake Charmer* (Island 1983)★★★, *Jah Wobble's Bedroom Album* (Lago 1983)★★, with Ollie Morland *Neon Moon* (Island 1985)★★★, *Psalms* (Wob 1987)★★★, with Invaders Of The Heart *Without Judgement* (Island 1990)★★★★, *Rising Above Bedlam* (Island 1991)★★★★, *Take Me To God* (Island 1994)★★★★, *Heaven & Earth* (Island 1995)★★★, with Eno *Spanner* (All Saints 1995)★★★, *The Inspiration Of William Blake* (All Saints 1996)★★★, *The Celtic Poets* (30 Hertz 1997)★★★.

JAMES

Championed initially by Morrissey of the Smiths, James signed with their hometown record label, Manchester's Factory Records, in 1983. Their early singles, 'What's The World?' and 'Hymn From A Village', were acclaimed for their unusual mixture of folk and new wave textures. The original line-up was Timothy Booth (b. 4 February 1960; vocals), James Glennie (b. 10 October 1963; bass), James Gott (guitar) and Gavan Whelan (drums). They signed to Sire Records in 1985 and began an unsettled three year relationship with the company. *Stutter* was a collection of strange but striking songs, followed two years later by *Strip Mine* which contained a stronger melodic edge. *One Man Clapping*, a live set recorded in Bath, England marked a return to independent status with Rough Trade Records. Dave Baynton-Power replaced Whelan and soon afterwards the group was augmented by Saul Davies (guitar/violin), Mark Hunter (keyboards) and Andy Diagram (trumpet). Fontana Records, with its policy of signing England's leading independent bands, re-released 'Come Home' and 'Sit Down', the latter single reaching number 2 in the UK charts. *Gold Mother* was more accessible than previous albums, the band writing in a more direct lyrical style, though there were still echoes of earlier eccentricities. The title track was a paean to mothers and the extreme physical pain they underwent during childbirth, and drew from Booth's personal exposure to the birth of his child. Although their recording career stretched back further than their contemporaries, they became part of an upsurge in talent from Manchester during the late 80s and early 90s and the media attention on the city made the transition

from independent to major league status that much easier. *Seven* saw the band digress further away from the immediacy of 'Sit Down', which up to that point was their most enduring and popular song. Instead the emphasis was on atmosphere and multi-layered, unconventional song structures. The upshot of this was a fall-off in commercial viability, although the group maintained a loyal fan base. *Laid*, meanwhile was a title presumably inspired by Booth's return from a life of celibacy, and its hit single of the same title was the first to make an impression in the US. The other contents were described as 'paranoid love songs, ecstatic laments and perverse lullabies' by *Select* magazine's reviewer. 1994's heavily experimental *Wah Wah* was seen by some critics as an attempt to steal U2's *Zooropa* thunder. It was recorded with Brian Eno during sessions for *Laid*, for release as an 'alternative' album. The move into ambient electronics had, however, been signposted by the 1993 Sabres Of Paradise remix of 'Jam J'. The group broke a three-year silence with the well-received *Whiplash* and the hit single 'She's A Star'.
●ALBUMS: *Stutter* (Sire 1986)★★★, *Strip Mine* (Sire 1988)★★★, *One Man Clapping* (Rough Trade 1989)★★★, *Gold Mother* (Fontana 1990)★★★★, *Seven* (Fontana 1992)★★★★, *Laid* (Fontana 1993)★★★, *Wah Wah* (Fontana 1994)★★, *Whiplash* (Fontana 1997)★★★.
●VIDEOS: *Come Home Live* (Polygram 1991), *Seven - The Live Video* (Polygram Video 1992).

JAMES, RICK

b. James Johnson, 1 February 1948, Buffalo, New York, USA. The nephew of Temptations vocalist Melvin Franklin, James pioneered a crossover style between R&B and rock in the mid-60s. In 1965, he formed the Mynah Birds in New York with two future members of the Buffalo Springfield, Neil Young and Bruce Palmer, plus Goldie McJohn, later with Steppenwolf. Motown Records signed the band as a riposte to the British wave of R&B artists then dominating the charts, before their career was aborted when James was arrested for draft evasion. Resuming his career in Britain in the early 70s, James formed the funk combo Main Line. Returning to the USA, he assembled a like-minded group of musicians to perform a dense, brash brand of funk influenced by Sly Stone and George Clinton. Signed to Motown in 1977, initially as a songwriter, he rapidly evolved a more individual style, which he labelled 'punk funk'. His first single, 'You And I', typified his approach, with its prominent bass riffs, heavy percussion, and sly, streetwise vocals. The record reached the US Top 20 and topped the specialist soul charts - a feat which its follow-up, 'Mary Jane', came close to repeating, though the song's blatant references to marijuana cut short any hopes of radio airplay. James chose to present himself as a social outlaw, with outspoken views on drugs and sex. In a move subsequently echoed by Prince, he amassed a stable of artists under his control at Motown, using the Stone City Band as his backing group, and the Mary Jane Girls as female pawns in his macho master plan. James also produced records by actor Eddie Murphy, vocalist Teena Marie, Val Young, and Process and the Doo-Rags.

His own recordings, predominantly in the funk vein, continued to corner the disco market, with 'Give It To Me Baby' and 'Super Freak' on which he was joined by the Temptations, achieving notable sales in 1981. Both tracks came from *Street Songs*, a Grammy-nominated record that catapulted James into the superstar bracket. Secure in his commercial standing, he revealed that he preferred recording ballads to the funk workouts which had made his name, and his drift towards a more conservative image was heightened when he duetted with Smokey Robinson on the hit single 'Ebony Eyes', and masterminded the Temptations' reunion project in 1983. James' flamboyant lifestyle took its toll on his health and he was hospitalized several times between 1979 and 1984. His career continued unabated, and he had major hits in 1984 and 1985 with the more relaxed '17' and 'The Glow'. The latter also provided the title for a highly acclaimed album, which reflected James' decision to abandon the use of drugs, and move towards a more laid-back soul style. He was angered by constant media comparisons of his work with Prince, and cancelled plans to star in an autobiographical film called *The Spice Of Life* in the wake of the overwhelming commercial impact of his rival's *Purple Rain*. After releasing *The Flag* in 1986, James ran into serious conflict with Motown over the status of his spin-off acts. When they refused to release any further albums by the Mary Jane Girls, James left the label, signing to Reprise Records, where he immediately achieved a soul number 1 with 'Loosey's Rap', a collaboration with Roxanne Shante. James' drug problems had not gone away and following years of abuse he was jailed in 1991, together with his girlfriend Tanya Hijazi, for various offences including dealing cocaine, assault and torture. The King Of Funk confessed to *Rolling Stone* that at least by being in prison he 'could not do drugs'. He was released in 1996.

●ALBUMS: *Come Get It* (Motown 1978)★★★, *Bustin' Out Of L Seven* (Motown 1979)★★★, *Fire It Up* (Motown 1979)★★★, *Garden Of Love* (Motown 1980)★★, *Street Songs* (Motown 1981)★★★★, *Throwin' Down* (Motown 1982)★★★, *Cold Blooded* (Motown 1983)★★, *The Glow* (Motown 1985)★★, *The Flag* (Motown 1986)★★, *Wonderful* (Reprise 1988)★★.
●COMPILATIONS: *Greatest Hits* (Motown 1993)★★★, *Bustin' Out: The Best Of Rick James* (Motown 1994)★★★, *Greatest Hits* (Spectrum 1996)★★★.

JAPAN

Formed in London in early 1974, this group comprised David Sylvian (b. David Batt, 23 February 1958, Lewisham, London, England; vocals), his brother Steve Jansen (b. Steven Batt, 1 December 1959, Lewisham, London, England; drums), Richard Barbieri (b. 30 November 1958; keyboards) and Mick Karn (b. Anthony Michaelides, 24 July 1958, London, England; saxophone). A second guitarist, Rob Dean, joined later and the group won a recording contract with the German record company Ariola-Hansa. During the same period, they signed to manager Simon Napier-Bell. The group's derivative pop style hampered their prospects during 1978, and they suffered a number of hostile reviews. Eminently unfashionable in the UK punk era, they first found success in Japan. After three albums with Ariola-Hansa, they switched to Virgin Records in 1980 and their fortunes improved a year later thanks to the surge of popularity in the new romantic movement. Japan's androgynous image made them suddenly fashionable and they registered UK Top 20 hits with 'Quiet Life', 'Ghosts' and a cover of Smokey Robinson And The Miracles' 'I Second That Emotion'. Their album, *Tin Drum*, was also well received. Disagreements between Karn and Sylvian undermined the group's progress, just as they were achieving some long-overdue success and they split in late 1982. Sylvian and Karn went on to record solo with varying degrees of success.
●ALBUMS: *Adolescent Sex* (Ariola-Hansa 1978)★★, *Obscure* (Ariola-Hansa 1978)★★, *Quiet Life* (Ariola-Hansa 1980)★★★, *Gentlemen Take Polaroids* (Virgin 1980)★★★, *Tin Drum* (Virgin 1981)★★★, *Oil On Canvas* (Virgin 1983)★★.
●COMPILATIONS: *Assemblage* (Hansa 1981)★★★, *Exorcising Ghosts* (Virgin 1984)★★★, *In Vogue* (Camden 1997)★★★.
●FURTHER READING: *A Tourist's Guide To Japan*, Arthur A. Pitt.

JARRE, JEAN-MICHEL

b. 24 August 1948, Lyon, France. This enigmatic composer and keyboard wizard has long been hailed as the premier exponent of European electronic music. From the age of five he took up the piano, and studied harmony and structure at the Paris Conservatoire, before abandoning classical music and joining Pierre Schaeffer's Musical Research group. Becoming gradually more fascinated with the scope offered by electronics, his first release comprised the passages 'La Cage' and 'Eros Machine' on EMI Pathe in France. He then contributed 'Aor' for the Paris Opera ballet, and the soundtrack for the film *Les Granges Bruless*, among others. After marrying actress Charlotte Rampling, he set about composing his first full scale opus, *Oxygene*. This reached number 2 in the UK charts, signalling Jarre's arrival as a commercial force. The subsequent *Equinoxe* continued in familiar style, exploring the emotive power of orchestrated electronic rhythms and melody. The first of several massive open air performances took place in Paris at the Place De La Concorde, with a world record attendance of over one million. However, it was not until 1981 and the release of *Magnetic Fields* that Jarre undertook his first tour, no small task considering the amount of stage equipment required. His destination was China where five concerts took place with the aid of 35 traditional Chinese musicians. A double album was released to document the event. 1983's *Music For Supermarkets* proved his most elusive release, recorded as background music for an art exhibition. Just one copy was pressed and sold at an auction for charity before the masters were destroyed. The *Essential Jean Michel Jarre*, compiled from earlier albums, proved more accessible for Jarre's legion of fans. *Zoolook* utilized a multitude of foreign language intonations in addition to the familiar electronic backdrop, but an unexpectedly lethargic reaction from the public prompted a two year absence from recording. He returned with another outdoor extravaganza, this time celebrating NASA's 25th anniversary in Houston. Viewed by over one million people this time, it was also screened on worldwide television. The release of *Rendezvous* the following month was hardly coincidental. His first concerts in the UK, advertised as 'Destination Docklands', were also televised in October 1988. Whatever the size of audience he attracted, he was still unable to woo the critics. *Revolutions* appeared in the shops shortly after, while one of its two singles, 'London Kid,' featured the Shadows' Hank B. Marvin on guitar. *Waiting For Cousteau* anticipated his most recent update on the world record for attendance at a music concert. This time two million crammed into Paris on Bastille Day to witness 'La Defence'. While Jarre continues to bewilder and infuriate music critics, statistical evidence shows he is far from short of advocates in the general public.

● ALBUMS: *Oxygene* (Polydor 1977)★★★★, *Equinoxe* (Polydor 1978)★★★, *Magnetic Fields* (Polydor 1981)★★★, *Concerts In China* (Polydor 1982)★★★, *Zoolook* (Polydor 1984)★★★, *Rendezvous* (Polydor 1986)★★, *Houston/Lyon* (Polydor 1987)★★, *Revolutions* (Polydor 1988)★★★, *Live* (Polydor 1989)★★, *Waiting For Cousteau* (Polydor 1990)★★, *Oxygene 7-13* (1997)★★.

● COMPILATIONS: *The Essential* (Polydor 1983)★★★.

● FURTHER READING: *The Unofficial Jean-Michel Jarre Biography*, Graham Needham.

JARREAU, AL

b. 12 March 1940, Milwaukee, Wisconsin, USA. Although Jarreau sang from childhood, it was many years before he decided to make singing his full-time occupation. Working outside music for most of the 60s, he began to sing in small west coast clubs and eventually achieved enough success to change careers. By the mid-70s he was becoming well known in the USA, and owing to records and a European tour greatly extended his audience. Singing a highly sophisticated form of vocalese, Jarreau's style displays many influences. Some of these come from within the world of jazz, notably the work of Jon Hendricks, while others are external. He customarily uses vocal sounds that include the clicks of African song and the plosives common in oriental speech and singing patterns. This range of influences makes him both hard to classify and more accessible to the wider audience for crossover music. More commercially successful than most jazz singers, Jarreau's work in the 70s and 80s consistently appealed to young audiences attuned to fusions in popular music. By the early 90s, when he was entering his 50s, his kinship with youth culture was clearly diminishing; but his reputation was by now firmly established.

● ALBUMS: *1965* (1965)★★, *We Got By* (Reprise 1975)★★★, *Glow* (Reprise 1976)★★, *Look To The Rainbow* (WEA 1977)★★, *All Fly Home* (WEA 1978)★★, *This Time* (WEA 1980)★★★, *Breakin' Away* (WEA 1981)★★★, *Jarreau* (WEA 1983)★★★,

Spirits And Feelings (Happy Bird 1984)★★★, *Ain't No Sunshine* (Blue Moon 1984)★★★, *High Crime* (WEA 1984)★★, *Al Jarreau Live In London* (WEA 1984)★★, *You* (Platinum 1985)★★★, *L As In Lover* (WEA 1986)★★★, *Hearts Horizon* (WEA 1988)★★★, *Manifesto* (Masters 1988)★★★, *Heaven And Earth* (WEA 1992)★★★, *Tenderness* (WEA 1994)★★★.

●FILMS: *Breakdance - The Movie* (1984).

JASON AND THE SCORCHERS

This country-rock 'n' roll styled US band was led by Jason Ringenberg (b. 22 November 1959; vocals, guitar, harmonica) who left his parents' farm in Sheffield, Illinois, in 1981 to travel to Nashville. There he teamed up with Warner Hodges (b. 4 June 1959, Nashville, Tennessee, USA; guitar) and Jeff Johnson (b. Nashville, Tennessee, USA; bass). Another original member was Jack Emerson, who went on to become the band's manager. Hodges' parents provided the band's pedigree, having been country musicians who toured with Johnny Cash. The band recruited Perry Bags (b. 22 March 1962, Nashville, Tennessee, USA; drums) and became Jason And The Nashville Scorchers, with the prefix later dropped, playing fast country rock ('cow punk' was the description coined in the UK). Their first EP for the Praxis label was 1982's *Reckless Country Soul* (USA only), followed by the mini-album *Fervor* a year later. This brought them well-deserved attention in the press and was subsequently re-released in 1984 on EMI-America. It was notable for the inclusion of Bob Dylan's 'Absolutely Sweet Marie', while a subsequent single tackled the Rolling Stones' '19th Nervous Breakdown'. *Lost And Found* included a cover of Hank Williams' 'Lost Highway'; the combination of these three covers gives a useful insight into the band's influences and sound.

After moving increasingly towards hard rock with *Thunder And Fire* in 1989, the Scorchers split up when that album failed to bring the expected commercial breakthrough. While guitarist Warner Hodges quit the music business in disgust, Jason Ringenberg took time to gather himself for an assault on the country market. His raunchy solo debut, *One Foot In The Honky Tonk* (released by Liberty Records and credited to 'Jason'), proved to be too traditional for country radio, but he remains an irrepressible live performer. They re-formed and released *A Blazing Grace*, and under the name Jason And the Nashville Scorchers they released *Reckless Country Soul* in 1996.

●ALBUMS: *Fervor* (EMI 1983)★★★, *Lost And Found* (EMI 1985)★★★, *Still Standing* (EMI 1986)★★★, *Thunder And Fire* (A&M 1989)★★★, *A Blazing Grace* (Mammoth 1995)★★★, *Reckless Country Soul* (Mammoth 1996)★★★, *Clear Impetuous Morning* (Mammoth 1996)★★★.

JAZZ BUTCHER

The Jazz Butcher are a prime example of British rock eccentricity. Formed in 1982 and hailing from Northampton, the group served as a vehicle for the idiosyncratic, melodic songwriting talents of Pat Fish (b. Patrick Huntrods; guitar/vocals), otherwise known as the Jazz Butcher. Although early group line-ups were erratic - including Rolo McGinty and Alice Thompson, (both later to emerge in the Woodentops) and ex-Bauhaus bassist David J. - the one constant member during much of the early years was lead guitarist Max Eider, whose light jazz/blues feel gave an eloquence to even the most heavy-handed of tunes. In terms of style, there was a large nod in the direction of Lou Reed and Jonathan Richman, while the songs' subject matter dealt with the diverse traumas of everyday life, taking in the joys and woes of small town living ('Living In A Village'), drink ('Soul Happy Hour'), fear and paranoia ('Death Dentist'), love ('Only A Rumour'/'Angels'), the virtues of public transport ('Groovin' In The Bus Lane'), film noir and Vladimir Ilyich Lenin. The classic Jazz Butcher line-up, including Max Eider, Felix Ray (bass) and 'Mr' O.P. Jones (drums), underwent a major upheaval in 1987 with the departure of Eider, resulting in the unit disintegrating. By the time of *Fishcotheque*, Fish was working virtually alone but for a new partner in guitarist Kizzy O'Callaghan. The Jazz Butcher (Conspiracy) model of the band was rebuilt to comprise Fish, O'Callaghan, Laurence O'Keefe (bass), Paul Mulreany (drums) and Alex Green (saxophone), and saw the group undergoing a change of label, moving from Glass to Creation Records. Subsequent albums saw an increasing use of cut-up film/television dialogue, and continued to garner encouraging reviews. While the Jazz Butcher has found a large audience in Europe, and more recently in the USA, substantial success in his homeland continues to elude him. 1995's *Illuminated* included the anti-Conservative government tract, 'Sixteen Years'. It saw some critics scoff at the way in which Creation's perseverence with the Jazz Butcher mirrored the British public's unwillingness to change administration.

●ALBUMS: *The Jazz Butcher In Bath Of Bacon* (Glass 1983)★★★, *A Scandal In Bohemia* (Glass

1984)★★★, *Sex And Travel* (Glass 1985)★★★, *The Jazz Butcher And The Sikkorskis From Hell - Hamburg - A Live Album* (Rebel 1985)★★★. As Jazz Butcher Conspiracy *Distressed Gentlefolk* (Glass 1986)★★★, *Fishcotheque* (Creation 1988)★★★, *Big Planet, Scary Planet* (Genius 1989)★★★, *Cult Of The Basement* (Rough Trade 1990)★★★, *Condition Blue* (Creation 1991)★★★, *Western Family (Live)* (Creation 1993)★★★, *Waiting For The Love Bus* (Creation 1993)★★★, *Illuminated* (Creation 1995)★★★. Solo: Max Eider *The Best Kisser In The World* (Big Time 1987)★★★.

●COMPILATIONS: *The Gift Of Music* (Glass 1985)★★★, *Bloody Nonsense* (Big Time 1986)★★★, *Big Questions - The Gift Of Music Vol. 2* (Glass 1987)★★★, *Edward's Closet* (Creation 1991)★★★, *Draining The Glass 1982-86* (Nectar 1997)★★★.

JENNINGS, WILL

b. 27 June 1944, Kilgore, East Texas, USA. He moved to Tyler when he was 12 and at that time took up the trombone as he had become fascinated with traditional jazz. Jennings is one of the leading lyric writers of the 80s, best known for his work with the Crusaders, B.B. King, Jimmy Buffett and Steve Winwood. As a teenager Jennings played guitar in rock bands; the most notable was Blue Mountain Marriage. He then became a literature teacher at the University of Wisconsin, Eau Claire. He moved to Nashville in 1971 and co-wrote four songs with Troy Seals for Dobie Gray's *Drift Away*. During the 70s he composed further material for country artists but had his first pop success co-writing with Richard Kerr. Together they composed 'Somewhere In The Night' for Barry Manilow and 'I Know I'll Never Love This Way Again' and 'No Night So Long' for Dionne Warwick. Next, Jennings forged a partnership with Joe Sample of the Crusaders to create the big hits 'Street Life' and 'One Day I'll Fly Away', recorded by Randy Crawford. He continued to write with Sample and B.B. King used their songs for three albums, *Midnight Believer*, *Take It Home* and *There's Always One More Time*. One of his biggest-selling pop-soul ballads, however, was 'Didn't We Almost Have It All', co-written with Michael Masser for Whitney Houston. Jennings' most fruitful long-lasting collaboration has been with Winwood, whom he met in 1981 following an introduction by Chris Blackwell. Their first success together was the US hit 'While You See A Chance', from *Arc Of A Diver*. Jennings co-composed a number of tracks from that album. Jennings subsequently wrote the lyrics for many tracks on all further Winwood solo

albums, including the hymn-like 'There's A River', 'Talking Back To The Night', 'And I Go', 'Back In The High Life', 'I Will Be Here', 'Valerie' (the subject of the latter is Valerie Carter) and the US hit singles 'Higher Love' (1986) and 'Roll With It' (1988). He met country star Jimmy Buffett in 1982 and wrote two albums with him, *Riddle In The Sand* and *Last Mango In Paris*. 'Up Where We Belong', the anthem of the film *An Officer And A Gentlemen*, was written with Buffy Saint-Marie and was a worldwide hit for Joe Cocker and Jennifer Warnes, and is Jennings' most lucrative copyright. He received a BMI award with Eric Clapton for 'Tears In Heaven' in 1996. He also struck up a friendship and musical partnership with Roy Orbison, writing a number of songs including 'Wild Hearts Run Out Of Time' from the Nicholas Roeg movie *Insignificance*. Hits and awards continued into the 90s as Jennings was commissioned to write songs for films and songs for established artists. His success is now self-perpetuating and he is one of the most sought after writers of the past two decades. Jennings is humble about working with talented musicians such as Winwood and Sample and yet he paints their music with colourful romantic lyrics. In 1996 he was collaborating with Winwood again and spent time working in Ireland with Paul Brady. Jennings states 'a great piece of (popular) music is so important, it deserves the very best I can write to it'. All this is maintained with a down-to-earth attitude, painful modesty, and a love of flat caps, British poetry and literature.

JESUS AND MARY CHAIN

Formed in East Kilbride, Scotland, this quartet comprised William Reid (vocals/guitar), Jim Reid (vocals/guitar), Douglas Hart (bass) and Murray Dalglish (drums). In the summer of 1984 they moved to London and signed to Alan McGee's label, Creation Records. Their debut, 'Upside Down', complete with trademark feedback, fared well in the independent charts and was backed with a version of Syd Barrett's 'Vegetable Man'. In November 1984, Dalglish was replaced on drums by Primal Scream vocalist Bobby Gillespie. By the end of the year, the group were attracting considerable media attention due to the violence at their gigs and a series of bans followed. Early the following year, the group signed to the WEA/Rough Trade label, Blanco y Negro. The Reid brothers publically delighted in the charms of amphetamine sulphate, which gave their music a manic edge. Live performances usually lasted 20 minutes, which brought more controversy and truculence from traditional gig habitués, who felt short-changed. 'Never Understand' further underlined comparisons with the anarchic school of 1977 in general and the Sex Pistols in particular. For their next release, however, the group surprised many by issuing the more pop-orientated 'Just Like Honey'. By October 1985, Gillespie had grown tired of the Jesus And Mary Chain and returned to his former group, Primal Scream. One month later, the Reid Brothers issued their highly acclaimed debut, *Psychocandy*. Full of multi-tracked guitar distortion, underscored with dark melodies, many critics proclaimed it one of rock's great debuts. The following August the group reached the UK Top 20 with the melodic 'Some Candy Talking', which received curtailed radio play when it was alleged that the subject matter concerned heroin. During the same period, the group found a new drummer, John Moore, and parted from their manager, Alan McGee. Further hits with 'April Skies' and 'Happy When It Rains' preceded their second album, *Darklands*. Again fawned over by the press, though not to quite the same extent as their debut, it was followed by a tempestuous tour of Canada and America, during which one brother was briefly arrested then acquitted on a charge of assaulting a fan. In the spring of 1988 a compilation of the group's various out-takes was issued. This assuaged demand before the arrival of *Automatic* at the turn of the decade. The band was effectively just a duo for this, with programmed synth drums as backing to the usual barrage of distortion and twisted lyrics (the best example of which was the single, 'Blues From A Gun'). *Honey's Dead* also housed a powerful lead single in 'Reverence', which brought the band back to the charts. After this, the Reid brothers changed tack for *Stoned & Dethroned*, with the feedback all but gone in favour of an acoustic, singer/songwriter approach. Self-produced and recorded at home, its more reflective texture was embossed by the appearance of guest vocalists Shane MacGowan (ex-Pogues) and Hope Sandoval from Mazzy Star.

●ALBUMS: *Psychocandy* (Blanco y Negro 1985)★★★★, *Darklands* (Blanco y Negro 1987)★★★, *Automatic* (Blanco y Negro 1990)★★, *Honey's Dead* (Blanco y Negro 1992)★★★, *Stoned & Dethroned* (Blanco y Negro 1994)★★★.

●COMPILATIONS: *Barbed Wire Kisses* (Blanco y Negro 1988)★★★, *Sound Of Speed* (Blanco y Negro 1993)★★★.

●FURTHER READING: *The Jesus and Mary Chain: A Musical Biography*, John Robertson.

JETT, JOAN, AND THE BLACKHEARTS

b. Joan Larkin, 22 September 1960, Philadelphia, Pennsylvania, USA. Jett was one of the most successful US female singers to emerge from the rock scene of the 70s. She spent most of her childhood in the Baltimore, Maryland, area, where she learned guitar as a child, playing along to favourite rock 'n' roll records. In 1972 her family relocated to Los Angeles, where she became enamoured with artists including David Bowie, Suzi Quatro, T. Rex and Gary Glitter. At the age of 15 she began infiltrating the Los Angeles rock scene and formed her first band. Producer Kim Fowley took the group under his wing and named it the Runaways, procuring a record contract with Mercury Records. The group recorded three punk-tinged hard rock albums which were unsuccessful in the USA but hits in Japan, where they recorded a live album. Also successful in England, they recorded their swansong, *And Now ... The Runaways*, in that territory in 1979. After the dissolution of the group, Jett moved to New York and teamed up with producer Kenny Laguna, who became her manager. Laguna had previously been involved with a number of 60s bubblegum hits. Laguna produced Jett's first solo album which was released on the European Ariola label. When no US label would pick it up they issued it themselves and the album sold well, becoming one of the best-selling US independent records of that time. That led to a contract with Neil Bogart's Boardwalk Records, who reissued it as *Bad Reputation* (a title inspired by the less than enthusiastic industry response to Jett after the Runaways) and saw it reach number 51 in the US charts. With her group the Blackhearts (guitarist Ricky Byrd, bassist Gary Ryan and drummer Lee Crystal), Jett recorded *I Love Rock 'N' Roll* in late 1981, produced by Laguna and Ritchie Cordell. The title track, originally an obscure b-side for UK group the Arrows, became a major hit, largely owing to a big push from MTV, and spent seven weeks at number 1 in the USA in early 1982. The follow-up single, a cover of Tommy James And The Shondells' 'Crimson And Clover', was itself a Top 10 hit, reaching number 7 in 1982. Also housed on the album was an update of a Jett song from the Runaways era, 'You're Too Possessive'. With Bogart's death the group signed to MCA, which then distributed Blackheart Records. Subsequent outings on that label were not nearly as successful as the Boardwalk releases, although *Album* did collect a gold award. *Glorious Results Of A Misspent*

Youth again retreated to Jett's past with the Runaways, this time on a revision of 'Cherry Bomb'. *Good Music* saw some intriguing collaborations, with members of the Beach Boys and Darlene Love guesting, and an unlikely rap duet with Scorpio of Grandmaster Flash And The Furious Five. The album also saw the departure of Lee Crystal and Gary Ryan, the former permanently replaced by Thommy Price. Jett meanwhile found time to make a second film appearance (following *We're All Crazy Now!*), playing Michael J. Fox's sister in *Light Of Day*. She also sang the Bruce Springsteen-penned theme. *Up Your Alley* brought another hit with 'I Hate Myself For Loving You', before 1990's *The Hit List*, an album of cover versions, which included a duet with Ray Davies on 'Celluloid Heroes'. *Notorious* saw her link up with Paul Westerberg of the Replacements for the co-written 'Backlash', but by the advent of *Pure And Simple* Byrd was no longer a permanent member of the band. This set saw a guest appearance from L7 on a track entitled 'Activity Grrrl', emphasizing Jett's influence on a new generation of female rockers (Jett had also produced Bikini Kill and late 70s LA punk band the Germs).

● ALBUMS: *Joan Jett* (Blackheart 1980)★★★, *Bad Reputation* reissue of debut (Boardwalk 1981)★★★ *I Love Rock 'n' Roll* (Boardwalk 1981)★★★★, *Album* (MCA/Blackheart 1983)★★★, *Glorious Results Of A Misspent Youth* (MCA/Blackheart 1984)★★★, *Good Music* (Columbia/Blackheart 1986)★★★, *Up Your Alley* (Columbia/Blackheart 1988)★★★, *The Hit List* (Columbia/Blackheart 1990)★★★, *Notorious* (Epic/Blackheart 1991)★★★, *Pure And Simple* (Blackheart/Warners 1994)★★★.

● COMPILATIONS: *Flashback* (Blackheart 1993)★★★★.

JIMMY JAM AND TERRY LEWIS

Based in Minneapolis, Minnesota, USA, Jimmy 'Jam' Harris and Terry Lewis are prolific producers of contemporary R&B, who first worked together in the early 80s as members of Time (formerly Flyte Time). Afterwards Harris (keyboards) and Lewis (bass) became black music's most consistently successful production duo. They had already formed their own record label, Tabu, in 1980. Tabu enjoyed enormous success with artists such as the S.O.S. Band throughout the 80s. Among the other early bands and artists to benefit from the duo's writing and production were Change, Cherrelle, the Force MD's, Johnny Gill and the former Time singer Alexander O'Neal. Their greatest success, however, came as the creative cat-

alysts behind Janet Jackson's career. The first album they recorded with her, *Control*, included five hit singles, and the follow-up, *Rhythm Nation 1814*, was similarly successful. In 1990 Jam and Lewis recorded once again with Time who had reformed to make *Pandemonium*, which was released on Prince's Paisley Park Records. Though the reunion was not widely regarded as a success, the duo's productions remained in the higher reaches of the charts. Their continued association with Jackson was never surpassed commercially but many others benefited from their expertise, from their pioneering work with what would become known as swingbeat to cross-genre productions with artists ranging from the Human League to Sounds Of Blackness. In the 90s they also established a new record label, Perspective Records, distributed by A&M Records.

JOBOXERS

This pop-soul group achieved minor fame in the early 80s with a sound built on fast beats and imagery from the film *On The Waterfront*. They comprised Dig Wayne (b. 20 July 1958, USA; vocals), Rob Marche (b. 13 October 1962, Bristol, England; guitar), Dave Collard (b. 17 January 1961, Bristol, England; keyboards), Chris Bostock (b. 23 November 1962, Bristol, England; bass) and Sean McLusky (b. 5 May 1961, Bristol, England; drums). All except Wayne were former members of Vic Goddard And The Subway Sect (*c*.1981 onwards), the last incarnation of a punk band who ended their career by backing Goddard's affected crooning. He met the rest of the band at a street market where both had second-hand clothes stalls. As JoBoxers they first attracted attention after appearing on the BBC television's *Oxford Roadshow* in 1982. Signed to RCA Records, in February 1983 they released 'Boxer Beat', which was a Top 5 hit in the UK. The follow-up 'Just Got Lucky' also went into the Top 10 but subsequent singles such as 'Johnny Friendly' did less well. The band split early in 1986, with Wayne going on to a brief solo career (one album, *Square Business*, 1987) with a band that featured Dave Collard of JoBoxers and Mark Reilly (ex-Matt Bianco).

● ALBUMS: *Like Gangbusters* (RCA 1983)★★, *Skin And Bone* (RCA 1985)★★.

JOHANSEN, DAVID

b. 9 January 1950, Staten Island, New York, USA. Johansen gained recognition in the early 70s as lead singer of the New York Dolls. An R&B/rock group taking inspiration from the likes of the

Rolling Stones, the Dolls' street attitude and outrageous sense of dress, thrust them into the glitter/glam scene, although their music had little in common with others of that nature. Prior to joining the Dolls, Johansen joined his first band, the Vagabond Missionaries, in high school. At the age of 17 he moved to Manhattan, New York, and briefly worked with a band called Fast Eddie And The Electric Japs. The Dolls came together in late 1971 and quickly built a devoted audience at New York clubs such as the Mercer Arts Center and Max's Kansas City. They recorded two albums for Mercury Records and held on until late 1976. After their demise they became an inspiration to numerous artists, from the newly forming punk bands such as the Sex Pistols to Kiss to the Smiths. Johansen launched a solo career in 1978, recording for Blue Sky Records. Less flamboyant than the Dolls' records, this was a solid rock effort that stressed Johansen's lyrical acumen. He released three other rock/R&B-oriented solo albums for Blue Sky and one for Passport Records before shifting career directions once again. In 1983 Johansen began booking small cabaret concert dates under the name Buster Poindexter, performing a slick, tightly arranged set of vintage R&B numbers, show tunes, and jump blues. Dressing in a formal tuxedo and playing the lounge lizard, Poindexter built a following of his own, until Johansen the rocker literally ceased to exist; he completely gave up his rock act to pursue the new image full-time. He recorded two albums as Buster Poindexter, *Buster Poindexter* (1987) and *Buster Goes Berserk* (1989), the first yielding a chart and club hit, a cover of Arrow's 1984 soca dance tune, 'Hot, Hot, Hot'. He was still popular as Poindexter in the early 90s, touring with a 10-piece band and packing clubs, his repertoire now including Caribbean-flavoured music, torch songs, blues, as well as the early R&B. He also launched an acting career in the late 80s, appearing in films including *Scrooged* and *Married To The Mob*.
● ALBUMS: *David Johansen* (Blue Sky 1978)★★★, *In Style* (Blue Sky 1979)★★★, *Here Comes The Night* (Blue Sky 1981)★★, *Live It Up* (Blue Sky 1982)★★★, *Sweet Revenge* (Passport 1984)★★★.

JOHNNY HATES JAZZ
Purveyors of super-slick UK pop, the band's line-up featured Calvin Hayes (b. 1963; keyboards/drums), Mike Nocito (b. 5 August 1963, Wiesbaden, Germany; guitar/bass) and Clark Datchler (vocals/keyboards), the son of former Stargazer Fred Datchler. Datchler was later replaced by multi-instrumentalist Phil Thornalley (b. 5 January 1964, Worlington, Suffolk, England; vocals/guitar). The connection between all four was RAK Records. The label was owned by Hayes' father, Mickie Most. Thornalley co-wrote the original single, 'Me And My Foolish Heart' that failed in 1986, but he could not front the band as he was producing Robbie Nevil. Hayes brought in ex-Hot Club team-mate Datchler, and some expensive suits. 'Shattered Dreams' (the Datchler-penned follow-up) was a UK Top 10 hit during 1987 and also fared well in the USA. Three further Top 20 hits followed during the next year: 'I Don't Want To Be A Hero', 'Turn Back The Clock' and 'Heart Of Gold'. The group's first album topped the UK charts, but they were unable to sustain that level of commercial appeal. Datchler went on to resume a largely unsuccessful solo career, releasing 'Crown Of Thorns' for JHJ stable Virgin Records.
● ALBUMS: *Turn Back The Clock* (Virgin 1988)★★, *Tall Stories* (Virgin 1991)★★. Solo: Clark Datchler *Raindance* (Virgin 1990)★★.
● COMPILATIONS: *The Very Best Of* (Virgin 1993)★★.
● VIDEOS: *The Video Singles* (1988).

JOLLEY, STEVE
In 1969, Jolley was guitarist with Sam Apple Pie. The following year, he joined Freedom, a Procol Harum splinter group, in whose ranks he remained until 1972. By the end of the decade, he had become principally a studio functionary. In partnership with Tony Swain, he worked on television's *Muppet Show* from 1975. However, it was after the pair's 'Body Talk' smash for Imagination that they emerged as a leading production team from 1982-84. Among their more feted clients were Truth, Bananarama - notably *Deep Sea Skiving* - Wang Chung, Louise Goffin, Diana Ross, Tom Robinson and Errol Brown. Jolley's career peaked commercially with 1983's *True*, a number 1 album (and title track single) in the UK for Spandau Ballet. Advantaged by a huge budget from CBS Records, Jolley and Swain also took on the award-winning *Alf*, Alison Moyet's chart-topping solo album debut, for which Jolley contributed and co-wrote all but one track. Since a subsequent break with Swain, Steve has continued to thrive in the record industry by forming his own label.

JONES, GRACE
b. 19 May 1952, Spanishtown, Jamaica, West Indies. Six feet of style, looks and attitude, Jones was raised in New York City, then became a suc-

cessful Paris model. After a flirtation with acting, she made some unexceptional disco records that sold on the strength of her image and her explicit stage show. Both were carefully crafted by her boyfriend, French artist Jean-Paul Goude. *Warm Leatherette* marked a major stylistic development. Recorded at Compass Point, Nassau, it featured top Jamaican session men Sly And Robbie, new wave material and half-spoken delivery that became the Grace Jones trademark. Her first hit was a cover of the Pretenders' 'Private Life' which made the UK Top 20. On *Nightclubbing* she turned her hand to writing and producing high-quality songs including 'Pull Up To The Bumper'. In 1984 she diversified into films, taking on Arnold Schwarzenegger in *Conan The Destroyer*. The following year she played alongside Roger Moore in *A View To A Kill*. A return to the recording studios with writer/producer Trevor Horn provided her most successful single to date, 'Slave To The Rhythm', and the album of extended versions and megamixes sold well. In 1986 the compilation *Island Life* was a big UK success, with 'Pull Up To The Bumper' and 'Love Is The Drug' reaching the charts the second time around. Although Chris Blackwell had faith in her as a musical artist the public always saw her as a personality. Her striking looks, outspoken nature and media coverage buried her musical aspirations and talent.

●ALBUMS: *Portfolio* (Island 1977)★★, *Fame* (Island 1978)★★, *Muse* (1979)★★, *Warm Leatherette* (Island 1980)★★★, *Nightclubbing* (Island 1981)★★★, *Living My Life* (Island 1982)★★★, *Slave To The Rhythm* (ZTT 1985)★★, *Inside Story* (EMI America 1986)★★, *Bullet Proof Heart* (Capitol 1990)★★.

●COMPILATIONS: *Island Life* (Island 1985)★★★.

●FURTHER READING: *Goude, Jean-Paul*, Jungle Fever. *Grace Jones: Ragged But Right*, Dolly Carlisle.

JONES, HOWARD

b. John Howard Jones, 23 February 1955, Southampton, Hampshire, England. Coming to prominence as a synthesizer-pop maestro in the mid-80s, Jones had been trying to succeed as a musician for almost 15 years. His childhood saw him on the move from country to country but by the time he reached his teens he was settled in High Wycombe, England. He joined his first band in 1976 and over the next few years played in Warrior, the Bicycle Thieves, and Skin Tight. In 1974 he went to music college in Manchester and after graduation he began performing solo in his home town. He soon introduced dancer Jed Hoile

to enliven his act by improvizing dance to his songs. Jones was offered a session by BBC disc jockey John Peel which led to tours with OMD and China Crisis. WEA Records signed him in the summer of 1983 and in September he charted with his first single 'New Song'. He won several Best New Artist awards and followed-up with hits like 'What Is Love', 'Hide And Seek', and 'Like To Get To Know You Well'. His debut *Human's Lib* topped the UK charts. Although he performed most of the music on his recordings in 1985 he formed a touring band with his brother Martin on bass, and Trevor Morais on drums. As the 80s drew to a close his singles charted lower and lower but he continues to record sporadically and even joined the unplugged with *Live Acoustic America* in 1996.

●ALBUMS: *Human's Lib* (WEA 1984)★★★, *The 12 Inch Album* (WEA 1984)★★, *Dream Into Action* (WEA 1985)★★★, *One To One* (WEA 1986)★★, *Cross That Line* (WEA 1989)★★★, *In The Running* (1992)★★, *Live Acoustic America* (Plump 1996)★★★.

●COMPILATIONS: *The Best Of Howard Jones* (WEA 1993)★★★.

JONES, STEVE

b. 3 September 1955, London, England. Formerly the provider of the guitar behind Johnny Rotten's sneer in the Sex Pistols, Jones's basic but powerful style was then employed as part of the under-achieving Professionals (with former Sex Pistol member Paul Cook). Before that he had worked with the Avengers in the USA. Later he played a substantial role in the creation of two records: Iggy Pop's *Blah Blah Blah* (1986), and ex-Duran Duran member Andy Taylor's *Thunder* (1987). His first solo venture, however, was a lacklustre affair, with Jones's rough Cockney voice spread thinly over a set which mingled rock numbers with, to the horror of old punks, ballads. The worst offender in this category was the comical version of 'Love Letters'. A capable fluent man with a rhythm guitar, given a microphone Jones came across as forced and inarticulate, a situation not helped by the clumsy moralism of tracks such as 'Drugs Suck'. Undeterred, Jones proceeded to make the same mistakes a second time with *Fire And Gasoline*. Co-produced and co-written with Ian Astbury of the Cult, and with a vocal contribution from Guns N'Roses' Axl Rose on the Pistols revival track, 'Did You No Wrong', it offered further evidence of Jones's decline. Billy Duffy of the Cult even managed to outgun the old-stager with his solo on 'Get Ready'. Collectively the albums offer a sad footnote to the career of one of rock and pop's most influential guitarists. Jones has since worked as part of The Neurotic Outsiders, alongside John Taylor (ex-Duran Duran) and Duff McLagan and Matt Sorum of Guns N'Roses, the group releasing an eponymous album for Madonna's Maverick label in 1996. The collaboration led to Jones replacing the departed Slash as Guns N'Roses' guitarist.

● ALBUMS: *Mercy* (Gold Mountain/MCA 1987)★★, *Fire And Gasoline* (Gold Mountain/MCA 1989)★★.

JORDAN, STANLEY

b. 31 July 1959, Chicago, Illinois, USA. Having absorbed a certain amount of theory from an early training on the piano, Jordan taught himself the guitar while in his teens, and performed with the numerous pop and soul groups working around Chicago in the mid-70s. However, winning a prize at the 1976 Reno Jazz Festival inspired Jordan to devote some time to a serious study of music. Studying electronic music, theory, and composition at Princeton University, his reputation quickly spread and he soon found himself playing with Dizzy Gillespie and Benny Carter. In 1982 he recorded his first album: *Touch Sensitive* was a relatively uninspiring solo collection which registered poor sales. But three years later, Jordan's second album *Magic Touch* was a huge commercial success. Produced by Al DiMeola, it featured Onaje Allen Gumbs, Charnett Moffett, and Omar Hakim, while retaining some unaccompanied tracks. Since *Magic Touch*, Jordan's band has become a regular feature of the major international jazz festivals. He is commonly known for his development of a complex technique of 'hammering-on' which has enabled him to accompany himself with bass lines and chords.

● ALBUMS: *Touch Sensitive* (1982)★★, *Magic Touch* (Blue Note 1985)★★★, *Standards* (Blue Note 1986)★★★, *Flying Home* (EMI Manhattan 1988)★★★, *Cornucopia* (Blue Note 1990)★★★, *Stolen Moments* (Blue Note 1991)★★★, *Bolero* (Arista 1994)★★★.

JOSEF K

This Edinburgh, Scotland-based band formed in the ashes of punk as TV Art and were influenced by New York bands such as Television, Talking Heads and the Velvet Underground. The original trio of Paul Haig (vocals), Malcolm Ross (guitar) and Ron Torrance (drums) were joined briefly by Gary McCormack (later with the Exploited), before a more permanent bassist was found in David Weddell. After a name change inspired by Franz Kafka's 1925 novel, *The Trial*, Josef K recorded a 10-track demo before committing 'Chance Meeting' to release on Steven Daly's Absolute label, in late 1979. Daly, who was also the drummer for Orange Juice, was the co-founder of Postcard Records, and thus signed Josef K to the newly formed label. 'Radio Drill Time' was more frantic than their debut, dominated by hectic, awkward chords and Haig's thin, nasal voice. After numerous support slots, 1980 ended with the more low-key, melodic sound of 'It's Kinda Funny'. The single fared well and Josef K were all set to release their debut *Sorry For Laughing* during the early months of 1981. Unhappy with its production, the band scrapped it at the test pressing stage and moved to a Belgian studio, in conjunction with the Les Disques du Crépescule label. The session yielded the re-recorded title track and their strongest single, 'Sorry For Laughing' (1981), which joined tracks from the unreleased album as a session for BBC radio disc jockey John Peel, while the band returned to Belgium to work on their album. Back at Postcard, they drafted Malcolm's brother Alistair to play trumpet on a new version of 'Chance Meeting', issued just two months later, coinciding with a full session for Peel. *The Only Fun In Town* emerged in July to a mixed reception. Its frantic, trebly live sound appeared hurried, and betrayed the fact that it had been recorded in just six days. Josef K announced their demise soon after, prompted by Malcolm Ross's invitation to join Orange Juice. Crépescule issued Josef K's farewell single, 'The Missionary', in 1982, while other tracks surfaced on various compilations. After Ross had joined Orange Juice, Haig worked with Rhythm Of Life before embarking on a solo career. In 1987, Scottish label Supreme International Editions followed the excellent 'Heaven Sent' with *Young And Stupid*, a collection of Peel sessions and tracks from the unreleased *Sorry For Laughing*. Then, in 1990, the entire recorded history of Josef K (plus tracks from their original demo) were compiled onto two definitive CDs by Les Temps Moderne.

● ALBUMS: *The Only Fun In Town* (Postcard 1981)★★.

● COMPILATIONS: *Young And Stupid* (Supreme International 1989)★★★, *The Only Fun In Town/Sorry For Laughing* (Les Temps Moderne 1990)★★★.

JOY DIVISION

Originally known as Warsaw, this Manchester post-punk outfit comprised Ian Curtis (b. July 1956,

Macclesfield, Cheshire, England, d. 18 May 1980; vocals), Bernard Dicken/Albrecht (b. 4 January 1956, Salford, Manchester, England; guitar/vocals), Peter Hook (b. 13 February 1956, Manchester, England; bass) and Steven Morris (b. 28 October 1957, Macclesfield, Cheshire, England; drums). Borrowing their name from the prostitution wing of a concentration camp, Joy Division emerged in 1978 as one of the most important groups of their era. After recording a regionally available EP, *An Ideal For Living*, they were signed to Manchester's recently formed Factory Records and placed in the hands of producer Martin Hannett. Their debut, *Unknown Pleasures*, was a raw, intense affair, with Curtis at his most manically arresting in the insistent 'She's Lost Control'. With its stark, black cover, the album captured the group still coming to terms with the recording process, but displaying a vision that was piercing in its clinical evocation of an unsettling disorder. With Morris's drums employed as a lead instrument, backed by the leaden but compulsive bass lines of Hook, the sound of Joy Division was distinctive and disturbing. By the time of their single, 'Transmission', the quartet had already established a strong cult following, which increased after each gig. Much of the attention centred on the charismatic Curtis, who was renowned for his neurotic choreography, resembling a demented marionette on wires. By the autumn of 1979, however, Curtis's performances were drawing attention for a more serious reason. On more than one occasion he suffered an epileptic seizure and blackouts onstage, and the illness seemed to worsen with the group's increasingly demanding live schedule. On 18 May 1980, the eve of Joy Division's proposed visit to America, Ian Curtis was found hanged. The verdict was suicide. A note was allegedly found bearing the words: 'At this moment I wish I were dead. I just can't cope anymore'. The full impact of the tragedy was underlined shortly afterwards, for it quickly became evident that Curtis had taken his life at the peak of his creativity. While it seemed inevitable that the group's posthumously released work would receive a sympathetic reaction, few could have anticipated the quality of the material that emerged in 1980. The single, 'Love Will Tear Us Apart', was probably the finest of the year, a haunting account of a fragmented relationship, sung by Curtis in a voice that few realized he possessed. The attendant album, *Closer*, was faultless, displaying the group at the zenith of their powers. With spine-tingling cameos such as 'Isolation' and the extraordinary 'Twenty-Four Hours', the album

eloquently articulated a sense of despair, yet simultaneously offered a therapeutic release. Instrumentally, the work showed maturity in every area and is deservedly regarded by many critics as the most brilliant rock album of the 80s. The following year, a double album, *Still*, collected the remainder of the group's material, most of it in primitive form. Within months of the Curtis tragedy, the remaining members sought a fresh start as New Order. In 1995 Curtis's widow, Deborah, published a book on her former huband and the band, while a compilation album and a re-released version of 'Love Will Tear Us Apart' were back on the shelves on the 15th anniversary of his death.

● ALBUMS: *Unknown Pleasures* (Factory 1979)★★★, *Closer* (Factory 1980)★★★★, *Still* (Factory 1981)★★★.
● COMPILATIONS: *The Peel Sessions* (Strange Fruit 1986)★★★, *Substance 1977-1980* (Factory 1988)★★★★, *Permanent: The Best Of Joy Division* (London 1995)★★★★.
● VIDEOS: *Here Are The Young Men* (IKON 1992).
● FURTHER READING: *An Ideal For Living: An History Of Joy Division*, Mark Johnson. *Touching From A Distance*, Deborah Curtis. *New Order & Joy Division*, Claude Flowers.

JUDAS PRIEST

This group was formed in Birmingham, England, in 1969, by guitarist K.K. Downing (b. Kenneth Downing) and close friend, bassist Ian Hill. As another hopeful, struggling young rock band, they played their first gig in Essington in 1971 with a line-up completed by Alan Atkins (vocals) and John Ellis (drums). The name Judas Priest came from Atkins' previous band (who took it from a Bob Dylan song, 'The Ballad Of Frankie Lee And Judas Priest') before he joined up with Hill and Downing, but it was retained as the best choice. Consistent gigging continued with Alan Moore taking over on drums only to be replaced at the end of 1971 by Chris Campbell. 1972 was spent mostly on the road in the UK, and in 1973 both Atkins and Campbell departed leaving the nucleus of Hill and Downing once more (in 1991 Atkins released a debut solo album, including 'Victim Of Changes', a song he co-wrote in Judas Priest's infancy). At this point their fortunes took a turn for the better. Vocalist and ex-theatrical lighting engineer Rob Halford (b. 25 August 1951, Walsall, England) and drummer John Hinch, both from the band Hiroshima, joined the unit. More UK shows ensued as their following grew steadily, culminating in the addition of second guitarist Glenn Tipton (b. 25 October 1948; ex-Flying Hat Band). In 1974 they toured abroad for the first time in Germany and the Netherlands, and returned home to a record contract with the small UK label, Gull. The band made their vinyl debut with *Rocka Rolla* in September 1974, but disappointed with the recording, the album failed to make any impact, and Hinch left to be replaced by the returning Alan Moore. In 1975 the band's appearance at the Reading Festival brought them to the attention of a much wider audience. *Sad Wings Of Destiny* was an improvement on the debut, with production assistance from Jeffrey Calvert and Max West. However, despite good reviews their financial situation remained desperate, and Alan Moore left for the second and final time. A worldwide contract with CBS Records saved the day, and *Sin After Sin* was a strong collection, with Simon Philips sitting in for Moore. The band then visited America for the first time with drummer Les Binks, who appeared on *Stained Class*, an album that showed Priest at a high watermark in their powers. *Killing Machine* yielded the first UK hit single, 'Take On The World', and featured shorter, punchier, but still familiar rock songs. *Unleashed In The East* was recorded on the 1979 Japanese tour, and in that year, Les Binks was replaced on drums by Dave Holland of Trapeze. After major tours with both Kiss and AC/DC, Priest's popularity was beginning to gather momentum. *British Steel* smashed into the UK album charts at number 3, and contained the hit singles 'Breaking The Law' and 'Living After Midnight'. After appearing at the 1980 Castle Donington Monsters Of Rock festival, they began recording *Point Of Entry*. It provided the hit single 'Hot Rockin', and was followed by sell-out UK and US tours. The period surrounding *Screaming For Vengeance* was phenomenally successful for the band. The hit single, 'You've Got Another Thing Comin'', was followed by a lucrative six-month US tour with the album going platinum in the USA. *Defenders Of The Faith* offered a similar, potent brand of headstrong metal to *Screaming For Vengeance*. *Turbo*, however, proved slightly more commercial and was poorly received, Judas Priest's traditional metal fans reacting with indifference to innovations including the use of synthesized guitars. *Ram It Down* saw a return to pure heavy metal by comparison, but by this time their popularity had begun to wane. Dave Holland was replaced by Scott Travis (b. Norfolk, Virginia, USA; ex-Racer X) for the return to form that was *Painkiller*. Although not as universally popular as before, Priest were still a major live attraction and

remained the epitome of heavy metal, with screaming guitars matched by screaming vocalist, with the protagonists clad in studs and black leather. The band were taken to court in 1990 following the suicide attempts of two fans (one successful) in 1985. Both CBS Records and Judas Priest were accused of inciting suicide through the 'backwards messages' in their recording of the Spooky Tooth classic, 'Better By You, Better Than Me'. They were found not guilty in June 1993 after a long court battle, Downing admitting: 'It will be another ten years before I can even spell subliminal'. Soon afterwards, Halford became disheartened with the band and decided to quit and form his own group, Fight. He had temporarily fronted an Ozzy-less Black Sabbath and recorded 'Light Comes Out Of The Black' with Pantera for the *Buffy The Vampire Slayer* soundtrack. Apparently still reeling from the shock the rest of Judas Priest have not been able to recover and seem to be waiting for Halford's return. This is unlikely as he debuted with his new band Halford in 1996. Ripper Owens is the present vocalist.

●ALBUMS: *Rocka Rolla* (Gull 1974)★★, *Sad Wings Of Destiny* (Gull 1976)★★, *Sin After Sin* (Columbia 1977)★★★, *Stained Class* (Columbia 1978)★★★, *Killing Machine* (Columbia 1978)★★, *Live-Unleashed In The East* (Columbia 1979)★★★★, *British Steel* (Columbia 1980)★★★★, *Point Of Entry* (Columbia 1981)★★★, *Screaming For Vengeance* (Columbia 1982)★★★, *Defenders Of The Faith* (Columbia 1984)★★★, *Turbo* (Columbia 1986)★★, *Priest Live* (Columbia 1987)★★, *Ram It Down* (Columbia 1988)★★★, *Painkiller* (Columbia 1990)★★★.

●COMPILATIONS: *Best Of* (Gull 1978)★★, *Hero Hero* (Telaeg 1987)★★, *Collection* (Castle 1989)★★★, *Metal Works '73 - '93* (Columbia 1993)★★★★, *Living After Midnight* (Columbia 1997)★★★.

●VIDEOS: *Fuel Of Life* (1986), *Judas Priest Live* (1987), *Painkiller* (1990), *Metal Works 73-93* (1993).

●FURTHER READING: *Heavy Duty*, Steve Gett.

JUDDS

Freshly divorced, Naomi Judd (b. Diana Ellen Judd 11 January 1946, Ashland, Kentucky, USA) migrated with her daughters Wynonna (b. Christina Ciminella, 30 May 1964, Ashland, Kentucky, USA) and Ashley (b. 1968) from California back to Morrill, Kentucky, where she worked as a nurse in a local infirmary. Outside working and school hours, she and the children would sing anything from bluegrass to showbiz standards for their own amusement. However, when Wynonna nurtured aspirations to be a professional entertainer, her mother lent encouragement to the extent of moving the family to Nashville in 1979. Naomi's contralto subtly underlined Wynonna's tuneful drawl. While tending a hospitalized relation of RCA Records producer Brent Maher, Naomi elicited an audition in the company's boardroom. With a hick surname and a past that read like a Judith Krantz novel, the Judds - so the executives considered - would have more than an even chance in the country market. An exploratory mini-album, which contained the show-stopping 'John Deere Tractor', proved the executives correct when, peaking at number 17, 'Had A Dream' was the harbinger of 1984's 'Mama He's Crazy', the first of many country chart-toppers for the duo. The Judds would also be accorded a historical footnote as the earliest commercial manifestation of the form's 'new tradition' - a tag that implied the maintenance of respect for C&W's elder statesmen. This was shown by the Judds adding their voices to Homecoming, a 1985 collaboration by Jerry Lee Lewis, Roy Orbison, Johnny Cash and Carl Perkins (who later co-wrote Naomi and Wynonna's 1989 smash, 'Let Me Tell You About Love').

The Judds' repertoire also contained revivals of Ella Fitzgerald's 'Cow Cow Boogie', Elvis Presley's 'Don't Be Cruel' and Lee Dorsey's 'Working In A Coal Mine'. Self-composed songs included Naomi's 1989 composition, 'Change Of Heart', dedicated to her future second husband (and former Presley backing vocalist) Larry Strickland. Maher, too, contributed by co-penning hits such as 1984's Grammy-winning 'Why Not Me', 'Turn It Loose', 'Girls Night Out' and the title track of the Judds' second million-selling album, Rockin' With The Rhythm Of The Rain. The team relied mainly on songsmiths such as Jamie O'Hara ('Grandpa Tell Me About The Good Old Days'), Kenny O'Dell ('Mama He's Crazy'), Mickey Jupp, Graham Lyle and Troy Seals ('Maybe Your Baby's Got The Blues') and Paul Kennerley ('Have Mercy', 'Cry Myself To Sleep'). Most Judds records had an acoustic bias - particularly on the sultry ballads selected for Give A Little Love. They also have an occasional penchant for star guests that have included the Jordanaires ('Don't Be Cruel'), Emmylou Harris 'The Sweetest Gift' (Heartland), Mark Knopfler on his 'Water Of Love' (River Of Time) and Bonnie Raitt playing slide guitar on Love Can Build A Bridge. In 1988, the pair became the first female country act to found their own booking agency

(Pro-Tours) but a chronic liver disorder forced Naomi to retire from the concert stage two years later. Naomi and Wynonna toured America in a series of extravagant farewell concerts, before Wynonna was free - conveniently, cynics said - to begin her long-rumoured solo career. This she did in style, with a remarkable album that touched on gospel, soul and R&B, and confirmed her as one of the most distinctive and powerful female vocalists of her generation.

● ALBUMS: The Judds: Wynonna & Naomi (RCA 1984)★★, Why Not Me? (RCA 1985)★★★, Rockin' With The Rhythm Of The Rain (RCA 1986)★★★, Give A Little Love (RCA 1986)★★★, Heartland (RCA 1987)★★, River Of Time (RCA/Curb 1989)★★★, Love Can Build A Bridge (Curb 1990)★★★. Solo: Wynonna Judd Wynonna (Curb 1992)★★★, Tell Me Why (Curb 1993)★★★, Revelations (Curb 1996)★★★.

● COMPILATIONS: Greatest Hits (RCA 1988)★★★★, The Judds Collection 1983 - 1990 (RCA 1991)★★★, Number One Hits (Curb 1995)★★★, The Essential Judds (RCA 1996)★★★★, The Judds Collection (Curb/The Hit 1996)★★★.

● VIDEOS: Their Final Concert (1992), The Farewell Tour (1994).

● FURTHER READING: The Judds: Unauthorized Biography, Bob Millard. Love Can Build A Bridge, Naomi Judd.

JUNGLE BROTHERS

Rap innovators and precursors to the sound later fine-tuned by De La Soul, PM Dawn et al. Following on from Afrika Bambaataa, the Jungle Brothers: Mike G (b. Michael Small, c.1969, Harlem, New York, USA), DJ Sammy B (b. Sammy Burwell, c.1968, Harlem, New York, USA) and Afrika Baby Bambaataa (b. Nathaniel Hall, c.1971, Brooklyn, New York, USA) were unafraid of cross-genre experimentation, the most famous demonstration being their version of Marvin Gaye's 'What's Going On', though their incorporation of house music on 'I'll House You' is another good example. They made their debut for Warlock/Idlers Records in October 1987, before signing to Gee Street Records. As part of the Native Tongues coalition with Queen Latifah, A Tribe Called Quest and others, they sought to enhance the living experiences of black men and women by educating them about their role in history and African culture. In many ways traditionalists, the Jungle Brothers carefully traced the lines between R&B and rap, their admiration of James Brown going beyond merely sampling his rhythms (including the basis of their name - which shares the godfather of soul's initials). A second album was slightly less funky and more soul-based, particularly effective on cuts like 'Beyond This World'. It has been argued that the Jungle Brothers' failure to break through commercially had something to do with the fact that they were initially signed to a New York dance label, Idlers. More likely is the assertion that audiences for macho skullduggery greatly outnumbered those for whom intelligent, discursive hip hop was a worthwhile phenomenon in the late 80s. By the time of 1993's *J Beez Wit The Remedy*, they had unfortunately succumbed to the former.

●ALBUMS: *Straight Out The Jungle* (Idlers/Warlock 1988)★★★, *Done By The Forces Of Nature* (Warners 1989)★★★★, *J Beez Wit The Remedy* (Warners 1993),★★ *Raw Deluxe* (Gee Street 1997)★★★.

K Klass

Four-piece dance troupe from Wrexham, Wales, who formed in late 1988 when Andy Williams (technical supervisor) and Carl Thomas (various instruments) dissolved their former outfit, Interstate. They had supported 808 State in their early days, forging links that would prove pivotal to their future. The duo recruited locals Paul Roberts (ideas and lyrics) and Russ Morgan (various instruments), more recently acquiring talented female vocalist Bobbi Depasois. Funded in part by an Enterprise Allowance grant and Roberts' British Telecom redundancy money, their debut *Wildlife* EP topped many dance charts in 1990, its extensive samples of Tony Soper's *Wildlife On One* television theme tune causing a strong subconscious hook with UK residents. After further supports with 808 State and hard gigging around the country, Martin Price of the aforementioned Manchester group released 'Rhythm Is A Mystery' on his Eastern Bloc shop's Creed label. Although it sold an impressive 13,000 copies, it took six months and a new label to launch it into the UK Top 10 at the tail end of 1991. Immediately they were heralded as one of the few house outfits with more than one song and two rhythm tracks: 'Anyone can learn how to use a synthesizer, anyone can make a dance record. But it's all about making good ones'. They continued in the same vein with 'Don't Stop' (1992) and 'Let Me Show' (1993), the latter prefacing their long-prepared debut album. This included, of all things, a guitar contribution from Johnny Marr (the Smiths) on 'Cassa' (he had obviously travelled a long way from that band's previous rallying call, 'Hang The DJ'). They have remixed for Oceanic ('Wicked Love'), New Order, Seven Grand Housing Authority and Denise Johnson.

●ALBUMS: *Universal* (DeConstruction 1993)★★★, *Remix And Additional Production* (DeConstruction 1996)★★★.

Kajagoogoo

Formed in Leighton Buzzard, Hertfordshire, England, this fresh-faced quartet comprised Nick

Beggs (b. 15 December 1961; vocals/bass), Steve Askew (guitar), Stuart Crawford (vocals/synthesizer) and lead singer Chris Hamill (b. 19 December 1958), better known as the anagrammatic Limahl. Emerging at a time when the 'New Pop' of Duran Duran, Adam Ant, Culture Club and Spandau Ballet was in the ascendant, Kajagoogoo was perfectly placed to reap instant chart rewards. Their debut single, 'Too Shy', had an irresistibly hummable pop melody and reached number 1 in the UK in early 1983. Significantly, the record was co-produced by Nick Rhodes, from their 'rivals' Duran Duran. Both groups relied on a strong visual image, but Kajagoogoo lacked the depth or staying power of their mid-80s contemporaries. They enjoyed two further hits, 'Ooh To Be Ah' and 'Hang On Now', before internal friction prompted Limahl's departure for a solo career. Kajagoogoo struggled on with Beggs taking lead vocals on the hits 'Big Apple' and 'The Lion's Mouth'. By 1985, however, they were suffering from diminishing chart returns and after briefly abbreviating their name to Kaja, they broke up early the following year. Beggs subsequently formed the Christian folk band Iona and more recently, in 1993 joined Phonogram Records UK as A&R manager.

●ALBUMS: *White Feathers* (EMI 1983)★★, *Islands* (EMI 1984)★★.

KAMEN, MICHAEL

b. 1948, New York, USA. A former member of the 60s band the New York Rock 'n' Roll Ensemble, a prolific composer, conductor, and arranger, particularly for films, from the 70s through to the 90s. After studying at the Juilliard School Of Music, Kamen contributed some music to the offbeat rock Western film *Zachariah* in 1971. Later in the 70s, he wrote the complete scores for *The Next Man*, *Between The Lines*, and *Stunts* (1977). During the 80s he co-composed the music for several films with some of contemporary pop music's most illustrious names, such as Eric Clapton (*Lethal Weapon*, *Homeboy*, and *Lethal Weapon II* (also with David Sanborn), George Harrison (*Shanghai Surprise*), David A. Stewart (*Rooftops*), and Herbie Hancock (*Action Jackson*). Subsequently, Kamen scored some of the period's most entertaining and diverting UK and US movies, which included *Venom*, *Pink Floyd - The Wall*, *Angleo, My Love*, *The Dead Zone*, *Brazil* (supposedly his favourite score), *Mona Lisa*, *Rita, Sue And Bob, Too*, *Someone To Watch Over Me*, *Suspect*, *Die Hard* and *Die Hard II*, *Raggedy Rawney*, *Crusoe*, *For Queen And Country*, *The Adventures Of Baron Munchausen*, *Dead-Bang*

(with Gary Chang), *Road House*, *Renegades*, and *Licence To Kill* (1989), Timothy Dalton's second attempt to replace Connery and Moore as James Bond. In the early 90s Kamen composed the music for *The Krays* and *Let Him Have It*, two films that reflected infamous criminal incidents in the UK, and others such as *Nothing But Trouble*, *Hudson Hawk*, *The Last Boy Scout*, *Company Business*, *Lethal Weapon 3*, *Shining Through* (1992), *Blue Ice*, *Splitting Heirs*, *Last Action Hero*, *The Three Musketeers*, *Circle Of Friends*, and *Don Juan DeMarco* (1995). In several instances, in addition to scoring the films, Kamen served as musical director, music editor, and played keyboards and other instruments. In 1991, he provided the music for the smash hit Kevin Costner movie, *Robin Hood: Prince Of Thieves*, and, with lyricists Bryan Adams and Robert John 'Mutt' Lange, composed the closing number, '(Everything I Do) I Do For You'. Adams' recording of the song enjoyed phenomenal success, staying at the top of the UK chart for an unprecedented 16 weeks. It was nominated for an Academy Award, and Kamen received two Grammys and a special Ivor Novello Award. Three years later the trio of songwriters repeated their success with 'All For Love', which was recorded by Adams, together with Sting and Rod Stewart, and turned up at the end of *The Three Musketeers* and at the top of the UK chart. Kamen has also composed music for tele-films such as *Liza's Pioneer Diary*, *S*H*E*, *Shoot For The Sun*, and two television miniseries, *The Duty Men* (theme: 'Watching You' (with Sashazoe)), and *Edge Of Darkness*. The theme from the latter, written with Eric Clapton, gained Kamen another Ivor Novello Award (1985). He has written a guitar concerto for Clapton, a saxophone concerto for David Sanborn, and composed several scores for the Joffrey Ballet and the La Scala Opera Company.

KARN, MICK

b. Anthony Michaelides, 24 July 1958, London, England. Formerly the bass player with early 80s UK art-pop band Japan, Karn released his debut solo album after that band's dissolution in 1982. Featuring several session musicians in addition to Karn on vocals, bass, keyboards and synthesizers, it reached number 74 in the UK charts. In June 1983 he joined Ultravox's Midge Ure for a one-off single, 'After A Fashion', which reached number 39 in the UK charts. In the following year he formed Dali's Car with former Bauhaus singer Pete Murphy and Paul Vincent Lawford, before resuming his solo career in 1986. 'Buoy' was credited to Mick Karn featuring David Sylvian (his former Japan colleague), and preceded the release of his second album, *Dreams Of Reason Produce Monsters*. Afterwards Karn concentrated on session work, his long list of clients including Kate Bush and Joan Armatrading, and his 'secondary' career, as a sculptor. His work has been exhibited in galleries in London, as well as Tokyo, Osaka and Sapporo in Japan and Turin in Italy. A long-delayed third collection, 1993's *Bestial Culture*, paired him with two former Japan members, Steve Jansen and Richard Barbieri, in addition to respected guitarist David Torn, to whose solo work Karn had previously contributed.

●ALBUMS: *Titles* (Virgin 1982)★★★, *Dreams Of Reason Produce Monsters* (Virgin 1987)★★★, *Bestial Cluster* (CMP 1993)★★★, with Steve Jansen, Richard Barbieri *Beginning To Melt* (Medium Productions 1994)★★★, with David Torn, Terry Bozzio *Polytown* (CMP 1994)★★★, *Tooth Mother* (CMP 1995)★★★.

KATRINA AND THE WAVES

This pop group enjoyed their major hit with 'Walking On Sunshine' in 1985, but were also well-known for their original version of 'Going Down To Liverpool', which was successfully covered by the Bangles. The band consisted of Katrina Leskanich (b. 1960, Topeka, Kansas, USA; vocals), Kimberley Rew (guitar), Vince De La Cruz (b. Texas, USA; bass) and Alex Cooper (drums). Leskanich and De La Cruz are Americans, but came to Britain during 1976 when their military fathers served in the UK. Based at Feltwell, Norfolk, the sight of the airforce base, Rew and Cooper were both graduates of Cambridge University. Rew was formerly in the Soft Boys and after leaving them released the solo *The Bible Of Pop*, in 1982. Many of the songs he wrote for his solo career were carried over into Katrina And The Waves, where he became the chief songwriter. The band was formed in 1982 but their first two albums were only released in Canada. They followed up 'Walking On Sunshine' with 'Sun Street', which was their last hit, although they remained a popular act on the college circuit for some time thereafter. 1993 brought a series of reunion gigs, at first in their 'adopted city' of Cambridge. Although it caused some surprise, the band were nominated by the British public as the UK entry for the 1997 Eurovision Song Contest. The mantric chorus in 'Love Shine A Light' appealed to the judges and it became the clear winner; obligatory chart success followed.

●ALBUMS: *Walking On Sunshine* (Canada 1983)★★★, *Katrina And The Waves 2* (Canada 1984)★★, *Katrina And The Waves* (Capitol 1985)★★, *Waves* (Capitol 1985)★★, *Break Of Hearts* (SBK 1989)★★.

KBC BAND

The potential of three ex-Jefferson Airplane colleagues joining together once again was enormous. With petty arguing and ego problems behind them the KBC Band announced an album to the world in 1986. Marty Balin (b. Martyn Jerel Buchwald, 30 January 1943, Cincinnati, Ohio, USA; vocals), Jack Casady (b. 13 April 1944, Washington DC, USA; bass) and Paul Kantner (b. 17 March 1941, San Francisco, California, USA; guitar/vocals) released an album that sounded jaded on release. Somehow, lyrically addressing political themes such as Lebanon and Nicaragua did not work (in 'America') and Marty Balin's old epic ballads paled against the new ('Mariel'). The addition of Keith Crossan (saxophone, guitar, vocals), Tim Gorman (guitar, vocals), Darrell Verdusco (drums) and Mark 'Slick' Aguilar (lead guitar, vocals) gave the unit a full AOR sound. The album probably charted in the USA on the strength of their names (number 75) and even produced a minor hit single with 'It's Not You, It's Not Me' (number 89). The unit disbanded shortly afterwards.

●ALBUMS: *KBC Band* (Arista 1986)★★.

KERSHAW, NIK

b. Nicolas David Kershaw, 1 March 1958, Bristol, Somerset, England. Diminutive singer, guitarist, songwriter Kershaw shone brightly for a couple of years in the mid-80s UK charts before taking a more behind the scenes role in the 90s. Son of a flautist father and opera-singing mother, Kershaw's first foray into the arts was as a 13-year-old student actor planning to go into repertory when he finished training. However, around 1974 he learned guitar and played Deep Purple covers in a school band called Half Pint Hogg (the name doubtless related to Kershaw's stature). Leaving school in 1976, he started work at the Department of Employment (and later the Co-op) but spent his evenings performing in the jazz-funk outfit Fusion. Fellow members were Reg Webb (keyboards), Ken Elson (bass), and Alan Clarke (drums). Signed to Plastic Fantastic Records and later to Telephone Records, they released one single and an album, respectively. The album, *'Til I Hear From You*, contained an early version of the track 'Human Racing', which Kershaw later re-recorded. When Fusion folded, Kershaw linked with Nine Below

Zero's manager Micky Modern, who helped him sign to MCA Records. The UK chart hits started to come in 1983 when his debut - 'I Won't Let The Sun Go Down On Me' - reached a modest number 47. However, early the next year the follow-up 'Wouldn't It Be Good' reached the Top 5. This perfect pop song justifiably gave Kershaw a high profile. That summer a reissue of his debut gave him his biggest success (number 2) and for the next 12 months a succession of his pleasant, simple tunes paraded through the upper reaches of the UK chart. On tour and record, Kershaw was backed by the Krew whose nucleus was Dennis Smith, Keiffer Airey (brother of Rainbow's Don Airey), Tim Moore, Mark Price and Kershaw's wife, Sheri. The first two albums featured guest appearances from Don Snow (ex-Squeeze; Sinceroes) and Mark King of Level 42. In 1985, Elton John - a big Kershaw fan - asked him to play guitar on his single 'Nikita'. Although the first two albums had been successes, the third proved a relative failure, and despite regular comebacks Kershaw's performing career has been in gradual decline ever since. In recent years he has returned as a songwriter of note behind other hit acts, notably Chesney Hawkes' massive hit 'The One And Only'.

●ALBUMS: *Human Racing* (MCA 1984)★★★, *The Riddle* (MCA 1984)★★★, *Radio Musicola* (MCA 1986)★★, *The Works* (MCA 1990)★★.
●COMPILATIONS: *The Collection* (MCA 1991)★★★.

KHAN, CHAKA

b. Yvette Marie Stevens, 23 March 1953, Great Lakes Naval Training Station, Illinois, USA. Having sung with several Chicago club bands, including Lyfe, Lock And Chains and Baby Huey And The Babysitters, Chaka Khan became acquainted with Ask Rufus, a group formed from the remnants of hit group the American Breed. When Khan replaced original singer, Paulette McWilliams, the line-up truncated its name to Rufus and as such released a succession of superior funk singles. Khan's stylish voice was the group's obvious attraction and in 1978 she began recording as a solo act. 'I'm Every Woman' topped the US R&B chart that year while subsequent releases, 'What Cha' Gonna Do For Me' (1981) and 'Got To Be There' (1982), consolidated this position. However, a 1984 release, 'I Feel For You' established the singer as an international act when it reached number 2 in the US and number 1 in the UK pop charts. This exceptional performance was written by Prince and featured contributions from Stevie Wonder and Melle Mel. It not only led to a platinum-selling album, but won a Grammy for Best R&B Female Performance. Khan has since continued to forge a successful career, working with David Bowie, Robert Palmer and duetting with Steve Winwood on his international smash, 'Higher Love'. In 1985 she enjoyed two Top 20 UK chart entries with 'This Is My Night' and 'Eye To Eye', while four years later a remix of 'I'm Every Woman' reached the Top 10 in the UK.

●ALBUMS: *Chaka* (Warners 1978)★★★, *Naughty* (Warners 1980)★★★, *What Cha' Gonna Do For Me* (Warners 1981)★★★, *Echoes Of An Era* (Elektra 1982)★★★, *Chaka Khan* (Warners 1982)★★★, *I Feel For You* (Warners 1984)★★★, *Destiny* (Warners 1986)★★, *CK* (Warners 1988)★★★, *Life Is A Dance - The Remix Project* (Warners 1989)★★, *The Woman I Am* (Warners 1992)★★★.
●COMPILATIONS: *Epiphany: The Best Of ... Vol. 1* (Reprise 1996)★★★★.
●FILMS: *Breakdance - The Movie* (1984).

KID CREOLE AND THE COCONUTS

b. August Darnell, 1951, Haiti. A relatively exciting entry into the UK charts at the height of New Romanticism in the early 80s, Kid Creole And The Coconuts introduced many to the dynamic pulse of Latin pop. Creole originally formed Dr. Buzzard's Original Savannah Band in the 70s with his brother Stoney Darnell. They would go on to create the Coconuts with the aid of 'Sugar Coated' Andy Hernandez (aka Coati Mundi), plus several multi-instrumentalists and a singing/dancing troupe. The group's fusion of salsa with disco pop was conducted with immense flair on their 1980 debut, *Off The Coast Of Me*. The follow-up album introduced a concept also pursued by three subsequent collections - namely a search by Kid and the Coconuts for Mimi, with nods to the various geographical stop-off points on the journey. The theme was not laboured, however, and proved entirely secondary to the bristling musical energy and zest beneath the surface. The Coconuts then hit a rich commercial vein with *Tropical Gangsters* (known as *Wise Guy* outside the UK). Three Top 10 chart placings followed for the album's singles; 'I'm A Wonderful Thing, Baby', 'Stool Pigeon' and 'Annie, I'm Not Your Daddy', the latter missing the top spot by just one place. Their live shows at this time were among the most propulsive and enchanting of the period, with outlandish dancing and cod theatricals garnishing the Latin beats. Afterwards the band's commercial profile declined, but there was no similar qualitative discount. *Doppelganger* returned to the grand theme as its premise - this time the cloning of Kid Creole by evil scientist King Nignat. Again such considerations proved secondary to the gripping music, particularly effective on 'The Lifeboat Party', which crept inside the UK Top 50. Elsewhere the selections spanned reggae, soul, scat jazz and funk, all flavoured by the familiar salsa rumble. The Coconuts also released an album of their own at this time, based on the dynamics of their powerful stage revue, while Hernandez released a solo album under his assumed title Coati Mundi. Kid Creole had become King Creole by the advent of *In Praise Of Older Women*, but this was another full-bodied work, and certainly far superior to 1987's *I, Too, Have Seen The Woods*. This introduced female vocalist Haitia Fuller on shared lead vocals, but the more laboured material made it a disappointing chapter. More promising was *Private Waters*, a return to form with inspired lyrics and buckets of the type of sexual innuendo that Creole had made his own.

●ALBUMS: *Off The Coast Of Me* (Ze 1980)★★★, *Fresh Fruit In Foreign Places* (Ze 1981)★★★, *Tropical Gangsters* aka *Wise Guy* (Ze 1982)★★★, *Doppelganger* (Ze 1983)★★★, *In Praise Of Older Women And Other Crimes* (Sire 1985)★★★, *I, Too, Have Seen The Woods* (Sire 1987)★★, *Private Waters In The Great Divide* (Columbia 1990)★★, *You Shoulda Told Me You Were . . .* (Columbia 1991)★★.

●COMPILATIONS: *Cre-Ole: Best Of Kid Creole And The Coconuts* (Island 1984)★★★, *The Best Of ...* (Island 1996)★★★. As The Coconuts: *Don't Take My Coconuts* (EMI 1983)★★★.

●VIDEOS: *Live At Hammersmith* (1984).

KID SENSATION

b. Steven Spence, Seattle, Washington, USA. Rapper who first came to fame as Sir Mix-A-Lot's DJ and keyboardist, before scoring a minor success with his own debut album. After graduating in 1988, he became part of the Sir Mix-A-Lot posse behind 1988's platinum-selling *Swass* set. It encouraged him to embark on his own career, which was soon rewarded when his debut album provided three hit singles, 'Back To Boom', 'Seatown Ballers' and 'Prisoner Of Ignorance'. His self-aggrandizing title was reflected in the cool braggadocio of much of the material on offer, but by the advent of a follow-up album there was a message behind the rhymes. 'I'm trying to show I'm a down to earth guy, it's more of what I'm all about'. The b-side of the album's promotional single, 'Ride The Rhythm', was 'The Way I Swing'. This was a duet with the Seattle Mariners' all-star centerfielder, and Sensation's sporting idol, Ken Friggy Jnr.

●ALBUMS: *Rollin' With Number One* (Nastymix 1990)★★★, *The Power Of Rhyme* (Nastymix 1992)★★★.

KIHN, GREG

b. 1952, Baltimore, USA. Kihn was a singer-songwriter who started out as a folk singer but switched to rock. He moved to Berkeley, California, in 1974, and the following year provided two solo songs for a compilation album on Matthew Kaufman's Beserkley Records. Afterwards, he became one of the first four acts signed to the label, adding backing vocals on label-mate Jonathan Richman's classic 'Road Runner'. Influenced by 60s pop such as the Yardbirds, he initially used another Beserkley signing Earth Quake to back him but then formed his own band in 1976 based initially around Earth Quake guitarist Ronnie Dunbar (brother of the Rubinoos' founder Tommy Dunbar). The initial line-up was Greg Kihn (vocals/guitar), Robbie Dunbar (lead guitar), Steve Wright (bass), and Larry Lynch (drums). They were based in the San Francisco Bay area from 1976, playing local clubs and bars. Dunbar left after the first album to concentrate on Earth Quake and was replaced by Dave Carpender. The second album, *Greg Kihn Again*, included cover versions of Bruce Springsteen's 'For You' and Buddy Holly's 'Love's Made A Fool Of You'. This line-up came closest to a hit with 'Moulin Rouge', before Gary Phillips (again ex-Earth Quake) joined on guitar in 1981. The change brought about a more commercial direction which found quick reward. 'The Breakup Song (They Don't Write 'Em)' reached the US Top 20 and *Kihntinued*, which housed it, became their biggest selling album, reaching number 4, after which Carpender was replaced by Greg Douglas (ex-Steve Miller Band). They managed a US number 2 in 1983 with the disco-styled 'Jeopardy', before Kihn dropped the band title and recorded solely as Greg Kihn. He has collaborated with bubblegum pop writer Kenny Laguna, and has become renowned for his punning album titles. In recent years he has additionally become a rock radio presenter, written a novel and still records.

●ALBUMS: *Greg Kihn* (Beserkley 1975)★★, *Greg Kihn Again* (Beserkley 1977)★★★, *Next Of Kihn* (Beserkley 1978)★★, *With The Naked Eye* (Beserkley 1979)★★★, *Glass House Rock* (Beserkley 1980)★★, *Rockihnroll* (Beserkley 1981)★★★★, *Kihntinued* (Beserkley 1982)★★★, *Kihnspiracy* (Beserkley 1983)★★★★, *Kihntageous*

(Beserkley 1984)★★★, *Citizen Kihn* (EMI 1985)★★, *Love And Rock And Roll* (EMI 1986)★★, *Unkihntrollable* (Rhino 1989)★★★, *Kihn Of Hearts* (FR 1992)★★★, *Mutiny* (Clean Cuts 1994)★★★, *Horror Show* (Clean Cuts 1996)★★★.
●COMPILATIONS: *Kihnsolidation: The Best Of Greg Kihn* (Rhino 1989)★★★★.
●FURTHER READING: *Horror Show*, Greg Kihn.

KILLDOZER

Killdozer were formed in Madison, Wisconsin, USA, and the music of the area is regularly celebrated in their primal country blues. The original line-up featured Michael Gerald (bass/vocals), plus the brothers Dan (guitar) and Bill Hobson (drums). Since formation the trio have released a steady stream of albums which often highlighted their distaste at what they saw as the social and political malaise of their native country. They were just as likely to turn the spotlight on smalltown weirdness, however, or their singer's rampant confusion about the state of the world. In a respite from this angst, *For Ladies Only* was a project dedicated to covers of classic songs of the 70s, including 'One Tin Soldier' and 'Good Lovin' Gone Bad'. Guitarist Paul Zagoras was recruited during the 90s in place of Dan Hobson, during which time Killdozer's formidable output was restrained somewhat due to Gerald taking accountancy exams (he is a former mathematics teacher). However, the band bounced straight back to form with albums in 1994 and 1995, both featuring further bizarre anecdotes. The band broke up at the end of 1996 with the aptly named 'fuck you we quit tour'.
●ALBUMS: *Intellectuals Are The Shoeshine Boys Of The Ruling Elite* (Bone Air 1984)★★★, *Snakeboy* (Touch & Go 1985)★★★, *Burl* mini-album (Touch & Go 1986)★★★, *Little Baby Buntin'* (Touch & Go 1987)★★★, *Twelve Point Buck* (Touch & Go 1988)★★★, *For Ladies Only* (Touch & Go 1989)★★★, *Uncompromising War On Art Under The Dictatorship Of The Proletariat* (Touch & Go 1994)★★★, *God Hears Pleas Of The Innocent* (Touch & Go 1995)★★★.
●VIDEOS: *Little Baby Buntin' Live* (1990).

KILLING JOKE

This immensely powerful post-punk UK band combined a furious rhythm section with near psychotic performances from Jaz Coleman (b. Jeremy Coleman, Cheltenham, England; vocals/keyboards). The band came about when Coleman, of Egyptian descent, was introduced to Paul Ferguson, then drumming for the Matt Stagger

Band. Coleman joined as a keyboard player, before they both quit to form their own group. This first incarnation added 'Geordie' (b. K. Walker, Newcastle, England; guitar) and Youth (b. Martin Glover Youth, 27 December 1960, Africa; bass), who had made his first public appearance at the Vortex in 1977 with forgotten punk band the Rage. After relocating to Notting Hill Gate they paid for a rehearsal studio and borrowed money from Coleman's girlfriend to release the *Turn To Red* EP. Picked up by UK disc jockey John Peel, the band provided a session which would become the most frequently requested of the thousands he has commissioned. Via Island Records the band were able to set up their own Malicious Damage label, on which they released 'Wardance' in February 1980, notable for its remarkably savage b-side, 'Psyche'. A succession of fine, aggressive singles followed, alongside live appearances with Joy Division. They were in a strong enough position to negotiate a three-album contract with EG, which allowed them to keep the name Malicious Damage for their records. After the release of a typically harsh debut album, the band were banned from a Glasgow gig when council officials took exception to posters depicting Pope Pius giving his blessing to two columns of Hitler's Brown Shirts (a genuine photograph). It was typical of the black humour that pervaded the band, especially on their record sleeves and graphics. After the recording of the third album was completed the band disintegrated when Coleman's fascination with the occult led him to the conclusion that apocalypse was imminent, and he fled to Iceland. He was followed later by Youth. When Youth returned it was to begin work with Ferguson on a new project, Brilliant. However, having second thoughts, Ferguson became the third Joker to flee to Iceland taking bass player Paul Raven (ex-Neon Hearts) with him. Brilliant continued with Youth as the only original member. The Killing Joke output from then on lacks something of the menace that had made them so vital. However, *Night Time* combined commercial elements better than most, proffering the hit single 'Love Like Blood'. While *Outside The Gate* was basically a Coleman solo album wrongly credited to the band, they returned with their best album for years with 1990's *Extremities, Dirt And Various Repressed Emotions*, which saw the drumming debut of Martin Atkins (ex-Public Image Limited). Regardless, the band broke up once more with bitter acrimony flying across the pages of the press the same year. While his former co-conspirators pronounced Killing Joke dead, Coleman pledged to continue under the name. He did just that after a brief sojourn into classical/ethnic music via a collaborative project with Anne Dudley which resulted in *Songs From The Victorious City* released on China Records in 1990. *Pandemonium* saw Youth return to join Geordie and Coleman, with the addition of new drummer Geoff Dugmore. This saw a revitalized Killing Joke, notably on 'Exorcism', recorded in the King's Chamber of the Great Pyramid in Cairo. They were welcomed back by a wide cross-section of critics (at least those who Coleman hadn't physically assaulted at some point) and friends. Indeed, bands claiming Killing Joke as a direct influence ranged from the Cult, Ministry and Skinny Puppy to Metallica and Soundgarden, while many noticed an uncanny similarity between the band's 'Eighties' and Nirvana's 'Come As You Are'. *Pandemonium* yielded two UK Top 20 singles, 'Millennium' and the title track, and sold in excess of 100,000 copies in the USA where they signed to Zoo Records. Meanwhile, Coleman's secondary career had evolved. In addition to scoring a second symphony alongside Youth and arranging classical interpretations of the music of Pink Floyd and the Who, he became composer in residence for the New Zealand Symphony Orchestra (a country where he spends most of his time). It led to him being hailed by conductor Klaus Tennstedt as 'the new Mahler'. For his part Youth had become one of the UK's top dance remixers, also recording with acts as diverse as Bananarama and Crowded House. He returned to Killing Joke in 1996 for *Democracy* - a cynical snipe at the build-up to election year in the UK.

● ALBUMS: *Killing Joke* (EG 1980)★★★, *What's THIS For ...!* (EG 1981)★★★, *Revelations* (Malicious Damage/EG 1982)★★★, *Ha! Killing Joke Live* (Malicious Damage/EG 1982)★★★, *Fire Dances* (EG 1983)★★★★, *Night Time* (EG 1985)★★★, *Brighter Than A Thousand Suns* (EG/Virgin 1986)★★★, *Outside The Gate* (EG/Virgin 1988)★★★, *Extremities, Dirt And Various Repressed Emotions* (RCA 1990)★★★, *Pandemonium* (Butterfly/Big Life 1994)★★★, *BBC In Concert* (Strange Fruit 1995)★★★, *Democracy* (Big Life 1996)★★★.

● COMPILATIONS: *An Incomplete Collection* (EG 1990)★★★, *Laugh? I Nearly Bought One* (EG 1992)★★★, *Wilful Days* (Virgin 1995)★★★.

KING

This Coventry-based group was formed in 1983 after the break-up of the Reluctant Stereotypes of which Paul King (vocals) was a member. The remainder of King comprised Tony Wall (bass), Mick Roberts (keyboards), James Jackel Lantsbery (guitar) and ex-Members Adrian Lillywhite (drums). They made their debut supporting the Mighty Wah! and signed to CBS Records. Despite extensive touring and a sizeable following, their first three singles and *Steps In Time* sold poorly. The break came late in 1984 when they supported Culture Club and reached a whole new teen audience. 'Love And Pride' was released early next year, and made number 2 in the UK chart, while the album went to number 6. The hits continued throughout the year, notably with the Top 10 hit, 'Alone Without You'. King abruptly disbanded in 1986. Paul King pursued a solo career, which at best gave him a minor hit with 'I Know' which reached number 59. The group will probably be remembered as much for their trademark spray-painted Dr. Martens boots and Paul King's affable personality than for their engaging pop songs. Paul King later became a video jockey for MTV.

● ALBUMS: *Steps In Time* (Columbia 1984)★★, *Bitter Sweet* (Columbia 1985)★★.

KING, DENIS

b. 25 July 1939, Hornchurch, Essex, England. In 1945, at the age of six, King (piano) and his elder brothers Tony (double and electric bass) and Michael (guitar), played local shows in Hornchurch. Five years later they were appearing professionally as a vocal-instrumental trio, the King III, but when they supported Max Bygraves at the London Palladium in 1955, their billing had changed to the King Brothers. After recording some tracks for the minor label Conquest, they had several hits on Parlophone Records in the late 50s, including 'A White Sports Coat', 'In The Middle Of An Island', 'Standing On The Corner', 'Mais Oui' and '76 Trombones'. In the 60s, their appeal waned, and they split up. Denis carved out a new career for himself as a composer of commercial jingles, television themes, film music and stage musicals. The possessor of a light touch, his best known music for television was probably 'Galloping Home', the theme for the successful BBC production of *The Adventures Of Black Beauty*. Other themes included *Lovejoy*, *Hannay* and *Taking The Floor*. He also composed the film music for *Sweeney!*, *Not Tonight Darling*, *The Spy's Wife*, *The Chairman's Wife* and *Holiday On The Buses*. In 1977, King provided the music, and served as musical director, for *Privates On Parade*, Peter Nicholls' hit vaudeville play about 'camp and colonialism in 1948 Malaya', which starred Denis Quilley, and eventually made it to New York, off-Broadway, in 1989, with Jim Dale in the leading role. During the 80s, King combined with Keith Waterhouse and Willis Hall for *Worzel Gummidge*, a theatrical spin-off from the popular television series, starring Jon Pertwee. King also collaborated with Benny Green for *Bashville*, adapted from a play by George Bernard Shaw, and wrote the music for two other Hall projects, *Wind In The Willows* and *Treasure Island*. In 1988, he was involved in the West End revue, *Re: Joyce*, an anecdotal biography of the British comedienne-actress, Joyce Grenfell, which starred Maureen Lipman. He served as her accompanist, comic foil, narrator of much of the biographical material, and impersonated several of the individuals in Grenfell's life, such as composer Richard Addinsell and Dame Myra Hess. King returned to the West End twice with *Re: Joyce*, and featured in the US production, plus the 1991 UK television version. Earlier that year, he had rejoined Benny Green for another attempt to set Bernard Shaw to music. For *Valentine's Day*, adapted from Shaw's *You Never Can Tell*, King's music 'reflected a move towards sweetness: slow waltz, quick waltz, here a touch of minuet', all of which was enhanced by the virtuoso performance of Edward Petherbridge.

KING, EVELYN 'CHAMPAGNE'

b 1 July 1960, Bronx, New York, USA. A former office cleaner at Gamble And Huff's Sigma Sound studios, King was nurtured by T. Life, a member of the company's writing and production staff. He coached the aspiring singer on recording technique and was instrumental in preparing King's career. Her debut single, 'Shame', was released in 1977 and after considerable success on the dance/club circuit - since regarded as a classic of its kind - it finally broke into the national pop charts the following year, reaching the US Top 10/UK Top 40. Evelyn's second hit, 'I Don't Know If It's Right', became the artist's second gold disc and she later enjoyed international hits with 'I'm In Love' (1981) and a UK Top 10 'Love Come Down' (1982). After a disappointing period during the mid-80s, her 1988 album *Flirt* was generally considered to be a return to form. King has remained a popular performer on the soul/dance music charts.

●ALBUMS: *Smooth Talk* (RCA 1977)★★★, *Music Box* (RCA 1979)★★★, *Call On Me* (RCA 1980)★★★, *I'm In Love* (RCA 1981)★★★, *Get Loose* (RCA 1982)★★★, *Face To Face* (RCA 1983)★★, *So Romantic* (RCA 1984)★★, *A Long Time Coming* (RCA 1985)★★, *Flirt* (EMI 1988)★★★.
●COMPILATIONS: *The Best Of Evelyn 'Champagne' King* (RCA 1990)★★★, *The Essential Works Of* (1992)★★★.

KINGS X

Initially known as the Edge and specializing in Top 40 cover versions, Doug Pinnick (bass/vocals), Ty Tabor (guitar) and Jerry Gaskell (drums) relocated to Houston, Texas, USA, in 1985, and were taken under the wing of ZZ Top video producer, Sam Taylor. Following Taylor's guidance, they concentrated on their own material and changed their name to Kings X. After recording demos and being turned down by several major record companies in the US, they finally secured a contract with the independent Megaforce label. *Out Of The Silent Planet*, with its unique sound and offbeat approach, emerged in 1988 to widespread critical acclaim. Fusing Beatles-style harmonies with hard rock and blues riffs, they encompassed a variety of genres that defied simple pigeon holing. *Gretchen Goes To Nebraska* was an even greater triumph, building on previous strengths, but adding depth in both a technical and lyrical sense. Preferring the 'positive' tag to that of Christian rockers, *Faith, Hope, Love*, released in 1990, scaled even greater heights with its state-of-the-art production and inspired compositions. After a long gap from recording *Ear Candy* was a pleasant surprise, both in quality and in the fact that their fans had not deserted them.

●ALBUMS: *Out Of The Silent Planet* (Megaforce 1987)★★★, *Gretchen Goes To Nebraska* (Megaforce 1989)★★★★, *Faith, Hope, Love* (Megaforce 1990)★★★★, *King's X* (Atlantic 1992)★★★★, *Dogman* (Atlantic 1994)★★★, *Ear Candy* (Atlantic 1996)★★★.

KITARÔ

b. Masanori Takahashi, 4 February 1953, Toyohashi, Japan. Soon after graduating from high school, Takahashi formed a rock band to perform in discos. He was converted to synthesizer music while visiting Asian countries including, in particular, India and the remoter reaches of his Japanese homeland. His debut, *Tenkai (The Heavens)*, a suite for synthesizer, prompted NHK (the Japanese broadcasting company) to commission Kitarô to write a score for the lengthy television documentary, *Silk Road*. This atmospheric, meditative piece full of simple melodies and unhurried tempos earned the composer national and international recognition. A resident of a small village in the Nagano prefecture in central Japan, Kitarô is able to pursue his work in contemplative surroundings, as reflected in his music. For much of the 80s Kitarô's distribution outlet in the west was handled by Polydor Records and the Kuckuck (Line) labels. However, in 1986 Kitarô signed a major contract with Geffen Records confirming his status as one of the world's leading 'new age' artists.

● ALBUMS: *Tenkai (The Heavens)* (Polydor 1978)★★, *Oasis* (Polydor 1979)★★★, *Silk Road I* (Polydor 1980)★★★★, *Silk Road II* (Polydor 1980)★★★, *Tonkô* (Polydor 1981)★★★, *Tenjiku (India, Or The Heavens)* (Polydor 1983)★★★, *Huin (Flying Clouds)* (Polydor 1983)★★, *From The Full Moon Story* (Polydor 1985)★★★, *Tanhaung* (Polydor 1986)★★★, *Towards The West* (Polydor 1986)★★★, *Tenkû (The Sky)* (Geffen 1986)★★★, *Silver Cloud* (Polydor 1986)★★★, *Ki* (Polydor 1986)★★★, *Live In Asia* (Geffen 1986)★★, *The Light Of The Spirit* (Geffen 1987)★★★, with the London Symphony Orchestra *Silk Road Suite* (Geffen 1987)★★★★, *Kojiki (The Legendary Stories Of Ancient Japan)* (Geffen 1990)★★★, *Music From The Motion Picture Soundtrack Heaven And Earth* (Geffen 1994)★★, *An Enchanted Evening* (Domo 1995)★★★, *Peace On Earth* (Domo 1996)★★★, *Kitarô's World Of Music Featuring Yu-Xiao Guang* (Domo 1996)★★★.

● COMPILATIONS: *Best Of Silk Road* (Polydor 1983)★★★, *Best Of Kitarô* (Kuckuck 1987)★★★, *Ten Years* (1988)★★★.

KLF

Since 1987 the KLF have operated under a series of guises, only gradually revealing their true nature to the public at large. The band's principal spokesman is Bill Drummond (b. William Butterworth, 29 April 1953, South Africa), who had already enjoyed a chequered music industry career. As co-founder of the influential Zoo label in the late 70s, he introduced and later managed Echo And The Bunnymen and Teardrop Explodes. Later he joined forces with Jimmy Cauty (b. 1954), an artist of various persuasions and a member of Brilliant in the mid-80s. Their first project was undertaken under the title JAMS (Justified Ancients Of Mu Mu - a title lifted from Robert Shea and Robert Anton Wilson's conspiracy novels dealing with the *Illuminati*). An early version of 'All You Need Is Love' caused little reaction compared to the provocatively titled LP which followed - *1987 - What The Fuck Is Going On?* Released under the KLF moniker (standing for Kopyright Liberation Front), it liberally disposed of the works of the Beatles, Led Zeppelin *et al* with the careless

abandon the duo had picked up from the heyday of punk. One of the disfigured super groups, Abba, promptly took action to ensure the offending article was withdrawn. In the wake of the emerging house scene the next move was to compromise the theme tune to well-loved British television show *Dr Who*, adding a strong disco beat and Gary Glitter yelps to secure an instant number 1 with 'Doctorin' The Tardis'. Working under the title Timelords, this one-off coup was achieved with such simplicity that its originators took the step of writing a book; *How To Have A Number One The Easy Way*. Returning as the KLF, they scored a big hit with the more legitimate cult dance hit 'What Time Is Love'. After the throwaway send-up of Australian pop, 'Kylie Said To Jason', they hit big again with the soulful techno of '3 A. M. Eternal'. There were further releases from the myriad of names employed by the duo (JAMS; 'Down Town', 'Its Grim Up North', Space; *Space*, Disco 2000; 'Uptight') while Cauty, alongside Alex Peterson, played a significant part in creating the Orb. Of the band's more recent work, perhaps the most startling was their luxurious video for the KLF's 'Justified And Ancient', featuring the unmistakable voice of Tammy Wynette. The song revealed the KLF at the top of their creative powers, selling millions of records worldwide while effectively taking the michael. They were voted the Top British Group by the BPI. Instead of lapping up the acclaim, the KLF, typically, rejected the comfort of a music biz career, and deliberately imploded at the BRITS award ceremony. There they performed an 'upbeat' version of '3AM Eternal', backed by breakneck speed punk band Extreme Noise Terror, amid press speculation that they would be bathing the ceremony's assembled masses with pig's blood. They contented themselves instead with (allegedly) dumping the carcass of a dead sheep in the foyer of the hotel staging the post-ceremony party, and Drummond mock machine-gunning the assembled dignitaries. They then announced that the proud tradition of musical anarchy they had brought to a nation was at a close: the KLF were no more. Their only 'release' in 1992 came with a version of 'Que Sera Sera' (naturally rechristened 'K Sera Sera', and recorded with the Soviet Army Chorale), which, they insisted, would only see the light of day on the advent of world peace. The KLF returned to their rightful throne, that of England's foremost musical pranksters, with a stinging art terrorist racket staged under the K Foundation banner. In late 1993, a series of advertisements began to appear in the quality press concerning the

Turner Prize art awards. While that body was responsible for granting £20,000 to a piece of non-mainstream art, the K Foundation (a new vehicle for messrs Drummond and Cauty) promised double that for the worst piece of art displayed. The Turner shortlist was identical to that of the KLF's. More bizarre still, exactly £1,000,000 was withdrawn from the National Westminster bank (the biggest cash withdrawal in the institution's history), nailed to a board, and paraded in front of a select gathering of press and art luminaries. The money was eventually returned to their bank accounts (although members of the press pocketed a substantial portion), while the £40,000 was awarded to one Rachel Whiteread, who also won the 'proper' prize. Urban guerrillas specializing in highly original shock tactics, the KLF offer the prospect of a brighter decade should their various disguises continue to prosper.

● ALBUMS: *Towards The Trance* (KLF 1988)★★★★, *The What Time Is Love Story* (KLF 1989)★★★, *The White Room* (KLF 1989)★★★, *Chill Out* (KLF 1989)★★★. As JAMS: *1987 - What The Fuck Is Going On?* (KLF 1987)★★★, *Who Killed The JAMS?* (KLF 1988)★★★, *Shag Times* (KLF 1989)★★★.

● VIDEOS: *Stadium House* (1991), *Trilogy* (PMI 1991).

● FURTHER READING: *Justified And Ancient: The Unfolding Story Of The KLF*, Pete Robinson. *Bad Wisdom*, Mark Manning and Bill Drummond.

KNOPFLER, MARK

b. 12 August 1949, Glasgow, Scotland. This homely ex-teacher is Dire Straits' main asset through his skill as a composer, a tuneful if detached vocal style - and a terse, resonant fretboard dexterity admired by Eric Clapton and Chet Atkins, both of whom sought his services for studio and concert projects in the 80s. Courted also by movie directors to score incidental music, he inaugurated a parallel solo career in 1983 with David Puttnam's film *Local Hero* from which an atmospheric tie-in album sold moderately well with its single 'Going Home' (the main title theme) a minor UK hit (which was incorporated into the band's stage act). Further film work included soundtracks to *Cal*, Bill Forsyth's *Comfort And Joy* and with Dire Straits' Guy Fletcher, *The Princess Bride*. After he and the group's Pick Withers played on Bob Dylan's *Slow Train Coming*, Knopfler was asked to produce the enigmatic American's *Infidels* in 1983. Further commissions included diverse acts such as Randy Newman, Willy (Mink) DeVille (*Miracle*), Aztec Camera (*Knife*) and Tina Turner, for whom he com-posed the title track of *Private Dancer*. Knopfler was also in demand as a session guitarist, counting Steely Dan (*Gaucho*), Phil Lynott (*Solo In Soho*), Van Morrison (*Beautiful Vision*) and Bryan Ferry (*Boys And Girls*) among his clients. By no means confining such assistance to the illustrious, he was also heard on albums by Sandy McLelland And The Backline and Kate And Anna McGarrigle (*Love Over And Over*). For much of the later 80s, he was preoccupied with domestic commitments and, in 1986, he was incapacitated by a fractured collar bone following an accident at a celebrity motor race during the Australian Grand Prix. In 1989, however, he and old friends Brendan Croker and Steve Phillips formed the Notting Hillbillies for an album and attendant tour, but neither this venture nor several nights backing Clapton during a 1990 Albert Hall season indicated an impending schism in Dire Straits' ranks. Throughout the first half of the 90s Knopfler sessioned on countless albums and it was only in 1996 that his 'official' solo career was announced. The debut *Golden Heart* featured support from slide blues guitarist Sonny Landreth, singer songwriter Paul Brady, the Chieftains and Vince Gill.

● ALBUMS: *Music From 'Local Hero'* soundtrack (Vertigo 1983)★★★, *Cal - Music From The Film* soundtrack (Vertigo 1984)★★★, *The Princess Bride* soundtrack (Warners 1987)★★, *Last Exit To Brooklyn* (Warners 1989)★★, with Chet Atkins *Neck And Neck* (Columbia 1990)★★★, *Golden Heart* (Mercury 1996)★★★.

● FURTHER READING: *Mark Knopfler: An Unauthorised Biography*, Myles Palmer.

KOOL AND THE GANG

Originally formed as a quartet, the Jazziacs, by Robert 'Kool' Bell (b. 8 October 1950, Youngstown, Ohio, USA; bass), Robert 'Spike' Mickens (b. Jersey City, New Jersey, USA; trumpet), Robert 'The Captain' Bell - later known by his Muslim name Amir Bayyan (b. 1 November 1951, Youngstown, Ohio, USA; saxophone/keyboards) and Dennis 'D.T.' Thomas (b. 9 February 1951, Jersey City, New Jersey, USA; saxophone). Based in Jersey City, this aspiring jazz group opened for acts such as Pharaoh Sanders and Leone Thomas. They were later joined by Charles 'Claydes' Smith (b. 6 September 1948, Jersey City, New Jersey, USA; guitar) and 'Funky' George Brown (b. 5 January 1949, Jersey City, New Jersey, USA; drums), and as the Soul Town Band, moderated their early direction by blending soul and funk, a transition completed by 1969 when they settled on the name Kool

And The Gang. The group crossed over into the US pop chart in 1973 and initiated a run of 19 stateside Top 40 hits on their own De-Lite label starting with 'Funky Stuff', a feat consolidated the following year with a couple of Top 10 hits, 'Jungle Boogie' and 'Hollywood Swinging'. They continued to enjoy success although their popularity momentarily wavered in the latter half of the 70s as the prominence of disco strengthened. In 1979 the Gang added vocalists, James 'J.T.' Taylor (b. 16 August 1953, Laurens, South Carolina, USA) and Earl Toon Jnr., with Taylor emerging as the key member in a new era of success for the group, which coincided with their employment of an outside producer. Eumire Deodato refined the qualities already inherent in the group's eclectic style and together they embarked on a series of highly successful international hits including 'Ladies Night' (1979), 'Too Hot' (1980), and the bubbling 'Celebration', a 1980 platinum disc and US pop number 1 - later used by the media as the home-coming theme for the returning American hostages from Iran. Outside the USA they achieved parallel success and proved similarly popular in the UK where 'Get Down On It' (1981), 'Joanna' (1984) and 'Cherish' (1985) each reached the Top 5. The arrival of Taylor also saw the group's albums achieving Top 30 status in their homeland for the first time, with *Celebrate!* (1980) reaching the Top 10. Their longevity was due, in part, to a settled line-up. The original six members remained with the group into the 80s and although newcomer Toon left, Taylor blossomed into an ideal frontman. This core was later supplemented by several auxiliaries, Clifford Adams (trombone) and Michael Ray (trumpet). This idyllic situation was finally undermined by Taylor's departure in 1988 and he was replaced by three singers, former Dazz Band member Skip Martin plus Odeen Mays and Gary Brown. Taylor released a solo album in 1989, *Sister Rosa*, while the same year the group continued recording with the album *Sweat*. The compilation set, *The Singles Collection* shows that Taylor left behind him one of the most engaging, and successful of soul/funk catalogues.

●ALBUMS: *Kool And The Gang* (1969)★★, *Live At The Sex Machine* (De-Lite 1971)★★, *Live At P.J.s* (De-Lite 1971)★★, *Music Is The Message* (1972)★★, *Good Times* (De-Lite 1973)★★★, *Wild And Peaceful* (De-Lite 1973)★★★, *Light Of Worlds* (De-Lite 1974)★★★, *Spirit Of The Boogie* (De-Lite 1975)★★, *Love And Understanding* (De-Lite 1976)★★, *Open Sesame* (De-Lite 1976)★★, *The Force* (De-Lite 1977)★★, *Everbody's Dancin'* (1978)★★, *Ladies' Night* (De-Lite 1979)★★★, *Celebrate!* (De-Lite 1980)★★★, *Something Special* (De-Lite 1981)★★, *As One* (De-Lite 1982)★★, *In The Heart* (De-Lite 1983)★★★★, *Emergency* (De-Lite 1984)★★, *Victory* (Curb 1986)★★, *Forever* (Mercury 1986)★★, *Sweat* (Mercury 1989)★★, *Kool Love* (Telstar 1990)★★, *State Of Affairs* (Curb 1996)★★.

●COMPILATIONS: *The Best Of ...* (De-Lite 1971)★★, *Kool Jazz* (De-Lite 1974)★★, *Kool And The Gang Greatest Hits!* (De-Lite 1975)★★★, *Spin Their Top Hits* (De-Lite 1978)★★★★, *Kool Kuts* (De-Lite 1982)★★★, *Twice As Kool* (De-Lite 1983)★★★★, *The Singles Collection* (De-Lite 1988)★★★★, *Everything's Kool And The Gang: Greatest Hits And More* (Mercury 1988)★★★★, *Great And Remixed 91* (Mercury 1992)★★★, *Collection* (Spectrum 1996)★★★.

KORGIS

The Korgis comprised two former members of Stackridge, James Warren (bass/guitar/vocals) and Andy Davis (drums/guitar), plus Phil Harrison (keyboards/percussion), and Stuart Gordon (guitar/violin). This UK group reached the Top 20 with their debut record 'If I Had You', but had problems when their next two singles failed. When their self-titled album also failed to make an impact it seemed they would end up as one-hit-wonders. However, 'Everybody's Gotta Learn Sometime' a classy love song, reached the UK Top 5 and was followed by a minor hit with 'If It's Alright With You Baby'. By 1983, the group had been dropped by their label Rialto and were basically down to a core of just Warren, who carried the name on for a few more years and a number of one-off record contracts. European success continued on a limited basis but at home the Korgis' success had ended. The unit of Warren and Davis reformed in 1990 with the addition of John Baker (b. 2 April 1961, Bath, Avon, England; guitar, keyboards, vocals; ex-Graduate). They recorded an album of new material together with a new version of 'Everybody's Gotta Learn Sometime'. During their career the band never performed live, so it came as a surprise when they announced their first tour, due for the summer of 1993.

●ALBUMS: *The Korgis* (Rialto 1979)★★★, *Dumb Waiters* (Rialto 1980)★★★, *Sticky George* (Rialto 1981)★★, *Burning Questions* (Sonet 1986)★★, *This World's For Everyone* (Dureco 1992)★★.

●COMPILATIONS: *The Best Of The Korgis* (1983)★★★.

KRAFTWERK

The word 'unique' is overused in rock music, but Kraftwerk have a stronger claim than most to the tag. Ralf Hutter (b. 1946, Krefeld, Germany; organ) and woodwind student Florian Schneider-Esleben (b. 1947, Düsseldorf, Germany; woodwind) met while they were studying improvised music in Düsseldorf, Germany. They drew on the influence of experimental electronic forces such as composer Karlheinz Stockhausen and Tangerine Dream to create minimalist music on synthesizers, drum machines and tape recorders. Having previously recorded an album with Organisation (*Tone Float*), Hutter and Schneider formed Kraftwerk with Klaus Dinger and Thomas Homann and issued *Highrail*, after which Dinger and Homann left to form Neu. Their first two albums, released in Germany, were later released in the UK as an edited compilation in 1972. Produced by Conny Plank (later to work with Ultravox and the Eurythmics), the bleak, spartan music provoked little response. After releasing a duo set, *Ralf And Florian*, Wolfgang Flur (electronic drums) and Klaus Roeder (guitar/violin/keyboards) joined the group. *Autobahn* marked Kraftwerk's breakthrough and established them as purveyors of hi-tech, computerized music. The title track, running at more than 22 minutes, was an attempt to relate the monotony and tedium of a long road journey. An edited version reached the Top 10 in the US and UK charts. In 1975, Roeder was replaced by Karl Bartos. *Radioactivity* was a concept album based on the sounds to be found on the airwaves. *Trans-Europe Express* and *The Man-Machine* were strong influences on new-wave groups such as the Human League, Tubeway Army (Gary Numan), Depeche Mode and OMD, while David Bowie claimed to have long been an admirer. The *New Musical Express* said of *Man Machine*: 'It is the only completely successful visual/aural fusion rock has produced so far'. Kraftwerk spent three years building their own Kling Klang studios in the late 70s, complete with, inevitably, scores of computers. The single 'The Model', from *Computer World*, gave the band a surprise hit when it topped the UK charts in 1981 and it led to a trio of hits, including 'Showroom Dummies' and 'Tour De France', a song that was featured in the film *Breakdance* and became the theme for the cycling event of the same name in 1983. *Electric Cafe* was seen as a pioneering dance record and the group was cited as a major influence on a host of dance artists from Afrika Bambaataa to the respected producer Arthur Baker. In 1990, Flur departed to be replaced by Fritz Hijbert. They achieved further UK chart success with 'The Robots' which was accompanied by the eerie display of Kraftwerk look-alike robots. Kraftwerk's best-known songs were collected together in 1991 on the double album *The Mix*, aimed chiefly at the dance market by EMI Records. 'I think our music has to do with emotions. Technology and emotion can join hands . . .' said Hutter in 1991.

●ALBUMS: *Highrail* (1971)★★, *Var* (1972)★★, *Ralf & Florian* (Philips 1973)★★★, *Autobahn* (Vertigo 1974)★★★★, *Radioactivity* (Capitol 1975)★★★, *Trans-Europe Express* (Capitol 1977)★★★★, *The Man-Machine* (Capitol 1978)★★★★, *Computer World* (EMI 1981)★★★★, *Electric Cafe* (EMI 1986)★★★.

●COMPILATIONS: *Kraftwerk* a UK compilation of the first two releases (Vertigo 1973)★★, *The Mix* (EMI 1991)★★★★.

●FURTHER READING: *Kraftwerk: Man, Machine & Music*, Pacal Bussy.

KROKUS

Formed in Soluthurn, Switzerland, Krokus appeared in 1974 playing symphonic rock similar to Yes, Genesis and Emerson, Lake And Palmer. After four years and two rather lacklustre albums, they switched to a hard rock style and dropped the frills in favour of a back-to-basics approach in the mode of AC/DC. The group originally comprised Chris Von Rohr (vocals), Fernando Von Arb (guitar), Jurg Naegeli (bass), Tommy Kiefer (guitar) and Freddy Steady (drums). The songs were formulaic numbers based on simple riffs and predictable choruses that were chanted repeatedly. With Von Rohr's voice lacking the necessary vocal range, he stepped down to became the bass player in favour of new arrival 'Maltezer' Marc (b. Marc Storace, Malta; ex-Tea). Naegeli occasionally played keyboards and subsequently took over the technical side of the band. *Metal Rendez-vous* was the turning point in the band's career; released in 1980, it was heavier than anything they had done before and coincided with the resurgence of heavy metal in Britain. They played the Reading Festival in 1980 and were well received, and their next two albums continued with an aggressive approach, though they streamlined their sound to make it more radio-friendly. *Hardware* and *One Vice At A Time* both reached the UK album charts, at numbers 44 and 28, respectively. Before *Headhunter* materialized a series of personnel changes took place. The most important of these was the replacement of Kiefer with ex-roadie Mark Kohler

(guitar), while Steve Pace stepped in on drums. Kiefer subsequently returned to replace Rohr. Produced by Tom Allom, *Headhunter*'s high-speed, heavy-duty approach propelled it to number 25 in the *Billboard* album charts. Further line-up changes (the temporary addition of ex-Crown guitarist Patrick Mason and the exit then return of Pace) delayed the release of *The Blitz*, an erratic album, which reached number 31 on the US chart mainly on the strength of its predecessor. Since 1985 there has been a continuing downward trend in the band's fortunes, with their personnel in a constant state of flux (Kesier committing suicide in 1986 and the introduction of guitarist Manny Maurer). Their music has progressed little during the last decade and relies heavily, even today, on the legacy of AC/DC and the Scorpions. In 1995 the band were touring with a line-up of Storace (vocals), Fernando Von Arb (bass), Maurer (guitar), Kohler (guitar) and Steady (drums), and recording sessions followed.

●ALBUMS: *Krokus* (Schmontz 1975)★★, *To You All* (Schmontz 1977)★★, *Painkiller* (Mercury 1978)★★, *Pay It In Metal* (Mercury 1979)★★, *Metal Rendezvous* (Ariola 1980)★★★, *Hardware* (Ariola 1981)★★★, *One Vice At A Time* (Ariola 1982)★★★, *Headhunter* (Arista 1983)★★★, *The Blitz* (Arista 1984)★★, *Change Of Address* (Arista 1985)★★, *Alive And Screamin'* (Arista 1986)★★, *Heart Attack* (MCA 1987)★★, *Stampede* (Ariola 1990)★★.

L.A. GUNS

This US group was formed by ex-Guns N'Roses guitarist Tracii Guns and Paul Black in Los Angeles in 1987, though the latter was soon replaced by ex-Girl/Bernie Torme vocalist Phil Lewis. Working on material that was a hybrid of metal, glam and blues-based rock 'n' roll, they signed with Polygram Records in the US the following year. With the addition of Mick Cripps (guitar), Kelly Nickels (bass) and Steve Riley (drums, ex-W.A.S.P.) the line-up was complete. However, with Riley arriving too late to appear on their self-titled debut, the group used the services of Nickey Alexander (formerly 'Nicky Beat' of punk legends the Weirdos). *Cocked And Loaded* was a marked improvement over its predecessor; the band had matured as songwriters and Lewis's vocals were stronger and more convincing. *Hollywood Vampires* saw them diversifying musically, but retaining the essential energy and rough edges for which they had become renowned. Touring as support to Skid Row in Europe, it at last seemed as if Guns' would no longer have to look longingly at the phenomenal success his former band had achieved in his absence. However, it was not to be. As the group disintegrated Guns went on to put together a new outfit, Killing Machine, while Lewis formed Filthy Lucre. However, L.A. Guns were soon reformed when both these bands failed. *Vicious Circle* continued the vampiric metaphors of the group's previous album with the track 'Crystal Eyes', a song originally included on *Hollywood Vampires*. Received as a strong return to the scene from a group still held in high regard, it was arguably the best recorded work yet by either Guns or Lewis.

●ALBUMS: *L.A. Guns* (Polygram 1988)★★, *Cocked And Loaded* (Polygram 1989)★★★, *Hollywood Vampires* (Polygram 1991)★★★, *Vicious Circle* (Polygram 1994)★★★.

●VIDEOS: *One More Reason* (1989), *Love, Peace & Geese* (1990).

LA'S

Formed in 1986 in Liverpool, Merseyside, England, the La's featured Lee Mavers (b. 2 August 1962, Huyton, Liverpool, England; guitar/vocals), John Power (b. 14 September 1967; bass), Paul Hemmings (guitar) and John Timson (drums). Early demo tapes resulted in their signing with Go! Discs in 1987. After a well-received debut single, 'Way Out', which hallmarked the group's effortless, 60s-inspired pop, they took a year out before issuing the wonderfully melodic 'There She Goes'. When this too eluded the charts, the La's, far from disillusioned, returned to the studio for two years to perfect tracks for their debut album. The line-up changed, too, with Lee's brother Neil (b. 8 July 1971, Huyton, Liverpool, England) taking up drums and ex-Marshmellow Overcoats guitarist Cammy (b. Peter James Camell, 30 June 1967, Huyton, Liverpool, England) joining the line-up. In the meantime, 'There She Goes' became a massive underground favourite, prompting a reissue two years on (after another single, 'Timeless Melody'). In October 1990 it reached the UK Top 20. *The La's* followed that same month, an invigorating and highly musical collection of tunes which matched, and some would argue outstripped, the Stone Roses' more garlanded debut. Its comparative lack of impact could be put down to Mavers truculence in the press, verbally abusing Go! Discs for insisting on releasing the record and disowning its contents: 'That's the worst LP I've ever heard by anyone.' Comparisons with the best of the 60s, notably the Byrds and Beach Boys, stemmed from the band's obsession with real instruments, creating a rootsy, authentic air. After 'Feelin'' was drawn from the album, the La's set about recording tracks for a new work and spent much of 1991's summer touring America and Japan. Little was then heard of the band for the next four years, which took few acquainted with Mavers' studio perfectionism by surprise. The delays proved too much for Power, however, who departed to set up Cast. Back in the notoriously insular La's camp rumours continued to circulate of madness and drug addiction. A collaboration with Edgar Summertyme of the Stairs was vaunted, but no public assignments were forthcoming. 1995 finally brought a Mavers solo acoustic set in support of Paul Weller, which went so badly awry that he had the plug pulled on him. In April he spoke to the *New Musical Express* about a 'second' La's album. Sessions were undertaken in the West London studio owned by Rat Scabies of the Damned, with Mavers playing all the instruments.

●ALBUMS: *The La's* (Go! Discs 1990)★★★★, *Strange Things Happening* (Rounder 1994)★★.

LABELLE, PATTI

b. Patricia Holte, 24 May 1944, Philadelphia, Pennsylvania, USA. The former leader of Labelle began her solo career in 1976. Although her first releases showed promise, she was unable to regain the profile enjoyed by her former group and at the beginning of the 80s Patti agreed to tour with a revival of the stage play, *Your Arms Are Too Short To Box With God*. The production reached Broadway in 1982 and, with Al Green as a co-star, became one of the year's hits. Having made her film debut as a blues singer in *A Soldier's Story* (1984), Patti resumed recording with 'Love Has Finally Come At Last', a magnificent duet with Bobby Womack. Two tracks from 1984's box-office smash, *Beverly Hills Cop*, 'New Attitude' (US Top 20) and 'Stir It Up', also proved popular. 'On My Own', a sentimental duet with Michael McDonald, was a spectacular hit in 1986. This million-selling single confirmed LaBelle's return and if some commentators criticize her almost operatic delivery, she remains a powerful and imposing performer. She made a return to the US stage in 1989, performing in various States with the 'lost' Duke Ellington musical, *Queenie Pie*.

●ALBUMS: *Patti LaBelle* (Epic 1977)★★★, *Tasty* (Epic 1978)★★★, *It's Alright With Me* (Epic 1979)★★★, *Released* (Epic 1980)★★★, *The Spirit's In It* (Philadelphia International 1981)★★★, *I'm In Love Again* (Philadelphia International 1983)★★★, *Patti* (Philadelphia International 1985)★★★, *The Winner In You* (MCA 1986)★★★, *Be Yourself* (MCA 1989)★★, *Starlight Christmas* (MCA 1990)★★★, *Burnin'* (MCA 1991)★★★, *Live!* (MCA 1992)★★, *Gems* (MCA 1994)★★★.

●COMPILATIONS: *Best Of ...* (Epic 1986)★★★, *Greatest Hits* (MCA 1996)★★★.

LADYSMITH BLACK MAMBAZO

The success of Paul Simon's album *Graceland* did much to give the music of black South Africa international recognition in the mid-80s, and in particular gave a high profile to the choral group Mambazo, who had sung on it. Founded by Joseph Shabalala in 1960, the group's name referred to Shabalala's home town of Ladysmith, while also paying tribute to the seminal 50s choral group Black Mambazo (black axe) led by Aaron Lerole (composer of the 1958 UK hit 'Tom Hark' by his brother Elias [Lerole] And His Zig Zag Flutes). The

group began working professionally in 1971, with a version of ingoma ebusukuk ('night music'), which Shabalala dubbed 'cothoza mfana' ('walking on tiptoe', an accurate description of Mambazo's ability to follow choruses of thundering intensity with split-second changes into passages of delicate, whisper-like intimacy). Until 1975, most of Mambazo's album output concentrated on traditional folk songs, some of them with new lyrics which offered necessarily coded, metaphorical criticisms of the apartheid regime. After 1975, and Shabalala's conversion to Christianity, religious songs were added to the repertoire - although, to non-Zulu speakers, the dividing line will not be apparent. In 1987, following the success of *Graceland*, the group's Warner Brothers Records debut album *Shaka Zulu*, produced by Paul Simon, reached the UK Top 40, and also sold substantially in the USA and Europe. In 1990, *Two Worlds One Heart* marked a radical stylistic departure for the group through its inclusion of tracks recorded in collaboration with George Clinton and the Winans. On 10 December 1991, as the result of what was described as a 'roadside incident' in Durban, South Africa, founder member Shabalala was shot dead.
●ALBUMS: *Amabutho* (BL 1973)★★★, *Isitimela* (BL 1974)★★★, *Amaqhawe* (BL 1976)★★★, *Ulwandle Olunggewele* (BL 1977)★★★, *Umthombo Wamanzi* (BL 1982)★★★, *Ibhayibheli Liyindlela* (BL 1984)★★★, *Unduku Zethu* (Shanachie 1984)★★★, *Inala* (Shanachie 1986)★★★, *Ezulwini Siyakhona* (1986)★★★, *Shaka Zulu* (Warners 1987)★★★★, *Journey Of Dreams* (Warners 1988)★★★★, with Danny Glover *How The Leopard Got His Spots* (Windham Hill 1989)★★★, *Two Worlds One Heart* (Warners 1990)★★★★, *Inkanyezi Nezazi* (1992)★★★, *Liph'Iqiniso* (Flame Tree 1994)★★★, *Gift Of The Tortoise* (Flame Tree 1995)★★★.
●COMPILATIONS: *Classic Tracks* (Shanachie 1991)★★★★, *Best Of* (Shanachie 1992)★★★★.

LAKE, GREG

b. 10 November 1948, Poole, Dorset, England. Greg Lake is a vocalist and bass guitarist of great ability. He started to play the guitar at the age of 12, earning small amounts of money by entertaining customers at his local bingo hall. At 15, he left school to pursue a career as a draughtsman, but by the age of 17 had played as a full-time musician with both Shame and the Gods. In 1968, he was contacted by Robert Fripp and Michael Giles (b. 1942, Bournemouth, England), who had heard of his musical abilities and of the peculiar choir-like tone of his voice, and was invited to form King Crimson with them. With King Crimson, Lake played at the Rolling Stones' Hyde Park, free concert on 5 July 1969, and the high profile of this occasion guaranteed the band almost overnight fame. However, during the recording of *In The Wake Of Poseidon*, he left to join Emerson, Lake And Palmer. This trio quickly gained a reputation for being one of the most technically skilled bands of the 70s. Keith Emerson (b. 1 November 1944, Todmorden, England; keyboards) and Carl Palmer (b. 20 March 1951, Birmingham, England; drums/percussion) made up the outfit which first played at the Isle of Wight festival in 1970. The band set up their own record label, Manticore, but despite considerable commercial success, they temporarily disbanded in 1974. Lake resurfaced around Christmas time 1975 when he released what was to become one of the most perennially-popular Christmas singles with 'I Believe In Father Christmas' (co-written with King Crimson/ELP lyricist Pete Sinfield) - the song carried on the ELP tradition of including a passage of popular classical music with Prokofiev's 'Sleigh Bell Ride'. This single, which reached number 2 in the UK, was so successful that it was re-released in both 1982 and 1983. 1977 saw Lake collaborating with Sinfield again to write blues-oriented songs such as 'Closer To Believing' on *Works, Volumes 1 And 2* by the reformed Emerson, Lake And Palmer. A huge tour followed this project, during the course of which the trio were accompanied by a full symphony orchestra. They disbanded for a second time in 1980, and Lake released the solo *Greg Lake* the following year. The album peaked at number 62 in both UK and US charts. The Greg Lake Band, which lasted from June 1981 to April 1982 included Gary Moore (guitar), Tommy Eyre (keyboards), Tristram Margetts (bass) and Ted McKenna (drums, former Rory Gallagher group and later MSG). Another solo album was released in 1983 for Chrysalis Records, but this time failed completely. In September 1983, Lake replaced John Wetton in Asia, but he left shortly afterwards. In 1984, he renewed his relationship with Emerson, and in 1985 *Emerson, Lake And Powell* was released, the latter name belonging to Cozy Powell who had played drums for bands such as Rainbow and Whitesnake. This combination lasted until 1987 when Powell departed. A new drummer, Richard Berry, was recruited for the release of the unsuccessful *To The Power Of Three*. By 1992, the original trio were recording and performing together again.
●ALBUMS: *Greg Lake* (Chrysalis 1981)★★, *Manoeuvres* (Chrysalis 1983)★★.

LAMB, ANNABEL

Although this UK pop vocalist is relegated to the one-hit-wonder category, her unusual vocal delivery of the Doors' hit 'Riders On The Storm' created considerable interest and made the UK Top 30. The brooding, breathy vocal style was used to great effect on this and her subsequent releases. Her backing musicians comprised: Robin Langridge (keyboards), Steve Greetham (bass), Chris Jarrett (guitar) and Jim Dvorak (trumpet). The hybrid of jazz, rock and reggae consistently produced by Wally Brill found only a loyal coterie of fans. Little has been heard of Lamb since 1988.
●ALBUMS: *Once Bitten* (A&M 1983)★★★, *The Flame* (A&M 1984)★★★, *Brides* (RCA 1987)★★★, *Justice* (1988)★★★.
●COMPILATIONS: *Heartland* (1988)★★★.

LAMBRETTAS

This English, Brighton-based band comprised Jez Bird (vocals/guitar), Doug Saunders (guitar/vocals), Mark Ellis (bass/vocals) and Paul Wincer (drums). Together with Secret Affair, the Merton Parkas and the Chords, they were part of the UK's short-lived mod revival of 1979-80. After securing a contract with Elton John's Rocket Records, they had 'Go Steady' included on the label's compilation *499 2139*, alongside fellow mod hopefuls the Act, the Escalators, Les Elite and the Vye. A month later, in November 1979, the same version of 'Go Steady' was released as a single, with little success, but drew much attention from the growing mod audiences. Success arrived with 'Poison Ivy', a catchy remake of the Leiber And Stoller-penned classic, reaching number 7 in the UK charts during 1980, eight places higher than the Coasters' original version of 1959. Their popularity continued with follow-up singles entering the charts, 'D-a-a-ance' climbed to number 12, and 'Another Day (Another Girl)' just managed to scrape into the UK Top 50, reaching number 49. The latter was originally called 'Page Three', but threatened legal action by *The Sun* newspaper, persuaded the band to rethink the title. Their debut *Beat Boys In The Jet Age* peaked at number 28 and was also their last glimpse of the charts. Successive releases: 'Steppin' Out', 'Good Times', 'Anything You Want', 'Decent Town' and 'Somebody To Love', had little impact on either critics or record-buying public, and by the time they issued *Ambience* in 1981, the mod revival was dead and buried and the band quickly folded. In 1985, Razor Records unearthed the Lambrettas' back catalogue,

releasing a compilation of their singles, entitled *Kick Start*.
●ALBUMS: *Beat Boys In The Jet Age* (Rocket 1980)★★★, *Ambience* (Rocket 1981)★★.
●COMPILATIONS: *Kick Start* (Razor 1985)★★★.

LANOIS, DANIEL

b. 1951, Hull, Canada. This esteemed producer rose to fame during the late 80s through his contribution to major releases by Peter Gabriel (*So*) and U2 (*The Unforgettable Fire* and *The Joshua Tree*). He subsequently produced *Robbie Robertson*, the widely acclaimed 'comeback' album by the former leader of the Band, and in 1989 undertook a similar role on Bob Dylan's *Oh Mercy*, widely regarded as the artist's finest work in several years. Lanois's love of expansive, yet subtle, sound, reminiscent of 'new age' styles, combines effectively with mature, traditional rock, as evinced on the artist's own album, *Acadie*. Drawing inspiration from French-Canadian heritage - Lanois used both his native country's languages, sometimes within the same song - he created a haunting tapestry combining the jauntiness of New Orleans music with soundscaped instrumentals. Contributions by Brian Eno and the Neville Brothers, the latter of whom Lanois also produced, added further weight to this impressive collection. Lanois and Eno co-produced U2's two aforementioned multi-million-selling studio albums and their combined influence has given the band's sound new dimensions. He was instrumental in redirecting Emmylou Harris' career with *Wrecking Ball* in 1995 and toured with her, leading his own band during the autumn of that year.
●ALBUMS: *Acadie* (Opal 1989)★★★★, *For The Beauty Of Wynona* (1993)★★★.

LASWELL, BILL

b. 14 February 1950. Laswell started playing guitar but later switched to bass. He was, he has said, more interested in being in a band than in playing music, but in the 70s he became more committed and has since organized some of the most challenging bands in recent popular music, including Material, Curlew (with Tom Cora, Nicky Skopelitis and George Cartwright) and Last Exit (with Sonny Sharrock, Peter Brötzmann and Ronald Shannon Jackson). He also established OAO and Celluloid, two adventurous record labels. For the latest Material album, *Third Power*, he assembled a band including Shabba Ranks, the Jungle Brothers, Herbie Hancock, Sly And Robbie and Fred Wesley. Laswell and Hancock had already worked together, in Last Exit (on *The Noise Of Trouble*) and on two

Hancock albums which he produced: on *Future Shock* in particular the 'backing band' was effectively Material. The list of albums below includes only those that Laswell has made under his own name; in addition he has produced for a wide range of people, including Iggy Pop, Motörhead, Laurie Anderson, Fela Kuti, Gil Scott-Heron, Yellowman, Afrika Bambaataa, Yoko Ono, Public Image Limited, Mick Jagger, Nona Hendryx, James 'Blood' Ulmer and Manu Dibango.

●ALBUMS: *Baselines* (Rough Trade 1984)★★★, with John Zorn *Points Blank/Metlable Snaps* (No Mans Land 1986),★★★ with Peter Brötzmann *Low Life* (1987)★★★, *Hear No Evil* (Venture 1988)★★★, *Outer Dark* (Fax 1994)★★★, with Pete Namlook *Outland* (Fax 1994)★★★, with Klaus Schulze, Pete Namlook *Dark Side Of The Moog IV* (Fax 1996)★★.

●COMPILATIONS: *The Best Of Bill Laswell* (Celluloid 1985)★★★.

LAUPER, CYNDI

b. Cynthia Anne Stephanie Lauper, 22 June 1953, Queens, New York, USA. Starting her career as a singer in Manhattan's clubs, Lauper began writing her own material when she met pianist John Turi in 1977. They formed Blue Angel and released a self-titled album in 1980 which included raucous versions of rock classics as well as their own numbers. She split with Turi and in 1983 began working on what was to become her multi-million-selling solo debut, *She's So Unusual*. It made number 4 in the USA and provided four hit singles - the exuberant 'Girls Just Want To Have Fun', which became a cult anthem for independent young women; 'Time After Time' (a US number 1 and later covered by Miles Davis on *You're Under Arrest* and by the jazz duo Tuck And Patti), 'She Bop' (which broached the unusual subject of female masturbation) and 'All Through The Night' (written by Jules Shear). The album also contained Prince's 'When You Were Mine'. At the end of 1984 *Billboard* magazine placed her first in the Top Female Album Artists and she was awarded a Grammy as Best New Artist.

Her image was one that adapted, for the American market, something of a colourful 'punk' image that would not offend parents too much, but at the same time still retain a sense of humour and rebelliousness that would appeal to youth. Pundits in the UK claimed to have seen through this straight away, yet they acknowledged Lauper's talent nonetheless. *True Colors* did not have the same commercial edge as its predecessor, yet the title track still provided her with an US number 1 and a Top 20 hit in the UK. In 1987, she took a role as a beautician in the poorly received film, *Vibes*. She made a brief return to the charts in 1990 with the single 'I Drove All Night' from *A Night To Remember*. Another lacklustre film appearance in *Off And Running* was not seen in the UK until two years later. Seen in some quarters as little more than a visual and vocal oddity, Lauper has nevertheless written several magnificent pop tunes ('Time After Time' is destined to become a classic) and, in 1985, boosted her credibility as a singer when she performed a stirring duet with Patti LaBelle at LaBelle's show at the Greek Theater in Los Angeles. Lauper was joined by her former writing partners Ron Hyman and Eric Brazilian for *Hat Full Of Stars*, a successful mix of soul/pop/hip hop with a smattering of ethnic/folk.

●ALBUMS: as Blue Angel *Blue Angel* (Polydor 1980)★★★, *She's So Unusual* (Portrait 1984)★★★★, *True Colors* (Portrait 1986)★★★, *A Night To Remember* (Epic 1989)★★, *Hat Full Of Stars* (Epic 1993)★★, *Sisters Of Avalon* (Epic 1997)★★★.

●COMPILATIONS: *12 Deadly Cyns* (Epic 1994)★★★★.

●VIDEOS: *Twelve Deadly Cyns ... And Then Some* (Epic 1994).

LEMONHEADS

From their origins in the Boston, USA hardcore scene, the Lemonheads and their photogenic singer/guitarist Evan Dando (b. Evan Griffith Dando, 4 March 1967, Boston, Massachusetts, USA) have come full circle; from sweaty back-street punk clubs to teen-pop magazines such as *Smash Hits*. The group first formed as the Whelps in 1985, with Jesse Peretz on bass and Dando and Ben Deily sharing guitar and drum duties. Enthused by DJ Curtis W. Casella's radio show, they pestered him into releasing their debut EP, *Laughing All The Way To The Cleaners*, in a pressing of 1000 copies, on his newly activated Taang! label. It featured a cover of Proud Scum's 'I Am A Rabbit', an obscure New Zealand punk disc often aired by the DJ. By January 1987 Dando had recruited the group's first regular drummer Doug Trachten, but he stayed permanent only for their debut album, *Hate Your Friends*, allegedly pressed in over seventy different versions by Taang! with an eye on the collector's market. This was a more balanced effort than the follow-up, which this time boasted the services of Blake Babies drummer John Strohm. *Creator* (reissued in 1996 with extra tracks) revealed Dando's frustration at marrying commercial punk-pop with a darker lyrical perspective, evident in the cover version of Charles Manson's 'Your Home Is Where You're Happy' (the first of several references to the 60s figurehead). The band broke up shortly afterwards, following a disastrous Cambridge, Massachusetts gig where Dando insisted on playing sections of Guns N'Roses' 'Sweet Child O Mine' during every guitar solo. However, the offer of a European tour encouraged him to reunite the band, this time with himself as drummer, adding second guitarist Coorey Loog Brennan (ex-Italian band Superfetazione; Bullet Lavolta). After *Lick* was issued in 1989, Deily, Dando's longtime associate and co-writer, decided to leave to continue his studies. He would subsequently put together his own group, Pods. However, for the second time Dando dissolved the Lemonheads, immediately following their acclaimed major label debut, *Lovey*. Peretz moved to New York to pursue his interests in photography and film, while new recruit David Ryan (b. 20 October 1964, Fort Wayne, Indiana, USA) vacated the drum stool. The new line-up featured Ben Daughtry (bass) and Byron Hoagland (drums, ex-Squirrel Bait). However, the new rhythm section was deemed untenable because Daughtry 'had a beard', so Jesse and David (both Harvard graduates) returned to the fold. The band, for some time hovering on the verge of a commercial breakthrough, finally achieved it by embarking on a series of cover versions; 'Luka' (Suzanne Vega) and 'Different Drum' (Michael Nesmith) were both *Melody Maker* singles of the week. There were also two covers on their *Patience And Prudence* EP; the old 50s chestnut 'Gonna Get Along Without You Now', plus a humorous reading of New Kids On The Block's 'Step By Step' - wherein Evan imitates each of the five vocal parts. Other choices have included Gram Parsons, hardcore legends the Misfits, and even a track from the musical *Hair*. However, the cover to make them cover stars proper was an affectionate reading of Simon And Garfunkel's 'Mrs Robinson'. By 1992 Nic Dalton (b. 6 June 1966, Canberra, Australia; ex-Hummingbirds and several other less famous Antipodeon bands) had stepped in on bass to help out with touring commitments, his place eventually becoming permanent. Dando had met him while he was in Australia, where he discovered Tom Morgan (ex-Sneeze, who had also included Dalton in their ranks), who would co-write several songs for the upcoming *It's A Shame About Ray* set. Dando's 'girlfriend' Juliana Hatfield (bass, ex-Blake Babies) also helped out at various points, notably on 'Bit Part'. She was the subject of 'It's About Time' on the follow-up, *Come On Feel The Lemonheads*, on

which she also sang back-up vocals. Other guests included Belinda Carlisle. The success of *It's A Shame About Ray* offered a double-edged sword: the more pressure increased on Dando to write another hit album, the more he turned to hard drugs. Sessions were delayed as he took time out to repair a badly damaged voice, allegedly caused through smoking crack cocaine. That *Come On Feel The Lemonheads* emerged at the tail-end of 1993 was surprise enough, but to hear Dando's songwriting continue in its purple patch was even more gratifying. *Car Button Cloth* came in the wake of Dando attempting to clean himself up. It was generally well received and contained some of his most mellow (some would say broody) songs to date.

● ALBUMS: *Hate Your Friends* (Taang! 1987)★★, *Creator* (Taang! 1988)★★, *Lick* (Taang! 1989)★★★, *Lovey* (Atlantic 1990)★★, *It's A Shame About Ray* (Atlantic 1992)★★★★, *Come On Feel The Lemonheads* (Atlantic 1993)★★★★, *Car Button Cloth* (Atlantic 1996)★★★.

● VIDEOS: *Two Weeks In Australia* (1993).

● FURTHER READING: *The Illustrated Story*, Everett True. *The Lemonheads*, Mick St. Michael.

LENNON, JULIAN

b. John Charles Julian Lennon, 8 April 1963, Liverpool, England. To embark on a musical career in the same sphere as his late father was a bold and courageous move. The universal fame of John Lennon brought the inevitable comparisons which quickly became more a source of irritation than pride. This awful paradox must have hampered the now low-profile career of a young star who began by releasing a commendable debut album in 1984. At times, Julian's voice uncannily and uncomfortably mirrored that of John's, nevertheless he was soon scaling the pop charts with excellent compositions like 'Valotte' and the reggae-influenced 'Too Late For Goodbyes'. The album was produced by Phil Ramone and showed a healthy mix of styles. Lennon was nominated for a Grammy in 1985 as the Best New Act. Success may have come too soon, and Julian indulged in the usual excesses and was hounded by the press, merely to find out what club he frequented and whom he was dating. *The Secret Value Of Daydreaming* was a poor album of overdone rock themes and was critically ignored. Lennon licked his wounds and returned in 1989 with *Mr. Jordan* and a change of style. The soul/disco 'Now You're In Heaven' was a lively comeback single, and the album showed promise. In 1991 Julian returned to the conventional activities of recording and promotion with the release of a single embracing 'green' issues, 'Salt Water', supported by an imaginative video and a heavy promotion schedule. With his last album Lennon seemed to be making a career on his own terms, rather than those dictated by the memories of his father. However, following the poor sales of his previous album, by 1995 Virgin had released Lennon from his contract, and he had joined a theatrical touring company's production of the play *Mr Holland's Opus* for which he sang the title song. After many years of legal wrangles Lennon received a financial settlement from his father's estate and the executor Yoko Ono. The sum of £20 million was alleged to have been agreed. Lennon was quoted as saying he needs the money to relaunch his rock career.

●ALBUMS: *Valotte* (Virgin 1984)★★★, *The Secret Value Of Daydreaming* (Virgin 1986)★★, *Mr Jordan* (Virgin 1989)★★, *Help Yourself* (Virgin 1991)★★.

LES MISÉRABLES

Opening in Paris in 1980, in the seemingly unlikely setting of a sports arena, *Les Misérables* brought light to the darkness of the European musical theatre. Taking as its improbable text, Victor Hugo's grim novel of one man's determined survival in the face of another's vengeful persecution, *Les Misérables* became a musical jewel. With music by Claude-Michel Schönberg, who also wrote the book with Alain Boublil, and lyrics by Herbert Kretzmer adapted into English from the French text by Boublil and Jean-Marc Natel, the show was originally staged at the Barbican in London on 30 September 1985 by Trevor Nunn and John Caird of the Royal Shakespeare Company. It subsequently transferred to the Palace Theatre and, after initially mixed reviews, settled in for a long run. Set in nineteenth-century France, the show was an impressive drama of political and social comment brimming with stirring music all impressively staged. The dramatic and memorable score included numbers such as 'I Dreamed A Dream', 'On My Own', 'Who Am I?', 'Come To Me', 'Do You Hear The People Sing?', 'Drink With Me To Days Gone By', and the grieving 'Empty Chairs At Empty Tables'. Starring Patti LuPone, Colm Wilkinson and Alun Armstrong, *Les Misérables* became the musical highlight of London's West End and ran on into the 90s as vivid proof that audiences were not deterred by musical shows with depth and that the musical theatre need not depend upon escapism for its continued existence. In January 1994, it overtook *Jesus Christ Superstar*

as the third-longest-running musical (after *Cats* and *Starlight Express*) in the history of the London musical theatre. At that time it was estimated that *Les Misérables* had played to 30 million people in more than 35 cities around the world, and taken £600 million at the box office, including £60 million in London alone. The American production, which opened at the Broadway Theatre in New York on 12 March 1987, soon became one of the hottest tickets in town, and won Tony Awards for best musical, score, book, featured actress (Frances Ruffelle), directors (Nunn and Caird), scenic design (John Napier), costumes (Andreane Neofitou), and lighting (David Hersey).

●VIDEOS: *10th Anniversary Concert* (VCI Columbia 1996), *Les Miserables In Concert* (Video Collection 1996).

●FURTHER READING: *The Complete Book Of Les Misérables*, Edward Behr.

LEVEL 42

Formed in 1980 as an instrumental jazz/funk unit, heavily influenced by the music of Stanley Clarke. The band comprised Mark King (b. 20 October 1958, England; bass/vocals), Phil Gould (b. 28 February 1957, England; drums), Boon Gould (b. 4 March 1955, England; guitar) and Mark Lindup (b. 17 March 1959; keyboards). By the release of their debut single, 'Love Meeting Love', King was urged to add vocals to give the band a more commercial sound. Their Mike Vernon-produced album was an exciting collection of dance and modern soul orientated numbers that made the UK Top 20. Cashing in on this unexpected success, their previous record company issued a limited edition album of early material, which their new record company Polydor Records repackaged the following year. Word had now got round that Level 42 was one of the most exciting new bands of the 80s, the focal point being Mark King's extraordinary bass-slapping/thumb technique, which even impressed the master of the style, Stanley Clarke. Most of their early singles were minor hits until 'The Sun Goes Down (Living It Up)' in 1984 made the UK Top 10. Their worldwide breakthrough came with *World Machine*, a faultless record that pushed their style towards straight, quality pop. King's vocals were mixed up-front and the group entered a new phase in their career as their fans left the dance floor for the football stadiums. This also coincided with a run of high-quality hit singles between 1985 and 1987, notably, 'Something About You', 'Leaving Me Now', 'Lessons In Love', the autobiographical 'Running In The Family' and the immaculate tear-jerker 'It's Over'. Both *Running In The Family* and *Staring At The Sun* were major successes, although the latter had no significant hit singles. At the end of 1987 the band had changed its line-up drastically with only King and Lindup remaining as the nucleus of the group. Jakko Jakszyk joined the band as lead guitarist in 1991 an added a stronger sound to their live performances. Their career had faltered by the mid-90s as both their recording and public activity took a lower profile. Mark King was taking life easy from his base in the Isle Of Wight. Level 42 have done much to bring quality jazz/funk music to the foreground by blending it with catchy pop melodies.

● ALBUMS: *Level 42* (Polydor 1981)★★★, *Strategy* (Elite 1981)★★★, *The Early Tapes: July-August 1980* (Polydor 1981)★★, *The Pursuit Of Accidents* (Polydor 1982)★★★, *Standing In The Light* (Polydor 1983)★★★, *True Colours* (Polydor 1983)★★★, *A Physical Presence* (Polydor 1985)★★, *World Machine* (Polydor 1985)★★★★, *Running In The Family* (Polydor 1987)★★★, *Staring At The Sun* (Polydor 1988)★★, *Guaranteed* (RCA 1991)★★, *Forever Now* (RCA 1994)★★. Solo: Mark King *Influences* (Polydor 1993)★★.

● COMPILATIONS: *Level Best* (Polydor 1989)★★★★, *The Remixes* (1992)★★★.

● VIDEOS: *Live At Wembley* (Channel 5 1987), *Family Of Five* (Channel 5 1988), *Level Best* (Channel 5 1989), *Fait Accompli* (1994).

● FURTHER READING: *Level 42: The Definitive Biography*, Michael Cowton.

LEWIS, HUEY, AND THE NEWS

The group was formed in Marin Country, California, USA, in 1980 by ex-Clover members singer and harmonica player Huey Lewis (b. Hugh Anthony Cregg III, 5 July 1951, New York, USA) and keyboards player Sean Hopper. They recruited guitarist and saxophonist Johnny Colla, Mario Cipollina (bass), Bill Gibson (drums) and Chris Hayes (lead guitar), all fellow performers at a regular jam session at local club Uncle Charlie's. A debut album produced by Bill Schnee was released by Chrysalis Records and a single from it, 'Do You Believe In Love', reached the US Top 10 aided by a tongue-in-cheek video. The band's easy-going rock/soul fusion reached its peak with *Sports*, which provided five US Top 20 hits. Among them were the Chinn And Chapman song 'Heart & Soul', 'The Heart Of Rock & Roll', 'If This Is It' and 'I Want A New Drug'. Lewis sued Ray Parker Jnr. over the latter song, claiming it had been plagiarized for the *Ghostbusters* theme. From 1985-86, three Lewis singles headed the US charts. They were 'The Power Of Love' (chosen as theme tune for Steven Spielberg's film *Back To The Future*), the Hayes-Lewis composition 'Stuck With You' and 'Jacob's Ladder', written by Bruce Hornsby. 'Perfect World' (1988) from the fifth album was also a success although *Hard At Play* did less well. Huey Lewis's status with AOR audiences was underlined when he was chosen to sing the national anthem at the American Bowl in the 80s. Although Lewis has had a much lower profile in the 90s, he did return with a beautiful a cappella version of Curtis Mayfield's 'Its All Right' in June 1993 followed by *Four Chords And Several Years Ago*, a tour through Lewis's musical mentors.

● ALBUMS: *Huey Lewis & The News* (Chrysalis 1980)★★, *Picture This* (Chrysalis 1982)★★★, *Sports* (Chrysalis 1983)★★★, *Fore!* (Chrysalis 1986)★★, *Small World* (Chrysalis 1988)★★, *Hard At Play* (Chrysalis 1991)★★, *Four Chords And Several Years Ago* (Elektra 1994)★★★.

● COMPILATIONS: *The Heart Of Rock & Roll: The Best Of* (Chrysalis 1992)★★★, *Time Flies: The Best Of Huey Lewis And The News* (East West 1996)★★★.

LILLYWHITE, STEVE

b. 1955, England. Lillywhite is a leading contemporary UK record producer, best known for his work with the Pogues and U2. He started out as a tape operator for Phonogram in 1972. After producing the demo tapes which won Ultravox a contract with Island Records, he joined the company as a staff producer. Lillywhite specialized in producing new wave bands such as Eddie And the Hot Rods, Siouxsie And the Banshees (the hit 'Hong Kong Garden'), the Members, Penetration, XTC and the Buzzards before he was approached to supervise Peter Gabriel's third solo album. By the early 80s, Lillywhite was widely recognized as one of the most accomplished of younger producers. Now a freelance Island brought him in to work on U2's debut *Boy*. He also produced the group's next two albums. In addition he worked with artists as varied as singer-songwriter Joan Armatrading, stadium rockers Simple Minds, art-punks Psychedelic Furs and the Rolling Stones (*Dirty Work*, 1987). In 1987, Lillywhite produced contrasting albums by the Pogues and Talking Heads (*Naked*), continuing with the Pogues' follow-up *Peace And Love* (1988) and with David Byrne's solo effort *Rei Momo*. Among Lillywhite's other productions was *Kite* by Kirsty MacColl whom he had married in 1984.

LIMAHL

b. Christopher Hamill, 19 December 1958. Limahl (an anagram of his surname) came to prominence as lead vocalist with Kajagoogoo. His rancorous exit from the group in 1983 was caused partly by guitarist Nick Beggs' increasing control over the outfit's destiny. However, a flamboyant performer and a friend of BBC pop presenter Paul Gambaccini, Limahl was well placed for solo success which began with 'Only For Love' in the UK Top 20. After a relative flop with 1984's 'Too Much Trouble', he touched number four with the film title theme, 'Never Ending Story'. This Giorgio Moroder opus was also Limahl's only US chart entry. Other than *Don't Suppose* flitting briefly into the UK charts, he has since been absent from charts in nearly all territories.
●ALBUMS: *Don't Suppose* (EMI 1984)★★.

LINDENBERG, UDO

b. 17 May 1946, Gronau, Germany. From the 70s' *Lindenberg* to the aiming of his output more directly at the English-speaking market in the late 80s, Lindenberg had sales of over 15 million albums in Germany alone. His early career included a spell as drummer in a local jazz group playing mainstream standards such as 'The Shadow Of Your Smile' which later found a place in his vocal repertoire. 'Lover Man (Where Can You Be)' would be performed with no lyrical alterations, to reflect what he called his 'flexible' sexuality. Further aspects of David Bowie's artistic presentation were noted in Lindenberg's multi-media concerts which featured wrestlers, trampolinists and similar non-musical support acts. Another influence was a less famous friend, Jean-Jacques Kravetz, whom Udo assisted willingly on three 70s albums. His interest in national left-wing politics manifested itself in active membership of the Green party and its peace movement - with compositions like 'Father You Should Have Killed Hitler' and 'They Don't Need Another Fuehrer' expressing concern over the renaissance of Nazism. This was balanced with the pride apparent in 1984's 'Germans' which lauded Goethe, Kafka, Mozart, Schumann and other cultural icons. Though this single - buttressed by a promotional visit - made ripples in Britain, a duet with Leata Galloway ('Gesang'), 'Berlin', the lighter 'Special Train To Pankow' (portraying a prominent East German leader 'as a closet rock 'n' roller') and other worthy singles together made less worldwide impact than his characteristically controversial

appearance, backed by the Panik Orchestra, as his country's representative on Live Aid. Nevertheless, though not neglecting a still huge home following, releases such as 1987's *All Clear!* (which embraced a revival of Steppenwolf's 'Born To Be Wild') demonstrate a continued wooing of a wider audience.
●ALBUMS: *Lindenberg* (1971)★★★, *Daumen Im Wind* (1972)★★★, *Alles Klar Auf Der Andrea Doria* (1973)★★★, *Ball Pompos* (1974)★★★, *Votan Wahnwitz* (1975)★★★, *Das Sind Die Herrn Vom Andern Stern* (1976)★★★, *Galaxo Gang* (1976)★★★, *Sister King Kong* (1977)★★★, *No Panic* (Decca 1977)★★★, *Lindenbergs Rock Revue* (1978)★★, *Droehnland Symphonie* (1978)★★★, *Odyssee* (1979)★★★, *Livehaftig* (1979)★★★, *Der Detektiv* (1979)★★★, *Panische Zeiten* (1980)★★★, *Udopia* (1981)★★★, *Intensivstationen* (1982)★★★, *Keule* (1982)★★★, *Lindstarke 10* (1983)★★★, *Gottewrhammerung* (1984)★★★, *Udo Lindenberg Und Das Panik Orchestra* (Teldec 1985)★★, *Feuerlamnd* (1987)★★★, *All Clear!* aka *Alles Klar!* (Teldec 1987)★★★, *Lieder Statt Briefe* (1988)★★★, *CasaNova* (1988)★★★, *Hermine* (1988)★★★, *Bunte Republik Deutschland* (1989)★★★, *Niemandsland* (1990)★★★, *Ich Will Dich Haben* (1991)★★★, *Gustav* (1991)★★★, *Panik-Panther* (1992).

LINX

One of the leading lights in the brief but high-profile Brit-funk movement of the early 80s (with Light Of The World, its spin-offs Beggar And Co, Imagination and Freeez), Linx were based around the duo of David Grant (b. 8 August, 1956, Kingston, Jamaica, West Indies; vocals) and Sketch Martin (b. 1954, Antigua, West Indies; bass), and completed by Bob Carter (keyboards) and Andy Duncan (drums). Grant came to the UK in the late 50s and grew up in north London. Sketch came over when he was four, and was based in West Ham, east London. They met while working in a hi-fi shop. Grant later opened a record shop with his cousin, and became a junior reporter on a local paper, before working at Island Records' press office. Martin worked for the civil service, a film company, and the Performing Rights Society. They had their debut single, 'You're Lying' released as a private pressing (1000 copies) and sold through a specialist funk shop before Chrysalis Records picked up on it and enabled it to be a hit. They were the first of the Brit Funk bands to make an impression in the USA, when 'You're Lying' made the R&B charts. Further singles included 'Intuition', and 'So This Is Romance'. The video for

'Intuition' featured the late Bertice Reading, while their stage performances harked back to the best traditions of the Glitter Band and Adam And The Ants by employing twin drummers. Grant moved on to a solo career with Chrysalis and had hit duets with Jaki Graham. He moved to Polydor Records in 1987 then Fourth and Broadway in 1990.

●ALBUMS: *Intuition* (Chrysalis 1981)★★★, *Go Ahead* (Chrysalis 1981)★★.

LITTLE SHOP OF HORRORS (STAGE MUSICAL)

After making its debut at the tiny WPA Theatre in New York, *Little Shop Of Horrors* moved to the Orpheum Theatre on the Lower East Side on 27 July 1982. The book, by Howard Ashman, was based on Charles Griffith's screenplay for the 1960 spoof of the horror movie genre, which had become a cult classic. Hardly the usual Broadway - or off-Broadway - fare, the grisly tale tells of Seymour Krelbourn (Lee Wilkof), an assistant at Mushnik's florist shop on Skid Row, who decides to boost sales by producing a strange houseplant. He names it Audrey II, because of his love for sales assistant Audrey (Ellen Greene), and finds that it grows faster if it is fed with a few drops of blood - and subsequently, human flesh. Things rapidly get out of hand as the monster - and the business - thrives, eventually devouring just about everything and everyone in sight. The amusing and imaginative score by Ashman and composer Alan Menken had some 'good rock in the Phil Spector Wall of Sound idiom', and included 'Grow For Me', 'Suddenly Seymour', 'Skid Row', 'Somewhere That's Green', and 'Little Shop Of Horrors'. The show's bizarre humour caught on in a big way, as Audrey II and Little Shop Of Horrors became a sort of phenomenon. It continued to amaze and delight off-Broadway audiences for 2209 performances, and was awarded the New York Drama Critics Circle Award for best musical. The 1984 London production, which ran for over a year, also received the Evening Standard prize for outstanding musical. Ellen Greene reprised her role in London, and for the 1986 film version which also starred Rick Moranis, Vincent Gardenia and Steve Martin. In 1994, a 'gorgeously funny' revival toured the UK starring Sue Pollard, better know for her role as Peggy, the zany chalet maid in the popular television comedy series *Hi-Di-Hi*.

LIVE AID

Millions saw the 1984 BBC Television news report narrated by Michael Buerk, showing the appalling famine in Ethiopia. Bob Geldof was so moved that he organized, promoted and produced a fund-raising enterprise like the world had never seen before. Geldof's likeable bullying and eloquently cheeky publicity endeared him to millions. The song 'Do They Know It's Christmas?', co-written with Midge Ure, assembled a cavalcade of rock and pop stars under the name Band Aid. It included members from: Status Quo, Culture Club, Bananarama, Style Council, Duran Duran, Spandau Ballet, Heaven 17 and U2. Solo stars included Phil Collins, Sting, George Michael, and Paul Young. Geldof brilliantly bludgeoned artists, record companies, pressing plants, distributors and record shops to forego their profit. The record scaled the UK charts and stayed on top for 5 weeks, eventually selling millions of copies. Geldof topped this masterstroke in July 1985 by organizing Live Aid. This spectacular rock and pop concert was televised worldwide, live from London and Philadelphia. Among the stellar cast were: Sade, Queen, Bob Dylan, Neil Young, the Cars, Beach Boys, Pat Metheny, Santana, Madonna, Kenny Loggins, Bryan Adams, Crosby, Stills And Nash, Eric Clapton, Phil Collins (who via Concorde appeared at both venues), Judas Priest, REO Speedwagon, Jimmy Page, Robert Plant, Status Quo, Elvis Costello, Bryan Ferry, Sting, Paul Young, Adam Ant, Simple Minds, U2, the Who, Paul McCartney, Mick Jagger, Tina Turner, Elton John, Spandau Ballet and David Bowie. The event had the largest television viewing figure of all time and raised over £50 million through pledged donations. Geldof carried through his sincere wish to help starving children with integrity, passion and a sense of humour. The Live Aid concert remains one of the greatest musical events of alltime.

●FURTHER READING: *Live Aid: The Greatest Show On Earth*, Peter Hillmore.

LIVING COLOUR

This US rock band was originally formed by Vernon Reid (b. 22 August 1958, London, England; guitar), Muzz Skillings (bass) and William Calhoun (b. 22 July 1964, Brooklyn, New York, USA; drums). Reid had studied performing arts at Manhattan Community College, having moved to New York at the age of two. His first forays were in experimental electric jazz with Defunk, before he formed Living Colour as a trio in 1984. Both Skillings and Calhoun were experienced academic musicians, having studied and received acclaim at City College and Berklee College Of Music, respectively. The line-up was completed by the induction of vocalist Corey Glover (b. 6 November 1964, Brooklyn, New York, USA), who had just finished his part in Oliver Stone's *Platoon* movie, and whom Reid had originally encountered at a friend's birthday party. Their first major engagement came when Mick Jagger saw them performing at CBGB's and invited them to the studio for his forthcoming solo album. Jagger's patronage continued as he produced two demos for the band, which would secure them a contract with Epic Records. Their debut, *Vivid*, earned them early critical favour and rose to number 6 in the US charts. Fusing disparate black musical formats like jazz, blues and soul, alongside commercial hard rock, its diversity was reflected in the support slots the band acquired to promote it, Cheap Trick, Robert Palmer and Billy Bragg among them. Musically, the band is aligned primarily to the first-named of that trio of acts, although their political edge more closely mirrors the concerns of Bragg.

In 1985 Reid formed the *Black Rock Coalition* pressure movement alongside journalist Greg Tate, and Living Colour grew to be perceived as their nation's most articulate black rock band. Two subsequent singles, 'Cult Of Personality' (which included samples of John F. Kennedy and won a Grammy award) and 'Open Letter (To A Landlord)' were both provocative but intelligent expressions of urban concerns. The ties with the Rolling Stones remained strong, with Reid collaborating on Keith Richards' solo album. They also joined the Stones on their *Steel Wheels* tour. After sweeping the boards in several Best New Band awards in such magazines as *Rolling Stone*, *Time's Up* was released in 1990, and afforded another Grammy Award. Notable contributions, apart from the omnipresent Jagger, included Little Richard on the controversial 'Elvis Is Dead'. In 1991 worldwide touring established them as a highly potent force in the mainstream of rock. Following Skillings' departure bassist Doug Wimbish (b. 22 September 1956, Hartford, Connecticut, USA) from Tackhead joined them for *Stain* which added a sprinkling of studio gimmickry on a number of tracks. The band announced its dissolution early in 1995. Vernon Reid issued a statement thus: '. . . Living Colour's sense of unity and purpose was growing weaker and fuzzier, I was finding more and more creative satisfaction in my solo projects. Finally it became obvious that I had to give up the band and move on'. An excellent retrospective, *Pride*, was released following their demise. Vernon Reid made an impressive solo debut in 1996.

●ALBUMS: *Vivid* (Epic 1988)★★★★, *Time's Up* (Epic 1990)★★★★, *Stain* (Epic 1993)★★★, *Dread* Japanese live release (Epic 1993)★★★.
●COMPILATIONS: *Pride* (Epic 1995)★★★★.

LIVING IN A BOX

This Sheffield, UK-based pop group comprised Richard Darbyshire (b. 8 March 1960, Stockport, Cheshire, England; vocal/guitar), Marcus Vere (b. 29 January 1962; keyboards) and Anthony Critchlow (drums). Their first single, the self-referential, 'Living In A Box' was a UK Top 10 hit in the spring of 1987 and further successes followed over the next two years, most notably, 'Blow The House Down' and 'Room In Your Heart'. Meanwhile, vocalist Richard Darbyshire guested on Jellybean's *Jellybean Rocks The House*. Having enjoyed a hit album with their self-titled debut, the group consolidated their success with *Gatecrashing*. However, the group sundered in 1990 as their chart fortunes declined. Darbyshire subsequently launched a solo career with Virgin Records.
●ALBUMS: *Living In A Box* (Chrysalis 1987)★★★, *Gatecrashing* (Chrysalis 1989)★★★.

LL COOL J

b. James Todd Smith, 16 August 1969, St. Albans, Queens, New York, USA. Long-running star of the rap scene, LL Cool J found fame at the age of 16, his pseudonym standing for 'Ladies Love Cool James'. As might be inferred by this, LL is a self-professed ladykiller in the vein of Luther Vandross or Barry White, yet he retains a superior rapping agility. Smith started rapping at the age of nine, after his grandfather bought him his first DJ equipment. From the age of 13 he was processing his first demos. The first to respond to his mail-outs was Rick Rubin of Def Jam Records, then a senior at New York University, who signed him to his fledgling label. The first sighting of LL Cool J came in 1984 on a 12-inch, 'I Need A Beat', which was the label's first such release. However, it was 'I Just Can't Live Without My Radio', which established his gold-chained, bare-chested B-boy persona. The song was featured in the *Krush Groove* film, on which the rapper also performed. In its wake he embarked on a 50 city US tour alongside the Fat Boys, Whodini, Grandmaster Flash and Run DMC. The latter were crucial to LL Cool J's development: his *modus operandi* was to combine their beatbox cruise control with streetwise B-boy raps, instantly making him a hero to a new generation of black youth. As well as continuing to tour with the trio, he would also contribute a song, 'Can You Rock It Like This', to Run DMC's *King Of Rock*. His debut album too, would see Rubin dose the grooves with heavy metal guitar breaks first introduced by Run DMC. LL Cool J's other early singles included 'I'm Bad', 'Go Cut Creator Go', 'Jack The Ripper' and 'I Need Love' (the first ballad rap, recorded with the Los Angeles Posse), which brought him UK Top 10 success. Subsequent releases offered a fine array of machismo funk-rap, textured with personable charm and humour. Like many of his brethren, LL Cool J's career has not been without incident. Live appearances in particular have been beset by many problems. Three people were shot at a date in Baltimore in December 1985, followed by an accusation of 'public lewdness' after a 1987 show in Columbus, Ohio. While playing rap's first concert in Cote d'Ivoire, Africa, fights broke out and the stage was stormed. Most serious, however, was an incident in 1989 when singer David Parker, body-guard Christopher Tsipouras and technician Gary Saunders were accused of raping a 15-year-old girl who attended a backstage party after winning a radio competition in Minneapolis. Though LL Cool J's personal involvement in all these cases was incidental, they undoubtedly have tarnished his reputation. He has done much to make amends, including appearances at benefits including Farm Aid, recording with the Peace Choir, and launching his *Cool School Video Program*, in an attempt to encourage children to stay at school. Even Nancy Reagan invited him to headline a 'Just Say No' concert at Radio City Music Hall. Musically, Cool is probably best sampled on his 1990 set, *Mama Said Knock You Out*, produced by the omnipresent Marley Marl, which as well as the familiar sexual braggadocio included his thoughts on the state of rap past, present and future. The album went triple platinum, though the follow-up, *14 Shots To The Dome*, was a less effective attempt to recycle the formula. Some tracks stood out: 'A Little Something', anchored by a sample of King Floyd's soul standard 'Groove Me', being a good example. Like many of rap's senior players, he has also sustained an acting career, with film appearances in *The Hard Way* and *Toys*, playing a cop in the former and a military man in the latter.

●ALBUMS: *Radio* (Columbia 1985)★★★, *Bigger And Deffer* (Def Jam 1987)★★, *Walking With A Panther* (Def Jam 1989)★★★, *Mama Said Knock You Out* (Def Jam 1990)★★★★, *14 Shots To The Dome* (Def Jam 1993)★★★, *Mr. Smith* (Def Jam 1995)★★★.

●COMPILATIONS: *Greatest Hits All World* (Def Jam 1996)★★★.

LLOYD WEBBER, ANDREW

b. 22 March 1948, London, England. The 'Sir Arthur Sullivan' of the rock age was born the son of a Royal College of Music professor and a piano teacher. His inbred musical strength manifested itself in a command of piano, violin and French horn by the time he had spent a year at Magdalen College, Oxford, where he penned *The Likes Of Us* with lyricist (and law student) Tim Rice. As well as his liking for such modern composers as Hindemith, Ligeti and Penderecki, this first musical also revealed a captivation with pop music that surfaced even more when he and Rice collaborated in 1967 on *Joseph And The Amazing Technicolor Dreamcoat*, a liberal adaptation of the scriptures. Mixing elements of psychedelia, country and French *chanson*, it was first performed at a London school in 1968 before reaching a more adult audience, via fringe events, the West End theatre (starring Paul Jones, Jess Conrad and Maynard Williams), an album, and, in 1972, national television.

In the early 70s, Lloyd Webber strayed from the stage, writing the music scores for two British films, *Gumshoe* and *The Odessa File*. His next major project with Rice was the audacious *Jesus Christ Superstar* which provoked much protest from religious groups. Among the studio cast were guest vocalists Michael D'Abo, Yvonne Elliman, Ian Gillan and Paul Raven (later Gary Glitter), accompanied by a symphony orchestra under the baton of André Previn - as well as members of Quatermass and the Grease Band. Issued well before its New York opening in 1971, the tunes were already familiar to an audience that took to their seats night after night as the show ran for 711 performances. A less than successful film version was released in 1976.

After the failure of *Jeeves* in 1975 (with Alan Ayckbourn replacing Rice) Lloyd Webber returned to form with *Evita*, an approximate musical biography of Eva Peron, self-styled 'political leader' of Argentina. It was preceded by high chart placings for its album's much-covered singles, most notably Julie Covington's 'Don't Cry For Me Argentina' and 'Oh! What A Circus' from David Essex. *Evita* was still on Broadway in 1981 when *Cats*, based on T.S. Eliot's *Old Possum's Book Of Practical Cats*, emerged as Lloyd Webber's most commercially satisfying work so far. It was also the composer's second musical without Rice, and included what is arguably his best-known song, 'Memory', with words by Eliot and the show's director, Trevor

Nunn. Elaine Paige, previously the star of *Evita*, and substituting for the injured Judi Dench in the feline role of Grizabella, took the song into the UK Top 10. Subsequently, it became popular for Barbra Streisand, amongst others. With *Song And Dance* (1982), which consisted of an earlier piece, *Tell Me On Sunday* (lyrics by Don Black), and *Variations* composed on a theme by Paganini for his cellist brother, Julian, Lloyd Webber became the only theatrical composer to have three works performed simultaneously in both the West End and Broadway. Two items from *Song And Dance*, 'Take That Look Off Your Face' and 'Tell Me On Sunday' became hit singles for one of its stars, Marti Webb. Produced by Cameron Mackintosh and Lloyd Webber's Really Useful Company, it was joined two years later by *Starlight Express* (lyrics by Richard Stilgoe), a train epic with music which was nicknamed 'Squeals On Wheels' because the cast dashed around on roller skates pretending to be locomotives. Diversifying further into production, Lloyd Webber presented the 1983 comedy *Daisy Pulls It Off*, followed by *The Hired Man*, *Lend Me A Tenor* and Richard Rodgers and Lorenz Hart's *On Your Toes* at London's Palace Theatre - of which he had become the new owner.

Like Sullivan before him, Lloyd Webber indulged more personal if lucrative artistic whims in such as *Requiem*, written for his father, which, along with *Variations*, became a best-selling album. A later set, *Premiere Collection*, went triple platinum. A spin-off from *Requiem*, 'Pie Jesu' (1985), was a hit single for Paul Miles-Kington and Sarah Brightman, the composer's second wife. She made the UK Top 10 again in the following year, with two numbers from Lloyd Webber's *The Phantom Of The Opera* (adapted from the Gaston Leroux novel), duetting with Steve Harley on the title theme, and later with Cliff Richard on 'All I Ask Of You'. The original 'Phantom', Michael Crawford, had great success with his recording of another song hit from the show, 'The Music Of The Night'. Controversy followed, with Lloyd Webber's battle to ensure that Brightman recreated her role of Christine in the Broadway production in 1988. His US investors capitulated, reasoning that future Lloyd Webber creations were guaranteed box office smashes before their very conception. Ironically, *Aspects Of Love* (lyrics by Charles Hart and Don Black), which also starred Brightman (by now Lloyd Webber's ex-wife), was rated as one of the failures (it did not recoup its investment) of the 1990/1 Broadway season, although it eventually ran for over 300 performances. In London, the show, which closed in 1992 after a three-year run, launched the career of Michael Ball, who had a UK number 2 with its big number, 'Love Changes Everything'. In April 1992, Lloyd Webber intervened in the Tate Gallery's attempt to purchase a Canaletto painting. Anxious, that it should remain in Britain, he bought the picture for £10 million. He was reported to have commented: 'I'll have to write another musical before I do this again'. That turned out to be *Sunset Boulevard*, a stage adaptation of Billy Wilder's 1950 Hollywood classic, with Lloyd Webber's music, and book and lyrics by Don Black and Christopher Hampton. It opened in London on 12 July 1993 with Patti LuPone in the leading role of Norma Desmond, and had its American premiere in Los Angeles five months later, where Desmond was played by Glenn Close. Legal wrangles ensued when Lloyd Webber chose Close to star in the 1994 Broadway production instead of LuPone (the latter is said to have received 'somewhere in the region of $1 million compensation'), and there was further controversy when he closed down the Los Angeles production after having reservations about the vocal talents of its prospective new star, Faye Dunaway. She too, is said to have received a 'substantial settlement'. Meanwhile, *Sunset Boulevard* opened at the Minskoff Theatre in New York on November 17 with a record box office advance of $37.5 million. Like *Cats* and *The Phantom Of The Opera* before it, the show won several Tony Awards, including best musical, score and book. Lloyd Webber was living up to his rating as the most powerful person in the American theatre in a list compiled by *TheaterWeek* magazine. His knighthood in 1992 was awarded for services to the theatre, not only in the USA and UK, but throughout the world - at any one time there are dozens of his productions touring, and resident in main cities. Among his other show/song honours have been Drama Desk, Grammy, Laurence Olivier, and Ivor Novello Awards. *Cats*, together with *Starlight Express* and *Jesus Christ Superstar*, gave Lloyd Webber the three longest-running musicals in British theatre history for a time, before the latter show was overtaken by *Les Misérables*. He is also the first person to have a trio of musicals running in London and New York. *Jesus Christ Superstar* celebrated its 20th anniversary in 1992 with a UK concert tour, and other Lloyd Webber highlights of just that one year included a series of concerts entitled *The Music Of Andrew Lloyd Webber* (special guest star Michael Crawford), a smash hit revival of *Joseph And The Amazing Technicolor Dreamcoat* at the London Palladium, and the recording, by Sarah

Brightman and José Carreras, of Lloyd Webber and Don Black's Barcelona Olympic Games anthem 'Friends For Life' ('Amigos Para Siempre').

Since those heady days, Lloyd Webber admirers have waited in vain for another successful theatrical project, although there has been no shortage of personal kudos. He was inducted into the Songwriters Hall of Fame, presented with the Praemium Imperiale Award for Music, became the first recipient of the ASCAP Triple Play Award, and in 1996 received the Richard Rodgers Award for Excellence in the Musical Theatre. In the same year a revised version of his 1975 flop, *Jeeves*, entitled *By Jeeves*, was well received during its extended West End season, but a new work, *Whistle Down The Wind* (lyrics: Jim Steinman, book: Patricia Knop), failed to transfer to Broadway following its Washington premiere. A revival of *Jesus Christ Superstar* re-opened the old Lyceum, just off the Strand, and a film version of *Evita*, starring Madonna, was finally released, containing a new Lloyd Webber-Rice song, 'You Must Love Me', for which they won Academy Awards. Elevated to the peerage in 1997, Baron Lloyd-Webber of Sydmonton disclosed that the New York and London productions of *Sunset Boulevard*, which both closed early in that year, 'lost money massively overall', and that his Really Useful Group had reduced its staff and suffered substantial financial setbacks. On the brighter side, in January 1996 the West End production of his most enduring show, *Cats*, took over from *A Chorus Line* as the longest-running musical of all time, and in June 1997, the show's New York production replaced *A Chorus Line* as the longest-running show (musical or play) in Broadway history.

●COMPILATIONS: *The Very Best Of … Broadway Collection* (Polydor 1996)★★★.

●VIDEOS: *The Premier Collection Encore* (1994).

●FURTHER READING: *Andrew Lloyd Webber*, G. McKnight. *Fanfare: The Unauthorized Biography Of Andrew Lloyd Webber*, J. Mantle. *Andrew Lloyd Webber: His Life And Works*, M. Walsh.

LOGGINS, KENNY

b. 7 January 1948, Everett, Washington, USA. Loggins came to prominence as a member of Loggins And Messina from 1972-77. After separating from Messina, he set out on a solo recording career, specializing in rock ballads such as 'Whenever I Call You Friend', a 1978 Top 10 hit in the US which was co-written by Melissa Manchester and had harmony vocals by Stevie Nicks. There was subsequent success with 'This Is

It' and Loggins co-wrote with Michael McDonald 'What A Fool Believes', a million-seller and a US number 1 for the Doobie Brothers. Don't Fight It' (1982) was a collaboration with Journey singer Steve Ferry. During the 80s, Loggins came to prominence as a writer and performer of theme songs for the new breed of Hollywood action movies. Beginning with 'I'm Alright' (from *Caddyshack*, 1980) and the chart-topping title song from *Footloose* (1984), he reached his peak with the soundtrack of *Top Gun* (1986). As well as co-writing several of the songs used in the film, Loggins recorded the best-selling 'Danger Zone'. This was followed by music for *Caddyshack II*, including another hit single, 'Nobody's Fool'. He had a minor hit with 'Convictions Of The Heart' in 1991.

●ALBUMS: *Celebrate Me Home* (Columbia 1977)★★★, *Nightwatch* (Columbia 1978)★★★, *Keep The Fire* (Columbia 1979)★★★, *Alive* (Columbia 1980)★★★, *High Adventure* (Columbia 1982)★★★, *Footloose* (1984)★★, *Vox Humana* (Columbia 1985)★★, *Top Gun* (1986)★★, *Back To Avalon* (Columbia 1988)★★, *Leap Of Faith* (Columbia 1991)★★, *Outside From The Redwoods - An Acoustic Afternoon* (Columbia 1993)★★★.

●COMPILATIONS: *At His Best* (Hollywood 1992)★★★, *Yesterday, Today, Tomorrow: The Greatest Hits Of Kenny Loggins* (Columbia 1997)★★★.

●VIDEOS: *Return To Pooh Corner* (Sony Wonder 1996).

●FILMS: *Footloose* (1984).

LONDONBEAT

This group featured a white English guitarist and three black American singers. Their line-up comprises Jimmy Chambers (b. 20 January 1946), Jimmy Helms (b. Florida, USA) and George Chandler (b. Atlanta, Georgia, USA), plus Willy M, (b. William Henshall, London, England). Helms was best known for his UK Top 10 hit in 1973 with 'Gonna Make You An Offer You Can't Refuse'. He released several other singles at the time, including 'Jack Horner's Holiday'. Chandler was in 60s soul group the Four Kents who were American but based in northern Italy as servicemen. He too had released solo singles in the 70s. They came together and settled in London where they signed to David A. Stewart's AnXious label. Much of their material was close to a cappella though they used session musicians when necessary. Their debut '9am (The Comfort Zone)' was a strong piece, and it reached the UK number 21 spot in 1988. It was 1990's 'I've Been Thinking About You' that gave the

band their biggest hit, rising to number 2. They also appeared with BBC Radio 1 disc jockeys Liz Kershaw and Bruno Brooks on the Christmas 1989 charity record 'It Takes Two Baby', which was a minor hit in the UK.
●ALBUMS: *Speak* (AnXious 1987)★★★, *In The Blood* (AnXious 1990)★★★, *Harmony* (1992)★★★.

LONE JUSTICE

This group of US country-rockers were fronted by Maria McKee (b. 17 August 1964, Los Angeles, California, USA) who is the half-sister of Love's Bryan Maclean. When she was just three years old her brother would take her to the various clubs along Los Angeles' Sunset Strip and she was befriended by the likes of Frank Zappa and the Doors. When she grew up, she and MacLean formed a duo initially called the Maria McKee Band, but later changed to the Bryan MacLean Band to cash in on *his* slightly higher profile. Heavily immersed in country music, McKee formed the first incarnation of Lone Justice with Ryan Hedgecock (guitar), Don Heffington (drums), Marvin Etzioni (bass) and Benmont Tench (keyboards, ex-Tom Petty And The Heartbreakers). The group were signed to the Geffen label at the recommendation of Linda Ronstadt. McKee's talents were also admired by artists such as Bob Dylan, U2's Bono, who offered them a support slot on tour, and Tom Petty, who donated songs to the first album. One of these, 'Ways To Be Wicked', while not achieving any notable chart status, was responsible for bringing the group to the attention of the UK audience via an imaginative black-and-white, cut-up-and-scratched video. The band's more established line-up transmuted to that of ex-patriot Brit Shayne Fontayne (guitar), Bruce Brody (keyboards, ex-Patti Smith; John Cale), Greg Sutton (bass) and Rudy Richardson (drums). They were managed by the respected producer, Jimmy Iovine. In 1985, former Undertones singer Feargal Sharkey scored a UK number 1 hit with McKee's 'A Good Heart'. Lone Justice split suddenly in 1987 with McKee going on to a solo career, taking only Brody with her from the remnants of Lone Justice.
●ALBUMS: *Lone Justice* (Geffen 1985)★★★, *Shelter* (Geffen 1987)★★, *Radio One Live In Concert* rec. 1986 (Windsong 1993)★★.

LONG RYDERS

Formed in November 1981, the Long Riders (as they were then known), initially included three ex-members of the Unclaimed - Sid Griffin (guitar/vocals), Barry Shank (bass/vocals) and Matt Roberts (drums). Steve Wynn completed this early line-up, but the guitarist was replaced by Stephen McCarthy on leaving to form the Dream Syndicate. Griffin and McCarthy remained at the helm throughout the group's turbulent history. As part of Los Angeles' 'paisley underground' movement, the Long Ryders' history is linked with, not only that of the Dream Syndicate, but also that of other guitar-orientated bands such as Rain Parade, (early) Bangles, Green On Red and Blood On The Saddle. A mini-album, *The Long Ryders*, was completed with Des Brewer (bass) and Greg Sowders (drums), although by the time the quartet secured a permanent deal, Tom Stevens had joined in place of Brewer. *Native Sons*, an excellent set influenced by Buffalo Springfield and Gram Parsons, suggested a promising future, but the Long Ryders were unable to repeat its balance of melody and purpose. They withered on record company indecision and, unable to secure a release from their contract, the group broke up in 1987. Griffin moved on to a dual career leading the Coal Porters and working as a music journalist.
●ALBUMS: *The Long Ryders* mini-album (1983)★★★, *Native Sons* (Zippo 1984)★★★★, *State Of Our Union* (Island 1985)★★★, *Two-Fisted Tales* (Island 1987)★★, *10-5-60* (Demon 1987)★★★, *BBC Radio One In Concert* (Windsong 1994)★★★.
●COMPILATIONS: *Metallic B.O.* early recordings (Overground 1989)★★.

LORDS OF THE NEW CHURCH

This rock band was made up of several well-known personalities, and often described as a punk 'supergroup'. The personnel was; Brian James (b. 18 February 1961; guitar, ex-Damned), Stiv Bators (b. 22 October 1956, Cleveland, Ohio, USA; vocals, ex-Dead Boys; Wanderers), Dave Treganna (b. 1954, Derby, England; bass, ex-Sham 69; Wanderers) and drummer Nicky Turner (b. 4 May 1959; ex-Barracudas). When Jimmy Pursey left Sham 69, the rest of the band had continued in the Wanderers, drafting in Stiv Bators. It was at this point that James contacted Bators with the view to setting up a group. Miles Copeland took on their management, their name coming from his original suggestion, Lords Of Discipline. They made their live debut in Paris in 1981. Their debut vinyl, 'New Church', helped to increase criticisms about the band's apparent blasphemy, hardly dispelled when the album appeared with lines like: 'Greed and murder is forgiven when in the name of the Church'. The self-titled debut premiered an authentic rock band with dark shades, flirting with apocalyptic and religious imagery. The single, 'Dance With Me', from *Is Nothing Sacred*, gained several MTV plays with a video directed by Derek Jarman. Unfortunately its success was scuppered after mistaken allegations about paedophilia saw it taken off air. Their final studio album, *Method To Our Madness*, revealed a band treading water with stifled heavy rock routines. They did not split officially until 1989, but before that Treganna had departed for Cherry Bombz, while Alistair Ward contributed some second guitar.

● ALBUMS: *Lords Of The New Church* (IRS 1982)★★, *Is Nothing Sacred* (IRS 1983)★★★, *Method To Our Madness* (IRS 1984)★★, *Live At The Spit* rec. 1982 (Illegal 1988)★★.
● COMPILATIONS: *Killer Lords* (IRS 1985)★★★.
● VIDEOS: *Holy War* (JE 1994).

LORI AND THE CHAMELEONS

Formed in 1979 in Liverpool, England, the group was a vehicle for the evocative teenage singer Lori Larty. With backing, production and songwriting provided by former Big In Japan alumni David Balfe and Bill Drummond, Lori emerged with an appealing, almost spoken-word tribute to Japan (the country), entitled 'Touch'. A sparkling arrangement, the disc entered the bottom of the UK charts and appeared to signal the emergence of a new talent. The concept of the group appeared to revolve vaguely around exotic, travelogue pop with each song title set in a specific geographical location: Japan, Peru, Russia and the Ganges River in India. The second single, 'The Lonely Spy', boasted another impressive, atmospheric vocal from Lori and an astonishing backing which emulated the bombastic scores associated with *James Bond* films. After four superb tracks, which represented some of the best UK pop of the period, the group ceased operating. The journeyman Troy Tate reappeared in the Teardrop Explodes, while Drummond turned to management and was later the brains behind a series of pseudonymous groups including the Justified Ancients Of Mu Mu (JAMS) and the Timelords who later emerged as the very successful KLF. Lori spurned imminent pop success by returning to art college and effectively retiring from the music business. Her fleeting career provided as much mystery and instant appeal as the extraordinary discs on which she appeared.

LOS LOBOS

This group were leaders of the Tex-Mex brand of rock 'n' roll, which is Latin-based Chicano music built around accordion and guitar. They were formed in 1974 in Los Angeles by Cesar Rosas (b. 1954, Los Angeles, California, USA; vocals/guitar/mandolin), David Hidalgo (b. c.1954, Los Angeles, California, USA; vocals/guitar/accordion), Luis (Louie) Perez (b. c.1953, Los Angeles, California, USA; drums/guitar/quinto), Conrad Lozano (b. c.1952, Los Angeles, California, USA; vocals/bass/guitarron) and Steve Berlin (b. c.1957, Philadelphia, Pennsylvania USA). Their mixture of Clifton Chenier zydeco and Richie Valens rock was a totally refreshing new sound. Their debut album came in 1978 with the self-financed *Just Another Band From East LA*, and although not a hit it was a critical success. The reviewers welcomed their second *How Will The Wolf Survive?* with open arms, but still it only made moderate sales. The superb title track vocal has an uncanny resemblance to Steve Winwood. The band continued to receive excellent reviews of their stage act, but it was not until 1987 that they found commercial success. Following their major contribution to the film soundtrack *La Bamba* the title single was released. It became an international number 1 and the first song in Spanish to top the pop charts. *La Pistola Y El Corazon* was a deliberate attempt to go back to their roots following their recent overwhelming profile. *Kiko* in 1992 was an excellent record, moving them back to a varied rock approach with delightful hints of cajun, straight rock and even soul music. *Colossal Head* in 1996 featured ex-Attractions drummer Pete Thomas

● ALBUMS: *Si Se Puede!* (Pan American 1976)★★★, *Just Another Band From East LA* (New Vista 1978)★★★, *. . . And A Time To Dance* (Slash 1983)★★★, *How Will The Wolf Survive?* (Slash 1984)★★★★, *By The Light Of The Moon* (Slash 1987)★★★★, *La Bamba* (Slash 1987)★★★, *La Pistola Y El Corazon* (Slash 1988)★★★, *The Neighbourhood* (Slash 1990)★★★★, *Kiko* (Slash 1992)★★★★, *Papa's Dream* (Warners 1995)★★★, *Colossal Head* (Warners 1996)★★★.
● COMPILATIONS: *Just Another Band From East L.A: A Collection* (Warners 1993)★★★★.

LOTUS EATERS

Rising from the ashes of the Wild Swans, Liverpool's Lotus Eaters enjoyed instant commercial success with a fragrant pop song, 'The First Picture Of You', their debut single from June 1983. Revolving around Peter Coyle (vocals) and Jeremy Kelly (guitar), plus Alan Wills (drums), Gerard Quinn (keyboards) and Phil (bass), the rhythm section was later replaced by Michael Dempsey (bass) and Steve Creese (drums). However, the band never managed to repeat their Top 20 status, despite four catchy follow-ups; 'You Don't Need Someone New' later in 1983, 'Set Me Apart' and 'Out On Your Own' (both 1984) and a final stab, 'It Hurts' (1985). Those who appreciate well-crafted, melodic pop should look no further than their only album, *No Sense Of Sin*, from 1984. Coyle and Kelly later reactivated the Wild Swans but were again unable to sustain significant interest.

●ALBUMS: *No Sense Of Sin* (Sylvan 1984)★★★.

LOVE AND ROCKETS

This *avant garde* UK rock band formed in Christmas 1985 from the ashes of Bauhaus. When David Jay (aka David J) had finished working with the Jazz Butcher on the *Sex And Travel* and *A Scandal In Bohemia* albums, he linked up once more with old colleague Daniel Ash, who had been working with Tones On Tail. Kevin Haskins also came with Ash, forming the band's nucleus of David Jay (vocals, bass, keyboards), Daniel Ash (vocals, guitar, keyboards) and Haskins (drums, keyboards). Early singles included 'Kundiluni Express', concerning Tuntric meditation, and a cover of the Temptations' 'Ball Of Confusion'. The band's debut, *Seventh Dream Of Teenage Heaven*, was a celebration of the rituals of youth, based loosely on their own experiences of going to rock concerts to see bands like Roxy Music. Like all of the post-Bauhaus projects, the band have failed to cultivate a UK audience to rival their previous standing. However, they enjoyed a big hit single in the USA with 'So Alive', where their work still sells moderately well.

●ALBUMS: *Seventh Dream Of Teenage Heaven* (Beggars Banquet 1986)★★, *Express* (Beggars Banquet 1986)★★★, *Earth Sun Moon* (Beggars Banquet 1987)★★★, *Love And Rockets* (Beggars Banquet 1989)★★★, *Hot Trip To Heaven* (American 1994)★★★, *Sweet F.A.* (Beggars Banquet 1996)★★★.

LOVERBOY

Loverboy were formed in Toronto, Canada, in 1980, by Mike Reno (vocals), Paul Dean (guitar), Doug Johnston (keyboards), Scott Smith (bass) and Matthew Frenette (drums). Reno was formerly with Moxy, and Dean and Frenette had been members of Sweetheart, a melodic AOR/heavy rock band. With this pedigree Loverboy were signed by CBS Records as soon as they were formed. Producer Bruce Fairbairn helped them record a self-titled album that was to set Loverboy's standard for years to come. It was an American-styled melodic hard rock collection that also dipped into reggae and jazz moods. With the hit singles 'Turn Me Loose' and 'The Kid Is Hot Tonite', *Loverboy* went platinum. After touring the group re-entered the studio in 1981, with Fairbairn again producing, to record the follow-up, *Get Lucky*. The album lived up to its name by selling over two million copies, helped by the singles chart progress of 'Working For The Weekend'. The only territory where the band had failed to take off was Europe.

After further touring Fairbairn produced the multi-platinum *Keep It Up* in 1983, from which 'Hot Girls In Love' charted. Loverboy's inviting blend of melodic AOR had now been honed to a fine art, the album's success keeping the band on the road for nearly two years. On *Lovin' Every Minute Of It* they were joined by Tom Allom, best known for his work with Judas Priest. The result was a musically tougher album that proved to be the band's least successful, though it still sold well over a million copies. The title track, released as a single, was written by Def Leppard producer, Robert John 'Mutt' Lange. Fairbairn had by now made his name as the producer of Bon Jovi, but returned to the helm for Loverboy's *Wildside*, released in 1987, and their most complete album to date. Bryan Adams, Richie Sambora and Jon Bon Jovi all co-wrote various tracks. 'Notorious' also proved the band's most successful single, achieving platinum status three times over. This was followed by a marathon two-year tour, their longest yet. They did, however, take a break for two months to record tracks with producer Bob Rock before they came over to support Def Leppard on their European tour in the spring of 1988. After this, Loverboy returned home to Canada and an uncertain future. Dean and Reno announced plans to record solo and this left the rest of the band in limbo. In 1989 a compilation album was released by Columbia, *Big Ones*, which also contained three new tracks that had been recorded with Bob Rock. Later that year Dean released a solo effort assisted by Loverboy drummer Frenette and Jon Bon Jovi on harmonica. The parent band, meanwhile, remained inactive.

●ALBUMS: *Loverboy* (Columbia 1980)★★★, *Get Lucky* (Columbia 1981)★★★, *Keep It Up* (Columbia 1983)★★★, *Lovin' Every Minute Of It* (Columbia 1985)★★★, *Wildside* (Columbia 1987)★★★. Solo: Paul Dean *Hard Core* (Columbia 1989)★★.

●COMPILATIONS: *Big Ones* (Columbia 1989)★★★.

LOVETT, LYLE

b. 1 November 1957, Houston, Texas, USA. Singer/songwriter Lovett grew up 25 miles north of Houston in the rural Klein community (an area largely populated by farmers of German extraction), which was named after his grandfather, Adam Klein. During his teenage years, as Houston's borders expanded, Lovett was exposed to more urban influences, and attended Texas A&M University where he studied journalism and then German. During this period (late 70s), he began writing songs; his early heroes included Guy Clark (who later wrote a dedication on the sleeve of Lovett's first album), Jerry Jeff Walker and Townes Van Zandt. Having visited Europe (to improve his German) in the late 70s, he met a local country musician named Buffalo Wayne (who apparently took his name from his favourite western heroes), and remained in touch after returning to Texas - when Wayne was organizing an event in Luxembourg in 1983, he booked Lovett, and also on the bill was an American band from Phoenix whose members included Matt Rollings (keyboards) and Ray Herndon (guitar) who were later involved with Lovett's albums.

Lovett worked the same Texas music circuit as Nanci Griffith, singing on two of her early albums, *Once In A Very Blue Moon* (1984, which included one of his songs, 'If I Were The Woman You Wanted') and *Last Of The True Believers* (1985), on which he is pictured on the front of the sleeve. When Guy Clark heard a demo tape by Lovett in 1984, he passed it on to Tony Brown of MCA Records, and by 1986, Lovett had signed to MCA/Curb. His self-titled debut album was idiosyncratic, to say the least, including both the song covered by Griffith and 'Closing Time', which was covered by Lacy J. Dalton, as well as a fine song he co-wrote with fellow singer/songwriter Robert Earl Keen Jnr., 'This Old Porch'. However, his acceptance was slow in US country music circles, and Lovett first received substantial critical acclaim when the album was eventually released in Europe. 1987 brought a follow-up, *Pontiac*, after Lovett had successfully toured Europe backed only by cellist John Hagen. The album made it clear that Lovett was rather more than a folk or country artist, with such songs as the surreal 'If I Had A Boat' and 'She's Hot To Go', while guests on the album included Emmylou Harris. By this time, Lovett was talking about both recording and touring with what he called His Large Band, with several saxophone players and a female backing singer, Francine Reed, as well as a regular rhythm section. His third album, released in 1989, was indeed titled *Lyle And His Large Band*. Including an insidiously straight cover of the Tammy Wynette standard 'Stand By Your Man', and a version of R&B oldie, 'The Glory Of Love', it again delighted critics by its very humour and eclecticism, but further confused record buyers, especially in the USA, who were unsure whether this was a country record or jazz or something quite different.

At this point Lovett moved away from Nashville, where he was regarded as too weird, and as a result, his fourth album, produced by Los Angeles heavyweight George Massenburg, was not released until early 1992. Its title, *Joshua Judges Ruth* (three consecutive books in the Old Testament, but meaning something very difference if read as a phrase), was symptomatic of Lovett's intelligence, but perhaps equally so of his idiosyncratic approach. As usual, critics loved it, although it included hardly any traces of country music, and seemed to portray him as a Tom Waits-like figure - ultra-sophisticated, but somewhat off the wall. In 1992, Lovett was chosen as the opening act for many of the dates on the first world tour during the 90s by Dire Straits. This exposed him to a huge international audience, but seems to have done little to extend his cult following. In the same year, Lovett met the Hollywood actress, Julia Roberts, on the set of *The Player*, a high-grossing film, in which Lovett played the role of a detective. They married in June 1993, the following year their marriage was floundering, by 1995 it appeared to be over. Presumably Lovett will now resume his career as one of the sharpest and wittiest songwriters to come out of America in recent times. He performed 'You've Got A Friend In Me' with Randy Newman for the soundtrack of the hugely successful movie *Toy Story*. *The Road To Ensenada* mixed Lovett's razor wit with pathos. Long-standing observers of Lovett's lyrics will read much into this album and pontificate for hours about their relevance to his relationship with Roberts.

● ALBUMS: *Lyle Lovett* (MCA/Curb 1986)★★★, *Pontiac* (MCA/Curb 1987)★★★★, *Lyle Lovett And His Large Band* (MCA/Curb 1989)★★★, *Joshua Judges Ruth* (MCA/Curb 1992)★★★, *I Love Everybody* (MCA/Curb 1994)★★★, *The Road To Ensenada* (MCA/Curb 1996)★★★.

LUDUS

Founded in 1978, this Manchester, England-based quartet was consistently fronted by the enigmatic lyricist/vocalist Linder (b. Linda Mulvey, 1954,

Liverpool, England). The backing was provided by Arthur Cadmon (b. Peter Sadler, Stockport, England), formerly of Manicured Noise and originally the musical genius behind the group. The line-up was completed by bassist Willie Trotter (b. 1959, Manchester, England) and drummer Phil 'Toby' Tolman (ex-Ed Banger And The Nosebleeds). With their jazz-influenced forays and Linder's strong, sloganeering, elliptical feminist lyrics, the group were one of the most interesting of the Manchester new wave of the late 70s. The departure of Cadmon and later Trotter, replaced by Ian Devine (Ian Pincombe), saw the group change direction, though the jazz influence remained. Linder, a former girlfriend of the Buzzcocks' Howard Devoto, later became a well-publicized confidante of Morrissey. In spite of some inspired moments with Ludus, the group almost wilfully avoided the mainstream. As manager Richard Boon concluded: 'Ludus were totally improvisational and their set list would read: bass, drums, voice, next number'. There was something self-limiting about Linder. Any time she seemed on the brink of a breakthrough, even if that meant selling 50 extra records, she would retreat, just like the poet Stevie Smith'. Ian Devine teamed up in 1989 with ex-Weekend singer, Alison Statton, to form Devine And Statton.

●ALBUMS: *Pickpocket* (New Hormones 1981)★★★.

LUSH

Though they made their live debut at the Camden Falcon on 6 March 1988, little was heard of London-based Lush's serene pop qualities and full-bodied guitar sound until their mini-album, *Scar*, was issued in October 1989 on 4AD Records. It was a critically acclaimed debut, and red-haired Miki Berenyi (b. 18 March 1967, St. Stephen's, London, England; vocals/guitar), Emma Anderson (b. 10 June 1964, Raynes Park, London, England; guitar/backing vocals), Steve Rippon (bass guitar) and Christopher Acland (b. 7 September 1966, Lancaster, Lancashire, England, d. 17 October 1996; drums) found themselves topping the independent charts. Previously Anderson, a former DHSS clerical assistant, had been bass player for the Rover Girls, Berenyi had played with I-Goat, Fuhrer Five and the Lillies, while Acland had been a member of Infection, Panik, A Touch Of Hysteria, Poison In The Machine and others. Tours with the Darling Buds and Loop followed Lush's initial breakthrough, plus an appearance on BBC2's *Snub TV* and a John Peel radio session. The EP *Mad Love*, issued in February 1990, was less raw but soared to new heights with the help of producer Robin Guthrie from the Cocteau Twins. Lush's consistent coverage in the music press, not least for their perpetual appearances at pre/post-gig parties, made them one of the leading UK independent groups of the year, one that was taken up with tours in the UK and Europe and an appearance at the Glastonbury Festival. Another EP, *Sweetness And Light*, offered a further move towards a commercial pop sound and only narrowly missed the national charts. The three EPs were compiled, originally for the US market, on *Gala*. Much of 1991 was spent recording the long-awaited full debut album, during which time they also issued an EP, *Black Spring* (which included a cover of Dennis Wilson's 'Fallin' In Love'). When *Spooky* was finally released, many were disappointed, some insisting that Guthrie's production had swamped the group sound. Nevertheless, the album reached the national Top 20 and number 1 in the UK independent chart. During the winter of 1991/2 the group line-up changed when bassist Steve Rippon left amicably, to be replaced by *New Musical Express* picture researcher, Phil King (b. 29 April 1960, Chiswick, London, England). His musical apprenticeship had already included stints in the Servants, Felt, Biff Bang Pow! and See See Rider. The critical reception that awaited 1994's second album, *Split*, was fervent, with its cool guitar textures winning over many who had doubted their staying power. Berenyi and Anderson, dismissed in some quarters as 'two pissheads from London', had dispelled not only that notion, but also that of them being a 'typically glacial post-punk 4AD band' with a stunningly evocative collection of pop songs. Although *Lovelife* failed to a certain degree in putting Lush in the premier league of pop bands (as was touted) it did contain the engaging 'Single Girl', an effortless classic pop song and '500', a paean to the tiny Fiat car. Anderson stated to the *NME,* 'I was sick of writing about bloody men, so I wrote about being in love with a car. They're more reliable than men'. Acland took his own life in October 1996.

●ALBUMS: *Spooky* (4AD 1992)★★, *Split* (4AD 1994)★★★, *Lovelife* (4AD 1996)★★★.
●COMPILATIONS: *Gala* (4AD 1990)★★★.

LYNCH, RAY

b. Texas, USA. One of the most prominent and influential of the new age musicians of the 80s, Lynch's initial training was on piano, before he switched to classical guitar at age 12 after hearing Adrés Segovia's work. Later he moved to

Barcelona, Spain, studying guitar technique for three years under Eduardo Sainz de la Maza. His studies continued back in America with a three year course at the University of Texas, learning composition of symphonic and chamber music. Some of these scores were later performed by the Dallas Symphony Orchestra. He also joined a group of madrigal singers as an auxiliary lutist. This led to an invitation to join the Renaissance Quartet in New York. He consequently relocated to the east coast and spent seven years performing with the Quartet and other sympathetic 'early music' groups, with interest in medieval and baroque music undergoing something of a revival. Purchasing a 125-acre farm in Maine, Lynch concurrently toured the country giving virtuoso solo performances, until he found something lacking in his life and dropped everything to move to California. His recording career was well underway at this point, having started in 1983 with *The Sky Of The Mind*, a reflective piece of mood music, with Tibetan bells merging with classically formed song structures. *Deep Breakfast* became a certified platinum album in the aftermath, mainly on the strength of the accompanying hit single, 'Celestial Soda Pop'. The five-year delay before *No Blue Thing* engendered a much expanded sound, with evocative melodies fashioning a full, adroit range of moods and atmospherics. It quickly became a runaway success in US new age circles, staying on *Billboard*'s genre chart for 122 weeks. Lynch also won *Billboard*'s award for New Age Album of The Year, an honour that the same record was awarded again the following year. 1993's *Nothing Above My Shoulders But The Evening* reflected on the trials of the human spirit, with Lynch commenting: 'The mind filters out so much of our humanity. Great art, if we participate fully in it, gives us permission to feel, and creates a space in which we can feel at a depth not ordinarily allowed.'

●ALBUMS: *The Sky Of Mind* (Ray Lynch Productions 1983)★★★, *Deep Breakfast* (Ray Lynch Productions 1984)★★★, *No Blue Thing* (Windham Hill 1989)★★★, *Nothing Above My Shoulders But The Evening* (Windham Hill 1993)★★★.

LYNNE, JEFF

b. 30 December 1947, Birmingham, England. Lynne's long and varied musical career began in 1966 when he joined the Nightriders, a popular beat group still reeling from the loss of their leader, Mike Sheridan, and guitarist, Roy Wood. Having completed all contractual obligations, the band took the name Idle Race and, under Lynne's guidance, became a leading exponent of classic late 60s pop. Frustrated at a lack of commercial success, the artist opted to join the Move in 1970, where he was teamed with the aforementioned Wood. Lynne's contributions to the unit's late-period catalogue included the riff-laden 'Do Ya', but this era is also marked by the duo's desire to form a more experimental outlet for their talents. This resulted in the launch of the Electric Light Orchestra, or ELO, of which Lynne took full control upon Wood's early and sudden departure. The group gradually developed from cult favourites into one of the 70s' leading recording acts, enjoying international success with several platinum-selling albums, including *A New World Record* and *Out Of The Blue*. Lynne's dual talents as a composer and producer ensured the group's status but, sensing an artistic sterility, he abandoned his creation in 1986. The artist then assumed an increasingly backroom role, but won praise for his production work with George Harrison (*Cloud Nine*), Randy Newman (*Land Of Dreams*) and Roy Orbison (*Mystery Girl*) and he has also contributed his distinctive production qualities to much of Tom Petty's recent output. Lynne's work with Orbison coincided with his position as 'Otis Wilbury' in the Traveling Wilburys, an informal 'supergroup' completed by Orbison, Harrison, Tom Petty and Bob Dylan. This particularly prolific period was also marked by his work with Brian Wilson on the ex-Beach Boy's first long-awaited solo album. In 1990, Lynne also unveiled his own solo debut, *Armchair Theatre*, on which his gifts for pop melody remained as sure as ever. In recent years Lynn has gained a measure of success (and some criticism) for his production of the Beatles' lost tapes, notably 'Free As A Bird' and 'Real Love'. He co-produced Paul McCartney's excellent *Flaming Pie* in 1997.

●ALBUMS: *Armchair Theatre* (Reprise 1990)★★.

●COMPILATIONS: *Message From The Country (The Jeff Lynne Years 1968-1973)* (Harvest 1979)★★★.

LYNOTT, PHIL

b. 20 August 1951, Dublin, Eire, d. 4 January 1986. Having enjoyed considerable success in Thin Lizzy, Lynott first recorded solo in 1980, the same year that he married Caroline Crowther, daughter of the television celebrity Leslie Crowther. Lynott's first single, 'Dear Miss Lonely Hearts', reached number 32 in the UK charts and was followed by an album, *Solo In Soho*. A tribute to Elvis Presley, 'King's Call', also reached number 35. Lynott had to wait until 1982 for his next hit, 'Yellow Pearl',

which reached the UK Top 20 after being used as the theme tune to television show *Top Of The Pops*. In the summer of 1983 Thin Lizzy broke up and it was widely anticipated that Lynott would go on to solo fame. A new group, Grand Slam, failed to develop and Lynott's subsequent solo single, 'Nineteen', did not sell. The last notable instalment in his career arrived in May 1985 when he partnered Gary Moore on the number 5 hit, 'Out In The Fields'. He played his last gig with Grand Slam at the Marquee in London on 3 December 1985. At the turn of the following year he suffered a drug overdose and, following a week in a coma, died of heart failure, exacerbated by pneumonia.
●ALBUMS: *Solo In Soho* (Vertigo 1981)★★★, *The Phillip Lynott Solo Album* (Vertigo 1992)★★.
●FURTHER READING: *Phillip Lynott: The Rocker*, Mark Putterford. *Songs For While I'm Away*, Phillip Lynott. *My Boy: The Philip Lynott Story*, Philomena Lynott.

M

M was the brainchild of former art school student and folk singer Robin Scott (b. 1 April 1947). He started out as manager of the R&B band Roogalator and formed the Do It label to release an album by them. Do It later found critical success with the band Adam And The Ants. Scott moved to Paris in 1978, where he produced the Slits and several French bands. It was here that he got the idea for the band M, the name taken from the signs for the Paris Metro. Their debut single 'Moderne Man' was not successful and was released at the same time as a single by Comic Romance on which Scott also featured. M's quirky and hook-laden second single 'Pop Musik' was a massive hit in the UK and the USA as well as across Europe. As a gimmick, some copies of the single featured both a and b-sides on the one playing surface with the listener taking pot luck as to which groove the needle dropped on to. An album was released to capitalize on the hit and, as well as the singles, also featured a re-recording of the track 'Cowboys And Indians' - previously the b-side of the 'Comic Romance' single. The album was recorded using session musicians Wally Badarov (keyboards), Gary Barnacles (saxophone/flute), Philip Gould (drums), Julian Scott (bass, ex-Roogalator), and Betty Vinchon (vocals). Among the musicians on the second album were Mark King of Level 42. After a couple of minor hit follow-ups, M's career slipped into rapid decline with subsequent singles (including a release on Stiff Records) failing to chart. Only a 1989 remix of 'Pop Musik' returned the name of M to the charts. Meanwhile, Scott worked with Ryûichi Sakamoto on two albums and put out his own solo album - *The Kiss Of Life* - in 1985.
●ALBUMS: *New York - London - Paris - Munich* (Sire 1979)★★, *The Official Secrets Act* (1980)★.
●COMPILATIONS: *Pop Muzik: The Very Best Of M* (Music Club 1997)★★.

MAAL, BAABA

b. 12 November 1960, Fouata, Senegal. Vocalist and guitarist Maal had humble origins, growing up in the sparsely populated town of Podor, where his father worked in the fields, but also had the honour of calling worshippers to the Mosque using song. The influence of Islam would remain central to his son's activities too, both father and son being members of the Fulani community, which originally brought the Muslim religion to the area. His mother was also a musician, writing her own songs, though the influence of imported western sounds (via transistor radio) such as Otis Redding and James Brown, then reggae ambassador Jimmy Cliff, would also have a profound influence. After winning a scholarship to the Ecole Des Beaux Arts in Dakar, the capital of Senegal, he travelled widely throughout Senegal and neighbouring Mali and Mauritania, studying the traditional musics of the area. 'It's very important for young modern musicians in Africa to do a lot of research. To know what is African music. You cannot say you are doing African music if you don't know exactly where this music comes from.' He spent a further two years of academic study at the Paris Conservatoire, learning European theory and composition, before returning to Dakar in the early 80s to form Daande Lenol ('the voice of the race'). This group was formed with his long-standing friend, musical accomplice and family 'griot', Mansour Seck. In 1982 he released the first of seven cassette-only albums which would, by mid-decade, establish him as a potential rival to Youssou N'Dour, the reigning king of Senegalese youth music. Disc jockey John Peel described one of these, *Djam Leelii*, as like 'listening to Muddy Waters for the first time.' The music employed the Pekan songs of Northern fishermen, Gumbala chants of ancient warriors and Dilere weaving tunes. Most pervasively, the musical framework was based on the Yela songs of indigenous women pounding grain - taught to him by his mother. In 1985, he signed to the Paris-based label Syllart, releasing three superb albums *Wango, Taara* and *Nouvelle Generationa*. In 1991 he moved to London-based Island Records subsidiary, Mango, ensuring his continued growth as an international artist. His debut for Mango, *Baayo*, featured a typically acoustic line-up, with Maal and Seck joined by Sayan Sissokho (guitar), Malick Sow (xalam) and Yakhoba Sissokho (kora). The emphasis here was on the experiences of his childhood, a delightful portrait of West African life which justified the award of several critical accolades. *Lam Toro*, dedicated to his mother who died young but remains a guiding influence, provided a more modern Senegalese sound, with synthesizers and pro-grammed percussion. It was later released in remixed form. *Firin' In Fouta* was also well received by the critics and introduced freeform jazz and reggae beats in an impressive marriage of the new and the old. It was partially based on a return journey to Podor when Maal made recordings of the traditional singers and musicians he had heard in his youth, mixing these into the final recording in Dakar.

● ALBUMS: *Djam Leelii* cassette (1984)★★★, *Wango* (Syllart 1988)★★★★, *Djam Leelii* reissue (Rogue 1989)★★★, *Taara* (Syllart 1990)★★★★, *Nouvelle Generation* (Syllart 1990)★★★, *Baayo* (Mango 1991)★★★, *Lam Toro* (Mango 1992)★★, *Lam Toro - The Remix Album* (Mango 1993)★★, *Firin' In Fouta* (Stern's 1994)★★★.

MacColl, Kirsty

b. 10 October 1959, England. The daughter of the celebrated folk singer Ewan MacColl, Kirsty has enjoyed success in her own right as an accomplished songwriter and pop vocalist. Originally signed to Stiff Records as a 16-year-old, she was most unfortunate not to secure a massive hit with the earnest 'They Don't Know'. Many years later, the television comedienne Tracey Ullman took an inferior rendition of the song to number 2 in the UK charts. MacColl had to wait until 1981 for her first chart hit. A change of label to Polydor Records brought her deserved UK Top 20 success with the witty 'There's A Guy Works Down The Chip Shop Swears He's Elvis'. Her interest in country and pop influences was discernible on her strong debut *Desperate Characters*. In 1984, MacColl married producer Steve Lillywhite, and during the same year she returned to the charts with a stirring version of Billy Bragg's 'A New England'. During the next couple of years, she gave birth to two children but still found herself in demand as a backing singer. She guested on recordings by a number of prominent artists, including Simple Minds, the Smiths, the Rolling Stones, Talking Heads, Robert Plant, Van Morrison and Morrissey. In December 1987, she enjoyed her highest ever chart placing at number 2 when duetting with Shane MacGowan on the Pogues' evocative vignette of Irish emigration, 'Fairytale Of New York'. In 1989, she returned to recording solo with the highly accomplished *Kite*. The album included the powerful 'Free World' and an exceptionally alluring version of the Kinks' 'Days', which brought her back to the UK Top 20. Smiths guitarist Johnny Marr guested on several of the album's tracks and appeared on the excellent follow-up released in 1991. *Electric Landlady*, an amusing pun on the Jimi Hendrix Experience's *Electric Ladyland*, was another strong album which demonstrated MacColl's diversity and songwriting talent. The haunting, dance-influenced 'Walking Down Madison' gave her another Top 40 UK hit. Her career to date was sympathetically compiled on *Galore*, which demonstrated a highly accomplished artist even though four albums in fifteen years is hardly prolific.

●ALBUMS: *Desperate Characters* (Polydor 1981)★★★, *Kite* (Virgin 1989)★★★★, *Electric Landlady* (Virgin 1991)★★★, *Titanic Days* (ZTT 1994)★★.
●COMPILATIONS: *Galore* (Virgin 1995)★★★★.

MACKINTOSH, CAMERON

b. 17 October 1946, Enfield, England. 'The Czar of theatrical producers' - that is what the American magazine *TheatreWeek* called him in 1993 when they rated him number 3 in their list of the 100 Most Powerful People in American Theatre. The son of a Maltese-born mother and a Scottish father, Mackintosh attended a small public school in Bath and became obsessed by the musical theatre at the age of eight after being taken to see a production of Julian Slade's *Salad Days* at Bristol Old Vic in 1954. After leaving school, where he was known as Darryl F. Mackintosh, he attended the Central School for Speech and Drama for a year before becoming an assistant stage manager at the Theatre Royal, Drury Lane, when *Camelot* was running. His first forays into producing came with some budget-priced touring shows before he moved into the West End in 1969 with a revival of *Anything Goes*. It proved to be a disaster and was withdrawn after 27 performances. *Trelawny* (1972) and *The Card* (1973) fared better, and, after a number of provincial productions of varying degrees of profitability, Mackintosh's breakthrough finally came in 1976 with *Side By Side By Sondheim*. During the next few years he mounted successful revivals of *Oliver!*, *My Fair Lady*, and *Oklahoma!*, before his meeting with Andrew Lloyd Webber resulted in *Cats* in 1981. The show transformed the lives of both men, and became the prototype for future productions that overthrew the old style of musical and provided a simple and vivid theatrical experience that did not rely on big name stars, and was easily exportable. In the 80s Mackintosh went from strength to strength with *Song And Dance*, *Les Misérables*, *The Phantom Of The Opera*, and *Miss Saigon* (1989). In 1990 the latter show provided an example of just how powerful Mackintosh had become when American Equity initially objected to the casting of Jonathan Pryce in the Broadway production 'because it would be an affront to the Asian community'. After the producer threatened to withdraw the show altogether - and one or two others as well - capitulation was more or less immediate. The incident did nothing to improve the producer's ruthless (he prefers 'relentless') reputation with the New York theatre community, many of whom objected to his dictatorial attitude and 'flashy' marketing methods. For some reason he deliberately did not use those ploys when his London hit, *Five Guys Named Moe*, transferred to Broadway, and that may well be one of the reasons for its relatively poor showing.

In 1992 Mackintosh was involved with a rare flop which some say marked the beginning of his decline. *Moby Dick* ('a damp squib . . . garbage') is reported to have cost him £1 million and a great deal of pride during its 15-week run, and he hinted at the time that he may be past his peak. However, the highly impressive monetary facts continued to emerge: a personal salary of over £8 million in 1991, the 39th richest man in Britain, and the acquisition of a substantial stake in two West End theatres, the Prince of Wales and the Prince Edward. His love of musicals - that is all he seems to be interested in producing - has caused Mackintosh to divert some of his reported £300 million wealth to a number of extremely worthy causes. As well as numerous donations to small theatrical projects, he provided £2 million to endow Oxford University's first professorship in drama and musical theatre, and his £1 million gift to the Royal National Theatre has enabled it to mount highly acclaimed revivals of *Carousel* and *Sweeney Todd*, the first two in a series of five classic musicals. It is not all philanthropy: Mackintosh is reported to retain the rights to the productions when they are eventually produced in the commercial sector. A knighthood is inevitable, but until then his kudos have included the 1991 *Observer* Award for Outstanding Achievement, and the prestigious Richard Rodgers Award for Excellence in Musical Theatre (1992). Previous recipients have been Harold Prince, Julie Andrews and Mary Martin. In 1994, Mackintosh's major revival of *Oliver!* opened at the London Palladium, starring Jonathan Pryce, and in 1995 his production company, Cameron Mackintosh Limited, earned a Queen's Award for Export Achievement. Two years earlier, for the benefit of an awe-struck journalist, he had attempted to remember all the musicals he had running in various parts of the world. They included six *Cats*, 20 *Phantom Of The Opera*, 12 *Les*

Misérables, seven *Miss Saigon*, four *Five Guys Named Moe*, two *Follies* . . . et cetera, et cetera, as Yul Brynner used to say.

MADNESS

This highly regarded UK ska/pop group evolved from the London-based Invaders in the summer of 1979. Their line-up comprised Suggs McPherson (b. Graham McPherson, 13 January 1961, Hastings, Sussex, England; vocals), Mark Bedford (b. 24 August 1961, London, England; bass), Mike Barson (b. 21 April 1958, London, England; keyboards), Chris Foreman (b. 8 August 1958, London, England; guitar), Lee Thompson (b. 5 October 1957, London, England; saxophone), Chas Smash (b. Cathal Smythe, 14 January 1959; vocals/trumpet) and Dan Woodgate (b. 19 October 1960, London, England; drums). After signing a one-off deal with 2-Tone they issued 'The Prince', a tribute to blue beat maestro Prince Buster (whose song, 'Madness', had inspired the group's name). The single reached the UK Top 20 and the follow-up, 'One Step Beyond' (a Buster composition) did even better, peaking at number 7, the first result of their new contract with Stiff Records. An album of the same title revealed Madness's charm with its engaging mix of ska and exuberant pop, a fusion they humorously dubbed 'the nutty sound'. Over the next two years the group enjoyed an uninter-rupted run of Top 10 UK hits, comprising 'My Girl', *Work Rest And Play* (EP), 'Baggy Trousers', 'Embarrassment', 'The Return Of The Los Palmas Seven', 'Grey Day', 'Shut Up' and 'It Must Be Love' (originally a hit for its composer, Labi Siffre). Although Madness appealed mainly to a younger audience and were known as a zany, fun-loving group, their work occasionally took on a more serious note. Both 'Grey Day' and 'Our House' showed their ability to write about working-class family life in a fashion that was piercingly accu-rate, yet never patronizing. At their best, Madness were the most able commentators on London life since the Kinks in the late 60s. An ability to tease out a sense of melancholy beneath the fun perme-ated their more mature work, particularly on the 1982 album, *The Rise And Fall*. That same year Suggs married singer Bette Bright and the group finally topped the charts with their 12th chart entry, 'House Of Fun' (which concerned the pur-chase of prophylactics and teenage sexuality). More UK hits followed, including 'Wings Of A Dove' and 'The Sun And The Rain', but in late 1983 the group suffered a serious setback when founding member Barson quit. The group con-

tinued to release some exceptional work in 1984 including 'Michael Caine' and 'One Better Day'. At the end of that year, they formed their own label, Zarjazz. Its first release was Feargal Sharkey's 'Listen To Your Father' (written by the group), which reached the UK Top 30. Madness continued to enjoy relatively minor hits by previous stan-dards with the contemplative 'Yesterday's Men', the exuberant 'Uncle Sam' and a cover of the former Scritti Politti success, 'The Sweetest Girl'. In the autumn of 1986, the group announced that they were splitting. Seventeen months later, they reunited as a four-piece under the name The Madness, but failed to emulate previous successes. One of Mark Bedford's projects was a collaboration with ex-Higson member Terry Edwards in Butterfield 8. Lee Thompson and Chris Foreman later worked under the appellation the Nutty Boys, releasing one album, *Crunch* (1990), and played to capacity crowds in London clubs and pubs. In June 1992 the original Madness re-formed for two open-air gigs in Finsbury Park, London, which resulted in *Madstock*, a 'live' document of the event. The group's renewed public image was rewarded with four chart entries during the year; three reissues, 'It Must Be Love', 'House Of Fun', and 'My Girl'; along with 'The Harder They Come'. In 1993, a 'musical about homelessness', One Step Beyond, by Alan Gilbey, incorporated 15 Madness songs when it opened on the London Fringe., further evidence, as if any was needed, of the enduring brilliance of Madness's irresistible songcraft.

● ALBUMS: *One Step Beyond* (Stiff 1979)★★★★, *Absolutely* (Stiff 1980)★★★, *Madness 7* (Stiff 1981)★★★, *The Rise And Fall* (Stiff 1982)★★★★, *Keep Moving* (Stiff 1984)★★★, *Mad Not Mad* (Zarjazz 1985)★★, as the Madness *The Madness* (Virgin 1988)★★, *Madstock* (Go! Discs 1992)★★★.
● COMPILATIONS: *Complete Madness* (Stiff 1982)★★★, *Utter Madness* (Zarjazz 1986)★★★, *The Peel Sessions* (Strange Fruit 1986)★★, *Divine Madness* (Virgin 1992)★★★★, *The Business - The Definitive Singles Collection* (Virgin 1993)★★★★.
● VIDEOS: *Complete Madness* (1984), *Utter Madness* (1988), *Complete And Utter Madness* (1988), *Divine Madness* (1992).
● FURTHER READING: *A Brief Case Of Madness*, Mark Williams. *Total Madness*, George Marshall.

MADONNA

b. Madonna Louise Veronica Ciccone, 16 August 1958, Rochester, Michigan, USA. Madonna excelled at dance and drama at high school and during brief periods at colleges in Michigan and North Carolina.

In 1977 she went to New York, studying with noted choreographer Alvin Ailey and taking modelling jobs. Two years later, Madonna moved to France to join a show featuring disco singer Patrick Hernandez. There she met Dan Gilroy and, back in New York, the pair formed club band the Breakfast Club. Madonna played drums and sang with the band before setting up Emmy in 1980 with Detroit-born drummer Steve Bray. Together, Madonna and Bray created dance tracks which led to a recording deal with Sire Records. With leading New York disc jockey Mark Kamins producing, she recorded 'Everybody', a US club hit in 1982. Madonna broke out from the dance scene into mainstream pop with 'Holiday' written and produced by John 'Jellybean' Benitez. It reached the US Top 20 and was a Top 10 hit across Europe in 1984. By now, her tough, raunchy persona was coming across to international audiences and the attitude was underlined by the choice of Tom Kelly and Billy Steinberg's catchy 'Like A Virgin' as a 1984 single. It was the first of ten US number 1 hits for Madonna. Among these was 'Material Girl', the video for which introduced one of her most characteristic visual styles, the mimicking of Marilyn Monroe's 'blonde bombshell' image. By the time of the *Live Aid* concert, at which she appeared, and her high-profile wedding to actor Sean Penn, Madonna had become an internationally recognized superstar, known to millions of tabloid newspaper readers without any interest in her music. Among the fans of her work were a growing number of 'wannabees', teenage girls who aped her independent and don't-care stance.

From 1985-87, she turned out a stream of irresistibly catchy hit singles. 'Crazy For You' was co-written by ex-Carpenters' collaborator John Bettis, while she and Steve Bray wrote 'Into The Groove'. These were followed by 'Dress You Up' and 'Papa Don't Preach', with its message of generational rebellion. 'True Blue', 'Open Your Heart' and 'La Isla Bonita' were later successes. Like an increasing number of her songs, 'Who's That Girl' (1987) was tied-in to a film - in this instance, a poorly received comedy in which she starred with Sir John Mills. Madonna's film career had begun in 1980 with a bit part in the b-movie *A Certain Sacrifice* before she starred in *Desperately Seeking Susan* (1985). In *Shanghai Surprise* (1986), Madonna appeared with Penn, from whom she separated in 1988. In that year, she also appeared on Broadway in the play *Speed The Plow* by David Mamet. Madonna continued to attract controversy when in 1989 the video for 'Like A Prayer', with its links between religion and eroticism, was condemned by the Vatican and caused Pepsi Cola to cancel a sponsorship deal with the star. The resulting publicity helped the album of the same title - co-produced with new collaborator Patrick Leonard - to become a global best-seller. In 1990 her career reached a new peak of publicity and commercial success. She starred with Warren Beatty in the blockbuster film *Dick Tracy* while the extravagant costumes and choreography of the Blond Ambition world tour were the apotheosis of Madonna's uninhibited mélange of sexuality, song, dance and religiosity. The tour was commemorated by a documentary film, *Truth Or Dare On The Band Behind The Scenes, And In Bed With Madonna*, released in 1991. Among the hits of the early 90s were 'Vogue', devoted to a short-lived dance craze, 'Justify My Love' (co-written with Lenny Kravitz) and 'Rescue Me', produced by Madonna and Shep Pettibone. Madonna's reputation as a strong businesswoman, in control of each aspect of her career, was confirmed in 1992 when she signed a multi-million dollar contractl with the Time-Warner conglomerate, parent company of Sire. This guaranteed the release of albums, films and books created by her own Maverick production company. The publication of her graphic and erotic book *Sex* put her back on top of the charts, though this time it was in the bestselling book lists. The book was an unprecedented success, selling out within hours and needing an immediate reprint. On *Bedtime Stories* she teamed up with Soul II Soul producer Nellee Hooper, who wrote the title track in conjunction with Björk. It was prefaced by the Top 10 performance of 'Secret', and boasted 11 tracks which combined, by her own description, pop, R&B, hip hop and Madonna. In 1996 her need to shock had mellowed considerably with a credible movie portrayel of Eva Peron. Later that year she became 'with child' on 14 October with the birth of Lourdes Maria Ciccone Leon.

●ALBUMS: *Madonna* (Sire 1983)★★★, *Like A Virgin* (Sire 1984)★★★, *True Blue* (Sire 1986)★★★★, *You Can Dance* (Sire 1987)★★★, *Who's That Girl* soundtrack (Sire 1987)★★, *Like A Prayer* (Sire 1989)★★★★, *I'm Breathless* (Sire 1990)★★★, *Erotica* (Maverick 1992)★★★, *Bedtime Stories* (Warners 1994)★★★, *Something To Remember* (Sire 1995)★★★, *Evita* soundtrack (Warners 1996)★★★.

●COMPILATIONS: *The Immaculate Collection* (Sire 1991)★★★★, *Best Of The Rest Vol. 2* (1993)★★★.

●VIDEOS: *The Virgin Tour* (1986), *Ciao Italia - Live From Italy* (1988), *Immaculate Collection* (1990),

Justify My Love (Warners 1991), *The Real Story* (1991), *Madonna Video EP* (1991), *In Bed With Madonna* (1991), *Madonna Exposed* (1993), *The Unauthorised Biography* (MIA Video 1994), *Madonna: The Girlie Show* (1994).

●FURTHER READING: *Madonna: Her Story*, Michael McKenzie. *Madonna: The New Illustrated Biography*, Debbi Voller. *Madonna: In Her Own Words*, Mick St Michael. *Madonna: The Biography*, Robert Matthew-Walker. *Madonna*, Marie Cahill. *Madonna: The Style Book*, Debbi Voller. *Like A Virgin: Madonna Revealed*, Douglas Thompson. *Sex*, Madonna. *Madonna Unathorized*, Christopher Anderson. *I Dream Of Madonna: Women's Dreams Of The Goddess Of Pop*, Kay Turner (compiled). *Madonna: The Girlie Show*, Glenn O'Brien. *Deconstructing Madonna*, Fran Lloyd. *Live!*, no author listed. *The Madonna Scrapbook*, Lee Randall.

MAISONETTES

Based in Birmingham, England, this 60s-influenced pop group reached number 7 in the UK chart in 1983 with 'Heartache Avenue' a particularly memorable song with strong influences of 60s soul music. The group consisted of Lol Mason (vocals), Elaine Williams (vocals), Denise Ward (vocals), Mark Tibbenham (keyboards), and Nick Parry (drums). Mason, the driving force behind the band, was no stranger to chart success, having previously been the singer with City Boy. Two follow-up singles, 'Where I Stand' and 'Say It Again', and an album, all on Birmingham independent label Ready Steady Go!, flopped, and the band broke up.
●ALBUMS: *For Sale* (Ready Steady Go! 1983)★★, *Heartache Avenue* (1993)★★.

MALMSTEEN, YNGWIE

b. 30 June 1963. This Swedish-born guitar virtuoso was the originator of the high-speed, technically precise, neo-classical style that developed during the 80s. Influenced by Jimi Hendrix, Ritchie Blackmore and Eddie Van Halen, Malmsteen first picked up a guitar at the age of five and had formed his first band, Powerhouse, by the time he entered his teens. At age 14 he formed Rising, named after Rainbow's second album, and recorded a series of demo tapes. One of these was picked up by producer and guitar specialist Mike Varney. Malmsteen was persuaded by Varney to relocate to Los Angeles and join Ron Keel's Steeler as lead guitarist, and went straight into the studio to record the band's debut album. He was then approached by Kiss, UFO and Ozzy Osbourne, but declined their offers in favour of teaming up with Graham

Bonnet in a new group called Alcatrazz. This association lasted for one studio album and a live set, recorded in Japan. After the dissolution of that band Malmsteen was immediately offered a solo contract by Polydor Records, just as his reputation and stature were beginning to escalate. He released the self-produced *Rising Force*, utilizing ex-Jethro Tull drummer Barriemore Barlow, vocalist Jeff Scott Soto and keyboardist Jens Johansson. This comprised a mixture of new songs and reworked demo material that had been available for several years. Deciding to work within a band framework once more, but this time exercising tight control, Malmsteen formed Rising Force with Soto and Johansson, plus bassist Marcel Jacob and drummer Anders Johansson. This basic formation recorded two albums (with Soto replaced by ex-Ted Nugent vocalist Mark Boals on *Trilogy*) that showcased Malmsteen's amazing virtuosity and ability to combine speed with melody. Following an 18-month break after a serious road accident involving Malmsteen, Rising Force was resurrected again with ex-Rainbow vocalist Joe Lynn Turner. Produced by Jeff Glixman and mixed by the Thompson/Barbiero team, *Odyssey* was released in 1988 to widespread acclaim. At last Malmsteen's guitar pyrotechnics had been anchored within commercial hard rock structures. The guitar solos were economical, and did not detract from the songs. The album reached number 40 on the US *Billboard* album chart and brought him many new fans. Eager to capitalize on this success, Malmsteen then issued a disappointing and self-indulgent live album recorded in Leningrad. The momentum was lost and Turner was dismissed, to be replaced by Goran Edman. *Eclipse* had weak vocals and an unusually restrained Malsteen on guitar, and it appeared that he was suppressing his real desires and ability in the search for commercial success. *Fire And Ice* debuted at number 1 in the Japanese charts, with a new vocalist Mike Vescera. He switched back to his old flamboyant style on *No Mercy*, which featured classical material and a string orchestra. In 1996 he joined with Jeff Scott Soto as Human Clay to issue their self-titled debut.
●ALBUMS: *Rising Force* (Polydor 1984)★★★, *Marching Out* (Polydor 1985)★★★, *Trilogy* (Polydor 1986)★★★, *Odyssey* (Polydor 1988)★★★, *Live In Leningrad* (Polydor 1989)★★, *Eclipse* (Polydor 1990)★★, *Fire & Ice* (Elektra 1992)★★, *Seventh Sign* (Elektra 1994)★★★, *No Mercy* (CMC International 1994)★★★.
●VIDEOS: *Rising Force Live 35* (1989), *Trial By Fire* (1989), *Collection* (1992).

MANNING, PHIL

b. 1948, Tasmania, Australia. Acoustic guitarist and singer Phil Manning came to prominence as part of one of Australia's top-rated rock/blues groups, Chain. Having been frustrated in his original intention to become a geologist he studied classical piano. However, when he heard the Beatles for the first time he switched to pop music, purchasing a Hofner Broadway guitar while still working in his father's electrical store. While at art school in Hobart in 1965 a visiting blues artist, Tony Worsley, arrived in town short of a guitar player for his band the Blue Jays. Manning, having previously played with the appropriately named Anonymous Unlimited, accepted the offer. However, after ill-paid work at showgrounds through Queensland, he formed Chain with Matt Taylor (vocals), Barry Sullivan (bass) and Barry Harvey (guitar). Their 1971 composition, 'Black'n'Blue', became an Australian number 1 for seven weeks. Despite the accompanying *Towards The Blues* album achieving gold status, the group fell from popularity as they began to experiment with jazz and fusion. Manning left in 1974 to record his debut solo album, *I Wish There Was A Way*. As well as occasional performances with a reformed Chain he then formed the Phil Manning Blues Band, with Mike Clarke (bass), Greg Cook (guitar) and Bruce Devinish (drums). He returned to solo status in 1986. Since then he has continued to record accomplished delta blues sets from his Brisbane mountain base. He has his own studio, fitted with antique recording equipment such as a 1937 Western Electric cardoid ribbon microphone, and his own record label, Tambourine Records.
●ALBUMS: *I Wish There Was A Way* (Mushroom 1974)★★★, *Manning* (Indigo 1978)★★★, *Live* (Mushroom 1979)★★★, with the Manning Taylor Band *Oz Blues* (Astor 1981)★★★, *LP* (Tambourine 1988)★★★, *It's Blues* (Tambourine 1989)★★★, *The Black Shed* (Tambourine 1995)★★★.

MARC AND THE MAMBAS

Formed by Marc Almond (b. Peter Marc Almond, 9 July 1956, Southport, Lancashire, England), Marc And The Mambas was a pseudonym that the singer employed for his more arcane and adventurous work. Weary of the restrictions that came with his pop star role in Soft Cell, the Mambas project enabled him to attempt more daring and original ideas without compromise. With the assistance of Annie Hogan, Almond completed *Untitled* in which he unveiled spirited revivals of material by artists

such as Lou Reed and Jacques Brel. By 1983, Almond was plunging far deeper into the Marc And The Mambas project, despite the continued success of Soft Cell. This phase culminated in the release of a double album, *Torment And Toreros*. This was unquestionably Almond's most extreme and personal recording, full of melodrama with a burningly revealing glimpse into the singer's darker side. When the album received a poor review in one music paper, Almond was so despondent and incensed that he announced his retirement. What that comment actually meant was the imminent dissolution of Marc And The Mambas and a final return to Soft Cell. When they, too, collapsed at the end of 1983, Almond embarked on a solo career, although his first post-Soft Cell recording, *Vermin In Ermine* was credited to Marc And The Willing Sinners and featured several musicians who had joined in the Mambas experiment.
●ALBUMS: *Untitled* (Some Bizzare 1982)★★, *Torment And Toreros* (Some Bizzare 1983)★★.

MARILLION

Front-runners of the short-lived UK progressive rock revival of the early 80s, Marillion survived unfavourable comparisons with Genesis to become a popular melodic rock group, notching up several successful singles plucked from their grandiose concept albums. The group formed in Aylesbury, Buckinghamshire, originally as Silmarillion, a name taken from the novel by J.R.R. Tolkien. The group featured Doug Irvine (bass), Mick Pointer (b. 22 July 1956; drums), Steve Rothery (b. 25 November 1959, Brampton, South Yorkshire, England; guitar) and Brian Jelliman (keyboards). After recording the instrumental demo, 'The Web', the band recruited Fish (b. Derek William Dick, 25 April 1958, Dalkeith, Edinburgh, Scotland; vocals) and Diz Minnett (bass) and began building a strong following through almost continuous gigging. Before recording their debut, 'Market Square Heroes', Jelliman and Minnitt were replaced by Mark Kelly (b. 9 April 1961; keyboards) and Pete Trewavas (b. 15 January 1959, Middlesbrough, Cleveland, England; bass). Fish wrote all the lyrics for *Script For A Jester's Tear* and became the focal point of the group, often appearing on stage in garish make-up, echoing the style, both visually and vocally, of Genesis's singer Peter Gabriel. In 1983 Pointer was sacked and replaced for brief stints by Andy Ward of Camel, then John Marter and Jonathan Mover before the arrival of Ian Mosley (b. 16 June 1953, London, England), a veteran of many progressive rock bands, including Curved Air and the Gordon Giltrap band. Marillion's second album embraced a more straightforward hard rock sound and yielded two hits, 'Assassin' and 'Punch And Judy'. 1985's *Misplaced Childhood* was Marillion's biggest-selling album - surprisingly so, as it featured an elaborate concept, being virtually one continuous piece of music based largely on Fish's childhood experiences. 'Kayleigh', a romantic ballad extracted from this mammoth work, reached number 2 in the UK charts. By 1988 Fish was becoming increasingly dissatisfied with the group's musical development and left to pursue a solo career. The live double album, *Thieving Magpie*, was his last recorded contribution, and provided a fitting overview of the group's past successes. Marillion acquired Steve Hogarth (b. Doncaster, Yorkshire, England), formerly of the Europeans, who made his debut on *Seasons End*, proving himself equal to the daunting task of fronting a well-established band. The 90s have found Marillion as popular as ever, with the ghost of Fish receding into the distance. With Hogarth fronting the band consistent success has continued to acrue, including chart status for 'Sympathy', 'The Hollow Man' and 'Alone Again In The Lap Of Luxury'. *Afraid Of Sunlight* tackled the subject of fame, with references to the recently deceased Nirvana vocalist, Kurt Cobain, John Lennon and O.J. Simpson, the former American footballer who at the time was on trial for murdering his wife (though he was later cleared). Unusually for a band rooted in the progressive rock subculture, a genre dominated by the album, Marillion continue to be distinguished as much for their singles.

●ALBUMS: *Script For A Jester's Tear* (EMI 1983)★★★, *Fugazi* (EMI 1984)★★, *Real To Real* (EMI 1984)★, *Misplaced Childhood* (EMI 1985)★★★, *Brief Encounter* (EMI 1986)★★, *Clutching At Straws* (EMI 1987)★★★, *B Sides Themselves* (EMI 1988)★★, *The Thieving Magpie* (EMI 1988)★★, *Seasons End* (EMI 1989)★★★, *Holidays In Eden* (EMI 1991)★★★, *Brave* (EMI 1994)★★★, *Afraid Of Sunlight* (EMI 1995)★★★, *Made Again* (EMI 1996)★★, *This Strange Engine* (Intact/Raw Power 1997)★★★.

●COMPILATIONS: *A Singles Collection* (EMI 1992)★★★, *The Best Of Both Worlds* (EMI 1997)★★★.

●VIDEOS: *1982-1986 The Videos* (1986), *Live From Lorely* (1987), *From Stoke Row To Ipanema* (1990), *Brave* (1995).

●FURTHER READING: *Market Square Heroes*, Mick Wall. *Marillion*, Carol Clerk. *The Authorized Story Of Marillion*, Mick Wall. *Marillion: The Script*, Clive Gifford.

MARILYN

b. Peter Robinson, 3 November 1962, Kingston, Jamaica, West Indies. Marilyn launched his UK singing career on the coat-tails of his friend Boy George as England's second cross-dressing pop star. Much photographed in the teenage press, he became a major celebrity in 1983 with the release of 'Calling Your Name', which became a number 4 hit in the UK charts (many critics suggested it sounded like a Culture Club offcut). The tabloids turned on him with barely concealed venom. As Marilyn complained later 'You just expect that, after Danny La Rue and Quentin Crisp and God knows who else, that people would be able to accept someone with a bit of make-up. England is like such a bunch of old drag-queens anyway. If you pick up a history book . . . I'm quite tame compared to a lot of people.' Afterwards, however, a succession of further singles for Mercury Records attained ever decreasing chart positions. The gospel-flavoured 'Cry And Be Free' reached 31 in February 1984. Exactly a year later 'You Don't Love Me' reached UK number 40. His record company dispatched him to Detroit, Michigan, to work with producer Don Was of Was (Not Was). However, when he arrived there he found nobody had paid for a room for him to stay in. Without personal funds, he cut his famous blonde hair (which gave him his name) and ceased to wear make-up, abandoning the image that had brought him his initial success. Despite this, 'Baby You Left Me' (one of two tracks recorded with Was) failed to re-ignite his career.

MARINE GIRLS

This UK quartet was formed by four Hertfordshire schoolfriends: Jane Fox (b. c.1963; bass/vocals), her sister Alice (b. c.1966; vocals/percussion), Tracey Thorn (b. 26 September 1962; guitar/vocals) and the soon-to-depart Gina (percussion/vocals). The Marine Girls recorded their homemade *Beach Party* in a garden shed. Musically competent, within limitations, their lyrics showed remarkable strength and eloquence in dealing with the age-old problems of difficult boyfriends, new love and loneliness, often using the symbolic context of the sea and all its mysteries. With initial encouragement from the Television Personalities, the album was released by the Whaam! label and was later picked up by Cherry Red Records, who

signed the group for a second album. By this time, Thorn had left school to go to Hull University, where she struck up a romantic and artistic relationship with Cherry Red stablemate Ben Watt. They recorded the Cole Porter song, 'Night And Day', under the name of Everything But The Girl. Thorn had also released a solo album in 1982, *A Distant Shore*, which was well received by the critics and public. Pursuing a parallel career as a Marine Girl and as a duettist with Watt at first proved comfortable, but with the increasing popularity and media attention of Everything But The Girl, an amicable split with the Fox sisters came in late 1983, after the release of the successful *Lazy Ways*. Continuing their seaside/oceanic fixation, the sisters formed Grab Grab The Haddock, which produced two fine EPs on Cherry Red before folding in 1986. The line-up of Grab Grab The Haddock was notable for the inclusion of Lester Noel, who later joined Norman Cook in Beats International.
●ALBUMS: *Beach Party* (Whaam! 1981)★★, *Lazy Ways* (Cherry Red 1983)★★★.

MARLEY, ZIGGY, AND THE MELODY MAKERS

b. 1968, Kingston, Jamaica, West Indies. Stephen Marley, one of Bob Marley's four children with his wife Rita Marley, started his career as one of the Melody Makers with siblings Sharon, Cedella and Stevie, whose appearance at their father's funeral in 1981 was their first introduction to the rest of the world. The following year 'What A Plot', released on Rita's label, was a big hit, and Ziggy's lead vocals sounded uncannily like his late father's. The Melody Makers were allowed the time and space to mature and practise before committing themselves needlessly to vinyl - unlike so many of their Jamaican counterparts where recording activities were an economic necessity - and by the late 80s they were a headline act - especially in the USA. Their *Play The Game Right* debut, the only album to be credited simply to the Melody Makers, included one notable excerpt from their father's songbook, 'Children Playing In The Street', which he had originally written for them. Despite their tender years, the record stands up to repeated listening and suggests that Marley's maturity and wisdom may well be hereditary. The album to confirm this was *Conscious Party*. Produced by Chris Frantz and Tina Weymouth from Talking Heads, and featuring an inspired selection of backing musicians, the set boasted high-calibre material like 'Tomorrow People' and 'We Propose', which

would not have disgraced any Wailers album. *One Bright Day* is a similarly delightful collection, comprising slick dance reggae with articulate rebuttals of the South African apartheid system.

The Melody Makers have resisted the obvious temptation to re-record too many of their father's songs, and instead forged a career in their own right. Stephen Davis recounts in his excellent book - *Bob Marley - Conquering Lion Of Reggae* - just how popular they are in America by detailing a short exchange between two youngsters after seeing Bob Marley on video. One's question: 'Who's that?', being met by the cursory response: 'Ziggy Marley's father'. In his own lifetime Bob and the Wailers never really cracked the American market in the way that the Melody Makers have done. It must be pointed out that they are also very popular in Jamaica too - and not just because of Ziggy's lineage, though his ability to sing over his father's songs as 'specials' for some of Kingston's top sound systems, adapting the lyrics to espouse the prowess of a particular system, has made him widely popular. Irie FM have been known to play their favourite Ziggy songs such as 'Garden' three times in a row when the vibes are right. Ziggy And The Melody Makers have transcended the 'famous parent' tag to become stars in their own right, following on from their father's tradition without ever leaning too heavily on it. As Bob once remarked: 'All a my family are music'.
●ALBUMS: *Play The Game Right* (EMI 1985)★★, *Hey World* (EMI 1986)★★, *Conscious Party* (Virgin 1988)★★★, *One Bright Day* (Virgin 1989)★★★, *Jahmekya* (Virgin 1991)★★★, *Joy & Blues - Ghetto Youths United* (Virgin 1993)★★★, *Free Like We Want 2 B* (Elektra 1995)★★★.
●COMPILATIONS: *Time Has Come: The Best Of Ziggy Marley And The Melody Makers* (EMI/Manhattan 1988)★★★.

MARRS

A collaboration between two 4AD bands, Colourbox and AR Kane which, though a one off, was enough to set both the independent, dance and national charts alight during autumn 1987. 'Pump Up The Volume' was augmented on the a-side by UK champion scratch mixer C.J. Mackintosh and London disc jockey/journalist Dave Dorrell. Primarily aimed at the dance market, the record was originally mailed to the 500 most influential regional club and dance DJs on an anonymous white label, in order that it received exposure six weeks prior to its stock version. On official release it entered the charts at number 35, a figure attained on 12-inch sales only. Daytime radio play ensured the single was the next week's highest climber, rising 24 places to number 11. The following two weeks it stayed at number 2 before reaching the number 1 spot on 28 September 1987. Originally the idea of 4AD supremo Ivo, the single featured samples of James Brown, a practice already common in hip hop which would soon come into vogue for an avalanche of dance tracks: 'We've used a lot of rhythms and time signatures from old records, classic soul records, but mixed that with modern electronic instruments and AR Kane's guitar sound', was how the single was described. The single was never followed up, apparently due to acrimony between the involved personnel over finance, which was a great shame. As such the MARRS discography is a brief but blemishless one. Dorrell would go on to manage Bush, and Mackintosh returned to the club circuit.

MARSALIS, BRANFORD

b. 26 August 1960, Breaux Bridge, Louisiana, USA. With their father, Ellis Marsalis, a bop pianist, composer and teacher, it is not surprising that his sons Branford, Delfeayo and Wynton Marsalis all took up music in childhood. Branford Marsalis's first instrument was the alto saxophone, which he played during his formative years and while studying at Berklee College Of Music. In 1981, he played in Art Blakey's Jazz Messengers and the following year began a spell with a small band led by Wynton. During this period Marsalis switched instruments, taking up both soprano and tenor saxophones. He also played on record dates with leading jazzmen such as Miles Davis and Dizzy Gillespie. After three years in his brother's band, he began a period of musical searching. Like many young musicians of his era, Marsalis often played in jazz-rock bands, including that led by Sting. He also formed his own small group with which he toured and recorded. By the late 80s he had established a reputation as a leading post-bop jazz saxophonist, but also enjoyed status in fusion and even classical circles (*Romances For Saxophone*). Like most jazzmen, Marsalis drew early inspiration from the work of other musicians, among them John Coltrane, Ben Webster, Wayne Shorter, Ornette Coleman and especially Sonny Rollins. In some of his recordings these influences have surfaced, leading to criticisms that he has failed to build a personal style. Closer attention reveals that these stylistic acknowledgements are merely that and not an integral part of his musical make-up. His 1993 outing with *I Heard You Twice The First*

Time showed a strong learning towards the blues; both John Lee Hooker and B.B. King are featured along with his brother. Perhaps of more significance to Marsalis's development as a musician is that his career appears fated to be constantly compared to and contrasted with his virtuoso brother Wynton. If this should result in his long-term overshadowing it will be, at least, unfortunate, because by the early 90s Branford Marsalis had proved himself to be an inventive soloist with considerable warmth. His best work contains many moments of powerful emotional commitment.

● ALBUMS: *Scenes In The City* (Columbia 1983)★★★★, with Dizzy Gillespie *New Faces* (1984)★★★, with Wynton Marsalis *Black Codes (From The Underground)* (Columbia 1985)★★★, with Sting *Bring On The Night* (A&M 1986)★★★, *Royal Garden Blues* (Columbia 1986)★★★, *Random Abstract* (Columbia 1987)★★★★, *Renaissance* (Columbia 1987)★★★, *Trio Jeepy* (Columbia 1988)★★★★, *Crazy People Music* (Columbia 1990)★★★★, *The Beautyful Ones Are Not Yet Born* (Columbia 1992)★★★★, *I Heard You Twice The First Time* (Columbia 1993)★★★, *Bloomington* (Columbia 1993)★★★, *Spike Lee's Mo Better Blues* (1993)★★★, with Ellis Marsalis *Loved Ones* (Columbia 1995)★★★, *The Dark Keys* (Columbia 1996)★★★★.

● VIDEOS: *Steep* (1989), *The Music Tells You* (1993).

MARSHALL, KEITH

Marshall was originally the guitarist for UK glam rock band Hello. When the band finally collapsed, he turned to singing and walked straight into a successful solo career in Germany with his first single 'Remember Me'. It was followed by another three chart contenders including the 1981 worldwide hit, 'Only Crying'. While Germany continued to hold him dear, Marshall was not content to spend the rest of his career rewriting his greatest hit and has continued to move on musically, releasing records mainly in Europe, leaving the UK with only the occasional single.

● ALBUMS: *Keith Marshall* (Arrival 1981)★★.

● COMPILATIONS: *Tonight We Dance* (Arrival 1988)★★★.

MARTYN, JOHN

b. Iain McGeachy, 11 September 1948, New Malden, Surrey, England, to musically minded parents. At the age of 17, he started his professional career under the guidance of folk artist Hamish Imlach. The long, often bumpy journey through Martyn's career began when he arrived in London, where he was signed instantly by the astute Chris Blackwell, whose fledgling Island Records was just finding major success. Martyn became the first white solo artist on the label. His first album, the jazz/blues tinged *London Conversation* (1968), was released amid a growing folk scene which was beginning to shake off its traditionalist image. The jazz influence was confirmed when, only nine months later, *The Tumbler* was released. A bold yet understated album, it broke many conventions of folk music, featuring the flute and saxophone of jazz artist Harold MacNair. The critics began the predictable Bob Dylan comparisons, especially as the young Martyn was not yet 20. Soon afterwards, Martyn married singer Beverly Kutner, and as John and Beverly Martyn they produced two well-received albums, *Stormbringer* and *Road To Ruin*. The former was recorded in Woodstock, USA, with a talented group of American musicians, including Levon Helm of the Band and keyboard player Paul Harris. Both albums were relaxed in approach and echoed the simple peace and love attitudes of the day, with their gently naïve sentiments. Martyn the romantic also became Martyn the drunkard, and so began his conflict. The meeting with jazz bassist Danny Thompson, who became a regular drinking companion, led to some serious boozing and Martyn becoming a 'Jack the Lad'. Hard work in the clubs, however, was building his reputation, but it was the release of *Bless The Weather* and *Solid Air* that established him as a concert hall attraction. Martyn delivered a unique combination of beautifully slurred vocals and a breathtaking technique using his battered acoustic guitar played through an echoplex unit, together with sensitive and mature jazz arrangements. The track 'Solid Air' was written as a eulogy to his friend, singer-songwriter Nick Drake, who had committed suicide in 1974. Martyn was able to pour out his feelings in the opening two lines of the song: 'You've been taking your time and you've been living on solid air. You've been walking the line, you've been living on solid air'. Martyn continued to mature with subsequent albums, each time taking a step further away from folk music. *Inside Out* and the mellow *Sunday's Child* both confirmed his important musical standing, although commercial success still eluded him. Frustrated by the music business in general, he made and produced *Live At Leeds* himself. The album could be purchased only by writing to John and Beverly at their home in Hastings; they personally signed every copy of the plain record sleeve upon despatch. Martyn's dark side was beginning to get the better of him, and his alcohol and drug intake put a strain on his marriage. *One World*, in 1977, has subtle references to these problems in the lyrics, and, with Steve Winwood guesting on most tracks, the album was warmly received. Martyn, however, was going through serious problems and did not produce a new work until three years later when, following the break up of his marriage, he delivered the stunning *Grace And Danger* produced by Phil Collins. This was the album in which Martyn bared all to his listeners, a painfully emotional work, which put the artist in a class of his own. Following this collection Martyn ended his association with Chris Blackwell. Martyn changed labels to WEA and delivered *Glorious Fool* and *Well Kept Secret*, also touring regularly with a full-time band including the experienced Max Middleton on keyboards and the talented fretless bassist, Alan Thompson. These two albums had now moved him firmly into the rock category and, in live performance, his much-revered acoustic guitar playing was relegated to only a few numbers, such as his now-classic song 'May You Never', subsequently recorded by Eric Clapton. Martyn's gift as a lyricist, however, had never been sharper, and he injected a fierce yet honest seam into his songs.

On the title track to *Glorious Fool* he wrote a powerful criticism of the former American president, Ronald Reagan (in just one carefully repeated line Martyn states, 'Half the lies he tells you are not true'). Following another home-made live album *Philentropy*, Martyn returned to Island Records and went on to deliver more excellent albums. *Sapphire*, with his evocative version of 'Somewhere Over The Rainbow', reflected a happier man, now re-married. The world's first commercially released CD single was Martyn's 'Angeline', a superbly crafted love song to his wife, which preceded the album *Piece By Piece* in 1986. With commercial success still eluding him, Martyn slid into another alcoholic trough until 1988, when he was given a doctor's ultimatum. He chose to dry out and live, returning in 1990 with *The Apprentice*. *Cooltide* was a fine album, expertly produced but contained songs that tended to last too long. This was also the case with *Couldn't Love You More* in 1992. The latter was a bonus for loyal fans as it was an album of re-recorded versions from Martyn's exquisite back catalogue. Perplexingly *No Little Boy* a year later was a re-recording of many of the songs on the former album. Martyn was unhappy with some of the tracks on *Couldn't Love You More* and his tolerant record company allowed him this luxury. Interestingly many of the versions were better especially a moody and lengthy return to 'Solid Air'. Following a move to Go! Discs in 1996 he recorded *And* (featuring Martyn's attempt at Thelonius Monk, with a cover art pose almost identical to *In Italy*), an album of new songs that features the cryptical 'Downward Pull Of Human Nature', an honest and sadly accurate observation of the attraction of infidelity with a strangely devastating punch line, 'did you ever look sideways at your best friend's wife'. Martyn has retained his loyal cult following for almost 30 years, and remains a critics' favourite. It is difficult to react indifferently to his challenging and emotional work. He now possesses a slurred voice that is a good octave lower than the young curly haired freshman of the 60s folk club circuit. He is a shambling genius of great originality and is by definition a major artist, although he has yet to receive major commercial success.

●ALBUMS: *London Conversation* (Island 1968)★★, *The Tumbler* (Island 1968)★★, *Stormbringer* (Island 1970)★★★, *The Road To Ruin* (Island 1970)★★★, *Bless The Weather* (Island 1971)★★★, *Solid Air* (Island 1973)★★★★, *Inside Out* (Island 1973)★★★, *Sunday's Child* (Island 1975)★★★, *Live At Leeds* (Island 1975)★★★, *One World* (Island 1977)★★★★, *Grace And Danger* (Island 1980)★★★★, *Glorious Fool* (Warners 1981)★★★★, *Well Kept Secret* (Warners 1982)★★★★, *Philentrophy* (1983)★★, *Sapphire* (Island 1984)★★★, *Piece By Piece* (Island 1986)★★★★, *Foundations* (Island 1987)★★★, *The Apprentice* (Island 1990)★★★, *Cooltide* (Permanent 1991)★★, *BBC Radio 1 Live In Concert* (Windsong 1992)★★★, *Couldn't Love You More* (Permanent 1992)★★★, *No Little Boy* (Permanent 1993)★★★, *And* (Go! Discs 1996)★★★.

●COMPILATIONS: *So Far So Good* (Island 1977)★★★, *The Electric John Martyn* (Island 1982)★★★, *Sweet Little Mysteries: The Island Anthology* (Island 1994)★★★★.

MARX, RICHARD

This Chicago, Illinois, USA-bred singer-songwriter began his career at the age of five, singing on US advertising jingles. This became his professional vocation until he moved on to become a backing singer for Lionel Richie. Afterwards, Marx embarked on a solo career in his own right. A string of hits began with 'Don't Mean Nothing' before he put together a run of three successive US number 1 hits with 'Hold On To The Nights', 'Satisfied' and 'Right Here Waiting'. He also wrote the Kenny Rogers hit 'What About Me'. Seemingly

unable to fail with his big ballad formula, Marx looks assured of continued success in the US market. He married Cynthia Rhodes of Animotion in August 1989.

●ALBUMS: *Richard Marx* (Manhattan 1987)★★★, *Repeat Offender* (EMI 1989)★★, *Rush Street* (Capitol 1991)★★★, *Paid Vacation* (Parlophone 1994)★★★.

MASSIVE ATTACK

This loose Bristol collective has grown to become one of the premier UK dance/rap outfits. The group features the talents of rapper '3D' Del Najo (b. c.1966), and Daddy G (b. c.1959) and Mushroom (b. c.1968, Knowle West, Bristol, England). They started in 1988 having spent several years working on various mobile sound systems, as well as releasing records under the Wild Bunch moniker ('Fucking Me Up', 'Tearing Down The Avenue'). Nellee Hooper, a former member of the Wild Bunch, left to work with Soul II Soul, while another original member, Milo Johnson, began work in Japan. 3D is also a well-respected graffiti artist, having his work featured in art galleries and a television survey on Channel 4. Liaisons with Neneh Cherry eventually led to a meeting with Cameron McVey, who produced Massive Attack's debut album. The resultant *Blue Lines* boasted three hit singles; 'Daydreaming', 'Unfinished Sympathy' (which also featured an orchestral score) and 'Safe From Harm'. The blend of rap, deep reggae and soul was provocative and rich in texture, and featured singing from Cherry and Shara Nelson. An outstanding achievement, it had taken eight months to create 'with breaks for Christmas and the World Cup'. 'Unfinished Sympathy' was particularly well received. *Melody Maker* magazine ranked it as the best single of 1991, and it remains a perennial club favourite. One minor hiccup arrived when they were forced, somewhat hysterically, to change their name during the Gulf War in order to maintain airplay. It was duly shortened to Massive. Their philosophy singled them out as dance music's new sophisticates, 'We don't ever make direct dance music. You've got to be able to listen and then dance.' That status was confirmed when U2 asked them to remix their single 'Mysterious Ways'. Despite *Blue Lines* being widely acclaimed, the band disappeared shortly afterwards. Shara Nelson had a solo career, with Massive Attack put on hold until the mid-90s. Another early contributor, Tricky, launched himself to considerable fanfare, with Massive Attack widely credited as an influence on fellow-Bristolians Portishead. A second Massive Attack album finally arrived in 1994, with former collaborator Nellee Hooper returning as producer. The featured singers this time included Tricky, Nigerian-born Nicolette, Everything But The Girl's Tracey Thorn and Horace Andy (who had also contributed to the debut) on a selection of tracks that sadly failed to capture the magic of *Blue Lines*. Many critics suggested that others had now run so far with the baton handed them by the collective that the instigators themselves were yet to catch up. A new album was due for release in August 1997.

●ALBUMS: *Blue Lines* (Wild Bunch/EMI 1991)★★★★, *Protection* (EMI 1994)★★★, Vs the Mad Professor *No Protection* (Circa 1995)★★★.

MASTERS OF REALITY

This New York, US-based quartet featured Chris Goss (vocals/guitar), Tim Harrington (guitar), Googe (bass) and Vinnie Ludovico (drums). Deriving their name from the title of Black Sabbath's third album, they fused a diverse array of rock styles into a form that clearly invoked names such as the Doors, Vanilla Fudge, Love and Deep Purple. The group originally formed as early as 1980, after which they embarked on a long-haul club touring policy that finally brought them serious attention. With the aid of producer Rick Rubin, who signed them originally to his Def Jam enterprise before it became Def American, they distilled their influences into a potent and powerful sound that had its roots in the 70s but was delivered with the technology of the present. Their self-titled debut was released to widespread critical acclaim in 1989, but fans had to wait another four years for a follow-up, *Sunrise On The Sufferbus*. This featured the legendary Ginger Baker joining only surviving original member, Goss. The first line-up had imploded following disastrous touring engagements in support of their debut, and the intervening period had seen Masters Of Reality put on ice. Harrington and Ludovico formed the Bogeymen.

●ALBUMS: *Masters Of Reality* (Def American 1989)★★★, *Sunrise On The Sufferbus* (Def American 1993)★★★.

MATT BIANCO

This UK jazz/pop group was formed in 1984 by ex-Blue Rondo A La Turk members Mark Reilly (b. 20 February 1960, High Wycombe, Buckinghamshire, England; lead vocals) and Daniel White (b. 26 August 1959, High Wycombe, Hertfordshire, England; keyboards), with Basia (b. Basha Trzetrzelewska, 30 September 1954, Jaworzno, Poland; vocals). They emerged in the latter part of the UK jazz/pop scene in the early 80s, inhabited by other acts such as Sade and Animal Nightlife. Signed to the WEA Records-distributed YZ label, they achieved a run of hits with the breezy, samba-laced 'Get Out Of Your Lazy Bed' (1984), 'Sneaking Out The Back Door'/'Matt's Moods' (1984), 'Half A Minute (1984) and a cover of Georgie Fame's 'Yeh Yeh' (1985). The initial employment of various session musicians was abandoned in favour of a full-time group, taking on Mark Fisher (who had connections to the group in the capacity of songwriter), as keyboard player, plus Kito Poncioni (b. Rio, Brazil; bass). Basia left in 1986 to forge her own solo career and was replaced by Jenni Evans. Daniel White also left around this time. Basia and White recorded *Time And Tide* together and, because of White's contractual problems the album, and various singles from it, came out as Basia solo releases. By now Matt Bianco was, in pop terms, unfashionable; yet Reilly's fascination, and adeptness with fusing Latin rhythms to pop, gave the group another UK hit in 1988 with the number 11 single, 'Don't Blame It On That Girl'. Increasingly driven to cater for a select audience, the group has continued to produce specialized, quality pop music.

●ALBUMS: *Whose Side Are You On?* (Warners 1984)★★★★, *Matt Bianco* (Warners 1986)★★★, *Indigo* (Warners 1988)★★★, *Samba In Your Casa* (East West 1991)★★.

●COMPILATIONS: *The Best Of Matt Bianco* (East West 1990)★★★★, *Yeah Yeah* (Warners 1993)★★.

MAYS, LYLE

b. 27 November 1953, Wausaukie, Wisconsin, USA. The varied keyboard talents of Mays are regularly heard together with Pat Metheny. They met in 1975, and have since forged a musical partnership built upon respect and admiration for each other's work. While it is Metheny who rightly takes the limelight, the integral backbone of the music has much to do with May's fluid keyboard playing, thoughtful arrangements and superb composing ability. In addition to sharing the credits on *As Falls Wichita, So Falls Wichita Falls*, he has played on virtually all of Metheny's impressive catalogue. He contributed to Eberhard Weber's *Later That Evening*, and has so far released two critically acclaimed solo albums. The 'Alaskan Suite', in particular, shows the vast range of capabilities possessed by this dedicated and unassuming musician.

●ALBUMS: *Lyle Mays* (Geffen 1986)★★★, *Street Dreams* (Geffen 1988)★★★★, with John DeJohnette, Marc Johnson *Fictionary* (Geffen 1993)★★★.

MAZE (FEATURING FRANKIE BEVERLY)

Frankie Beverly (b. 6 December 1946, Philadelphia, Pennsylvania, USA) had an apprenticeship in several Philadelphia groups. One such unit, Frankie Beverly And The Butlers, recorded several well-received singles in the 60s, but never managed to get more than local play. By the early 70s, however, impressed by Santana and Sly And The Family Stone, he formed a self-contained band, Raw Soul, and they moved to San Francisco where they became the house band at a local club, the Scene. Discovered by a girlfriend of Marvin Gaye, the group subsequently supported the singer in concert, and it was he who suggested they change their name in deference to their now cooler sound. The septet, which featured Wayne aka Wuane Thomas, Sam Porter, Robin Duke, Roame Lowery, McKinley Williams, Joe Provost plus Beverly, thus became Maze. Their debut was issued in January 1977, since which time Maze have remained one of soul's most consistent live attractions. Indeed, the group sold out six consecutive nights at London's Hammersmith Odeon during their 1985 tour. However, Beverly's brand of funk/R&B has failed to achieve the wider recognition it deserves and he remains something of a cult figure.

●ALBUMS: *Maze Featuring Frankie Beverly* (Capitol 1977)★★★, *Golden Time Of Day* (Capitol 1978)★★★, *Inspiration* (Capitol 1979)★★★, *Joy And Pain* (Capitol 1980)★★★, *Live In New Orleans* (Capitol 1981)★★★, *We Are One* (Capitol 1983)★★★, *Can't Stop The Love* (Capitol 1985)★★★, *Live In Los Angeles* (Capitol 1986)★★★★, *Silky Soul* (Warners 1989)★★★, *Back To Basics* (1993)★★★.

●COMPILATIONS: *Lifelines Volume One* (Capitol 1989)★★★.

McFERRIN, BOBBY

b. 11 March 1950, New York City, New York, USA. To call Bobby McFerrin a jazz vocalist is hardly to do him justice, for when McFerrin performs - he usually appears solo in lengthy concerts - he uses his entire body as a sound-box, beating noises out of his slender frame while emitting a constant accompaniment of guttural noises, clicks and popping sounds. To all this he adds a vocal technique that owes a slight debt to the bop vocalist Betty Carter and her daring swoops and scat vocals. McFerrin was brought up in a musical family - both his parents are opera singers, his father performing on the film soundtrack of *Porgy And Bess* in 1959 - but his main jazz influence came from Miles Davis's *Bitches Brew* album. Training as a pianist at the Juilliard School and later at Sacramento State College, he worked first as an accompanist, then as a pianist and singer during the 70s. He came to public notice in 1979, when he performed in New York with the singer Jon Hendricks, from whom he learnt much, but it was his unaccompanied appearance at the 1981 Kool Jazz Festival which brought him widespread acclaim. By 1983, he had perfected his solo style of wordless, vocal improvisations. His debut album contained a dramatic reworking of Van Morrison's 'Moondance', while *The Voice* mixed his fondness for pop classics - this time, the Beatles' 'Blackbird' - with more adventurous pieces, notably the self-descriptive 'I'm My Own Walkman'. The 1988 album *Simple Pleasures* shows off his wide range with its mixture of pop classics and self-composed material. The highlight of the album was his idiosyncratic version of Cream's 'Sunshine Of Your Love', complete with a vocal electric guitar. That recording also spawned a huge hit single 'Don't Worry Be Happy' which was featured in the movie *Cocktail*. It reached number 1 in the USA and number 2 in the UK. Further hit success came when Cadbury's chocolate used 'Thinkin' About Your Body' in a major advertising campaign (substituting the word chocolate for body). This moved him away from a jazz audience although *Paper Music* was an impressive venture with McFerrin attempting the music of Bach, Mozart and Mendelsohn. He joined forces with Yellowjackets on *Bang!Zoom*, arguably his finest album to date. McFerrin is a true original, blessed with a remarkable vocal ability that goes beyond the human voice.

●ALBUMS: *Bobby McFerrin* (Elektra Musician 1982)★★★, *The Voice* (Elektra Musician 1984)★★★, *Spontaneous Inventions* (Blue Note 1986)★★★, *Simple Pleasures* (EMI Manhattan 1988)★★★, *Medicine Music* (EMI Manhattan 1990)★★★, with Chick Corea *Play* (Blue Note 1992)★★★, *Paper Music* (Sony 1995)★★★, *Bang!Zoom* (Blue Note 1996)★★★, *Circle Songs* (Sony 1997)★★★.

McLAREN, MALCOLM

b. 22 January 1946, London, England. After a tempestuous childhood, during which he was reared by his eccentric grandmother, McLaren spent the mid to late 60s at various art colleges. In 1969 he became romantically involved with fashion designer Vivienne Westwood and they subsequently had a son together, Joseph. McLaren was fascinated by the work of the Internationale Situationist, a Marxist/Dadaist group which espoused its doctrines through sharp political slogans such as 'be reasonable - demand the impossible'. Their use of staged 'situations', designed to gain the attention of and ultimately enlighten the proletariat, impressed McLaren, and would significantly influence his entrepreneurial career. In 1971 he opened the shop Let It Rock in Chelsea's Kings Road, which catered for Teddy Boy fashions. Among the shop's many visitors were several members of the New York Dolls, whose management McLaren took over in late 1974. It was to prove an ill-fated venture, but McLaren did spend some time with them in New York and organized their 'Better Dead Than Red' tour. After returning to the UK, he decided to find a new, young group whose power, presence and rebelliousness equalled that of the Dolls. The result was the Sex Pistols, whose brief spell of public notoriety ushered in the era of punk. McLaren was at the peak of his powers during this period, riding the wave of self-inflicted chaos that the Pistols spewed forth. The highlights included McLaren taking sizeable cheques from both EMI and A&M Records, who signed then fired the group in quick succession. The creation of the tragic caricature Sid Vicious, the conflict with Johnny Rotten, the involvement with Great Train Robber Ronnie Biggs and, finally, a self-glorifying film *The Great Rock 'n' Roll Swindle*, were all part of the saga. Following the Sex Pistols' demise, McLaren launched Bow Wow Wow, heavily promoting the 14-year-old singer Annabella Lu Win. Although their recordings were highly original for the period, the dividends proved unimpressive and the group split. In the meantime, McLaren had served as 'advisor' to and let slip through his hands 80s stars such as Adam Ant and Boy George (Culture Club). Eventually, he decided to transform himself into a recording star, despite the fact that he could not sing (ample evidence of which had appeared on his *Great Rock 'n' Roll Swindle* out-take, 'You Need Hands'). His singular ability to predict trends saw him assimilating various styles of music, from the Zulu tribes in Africa to the ethnic sounds of the Appalachian Mountains. The arduous sessions finally came to fruition with *Duck Rock*, which featured two UK Top 10 singles, 'Buffalo Girls' and 'Double Dutch'.

The work pre-empted rock's interest in world music, as exemplified on *Graceland* by Paul Simon. McLaren next persisted with the music of urban New York and was particularly interested in the 'scratching' sounds of street hip hop disc jockeys. *Would Ya Like More Scratchin'* again anticipated the strong dance culture that would envelop the UK pop scene in the late 80s. Ever restless, McLaren moved on to a strange fusion of pop and opera with *Fans*, which featured a startling version of 'Madam Butterfly' that became a UK Top 20 hit. Following his experimental forays in the music business, McLaren relocated to Hollywood for a relatively unsuccessful period in the film industry. Nothing substantial emerged from that sojourn, but McLaren remains as unpredictable and innovative as ever.
●ALBUMS: *Duck Rock* (Island 1983)★★, *Would Ya Like More Scratchin'* (Island 1984)★★, *Fans* (Island 1984)★★★, *Swamp Thing* (Island 1985)★, *Waltz Darling* (Epic 1989)★★. As Malcolm McLaren Presents The World Famous Supreme Team Show *Round The Outside! Round The Outside!* (Virgin 1990)★★, *Paris* (Disques Vogue 1994)★★★, *The Largest Movie Houses In Paris (The Ambient Remixes)* (World Attractions 1996)★★.
●FURTHER READING: *Starmakers & Svengalis: The History Of British Pop Management*, Johnny Rogan. *The Wicked Ways Of Malcolm McLaren*, Craig Bromberg.

MEKONS
Although initially based in Leeds, England, the Mekons made their recording debut for the Edinburgh-based Fast Product label in 1978. 'Never Been In A Riot', the outlet's first release, was the subject of effusive music press praise, and its joyous amateurism set the standard for much of the group's subsequent work. Having completed a second single, 'Where Were You', the Mekons were signed to Virgin Records where a line-up of Andy Carrigan (vocals), Mark White (vocals), Kevin Lycett (guitar), Tom Greenhalgh (guitar), Ross Allen (bass) and Jon Langford (drums, later guitar/vocals) completed *The Quality Of Mercy Is Not Strnen*. This unusual title was drawn from the axiom that, if you give a monkey a typewriter and an infinite amount of time, it would eventually produce the complete works of Shakespeare, a wry comment on the group's own musical ability. Nonetheless, the Mekons' enthusiasm, particularly in a live setting, was undoubtedly infectious and has contributed greatly to their long career. Despite numerous personnel changes (over 30 dif-

ferent members to 1995), they have retained a sense of naïve adventurism, embracing world music, folk and roots material in their customarily ebullient manner. In the 90s three of the core members of the band (Greenhaigh, Langford and Sara Corina, Greenhaigh's violinist partner who joined in 1991) had relocated to Chicago, Illinois, USA, where the group enjoyed a loose recording contract with Quarterstick Records. This followed an unfortunate major label coalition with A&M Records. Other important contributors to the Mekons' legacy include Sally Timms, vocalist and full-time member since the late 80s, who has released a brace of solo albums and is based in New York, and drummer Steve Goulding (ex-Graham Parker And The Rumour), a part-time journalist who has worked with Pig Dog Pondering. Langford also worked with Goulding on his part-time country band, Jon Langford And The Pine Valley Cosmonauts, who issued an album in Germany in 1994. He has also had numerous exhibitions of his paintings.

● ALBUMS: *The Quality Of Mercy Is Not Strnen* (Virgin 1979)★★, *Mekons* (Red Rhino 1980)★★, *Fear And Whiskey* (Sin 1985)★★★, *The Edge Of The World* (Sin 1986)★★★, *Honky Tonkin'* (Sin 1987)★★★, *New York Mekons* cassette only (ROIR 1987)★★, *So Good It Hurts* (Twin/Tone 1988)★★★, *Mekons Rock 'N' Roll* (A&M 1989)★★★, *F.U.N. '90 EP* (A&M 1990)★★★, *The Curse Of The Mekons* (Blast First 1991)★★★, *I Love Mekons* (Quarterstick 1993)★★★, *Retreat From Memphis* (Quarterstick 1994)★★★, with Kathy Acker *Pussy, King Of The Pirates* (Quarterstick 1996)★★★, *Mekons United* CD/novel (Touch And Go 1996)★★.

● COMPILATIONS: *Mekons Story* (CNT 1982)★★★, *Original Sin* (RTD 1989)★★★.

● FURTHER READING: *Mekons United*, no author listed.

MELLE MEL AND THE FURIOUS 5

Melle Mel (b. Melvin Glover, New York City, New York, USA) was a typical black 'ghetto child' whose interest in music originally stemmed from the Beatles. He soon embraced the earliest sounds of hip hop in the mid 70s, becoming a breakdancer with the D-Squad. As a DJ with his brother Kid Creole he was influenced by others in the profession like Klark Kent and Timmy Tim who used to talk rhymes whilst playing music. The pair started their own brand of rapping and around 1977 set up with another DJ, Grandmaster Flash - who gave Melle Mel his new name. Flash already had one MC - Cowboy - with him, and so the new team

became Grandmaster Flash and the 3MCs. Over the next couple of years they were joined by Scorpio and then Rahiem. Spurred by the success of 'Rapper's Delight' by the Sugarhill Gang, Flash's team recorded 'We Rap More Mellow' under the name The Young Generation. Both it and a second single ('Sugar Rappin') flopped but then they signed to Sugarhill Records as Grandmaster Flash and the Furious Five. Together they recorded one of rap's greatest standards, 'The Message'. A hugely significant record which took hip hop away from braggadocio into social commentary, the featured vocalist was Melle Mel. Subsequent releases over the next few years came out under a wide variety of names and the battle for best billing plus squabbles with management and record company eventually led to the group splitting in two in 1984. A deep rift between Flash and Mel came about because, according to the latter: 'We'd known that Sugarhill was crooks when we first signed with 'em, so the plan had always been to build it up to a certain point where . . . they couldn't keep on taking the money that they was taking! That's what I'd been banking on, but those that left didn't seem to see it the same way'. Mel retained Cowboy and Scorpio and recruited another of his brothers King Louie III plus Tommy Gunn, Kami Kaze, and Clayton Savage. Flash had inaugurated a $5 million court action against Sylvia Robinson's Sugarhill label to attain full rights to the Grandmaster Flash name, which he lost. The group's new operating title was thus Grandmaster Melle Mel & The Furious Five. The name was forced on the band by Sugarhill, though it infuriated Flash and Mel himself was unhappy with it. Singles like 'Beat Street Breakdown Part 1', and 'We Don't Work For Free' would fail to break the upper echelons of the charts, though Mel did appear on the intro to Chaka Khan's worldwide smash 'I Feel For You'. There was also a UK Top 10 hit with 'Step Off', after which his popularity cooled. By 1987 the mutual lack of success encouraged the separated parties to reunite as Grandmaster Flash, Melle Mel And The Furious Five for a Paul Simon-hosted charity concert in New York. The intervening years between then and Mel's appearance on Quincy Jones' 'Back On The Block' were lost to drug addiction, painfully ironic, considering that Mel's best-known record remains 'White Lines (Don't Do It)', an anti-drug blockbuster which was credited to Grandmaster Flash and Melle Mel. It first hit the charts in 1983 and re-entered on several occasions. Originally targeted specifically at cocaine, it was revamped in 1989 by Sylvia Johnson because of the crack boom. Its pro-abstinence stance was not physically shared by the protagonists. When Mel was in the studio in 1982, laying down the vocal track, he admits that the 'only thing I was thinking about in that studio was listening to the record, joking and getting high'. In 1994 news broke that Mel was back and fighting fit (taking the trouble to perform press-ups for interviewers to prove the point), and working on a new album with former Ice-T collaborator Afrika Islam. He also linked with Flash for his 'Mic Checka' radio show.

●ALBUMS: *Work Party* (Sugarhill 1984)★★★, *Stepping Off* (Sugarhill 1985)★★★.

MELLENCAMP, JOHN

b. 7 October 1951, Seymour, Indiana, USA. Mellencamp survived an early phase as a glam-rocker to become one of America's most successful mainstream rock singers of the past two decades. He played in local band Trash with guitarist Larry Crane (b. 1953), who remained with Mellencamp throughout the 80s. In 1976, David Bowie's manager Tony de Fries signed him to a recording contract. His name was changed to Johnny Cougar, he was given a James Dean-style image and a debut album was rush-released. *Chestnut Street Incident*, released as a demo and consisting of mainly cover versions, was credited to Johnny Cougar and did not chart. He left MainMan and moved back to Indiana, formed the Zone and recorded the self-penned *The Kid Inside*. Shortly afterwards he signed to Riva Records, owned by Rod Stewart's manager Billy Gaff who presented him as 'the next Bruce Springsteen'. His first chart action came courtesy of *John Cougar*, which included the US Top 30 single 'I Need A Lover' in December 1979. Cougar and his band toured constantly, a strategy which paid off in 1982 when *American Fool* headed the US album chart (USA sales by 1996 were 5 million) while both 'Hurts So Good' and 'Jack And Diane' were million-sellers.

The following year he became John Cougar Mellencamp, eventually dropping 'Cougar' in 1989. With many of his songs dealing with social problems, Mellencamp was one of the organisers of the Farm Aid series of benefit concerts. His straight-ahead rock numbers also brought a string of big hits in the second half of the 80s. Among the most notable were 'Small Town', 'R.O.C.K. In The USA', 'Paper In Fire' (1987) and 'Cherry Bomb' (1988). *Lonesome Jubilee* used fiddles and accordions to illustrate bleak portraits of America in recession, while 'Pop Singer' from *Big Daddy* expressed Mellencamp's disillusionment with the current state of the music business. He took time off to concentrate on painting but returned with *Whenever We Wanted,* which recaptured the muscular rock sound of his earlier albums. In 1991, Mellencamp directed and starred in the film *Falling From Grace.* He has continued to hit the US charts with amazing rapidity and, up until early 1991, he had charted 21 singles in the US Hot 100 of which nine were Top 10, with one number 1, 'Jack And Diane' in 1982.

●ALBUMS: *Chestnut Street Incident* (Mainman 1976)★★, *The Kid Inside* (Castle 1977)★★, *A Biography* (Riva 1978)★★, *John Cougar* (Riva 1979)★★★, *Nothing Matters And What If It Did* (Riva 1981)★, *American Fool* (Riva 1982)★★★, *Uh-Huh* (Riva 1983)★★★, *Scarecrow* (Riva 1985)★★★, *The Lonesome Jubilee* (Mercury 1987)★★★, *Big Daddy* (Mercury 1989)★★★, *Whenever We Wanted* (Mercury 1991)★★★, *Human Wheels* (Mercury 1993)★★, *Dance Naked* (Mercury 1994)★★, *Mr. Happy Go Lucky* (Mercury 1996)★★★.

●COMPILATIONS: *Early Years* (Rhino 1986)★★, *The John Cougar Collection* (Castle 1986)★★★.

●VIDEOS: *John Cougar Mellencamp: Ain't That America* (Embassy 1984).

●FURTHER READING: *American Fool: The Roots And Improbable Rise Of John Cougar Mellencamp*, Torgoff.

MEN AT WORK

Formed in Melbourne, Australia, in 1979, by singer Colin Hay (b. 29 June 1953, Scotland - emigrated to Australia aged 14) and guitarist Ron Strykert (b. 18 August 1957, Australia), initially as an acoustic duo. With the later addition of Greg Ham (b. 27 September 1953, Australia), John Rees (bass) and Jerry Speiser (drums), Men At Work performed for two years in small, inner-suburban pubs before being discovered and signed by CBS Records executive Peter Karpin. In 1981, the first single, 'Who Can It Be Now?', was an enormous Australian hit, soon followed by 'Down Under' and the album *Business As Usual.* The band's success surprised and infuriated home critics, who had written them off as derivative and insipid. However, blessed with three songwriters and supported by videos which showcased the band's sense of humour (and as a support act to Fleetwood Mac), Men At Work were able to achieve two US number 1 hits in 1982 with 'Who Can It Be Now?' and 'Down Under' and a US number 1 album that same year. Success followed again in the UK where 'Down Under' reached number 1 in early 1983, accompanied by *Business As Usual* topping the charts. By now, Men At Work could comfortably claim to be the world's most successful Australian pop group. The follow-up album, *Cargo,* sold well in the USA, reaching number 3, and provided two Top 10 singles in 'Overkill' and 'It's A Mistake'. Despite the album reaching the Top 10 in the UK, single success there was harder to sustain, with three singles reaching Top 40 status only. The third album, *Two Hearts,* sold less well, although it did achieve gold status in the USA, peaking at number 50. The original personnel had by now disintegrated, leaving Hay as the sole surviving member. The break-up in 1985 followed arguments over management and writing, and each member followed his own path. Hay, after recording a solo album, *Looking For Jack* (1987), recorded another, *Wayfaring Sons,* on MCA in 1990, as the Colin Hay Band, using Celtic music as its base.

●ALBUMS: *Business As Usual* (Epic 1981)★★★, *Cargo* (Epic 1983)★★★, *Two Hearts* (Epic 1985)★★.

MEN WITHOUT HATS

Formed in Montreal, Canada, in 1980, this act was the brainchild of siblings Ivan (vocals) and Jeremy (drums) Arrobas, who manufactured the remaining accompaniment on their records with synthesizers. An independent EP, *Folk Of The 80s,* created overseas cult interest to the extent that it was reissued on Britain's Stiff Records, along with an edit of its 'Antarctica' track as a single. However, just after the release of 1981's 'Nationale Seven', Jeremy left to allow composer Ivan to front a Men Without Hats with the brothers Stefan (guitar/violin) and Colin Doroschuk (keyboards) plus Allan McCarthy (drums). Produced by manager Marc Durand, *Rhythm Of Youth* reached number 14 in the USA in the wake of 'Safety Dance', a global smash born of a truce between electro-pop and medieval jollity that carried an anti-nuclear message over into an arresting video. A sure sign of its impact was a parody by 'Weird Al' Yankovic. No more hits came the group's way, but their recordings still received a fair critical consideration.

●ALBUMS: *Rhythm Of Youth* (Statik 1982)★★★, *Folk Of the 80s Part III* (Statik 1984)★★★, *Pop Goes The Word* (Mercury 1987)★★.

MERCURY, FREDDIE

b. Frederick Bulsara, 5 September 1946, Zanzibar, Africa, d. 24 November 1991, London, England. Best known as the flamboyant lead singer of the multi-million-selling UK group Queen, Mercury also branched out into extra-curricular musical activities. In 1973, while Queen were about to release their debut album, Mercury recorded a revival of the Beach Boys' 'I Can Hear Music' under the glam rock name Larry Lurex. It was not until late 1984 that he again attempted a solo work, this time with the UK Top 20 hit 'Love Kills', from the Giorgio Moroder soundtrack to the film *Metropolis*. A second solo single, 'I Was Born To Love You', reached the UK Top 20 early the next year. A solo album and some lowly placed solo singles followed. In 1986, Mercury contributed some tracks to the cast recording of Dave Clark's musical *Time*. His greatest solo success, however, came in 1987, with a kitsch revival of the Platters' 'The Great Pretender', which reached the UK Top 5. Later that year, Mercury emphasized his immemorial love of opera by teaming up with Monserrat Caballe for the grandiloquent 'Barcelona', another Top 10 success. An album of the same title was also successful and, in late 1988, the operatic duo played a major show at the Avinguda De Maria Cristina Stadium in Barcelona. Mercury retained a low profile thereafter, and, following much speculation over his health in November 1991 he finally admitted that he was suffering from AIDS. Within forty-eight hours, on 24 November, he died from bronchial pneumonia at his Knightsbridge home. A major concert was arranged in April 1992 at London's Wembley stadium. Known as the Freddy Mercury Aids Benefit, it attracted the largest ever worldwide viewing audience when televised live.

●ALBUMS: *Mr Bad Guy* (Columbia 1985)★★, with Monserrat Caballe *Barcelona* (Polydor 1988)★★.

●FURTHER READING: *The Show Must Go On: The Life Of Freddie Mercury,* Rick Sky. *A Kind Of Magic: A Tribute To Freddie Mercury,* Ross Clarke. *Mercury And Me,* Jim Hutton with Tim Wapshott.

METHENY, PAT

b. 12 August 1954, Kansas City, Missouri, USA. Although classed as a jazz guitarist, Metheny has bridged the gap between jazz and rock music in the same way that Miles Davis did in the late 60s and early 70s. Additionally, he has played a major part in the growth of jazz with the younger generation of the 80s. His first musical instrument was a French horn, and surprisingly he did not begin with the guitar until he was a teenager. His outstanding virtuosity soon had him teaching the instrument at the University Of Miami and the Berklee College Of Music in Boston. He joined Gary Burton in 1974, and throughout his three-album stay, he contributed some fluid Wes Montgomery-influenced guitar patterns. Manfred

Eicher of ECM Records saw the potential and initiated a partnership that lasted for 10 superlative albums. He became, along with Keith Jarrett, ECM's biggest-selling artist, and his albums regularly topped the jazz record charts. Metheny is one of the few artists to make regular appearances in the pop album charts, such is the accessibility of his music. Both *Bright Size Life*, featuring the late Jaco Pastorious and *Watercolours*, though excellent albums, still showed a man who was feeling his way. His own individualistic style matured with *Pat Metheny Group* in 1978.

Together with his musical partner (and arguably, his right arm), the brilliant keyboardist Lyle Mays, he initiated a rock group format that produced album after album of melodious jazz/rock. Following a major tour with Joni Mitchell and Pastorious (*Shadows And Light*), Metheny released *New Chautauqua* and demonstrated an amazing dexterity on 12-string guitar and, against the fashion of the times, made the US Top 50. He returned to the electric band format for *American Garage*, which contained his country-influenced '(Cross The) Heartland'. The double set *80/81* featured Michael Brecker, Jack DeJohnette, Charlie Haden and Dewey Redman, and was more of a typical jazz album, featuring in particular the moderately *avant garde* 'Two Folk Songs'. The record still climbed the popular charts. During this time, Metheny constantly won jazz and guitarist polls. Mays' keyboards featured prominently in the group structure, and he received co-authorship credit for the suite *As Falls Wichita, So Falls Wichita Falls*. Metheny had by now become fascinated by the musical possibilities of the guitar synthesizer or synclavier. He used this to startling effect on *Offramp*, notably on the wonderfully contagious and arresting 'Are You Going With Me?' The double set *Travels* showed a band at the peak of its powers, playing some familiar titles with a new freshness. The short piece 'Travels', stands as one of his finest compositions, the low-level recording offers such subtle emotion that it becomes joyously funereal. *Rejoicing* was a modern jazz album demonstrating his sensitive interpretations of music by Horace Silver and Ornette Coleman. *First Circle* maintained the standard and showed a greater leaning towards Latin-based music, still with Metheny's brilliant ear for melody; additionally the track 'If I Could' displayed the same sparse subtlety of *Travels*. In 1985, he composed the film score for *The Falcon And The Snowman* which led to his recording 'This Is Not America' with David Bowie. The resulting Top 40 US hit (number 12 in the UK),

brought Metheny many new young admirers. The concert halls found audiences bedecked in striped rugby shirts, in the style of their new hero.

Ironically, at the same time, following a break with ECM, Metheny turned his back on possible rock stardom and produced his most perplexing work, *Song X*, with free-jazz exponent Ornette Coleman. Reactions were mixed in reviewing this difficult album - ultimately the general consensus was that it was brilliantly unlistenable. He returned to more familiar ground with *Still Life (Talking)* and *Letter From Home*, although both showed a greater move towards Latin melody and rhythm. In 1990, *Reunion* was released, a superb meeting with his former boss Gary Burton and a few months later, together with Dave Holland and Roy Haynes, he made *Question And Answer*. Additionally he was heavily featured, along with Herbie Hancock, on the excellent Jack DeJohnette album, *Parallel Realities*.

He continued into the 90s with *Secret Story*, an album of breathtaking beauty. Although the album may have made jazz purists cringe it was a realization of all Metheny's musical influences. His second live album *The Road To You* did not have the emotion of *Travels*. It was something to keep the fans quiet before he unleashed an exciting recording with John Scofield, both guitarists having been sharing the honours at the top of jazz polls for the past few years. *Zero Tolerence For Silence* can only be described as astonishing - for many this wall of sound guitar was a self-indulgent mess. After repeated play the music does not get any easier, but at least we can understand his motives more and appreciate what a bold move this thrash metal outing was. Metheny found himself reviewed in the heavy metal press for the first (and last) time. *We Live Here* was a return to familiar ground, and a familiar position at the top of the jazz charts. He has an extraordinary sense of melody and his work neither rambles nor becomes self-indulgent; much credit must also be given to the like-minded Lyle Mays, whose quiet presence at the side of the stage is the backbone for much of Metheny's music.

●ALBUMS: *Bright Size Life* (ECM 1976)★★★★, *Watercolours* (ECM 1977)★★★, *Pat Metheny Group* (ECM 1978)★★★★, *New Chautauqua* (ECM 1979)★★★★, *American Garage* (ECM 1979)★★★★, *80/81* (ECM 1980)★★★, *As Falls Wichita, So Falls Wichita Falls* (ECM 1981)★★★★, *Offramp* (ECM 1982)★★★★, *Travels* (ECM 1983)★★★★, with Charlie Haden and Billy Higgins *Rejoicing* (ECM 1983)★★★, *First Circle* (ECM 1984)★★★, *The*

Falcon And The Snowman film soundtrack (EMI America 1985)★★, with Ornette Coleman *Song X* (Geffen 1986)★★★, *Still Life (Talking)* (Geffen 1987)★★★★, *Letter From Home* (Geffen 1989)★★★, with Gary Burton *Reunion* (Geffen 1990), *Question And Answer* (Geffen 1990)★★★★, with Jack DeJohnette *Parallel Realities* (Geffen 1990)★★★, *Secret Story* (Geffen 1992)★★★★, *The Road To You - Recorded Live In Europe* (Geffen 1993)★★★, with John Scofield *I Can See Your House From Here* (Blue Note 1994)★★★, *Zero Tolerance For Silence* (Geffen 1994)★★, *We Live Here* (Geffen 1995)★★★, *Quartet* (Geffen 1997)★★★, with Charlie Haden *Beyond The Missouri Sky (Short Stories)* (Verve 1997)★★★.

●COMPILATIONS: *Works* (ECM 1983)★★★★, *Works 2* (ECM 1988)★★★★.

●VIDEOS: *More Travels* (1993).

MEZZOFORTE

Until the arrival of the Sugarcubes, jazz-fusion band Mezzoforte were Iceland's best-known musical export. The group was formed in 1977 at a Rekjavik high school by Fridrik Karlsson (guitar), Eythor Gunnarsson (keyboards), Johann Asmundsson (bass), Gunnlaugur Briem (drums) and Kristin Svararsson (saxophone). They signed a recording contract with local label Steinar and the second album contained the exuberant 'Garden Party' which was a Top 20 hit in the UK in 1983. The tune was covered in the USA by Herb Alpert who performed it at half-speed, reportedly because he had learned the piece from a 45 rpm single accidentally played at 33. The follow-up 'Rockall' was only a minor hit but it was adopted as a signature tune by radio chart shows in The Netherlands and Britain. For a brief period, the group was based in London and in the mid-80s Mezzoforte played the European jazz festival circuit with vocalists Chris Cameron and Noel McCalla, formerly with Moon and Mike Rutherford's group. In 1990, Karlsson formed a jazz/funk band Point Blank featuring singer Ellen Kristjansdottor and members of Mezzoforte.

●ALBUMS: *Mezzoforte* (Steinar 1981)★★★, *I Hakanum* (Steinar 1982)★★★, *Thvilkt Og Annadeins* (1983)★★★, *Catching Up With Mezzoforte* (Steinar 1983)★★, *Surprise Surprise* (Steinar 1983)★★, *Observations* (Steinar 1984)★★★, *Rising* (Steinar 1984)★★, *No Limit* (Steinar 1987)★★★, *Playing For Time* (Steinar 1989)★★★.

MICHAEL, GEORGE

b. Georgios (Yorgos) Kyriacos Panayiotou, 25 June 1963, Finchley, London, England. Michael first served his pop apprenticeship in the million-selling duo Wham!, the most commercially successful, teen-orientated group of the 80s. His solo career was foreshadowed in 1984's 'Careless Whisper', a song about a promiscuous two-timer with the oddly attractive line: 'Guilty feet have got no rhythm'. By the time Wham! split in 1986, Michael was left with the unenviable task of reinventing himself as a solo artist. The balladeering 'Careless Whisper' had indicated a possible direction, but the initial problem was one of image. As a pin-up pop idol, Michael had allowed himself to become a paste-board figure, best remembered for glorifying a hedonistic lifestyle and shoving shuttlecocks down his shorts in concert. The rapid transition from dole queue reject to Club Tropicana playboy had left a nasty taste in the mouths of many music critics. Breaking the Wham! icon was the great challenge of Michael's solo career, and his finest and most decisive move was to take a sabbatical before recording an album, to allow time to put his old image to rest. In the meantime, he recorded the chart-topping 'A Different Corner', a song stylistically similar to 'Careless Whisper' and clearly designed to show off his talent as a serious singer-songwriter. Enlivening his alternate image as a blue-eyed soul singer, he teamed up with Aretha Franklin for the uplifting 'I Knew You Were Waiting', a transatlantic chart topper. Michael's re-emergence came in 1988, resplendent in leather and shades and his customary designer stubble. A pilot single, 'I Want Your Sex', was banned by daytime radio stations and broke his string of number 1s in the UK. *Faith* followed, and was not only well-received but sold in excess of 10 million copies. The album spawned a plethora of hit singles in the USA, including the title track, 'Father Figure', 'One More Try' and 'Monkey'. Equally adept at soul workouts and ballads, and regarded by some as one of the best new pop songwriters of his era, Michael seemed set for a long career. In 1990, he released his second album, *Listen Without Prejudice, Vol 1*, a varied work which predictably sold millions. The first single from the album 'Praying For Time' reached number 1 in the USA. In the UK, however, the comeback single was merely a Top 10 hit, suggesting that his status as a singles exponent in his homeland had markedly declined. Still dissatisfied with his media image, Michael announced that he would cease conducting interviews in future and concentrate on pursuing his career as a serious songwriter and musician. In 1992 the *Sunday Times* announced his arrival as one of the richest men in the UK. However, a court clash with his record label Sony dominated his activities in 1993 and 1994 (and was estimated to have cost him $7 million), with Michael arguing that his contract rendered him a 'pop slave' and demanding to be released from it. Mr Justice Jonathan Parker ruled in Sony's favour and Michael stated he would appeal, and also insisted that he would never again record for the label. In July 1995 it looked likely that Michael had managed to free himself from Sony - but only at the cost of $40 million. The buy-out was financed by David Geffen's new media empire, Dreamworks, and Virgin Records, who were also reputed to have paid him an advance of £30 million for two albums. The first was *Older*, one of the decade's slickest productions. Although the album became a huge success there was no great depth to the songs underneath the immaculate production. Michael announced the formation of his own record label Aegean Records, in February 1997.

●ALBUMS: *Faith* (Epic 1987)★★★★, *Listen Without Prejudice, Vol. 1* (Epic 1990)★★★, *Older* (DreamWorks 1996)★★★.

●VIDEOS: *Faith* (1988), *George Michael* (1990).

●FURTHER READING: *Wham! (Confidential) The Death Of A Supergroup*, Johnny Rogan. *Bare*, George Michael with Tony Parsons. *George Michael: The Making Of A Super Star*, Bruce Dessau, *In His Own Words*, Nigel Goodall.

MICRODISNEY

This incendiary pop/folk group were formed in Cork, Eire, in 1980. There was little cohesion in their early formations; 'We used to be much more frenzied in those days, a Fall-type mess, and our line-up was always changing. Originally Sean (O'Hagan) was going to play guitar and I (Cathal Coughlan) was going to recite poetry, then one week it was guitar, bass, drums, then guitar key-board and violin, then we had a drum machine . . ! After settling on the more traditional formation of drums, guitars, bass and keyboards, the band began releasing singles which were eventually collected together on *We Hate You White South African Bastards*. The title was typically inflammatory, and in direct opposition to that of their long-playing debut, *Everybody Is Fantastic*. An early clue to their subversive nature, on the surface Microdisney were purveyors of accessible and restrained pop music. This attracted Virgin Records, but the band

had a dark edge in Coughlan's bitter lyricism. Their Virgin debut, 'Town To Town', dented the lower regions of the charts and was quickly followed by *Crooked Mile*. However, Microdisney elected to bite the hand that fed them with the near hit 'Singer's Hampstead Home', which thinly masked an attack on Virgin's fallen idol, Boy George. They bowed out with *39 Minutes,* by which time the vitriol was really flowing, counter-balanced as ever by O'Hagan's delicate country guitar. Despite critical acclaim, Microdisney's sales had remained disappointingly in the cult bracket. O'Hagan went on to release a solo album in 1990 (*High Llamas*), and then record as the High Llamas, while Coughlan's Fatima Mansions have done much to spice up the late 80s and early 90s.

●ALBUMS: *Everybody Is Fantastic* (Rough Trade 1984)★★, *We Hate You White South African Bastards* (Rough Trade 1984)★★, *The Clock Comes Down The Stairs* (Rough Trade 1985)★★★, *Crooked Mile* (Virgin 1987)★★★, *39 Minutes* (Virgin 1988)★★★, *Peel Sessions* (Strange Fruit 1989)★★★.

●COMPILATIONS: *Big Sleeping House* (Virgin 1995)★★★★.

MIDNIGHT OIL

Formed in Sydney, New South Wales, in 1975, and known as Farm, this strident band has pioneered its own course in Australian rock without relying on the established network of agencies and record companies. The original nucleus of the band comprised Martin Rotsey (guitar), Rob Hirst (drums) and Jim Moginie (guitar). They were later joined by law student Peter Garrett (lead vocals). The group became notorious for always insisting on total control over its recorded product and media releases, including photos, and when booking agencies denied the band gigs, the members organized their own venues and tours, taking advantage of the group's large following on the alternative rock scene. Joined by Dwayne 'Bones' Hillman (bass) in 1977 and changing their name to Midnight Oil, the group took a couple of album releases to refine its songwriting style, principally by Moginie and Hirst. As *Head Injuries* went gold in Australia, the imposing shaven-headed Garrett, who had by now received his law degree, began to make known his firm views on politics. Having signed a worldwide deal with CBS/Columbia Records, it was *10,9,8,7,6,5,4,3,2,1*, which saw the band gain mainstream radio airplay. Featuring songs about the environment, anti-nuclear sentiments, anti-war songs and powerful anthems of anti-establishment, it also propelled the band into the international market place. The band performed at many charity concerts, promoting Koori (Australian aborigines) causes in Australia and the loquacious Garrett almost gained a seat in the Australian Parliament in 1984 while standing for the Nuclear Disarmament Party. The following album saw the band tour the USA and Europe, and *Rolling Stone* writers voted the album one of the best of 1989, despite a low profile there. While many regard *Red Sails In The Sunset* as their best work, the subsequent albums have been equally highly regarded. The group's peak album chart positions in the UK and USA were achieved with *Diesel And Dust* reaching the UK Top 20 and US number 21, while in the US the follow-up, *Blue Sky Mining* emulated that position. The group continued its antagonistic attitude towards major industrial companies in 1990, by organizing a protest concert outside the Manhattan offices of the Exxon oil company which was responsible for the Valdez oil slick in Alaska.

●ALBUMS: *Midnight Oil* (Powderworks 1978)★★, *Head Injuries* (Powderworks 1979)★★★, *Place Without A Postcard* (Columbia 1981)★★★, *10,9,8,7,6,5,4,3,2,1* (Columbia 1982)★★★, *Red Sails In The Sunset* (Columbia 1985)★★★★, *Diesel And Dust* (Columbia 1987)★★★★, *Blue Sky Mining* (Columbia 1990)★★★★, *Scream In Blue-Live* (Columbia 1992)★★★, *Earth And Sun And Moon* (Columbia 1993)★★★, *Breathe* (Columbia 1996)★★★.

●FURTHER READING: *Strict Rules*, Andrew McMillan.

MILLI VANILLI

This soul duo consisted of Rob Pilatus, who was brought up in an orphanage, and Fabrice Morvan, who was training to be a trampoline athlete until a fall damaged his neck. Based in Germany, they worked as backing singers for various German groups, before forming their own duo combining rap and soul, taking their name from a New York club. They enjoyed big hits with 'Girl, You Know It's True' and the similar 'Girl, I'm Gonna Miss You' before they suffered a major backlash when they were exposed as frontmen for a 'group' fabricated by producer Frank Farian. The duo had apparently been chosen for their looks and were effectively locked out of the studio when recording took place. After handing back music industry awards, they promised to return with a new contract and their own voices.

●ALBUMS: *All Or Nothing* (Cooltempo 1988)★★, *Two X Two* (Cooltempo 1989)★.

MINOGUE, KYLIE

b. 23 May 1968, Melbourne, Australia. Coming from a stage family, Minogue passed an audition for the Australian soap opera *Neighbours*, which eventually led to her recording debut with Little Eva's hit, 'The Locomotion. When the television series was successfully screened in Britain, prolific hit producers Stock, Aitken And Waterman intervened to mould Minogue's attractive, wholesome, anodyne image to their distinctive brand of radio-centred pop. The first UK single, 'I Should Be So Lucky', soon reached number 1, presaging an impressive chart run of instantly hummable hits, including 'Got To Be Certain', 'Je Ne Sais Pas Pour quoi', 'Hand On Your Heart', 'Wouldn't Change A Thing' and 'Never Too Late'. With solo success enhanced by duets with co-star Jason Donovan, Minogue has emerged as one of the most successfully marketed acts of the late 80s, with books and films, including *The Delinquents*. In 1991, the former soap star drastically changed her girl-next door image and adopted a sexier persona, which won her even more media coverage - particularly when she became romantically involved with INXS lead singer, Michael Hutchence. Surprisingly, she even won some acclaim in the music press and found herself championed as an unlikely 'pop goddess'. In 1996 she recorded with Nick Cave and the following year was working in the recording studio with the Manic Street Preachers.

●ALBUMS: *Kylie* (PWL 1988)★★, *Enjoy Yourself* (PWL 1989)★★, *Kylie* (PWL 1991)★★, *Kylie Minogue* (DeConstruction 1994)★★.

●COMPILATIONS: *Greatest Hits* (PWL 1992)★★★.

●FURTHER READING: *The Superstar Next Door*, Sasha Stone.

MINT JULEPS

This a cappella soul group from the East End of London, England, consisted of sisters Debbie, Lizzie, Sandra and Marcia Charles plus their friends Debbie and Julie. They all formerly worked together at the Half Moon Theatre in Putney, where they decided to form a group. They played at various benefits and toured with Sister Sledge and Billy Bragg, and worked as backing singers for Bob Geldof, the Belle Stars and Dr. Feelgood. They signed to Stiff Records, and were managed by former Darts members Rita Ray and Rob Fish. The Mint Juleps recorded vocal versions of Neil Young's 'Only Love Can Break Your Heart', Robert Palmer's 'Every Kinda People', and the original 'Girl To The Power Of 6' (produced by Trevor Horn). They later moved away from a cappella into a kind of light-weight rap in the vein of Salt 'N' Pepper. They appeared on ex-Grateful Dead drummer Mickey Hart's *Mystery Box* in 1996

●ALBUMS: *One Time* (Stiff 1985)★★★.

MINUTEMEN

Formed in 1980 in San Pedro, California, USA, and originally known as the Reactionaries. This influential hardcore trio initially comprised D. Boon (guitar/vocals), Mike Watt (bass) and Frank Tonche (drums), but the last named was replaced by George Hurley prior to recording. Although the trio donated tracks to several independent compilations, notably for the pivotal Radio Tokyo Tapes and the Posh Boy and New Alliance labels, their association with SST Records resulted in some of the genre's most impressive recordings. The unfettered rage of their early work was less apparent on *Buzz Or Howl Under The Influence Of Heat* and *Project: Mersh* ('Mersh' is San Pedro slang for 'commercial'), but *Double Nickels On The Dime* and *3-Way Tie (For Last)* showed an undeterred passion and commitment. The Minutemen came to a premature end in 1986 following the death of D. Boon. Watt and Hurley decided to drop the group's name, and in its place formed Firehose with guitarist Ed Crawford.

●ALBUMS: *The Punchline* (SST 1980)★★, *Bean Spill* (SST 1982)★★, *What Makes A Man Start Fires?* (SST 1983)★★, *Buzz Or Howl Under The Influence Of Heat* (SST 1983)★★★, *Politics Of Time* (SST 1984)★★★, *Double Nickels On The Dime* (SST 1984)★★★, *Project: Mersh* (SST 1985)★★★, *3-Way Tie (For Last)* (SST 1986)★★★, *Ballot Result* (SST 1987)★★★.

●COMPILATIONS: *My First Bells 1980-1983* (SST 1985)★★★, *Post-Mersh Volume 1* (SST 1987)★★, *Post-Mersh Volume 2* (SST 1987)★★★, *Post-Mersh Volume 3* (SST 1989)★★★.

MISSION

UK rock band who evolved from the Sisters Of Mercy, when Wayne Hussey (b. 26 May 1959, Bristol, England; ex-Walkie Talkies; Dead Or Alive) and Craig Adams split from Andrew Eldritch. They quickly recruited drummer Mick Brown (ex-Red Lorry, Yellow Lorry) and guitarist Simon Hinkler (ex-Artery). The original choice of title was the Sisterhood, which led to an undignified series of exchanges in the press between the band and Eldritch. In order to negate their use of the name, Eldritch put out a single under the name Sisterhood on his own Merciful Release label. Thus

the title the Mission was selected instead. After two successful independent singles on the Chapter 22 label, they signed to Mercury Records in the autumn of 1986. Their major label debut, 'Stay With Me', entered the UK singles charts while the band worked on their debut album. *God's Own Medicine* was the outcome, revealing a tendency towards straightforward rock, and attracting criticism for its bombast. A heavy touring schedule ensued, with the band's offstage antics attracting at least as much attention as their performances. A particularly indulgent tour of America saw Adams shipped home suffering from exhaustion. His temporary replacement on bass was Pete Turner. After headlining the Reading Festival, they began work on a new album under the auspices of Led Zeppelin bass player John Paul Jones as producer. *Children* was even more successful than its predecessor, reaching number 2 in the UK album charts, despite the customary critical disdain. 1990 brought 'Butterfly On A Wheel' as a single, providing further ammunition for accusations that the band were simply dredging up rock history. In February, the long-delayed third album, *Carved In Sand*, was released, revealing a more sophisticated approach to songwriting. During the world tour to promote the album, both Hinkler and Hussey became ill because of the excessive regime. Hinkler departed suddenly when they reached Toronto, leaving Dave Wolfenden to provide guitar for the rest of the tour. On their return, Paul Etchells took over the position on a more permanent basis. Hussey had meanwhile joined with the Wonder Stuff in proposing a fund-raising concert in London under the banner The Day Of Conscience, but the event self-destructed with a barrage of allegations about commercial intrusion. In a similar vein over the Christmas period, members of the band joined with Slade's Noddy Holder and Jim Lea to re-record 'Merry Xmas Everybody' for charity. However, 1992 would bring numerous further personnel difficulties. Craig Adams returned to Brighton, while Hussey brought in Andy Hobson (bass), Rik Carter (keyboards) and Mark Gemini Thwaite (guitar). A reflective Hussey, promoting the *Sum And Substance* compilation, conceded: 'We had an overblown sense of melodrama. It was great - pompous songs, big grand statements. We've never attempted to do anything that's innovative'. A nation of rock critics found something on which to agree with Hussey at last.

●ALBUMS: *God's Own Medicine* (Mercury 1986)★★, *Children* (Mercury 1988)★★★, *Carved In Sand* (Mercury 1990)★★★, *Masque* (Mercury

1992)★★, *Neverland* (Neverland 1995)★★.
●COMPILATIONS: *The First Chapter* (Mercury 1987)★★, *Grains Of Sand* (Mercury 1990)★★, *Sum And Substance* (Vertigo 1994)★★★, *Salad Daze* (Nighttracks 1994)★★, *Blue* (Equator 1996)★★.
●VIDEOS: *South America* (1989), *Crusade* (1991), *From Dusk To Dawn* (1991), *Waves Upon The Sand* (1991), *Sum And Substance* (1994).
●FURTHER READING: *The Mission - Names Are Tombstones Baby*, Martin Roach with Neil Perry.

MISSION OF BURMA

Once cited as 'the ultimate collision of punk and pop', Boston, Massachusetts band Mission Of Burma were compared by others to the UK's art terrorists Wire. Certainly, they invoked a similar level of rapture among US critics and, much like Wire, self-consciously avoided the glare of the mainstream. The original line-up of Clint Conley (bass), Peter Prescott (drums), and Roger Miller (guitar) were greatly influential to a number of more commercially viable outfits. They formed in 1979, when Miller and Conley moved to Boston from Ann Arbor and New York, respectively. They briefly put together Moving Parts before joining with resident Bostonian Prescott. Burma kicked off with supports for the UK's Gang Of Four. These went well and the Leeds funksters continued to sponsor them early in their development. They broke up in 1985 after a career that embraced well-defined but chaotic live and recorded work. Through a series of reissues on the venerated underground label, Taang! Records, critics have now reassessed their historical importance. Among their staunchest admirers are R.E.M., who regularly covered 'Academy Flight Song' in their live sets. Prescott went on to SST recording artists Volcano Suns.
●ALBUMS: *Signals, Calls, And Marches* (Ace Of Hearts 1981)★★★, *Vs* (Ace Of Hearts 1982)★★★★, *The Horrible Truth About Burma Live* (Ace Of Hearts 1985)★★★, *Forget* (Taang! 1988)★★★, *Let There Be Burma* (Taang! 1990)★★★.
●COMPILATIONS: *Mission Of Burma* (Rykodisc 1988)★★★★.

MO-DETTES

Despite the name, the timing of their appearance on the music scene, and the fact that they covered the Rolling Stones' 'Paint It Black', the Mo-Dettes were not modettes and disliked anyone who said they were. They were originally formed for a one-off gig at the Acklam Hall, supporting the Vincent Units. Their line-up was built around Kate Korus (b. Katherine Corris, New York, USA; guitar), who played with the Castrators before lasting just three gigs with the earliest line-up of the Slits. She left (to be replaced by Viv Albertine) and attempted to form several bands. Korus took a long time finding musicians with whom she was happy, but gradually she came across (on the set of *The Great Rock 'N' Roll Swindle* where both had non-acting jobs) drummer June Miles-Kingston (the sister of Bob Kingston of Tenpole Tudor) and bassist Jane Crockford. Crockford had previously played in the Banks Of Dresden with Richard Dudanski. Through a mutual friend they met Ramona Carlier, a singer from Switzerland whose experience to date had been backing vocals at a few sessions plus a one-off party gig with a band called the Bomberettes, and had been in England about a year. The first product of their labours was 'White Mice' - on their own Mode label through Rough Trade Records. Ramona left late in 1981 to start a solo career, and was replaced by Sue Slack. Soon after, Korus split to be replaced by Melissa Ritter. The final split came shortly afterwards in 1982, owing to further internal friction. Miles-Kingston moved on to Fun Boy Three's backing band, before she produced a solo single for Go! Discs, joined the Communards and sang on various sessions. Kate Korus also released a single with Jenny of the Belle Stars.
●ALBUMS: *The Story So Far* (Mode 1980)★★.
●COMPILATIONS: *Loved By Thousands ... Hated By Millions* (Bullet Proof 1995)★★.

MODERN ENGLISH

Formed in Colchester, Essex, England, in 1979, Modern English's debut, *Mesh And Lace* was released in suitably arty packaging by 4AD Records two years later. It drew heavily on the gloom rock sound already patented by bands like Joy Division, and had little originality or focus. *After The Snow*, recorded by the same line-up of Robbie Gray (vocals), Gary McDowell (guitar/vocals), Richard Brown (drums), Mick Conroy (bass /vocals) and Stephen Walker (keyboards) was a minor revelation, as they introduced warmth and strong guitar harmonies, rejecting the tinny bleakness of the debut It was well received in the USA, and the band relocated to New York to consolidate a popularity encouraged by college radio. *Richochet Days* had a crisper production but less creative experimentation. By *Stop Start*, released by Sire Records in 1986, Stephen Walker and Richard Brown had left, and Aaron Davidson (keyboards/guitar) had joined. The band had tried too hard for commercial approval and was left with an unspecific rock/pop sound that caused them to split soon afterwards. Robbie Gray returned to England to form a new group. They reconvened in 1990 for *Pillow-Lips*, but to little interest

●ALBUMS: *Mesh And Lace* (4AD 1981)★★, *After The Snow* (Sire 1982)★★★, *Richochet Days* (Sire 1984)★★★, *Stop Start* (Sire 1986)★★, *Pillow-Lips* (TVT 1990)★★.

MODERN ROMANCE

From the remnants of UK punk band the (Leyton) Buzzards, crawled Geoff Deanne and David Jaymes. After becoming involved in the London club scene (alongside luminaries like Steve Strange), they formed a company called Business Art Productions with manager Brian O'Donoughue. Signed to WEA, they released 'Tonight'. This flopped, so in late 1980, Jaymes and Deanne formed a new line-up featuring Deanne (b. 10 December 1954; vocals), Jaymes (b. 28 November 1954; bass), brother Robbie Jaymes (b. 3 October 1962; keyboards), Paul Gendler (b. 11 August 1960; guitar) and Andy Kyriacou (b. 19 April 1958; drums, ex-Linx; Central Line). John Du Prez also featured on trumpet. Through their club connections they came across the Latin-American music salsa, which was set to be all the craze in the summer of 1981. They quickly recorded 'Everybody Salsa', which gave them their first hit. It was followed by other successful material in a similar vein; 'Ay Ay Ay Ay Moosey', 'Queen Of The Rapping Scene', and 'Cherry Pink And Apple Blossom White'. At this point Deanne left to release several solo singles and write for camp club act Divine. Former fireman Michael J. Mullins (b. 9 November 1956) was his replacement. Their hit run continued in 1983, with 'Best Years Of Our Life', 'High Life' and 'Walking In The Rain'. A cover of Baltimora's 'Tarzan Boy' the following year fared less well. They disbanded shortly afterwards. David Jaymes released a solo single in 1988, while Deanne now writes comedy scripts. John Du Prez currently lives in Hollywood where he plays on film scores.

●ALBUMS: *Adventures In Clubland* (Warners 1981)★★, *Trick Of The Light* (Warners 1983)★★, *Party Tonight* (Ronco 1983)★★, *Move On* (RCA 1985)★★.

MOLLY HATCHET

This Lynyrd Skynyrd-style, blues-rock boogie outfit emerged from the USA's deep south. The name is taken from a lady who beheaded her lovers with an axe after sleeping with them in seventeenth-century Salem. The initial line-up comprised guitarists Dave Hlubek, Steve Holland and Duane Roland plus bassist Bonner Thomas, vocalist Danny Joe Brown and drummer Bruce Crump. Their debut album, produced by Tom Werman (of Cheap Trick and Ted Nugent fame), was an instant success, with its three-pronged guitar onslaught and gut-wrenching vocals. Brown was replaced by Jimmy Farrar in 1980, before the recording of *Beatin' The Odds*. Farrar's vocals were less distinctive than Brown's, and an element of their identity was lost while the former fronted the band. Nevertheless, commercial success ensued, with both *Beatin' The Odds* and *Take No Prisoners* peaking on the *Billboard* album chart at numbers 25 and 36, respectively. In 1982 Danny Joe Brown rejoined the band, while Thomas was replaced by Riff West on bass. *No Guts ... No Glory* emerged and marked a return to their roots: explosive guitar duels, heart-stopping vocals and steadfast rock 'n' roll. Surprisingly the album flopped and Hlubek insisted on a radical change in direction. Steve Holden quit and keyboardist John Galvin was recruited for the recording of *The Deed Is Done*. This was a lightweight pop-rock album, devoid of the band's trademarks. Following its release the band retired temporarily to lick their wounds and reassess their future. In 1985 *Double Trouble Live* marked a return to former styles. It included versions of their best-known songs plus a Skynyrd tribute in the form of 'Freebird'. Founder member Dave Hlubek departed, to be replaced by Bobby Ingram in 1989. They signed a new contract with Capitol Records and released *Lightning Strikes Twice*. This leaned away from their southern roots towards highly polished AOR. It featured covers of Paul Stanley's 'Hide Your Heart' and Miller/Burnette's 'There Goes The Neighbourhood', but was poorly received by fans and critics alike, despite the return of Danny Joe Brown, who had been plagued by illness due to diabetes.

●ALBUMS: *Molly Hatchet* (Epic 1978)★★★, *Flirtin' With Disaster* (Epic 1979)★★★, *Beatin' The Odds* (Epic 1980)★★, *Take No Prisoners* (Epic 1981)★★, *No Guts ... No Glory* (Epic 1983)★★★, *The Deed Is Done* (Epic 1984)★★, *Double Trouble Live* (Epic 1985)★★, *Lightning Strikes Twice* (Capitol 1989)★★, *Devil's Canyon* (SPV 1996)★★.

●COMPILATIONS: *Greatest Hits* (Epic 1990)★★★.

MONEY, EDDIE

Legend has it that Brooklyn native Eddie Mahoney was a New York police officer when first discovered by promoter Bill Graham (he was, in fact, a NYPD typist). Nevertheless, under Graham's managerial wing, Mahoney became Eddie Money and produced two hit singles in 'Baby Hold On' and 'Two Tickets To Paradise' from his self-titled debut, to begin a career that has seen him maintain arena headlining status in America with a series of consistently fine R&B-flavoured AOR records. *Life For The Taking* produced two more hits, 'Rock And Roll The Place' and 'Maybe I'm A Fool', as Money built a strong live following which set him free from the constraining need for radio or MTV airplay to sell albums or concert tickets, although the hits continued to come. *Where's The Party?* saw a slight dip in form, but Money stormed back with perhaps his best 80s album, *Can't Hold Back*, producing three huge hits in the title track, 'I Wanna Go Back' and 'Take Me Home Tonight', where his warm, soulful vocals were augmented by Ronnie Spector's production. In 1991, *Right Here* saw Money move away from the keyboard-dominated sound of preceding albums towards the rootsier feel of his early work, producing another hit in a cover of Romeo's Daughter's 'Heaven In The Backseat'. While European success continues to elude him, Money's future in his homeland seems secure.

●ALBUMS: *Eddie Money* (Columbia 1977)★★, *Life For The Taking* (Columbia 1978)★★, *Playing For Keeps* (Columbia 1980)★★, *No Control* (Columbia 1982)★★, *Where's The Party?* (Columbia 1984)★★, *Can't Hold Back* (Columbia 1986)★★★, *Nothing To Lose* (Columbia 1988)★★, *Right Here* (Columbia 1991)★★.

●COMPILATIONS: *Greatest Hits: The Sound Of Money* (Columbia 1989)★★★.

●FILMS: *Americation* (1979).

MONOCHROME SET

Any all-encompassing classification of the Monochrome Set's music would be difficult. During a sporadic career that has spanned as many musical styles as it has record labels, they have been on the verge of breaking to a wider audience on a number of occasions. Formed in the UK during late 1976, Andy Warren (bass), Lester Square (guitar) and Bid (guitar/vocals) were playing in the B-Sides with Adam Ant. When the B-Sides became Adam And The Ants, Bid and Lester Square left. They formed the Monochrome Set in January 1978, later joined by Warren in 1979 after his role on the debut Ants album. With Jeremy Harrington (bass, ex-Gloria Mundi; Mean Street) and J.D. Haney (drums, ex-Art Attacks), the band issued singles during 1979-80 for Rough Trade

Records including 'He's Frank', 'Eine Symphonie Des Graeuns', 'The Monochrome Set' and 'He's Frank (Slight Return)', each completely different in style and content. Their debut, *The Strange Boutique*, skirted the UK charts. After the title track came further singles '405 Lines' and 'Apocalypso', and a second album, *Love Zombies*. Lex Crane briefly sat in on drums before ex-Soft Boys member Morris Windsor joined for the release of the brilliant sex satire, 'The Mating Game', in July 1982, followed by 'Cast A Long Shadow' and the memorable *Eligible Bachelors*. By this time Carrie Booth had joined on keyboards while Nick Wesolowski took up the drums and Foz the guitar soon after. *Volume, Brilliance, Contrast*, compiled their Rough Trade recordings and selected BBC Radio 1 sessions, and coincided with another indie hit, 'Jet Set Junta' (like many Monochrome Set compositions deflating class/monetary division). 'Jacob's Ladder' seemed a sure-fire hit for 1985, but like 'Wallflower' later that year and the charming *The Lost Weekend*, eluded the charts. Disheartened, the band split and it was left to Cherry Red Records' El subsidiary to issue a sympathetic retrospective, *Fin! Live*, a year later. Various collections filtered out over the next three years (*Colour Transmission* featured much of the DinDisc material, while *Westminster Affair* highlighted their earliest recordings). In December 1989 the band re-formed, with Bid, Lester and Warren joined by Orson Presence on guitar and keyboards, marking their return with *Dante's Casino*. From there on they have concentrated primarily on their cult following in the Far East, with frequent tours there.

●ALBUMS: *The Strange Boutique* (DinDisc 1980)★★, *Love Zombies* (DinDisc 1980)★★, *Eligible Bachelors* (Cherry Red 1982)★★★, *The Lost Weekend* (Blanco y Negro 1985)★★★, *Dante's Casino* (Vinyl Japan 1990)★★★, *Charade* (Cherry Red 1993)★★★, *Misere* (Cherry Red 1994)★★★, *Trinity Road* (Cherry Red 1995)★★★.

●COMPILATIONS: *Volume, Brilliance, Contrast* (Cherry Red 1983)★★★, *Fin! Live* (El 1985)★★★, *Colour Transmission* (Virgin 1987)★★★, *Westminster Affair* (Cherry Red 1988)★★, *Black & White Minstrels* (Cherry Red 1995)★★★.

●VIDEOS: *Destiny Calling* (Visionary 1994).

MOORE, CHRISTY

b. 7 May 1945, Dublin, Eire. Moore's beginnings were fairly typical for a solo folk performer in the 60s: playing the club circuit in Eire, subsequently doing likewise in England while in-between working on building sites and road gangs.

Influenced by the American styles of Woody Guthrie, Bob Dylan and the British folk giant, Ewan MacColl, Moore performed in the UK folk clubs alongside the rising stars of the period. It was in England, in 1969, that he recorded his first album, a collaboration with Dominic Behan, *Paddy On The Road*. His first solo album led to the forming of Planxty, where he stayed until 1975. Having once again embarked on a solo career, he became involved in the mid-70s with the Anti-Nuclear Roadshow which featured performers, environmental activists and politicians. The 'Roadshow' established Moore's reputation as a campaigning and political performer and the ensemble's success made a heavy contribution to undermining the plans for a Irish nuclear power programme.

After a brief reunion with Planxty in the late 70s, Moore and fellow Planxty member Donal Lunny split in 1981 to form Moving Hearts. This progression from the former group fused folk with rock. Despite the group taking a similar ideologically agit-prop stance, Moore eventually felt uncomfortable within a group set-up and once again returned to solo work in 1982. Since that time, Moore's mixture of traditional songs with contemporary observations of Irish life, social and political, has also tackled the political problems of Central America and South Africa as well as the problems in his homeland and Ulster. His songs are notable not only for their spiky commentary but also an engaging humour. Christy Moore's standing in Irish folk music is of a stature unparalleled and his influence spills over into the field of pop and rock, winning critical favour, respect and debt, from such contemporary pop performers as the Pogues, Elvis Costello, Billy Bragg and U2.

●ALBUMS: with Dominic Behan *Paddy On The Road* (1969)★★★, *Prosperous* (Trailer 1971)★★★, *Whatever Tickles Your Fancy* (Polydor 1975)★★★, *Christy Moore* (1976)★★★, *The Iron Behind The Velvet* (1978)★★★, *Live In Dublin* (1978)★★★, *The Spirit Of Freedom* (Warners 1983)★★★, *The Time Has Come* (Warners 1983)★★★, *Ride On* (Warners 1984)★★★, *Ordinary Man* (Warners 1985)★★★, *Nice 'N' Easy* (Polydor 1986)★★★, *Unfinished Revolution* (Warners 1987)★★★, *Voyage* (Warners 1989)★★★, *Smoke And Strong Whiskey* (Newberry 1991)★★★, *King Puck* (Equator 1993)★★★, *Live At The Point* (Grapevine 1994)★★★, *Graffiti Tongue* (Grapevine 1996)★★★★.

●COMPILATIONS: *The Christy Moore Collection '81-'91* (East West 1991)★★★★.

●VIDEOS: *Christy* (SMV 1995).

MORRICONE, ENNIO

b. 11 October 1928, Rome, Italy. A distinguished and prolific composer, whose revolutionary scores for 'spaghetti Westerns' have made him one of the most influential figures in the film music world. He studied trumpet and composition before becoming a professional writer of music for radio, television and the stage as well as the concert hall. During the 50s he wrote songs and arrangements for popular vocalist Gianni Morandi and he later arranged Paul Anka's Italian hit 'Ogni Volta' (1964). Morricone's first film score was for the comedy *Il Federale* in 1961. Three years later he was hired by Sergio Leone to compose music for *A Fistful Of Dollars*. Using the pseudonym Dan Savio, Morricone created a score out of shouts, cries and a haunting whistled phrase, in direct contrast to the use of pseudo-folk melodies in Hollywood westerns. His work on Leone's trilogy of Italian westerns led to collaboration with such leading European directors as Pontecorvo (*Battle Of Algiers* 1966), Pasolini (*Big Birds, Little Birds*, 1966) and Bertolucci (*1900*, 1976). In the 70s he began to compose for US films, such as *Exorcist II* (1977), *Days Of Heaven* (1978), *The Untouchables* (1987) and *Frantic* (1988). Morricone won an Oscar for Roland Joffe's *The Mission* (1986), where he used motifs from sacred music and native Indian melodies to create what he called 'contemporary music written in an ancient language'. In 1992 Morricone's score for *Bugsy* received an Oscar nomination. The composer's other scores in the early 90s included *Husbands And Lovers, City Of Joy, Tie Me Up! Tie Me Down!, Everybody's Fine, Hamlet, State Of Grace, Octopus 6 - The Force Of The Mafia, Jonah Who Lived In A Whale, In The Line Of Fire*, and *Cinema Paradiso - The Special Edition, La Scorta, Wolf*, and *Disclosure* (1994). The Spaghetti western sound has been a source of inspiration and samples for a number of rock artists including BAD, Cameo and John Zorn (*Big Gundown*, 1987). Morricone has recorded several albums of his own music and in 1981 he had a hit with 'Chi Mai', a tune he composed for a BBC Television series. A double album for Virgin Records in 1988 included Morricone's own selection from more than 100 films that he has scored, while in the same year Virgin Venture issued a recording of his classical compositions.

●ALBUMS: *Moses* soundtrack (Pye 1977)★★★, *This Is ...* (EMI 1981)★★★, *Chi Mai* (BBC 1981)★★★, *The Mission* film soundtrack (Virgin 1986)★★★★, *Chamber Music* (Venture 1988)★★★, *Frantic* film soundtrack (Elektra 1988)★★★, *The*

Endless Game television soundtrack (Virgin 1989)★★★, *Live In Concert* (Silva Screen 1989)★★★, *Casualties Of War* (1990)★★★, *Morricone '93 Movie Sounds* (1993)★★★, *Wolf* film soundtrack (Columbia 1994)★★★, *Disclosure* film soundtrack (Virgin 1995)★★★, *Ninfa Plebea* film soundtrack (AM Original Soundtracks 1995)★★★, *Concerto: Premio Rota 1995* (AM Original Soundtracks 1996)★★★.

●COMPILATIONS: *Film Hits* (RCA 1981)★★★, *Film Music 1966-87* (Virgin 1988)★★★★, *The Very Best Of* (1992)★★★, *The Ennio Morricone Anthology (A Fistfull Of Film Music)* (Rhino 1995)★★★★, *His Greatest Themes* (Allegro 1995)★★★.

MORRISSEY

b. Steven Patrick Morrissey, 22 May 1959, Davyhulme, Manchester, England. Morrissey began his career with the vague intention of succeeding as a music journalist. Unemployed in Manchester during the late 70s, he frequently wrote letters to the music press and was eventually taken on by *Record Mirror* as a freelance local reviewer. During this period, he also ran a New York Dolls fan club and wrote a booklet about them. Another small illustrated volume, *James Dean Is Not Dead*, briefly catalogued the career of another Morrissey obsession. Two other projects, on girl groups and minor film stars, failed to reach the printed page. In the meantime, Morrissey was attempting unsuccessfully to progress as a performer. He had played a couple of gigs with local group the Nosebleeds and failed a record company audition with a relaunched version of Slaughter And The Dogs. In 1982 he was approached by Wythenshawe guitarist Johnny Maher (later Marr) with the idea of forming a songwriting team. They soon developed into the Smiths, the most important and critically acclaimed UK group of the 80s. Morrissey's arch lyrics, powerful persona and general newsworthiness made him a pop figure whose articulacy was unmatched by any of his contemporaries. By the late summer of 1987, the Smiths had disbanded, leaving Morrissey to pursue a solo career. Early the following year he issued his first post-Smiths single, 'Suedehead', with Vini Reilly (Durutti Column) filling the guitarist's spot. The track was irresistibly commercial and reached the UK Top 5. The subsequent *Viva Hate* hit number 1 in the UK album charts soon after, indicating a long and successful future with EMI Records. A further UK Top 10 single with the John Betjemen-influenced 'Everyday Is Like Sunday' reiterated that point. In spite of his successes, Morrissey was ini-

tially keen on promoting a Smiths reunion but the closest this reached was the equivalent of a farewell concert in the unlikely setting of Wolverhampton Civic Hall. On 22 December 1988, Morrissey performed alongside former Smiths, Andy Rourke, Mike Joyce and Craig Gannon for a 1700 capacity audience, many of whom had queued for days in order to gain admittance to the venue. The following year brought several problems. Although he continued to release strong singles such as 'The Last Of The Famous International Playboys' and 'Interesting Drug', both reviews and chart placings were slightly less successful than expected. By the time of 'Ouija Board, Ouija Board', Morrissey suffered the most disappointing reviews of his career and, despite its charm, the single only reached number 18. Financial wrangles and management changes, which had characterized the Smiths' career, were repeated by Morrissey the soloist. A projected album, *Bona Drag*, was delayed and eventually cancelled, although the title served for a formidable hits and b-side compilation. In the meantime, Morrissey concentrated on the singles market, issuing some fascinating product, most notably the macabre 'November Spawned A Monster' and controversial 'Piccadilly Palare'. In March 1991, Morrissey issued the long-awaited *Kill Uncle*, a light yet not unappealing work, produced by Clive Langer and Alan Winstanley. By this time, the artist had not toured since the heyday of the Smiths, and there were some critics who wondered whether he would ever perform again. That question was answered in the summer and winter of 1991 when the singer embarked on a world tour, backed by a rockabilly group, whose raw energy and enthusiasm brought a new dimension to his recently understated studio work. The fruits of this collaboration were revealed on *Your Arsenal*, a neat fusion of 50s rockabilly influences and 70s glam rock. The presence of former David Bowie acolyte Mick Ronson as producer added to its impetus. During 1992 Morrissey again hit the headlines when he issued a bitter attack on author Johnny Rogan. Prior to the publication of a book on the Smiths, which he had yet to read, Morrissey decreed: 'Personally, I hope Johnny Rogan ends his days very soon in an M3 pile-up.' The much-publicized and long-running dispute merely served to focus attention on the book and heighten appreciation of his Smiths work. *Beethoven Was Deaf*, a live album which disappeared after only two weeks in the charts was a dismal failure. However, Morrissey was now beginning to cultivate a following in the USA substantially beyond the cult devotees who had followed the Smiths there. This offered welcome succour at a time when UK critics were predicting his imminent downfall. Then came the Madstock disaster - a live appearance in support of a reformed Madness that saw Morrissey bedecked in a Union Jack - which, when combined with song titles such as 'Bengali In Platforms' and 'The National Front Disco', saw a huge debate rage in the media over the artist's interpretation of 'Englishness'. *Vauxhall And I*, a chilling treatise of pained reflection proved Morrissey's most out-standing release to date, reaching number 1 in the UK. With the more sedate production from Steve Lillywhite, this was the closest the artist had come since the Smiths to matching his lyricism with the right material components. Indeed, as *Select* maga-zine decreed: 'If he keeps making albums like this, you won't want the Smiths back'. However, it was his last album with EMI/HMV Records, apart from the much-criticized compilation *The World Of Morrissey*. Meanwhile a collaboration with Siouxsie Sioux on the single 'Interlude', fell outside the UK Top 40. Morrissey next moved to BMG Records as they chose to revive another old label, this time RCA Victor for 1995's *Southpaw Grammar*. This set opened with 'The Teachers Are Afraid Of The Pupils', an arresting 11-minute update to the Smiths' 'The Headmaster Ritual', which placed the secondary school teacher in the role of victim. Critics were not overly impressed and the album disappeared from the playlists and people's minds after a few weeks. Morrissey made the headlines in 1997 with the long-standing court case over Mike Joyce's claim against royalties. The judge ruled against Morrissey and Marr. This must have been his absolute nadir; even his tracker-dog biographer Rogan was able to confront him at the court rooms.

●ALBUMS: *Viva Hate* (HMV 1988)★★★★, *Kill Uncle* (HMV 1991)★★, *Your Arsenal* (HMV 1992)★★★★, *Beethoven Was Deaf* (HMV 1993)★★, *Vauxhall And I* (HMV 1994)★★★★, *Southpaw Grammar* (RCA Victor 1995)★★★.

●COMPILATIONS: *Bona Drag* (HMV 1990)★★★★, *The World Of Morrissey* (EMI 1995)★★.

●VIDEOS: *Live In Dallas* (1993), *Introducing Morrissey* (Warner Music Video 1996).

●FURTHER READING: *Morrissey In His Own Words*, John Robertson. *Morrissey Shot*, Linder Sterling. *Morrissey & Marr: The Severed Alliance*, Johnny Rogan. *Peepholism: Into The Art Of Morrissey*, Jo Slee. *Landscapes Of The Mind*, David Bret.

MOTELS

Formed in Berkeley, California, in the early 70s, the Motels comprised Martha Davis (vocals), Jeff Jourard (guitar), his brother Martin (keyboards/saxophone), former jazzer Michael Goodroe (bass) and UK session drummer Brian Glascock (ex-Toe Fat). Transferring to Los Angeles, the group assembled for appearances at Hollywood's Whiskey club throughout July 1978, attracting a modicum of music industry interest in the process. In 1979 their stunning debut album was issued by Capitol Records. Like its remaining tracks, the hit ballad, 'Total Control', was produced by John Carter and composed by central figure Davis, whose eclectic tastes included blues, Broadway musicals and Stravinsky. Her onstage presence was 'exceptionally charismatic', wrote *The Los Angeles Times*, wrongly predicting that she 'could become one of the most influential female performers in rock'. Her boyfriend, Tim McGovern (ex-Captain Kopter And The Fabulous Twirlybirds), replaced Jeff Jourard during sessions for *Careful*, with a sleeve adorned with a print of a Dougie Fields' painting. Though its singles, 'Whose Problem' and 'Days Are OK', flitted into the US and UK charts, they fared well in regional charts in Australasia, a territory where the group made its strongest impact. Their albums and tie-in singles tended to hover around the lower half of the UK Top 40 after *All Four One*, at number 16, marked the Motels' commercial zenith. In their homeland they enjoyed two US Top 10 hits with 'Only The Lonely' (1982) and 'Suddenly Last Summer' (1983), but folded in 1987.

●ALBUMS: *The Motels* (Capitol 1979)★★★★, *Careful* (Capitol 1980)★★★, *All Four One* (Capitol 1982)★★★, *Little Robbers* (Capitol 1983)★★, *Shock* (Capitol 1985)★★.

MÖTLEY CRÜE

This heavy rock band was formed in 1980 by Nikki Sixx (b. Frank Faranno, 11 December 1958, California, USA; bass) and consisted of former members of several other Los Angeles-based groups. Tommy Lee (b. 3 October 1962, Athens, Greece; drums) was recruited from Suite 19; Vince Neil (b. Vince Neil Wharton, 8 February 1961, Hollywood, California, USA; vocals) from Rocky Candy; while Nikki himself had recently left London. Mick Mars (b. Bob Deal, 3 April 1956, USA; guitar) was added to the line-up after Sixx and Lee answered an advertisement announcing 'Loud, rude, aggressive guitarist available'. Their first single, 'Stick To Your Guns'/'Toast Of The Town', was issued in 1981 on their own Leathür label, followed by their self-produced debut, *Too Fast For Love*. The band signed to Elektra Records in 1982, and the album was remixed and reissued that August. The following year they recorded a new set, *Shout At The Devil*, with producer Tom Werman. He stayed at the helm for the two albums that broke them to a much wider audience in the USA, *Theatre Of Pain* (which sold more than two million copies) and *Girls, Girls, Girls*, which achieved the highest entry for a heavy metal album on *Billboard*'s album chart since *The Song Remains The Same* by Led Zeppelin in 1976. These albums refined the raw sound of earlier releases, without hiding the influence that Kiss and Aerosmith have exerted on their work. This change in style, which saw Mötley Crüe experimenting with organs, pianos and harmonicas in addition to their traditional instruments, has been described as a move from 'club-level metal glam' to 'stadium-size rock 'n' roll'. The band have not been without their setbacks: in 1984, Vince Neil was involved in a major car crash in which Hanoi Rocks drummer Razzle was killed. The subsequent *Theatre Of Pain* was dedicated to his memory, and this grim incident helped inform the mood of the recording. Three years later, Nikki Sixx came close to death after a heroin overdose following touring with Guns N'Roses. Feuding with that same band, particularly that between Neil and Axl Rose, later provided the group with many of their column inches in an increasingly disinterested press. The band survived to appear at the Moscow Peace Festival in 1989 before more than 200,000 people, and then in 1991 to issue *Dr. Feelgood*, which gave them their first US number 1 chart placing. Vince Neil was ejected from the band's line-up, unexpectedly, in 1992, starting the Vince Neil Band shortly thereafter. His replacement for 1994's eponymous album would be John Corabi (ex-Scream), though the band's problems continued with a record label/management split and disastrous North American tour. Neil was working with the band again in autumn 1996.

●ALBUMS: *Too Fast For Love* (Leathur 1981)★★, *Shout At The Devil* (Elektra 1983)★★, *Theatre Of Pain* (Elektra 1985)★★, *Girls, Girls, Girls* (Elektra 1987)★★★, *Dr. Feelgood* (Elektra 1989)★★★, *Mötley Crüe* (Elektra 1994)★★★.

●COMPILATIONS: *Raw Tracks* (Elektra 1988)★★★, *Decade Of Decadence* (Elektra 1991)★★★★.

●VIDEOS: *Uncensored* (WEA Music Video 1987), *Dr. Feelgood, The Videos* (Warner Music Video 1989), *Decade Of Decadence* (Warner Music Video 1991).

●FURTHER READING: *Lüde, Crüde And Rüde*, Sylvie Simmons and Malcolm Dome.

MOTÖRHEAD

In 1975 Lemmy (b. Ian Fraiser Kilmister, 24 December 1945, Stoke, England; vocals/bass) was sacked from Hawkwind after being detained for five days at Canadian customs on possession charges. The last song he wrote for them was entitled 'Motörhead', and, after ditching an earlier suggestion, Bastard, this became the name of the band he formed with Larry Wallis of the Pink Fairies on guitar and Lucas Fox on drums. Together they made their debut supporting Greenslade at the Roundhouse, London, in July. Fox then left to join Warsaw Pakt, and was replaced by 'Philthy' Phil Taylor (b. 21 September 1954, Chesterfield, England; drums), a casual friend of Lemmy's with no previous professional musical experience. Motörhead was a four-piece band for less than a month, with Taylor's friend 'Fast' Eddie Clarke (b. 5 October 1950, Isleworth, Middlesex, England) of Continuous Performance as second guitarist, until Wallis returned to the Pink Fairies. The Lemmy/Taylor/Clarke combination would last six years until 1982, in which time they became the most famous trio in hard rock. With a following made up initially of hell's angels (Lemmy had formerly lived with their president, Tramp, for whom he would write the biker epic 'Iron Horse'), the band made their debut with the eponymous 'Motörhead'/'City Kids'. A similarly titled debut album charted, before the group moved over to Bronze Records. *Overkill* and *Bomber* firmly established the group's *modus operandi*, a fearsome barrage of instruments topped off by Lemmy's hoarse invocations. They toured the world regularly and enjoyed hit singles with 'Ace Of Spades' (one of the most definitive heavy metal performances ever, it graced a 1980 album of the same name which saw the band at the peak of their popularity) and 'Please Don't Touch' (as Headgirl). Their reputation as the best live band of their generation was further enhanced by the release of *No Sleep 'Til Hammersmith*, which entered the UK charts at number 1. In May 1982 Clarke left, citing musical differences, and was replaced by Brian Robertson (b. 12 September 1956, Glasgow, Scotland), who had previously played with Thin Lizzy and Wild Horses. This combination released *Another Perfect Day*, but this proved to be easily the least popular of all Motörhead line-ups. Robertson was replaced in November 1983 by Wurzel (b. Michael Burston, 23 October 1949, Cheltenham, England; guitar) - so-called on account of his scarecrow-like hair - and Philip Campbell (b. 7 May 1961, Pontypridd, Wales; guitar; ex-Persian Risk), thereby swelling the Motörhead ranks to four. Two months later and, after a final appearance on television's *The Young Ones*, Taylor left to join Robertson in Operator, and was replaced by ex-Saxon drummer Pete Gill. Gill remained with the band until 1987 and played on several fine albums including *Orgasmatron*, the title track of which saw Lemmy's lyric-writing surpass itself. By 1987 Phil Taylor had rejoined Motörhead, and the line-up remained unchanged for five years during which time Lemmy made his acting debut in the *Comic Strip* film *Eat The Rich*, followed by other celluloid appearances including the role of taxi driver in *Hardware*. In 1992 the group released *March Or Die*, which featured the American Mikkey Dee (ex-King Diamond) on drums and guest appearances by Ozzy Osbourne and Slash (Guns N'Roses). The title track followed on from '1916' and revealed a highly sensitive side to Lemmy's lyrical and vocal scope, both songs dealing with the horrors of war. The idiosyncratic Lemmy singing style, usually half-growl, half-shout, and with his neck craned up at 45 degrees to the microphone, remained as ever. On a more traditional footing they performed the theme song to the horror film *Hellraiser 3*, and convinced the film's creator, Clive Barker, to record his first promotional video with the band. Lemmy also hammered his way through insurance adverts, taking great delight in his press image of the unreconstructed rocker. Wurzel left the band and formed Wvkeaf in 1996.

●ALBUMS: *Motörhead* (Chiswick 1977)★★★, *Overkill* (Bronze 1979)★★★, *Bomber* (Bronze 1979)★★★, *On Parole* (United Artists 1979)★★★, *Ace Of Spades* (Bronze 1980)★★★★, *No Sleep Till Hammersmith* (Bronze 1981)★★★★, *Iron Fist* (Bronze 1982)★★★, *Another Perfect Day* (Bronze 1983)★★, *What's Wordsworth* (Big Beat 1983)★★, *Orgasmatron* (GWR 1986)★★★, *Rock 'N' Roll* (GWR 1987)★★★, *Eat The Rich* (GWR 1987)★★★, *No Sleep At All* (GWR 1988)★★★, *1916* (Epic 1991)★★★, *March Or Die* (Epic 1992)★★★, *Bastards* (ZYX 1993)★★★, *I* (SPV 1996)★★, *Overnight Sensation* (SPV 1996)★★★.

●COMPILATIONS: *No Remorse* (Bronze 1984)★★★★, *Anthology* (Raw Power 1986)★★, *Dirty Love* (Receiver 1989)★★, *From The Vaults* (Sequel 1990)★★, *Best Of* (Action Replay 1990)★★, *Collection* (Castle 1990)★★★, *Meltdown* 3-CD box set (Castle 1991)★★★, *All The Aces* (Castle 1993)★★, *The Best Of ...* (Castle 1993)★★★.

●VIDEOS: *Deaf Not Blind* (1984), *Birthday Party* (1986), *Eat The Rich* (1988, film), *Toronto Live* (1989), *Best Of* (1991), *Everything Louder Than Everything Else* (1991).

●FURTHER READING: *Motörhead*, Alan Burridge. *Born To Lose*, Alan Burridge. *Motorhead*, Giovanni Dadomo.

MOULD, BOB

b. 16 October 1960, Malone, New York, USA. The former guitarist, vocalist and co-composer of Hüsker Dü, Mould surprised many of that leading hardcore act's aficionados with his reflective solo debut, *Workbook*. Only one track, 'Whichever Way The Wind Blows', offered the maelstrom of guitars customary in the artist's work and instead the set was marked by a predominantly acoustic atmosphere. Cellist Jane Scarpantoni contributed to its air of melancholy, while two members of Pere Ubu, Tony Maimone (bass) and Anton Fier (drums; also Golden Palominos), added sympathetic support, helping to emphasize the gift for melody always apparent in Mould's work. Maimone and Fier also provided notable support on *Black Sheets Of Rain*, which marked a return to the uncompromising power of the guitarist's erstwhile unit. The set included the harrowing 'Hanging Tree' and apocalyptical 'Sacrifice Sacrifice/Let There Be Peace', but contrasted such doom-laden material with a brace of sprightly pop songs in 'It's Too Late' and 'Hear Me Calling', both of which echoed R.E.M. Mould also formed his own record company, SOL (Singles Only Label), which has issued material by, among others, William Burroughs. The artist abandoned his solo career in 1993, reverting to the melodic hardcore trio format with Sugar. By 1995 following the apparent demise of Sugar he had reverted once again to his solo career. *Bob Mould* was an excellent album, even though he refused to promote it. Not surprisingly it sounded like a cross between Hüsker Dü and Sugar, with sparkling tracks such as the venomous 'I Hate Alternative Rock' and the Tom Pettyesque 'Fort Knox, King Solomon'.

●ALBUMS: *Workbook* (Virgin 1989)★★★, *Black Sheets Of Rain* (Virgin 1990)★★, *Bob Mould* (Creation/Rykodisk 1996)★★★★.

●COMPILATIONS: *Poison Years* (Virgin 1994)★★★★.

MOYET, ALISON

b. 18 June 1961, Basildon, Essex, England. The former singer of the synthesizer duo Yazoo, Moyet embarked on a solo career in 1983, after critics had consistently praised her outstanding natural blues voice. The debut *Alf* was a superb recording, produced and co-written by Tony Swain and Steve Jolley. 'Invisible', 'Love Resurrection' and 'All Cried Out' were all UK hits, while the album made number 1 and took root in the charts for nearly two years. In 1985 she abandoned pop and toured with a jazz band led by John Altman, performing standards that included a version of Billie Holiday's 'That Ole Devil Called Love', which became her biggest hit to date. The tour was not well received and following her performance with Paul Young at the Live Aid concert, little was seen or heard of her, apart from a major UK hit with 'Is this Love' in 1986. During this time she gave birth to a daughter and experienced the break-up of her marriage. *Raindancing* appeared in 1987 and narrowly missed the number 1 position in the UK chart. Two single successes were the driving 'Weak In The Presence Of Beauty' and a sensitive cover of Ketty Lester's 'Love Letters'. Once again Alison disappeared and resurfaced in 1991. During this second hibernation she had another child and experienced a bout of lack of self-confidence. She embarked on a UK tour and released a new album. *Hoodoo* was a diverse record that broke Moyet away from the mould she was anxious to escape. It was artistically satisfying, although commercially pedestrian and effectively enabled this highly talented singer to start again. *Essex* failed to redress the balance with material that was nowhere near as strong as her outstanding voice deserves. We were reminded of the quality of her past songs on *Singles*, a well-compiled retrospective that reached number 1 in the UK album chart.

●ALBUMS: *Alf* (Columbia 1984)★★★★, *Raindancing* (Columbia 1987)★★, *Hoodoo* (Columbia 1991)★★★, *Essex* (Columbia 1994)★★.
●COMPILATIONS: *Alison Moyet Singles* (Columbia 1995)★★★.

MR. MISTER

Although formed in Phoenix, Arizona, USA, soft metal artists Mr Mister were based in Los Angeles and were the brainchild of Richard Page (bass/vocals) and Steve George (b. 20 May 1955, keyboards) who had previously played together in the Pages. They were both also experienced session men, working alongside REO Speedwagon and John Parr. 'It became really frustrating. We were having the big US hits, but weren't getting any of the credit'. The band were completed when Steve Farris (guitar) and Pat Mastelotto (drums) joined in 1982. Their debut in 1984, *I Wear The Face*, provided the minor US hit 'Hunters Of The Night'. The album was released in the UK two years later. The next album broke the band by scaling the top of the charts and delivering 2 US number 1 singles in 'Broken Wings' and 'Kyrie'. Its release coincided with a marathon Tina Turner support tour. Both singles also made the UK Top 20. After one more album Farris left and was replaced by the well-known session guitarist Buzzy Feiten. Page has since resisted offers to become vocalist for both Toto and Chicago.

●ALBUMS: *I Wear The Face* (RCA 1984)★★, *Welcome To The Real World* (RCA 1985)★★, *Go On* (RCA 1987)★★.

MTV

The first television channel entirely devoted to music was launched in the USA in 1981. MTV was also *the* major influence on the growth of music video during the 80s. Although there had been numerous US rock television shows since *American Bandstand* in the 50s, the immediate predecessor of MTV was *Popclips*, a 30-minute show combining comedy with music videos. It was produced by Michael Nesmith's Pacific Arts company in 1981 for the Nickelodeon cable television channel. In that year, Nickelodeon's owners Warner-Amex Television launched MTV (Music Television) with Buggles' 'Video Killed The Radio Star' as its first offering. Headed by Robert Pittman, the 24-hour station hired five VJs (video-jockeys) from radio and the theatre to announce the videos. Starting from a small audience base, the station used 'I Want My MTV' promotional spots by artists such as Pete Townshend, David Bowie, Mick Jagger and Pat Benetar to increase its reach. (In 1986, Dire Straits affectionately parodied the slogan in 'Money For Nothing', which duly won that year's MTV Award for best video.) Soon, MTV plays for their promotional videos were boosting record sales for bands like the Human League ('Don't You Want Me'), Duran Duran ('Hungry Like The Wolf', 'Rio') and the US success in 1983/4 of such UK artists as Haircut 100 and A Flock Of Seagulls was widely attributed to MTV airplay. The impact of MTV led to the formation of specialist cable channels for black music (Black Entertainment TV) and country (the Nashville Network). But a direct competitor launched by Ted Turner failed to dislodge

MTV from its pre-eminence. Meanwhile, the growth in television video programming and its influence on the charts forced record companies to produce accompanying videos for almost every new single they issued.

By 1984, MTV was making annual profits of six million dollars and it began a programme of international expansion with outlets in Japan (1984), Australia (1987) and Brazil (1990). Opened in 1987, MTV Europe had built up a reach of 30 million households in 28 countries by 1991, and operated its own programming policy, using videos by local artists as well as programmes imported from the USA. In 1991, MTV Asia was launched from Hong Kong as a satellite channel, also with a pledge to feature local acts. Expansion in the USA took the form of the creation of VH-1, devoted to album and adult-orientated rock in 1987, shortly after MTV Networks was purchased by Viacom Ltd. In 1991, plans were announced for a further splitting of MTV itself into three separate musical strands. By then, the global audience for MTV was said to be 52 million.

●VIDEOS: *MTV's Greatest Hits* (1993).

●FURTHER READING: *MTV unplugged: First Edition*, Sarah Malarkey (ed.).

MUDHONEY

Mudhoney, forged from a host of hobbyist bands, can lay claim to the accolade 'godfathers of grunge' more legitimately than most - whether or not they desire that title. The band comprises brothers Mark Arm (b. 21 February 1962, California, USA; vocals) and Steve Turner (b. 28 March 1965, Houston, USA; guitar), plus Matt Lukin (b. 16 August 1964, Aberdeen, Washington, USA; bass) and Dan Peters (b. 18 August 1967, Seattle, Washington, USA; drums). Arm and Turner were both ex-Green River, the band that also gave birth to Pearl Jam, and the less serious Thrown Ups. Lukin was ex-Melvins, Peters ex-Bundles Of Piss. Mudhoney were the band that first imported the sound of Sub Pop Records to wider shores. In August 1988 they released the fabulous 'Touch Me I'm Sick' single, one of the defining moments in the evolution of 'grunge', followed shortly by their debut mini-album. Contrary to popular belief, Turner chose the name *Superfuzz Bigmuff* after his favourite effects pedals rather than any sexual connotation. Early support included the admiration of Sonic Youth who covered their first a-side while Mudhoney thrashed through Sonic Youth staple 'Halloween' on the flip side of a split single. The first album was greeted as a comparative disap-

pointment by many, though there were obvious standout tracks ('When Tomorrow Hits'). The EP *Boiled Beef And Rotting Teeth* contained a cover of the Dicks' 'Hate The Police', demonstrating a good grasp of their 'hardcore' heritage. They had previously demonstrated an ability to nominate a sprightly cover tune when Spacemen 3's 'Revolution' had appeared on the b-side to 'This Gift'. The band also hold the likes of Celibate Rifles and Billy Childish in high esteem. Members of the former have helped in production of the band, while on trips to England they have invited the latter to join as support. It was their patronage that led to Childish's Thee Headcoats releasing material through Sub Pop. Meanwhile, Mudhoney's shows were becoming less eye-catching, and progressively close to eye-gouging. Early gigs in London saw Arm invite the audience, every single one of them, on to the stage, with the resultant near destruction of several venues. *Every Good Boy Deserves Fudge* was a departure, with Hammond organ intruding into the band's accomplished rock formula. It demonstrated their increasing awareness of the possibilities of their own songwriting. They are certainly not the wooden-headed noise dolts they are sometimes portrayed as: each comes from a middle-class background, and while Arm is an English graduate, Turner has qualifications in anthropology. After much speculation Mudhoney became the final players in the Sub Pop empire to go major when they moved to Warner Brothers Records, though many would argue that none of their efforts thus far have managed to reproduce the glory of 'Touch Me I'm Sick' or other highlights of their independent days. *My Brother The Cow*, however, revealed a band nearly back at its best. Released after extensive worldwide touring with Pearl Jam, songs such as 'Into Your Schtick' reflected on the passing of one-time friend Kurt Cobain. Jack Endino's production added lustre and managed to capture the band's compelling live sound better than had previously been the case. The future of the band was in doubt when Mark Arm formed the offshoot Bloodloss in early 1996.

●ALBUMS: *Superfuzz Bigmuff* (Sub Pop 1988)★★★, *Mudhoney* (Sub Pop 1989)★★, *Every Good Boy Deserves Fudge* (Sub Pop 1991)★★★, *Piece Of Cake* (Warners 1992)★★★, *Five Dollar Bob's Mock Cooter Stew* (Warners 1993)★★, *My Brother The Cow* (Warners 1995)★★★.

●COMPILATIONS: *Superfuzz Bigmuff Plus Early Singles* (Sub Pop 1991)★★★.

●VIDEOS: *Absolutely Live* (Pinnacle 1991), *No 1 Video In America This Week* (Warner Video 1995).

MUSICAL YOUTH

Formed at Duddeston Manor School, Birmingham, England, this pop/reggae-influenced group featured two sets of brothers, Kelvin and Michael Grant and Junior and Patrick Waite (b. c.1969, d. 18 February 1993). The latter pair's father, Fred Waite, was a former member of Jamaican group the Techniques, and sang lead with Junior at the start of the group's career in the late 70s. Although schoolboys, the group managed to secure gigs at certain Birmingham pubs and released a single, 'Political'/'Generals' on local label 021 Records. An appearance on BBC disc jockey John Peel's evening show brought further attention to the group and they were signed to MCA Records. By that time, founding father Fred Waite had backed down to be replaced by Dennis Seaton as lead singer. During the winter of 1982, the group issued one of the fastest selling singles of the year in 'Pass The Dutchie'. Based on the Mighty Diamonds' 'Pass The Kouchie' (a song about marijuana), the title had been subtly altered to feature the patois 'Dutchie' (literally a 'cooking pot'). The infectious enthusiasm of the group's performance captured the public's imagination and propelled the record to number 1 in the UK charts. A US Top 10 hit also followed. The catchy follow-up 'Youth Of Today' also reached the UK Top 20 and early in 1983 'Never Gonna Give You Up' climbed to number 6. Minor successes with 'Heartbreaker' and 'Tell Me Why' were succeeded by a surprise collaboration with Donna Summer on the UK Top 20 hit 'Unconditional Love'. A revival of Desmond Dekker's '007' saw them back in the Top 30, but after one final hit with 'Sixteen', they fell from commercial grace and subsequently split up in 1985 when Seaton left the band. Plans to reform were scotched when Patrick Waite, who had gone on to a career of juvenile crime, died of natural causes while awaiting a court appearance on drug charges. The Grant brothers remain involved in music, while Seaton has released a solo set and formed his own band, XMY.
● ALBUMS: *The Youth Of Today* (MCA 1982)★★★, *Different Style* (MCA 1983)★★. Solo: Dennis Seaton *Imagine That* (Bellaphon 1989)★★.
● FURTHER READING: *Musical Youth: Their Own Story*, no editor listed.

MUTE RECORDS

Daniel Miller's brainchild was originally set up for a single under the guise of the Normal. 'T.V.O.D.'/'Warm Leatherette' became the first Mute single in early 1978, a pioneering utilization of electronics that paved the way for Mute's alignment with synthesized and hi-tech sounds. Several hundred albums later, Mute's singular artistic identity and experimental approach still cuts a distinctive chord through an apathetic music industry. Along with Factory and Rough Trade Records, Mute has demonstrated an ability to combine aesthetic autonomy with survival. Among the label's early group roster were Fad Gadget, DAF and Depeche Mode. It was the success of the latter that convinced many that a post-punk independent label could succeed in producing a consistent chart act. Despite the offers made to the group from major labels, Depeche Mode resisted any temptation to move - a tribute to Miller's business acumen and his faith in Depeche Mode's artistic growth. The label has also been greatly assisted by ex-Depeche Mode member Vince Clark's series of projects from Yazoo through to Erasure. Owing to Depeche Mode and Erasure's continuing international success, Mute has been able to finance less commercial acts such as Laibach, Crime And The City Solution, Diamanda Galas and Nitzer Ebb. The label's acquisition of the back catalogues of Cabaret Voltaire, Can and Throbbing Gristle also ensured the continued availability of these seminal artists' output. In the 90s a subsidiary operation dealing with dance and techno, Novamute, was established, dealing with forerunning experimental artists such as Moby. On a more conventional front the parent label also signed the Inspiral Carpets, but the long-standing artist who has best combined critical and commercial approbation has undoubtedly been Nick Cave.
● COMPILATIONS: *International* (Mute 1991)★★★.

MY BLOODY VALENTINE

It took several years for My Bloody Valentine to capture their ground-breaking hybrid of ethereal melodies and studio-orientated, discordant sounds which proved so influential on the independent scene of the late 80s. Their roots lay in Dublin, where singer/guitarist Kevin Shields joined drummer Colm O'Ciosoig in the short-lived Complex. Forming My Bloody Valentine in 1984, the pair moved to Berlin, joined by vocalist Dave Conway (vocals) and Tina (keyboards). A mini-album, *This Is Your Bloody Valentine*, on the obscure German Tycoon label in 1984, made little impression (although it was later reissued in the UK), so the band returned to London and recruited bassist Debbie Googe. The 12-inch EP, *Geek!* (and the accompanying 'No Place To Go') emerged on

Fever in mid-1986 which, like their debut, was strongly influenced by the Cramps and the Birthday Party. Later that year, the band signed with Joe Foster's fledgling Kaleidoscope Sound label for *The New Record By My Bloody Valentine* EP, which revealed a new influence, the Jesus And Mary Chain. A switch to the Primitives' label Lazy, produced 'Sunny Sundae Smile' (1987), which meshed bubblegum pop with buzzsaw guitars, a formula that dominated both the mini-album, *Ecstasy*, and 'Strawberry Wine', released later that year. The departure of Conway signalled a change in musical direction, reinforced by the arrival of vocalist Belinda Butcher. A further move to Creation Records allowed for a drastic reappraisal in recording techniques, first apparent on the formidable *You Made Me Realise* EP in 1988. Enticing melodic structures contrasted with the snarling, almost unworldly collage of noise, developed more fully that year on My Bloody Valentine's pivotal *Isn't Anything*, from which was drawn the barrage of guitars, 'Feed Me With Your Kiss'. At last, the group had unearthed a completely new sound. Since then, their status has mushroomed. The release of an EP, *Glider* (1990), alongside a remix from the in-demand DJ Andy Weatherall, flirted with both dance music and the charts while 'Tremelo' (1991) must rank as arguably the most extreme piece of music to reach the Top 30. To quote the band, it 'sounded like it was being played through a transistor radio'. My Bloody Valentine's increasing maturity saw the meticulously produced *Loveless* album reinforce their reputation as one of the prime influences on the late 80s UK independent scene; one that groups such as Slowdive, Lush and Chapterhouse owe a great deal. However, the massive studio bills run up during that time saw My Bloody Valentine leave Creation, moving instead to Island Records. At this point another agonizing gestation period was embarked upon, allegedly due to difficulty installing equipment in their own purpose-built studio in south London.

●ALBUMS: *This Is Your Bloody Valentine* (Tycoon 1984)★★, *Ecstasy* mini-album (Lazy 1987)★★, *Isn't Anything* (Creation 1988)★★★★, *Loveless* (Creation 1991)★★★.

NAKED RAYGUN

Formerly Negro Commander, a band whose life span extended to a single show, Chicago, Illinois, USA's Naked Raygun were their city's premier hardcore band of the early 80s. Despite appearances to the contrary, their name was chosen prior to the election of US President Ronald Reagan. Dropping bass player Marco Pezzati for Camilo Gonzalez of the Wayouts at the same time as they lost their original name, the rest of the band comprised Jeff Pezzati (vocals) and Santiago Durango (guitar). No drummer featured in the original line-up until Jim Colao was recruited. Santiago then moved on to Big Black and Arsenal, and was replaced by John Haggerty who had already played saxophone at early shows. Their recording career had begun with the documentary 1981 Chicago live compilation, *Busted At Oz*, released on Autumn Records (it also featured the Effigies and Strike Under, from whom later members would come). New drummer Eric Spicer (ex-DVA) was drafted in 1983 as the group began to take shape. 'The old line-up didn't have a common, long-term goal. We just had practices, we just played some songs we had in our heads . . . We never talked about records, we played any show in Chicago we could get . . .' They played their first New York date at Gildersleeves later that year. It had taken the band three years to complete their first tour, after which they announced two further tours in 1984. Their first record release had been 1983's cacophonous *Basement Screams* EP on Ruthless Records (run by Big Black and the Effigies, and entirely different to the label of the same name operated by rapper Eazy E). However, their debut album was a vastly superior artefact in showcasing their talents, with individual songs of great quality including 'Surf Combat' and 'Gear', while 'Metastasis' benefited from Pezatti's trademark malevolent vocal inflections. The jazzy intonations of 'Libido', meanwhile, served as an early indication of a willingness to change their mode of address. In 1986 Pierre Kezdy deputized for Camillo on bass, and their *All Rise* album of that year proved to be their finest moment. The group then moved from

Homestead Records to set up their own Sandpunder label, before a further shift to Caroline Records. Their admiration for the work of the Buzzcocks was compounded when they were joined by a drunken Steve Diggle onstage on their 1989 UK tour, to promote *Understand?*, their second album for Caroline. After an emotional final gig at Chicago's Maxwell's venue Haggerty left (to join Pegboy) to be replaced by Bill Stephens (ex-Product 19). However, his contribution to 1990's *Raygun ... Naked Raygun* failed to fill the gap adequately, and Naked Raygun subsequently ground to a halt.

●ALBUMS: *Throb Throb* (Homestead 1985)★★★, *All Rise* (Homestead 1986)★★★★, *Jettison* (Caroline 1988)★★★, *Understand?* (Caroline 1989)★★★, *Raygun ... Naked Raygun* (Caroline 1990)★★.

NAPALM DEATH

This quintet from Birmingham, England, was formed in 1981. Dispensing with their original style by the mid-80s, they then absorbed punk and thrash metal influences to create the new sub-genre of grindcore, arguably the most extreme of all musical forms. Side one of their debut album featured Justin Broadrick (guitar), Mick Harris (drums) and Nick Bullen (bass/vocals), but by side two this had switched to Bill Steer (guitar), Jim Whitely (bass) and Lee Dorrian (vocals), later replaced by Barney Greenway, with Harris the only survivor from that first inception (though that too had been subject to numerous changes). Broadrick would go on to Head Of David and Godflesh. *Scum* largely comprised sub-two minute blasts of metallic white noise, overridden by Dorrian's unintelligible vocal tirade. The lyrics dealt with social and political injustices, but actually sounded like somebody coughing up blood. Their main advocate was Radio 1 disc jockey John Peel, who had first picked up on *Scum*, playing the 0.75 second-long track 'You Suffer' three times before inviting them to record a session for the programme in September 1987. This would come to be acknowledged as one of the 'Classic Sessions' in Ken Garner's 1993 book on the subject, and introduced new bass player Shane Embury (also Unseen Terror, who split after one album in 1988). Elsewhere Napalm Death were the subject of derision and total miscomprehension. They were, however, the true pioneers of the 'blast-snare' technique - whereby the tempo of a given beat is sustained at the maximum physical human tolerance level. They went on to attract a small but loyal cult following on the underground heavy metal scene.

From *Enslavement To Obliteration*, consisting of no less than 54 tracks on the CD, was a state of the artless offering which easily bypassed previous extremes in music. However, following a Japanese tour in 1989 both Dorrian and Steer elected to leave the band, the former putting together Cathedral, the latter Carcass. Despite the gravity of the split replacements were found in vocalist Mark 'Barny' Greenway (ex-Benediction) and US guitarist Jesse Pintado (ex-Terrorizer). To maintain their profile the band embarked on the European *Grindcrusher* tour (in their wake grindcore had developed considerably and found mass acceptance among the rank and file of the metal world) with Bolt Thrower, Carcass and Morbid Angel, before playing their first US dates in New York. A second guitarist, Mitch Harris (ex-Righteous Pigs) was added in time for *Harmony Corruption*, which, along with the 12-inch 'Suffer The Children', saw Napalm Death retreat to a purer death metal sound. During worldwide touring in 1992 sole surviving original member Mick Harris became disillusioned with the band and left, making way for Danny Herrara a friend of Pintado's from Los Angeles. A fourth album, *Utopia Banished*, celebrated the band's remarkable survival instincts, while the heady touring schedule continued unabated. By 1993 the band had played in Russia, Israel, Canada and South Africa in addition to the more familiar European and US treks. A cover of the Dead Kennedys' 'Nazi Punks Fuck Off', issued as a single, reinstated their political motives. As *Fear, Emptiness, Despair* confirmed, however, they remain the antithesis of style, melody and taste - the punk concept taken to its ultimate extreme, and a great band for all the difficulty of listening to them. Greenway was sacked in October 1996 and replaced a few months later by Phil Vane.

●ALBUMS: *Scum* (Earache 1987)★★, *From Enslavement To Obliteration* (Earache 1988)★★★, *The Peel Sessions* (Strange Fruit 1989)★★★, *Harmony Corruption* (Earache 1990)★, *Live Corruption* (Earache 1990)★, *Utopia Banished* (Earache 1992)★★, *Fear, Emptiness, Despair* (Earache 1994)★★, *Greed Killing* mini-album (Earache 1995)★★, *Diatribes* (Earache 1996)★★.

●COMPILATIONS: *Death By Manipulation* (Earache 1992)★★.

●VIDEOS: *Live Corruption* (1990).

NELSON, BILL

b. William Nelson, 18 December 1948, Wakefield, West Yorkshire, England. Although noted chiefly for his innovative guitar work with Be-Bop Deluxe, his solo releases actually form more than four-fifths of his total output. *Smile* was a dreamy, acoustic debut after he had played throughout his home county with pre-progressive rock outfits such as the Teenagers, Global Village and Gentle Revolution. He fronted Be-Bop Deluxe for most of the 70s before responding to punk and techno-rock forces by assembling Bill Nelson's Red Noise. *Sound On Sound*, released in 1979, was an agitated but confused debut from Red Noise, and Nelson returned to solo work. The single 'Do You Dream In Colour?' provided his highest UK solo chart placing at number 52. It was released on his own label, Cocteau Records. Following a short-lived contract with Mercury Records he continued to release introspective, chiefly home-recorded albums. He was in demand as a producer and worked on sessions with many new wave bands including the Skids and A Flock Of Seagulls. Surprisingly, after the demise of Be-Bop Deluxe he showed little inclination to use the guitar and preferred to experiment with keyboards and sampled sounds, composing thematic pieces which have been used in films and plays. He recorded backing music for the Yorkshire Actors Company's version of both *Das Kabinett* and *La Belle Et La Bette*, issued later as albums. Many of his releases throughout the 80s were of a whimsical, self-indulgent nature and missed the input of other musicians. Numerous albums were issued via his fan club and the quality was rarely matched by the prolificacy, which twice ran to four-album boxed sets, *Trial By Intimacy* and *Demonstrations Of Affection*. In 1991 he moved markedly towards a stronger and more defined melodic style with *Luminous* on Manchester's independent label, Imaginary, and also spoke of returning to his first love, the guitar. He is the main figure behind Channel Light Vessel.

●ALBUMS: *Smile* (1971)★★, *Sound On Sound* (Harvest 1979)★★, *Quit Dreaming And Get On The Beam* (Mercury 1981)★★★★, *Sounding The Ritual Echo* (Harvest 1981)★★★, *Das Kabinett* (Cocteau 1981)★★, *La Belle Et La Bette* (1982)★★★, *The Love That Whirls* (Mercury 1982)★★★, *Chimera* (Mercury 1983)★★★, *The Two Fold Aspect Of Everything* (Cocteau 1984)★★★, *Trial By Intimacy* (Cocteau 1984)★★★, *Map Of Dreams* (Cocteau 1984)★★★, *Aconography* (Cocteau 1986)★★★, *Chamber Of Dreams* (Cocteau 1986)★★★, *Summer Of God's Piano* (Cocteau 1986)★★★, *Getting The Holy Ghost Across* (Portrait 1986)★★★, *Chance Encounters In The Garden Of Light* (Cocteau 1988)★★★, *Optimism* (Cocteau 1988)★★★, *Pavillions Of The Heart And Soul* (Cocteau 1989)★★★, *Demonstrations Of Affection* (Cocteau 1989)★★★, *Luminous* (Imaginary 1991)★★★, *Blue Moons And Laughing Guitars* (1992)★★★, *After The Satellite Sings* (Resurgence 1996)★★★, with Culturemix *Culturemix With Bill Nelson* (Resurgence 1996)★★★.

●COMPILATIONS: *Duplex: The Best Of Bill Nelson* (Cocteau 1989)★★★.

NEVILLE BROTHERS

The Nevilles represented the essence of 40 years of New Orleans music distilled within one family unit. The Nevilles comprised Art (b. Arthur Lanon Neville, 17 December 1937, New Orleans, Louisiana, USA; keyboards/vocals), Charles (b. 28 December 1938, New Orleans, Louisiana, USA; saxophone/flute), Aaron (b. 24 January 1941, New Orleans, Louisiana, USA; vocals/keyboards) and Cyril (b. 10 January 1948, New Orleans, Louisiana, USA; vocals). Each member was also a capable percussionist. They have, individually and collectively, been making an impression on R&B, rock 'n' roll, soul, funk and jazz since the early 50s. Art was the leader of the Hawkettes, whose 1954 Chess Records hit 'Mardi Gras Mambo' has become a New Orleans standard, reissued every year at Mardi Gras time. From 1957 he released solo singles on Speciality Records, and in the early 60s, both he and Aaron worked (separately) for the legendary producer Allen Toussaint. Aaron had emerged from vocal group the Avalons, and although he scored a minor R&B hit in 1960 with Toussaint's 'Over You', it was not until 1967 that he achieved fame with the soul ballad 'Tell It Like It Is', a million-seller which reached number 2 in the charts. Charles Neville, meanwhile, had been working - on the road, or back home as part of the Dew Drop Inn's houseband - with many legendary names: B.B. King, Bobby Bland and Ray Charles among them. In 1968 Art formed the Meters, one of the Crescent City's most innovative and respected outfits. Featuring Leo Nocentelli (guitar), George Potter Jnr. (bass), Joseph Modeliste (drums) and, later, Cyril Neville (percussion), they were New Orleans' answer to Booker T. And The MGs, and besides their own albums, they could be heard on early 70s releases by Paul McCartney, Robert Palmer, LaBelle and Dr. John. 1976's *The Wild Tchoupitoulas* was a transitional album, featuring the Meters' rhythm section and all four Neville Brothers; by 1978 they were officially a group. Despite a considerable 'cult' following, particularly among fellow musicians, it took them until 1989, and the release of the Daniel Lanois-produced

Yellow Moon, to find a wider audience. A single, 'With God On Our Side' was extracted and became a minor hit; Aaron, duetting with Linda Ronstadt, achieved his greatest chart success since 'Tell It Like It Is', when 'Don't Know Much' reached US and UK number 2 and won them the first of two Grammy awards. In 1990, as a band, they released *Brother's Keeper* and appeared on the soundtrack of the movie *Bird On A Wire*.

●ALBUMS: *The Wild Tchoupitoulas* (1976)★★★, *The Neville Brothers* (Capitol 1978)★★★, *Fiyo On The Bayou* (A&M 1981)★★★★, *Neville-ization* (Black Top 1984)★★★★, *Live At Tipitina's* (Spindletop 1985)★★★, *Neville-ization II* (1987)★★★, *Uptown* (EMI America 1987)★★, *Yellow Moon* (A&M 1989)★★★★, *Brother's Keeper* (A&M 1990)★★★★, *Family Groove* (A&M 1992)★★★, *Live On Planet Earth* (A&M 1994)★★★, *Mitakuye Oyasin Oyasin/All My Relations* (A&M 1996)★★★.

●COMPILATIONS: *Treacherous: A History Of The Neville Brothers 1955-1985* (Rhino 1986)★★★★, *Treacherous Too!* (Rhino 1991)★★★, *Legacy: A History Of The Nevilles* (Charly 1990)★★★★.

NEVILLE, AARON

b. 24 January 1941, New Orleans, Louisiana, USA. Neville began performing in the Hawkettes, a group that also featured his brother, Art. Aaron was signed to Minit Records as a solo artist, but despite a minor hit with 'Over You' (1960), remained largely unknown until the release of 'Tell It Like It Is' (1966). This simple, haunting ballad showcased the singer's delicate delivery while the song's slogan-like title echoed the sentiments of the rising Black Power movement. Sadly, the single's outlet, Par-Lo, went bankrupt, and despite subsequent strong releases, Neville was unable to repeat its commercial success. In 1978, following the break-up of the Meters, Aaron joined Art, Cyril and Charles in the Neville Family Band; later they renamed themselves the Neville Brothers. He continued a parallel solo career and in 1989 had an international hit with 'Don't Know Much', a duet with Linda Ronstadt.

●ALBUMS: *Tell It Like It Is* (Par-Lo 1967)★★, *Orchid In The Storm* (Demon 1986)★★★, *Warm Your Heart* (A&M 1991)★★★, *The Grand Tour* (1993)★★, *Soulful Christmas* (1993)★★, *The Tattooed Heart* (A&M 1995)★★.

●COMPILATIONS: *Like It 'Tis* (Minit 1967)★★, *Humdinger* (Stateside 1986)★★, *Make Me Strong* (Charly 1986)★★★, *Show Me The Way* (1989)★★★, *My Greatest Gift* (Rounder 1990)★★★.

NEW KIDS ON THE BLOCK

Formed in 1985, this pop group from Boston, Massachusetts, USA, featured Joe McIntyre (b. 31 December 1972, Needham, Massachusetts, USA), Jordan Knight (b. 15 May 1970, Worcester, Massachusetts, USA), Jonathan Knight (b. 29 November 1968, Worcester, Massachusetts, USA), Daniel Wood (b. 14 May 1969, Boston, Massachusetts, USA) and Donald Wahlberg (b. 17 August 1969, Boston, Massachusetts, USA). They were discovered by producer/writer Maurice Starr, who had previously moulded the career of New Edition. It was Starr who presented his protégés with a rap song titled 'New Kids On The Block' from which they took their name. Their self-titled album, released in 1986, fused rap and pop and brought them popularity among a predominantly white teenage audience. However, it was not until 1988 that they broke through to the US charts with 'Please Don't Go Girl'. In 1989, they became the biggest-selling group in America, enjoying sizeable hits with 'You Got It (The Right Stuff)', 'I'll Be Loving You (Forever)', 'Cover Girl' and 'Didn't I'. A reissue of 'You Got It (The Right Stuff)' climbed to number 1 in the UK, thereby establishing the quintet as an act of international teen appeal.

●ALBUMS: *New Kids On The Block* (Columbia 1986)★★, *Hangin' Tough* (Columbia 1988)★★, *Merry Merry Christmas* (Columbia 1989)★, *Step By Step* (Columbia 1990)★★, *No More Games/Remix Album* (Columbia 1991)★★.

●COMPILATIONS: *H.I.T.S* (Columbia 1991)★★★.

●FURTHER READING: *New Kids On The Block: The Whole Story By Their Friends*, Robin McGibbon. *New Kids On The Block*, Lynn Goldsmith.

NEW MODEL ARMY

With their roots embedded in the punk era, New Model Army were formed in Bradford, Yorkshire, in 1980, and immediately outlined their manifesto by naming themselves after the Sir Thomas Fairfax/Oliver Cromwell revolutionary army. The group was and is led by Justin 'Slade The Leveller' Sullivan (b. 1956, Buckinghamshire, England; guitar/vocals), a former platform sweeper and Mars Bar production line worker, with the help of Jason 'Moose' Harris (b. 1968; bass/guitar) and Robb Heaton (b. 1962, Cheshire, England; drums/guitar). Their brand of punk folk/rock attracted a loyal cult following, much of whom shared the band's grievances towards the Conservative government policies of the 80s. This was best executed on their debut album, which combined militant themes such as 'Spirit Of The Falklands' and 'Vengeance' (a vitriolic anthem about getting even with one's trespassers) with the haunting lament for childhood, 'A Liberal Education'. The group's championing of traditional working-class ethics saw an unexpected boost for a dying art and trade; that of the clog. New Model Army made their first public appearance at Scamps Disco in Bradford in October 1980. After releasing singles on Abstract Records, and enjoying a number 2 UK independent chart hit with 'The Price' in 1984, they formed an unlikely alliance with the multi national EMI Records, which saw the band acquire a higher profile and a significantly increased recording budget. They eventually broke through to a wider audience with 'No Rest' which peaked at number 28 on the UK singles chart in 1985 - a position they were never to beat in an impressive run of 12 UK chart singles between 1985 and 1991. With often inflammatory lyrics, the band have never compromised their beliefs for commercial gain. They ran into trouble with the BBC's *Top Of The Pops* chart show for donning T-shirts with the (albeit laudable) slogan, 'Only Stupid Bastards Use Heroin'. This attracted some derision from the 'anarcho-punk' traditionalists Conflict, who replied with their own motif: 'Only Stupid Bastards Help EMI'. They subsequently continued to release high quality albums, with considerable crossover potential, always maintaining credibility with their original fan base. In December 1991 the group left EMI, eventually finding a new home on Epic Records. Their first single for the label revealed few concessions to the mainstream: 'Here Comes The War' featured a picture of a charred body, and a pull-out poster instructing the user in how to prepare a nuclear bomb.

●ALBUMS: *Vengeance* (Abstract 1984)★★★, *No Rest For The Wicked* (EMI 1985)★★★, *Ghost Of Cain* (EMI 1986)★★, *Radio Sessions* (Abstract 1988)★★, *Thunder And Consolation* (EMI 1989)★★★, *Impurity* (EMI 1990)★★★, *Raw Melody Men* (EMI 1990)★★★, *The Love Of Hopeless Causes* (Epic 1993)★★★, *BBC Radio One - Live In Concert* (Windsong 1994)★★.

●COMPILATIONS: *The Independent Story* (Abstract 1987)★★★, *History* (EMI 1992)★★★.

●VIDEOS: *History: The Videos 85-90* (PMI 1993).

NEW MUSIK

This UK pop group comprised Tony Mansfield (guitar/keyboards/vocals), Tony Hibbert (bass), Phil Towner (drums) and Clive Gates (keyboards).

They came to prominence after a minor hit in 1979 with 'Straight Lines', during 1980 with three pop/synthesizer hits on the GTO label, 'Living By Numbers', 'The World Of Water' and 'Sanctuary'. Mansfield regarded their debut *From A To B* as rudimentary, but the succeeding *Anywhere* fared less well, despite its evident maturity. The change in style also took its toll on the band with the departure of Hibbert and Towner soon after its release. They were replaced by electronic percussionist Cliff Venner for the band's final and rather uninspired *Warp*. Full of empty electronic dance tracks it was notable for an daring attempt at the Beatles' *All You Need Is Love*. However, sales were very poor and they soon disbanded. Mansfield went on to produce hits for Captain Sensible, Mari Wilson, Naked Eyes and worked on A-Ha's debut album *Hunting High And Low*.

●ALBUMS: *From A To B* (GTO 1980)★★★, *Anywhere* (GTO 1981)★★★, *Warp* (GTO 1982)★★.

NEW ORDER

When Joy Division's Ian Curtis committed suicide in May 1980 the three remaining members, Bernard Sumner (b. Bernard Dicken, 4 January 1956, Salford, Manchester, England; guitar/vocals), Peter Hook (b. 13 February 1956, Manchester, England; bass) and Stephen Morris (b. 28 October 1957, Macclesfield, Cheshire, England; drums) continued under the name New Order. Sumner took over vocal duties and the trio embarked upon a low-key tour of the USA, intent on continuing as an entity independent of the massive reputation Joy Division had achieved shortly before their demise. Later that same year they recruited Morris's girlfriend, Gillian Gilbert (b. 27 January 1961, Manchester, England; keyboards/guitar) and wrote and rehearsed their debut, *Movement*, which was released the following year. Their first single, 'Ceremony', penned by Joy Division, was a UK Top 40 hit in the spring of 1981, and extended the legacy of their previous band. Hook's deep, resonant bass line and Morris's crisp, incessant drumming were both Joy Division trademarks. The vocals, however, were weak, Sumner clearly at this stage feeling uncomfortable as frontman. Much was made, in 1983, of the band 'rising from the ashes' of Joy Division in the music press, when *Power, Corruption And Lies* was released. Their experimentation with electronic gadgetry was fully realized and the album contained many surprises and memorable songs. The catchy bass riff and quirky lyrics of 'Age Of Consent' made it an instant classic, while the sign-off line, on the otherwise elegiac 'Your Silent Face', 'You've caught me at a bad time/So why don't you piss off', showed that Sumner no longer felt under any pressure to match the poetic, introspective lyricism of Ian Curtis. As well as redefining their sound they clearly now relished the role of 'most miserable sods in pop'. 'Blue Monday', released at this time in 12-inch format only, went on to become the biggest-selling 12-inch single of all time in the UK. In 1983 'disco' was a dirty word among the independent fraternity and 'Blue Monday', which combined an infectious dance beat with a calm, aloof vocal, was a brave step into uncharted territory. As well as influencing a legion of UK bands, it would be looked back upon as a crucial link between the disco of the 70s and the dance/house music wave at the end of the 80s. New Order had now clearly established themselves, and throughout the 80s and into the 90s they remained the top independent band in the UK, staying loyal to Manchester's Factory Records. Their subsequent collaboration with 'hot' New York hip hop producer Arthur Baker spawned the anti-climactic 'Confusion' (1983) and 'Thieves Like Us' (1984). Both singles continued their preference for the 12-inch format, stretching in excess of six minutes, and stressing their lack of concern for the exposure gained by recording with mainstream radio in mind. *Low Life* appeared in 1985 and is perhaps their most consistently appealing album to date. While the 12-inch version of *Low Life*'s 'Perfect Kiss' was a magnificent single, showing the band at their most inspired and innovative, the collaboration with producer John Robie on the single version of 'Subculture' indicated that their tendency to experiment and 'play around' could also spell disaster. Their next album, 1986's *Brotherhood*, although containing strong tracks such as 'Bizarre Love Triangle', offered nothing unexpected. It was not until the UK Top 5 single 'True Faith' in 1987, produced and co-written by Stephen Hague hot on the heels of his success with the Pet Shop Boys and accompanied by an award-winning Phillipe Decouffle video, that New Order found themselves satisfying long-term fans and general public alike. The following year Quincy Jones' remix of 'Blue Monday' provided the group with another Top 5 hit. If the recycling of old songs and proposed 'personal' projects fuelled rumours of a split then 1989's *Technique* promptly dispelled them. The album, recorded in Ibiza, contained upbeat bass-and-drums-dominated tracks that characterized the best of their early output. Its most striking feature, however, was their flirtation with the popular Balearic style, as in the hit single, 'Fine Time', which contained lines like 'I've met a lot of cool chicks, But I've never met a girl with all her own teeth', delivered in a voice that parodied Barry White's notoriously sexist, gravelly vocals of the 70s. Meanwhile the band had changed significantly as a live act. Their reputation for inconsistency and apathy, as well as their staunch refusal to play encores, was by now replaced with confident, crowd-pleasing hour-long sets. In the summer of 1990 they reached the UK number 1 position with 'World In Motion', accompanied by the England World Cup Squad, with a song that earned the questionable accolade of best football record of all time, and caused a band member to observe that 'this is probably the last straw for Joy Division fans'. Rather than exploiting their recent successes with endless tours, the group unexpectedly branched out into various spin-off ventures. Hook formed the hard-rocking Revenge, Sumner joined former Smiths guitarist Johnny Marr in Electronic and Morris/Gilbert recorded an album under the self-effacing title, the Other Two. The extra-curricular work prompted persistent rumours that New Order had irrevocably split, but no official announcement or press admission was forthcoming. In the summer of 1991 the group announced that they had reconvened for a new album which was eventually released in 1993. *Republic* consequently met with mixed reviews reflecting critical confusion about their status and direction. While retaining the mix of rock and dance music successfully honed on *Technique*, the tone was decidedly more downbeat, even sombre. Sadly it arrived too late to help the doomed Factory label, and afterwards the band's membership would return to varied solo projects. Hook formed Monaco in 1996

●ALBUMS: *Movement* (Factory 1981)★★★, *Power, Corruption And Lies* (Factory 1983)★★★, *Low Life* (Factory 1985)★★★★, *Brotherhood* (Factory 1986)★★★★, *Technique* (Factory 1989)★★★, *Republic* (London 1993)★★★.

●COMPILATIONS: *Substance* (Factory 1987)★★★★, *The Peel Sessions* (Strange Fruit 1990)★★★, *Live In Concert* (Windsong 1992)★★★, *(The Best Of) New Order* (London 1995)★★★★, *(The Rest Of) New Order* (London 1995)★★★.

●VIDEOS: *Taras Shevenko* (1984), *Pumped Full Of Drugs* (1988), *Substance 1989* (1989), *Brixton Academy April 1987* (1989), *Neworderstory* (1993).

●FURTHER READING: *New Order & Joy Division: Pleasures And Wayward Distractions*, Brian Edge. *New Order & Joy Division: Dreams Never End*, Claude Flowers.

NEW ROMANTICISM

New romanticism emerged in the UK music scene in the early 80s as a direct backlash against the austerity of the punk movement. At various times it became a catch-all term for quite disparate bands working within the pop world, and consequently works better as a description of a specific time rather than sound or style. Where punk railed against life on England's council estates, the new romantics celebrated glamour, ostentatious clothes and hedonism. The coming of age of the video as a promotional tool was important to the development of new romanticism, as were the outlandish haircuts (A Flock Of Seagulls), the frilled shirts (Duran Duran, Spandau Ballet) and the fact that men could be seen wearing mascara (practically everyone involved). Guitars, though present, were subordinate to synthesizers. The movement's early fulcrum was Stevo (Steven Pearse), whose *Some Bizzare Album* compilation in 1980 introduced such artists as Classix Nouveaux, Blancmange, Depeche Mode and Soft Cell. Centred on London clubs such as Blitz, this new gaggle of groups was at first termed 'futuristic'. The Human League had been active for some time in Sheffield but in a new incarnation perfectly amalgamated simple song ideas with basic keyboard skills to define the essential new romantic blueprint. Adam And The Ants were historically linked with punk, as were, more obliquely, Culture Club, though both found a place on the fringe of the movement as a platform for major chart success. If the most obvious historical ancestor of new romanticism was David Bowie, then Japan were his closest living relatives, aping even his fascination with the Orient. The two biggest stars were undoubtedly Duran Duran and Spandau Ballet. The former wrote classic pop hooks with casual ease for much of the period, though Spandau Ballet were always more visually than aurally appealing, despite the occasional winning single (the melodrama of 'True' was resonant enough for PM Dawn to make it rap's first new romantic sample). Of less enduring fame or substance were Classix Nouveaux, Visage and A Flock Of Seagulls, despite the latter breaking through in the American market. Nevertheless, several exceptional singles were left behind that effectively defined the times, and it was to no great surprise that the movement was revisited in 1995 with the development of the 'Romo' scene.

●FURTHER READING: *Like Punk Never Happened - Culture Club And The New Pop*, Dave Rimmer.

NEW WAVE OF BRITISH HEAVY METAL

The names speak for themselves - Iron Maiden, Def Leppard, Saxon, Samson, Venom, Diamond Head, Girlschool and Praying Mantis. Just a handful of the bands who made it during the period 1979 to 1981. The phrase was first coined by Geoff Barton at *Sounds*, but much credit is also due to DJ Neal Kay, whose help in giving bands like Iron Maiden and Praying Mantis (as well as many others) their first break was crucial. EMI Records were quick off the mark and with Kay's help they produced the compilation album, *Metal For Muthas*, which put many bands on the road to fame and others, like Toad The Wet Sprockett, on the road to obscurity. Well over 200 bands emerged during this period and many released records on their own labels - even more never got past the rehearsal stage, while others remained strictly 'bedroom' bands. This enthusiasm also helped to revitalize older bands and some, like Gillan and Motörhead, became spearheads for the movement. Yet by 1981 the corporate machine began to eat up the talent and American influences crept in to destroy the movement's identity. If, as has often been stated, the movement started with Iron Maiden's *Soundhouse Tapes* EP in 1979, then it would be equally true to say that the final nail in its coffin came in September 1981 when Paul Di'Anno left them. Just like punk in 1977, the ideas and attitude fell victim to clean living and commerciality.

●COMPILATIONS: *Metal For Muthas Volume 1* (EMI 1980)★★★, *Metal For Muthas Volume 2 Cut Loud* (EMI 1980)★★, *Brute Force* (MCA 1980)★★, *New Electric Warriors* (Logo 1980)★★★, *The NWOBHM '79 Revisisted* (Vertigo 1990)★★.

NICKS, STEVIE

b. Stephanie Nicks, 26 May 1948, Phoenix, Arizona, USA. When Stevie Nicks joined Fleetwood Mac in January 1975, she not only introduced her talents as a singer and songwriter, but provided a defined focal point during the group's live appearances. A former vocalist with Fritz, a struggling San Francisco band, Nicks moved to Los Angeles with her boyfriend and fellow ex-member Lindsey Buckingham. Together they recorded *Buckingham-Nicks*, a promising but largely neglected album, at the Second City Studio in Van Nuys, which was then used to demonstrate the facilities to Mick Fleetwood. By coincidence both Nicks and Lindsey were in a nearby room and were introduced to the

Fleetwood Mac drummer when he showed interest in their work. Within weeks the duo were invited to join his group to replace the departing Bob Welch. Their arrival brought a change in Fleetwood Mac's commercial fortunes. Nicks provided many of the group's best-known and successful songs, including the atmospheric 'Rhiannon' and the haunting 'Dreams'. The latter was one of several excellent compositions which graced the multi-million-selling *Rumours*, although the album itself signalled the collapse of two in-house relationships, including that of Buckingham and Nicks. In 1980, following the release of Fleetwood Mac's much-maligned *Tusk*, she began recording a solo album. *Bella Donna*, released the following year, that achieved platinum sales and remained on the *Billboard* album chart for over two years. It also spawned two US Top 10 singles in 'Stop Dragging My Heart Around', a duet with Tom Petty and 'Leather And Lace', which featured former Eagles drummer, Don Henley. A second selection, *The Wild Heart*, followed in 1983 and this best-seller produced two major hits in 'Stand Back' and 'Nightbird'. Her third album, *Rock A Little*, was less successful, artistically and commercially, and following its release Nicks entered the Betty Ford Clinic to be treated for drug dependency. She then rejoined Fleetwood Mac for *Tango In The Night*, which marked the departure of Lindsey Buckingham. Although his absence has created more space within the band's framework, a revitalized Nicks continued her solo activities, as exemplified by 1989's *The Other Side Of The Mirror*. She rejoined Buckingham in Fleetwood Mac when the *Rumours* line-up reconvened in 1997.

●ALBUMS: with Lindsey Buckingham *Buckingham-Nicks* (Polydor 1973)★★, *Bella Donna* (Warners 1981)★★★, *The Wild Heart* (Warners 1983)★★★, *Rock A Little* (Modern 1985)★★, *The Other Side Of The Mirror* (EMI 1989)★★★, *Street Angel* (EMI 1994)★★.

●COMPILATIONS: *Timespace: The Best Of Stevie Nicks* (EMI 1991)★★★.

NIGHTINGALES

After a series of low-key UK school bands, Robert Lloyd (b. 1959, Cannock, Staffordshire, England) formed the Prefects - one of the earliest punk bands - who toured with the Clash. They split up in 1979 and Lloyd assembled the Nightingales using the best of the musicians who had passed through the ranks of the Prefects. The first of many subsequent Nightingales line-ups were Alan and Paul Apperley, Joe Crow, Eamonn Duffy and Lloyd

himself. They were ably championed by BBC disc jockey John Peel, for whom Lloyd has recorded more sessions under various guises than any other artist. Peel himself said of them: '(their performances) will serve to confirm their excellence when we are far enough distanced from the 1980s to look at the period rationally, and other, infinitely better known bands stand revealed as charlatans'. The Nightingales' debut single, 'Idiot Strength', was released in 1981 on the band's own Vindaloo label in association with Rough Trade Records. Joe Crow then departed and his replacements, Nick Beales and Andy Lloyd, two of 15 personnel who would pass through the ranks, brought a totally different sound to the band. Cherry Red Records picked them up and the band's career began in earnest. Lloyd soon established himself as one of the more interesting lyricists of the independent chart. Most of his tirades were draped in humour: 'I'm too tired to do anything today, but tomorrow I'll start my diet, and answer some of my fan mail' ('Elvis: The Last Ten Days'). Alternatively: 'I worked in a bakery . . . the jokes were handed down like diseases, I only worked there for the bread.' The lack of success of subsequent releases led Lloyd and friends to the new Red Flame label started by Dave Kitson, the promoter of the Moonlight Club in London's Hampstead. Still unhappy with the way record companies were handling his band's career, Lloyd decided to reactivate the Vindaloo label. Ironically, this led to the demise of the Nightingales as Lloyd needed to spend more time as songwriter, producer and label boss for his relatively successful roster of artists such as We've Got A Fuzzbox And We're Gonna Use It and comedian Ted Chippington. When Fuzzbox toured America, taking the Nightingales' keyboard player with them, Lloyd dissolved the group and concentrated on a solo career. The Nightingales' legacy was wrapped up in 1991 with a compilation album for Mau Mau Records with sleevenotes written by a still devoted John Peel.

●ALBUMS: *Pigs On Purpose* (Cherry Red 1982)★★★, *Hysterics* (Red Flame 1983)★★★, *Just The Job* (Vindaloo 1983)★★★, *In The Good Old Country Ways* (Vindaloo 1986)★★★.

●COMPILATIONS: *What A Scream* (Mau Mau 1991)★★★.

NINE BELOW ZERO

A powerful and exciting UK R&B band of the late 70s, the group took its name from a song by Sonny Boy 'Rice Miller' Williamson and was led by guitarist/singer Dennis Greaves and virtuoso har-

monica player Mark Feltham. With Peter Clark (bass/vocals) and Kenny Bradley (drums), Feltham recorded the EP *Packed Fair And Square* (1979). This led to a recording contract with A&M Records and a live recording at London's Marquee Club where Nine Below Zero had a residency. The producer was Glyn Johns. With Stix Burkey replacing Bradley, the second album included some original songs while *Third Degree* was a minor UK hit. The band dissolved in the mid-80s as Feltham concentrated on session work and Greaves went on to a solo career and became a member of the Truth. However, Feltham revived Nine Below Zero at the end of the decade, signing a new recording contract with the China label. By the mid-90s they were recording with the mighty A&M as roots blues was experiencing a small rebirth.
●ALBUMS: *Live At The Marquee* (A&M 1980)★★★, *Don't Point Your Finger* (A&M 1981)★★★, *Third Degree* (A&M 1982)★★★, *Live At The Venue* (China 1990)★★★, *Off The Hook* (China 1992)★★★, *Live In London* (Indigo 1995)★★★, *Ice Station Zebro* (A&M 1996)★★★.

NITZER EBB

The driving force behind this electronic based band are Douglas McCarthy (b. 1 September 1966, Chelmsford, Essex, England; vocals) and Bon Harris (b. 12 August 1965, Chelmsford, Essex, England; percussion/vocals). Frustrated by their environment at school in Chelmsford, and inspired by bands like DAF, Bauhaus and the Birthday Party, they began their first experiments with synthesizers and drum machines in 1983. They were joined in their strictly amateur pursuits by schoolmate David Gooday. They had summoned enough experience and confidence to release their first single the next year, 'Isn't It Funny How Your Body Works', on Power Of Voice Communications. They were nothing if not prolific, releasing a further five singles over the next twelve months, which led to a contract with the premier UK independent stable, Mute Records, and Geffen Records in the USA. Their first album appeared in 1987, *That Total Age*, home to surging minimalist aggression, and the beginning of a long-term relationship with producer Flood, who would remix the single 'Join In The Chant'. On Gooday's departure Julian Beeston was enrolled. After a lengthy European trek with Depeche Mode, the band recorded *Belief*, and in 1989 followed up their own world tour with *Showtime*. Their third album revealed a swing in attitude, with music that was less confrontational and more consumer friendly. This was particularly

true in the USA, where the single 'Fun To Be Had' peaked at number 2 in the US dance charts. Their most recent album has confirmed their popularity with fans and a previously reluctant press. As McCarthy puts it: 'With the advent of *Ebbhead*, I think we've managed to twist listenability around to our way of thinking'.
●ALBUMS: *That Total Age* (Mute 1987)★★, *Belief* (Mute 1988)★★, *Showtime* (Mute 1989)★★★, *Ebbhead* (Mute 1991)★★★, *Big Hit* (Mute 1995)★★★.

NO FX

No FX were formed in Los Angeles, California, USA, in 1983. Immediately it was obvious they were one of the few bands in the hardcore scene to embrace humorous lyrical fare to genuinely amusing effect. The band, whose present line-up features 'Fat' Mike (vocals/bass), Eric Melvin (guitar/vocals), El Hefe (guitar/trumpet) and Erik Sandon (drums), set their agenda with their debut EP for Mystic Records, *The PMRC Can Suck On This*. Afterwards, they addressed accusations about being on this most unfashionable of labels (which was completely injudicious in releasing material by any hardcore band which came its way), with the *So What If We're On Mystic* EP. It was via a contract with Epitaph Records and the *Ribbed* album that No FX became a productive unit in terms of worldwide sales. *Ribbed* featured a blemishless collection of genuinely funny songs, notably the male-hygiene-bonding epic, 'Shower Day'. The full musicianship and clean production only helped to illuminate their witty, everyday intrigues, with lyrics written by 'Fat' Mike, a graduate of San Francisco University. With the breakthrough of groups such as Offspring and Rancid, No FX, significantly older than either, became a mainstream group by the mid-90s, though in truth they had not altered musical direction since their inception. Instead each album offered increasingly savage witticisms and a disciplined but flexible musical attack, able to vary pace from anything between outright thrash and ska.
●ALBUMS: *Liberal Animation* (Epitaph 1988)★★, *S+M Airlines* (Epitaph 1990)★★, *Ribbed* (Epitaph 1991)★★★, *White Trash, Two Heebs And A Bean* (Epitaph 1992)★★★, *Punk In Drublic* (Epitaph 1994)★★, *We Heard They Suck Live* (Epitaph 1995)★★, *Heavy Petting Zoo* (Epitaph 1996)★★.

NOTTING HILLBILLIES

On 31 May 1986, Mark Knopfler played a low key gig at the Grove pub in Holbeck, Leeds, with old friends Steve Phillips and Brendan Croker. They were billed as the Notting Hillbillies and each received the princely sum of £22 for their performance. Phillips first met Knopfler in 1968 when both interviewed a local blues and country guitarist (also called Steve Phillips) for the *Yorkshire Post*. As both journalists played guitar they formed the Duolian String Pickers duo and played together during the late 60s. They split when Knopfler went to university in 1970. When he finished studying three years later he went to London and eventually formed Dire Straits. Meanwhile, Phillips formed the Steve Phillips Juke Band to play rockabilly. In 1976 Bradford-born Croker met Phillips and when the Juke Band split they toured as Nev And Norriss. In 1980, Phillips temporarily retired from music to concentrate on art. Croker eventually got the 5 O'Clock Shadows together. In 1986 Knopfler, flushed with success through Dire Straits, decided the time was right to do something a little different and all three musicians came together. Dire Straits manager Ed Bicknell was recruited as drummer (he had previously played in Mogul Thrash) and with backing musicians like Guy Fletcher (guitar), Paul Franklin (pedal steel) and Marcus Cliff (bass, of the 5 O'Clock Shadows), they set out on a tour. They made just one album before returning to concentrate on their main bands.

●ALBUMS: *Missing ... Presumed Having A Good Time* (Vertigo 1990)★★★.

NUMAN, GARY

b. Gary Anthony James Webb, 8 March 1958, Hammersmith, London, England. Originally appearing under the group name Tubeway Army, Numan enjoyed enormous success in the UK at the close of the 70s. His Kraftwerk/David Bowie-influenced electronic music saw Tubeway Army top the UK charts in May 1979 with 'Are Friends Electric?' By September 1979 Numan abandoned the group pseudonym for the follow-up single 'Cars' which also topped the UK charts and reached the US Top 10. At his peak, Numan was one of the bestselling artists in Britain and his albums *The Pleasure Principle* and *Telekon* both entered the charts at number 1. His science fiction-orientated lyrics and synthesizer-based rhythms brought further Top 10 successes with 'We Are Glass', 'I Die: You Die', 'She's Got Claws' and 'We Take Mystery (To Bed)'. As the decade progressed his record sales steadily declined and his glum-robotic persona was replaced by that debonair man-about-town who also enjoyed aviation. In March 1982 he attempted to fly around the world in his light aircraft and was

arrested in India on suspicion of spying. The charge was later dropped. While his reputation among music critics atrophied amid accusations of anachronism, his fan base remained solid and his recordings continue to reach the lower placings in the UK charts. His career took an upturn in 1996 following the use of 'Cars' in a television beer ad. Numan promoted the greatest hits album with gusto. Nothing had changed except his hair, which had become much thicker and darker.

●ALBUMS: as Tubeway Army *Tubeway Army* (Beggars Banquet 1979)★★, as Tubeway Army *Replicas* (Beggars Banquet 1979)★★, *The Pleasure Principle* (Beggars Banquet 1979)★★★, *Telekon* (Beggars Banquet 1980)★★★, *Living Ornaments 1979-80* (Beggars Banquet 1981)★★, *Dance* (Beggars Banquet 1981)★★, *I Assassin* (Beggars Banquet 1982)★★, *Warriors* (Beggars Banquet 1983)★★, *The Plan* (Beggars Banquet 1984)★★, *Berserker* (Numa 1984)★★, *White Noise - Live* (Numa 1985)★★, *The Fury* (Numa 1985)★★, *Strange Charm* (Numa 1986)★★, *Exhibition* (Beggars Banquet 1987)★★, *Metal Rhythm* (Illegal 1988)★★, *The Skin Mechanic* (IRS 1989)★★, *Outland* (IRS 1991)★★, *Machine And Soul* (Numa 1992)★★, *Dream Corrosion* (Numa 1994)★★.

●COMPILATIONS: *New Man Numan - The Best Of Gary Numan* (TV 1982)★★★, *Document Series Presents* (Document 1992)★★, *The Best Of ...* (Beggars Banquet 1993)★★★★, *The Premier Hits* (Polygram 1996)★★★★, *The Best Of ...* (Emporio 1997)★★★, *Archive* (Rialto 1997)★★, tribute album *Random* various artists (Beggars Banquet 1997)★★★.

●VIDEOS: *Dream Corrosion* (Numa 1994).

●FURTHER READING: *Gary Numan By Computer*, Fred and Judy Vermorel *Gary Numan: The Authorized Biography*, Ray Coleman.

NWA

The initials stand for Niggers With Attitude, which was the perfect embodiment of this Los Angeles group's outlook. They comprised Dr. Dre (b. Andre Young), DJ Yella (b. Antoine Carraby), MC Ren (b. Lorenzo Patterson) and Eazy E (b. Eric Wright, 7 September 1973, Compton, California, USA, d. 26 March 1995, Los Angeles, California, USA). Founder-member Ice Cube (b. Oshea Jackson, c 1970, South Central, Los Angeles, California, USA), arguably the most inspiring of the rapping crew, departed for a solo career after financial differences with the band's manager (which would later be recorded in a highly provocative song which attacked him for, among other things, being

Jewish). However, all the band's members had long CVs: Dr. Dre had DJed for World Class Wreckin' Crew, and had produced Ice Cube's first band, CIA. Both Eazy E and DJ Yella had recorded and produced several rap discs under their own names, the former funding his Ruthless Records label allegedly through illegal activities. Other early members of the posse included Arabian Prince and D.O.C. NWA's first single was 'Boyz N' The Hood', marking out their lyrical territory as guns, violence and 'bitches'. Though *N.W.A. And The Posse* was their debut album, they only performed four of the raps on it, and to all intents and purposes *Straight Outta Compton* counts as their first major release. For those attracted to the gangsta rappers first time round, this was more of the same only sharper and more succinct. A landmark release, in its aftermath rap became polarized into two distinct factions; traditional liberal (reflecting the ideas of Martin Luther King) and a black militancy redolent of Malcolm X, albeit much less focused and reasoned. In 1989 the FBI investigated *Straight Outta Compton*'s infamous 'Fuck Tha Police', after which Cube left the group. It set a precedent for numerous actions against NWA, including the first time anyone in the music industry had received a threatening letter from the FBI. *Efil4zaggin* (Niggaz4life spelt backwards) which made US number 1, also topped the outrage factor of its predecessor by addressing gang rape and paedophilia, alongside the established agenda of oral sex, cop killing and prostitution. Musically it contained furious blasts of raggamuffin and 70s funk, but that was somehow secondary. It did reveal some humour in the band, i.e., on 'Don't Drink That Wine' (which jokingly encourages drug abuse instead), or lines like; 'Why do I call meself a nigger, you ask me? Because my mouth is so muthafuckin' nasty, Bitch this bitch that nigger this nigger that, In the meanwhile my pockets are getting fat.' Such wit was stretched paper thin over a clutch of expletives and obscenities. The UK government used the Obscene Publications Act to seize copies but were forced to return them following legal action. Ultimately the BPI withdrew their support from Island Marketing's successful action. Counsel for the defence was Geoffrey Robertson QC, who had played a similar role in the infamous *Oz* trial of 1971. Expert testimony from Wendy K of Talkin' Loud Records, rap author David Toop and psychologist Guy Cumberbatch of Aston University swung the case. This prompted a variety of statements from British MPs outlining their intention to toughen up the law. However, even the anti-censorship lobby must concede that NWA's by turns ludicrous ('Find 'Em Fuck 'Em And Flee') and dangerous ('To Kill A Hooker') songs have blurred the generally positive influence of the rap movement. As the decade progressed it became obvious that the members of NWA were spending more time on their solo projects, Dr. Dre enjoying huge success as an artist and producer. His acrimonious parting from Eazy E over monies owed through Ruthless Records was celebrated in records by both artists. Yella has been quiet, co-production credits on Ruthless aside, while Ren released a disappointing solo album and EP.

● ALBUMS: *NWA And The Posse* (Ruthless 1987)★★★, *Straight Outta Compton* (Ruthless 1989)★★★★, *Efil4zaggin'* (Ruthless 1991)★.
● COMPILATIONS: *Greatest Hits* (Virgin 1996)★★★.

NYLONS

Formed in Toronto, Canada, in 1979, the Nylons' line-up comprised three erstwhile actors: Paul Cooper, Marc Connors and Claude Morrison, with Arnold Robinson (b. Wilmington, North Carolina, USA), who had spent several years in Sonny Turner's Platters (aka Sounds Unlimited). Originally harmonizing a cappella, their material was one third original, one third classic doo-wop and one third contemporary pop covers. Their debut album featured bare rhythmic accompaniment underpinning the group's elegant harmonies. *One Size Fits All* housed the single 'Silhouettes', which gained a number of plays on mainstream US radio. The Tokens' 'The Lion Sleeps Tonight' and Steam's 'Na Na Hey Hey (Kiss Him Goodbye)' were reprised on *Seamless* and *Happy Together*, respectively, and again sold well in their domestic market, while the latter single also made the US charts at number 12 in 1987. They then collaborated on their expansive *Rockapella* project, while their version of the Turtles' 'Happy Together' peaked at number 75 in the US charts. Paul Cooper departed in 1990 to be replaced by Micah Barner, but by the following year Marc Connors had died prompting a further line-up shuffle, with Billy Newton-Davis stepping into the breach.

● ALBUMS: *The Nylons* (Attic 1982)★★, *One Size Fits All* (Attic 1984)★★, *Seamless* (Attic 1986)★★★, *Happy Together* (Attic 1987)★★, *Rockapella* (Attic 1987)★★, *Four On The Floor* (Attic 1991)★★.

O'CONNOR, HAZEL

b. 16 May 1955, Coventry, England. O'Connor's introduction to showbusiness involved working as a dancer and starring with a minor movie role in *Girls Come First*. At the close of the 70s, she signed to the Albion label and issued the single 'Ee-I-Adio', which failed to sell. Her profile increased when she appeared in the film *Breaking Glass*, a melodramatic portrayal of a fictional rock star. O'Connor's aggressive singing style and confrontational appearance was used to good effect on the Tony Visconti produced 'Eighth Day' (complete with 'robotic' intonation) which reached the UK Top 5. The following year, she registered two further Top 10 singles, 'D-Days' and the uncharacteristic ballad 'Will You'. Various disputes with her record company and management slowed down her career. In 1984, she recorded *Smile* for RCA Records but the record sold poorly and the label declined to renew her option. O'Connor subsequently appeared in the musical *Girlfriends* in 1987.

●ALBUMS: *Breaking Glass* soundtrack (A&M 1980)★★, *Sons And Lovers* (A&M 1980)★★, *Glass Houses* (A&M 1980)★★, *Cover Plus* (Albion 1981)★★, *Smile* (RCA 1984)★★, *Live In Berlin* (Start 1997)★.

●FURTHER READING: *Hazel O'Connor: Uncovered Plus*, Hazel O'Connor.

●FILMS: *Breaking Glass* (1980).

O'DONNELL, DANIEL

b. 12 December, 1961, Kincasslagh, Co. Donegal, Eire. O'Donnell is without doubt the biggest-selling act ever in the musical genre known as 'Country 'n' Irish'. He is a clean-cut and gimmick-free vocalist with leanings towards sentimental MOR material. He first emerged in Britain in 1985, although he was already popular in Ireland. His first attempts at singing came when he worked as backing vocalist in the band that backed his sister, folk/country singer Margo O'Donnell, during the early 80s, and his popularity among the female audiences increased at high speed. After a handful of early recordings (later released after he came to fame as 'The Boy From Donegal'), he signed to Michael Clerkin's Ritz Records, an Irish label based in London, and *Two Sides Of Daniel O'Donnell* was released in 1985. It was promoted by the first in a continuing series of nationwide UK tours which attracted capacity audiences (largely composed of fans of artists like the late Jim Reeves; O'Donnell usually features in his stage show a medley of songs connected with Reeves). 1986 brought a second O'Donnell release, *I Need You*, which was his first to reach the UK country album charts (which it did in March 1987). That year's album *Don't Forget To Remember* (featuring a cover of the hit by the Bee Gees as its title track), was O'Donnell's first to enter the UK country chart at number 1, which has also occurred with his five subsequent original albums, although the next one to be released in chronological terms, *The Boy From Donegal*, consisted mainly of material recorded in 1984 before he signed to Ritz, and was released in the UK by Prism Leisure.

In 1988, Ritz licensed O'Donnell's next release, *From The Heart*, to Telstar Records, a television marketing company, and as well as entering the UK country chart at number 1, the album also reached the UK pop album chart in the autumn of that year, while a video, *Daniel O'Donnell Live In Concert*, was released. 1989 brought *Thoughts Of Home*, an album and video which were both advertised on television by Telstar - the album made the Top 40 of the pop chart and the video became O'Donnell's first to reach the UK Music Video chart; once again, all subsequent videos have featured in the latter chart, which the original *Live In Concert* also entered in the wake of *Thoughts From Home*. By 1990, O'Donnell was back with an album, *Favourites*, (and a companion video, *TV Show Favourites*), which was composed of material filmed for a hugely successful Irish television series. However, of far greater interest in 1990 was the news that he was making an album with noted producer Allen Reynolds (who had enjoyed major success with Don Williams, Crystal Gayle, Kathy Mattea and latterly, Garth Brooks) in Nashville - the first since O'Donnell's breakthrough that he had recorded with his original producer John Ryan. Released in late 1990, *The Last Waltz* was somewhat closer to genuine country music than its predecessors, and once again entered the UK country album charts at the top and charted strongly in the UK pop equivalent, while another video, *An Evening With Daniel O'Donnell*, was in the Top 20 of the UK Music Video chart for 18 months. During 1991, it was decided that nearly all of

O'Donnell's album catalogue was MOR rather than country, and at a stroke, a UK country album chart - in which O'Donnell occupied the majority of the Top 10 - hardly featured his albums at all. This produced an avalanche of complaints (including one from a nun) and public demonstrations urging that the decision be reversed and his albums reinstated in the country list, which eventually occurred in late 1991. Another release, *The Very Best Of Daniel O'Donnell*, a compilation composed partly of previously released items along with some newly recorded material, continued O'Donnell's remarkable success story. In musical terms, what O'Donnell records is unadventurous, yet his immense popularity in the UK and Eire makes it clear that his output has been brilliantly targeted. As yet, he has not released an album in the USA, although imported albums have been sold prodigiously in areas with population composed of large numbers of people of Irish extraction, and several concert appearances, including one at New York's Carnegie Hall in 1991, have been commercial triumphs.

●ALBUMS: *Two Sides Of Daniel O'Donnell* (Ritz 1985)★★★, *I Need You* (Ritz 1986)★★★, *Don't Forget To Remember* (Ritz 1987)★★★, *The Boy From Donegal* rec. 1984 (Ritz 1987)★★★, *From The Heart* (Telstar 1988)★★★, *Thoughts From Home* (Telstar 1989)★★★, *Favourites* (Ritz 1990)★★★, *The Last Waltz* (Ritz 1990)★★★, *Follow Your Dream* (Ritz 1992)★★★, *Especially For You* (Ritz 1994)★★★, with Mary Duff *Timeless* (Ritz 1996)★★★, *Songs Of Inspiration* (Ritz 1996)★★★.

●COMPILATIONS: *The Very Best Of Daniel O'Donnell* (Ritz 1991).

●VIDEOS: *Live In Concert* (1988)★★★, *Thoughts Of Home* (1989)★★★, *TV Show Favourites* (1990)★★★, *An Evening With* (1990)★★★, *Follow Your Dream* (1992)★★★, *And Friends Live* (1993)★★★, *Just For You* (1994)★★★.

O'NEAL, ALEXANDER

b. 14 November 1954, Minneapolis, Minnesota, USA. O'Neal was one of the best-known soul crooners of the late 80s. In 1978, he joined Flyte Tyme with future producers Jimmy Jam And Terry Lewis. The group became the backing band for Prince, although O'Neal was soon dismissed for insubordination. During the early 80s he began a solo career as a vocalist, making his first recordings with Jam and Lewis producing in 1984. The resulting album was issued by the local Tabu label, and contained R&B hits with 'A Broken Heart Could Mend', 'Innocent' (a duet with Cherrelle)

and 'If You Were Here Tonight'. The latter reached the UK Top 20 in 1986, after Cherrelle's 'Saturday Love' (which featured O'Neal) had been an even bigger success there. His career was interrupted by treatment for drug and alcohol addiction, but O'Neal broke through to the mainstream US audience 1987-88 with his second album and the singles 'Fake' and 'Never Knew Love Like This', another collaboration with Cherrelle. He remained very popular in the UK with live performances (including a Prince's Trust concert) and a BBC television special. When, in 1991, he released his first album of new material for three years, it went straight into the UK Top 10. Jam and Lewis were again the producers.

●ALBUMS: *Alexander O'Neal* (Tabu 1985)★★★, *Hearsay* (Tabu 1987)★★★★, *My Gift To You* (Tabu 1988)★★★, *All Mixed Up* (Tabu 1989)★★★, *All True Man* (Tabu 1991)★★★★, *Love Makes No Sense* (Tabu 1993)★★★, *Lovers Again* (One World/EMI Premier 1996)★★★.

●COMPILATIONS: *This Thing Called Love, The Greatest Hits* (Tabu 1992)★★★★.

OCEAN, BILLY

b. Leslie Sebastian Charles, 21 January 1950, Trinidad, West Indies. Raised in England, Ocean worked as a session singer between employment at the Dagenham Ford Motor Company plant before being signed by the GTO label as a solo artist. His early hits included 'Love Really Hurts Without You' (1976) and 'Red Light Spells Danger' (1977), two purposeful, if derivative performances. The singer's subsequent releases fared less well and for four years, between 1980 and 1984, Ocean was absent from the UK charts. Paradoxically, it was during this period that he began to win an audience in America. Ocean moved there at the turn of the decade and several R&B successes prepared the way for 'Caribbean Queen (No More Love On The Run)', his first national US pop number 1. Now signed to the Jive label, this million-selling single introduced an impressive run of hits, including two more US chart toppers, 'There'll Be Sad Songs (To Make You Cry)' (1986) and 'Get Outta My Dreams, Get Into My Car' (1988). Despite securing a UK number 1 with 'When The Going Gets Tough, The Tough Get Going', (which was featured in the film *The Jewel Of The Nile*) Ocean's luck with chart success in Britain constantly fluctuated. However, his popular appeal secured him three UK Top 5 albums during this period including the *Greatest Hits* collection in 1989.

●ALBUMS: *Billy Ocean* (GTO 1977)★★, *City Limit*

(GTO 1980)★★, *Nights (Feel Like Getting Down)* (GTO 1981)★★★, *Inner Feelings* (GTO 1982)★★★, *Suddenly* (Jive 1984)★★★, *Love Zone* (Jive 1986)★★, *Tear Down These Walls* (Jive 1988)★★, *Time To Move On* (1993)★★.
●COMPILATIONS: *Greatest Hits* (Jive 1989)★★★, *Lover Boy* (Spectrum 1993)★★★.

ODYSSEY

Formed in New York City, vocalists Lillian, Louise and Carmen Lopez were originally known as the Lopez Sisters. Their parents came from the Virgin Islands, but they were born and raised in Stamford, Connecticut, USA. Carmen left the group in 1968 and was replaced by Tony Reynolds (b. Manila), who after the group's first album was replaced by Bill McEachern. Odyssey's 1977 release, 'Native New Yorker', reached the US Top 20, but the song proved more popular in the UK where it peaked at number 5. It was not until 1980 that Odyssey appeared again in the UK chart with the first of several UK hits. 'Use It Up And Wear It Out' topped the chart in June of that year, while the beautiful soulful ballad, 'If You're Looking For A Way Out' gave them their third Top 10 hit. Two more effortless pop/soul offerings, 'Going Back To My Roots' (1981) and 'Inside Out' (1982), reached the Top 5. However, the lack of a sustained success at home hampered the group's wider progress and they latterly broke up.
●ALBUMS: *Odyssey* (RCA 1977)★★★, *Hollywood Party Tonight* (RCA 1978)★★★, *Hang Together* (RCA 1980)★★★, *I Got The Melody* (RCA 1981)★★, *Happy Together* (RCA 1982)★★, *A Piping Journey* (Mannick Music 1987)★★.
●COMPILATIONS: *Best Of Odyssey* (RCA 1981)★★★, *Magic Touch Of Odyssey* (Telstar 1982)★★, *Greatest Hits* (Stylus 1987)★★★.

OINGO BOINGO

An eight-piece band from Los Angeles, California, USA, Oingo Boingo's prolific if unspectacular career has always been centred on the compositional skills of leader Danny Elfman. Their early recordings for A&M Records were mainly synthesizer-led songs accompanied by a three piece horn section, and many compared them to a 'west coast Devo'. They developed their sound, however, and on *Nothing To Fear*, for example, they attempted to achieve commercial recognition with electronic funk. *Good For Your Soul*, produced by Robert Margouleff, was more effective and included the notable 'Wake Up (It's 1984)', although too many of the band's songs remained slight and insubstantial.

Elfman's solo debut, *So-Lo*, on which other members of the band played, gave prominence to his sometimes grandiose vocals and lyrical themes, but made little impression on the charts or the critics. *Dead Man's Party* anticipated Elfman's future solo career with material suited to film soundtracks (most obviously on 'Weird Science', which accompanied the movie of the same name and was released as a single). With forceful songs such as 'Help Me' and 'Stay', many see *Dead Man's Party* as Oingo Boingo's finest hour. *Boi-ngo* retreated to a more experimental stance, offering an intricate but difficult listening climate in which instruments vied with each other and stereo effects in an aural collage, but not one destined for repeated listening. In the 90s Elfman concentrated increasingly on film and television soundtrack work, finding particular success with *Batman*, *Dick Tracy*, *Scrooged* and *The Simpsons*. Despite this, he has continued to return to the Oingo Boingo format, releasing a double live album before a new studio set, *Dark At The End Of The Tunnel*, under his own name, in 1990.
●ALBUMS: *Oingo Boingo* mini-album (IRS 1980)★★, *Only A Lad* (A&M 1981)★★, *Nothing To Fear* (A&M 1982)★★, *Good For Your Soul* (A&M 1983)★★, *Dead Man's Party* (MCA 1985)★★★, *BOINGO* (MCA 1987)★★, *Boingo Alive: Celebration Of A Decade 1979-1988* (MCA 1988)★★, *Dark At The End Of The Tunnel* (MCA 1990)★★. Solo: Danny Elfman *So-lo* (MCA 1984)★★, *Music For A Darkened Theatre* (MCA 1990)★★.
●COMPILATIONS: *Skeletons In The Closet: The Best Of Oingo Boingo* (A&M 1989)★★, *Farewell* (A&M 1996)★★★.
●VIDEOS: *Farewell* (A&M Video 1996).

OLDFIELD, SALLY

This UK-born vocalist was the sister of Mike Oldfield. Together with her brother she formed Sallyangie and released an album and a couple of singles to little success. By the early 70s the duo had gone their separate ways professionally. While Mike was making a name for himself with albums like *Tubular Bells* and *Hergest Ridge*, Sally joined a number of small bands and appeared as guest vocalist on her brother's first four albums. In 1978 she released a solo album which included her debut and only hit, 'Mirrors'. Four other albums appeared on the Bronze label, all to mixed reactions and little success. She re-emerged in 1987 with the backing of a major label and considerable press backing, but still she could not add to her initial success. She remains highly popular in Europe, notably Germany and the Netherlands.

●ALBUMS: with Mike Oldfield *Sallyangie* (Transatlantic 1968)★★, *Water Bearer* (Bronze 1978)★★, *Easy* (Bronze 1979)★★, *Celebration* (Bronze 1980)★★, *Playing With The Flame* (Bronze 1981)★★, *Strange Day In Berlin* (Bronze 1983)★★, *Femme* (Columbia 1987)★★.

●COMPILATIONS: *The Collection* (Castle 1988)★★, *Mirrors* (Spectrum 1995)★★.

OMD

This UK synthesizer pop duo comprised Paul Humphreys (b. 27 February 1960, Liverpool, England) and Andy McCluskey (b. 24 June 1959, Liverpool, England). Originally combining in school band Equinox they moved on through VCL XI and Hitlerz Underpantz, and finally the Id. When that band broke up in 1978 McCluskey spent a short time with Dalek I Love You before he and Humphreys, together with Paul Collister, performed live in October 1978 under their full title Orchestral Manoeuvres In The Dark. Tony Wilson of Factory Records became interested in the band, releasing their debut 'Electricity'. It was quickly re-released when Virgin Records subsidiary DinDisc signed them. Its success subsequently allowed the group the chance to build their own studio. They replaced their 4-track recorder ('Winston') with real personnel Malcom Holmes (ex-Equinox and the Id) and Dave Hughes (Dalek I Love You). 1980 saw 'Red Frame/White Light' released as a single to preface the band's first, self-titled album. Their breakthrough, however, came with the re-recorded 'Messages' and was followed by the UK Top 10 'Enola Gay', and its familiar nuclear war sentiments. *Organisation* followed quickly, with Martin Cooper replacing Dave Hughes shortly afterwards. The more sophisticated *Architecture And Morality* showed a new romanticism particularly in the singles 'Joan Of Arc' and 'Maid Of Orleans'. *Dazzle Ships* was a flawed attempt at progression, highlighting dilemmas forced on them by popularity and DinDisc's collapse (the band transferred to Virgin). *Junk Culture* faced similar critical disdain, and boasted the presence of a hit single 'Locomotion'. *Crush* was a less orchestrated and more immediate affair, featuring the return of political commentary alongside the permanent insertion of Graham and Neil Weir into the line-up. *The Pacific Age* was premiered on another of the band's frequent worldwide touring endeavours, but it was obvious from its chart position that their domestic popularity was slipping. The six-piece line-up was proving too cumbersome and the Weir

brothers departed shortly afterwards. The rift was compounded when Holmes and Cooper and, importantly, Humphreys joined the list of departures. McCluskey retained the name and, after a long restorative period, resurfaced in 1991 with 'Sailing On The Seven Seas'. The resultant album harkened back to the era of *Architecture And Morality*, including the use of choral effects. Humphreys, Holmes and Cooper formed a new band under the name the Listening Pool.

●ALBUMS: *Orchestral Manoeuvres In The Dark* (DinDisc 1980)★★★, *Organisation* (DinDisc 1980)★★★, *Architecture And Morality* (DinDisc 1981)★★★, *Dazzle Ships* (Telegraph 1983)★★, *Junk Culture* (Virgin 1984)★★★, *Crush* (Virgin 1985)★★★, *The Pacific Age* (Virgin 1986)★★, *Sugar Tax* (Virgin 1991)★★, *Liberator* (Virgin 1993)★★★, *Universal* (Virgin 1996)★★★.

●COMPILATIONS: *The Best Of OMD* (Virgin 1988)★★★★.

●FURTHER READING: *Orchestral Manoeuvres In The Dark*, Mike West.

ONE LITTLE INDIAN RECORDS

The roots of the UK One Little Indian record label lie in the anarcho-punk scene of the early 80s particularly in one of its pioneering bands, Flux Of Pink Indians. The precursor to One Little Indian was Spiderleg, which released records by the System, Subhumans, and Amebix in addition to Flux's own material. Both labels were run by Derek Birkett (b. 18 February 1961, London, England), Flux's bass player, alongside friends and colleagues from the independent punk scene. Early releases included ones by Annie Anxiety, D&V and the Very Things. Reflecting on the mistakes made earlier, the label used expensive and tasteful cover art by Paul White's Me Company. When the Sugarcubes, a band Birkett previously knew when they were Kukl, broke through, financial security was assured. While One Little Indian retains its identity as the 'ethical indie', the operation is constructed on level-headed business practices: 'Our motives are artistic and business is reality'. Unlike many labels, the roster of bands does not have a uniform image or sounds. Music on the label includes the bright and breezy pop of the Popinjays, Heart Throbs and the Sugarcubes, the dance sound of the Shamen and Finitribe, the delicate, crafted pop of Kitchens Of Distinction and the shattering volume of What? Noise. The label was also the temporary home for They Might Be Giants, who released *Lincoln* and two singles. The recent mainstream success of the Shamen has con-

solidated their position in the independent charts. The massive success of Björk was long overdue and was financially very welcome, although other outfits, like Daisy Chainsaw, failed to fulfil expectations. Recent signings include Compulsion, Credit To The Nation and a revitalized Chumbawamba. The label has released several 'Best Of' compilations to date which act as good introductions.
●VIDEOS: *One Little Indian* (Virgin Vision 1990).

ORANGE JUICE

Formed in Scotland at the end of the 70s, this engaging and, in some quarters, revered, pop group comprised Edwyn Collins (b. 23 August 1959, Edinburgh, Scotland; vocals/lead guitar), James Kirk (vocals/rhythm guitar), David McClymont (bass) and Steven Daly (drums). They began their career on the cult independent label Postcard Records where they issued some of the best pop records of the early 80s, including 'Blue Boy' and 'Falling And Laughing'. Collins' coy vocal and innocent romanticism gave them a charm that was matched by strong musicianship. After signing to Polydor Records they issued *You Can't Hide Your Love Forever*, a highly accomplished effort that augured well for the future. At that point, the group suffered an internal shake-up with Kirk and Daly replaced by Malcolm Ross and Zeke Manyika. *Rip It Up* was another strong work, and the insistent title track reached the UK Top 10. Further musical differences saw the group reduced to Collins and Manyika as they completed an energetic minialbum, *Texas Fever*, and an eponymous third album, which included the wistful 'What Presence?' Collins subsequently recorded a couple of singles with Paul Quinn, after which he embarked on a solo career that has only begun to fulfil its early promise in the mid-90s. Ross joined the line-up of Roddy Frame's Aztec Camera. Manyika also spawned solo projects on Polydor and Parlophone Records.
●ALBUMS: *You Can't Hide Your Love Forever* (Polydor 1982)★★★, *Rip It Up* (Polydor 1982)★★★★, *Texas Fever* (Polydor 1984)★★★, *Orange Juice* (Polydor 1984)★★★, *Ostrich Churchyard* (Postcard 1992)★★.
●COMPILATIONS: *In A Nutshell* (Polydor 1985)★★★, *The Very Best Of* (Polydor 1992)★★★★, *The Heather's On Fire* (Postcard 1993)★★★.
●VIDEOS: *Dada With Juice* (Hendring Video 1989).

OREGON

This inventive and influential progressive jazz chamber group were formed in 1970 from the nucleus of the Paul Winter Consort, an aggregation led by Paul Winter. Oregon comprised Ralph Towner (b. 1 March 1940, Chehalis, Washington, USA; guitar/keyboards), Collin Walcott (b. 24 April 1945, New York City, USA; d. 8 November 1984; percussion/sitar/tabla/clarinet), Glen Moore (bass/violin/piano/flute) and Paul McCandless (b. 24 March 1947, Indiana, Pennsylvania, USA; alto saxophone/oboe/bass clarinet). Walcott's death from a car accident in 1984 seemed a fatal blow to the band, but after a year in mourning they returned. The recruitment of Walcott's friend Trilok Gurtu (b. 30 October 1951, Bombay, India; tabla/drums/percussion) gave them a fresh incentive. Their debut on ECM Records in 1983 was an eclectic, part-electric album. Oregon explore the boundaries of jazz, using uniquely disparate influences of classical, folk, Indian and other ethnic music. Their chamber-like approach encourages hushed auditoriums and intense concentration, which is required to get maximum benefit from their weaving style. Occasionally they will burst into a song of regular form and pattern, as if to reward a child with a treat. One such number is the evocatively rolling 'Crossing' from the same album. Another outstanding piece from their immense catalogue is 'Leather Cats'. Their refusal to compromise leaves them a lone innovative force and one of the most important jazz-based conglomerations of the past three decades.
●ALBUMS: *Music Of Another Present Era* (Vanguard 1972)★★, *Distant Hills* (Vanguard 1973)★★★, *Winter Light* (Vanguard 1974)★★, *In Concert* (1975)★★, with Elvin Jones *Oregon/Jones Together* (Vanguard 1976)★★★, *Friends* (Vanguard 1977)★★★, *Out Of The Woods* (Elektra 1978)★★★★, *Violin* (Vanguard 1978)★★★, *Roots In The Sky* (Elektra 1979)★★★, *Moon And Mind* (Vanguard 1979)★★, *In Performance* (Elektra 1980)★★, *Oregon* (ECM 1983)★★★, *Crossing* (ECM 1985)★★★★, *Ecotopia* (ECM 1987)★★★, *45th Parallel* (Verabra 1989)★★, *Always, Never, And Forever* (Verabra 1991)★★★, *Beyond Words* (Chesky 1995)★★★.

OSBORNE, JEFFREY

b. 9 March 1948, Providence, Rhode Island, USA. Osborne sang with LTD (Love, Togetherness And Devotion) from 1970 until its disbandment 12 years later. However, he remained subject to the LTD contract with A&M Records for whom he recorded five albums as a solo soul executant. Under George Duke's supervision, the first of these contained the singles 'I Really Don't Need No Light' and 'On The

Wings Of Love' which both reached the US Top 40 - and the latter was a 'sleeper' hit in the UK, when 'Don't You Get So Mad' and the title track of *Stay With Me Tonight* had made slight headway there. In 1984 'Don't Stop' was, nevertheless, his last UK chart entry. The album of the same name featured a duet with Joyce Kennedy - duplicated on her *Lookin' For Trouble*, which was produced by Osborne. *Emotional* was a strong album, as were the subsequent singles, among them 'You Should Be Mine (The Woo Woo Song)', which reached number 13, becoming his biggest US hit. For two years, he chose, perhaps unwisely, to rest on his laurels. He returned with *One Love One Dream* (co-written with Bruce Roberts) and, just prior to a transfer to Arista Records, he teamed up with Dionne Warwick for 1990's 'Love Power'. Airplay for his increasingly more predictable output was no longer automatic - and consumers had not restored him, even temporarily, to his former moderate glory.

●ALBUMS: *Jeffrey Osborne* (A&M 1982)★★★, *Stay With Me Tonight* (A&M 1983)★★★, *Don't Stop* (A&M 1984)★★★, *Emotional* (A&M 1986)★★★, *One Love One Dream* (A&M 1988)★★, *Only Human* (Arista 1991)★★★.

OSBOURNE, OZZY

b. John Osbourne, 3 December 1948, Birmingham, England. In 1979 this highly individual and by now infamous vocalist and songwriter left Black Sabbath, a band whose image and original musical direction he had helped shape. His own band was set up with Lee Kerslake, formerly of Uriah Heep, on drums, Rainbow's Bob Daisley (bass) and Randy Rhoads, fresh from Quiet Riot, on guitar. Rhoads' innovative playing ability was much in evidence on the debut, *Blizzard Of Oz*. By the time of a second album, Daisley and Kerslake had left to be replaced by Pat Travers drummer Tommy Aldridge, and Rudy Sarzo (bass). Throughout his post-Black Sabbath career, Osbourne has courted publicity, most famously in 1982 when he had to undergo treatment for rabies following an onstage incident when he bit the head off a bat. In the same year his immensely talented young guitarist, Rhoads, was killed in an air crash. In came Brad Gillis, former guitarist in Night Ranger, but, so close was Rhoads' personal as well as musical relationship to Osbourne, many feared he would never be adequately replaced. *Speak Of The Devil* was released later in 1982, a live album which included Sabbath material. Following a tour that saw Sarzo and Gillis walk out, Osbourne was forced to re-

think the line-up of his band in 1983 as Daisley rejoined, along with guitarist Jake E. Lee. Aldridge left following the release of *Bark At The Moon*, and was replaced by renowned virtuoso drummer Carmine Appice. This combination was to be short-lived, however, Randy Castillo replacing Appice, and Phil Soussan taking on the bass guitar. Daisley appears on *No Rest For The Wicked*, although Sabbath bassist Geezer Butler played on the subsequent live dates. The late 80s were a trying time for Osbourne. He went on trial in America for allegedly using his lyrics to incite youngsters to commit suicide; he was eventually cleared of these charges. His wife, Sharon (daughter of Don Arden), also became his manager, and has helped Osbourne to overcome the alcoholism which was the subject of much of his work. His lyrics, however, continue to deal with the grimmest of subjects such as the agony of insanity, and *The Ultimate Sin* is concerned almost exclusively with the issue of nuclear destruction. In later years Osbourne has kept to more contemporary issues, rejecting to a certain extent the satanic, werewolf image he constructed around himself in the early 80s. He embarked on a farewell tour in 1992, but broke four bones in his foot which inhibited his performances greatly. He also donated $20,000 to the Daughters Of The Republic Of Texas appeal to help restore the Alamo, and performed his first concert in the city of San Antonio since being banned for urinating on a wall of the monument in 1982. Predictably neither retirement nor atonement sat too comfortably with the man, and by late 1994 he was announcing the imminent release of a new solo album, recorded in conjunction with Steve Vai. He also teamed up with Therapy? to sing lead vocals on the track 'Iron Man' for the Black Sabbath tribute album, *Black Nativity*. Far less likely was his pairing with Miss Piggy of *The Muppet Show* on 'Born To Be Wild', for a bizarre Muppets compilation album. He also confesssed that his original partner on his 1992 Don Was-produced duet with actress Kim Basinger, 'Shake Your Head', was Madonna, although he had not actually recognized her. Other strange couplings included one with the Scottish comedian Billy Connolly and the popular UK boxer Frank Bruno on the 'Urpney Song', written by Mike Batt for the cartoon series *Dreamstone*. *Ozzmosis* is arguably his best album, and it was a major success. It opens with the tale of the fiction and television character 'Perry Mason'; never has Raymond Burke been eulogized by such chrunching power chords. The line-up on *Ozzmosis* was: Geezer Butler (bass), Rick Wakeman (key-

boards), Zakk Wylde, who co-wrote six tracks, (guitar) and Deen Castronovo (drums). Osbourne is one hard rocker who has tried every excess known and has lived. Amazingly his work still sounds inspired and exciting.
●ALBUMS: *Blizzard Of Oz* (Jet 1980)★★★, *Diary Of A Madman* (Jet 1981)★★★, *Talk Of The Devil* (Jet 1982)★★, *Bark At The Moon* (Jet 1983)★★, *The Ultimate Sin* (Epic 1986)★★, *Tribute* (Epic 1987)★★★, *No Rest For The Wicked* (Epic 1988)★★, *Just Say Ozzy* (Epic 1990)★★, *No More Tears* (Epic 1991)★★★, *Live & Loud* (Epic 1993)★★, *Ozzmosis* (Epic 1995)★★★★.
●VIDEOS: *The Ultimate Ozzy* (1987), *Wicked Videos* (1988), *Bark At The Moon* (1990), *Don't Blame Me* (1992), *Live & Loud* (1993).
●FURTHER READING: *Diary Of A Madman*, Mick Wall. *Ozzy Osbourne*, Garry Johnson.

OTTAWAN

This European disco duo consisted of Annette (b. 1960, Guadeloupe Islands, West Indies) and Patrick (b. 1956, Guadeloupe Islands, West Indies). Patrick moved to Paris in 1966 and Annette in 1976. He was already a star in France when they met and formed Ottawan. 'D.I.S.C.O.' was a hit on the continent in 1979 and was requested by returning holiday makers who helped make it a UK hit in 1980. Only the combined efforts of the Police ('Don't Stand So Close To Me') and Barbra Streisand ('Woman In Love') managed to hold Ottawan at number 2 for three weeks. The follow-ups, all in a very similar vein, were 'You're OK', 'Hands Up (Give Me Your Heart)' (which reached number 3), and 'Help, Get Me Some Help!' By this time their audience was growing tired of their material, and Ottawan disbanded.
●ALBUMS: *Ottawan* (Carrere 1980)★.
●COMPILATIONS: *Ottawan's Greatest Hits* (Carrere 1981)★, *The Very Best Of Ottawan* (Carrere 1993)★.

OYSTER BAND

The Oyster Band entry was withdrawn at the request of band member John James.
●ALBUMS: *Jack's Alive* (1980)★★, *English Rock 'N' Roll - The Early Years 1800-1850* (Pukka 1982)★★★★, *Lie Back And Think Of England* (Pukka 1983)★★★, *20 Golden Tie-Slackeners* (1984)★★★, *Liberty Hall* (Pukka 1985)★★★, *Step Outside* (Cooking Vinyl 1986)★★★, *Wide Blue Yonder* (Cooking Vinyl 1987)★★★, *Freedom And Rain* (Cooking Vinyl 1990)★★★, *Deserters* (Cooking Vinyl 1992)★★★★, *Holy Bandits* (Cooking Vinyl 1993)★★★, *The Shouting End Of*

Life (Cooking Vinyl 1995)★★★.
●COMPILATIONS: *Trawler* (Cooking Vinyl 1994)★★★★.

OZRIC TENTACLES

Predominantly an 80s UK festival band, Ozric Tentacles was originally a name conjured up by the band for a psychedelic breakfast cereal. Their original line-up featured Ed Wynne (guitar), his brother Roly (bass), Nick 'Tig' Van Gelder (drums), Gavin Griffiths (guitar) and Joie 'Ozrooniculator' Hinton (keyboards). They met at an open camp fire at Stonehenge in 1982. By the following year a second synthesizer player Tom Brookes, had joined. They started gigging in clubs such as the 'Crypt' in Deptford, south-east London. There they met their second percussionist, Paul Hankin. They soon became regulars at another psychedelic 'head' venue, the Club Dog, at the George Robey pub in Finsbury Park, north London. The band's long existence has seen a number of shifts in personnel. In 1984 Griffiths left to form the Ullulators, and Brookes left a year later. Hinton remained but also played for the aforementioned Ullulators and also the Oroonies. The next major change arrived in 1987 when Merv Pepler replaced Van Gelder. More recently Steve Everett has replaced Brookes on synthesizers, while Marcus Carcus and John Egan have added extra percussion and flute. Considering their lengthy career it might appear that the band has had a relatively sporadic, and recent, recording output. However, much of their work from the mid-80s onwards was made available on six cassette-only albums. Into the early 90s, with the British neo-hippy new age travellers receiving a higher media profile and their role in organizing music festivals becoming increasingly important, bands such as the Ozric Tentacles and the Levellers benefited greatly and began to widen their audience. Hinton and Pepler left the band in 1994 and devoted their energies to Eat Static full time. New members Rad and Seaweed joined in time for *Become The Other*.
●ALBUMS: *Pungent Effulgent* (Dovetail 1989)★★★, *Erp Land* (Dovetail 1990)★★★, *Strangeitude* (Dovetail 1991)★★★, *Jurassic Shift* (Dovetail 1993)★★★, *Arborescence* (Dovetail 1994)★★, *Become The Other* (Dovetail 1995)★★.

P

PABLO

b. Pablo Lubadika Porthos, 1952, Inongo, Zaire. Vocalist and guitarist Pablo first came to the attention of European African music enthusiasts in the early 80s, following the release of Island Records' soukous compilation album, *Sound D'Afrique*, and the tracks 'Mbanda' and 'Madeleina'. By this time he was already a major star in Zaire, having worked during the 70s with such bands as Orchestre Kara, Kim Bantous and Lovy Du Zaire. He was also featured on Sam Mangwana's first major hit, 'Georgette Eckins'. Having been invited to join Les Quatre Etoiles in 1984, he declined, preferring to pursue a solo career as a vocalist, and a session career as a guitarist. His first UK release was *Pablo Pablo Pablo* in 1985, but afterwards he would concentrate almost exclusively on session work in Paris.

●ALBUMS: *Idie* (AMR 1981)★★★, *Concentration* (Syllart 1982)★★★, *Revient En Force* (COSIC 1983)★★★, *En Action* (Darl 1984), *Pablo Pablo Pablo* (Globestyle 1985)★★★, with Tutu *Safula* (BIZ 1987)★★★.

PAIGE, ELAINE

b. Elaine Bickerstaff, 5 March 1951, Barnet, Hertfordshire, England. An actress and singer, often called the first lady of contemporary British musical theatre, Elaine Paige was trained at the Aida Foster Stage School in Golders Green, north London. She had already appeared in several stage musicals in the 60s and 70s, including *The Roar Of The Greasepaint-The Smell Of The Crowd*, *Hair* (her first West End show), *Maybe That's Your Problem*, *Rock Carmen*, *Jesus Christ Superstar*, *Grease*, *Billy*, and before she was chosen to portray Eva Peron in Tim Rice and Andrew Lloyd Webber's *Evita* in 1978. Although Julie Covington had sung the part on the original concept album and had a UK number 1 hit with 'Don't Cry For Me Argentina', Paige went on to make the role her own. In spite of the disappointment of being unable to play the part on Broadway (because of American union rules), *Evita* made Paige into a star almost overnight. She won a Society of West End Theatres Award for her outstanding performance, and was also voted Show Business Personality of the Year. In the 80s she starred in *Cats* (as Grizabella, singing 'Memory'), *Abbacadabra*, *Chess*, and a West End revival of Cole Porter's *Anything Goes*. She topped the UK chart with a number from *Chess*, 'I Know Him So Well', in a duet with Barbara Dickson. Her first solo album, which came in 1981, featured a variety of songs, mostly with lyrics by Tim Rice. It was recorded with the assistance of Stuart Elliot (ex-Cockney Rebel), Ian Bairnson and David Paton from Pilot, and Mike Moran. As well as a version of Paul Simon's 'How The Heart Approaches What It Yearns', there was a rare Paul McCartney instrumental ('Hot As Sun') with words by Rice. She was voted 'Recording Artist of the Year' by the Variety Club of Great Britain. Her most unusual album was released in 1988, and consisted of cover versions of Queen songs. In 1989 she turned her attention more to straight acting, and made two films for the BBC including the acclaimed *Unexplained Laughter*, with Diana Rigg. She had previously worked in television programmes such as *Crossroads*, *Lady Killers*, *Ladybirds*, *A View Of Harry Clark*, and *Tales Of The Unexpected*, as well as musical specials such as *Elaine Paige In Concert*. In 1990 her long-term relationship with Tim Rice dissolved and she threw herself into her work. During the 80s and 90s she embarked on concert tours of Europe, the Middle East, Scandanavia and the UK, most recently accompanied by a 26-piece symphony orchestra. In 1993 she was highly acclaimed for her powerful and dramatic performance as the legendary Edith Piaf in Pam Gems' play with music, *Piaf*, at the Piccadilly Theatre in London. In May 1995, she took over from Betty Buckley in the leading role of Norma Desmond in the West End hit musical *Sunset Boulevard*, and later in the year received an OBE in the Queen's Birthday Honours List. In 1996 she finally appeared on Broadway when she replaced Betty Buckley in the New York production of *Sunset Boulevard*.

●ALBUMS: with Peter Oliver *Barrier* (Euro Disk 1978)★★, *Elaine Paige* (Warners 1982)★★★, *Stages* (K-Tel 1983)★★, *Cinema* (K-Tel 1984)★★, *Sitting Pretty* (Warners 1985)★★, *Love Hurts* (Warners 1985)★★, *Christmas* (Warners 1986)★★, *The Queen Album* (Virgin 1988)★★, *Love Can Do That* (1991)★★, with Barbara Dickson *Together* (1992)★★, *Romance And The Stage* (RCA 1993)★★, *Piaf* (Warners 1995)★★★, *Encore* (Warners 1995)★★★, and Original Cast recordings.

●COMPILATIONS: *Memories - The Best Of Elaine Paige* (Telstar 1987)★★★, *The Collection* (Pickwick 1990)★★★.

PALE FOUNTAINS

Formed in Liverpool in the early 80s by songwriter Michael Head (guitar/vocals) and Chris McCaffrey (bass) with Thomas Whelan (drums) and Andy Diagram, formerly of Dislocation Dance and the Diagram Brothers. Having been assimilated into the early 80s 'quiet pop'/'Bossa Nova' movement, Pale Fountains also drew upon such influences as the Beatles, the Mamas And The Papas and Love, but were probably better known for wearing short baggy trousers. Previously on the Operation Twilight label, the group attempted to break into the big time when they signed to Virgin Records. Despite this lucrative move, this highly touted group never broke out of their cult status. Their highest national chart position was the UK Top 50 'Thank You' in 1982.
●ALBUMS: *Pacific Street* (Operation Twilight 1984)★★★, *From Across The Kitchen Table* (Virgin 1985)★★★.

PARIS, MICA

b. Michelle Wallen, 27 April 1969, London, England. Having written, recorded and produced with the aid of heavyweights like Nile Rodgers (Chic), Prince and Rakim (Eric B And Rakim), Paris remains one of the UK's biggest talents to never make the great leap forward. It has not been for want of effort or ability, yet somehow no-one has yet found a way of getting the most out of one of the world's most delightful soul-dance performers. Stronger material would certainly help. There are examples from her debut album when she hits a perfect beat, as when she matches the tenor sax of Courtney Pine for its dexterity on 'Like Dreamers Do'. Her second album chose new, hot producers as a remedy (Charles Mantronik of Mantronix, and Dancin' Danny D of D-Mob). A sense of frustration still pervades her career, however.
●ALBUMS: *So Good* (4th & Broadway 1989)★★★, *Contribution* (4th & Broadway 1990)★★.
●VIDEOS: *Mica Paris* (1991).

PARR, JOHN

b. 18 November 1954. This vocalist, guitarist, composer and producer specializes in highly melodic AOR. Though British his success had been drawn largely from the US where his recordings for Atlantic Records have been compared to Rick Springfield and Eddie Money. Parr composed the themes for the movies *American Anthem* and *St. Elmo's Fire*, the second of which made the UK Top 10 singles chart in 1985. The follow-up, 'Naughty Naughty', achieved a paltry number 58. He also duetted with Meat Loaf on 'Rock 'N' Roll Mercenaries', but this failed to embellish either artist's profile, stopping just short of the Top 30. Producing two solo albums, his self-titled debut in 1985 and *Running The Endless Mile* in 1986, both fared poorly with the critics. His finest moment remains the energetic 'St. Elmo's Fire (Man In Motion)', to give it its full title.
●ALBUMS: *John Parr* (Atlantic 1985)★★, *Running The Endless Mile* (Atlantic 1987)★.

PASSIONS (UK)

This English post-punk group, with definite pop leanings, was formed in June 1978 and comprised Barbara Gogan (b. Dublin, Eire; vocals/guitar), Mitch Barker (vocals), Clive Timperley (guitar/vocals), Claire Bidwell (bass/vocals) and Richard Williams (drums). All save Timperley had featured in Rivers Of Passion, while all except Bidwell had spent time in the various incarnations of the Derelicts between 1974-76. During this time Timperley also played with Joe Strummer's 101ers. Gogan left her Dublin home at the age of 18 and settled in France within a Marxist commune. She came to London in 1972 and moved into a 'squat' near Ladbroke Grove, where she became involved with the Derelicts, a loose collection of like-minded left-wingers. Evolving into the Passions they released their first single, 'Needles And Pins', on the tiny Soho label, also home of the Nips and the Inmates. They lost Barker in 1979 when a broken leg put paid to his musical activities. Continuing as a four-piece they signed to Fiction Records for their debut album, and one single, 'Hunted'. Bidwell left in July 1980 to form Schwarze Kapelle and then joined the Wall. David Agar, once a member of the fledgling Spandau Ballet, replaced her. Three days later they were dropped by Fiction but fell immediately on their feet with a contract for Polydor Records. They finally found success in 1981 with their second single for the label, 'I'm In Love With A German Film Star'. It would be their only hit, despite the eloquence and strength of later material. Timperley left to run a health shop in December 1981, while the recruitment of Kevin Armstrong (ex-Local Heroes SW9) on guitar and Jeff Smith (ex-Lene Lovich band) on keyboards failed to put the brakes on their commercial slide. Armstrong himself left in August 1982 to be replaced by Steve

Wright, but by this time the band was in its death throes.

●ALBUMS: *Michael And Miranda* (Fiction 1980)★★, *Thirty Thousand Feet Over China* (Polydor 1981)★★★, *Sanctuary* (Polydor 1982)★★.

PASTELS (UK)

Formed in Glasgow, Scotland, in 1982, the Pastels were one of the prime movers in the 80s 'shambling'/'anorak' independent scene that influenced later luminaries such as the Flatmates and Talulah Gosh. Group leader Stephen Pastel (b. Stephen McRobbie, Scotland; guitar/vocals) has since gone to great lengths to distance the Pastels from their past idolaters. Today they serve as a major influence on emerging Scottish bands such as Teenage Fanclub (whose Norman Blake is a fan club member and later played in the Pastels) and Captain America/Eugenius. However, their history has been characterized by the kind of lethargy that has doomed them to mere cultism: 'I just find careerism and naked ambition really ugly'. The Pastels themselves were motivated by a conglomeration of the Monkees and the Ramones. The early line-up also comprised Brian Superstar (b. Brian Taylor; guitar) and Chris Gordon (drums), but the latter's early departure signalled a recurring instability in the group's rhythm section. Their first release on the Television Personalities' Whaam! label, the *Songs For Children* EP, was the beginning of an unsettled relationship with a variety of labels including Glass, Rough Trade, and Creation Records. Appearances on various compilations, not least a prestigious slot on the seminal *C86* collection ('Breaking Lines') from the *New Musical Express* increased their standing in the independent market, while their music combined ambitious vision with naïve ability. A settled line-up; Pastel, Superstar, Aggi Wright (vocals), Martin Hayward (bass) and Bernice Swanson (drums) - completed two albums, *Up For A Bit With The Pastels* and *Sittin' Pretty*, wherein the group matured from the charming innocence of early releases to embrace a myriad of contrasting styles held together by McRobbie's commited vision. Material ranged from the bouyant 'Nothing To Be Done' to the lengthy 'Baby Honey' and 'Ditch The Fool', as the Pastels expanded their musical horizons with the temporary aid of Eugene Kelly (ex-Vaselines), Norman Blake and David Keegan, formerly of the Shop Assistants and Pastel's partner in the pivotal 53rd & 3rd Records label. By the early 90s Keegan had become a full-time member of the Pastels which, following a series of alterations, re-emerged centred around McRobbie, Wright (now on bass) and Katrina Mitchell (drums), the latter pursuing a concurrent path as a member of Melody Dog. Against the odds this trio was still in place for 1995's *Mobile Safari*, an enjoyable collection of raggamuffin odes to life in and outside of an under-achieving indie band, punctuated by songs such as 'Yoga' and 'Classic Lineup'.

●ALBUMS: *Up For A Bit With The Pastels* (Glass 1987)★★★, *Sittin' Pretty* (Chapter 22 1989)★★★, *Mobile Safari* (Domino 1995)★★★.

●COMPILATIONS: *Suck On The Pastels* (Creation 1988)★★★, *1986-1993 Truckload Of Trouble* (Seed 1993)★★★★.

PEARL HARBOR AND THE EXPLOSIONS

Formed in San Francisco, California in 1979, this much-touted attraction was centred on vocalist Pearl Harbor (b. 1958, Germany, of a Filipino mother), who, as Pearl E. Gates, had previously been a dancer in the Tubes' live show. She subsequently joined Jane Dornacker in Leila And The Snakes, before taking the group's rhythm section - Hilary Stench (bass) and John Stench (drums) - in this new act. Their act continued the theatricality of the Tubes, but Gates was now more interested in conventional rock 'n' roll. To this end she recruited Peter Bilt (guitar) and formed Pearl Harbor And The Explosions in October 1978. They specialized in old fashioned rock 'n' roll/rockabilly spiced with 'new wave' energy. Their debut single 'Drivin'' (which was later covered by Jane Aire And The Belvederes) came out on the independent 415 Records label and became a cult hit. Its success encouraged Warner Brothers Records to sign the group. Their self-titled debut was a strong, promising work, but the group failed to complete a follow-up. They split in June 1980 leaving Pearl to continue with a desultory solo album *Don't Follow Me I'm Lost* under her new name Pearl Harbor. The album was produced by Nicky Gallagher (a former member of Ian Dury's Blockheads). The Stench brothers joined ex-Jefferson Airplane guitarist Jorma Kaukonen in Vital Parts, before then embarking on an association with cult *avant garde* act Chrome.

●ALBUMS: *Pearl Harbor And The Explosions* (Warners 1979)★★★, as Pearl Harbor *Don't Follow Me, I'm Lost* (Warners 1981)★★, *Here Comes Trouble* (Backtrip 1996)★★.

PENGUIN CAFE ORCHESTRA

This collection of accomplished musicians was inaugurated in the late 70s to cater for the musical eclecticism of leader Simon Jeffes (b. 1948). Ex-London music student Jeffes nurtured a desire to create an ensemble capable of fusing musics from around the world, of different styles and cultures - literally an Utopian dream which came to him while suffering from food poisoning in the early 70s. After working on the fringes of the pop world, involving himself with production work with such groups as Caravan and Camel, Jeffes found a champion for his musical vision in Brian Eno. The Orchestra, which includes within its line-up Elizabeth Perry, Gavyn Wright, Bob Loveday (violins), Helen Liebmann (cello), Steve Nye (keyboards) and Neil Rennie (cuatro/ukulele), recorded their debut album on Eno's esoteric Obscure label. Jeffes continued his studio work, being hired at various points by the Clash and Malcolm McLaren with Sid Vicious. A follow-up did not appear until almost five years later, and using such esoteric song titles as 'The Ecstacy Of Dancing Fleas' and 'Cutting Branches For A Temporary Shelter' they betrayed a degree of pretentiousness. The music, however, swayed between a studied seriousness and a sense of jolliness. The group have also drawn criticism over the years on account of being *too* clever and employing a dry approach to their music - an observation often levelled at classically trained musicians seen to be straying outside their boundaries.

●ALBUMS: *Music From The Penguin Cafe* (Obscure 1977)★★★, *Penguin Cafe Orchestra* (Editions EG 1981)★★★, *Broadcasting From Home* (Editions EG 1984)★★★, *Signs Of Life* (Editions EG 1987)★★★, *When In Rome - Live* (Editions EG 1988)★★★, *Union Cafe* (1993)★★★, *Concert Program* (Windham Hill 1995)★★★, *Preludes, Airs And Yodels* (Virgin 1996)★★★.

PEPSI AND SHIRLIE

Former backing singers to Wham!, Lawrie 'Pepsi' Damacque (b. 10 December 1958, Paddington, London, England) and Shirlie Holliman (b. 18 April 1962, Watford, Hertfordshire, England) embarked on a solo career after that group's break-up in 1986. This connection was put to great use in the UK teenage magazine market where their pop/dance style appealed to suburban audiences. Signing a deal with Polydor Records, the duo recorded two UK Top 10 singles in 1987 with 'Heartache' (a number 2 hit) and 'Goodbye Stranger'. Later singles fared less well and *Change* was released over three years after their debut. Though it included one song George Michael had written for them, 'Someday', it was apparent that Pepsi And Shirlie's following had moved on. The album failed to chart and no single success resulted. Their lame attempts to rehabilitate their image to that of rave club divas on 1993's *Heartache* fooled neither the critics nor the public..

●ALBUMS: *All Right Now* (Polydor 1987)★★, *Change* (Polydor 1991)★★, *Heartache* (1993)★.

PERFECT DISASTER

Having tested the water as Orange Disaster, then the Architects Of Disaster, these calamitously inclined types finally settled on the Perfect Disaster in 1984 as the original rhythm section departed to form Fields Of The Nephilim. The initial UK-based line-up consisted of Phil Parfitt, Allison Pates, John Saltwell and Malcolm Catto, although personnel changes were to plague the band's career. Ignored by the British music scene, the Perfect Disaster took their twisted, broody guitar sound to France for their self-titled debut album in 1985. There followed a couple of years of blank struggle on both sides of the English Channel before the band signed to Fire Records at home and released the critically acclaimed *Asylum Road*. Prior to this, Saltwell and Pates both left, disillusioned, to be replaced by bassist Josephine Wiggs (b. Josephine Miranda Cordelia Susan Wiggs, 26 February 1965, Letchworth, Hertfordshire, England) and long-term guitarist Dan Cross. In 1989 better prospects lurked over the horizon: the *Up* album, which stretched splendidly from fiery two-chord blasts to near-suicidal ramblings, coincided with prestigious live shows with the likes of the Jesus And Mary Chain; and the band's initial inspiration, based upon singer Parfitt's spell working at a Victorian mental institution, looked set to reap rewards. The public, alas, did not share the critics' enthusiasm for the band. The *Heaven Scent* album continued the Perfect Disaster's foray into the darker side of alternative music, but rumours of the band's demise, which persisted throughout 1991, were finally confirmed. Wiggs left to spend more time on the Breeders, a side project that also involved Tanya Donelly from Throwing Muses and Kim Deal of the Pixies, allowing John Saltwell to return on bass and Jon Mattock was borrowed from Spacemen 3 to contribute the drumming for *Heaven Scent*. Parfitt went on to write alongside Jason Pierce (Spiritualized) before forming Oedipussy.

●ALBUMS: *The Perfect Disaster* (Kampa 1985)★★, *Asylum Road* (Fire 1988)★★★, *Up* (Fire 1989)★★★, *Heaven Scent* (Fire 1990)★★★.

PETRA

One of the first US Christian hard rock bands, Petra (named after the ancient city in Jordan) are an excellent musical unit who have never been swayed by passing trends and have stuck fast to their own ideals and beliefs. The group was formed in 1972 by vocalist Greg Volz and guitarist Bob Hartman, recruiting Mark Kelly (bass), John Slick (keyboards) and Louie Weaver (drums) to their cause. Petra specialized in a varied musical approach that incorporated elements of the Eagles, Joe Walsh, Kansas and Deep Purple. They have released well over a dozen albums to date, with their popularity having gradually waned from its peak in 1984. At this time, they appeared in the US Top 12 best-attended bands list in *Performance* magazine, while *Not Of This World* sold in excess of a quarter of a million units. John Schlitt (ex-Head East) replaced Volz after 1986's *Back To The Street* and the band adopted a heavier direction thereafter. John Lawry and Ronnie Cates replaced Slick and Kelly on keyboards and bass, respectively, in 1988. David Lichens (guitar) and Jim Cooper (keyboards) have also joined and departed. Their two most recent releases owe much to Kiss and Stryper and are more aggressive than their earlier material. In 1996 the new line-up consisted of Pete Orta (lead guitar), Kevin Brandow (keyboards) and Lonnie Chapin (bass) together with longstanding members Weaver and Schlitt. Hartman is still very much part of the organization although he no longer tours; instead he prefers to take a Brian Wilson-style role as writer and producer.

●ALBUMS: *Petra* (Myrrh 1974)★★, *Come And Join Us* (Myrrh 1977)★★, *Washes Whiter Than* (Star Song 1979)★★, *Never Say Die* (Star Song 1981)★★★, *More Power To Ya* (Star Song 1982)★★★, *Not Of This World* (Kingsway 1983)★★★, *Beat The System* (Kingsway 1985)★★★, *Captured In Time And Place* (Star Song 1986)★★★, *Back To The Street* (Star Song 1986)★★★, *This Means War* (Star Song 1987)★★★, *On Fire* (Star Song 1988)★★★, *Petra Means Rock* (Star Song 1989)★★★, *Petra Praise - The Rock Cries Out* (Dayspring 1989), *Beyond Belief* (Star Song 1990)★★★, *Petra Praise 22: We Need Jesus* (Word 1997)★★★.

●VIDEOS: *Captured In Time And Space* (1989).

PETTY, TOM, AND THE HEARTBREAKERS

The Heartbreakers were formed from the ashes of Petty's first professional band, Mudcrutch, in 1971. In addition to Tom Petty (b. 20 October 1953, Florida, USA; guitar) the band comprised; Mike Campbell (b. 1 February 1954, Florida, USA; guitar), Benmont Tench (b. 7 September 1954, Gainesville, Florida, USA; keyboards), Stan Lynch (b. 21 May 1955, Gainesville, Florida, USA; drums) and Ron Blair (b. 16 September 1952, Macon, Georgia, USA; bass). Armed with a Rickenbacker guitar and a Roger McGuinn voice, Petty's debut was accepted more in England where anything Byrds-like would find an audience. McGuinn in fact later recorded 'American Girl' (and did a fine Petty impersonation). The tight-structured rock formula of the first album showed great promise and eventually it made a substantial impression on the US charts, over a year after release. Having received rave reviews following his visit to Europe he released a second collection *You're Gonna Get It* to excellent reviews. Petty was able to appeal both to the new wave and lovers of American west coast rock with his rock songs. *Damn The Torpedoes* followed after a lengthy legal battle during which time he filed for bankruptcy. His cash flow soon improved as the album was only kept from the top of the US charts by Pink Floyd as it went platinum. Petty's subsequent albums have been similarly satisfying although not as successful. In 1981 he duetted with Stevie Nicks on 'Stop Draggin My Heart Around', complete with an MTV-style video, and in 1983 he was one of the artists to encourage Del Shannon to record again, producing his album *Drop Down And Get Me*. In 1985 he had another major hit with 'Don't Come Around Here No More' aided by an imaginative and award-winning *Alice in Wonderland* video depicting him as the Mad Hatter. During the recording of *Southern Accents* Petty smashed his hand (in anger) on the recording console and had to have a metal splint permanently fixed as the bones were too badly broken. Petty's outburst failed to stop the album becoming another million-seller. That same year he played Live Aid in Philadelphia. The following year he reunited with Nicks for a remake of the Searchers' 'Needles And Pins'. His association with Bob Dylan prospered and they toured together; additionally, Petty performed on Dylan albums and co-wrote with him. The live album *Pack Up The Plantation* delighted old fans, but failed to break any new ground. Tradegy struck that year when Petty's home was burnt down. In 1988 Jeff Lynne and Petty struck up a friendship and together with George Harrison, Roy Orbison and Dylan, they formed the Traveling Wilburys. Lynne's high-tech and over-crisp production was in evidence on *Full Moon Fever* (a solo project) and *Into The Great Wide Open*, and fortunately the strength of Petty's songs won through. Both albums combined much of Petty's great gift for melody and irresistible 'middle eights' while acknowledging his influences including the Beatles, Byrds, R.E.M. and the Searchers. A greatest hits album was released in 1993 and became a huge hit in his homeland (3 million sales to date). It served as an introduction to a younger audience who had seen Petty cited as a major influence on some of the 90s guitar-based rock bands. This new wave of success seemed to have inspired Petty to deliver *Wildflowers*, probably his most satisfying album. This overtly acoustic and mellow collection gave his lyrics a chance to be heard clearly and together with a lower and more mature vocal delivery it is a stunning work. Seasoned session drummer Steve Ferrone replaced the long-serving Stan Lynch and together with Howie Epstein (bass) they have bolstered the permanent band members of Petty, Tench and Campbell into an unbeatable live band. Petty has succeeded in a fickle marketplace by playing honest, unpretentious catchy rock with irresistible hook lines. He is one of the most durable American artists of the past two decades and one that is still being creative and not dwelling on his past glory.

●ALBUMS: *Tom Petty And The Heartbreakers* (Shelter 1976)★★★, *You're Gonna Get It* (Shelter 1978)★★★★, *Damn The Torpedoes* (MCA 1979)★★★★, *Hard Promises* (MCA 1981)★★★, *Long After Dark* (MCA 1982)★★★, *Southern Accents* (MCA 1985)★★★★, *Pack Up The Plantation: Live!* (MCA 1985)★★★, *Let Me Up (I've Had Enough)* (MCA 1987)★★★, Tom Petty solo *Full Moon Fever* (MCA 1989)★★★, *Into The Great Wide Open* (MCA 1991)★★★, *Wildflowers* (Warners 1994)★★★★, *She's The One* (Warners 1996)★★★.

●COMPILATIONS: *Greatest Hits* (MCA 1993)★★★★, *Playback* 6-CD box set (MCA 1995)★★★★.

●VIDEOS: *Playback* (MCA Music Video 1995).

PHD

This UK pop duo comprised Jim Diamond (vocals) and Tony Hymas (keyboards). Their debut album included the single 'I Won't Let You Down', which initially failed to chart. Convinced that the band

had potential an extra push from WEA Records was put behind the record and finally it paid off when the single reached number 3 in the UK charts and repeated its success in Europe. However they found life hard afterwards with their second and final album, which did not sell as well. The duo went their separate ways and Diamond signed a solo deal with A&M Records and found further chart success.

●ALBUMS: *PhD* (Warners 1981)★★, *Is It Safe?* (Warners 1983)★★.

PIGBAG

Pigbag will be forever linked with their debut single, and only hit, 'Papa's Got A Brand New Pigbag' (a play on words on the mid-60s James Brown classic, 'Papa's Got A Brand New Bag'). A quirky, but nevertheless, catchy funk/soul instrumental, the single was first released in May 1981, but took almost a year to reach the charts, peaking at number 3. Word had it that their label, Y, had deleted the single and then reactivated it when the demand was sufficient. The band had formed around the Gloucestershire and Avon region from the ashes of hardline militant funk act the Pop Group; Simon Underwood (bass) joined up with James Johnstone (guitar/keyboards), Ollie Moore (saxophone), Chip Carpenter (drums) and Roger Freeman (percussion). By the time of their hit, Pigbag already issued two further singles, 'Sunny Day' and 'Getting Up'. The debut album, *Dr Heckle And Mr Jive*, subsequently reached the UK Top 20. Despite shrewd promotion, Pigbag's heyday was short-lived. 'Big Bean' (1982) peaked at number 40 and 'Hit The "O" Deck' (1983) failed to make any impact. After a live album, the band broke up, although 'Papa's Got A Brand New Pigbag' was later re-recorded in 1987, to coincide with *The Best Of Pigbag*.

●ALBUMS: *Dr Heckle And Mr Jive* (Y 1982)★★, *Pigbag - Live* (Y 1983)★★.

●COMPILATIONS: *The Best Of Pigbag* (Kaz 1987)★★.

PIL

(see Public Image Limited)

PINE, COURTNEY

b. 18 March 1964, London, England. Like many of his generation of young, black, UK jazz musicians, Pine came from a reggae and funk background. Pine is a dazzling performer on many instruments, notably saxophone, clarinet, flute and keyboards. He had been a member of Dwarf Steps, a hard-bop band consisting of Berklee College Of Music graduates, before joining reggae stars Clint Eastwood and General Saint. His interest in jazz was fostered when he participated in workshops run by John Stevens. In 1986 he deputized for Sonny Fortune in Elvin Jones's band, and was involved in setting up the Jazz Warriors. He came to wider public notice as a result of playing with Charlie Watts' Orchestra, George Russell's European touring band and with Art Blakey at the Camden Jazz Festival. Blakey invited him to join the Messengers, but he decided to stay in Britain.

In 1987 he played at the Bath Festival with the Orchestre National de Jazz. By that time his reputation had spread far beyond jazz circles, and his first album was a massive seller by jazz standards. He appeared before a huge worldwide audience in the Nelson Mandela 70th Birthday Concert at Wembley, backing dancers IDJ, and was the main subject of a number of television arts programmes about jazz in the late 80s, his smart image and articulate seriousness about his music enabling him to communicate with many people who had never before given jazz a hearing. He became much in demand for film and television, and appeared, for example, on the soundtrack of Alan Parker's *Angel Heart* and over the titles of BBC television's *Juke Box Jury*. His quartet comprised of young American luminaries Kenny Kirkland (piano), Charnett Moffett (bass) and Marvin 'Smitty' Smith (drums). Many of his admirers feel that in some ways his high media profile has hindered his development, but his talent, dedication and level-headedness have ensured that he has never been diverted by the hype, and his most recent work illustrates an emotional depth matching his undoubted technical brilliance. He has also continued to play in reggae and other pop contexts (*Closer To Home*), and is a frequent collaborator with UK soul singer Mica Paris. *Modern Day Jazz Stories* showed a strong rap/hip hop influence and featured a funky support trio of Ronnie Burrage (drums), Charnett Moffett (bass) and Geri Allen (piano).

●ALBUMS: *Journey To The Urge Within* (Island 1986)★★, *Destiny's Song And The Image Of Pursuance* (Island 1988)★★, *The Vision's Tale* (Island 1989)★★★, *Within The Realms Of Our Dreams* (Island 1991)★★★, *Closer To Home* (Island 1992)★★★, *To The Eyes Of Creation* (Island 1992)★★★★, *Modern Day Jazz Stories* (Verve/Talkin' Loud 1996)★★.

PIXIES

This US group was formed in Boston, Massachusetts, by room-mates Charles Michael Kittridge Thompson IV aka Black Francis (b. Long Beach, California, USA; vocals, guitar) and Joey Santiago (guitar). A newspaper advertisement, requiring applicants for a 'Hüsker Dü/Peter, Paul And Mary band', solicited bassist Kim Deal who in turn introduced drummer David Lovering. Originally known as Pixies In Panoply, the quartet secured a recording deal on the UK independent label 4AD Records on the strength of a series of superior demo tapes. Their debut release, *Come On Pilgrim*, introduced the band's abrasive, powerful sound and Francis's oblique lyrics. *Surfer Rosa*, produced by Big Black's Steve Albini, exaggerated the savage fury of its predecessor and the set was acclaimed Album Of The Year in much of the UK rock press. The superlative *Doolittle* emphasized the quartet's grasp of melody, yet retained their drive, and this thrilling collection scaled the national Top 10, aided and abetted by the band's most enduring single, 'Monkey Gone To Heaven'. The Pixies were now a highly popular attraction and their exciting live performances enhanced a growing reputation, establishing clear stage favourites in 'Debaser', 'Cactus', 'Wave Of Mutilation' and 'Bone Machine'. 1990's *Bossanova* showed an undiminished fire with a blend of pure pop with 'Allison' and sheer ferocity in 'Rock Music'. The band found themselves the darlings of the rock press and were once again widely regarded for recording one of the top albums of the year. Kim Deal, meanwhile, attracted glowing reviews for her offshoot project, the Breeders. *Trompe Le Monde* was, if anything, an even harsher collection than those that had preceded it, prompting some critics to describe it as the 'Pixies' heavy metal album'. Following the rechristened Frank Black's departure for a solo career in early 1993 the band effectively folded, but the group's reputation continues to outshine any of the membership's concurrent or subsequent projects.

●ALBUMS: *Come On Pilgrim* (4AD 1987)★★★, *Surfer Rosa* (4AD 1988)★★★★, *Doolittle* (4AD 1989)★★★★, *Bossanova* (4AD 1990)★★★, *Trompe Le Monde* (4AD 1991)★★★.

PLANXTY

This early 70s Irish group originally featured Christy Moore (b. 7 May 1945, Dublin, Eire; guitar/vocals), Donal Lunny (guitar/bouzouki/synthesizer), Liam O'Flynn (uillean pipes) and

Andy Irvine (guitar/mandolin/bouzouki/vocals). After two albums, Lunny left, to be replaced by Johnny Moynihan (bouzouki). In 1974, Moore left and was replaced by Paul Brady (b. 19 May 1947, Co. Tyrone, Northern Ireland; vocals/guitar). The name Planxty is an Irish word for an air that is written to thank or honour a person. The group remained highly popular throughout its existence and their records sold well. Moynihan then left to join De Dannan. After splitting up, the original group re-formed, this time with Matt Molloy (flute), who later joined the Chieftains in September 1979. Moore and Lunny departed once more in 1981 to form Moving Hearts. *Words And Music* featured the Bob Dylan song 'I Pity The Poor Immigrant'. The group were only ever formed as an extension of the various group members' solo commitments, and though they were always in demand at festivals, personal career moves saw an end to the line-up. By the time *The Best Of Planxty Live* emerged, they were pursuing solo projects.

●ALBUMS: *Planxty* (Polydor 1972)★★★, *The Well Below The Valley* (Polydor 1973)★★★★, *Cold Blow And The Rainy Night* (Polydor 1974)★★★, *After The Break* (Tara 1979)★★★, *The Woman I Loved So Well* (Tara 1980)★★★, *Timedance* (1981)★★★, *Words And Music* (1983)★★★.

●COMPILATIONS: *The Planxty Collection* (Polydor 1976)★★★★, *The High Kings Of Tara* (Tara 1980)★★, *Ansi!* (1984)★★, *The Best Of Planxty Live* (1987)★★.

PLIMSOULS

One of a group of bands from Los Angeles, California, USA, playing power-pop in the mid-80s, the Plimsouls consisted of Peter Case (vocals/guitar, ex-Nerves), plus Lou Ramirez (drums), Dave Pahoa (bass) and Eddie Munoz (lead guitar). Formed in 1979, they originally worked as Tone Dogs before changing names and earning a strong local live reputation. This culminated in the low-budget recording in 1980 of a debut EP *Zero Hour* on the band's own Beat Records which captured their live energy despite its lo-fi recording quality. Their love of 60s pop was more fully realised on *The Plimsouls*, whose vibrant pop tunes were given a clearer production. However, disappointed by record sales the group's relationship with Planet deteriorated, and they signed to Geffen Records. Again the band stayed long enough to produce only a single recording, the widely acclaimed *Everywhere At Once*, which included 'A Million Miles Away', issued as a 12-inch single while the band were between labels. One of the album's most

enduring tracks 'How Long Will It Take?', seemed to amplify the Plimsouls' long-standing role as commercial underachievers, and it was to be their last studio release. Case went on to a solo career while the Plimsouls' legacy was wrapped up with the 1988 release of a 1981 live gig by French label Fan Club.

●ALBUMS: *The Plimsouls* (Planet 1981)★★★, *Everywhere At Once* (Geffen 1983)★★★★, *One Night In America* (Fan Club 1988)★★★.

POGUES

The London punk scene of the late 70s inspired some unusual intermingling of styles, and the Pogues (then known as Pogue Mahone) performed punky versions of traditional Irish folk songs in pubs throughout the capital. They were fronted by singer Shane MacGowan (b. 25 December 1957, Kent, England) and also included Peter 'Spider' Stacy (tin whistle), Jem Finer (banjo/mandolin), James Fearnley (guitar/piano accordion), Cait O'Riordan (bass) and Andrew Ranken (drums). MacGowan had spent his late teen years singing in a punk group called the Nipple Erectors (aka the Nips) which also contained Fearney. After several complaints the band changed their name (Pogue Mahone is 'kiss my arse' in Gaelic) and soon attracted the attention of the Clash who asked them to be their opening act. Record companies were perturbed by the band's occasionally chaotic live act where they would often fight onstage and Stacy kept time by banging his head with a beer tray. In 1984 Stiff Records signed them and recorded *Red Roses For Me*, containing several traditional tunes as well as excellent originals like 'Streams Of Whiskey' and 'Dark Streets Of London'. It announced a major songwriting talent in McGowan's evocative descriptions of times and places he had often visited first-hand. Elvis Costello produced *Rum, Sodomy And The Lash* on which Philip Chevron, formerly a guitarist with the Radiators From Space, replaced Finer who was on 'paternity leave'. The group soon established themselves as a formidable and unique live act and the record entered the UK Top 20. There were further changes when the multi-instrumentalist Terry Woods (a co-founder of Steeleye Span) joined and Cait O'Riordan was replaced by Darryl Hunt. O'Riordan later married Elvis Costello. The group's intrinsicly political stance resulted in their video to accompany the single 'A Pair Of Brown Eyes', having to be re-edited because the group were filmed spitting on a poster of Prime Minister, Margaret Thatcher. 'We represent the people who don't get the breaks. People can look at us and say, "My God, if that bunch of tumbledown wrecks can do it, so can I'", explained Chevron in a press interview. The band would later have their protest ballad, 'Birmingham Six', banned from airplay. The album on which this was to be found, *If I Should Fall From Grace With God*, was produced by Steve Lillywhite and embraced Middle Eastern and Spanish sounds. It sold more than 200,000 copies in the USA and 'Fairytale Of New York', a rumbustuous but poignant duet by MacGowan and Lillywhite's wife, Kirsty MacColl, was a Christmas number 2 hit in the UK in 1987. In the autumn of 1989 there were fears for the future of the group when MacGowan's heavy drinking led to him pulling out of several shows. He was due to join the band in the USA for a prestigious tour with Bob Dylan when he collapsed at London's Heathrow Airport. He missed all the support spots with Dylan and the band played without him. 'Other groups in a situation like that would've either said, "Let's get rid of the guy" or "Let's split up", but we're not the sort to do that. We're all part of each other's problems whether we like it or not', said Chevron. *Peace And Love* featured songs written by nearly every member of the group and its eclectic nature saw them picking up the hurdy-gurdy, the cittern and the mandola. Its erratic nature drew criticism from some quarters, mainly from original fans who had preferred the early folk-punk rants. While the rest of the group were clearly strong players it was widely accepted that MacGowan was the most talented songwriter. His output had always been highly sporadic but there were now fears that the drinking that fuelled his earlier creativity may have slowed him to a standstill. In an interview in 1989 he said he had not been 'dead-straight sober' since he was 14 and that he drank in quantity because 'it opened his mind to paradise'. It was announced in September 1991 that MacGowan had left the band and had been replaced by the former Clash singer, Joe Strummer. This relationship lasted until June the following year when Strummer stepped down and the lead vocalist job went to Spider Stacy. McGowan later re-emerged with his new band, the Popes, while his erstwhile colleagues continued to tour heavily, recording competent new material that lacked the flair of old.

●ALBUMS: *Red Roses For Me* (Stiff 1984)★★★, *Rum, Sodomy And The Lash* (Stiff 1985)★★★★, *If I Should Fall From Grace With God* (Stiff 1988)★★★★, *Peace And Love* (Warners 1989)★★★, *Hell's Ditch* (Pogue Mahone 1990)★★★, *Waiting For Herb* (PM 1993)★★, *Pogue Mahone* (Warners 1995)★★.

●COMPILATIONS: *The Best Of The Pogues* (PM 1991)★★★, *The Rest Of The Best* (PM 1992)★★★.

●VIDEOS: *Completely Pogued* (Start 1991), *Poguevision* (Warners 1991).

●FURTHER READING: *The Pogues: The Lost Decade*, Ann Scanlon. *Poguetry: The Illustrated Pogues Songbook*, Hewitt McGowan and Pike.

POLICE

The reggae-influenced minimalist pop sound of this highly talented UK trio was one of the musical high points of the late 70s and early 80s. Their individual talent and egos ultimately got the better of them and they fragmented, although each of the strong-willed former members has never ruled out the possibility of a re-match. The group comprised Stewart Copeland (b. 16 July 1952, Alexandria, Egypt; drums/percussion/vocals), Andy Summers (b. Andrew Somers, 31 December 1942, Poulton Le Fylde, Lancashire, England; guitar) and Sting (b. Gordon Sumner, 2 October 1951, Wallsend, Tyne And Wear, England; bass/vocals). Masterminded by Miles Copeland, ex-Curved Air member Stewart and ex-Last Exit bassist Sting came together with the vastly experienced Summers, leaving the original member Henry Padovani no alternative but to leave. He had previously played on their independent chart hit 'Fall Out', released on Miles' Illegal label. Summers, a former session musician and ex-Zoot Money, Dantalians Chariot, Eric Burdon And The New Animals, Soft Machine and Kevin Ayers, blended instantly with Copeland's back-to-front reggae drum technique and Sting's unusual and remarkable voice. Summers added a sparse, clean guitar utilizing a flanger with echo, a sound he arguably invented and most certainly popularized; he found many imitators during his career with the Police. The mixture of such unusual styles gave them a totally fresh sound which they honed and developed over five outstanding albums; each record was a step forward both in musical content and sales.

Astonishingly, their A&M Records debut 'Roxanne' failed to chart when first released, but this now-classic tale of a prostitute was a later success on the back of 'Can't Stand Losing You'. Their heavily reggae-influenced *Outlandos D'Amour* and *Regatta De Blanc* dominated the UK charts for most of 1979 and contained such chart-toppers as 'Message In A Bottle' and 'Walking On The Moon'. Sting's simple but intelligently written lyrics were complete tales. *Zenyatta Mondatta* was their big breakthrough in America, Europe, Japan and indeed the rest of the world. The group's third number 1, 'Don't Stand So Close To Me', a tale of the temptations of being a schoolteacher (which Sting had been previously), was closely followed by the lyrically rich yet simply titled 'De Do Do Do De Da Da Da'. The following year, having now conquered the world, they released the outstanding *Ghost In The Machine*, which contained Sting's most profound lyrics to date and was enriched by Hugh Padgham's fuller production. The major hit singles from this album were the thought-provoking 'Spirits In The Material World', 'Invisible Sun', a brooding atmospheric comment on Northern Ireland and the joyous Caribbean carnival sound of 'Every Little Thing She Does Is Magic' which provided their fourth UK number 1.

Following yet another multi-million-seller, the band relaxed in 1982 to concentrate on solo projects. Copeland resurrected his Klark Kent *alter ego*, releasing *Klark Kent*, and wrote the music for the film *Rumblefish*. Summers had a book of photographs published to coincide with an exhibition of his camera work and also made an album with Robert Fripp. Sting appeared in the film adaptation of Dennis Potter's *Brimstone And Treacle* and had the UK gutter press speculate on his sexual preferences. The Police reconvened in 1983 and released the carefully crafted *Synchronicity*; almost as if they knew this would be their last album. The package was stunning, a superb album containing numerous potential hit singles and a series of expertly made accompanying videos. The magnificent 'Every Breath You Take', arguably their greatest song, stayed at number 1 in the UK for four weeks, and for twice as many weeks in the USA, while the album stayed at the top for an astonishing 17 weeks. The collection varies from gentle songs like 'Tea In The Sahara' and 'Wrapped Around Your Finger', to the mercurial energy of 'Synchronicity II'.

●ALBUMS: *Outlandos D'Amour* (A&M 1978)★★★, *Regatta De Blanc* (A&M 1979)★★★★, *Zenyatta Mondatta* (A&M 1980)★★, *Ghost In The Machine* (A&M 1981)★★★★, *Synchronicity* (A&M 1983)★★★★, *Live!* rec. 1979 (A&M 1996)★★.

●COMPILATIONS: *Every Breath You Take - The Singles* (A&M 1986)★★★★, *Greatest Hits* (A&M 1992)★★★★.

●VIDEOS: *Outlandos To Synchronicities: A History Of The Police* (1995).

●FURTHER READING: *The Police Released*, no editor listed. *Message In A Bottle*, Rossetta Woolf. *The Police: L'Historia Bandido*, Phil Sutcliffe and Hugh Fielder. *The Police: A Visual Documentary*, Miles. *The Police*, Lynn Goldsmith. *Complete Guide To The Music Of The Police And Sting*, Chris Welch.

POP GROUP

This seminal UK punk group operated from Bristol, Avon, in the late 70s, combining abstracted funk with chaos and expressionist vocals courtesy of Mark Stewart. The topics under consideration - starvation, war, exploitation - were similar to those expounded by anarcho-punks Crass, but the Pop Group's music was much more sophisticated. Their records are by turns inspirational and intolerable, some of the most extreme music to have been pressed onto vinyl. The masterpiece was *For How Much Longer Must We Tolerate Mass Murder*. No one is able to maintain such a pitch of intensity: bassist Simon Underwood left to form Pigbag, a welcome relief from the drabness punk conformity had created, a riot of bright shirts, ethnic rhythms and James Brown references. He now works in A&R and band management. Guitarist and saxophonist Gareth Sagar formed the irrepressible Rip Rig And Panic Float Up CP, Head, Pork And Opium and in 1995 formed Pregnant. Only singer Mark Stewart kept to his bleak viewpoint, forming the Maffia with the rhythm team from Sugarhill Records and working with producer Adrian Sherwood. Guitarist John Waddington formed Maximum Joy and drummer Bruce Smith moved through Rip Rig And Panic and worked with numerous top names on sessions including Terence Trent D'Arby and Soul II Soul.

●ALBUMS: *Y* (Radar 1979)★★, *For How Much Longer Must We Tolerate Mass Murder* (Rough Trade 1980)★★★, *We Are Time* (Rough Trade 1980)★★.

POPINJAYS

Formed in London in 1988 by songwriters Wendy Robinson (b. 6 April 1964, Huddersfield, Yorkshire, England; vocals), Polly Hancock (b. 16 July 1964, Berkshire, England; guitar/vocals) and a drum machine, the Popinjays evolved out of the influential Timebox Club at the Bull & Gate pub in Kentish Town, north London (the duo later ran their own Pop Club at the same venue), by striving to perfect the ultimate pop formula. Dana Baldinger (b. 26 December 1963 California, USA; bass) joined in 1989 as the offer of a combination of sweets, comics and biscuits won the band a record deal with One Little Indian Records. Dana departed after one single, to be replaced by fellow countrywoman Anne Fogers (b. 17 October 1962, New York, USA) a move that was followed by a multitude of critical recommendations for the debut album, *Bang Up To Date With The Popinjays*. Ever conscious of the importance of fun in music, their promo video for the 'Vote Elvis' single featured much Monkees-style running around with special guest Cathal Coughlan from Fatima Mansions. Drummer Seamus Feeney (b. 19 November 1964, Middlesex, England), caused the drum machine to be sacked at the close of 1990, just as the Popinjays were beginning to garner appreciative attention from America. *Flying Down To Mono Valley* did little to embellish their reputation, and it was left to their 1994 album to produce a significant stylistic departure. *Tales From The Urban Prairie* saw forays into country rock and singer songwriter melancholia, an affecting performance but one that left their traditional fan base in some degree of confusion.

●ALBUMS: *Bang Up To Date With The Popinjays* (One Little Indian 1990)★★★, *Flying Down To Mono Valley* (One Little Indian 1992)★★★, *Tales From The Urban Prairie* (One Little Indian 1994)★★★.

POWER STATION

This commercial rock band started out as a Tony Thompson (drums, ex-Patti LaBelle; Chic) solo project, but came to be viewed as a spin-off from Duran Duran. Andy Taylor (b. 16 February 1961, Cullercoats, Newcastle-upon-Tyne, England; guitar) saw it as a cross between Chic and the Sex Pistols, and was joined by fellow Duran Duran member John Taylor (b. 20 June 1960, Birmingham, England; bass) and vocalist Robert Palmer (b. 19 January 1949, Batley, Yorks, England). Thompson's Chic partner Bernie Edwards (b. 31 October 1952, Greenville, North Carolina, USA) handled production duties. Palmer had previously met the Duran Duran members at a MENCAP charity concert. They hit almost immediately with 'Some Like It Hot' and a cover of T. Rex's 'Get It On'. Both tracks reached the US Top 10. Then, after a subsequent minor hit with 'Communication' marking their third success of 1985, they split. Their sole album was recorded at the Power Station Studio in New York, from which they took their name. Palmer did not want to tour so he was replaced by former Silverhead and Detective vocalist Michael Des Barres. Following the band's quick exit John Taylor returned to Duran Duran while Andy Taylor went on to attempt a solo career. He invited Steve Jones to guest on his debut solo album, fulfilling the prophecy of his stated ambition that Power Station should fuse the Sex Pistols and Chic by eventually working with members of both.

The reunion in 1996 was unexpected, as major problems were encountered during the recording sessions for the second coming. John Taylor's replacement Bernard Edwards died during the sessions. He had produced the first album and stepped in after Taylor jumped ship midway through recording. *Living In Fear*, although well-produced and full sounding, was a record out of its time. Very much an 80s sound, these songs sounded dated in the context of 90s alternative rock and pop. The public voted by keeping their hands on their wallets.

●ALBUMS: *The Power Station* (Parlophone 1985)★★, *Living In Fear* (Chrysalis 1996)★★.

PRAYING MANTIS

Formed in London, England, in 1977, Praying Mantis were at the forefront of the New Wave Of British Heavy Metal. The original line-up consisted of Tino 'Troy' Neophytou (guitar/vocals), Robert Angelo (guitar), Tino's brother Chris 'Troy' Neophytou (bass/vocals) and Mick Ransome (drums). Through early demo recordings the band attracted the attention of the heavy metal club DJ Neal Kay, who helped them release an independent three-track EP, *The Soundhouse Tapes Vol. 2*, a title also used by Iron Maiden for their first release. The band's career can be closely linked with Iron Maiden during those early years as, in addition to both bands appearing on the *Metal For Muthas* compilation released by EMI Records in 1980, they also toured England together. Signing to Arista Records and replacing Robert Angelo (who joined Weapon in July 1981) and Mick Ransome with guitarist/vocalist Steve Carroll and ex-Ten Years After drummer Dave Potts, the band's debut, *Time Tells No Lies*, was released in 1981. However, it was not well received due to the lacklustre production and basic melodic rock sound. The band decided a line-up change was needed, and replaced the departed Steve Carroll with ex-Grand Prix vocalist Bernie Shaw, and they also recruited keyboard player Jon Bavin. This line-up went on to record 'Turn The Tables' for a compilation album released on the Yet Records label in the mid-80s. Through a lack of media interest the band metamorphosized into Stratus, who specialized in standard melodic rock and also featured ex-Iron Maiden drummer Clive Burr. To celebrate the 10th anniversary of the NWOBHM the band re-formed early in 1990 to tour Japan as part of the British All Stars. This new line-up consisted of founder-members Tino and Chris Troy, ex-Iron Maiden vocalist Paul Di'anno, ex-Iron

Maiden guitarist Dennis Stratton and ex-Weapon drummer Bruce Bisland.

●ALBUMS: *Time Tells No Lies* (Arista 1981)★★, *Predator In Disguise* (1993)★★.

PREFAB SPROUT

The intricate tales and thoughts in the lyrics of songwriter Paddy McAloon indicate a major songwriter. His Bob Dylan imagery and Elvis Costello bluntness have made Prefab Sprout one of the most refreshing pop bands of the late 80s and beyond. The band was formed in 1982 and comprised: Paddy McAloon (b. 7 June 1957, Durham, England; guitar/vocals), Martin McAloon (b. 4 January 1962, Durham, England; bass), Wendy Smith (b. 31 May 1963, Durham, England; vocals/guitar) and Neil Conti (b. 12 February 1959, London, England). Following a self-pressed single, 'Lions In My Own Garden', Paddy attracted the attention of the independent label Kitchenware. They had further hits in the UK independent charts and their debut *Swoon* made the national chart. *Swoon* was a wordy album featuring songs with many chord changes that ultimately concentrated on lyrics rather than melody. Later that year the excellent 'When Love Breaks Down' failed to excite the single-buying public. A remixed version by Thomas Dolby was released the following year, but once again it failed. When *Steve McQueen* was issued in 1985 the band became media darlings, with Paddy McAloon coming near to over-exposure. The album was a critics' favourite and displayed hummable songs with fascinating lyrics, and it made a respectable showing in the charts. At the end of the year 'When Love Breaks Down' was issued for a third time and finally became a hit.

In the USA, *Steve McQueen* was forcibly retitled *Two Wheels Good*. A striking work, the album included a tribute to Faron Young and the arresting 'Goodbye Lucille # 1' (aka 'Johnny Johnny'). *From Langley Park To Memphis* in 1988 was a major success worldwide; Paddy had now refined his art to produce totally accessible yet inventive pop music. The album represented a courageous change of direction with McAloon employing strings and composing melodies that recalled the great show musical writers of the pre-rock 'n' roll era. 'Nightingales' was very much in this vein, and the work ended with the strikingly melodramatic 'Nancy (Let Your Hair Down For Me)' and 'The Venus Of The Soup Kitchen'. Already the band had reached the stage of having superstar guests 'turning up on the album'. Both Stevie Wonder (harmonica solo on 'Nightingales') and Pete

Townshend put in appearances. 'The King Of Rock 'N' Roll' became their biggest hit to date. *Protest Songs* was a collection scheduled to appear before their previous album and its success was muted by the continuing sales of both *Steve McQueen* and *From Langley Park To Memphis*. McAloon unleashed *Jordan: The Comeback* in 1990, and for many critics it was the album of the year. All McAloon's talents had combined to produce a concept album of magnificence. Over 64 minutes in length, the album boasted 19 tracks, full of striking melodies and fascinatingly oblique lyrics. The ghost of Elvis Presley haunted several of the songs, most notably the elegiac 'Moon Dog'. McAloon spent the next few years tinkering with various new projects, paying the bills by writing songs for actor/singer Jimmy Nail. A new album, *Andromeda Heights*, finally appeared in 1997. Sophisticated and intelligent mood music, it met with a polite response from critics still entranced by McAloon's intricate musical and lyrical conceits.

●ALBUMS: *Swoon* (Kitchenware 1984)★★★, *Steve McQueen* (Kitchenware 1985)★★★★, *From Langley Park To Memphis* (Kitchenware 1988)★★★, *Protest Songs* (Kitchenware 1989)★★★, *Jordan: The Comeback* (Kitchenware 1990)★★★, *Andromeda Heights* (Columbia 1997)★★★.

●COMPILATIONS: *A Life Of Surprises: The Best Of* (Kitchenware 1992)★★★★.

●FURTHER READING: *Myths, Melodies & Metaphysics, Paddy McAloon's Prefab Sprout*, John Birch.

●VIDEOS: *A Life Of Surprises: The Video Collection* (SMV 1997).

PRETENDERS

Chrissie Hynde (b. 17 September 1951, Akron, Ohio, USA), came to England to seek her fortune during the early 70s. After meeting with *New Musical Express* writer and future boyfriend Nick Kent she joined the paper and gained entrance into the world of rock. During her pre-Pretenders days she worked at Malcolm McLaren's shop, SEX, played with Chris Spedding, joined Jack Rabbit, formed the Berk Brothers and made a tasteless, unreleased single as the Moors Murderers. By the time she assembled the band in 1978, Hynde had gained a great deal of experience. The classic Pretenders line-up comprised: Pete Farndon (b. 2 June 1952, Hereford, England, d. 14 April 1983; bass), James Honeyman-Scott (b. 4 November 1956, Hereford, England d. 16 June 1982; guitar) and Martin Chambers (b. 4 September 1951,

Hereford, England; drums). Their debut was a Nick Lowe-produced version of the Kinks' 'Stop Your Sobbing' in 1978. It scraped into the UK Top 40 the following year, having received critical praise and much interest. 'Kid' and the superb 'Brass In Pocket' followed. The latter was accompanied by a superb black and white video with Hynde portrayed as a waitress, and reached the number 1 position in the UK. It was their debut album that eventually put them on the road to becoming one of the decade's most important groups. *Pretenders* was a *tour-de-force* and remains their finest work. In addition to their previous singles the album contained the reggae-styled 'Private Life' (later recorded by Grace Jones), the frenetic 'Precious', the Byrds-like 'Talk Of The Town' and the beautiful ballad 'Lovers Of Today'.

Throughout 1980 they became a major stadium attraction in the USA; it was in America that Hynde met and fell in love with her musical idol, the Kinks' Ray Davies. *Pretenders II* came in 1982; it was another collection of melodious rock played with new wave enthusiasm. Stand-out tracks were 'Message Of Love', the brilliantly confessional 'The Adulteress' and another Davies' chestnut, 'I Go To Sleep', first recorded by the Applejacks in 1964. During the turbulent month of June, Pete Farndon, whose drug abuse had been a problem for some time, was fired. Two days later Honeyman-Scott was found dead from a deadly concoction of heroin and cocaine. Nine months later Hynde gave birth to a daughter; the father was Ray Davies. Two months after this happy event, tragedy struck again. Pete Farndon was found dead in his bath from a drug overdose.

The new full-time Pretenders were Robbie McIntosh (ex-Average White Band) on lead guitar, and bassist Malcolm Foster. They set about recording a third album and the band ended the year with another hit single, the Christmassy '2000 Miles'. *Learning To Crawl* was released at the beginning of another successful year. The album was erratic, but it did contain some gems, notably the epic 'Thin Line Between Love And Hate', the powerful 'Middle Of The Road' and the melodic, yet poignant tribute to Honeyman-Scott, 'Back On The Chain Gang'. The band embarked on another US tour, but Hynde refused to be parted from her baby daughter who accompanied her, while Davies and his band were touring elsewhere. In May 1984, following a whirlwind affair, Hynde married Jim Kerr of Simple Minds. Back with the Pretenders she appeared at Live Aid at the JFK stadium in Philadelphia, and would enjoy success under her

own name duetting with UB40 on the chart-topping reggae remake of Sonny And Cher's 'I Got You Babe'. Following the birth of another daughter (Jim Kerr was the father), Hynde effectively dismantled the band. *Get Close* was released at the end of 1987 and was well received. Both 'Don't Get Me Wrong' and 'Hymn To Her' were substantial hits. In 1988 a solo Hynde performed with UB40 at the Nelson Mandela Concert and the subsequent duet 'Breakfast In Bed' was a Top 10 UK hit. Hynde has since spent much of her time campaigning for Animal Rights. Her marriage to Kerr collapsed and in 1990 she returned with a new album, *Packed*, still as the Pretenders. It was another critical and commercial success, demonstrating Hynde's natural gift for writing tight, melodic rock songs. *Last Of The Independents* was released in 1994, seeing Hynde reunited with drummer Martin Chambers, alongside Adam Seymour (guitar) and Andy Hobson (bass).

●ALBUMS: *Pretenders* (Warners 1980)★★★★, *Pretenders II* (Warners 1981)★★★★, *Learning To Crawl* (Warners 1984)★★★★, *Get Close* (Warners 1986)★★, *Packed* (Warners 1990)★★, *Last Of The Independents* (Sire/Warners 1994)★★★, *Isle Of View* (Warners 1995)★★★.

●COMPILATIONS: *The Singles* (Warners 1987)★★★★.

●VIDEOS: *The Isle Of View* (Warner Music Vision 1995).

●FURTHER READING: *Pretenders*, Miles. *The Pretenders*, Chris Salewicz. *The Pretenders: With Hyndesight*, Mike Wrenn.

PRIEST, MAXI

b. Max Elliot, 10 June 1962, Lewisham, London, England. Former carpenter Maxi Priest is now a hugely successful solo reggae artist. Named by his mother after her fondness for Max Bygraves, Elliot took his new name upon his conversion to Rastafarianism (from Priest Levi, one of the figureheads of the 12 tribes of Israel). He made his initial music industry breakthrough by employing his artisan's skills in building sound systems. He went on to tour with Saxon International, the UK's premier reggae assembly, where he rubbed shoulders with Peter King, Phillip Levi, Smiley Culture and Asher Senator. He made his name and reputation as a 'singing' DJ, vocalizing off the cuff observations over prime 70s roots music, but he soon progressed to a more soulful style which was captured by producer Paul Robinson (aka Barry Boom) on his debut, *You're Safe*. After recording this album, he started a run of hits in 1986 with 'Strollin' On',

'In The Springtime' and 'Crazy Love'. In 1987 he enjoyed a minor hit single with a cover of Robert Palmer's 'Some Guys Have All The Luck'. However, most successful was his 1988 cover of Cat Stevens' 'Wild World', though it owed more of a debt to the Jimmy Cliff reggae version. Further chart appearances followed with 'Close To You', 'Peace Throughout The World' and 'Human Work Of Art'. 1990's *Bona Fide* included contributions from, among others, Soul II Soul, a group undoubtedly influenced by Priest's mellow but evocative brand of lovers rock.

●ALBUMS: *You're Safe* (Virgin 1985)★★, *Intentions* (Virgin 1986)★★, *Maxi* (Ten 1987)★★, *Bona Fide* (Ten 1990)★★★, *Fe Real* (Ten 1992)★★, *Man With The Fun* (Virgin 1996)★★.
●COMPILATIONS: *The Best Of Me* (Ten 1991)★★★.

PRINCE

b. Prince Rogers Nelson, 7 June 1958, Minneapolis, Minnesota, USA. A prodigiously talented singer-songwriter, multi-instrumentalist and producer, Prince was named after the Prince Roger Trio, of whom his father John Nelson was a member. After running away from his mother and stepfather he briefly joined up with John, who bought him his first guitar. He was later adopted by the Andersons, and became a close friend of Andre Anderson (later Andre Cymone). Prince was already conversant with piano and guitar and had written his own material from an early age. Together with Andre he joined Anderson's cousin Charles Smith in a junior high school band titled Grand Central. As Prince progressed to high school, Grand Central became Champagne, and he introduced original material into his sets for the first time. His musical development continued with the emergence of 'Uptown', a musical underground scene that included Flyte Time as well as other important influences including Jellybean Johnson, Terry Lewis and Alexander O'Neal. Prince's first demos were recorded in 1976 with Chris Moon, who gave him guidance in the operation of a music studio, and free reign to experiment at weekends. Moon also introduced him to backer Owen Husney, after which Prince provided interested parties with a superior quality demo. Husney and partner Levinson set about a massive 'hyping' campaign, the results of which secured him a long term, flexible contract with Warner Brothers Records after a great deal of scrambling amongst the majors.

Debuting with *Prince For You*, Prince sent shock waves through his new sponsors by spending double his entire advance on the production of a single album. It sold moderately (USA number 163), with the single 'Soft And Wet' making a big impact in the R&B charts. The album's blend of deep funk and soul was merely an appetizer in comparison to his later exploits, but enough to reassure his label that their investment had been a solid one. By 1979 Prince had put together a firm band (his debut was recorded almost exclusively by himself). This featured Cymone (bass), Gayle Chapman and Matt Fink (both keyboards), Bobby Z (drummer) and Dez Dickerson (guitar). Despite lavishing considerably less time and money on it than its predecessor, *Prince* nevertheless charted (USA number 22) and boasted two successful singles, 'Why You Wanna Treat Me So Bad?' and 'I Wanna Be Your Lover'. A succession of live dates promoting the new album *Dirty Mind* saw Lisa Coleman replacing Chapman. The album was the first to fully embody Prince's sexual allure, and the phallic exhortations on his Fender Telecaster and explicit material like 'Head' appalled and enticed in equal proportions. Artists like Rick James, whom Prince supported in 1980, were among those who mistrusted Prince's open, androgynous sexuality. Returning to Minneapolis after an aborted UK tour, Cymone departed for a solo career while former members of Flyte Time and others released a self-titled album under the band name the Time. It transpired later that their songs had been written by Prince, who was the motivation behind the entire project. Prince was nothing if not prolific, and both *Controversy* and *1999* followed within 12 months. *Controversy* attempted to provide a rationale for the sexual machinations that dominated *Dirty Mind*, falling unhappily between the two stools of instinct and intellect. It was a paradox not entirely solved by *1999*, a double album which had enough strong material to make up two sides of excellence but no more.

The promotional tour featured a special revue troupe. Prince And The Revolution headlined above the Time and Vanity 6 (an all-girl Prince creation). The single 'Little Red Corvette' was lifted from the album and was the first to gain significant airplay on MTV. The song was almost entirely constructed for this purpose, using a strong 'white' metaphor as leverage. After internal disputes with the Time, Prince began work on the *Purple Rain* film, a glamorized autobiographical piece in which he would star. The potent social commentary of 'When Doves Cry' was lifted from the soundtrack and became the first Prince song to grace the top of the US charts. 'Let's Go Crazy' and 'Purple Rain' (numbers 1 and 2, respectively) further established him as a figurehead for the 80s. The latter saw him turn his hand to Jimi Hendrix pyrotechnics and textures in the song. After the finish of a huge and successful tour, Prince returned to the studio for a duet with Apollonia, the latest in a seemingly endless succession of female protégées. He also found time to revitalize the career of Scottish pop singer Sheena Easton by composing her US Top 10 effort 'Sugar Walls'. When *Around The World In A Day* emerged in 1985 it topped the US charts for a three-week run, despite a deliberate lack of promotion. Drowning in quasi-psychedelia and 60s optimism, it was a diverting but strangely uneventful, almost frivolous, jaunt. It preceded the announcement that Prince was retiring from live appearances. Instead he had founded the studio/label/complex Paisley Park in central Minneapolis, which would become the luxurious base for his future operations. As work began on a second movie, *Under The Cherry Moon*, 'Kiss' was released to become his third US number 1. Held one place beneath it was the Bangles' 'Manic Monday', written by Prince under one of his numerous pseudonyms, in this case, Christopher.

He quickly overturned his decision not to perform live, and set out on the *Parade* tour to promote the number 1 album of the same name. Unfortunately, if 'Kiss' and 'Girls And Boys' represented classic Prince innuendo, the rest of the album lacked focus. The shows, however, were spectacular even by Prince standards, but his backing band the Revolution were nevertheless disbanded at the end of the tour. 1987 saw a new line-up for the latest live engagements. While retaining the backbone of the Revolution (Fink, Leeds, Brooks and Safford) he added Sheila E, Marco Weaver, and Seacer. The new album was to be a radical departure from the laconic, cosseted atmosphere that pervaded *Parade*. 'Sign 'O' The Times', the title track, was a hard-hitting testimony to urban dystopia, drug-related violence and human folly. The vast majority of tracks on the double album revisited the favoured territory of sex and sensuality. The follow-up album would elaborate on the darker shades of 'Sign 'O' The Times' apocalyptic vision. However, the *Black Album* was recalled by Prince before it reached the shops. Combining primal funk slices with sadistic overtones, Prince's decision to suspend it ensured that it would become the 80s' most coveted bootleg. The mythology surrounding its non-release has it that the *Black Album* was the work of Prince's 'dark' side - 'Spooky Electric'. This was given credence by the subse-

quent *Lovesexy*, apparently the result of the pre-eminence of 'Camille' - Prince's 'good' side. Playing both albums side by side certainly reveals a sharp dichotomy of approach.

His next tour, meanwhile, saw the inclusion of a huge Pink Cadillac as a mobile part of the set. Exhausted musicians testified to the difficulty of backing their leader, rushing from orchestrated stadium performances to private club dates where entire sets would be improvised, all of which Prince, naturally, took in his stride. 1989 closed with a duet with Madonna, who, alongside Michael Jackson, was the only artist able to compete with Prince in terms of mass popularity. The following year was dominated by the soundtrack album for the year's biggest film, *Batman*. If the album was not his greatest artistic success, it proved a commercial smash, topping the US charts for six weeks. He had also written and produced an album for singer Mavis Staples. At first glance it seemed an unlikely combination, but Prince's lyrics tempered the sexual with the divine in a manner that was judged acceptable by the grand lady of gospel. *Graffiti Bridge* was his first commercial let-down for some time, peaking at number 6 in the USA (although it made number 1 in the UK). Prince, as usual, was already busy putting together new projects. These included his latest backing outfit the New Power Generation, featuring Tony M (rapper), Rosie Gaines (vocals), Michael Bland (drums), Levi Seacer (guitar), Kirk Johnson (guitar), Sonny T (bass) and Tommy Barbarella (keyboards). They were in place in time for the sessions for *Diamonds And Pearls*, a comparatively deliberate and studied body of work. In February 1990 Sinead O'Connor recorded a version of Prince's composition, 'Nothing Compares 2 U', which topped both the US and UK charts. In September he released *Graffiti Bridge*, which accompanied a film release of the same title. The album was composed entirely of Prince compositions of which he sang just over half - other guests included Tevin Campbell, Mavis Staples and the Time. Both album and film were critical and commercial failures, however. *Diamonds And Pearls* was released in October 1991, and showcased the New Power Generation, his latest backing band. Greeted by most critics as a return to form, the New Power Generation were also considered his most able and vibrant collaborators since the mid-80s. Taken from it, 'Cream' became a US number 1. 1992's 'Money Don't Matter 2 Night' featured a video directed by filmmaker Spike Lee, while 'Sexy MF' was widely banned on UK radio because of its suggestive lyrics. Both 'Sexy MF' and 'My Name Is Prince' were included on the *Love Symbol Album* - which introduced the cryptic 'symbol' which he would later legally adopt as his name in June 1993. Much of the attention subsequently surrounding the artist concerned his protracted battle against his record company, Warner Brothers. His behaviour became increasingly erratic - speaking only through envoys, he appeared at the 1995 BRIT Awards ceremony with the word 'slave' written across his forehead in protest at the record industry. In October he abandoned the symbol moniker and from now on would be known as the 'Artist Formerly Known As Prince'. Naturally, this produced enough running gags to fill a book and his credibility was in serious danger. In 1995 he released *The Gold Experience*, a return to the raunchy funk of his 80s prime in tracks such as 'Pussy Control' and 'I Hate You'. It also included the smoothly accessible 'The Most Beautiful Girl In The World', his best-selling single for many years. Following the release of *Chaos And Disorder* in July 1996 he sacked his band the New Power Generation and announced that he would not be touring, preferring to spend more time with his wife and new baby (who tragically died months after birth). Although the 'Artist Formerly Known As Prince' has yet to provide the definitive album of which he is so obviously capable, the continued flow of erratic, flawed gems suggests the struggle will continue to captivate his audience through the 90s. It it universally hoped that he reverts to his real name.

●ALBUMS: *Prince For You* (Warners 1978)★★★, *Prince* (Warners 1979)★★★, *Dirty Mind* (Warners 1980)★★★, *Controversy* (Warners 1981)★★★, *1999* (Warners 1982)★★★★, *Purple Rain* soundtrack (Warners 1984)★★★★, *Around The World In A Day* (Paisley Park 1985)★★★, *Parade - Music From Under The Cherry Moon* film soundtrack (Paisley Park 1986)★★★, *Sign 'O' The Times* (Paisley Park 1987)★★★★, *Lovesexy* (Paisley Park 1988)★★★, *Batman* film soundtrack (Warners 1989)★★★, *Graffiti Bridge* (Paisley Park 1990)★★, *Diamonds And Pearls* (Paisley Park 1991)★★★, with The New Power Generation *Symbol* (Paisley Park 1993)★★★, *Come* (Paisley Park 1994)★★, *The Gold Experience* (Warners 1995)★★★, *Chaos And Disorder* (Warners 1996)★★, *Emancipation* (New Power Generation 1996)★★.

●COMPILATIONS: *The Hits: Volume I & II* (Paisley Park/Warners 1993)★★★★.

●VIDEOS: *Double Live* (1986), *Prince And The Revolution; Live* (1987), *Sign O' The Times* (1988), *Lovesexy Part 2* (1989), *Lovesexy Part 1* (1989), *Get Off* (1991), *Prince: The Hits Collection* (1993), *3 Chains O' Gold* (Warner Reprise 1994), *Billboards* (Warner Vision 1994).

●FURTHER READING: *Prince: Imp Of The Perverse*, Barney Hoskyns. *Prince: A Pop Life*, Dave Hill. *Prince By Controversy*, The 'Controversy' Team. *Prince: A Documentary*, Per Nilsen. *Prince: An Illustrated Biography*, John W. Duffy. *Prince*, John Ewing.

PROPAGANDA

This Euro pop/synthesizer band left their native Germany to arrive in England in 1983. Comprising Claudia Brücken (vocals, ex-Eggolinos), Michael Mertens (percussion, ex-Dusseldorf Symphony Orchestra), Susanne Freytag and Ralf Dorper (keyboards), they found an early advocate in Paul Morley of ZTT Records. Their first release, 'Dr. Mabuse' reached number 27 in the UK charts. However, due to the label, and Trevor Horn's commitment to Frankie Goes To Hollywood, the follow-up would not be released until over a year later. 'Duel'/'Jewel' was more successful still as Brücken moved permanently to England to wed Morley. The group's first live performance in June 1985 saw their line-up bolstered by Derek Forbes (ex-Simple Minds) on bass and Steve Jansen (ex-Japan) on drums. *A Secret Wish* and the single from it, 'P-Machinery', emerged a month later. Their European tour saw another line-up shuffle with Brian McGee (also ex-Simple Minds) taking over drums, and Kevin Armstrong on guitar, alongside Brücken, Mertens, Freytag and Forbes. Dorper had departed on the advent of the tour, and eventually only Mertens remained from the original line-up. They became involved in a huge legal battle with ZTT, and Brücken decided to stay with her husband's label. She formed Act with Thomas Leer in 1987. When the litigation had finished in 1988 the new Propaganda line-up featured Besti Miller, an American expatriate based in Germany on vocals. They released *1-2-3-4* in 1990, with contributions from old hands Freytag and Dorper, as well as Howard Jones and David Gilmour. Meanwhile, Brücken had embarked on a solo career and released *Love; And A Million Other Things* in 1991.

●ALBUMS: *A Secret Wish* (ZTT 1985)★★, *Wishful Thinking* (ZTT 1985)★★, *1-2-3-4* (Virgin 1990)★★.

PSYCHEDELIC FURS

Until the recruitment of a drummer (Vince Ely) in 1979, Richard Butler (b. 5 June 1956, Kingston-upon-Thames, Surrey, England; vocals), Roger

Morris (guitar), ex-Photon John Ashton (b. 30 November 1957; guitar), Duncan Kilburn (woodwinds) and Tim Butler (b. 7 December 1958; bass) had difficulties finding work. The group were also dogged by an unprepossessing sullenness in interview, an equally anachronistic group name - inspired by the 1966 Velvet Underground track, 'Venus In Furs' - and Richard Butler's grating one-note style. It was not until a session on John Peel's BBC Radio 1 programme that they were invested with hip credibility - and a CBS Records recording contract. Under Steve Lillywhite's direction, their bleak debut album was followed by minor singles chart entries with 'Dumb Waiter' and 'Pretty In Pink', both selections from 1981's more tuneful and enduring *Talk Talk Talk*. Creeping even closer to the UK Top 40, 'Love My Way' was the chief single from *Forever Now*, produced in the USA by Todd Rundgren. On replacing Ely with Philip Calvert (ex-Birthday Party) in 1982, the outfit traded briefly as just 'the Furs' before *Mirror Moves* emitted a UK Top 30 hit with 'Heaven' (which was underpinned with a fashionable disco rhythm). Lucrative, too, were 'Ghost In You' and a re-recording of 'Pretty In Pink' for inclusion on 1986's film of the same title. That same year, they appeared at the mammoth Glastonbury Fayre festival - which, to many of their fans, remains the most abiding memory of the Psychedelic Furs as performers. By 1990, Ashton, the Butler brothers and hired hands were all that remained of a band that had become mostly a studio concern. Three years later the band were just a very fond memory, with Richard Butler moving on to recapture 'the spark of surprise' with new outfit, Love Spit Love.

●ALBUMS: *Psychedelic Furs* (Columbia 1980)★★★, *Talk Talk Talk* (Columbia 1981)★★★, *Forever Now* (Columbia 1982)★★★, *Mirror Moves* (Columbia 1984)★★★, *Midnight To Midnight* (Columbia 1987)★★, *Book Of Days* (Columbia 1989)★★, *World Outside* (Columbia 1991)★★, *Radio 1 Sessions* (Strange Fruit 1997)★★★.

●COMPILATIONS: *All Of This And Nothing* (Columbia 1988)★★★★, *The Collection* (Columbia1991)★★★.

PUBLIC IMAGE LIMITED

Public Image Ltd (PiL) was the 'company' formed by John Lydon (b. 31 January 1956, Finsbury Park, London, England) when he left behind both the Sex Pistols and previous moniker, Johnny Rotten, in January 1978. With Lydon on vocals, classically trained pianist and early Clash guitarist Keith Levene on guitar, reggae-influenced bass player

Jah Wobble (b. John Wardle), and Canadian drummer Jim Walker (ex-Furies), the band were put together with the working title of the Carnivorous Buttock Flies. By the time the debut single - the epic 'Public Image' - was released in its newspaper sleeve in September, they had adopted the less ridiculous name. Their live debut followed in Brussels on 12 December, and they played the UK for the first time on Christmas Day. In January 1979 ex-101ers and Raincoats drummer Richard Dudanski replaced Walker, who went on to punk band the Straps. The *Metal Box* set came out later that year as a set of 12-inch records housed in tin 'film' cans (it was later reissued as a normal album). One of the most radical and difficult albums of its era, its conception and execution was a remarkable blend of Lydon's antagonism and Levene's climatic guitar. The single 'Death Disco' also reached the UK charts. With Dudanski leaving, Fall drummer Karl Burns was enlisted until Martin Atkins (b. 3 August 1959, Coventry, England) from Mynd, joined in time to tour the USA in the spring of 1980. A live album, *Paris Au Printemps*, was recorded after which both Wobble and Atkins left. Wobble went on to record solo material and work briefly in 1987 for London Transport as a train guard, while Atkins formed Brian Brain. In May 1981 Lydon and Levene, augmented by hired musicians, played from behind an onstage screen at the New York Ritz. The crowd failed to grasp the concept and 'bottled' the band. After *Flowers Of Romance* Pete Jones (b. 22 September 1957) became bass player, and Atkins returned on drums. Around this time subsidiary members Dave Crowe and Jeanette Lee, who had been with the band since the beginning in business roles, both departed and the group started a new era as Lydon decided to settle in Los Angeles. In 1983 Jones left as the hypnotic 'This Is Not A Love Song' became PiL's Top 5 hit, and Levene also departed as it was climbing the chart. In a relatively quiet period when Lydon collaborated with Afrika Bambaataa on the Time Zone single, 'World Destruction', PiL released only the 1984 album *This Is What You Want, This Is What You Get*, and another set of live recordings from foreign fields. Lydon also made his first feature film appearance in *Order Of Death* (1983). They returned to the forefront with 1986's *Album*, from which came 'Single' aka 'Rise', featuring the drumming talents of Ginger Baker. The album included numerous guest/session musicians such as Steve Vai, Ryûichi Sakamoto and Tony Williams. The next year, Lydon assembled a permanent band once again, this time drawing on guitarists John McGeogh (ex-Magazine; Siouxsie And The Banshees; Armoury Show) and Lu Edmunds (ex-Damned; Mekons; 3 Mustaphas 3), bass player Allan Dias from America (formerly in nightclub backing bands and working with stars such as Tyrone Ashley and the *avant garde* Sun Ra), and drummer Bruce Smith (ex-Pop Group and various sessions). Lu Edmunds was forced to leave in 1989 because he was suffering from tinnitus (Ted Chau was a temporary replacement), and Smith left in 1990 as the band fell into inactivity again. The three remaining members came back to life in 1990 when Virgin Records put out a *Greatest Hits ... So Far* compilation, confidently including the new single 'Don't Ask Me' - Lydon's nod to the environmental problems of the world. After several years and countless line-ups, Lydon has remained the *enfant terrible* of the music industry, a constant irritant and occasional source of brilliance: 'I've learnt to manipulate the music business. I have to deal with all kinds of stupid, sycophantic people. I've just learnt to understand my power. Everyone should learn that, otherwise they lose control'. PiL then recruited new drummer Mike Joyce (ex-Smiths; Buzzcocks), but Lydon concentrated more on his autobiography and other musical projects (such as the Leftfield collaboration, 'Open Up') than PiL in the 90s.

●ALBUMS: *Public Image* (Virgin 1978)★★★, *Metal Box* UK title *Second Edition* USA title (Virgin 1979)★★★★, *Paris Au Printemps* (Virgin 1980)★★, *Flowers Of Romance* (Virgin 1981)★★, *Live In Tokyo* (Virgin 1983)★★, *Commercial Zone* (PIL/Virgin 1983)★★, *This Is What You Want, This Is What You Get* (Virgin 1984)★★★, *Album* (Virgin 1986)★★★, *Happy?* (Virgin 1987)★★★, *9* (Virgin 1989)★★, *That What Is Not* (Virgin 1992)★★.

●COMPILATIONS: *Greatest Hits ... So Far* (Virgin 1990)★★★.

●VIDEOS: *Live In Toyko* (Virgin 1983), *Videos* (Virgin 1986).

●FURTHER READING: *Public Image Limited: Rise Fall*, Clinton Heylin.

PYLE, ARTIMUS, BAND

Following his departure from Lynyrd Skynyrd, drummer Artimus Pyle put his own outfit together and they debuted in 1982 with an album that was, unsurprisingly, reminiscent of both his previous band and Pat Travers. With a line-up of Pyle, Darryll Otis Smith (vocals), John Boerstler (guitar), Steve Brewington (bass) and Steve Lockhart (guitar/keyboards), they played a mixture of souped-up rock 'n' roll and heavy rock with a pro-nounced southern flavour, and the first album showed much promise, which was sacrificed for commercial appeal a year later. Renaming themselves APB, *Nightcaller* saw Lockhart replaced by Russ Milner and featured a new vocalist in Karen Blackmon. This album contained an undistinguished set of pop-rock tunes with a new wave leaning. Lacking any real hope of a commercial breakthrough, it was no surprise that APB released no further albums.

●ALBUMS: *Artimus Pyle Band* (MCA 1982)★★★, as APB *Nightcaller* (MCA 1983)★★.

Q-Tips

Fronted by Paul Young (b. 17 January 1956, Luton, Bedfordshire, England), Q-Tips was one of the most renowned live bands on the UK club circuit in the early 80s, playing an estimated 800 gigs in under three years. The group was formed in 1979 by Young and other ex-members of Streetband, John Gifford (guitar/vocals) and Mick Pearl (bass/vocals). In place of their former band's rock sound, Q-Tips was organized as a classic soul group with an experienced brass section of Tony Hughes (trumpet), and saxophonists Steve Farr and Stewart Blandamer who had worked with Johnny Wakelin's Kinshasa Band, Jimmy James And The Vagabonds and the Flirtations. Other members were Barry Watts drums and Ian Kewley (keyboards) from Samson and latterly hard rock band Limey. With matching suits and arrangements out of the Tamla/Motown and Stax songbooks, Q-Tips were seen as part of a mod revival. After releasing a frantic version of Joe Tex's 'SYSLJFM (The Letter Song)' on the independent Shotgun label, the group signed to Chrysalis Records and covered the Miracles' 'Tracks Of My Tears'. By now Clifford had been replaced by Garth Watt-Roy, whose career had included spells with Greatest Show On Earth, Fuzzy Duck, Marmalade and Limey. The self-titled debut album included Blandamer originals like 'A Man Can't Lose' as well as cover versions, but its lack of sales led to Chrysalis dropping the band. They then signed to Rewind Records which chose a version of Boudleaux Bryant's 'Love Hurts' as a single. Although this also failed to sell, it served to bring Young to the notice of CBS Records, resulting in him being signed to the label as a solo artist at the start of 1982. This was the signal for the break-up of Q-Tips, and they disbanded after a farewell tour and the release of a live album. *Live At Last* included 'Broken Man', the first song co-written by Young and Kewley, who would continue their partnership during the first phase of the singer's triumphant solo career. A BBC concert recording of the Q-Tips was released in 1991.

●ALBUMS: *Q-Tips* (Chrysalis 1980)★★★, *Live At Last* (Rewind 1982)★★★, *BBC Radio 1 Live In Concert* (Windsong 1991)★★.

Quarterflash

This band from Portland, Oregon, USA, were most renowned for their massive US/UK hit single 'Harden My Heart'. This track was a prime example of the group's sound, delivering passionate guitars, wailing saxophone, emotive vocals and an enormous chorus. Primarily described as AOR, Quarterflash boasted the talents of Cindy Ross (vocals/saxophone), Marv Ross (guitar), Jack Charles (vocals/guitar), Rich Gooch (bass), Rick DiGiallonardo (keyboards) and Brian Willis (drums). They recorded three strong albums, although their debut met with most commercial success, particularly in the USA. The group split in 1985 after the release of *Black Into Blue* but reformed in 1990 much to the delight of classic AOR fans.

●ALBUMS: *Quarterflash* (Geffen 1982)★★★, *Take Another Picture* (Geffen 1983)★★★, *Black Into Blue* (Geffen 1985)★★★.

Queen Latifah

b. Dana Owens, 18 March 1970, East Orange, New Jersey, USA. Rap's first lady, Queen Latifah, broke through in the late 80s with a style that picked selectively from jazz and soul traditions. The former Burger King employee has maintained her early commitment to answer the misognyist armoury of her male counterparts, and at the same time impart musical good times to all genders. After working as the human beatbox alongside female rapping crew Ladies Fresh, she was just 18 years old when she released her debut single, 'Wrath Of My Madness', in 1988. A year later her debut long-player enjoyed fevered reviews: an old, wise head was evident on the top of her young shoulders. Production expertise from Daddy-O, KRS-1, DJ Mark The 45 King and members of De La Soul doubtlessly helped as well. By the time of her third album she had moved from Tommy Boy Records to a new home, Motown Records, and revealed a shift from the soul and ragga tones of *Nature Of A Sista* to sophisticated, sassy hip hop. She has subsequently embarked on a career as an actress, notably in the hit streetwise black comedy, *Living Single*, where she plays magazine boss Khadijah James. He film credits already include *Juice*, *Jungle Fever* and *House Party 2*. As if that was not enough, she additionally set up her own Flavor Unit record label and management company in

1993, as an outlet for new rap acts as well as her own recordings. Its first release, 'Roll Wit Tha Flava', featured an all-star cast including Naughty By Nature's Treach, Fu-Schnickens' Chip-Fu, Black Sheep's Dres and D-Nice. She also guested on the Shabba Ranks single, 'Watcha Gonna Do'. Previous collaborations had included those with De La Soul ('Mama Gave Birth To The Soul Children', in that band's infancy) and Monie Love (the agenda-setting 'Ladies First'). Queen Latifah represents an intelligent cross-section of hip hop influences. Though she is a forthright advocate of her race's struggle, she is also the daughter of and brother to policemen. *Black Reign*, in fact, is dedicated to the death of that same brother: 'I see both sides. I've seen the abuse and I've been the victim of police who abuse their authority. On the other side you've got cops getting shot all the time, you got people who don't respect them at all'. While a little too strident to live up to the Arabic meaning of her name (Latifah equates to delicate and sensitive), Queen Latifah is one of the most positive role models for young black women (and men) in hip hop culture: 'Aspire to be a doctor or a lawyer, but not a gangster'. As one of the singles lifted from *Black Reign* advocates: 'UNITY (Who You Calling A Bitch?)'.

●ALBUMS: *All Hail The Queen* (Tommy Boy 1989)★★★★, *Nature Of A Sista* (Tommy Boy 1991)★★★, *Black Reign* (Motown 1993)★★★.

QUEENSRŸCHE

Queensrÿche were formed in Seattle, USA, by Geoff Tate (vocals), Chris DeGarmo (guitar), Michael Wilton (guitar), Eddie Jackson (bass), and Scott Rockenfield (drums), from the ashes of club circuit band the Mob and, in Tate's case, the Myth. Immediately Tate offered them a distinctive vocal edge, having studied opera but turned to hard rock because of the lyrical freedom it offered. A four-track demo tape recorded in the basement of Rockenfield's parents' house in June 1982 led to record store owners Kim and Diana Harris offering to manage the band. The tape itself took on a life of its own, circulating throughout the north west of America, and in May 1983 the band launched their own 206 Records label to house the songs on a self-titled 12-inch EP (lead track, 'Queen Of The Reich', had long since given them their name). The EP caused quite a stir in rock circles and led to EMI Records offering them a seven-album contract. The record was quickly re-released and grazed the UK Top 75, although the band's sound was still embryonic and closer to Britain's New Wave Of British Heavy Metal than the progressive rock flavour that would become their hallmark. Their first full album for EMI, *The Warning*, was comparatively disappointing, failing to live up to the promise shown on the EP, particularly in the poor mix which was the subject of some concern for both the record company and band. Only 'Road To Madness' and 'Take Hold Of The Flame', two perennial live favourites, met expectations. *Rage For Order* followed in 1986 and saw the band creating a more distinctive style, making full use of modern technology, yet somehow the production (this time from Neil Kernon) seemed to have over-compensated. Although a dramatic improvement, and the first genuine showcase for Tate's incredible vocal range and the twin guitar sound of DeGarmo and Wilton, the songs emerged as clinical and neutered. 1988 saw the Peter Collins-produced *Operation Mindcrime*, a George Orwell-inspired concept album that was greeted with enthusiastic critical acclaim on its release. With some of the grandiose futurism of earlier releases dispelled, and additional orchestration from Michael Kamen, worldwide sales of over one million confirmed this as the album to lift the band into rock's first division. In the wake of its forerunner, there was something positively minimal about *Empire*, which boasted a stripped-down but still dream like rock aesthetic best sampled on the single, 'Silent Lucidity', a Top 5 US hit, which was also nominated for a Grammy. The album itself earned Top 10 placings on both sides of the Atlantic. Only single releases broke a four-year recording gap between *Empire* and 1994's *Promised Land*, the most notable of which was 1993's 'Real World', included on the soundtrack to the Arnold Schwarzenegger flop *Last Action Hero*. Though a more personal and reflective set, *Promised Land* continued the band's tradition of dramatic song structures, this time without Kamen's arranging skills. Well over a decade into a career which at first seemed of limited appeal, Queensrÿche's popularity continues to grow.

●ALBUMS: *The Warning* (EMI 1984)★★, *Rage For Order* (EMI 1986)★★, *Operation Mindcrime* (EMI 1988)★★★, *Empire* (EMI 1990)★★★, *Promised Land* (EMI 1994)★★★, *Hear In The New Frontier* (EMI 1997)★★★.

●COMPILATIONS: *Queensrÿche* includes *Queensrÿche* and *Prophecy* EPs (EMI 1988).

●VIDEOS: *Live In Tokyo* (1985), *Video Mindcrime* (1989), *Operation Live Crime* (1991), *Building Empires* (1992).

QUIET RIOT

Heavy metal band Quiet Riot had their 'five minutes' of fame in 1983 with a remake of a Slade song, 'Cum On Feel The Noize', and a US number 1 album, *Metal Health* - the first metal album to reach that position in the US charts. However, they were unable to maintain that momentum with subsequent releases. The band formed in 1975 with lanky vocalist Kevin DuBrow (b. 1955), Randy Rhoads (guitar), Drew Forsyth (drums) and Kelly Garni (bass), taking their name from a suggestion made by Status Quo's Rick Parfitt. They recorded two albums with that line-up, released only in Japan, which are now collector's items. Rudy Sarzo then replaced Garni. Rhoads left in 1979 to join Ozzy Osbourne and was later tragically killed in a plane crash in March 1982. At that point the band briefly split up, with some members joining the vocalist in a band called DuBrow, Sarzo also working with Ozzy. Quiet Riot regrouped around DuBrow, Sarzo, guitarist Carlos Cavazo and drummer Frankie Banali and signed to the Pasha label for their breakthrough album and single in 1983, their musical and visual style fashioned after the harder rocking glam acts of the 70s. Friction within the group followed their quick success and resultant publicity affected sales of the follow-up, *Condition Critical*, which reached number 15 in the US charts but was considered disappointing. After several personnel changes Quiet Riot recorded another album in 1986, which reached number 31 but showed a marked decline in the group's creativity. DuBrow was subsequently ejected from the band and a self-titled 1988 album, with new vocalist Paul Shortino (ex-Rough Cutt), barely made the charts. The group then disbanded, with DuBrow going on to form Little Women. Banali later worked with W.A.S.P.

●ALBUMS: *Quiet Riot* (Columbia Japan 1977)★★, *Quiet Riot II* (Columbia Japan 1978)★★, *Metal Health* (Epic 1983)★★★, *Condition Critical* (Epic 1984)★★, *QRIII* (Epic 1986)★, *Quiet Riot* (Pasha 1988)★.

●COMPILATIONS: *Wild Young And Crazee* (Raw Power 1987)★★, *The Randy Rhoads Years* (Rhino 1993)★★.

●FILMS: *Footloose - (Soundtrack Song)* (1984).

R. CAJUN AND THE ZYDECO BROTHERS

R. Cajun were formed in 1979 by Chris Hall, a former member of Shufflin' Sam and a keen enthusiast of Cajun music. The original line-up was Chris Hall (b. 2 July 1952, Sheffield, Yorkshire, England; accordion/vocals), Tony Dark (fiddle), Alf Billington (guitar/vocals), and Veronica Matthews (triangle). The following year, Trevor Hopkins (bass) joined the line-up, but was soon replaced by Beeds (b. 13 October 1947, Derby, Derbyshire, England; guitar/harmonica). The line-up, which started to make some impact on the folk circuit in 1982, consisted of Hall, Billington, John Squire (fiddle/guitar/mandolin), who joined that year, as did Beeds, and Jan Hall (b. 17 January 1953, Sheffield, Yorkshire, England; triangle/percussion). *Bayou Rhythms* included the Zydeco Brothers, Graham Jones (bass) and Neil 'Freddy' Hopwood (b. 23 April 1947, Lichfield, Staffordshire, England; drums). Hopwood had formerly been a member of Dr. Strangely Strange, and the Sutherland Brothers bands. The album contained some infectious pieces such as 'Cajun Two-Step', and 'Bayou Pom Pom Special', as well as standards such as 'Jambalaya' and 'Deportees', and quickly established them as a popular group at festivals. In 1984, Dave Blant (b. 27 November 1949, Burton Upon Trent, Staffordshire, England; bass/vocals) joined, replacing Graham Jones. Having previously left the group, Tony Dark rejoined them in 1986, in turn replacing John Squire. The same year, Clive Harvey (b. 27 November 1945, Watford, Hertfordshire, England; guitar/vocals), was added. It was this line-up that recorded *Pig Sticking In Arcadia*. Three years later, Dark again left the group, to be replaced by Derek Richardson (fiddle), then Dave 'Mitch' Proctor (b. 8 December 1952, Heanor, Derbyshire, England; fiddle) joined in 1990, replacing Richardson. Despite the various personnel changes, the overall sound of the group has remained remarkably constant. Their blend of cajun and zydeco, apart from being unusual, has added to the band's original sound and style. They continue playing festivals, both at home and abroad, where they are equally popular. Chris Hall is the co-owner of Swamp, an organization that runs Bearcat Records and the UK's top cajun venue, The Swamp Club, in Derby.

●ALBUMS: *Bayou Rhythms* (Moonraker 1984)★★★, *Pig Sticking In Arcadia* (Disc Ethnique 1987)★★★, *Out Of The Swamp* (1990)★★★, *No Known Cure* (1993)★★★, *That Cajun Thing* (Bearcat 1994)★★★.

R.E.M.

R.E.M. played their first concert in Athens, Georgia, USA, on 19 April 1980. Their line-up, then as now, consisted of four drop-outs from the University of Georgia; Michael Stipe (b. 4 January 1960, Decatur, Georgia, USA; vocals), Peter Buck (b. 6 December 1956, Los Angeles, California, USA; guitar), Mike Mills (b. 17 December 1958, Orange County, California, USA; bass) and Bill Berry (b. 31 July 1958, Duluth, Minnesota, USA; drums). Without the charisma of Stipe and his eccentric onstage behaviour, hurling himself about with abandon in-between mumbling into the microphone, they could easily have been overlooked as just another bar band, relying on the harmonious guitar sound of the Byrds for their inspiration. Acquiring a healthy following among the college fraternity in their hometown, it was not long before they entered the studio to record their debut single 'Radio Free Europe', to be released independently on Hibtone Records. This was greeted with considerable praise by critics who conceded that the band amounted to more than the sum of their influences. Their country/folk sound was contradicted by a driving bassline and an urgency that put the listener more in mind of the Who in their early mod phase. Add to this the distinctive voice of Stipe and his, on the whole, inaudible, perhaps even non-existent, lyrics, and R.E.M. sounded quite unlike any other band in the USA, in the post-punk era of the early 80s. Gaining further favourable notices for the *Chronic Town* mini-LP, their debut full-length album was now eagerly anticipated; when it arrived in 1983 it surpassed all expectations, and was eventually made Album Of The Year by *Rolling Stone* magazine. As in the USA, the band earned a devoted cult following in Europe, largely comprised of college students, as a result of *Murmur*.

Reckoning appeared the following year and was permeated by a reckless spontaneity that had been missing from their earlier work. Recorded in only 12 days, the tracks varied in mood from frustration,

as on 'So. Central Rain', to the tongue-in-cheek singalong '(Don't Go Back To) Rockville'. The songs were accessible enough but, as would be the case for most of the 80s, the singles culled from R.E.M.'s albums were generally deemed uncommercial by mainstream radio programmers. However, their cult reputation benefited from a series of flop singles on both sides of the Atlantic. Although received enthusiastically by critics, *Fables Of The Reconstruction* was a stark, morose album that mirrored a period of despondency within the band. Peter Buck summed it up in the 90s - 'If we were to record those songs again, they would be very different'. *Life's Rich Pageant*, in 1986, showed the first signs of a politicization within the band that would come to a head, and coincide with their commercial breakthrough, in the late 80s. Stipe's lyrics began to dwell increasingly on the prevailing amorality in the USA and question its inherited ethics, while still retaining their much vaunted obliqueness. Tracks such as 'These Days' and 'Cuyahoga' were rallying cries to the young and disaffected; although the lyrics were reflective and almost bitter, the music was the most joyous and uplifting the band had recorded to date. This ironic approach to songwriting was typified by 'It's The End Of The World As We Know It (And I Feel Fine)', from the equally impressive *Document*. Released also as a single, it intentionally trivialized its subject matter with a witty and up-tempo infectiousness, more characteristic of the Housemartins.

Green arrived in 1988 and sold slowly but steadily in the USA, the attendant single 'Stand' reaching number 6 there, while 'Orange Crush' entered the UK Top 30. Apart from demonstrating their environmental awareness, particularly in 'You Are The Everything', the album laid more emphasis than previously on Stipe's vocals and lyrics. This, to the singer's dismay, led to his elevation as 'spokesman for a generation'. Already hero-worshiped by adoring long-term fans, Stipe insists 'Rock 'n' roll is a joke, people who take it seriously are the butt of the joke'. The world tour that coincided with the album's release saw R.E.M. making a smooth transition from medium-size venues to the stadium circuit, due as much to Stipe's individual choreography as to the elaborate projected backdrops. After a break of two years the band re-emerged in 1991 with *Out Of Time*. Their previous use of horns and mandolins to embroider songs did not prepare their audience for the deployment of an entire string section, nor were the contributions from B-52s singer Kate Pierson and Boogie Down

Productions' KRS-1 expected. Ostensibly all love songs, the album was unanimously hailed as a masterpiece and entered the UK Top 5 on its release, topping both US and UK album charts shortly afterwards. The accompanying singles from that album 'Losing My Religion', 'Shiny Happy People', and 'Near Wild Heaven' gave them further hits. After picking up countless awards during the early 90s the band has maintained the high standard set by *Out Of Time*. *Automatic For The People* was released in October 1992, to universal favour. It reached the top of the charts in the UK and USA. Michael Stipe was seen both as pin-up and creative genius. The album produced a number of memorable singles including the moody 'Drive' and the joyous 'Man In The Moon', with its classic Elvis Presley vocal inflections from Stipe and an accompanying award-winning monochrome video. *Monster* showed the band in grungelike mode, not letting any accusations of selling out bother them, and certainly letting fans and critics alike know that they had not gone soft. 'What's The Frequency Kenneth?' started a run of further hit singles taken from the album and further awards were heaped upon them. Following the collapse of Bill Berry in Switzerland while on a major tour in 1995 the band were forced to rest. Berry was operated on for a ruptured aneurysm and he made a full recovery. In August 1996 the band re-signed with Warner Brothers Records for the largest recording contract advance in history. $80 million was guaranteed for a five album contract. *New Adventures In Hi-Fi* was released in September. Retaining the harder edged sound of Monster on most tracks it was another excellent collection. From the epic chord changes of 'Be Mine' to the cool understated calm of 'How the West Was Won And Where It Got Us', the band have remarkable depth and ideas. The critical praise heaped upon the band has been monumental, and through all the attention the band appear united, reasonably unaffected and painfully modest. They are one of the most important and popular groups to appear over the past three decades, and still retain massive credibility.
●ALBUMS: *Chronic Town* mini-album (IRS 1982)★★★, *Murmur* (IRS 1983)★★★★, *Reckoning* (IRS 1984)★★★, *Fables Of The Reconstruction* (IRS 1985)★★★, *Life's Rich Pageant* (IRS 1986)★★★, *Document* (IRS 1987)★★★, *Green* (Warners 1988)★★★★, *Out Of Time* (Warners 1991)★★★★, *Automatic For The People* (Warners 1992)★★★★, *Monster* (Warners 1994)★★★★, *New Adventures In Hi-Fi* (Warners 1996)★★★★★.

●COMPILATIONS: *Dead Letter Office* (IRS 1987)★★★, *Eponymous* (IRS 1988)★★★.
●VIDEOS: *Athens, Ga - Inside Out* (A&M 1986), *Succumbs* (A&M 1987), *Pop Screen* (Warner 1990), *This Film Is On* (Warner Reprise 1991), *Tour Film* (Warner Reprise 1991), *Parallel* (Warner Music Vision 1995), *Road Movie* (Warner Vision 1996).
●FURTHER READING: *Remarks: Story Of R.E.M.*, Tony Heylin Fletcher. *R.E.M.: Behind The Mask*, Jim Greer. *R.E.M.: File Under Water, The Definitive Guide To 12 Years Of Recordings And Con*, Jon Storey. *An R.E.M. Companion: It Crawled From The South*, Marcus Gray. *The Rolling Stone Files*, no editor listed. *Talk About The Passion: R.E.M. An Oral History*, Denise Sullivan. *R.E.M. Documental*, Dave Bowler and Bryan Dray.

RAIN

This group originated in Liverpool, England in the late 80s and adopted the heritage of harmony pop in the vein of the Byrds. Rain were initially notable by dint of having three good harmony singers to back up their Rickenbacker guitar sound. They formed at the Merseyside Trade Union Community And Unemployed Resource Centre in Liverpool, set up with a £100,000 grant. The band's original locale was the severely depressed Huyton area, but eight months later they were signed to CBS Records and worked on album sessions with Nick Lowe. After a debut single, 'Lemonstone Desired', they courted controversy with the provocative nudity featured on the cover of 'Taste Of Rain'. Their debut album was honed by months of rehearsal with guest appearances by Green On Red and blues musician Joe Louis Walker. The band comprise Ned Clark, Colin Murphy (singers, guitarists and songwriters), Martin Campbell and Tony McGuigan (bass and drums).
●ALBUMS: *A Taste Of Rain* (Columbia 1991)★★★.
●FILMS: *Birth Of The Beatles* (1979).

RAIN PARADE

Part of Los Angeles' rock renaissance of the early 80s, the Rain Parade drew from late 60s influences to forge a new brand of psychedelia-tinged rock. After a promising debut single, 'What She's Done To Your Mind', on their own Llama label, the band - David Roback (vocals/guitar/percussion), brother Steve (vocals/bass), Matthew Piucci (vocals/guitar/sitar), Will Glenn (keyboards/violin) and Eddie Kalwa (drums) - issued *Emergency Third Rail Power Trip* to critical acclaim in 1983, followed by the excellent 'You Are My Friend' in 1985. Such was their impetus that the Rain Parade signed with

Island Records, despite the loss of key figure David Roback (who then formed Opal with partner and original Rain Parade bassist Kendra Smith, eventually re-emerging in Mazzy Star). His replacement, John Thoman, arrived alongside new drummer Mark Marcum in time for *Beyond The Sunset*, drawn from live performances in Japan. A second studio set, *Crashing Dream*, emerged later in the year, but some of the original Rain Parade's otherworldly, evocative nature had been lost. Piucci would go on to form Gone Fishin'. He also recorded an album with Neil Young's Crazy Horse.

● ALBUMS: *Emergency Third Rail Power Trip* (Enigma 1983)★★★, *Beyond The Sunset* (Restless 1985)★★★, *Crashing Dream* (Island 1985)★★★.

RAINCOATS

This female outfit epitomized the experimental approach that characterized much of punk's aftermath. The group were formed at Hornsey Art College, London, in 1976 by Gina Birch and Ana Da Silva. Augmented by Vicky Aspinall and manager Shirley O'Loughlin, they were originally joined by Palmolive before she left to concentrate on the Slits. This line-up was merely a nucleus for a flexible structure that involved numerous other musicians. As Birch recalls: 'We didn't exactly ignore the audience, but for us, playing was an emotional thing. We would struggle, we would cry, we didn't really know what we were doing half the time'. The Raincoats' debut, 'Fairytale In The Supermarket', appeared on Rough Trade Records (a label that shared their ground-breaking stance) in 1979. It would sell a healthy 25,000 copies. A self-titled album that same year boasted a similarly distinctive sound and both were revered by critics and a hardcore of admirers alike. *Odyshape* followed in 1981, but was less direct than their debut. Two further singles, a cover of Sly Stone's 'Running Away' (1982) and 'Animal Rhapsody' (1983) both hinted at unfulfilled potential. The Raincoats eventually delivered their swansong in 1984 with *Moving*. However, as fitting an epitaph as any can be found on *The Kitchen Tapes*, on the ROIR label, originally released in 1983. The group may have remained of historical interest only had not one of their biggest US fans, Kurt Cobain of Nirvana, tracked down Ana Da Silva to an antique shop in Notting Hill, London. In exchange for a customized original of the band's debut album, Cobain offered the Raincoats the chance to reform and support Nirvana on upcoming UK dates (he would also write sleevenotes for the CD reissues of their albums). Thus the 1994 model Raincoats, who featured Da Silva with Birch, joined by violinist Anne Wood and drummer Steve Shelley (a stand-in on loan from Sonic Youth). Palmolive was said to have departed for a life of religious evangelicism in Texas, while Aspinall was busy running a dance label. The band reformed in late 1995 and issued *Looking In The Shadows* in 1996. The original members De Silva and Gina Birch were augmented by ex-Bratmobile Heather Dunn (drums) and Anne Wood (violin).

● ALBUMS: *The Raincoats* (Rough Trade 1979)★★★, *Odyshape* (Rough Trade 1981)★★, *The Kitchen Tapes* (ROIR 1983)★★★, *Moving* (Rough Trade 1984)★★★, *Looking In The Shadows* (Geffen 1996)★★★.

● COMPILATIONS: *Fairytales* (Tim/Kerr 1995)★★★.

RAMONE, PHIL

b. USA. One of his country's most venerable and talented producers, Phil Ramone's interests in music began at the age of three, when he undertook violin and piano lessons. A child prodigy, his studies of classical violin brought him to world renown before he was even a teenager, including a command performance for Queen Elizabeth II aged just 10. During his adolescence he was enticed away from classical music by pop and rock 'n' roll, leading to his first job as an engineer in New York, where he cut his musical teeth. In this discipline he worked on landmark recordings such as Arlo Guthrie's 'Alice's Restaurant', João and Astrud Gilberto's 'The Girl From Ipanema', Wings' 'Uncle Albert/Admiral Halsey' and B.J. Thomas's 'Raindrops Keep Fallin' On My Head'. His production work is even more extensive, encompassing work with Billy Joel, Frank Sinatra, Paul Simon, Julian Lennon, Barbra Streisand, Gloria Estefan, Bob Dylan, Dionne Warwick, Sinéad O'Connor, Peter, Paul And Mary and Chicago. His soundtrack work on films his other great passion, includes *Midnight Cowboy*, *Flashdance* and *A Star Is Born*. His theatrical commissions include *Hair* and *Promises, Promises*, while producing cast albums of productions including *Little Shop Of Horrors* and *Starlight Express*. Ramone's most distinctive quality is his ability to combine a love of music's essence with a keen interest in emerging technology - he was one of the earliest and most vocal acolytes of compact discs when they were first introduced in the 80s. Indeed, the first CD single ever released, Billy Joel's 'The Stranger', was a Ramone production. Despite accruing substantial wealth from his production work, in the 90s he showed no signs of slowing down, working with Johnny Mathis, Patricia Kaas, Michael Crawford, Barry Manilow and many others in 1995 and 1996. By this time he had received eight Grammy awards for his work, a total exceeded by only one other producer, Quincy Jones.

RATT

This heavy metal group formed in Los Angeles, California, USA, and featured Stephen Pearcy (vocals), Robbin Crosby (guitar), Warren DeMartini (guitar), Juan Croucier (bass) and Bobby 'The Blotz' Blotzer (drums). They evolved out of 70s band Mickey Ratt, transmuting into their present form in 1983, with a hint of pop about their brand of metal similar to Cheap Trick or Aerosmith. They released a self-titled mini-album in 1983 on a local label, and struck up a close personal friendship with members of Mötley Crüe, which no doubt helped them to sign to Atlantic Records the following year. They made their breakthrough with their first full album, *Out Of The Cellar*, which stayed in the *Billboard* Top 20 for six months. They toured with Ozzy Osbourne before joining a Billy Squier jaunt where they were apparently 'thrown off' because they were more popular than the headline act. Their subsequent output has seen them follow a familiar heavy metal route with accusations over sexist videos contrasting with their ability to sell out concert halls and produce recordings that regularly received gold discs. *Decimater* featured several songs co-written with Desmond Child and proved their most adventurous recording to date, though Crosby would depart after *Rat 'n' Roll*. In 1993 Pearcy unveiled his new outfit, Arcade, confirming the dissolution of the band. In 1996 Pearcy formed Vertex.
●ALBUMS: *Ratt* (Time Coast 1983)★★, *Out Of The Cellar* (Atlantic 1984)★★, *Invasion Of Your Privacy* (Atlantic 1985)★★, *Dancing Undercover* (Atlantic 1986)★★, *Reach For The Sky* (Atlantic 1988)★★★, *Decimater* (Atlantic 1990)★★★, *Rat 'n' Roll* (East West 1991)★★★.
●VIDEOS: *The Video* (1986).

RATTLESNAKE ANNIE

b. Rosan Gallimore, 26 December 1941, Paris, Tennessee, USA. Rattlesnake Annie, of Cherokee heritage, was born into a family of tobacco and cotton farmers. They had no electricity or modern conveniences, apart from a radio, on which Gallimore would hear country music from Nashville. Many of her songs are about those years. and laterly about her heritage. As part of the

Gallimore Sisters, she appeared on the *Junior Grand Ole Opry*. In 1954 she married Max McGowan. Her first album was self-financed and featured Nashville musicians and established her as both a performer and a songwriter. She has been accepted in the UK and even more so in Czechoslovakia where her album with local country star, Michal Tucny, went platinum. She recorded 'Long Black Limousine' with Willie Nelson - a friend of several decades.
●ALBUMS: *Rattlesnakes And Rusty Water* (Rattlesnake 1979)★★★, *Country Livin'* (Rattlesnake 1981)★★★★, with Michal Tucny *Rattlesnake Annie And The Last Cowboy* (Supraphon 1982)★★★, *Rattlesnake Annie* (Sony/Columbia 1987)★★★, *Rattlesnake Annie Sings Hank Williams* (Rattlesnake 1988)★★★★, *A Time For Feelings* (Dino 1992)★★★, *Crossroads* (Sony/Columbia 1993)★★★, *Indian Dreams* (Sony 1993)★★★, *Painted Bird* (Rattlesnake 1994)★★★, *Adios Last Cowboy* (Sony 1995)★★★, *Troubadour* (Sony 1996)★★★, *Some Stories Never End* (Sony 1997)★★★.

RAVEN, EDDY

b. Edward Garvin Futch, 19 August 1944, Lafayette, Louisiana, USA. Eddy, one of 11 children, was raised in bayou country. His father, a truck driver and blues guitarist, would take him to honky tonks. He was given a guitar, and by the time he was 13 years old, he was playing in a rock 'n' roll band. When the family moved to Georgia in 1960, he worked for a radio station and recorded his own song as Eddy Raven, 'Once A Fool', for the small Cosmo label. They returned to Lafayette in 1963 and Eddy worked in La Louisianne record store and also made singles for the owner's label. In 1969 he recorded *That Crazy Cajun Sound*, which impressed Jimmy C. Newman, who secured Raven a songwriting contract in Nashville with Acuff-Rose. He also worked as lead singer for Jimmie Davis's band and toured with him during an election campaign for Governor of Louisiana. In 1971 Don Gibson had a Top 5 US country hit with Raven's 'Country Green', which was followed by Jeannie C. Riley's 'Good Morning, Country Rain'. He also wrote 'Back In The Country' (Roy Acuff), 'Sometimes I Talk In My Sleep' (Randy Cornor) and 'Touch The Morning' (Don Gibson). He had his first US country chart entry with 'The Last Of The Sunshine Cowboys' in 1974 for ABC Records and then recorded for Monument ('You're A Dancer') and Dimension ('Sweet Mother Texas', 'Dealin' With The Devil'). He had four country hits from his

Elektra album, *Desperate Dreams*, including 'Who Do You Know In California?' and 'She's Playing Hard To Forget'. A second album for Elektra was never released and Raven spent two years resolving management problems. He wrote a Top 5 country record for the Oak Ridge Boys, 'Thank God For Kids'. He came back on RCA Records in 1984 with the escapist theme of 'I Got Mexico', a style to which he returned in 1988 for 'Joe Knows How To Live'. Other hits followed, including 'I Could Use Another You', 'Shine Shine Shine' and 'You're Never Too Old For Young Love'. He went to number 1 with a bluesy song written by Dennis Linde and first recorded by Billy Swan, 'I'm Gonna Get You'. Linde also wrote his 1989 number 1, 'In A Letter To You', for the new Universal label. That year he also returned to the cajun sounds of his youth for 'Bayou Boys' in a mixture he describes as 'electric cajun'. In 1991 he moved to the ninth label of his career, Capitol Records.

●ALBUMS: *That Cajun Country Sound* (La Louisianne 1969)★★★, *This Is Eddy Raven* (ABC/Dot 1976)★★★, *Eyes* (Dimension 1979)★★★, *Desperate Dreams* (Elektra 1981)★★★★, *I Could Use Another You* (RCA 1985)★★★, *Love And Other Hard Times* (RCA 1986)★★★, *Right Hand Man* (RCA 1987)★★★, *Temporary Sanity* (Universal 1989)★★★, *Right For The Flight* (Capitol 1991)★★★, *Wide Eyed And Crazy* (Intersound 1994)★★★.

REA, CHRIS

b. 4 March 1951, Middlesborough, Cleveland, England. Rea is a songwriter, singer and guitarist with a wide following throughout Europe. Of Irish/Italian parentage, he grew up in the northeast of England where his family owned an ice cream parlour. Rea's first group was Magdalene, a local band in which he replaced David Coverdale, who had joined Deep Purple. As Beautiful Losers, the band won a national talent contest in 1975 but remained unsuccessful. Rea went solo, signing to Magnet Records where Gus Dudgeon produced his first album. With a title referring to a suggested stage-name for Rea, it included the impassioned 'Fool (If You Think It's Over)' which reached the Top 20 in the US and was later covered successfully in Britain by Elkie Brooks. With the UK in the grip of punk and new wave, Rea's earliest supporters were in Germany, and throughout the first part of the 80s he steadily gained in popularity across the Continent through his gruff, bluesy singing and rock guitar solos, notably the instrumental track, 'Deltics'. His backing group was led by experienced

keyboards player Max Middleton. Rea's most successful record at this time was 'I Can Hear Your Heartbeat' from *Water Sign* In Britain, the breakthrough album proved to be *Shamrock Diaries*. Both it and 'Stainsby Girls' (a slice of nostalgia for the northern England of his adolescence) reached the Top 30 in 1985. Two years later, *Dancing With Strangers* briefly went to number 2 in the UK charts although the gritty 'Joys Of Christmas' was commercially unsuccessful.

In 1988, WEA acquired Rea's contract through buying Magnet, and issued a compilation album that sold well throughout Europe. The album reached the Top 5 in the UK and suddenly Rea was fashionable, something that this unpretentious artist has been trying to live down ever since. This was followed by his first UK number 1, *The Road To Hell*, one of the most successful albums of 1989-1990. The powerful title track told of an encounter with the ghost of the singer's mother and a warning that he had betrayed his roots. Like its predecessor, *Auberge* topped the UK chart while its title track reached the UK Top 20. 'Julia', a track from *Espresso Logic*, became his 27th UK hit in November 1993. Rea remains loyal to his roots and refuses to join the rock *cognoscenti*.

●ALBUMS: *Whatever Happened To Benny Santini* (Magnet 1978)★★★, *Deltics* (Magnet 1979)★★, *Tennis* (Magnet 1980)★★, *Chris Rea* (Magnet 1982)★★, *Water Sign* (Magnet 1983)★★, *Wired To The Moon* (Magnet 1984)★★, *Shamrock Diaries* (Magnet 1985)★★, *On The Beach* (Magnet 1986)★★★★, *Dancing With Strangers* (Magnet 1987)★★★★, *The Road To Hell* (Warners 1989)★★★★, *Auberge* (Atco 1991)★★★★, *God's Great Banana Skin* (East West 1992)★★★, *Espresso Logic* (1993)★★★, *La Passione* soundtrack (East West 1996)★★.

●COMPILATIONS: *New Light Through Old Windows* (Warners 1988)★★★.

RED DOGS

This blues-based UK rock 'n' roll quintet was formed in 1989 by Mickey 'The Vicar' Ripley (vocals) and Chris John (guitar). Enlisting the services of Mick Young (bass), Paul Guerin (guitar) and Stow (drums), the band signed to Episode Records the following year. They debuted with *Wrong Side Of Town*, a six-track offering which took the Rolling Stones as its primary influence. The Red Dogs raised their profile by supporting Cheap And Nasty and UFO on their 1991 UK tours. Taking their infectious brand of bar-room boogie to a larger stage proved initially successful, though afterwards they failed to heighten their profile significantly. Ripley departed and formed Josh in 1996.

●ALBUMS: *Wrong Side Of Town* mini-album (Episode 1989)★★★.

REDD KROSS

This Los Angeles, California, USA band was formed in 1979. Redd Kross melded elements of 70s glam-rock, 60s psychedelia and 80s heavy metal to become a popular 'alternative' act in the 80s. Originally called the Tourists, the band changed its name to Red Cross. (They were later forced to change the spelling after the International Red Cross organization threatened to sue.) At the beginning, the band consisted of 15-year-old Jeff McDonald as singer, his 11-year-old brother Steve on bass, Greg Hetson on guitar and Ron Reyes on drums. After gaining local recognition opening for such punk outfits as Black Flag, Red Cross made its first recordings in 1980 for a compilation album on the punk label Posh Boy Records. Shortly afterwards Hetson left to form the Circle Jerks and Reyes joined Black Flag. The band signed with manager John Silva and he went on to manage Nirvana and Sonic Youth following introductions by members of Red Kross. Other musicians came and went throughout the band's history, the McDonald brothers being the only mainstay. The group's popularity grew steadily, particularly among those who listened to college radio stations, and by the end of the 80s they had recorded three albums in addition to the debut. Some featured cover versions of songs by such influences as the Rolling Stones and Kiss, while elsewhere the group's originals seemed to cross 70s punk with the bubblegum hits of the 60s. The group resurfaced in the autumn of 1990 with *Third Eye*, their first album for a major label, Atlantic Records. However, it was 1993's *Phaseshifter* that brought about their commercial breakthrough, with the band continuing to record catchy post-punk homages to 70s kitsch.

●ALBUMS: *Born Innocent* (Smoke 7 1982)★★, *Teen Babes From Monsanto* (Gasatanka 1984)★★★, *Neurotica* (Big Time 1987)★★★, *Third Eye* (Atlantic 1990)★★, *Phaseshifter* (This Way Up 1993)★★★, *Showtime* (This Way Up 1997)★★★, *Show World* (This Way Up 1997)★★★★.

REEVES, DIANNE

b. 1956, Detroit, Michigan, USA. A vocalist with an international reputation and following, Dianne Reeves made her name in the late 80s, when she was discovered by Blue Note Records during a worldwide revival of interest in jazz. A gifted technician with a genuine swing feel, Reeves' career has tended to reflect the difficult fortunes of the singer trying to find a voice in contemporary jazz, without succumbing to the financially dominant worlds of soul or R&B. Born in Detroit but raised from the age of two in Denver, Reeves was still in high school, singing with the high school big band, when she was spotted by swing trumpeter Clark Terry at the National Association of Jazz Educators Conference in Chicago. Terry's encouragement and advice led her to study at the University of Colorado, where she was able to perform with him, and later to move to California and pursue music full time. In Los Angeles in the mid-70s, Reeves' range and rich, expressive natural voice, led her quickly into the west coast's famous studio scene, where she became very much in demand, recording for drummer Lenny White, saxophonist Stanley Turrentine and drummer Alphonzo Johnson. Between 1978 and 1980, she worked full-time with Los Angeles-based pianist Billy Childs, whom Reeves still credits for giving her a chance to experiment and grow, whilst working almost nightly. Still studying (under vocal coach Phil Moore), she had her first big international exposure in 1981, touring with Sergio Mendes. Reeves recorded her first album a year later. *Welcome To My Love*, co-produced by Childs and released on Palo Alto Jazz, set the trend for the original material that helped distinguish much of Reeves' work in later years. But it was in 1987 that she got her biggest break, when Blue Note Records president Bruce Lundvall spotted her at an Echoes Of Ellington concert in Los Angeles, and wasted no time in setting up her first major session. The resulting *Dianne Reeves* features George Duke, Freddie Hubbard, Herbie Hancock, Tony Williams, Stanley Clarke and her old friend Billy Childs, and rocketed Reeves onto the international festival circuit. Despite a long-running flirtation with R&B and soul (her discography is split almost exactly down the middle), Reeves has managed to retain her jazz credibility, most recently releasing *Quiet After The Storm*, a superb world music-influenced jazz record with guest contributions by saxophonist Joshua Redman, trumpeter Roy Hargrove, flautist Hubert Laws, guitarist Kevin Eubanks and percussionist Airto Moreira.

●ALBUMS: *Welcome To My Love* (Palo Alto Jazz 1982)★★★, *For Every Heart* (Palo Alto Jazz 1985)★★★, *Dianne Reeves* (Blue Note 1987)★★★, *Never Too Far* (EMI 1989)★★★, *I Remember* (EMI

1990)★★★, *Art And Survival* (EMI 1994)★★★, *Quiet After The Storm* (Blue Note 1995)★★★★, *The Grand Encounter* (Blue Note 1996)★★★★.

REMLER, EMILY

b. 18 September 1957, New York City, New York, USA, d. 4 May 1990, Australia. Emily Remler began playing guitar as a small child and her early preference for rock was superseded by jazz while studying at Berklee College Of Music. After leaving Berklee in 1976 she began performing professionally, playing club, concert and festival engagements across the USA. A residency in New Orleans attracted attention when she was called upon to accompany important visiting instrumentalists and singers. She was heard by Herb Ellis, who actively encouraged her career, helping her to obtain her first recording date, for Concord, and an appearance at the Concord Jazz Festival. She continued to tour, particularly with Astrud Gilberto, and made a fine duo album, *Together*, with Larry Coryell. Other guitarists with whom she worked were Barney Kessel and Charlie Byrd. A strikingly gifted performer with eclectic musical tastes, she played with flair and her dazzling technique was built upon a deep knowledge and understanding of all forms of jazz. Appealing alike to audiences, critics and her fellow musicians, she rapidly gained respect and admiration for her dedication, enthusiasm and remarkable skills. That someone as gifted as this should have died so young (although she was addicted to heroin) and so unexpectedly was a major loss to the jazz world. Her death, at the age of 32, came while she was on tour in Australia. Remler had played on David Benoit's *Waiting For Spring* and he wrote the beautiful 'Six String Poet' in her memory on his *Inner Motion*.
●ALBUMS: *The Firefly* (Concord 1981)★★, *Take Two* (Concord 1982)★★, *Transitions* (Concord 1983)★★★, *Catwalk* (Concord 1985), with Larry Coryell *Together* (1985)★★★, *East To Wes* (Concord 1988)★★★★.
●COMPILATIONS: *Retrospective Vols 1 & 2* (Concord 1989)★★★★, various artists *Just Friends: A Gathering In Tribute To Emily Remler Vol. 2* (1992)★★★, *This Is Me* (Justice 1992)★★★.

REPLACEMENTS

This pop-punk group was formed in Minneapolis, Minnesota, USA, in 1979, with Paul Westerberg (b. 31 December 1960, Minneapolis, USA; guitar/vocals), Tommy Stinson (b. 6 October 1966, San Diego, California, USA; bass), Bob Stinson (b. 17 December 1959, Mound, Minnesota, USA, d. 18

February 1995; guitar) and Chris Mars (b. 26 April 1961, Minneapolis, USA; drums). Originally the Impediments, their early shambolic, drunken gigs forced a name change to secure further work. Their debut album for the local Twin/Tone label showcased their self-proclaimed power trash style, earning comparisons with hardcore legends Hüsker Dü. Subsequent albums saw the group diversifying to encompass influences from folk, country, and blues without straying far from their winning formula of rock 'n' roll married to the raw passion of punk rock. Beloved by critics on both sides of the Atlantic, the group appeared on the verge of mainstream success in America with the release of *Pleased To Meet Me*. Bob Stinson was replaced by Slim Dunlap and Westerberg was at the height of his songwriting powers on the suicide anthem, 'The Ledge', and the achingly melodic 'Skyway'. Greater success somehow eluded them and *All Shook Down* was a largely subdued affair, hinting at an impending solo career for Westerburg. However, it was Mars who would become the first ex-Replacement to record following the band's dissolution in 1990. Westerberg too would go on to sign under his own name, while Tommy Stinson formed his own bands, Bash And Pop and then Perfect. Dunlap reappeared on Dan Baird's debut solo album. Bob Stinson died in 1995 of a suspected drug overdose.
●ALBUMS: *Sorry, Ma, Forgot To Take Out The Trash* (Twin/Tone 1981)★★, *Hootenanny* (Twin/Tone 1983)★★★, *Let It Be* (Twin/Tone 1984)★★★★, *The Shit Hits The Fans* cassette only (Twin/Tone 1985)★★, *Tim* (Sire 1985)★★★, *Pleased To Meet Me* (Sire 1987)★★★★, *Don't Tell A Soul* (Sire 1989)★★★, *All Shook Down* (Sire 1990)★★★.
●COMPILATIONS: *Boink!!* (Glass 1986)★★★.

RESIDENTS

Despite a recording career spanning two decades, the Residents have successfully - and deliberately - achieved an air of wilful obscurity. Mindful of the cult of personality, they studiously retain an anonymity and refuse to name personnel, thus ensuring total artistic freedom. Their origins are shrouded in mystery and mischief, although common currency agrees the group was founded in Shrieveport, Louisiana, USA. They later moved to San Mateo, California, where a series of home-recorded tapes was undertaken. In 1971 the group collated several of these performances and sent the results to Hal Haverstadt of Warner Brothers Records, who had signed Captain Beefheart. No name had been included and thus the rejected package was returned marked 'for the attention of the residents', which the collective accepted as a sign of distinction. In 1972 the group was resettled in San Francisco where they launched Ralph Records as an outlet for their work. *Meet The Residents* established their unconventional style, matching bizarre reconstructions of 60s pop favourites with ambitious original material. Critics drew comparisons with the Mothers Of Invention, but any resemblance was purely superficial as the Residents drew reference from a wider variety of sources and showed a greater propensity for surprise. *Third Reich Rock 'N' Roll* contained two suites devoted to their twisted vision of contrasting cover versions, whereas *Not Available* comprised material the group did not wish to release. It had been recorded under the Theory Of Obscurity, whereby a record should not be issued until its creators had forgotten its existence, but appeared as a stop-gap release during sessions for the ambitious *Eskimo*. *The Commercial Album* consisted of 40 tracks lasting exactly 1 minute and contrasted with the Residents' next project, the *Mole Trilogy*, which comprised *Mark Of The Mole*, *The Tunes Of Two Cities* and *The Big Bubble*. The group undertook extensive live appearances in the US and Europe to promote this expansive work, which in turn spawned several in-concert selections and an EP devoted to music played during the shows' intermissions. Their subsequent *American Composers Series* has included *George And James*, a homage to George Gershwin and James Brown, *Stars And Hank Forever*, a celebration of Hank Williams and John Phillip Sousa, and *The King And Eye*, an album of Elvis Presley hits. If this suggests a paucity of original material, it is worth recalling that the Residents' strength lies in interpretation and use of cultural icons as templates for their idiosyncratic vision.

●ALBUMS: *Meet The Residents* (Ralph 1974)★★★★, *Third Reich Rock 'N' Roll* (Ralph 1976)★★★, *Fingerprince* (Ralph 1976)★★★, *Not Available* (Ralph 1978)★★★, *Duck Stab/Buster And Glen* (Ralph 1978)★★★★, *Eskimo* (Ralph 1979)★★★, *The Commercial Album* (Ralph 1980)★★★★, *Mark Of The Mole* (Ralph 1981)★★★, *Intermission* (Ralph 1982)★★, *The Tunes Of Two Cities* (Ralph 1982)★★, *George And James* (Ralph 1984)★★★, *Whatever Happened To Vileness Fats* (Ralph 1984)★★, *The Big Bubble* (Ralph 1985)★★, *Stars And Hank Forever* (Ralph 1986)★★, *13th Anniversary Show Live In Holland* (Torso 1986)★★, *13th Anniversary Show Live In Japan* (Ralph 1986)★★, *13th Anniversary Show Live In The USA* (Ralph 1986)★★, *The Mole Show Live In Holland* (Ralph 1987)★★, *God In Three Persons* (Rykodisc 1988)★★, *God In Three Persons: Original Soundtrack Recording* (Rykodisc 1988)★★, *The King And Eye* (Enigma 1989)★★, *Freakshow* (Official Product 1991)★★, *Our Finest Flowers* (Ralph 1993)★★, *Gingerbread Man* (Euroralph 1995)★★.

●COMPILATIONS: *Nibbles* (Virgin 1979)★★★, *Ralph Before '84 Volume 1* (Ralph 1984)★★★, *Ralph Before '84 Volume 2* (Ralph 1985)★★★, *Heaven?* (Rykodisc 1986)★★★, *Hell?* (Rykodisc 1986)★★★.

●FURTHER READING: *Meet The Residents*, Ian Shirley.

REVILLOS

Formed in March 1979 by Eugene Reynolds and Fay Fife, previously vocalists with the Rezillos. HiFi Harris (guitar), Rocky Rhythm (drums) and three backing singers - Jane White, Jane Brown and Tricia Bryce - completed the group's original line-up, but within months the latter trio had been replaced by Babs and Cherie Revette. The Revillos made their debut with 'Where's The Boy For Me' (1979), but although this exciting performance recalled the best of the previous group, it failed to emulate their success. Internal friction undermined the unit's undoubted potential - guitarists, bassists and singers were replaced with regularity as Reynolds, Fife and Rhythm pursued their uncompromising vision. An album, *Rev-Up*, captured the Revillos' enchanting mixture of girl-group, beat and science fiction, but they were subsequently dropped by their record company. Undeterred, the group inaugurated Superville for ensuing releases and embarked on two gruelling tours of the USA and Canada which they financed themselves. However, an anticipated deal failed to materialize and this ebullient act later disintegrated.

●ALBUMS: *Rev-Up* (Dindisc 1980)★★★, *Attack* (Superville 1983)★★, *Live And On Fire In Japan* (Vinyl Japan 1995)★★.

●COMPILATIONS: *Motorbike Beat* (Mau Mau 1995)★★★, *From The Freezer* (Damaged Goods 1996)★★.

RICH KIDS

Formed in London, England, during September 1977, the Rich Kids were the subject of exceptional initial interest. Centred on bassist Glen Matlock (b. 27 August 1956), a former member of the seminal Sex Pistols, his eminent role was emphasized by the inclusion of two 'unknown' musicians, Steve New (guitar/vocals) and Rusty Egan (drums). The group was later completed by Midge Ure, disillusioned frontman of struggling pop group Slik, and this unusual mixture engendered criticism from unsympathetic quarters. The Rich Kids distanced themselves from punk, and their meagre releases were generally mainstream in execution. Indeed the group's ebullience recalled a 60s bonhomie, but this merely compounded criticism of their 'power pop' approach. The quartet was unable to transform their energy to record, while tension between Matlock and Ure increased to the extent that they were constantly squabbling. The group broke up in November 1978, but denied the fact until free of contractual obligations. Egan and Ure later formed Visage, while their former colleagues pursued several low-key projects. Ure would find the greatest subsequent success as singer with Ultravox, also playing a significant part in the launch of Band Aid.

●ALBUMS: *Ghosts Of Princes In Towers* (EMI 1978)★★.

RICHIE, LIONEL

b. 20 June 1949, Tuskegee, Alabama, USA. Richie grew up on the campus of Tuskegee Institute, where he formed a succession of R&B groups in the mid-60s. In 1968 he became the lead singer and saxophonist of the Commodores. They signed to Atlantic Records in 1968 for a one-record contract, before moving to Motown Records, being schooled as support act to the Jackson Five. The Commodores became established as America's most popular soul group of the 70s, and Richie was responsible for writing and singing many of their biggest hits, specializing in romantic, easy listening ballads such as 'Easy', 'Three Times A Lady' and 'Still'. His mellifluous vocal tones established him as the most prominent member of the group, and by the late 70s he had begun to accept songwriting commissions from other artists. He composed Kenny Rogers' 1980 number 1 'Lady', and produced his *Share Your Love* the following year. Also in 1981, he duetted with Diana Ross on the theme song for the film *Endless Love*. Issued as a single, the track topped the UK and US charts, and became one of Motown's biggest hits to date. Its success encouraged Richie to branch out into a fully fledged solo career in 1982. His debut album, produced another chart-topping single, 'Truly', which continued the style of his ballads with the Commodores.

In 1983, he released *Can't Slow Down*, which catapulted him into the first rank of international superstars, eventually selling more than 15 million copies worldwide. The set also won two Grammy awards, including Album Of The Year. It spawned the number 1 hit 'All Night Long', a gently rhythmic dance number which was promoted by a startling video produced by former Monkee Michael Nesmith. Several more Top 10 hits followed, the most successful of which was 'Hello', a sentimental love song that showed how far Richie had moved from his R&B roots. Now described by one critic as 'the black Barry Manilow', Richie wrote and performed a suitably anodyne theme song, 'Say You, Say Me', for the film *White Nights* - winning an Oscar for his pains. He also collaborated with Michael Jackson on the charity single 'We Are The World' by USA For Africa.

In 1986, he released *Dancing On The Ceiling*, another phenomenally popular album which produced a run of US and UK hits. The title track, which revived the sedate dance feel of 'All Night Long', was accompanied by another striking video, a feature that has played an increasingly important role in Richie's solo career. The critical consensus was that this album represented nothing more than a consolidation of his previous work, though Lionel's collaboration with the country group Alabama on 'Deep River Woman' did break new ground. Since then, his ever more relaxed schedule has kept his recording and live work to a minimum. He broke the silence in 1996 with *Louder Than Words* on which he resisted any change of style or musical fashion-hopping of the past decade. Instead he stuck with his chosen path of well-crafted soul music, which in the intervening years has become known as 'Urban R&B'.

●ALBUMS: *Lionel Richie* (Motown 1982)★★★, *Can't Slow Down* (Motown 1983)★★★★, *Rockin And Romance* (Motown 1985)★★, *The Composer* (Motown 1985)★★, *Dancing On The Ceiling* (Motown 1986)★★★, *Back To Front* (Motown 1992)★★, *Louder Than Words* (Mercury 1996)★★.

●FURTHER READING: *Lionel Richie: An Illustrated Biography*, David Nathan.

RILEY, MARC, AND THE CREEPERS

b. Manchester, England. Riley started playing in a band when he was aged 15, 'then I sort of wormed my way into the Fall when I was 16'. He left to form the Creepers, with Eddie Fenn (drums), Paul Fletcher (guitar) and Pete Keogh (bass). The last two were later replaced by Mark Tilton (guitar) and Phil Roberts (bass). The records that followed were full of hard-hitting humour and remained as opinionated as those of Riley's former boss, Mark E. Smith (who apparently wrote the sarcastic 'Middle

Mass' about Riley). Examples included the anti-Paul Weller rallying cry, 'Bard Of Woking'. Riley formed In Tape records with keyboardist Jim Khambatta, who also managed the Creepers. Starved of commercial success, and burdened by his heritage, Riley disbanded the Creepers in 1987 and formed the Lost Soul Crusaders, later undertaking a career in radio.

●ALBUMS: *Cull* (In Tape 1984)★★, *Gross Out* (In Tape 1984)★★, *Fancy Meeting God* (In Tape 1985)★★, *Warts 'n' All* (In Tape 1985)★★. The Creepers: *Miserable Sinners* (In Tape 1986)★★, *Rock 'N' Roll Liquorice Flavour* (Red Rhino 1987)★★.

●COMPILATIONS: *Sleeper: A Retrospective* (Bleed 1989)★★★.

RIP RIG AND PANIC

Evolving out of Bristol's the Pop Group, Rip Rig And Panic was formed in 1981 as a conceptual musicians' collective, taking its name from an album by Roland Kirk. The group's prime movers were multi-instrumentalist and songwriter Gareth Sager, jazz trumpeter Don Cherry's stepdaughter Neneh Cherry (b. Stockholm, Sweden; vocals), Cherry's partner and drummer Bruce Smith, Sean Oliver (bass) and Mark Springer (piano). Powerful and disturbing live, their playful, anarchic jazz-funk was well-captured on the irreverent 1981 debut album, *God*, which appeared as two 45rpm discs, but was too radical for daytime airplay or significant sales. They performed at the first WOMAD festival in 1982 shortly before Cherry returned to Sweden to have her first baby. Sean Oliver's sister Andrea temporarily took over vocals, and Louis Moholo joined on drums. The equally experimental second album, *I Am Cold*, appeared in 1982, followed by the more accessible *Attitude* in 1983. Unwilling to compromise further, but feeling the strain of constant innovation, they split in 1985, only to realign as the smaller outfit, Float Up CP and, briefly, God Mother And Country, before Cherry went on to a successful solo career with Andrea Oliver contributing to some of her songs.

●ALBUMS: *God* (Virgin 1981)★★★, *I Am Cold* (Virgin 1982)★★★, *Attitude* (Virgin 1983)★★★.

ROBERTSON, ROBBIE

b. Jaime Robbie Robertson, 5 July 1943, Toronto, Canada. Robertson's professional career began in 1960 when he replaced guitarist James Evans in Ronnie Hawkins' backing group, the Hawks. Robertson's rough, but exciting style prevails on several of Hawkins' releases, including 'Matchbox', 'Bo Diddley' and 'Who Do You Love', the last of which boasts an arresting solo. The group then left Hawkins and by 1964 was barnstorming tiny American venues, firstly as the Canadian Squires, then as Levon And The Hawks. They recorded a handful of singles including Robertson's 'The Stones I Throw', which showed the genesis of a remarkable compositional talent. The compulsive backing the Hawks had provided on sessions by blues singer John Hammond led to their association with Bob Dylan. Their emphatic drive underscored Robertson's raging guitar work and helped complete the one-time folksinger's transformation from acoustic sage to electric guru. Robertson's songwriting blossomed during their relationship. His lyrics assumed a greater depth, suggesting a pastoral America, while the music of the group, now dubbed simply the Band, drew its inspiration from a generation of rural styles, both black and white, as well as contemporary soul music peers. Such skill resulted in a body of work which, by invoking the past, created something familiar, yet original. The Band broke up in 1976 following a farewell concert at San Francisco's Winterland Ballroom. The event was captured in the celebratory film *The Last Waltz*, directed by Martin Scorsese, which in turn inspired Roberston's cinematic ambitions. *Carny*, which he also produced, provided his sole starring role to date, although he maintained a working relationship with Scorsese by scoring several of his films, including *Raging Bull* and *The Color Of Money*.

A 1983 collaboration, *King Of Comedy*, was notable for Robertson's solo track, 'Between Trains'. This understated performance was the prelude to the artist's 'comeback' album. *Robbie Robertson*, released in 1987, was an exceptional collection and offered a full, state-of-the-art production and notable guest contributions by U2, Peter Gabriel, Daniel Lanois and the late Gil Evans, as well as his former Band colleagues Rick Danko and Garth Hudson. Such appearances enhanced a work that compared favourably with Robertson's previous recordings and included two exceptional compositions in 'Fallen Angel' and 'Broken Arrow'. This artistic rebirth bodes well for the 90s, although *Storyville* was a disappointing album for those expecting a repeat of his solo debut. He was not part of the reformation of the Band in 1993. His most interesting project to date (although uncommercial) was in 1994 with the Red Road Ensemble, a group of native Americans. Robertson is passionate about their continuing plight and much of his time in the mid-90s was spent working on their behalf. In 1995 he collaborated with film director

Martin Scorsese again by writing the soundtrack for *Casino*.

●ALBUMS: *Robbie Robertson* (Geffen 1987)★★★★, *Storyville* (Geffen 1991)★★, with the Red Road Ensemble *Music For The Native Americans* (Capitol 1994)★★★.

ROCHES

Sisters Maggie (b. 26 October 1951, Detroit, Michigan, USA) and Terre Roche (b. 10 April 1953, New York City, New York, USA) began singing a mixture of traditional, doo-wop and barbershop quartet songs in New York clubs in the late 60s. Their first recording was as backing singers on Paul Simon's 1972 album, *There Goes Rhymin' Simon*. Through Simon, the duo recorded an album for CBS Records in 1975 that attracted little attention. The following year, the Roches became a trio with the addition of the distinctive voice of younger sister Suzzy (b. New York City, New York, USA) to Terre's soprano and Maggie's deep alto. With Maggie's compositions, by turns whimsical and waspish, featuring strongly they became firm favourites on New York's folk club scene. A Warner Brothers Records recording contract followed and Robert Fripp produced the self-titled second album, which included compositions by each of the sisters and remains their strongest recording. Among the many lyrical extravaganzas were Maggie's best-known song of infidelity 'The Married Men' (later covered by Phoebe Snow), Terre's poignant and autobiographical 'Runs In The Family' and 'We', the trio's a cappella opening number at live performances. The highly commercial 'Hammond Song' was arguably the star track (featuring a fine Fripp solo). *Nurds*, another Fripp production, featured the extraordinary 'One Season' wherein the trio manage to sing harmony almost a cappella but totally (and deliberately) out of tune. (Harmony vocalists will appreciate that this is extremely difficult.) *Keep On Doing* maintained a high standard including a refreshing burst of Handel's 'Hallelujah Chorus' and Maggie's tragic love song 'Losing You'. If the Roches ever had strong desires on the charts *Another World* was potentially the album to do it. Featuring a full rock-based sound this remains an undiscovered gem including the glorious title track and a cover of the Fleetwoods' 'Come Softly To Me'. Throughout the 80s, the Roches continued to perform in New York and appeared occasionally at European folk festivals. They also wrote and performed music for theatre productions and the 1988 film *Crossing Delancy*. *Speak* went largely unnoticed in 1989.

Three Kings was a memorable Christmas gift; containing traditional yuletide songs and carols it displayed clearly the Roches' exceptional harmony. *A Dove* in 1992 featured the 'Ing' Song' a brilliant lyrical exercise with every word ending with ing. They remain a highly original unit with a loyal cult following. Quirky is a description at which the Roches would probably squirm, but no other word better describes their style. 'My Winter Coat' from *Can We Go Home Now?* is a perfect example; few artists would attempt an eight-minute song about a coat. The album also featured several songs informed by the death of the sisters' father from Alzheimer's disease.

●ALBUMS: *Seductive Reasoning* (Columbia 1975)★★, *The Roches* (Warners 1979)★★★★, *Nurds* (Warners 1980)★★★, *Keep On Doing* (Warners 1982)★★★, *Another World* (Warners 1985)★★★, *No Trespassing* (Rhino 1986)★★, *Crossing Delancey* soundtrack (Varese Sarabande 1988)★★★, *Speak* (MCA/Paradox 1989)★★★, *Three Kings* (MCA 1990)★★★, *A Dove* (MCA 1992)★★, *Will You Be My Friend* children's album (Baby Boom 1994)★★, *Can We Go Home Now?* (Rykodisc 1995)★★★.

ROCKET 88

This part-time attraction was drawn from the ranks of the UK's finest R&B/jazz musicians. Formed in 1979, the unit revolved around singer/guitarist Alexis Korner, bassist/vocalist Jack Bruce and three members of the Rolling Stones' circle, Ian Stewart (piano), Bill Wyman (bass) and Charlie Watts (drums). The unit took its name from a 1951 recording by Jackie Brenson, often cited as the first rock 'n' roll single, although the music offered by this *ad hoc* collective invoked the earlier, boogie-woogie style of Meade 'Lux' Lewis. Their lone album, recorded live in Hannover, Germany, included versions of 'St. Louis Blues' and 'Roll 'Em Pete' and, while undeniably low-key, was nonetheless an enthralling glimpse into the artistic preferences of musicians freed from perceived commercial restraints. Korner's premature death ended speculation that Rocket 88 might blossom into a full-time commitment.

●ALBUMS: *Rocket 88* (Atlantic 1981)★★★.

RODRIGUEZ, JOHNNY

b. Juan Raul Davis Rodriguez, 10 December 1951, Sabinal, Texas, USA. Rodriguez grew up with a large family living in a shanty town 90 miles from the Mexican border. He was given a guitar when he was seven and, as a teenager, he sang with a beat group. His troubles with the law included goat rustling (he barbecued the goats). A Texas ranger, who heard him singing in his cell, found him a job at the Alamo village and he drove stagecoaches, rode horses and entertained tourists. Tom T. Hall recognized his talent and employed him as lead guitarist with his road band, the Storytellers. He was signed to Mercury Records who particularly liked the way he could switch from English to Spanish. Rodriguez went to number 9 in the US country chart with his first release, 'Pass Me By' in 1972 and then had three consecutive number 1 records, 'You Always Come Back (To Hurting Me)', 'Riding My Thumb To Mexico' and 'That's The Way Love Goes'. He wrote many of his songs and occasionally wrote with Hall. In 1975 he had further number 1 country records with 'I Just Can't Get Her Out Of My Mind', 'Just Get Up And Close The Door' and 'Love Put A Song In My Heart'. In 1977, he had a Top 10 country hit with a revival of the Eagles' 'Desperado'. He moved to Epic Records in 1979 and scored by singing 'I Hate The Way I Love It' with newcomer Charly McClain. Drug addiction made him more erratic, and he started to take less care over his records. In 1983, he sacked his band, but realized he could only get a new one by adopting a more responsible attitude. He moved to Capitol Records in 1988 and had a country hit with a classy ballad, 'I Didn't (Every Chance I Had)'. He then had a further four minor hits with Capitol over a two-year period; 'I Wanta Make Up With You', 'You Might Want To Use Me Again', 'No Chance To Dance' and 'Back To Stay'. He recorded only one album for Capitol. His 1994 album, *Run For The Border*, smacks of desperation - a few new songs and reworkings of his former glories.

●ALBUMS: *Introducing Johnny Rodriguez* (Mercury 1973)★★★, *All I Ever Meant To Do Was Sing* (Mercury 1973)★★★, *My Third Album* (Mercury 1974)★★★, *Songs About Ladies In Love* (Mercury 1974)★★, *Just Get Up And Close The Door* (Mercury 1975)★★★, *Love Put A Song In My Heart* (Mercury 1975)★★★, *Reflecting* (Mercury 1976)★★, *Practice Makes Perfect* (Mercury 1977)★★, *Just For You* (Mercury 1977)★★, *Love Me With All Your Heart* (Mercury 1978)★★, *Rodriguez Was Here* (1979)★★, *Rodriguez* (1979)★★, *Sketches* (1979)★★, *Gypsy* (Epic 1980)★★, *Through My Eyes* (Epic 1980)★★, *After The Rain* (Epic 1981)★★, *For Every Rose* (Epic 1983)★★, *Fooling With Fire* (Epic 1984)★★, *Full Circle* (Epic 1986)★★★, *Gracias* (Capitol 1988)★★★, *Run For The Border* (Intersound 1994)★★, *You Can Say That Again* (High Tone 1996)★★.

ROOMFUL OF BLUES

Formed as a seven-piece band in the Boston, Massachusetts, area in the late 70s. Roomful Of Blues quickly established first a national reputation in the USA with their very authentic-sounding, swing big band R&B, and then broke through on the international scene in the 80s. The group honed their first-hand knowledge of the music by playing with many of the originators, as well as having numerous recordings in their own right. They also recorded behind 'Big' Joe Turner, Eddie 'Cleanhead' Vinson, and Earl King. The group's main successful alumni included guitarists Duke Robillard (b. Michael Robillard, 4 October 1948, Woonsocket, Rhode Island, USA) and Ronnie Earl (b. Ronald Earl Horvath, 1953, New York City, USA), vocalist Curtis Salgado, pianist Al Copley, and saxophonist Greg Piccolo. Despite personnel changes, the group continues to work regularly, although their impact has lessened, due to the numbers of similar groups that have followed in their wake.

Hopes for a new era of interest for the band rose in 1994 when they signed a three-album contract with the Bullseye Blues label under the leadership of Carl Querfurth (trombone). A stable line-up ensued for the excellent *Turn It On, Turn It Up* in 1995. Upon its release on 13 October 1995, the Governor of Rhode Island announced an official annual Roomful Of Blues day for the state of Rhode Island. The present band comprises; Carl Querfurth (b. 3 February 1956, Camden, New Jersey, USA; trombone), John 'JR' Rossi (b. 13 November 1942; drums), Doug James (b. Douglas James Schlecht, 1953, Turlock, California, USA; saxophone), Matt McCabe (b. 6 June 1955, Devon, England; keyboards), Chris Vachon (b. 4 October 1957, South County, Rhode Island, USA; guitar), Sugar Ray Norcia (b. 6 June 1954, Westerly, Rhode Island, USA; vocals/harmonica), Kenny 'Doc' Grace (b. 11 March 1951, Providence, Rhode Island, USA; bass), Bob Enos (b. 4 July 1947, Boston, Massachussetts, USA; trumpet) and Rich Lataille (b. 29 October 1952, Providence, Rhode Island, USA; saxophone). *Under One Roof*, released in 1997, was a less successful album.

●ALBUMS: *The First Album* (Island 1977)★★, *Let's Have A Party* (Antilles 1979)★★, *Hot Little Mama* (Blue Flame 1981)★★★, *Eddie 'Cleanhead' Vinson & Roomful Of Blues* (Muse 1982)★★★, *Blues Train/Big Joe Turner & Roomful Of Blues* (Muse 1983)★★★, *Dressed Up To Get Messed Up* (Rounder 1984)★★★, *Live At Lupo's Heartbreak Hotel* (Rounder

1986)★★★, with Earl King *Glazed* (Black Top 1988)★★★, *Dance All Night* (Rounder 1994)★★★, *Turn It On, Turn It Up* (Bullseye Blues 1995)★★★★, *Under One Roof* (Bullseye Blues 1997)★★★.

ROTH, DAVID LEE

b. 10 October 1955, Bloomington, Indeanapolis, USA. Roth, the former lead vocalist with Van Halen, first expressed his desire to go solo during a period of band inactivity during 1985. He subsequently recorded a mini-album, *Crazy From The Heat*, featuring a varied selection of material that was a departure from the techno-metal approach of Van Halen. The album was favourably reviewed and after much speculation, he finally broke ranks in the autumn of 1985. Roth soon found himself in the US Top 3 with an unlikely version of the Beach Boys' 'California Girls' (complete with a suitably tacky video) and an even stranger cover of 'I Ain't Got Nobody'. This bizarre change must have baffled and bemused his fans, but he soon assembled an impressive array of musicians, notably guitar virtuoso Steve Vai (ex-Zappa; Alcatrazz), bassist Billy Sheehan (ex-Talas) and drummer Greg Bissonette to record *Eat 'Em And Smile*. This featured an amazing selection of blistering rockers and offbeat, big production numbers. It proved that Roth was still a great showman; the album was technically superb and infused with an irreverent sense of 'Yankee' humour.

Skyscraper, released two years later, built on this foundation, but focused more on an elaborately produced hard rock direction. Billy Sheehan departed shortly after its release to be replaced by Matt Bissonette. Brett Tuggle on keyboards was also recruited to expand the line-up to a five piece and add an extra dimension to their sound. Steve Vai left in 1989 to pursue a solo career, but was only temporarily missed as Jason Becker stepped in, a new six-string whizz kid of the Yngwie Malmsteen school of guitar improvisation. *A Little Ain't Enough* emerged in 1991 and, although technically faultless, it tended to duplicate ideas from his previous two albums. *Your Filthy Little Mouth* appeared after a three year gap during which Roth had relocated to New York. This time, amid the histrionics about girls and cars, were odes to the Los Angeles riots, and the unutterably horrible pseudo reggae of 'No Big 'Ting'. In 1996, following Sammy Hagar's departure (sacking) from Van Halen, Roth rejoined the band 10 years after he originally left.

●ALBUMS: *Crazy From The Heat* (Warners 1985)★★★, *Eat 'Em And Smile* (Warners 1986)★★,
Skyscraper (Warners 1988)★★, *A Little Ain't Enough* (Warners 1991)★★, *Your Filthy Little Mouth* (Warners 1994)★★.
●VIDEOS: *David Lee Roth* (1987).

ROWAN, PETER

b. 4 July 1942, Boston, Massachusetts, USA. Rowan's long career began as a member of the Cupids, a college band that developed his interest in an amalgam of Tex-Mex and roots music. After he graduated he played mandolin with the Mother Bay State Entertainers and later on joined two influential groups, the Charles River Valley Boys and Bill Monroe's Bluegrass Boys. For two years he led the critically acclaimed progressive rock band Earth Opera with fellow traditional acolyte David Grisman, before joining Sea Train in 1970. Although both units were rock-based, Rowan maintained his bluegrass roots as a member of Muleskinner, Old And In The Way which also featured the late Jerry Garcia and the Free Mexican Airforce. His subsequent solo work has placed the performer firmly within America's folk heritage. A prolific and engaging artist, he is now established as one of the leaders in his field of music; his recordings have embraced Tex-Mex, country, folk, acid rock and ethnic material, each of which has been performed with empathy and purpose. His vast catalogue also includes albums with his siblings, the Rowan Brothers.

●ALBUMS: *Peter Rowan* (Flying Fish 1979)★★★, *Mediciane Trail* (Flying Fish 1980)★★★, *Peter Rowan* (Flying Fish 1980)★★★, *Hiroshima Mon Amour* (1980)★★★, *Peter Rowan, Richard Green And The Red Hot Pickers* (1980)★★★★, *Texican Badman* (Appaloosa 1981)★★★, *The Walls Of Time* (Sugar Hill 1981)★★★, *The Usual Suspect* (1982)★★, *Peter Rowan And The Wild Stallions* (Apaloosa 1983)★★★, *Peter Rowan And The Red Hot Pickers* (Sugar Hill 1984)★★★★, *Revelry* (Waterfront 1984)★★★, *Festival Tapes* (1985)★★★, *T Is For Texas* (Waterfront 1985)★★★, *The First Whipoorwill* (Sugar Hill 1985)★★★, with David Grisman, Keith, Greene And White *Muleskinner* (1987)★★★★, *New Moon Rising* (Special Delivery 1988)★★★, *Dust Bowl Children* (Sugar Hill 1989)★★★, *All On A Rising Day* (Special Delivery 1991)★★★, *Awake Me In The New World* (1993)★★★, as the Rowan Brothers *Tree On A Hill* (Sugar Hill 1994)★★★, *Bluegrass Boy* (Sugar Hill 1996)★★★.
●VIDEOS: *Muleskinner - Live The Video* (1991).

Run DMC

New York rappers Joe Simmons (b. 24 November 1966, New York, USA; the brother of Russell Simmons, their Rush Management boss), Darryl 'DMC' McDaniels (b. 31 May 1964, New York, USA) and DJ 'Jam Master Jay' (b. Jason Mizell, 1965, New York, USA) originally came together as Orange Crush in the early 80s, becoming Run DMC in 1982 after graduating from St. Pascal's Catholic School. They had known each other as children in Hollis, New York, Mizell and McDaniels even attending the same kindergarten. After circulating demos the group signed to Profile Records for an advance of $2500, immediately enjoying a US underground hit with 'It's Like That'. However, it was the single's b-side, 'Sucker MCs', that created the stir. It single-handedly gave birth to one of rap's most prevalent terms, and almost became a genre in its own right. Many critics signpost the single as the birth of modern hip hop, with its stripped-down sound (no instruments apart from a drum machine and scratching from a turntable, plus the fashion image of the B-boy: street clothing, chiefly sportswear, and street language). In the wake of the single's success their debut album went gold in 1984, the first time the honour had been bestowed upon a rap act. They cemented their position as hip hop's men of the moment with furious touring, and appearances on the *Krush Groove* film, a fictionalized account of the life of Russell Simmons, who was now joint-head of Def Jam with Rick Rubin. They also took a hand at the prestigious King Holliday (a Martin Luther King tribute) and Sun City (Artists Against Apartheid) events. They broke further into the mainstream on both sides of the Atlantic in 1986 when, via Rubin's auspices, they released the heavy metal/rap collision 'Walk This Way' (featuring Steven Tyler and Joe Perry of Aerosmith). Its distinctive video caught the imaginations of audiences on both sides of the Atlantic. The partnership had been predicted by earlier singles, 'Rock Box' and 'King Of Rock', both of which fused rap with rock. By 1987 *Raisin' Hell* had sold three million copies in the US, becoming the first rap album to hit the R&B number 1 mark, the first to enter the US Top 10, and the first to go platinum. Run DMC also became the first rap group to have a video screened by MTV, the first to feature on the cover of *Rolling Stone*, and the first non-athletes to endorse Adidas products (a sponsorship agreement that followed rather than preceded their 'My Adidas' track). Sadly, a projected collaboration with Michael Jackson never took place, though they did duet with Joan Rivers on her television show, and held street seminars to discuss inter-gang violence. Subsequent efforts have been disappointing, although both *Tougher Than Leather* and *Back From Hell* contained a few tough-like-the-old-times tracks ('Beats To The Ryhme', 'Pause' etc.) among the fillers. The former album was tied to a disastrous film project of similar title. In the 90s Daniels and Simmons experienced religious conversion, after the former succumbed to alcoholism and the the latter was falsely accused of rape in Cleveland. Singles continued to emerge sporadically, notably 'What's It All About', which even sampled the Stone Roses. Despite an obvious effort to make *Down With The King* their major comeback album, with production assistance offered by Pete Rock, EPMD, the Bomb Squad, Naughty By Nature, A Tribe Called Quest, even Rage Against The Machine, and guest appearances from KRS-1 and Neneh Cherry, it is hard to shake the view of Run DMC as a once potent, now spent force. Unsurprisingly, this is not their own outlook, and as Simmons is keen to point out: 'The Run DMC story is an exciting story. It's a true legend, it's the sort of life you want to read about'.

●ALBUMS: *Run DMC* (Profile 1984)★★★★, *King Of Rock* (Profile 1985)★★★★, *Raising Hell* (Profile 1986)★★★★, *Tougher Than Leather* (Profile 1988)★★★, *Back From Hell* (Profile 1990)★★★, *Down With The King* (Profile 1993)★★★.

●COMPILATIONS: *Together Forever: Greatest Hits 1983-1991* (Profile 1991)★★★★.

●FURTHER READING: *Run DMC*, B. Adler.

Runrig

The phenomenon of Runrig is an extraordinary example of cultural differences. This premier Scottish group has emerged from a folk background to a higher profile in the pop/rock field and is arguably the most popular band north of Carlisle. The group made its debut - as the Run Rig Dance Band - at the Kelvin Hall, Glasgow, in 1973. Initially a trio comprising of brothers Rory MacDonald (b. 27 July 1949, Dornoch, Sutherland, Scotland; guitar/bass/vocals, ex-Skyevers), Calum MacDonald (b. 12 November 1953, Lochmaddy, North Uist, Scotland; drums/percussion/vocals) and Blair Douglas (accordion), the group was viewed as a part-time venture, 'Something to do during the holidays,' as Calum later stated. Donnie Munroe (b. 2 August 1953, Uig, Isle Of Skye, Scotland; vocals/guitar) joined the following year as the group took on a more serious perspective. At this point their repertoire consisted of cover versions - Creedence Clearwater Revival was a particular favourite - and traditional material played in a folk/rock manner, reminiscent of Horslips and Fairport Convention. Although the MacDonald siblings were writing material, Runrig demurred from playing them live until 1978 and the release of *Play Gaelic*. Issued on the Scottish Lismor Record label, this pastoral set introduced newcomer Robert MacDonald (no relation) who had replaced Blair Douglas. A higher profile ensued and, with the extra credibility of an album behind them, the group set up their own label, Ridge Records. Malcolm Jones (b. 12 July 1958, Inverness, Scotland; guitar/mandolin/accordion) replaced Robert MacDonald who was unwilling to turn professional. Sadly, Robert died of cancer in 1986. *Highland Connection* introduced a greater emphasis on electric styles and in 1980 Iain Bayne (b. 22 January 1960, St. Andrews, Fife, Scotland) took over as the drummer, freeing Calum to concentrate on vocals and percussion. By the release of *Recovery*, produced by Robert Bell of the Blue Nile, it was clear the band was more than just another folk/rock act. The music still retained its rural feel and traditions, with many songs being sung in Gaelic, but the sound took Runrig outside the narrow bounds of the traditional arena. English keyboard player Richard Cherns joined the group for its first European tour, but left following the release of *Heartland*. He was replaced by former Big Country member Peter Wishart (b. 9 March 1962, Dunfermline, Fife, Scotland). Runrig performed successful concerts in Canada and East Berlin in 1987 and played support to U2 at Murrayfield, Edinburgh, Scotland. After the release of *The Cutter And The Clan*, the group signed to Chrysalis Records, who immediately re-released the album. Chart success followed in 1989 with *Searchlight* almost making the Top 10 in the UK charts. Constant touring - the secret of Runrig's appeal - ensued and in 1990 the *Capture The Heart* EP entered the UK Top 50. A television broadcast of a live performance elicited huge response from viewers to the extent that five concerts at Glasgow's Royal Concert Hall sold out. A subsequent video, *City Of Lights*, reached the Top 10 best-selling videos in the UK. The highly acclaimed *The Big Wheel* reached number 4 in the UK charts and an open-air concert at Loch Lomond was attended by 45,000 people. The EP *Hearthammer* broached the UK Top 30 in September 1991, followed by 'Flower Of The West' (UK number 43). The acceptance of Runrig outside Scotland now seems certain and having combined their national and cultural pride with stadium rock, they have awoken the world to Scottish popular music and traditions, without hint of compromise.

●ALBUMS: *Play Gaelic* (Lismor 1978)★★★, *Highland Connection* (Ridge 1979)★★★, *Recovery* (Ridge 1981)★★★, *Heartland* (Ridge 1985)★★★, *The Cutter And The Clan* (Ridge 1987)★★★, *Once In A Lifetime* (Chrysalis 1988)★★★, *Searchlight* (Chrysalis 1989)★★★, *The Big Wheel* (Chrysalis 1991)★★★★, *Amazing Things* (Chrysalis 1993)★★★, *Transmitting Live* (Chrysalis 1994)★★, *Mara* (Chrysalis 1995)★★.

●FURTHER READING: *Going Home: The Runrig Story*, Tom Morton.

RUSH

This Canadian heavy rock band comprised Geddy Lee (b. Gary Lee Weinrib, 29 July 1953, Willowdale, Toronto, Canada; keyboards/bass/vocals), Alex Lifeson (b. Alex Zivojinovich, 27 August 1953, British Columbia, Canada; guitar) and John Rutsey (drums). From 1969-72 they performed in Toronto playing a brand of Cream-inspired material, honing their act on the local club and bar circuit. In 1973 they recorded a version of Buddy Holly's 'Not Fade Away' as their debut release, backing it with 'You Can't Fight It', for their own label, Moon Records. Despite failing to grab the attention as planned, the group pressed ahead with the recording of a debut album, which was remixed by Terry 'Broon' Brown. Brown would continue to work with the band until 1984's *Grace Under Pressure*. With no bite from the majors, once again this arrived via Moon, with distribution by London Records. However, at least the quality of the group's live appointments improved, picking up support slots with the New York Dolls in Canada and finally crossing the US border to play gigs with ZZ Top. Eventually Cliff Burnstein of Mercury Records (who would later also sign Def Leppard) heard the band, and his label reissued the group's debut. At this point Neil Peart (b. 12 September 1952, Hamilton Ontario, Canada; drums, ex-Hush), who was to be the main songwriter of the band, replaced Rutsey, and Rush undertook their first full tour of the USA. Rush's music was typified by Lee's oddly high-pitched voice, a tremendously powerful guitar sound, especially in the early years, and a recurrent interest in science fiction and fantasy from the pen of Neil Peart. Later he would also conceptualize the work of authors such as John Barth, Gabriel Garcia Marquez and John Dos Passos. This approach reached its zenith in the group's 1976 concept album, *2112*, based on the work of novelist/philosopher Ayn Rand, which had as its central theme the concept of individual freedom and will. Including a 20-minute title track that occupied all of side one, it was a set that crystallized the spirit of Rush for both their fans and detractors. However, the band's most popular offering, *A Farewell To Kings*, followed by *Hemispheres* in 1978, saw Peart finally dispense with his 'epic' songwriting style. By 1979 Rush were immensely successful worldwide, and the Canadian Government awarded them the title of official Ambassadors of Music. As the 80s progressed Rush streamlined their image to become sophisticated, clean-cut, cerebral music-makers. Some early fans denigrated their determination to progress musically with each new album, though in truth the band had thoroughly exhausted its earlier style. They enjoyed a surprise hit single in 1980 when 'Spirit Of Radio' broke them out of their loyal cult following, and live shows now saw Lifeson and Lee adding keyboards for a fuller sound. Lee's vocals had also dropped somewhat from their earlier near-falsetto. The best recorded example of the band from this period is the succinct *Moving Pictures* from 1981, a groundbreaking fusion of technological rock and musical craft that never relied on the former at the expense of the latter. However, their career afterwards endured something of a creative wane, with the band at odds with various musical innovations. Despite this, live shows were still exciting events for the large pockets of fans the band retained all over the world, and in the powerful *Hold Your Fire* in 1987 they proved they were still able to scale former heights. This was repeated in 1996 with *Test For Echo*. Often criticized for lyrical pretension and musical grandstanding - unkind critics have suggested that Rush is exactly what you get if you let your drummer write your songs for you; they nevertheless still remain Canada's leading rock attraction.

●ALBUMS: *Rush* (Moon 1974)★★, *Fly By Night* (Moon 1975)★★, *Caress Of Steel* (Mercury 1975)★★, *2112* (Mercury 1976)★★, *All The World's A Stage* (Mercury 1976)★★, *A Farewell To Kings* (Mercury 1977)★★, *Hemispheres* (Mercury 1978)★★, *Permanent Waves* (Mercury 1980)★★★, *Moving Pictures* (Mercury 1981)★★★, *Exit: Stage Left* (Mercury 1981)★★★, *Signals* (Mercury 1982)★★★, *Grace Under Pressure* (Mercury 1984)★★, *Power Windows* (Mercury 1985)★★, *Hold Your Fire* (Mercury 1987)★★, *A Show Of Hands* (Mercury 1989)★★, *Presto* (Atlantic 1989)★★, *Roll The Bones* (Atlantic 1991)★★, *Counterparts* (Mercury 1993)★★, *Test For Echo* (Atlantic 1996)★★. Solo: Alex Lifeson *Victor* (East West 1996).

●COMPILATIONS: *Archives* 3-CD set (Mercury 1978)★★★, *Rush Through Time* (Mercury 1980)★★, *Chronicles* (Mercury 1990)★★★.

●VIDEOS: *Grace Under Pressure* (1986), *Exit Stage Left* (1988), *Thru' The Camera's Eye* (1989), *A Show Of Hands* (1989), *Chronicles* (1991).

●FURTHER READING: *Rush*, Brian Harrigan. *Rush Visions: The Official Biography*, Bill Banasiewicz.

RUSH, JENNIFER

b. Heidi Stern, 29 September 1960, New York City, New York, USA. Rush studied piano, violin and singing before starting her pop career. She went to Europe in 1969, when her father, the opera singer Maurice Stern, took an engagement at the Flensburg Opera in northern Germany. She subsequently settled in Wiesbaden, Germany, but moved back to America in the early 70s. A return to Germany came at the beginning of the 80s, working as a secretary for the US Army in Harlaching, Bavaria. Her career in popular music was hallmarked by the spectacular 1986 success of 'Power Of Love', an emphatic MOR ballad that became a major worldwide hit. It reached number 1 in the UK charts in June 1985, re-entering the Top 60 nearly 18 months later in December 1986. Further success arrived via duets with Elton John and Michael Bolton, before teaming up with Placido Domingo, in many ways a salute to her operatic roots, for the 1989 hit, 'Till I Loved You'. She also enjoyed solo success with '25 Lovers', 'Ring Of Ice' and 'I Come Undone'. By the 90s she had become a fixture on AOR radio in the USA, with each of her albums selling strongly. She has over 50 gold records to date, and numerous platinum albums (four of which went 'double platinum').

●ALBUMS: *Jennifer Rush* (Columbia 1979)★★, *Moving* (Columbia 1985)★★, *Passion* (Columbia 1988)★★, *Wings Of Desire* (Columbia 1989)★★, *Jennifer Rush* (Columbia 1992)★★.

RUTHERFORD, MIKE

b. 2 October 1950, Guildford, Surrey, England. While working in Genesis, guitarist Rutherford has had a solo career broken into two distinct phases. *Smallcreep's Day* was a concept album based on Peter C. Brown's novel, featuring vocalist Noel McCalla, formerly with Moon who made two Epic albums in 1976/7. But neither that nor the follow-up were commercially successful. Rutherford resumed his solo activity in 1985, under the name Mike And The Mechanics. He had two new song-writing partners - producer Chris Neil and former hitmaker B.A. Robertson. The group also had twin lead vocalists in Paul Carrack (ex-Ace; Squeeze) and Paul Young from Sad Cafe. The new formation created two US hit singles, 'Silent Running' and 'All I Need Is A Miracle' and a million-selling album. The same line-up was retained for *Living Years*, whose title track was both an international best seller and an Ivor Novello award winner. Co-written by Rutherford and Robertson it was strongly autobiographical in its theme of the death of a parent. During the late 80s and 90s, the group was also a touring band, with the addition of Peter Van Hooke (drums) and Adrian Lee (bass).

●ALBUMS: *Smallcreep's Day* (Charisma 1980)★★, *Acting Very Strange* (Warners 1982)★★, *Mike And The Mechanics* (WEA 1985)★★, *The Living Years* (WEA 1988)★★★, *Word Of Mouth* (Virgin 1991)★★★, *Beggar On A Beach Of Gold* (Virgin 1995)★★★.

Rypdal, Terje

b. 23 August 1947, Oslo, Norway. The son of a nationally famous conductor, Rypdal had piano lessons as a child, but taught himself the electric guitar. Studying composition at Oslo University, he also studied George Russell's theories of improvisation with Russell himself, and then played in his big band and sextet. In the late 60s he began to collaborate with Jan Garbarek, and played on Garbarek's first two albums for ECM Records; but he received more exposure in the 1969 German Free Jazz Festival, playing with musicians from the burgeoning Chicago free jazz scene in a band led by Lester Bowie. Forming Odyssey in the 70s, Rypdal, now recording, also began touring, which he has continued strenuously ever since. Odyssey made a highly successful tour which included the USA, and since then he has made annual appearances at the major European jazz festivals, leading a trio in the mid-80s with Bjorn Kjellemyr and Audun Kleive, and performing with Palle Mikkelborg in Norway. Rypdal is making an an important contribution to the European genre. Writing for orchestra as well as jazz ensemble, he is noted for his system of bowing the guitar in the manner of violin. On *If Mountains Could Sing* the violin is featured strongly, not by the guitarist but by Terje Tonnesen, Lars Anders Tomter and Oystein Birkland. It is however in rolling and uplifting pieces such as 'The Return Of Per Ulv' that Rypdal is renowned.

●ALBUMS: *What Comes After* (ECM 1974)★★, with Jan Garbarek *Afric Pepperbird* (ECM 1974)★★★, *Odyssey* (ECM 1975)★★★, *Whenever I Seem To Be Far Away* (ECM 1975)★★★, *After The Rain* (ECM 1976)★★★, *Waves* (ECM 1978)★★★, *To Be Continued* (ECM 1981)★★★, *Eos* (ECM 1984)★★★, *Chaser* (ECM 1985)★★★, *Sunrise* (1985)★★★, *Terje Rypdal/Miroslav Vitous/Jack DeJohnette* (ECM 1985)★★★★, *Descendre* (ECM 1986)★★★, *Blue* (ECM 1987)★★★, *The Singles Collection* (ECM 1989)★★★, *Undisonus* (1990)★★★, *Q.E.D.* (1993)★★★, *If Mountains Could Sing* (ECM 1995)★★★.

●COMPILATIONS: *Works* (ECM 1989)★★★.

S

S-K-O

This US group comprised three songwriters, Thom Schuyler, Fred Knobloch and Paul Overstreet, who decided to work together as an occasional band. Schuyler (b. 1952, Bethlehem, Pennsylvania, USA) was, by trade, a carpenter, whose songwriting abilities were discovered by Eddie Rabbitt when he was making alterations to the latter's studio. Schuyler wrote '16th Avenue', 'Hurricane' and 'I Don't Know Where To Start' and had *Blue Heart* released by Capitol Records, which led to some entries on the US country chart. With Paul Overstreet, he wrote 'I Fell In Love Again Last Night' (the Forester Sisters), and 'A Long Line Of Love' (Michael Martin Murphey), both US country number 1 hits. Knobloch, pronounced 'no-block', (b. Jackson, Mississippi, USA) worked in Atlanta, Georgia, and Los Angeles, California, before moving to Nashville, Tennessee in 1983. He wrote 'The Whole World's In Love When You're Lonely' and 'Julianne' (the Everly Brothers). As Fred Knoblock (sic), he had a US pop hit with 'Why Not Me' and country hits with 'Memphis' and, with Susie Allanson, 'Killin' Time'. Overstreet (b. VanCleave, Mississippi, USA), a more traditional country songwriter, wrote both 'On The Other Hand' and 'Forever And Ever, Amen' with Don Schlitz (both US country number 1 hits for Randy Travis); 'Diggin' Up Bones' with Al Gore (also a number 1 for Travis); and 'You're Still New To Me' with Paul Davis (a US country number 1 for Marie Osmond and Paul Davis). Knobloch was briefly married to Dolly Parton's sister, Freida. The first S-K-O release, 'You Can't Stop Love', made the US country Top 10. Their second single, 'Baby's Got A New Baby', topped the US country chart in 1987. At that time, Overstreet opted for a solo career and he had a further US country number 1 with Tanya Tucker and Paul Davis with a song he wrote with Don Schlitz, 'I Won't Take Less Than Your Love'. He also wrote 'You Again' (the Forester Sisters), 'When You Say Nothing At All' (Keith Whitley) and 'Deeper Than The Holler' (Randy Travis), all with Don Schlitz and all US country number 1 hits. His

place was taken by songwriter Craig Bickhardt (b. Pennsylvania, USA), thus making the group S-K-B. Bickhardt's band, Wire And Wood, opened for many well-known acts in the early 70s. He wrote or co-wrote 'Finally Found A Reason' (Art Garfunkel), 'I'm Falling In Love Tonight' (the Judds), 'Never Been In Love' (Randy Meisner), 'You're The Power' (Kathy Mattea), 'Give A Little Love To Me' (the Judds), 'I Know Where I'm Going' (the Judds), and songs for the film, *Tender Mercies*. S-K-B finally had a US Top 10 country single with 'Givers And Takers' before disbanding in 1989.

●ALBUMS: *S-K-O* (1987)★★, Thom Schuyler, Fred Knobloch with Craig Bickhardt *No Easy Horses* (1987)★★.

S.O.S. BAND

Formed in Atlanta, Georgia, USA, in 1977, the S.O.S. Band enjoyed a long run of hits on the US R&B charts during the 80s. The group originally consisted of Mary Davis (vocals/keyboards), Jason 'T.C.' Bryant (keyboards), Billy R. Ellis (saxophone) and James Earl Jones III (drums). They performed regularly, as Sounds Of Santa Monica, at Lamar's Regal Room in Atlanta where they were discovered by Milton Lamar, the club's owner, who later became their manager. The group were signed to the independent Tabu Records and soon added new members Willie 'Sonny' Killebrew (saxophone/flute), John Simpson III (bass/keyboards) and Bruno Speight (guitar). The group then changed its name to the S.O.S. Band. Performing in the then popular funk style, the band began to amass a catalogue of US hits in 1980, with 'Take Your Time (Do It Right) Part 1' rising to number 1 on the R&B chart and number 3 national pop chart. They returned to the pop singles chart four more times throughout their career, but never again rose close to that initial position. On the R&B chart, however, they were mainstays through 1987, returning to the Top 10 four more times: in 1983 with 'Just be Good To Me' (number 2) and 'Tell Me If You Still Care' (number 5), in 1984 with 'Just The Way You Like It' (number 6), and in 1986 with 'The Finest' (number 2). Five S.O.S. Band albums also charted in the US, the debut, *S.O.S.*, faring the best at number 12. There were a number of personnel changes throughout the decade, with vocalist Davis leaving for a solo career in 1987. The S.O.S. Band was still recording for Tabu and performing at the end of the 80s.

●ALBUMS: *S.O.S.* (Tabu 1980)★★, *Too* (Tabu 1981)★★, *S.O.S. III* (Tabu 1982)★★, *On The Rise* (Tabu 1983)★★★, *Just The Way You Like It* (Tabu

1984)★★★, *Sands Of Time* (Tabu 1985)★★★, *Diamonds In the Raw* (Tabu 1989)★★, *One Of Many Nights* (Arista 1991)★★★.

SAGA

Drawing on a variety of influences from Rush to Emerson, Lake And Palmer, multi-talented musician Mike Sadler and drummer Steve Negus put together their first line-up in Toronto, Canada, in 1977, with the guitar/keyboard playing brothers Jim and Ian Crichton. A self-financed album was then released on their own label. In 1980 they signed to Polydor Records and, with additional musicians, produced *Images At Twilight*, which continued the science fiction themes of their debut. A 12-inch EP was released in the UK to promote the album and, receiving a good deal of positive reaction, they set out on tour, supported for many shows by Magnum. Later that year they added another keyboard player, Jim Gilmore, and began work on the next album. Released in 1981, this elevated them into the major concert circuit where they proved a big attraction in America. Their record company lost interest, but Epic came to the rescue until a more lasting contract was set up with Portrait Records. However, the band lost direction and the founder members became disillusioned and soon left to pursue a new venture. The rest of the group continue and attempted to recapture former glories. They returned to the sci-fi concept for their album in 1989.

● ALBUMS: *Saga* (Maze 1978)★★, *Images At Twilight* (Polydor 1980)★★★, *Silent Knight* (Polydor 1980)★★★, *Worlds Apart* (Polydor 1981)★★, *In Transit* (Polydor 1982)★★, *Head Or Tails* (Epic 1983)★★, *Behaviour* (Portrait 1984)★★, *Wildest Dreams* (Atlantic 1987)★★, *The Beginners Guide To Throwing Shapes* (Bonaire 1989)★★, *Security Of Illusion* (1992)★★, *Steel Umbrellas* (1995)★★, *Generation 13* (Bonaire 1995)★★.

SAGER, CAROLE BAYER

b. 8 March 1946, New York City, New York, USA. Sager's career as a hit songwriter stretches over three decades, from the catchy pop of 'A Groovy Kind Of Love' to the charity ballad 'That's What Friends Are For', which has raised over $1 million for AIDS research. She began writing songs in the early 60s while a student at New York's High School of Music and Art. Sager was subsequently spotted by Don Kirshner who signed her to his Screen Gems publishing company. She had her first big hit in 1966 with 'A Groovy Kind Of Love'. Co-written by Toni Wine, the song was first recorded by Patti Labelle And The Bluebelles, but it became an international best-seller in the version by the Mindbenders. It was equally successful when revived by Phil Collins for the soundtrack of *Buster* in 1989. In 1970, Sager provided the lyrics for the off Broadway musical *Georgy*, before co-writing 'Midnight Blue' with Melissa Manchester, who took it into the US Top 10 in 1975. Her own recording career had begun in 1972, and, four years later, Richard Perry produced 'You're Moving Out Today', which she wrote with Bette Midler and Bruce Roberts. It was a UK Top 10 hit for Sager on Elektra Records. Even more impressive was the dramatic 'When I Need You' (with Albert Hammond), a chart-topper for Leo Sayer on both sides of the Atlantic. In the late 70s Sager collaborated with Marvin Hamlisch on the successful Broadway musical *They're Playing Our Song*, a semi-autobiographical piece about the romantic entanglement of a songwriting team. In 1981, she recorded for CBS Records, having her biggest US hit with 'Stronger Than Before'. Her most important partnership, with Burt Bacharach, produced the Oscar-winning 'Arthur's Theme (Best That You Can Do)', which was a US number 1 in 1981 for Christopher Cross, who collaborated on the number along with Peter Allen. She subsequently married Bacharach (they parted in 1991) and worked with him on 'Love Is My Decision' (from *Arthur 2: On The Rocks*) and 'That's What Friends Are For', which became a US number 1 hit in 1986 when recorded by Dionne Warwick And Friends. Other notable Sager compositions include 'Don't Cry Out Loud' and 'I'd Rather Leave While I'm In Love' (both with Peter Allan); 'Better Days', 'Come In From The Rain' (with Melissa Manchester); two numbers with Hamlisch, 'Better Than Ever' and 'Nobody Does It Better' (the James Bond film theme recorded by Carly Simon), the Patti Labelle/Michael McDonald duet 'On My Own' (with Bacharach), and two 90s film songs, 'The Day I Fell In Love' (from *Beethoven's 2nd*, with James Ingram, and Cliff Magness) and 'Look What Love Has Done' (from *Junior*, with Ingram, James Newton Howard, and Patty Smyth).

● ALBUMS: *Carole Bayer Sager* (Elektra 1977)★★★, *Too* (Elektra 1978)★★★, *Sometimes Late At Night* (Columbia 1981)★★★.

SAINT ETIENNE

By far the most dextrous of those bands cursed with the 'indie-dance' label, and one of the few to maintain genuine support in both camps. Pete Wiggs (b. 15 May 1966, Reigate, Surrey, England)

and music journalist Bob Stanley (b. 25 December 1964, Horsham, Sussex, England) grew up together in Croydon, Surrey, England. In the early 80s, the pair began to experiment with party tapes, but did not make any serious inroads into the music business until forming Saint Etienne in 1988, taking their name from the renowned French football team. Relocating to Camden in north London, the pair recruited Moira Lambert of Faith Over Reason for a dance/reggae cover of Neil Young's 'Only Love Can Break Your Heart'. Issued in May 1990 on the aspiring Heavenly Records label, the single fared well in the nightclubs and surfaced on a magazine flexidisc remixed by label mates Flowered Up (who appeared on the b-side) in July. Another cover, indie guitar band the Field Mice's 'Kiss And Make Up', was given a similar dance pop overhaul for Saint Etienne's second single, fronted this time by New Zealand vocalist Donna Savage of Dead Famous People. Then came the infectious northern soul-tinged 'Nothing Can Stop Us' in May 1991. Its strong European feel reflected both their name, which helped attract strong support in France, and their logo (based on the European flag). It also benefited from Sarah Cracknell's (b. 12 April 1967, Chelmsford, Essex, England) dreamy vocals, which would dominate Saint Etienne's debut, *Foxbase Alpha*, released in the autumn. Cracknell had formerly recorded with Prime Time. 'Only Love Can Break Your Heart' was reissued alongside the album, and provided them with a minor chart hit. Throughout the 90s the only critical barb that seemed to stick to Saint Etienne with any justification or regularity was that they were simply 'too clever for their own good', criticism that Stanley clearly could not abide: 'The image that the media has built up of us as manipulators really makes us laugh'. *So Tough* revealed a rich appreciation of the vital signs of British pop, paying homage to their forerunners without ever indulging in false flattery. *Tiger Bay*, toted as a folk album, transcended a variety of musical genres with the sense of ease and propriety that Saint Etienne had essentially patented. The medieval folk/trance ballad, 'Western Wind', and the instrumental 'Urban Clearway', redolent but not traceable to a dozen prime time television themes, were just two of the bookends surrounding one of the greatest albums of that year. It was followed by a fan club only release, *I Love To Paint*, limited to 500 copies. However, in 1995 Sarah Cracknell was said to be working on a solo album, having already recorded a duet with Tim Burgess of the Charlatans, 'I Was Born On Christmas Day',

released at the end of 1993 in a failed attempt to mug the Christmas singles market.
● ALBUMS: *Foxbase Alpha* (Heavenly 1991)★★★, *So Tough* (Heavenly 1993)★★★, *Tiger Bay* (Heavenly 1994)★★★, *Too Young To Die - The Singles* (Heavenly 1995)★★★★, *Too Young To Die - The Remix Album* (Heavenly 1995)★★★, *Casino Classics* (Heavenly 1996)★★★.
● COMPILATIONS: *You Need A Mess Of Help To Stand Alone* (Heavenly 1993)★★★.
● VIDEOS: *Too Young To Die* (Wienerworld 1995).

SAKAMOTO, RYÛICHI

b. 17 January 1952, Tokyo, Japan. Sakamoto studied composition and electronic music at Tokyo College of Arts and took a Master of Arts degree in 1976 before forming the Yellow Magic Orchestra with Haruomi Hosono and Yukihiro Takahashi two years later. It was with the YMO that he first achieved international recognition with 'Computer Game (Theme From The Invaders)' reaching number 17 in the UK charts in 1980. Sakamoto's first solo *One Thousand Knives*, was recorded in 1978, but not released until 1982 and only then in The Netherlands. The first widely distributed recording was *B-2 Unit*, made while he was still a member of the Yellow Magic Orchestra in 1980 with the help of Andy Partridge (XTC) and Dennis Bovell. Robin Scott was given equal billing on *Left Handed Dream* on which he provided vocals, with US session guitarist Adrian Belew (Talking Heads, Frank Zappa and David Bowie) also featured. *The End Of Asia* was recorded with Danceries, a Japanese classical ensemble which specialized in recreating medieval music. Working alongside David Sylvian (to whose work Sakamoto became a key contributor), he enjoyed two UK hit singles with 'Bamboo Houses' (1982) and 'Forbidden Colours' (1983). Since the mid-80s, Sakamoto has established a successful career as a solo recording artist, a film composer and an film actor. Sakamoto's evocative soundtrack to Nagisa Oshima's *Merry Christmas, Mr Lawrence* - in which he made his acting debut - received critical acclaim; his contribution to the soundtrack of Bernardo Bertolucci's *The Last Emperor* (with David Byrne and Cong Su), earned him an Academy Award. In September 1985 at the Tsukaba Expo, he collaborated with Radical TV on a spectacular live performance of *TV WAR*, a science fiction show involving music, video and computer graphics. He has constantly attracted a variety of leading musicians in studio work, varying from Iggy Pop to Brian Wilson and Robbie Robertson and was assisted by Thomas Dolby on *Musical Encyclopedia* and the single 'Field Work' (1986). He has also contributed to Public Image Limited's *Album* and Arto Lindsey's *Esperanto*. His own solo albums have consistently displayed a hi-tech integration of western pop music with traditional music from Japan, the Middle East and Africa. After releasing *Beauty*, which incorporated Okinawan music, Sakamoto toured the USA and Europe and established his international fame with his highly eclectic style. He conducted and arranged the music at the opening ceremony for the 1992 Barcelona Olympic Games.

●ALBUMS: *B-2 Unit* (Island 1980)★★, *Hidariudeno (A Dream Of The Left Arm)* (1981)★★★, *Merry Christmas, Mr. Lawrence* soundtrack (Virgin 1983)★★, *Coda* (1983)★★★, *Ongaku Zukan (A Picture Book Of Music)* (1984)★★★, *Esperanto* (1985)★★★, *Miraiha Yarô (A Futurist Chap)* (1986)★★★, *Media Bahn Live* (1986)★★, *Oneamisno Tsubasa (The Wings Of Oneamis)* (1986)★★★, *Illustrated Musical Encyclopedia* (Ten 1986)★★, *Neo Geo* (CBS 1987)★★★, with David Byrne, Cong Su *The Last Emperor* soundtrack (Virgin 1987)★★★, *Playing The Orchestra* (1988)★★, *Gruppo Musicale* (1989)★★★, *Beauty* (Virgin 1989)★★★, *Heartbeat* (Virgin 1991)★★★, *Wild Palms* soundtrack (1993)★★★, *Sweet Revenge* (Elektra 1994)★★★, *1996* (Milan 1996)★★★, *Smoochy* (Milan 1997)★★★.

●COMPILATIONS: *Tokyo Joe* (Denon 1988)★★★, *Sakamoto Plays Sakamoto* (Virgin 1989)★★★.

●FURTHER READING: *Otowo Miru, Tokiwo Kiku (Seeing Sound And Hearing Time)*, Ryûichi Sakamoto and Shôzô Omori. *Seldom-Illegal*, Ryûichi Sakamoto.

SANBORN, DAVID

b. 30 July 1945, Tampa, Florida, USA. Sanborn's virtuosity has now spanned four decades, taking him from being a band member (with the seminal Paul Butterfield) to a leading session player for artists such as David Bowie, James Taylor and Stevie Wonder. His is the alto saxophone solo on Bowie's 'Young Americans'. He grew up in St. Louis and played with some of the finest Chicago school bluesmen, including Albert King. Nowadays, under his own name, Sanborn records and performs regularly. His blistering alto saxophone style competes somewhere between Junior Walker and Dick Heckstall-Smith, and is all the more remarkable because for many years as a child he suffered from polio and had breathing difficulties. Sanborn does not flirt with his instrument, he blows it hard. His

solo debut was in 1975 with *Taking Off*. Over the next decade he produced a series of albums that were all successful, and won a Grammy for *Voyeur*. In 1985, *A Change Of Heart* proved to be a big hit in the jazz charts, although much of it was in the rock style, notably the unrelenting and powerful 'Tintin' along with the pure funk of 'High Roller'. *Close Up* featured a sensitive (though raucous) reading of the Diana Ross and Marvin Gaye hit 'You Are Everything'. In 1991 Sanborn made his first ever 'pure jazz album' and achieved the esteem of the jazz reviewers. *Another Hand* and more recently *Pearls* have lifted Sanborn to the peak of his already lengthy career. The latter album was lodged at the top of the *Billboard* jazz chart for many weeks in 1995.

●ALBUMS: *Taking Off* (Warners 1975)★★, *Sanborn* (Warners 1976)★★, *David Sanborn Band* (1977)★★★, *Heart To Heart* (Warners 1978)★★★, *Hideaway* (Warners 1980)★★★, *Voyeur* (Warners 1981)★★★, *As We Speak* (Warners 1982)★★★, *Backstreet* (Warners 1983)★★★, *Let It Speak* (Warners 1984)★★★, *Love And Happiness* (1984)★★★, *Straight To The Heart* (Warners 1985)★★★★, *A Change Of Heart* (Warners 1987)★★★, *Close Up* (Reprise 1988)★★★, *Another Hand* (Elektra 1991)★★★★, *Upfront* (Elektra 1992)★★★, *Hearsay* (Elektra 1993)★★★, *Pearls* (Elektra 1995)★★★★, *Love Songs* (Warners 1995)★★★, *Songs From The Night Before* (Elektra 1996)★★★.

SATRIANI, JOE

Joe Satriani grew up in Long Island, New York, USA, and is a skilled guitarist responsible for teaching the instrument to, among others, Kirk Hammett of Metallica, and Steve Vai. After travelling abroad extensively in his youth he returned to the USA to form the Squares. This project folded in 1984 through an abject lack of commercial recognition, giving Satriani the opportunity to concentrate on his experimental guitar playing. The outcome of this was the release of an EP, *Joe Satriani*. Following a spell with the Greg Kihn band, appearing on *Love And Rock 'N' Roll*, Satriani released *Not Of This Earth*, an album which was less polished than its successor, *Surfing With The Alien*. Despite offering no vocal accompaniment, this set was a major seller and brought mainstream respect to an artist often felt to be too clinical or technical for such reward. In 1988 he was joined more permanently by Stu Hamm (bass) and Jonathan Mover (drums), also working for a spell on Mick Jagger's late 80s tour. Never afraid to push his considerable musical skills to the limit, Satriani has played the banjo and harmonica on his albums, as well as successfully attempting vocals on *Flying In A Blue Dream*. In 1993 he released *Time Machine*, a double CD that contained a mixture of new and previously unreleased tracks dating back to 1984, and also live material from his 1993 Extremist world tour. The guitarist then replaced Ritchie Blackmore in Deep Purple in 1994 while maintaining his own solo recording carreer.

●ALBUMS: *Not Of This Earth* (Relativity 1986)★★★, *Surfing With The Alien* (Relativity 1987)★★★★, *Dreaming 11* (Relativity 1988)★★★, *Flying In A Blue Dream* (Relativity 1990)★★★, *Time Machine* (1993)★★★, *Joe Satriani* (Epic 1995)★★★.

SAXON

Formed in the north of England in the late 70s, Saxon were originally known as Son Of A Bitch and spent their early days paying dues in clubs and small venues up and down the UK, with Peter 'Biff' Byford (vocals), Graham Oliver (guitar), Paul Quinn (guitar), Steve Dawson (bass) and Pete Gill (drums) building a strong live reputation. After the name switch they signed a contract with French label Carrere, better known for its disco productions than its work with heavy metal bands. During the late 70s many young metal bands were emerging in a UK scene that became known as the New Wave Of British Heavy Metal. These bands challenged the supremacy of the old guard of heavy metal bands, and Saxon were at the head of this movement along with Iron Maiden and Diamond Head. The first album was a solid, if basic, heavy rock outing, but the release of *Wheels Of Steel* turned the tide. Saxon's popularity soared, earning themselves two UK Top 20 hits with 'Wheels Of Steel' and '747 (Strangers In The Night)'. They capitalized on this success with the release in the same year of *Strong Arm Of The Law*, another very heavy, surprisingly articulate, metal album. A further Top 20 hit arrived with 'And The Bands Played On', drawn from the following year's *Demin And Leather*, which also produced 'Never Surrender'. They toured the USA to great acclaim and appeared at the Castle Donington 'Monsters Of Rock' festival. By the time of 1982's *The Eagle Has Landed*, which gave Saxon their most successful album, reaching the UK Top 5, the group were at their peak. That same year, Pete Gill was replaced by drummer Nigel Glockler, who had previously worked with Toyah. At this point Saxon counted among their rivals only the immensely popular Iron Maiden. The release of *Power And The Glory*

enforced their credentials as a major rock band. The follow-up, *Innocence Is No Excuse*, was a more polished and radio-friendly production but it stalled just inside the Top 40. It heralded an uncertain time for the band and a resulting slide in their popularity. The departure of Steve Dawson contributed to their malaise. *Rock The Nations* was as punishing as old, but the chance to recapture former glories had now expired. In 1990 Saxon returned to the public eye with a UK tour that featured a set-list built on their popular older material. *Solid Ball Of Rock* was their most accomplished album for some time, but in early 1995 Oliver, Dawson and Gill played live together while contesting the rights to the name Saxon with Byford. The issue was soon resolved, however, and Byford was back in place for *Dogs Of War*, with Oliver having taken his leave. A workmanlike record harking back to the band's mid-80s propensity for epic choruses, it was neither awful nor progressive. Oliver, Dawson and Gill subsequently formed Son Of A Bitch.

●ALBUMS: *Saxon* (Saxon Carrere 1979)★★★, *Wheels Of Steel* (Saxon Carrere 1980)★★★, *Strong Arm Of The Law* (Carrere 1980)★★★, *Denim And Leather* (Carrere 1981)★★★, *The Eagle Has Landed* (Carrere 1982)★★★, *Power And The Glory* (Carrere 1983)★★★, *Crusader* (Carrere 1984)★★★, *Innocence Is No Excuse* (Parlophone 1985)★★, *Rock The Nations* (EMI 1986)★★, *Destiny* (EMI 1988)★★★, *Rock 'N' Roll Gypsies* (Roadrunner 1990)★★, *Solid Ball Of Rock* (Virgin 1991)★★★, *Dogs Of War* (HTD/Virgin 1995)★★.

●COMPILATIONS: *Anthology* (Raw Power 1988)★★★, *Back On The Streets* (Connoisseur 1990)★★★, *Greatest Hits Live* (Essential 1990)★★, *Best Of* (EMI 1991)★★★★.

●VIDEOS: *Live Innocence* (1986), *Power & The Glory - Video Anthology* (1989), *Saxon Live* (1989), *Greatest Hits Live* (1990).

SCHENKER, MICHAEL

b. 10 January 1955, Sarstedt, Germany. Schenker began his musical career in 1971 at the age of 16, when, along with brother Rudolf, he formed the Scorpions. After contributing impressive guitar-work on the band's *Lonesome Crow* debut, he was offered the chance to replace Bernie Marsden in UFO. Schenker joined the group in June 1973 and their resultant musical direction swung to hard rock. *Phenomenon*, released in 1974, featured the metal classics 'Doctor, Doctor' and 'Rock Bottom', with Schenker's performance on his Gibson 'Flying V' hammering home the band's new identity. A series of strong albums followed before Schenker eventually quit in 1978 after the recording of *Obsession*. The split had been predicted for some time following personal conflicts between Schenker and vocalist Phil Mogg. The guitarist moved back to Germany and temporarily rejoined the Scorpions, contributing to *Lovedrive*, released in 1979. Soon afterwards he formed his own band, the Michael Schenker Group, which was later abbreviated to MSG. MSG's personnel has remained in a constant state of flux, with Schenker hiring and firing musicians seemingly at will. In 1991 Schenker also took time out between MSG albums to contribute to the Contraband project, a one-off collaboration between members of Shark Island, Vixen, Ratt and L.A. Guns.

●ALBUMS: as MSG *The Michael Schenker Group* (Chrysalis 1980)★★, *MSG* (Chrysalis 1981)★★, *One Night At Budokan* (Chrysalis 1982)★★, *Assault Attack* (Chrysalis 1982)★★, *Built To Destroy* (Chrysalis 1983)★★, *Rock Will Never Die* (Chrysalis 1984)★★, *Perfect Timing* (EMI 1987)★★, *Save Yourself* (Capitol 1989)★★, *MSG* (EMI 1992)★★, *BBC Radio One Live In Concert* rec. 1982 (Windsong 1993)★★.

SCHNEIDER, JOHN

b. 8 April 1954, Mount Kisco, Westchester County, New York, USA. Schneider, a gifted musician and actor, has appeared in musicals from the age of 14. He played Bo Duke in the long-running US television series about a disaster-prone, hillbilly family, *The Dukes Of Hazzard* from 1979-85. He is featured on the 1982 cast album of the same name. In 1981 he had his first US hit (pop chart number 14, country number 4) with a revival of Elvis Presley's 'It's Now Or Never', and proved himself to be one television star who could sing. However, despite other successes on the US country chart, he was not accepted as a bona fide artist by country disc jockeys. In 1984, the disc jockeys were given unmarked copies of 'I've Been Around Enough To Know', and many of them played the record believing it to be by George Strait. Schneider's identity was revealed and the single topped the US country chart. He had further number 1s with 'Country Girls', 'What's A Memory Like You (Doing In A Love Like This)?' and 'You're The Last Thing I Needed Tonight'. Schneider though, unlike most country stars, did not care for touring and his final US Top 10 country hit was in 1987 with 'Love, You Ain't Seen The Last Of Me', at a time when he was planning to do just that. He returned to acting and was in a successful series, *Grand Slam*, in 1990.

●ALBUMS: *Now Or Never* (Scotti Bros 1981)★★★, *White Christmas* (Scotti Bros 1981)★★, *Dukes Of Hazzard* television cast (Scotti Bros 1982)★★, *Quiet Man* (1982)★★, with Jill Michaels *If You Believe* (1983)★★, *Too Good To Stop Now* (MCA 1984)★★★, *Trying To Outrun The Wind* (MCA 1985)★★★, *A Memory Like You* (MCA 1986)★★★, *Take The Long Way Home* (MCA 1986)★★★, *You Ain't Seen The Last Of Me* (MCA 1987)★★★.

SCRITTI POLITTI

Scritti Politti was founded by a group of Leeds art students in 1978. By the time of their first single, 'Skank Bloc Bologna', the nucleus of the band was Green Gartside (b. 'Green' Strohmeyer-Gartside, 22 June 1956, Cardiff Wales; vocals/guitar - who refuses to reveal his actual first name), Matthew Kay (keyboards/manager), Tom Morley (drums) and Nial Jinks (bass, departed 1980). At this stage, the group was explicitly political (Green had been a Young Communist), encouraging listeners to create their own music in the face of the corporate record industry. Gartside also gained a reputation for convoluted wordplay within his lyrics. This early *avant garde* phase gave way to a smooth sound that brought together elements of pop, jazz, soul and reggae on songs like 'The Sweetest Girl' (with Robert Wyatt on piano) and 'Asylums In Jerusalem'/'Jacques Derrida', which appeared on their debut album for Rough Trade Records, produced by Adam Kidron. Morley departed from the group in November 1982, by which time Gartside was Scritti Politti. *Songs To Remember* became Rough Trade's most successful chart album; number 1 in the UK independent and, in the national chart, peaking at number 12 (beating Stiff Little Fingers' previous effort at number 14). After moving on to Virgin Records, Green linked up with New York musicians David Gamson (keyboards/programming) and Fred Maher (drums), who formed the basis of the group that made a series of UK hits in the years 1984-88. Produced by Arif Mardin, these included 'Wood Beez (Pray Like Aretha Franklin)' (number 10), 'Absolute' (number 17) and 'The Word Girl' (number 6). A three-year silence was broken by 'Oh Patti (Don't Feel Sorry For Loverboy)' (number 13), lifted from *Provision*, and boasting a trumpet solo by Miles Davis. Gartside again maintained a low profile for two years after 'First Boy In This Town (Love Sick)', failed to break into the UK Top 60 in late 1988. He returned in 1991 with a revival of the Beatles' 'She's A Woman' (number 20), featuring leading reggae star Shabba Ranks, while another Jamaican star, Sweetie Irie, guested on a version of Gladys Knight And The Pips' 1967 hit, 'Take Me In Your Arms And Love Me'.

●ALBUMS: *Songs To Remember* (Rough Trade 1982)★★★, *Cupid And Psyche* (Virgin 1985)★★★, *Provision* (Virgin 1988)★★.

●VIDEOS: *Scritti Politti* (Virgin 1985), *Boom! There She Was* (Virgin 1988).

SEALS, DAN

b. 8 February 1950, McCamey, Texas, USA. Leaving successful pop duo England Dan And John Ford Coley was, at first, a disastrous career move for Dan Seals. His management left him with unpaid tax bills and mounting debts and he lost his house, his van and his money. He says, 'I was bankrupt, separated and living at friends' places. My kids were with friends. It was a real bad time'. Furthermore, the two albums that he made for Atlantic Records as a solo artist, *Stones* and *Harbinger*, meant little. However, Kyle Lehning, who produced his hits with England Dan And John Ford Coley, never lost faith and helped to establish him on the US country charts with 'Everybody's Dream Girl' in 1983. Further country hits followed and he had a US number 1 hit with 'Meet Me In Montana', a duet with Marie Osmond, in 1985. Seals then had an extraordinary run of nine consecutive US number 1 country singles: the dancing 'Bop', the rodeo story 'Everything That Glitters (Is Not Gold)', 'You Still Move Me', 'I Will Be There', 'Three Time Loser', the wedding song 'One Friend', 'Addicted' and 'Big Wheels In The Moonlight', many of which he wrote himself. Two further number 1 hits in 1990 included a re-working of soul singer Sam Cooke's 'Good Times'. *Won't Be Blue Anymore* sold half a million copies in the USA, while another big-selling record, *On The Front Line*, included an exquisite duet with Emmylou Harris, 'Lullaby'.

●ALBUMS: *Stones* (Atlantic 1980)★★, *Harbinger* (Atlantic 1982)★★, *Rebel Heart* (1983)★★, *San Antone* (EMI America 1984)★★, *Won't Be Blue Anymore* (EMI America 1985)★★, *On The Front Line* (EMI America 1986)★★, *Rage On* (Capitol 1988)★★, *On Arrival* (Capitol 1990)★★, *Walking The Wire* (1992)★★, *In A Quiet Room* (Intersound 1995)★★.

●COMPILATIONS: *The Best Of Dan Seals* (Capitol 1987)★★★.

SECRET AFFAIR

Led by Ian Page (b. Ian Paine, 1960, England; vocals/trumpet/piano/organ), and Dave Cairns (b.

1959, England; guitar/vocals), Secret Affair, one of the most creative neo-mod groups of the late 70s, emerged out of the lightweight UK new wave band New Hearts who folded in 1978. New Hearts released two lacklustre singles. The Secret Affair line-up was completed by Dennis Smith (bass/vocals, ex-Advertising), and Chris Bennett (drums, ex-Alternative TV). Bennett did not work out and was replaced by Seb Shelton (ex-Young Bucks). They debuted supporting the Jam (as the New Hearts had once done), but made their name at the Bridge House Tavern in Canning Town, London, centre of the mod revival. They appeared on the *Mods Mayday* live compilation but then set up their own I-Spy label through Arista Records. Subsequently they toured with Purple Hearts and Back To Zero under the banner 'March Of The Mods'. Their first single, 'Time For Action', was an immediate success for both band and label, featuring Chris Gent (of the Autographs) on saxophone. They also signed Squire to the I-Spy label. Further singles in differing styles charted and the debut album was well received, particularly the epic title track which referred to their fan following. However, Shelton left late in 1980 to join the Up-Set, then Dexys Midnight Runners and was replaced by Paul Bultitude. After two singles from the final Secret Affair album failed commercially, they disbanded. Dave Cairns went on to form the duo Flag, with Archie Brown, his former colleague from the Young Bucks. He subsequently formed another band called Walk On Fire with Dennis Smith. Page, who now writes fantasy books, formed Ian Page and Bop whose single 'Unity Street' created some interest. Bultitude joined the Mari Wilson's Wilsations and later founded the Dance Network label. Smith threw in his lot with Nik Kershaw's Krew, and Seb Shelton went on to manage, among others, the Woodentops.

●ALBUMS: *Glory Boys* (I-Spy 1979)★★★, *Behind Closed Doors* (I-Spy 1980)★★, *Business As Usual* (I-Spy 1982)★★.

SELECTER

When Coventry's Specials needed a b-side for their own debut, 'Gangsters', they approached fellow local musician Noel Davies. With the assistance of John Bradbury aka Prince Rimshot (drums), and Barry Jones (trombone), Davies concocted the instrumental track 'The Selecter'. Released on the Specials own 2-Tone label, the single took off with both sides receiving airplay. This meant that a band had to be formed to tour. Bradbury was busy drumming for the Specials and Jones had returned to his newsagent business so Davies assembled the Selecter Mk II. This consisted of Pauline Black (vocals), Noel Davis (guitar), Crompton Amanor (drums/vocals), Charles H. Bainbridge (drums), Gappa Hendricks, Desmond Brown (keyboards) and Charlie Anderson (bass). Anderson claims the original ska superstar, Prince Buster, among his ancestors. The debut album featured the renowned ska trombonist Rico Rodriquez. Like many of the bands who first found fame on 2-Tone, the Selecter departed for pastures new - in this case 2-Tone's distributors, Chrysalis Records. They managed a string of successful singles such as 'On My Radio', 'Three Minute Hero', and 'Missing Words'. Black left in 1981 and recorded the single 'Pirates Of The Airwaves', with Sunday Best before concentrating on acting. She would reappear to the general public as hostess of the children's pop/games show, *Hold Tight*. However, more impressive performances included a one-woman show, *Let Them Call It Jazz*, plus portrayals of Cleopatra and Billie Holiday, the latter bringing her the *Time Out* award for best actress in 1990. Black rejoined Selecter on tour in 1991 as signs of a ska revival in London gained ground, though she also found time to host Radio 5's *Black To The Future* and complete her first novel, *The Goldfinches*. A phone call from Doug Trendle (aka Buster Blood Vessel from Bad Manners) had prompted the Selecter's reformation, which culminated in the release of their first new material for over a decade in 1994.

●ALBUMS: *Too Much Pressure* (2-Tone 1980)★★★★, *Celebrate The Bullet* (Chrysalis 1981)★★★, *Out On The Streets: Live In London* (Triple X 1992)★★, *The Happy Album* (Triple X 1994)★★★, *Hairspray* (Triple X 1995)★★★, *Live At Roskilde Festival* (Magnam Music 1997)★★.

●COMPILATIONS: *The Selecter & The Specials: Live In Concert* (1993)★★, *Prime Cuts* (Magnum 1995)★★★, *Selecterized: The Best Of The Selecter 1991-1996* (Dojo 1997)★★★.

Sex Gang Children

This London-based post punk/gothic band were briefly in vogue in the early 80s. They were built around vocalist Andi Sex Gang, who talked himself into support slots for which he needed to quickly assemble a new band. He eventually settled on Dave Roberts (bass), Terry McLeay (guitar) and Rob Stroud (drums), who played their first gig under the name Panic Button. The name Sex Gang Children was lifted from a William Burroughs book and was actually on a list of names with which fellow King's Road fashion victim Boy George was

toying. It later transpired that Boy George had in turn taken it from Malcolm McLaren's original suggestion for a moniker for the band which would become Bow Wow Wow. By 1982 a number of bands in the same mould began breaking through in the capital. Sex Gang Children's first vinyl release was a 12-inch titled 'Beasts', produced by Nicky Garrett (ex-UK Subs), after which Tony James (Generation X, later Sigue Sigue Sputnik) began to take an interest in the band. Their most fondly remembered release, 'Into The Abyss', closed 1982 with their debut long player arriving early the next year. The single lifted from it, 'Sebastiane', featured Jinni Hewes from Marc And The Mambas on violin. Andi then performed a debut with Marc Almond ('The Hungry Years') for the compilation *The Whip*, which also included a contribution from Roberts' other band, Car Crash International. Stroud left to join Pink And Black (featuring future All About Eve bass player Andy Cousins), and was replaced by Nigel Preston (ex-Theatre Of Hate). He stayed long enough to record the single 'Mauritia Mayer', before he took part in a bizarre 'drummers' swap with Ray Mondo of Death Cult. Events took a further strange turn when the latter was deported back to Sierra Leone for passport irregularities after a US tour. Roberts also departed, leaving Andi and McLeay to recruit Cam Campbell (bass), and Kevin Matthews (drums). However, only one single, 'Deiche', was released before the band disintegrated and Andi set out on a solo career.

●ALBUMS: *Song And Legend* (Illuminated 1983)★★, *Beasts* (Illuminated 1984)★★, *Live* (Arkham 1984)★, *Re-enter The Abyss* (Dojo 1986)★, *Blind* (Jungle 1993)★★.

Shack

Formed in 1986 by brothers Mick (b. 28 November 1961, Liverpool, England) and John Head (b. 4 October 1965). Shack emerged from the ashes of the Pale Fountains. Having had their fingers burnt by the major records industry - the Pale Fountains reached number 46 in the UK charts with 'Thank You', but were generally misunderstood by their employers - Shack joined up with independent label the Ghetto Recording Company. Experts at the cleverly understated melodic guitar pop song, 1988 saw the release of their acclaimed debut album, *Zilch*. Yet instead of persevering with their commercial instincts, Shack laid low until reappearing with a single in 1991 and a planned second album for the year after, which was finally issued in 1995. Much of what Shack were doing in 1990 can be heard in the current wave of mid-90s guitar-based indie bands. It is hoped that they will be both credited and remembered for their originality.

●ALBUMS: *Zilch* (Ghetto 1988)★★★★, *Water Pistol* (Marina 1995)★★★.

SHAKATAK

This UK group were one the original benefactors of the early 80s British jazz/funk boom (alongside contemporaries Level 42). The group comprised Bill Sharpe (keyboards), George Anderson (bass), Keith Winter (guitar), Roger Odell (drums), Nigel Wright (keyboards/synthesizers) and Gil Seward (vocals). Between 1980 and 1987, Shakatak had 14 UK chart singles. Since their chart debut with 'Feels Like The First Time' on Polydor Records (a long-standing partnership), other notable hits have been 'Easier Said Than Done' (1981), 'Night Birds' (UK Top 10 - 1982), 'Dark Is The Night' (1983) and 'Down On The Street' (UK Top 10 - 1984). This understated group proved their reputation as one of the finest purveyors of classy jazz/funk with the successful K-Tel compilation, *The Coolest Cuts*. The later half of the 80s have shown Shakatak leaving behind the demands of instant pop chart hits and they allowed themselves to mature, honing their jazz influences. - most evident on the 1989 set, *Turn The Music Up*, their first studio effort in almost five years. In addition to releasing a solo album in 1988, Sharpe has also collaborated with Gary Numan on what was a one-off single, 'Change Your Mind', in 1985. On reaching the UK Top 20, it was not until four years later that the duo released a full album, *Automatic*.

●ALBUMS: *Drivin' Hard* (Polydor 1981)★★★, *Nightbirds* (Polydor 1982)★★★, *Invitations* (Polydor 1982)★★★, *Out Of This World* (Polydor 1983)★★★, *Down On The Street* (Polydor 1984)★★★, *Live!* (Polydor 1985)★★, *Turn The Music Up* (Polydor 1989)★★★, *Bitter Sweet* (Polydor 1991)★★★, *Street Level* (1993)★★. Solo: Bill Sharpe *Famous People* (Polydor 1988)★★, with Gary Numan *Automatic* (Polydor 1989)★★.

●COMPILATIONS: *The Coolest Cuts* (K-Tel 1988)★★★, *The Remix Best Album* (1992)★★.

SHARKEY, FEARGAL

b. 13 August 1958, Derry, Northern Ireland. Sharkey first found fame as the lead singer of the Irish pop-punk group, the Undertones, whose singles provided some of the best pop of the late 70s. The group's reign lasted from 1976-83 after which Sharkey teamed up with Vince Clarke in the short-lived Assembly. The plaintive 'Never Never' was a

Top 10 hit for the group and highlighted the power of Sharkey's distinctive, quavering vocal style. In 1984, Sharkey recorded the underrated 'Listen To Your Heart' for Madness's label Zarjazz and this was followed by his biggest success, 'A Good Heart'. This insistent tune established him as a potential major act by reaching number 1 in the UK charts. The Top 10 follow-up 'You Little Thief' was almost equally distinctive and Sharkey's debut album, produced by the Eurythmics' David A. Stewart, was very well received. Sharkey subsequently moved to America, where he recorded *Wish*. A long-delayed third album, *Songs From The Mardi Gras*, continued Sharkey's slow drift away from the mainstream, although it did spawn a surprise Top 20 hit, 'I've Got News For You'. In 1993 Sharkey was working as an A&R manager for Polydor Records and in 1995 it was announced that he was forming a new UK record label.

●ALBUMS: *Feargal Sharkey* (Virgin 1985)★★★, *Wish* (Virgin 1987)★★, *Songs From The Mardi Gras* (Virgin 1991)★★.

SHELTON, RICKY VAN

b. 2 January 1952, Grit, near Lynchburg, Virginia, USA. Shelton was raised in a church-going family and he learned to love gospel music. His brother worked as a musician and through travelling with him, he also acquired a taste for country music. He worked as a pipefitter but his prospective wife, Bettye, realized his singing potential and, in 1984, suggested that they went to Nashville where she had secured a personnel job. In 1986 he impressed producer Steve Buckingham during a club performance, and his first recording session yielded a US Top 30 country hit in 'Wild-Eyed Dream'. He then made the country Top 10 with one of his best records, the dramatic story-song, 'Crimes Of Passion'. In 1987 he had a US country number 1 by reviving a song from a Conway Twitty album, 'Somebody Lied'. In 1988 he had another number 1 by reviving Harlan Howard's song, 'Life Turned Her That Way', which, unlike Merle Tillis, he performed in its original 4/4 tempo. His revival of an obscure Roger Miller song, 'Don't We All Have The Right', also went to number 1, thus giving him five country hits from his first album. Since then, he has had US country number 1s with revivals of 'I'll Leave This World Loving You', Ned Miller's 'From A Jack To A King' and a new song, 'Living Proof'. Although Shelton has much in common with his hard-nosed contemporaries, he succumbed to a middle-of-the-road album of familiar Christmas songs. He recorded a duet of 'Sweet Memories' with Brenda Lee, while 'Rockin' Years' with Dolly Parton was a number 1 country single in 1991. To help his career, Shelton's wife studied law, while he attempted to conquer his fear of flying. In 1992, Shelton recorded an album of semi-spiritual material, *Don't Overlook Salvation*, as a gift to his parents, before enjoying more hits with the new recordings included on *Greatest Hits Plus*. From then on, Shelton has lost ground, not achieving country hits with the same regularity. He recorded an ironic song, 'Still Got A Couple Of Good Years Left', which became a US country Top 50 hit in 1993.

●ALBUMS: *Wild-Eyed Dream* (Columbia 1987)★★★, *Loving Proof* (Columbia 1988)★★★, *Ricky Van Shelton Sings Christmas* (1989)★★, *Ricky Van Shelton III* (Columbia 1990)★★★, *Backroads* (Columbia 1991)★★★, *Don't Overlook Salvation* (Columbia 1992)★★★, *A Bridge I Didn't Burn* (Columbia 1993)★★★, *Love And Honor* (Columbia 1994)★★★.

●COMPILATIONS: *Greatest Hits Plus* (Columbia 1992)★★★.

●VIDEOS: *Where Was I, Live* (1993), *To Be Continued ...* (1993).

SHEPPARD, ANDY

b. 20 January 1957, Bristol, Avon, England. Sheppard attempted to learn saxophone at school, but was told he would have to take up clarinet first. In disgust he bought a guitar instead, but began on tenor saxophone after hearing John Coltrane. He also played the flute and sang solo in the choir while at school. He later discovered that he had perfect pitch, and only learned to read music in his late 20s. He took up the soprano under the influences of Steve Lacy and alcohol, having sold his tenor to a friend when drunk. Before moving to London Sheppard played with Sphere (not to be confused with the US band of the same name). He also played in Klaunstance, then spent two years in Paris working with Laurent Cugny's big band, Lumiere, and Urban Sax. Returning to the UK he played with Paul Dunmall and Keith Tippett. In early 1987 Sheppard formed his own small band, recording two acclaimed albums and undertaking several successful tours. He also became a regular performer in bands led by Carla Bley, Gil Evans and George Russell. In 1990 he set up the Soft On The Inside big band, which produced an album and a video, and he also recorded an acclaimed set of duo improvisations with Tippett. Since early 1991 Sheppard has run an electric small group, In Co-Motion (featuring the fine trumpeter Claude Deppa), alongside the big band, and he recently

composed a piece for ice-dancers Torville and Dean. He also played in an occasional trio with Bley and Steve Swallow (producer on most of his albums). Sheppard is one of the most assured and versatile (and least flashy) saxophonists on the scene today.

●ALBUMS: *Andy Sheppard* (Antilles 1987)★★★, with Sphere *Sphere* (Cadillac 1988)★★★, with Sphere *Present Tense* (Cadillac 1988)★★★, *Introductions In The Dark* (Antilles 1989)★★, *Soft On The Inside* (Antilles 1990)★★★, with Keith Tippett *66 Shades Of Lipstick* (Editions EG 1990)★★, *In Co-Motion* (Antilles 1991)★★★★, *Rhythm Method* (Blue Note 1993)★★★, *Delivery Suite* (Blue Note 1994)★★★, with Nana Vasconcelos, Steve Lodder *Inclassifible* (Label Bleu 1995)★★★, with Lodder *Moving Image* (Verve 1996)★★★.

SHOCKED, MICHELLE

b. Karen Michelle Johnson, 1962, Dallas, Texas, USA. This roots singer-songwriter's music draws on frequently tough experiences of a nomadic lifestyle. Her childhood had been divided between a religiously inclined mother (Catholic then Mormon), and her estranged father, a sometime mandolin player. She originally came to prominence via a Walkman-recorded gig, taped around a campfire, complete with crickets on backing vocals. *Short Sharp Shocked* highlighted more varied and less self-conscious stylings than the more mainstream Suzanne Vega/Tracy Chapman school. *Captain Swing* was her 'big band' record, where she was joined once more by Dwight Yoakam's producer/guitarist Pete Anderson, as well as many famous extras (Fats Domino, Bobby Bland, Randy Newman). Despite songs with titles like 'God Is A Real Estate Developer', its jazzy rhythms and swishing brass made it her most commercially accessible. The album's title was taken from the 19th-century leader of a farm labourer's revolt, the type of subject matter which put her in good company with touring companion Billy Bragg. The recording of *Arkansas Traveller* was completed by travelling across the USA and further afield with a portable studio. Hence, musicians such as Taj Mahal, Doc Watson, Levon Helm, Clarence 'Gatemouth' Brown and Hothouse Flowers made their contributions in Ireland, Australia and elsewhere. Shocked had spent time researching the origins of American music and in particular the black-faced minstrel legacy, which she attacked with her own traditional songs. In the summer of 1995 Shocked filed a suit to be released from her contract with Polygram/Mercury Records following a number of accusations from both parties. When this was resolved she signed with BMG and released *Kind Hearted Woman* in October 1996. Shocked is one of the most interesting of the new /*generation of folk artists.

●ALBUMS: *The Texas Campfire Tapes* (Cooking Vinyl 1987)★★, *Short Sharp Shocked* (Cooking Vinyl 1988)★★★, *Captain Swing* (Cooking Vinyl 1989)★★, *Arkansas Traveller* (London 1992)★★★, *Kind Hearted Woman* (BMG 1996)★★★, *Stillborn* (Private 1996)★★★.

●COMPILATIONS: *Mercury Poise: 1988-1995* (Mercury 1997)★★★.

SHRIEKBACK

Shriekback originally evolved around a three-man nucleus of ex-Gang Of Four member Dave Allen, Carl Marsh (fresh from his own band, Out On Blue Six), plus Barry Andrews, previously with XTC, League Of Gentlemen and Restaurant For Dogs. The trio fused funk and rock with a unique and complex rhythmic approach, creating a distinctive and influential sound. The first fruits of this project came in 1982 with the EP *Tench* and then 'Sexthinkone' on the Y label, but it was the next two singles, 'My Spine Is the Bassline' (1982) and 'Lined Up' (1983) that established the band. Two further singles, 'Working On The Ground' and 'Accretions', were enough to secure a contract with Arista Records, releasing *Jam Science* in 1984. The album also spawned two excellent singles, 'Hand On My Heart' and 'Mercy Dash'. The following year saw the release of *Oil And Gold*, which included 'Nemesis' and 'Fish Below The Ice'. Although more commercially based, the band had lost that hard, infectious funk vein that was previously so predominant. A move to Island Records yielded *Big Night Music*, early in 1987, accompanied by 'Gunning For Buddha' a month earlier. 'Get Down Tonight' followed in 1988, but this presaged the last Shriekback album proper, *Go Bang*. Those looking for an introduction to Shriekback might opt for *The Infinite*, a collection of the Y singles released on the Kaz label. Since then, there have been two further collections, summarizing the band's time with Arista and Island, respectively.

●ALBUMS: *Care* (Warners 1983)★★, *Jam Science* (Arista 1984)★★★, *Oil And Gold* (Arista 1985)★★★, *Big Night Music* (Island 1987)★★★, *Go Bang* (Shriekback 1988)★★, *Sacred City* (Shriekback 1994)★★.

●COMPILATIONS: *The Infinite - The Best Of Shriekback* (Kaz 1985)★★★, *The Best Of Shriekback, Volume 2* (Shriekback 1988)★★★, *The Best Of Shriekback* (Shriekback 1990)★★★.

SIBERRY, JANE

b. 12 October 1955, Toronto, Canada. This singer/composer stands outside the traditional boundaries of folk music, being compared to such artists as Laurie Anderson, Joni Mitchell and Suzanne Vega. Having graduated from the University of Guelph with a degree in Microbiology, Siberry began by performing on the local coffee house circuit in Canada. Her first, independently produced album, in 1981, was followed by a Canadian tour. She financed the project by earning tips as a waitress. *No Borders Here* included 'Mimi On The Beach', an underground hit at home in Canada. *The Speckless Sky* went gold in Canada, and won two CASBYS, Canada's People Choice Award, for both album and producer of the year. Siberry made her first live appearance in Europe, following the release of *The Walking*, at the ICA in London. *The Walking* marked her recording debut for Reprise Records. Having recorded her earlier production demos in a 16-track studio located in an apple orchard near Toronto, she decided to record the whole of *Bound By The Beauty* at Orchard Studio. For the task, a 24-track unit was parachuted into the studio. The whole album was recorded in a matter of weeks, and included Teddy Borowiecki, who had played with k.d. lang (piano/accordion), Stich Winston (drums), John Switzer (bass), and Ken Myhr (guitar). The album was mixed by Kevin Killen, known for work with both Kate Bush and Peter Gabriel and was greeted with considerable critical acclaim. The belated follow-up saw her work with Brian Eno on two tracks. Commenting on its distinctive title and character, she noted: 'I think this record is more whole in a funny way . . . It is also more masculine. Before, my work has always had a sense of graciousness and hospitality, like the good mother. I don't think I could be called a female singer/songwriter with this record'.

●ALBUMS: *Jane Siberry* (Street 1980)★★★, *No Borders Here* (Open Air 1984)★★★, *The Speckless Sky* (Reprise 1985)★★★, *The Walking* (Duke Street 1987)★★, *Bound By The Beauty* (Reprise 1989)★★★★, *When I Was A Boy* (Reprise 1993)★★★, *Maria* (Warners 1995)★★★, *Teenager* (Sheeba 1996)★★★.

●COMPILATIONS: *Summer In The Yukon* (Reprise 1992)★★★, *A Collection 1984-1989* (Duke Street 1993)★★★.

SIGUE SIGUE SPUTNIK

These UK punk/glam revivalists engineered themselves a briefly prosperous niche in the mid-80s. The creation of Tony James (ex-Chelsea; Generation X), Sigue Sigue Sputnik artlessly copied the shock tactics of Sex Pistols manager Malcolm McLaren. Instead of taking on board the Pistols' nihilism, James poached from cyberpunk novels and films (particularly *Blade Runner*) for their image. This consisted of dyed hair piled high, bright colours and an abundance of eye-liner. James had also recruited clothes designer Martin Degville (vocals), Neal X (b. Neil Whitmore; guitar), Ray Mayhew (drums) and Chris Kavanagh (b. 4 June 1964; drums), taking pride in their apparent lack of musical experience. Taking their name from a Moscow street gang, they set about a publicity campaign that resulted in EMI Records, understandably keen not to let the next Pistols slip through their hands again, signing them for a reported £4 million. The figure, however, was deliberately exaggerated in order to provoke publicity. Their first single was 'Love Missile F1-11', which soared to number 3 in the UK charts in February 1986. However, although 'Twenty-First Century Boy' also made the Top 20, and a debut album sold advertising space between tracks, James's money-making ruse soon ended. Despite an avalanche of intentionally lurid press, the band dissolved, and Tony James subsequently, albeit briefly, joined the Sisters Of Mercy in 1991. Kavanagh would go on to Big Audio Dynamite, though James would make another attempt at resurrecting Sigue Sigue Sputnik later in the 90s. Degville recorded a dreadful solo album in the interim.

● ALBUMS: *Flaunt It* (Parlophone 1986)★★, *Dress For Excess* (EMI 1988)★.
● COMPILATIONS: *First Generation* (Jungle 1990)★.
● FURTHER READING: *Ultra*, no author listed.

SIMPLE MINDS

This Scottish group was formed in 1978 by Jim Kerr (b. 9 July 1959, Glasgow, Scotland; vocals), Charlie Burchill (b. 27 November 1959, Glasgow, Scotland; guitar), Tony Donald (bass) and Brian McGee (drums), former members of Glasgow punk group Johnny And The Self-Abusers. A second guitarist, Duncan Barnwell, was recruited following a newspaper advertisement. The unit was augmented by keyboard player Mick McNeil (b. 20 July 1958) before Derek Forbes (b. 22 June 1956) replaced a disaffected Donald. The upheavals of this initial era were completed with Barnwell's departure. Having established themselves as one of Scotland's leading live attractions, Simple Minds were signed to Zoom, an Edinburgh-based independent label marketed by Arista Records. 'Life In A Day', the group's debut single, broached the UK Top 50 in March 1979 while the attendant album reached number 30. Critics were divided over its merits, although a consensus deemed the set derivative. Within weeks the quintet began decrying their creation and embarked on a more radical direction. *Real To Real Cacophony* unfolded within the recording studio in an attempt to regain an early spontaneity and while this largely experimental collection was a commercial flop, it reinstated the group's self-respect and won unanimous music press approbation.

Empires And Dance was released in September 1980. The set fused the flair of its predecessor to a newly established love of dance music and reflected influences garnered during European tours. It included 'I Travel', a pulsating travelogue that became a firm favourite throughout the club circuit and helped engender a new sense of optimism in the group's career. Now free of Arista, Simple Minds were signed to Virgin Records in 1981, and paired with producer Steve Hillage. The resultant sessions spawned two albums, *Sons And Fascination* and *Sister Feelings Call*, which were initially released together. It became the group's first UK Top 20 entrant, spawning three minor hit singles with 'The American', 'Love Song' and 'Sweat In Bullet' and began Simple Minds' transformation from cult to popular favourites. This very success unnerved Brian McGee, who abhorred touring. In August 1981 he was replaced by former Slik and Skids drummer Kenny Hyslop (b. 14 February 1951, Helensburgh, Strathclyde, Scotland), although the newcomer's recorded contribution was confined to 'Promised You A Miracle'. This powerful song reached number 13 in Britain, and proved popular in Europe and Australia where the group enjoyed an almost fanatical following.

Although Mike Ogletree joined on Hyslop's departure, a former musician, Mel Gaynor (b. 29 May 1959), eventually became the quintet's permanent drummer. Both musicians were featured on *New Gold Dream*, Simple Minds' most successful album to date which peaked at number 3. Here the group was harnessing a more commercial sound, and they achieved a series of hits with its attendant singles, 'Glittering Prize' and 'Someone, Somewhere In Summertime'. A sixth collection, *Sparkle In The*

Rain, united the quintet with producer Steve Lillywhite, inspiring comparisons with his other protégés, U2. 'Waterfront', a brash, pulsating grandiose performance, and 'Speed Your Love To Me', prefaced its release, and the album entered the UK chart at number 1. The set also featured 'Up On The Catwalk', a further Top 30 entrant, and a version of Lou Reed's 'Street Hassle', a long-established group favourite.

Jim Kerr married Pretenders' singer Chrissie Hynde in 1984, but their relationship did not survive the rigours of touring. The following year Simple Minds chose to record in America under the aegis of Jimmy Iovine and Bob Clearmountain. It was during this period that the group contributed 'Don't You (Forget About Me)' to the soundtrack of the film *The Breakfast Club*. The quintet remained ambivalent about the song, which was written by Keith Forsey and Steve Schiff, but it paradoxically became a US number 1 when issued as a single. Although the group initially vetoed a worldwide release, they reneged in the light of this achievement whereupon the record became a massive international hit and confirmed the group's world-beating status. However, the track did not appear on the ensuing *Once Upon A Time* which, despite international success, drew considerable criticism for its bombastic approach. Three tracks, 'Alive And Kicking', 'Sanctify Yourself' and 'All The Things She Said', nonetheless reached the UK Top 10, while a concurrent world tour, documented on *Live In The City Of Light*, was one of the year's major events. The proceeds of several dates were donated to Amnesty International, reflecting a growing politicization within the group. In 1988 they were a major inspiration behind the concert celebrating Nelson Mandela's 70th birthday, but although a new composition, 'Mandela Day', was recorded for the event, Simple Minds refused to release it as a single, fearful of seeming opportunistic. The song was later coupled to 'Belfast Child', a lengthy, haunting lament for Northern Ireland based on a traditional folk melody, 'She Moved Through The Fair'. This artistically ambitious work topped the UK chart in February 1989 and set the tone for the group's subsequent album, *Street Fighting Years*, their first studio set in four years. Although it achieved platinum status within five days, sales then dropped rather dramatically, reflecting the uncompromising nature of its content. Three further singles entered the UK Top 20, while *The Amsterdam EP*, which included a version of Prince's 'Sign 'O' The Times', reached number 18 at the end of the year. This contradictory period

closed with the rancorous departure of Mick McNeil, replaced by Peter Vitesse, and the ending of the group's ten-year association with Schoolhouse Management. Simple Minds entered the 90s with an official line-up of Jim Kerr and Charlie Burchill and a development almost impossible to predict. *Real Life* saw the band re-introducing more personal themes to their songwriting after the political concerns of previous albums. The new material recaptured the grand, epic sound that is Simple Minds' trademark. Kerr married Patsy Kensit in January 1992. The highly commercial 'She's A River' came in advance of *Good News From The Next World* in 1995; just as the next world was beginning to think Simple Minds were from an age past, this timely album re-awoke memories of the early 80s.

●ALBUMS: *Life In A Day* (Zoom 1979)★★, *Real To Real Cacophony* (Arista 1979)★★, *Empires And Dance* (Arista 1980)★★, *Sons And Fascination/Sister Feelings Call* (Virgin 1981)★★★, *New Gold Dream (81, 82, 83, 84)* (Virgin 1982)★★★★, *Sparkle In The Rain* (Virgin 1984)★★★★, *Once Upon A Time* (Virgin 1985)★★★★, *Live In The City Of Light* (Virgin 1987)★★, *Street Fighting Years* (Virgin 1989)★★, *Real Life* (Virgin 1991)★★, *Good News From The Next World* (Virgin 1995)★★★.

●COMPILATIONS: *Celebration* (Arista 1982)★★, *Themes For Great Cities* (Stiff 1982)★★, *Glittering Prizes 81/92* (Virgin 1992)★★★★.

●FURTHER READING: *Simple Minds: Glittering Prize*, Dave Thomas. *Simple Minds*, Adam Sweeting. *Simple Minds: A Visual Documentary*, Mike Wrenn. *Simple Minds: Street Fighting Years*, Alfred Bos.

SIMPLY RED

This 80s soul-influenced group was led by Manchester-born vocalist Mick Hucknall (b. Michael James Hucknall, 8 June 1960, Denton, Gt. Manchester, England). Hucknall's first recording group was the punk-inspired Frantic Elevators, who recorded a handful of singles, including an impressive vocal ballad, 'Holding Back The Years'. When they split up in 1983, the vocalist formed Simply Red with a fluid line-up that included Ojo, Mog, Dave Fryman and Eddie Sherwood. After signing to Elektra Records the group had a more settled line-up featuring Hucknall, Tony Bowers (bass), Fritz McIntyre (b. 2 September 1958; keyboards), Tim Kellett (brass), Sylvan Richardson (guitar) and Chris Joyce (drums). Their debut album *Picture Book* climbed to number 2 in the UK charts, while their enticing cover of the Valentine Brothers' 'Money's Too Tight To Mention' was a Top

20 hit. Although the group registered a lowly number 66 with the follow-up 'Come To My Aid', they rediscovered the hit formula with a sterling re-recording of the minor classic 'Holding Back The Years' which peaked at number 2. The song went on to top the US charts, which ushered in a period of international success. Their next album, *Men And Women*, included collaborations between Hucknall and former Motown Records composer Lamont Dozier (of Holland/Dozier/Holland fame). Further hits followed with 'The Right Thing', 'Infidelity' and a reworking of the Cole Porter standard, 'Ev'ry Time We Say Goodbye'. Having twice reached number 2 in the album charts, Simply Red finally scaled the summit in 1989 with the accomplished *A New Flame*. The album coincided with another hit, 'It's Only Love', which was followed by a splendid reworking of Harold Melvin And The Bluenotes' 'If You Don't Know Me By Now', which again climbed to number 2 in the UK. Since then, Simply Red have consolidated their position as the one of the most accomplished blue-eyed soul outfits to emerge from the UK in recent years. The 1991 album *Stars* showed them pursuing hip hop-inspired rhythms, alongside their usual soul-inspired style. It topped the British charts over a period of months, outselling much-hyped efforts by Michael Jackson, U2, Dire Straits and Guns N' Roses. The much awaited follow-up *Life* was also a big seller, although it showed little sign of creative development.

●ALBUMS: *Picture Book* (Elektra 1985)★★★, *Men And Women* (Warners 1987)★★, *A New Flame* (Warners 1989)★★★, *Stars* (East West 1991)★★★★, *Life* (East West 1995)★★★.

●COMPILATIONS: *Greatest Hits* (East West 1996)★★★.

●VIDEOS: *Greatest Video Hits* (Warner Vision 1996).

●FURTHER READING: *Simply Mick: Mick Hucknall Of Simply Red. The Inside Story*, Robin McGibbon and Rob McGibbon. *The First Fully Illustrated Biography*, Mark Hodkinson.

SIMPSON, MARTIN

b. 5 May 1953, Scunthorpe, South Humberside, England. Having started playing guitar at the age of 12, Simpson played the proverbial 'floor spots' at local folk clubs, and received his first paid booking at the age of 14. By the age of 18 Simpson had become a full-time professional on the folk club circuit. He came to the attention of a number of influential people, one of whom was Bill Leader who recorded Simpson's debut *Golden Vanity* for

his own Trailer label. The album mixed such folk standards as 'Pretty Polly' and 'Soldiers Joy', with contemporary works such as Bob Dylan's 'Love Minus Zero/No Limit'. That same year, Simpson opened for Steeleye Span on their UK tour, and, not long after became an accompanist for June Tabor. In 1979 he joined the Albion Band at the National Theatre and played with them on two subsequent tours. *A Cut Above*, recorded with Tabor on Topic Records, is still highly regarded. There followed a succession of fine albums, but without a great degree of commercial success. Since 1987, Simpson has lived in the USA with his American wife Jessica Radcliffe Simpson (b. 18 February 1952, Los Angeles, California, USA). The two also work as a duo, having released *True Dare Or Promise* in 1987. *The Pink Suede Bootleg* was released as a limited edition. Noted for his style of playing, Simpson is not in the limelight as often as he was in the 70s and 80s, but a tour of the UK in 1991 showed that he was still a talent of great merit. In addition to solo and duo work, Simpson played briefly with Metamora in the USA, and has also been working with Henry Gray, the Louisiana born blues pianist. Simpson also played on *Abbysinians* and *Aqaba* by June Tabor, and *Earthed In Cloud Valley* and *'Til The Beasts Returning* by Andrew Cronshaw. In 1991, he was made honorary guitarist of the American Association of Stringed Instrument Artisans (ASIA). A new album from Martin and Jessica was released, featuring their New York-based band of Eric Aceto (violect), Hank Roberts (cello), Doug Robinson (bass), and Tom Beers (harmonica). *Smoke And Mirrors* was a successful excursion into acoustic blues with a notable version of Willie Dixon's 'Spoonful'

●ALBUMS: *Golden Vanity* (Trailer 1976)★★★, with June Tabor *A Cut Above* (Topic 1981)★★★★, *Special Agent* (1981)★★★, *Grinning In Your Face* (Topic 1983)★★★, *Sad Or High Kicking* (Topic 1985)★★★, *Nobody's Fault But Mine* (Dambuster 1986)★★★, with Jessica Radcliffe Simpson *True Dare Or Promise* (Topic 1987)★★★, *Leaves Of Life* (Shanachie 1989)★★★, *When I Was On Horseback* (1991)★★★, *A Closer Walk With Thee* (Gourd 1994)★★★, with Radcliffe Simpson *Red Roses* (Rhiannon 1994)★★★, *Smoke And Mirrors* (Thunderbird 1995)★★★.

●COMPILATIONS: *The Collection* (Topic 1992)★★★★.

●VIDEOS: *The Acoustic Guitar Of Martin Simpson* (1994), *Acoustic Guitar Instrumentals* (1994).

SINITTA

b. Sinitta Renay Malone, 19 October 1966, Seattle, Washington, USA. The daughter of singer Miquel Brown, Sinitta's brand of manufactured disco-pop was aided by competent studio production and songwriting assistance by a variety of talent, namely the Stock, Aitken And Waterman team, plus, at various times, Ralf Rene Maue, Paul Hardcastle and James George Hargreaves. Sinitta's pleasant appearance went a long way in securing, for a while, constant coverage in the British teen pop magazines. This was reflected in her run of UK hits on the Fanfare label in the latter half of the 80s which was launched by 'So Macho'/'Cruising', (number 2, 1986) and was distinguished by three further Top 10 hits, 'Toy Boy' (1987), 'Cross My Broken Heart' (1988), and 'Right Back Where We Started From' (1989). Later chart positions boasted a Top 20 hit with a cover version of the 1973 Robert Knight hit 'Love On A Mountain Top' (number 20, 1989). In early 1993 Sinitta released *The Supremes EP*, which as the name suggests is a collection of Supremes covers.

●ALBUMS: *Sinitta!* (Fanfare 1987)★★, *Wicked!* (Fanfare 1989)★★.

SIOUXSIE AND THE BANSHEES

Siouxsie Sioux (b. Susan Dallion, 27 May 1957, London, England) was part of the notorious 'Bromley contingent', including Steve Severin (b. Steven Bailey, 25 September 1955), which followed the Sex Pistols in their early days. Siouxsie had also taken part in the 100 Club Punk Festival, singing an elongated version of 'The Lord's Prayer' with a group that included Sid Vicious on drums. The fledgling singer also achieved some minor fame after a verbal exchange with television presenter Bill Grundy which unwittingly prompted the Sex Pistols' infamous swearing match on the *Today* programme. Within months of that incident Siouxsie put together her backing group the Banshees, featuring Pete Fenton (guitar), Steve Severin (bass) and Kenny Morris (drums). Siouxsie flirted with Nazi imagery, highlighted by black make-up and frequently exposed breasts. By mid-1977 Fenton was replaced by John McGeogh, and the group supported Johnny Thunders And The Heartbreakers as well as recording a session for the BBC disc jockey, John Peel. By 1978, the group had signed to Polydor Records (the last of the important punk bands of the era to be rounded up by a major) and released their first single, the sublime 'Hong Kong Garden', which reached the UK Top 10. *The Scream* soon followed, produced by Steve Lillywhite. Less commercial offerings ensued with 'The Staircase (Mystery)' and 'Playground Twist', which were soon succeeded by *Join Hands*. During a promotional tour, Morris and McKay abruptly left, to be replaced by former Slits drummer Budgie (b. Peter Clark, 21 August 1957) and temporary Banshee Robert Smith, on leave from the Cure. Siouxsie's Germanic influences were emphasized on the stark 'Mittageisen (Metal Postcard)', which barely scraped into the Top 50. Both 'Happy House' and 'Christine' were more melodic offerings, deservedly bringing greater commercial success. After the success of *Kaleidoscope*, the group embarked on a world tour, including a concert behind the 'Iron Curtain'. Another Top 10 album, *Juju*, was followed by some extra-curricular activities. Siouxsie and Budgie formed an occasional off-shoot group, the Creatures, who enjoyed Top 10 success in their own right, as well as recording an album. Smith and Severin also recorded successfully together as the Glove. After the string-accompanied *A Kiss In The Dreamhouse*, the group reconvened in the autumn of 1983 to play a concert for Italy's Communist Party. A highly commercial version of the Beatles' 'Dear Prudence' provided the group with their biggest UK hit, peaking at number 3. Early in 1984 the evocative 'Swimming Horses' maintained their hit profile, while further personnel changes ensued with the enlistment of John Carruthers from Clock DVA. He, in turn, was replaced by Jon Klein. Regular albums during the mid-80s showed that the group had established a loyal cult following and could experiment freely in the studio without a significant loss of commercial appeal. Having already enjoyed success with a cover version, Siouxsie then tackled Bob Dylan's 'This Wheel's On Fire', which reached the UK Top 20. An entire album of cover versions followed though *Through The Looking Glass* received the most awkward reviews of the band's career. A change of direction with *Peep Show* saw the band embrace a more sophisticated sound, maintaining the eastern nuances of yore but doing so within an elaborate musical scheme. 1991 returned them to the charts with the evocative 'Kiss Them For Me' and *Superstition*, an album of light touch but contrastingly dense production. Arguably their greatest achievement of the 90s, however, was the much-delayed *The Rapture*. Adding musical adventurism (notably the heavily orchestrated three movements of the title track) to familiar but entertaining refractions from their earlier career ('Not Forgotten'), the approach of middle age had evidently not weakened their resolve. Some criticism was received that the album was a sell-out and the band announced in April 1996 that they were 'going out with dignity'.

●ALBUMS: *The Scream* (Polydor 1978)★★★, *Join Hands* (Polydor 1979)★★★, *Kaleidoscope* (Polydor 1980)★★★, *Juju* (Polydor 1981)★★★, *A Kiss In The Dreamhouse* (Polydor 1982)★★★, *Nocturne* (Polydor 1983)★★★, *Hyaena* (Polydor 1984)★★★, *Tinderbox* (Polydor 1986)★★★, *Through The Looking Glass* (Polydor 1987)★★, *Peep Show* (Polydor 1988)★★★, *Superstition* (Polydor 1991)★★★, *The Rapture* (Polydor 1995)★★★.

●COMPILATIONS: *Once Upon A Time - The Singles* (Polydor 1981)★★★★, *The Peel Sessions* (Strange Fruit 1991)★★★, *Twice Upon A Time* (Polydor 1992)★★★.

●VIDEOS: *Greetings From Zurich* (1994).

●FURTHER READING: *Siouxsie And The Banshees*, Mike West. *Entranced: The Siouxsie & The Banshees Story*, Brian Johns.

●FILMS: *Jubilee* (1978).

SKAGGS, RICKY

b. Ricky Lee Skaggs, 18 July 1954, Brushey Creek, near Cordell, Kentucky, USA. His father, Hobert, was a welder, who enjoyed playing the guitar and singing gospel songs with Skaggs' mother, Dorothy. Skaggs later recorded one of her songs, 'All I Ever Loved Was You'. Hobert came back from a welding job in Ohio with a mandolin for the five-year-old Skaggs, but had to return before he could show him how to play it. Within two weeks, Skaggs had figured it out for himself. In 1959 he was taken onstage during one of Bill Monroe's concerts and played 'Ruby' on Monroe's mandolin to rapturous applause. At the age of seven, he played mandolin on Flatt And Scruggs' television show, and then learnt guitar and fiddle. Whilst working at a square dance with his father, he met Keith Whitley; they were to form a trio with Whitley's banjo-playing brother, Dwight, recording bluegrass and gospel shows for local radio. In 1970 they opened for Ralph Stanley, formerly of the Stanley Brothers, who was so impressed that he invited them to join his band, the Clinch Mountain Boys. They both made their recording debuts on Stanley's *Cry From The Cross*. The youngsters made two albums together, but Skaggs soon left in 1972, discouraged by the long hours and low pay.

Skaggs married Stanley's cousin and worked in a boiler room in Washington, DC. However, he returned to music by joining the Country Gentlemen, principally on fiddle. Then, from 1974-75, he played in the modern bluegrass band, J.D. Crowe And The New South. He later recorded a duet album with another member of the band, Tony Rice. Skaggs' first solo, *That's It*, includes contributions from his own parents. He formed his own band, Boone Creek, and recorded bluegrass albums, although they also touched on western swing and honky tonk. He was then offered a job in Emmylou Harris's Hot Band. 'Emmy tried to get me to join three times before I went. I wanted to stay in bluegrass and learn as much about the music as I could, but when Rodney Crowell left, I had an incentive to join her because I knew I'd be able to sing a lot.' From 1977-80, Skaggs encouraged Harris's forays into traditional country music via her *Blue Kentucky Girl*, *Light Of The Stable* and, especially, *Roses In The Snow*. Although Skaggs had rarely been a lead vocalist, his clear, high tenor was featured on an acoustic-based solo album, *Sweet Temptation*, for the North Carolina label, Sugar Hill. Emmylou Harris and Albert Lee were amongst the guest musicians. While he was working on another Sugar Hill album, *Don't Cheat In Our Hometown*, Epic Records took an interest in him. He switched to Epic and made his debut on the US country charts with a revival of Flatt And Scruggs' 'Don't Get Above Your Raising', which he later re-recorded in concert with Elvis Costello. *Rolling Stone* likened Skaggs' first Epic release, *Waitin' For The Sun To Shine*, to Gram Parsons' *Grievous Angel* as they both represented turning-points in country music.

Skaggs was putting the country back into country music by making fresh-sounding records that related to the music's heritage. As if to prove the point, he had US number 1 country hits by reviving Flatt and Scruggs' 'Crying My Heart Out Over You' and Webb Pierce's 'I Don't Care'. He was the Country Music Association Male Vocalist of the Year for 1982, and became the sixty-first - and youngest - member of the *Grand Ole Opry*. Despite the old-time feeling, he appealed to rock fans in a sell-out concert at London's Dominion Theatre, which was released on a live album. Skaggs had played on Guy Clark's original version of 'Heartbroken' and his own recording of the song gave him another country chart-topper. He also completed his *Don't Cheat In Our Hometown*, which was released, after much negotiation, by Epic. Skaggs is a principled performer who leaves drinking or cheating songs to others, but he justified the title track, originally recorded by The Stanley Brothers, by calling it a 'don't cheat' song. Skaggs played on Albert Lee's first-class solo

Hiding, and he had another number 1 with his own version of Lee's 'Country Boy', although the whimsical lyric must have baffled American listeners. With a revival of Bill Monroe's 'Uncle Pen', Skaggs is credited as being the first performer to top the country charts with a bluegrass song since Flatt And Scruggs in 1963, although he says, "Uncle Pen' would not be a bluegrass single according to law of Monroe because there are drums and electric instruments on it.' Skaggs won a Grammy for the best country instrumental, 'Wheel Hoss', which was used as the theme music for his BBC Radio 2 series, *Hit It, Boys*. In 1981 Skaggs, now divorced, married Sharon White of the Whites. They won the Vocal Duo of the Year award for their 1987 duet, 'Love Can't Ever Get Better Than This'. He also recorded a playful duet of 'Friendship' with Ray Charles, and says, 'The people who call me Picky Ricky can't have met Ray Charles. He irons out every wrinkle. I would sing my lead part and he'd say, "Aw, honey, that's good but convince me now: sing to your ol' daddy."' Skaggs has worked on albums by the Bellamy Brothers, Rodney Crowell, Exile and Jesse Winchester. Johnny Cash had never previously used a fiddle player until Skaggs worked on *Silver*. Skaggs' busy career suffered a setback when his son Andrew was shot in the mouth by a drug-crazed truckdriver, but returned in 1989 with two fine albums in the traditional mould: *White Limozeen*, which he produced for Dolly Parton, and his own *Kentucky Thunder*. *My Father's Son* in 1991 was his most consistent album in years, but its poor sales led Columbia Records to drop him from their roster in 1992. Skaggs is modest about his achievements, feeling that he is simply God's instrument. He has rekindled an interest in country music's heritage, and many musicians have followed his lead. He remains one of the best performers in country music today.

●ALBUMS: with Keith Whitley *Tribute To The Stanley Brothers* (1971)★★★, with Whitley *Second Generation Bluegrass* (1972)★★★, *That's It* (1975)★★★, as Boone Creek *Boone Creek* (1977)★★★, as Boone Creek *One Way Track* (1978)★★★, with Tony Rice *Take Me Home Tonight In A Song* (1978)★★★, *Sweet Temptation* (Sugar Hill 1979)★★★★, with Rice *Skaggs And Rice* (Sugar Hill 1980)★★★, *Waitin' For The Sun To Shine* (Epic 1981)★★★, *Family And Friends* (Rounder 1982)★★★, *Highways And Heartaches* (Epic 1982)★★★, *Don't Cheat In Our Hometown* (Epic 1983)★★★★, *Country Boy* (Epic 1984)★★★, *Live In London* (Epic 1985)★★★, *Favorite Country Songs* (Epic 1985)★★★★, *Love's Gonna Get Ya!* (Epic

1986)★★★, *Comin' Home To Stay* (Epic 1988)★★★, *Kentucky Thunder* (Epic 1989)★★★, *My Father's Son* (Columbia 1991)★★★★, *Solid Ground* (Atlantic 1996)★★★.

SKID ROW (USA)

Skid Row were formed in New Jersey, USA, in 1986 by Dave 'The Snake' Sabo (b. 16 September 1964; guitar) and Rachel Bolan (b. 9 February 1964; bass). Sebastian Bach (b. 3 April 1968, Freeport, Bahamas; vocals, ex-Madam X), Scotti Hill (b. 31 May 1964; guitar) and Rob Affuso (b. 1 March 1963; drums) completed the line-up. Influenced by Kiss, Sex Pistols, Ratt and Mötley Crüe, the band's rise to fame was remarkably rapid. The break came when they were picked up by Bon Jovi's management (Sabo was an old friend of Jon Bon Jovi) and offered the support slot on their US stadium tour of 1989. Bach's wild and provocative stage antics established the band's live reputation. Signed to Atlantic Records, they released their self-titled debut album to widespread critical acclaim the same year. It peaked at number 6 on the *Billboard* album chart and spawned two US Top 10 singles with '18 And Life' and 'I Remember You'. *Slave To The Grind* surpassed all expectations, debuting at number 1 in the US charts. Their commercial approach had been transformed into an abrasive and uncompromising barrage of metallic rock 'n' roll, delivered with punk-like arrogance. Afterwards, however, progress was halted by squabbling which threatened to break the group. As Bach admitted to the press: 'I know I can be overbearing. But that's all changed now. Now people are in my face, giving their two cents' worth, making sure that everybody's vision is realised.' 1994's *Subhuman Race* was produced by Bob Rock.

●ALBUMS: *Skid Row* (Atlantic 1989)★★, *Slave To The Grind* (Atlantic 1991)★★★, *B-Sides Ourselves* mini-album (Atlantic 1992)★★, *Subhuman Race* (Atlantic 1995)★★.

●VIDEOS: *Oh Say Can You Scream?* (1991), *No Frills Video* (1993), *Roadkill* (1993).

SKY

A UK instrumental group founded in 1979 and devoted to fusing classical, jazz and rock music, Sky was led by virtuoso classical guitarist John Williams (b 24 April 1941, Melbourne, Victoria, Australia). Having already played concerts at Ronnie Scott's jazz club, Williams formed the group with rock guitarist Kevin Peek, classical percussionist Tristram Fry, ex-Curved Air keyboards player Francis Monkman and Herbie Flowers, a versatile session bass player and composer of the novelty UK number 1 'Grandad'. In 1981, Monkman was replaced by Steve Gray. The group made an instant impact in Britain. Mixing original compositions with inventive adaptations of classical pieces, each of the first four albums reached the UK Top 10. *Sky 2* even headed the UK chart in 1980, aided by 'Toccata' a hit single taken from a Bach theme. European and Japanese concert tours were equally successful. *Cadmium* was more pop-orientated, containing the Alan Tarney compositions 'The Girl In Winter' and 'Return to Me'. After its release, Williams left the group which continued to record sporadically until 1987 when it folded.

●ALBUMS: *Sky* (Ariola 1979)★★★, *Sky 2* (Ariola 1980)★★, *Sky 3* (Ariola 1981)★★★, *Forthcoming* (Ariola 1982)★★, *Sky 5 Live* (Ariola 1983)★★, *Cadmium* (Ariola 1983)★★, *The Great Balloon Race* (Epic 1985)★★, *Mozart* (1987)★★.

●COMPILATIONS: *Masterpieces - The Very Best Of Sky* (Telstar 1984)★★★, *The Best Of ...* (Music Club 1995)★★★.

SLAYER

This intense death/thrash metal quartet was formed in Huntington Beach, Los Angeles, USA, during 1982. Comprising Tom Araya (bass/vocals), Kerry King (guitar), Jeff Hanneman (guitar) and Dave Lombardo (drums) they made their debut in 1983, with a track on the compilation *Metal Massacre III*. This led to Metal Blade signing the band and releasing their first two albums. *Show No Mercy* and *Hell Awaits* were undiluted blasts of pure white metallic noise. The band played at breakneck speed with amazing technical precision, but the intricacies of detail were lost in a muddy production. Araya's lyrics dealt with death, carnage, satanism and torture, but were reduced to an indecipherable guttural howl. Rick Rubin, producer and owner of the Def Jam label teamed up with the band in 1986 for the recording of *Reign In Blood*. Featuring 10 tracks in just 28 minutes, it took the concept of thrash to its ultimate conclusion. The song 'Angel Of Death' became notorious for its references to Joseph Mengele, the Nazi doctor who committed atrocities against humanity (ironic, given that Araya has obvious non-Aryan origins). They themselves admitted to a right-wing stance on matters of society and justice, despite being the subject of virulent attacks from that quarter over the years. *Hell Awaits* saw Rubin achieve a breakthrough in production with a clear

and inherently powerful sound, and opened up the band to a wider audience. *South Of Heaven* was Slayer applying the brakes and introducing brain-numbing bass riffs similar to Black Sabbath, but was delivered with the same manic aggression as before. The guitars of Hanneman and King screamed violently and Araya's vocals were clearly heard for the first time. *Seasons In The Abyss* pushed the band to the forefront of the thrash metal genre, alongside Metallica. A state-of-the-art album in every respect, although deliberately commercial it is the band's most profound and convincing statement. A double live album followed, recorded in London, Lakeland and San Bernadino between October 1990 and August 1991. It captured the band at their brutal and uncompromising best and featured definitive versions of many of their most infamous numbers. However, it saw the permanent departure of Lombardo after many hints of a separation, with ex-Forbidden drummer Paul Bostaph stepping in. Lombardo went on to form Grip Inc., working with Death leader Chuck Shuldiner. 1994 saw the group work alongside Ice-T on a cover of the Exploited's 'Disorder' for the *Judgement Night* soundtrack, before the unveiling of their sixth studio album, *Divine Intervention*. Bostaph departed from the band in 1995 and was replaced by ex-Testament John Dette in January 1996. *Undisputed Attitude* was closer to punk than heavy metal and featured a particularly inspired version of the Stooges' 'I Wanna Be Your Dog'.

●ALBUMS: *Show No Mercy* (Metal Blade 1984)★★, *Hell Awaits* (Metal Blade 1985)★★, *Reign In Blood* (Def Jam 1986)★★★, *Live Undead* (Enigma 1987)★★, *South Of Heaven* (Def American 1988)★★★, *Seasons In The Abyss* (Def American 1990)★★★, *Decade Of Aggression-Live* (Def American 1991)★★★, *Divine Intervention* (American 1994)★★★, *Undisputed Attitude* (American 1996)★★★.

●VIDEOS: *Live Intrusion* (American Visuals 1995).

SLY AND ROBBIE

Sly Dunbar (b. Lowell Charles Dunbar, 10 May 1952, Kingston, Jamaica; drums) and Robbie Shakespeare (b. 27 September 1953, Kingston, Jamaica; bass). Dunbar, nicknamed 'Sly' in honour of his fondness for Sly And The Family Stone, was an established figure in Skin Flesh And Bones when he met Shakespeare. They have probably played on more reggae records than the rest of Jamaica's many session musicians put together. The pair began working together as a team in 1975 and they quickly became Jamaica's leading, and most distinctive, rhythm section. They have played on numerous releases, including those by U-Roy, Peter Tosh, Bunny Wailer, Culture and Black Uhuru, while Dunbar also made several solo albums, all of which featured Shakespeare. They have constantly sought to push back the boundaries surrounding the music with their consistently inventive work. Sly drummed his first session for Upsetter Lee Perry as one of the Upsetters; the resulting 'Night Doctor' was a big hit both in Jamaica and the UK. He next moved to Skin, Flesh And Bones, whose variations on the reggae-meets-disco/soul sound gave them much session work and a residency at Kingston's Tit for Tat club. Sly was still searching for more, however, and he moved onto another session group in the mid-70s, the Revolutionaries. This move changed the course of reggae music through their work at Joseph 'Joe Joe' Hookim's Channel One Studio and their pioneering rockers sound. It was with the Revolutionaries that he teamed up with bass player Robbie Shakespeare who had gone through a similar apprenticeship with session bands, notably Bunny Lee's Aggrovators. The two formed a friendship that turned into a musical partnership, and that dominated reggae music throughout the remainder of the 70s, 80s and on into the 90s.

Known now simply as Sly And Robbie (and occasionally Drumbar & Basspeare), they not only formed their own label Taxi, which produced many hit records for scores of well-known artists but also found time to do session work for just about every important name in reggae. They toured extensively as the powerhouse rhythm section for Black Uhuru and, as their fame spread outside of reggae circles, they worked with Grace Jones, Bob Dylan, Ian Dury and Joan Armatrading among a host of other rock stars. In the early 80s they were among the first to use the burgeoning 'new technology' to musical effect; they demonstrated that it could be used to its full advantage without compromising their musicianship in any way. In a genre controlled by producers and 'this week's star', reggae musicians have never really been given their proper respect, but the accolades heaped on Sly And Robbie have helped to redress the balance. Sly And Robbie's mastery of the digital genre coupled with their abiding love and respect for the music's history has placed them at the forefront of Kingston's producers of the early 90s, and their 'Murder She Wrote' cut for Chaka Demus And Pliers set the tone for 1992, while 'Tease Mi' for the same duo, built around a sample from the Skatalites 60s hit, 'Ball Of Fire', was another signif-

icant UK chart success in 1993. Quite remarkable for a team whose successful career has already spanned three decades, with the promise of yet more to come. Their productions include: Various *Present Taxi* (Taxi 1981)★★★★, *Crucial Reggae* (Taxi 1984)★★★, *Taxi Wax* (Taxi 1984)★★★, *Taxi Gang* (Taxi 1984)★★★, *Taxi Connection Live In London* (Taxi 1986)★★★, *Taxi Fare* (Taxi 1987)★★★, *Two Rhythms Clash* (RAS 1990)★★★, *DJ Riot* (Mango/Island 1990)★★★, *Sound Of The 90s* (1990)★★★, *Carib Soul* (1990)★★★, *Present Sound Of Sound* (Musidisc 1994)★★★, *Present Ragga Pon Top* (Musidisc 1994)★★★.
●ALBUMS: *Disco Dub* (Gorgon 1978)★★, *Gamblers Choice* (Taxi 1980)★★★, *Raiders Of The Lost Dub* (Mango/Island 1981)★★★, *60s, 70s Into The 80s* (Mango/Island 1981)★★★, *Dub Extravaganza* (CSA 1984)★★★, *A Dub Experience* (Island 1985)★★★, *Language Barrier* (Island 1985)★★★, *Electro Reggae* (Island 1986)★★★, *The Sting* (Taxi 1986)★★★, *Rhythm Killers* (4th & Broadway 1987)★★★★, *Dub Rockers Delight* (Blue Moon 1987)★★★, *The Summit* (RAS 1988)★★★, *Silent Assassin* (4th & Broadway 1990)★★★.
●COMPILATIONS: *Reggae Greats* (Island 1985)★★★, *Hits 1987-90* (Sonic Sounds 1991)★★★★.

SMILEY CULTURE

b. David Emmanuel, *c*.1960, London, England, of a Jamaican father and South American mother. Smiley gained his nickname at school where his method of chatting up girls was simply to ask for a smile. He served his apprenticeship with a number of local sounds before hitting the big time with south London's Saxon sound system, the home of a formidable amount of British reggae talent including Maxi Priest, Tippa Irie and Phillip Papa Levi. His live reputation attracted the attention of record producers and his first recording for Fashion Records, 'Cockney Translation', featuring Smiley slipping effortlessly from Jamaican patois to a south London accent, touched a nerve and sold an unprecedented 40,000 copies. His follow-up 'Police Officer', again featuring the cockney and 'yardy' voices, did even better and reached the national Top 20 in early 1985. Appearances on BBC Television's *Top Of The Pops* followed - a first for a reggae DJ - and Smiley was a 'star'. A major recording contract with Polydor Records followed. As well as hosting his own television show *Club Mix*, Smiley also found the time for a cameo appearance in the film *Absolute Beginners* singing Miles Davis' 'So What'. He continued to record, including some interesting collaborations with American hip hop artists. Smiley's importance is that he was among the first English-based reggae artists to challenge the Jamaicans and succeed. The British public also took him to their hearts while the lyrics of 'Cockney Translation' are now used by teachers and lecturers to illustrate the effects and influence of immigration on the 'mother tongue'.

●ALBUMS: *The Original* (Top Notch 1986)★★★, *Tongue In Cheek* (Polydor 1986)★★★.

SMITH, TOMMY

b. 27 April 1967, Luton, Bedfordshire, England. Smith grew up in Edinburgh and started playing saxophone at the age of 12. He wowed the jazz clubs with his precocious brilliance and appeared on television in 1982, backed by pianist Gordon Beck and bassist Niels-Henning Ørsted Pedersen. The next year, aged only 16, he recorded *Giant Strides* for Glasgow's GFM Records. It was an astonishing debut. The young tenor made mistakes, but the stark recording honed in on his major assets: a full, burnished tone and a firm idea of the overall shape of his solos. It shone out of the British jazz of the time like a beacon, a herald of the 'jazz revival' among younger players. In 1983 he played the Leverkusen Jazz Festival in Germany. The Scottish jazz scene helped to raise the money to send him to Berklee College Of Music, where he enrolled in January 1984. Jaco Pastorius invited him to join his group for club dates, as did vibist Gary Burton. In 1985 Smith formed Forward Motion, with Laszlo Gardonyi (piano), Terje Gewelt (bass) and Ian Froman (drums), and began international tours, playing a spacious, reflective jazz. It was no surprise when ECM Records' Manfred Eicher asked him to play on Burton's *Whiz Kids* in 1986, as Smith was sounding more and more like the label's established saxophone maestro, Jan Garbarek. In 1988 he toured under his own name with Froman from Forward Motion, pianist John Taylor and bassist Chris Laurence. In 1989 he introduced a series of 10 jazz television broadcasts and in 1990 worked with pop band Hue And Cry. In May 1990 he premiered a concerto for saxophone and string ensemble commissioned by the Scottish Ensemble. Signed to Blue Note Records in the late 80s, he released three albums on the label before a move to the audiophile label Linn.

●ALBUMS: *Giant Strides* (GFM 1983)★★★, with Forward Motion *Progressions* (1985)★★★, with Forward Motion *The Berklee Tapes* (1985)★★★, *Step By Step* (Step By Step 1989)★★★★, *Peeping Tom* (Blue Note 1990)★★★★, *Standards* (Blue Note 1991)★★★★, *Paris* (Blue Note 1992)★★★, *Reminiscence* (Linn 1994)★★★, *Misty Morning & No Time* (Linn 1995)★★★, *Beasts Of Scotland* (Linn 1996)★★★.

SMITHEREENS

Influenced by the 60s pop of the Beatles, Beach Boys and the Byrds, the Smithereens formed in New Jersey in 1980. Members Jim Babjak (guitar) and Dennis Diken (drums) had played together since 1971; Mike Mesaros (bass) was recruited in 1976 and finally Pat DiNizio (vocals). After recording two EPs, they backed songwriter Otis Blackwell ('Great Balls Of Fire') on two obscure albums. In 1986 the group signed to Enigma Records and released their first full album, *Especially For You*, which fared well among both college radio and mainstream rock listeners, as did the single 'Blood And Roses'. After a lengthy tour, the Smithereens recorded their second album, *Green Thoughts*, in 1988, this time distributed by Capitol Records. *Smithereens 11* was their biggest selling album to date, reaching number 41 in the US chart. The group's music has also been featured in several movie soundtracks including the teen-horror film, *Class Of Nuke 'Em High*. Their career faltered in 1991 with the poorly received *Blow Up* (US number 120) leaving critics to ponder if the band had run out of ideas.

●ALBUMS: *Especially For You* (Enigma 1986)★★★, *Green Thoughts* (Capitol 1988)★★★★, *Smithereens 11* (Enigma 1990)★★★★, *Blow Up* (Capitol 1991)★★, *A Date With The Smithereens* (RCA 1994)★★, *Attack Of The Smithereens* (Capitol 1995)★★.

SMITHS

Acclaimed by many as the most important UK group of the 80s, the Smiths were formed in Manchester during the spring of 1982. Morrissey (b. Steven Patrick Morrissey, 22 May 1959, Davyhulme, Manchester, England) and Johnny Marr (b. John Maher, 31 October 1963, Ardwick, Manchester, England) originally combined as a songwriting partnership, and only their names appeared on any contract bearing the title 'Smiths'. Morrissey had previously played for a couple of months in the Nosebleeds and also rehearsed and auditioned with a late version of Slaughter And The Dogs. After that he wrote reviews for *Record Mirror* and penned a couple of booklets on the New York Dolls and James Dean. Marr, meanwhile, had played in several Wythenshawe groups including the Paris Valentinos, White Dice, Sister Ray and Freaky Party. By the summer of 1982, the duo decided to form a group and recorded demos with drummer Simon Wolstencroft and a recording engineer named Dale. Wolstencroft subsequently declined an offer to join the Smiths and in later years became a member of the Fall. Eventually, Mike Joyce (b. 1 June 1963, Fallowfield, Manchester, England) was recruited as drummer, having previously played with the punk-inspired Hoax and Victim. During their debut gig at the Ritz in Manchester, the group was augmented by go-go dancer James Maker, who went on to join Raymonde and later RPLA. By the end of 1982, the group appointed a permanent bassist. Andy Rourke (b. 1963, Manchester, England) was an alumnus of various past groups with Marr. After being taken under the wing of local entrepreneur Joe Moss, the group strenuously rehearsed and after a series of gigs, signed to Rough Trade Records in the spring of 1983. By that time, they had issued their first single on the label, 'Hand In Glove', which failed to reach the Top 50. During the summer of 1983, they became entwined in the first of several tabloid press controversies when it was alleged that their lyrics contained references to child molesting. The eloquent Morrissey, who was already emerging as a media spokesperson of considerable power, sternly refuted the rumours. During the same period the group commenced work on their debut album with producer Troy Tate, but the sessions were curtailed, and a new set of recordings undertaken with John Porter. In November 1983 the group issued their second single, 'This Charming Man', a striking pop record that infiltrated the UK Top 30. Following an ill-fated trip to the USA at the end of the year, the quartet began 1984 with a new single, the notably rockier 'What Difference Does It Make?', which took them to number 12. *The Smiths* ably displayed the potential of the group, with Morrissey's oblique genderless lyrics coalescing with Marr's spirited guitar work. The closing track of the album was the haunting 'Suffer Little Children', a requiem to the child victims of the 60s Moors Murderers. The song later provoked a short-lived controversy in the tabloid press, which was resolved when the mother of one of the victims came out on Morrissey's side. A series of college gigs throughout Britain established the group as a cult favourite, with Morrissey displaying a distinctive image, complete with National Health spectacles, a hearing aid and bunches of gladioli. A collaboration with Sandie Shaw saw 'Hand In Glove' transformed into a

belated hit, while Morrissey dominated music press interviews. His celibate stance provoked reams of speculation about his sexuality and his ability to provide good copy on subjects as various as animal rights, royalty, Oscar Wilde and 60s films, made him a journalist's dream interviewee. The singer's celebrated miserabilism was reinforced by the release of the autobiographical 'Heaven Knows I'm Miserable Now', which reached number 19 in the UK. Another Top 20 hit followed with 'William, It Was Really Nothing'. While the Smiths commenced work on their next album, Rough Trade issued the interim *Hatful Of Hollow*, a bargain-priced set which included various flip sides and radio sessions. It was a surprisingly effective work, which captured the inchoate charm of the group. By 1984 the Smiths found themselves feted as Britain's best group by various factions in the music press. The release of the sublime 'How Soon Is Now?' justified much of the hyperbole and this was reinforced by the power of their next album, *Meat Is Murder*. This displayed Morrissey's increasing tendency towards social commentary, which had been indicated in his controversial comments on Band Aid and the IRA bombings. The album chronicled violence at schools ('The Headmaster Ritual'), adolescent thuggery ('Rusholme Ruffians'), child abuse ('Barbarism Begins At Home') and animal slaughter ('Meat Is Murder'). The proseletyzing tone was brilliantly complemented by the musicianship of Marr, Rourke and Joyce. Marr's work on such songs as 'The Headmaster Ritual' and 'That Joke Isn't Funny Anymore' effectively propelled him to the position of one of Britain's most respected rock guitarists. Despite releasing a milestone album, the group's fortunes in the singles charts were relatively disappointing. 'Shakespeare's Sister' received a lukewarm response and stalled at number 26, amid ever growing rumours that the group were dissatisfied with their record label. Another major UK tour in 1985 coincided with various management upheavals, which dissipated the group's energies. A successful trek across the USA was followed by the release of the plaintive summer single 'The Boy With The Thorn In His Side', which, despite its commerciality, only reached number 23. A dispute with Rough Trade delayed the release of the next Smiths album, which was preceded by the superb 'Big Mouth Strikes Again', another example of Marr at his best. During the same period, Rourke was briefly ousted from the group due to his flirtation with heroin. He was soon reinstated, however, along with a second guitarist Craig Gannon, who had previously played with Aztec Camera, the Bluebells and Colourfield. In June 1986 *The Queen Is Dead* was issued and won immediate critical acclaim for its diversity and unadulterated power. The range of mood and emotion offered on the album was startling to behold, ranging from the epic grandeur of the title track to the overt romanticism of 'There Is A Light That Never Goes Out' and the irreverent comedy of 'Frankly Mr Shankly' and 'Some Girls Are Bigger Than Others'. A superb display of Morrissey/Marr at their apotheosis, the album was rightly placed alongside *Meat Is Murder* as one of the finest achievements of the decade. A debilitating stadium tour of the USA followed and during the group's absence they enjoyed a formidable Top 20 hit with the disco-denouncing 'Panic'. The sentiments of the song, coupled with Morrissey's negative comments on certain aspects of black music, provoked further adverse comments in the press. That controversy was soon replaced by the news that the Smiths were to record only one more album for Rough Trade and intended to transfer their operation to the major label, EMI Records. Meanwhile, the light pop of 'Ask' contrasted with riotous scenes during the group's 1986 UK tour. At the height of the drama, the group almost suffered a fatality when Johnny Marr was involved in a car crash. While he recuperated, guitarist Craig Gannon was fired, a decision that prompted legal action. The group ended the year with a concert at the Brixton Academy supported by fellow Mancunians, the Fall. It was to prove their final UK appearance. After another hit with 'Shoplifters Of The World Unite' the group completed what would prove their final album. The glam-rock inspired 'Sheila Take A Bow' returned them to the Top 10 and their profile was maintained with the release of another sampler album, *The World Won't Listen*. Marr was growing increasingly disenchanted with the group's musical direction, however, and privately announced that he required a break. With the group's future still in doubt, press speculation proved so intense that an official announcement of a split occurred in August 1987. *Strangeways, Here We Come*, an intriguing transitional album, was issued posthumously. The work indicated the different directions towards which the major protagonists were progressing during their final phase. A prestigious television documentary of the group's career followed on *The South Bank Show* and a belated live album, '*Rank*', was issued the following year. The junior members Rourke and Joyce initially appeared with Brix Smith's Adult Net, then backed Sinead O'Connor, before Joyce joined the Buzzcocks. Morrissey pursued a solo career, while Marr moved from the Pretenders to The The and Electronic, as well as appearing on a variety of sessions for artists as diverse as Bryan Ferry, Talking Heads, Billy Bragg, Kirsty MacColl, the Pet Shop Boys, Stex and Banderas. In 1992 there was renewed interest in the Smiths following the furore surrounding Johnny Rogan's controversial biography of the group, and Warner Brothers acquisition of the group's back-catalogue from Rough Trade. In 1996 the long-standing legal action taken by Mike Joyce was resolved by both Morrisey and Marr losing the case. Joyce was awarded damages of £1 million.

●ALBUMS: *The Smiths* (Rough Trade 1984)★★★, *Meat Is Murder* (Rough Trade 1985)★★★★, *The Queen Is Dead* (Rough Trade 1986)★★★★, *Strangeways, Here We Come* (Rough Trade 1987)★★★, '*Rank*' (Rough Trade 1988)★★.
●COMPILATIONS: *Hatful Of Hollow* (Rough Trade 1984)★★★, *The World Won't Listen* (Rough Trade 1987)★★★, *Louder Than Bombs* (Rough Trade 1987)★★★, *The Peel Sessions* (Strange Fruit 1988)★★, *Best .. I* (Warners 1992)★★★, *Best ... II* (Warners 1992)★★, *Singles* (Warners 1995)★★★★.
●VIDEOS: *The Complete Picture* (1993).
●FURTHER READING: *The Smiths*, Mick Middles. *Morrissey & Marr: The Severed Alliance*, Johnny Rogan. *The Smiths: The Visual Documentary*, Johnny Rogan. *The Smiths: All Men Have Secrets*, Tom Gallagher, M. Chapman and M. Gillies.

SMURFS (FATHER ABRAHAM AND THE)

If ever popular music veers too close to being a serious topic of academic cultural discussion, one only has to remember episodes like those of the Smurfs in the late 70s. While the punk wars raged around them, Father Abraham And The Smurfs formed in the Netherlands and mounted their chart bid with 'The Smurf Song', released on Decca Records in May 1978. Conducted in a semi-duet fashion, with Father Abraham leading the assembled midget characters in call-response chants, delivered in their eminently silly, high-pitched voices, it served to introduce the concept of Smurf culture to the nation. The Smurfs, also depicted in a cartoon series, lived in forests and promoted pre-environmental awareness sentiments while hiding from human beings. Similar to the Wombles concept of a few years earlier, Father Abraham And The Smurfs enjoyed two further UK charts hits,

'Dippety Day' (number 13) and 'Christmas In Smurfland' (number 19). This prompted music business maverick Jonathan King to release the cash-in novelty record, 'Lick A Smurf For Christmas (All Fall Down)', credited to Father Abraphart And The Smurfs. There were also a clutch of dreadful albums for the more masochistic fans. In the 90s a re-awakening of Smurfmania occurred, leaving those who were old enough to remember the first wave to ponder; why?

●ALBUMS: *Smurfing Sing Song* (Decca 1979)★, *Merry Christmas With The Smurfs* (Dureco 1983)★, *Smurfs Party Time* (Dureco 1983)★, *The Smurfs Go Pop* (EMI 1996)★, *Christmas Party* (EMI 1996)★, *Hits '97 - Volume One* (EMI 1997)★.

SNFU

From Edmonton, Alberta, Canada, SNFU are a hardcore punk band who took obvious influence from both the Subhumans and DOA Their line-ups have always centred around Mr Chi Pig (vocals), and Brent (guitar), with the rhythm section changing with almost every successive album. One of their early drummers, John Card, would later join DOA. SNFU have persevered over the years with a formula encompassing largely headlong adrenaline rushes. The most significant interlude was *If You Swear You'll Catch No Fish*, slick titles such as 'Better Homes And Gardens' indicating a growing maturity in the way they conveyed their lyrical gaze. Previously, overtly obvious joke anthems like 'Cannibal Cafe' had been their let-down. By the next album, they were speeding along at a furious rate once more, though some of the early angst had disappeared; 'It's hard to be angry when you live in an environment like this; the physical aspect of Edmonton is so comfortable'. They had definitely not grown in self-importance, however; 'We're still the same awful band we were in '81'. Still active, SNFU encapsulate the best traditions of Canadian hardcore; energy, verve and humour. They moved over to Epitaph Records in 1995 for another splintering punk rock album.

●ALBUMS: *And No One Else Wanted To Play* (BYO 1984)★★, *If You Swear You'll Catch No Fish* (BYO 1986)★★★, *Better Than A Stick In The Eye* (BYO 1988)★★, *Last Of The Big Time Suspenders* (Skullduggery 1992)★★, *The Ones Most Likely To Succeed* (Epitaph 1995)★★, *Fyulaba* (Epitaph 1996)★★.

SNIPER

This Japanese heavy metal group was formed in 1981 by guitarist Mansanori Kusakabe. Enlisting the services of Shigehisa Kitao (vocals), Romy Murase (bass) and Shunji Itoh (drums), their brand of heavy metal drew strongly on the styles of UFO and Deep Purple. Debuting with the single 'Fire' in 1983, they contributed 'Crazy Drug' to the *Heavy Metal Forces* compilation album the following year. Their first album was recorded live at the Electric Ladyland Club in Nagoya in 1984 and featured new recruit Ravhun Othani (ex-Frank Marino Band) as a second guitarist. The album was a limited edition of 1000, which sold out, only to be re-pressed twice, with similar success. The band disintegrated shortly after its release, but was resurrected in 1985 by Kusakabe. The new line-up included Noburu Kaneko (vocals), Takeshi Kato (keyboards), Tsukasa Shinohara (bass) and Toshiyuki Miyata (drums). They produced *Quick And Dead*, but it made little impact outside Japan. A proposed tour of the Netherlands to support it was cancelled and the band have been inactive since.

●ALBUMS: *Open The Attack* (Electric Ladyland 1984)★★, *Quick And Dead* (Megaton 1985)★★.

SOFT BOYS

When Syd Barrett gave up music for art, another Cambridge musician emerged to take on his mantle. Robyn Hitchcock started out as a solo performer and busker before becoming a member of B.B. Blackberry And The Swelterettes, then the Chosen Few, the Worst Fears, and Maureen And The Meatpackers. It was with the last-named that Hitchcock first recorded (in 1976), although the results were not released until much later. His next group, Dennis And The Experts became the Soft Boys in 1976. The Soft Boys' first recording session was in March 1977 by which point the line-up was Hitchcock (vocals/guitar/bass), Alan Davies (guitar), Andy Metcalfe (bass), and Morris Windsor aka Otis Fagg (drums). The original sessions remain unreleased but the same line-up also recorded a three-track single - known as the *Give It To The Soft Boys* EP - for the notorious local Cambridge label, Raw Records (or rip-off records, to those who knew its owner well). This was released in the autumn of 1977 after which Davies left and Kimberley Rew was installed on guitar, harmonica, and vocals. The Soft Boys, now signed to Radar Records, released the single '(I Wanna Be An) Anglepoise Lamp', but it was not considered representative of their innovative live work. Forming their own Two Crabs label they released *Can Of Bees* in 1979 after which they replaced Metcalfe with Matthew Seligman. Jim Melton, who had been playing harmonica for a while, also left.

Their remaining releases came on the Armageddon label and included *Underwater Moonlight*, which is considered among Hitchcock's finest moments. They broke up early in 1981 and Hitchcock went on to enjoy an erratic solo career, recruiting along the way Metcalfe and Windsor to form the Egyptians. Rew joined Katrina And The Waves and wrote the classic 'Going Down To Liverpool', while Seligman joined Local Heroes SW9 and continued to contribute to Hitchcock's solo efforts.

●ALBUMS: *A Can Of Bees* (Two Crabs 1979)★★★, *Underwater Moonlight* (Armageddon 1980)★★★★, *Two Halves For The Price Of One* (Armageddon 1981)★★★, *Invisible Hits* (Midnight 1983)★★★, *Live At The Portland Arms* cassette only (Midnight 1987)★★★.

●COMPILATIONS: *Raw Cuts* mini-album (Overground 1989)★★, *The Soft Boys 1976-81* (Rykodisc 1994)★★★★.

SOFT CELL

Formed in Leeds, England, in 1980 this duo featured vocalist Marc Almond (b. Peter Marc Almond, 9 July 1956, Southport, Lancashire, England) and synthesizer player David Ball (b. 3 May 1959, Blackpool, Lancashire, England). The art school twosome came to the attention of Some Bizzare Records entrepreneur Stevo following the release of their self-financed EP *Mutant Moments*. He duly included their 'Girl With The Patent Leather Face' on the compilation *Some Bizzare Album* and negotiated a licensing deal with Phonogram Records in Europe and Sire Records in the USA. Their debut single, 'Memorabilia', produced by Mute Records boss Daniel Miller, was an underground hit paving the way for the celebrated 'Tainted Love'. Composed by the Four Preps' Ed Cobb and already well known as a northern soul club favourite by Gloria Jones, 'Tainted Love' topped the UK charts, became the best selling British single of the year and remained in the US charts for an astonishing 43 weeks. Produced by the former producer of Wire, Mike Thorne, the single highlighted Almond's strong potential as a torch singer, a role that was developed on subsequent hit singles including 'Bedsitter, 'Say Hello Wave Goodbye', 'Torch' and 'What'. Almond's brand of erotic electronic sleaze could only partially be realized in the Soft Cell format and was more fully developed in the offshoot Marc And The Mambas. Implicit in Soft Cell's rise was a determined self-destructive streak, which meant that the group was never happy with the pop machinery of which it

had inevitably became a part. The title of *The Art Of Falling Apart* indicated how close they were to ending their hit collaboration. At the end of 1983 the duo announced their proposed dissolution and undertook a final tour early the following year, followed by a farewell album, *This Last Night In Sodom*. Almond embarked on a solo career, while Ball would eventually become one half of the Grid.

●ALBUMS: *Non-Stop Erotic Cabaret* (Some Bizzare 1981)★★★, *Non-Stop Ecstatic Dancing* (Some Bizzare 1982)★★, *The Art Of Falling Apart* (Some Bizzare 1983)★★, *This Last Night In Sodom* (Some Bizzare 1984)★★.

●COMPILATIONS: *The Singles 1981-85* (Some Bizzare 1986)★★★, *Their Greatest Hits* (Some Bizzare 1988)★★★, *Memorabilia* (Mercury 1991)★★, *Say Hello To Soft Cell* (Spectrum 1996)★★.

●FURTHER READING: *Soft Cell*, Simon Tebbutt.

SONIC YOUTH

A product of New York's experimental 'No-Wave' scene, Sonic Youth first recorded under the auspices of *avant garde* guitarist Glenn Branca. Thurston Moore (b. 25 July 1958, Coral Gables, Florida, USA; guitar), Lee Ranaldo (b. 3 February 1956, Glen Cove New York, USA; guitar) and Kim Gordon (b. 28 April 1953, Rochester, New York, USA; bass) performed together on Branca's *Symphony No. 3*, while the group debuted in its own right on his Neutral label. *Sonic Youth* was recorded live at New York's Radio City Music Hall in December 1981 and featured original drummer Richard Edson. Three further collections, *Confusion Is Sex*, *Sonic Death* and a mini-album, *Kill Yr Idols*, completed the quartet's formative period which was marked by their pulsating blend of discordant guitars, impassioned vocals and ferocious, compulsive drum patterns, courtesy of newcomer Jim Sclavunos, or his replacement, Bob Bert. *Bad Moon Rising* was the first Sonic Youth album to secure a widespread release in both the USA and Britain. This acclaimed set included the compulsive 'I'm Insane' and the eerie 'Death Valley '69', a collaboration with Lydia Lunch, which invoked the horror of the infamous Charles Manson murders. Bob Bert was then replaced by Steve Shelley (b. 23 June 1962, Midland, Michigan, USA), who has remained with the line-up ever since. In 1986 the group unleashed *Evol*, which refined their ability to mix melody with menace, particularly on the outstanding 'Shadow Of A Doubt'. The album also introduced the Youth's tongue-in-cheek fascination with Madonna. 'Expressway To Yr Skull' was given two alternative titles, 'Madonna, Sean And Me' and 'The Cruxifiction Of Sean Penn', while later in the year the band were joined by Mike Watt from Firehose in a spin-off project, Ciccone Youth, which resulted in a mutated version of 'Into The Groove(y)'. (In 1989 this *alter ego* culminated in *Ciccone Youth*, which combined dance tracks with experimental sounds redolent of German groups Faust and Neu.) Sonic Youth's career continued with the highly impressive *Sister*, followed in 1988 by *Daydream Nation*, a double set that allowed the group to expand themes when required. Once again the result was momentous. The instrumentation was powerful, recalling the intensity of the Velvet Underground or Can while the songs themselves were highly memorable. In 1990 Sonic Youth left the independent circuit by signing with the Geffen Records stable, going on to establish a reputation as godfathers to the alternative US rock scene. Thurston Moore was instrumental in the signing of Nirvana to Geffen Records, while Kim Gordon was similarly pivotal in the formation of Hole. Steve Shelley would also work closely with Geffen on a number of acts. Successive stints on Lollapalooza tours helped to make Sonic Youth the nation's best known underground band, while the group's members continued to collaborate on music and soundtrack projects to a degree that ensured the continuation of an already vast discography.

●ALBUMS: *Confusion Is Sex* (Neutral 1983)★★★, *Kill Yr Idols* (Zensor 1983)★★, tape only *Sonic Death: Sonic Youth Live* (Ecstatic Peace! 1984)★★, *Bad Moon Rising* (Homestead 1985)★★★, *EVOL* (SST 1986)★★★★, *Sister* (SST 1987)★★★★, *Daydream Nation* (Blast First 1988)★★★★, *Goo* (Geffen 1990)★★★, *Dirty* (Geffen 1992)★★★★, *Experimental Jet Set, Trash And No Star* (Geffen 1994)★★★, *Washing Machine* (Geffen 1995)★★★, *Made In USA* film soundtrack rec. 1986 (Rhino/Warners 1995)★★. Solo: Lee Renaldo *From Here To Infinity* (SST 1987)★★. Thurston Moore *Psychic Hearts* (Geffen 1995)★★★.

●COMPILATIONS: *Screaming Fields Of Sonic Love* (Blast First 1995)★★★.

●VIDEOS: *Goo* (DGC 1991).

●FURTHER READING: *Confusion Is Next: The Sonic Youth Story*, Alec Foego.

SPACEMEN 3

Spacemen 3 were instigated in Rugby, Warwickshire, England, in 1982 by Sonic Boom (b. Pete Kember, 19 November 1965) and regional soulmate Jason Pierce (also, strangely enough, b.

19 November 1965). Augmented by the rhythm section of Rosco and Pete Baines, it took Spacemen 3 four full years to blossom onto record. Initially crying shy of sounding too much like the Cramps, the band carefully evolved into one-chord wonders; masters of the hypnotic, blissed-out groove. Such was their languid approach to working, and so dream-inspiring was their music, Spacemen 3 made a habit of sitting down for the entirety of their gigs. 1989's *Playing With Fire* included the intensely repetitive blast of 'Revolutions'. The free live album given with the first 2000 copies of the previous album, featured superior versions of some of their recorded live material. By this time Baines and Rosco had formed what was tantamount to a Spacemen 3 spin-off in the Darkside, allowing Will Carruthers and John Mattock to step into their places, and although this was the peak of the band's career, fundamental problems were still inherent: Sonic Boom made no secret of his drug dependency, having replaced heroin with methadone, and he and Jason Pierce were gradually growing apart to the point where they were chasing different goals. The relationship became so strained that *Recurring*, although still a Spaceman 3 effort, saw the two forces working separately, Boom being attributed with side one and Pierce with side two. By this stage Boom had embarked upon a solo career and Pierce was working with Mattock and Carruthers in another band, Spiritualized, a situation that further fanned the flames. When *Recurring* finally saw the light of day Spaceman 3's creative forces refused even to be interviewed together. A petty demise to what was, for some time, a creatively intense band.

●ALBUMS: *Sound Of Confusion* (Glass 1986)★★, *The Perfect Prescription* (Glass 1987)★★★, *Performance* (Glass 1988)★★, *Playing With Fire* (Fire 1989)★★★, *Dreamweapon: An Evening Of Contemporary Sitar Music* (Fierce 1990)★★, *Recurring* (Fire 1991)★★★, *For All The Fucked Up Children Of This World We Give You Spacemen 3* first recording session (Sympathy For The Record Industry 1995)★, *Live In 89* (Orbit 1995)★★.

●COMPILATIONS: *Taking Drugs To Make Music To Take Drugs To - The Northampton Demos* (Bomp 1990)★★★, *Translucent Flashbacks (The Glass Singles)* (Fire 1995)★★★.

SPAGNA, IVANA

b. Italy. Disco singer Ivana Spagna first rose to fame outside her native Italy with the European success of 'Easy Lady' in the 80s. However, by the 90s she had remodelled herself as an altogether more sophisticated, adult-orientated artist. As evidence of this, her 1996 release for Epic Records, *Lupid Solitari (Lone Wolves)*, was entirely self-produced and written. By this time she had re-established local popularity by making an Italian language version of the Elton John song 'Circle Of Life', from the 1994 Walt Disney film, *The Lion King*. Her 1995 set, *Siamo In Due*, achieved triple platinum (300,000 sales) status as a result, making her Italy's best-selling artist of the year. In 1996 she also reached third place in the San Remo Song Festival with 'E Lo Penso A Te' ('And I Think Of You'), as her record label attempted to launch her as a pan-European star.

●ALBUMS: *Siamo In Due* (Epic 1995)★★, *Lupid Solitari* (Epic 1996)★★.

SPANDAU BALLET

Evolving from a school group, the Makers, this UK New Romantic group was founded in 1979 with a line-up comprising Gary Kemp (b. 16 October 1960, London, England; guitar), his brother Martin Kemp (b. 10 October 1961, London, England; bass), Tony Hadley (b. 2 June 1960, London, England), John Keeble (b. 6 July 1959, London, England; drums) and Steve Norman (b. 25 March 1960, London, England; rhythm guitar/saxophone/percussion). Another school colleague, Steve Dagger, became the group's long-standing manager. The group originally came to prominence as part of the new romantic scene revolving around a handful of fashionable London clubs, at which the habitués would dress in outlandish clothes and make-up. Such was the interest in this unknown group that Spandau Ballet were offered a contract by Island Records proprietor Chris Blackwell. This was rejected and, instead, the group set up their own label, Reformation. During early 1980, they were filmed for a television documentary and soon after licensed their label through Chrysalis Records. Their powerful debut, the harrowing 'To Cut A Long Story Short' reached the UK Top 5. With their kilts and synthesizers, it was easy to assume that the group were just part of a passing fashion and over the next year their singles 'The Freeze' and 'Musclebound' were average rather than exceptional. The insistent 'Chant Number 1 (I Don't Need This Pressure On)' revealed a more interesting soul/funk direction, complete with added brass and a new image. The single reached the UK Top 3, but again was followed by a relatively fallow period with 'Paint Me Down' and 'She Loved Like Diamond' barely scraping into the charts. The group completed a couple of albums and employed

various producers, including Trevor Horn for 'Instinction' and Tony Swain and Steve Jolley for 'Communication'. By 1983 the group pursued a more straightforward pop direction and pushed their lead singer as a junior Frank Sinatra. The new approach was demonstrated most forcibly on the irresistibly melodic 'True', which topped the UK charts. The album of the same name repeated the feat, while the follow-up 'Gold' reached number 2. The obvious international appeal of a potential standard like 'True' was underlined when the song belatedly climbed into the US Top 10. During the mid-80s, the group continued to chart regularly with such hits as 'Only When You Leave', 'I'll Fly For You', 'Highly Strung' and 'Round And Round'. A long-running legal dispute with Chrysalis forestalled the group's progress until they signed to CBS/Columbia Records in 1986. The politically conscious *Through The Barricades* and its attendant hit single 'Fight For Yourselves' partly re-established their standing. Their later work, however, was overshadowed by the acting ambitions of the Kemp brothers, who appeared to considerable acclaim in the London gangster movie, *The Krays*.

●ALBUMS: *Journey To Glory* (Reformation 1981)★★, *Diamond* (Reformation 1982)★, *True* (Reformation 1983)★★, *Parade* (Reformation 1984)★★, *Through The Barricades* (Reformation/Columbia 1986)★★, *Heart Like A Sky* (Columbia 1989)★★. Solo: Tony Hadley *State Of Play* (1993)★★.

●COMPILATIONS: *The Best Of ...* (Chrysalis 1991)★★★.

SPEAR OF DESTINY

Formed from the ashes of Theatre Of Hate in early 1983, Spear Of Destiny took their name from the mythological weapon that pierced the body of Christ, and was supposedly acquired over the years by Attila The Hun, Napoleon and Hitler. This helped the band to attract quite a volume of destructive commentary in the press. The original line-up featured mainstay Kirk Brandon (b. 3 August 1956, Westminster, London, England; vocals/guitar), Chris Bell (drums), Lasettes Ames (saxophone) and Stan Stammers (ex-Theatre Of Hate; bass). They signed to CBS Records, but maintained their own label design, 'Burning Rome', which had appeared on previous Theatre Of Hate releases. The first single, 'Flying Scotsman', arrived in 1983, and was featured on *The Grapes Of Wrath* alongside the relentless single 'The Wheel'. Critical response to the group was divided. By July, Bell and Ames had left, for reasons described by Bell as personal and religious. Brandon and Stammers brought in former Theatre Of Hate saxophonist John Lennard (b. Canada; ex-Diodes) and Nigel Preston (ex-Theatre Of Hate; Sex Gang Children). A third line-up added Alan St. Clair (guitar) and Neil Pyzor (keyboards/saxophone, ex-Case), Dolphin Taylor (drums, ex-Tom Robinson Band; Stiff Little Fingers) and Nicky Donnelly (saxophone, ex-Case). It was this formation that recorded *One Eyed Jacks*, arguably the band's best album, and the singles 'Rainmaker', 'Liberator' and 'Prisoner Of Love', the latter signalling a change in direction that was more fully realized on the follow-up album. When *World Service* arrived, there was considerable disappointment from fans and critics alike. Having built an enviable reputation as a lyricist of considerable vigour, tracks like 'Mickey' seemed grotesque and clumsy. Further personnel changes became commonplace, and by 1987 and *Outlands* the line-up comprised Pete Barnacle (drums), Volker Janssen (keyboards) and Chris Bostock (bass) alongside Brandon. The summer of that year saw Brandon incapacitated for six months with an ankle injury that left him unable to walk, an affliction from which he still carries a limp. However, the band were soon back in the charts with 'Never Take Me Alive', and a support tour with U2. Their 1988 singles 'So In Love With You' and 'Radio Radio' saw them switch from Epic to Virgin Records. By December 1990, old colleague Stan Stammers returned on bass, alongside new drummer and guitarist Bobby Rae Mayhem and Mark Thwaite. 1991 opened with Brandon touring once more under the joint Theatre Of Hate/Spear Of Destiny banner. In 1996 Brandon dropped the name of his latest band 10:51 and reverted to Theatre Of Hate. He embarked on an unsuccessful litigation with Boy George that year over allegations of a homosexual relationship, revealed in George's autobiography.

●ALBUMS:*The Grapes Of Wrath* (Epic 1983)★★, *One Eyed Jacks* (Burning Rome 1984)★★★, *World Service* (Burning Rome 1985)★★, *Outlands* (Ten 1987)★★, *The Price You Pay* (Virgin 1988)★★, *S.O.D.'s Law* (Virgin 1992)★★, *Live At The Lyceum* (1993)★, *BBC Radio One Live In Concert* rec. 1987 (Windsong 1994)★.

●COMPILATIONS: *S.O.D. The Epic Years* (Epic 1987)★★★.

SPINAL TAP

The concept for Spinal Tap - a satire of a fading British heavy metal band - was first aired in a late 70s television sketch. Christopher Guest, formerly of parody troupe *National Lampoon*, played the part of lead guitarist Nigel Tufnell, while Harry Shearer (bassist Derek Smalls) and actor Michael McKean (vocalist David St. Hubbins) had performed with the Credibility Gap. Their initial sketch also featured Loudon Wainwright III and drummer Russ Kunkel, but these true-life musicians dropped out of the project on its transformation to full-length film. *This Is Spinal Tap*, released in 1984, was not a cinematic success, but it has since become highly popular through the medium of video. Its portrayal of a doomed US tour is ruthless, exposing incompetence, megalomania and sheer madness, but in a manner combining humour with affection. However, rather than incurring the wrath of the rock fraternity, the film has been lauded by musicians, many of whom, unfathomably, claim inspiration for individual scenes. The contemporary UK comedy team, the Comic Strip, used elements of Spinal Tap's theme in their second film, *More Bad News*. Spinal Tap reunited as a 'real' group and undertook an extensive tour in 1992 to promote *Break Like The Wind*, which featured guest appearances by Jeff Beck, Nicky Hopkins and Slash (Guns N'Roses). At this stage it seems Spinal Tap's jokes at metal's expense are too deep-rooted in truth to ever wear thin.

●ALBUMS: *This Is Spinal Tap* (Polydor 1984)★★★, *Break Like The Wind* (MCA 1992)★★★.

●VIDEOS: *This Is Spinal Tap* (1989).

●FURTHER READING: *Inside Spinal Tap*, Peter Occhiogrosso.

SPYRO GYRA

Formed in 1975 by saxophonist Jay Beckenstein and pianist Jeremy Wall, the original Spyro Gyra comprised Chet Catallo (electric guitar), David Wolford (electric bass), Eli Konikoff (drums), and Gerardo Velez (percussion). After a modest start in Buffalo, New York, and an album on a small independent label, Beckenstein's hard work and commitment through countless changes of personnel resulted in appearances at major international jazz festivals in the 80s, and several gold albums. In addition to having four hits in the USA the band found considerable success in the UK with the infectious 'Morning Dance'. The band's mainstream treatment of a mixture of funk, Latin, and jazz remains popular today.

●ALBUMS: *Spyro Gyra* (Infinity 1978)★★, *Morning Dance* (Infinity 1979)★★★★, *Catching The Sun* (MCA 1980)★★, *Carnival* (MCA 1980)★★★, *Freetime* (MCA 1981)★★, *Incognito* (MCA 1982)★★, *City Kids* (MCA 1983)★★, *Access All Areas* (MCA

1984)★★, *Alternating Currents* (GRP 1985)★★, *Breakout* (MCA 1986)★★, *Stories Without Words* (MCA 1987)★★, *Rites Of Summer* (GRP 1988)★★, *Point Of View* (MCA 1989)★★, *Fast Forward* (GRP 1990)★★, *Three Wishes* (GRP 1992)★★, *Dreams Beyond Control* (GRP 1993)★★, *Love And Other Obsessions* (GRP 1994)★★, *Heart Of The Night* (GRP 1996)★★.
●COMPILATIONS: *The Collection* (GRP 1991)★★★.
●VIDEOS: *Graffiti* (GRP 1992).

SQUADRON

This American glam-rock quartet was formed in 1981 by Kevin (guitar/vocals) and Shawn Duggan (guitar/vocals). With the addition of bassist Bob Catalano and drummer John Blovin, they drew inspiration from the New York Dolls, Marc Bolan and Mötley Crüe. Dressed in red plastic clothes, with their hair sprayed grey, the visuals were always more interesting than the music. They released one album but disbanded soon after its release.
●ALBUMS: *First Mission* (1982)★★.

SQUEEZE

Formed in the south-east London area of Deptford in 1974, Squeeze came to prominence in the late 70s riding on the new wave created by the punk movement. Original members Chris Difford (b. 4 November 1954, London, England; guitar/lead vocals), Glenn Tilbrook (b. 31 August 1957, London, England; guitar/vocals) and Jools Holland (b. 24 January 1958; keyboards) named the group after a disreputable Velvet Underground album. With the addition of Harry Kakoulli (bass), and original drummer Paul Gunn replaced by session drummer Gilson Lavis (b. 27 June 1951, Bedford, England), Squeeze released an EP, *Packet Of Three*, in 1977 on the Deptford Fun City label. It was produced by former Velvets member John Cale. The EP's title in itself reflected the preoccupation of the group's main songwriters, Chris Difford and Glenn Tilbrook, with England's social underclass. It led to a major contract with A&M Records and a UK Top 20 hit in 1978 with 'Take Me I'm Yours'. Minor success with 'Bang Bang' and 'Goodbye Girl' that same year was followed in 1979 by two number 2 hits with 'Cool For Cats' and 'Up The Junction'. Difford's lyrics were by now beginning to show an acute talent in capturing the flavour of contemporary south London life with a sense of the tragi-comic. This began to flower fully with the release of 1980's *Argy Bargy* which spawned the singles 'Another Nail In My Heart' (UK Top 20) and the

sublime 'Pulling Mussels (From A Shell)'. The set was Squeeze's most cohesive album to date; having finally thrown off any remaining traces of a punk influence they now displayed some of the finest 'kitchen sink' lyrics since Ray Davies' peak. The album also featured the group's new bass player, John Bentley (b. 16 April 1951). In 1980 Holland left for a solo career that included performing and recording with his own band, Jools Holland And The Millionaires (which displayed his talent for the 'boogie-woogie' piano style) and, to a larger extent, hosting the UK television show *The Tube*. His replacement was singer/pianist Paul Carrack, formerly with pub-rock band Ace. He appeared on *East Side Story* which was co-produced by Elvis Costello. Carrack stamped his mark on the album with his performance on 'Tempted' and with the success of 'Labelled With Love', a UK Top 5 hit, the album became the band's most successful to date. Carrack departed soon after to join Carlene Carter's group and was replaced by Don Snow (b. 13 January 1957, Kenya; ex-Sinceros). The follow-up, *Sweets From A Stranger*, was an uneven affair, although it did spawn the superb 'Black Coffee In Bed'. At the height of the group's success, amid intense world tours, including selling out New York's Madison Square Garden, Difford And Tilbrook dissolved the group. However, the duo continued to compose together releasing an album in 1984. The following year they re-formed the band with Lavis, the returning Holland and a new bass player, Keith Wilkinson. *Cosi Fan Tutti Frutti* was hailed as a return to form, and although not supplying any hit singles, the tracks 'King George Street', 'I Learnt How To Pray' and Difford/Holland's 'Heartbreaking World' stood out. In 1987 Squeeze achieved their highest position in the UK singles chart for almost six years when 'Hourglass' reached number 16 and subsequently gave the group their first US Top 40 hit, reaching number 15. '853-5937' repeated the transatlantic success. The accompanying album, *Babylon And On*, featured contributions from former Soft Boys' Andy Metcalfe (horns/keyboards/moog). After the release of 1989's *Frank*, which contained one of the most sensitive lyrics ever written by a man about menstruation ('She Doesn't Have To Shave'), Holland departed once again to concentrate on television work. With Matt Irving joining as a second keyboard player, Squeeze released a live album, *A Round And A Bout*, on their old Deptford Fun City label in 1990, before signing a new record contract with Warner Brothers Records. The release of *Play* confirmed and continued Chris

Difford and Glenn Tilbrook's reputation as one of the UK's finest songwriting teams, with 'Gone To The Dogs' and 'Wicked And Cruel' particularly resonant of earlier charms. *Some Fantastic Place* saw them reunited with A&M Records, although there was some critical carping about their insistence on a group format which did not always augur well for their more adroit and sober compositions. *Ridiculous* was their strongest album in years, back to writing sharp, humourous yet provocative lyrics on the up-tempo tracks and poignant love songs on the ballads. The lively 'Electric Trains' for example, managed to combine the unlikely pairing of Julie Andrews and Jerry Garcia in one lyric! 'Grouch Of The Day' cleverly delivered self deprecating honesty while the minor hit 'This Summer' has the wonderful coupling lyric 'nights we spent out of control like two flags wrapped around a pole', a tremendous set of songs that strangely missed the record buying public by a mile and was not released in the USA. Hits or not like Andy Partridge of XTC and Ray Davies of the Kinks, Difford And Tillbrook are prized possessions of the great English pop song tradition.
●ALBUMS: *Squeeze* (A&M 1978)★★★, *Cool For Cats* (A&M 1979)★★★★, *Argy Bargy* (A&M 1980)★★★★, *East Side Story* (A&M 1981)★★★★, *Sweets From A Stranger* (A&M 1982)★★★, *Cosi Fan Tutti Frutti* (A&M 1985)★★★, *Babylon And On* (A&M 1987)★★★, *Frank* (A&M 1989)★★, *A Round And About* (Deptford Fun City 1990)★★, *Play* (Reprise 1991)★★, *Some Fantastic Place* (A&M 1993)★★★, *Ridiculous* (A&M 1995)★★★★.
●COMPILATIONS: *Singles 45 And Under* (A&M 1982)★★★★, *Excess Moderation* (A&M 1996)★★★.

STARSOUND

The credit for the Starsound phenomenon arguably belongs to an unknown European bootlegger who created a medley of songs by original artists for use in discotheques during 1980. One of the tunes in the sequence was Shocking Blue's 'Venus' and its appearance so outraged publisher William van Kooten that he was determined to record a rival legal version. Producer Jaap Eggermont, formerly a drummer in Golden Earring, elected to retain 'Venus' followed by the Archies' 'Sugar Sugar' and a wealth of Beatles oldies. Three Fab Four soundalikes, Bas Muys, Okkie Huysdens and Hans Vermoulen, took on the roles of John Lennon, Paul McCartney and George Harrison, respectively. In the UK, the track was titled 'Stars On 45' and credited to Starsound, but in the USA, Stars On 45 were the registered artists and the song sub title was the

longest in chart-topping history: 'Medley: Intro/Venus/Sugar Sugar/No Reply/I'll Be Back/Drive My Car/Do You Want To Know A Secret/We Can Work It Out/I Should Have Known Better/Nowhere Man/You're Going To Lose That Girl/Stars On 45'. In the UK, 'Stars On 45, Volume 2' featured a medley of Abba songs and, like its predecessor, reached number 2. Before long, the idea was ruthlessly milked and other record companies took note by releasing medley tributes by such artists as the Beach Boys and Hollies. A decade later, the medley art was resurrected and perfected by the multi-chart-topping Jive Bunny And The Mastermixers.
●ALBUMS: *Stars On 45* (Columbia 1981)★★, *Stars On 45 - Volume 2* (Columbia 1981)★★, *Stars Medley* (Columbia 1982)★★.

STEINMAN, JIM

American songwriter/producer/musician Steinman first came to the public's attention in 1975 as musical arranger for the comedy company National Lampoon. He was also a playwright and it was at an audition that he first met Dallas singer/actor Meat Loaf. Together they conceived one of the biggest rock albums of all time, *Bat Out Of Hell*. Steinman's songs with their unique Wagnerian production technique was later to grace countless other artists from Bonnie Tyler ('Total Eclipse Of The Heart') to Barry Manilow. With Meat Loaf unable to record a follow-up Steinman grew impatient and decided to record the album himself. Released in 1981, *Bad For Good* lacked the vocal impact of Meat Loaf and was not a best-seller - it was, however, still a superb album featuring Todd Rundgren as guitarist and co-producer. Many of the songs would later appear on the *Bat Out Of Hell 2* album which heralded a reunion with Meat Loaf, having parted company after the latter's *Deadringer* set, also from 1981. Perhaps the most stunning track from *Bad For Good* was a spoken-word piece titled 'Love And Death And An American Guitar', where Steinman proclaims in a style reminiscent of Jim Morrison's 'Horse Latitudes', that 'I once killed a Fender guitar'. He was also the mastermind for the 1990 double album project, *Original Sin*, a concept piece based on sexuality - at times almost operatic in construction; it was not taken seriously and so he returned to production work where he remains most in demand. Steinman produced Bonnie Tyler's *Free Spirit* in 1996, the same year that he negotiated a long-term publishing contract with Polygram. One of the first fruits is the rock opera *Dance Of The*

Vampires. That year he also worked with Andrew Lloyd Webber on a project based upon the 60s movie *Whistle Down The Wind*.

●ALBUMS: *Bad For Good* (Epic 1981)★★★, *Original Sin* (Virgin 1990)★★.

STEVO

b. Steven Pearse, 26 December 1962, Dagenham, Essex, England. One of the most outspoken, adventurous and original discoverers of arcane talent, Stevo came to the fore of the British music scene during the early 80s. A misfit and underachiever at school, he was virtually illiterate and underwent a self-improving course that coincided with his rise to prominence in the music industry. Originally a disc jockey, he compiled an 'electronic music' and 'futurist' chart for the music press which led to him being bombarded with roughly hewn demos from unknown artists. During 1980, Stevo packaged the best of this material as the *Some Bizzare Album* (its misspelling was unintentional but apposite). Among the artists included were Throbbing Gristle, Classix Noveaux, Clock DVA, Cabaret Voltaire, Blancmange, Depeche Mode, Soft Cell and The The. The latter two artists came under Stevo's management and joined his innovative Some Bizzare record label. Stevo received instant recognition for his brusque behaviour and eccentric business dealings. After the chart-topping success of Soft Cell, major record companies anxious to license his acts were forced to endure the teenage entrepreneur's strange whims, which included signing a contract in the pouring rain while sitting on one of the lions in Trafalgar Square. With similar eccentricity, the contract for the hand of Psychic TV included a clause demanding a year's supply of baby food. It said much for Stevo's power and persuasion that he managed to license so many wilfully uncommercial acts to the major labels. His strength lay in an ability to capture innovative acts at an early stage when they were merely regarded as weird. In the case of Soft Cell and later The The, Stevo showed that he had the ear to nurture potentially major artists. Many other acts were a testament to his love of the unusual. Berlin's Einsturzende Neubaten decried conventional rock instruments in favour of industrial sounds, and the scream of clanging metal as percussion could also be heard via Test Department. The unremitting aural depravity of Foetus threatened to complete Stevo's journey into the darker areas of the soul, and with commercial acts on the wane the future of his label was perpetually in doubt. In the early 90s, however, Stevo is still stalking the musical boundaries with a stream of new signings including Stex, Tim Hutton, Kandis King and Vicious Circle.

●FURTHER READING: *Starmakers And Svengalis: The History Of British Pop Management*, Johnny Rogan.

STEWART, DAVE, AND BARBARA GASKIN

One of the surprise hits of the early 80s was a UK number 1 cover of Leslie Gore's 'Its My Party' by two former members of several UK progressive bands. Dave Stewart was originally organist in Uriel in late 1967 (with Steve Hillage). When Hillage left, Stewart and Uriel's other members Clive Brooks and Mont Campbell formed Egg who released a couple of albums in the late 60s and early 70s. At the same time Stewart often guested on keyboards with Steve Hillage's new band Khane. In 1973 he replaced David Sinclair in Hatfield And The North who included a female backing group the Northettes, consisting of Barbara Gaskin (ex-Spyrogyra; not the chart act of the late 70s but a Canterbury folk rock assembly), Amanda Parsons, and Ann Rosenthal. Hatfield And The North metamorphosized into National Health in 1975 but eventually folded later in the decade. Stewart formed his own record label Broken Records and recorded a version of the Jimmy Ruffin hit, 'What Becomes Of The Broken Hearted', featuring Colin Blunstone on vocals. The record (and label) were picked up by Stiff Records and became a Top 20 UK hit. For the follow-up Stewart chose his former Hatfield And The North colleague (and by now, lover) Barbara Gaskin to sing lead with Northette Amanda Parsons on backing vocals. The record - 'It's My Party' - reached number 1. Subsequent singles, 'Johnny Rocco' and 'The Siamese Cat Song' (from *Lady And The Tramp*), flopped, though 'Busy Doin' Nothin' (from *A Connecticut Yankee In The Court Of King Arthur*) made the Top 50. 'Leipzig' and 'I'm In A Different World' were further failures but in 1986 they returned with another oldie - Little Eva's 'The Locomotion', which reached the bottom end of the charts.

●ALBUMS: *The Big Idea* (Rykodisc 1991)★★.

STEWART, DAVID A.

b. 9 September 1952, Sunderland, Tyne & Wear, England. At the age of 15, the fledgling guitarist Stewart introduced himself to the world of rock music by stowing away in the back of Amazing Blondel's tour van, after the group had given a performance in Stewart's home town of Newcastle. He later teamed up with guitarist Brian Harrison to form a duo, which after releasing *Deep December* went on to form Longdancer on Elton John's Rocket label in 1973. During this time, Stewart had met ex-Royal Academy of Music student Annie Lennox in London, where the couple co-habited. In 1977, together with friend Peter Coombes, they first recorded as a trio, the Catch, which developed into the Tourists. After establishing a following on the European continent, the Tourists achieved fame in the UK with minor hit singles, culminating in the number 4 hit cover version of Dusty Springfield's 1979 'I Only Want To Be With You' and 'So Good To Be Back Home Again'. This popularity with the public, however, was at odds with the particularly virulent and antagonistic attitude of the popular music press who viewed the band as 'old wave' cashing in on the 'new wave'. When the band split in late 1980, Stewart and Lennox, who had now ended their romantic relationship, continued working together and formed the Eurythmics. After a spell spent shaking off their reputation left over from the Tourists, the duo gradually won favourable reviews to eventually emerge as one of the world's major pop acts of the 80s. They were awarded the Ivor Novello award for Songwriter Of The Year in 1984 and Stewart received the Best British Producer award at the BRITS ceremony in 1986. He increased his role and reputation as a producer by working with, among others, Bob Dylan, Feargal Sharkey and Mick Jagger. A flurry of awards followed the next year for songwriting and production and in August, Stewart married Siobhan Fahey of Bananarama. In 1989 Boris Grebenshikov, the first Russian rock artist to record and perform in the west, travelled to the USA and UK to record *Radio Silence* with Stewart. After the recording of the Eurythmics' *We Too Are One*, the group's activities were put on hold while the duo allowed themselves time to rest and indulge in other projects. For Stewart, this included forming his own record label, Anxious, working with saxophonist Candy Dulfer on the UK Top 10 hit 'Lily Was Here' (1990), and the formation of his new group, the Spiritual Cowboys, who achieved a minor UK chart placing for 'Jack Talking' (1990). Comprising Martin Chambers (drums, ex-Pretenders), John Turbull (guitar) and Chris James (bass), the group toured and recorded as a full-time project, and their debut album reached the UK Top 40. Stewart is now regarded as one of the major figures of the pop establishment, and despite the attacks of a personal and artistic nature from the more radical quarters of the British press, it can be said that he has been responsible for some of the finest pop music produced throughout the 80s and early 90s. On his solo album in 1994 he enlisted the services of a wide-ranging group of artists, including Carly Simon, Lou Reed, Bootsy Collins, David Sanborn, Laurie Anderson, Mick Jagger and his wife Siobhan Fahey.

●ALBUMS: *Lily Was Here* film soundtrack (AnXious 1990)★★, with the Spiritual Cowboys *Dave Stewart And The Spiritual Cowboys* (RCA 1990)★★, with the Spiritual Cowboys *Honest* (RCA 1991)★★, *Greetings From The Gutter* (East West 1994)★★.

STING

b. Gordon Sumner, 2 October 1951, Wallsend, Tyne & Wear, England. Sting's solo career began in 1982, two years before the break-up of the Police, for whom he was lead singer and bassist. In that year he starred in the film *Brimstone And Treacle* and from it released a version of the 30s ballad, 'Spread A Little Happiness', composed by Vivian Ellis. Its novel character and Sting's own popularity ensured Top 20 status in Britain. While continuing to tour and record with the Police, he also co-wrote the Dire Straits hit 'Money For Nothing' and sang harmonies on Phil Collins' *No Jacket Required*. By 1985, however, the other members of the Police were pursuing solo interests and Sting formed a touring band, the Blue Turtles. It included leading New York jazz figures such as Branford Marsalis (alto saxophone), Kenny Kirkland (keyboards) and Omar Hakim (drums). The group recorded his first solo album at Eddy Grant's studio in Jamaica before Marsalis and Sting performed at the Live Aid concert with Phil Collins. *Dream Of The Blue Turtles* found Sting developing the more cerebral lyrics to be found on the final Police album, *Synchronicity*. It also brought him three big international hits with 'If You Love Somebody Set Them Free', 'Fortress Around Your Heart' and 'Russians'. 'An Englishman In New York' (inspired by English eccentric Quentin Crisp) became a UK hit in 1990 after being remixed by Ben Liebrand. In 1985, Michael Apted directed *Bring On The Night*, a film about Sting and his group.

After touring with the Blue Turtles, Sting recorded *Nothing Like The Sun* (a title taken from a Shakespeare sonnet) with Marsalis and Police guitarist Andy Summers plus guests Ruben Blades, Eric Clapton and Mark Knopfler. The album was an instant success internationally and contained 'They Dance Alone (Gueca Solo)', Sting's tribute to the victims of repression in Argentina, in addition to a notable recording of Jimi Hendrix's 'Little Wing'. This track featured one of the last orchestral arrangements by the late Gil Evans. In 1988, Sting took part in Amnesty International's *Human Rights Now!* international tour and he devoted much of the following two years to campaigning and fundraising activity on behalf of environmental causes, notably highlighting the plight of the Indians of the Brazilian rainforest. He set up his own label, Pangaea, in the late 80s to release material by jazz and *avant garde* artists, and returned in 1991 with the autobiographical *The Soul Cages* from which 'All This Time' was a US Top 10 hit. He continued in a similar vein with *Ten Summoner's Tales*, which contained further high quality hit singles including 'If I Ever Lose My Faith In You' and 'Fields Of Gold'. Gordon 'Mr Sheer Profundity' Sumner has become one of the finest quality songwriters to appear out of the second UK 'new wave' boom (post 1977). The collection *Fields Of Gold* highlights his considerable accomplishment. Sting spent a traumatic time during the summer of 1995 when he had to testify in court after accusing his accountant of stealing vast sums of his income. The outcome was in Sting's favour and the accountant Keith Moore was jailed for six years. *Mercury Falling* was very much a marking-time album, not as strong as *Ten Summoner's Tales* but good enough to satisfy his fans and placate most reviewers.

●ALBUMS: *Dream Of The Blue Turtles* (A&M 1985)★★★, *Bring On The Night* (A&M 1986)★★, *Nothing Like the Sun* (A&M 1987)★★★★, *The Soul Cages* (A&M 1991)★★★, *Acoustic - Live In Newcastle* (A&M 1991)★★★, *Ten Summoner's Tales* (A&M 1993)★★★★, *Mercury Falling* (A&M 1996)★★★.

●COMPILATIONS: *Fields Of Gold 1984-1994* (A&M 1994)★★★★.

●VIDEOS: *Bring On The Night* (1987), *The Videos* (1988), *The Soul Cages* (1991), *Live At The Hague* (1991), *Fields Of Gold: The Best Of Sting 1984-94* (1994).

●FURTHER READING: *Sting: A Biography*, Robert Sellers.

STOCK, AITKEN AND WATERMAN

Modelling themselves on the Motown Records hit factory of the 60s, Mike Stock (b. 3 December 1951), Matt Aitken (b. 25 August 1956), and Pete Waterman (b. 15 January 1947) were the most successful team of UK writer/producers during the 80s. Waterman had been a soul disc jockey, promoter, producer and remixer (Adrian Baker's 'Sherry', Susan Cadogan's 'Hurts So Good'). In

1984, he joined forces with Stock and Aitken, members of pop band Agents Aren't Aeroplanes. The trio first designed records for the thriving British disco scene, having their first hits with singles by Dead Or Alive ('You Spin Me Round', UK number 1, 1984) Divine, Hazell Dean and Sinitta ('So Macho', 1986). The team specialized in designing songs for specific artists and they gained further UK number 1s in 1987 with 'Respectable' by Mel And Kim and Rick Astley's 'Never Gonna Give You Up'. In that year, too they released a dance single under their own names. 'Roadblock' reached the UK Top 20. In 1988, SAW, as they were now referred to, launched their own PWL label and shifted their attention to the teenage audience. Their main vehicles were Australian soap opera stars Kylie Minogue and Jason Donovan. Minogue's 'I Should Be So Lucky' was the first of over a dozen Top 10 hits in four years and the epitome of the SAW approach, a brightly produced, tuneful and highly memorable song. Donovan had similar success both with SAW compositions like 'Too Many Broken Hearts' and revivals (Brian Hyland's 'Sealed With A Kiss'). The Stock, Aitken Waterman formula was applied to other artists such as Sonia, Brother Beyond, Big Fun and Donna Summer but by 1991, a change of direction was apparent. Following Astley's example, Jason Donovan had left the fold in search of artistic freedom. Equally significantly, the SAW team was hit by the departure of its main songwriter Matt Aitken. Meanwhile, Waterman was busy with three new labels, PWL America, PWL Continental and PWL Black. The list of further hits goes on and on; clearly they now command enormous respect.

●ALBUMS: *Hit Factory* (1987)★★★, *Hit Factory, Volume 2* (1988)★★★, *Hit Factory, Volume 3* (1989)★★★.

●COMPILATIONS: *The Best Of Stock, Aitken And Waterman* (1990)★★★.

●VIDEOS: *Roadblock* (Touchstone Video 1988).

STONE ROSES

A classic case of an overnight success stretched over half a decade, the UK band Stone Roses evolved through a motley collection of Manchester-based non-starters such as the Mill, the Patrol and English Rose before settling down as Stone Roses in 1985. Acclaimed for their early warehouse gigs, at this time the line-up consisted of Ian Brown (b. Ian George Brown, 20 February 1963, Ancoats, Gt. Manchester, England; vocals), John Squire (b. 24 November 1962, Broadheath, Gt. Manchester, England; guitar), Reni (b. Alan John

Wren, 10 April 1964, Manchester, England; drums), Andy Couzens (guitar) and Pete Garner (bass). In their hometown, at least, the band had little trouble in working up a following, in spite of their prediliction for juxtaposing leather trousers with elegant melodies. In 1987 guitarist Andy Couzens left, later to form the High, and Pete Garner followed soon after, allowing Gary 'Mani' Mounfield (b. 16 November 1962, Crumpsall, Gt. Manchester, England) to take over bass guitar. By this time the band had already made a low-key recording debut, with the ephemeral 45, 'So Young'. By the end of the year the reconstituted foursome were packing out venues in Manchester, but finding it difficult to get noticed in the rest of the country. A contractl with the Silvertone Records label in 1988 produced 'Elephant Stone', and showed its makers to be grasping the essence of classic 60s pop. A year later they had carried it over the threshold of the independent scene and into the nation's front rooms. When the follow-up, 'Made Of Stone', attracted media attention, the Stone Roses' ball started rolling at a phenomenal pace. Their debut album was hailed in all quarters as a guitar/pop classic, and as the Manchester 'baggy' scene infiltrated Britain's consciousness, Stone Roses - alongside the funkier, grubbier Happy Mondays - were perceived to be leaders of the flare-wearing pack. By the close of 1989, the Roses had moved from half filling London's dingiest clubs to playing to 7500 people at Alexandra Palace. Having achieved such incredible success so quickly, when the band vanished to work on new material, the rumour mongers inevitably came out in force. In 1990 'One Love' reached the UK Top 10, but aside from this singular vinyl artefact, the media was mainly concerned with the Roses' rows with a previous record company, who had reissued old material accompanied by a video made without the band's permission. This resulted in the group vandalizing the company's property, which in turn led to a much-publicized court case. As if this was not enough, Stone Roses were back in court when they tried to leave Silvertone, who took out an injunction against their valuable protégés. This prevented any further Stone Roses material from being released, even though the band eventually won their case and signed to Geffen Records for a reported $4 million. At the end of 1991, their eagerly awaited new product was still stuck somewhere in the pipeline while, in true Stone Roses fashion, after their live extravaganzas at Spike Island, Glasgow, London and Blackpool, plans were afoot for a massive open-air comeback gig for the following spring. It never happened that year, nor the next. In fact the Stone Roses' absence from the limelight - initially through contractual problems with Silvertone and management squabbles, then seemingly through pure apathy - became something of an industry standing joke. Had their debut album not had such a huge impact on the public consciousness they would surely have been forgotten. Painstaking sessions with a series of producers finally saw the immodestly titled *Second Coming* released in 1995. It was announced in an exclusive interview given to the UK magazine dedicated to helping the homeless, *The Big Issue*, much to the chagrin of a slavering British music press. Almost inevitably, it failed to meet expectations, despite the fact that the US market was now opening up for the band. They also lost drummer Reni, who was replaced within weeks of its release by Robbie Maddix, who had previously played with Manchester rapper Rebel MC. Promotional gigs seemed less natural and relaxed than had previously been the case, while Silvertone milked the last gasp out of the band's legacy with them to compile a second compilation album (from only one original studio set). The tour they undertook in late 1995 dispelled any further gossip about loss of form or break-ups and nudged them back into the minds of critics who were beginning to see the band in a less than favourable light. Amid interviews it was clear that Squire was becoming disenchanted; he did not always show a united front in admitting that they had lost much by having such a gap between releases. It was therefore not too big a shock when he announced his departure in April 1996. Squire's carefully worded official statement read, 'It is with great regret that I feel compelled to announce my decision to leave. I believe all concerned will benefit from a parting of the ways at this point and I see this as the inevitible conclusion to the gradual social and musical separation we have undergone in the past few years. I wish them every success and hope they go on to greater things'. This now forced Ian Brown and company to decide on a concrete plan of action or become another memorable rock legend. They chose the former and only commented on Squire's departure at the 1996 Reading Festival, where they were headlining. Speaking positively, Brown said that Squire had been a barrier for the band playing live. With new members Aziz Ibrahim (guitar) and Nigel Ippinson (keyboards) they planned to be much more active. The press reports, however, were a different matter. Most sources confirmed that Brown's vocals were so off-key it was excruciating to have to listen.

They made the right decision in October 1996 by announcing their demise. Mani joined Primal Scream full-time and ex-guitarist John Squire went on to form the Seahorses. Too much was against them to survive either creatively or socially.

●ALBUMS: *The Stone Roses* (Silvertone 1989)★★★★, *Second Coming* (Geffen 1995)★★★.

●COMPILATIONS: *Turns Into Stone* (Silvertone 1992)★★★, *The Complete Stone Roses* (Silvertone 1995)★★★, *Garage Flower* (Silvertone 1996)★★.

●VIDEOS: *The Complete Stone Roses* (Wienerworld 1995).

STRAIT, GEORGE

b. 18 May 1952, Poteet, Texas, USA. Strait, the second son of a school teacher, was raised in Pearsall, Texas. When his father took over the family ranch, he developed an interest in farming. Strait heard country music throughout his youth but the record that cemented his love was Merle Haggard's *A Tribute To The Best Damn Fiddle Player In The World (Or, My Salute To Bob Wills)*. Strait dropped out of college to elope with his girlfriend, Norma, and then enlisted in the US Army. While there, he began playing country music. Then, at university studying agriculture, he founded the Ace In The Hole band. (His 1989 US country number 1, 'Ace In The Hole', was not about his band, nor did it feature them.) In 1976, he briefly recorded for Pappy Daily's D Records in Houston, one title being 'That Don't Change The Way I Feel About You'. Starting in 1977, Strait made trips to Nashville, but he was too shy to do himself justice. Disillusioned, he was considering a return to Texas but his wife urged him to keep trying. A club owner he had worked for, Erv Woolsey, was working for MCA Records: he signed him to the label and then became his manager.

In 1981, Strait's first single, 'Unwound', made number 6 in the US country charts. After two further hits, 'Fool Hearted Memory', from the film in which he had a cameo role, *The Soldier*, went to number 1. Strait was unsure about the recitation on 'You Look So Good In Love', but it was another chart-topper and led to him naming a racehorse Looks Good In Love. Strait's run of 18 US country number 1 hits also included 'Does Fort Worth Ever Cross Your Mind?' (1985), 'Nobody In His Right Mind Would've Left Her' (1986), 'Am I Blue' (1987), 'Famous Last Words Of A Fool' (1988) and 'Baby's Gotten Good At Goodbye' (1989). Strait was a throwback to the 50s honkytonk sound of country music. He used twin fiddles and steel guitar and his strong, warm delivery was similar to Haggard

and Lefty Frizzell. He made no secret of it as he recorded a fine tribute to Frizzell, 'Lefty's Gone'. Strait suffered a personal tragedy when his daughter, Jennifer, died in a car accident in 1986. Managing to compose himself, *Ocean Front Property* became the first album to enter *Billboard*'s country music chart at number 1, and it included another classic single, 'All My Ex's Live In Texas', which also demonstrated his love of western swing. The white-stetsoned Strait, who also manages to run a large farm, became one of the USA's top concert attractions, winning many awards from the Country Music Association, but it was only in 1989 that he became their Entertainer of the Year. After the impressive *Chill Of An Early Fall*, Strait enjoyed a major commercial success with a starring role in the film *Pure Country*. The magnificent box set *Strait Out Of The Box* demonstrates how consistent he has been over the years. Among the previously unissued tracks is a bizarre duet of 'Fly Me To The Moon', featuring that well-known honky tonk singer Frank Sinatra. A box-set retrospective often indicates that a career is nearing its end but *Lead On* in 1994 and *Clear Blue Sky* in 1996 are as as good as anything he has recorded, the latter making it's debut at number 1 on the *Billboard* country chart. The title track also became his 26th US country number 1.

●ALBUMS: *Strait Country* (MCA 1981)★★★★, *Strait From Your Heart* (MCA 1982)★★★, *Right Or Wrong* (MCA 1983)★★★, *Does Fort Worth Ever Cross Your Mind?* (MCA 1984)★★★★, *Something Special* (MCA 1985)★★, *No. 7* (MCA 1986)★★★, *Merry Christmas Strait To You* (MCA 1986)★★★, *Ocean Front Property* (MCA 1987)★★★★, *If You Ain't Lovin' (You Ain't Livin')* (MCA 1988)★★★, *Beyond The Blue Neon* (MCA 1989)★★★, *Livin' It Up* (MCA 1990)★★, *Chill Of An Early Fall* (MCA 1991)★★★★, *Holding My Own* (MCA 1992)★★★, *Pure Country* soundtrack (1992)★★★, *Easy Come, Easy Go* (MCA 1993)★★★, *Lead On* (MCA 1994)★★★★, *Clear Blue Sky* (MCA 1996)★★★★.

●COMPILATIONS: *Greatest Hits* (MCA 1986)★★★★, *Greatest Hits, Volume 2* (MCA 1987)★★★★, *Strait Out Of The Box* 4-CD box set (MCA 1995)★★★★.

●VIDEOS: *The Man In Love With You* (1994), *Pure Country* (1995).

STRAWBERRY SWITCHBLADE

This colourful duo comprising Jill Bryson (vocals/guitar) and Rose McDowell (vocals/guitar), emerged as a product of the late 70s Glasgow, Scotland punk scene. Their appearance in polka-dotted frocks with frills, ribbons, flowers and cheap jewellery unfortunately distracted attention from their songwriting. Despite sounding like a happy pop band, their lyrics expressed sadness. The debut single in 1983, 'Trees And Flowers', was written as a result of Jill's agoraphobia. Signed to the independent Ninety-Two Happy Customers label (under the aegis of producers David Balfe and Bill Drummond), this melancholy song was given a pastoral feel by the oboe playing of former Ravishing Beauties member Kate St. John. With added studio assistance from Roddy Frame (guitar) of Aztec Camera and Madness's Mark Bedford (bass), the single reached number 4 in the UK independent chart. The duo found national success in late 1984 with the chirpy 'Since Yesterday' and were feted by the music media. An over-produced debut album, far removed from the simplicity of 'Trees And Flowers', entered the UK Top 25 but failed to supply the duo with the expected run of hit singles. Their last hit came in 1985 with a cover of Dolly Parton's classic, 'Jolene'. Following the break-up of the group, Rose attempted to revive her career without Jill in the late 80s for a time working under the name Candy Cane, but met with little success.

●ALBUMS: *Strawberry Switchblade* (Korova 1985)★★.

STRAY CATS

With high-blown quiffs and 50s 'cat' clothes, Brian Setzer (b. 10 April 1959, New York, USA; guitar/vocals), Lee Rocker (b. Leon Drucher, 1961; double bass) and Slim Jim Phantom (b. Jim McDonnell, 20 March 1961; drums) emerged from New York's Long Island as the most commercially viable strand of the rockabilly resurgence in the early 80s - though they had to migrate to England to find a short but intense period of chart success. Their exhilarating repertoire was dominated by the works of artists such as Carl Perkins and Eddie Cochran in addition to some stylized group originals, but their taste was sufficiently catholic to also acknowledge the influence of later rock 'n' roll practitioners such as Creedence Clearwater Revival and Joe Ely. Probably their most iconoclastic reworking, however, was their arrangement of the Supremes' 'You Can't Hurry Love', which appeared on the b-side of their second single, 1981's 'Rock This Town'. This shared the same UK chart position as their earlier, debut hit, 'Runaway Boys', reaching number 9. 'Stray Cat Strut', produced by Dave Edmunds, was a similar success - as was the trio's debut album, but 1981 closed with

the comparative failure of both *Gonna Ball* and 'You Don't Believe Me' - as well as 'The Race Is On', a joint effort with Edmunds. When the group split shortly after '(She's) Sexy And 17' reached only number 29 in 1983, Rocker and Phantom amalgamated - as 'Phantom, Rocker And Slick' - with guitarist Earl Slick with whom they appeared on a star-studded televised tribute to Carl Perkins, organized by Edmunds in 1985. The band returned to the lower reaches of the charts in 1989 with 'Bring It Back Again'.

●ALBUMS: *Stray Cats* (Arista 1981)★★★, *Gonna Ball* (Arista 1981)★★★, *Built For Speed* US release - mixture of tracks from first two albums (EMI America 1982)★★★, *Rant 'N' Rave With The Stray Cats* (EMI America 1983)★★★, *Blast Off* (EMI America 1989)★★, *Choo Choo Hot Fish* (Dino 1992)★★, *Original Cool* (Essential 1994)★★★. Solo: Brian Setzer *The Knife Feels Like Justice* (EMI America 1984)★★★, *Live Nude Guitars* (EMI 1988). Phantom, Rocker And Slick *Phantom, Rocker And Slick* (EMI America 1985)★★★, *Cover Girl* (EMI America 1986)★★.

STYLE COUNCIL

Founded in 1983 by Paul Weller (b. 25 May 1958, Woking, Surrey, England) and Mick Talbot (b. 11 September 1958). Weller had been lead singer of the Jam while Talbot was the former keyboards player with the Merton Parkas and the Bureau. Another constant collaborator was singer D.C. Lee, whom Weller married. Weller's avowed aim with the group was to merge his twin interests of soul music and social comment. In this, his most important model was Curtis Mayfield, who appeared on Style Council's 1987 album. The continuing popularity of the Jam ensured that Style Council's first four releases, in 1983, were UK hits. They included the EP *Paris*, 'Speak Like A Child' and 'Long Hot Summer'. Tracey Thorn from Everything But The Girl was a guest vocalist on the band's first album. Perhaps the most effective Style Council song was the evocative 'My Ever Changing Moods', the first of three Top 10 hits in 1984 and the band's only US hit. During the mid-80s, Weller's political activism was at its height as he recorded 'Soul Deep' as the Council Collective with Jimmy Ruffin and Junior Giscombe to raise funds for the families of striking coal miners and became a founder-member of Red Wedge, an artists' support group for the Labour Party. Style Council appeared at Live Aid in 1985 and in 1986 made a short film, *JerUSAlem*, a satirical attack on the pop music industry. There were continuing British hits, notably 'The Walls Come

Tumbling Down' (1985), 'Have You Ever Had It Blue' (featured in the 1986 film *Absolute Beginners*) and 'Wanted' (1987). With its eclectic mix of soul, classical and pop influences, the 1988 album was less of a commercial success and by 1990, Style Council was defunct. Weller re-emerged the next year with a new band, the Paul Weller Movement, recording for his own Freedom High label, and subsequently became one of the 90s' most acclaimed solo artists.

●ALBUMS: *Cafe Bleu* (Polydor 1984)★★, *Our Favourite Shop* (Polydor 1985)★★★, *Home And Abroad* (Polydor 1986)★★, *The Cost Of Loving* (Polydor 1987)★★, *Confessions Of A Pop Group* (Polydor 1988)★★, *Here's Some That Got Away* (Polydor 1993)★★.

●COMPILATIONS: *Singular Adventures Of The Style Council* (Polydor 1989)★★★, *The Style Council Collection* (Polydor 1996)★★★.

●VIDEOS: *What We Did On Our Holidays* (Polygram 1983), *Far East And Far Out - Council Meeting In Japan* (Polygram 1984), *What We Did The Following Year* (Polygram 1985), *Showbiz!, The Style Council Live* (Polygram 1986), *JerUSAlem* (Palace 1987), *Confessions Of A Pop Group* (Channel 5 1988), *The Video Adventures Of ... Greatest Hits Vol. 1* (Channel 5/Polygram 1991).

●FURTHER READING: *Mr Cool's Dream - The Complete History Of The Style Council*, Ian Munn.

SUBWAY SECT
(see Godard, Vic, And The Subway Sect)

SUGARCUBES
This offbeat pop band was formed in Reykjavik, Iceland on 8 June 1986, the date taken from the birth of Björk's son, Sindri. The settled line-up featured Björk Gundmundsdottir (b. 1966, Reykjavik, Iceland; vocals/keyboards), Bragi Olaffson (bass), Einar Orn Benediktsson (vocals/trumpet), Margret 'Magga' Ornolfsdottir (keyboards, replacing original keyboard player Einar Mellax) Sigtryggur 'Siggi' Balduresson (drums) and Thor Eldon (guitar). Björk's step father was in a rock showband, and after early stage appearances she completed her first album at the age of 11. She was also the singer for prototype groups Toppie Tikarras then Theyr, alongside Siggi Balduresson. The latter band shot to prominence when Jaz Coleman and Youth (Killing Joke) mysteriously appeared in Iceland in March 1982, paranoid about an impending apocalypse, and collaborated on several projects with Theyr. Björk, Einar and Siggi then went on to form Kukl, who toured Europe and

released two records on the Crass label, establishing a link with the UK anarcho-punk scene that would be cemented when the band joined UK independent label One Little Indian Records. Their debut single, 'Birthday', and album, *Life's Too Good*, saw the band championed in the UK press. In particular, praise was heaped on Björk's distinctive and emotive vocals. The Sugarcubes ran their own company in Iceland called Bad Taste, an organization that encompassed an art gallery, poetry bookshop, record label, radio station and publishing house. Björk's ex-husband, Thor, a graduate in Media Studies from London Polytechnic and the band's guitarist, sired their son Sindri under a government incentive scheme to boost the island's population, the financial rewards for this action allowing him to buy a pair of contact lenses. He then married Magga Ornolfsdottir (ex-the Giant Lizard), who joined the band in time for their second album. In addition, Siggi Balduresson and Bragi Olaffson, the band's rhythm section, were brother-in-laws, having married twin sisters. Most bizarre of all, however, was the subsequent marriage of Einar and Bragi in Denmark in 1989, the first openly gay marriage in pop history. *Here Today, Tomorrow, Next Week*, its title taken from Kenneth Graeme's book *Wind In The Willows*, was a more elaborate album, with a full brass section on 'Tidal Wave' and strings on the single 'Planet'. Compared with the rapturous reception granted their first album. *Here Today* took a critical pasting. Even label boss Derek Birkett conceded that it was far too deliberate. The press was also quick to seize on the fact that Einar's vocal interjections detracted from the band's performance. After much touring the group returned to Reykjavik, where they followed their own interests for a time. Björk collaborated on the Bad Taste album *Gling Glo*; 'Just Icelandic pop songs from the 50s with jazz influences'. Balduresson contributed drums. Members of the band spent time as an alternative jazz orchestra. They then played a concert for President Mitterand of France, in Reykjavik, and Björk joined 808 State on their *Ex:El* album and single, 'Oops'. The group's third album found them back in favour with the music press and back in the charts with 'Hit', but the inevitable happened shortly afterwards, with Björk heading for a critically and commercially rewarding solo career.

●ALBUMS: *Life's Too Good* (One Little Indian 1988)★★★★, *Here Today, Tomorrow, Next Week* (One Little Indian 1989)★★, *Stick Around For Joy* (One Little Indian 1992)★★★, *It's It* remixes (One Little Indian 1992)★★.

SUGARHILL GANG

Englewood, New Jersey troupe, whose 'Rapper's Delight' was hip hop's breakthrough single. They gave the music an identity and a calling card in the first line of the song: 'A hip-hop, The hi-be, To the hi-be, The hip-hip-hop, You don't stop rockin'. Master Gee (b. Guy O'Brien, 1963), Wonder Mike (b. Michael Wright, 1958) and Big Bank Hank (b. Henry Jackson, 1958) saw massive international success in 1979 with 'Rappers Delight', based on the subsequently widely borrowed rhythm track from Chic's 'Good Times', over which the trio offered a series of sly boasts which were chatted rather than sung. Joe Robinson remembers the song's elevation to commercial status: 'Sylvia brought this to me, a 15 minute record on a 12-inch disc. No 15 minute record has ever got played on the radio, so I said, what am I gonna do with this? But all I had to do with it was get one play anywhere and it broke'. Considered at the time to be something of a novelty item, 'Rapper's Delight' was significantly more than that. Sylvia and Joe Robinson had recruited the three rappers on an *ad hoc* basis. Hank was a former bouncer and pizza waiter, and brought fresh rhymes from his friend Granmaster Caz (see Cold Crush Brothers). The backing was offered by Positive Force, a group from Pennsylvania who enjoyed their own hit with 'We Got The Funk', but became part of the Sugarhill phenomenon when 'Rapper's Delight' struck. They would go on to tour on the Gang's early live shows, before the Sugarhill house band took over. Smaller hits followed with 'The Love In You' (1979) and 'Kick It Live From 9 To 5' (1982), before the group faded and fell apart in the early 80s. The Sugarhill Gang were already assured of their place in hip hop's history, even if reports that Big Bank Hank was working as a Englewood garbage man in the 90s are correct.
●ALBUMS: *Rappers Delight* (Sugarhill 1980)★★★, *8th Wonder* (Sugarhill 1982)★★.

SUMMERS, ANDY

b. Andrew Somers, 31 December 1942, Poulton-le-Fylde, Lancashire, England. Raised in Bournemouth, Dorset, Summers was performing in the city's clubs and coffee-bars while still a teenager. He first encountered Zoot Money in the Don Robb Band, a local cabaret attraction, and later joined the ebullient singer in his Big Roll Band. This excellent soul/R&B group became one of the leading acts of the London club circuit during the mid-60s. Summers retained his association with Money in Dantalion's Chariot and the US-based New Animals. When the latter broke up in 1968, the guitarist remained in California where he studied classical styles, joined a latino-rock band and acted with various Hollywood theatre groups. He returned to England in 1973 and over the next four years Summers toured with several contrasting artists, including Neil Sedaka, David Essex, Kevin Coyne and Kevin Ayers. In May 1977, he played guitar in a temporary unit, Strontium 90, which also included Sting (bass) and Stewart Copeland (drums). Summers so impressed the duo they asked him to join their full-time group, the Police, with whom the guitarist remained until they disbanded. A superbly inventive musician, he did much to popularize the use of the 'flanging' effect. Summers embarked on several projects; his finely honed skills were more fully developed on *I Advance Unmasked*, a collaboration with King Crimson's Robert Fripp. Ensuing solo albums have enhanced the guitarist's reputation for both excellence and imagination. Ginger Baker collaborated with him on *Synaesthesia* in 1996.
●ALBUMS: with Robert Fripp *I Advance Unmasked* (A&M 1982)★★★★, with Fripp *Bewitched* (A&M 1984)★★★, *XYZ* (MCA 1987)★★, *Mysterious Barricades* (Private Music 1988)★★★, *The Golden Wire* (Private Music 1989)★★★★, *Charming Snakes* (Private Music 1990)★★★★, *World Gone Strange* (Private Music 1991)★★, with John Etheridge *Invisible Threads* (Mesa 1994)★★★, *Synaesthesia* (CMP 1996)★★★.

SUNDAYS

Indie band formed in London, England, in the summer of 1987, by songwriters David Gavurin (b. 4 April 1963, England; guitar) and Harriet Wheeler (b. June 26 1963, England; vocals), who had already gained prior singing experience in a band called Jim Jiminee. Later joined by the rhythm section of Paul Brindley (b. 6 November 1963, England; bass) and Patrick Hannan (b. 4 March 1966, England; drums), the Sundays' first ever live performance at the seminal Falcon 'Vertigo Club' in Camden Town, London, in August 1988, sparked off abnormally excessive interest from both media and record business circles. Playing what many perceived to be a delicate, flawless mix of the Smiths' guitars and the Cocteau Twins' vocal acrobatics, the band's high profile ensured a Top 50 place in the UK charts for their debut single, 'Can't Be Sure', in January 1989. Despite this dramatic arrival, the Sundays did not capitalize on their success until exactly a year later, when *Reading,*

Writing, Arithmetic took everyone by surprise by entering the UK charts at number 4. Despite these rapid advances, the Sundays are notorious for being slow songwriters - legend has it that their label, Rough Trade Records, wanted to release a single from the album but the band did not have any other material for a b-side. This was to be their last release for two years, as touring commitments took the quartet to Europe, Japan and the equally reverential America, where *Rolling Stone* magazine had voted the Sundays Best Foreign Newcomer. Financial difficulties at their label also held up proceedings while they sought a new record contract during 1991, eventually signing to Parlophone Records in January 1992. A second album was not completed before October of that year, and reactions, though not unkind, lacked the fervour that had greeted their debut. Their debut was reissued on Parlophone in 1996.

●ALBUMS: *Reading, Writing, Arithmetic* (Rough Trade 1990)★★★, *Blind* (Parlophone 1992)★★.

SURVIVOR

This sophisticated melodic US rock group was put together by guitarists Jim Peterik (formerly of Ides Of March) and Frankie Sullivan in 1978. Recruiting vocalist Dave Bickler, they recorded their self-titled debut as a three-piece. This featured a *pot-pourri* of ideas that had no definite direction or style. They expanded the band to a quintet in 1981, with the addition of Marc Doubray (drums) and Stephen Ellis (bass). From this point on, the band were comparable in approach to the AOR rock styles of Styx, Foreigner and Journey, but never achieved the same degree of recognition or success. Their first short-lived affair with glory came with the song 'Eye Of The Tiger', used as the theme to the *Rocky III* film. The single, with its heavy drumbeat and rousing chorus, became a worldwide number 1 hit, and is still a staple of FM radio and various advertising campaigns. Unfortunately, the rest of the songs on the album of the same name were patchy in comparison. Nevertheless, the work succeeded on the strength of the title song, peaking at numbers 2 and 12 on the US and UK album charts, respectively. *Caught In The Game*, released the following year, was a more satisfying album. It adopted a heavier approach and featured a more up-front guitar sound from Sullivan, but did not find favour with the record-buying public. Bickler was fired at this stage and replaced by ex-Cobra vocalist Jimi Jamison, whose vocals added an extra, almost soulful dimension to the band. The resulting *Vital Signs* gave the band their second

breakthrough. It enjoyed a six-month residency on the *Billboard* album chart, reaching number 16 as its highest position, and also spawned two Top 10 hits with 'High On You' and 'The Search Is Over'. They recorded 'Burning Heart' (essentially a retread of 'Eye Of The Tiger') as the theme song to *Rocky IV* in 1986 and achieved another international hit, reaching number 5 on the UK singles chart. Surprisingly, the song was not included on *When Seconds Count*, which pursued a heavier direction once more. The band had contracted to a three-piece nucleus of Jamison, Sullivan and Peterik at this juncture and had used session musicians to finish the album. *Too Hot To Sleep* was probably the most consistent and strongest album of the band's career, featuring a collection of commercially minded, hard rock anthems. The album made little commercial impact and the band finally disbanded in 1989.

●ALBUMS: *Survivor* (Scotti Bros 1979)★★, *Premonition* (Scotti Bros 1981)★★, *Eye Of The Tiger* (Scotti Bros 1982)★★, *Caught In The Game* (Scotti Bros 1983)★★, *Vital Signs* (Scotti Bros 1984)★★★, *When Seconds Count* (Scotti Bros 1986)★★, *Too Hot To Sleep* (Scotti Bros 1988)★★★.

●COMPILATIONS: *Best Of* (Scotti Bros 1989)★★★.

SWAIN, TONY

b. 20 January 1952, London, England. Record producer, musician and songwriter Swain started his career as a television cameraman, where he met Steve Jolley in 1975. They worked together on the *Muppet Show* until Tony left to work in a recording studio as a writer/producer. In 1981, reunited with Jolley, they built a reputation when their song 'Body Talk' became a major hit for Imagination. The formula continued through a run of eight further hit singles, including 'Just An Illusion' which narrowly missed the UK number 1 spot. In addition to four albums with Imagination, their high standing in the music business gave them an impressive list of productions with major success with Bananarama, Spandau Ballet and Alison Moyet, including the multi-million-selling number 1 albums *True*, *Parade* (Spandau Ballet) and *Alf* (Moyet). Swain co-wrote all the tracks bar one on the last, and played keyboards on this classic pop album including the major hit 'Love Resurrection'. Swain and Jolley were nominated for a BPI award following its success. Since then they have worked with the Truth, Diana Ross, Tom Robinson, Errol Brown, Wang Chung and Louise Goffin, and following their mutual break Tony went on to produce Kim Wilde's *Close* which became another million-seller. Towards the end of a highly lucrative decade, Swain saw the completion of his own 'state of the art' recording studio at his home in Hertfordshire. He was a major contributor to quality UK pop music throughout the 80s.

SWEETHEARTS OF THE RODEO

Sisters Janis and Kristine Oliver grew up in California and spent much time harmonizing. In 1973 they started working as an acoustic duo, taking their name from a Byrds album. Although they mostly performed contemporary country rock songs, they also had some traditional country leanings. They both married, becoming Janis Gill and Kristine Arnold. Janis went to Nashville with her husband, Vince Gill, who became one of the first of the 'new country' singers. Janis invited her sister to Nashville, where they won a major talent contest. In 1986, they recorded their first album, *Sweethearts Of The Rodeo*, which yielded five US country singles including 'Hey Doll Baby'. By and large, Kristine is the lead singer and Janis the songwriter, although their wide repertoire includes 'I Feel Fine' and 'So Sad (To Watch Good Love Go Bad)'. The long delay before Columbia Records released *Sisters* led to rumours that the duo's time at the label was drawing to a close. The 1993 album was released on Sugar Hill Records.

●ALBUMS: *Sweethearts Of The Rodeo* (Columbia 1986)★★★, *One Time One Night* (Columbia 1988)★★★, *Buffalo Zone* (Columbia 1990)★★★, *Sisters* (Columbia 1992)★★★, *Rodeo Waltz* (Sugar Hill 1993)★★★, *Beautiful Lies* (Sugar Hill 1996)★★★.

SYLVIAN, DAVID

b. David Batt, 23 February 1958, Beckenham, Kent, England. Sylvian first established himself as a singer with Japan. His androgynous image and ethereal vocals made him a prominent figure in that group. Just before their break-up in late 1982, he branched out into a new venture recording with Ryûichi Sakamoto of the Yellow Magic Orchestra. The duo's 'Bamboo House' reached the UK Top 30 and the collaboration continued the following year with 'Forbidden Colours', the haunting theme to the David Bowie film *Merry Christmas Mr Lawrence*. Sylvian's own 'Red Guitar' also reached the Top 20 and he soon gained a reputation as an uncompromising artist, intent on working at his own pace, and to his own agenda. The atmospheric *Brilliant Trees* reached the UK Top 5 and was widely acclaimed. Over two years elapsed before the double album follow-up *Gone To Earth*, which fared

less well. By the time of *Let The Happiness In*, Sylvian had virtually returned to the pop fringe but his love of experimentation was still present. A collaboration with former Can member Holgar Czukay on the atmospherically ambient *Plight And Premonition* and *Flux And Mutability* emphasized this point. Sylvian subsequently joined his former Japan colleagues for their 1991 reunion project under the guise of Rain Tree Crow. Following his collaboration with Ryûichi Sakamoto in 1992, Sylvian was back in the charts with 'Heartbeat (Tainai Kaiki II)', after which he worked on an album with Robert Fripp.

●ALBUMS: *Brilliant Trees* (Virgin 1984)★★★, *Alchemy (An Index Of Possibilities)* cassette release (Virgin 1985)★★, *Gone To Earth* double album (Virgin 1986)★★★, *Secrets Of The Beehive* (Virgin 1987)★★★, with Holgar Czukay *Plight And Premonition* (Virgin 1988)★★, *Flux And Mutability* (Virgin 1989)★★, *The Weather Box* (Virgin 1989)★★★, *Ember Glance* (1991), with Robert Fripp *The First Day* (Virgin 1993)★★★, with Fripp *Damage* (Damage 1994)★★★.

●FURTHER READING: *David Sylvian: 80 Days*, D. Zornes, H. Sawyer and H. Powell.

T'PAU

Formed in 1986, this UK group began as a song-writing partnership between vocalist Carol Decker (b. 10 September 1957, London, England) and guitarist Ronnie Rogers (b. 13 March 1959, Shrewsbury, England). While recording a demonstration disc, they were joined by session musicians Michael Chetwood (b. 26 August 1954, Shrewsbury, England; keyboards), Paul Jackons (b. 8 August 1961; bass) and Tim Burgess (b. 6 October 1961, Shrewsbury, England; drums). The group then signed to Siren Records as T'Pau, the name being taken from a character in the science fiction television series *Star Trek*. Having acquired the services of producer Roy Thomas Baker, T'Pau recorded their first sessions in Los Angeles. The group's first two singles failed to make any impact in the UK market, until 'Heart And Soul' abruptly established them in the US charts, where it climbed to number 4 in 1987. The song was re-promoted in Britain and repeated that chart placing. In order to bolster the line-up, lead guitarist Dean Howard was recruited and a major UK tour followed. Decker's strong, expressive vocals were highlighted on 'China In Your Hand', which topped the UK charts, a feat repeated by *Bridge Of Spies*. Further Top 20 hits with 'Valentine', 'I Will Be With You' and 'Secret Garden' and two more albums consolidated their standing, without threatening a return to peak form. Following their break-up Decker embarked on a solo career in 1994.

●ALBUMS: *Bridge Of Spies* (Siren 1987)★★, *Rage* (Siren 1988)★★, *Promise* (Siren 1991)★★.
●COMPILATIONS: *Heart And Soul - The Very Best Of* (Virgin 1992)★★★.

TABOR, JUNE

b. 31 December 1947, Warwick, England. Tabor is a fine interpreter of both contemporary and traditional songs. Her acclaimed debut, *Airs And Graces*, immediately made her a favourite singer for numerous session appearances. She has collaborated with Martin Simpson on several occasions, resulting in *A Cut Above*, as well as with Maddy Prior from Steeleye Span with whom she has recorded as the Silly Sisters. *Freedom And Rain* was recorded with the Oyster Band, which saw Tabor departing into more of a rock format that many felt was long overdue. In addition, following a period of working with Huw Warren (piano), Tabor recorded *Some Other Time* which included jazz standards such as 'Round Midnight'. Other collaborations utilizing her exceptional voice have been with Nic Jones, Martin Carthy, Peter Bellamy, the Albion Band and Fairport Convention. A number of her earlier albums have recently been re-released, and the excellent Conifer compilation *Aspects* was well received.

●ALBUMS: *Airs And Graces* (Topic 1976)★★★★, *Ashes And Diamonds* (Topic 1977)★★★★, *Bees On Horseback* (Free Reed 1977)★★★, with Martin Simpson *A Cut Above* (Topic 1980)★★★★, *Abyssinians* (Topic 1983)★★★, *Theme From 'Spy Ship'* (1983)★★★, *The Peel Sessions* (Strange Fruit 1986)★★★, with Maddy Prior *Silly Sisters* (1986)★★★, *Aqaba* (Topic 1988)★★★, *Some Other Time* (Hannibal 1989)★★★, with Maddy Prior *No More To The Dance* (1990)★★★, *Angel Tiger* (Cooking Vinyl 1992)★★★★, *Against The Streams* (Cooking Vinyl 1994)★★.
●COMPILATIONS: *Aspects* (Conifer 1990)★★★★, *Anthology* (Music Club 1993)★★★.

TALK TALK

Formed in 1981, this UK pop group comprised Mark Hollis (b 1955, Tottenham, London, England; vocals), Lee Harris (drums), Paul Webb (bass), Simon Brenner (keyboards). They were soon signed to EMI Records who were intent on moulding them into the same league as stablemates Duran Duran. In fact, they could not have been more different. They went along with their company's ideas for the first album which produced a number of hit singles, including 'Talk Talk' and 'Today'. Labelled as a 'New Romantic' band, they were very keen to shake off the tag and dismissed their keyboard player to make them a looser, more flexible creative unit. For the next couple of years Hollis spent the time writing new material and assembling a pool of musicians to record a second album. The format was repeated with the highly accessible *The Colour Of Spring*, both records were critically acclaimed and showed the band as a more creative and imaginative act than their debut had suggested. It was their fourth album *Spirit Of Eden* that showed their true musical preferences. A solemn six-track record, it had no commercial appeal, and no obvious single.

Its poor showing led to EMI dropping the band who signed with Polydor Records. It was three years before a new studio album appeared, and to fill in the gap a greatest hits compilation was issued without the band's permission. It nevertheless managed to sell over a million copies and give them three more hit singles. Ironically, their biggest success so far was an EMI reissue of their previous hit 'Its My Life'. *Laughing Stock* picked up where they had left off although they have failed to match the catchy commercial appeal of *The Colour Of Spring*.

Albums; *The Party's Over* (EMI 1982)★★, *Its My Life* (EMI 1984)★★★, *Its My Mix* (EMI 1984)★★, *The Colour Of Spring* (EMI 1986)★★★★, *Spirit Of Eden* (Parlophone 1988)★★★★, *Laughing Stock* (Verve 1991)★★★.

●COMPILATIONS: *Natural History: The Very Best Of Talk Talk* (Parlophone 1990)★★★, *History Revisited: The Remixes* (Parlophone 1991)★★, *The Very Best Of Talk Talk* (EMI 1997)★★★.

TALKING HEADS

One of the most critically acclaimed groups of the past two decades, Talking Heads pursued an idiosyncratic path of (often) uncompromising brilliance. After graduating from the Rhode Island School of Design, students David Byrne (b. 14 May 1952, Dumbarton, Scotland; vocals/guitar), Chris Frantz (b. Charlton Christopher Frantz, 8 May 1951, Fort Campbell, Kentucky, USA; drums) and Tina Weymouth (b. Martina Weymouth, 22 November 1950, Coronado, California, USA; bass) relocated to New York. In 1975, they lived and rehearsed in Manhattan and named themselves Talking Heads. After appearing at the club CBGB's, they were approached by Seymour Stein of Sire Records, who would eventually sign the group. Early in 1976, the line-up was expanded to include pianist Jerry Harrison (b. Jeremiah Harrison, 21 February 1949, Milwaukee, Wisconsin, USA), a former member of Jonathan Richman's Modern Lovers. The group's art school background, witty invention and musical unorthodoxy were evident on their intriguingly titled debut, 'Love Goes To Building On Fire'. After touring extensively, they issued *Talking Heads '77*, an exhilarating first album, which was widely praised for its verve and intelligence. The highlight of the set was the insistent 'Psycho Killer', a *tour de force*, in which singer Byrne displayed his deranged vocal dramatics to the full. His wide-eyed stare, jerky movements and onstage cool reminded many commentators of Anthony Perkins, star of Hitchcock's movie *Psycho*.

For their second album, the group turned to Brian Eno as producer. *More Songs About Buildings And Food* was a remarkable work, its title echoing Talking Heads' anti-romantic subject matter. Byrne's eccentric vocal phrasing was brilliantly complemented by some startling rhythm work and the songs were uniformly excellent. The climactic 'The Big Country', a satiric commentary on consumerist America, featured the scathing aside: 'I wouldn't live there if you paid me'. The album also featured one cover version, an interesting reading of Al Green's 'Take Me To The River', which was a minor hit. Eno's services were retained for the more opaque *Fear Of Music*, which included the popular 'Life During Wartime'. Byrne next collaborated with Eno on *My Life In The Bush Of Ghosts*, before the group reunited for *Remain In Light*. The latter boasted the superb 'Once In A Lifetime', complete with 'found voices' and African polyrhythms. An edited version of the song provided one of the best hit singles of 1981. During the early 80s, the group's extra-curricular activities increased and while Byrne explored ballet on *The Catherine Wheel*, Frantz and Weymouth found success with their spin-off project, Tom Tom Club. The live double *The Name Of This Band Is Talking Heads* served as a stop gap until *Speaking In Tongues* appeared in the summer of 1983. As ambitious as ever, the album spawned the group's UK Top 10 single, 'Burning Down The House'. While touring with additional guitarist Alex Weir (formerly of the Brothers Four), the group were captured on film in *Stop Making Sense*, the soundtrack of which sold well. The excellent *Little Creatures*, a more accessible offering than their more experimental work, featured three strong singles in the title track, 'And She Was' and 'Road To Nowhere'. The latter brought the group their biggest chart hit and was accompanied by an imaginative and highly entertaining video. In 1986, Byrne moved more forcibly into movies with *True Stories*, for which Talking Heads provided the soundtrack; it was two more years before the group reconvened for *Naked*. Produced by Steve Lillywhite, the work included musical contributions from Level 42 producer Wally Badarou and guitarists Yves N'Djock and Johnny Marr (from the Smiths). Since then Talking Heads have branched out into various offshoot ventures; there was an official announcement of their break-up at the end of 1991. The single- and double-album retrospectives released in October 1992 provided a fairly definitive assessment of their career, including some interesting rarities, but without doing justice to a band rightly regarded as one of the best and most influential of their time. In 1996 Weymouth, Frantz and Harrison launched the Heads.

●ALBUMS: *Talking Heads '77* (Sire 1977)★★★, *More Songs About Buildings And Food* (Sire 1978)★★★, *Fear Of Music* (Sire 1979)★★★, *Remain In Light* (Sire 1980)★★★★, *The Name Of This Band Is Talking Heads* (Sire 1982)★★★, *Speaking In Tongues* (EMI 1983)★★★, *Stop Making Sense* (EMI 1984)★★★, *Little Creatures* (EMI 1985)★★★★, *True Stories* soundtrack (EMI 1986)★★★, *Naked* (EMI 1988)★★, as the Heads *No Talking Just Heads* (MCA 1996)★★.

●COMPILATIONS: *Once In A Lifetime: The Best Of* (EMI 1992)★★★, *Popular Favorites 1976 - 1992 (Sand In The Vaseline)* (EMI 1992)★★★.

●VIDEOS: *Stop Making Sense* (1986), *Storytelling Giant* (1988).

●FURTHER READING: *Talking Heads*, Miles. *The Name Of This Book Is Talking Heads*, Krista Reese. *Talking Heads: The Band And Their Music*, David Gans. *Talking Heads: A Biography*, Jerome Davis.

TEARDROP EXPLODES

This Liverpool group was assembled by vocalist Julian Cope (b. 21 October 1957, Bargoed, Wales), a former member of the Crucial Three, which had featured Ian McCulloch (later of Echo And The Bunnymen) and Pete Wylie (later of Wah!). The Teardrop Explodes took their name from a page in a Marvel comic and the original group came together in late 1978 with a line-up featuring Cope, Michael Finkler (guitar), Paul Simpson (keyboards) and Gary Dwyer (drums). After signing to Bill Drummond and Dave Balfe's Liverpool record label Zoo, they issued 'Sleeping Gas' in early 1979. It was soon followed by the eccentric but appealing 'Bouncing Babies'. By then, Simpson had left to be replaced by Balfe, who had previously appeared in the short-lived Lori And The Chameleons. The exuberant 'Treason (It's Just A Story)' was the Teardrop Explodes' most commercial and exciting offering to date, and was unlucky not to chart. The shaky line-up next lost Finkler, who was replaced by Alan Gill, formerly of Dalek I Love You. A distribution agreement with Phonogram Records coincided with a higher press profile for Cope, which was rewarded with the minor hit, 'When I Dream'. *Kilimanjaro* followed and displayed the group as one of the most inventive and intriguing of their era. A repromoted/remixed version of 'Treason' belatedly charted, as did the stirring 'Passionate Friend'. By late 1981, Cope was intent on restructuring the group; new members included

Alfie Agius and Troy Tate. *Wilder* further displayed the wayward talents of Cope and revealed a group bristling with ideas, unusual melodies and strong arrangements influenced by late 60s psychedelia. When the sessions for a third album broke down, Cope curtailed the group's activities and in 1984 embarked on an erratic yet often inspired solo career. The irreverently titled *Everybody Wants To Shag The Teardrop Explodes* was posthumously exhumed for release in 1990, using the sessions for that projected third collection.

●ALBUMS: *Kilimanjaro* (Mercury 1980)★★★, *Wilder* (Mercury 1981)★★★, *Everybody Wants To Shag The Teardrop Explodes* (Fontana 1990)★★.

●COMPILATIONS *Piano* (Document 1990)★★★.

TEARS FOR FEARS

Schoolfriends Roland Orzabal (b. 22 August 1961, Bath, England) and Curt Smith (b. 24 June 1961, Bath, England) formed Tears For Fears after they had spent their teenage years in groups together, including a ska revivalist combo called Graduate. The name Tears For Fears was drawn from a book written by Arthur Janov. They signed to Phonogram in 1981 while other synthesizer groups such as the Human League and Depeche Mode were breaking through into the pop field. Their first two singles were unsuccessful but 'Mad World' made number 3 in the UK charts in 1982. Curt Smith, dressed in long overcoats and sporting a pigtail, was touted in the UK as a vaguely alternative teen idol. *The Hurting* showcased a thoughtful, tuneful band and it topped the UK charts, supplying further Top 10 singles with 'Change' and 'Pale Shelter'. During this time the duo was augmented by Ian Stanley on keyboards and Manny Ellis on drums. By *Songs From The Big Chair* Orzabal was handling most of the vocal duties and had taken on the role of chief songwriter. 'Shout' and 'Everybody Wants To Rule The World' were number 1 hits in the USA and the album also reached number 1. 'Everybody Wants To Rule The World' was adopted as the theme tune for the Sport Aid famine relief event in 1986 (with a slight change in the title to 'Everybody Wants To Run The World') and it gave the group massive exposure. They took a lengthy break after 1985 and reappeared four years later with a highly changed sound on *The Seeds Of Love*. They shunned their earlier electronic approach and attempted to weave together huge piano and vocal chords in a style reminiscent of the Beatles. Its release was delayed many times as the pair constantly remixed the material. Many top names played on the album including Phil Collins and Oleta Adams, whom Orzabal later produced. Both the album and single, 'Sowing The Seeds Of Love', were Top 10 hits in the USA but in the UK the lavish arrangements did not receive the same critical and commercial approval. Smith left the band in the early 90s to begin a solo career. Retaining the name of the band Orzabal released *Elemental*, the first album after Smith's departure. A muted response greeted *Raoul And The Kings Of Spain* in 1995.

●ALBUMS: *The Hurting* (Mercury 1983)★★★, *Songs From The Big Chair* (Mercury 1985)★★★, *The Seeds Of Love* (Fontana 1989)★★★, *Elemental* (Mercury 1993)★★, *Raoul And The Kings Of Spain* (Epic 1995)★★. Solo: Curt Smith *Soul On Board* (Mercury 1993)★.

●COMPILATIONS: *Tears Roll Down (Greatest Hits 82-92)* (Fontana 1992)★★★★, *Saturnine Martial & Lunatic* (Fontana 1996)★★★.

●VIDEOS: *Scenes From The Big Chair* (4 Front Video 1991).

●FURTHER READING: *Tears For Fears*, Ann Greene.

TECHNO

An easy definition of techno would be percussion-based electronic dance music, characterized by stripped-down drumbeats and basslines. However, the real roots of techno can be traced back to the experimental musicologists like Karl Heinz Stockhausen. In terms of equipment there was no greater precedent than that set by Dr Robert Moog, who invented the synthesizer in California, and provoked the first fears of the 'death of real music' which have shadowed electronic recordings ever since. If Chicory Tip's 'Son Of My Father' was the first to employ the Moog in 1972, then Kraftwerk were certainly the first to harness and harvest the possibilities of the synthesizer and other electronic instruments. Kraftwerk served as godfathers to UK electro pop outfits like the Human League (in their early experimental phase) and Depeche Mode. It is hard to imagine now but groups such as these and even Gary Numan proved a huge influence on the US hip hop scene and the development of New York 'electro' in the early 80s (particularly Afrika Bambaataa's 'Planet Rock'). However, techno as we now know it descended from the Detroit region, which specialized in a spartan, abrasive sound, maintaining some of the soulful elements of the Motown Records palate, over the innovations that hip hop's electro period had engendered. Techno also reflected the city's decline, as well as the advent of technology, and this tension was crucial

to the dynamics of the sound. As Kevin Saunderson recounts: 'When we first started doing this music we were ahead. But Detroit is still a very behind city when it comes to anything cultural'. Techno as an umbrella term for this sound was first invoked by an article in *The Face* in May 1988, when it was used to describe the work of Saunderson (particularly 'Big Fun'), Derrick May (who recorded techno's greatest anthem, 'Strings Of Life') and Juan Atkins ('No UFO's'). The Detroit labels of note included May's Transmat, Juan Atkins' Metroplex, Saunderson's KMS, Underground Resistance, Planet E, Red Planet, Submerge and Accelerate. Much like house, the audience for techno proved to be a predominantly British/European one. Labels such as Rising High and Warp in the UK, and R&S in Belgium helped build on the innovations of May, Atkins and Carl Craig. UK artists such as the Prodigy and LFO took the sound to a new, less artful but more direct level. According to Saunderson, the difference between most Detroit techno and its English re-interpreters was that it lacked the 'spirituality' of the original. Had he wished to produce more controversy, he might have substituted 'blackness' - nearly all of the main Detroit pioneers were black. Most UK techno, conversely, at least until the advent of jungle, were white. Most techno utilizes the establishment of a groove or movement by repetition, building a framework that does not translate easily into more conventional musical terms. Some obviously find this adjustment difficult, but the variations in texture and tempo are at least as subtle as those in rock music - often more so, due to the absence of a lyrical focus.

TELEVISION PERSONALITIES

A crass meeting of 60s pastiche and a tongue-in-cheek nod towards punk have characterized Dan Treacy's Television Personalities over their long, erratic career. Treacy teamed up with Edward Ball (b. 23 November 1959, Chelsea, London, England) back in 1977, releasing the privately pressed '14th Floor' the following year. After Ball's solo single as O Level, the pair issued what was to be seen as a pivotal artefact of the time, the EP *Where's Bill Grundy Now?* (1978). BBC disc jockey John Peel latched onto one of the tracks, 'Part Time Punks' (a cruel send-up of a rapidly decaying London scene), and this exposure attracted the interest of Rough Trade Records. Ball spent some time working on his solo projects in the early 80s, the Teenage Filmstars and the Times. The TV Personalities' debut album, *And Don't The Kids Just Love It,* extended Treacy's exploration of 60s influences. From it came the whimsical 'I Know Where Syd Barrett Lives' as a single, their last for Rough Trade. Treacy then teamed up with Ed Ball to form the Whaam! label, for TVPs and Times products plus other signings, including the Marine Girls. 1982, the group's busiest recording year, saw *Mummy You're Not Watching Me* share the instant appeal of the group's debut. 'Three Wishes' followed, and coincided with a minor psychedelic revival in London. *They Could Have Been Bigger Than The Beatles* was a surprisingly strong collection of demos and out-takes. The band were soon expanded by Mark Flunder (bass), Dave Musker (organ) and Joe Foster (12-string guitar) for a tour of Italy, with Flunder replaced by ex-Swell Maps bass player Jowe Head for a similar tour of Germany. 1983's 'A Sense Of Belonging' saw a one-off return to Rough Trade and caused a minor scandal over its sleeve. However, delays meant that *The Painted Word* was not issued until January 1985. Foster and Musker soon left to work at Creation Records. With a new drummer, Jeff Bloom, Treacy set up a new label, after Whaam! was folded due to pressure from pop duo Wham! In the meantime, the German album *Chocolat-Art (A Tribute To James Last)*, captured one of their European live gigs. It was not until early 1990 that the next album emerged. *Privilege* included the catchy 'Salvador Dali's Garden Party'. The band laid low for a further two years (punctuated by a live album for Overground Records) until the release of *Closer To God*. Ball signed with Creation as a solo artist and had his first hit in 1997 with 'Love is Blue'.

●ALBUMS: *And Don't The Kids Just Love It* (Rough Trade 1981)★★, *Mummy You're Not Watching Me* (Whaam! 1982)★★, *They Could Have Been Bigger Than The Beatles* (Whaam! 1982)★★, *The Painted Word* (Illuminated 1985)★★★, *Chocolat-Art (A Tribute To James Last)* (Pastell 1985)★★, *Privilege* (Fire 1990)★★★, *Camping In France* (Overground 1991)★★, *Closer To God* (Fire 1992)★★★, *I Was A Mod Before You Were A Mod* (Overground 1995)★★★, *Paisley Shirts And Mini-Skirts* live 1980 recording (1995)★, *Top Gear* (Overground 1996)★★, *Made In Japan* (Little Teddy 1996)★★.

●COMPILATIONS: *Yes Darling, But Is It Art? (Early Singles And Rarities)* (Fire 1995)★★★.

TENPOLE TUDOR

This theatrical UK punk-pop group was led by the inimitable Edward Tudor-Pole (b. 6 December 1955, London, England) who first took to the stage at the age of nine when he appeared in *A Christmas Carol*. After a course at Chiswick Polytechnic he went to train at the Royal Academy of Dramatic Arts. In 1977 he joined a band called the Visitors which also included future *Riverside* BBC Television host Mike Andrews. Tudor formed the band Tenpole Tudor with Visitors Gary Long (drums), Dick Crippen (bass) and Bob Kingston (guitar). Kingston came from a musical family and had previously been a member of Sta-Prest with his brother Ray, himself later in the Temper. His sister June would soon become a member of the Mo-Dettes. Tudor appeared in the film *The Great Rock 'N' Roll Swindle* (Malcolm McLaren had been an early mentor) and performed 'Who Killed Bambi', which appeared on the b-side of the Sex Pistols' 'Silly Thing'. He also helped Paul Cook and Steve Jones write the title song to the film. His first single under their own name was 'Real Fun', which came out on Korova Records. After signing to Stiff Records the group released 'Three Bells In A Row'. Over the next few months they took part on the *Sons Of Stiff* tour, hit the charts three times starting with the raucous 'Swords Of A Thousand Men', recruited a second guitarist in the form of Munch Universe, and released two albums, before they suddenly went out of fashion again. In 1982 Tudor decided to split up the band. Crippen, Long, and Kingston became the Tudors and released 'Tied Up With Lou Cool' whilst Tudor formed a new cajun-style Tenpole Tudor and put out the 'Hayrick Song'. He then left Stiff and moved into jazz and swing-style bands while also reviving his acting career. In 1985 he formed an old-style Tenpole Tudor and toured the country dressed in armour but left the following year to concentrate on acting. He subsequently appeared on stage (*The Sinking Of The Belgrano*), film (*Straight To Hell, Absolute Beginners* and *Walker*) and television (in the comedy *Roy's Raiders*). He also re-formed Tenpole Tudor again in 1989 and it seemed likely that he would continue to do so at regular intervals until his acting career took off. Memorably playing the narrator in stage play *The Road*, Tudor then took over the host's role in Channel 4 television's *The Crystal Maze*.

●ALBUMS: *Eddie, Old Bob, Dick And Gary* (Stiff 1981)★★, *Let The Four Winds Blow* (Stiff 1981)★★.

●COMPILATIONS: *Wunderbar* (Dojo 1992)★★.

TEXAS

The Scottish guitar pop band with the American name originally consisted of Italian-descended Sharleen Spiteri (b. c.1970, Glasgow, Scotland; vocals/guitar), Ally McErlaine (b. 1969; guitar),

Johnny McElhone (bass, ex-Altered Images) and Stuart Kerr (drums, ex-Friends Again; Love And Money). The band were formed in 1986 around McElhone who formerly played bass in Altered Images and Hipsway, though Spiteri and McErlaine quickly became the focal point, partly due to McErlaine's fluent guitar playing and their joint mastery of Ry Cooder-inspired slide guitar. It was the latter style that distinguished the UK number 8 single, 'I Don't Want A Lover', the very first song they had written together. It helped to break them nationwide as one of a clutch of Scottish bands occupying a slightly awkward space between commercial rock and pop. The group made its live debut at Dundee University in March 1988, signing to Phonogram subsidiary Vertigo Records through McElhone's former connections with Hipsway. Their first album, 1989's *Southside*, continued to explore the theme of doomed relationships, though the original sessions with Chic's Bernard Edwards were abandoned as 'too heavy handed'. When eventually released it sold over two million copies worldwide, peaking at number 3 in the UK album charts. Richard Hynd replaced Kerr on drums in 1991 and the band was also augmented by the presence of Eddie Campbell. *Mother's Heaven* failed to repeat the success of their debut, though by now the group had established itself as a strong concert attraction throughout Europe. 1992 brought their second Top 20 hit when a version of Al Green's 'Tired Of Being Alone' was released. *Rick's Road* was completed with new producer Paul Fox after the band stated their fondness for his work with 10,000 Maniacs and the Wallflowers. It included backing vocals from Rose Stone, sister of Sly Stone, and was recorded at Bearsville Studios in Woodstock. In 1997 after another lengthy gap they had a major UK hit with 'Say What You Want'. The following album showed a number of styles as the band found more mainstream success.

●ALBUMS: *Southside* (Vertigo 1989)★★, *Mother's Heaven* (Vertigo 1991)★★, *Rick's Road* (Vertigo 1993)★★★, *White On Blonde* (Mercury 1997)★★★.

THAT PETROL EMOTION

This critically lauded and highly skilled pop group's efforts to break into the mainstream were been consistently thwarted despite a splendid arsenal of songs. The band was originally formed when the O'Neill brothers (Sean; guitar, Damian; bass) parted from the fragmenting Undertones. A new approach was immediate with Sean reverting to his Irish name (having always appeared as John in his former band), and Damian switching to bass instead of guitar. They added Ciaran McLaughlin (drums), Reamann O'Gormain (guitar, ex-Bam Bam And The Calling), and, most importantly, dynamic Seattle-born frontman Steve Mack (vocals). They debuted with a single, 'Keen', on the small independent label, Pink. Both that and the subsequent 'V2' proved radical departures for those clamouring for a rerun of the Undertones, with frothing guitar and a fuller sound. There was now a political agenda too, ironic in view of the press bombardment of the Undertones as to why they did not write songs about the troubles in Northern Ireland. The questioning of British imperialism, explored through factors like 'racist' jokes and the fate of political prisoners, would became a tenet of their music (and more particularly record sleeves). Both their pop-based debut and *Babble* were dominated by frantic guitar and Mack's wholehearted delivery. However, their one-album contract with Polydor Records ended with *Babble* and they moved on to Virgin Records for the more diverse *End Of The Millenium Psychosis Blues*. This included the controversial but poignant ballad 'Cellophane', bone-shattering disco of 'Groove Check', and Sonic Youth-tainted 'Under The Sky'. Big Jimmy (trombone) and Geoff Barrett (saxophone), ex-Dexys Midnight Runners, had been added to bolster the sound but finances could not stretch to taking them on tour. McLaughlin was beginning to step out as a major songwriting force, as Sean O'Neill elected to give family matters more prominence and returned to Derry. His brother switched to guitar with John Marchini taking over on bass. *Chemicrazy* which followed was exceptionally strong, especially on singles 'Hey Venus' and 'Sensitize'. In the light of its commercial failure the group were dropped by Virgin, going on to release a final album on their own label, Koogat. However, its lack of sales again contrasted with its critical reception, and in March 1994 press announcements of the band's split reached the music press (though the group had already been inactive for some time). Despite constant campaigning on their behalf by the press, 'Big Decision', a direct call to political activism which reached a paltry UK number 42, remained their biggest chart success.

●ALBUMS: *Manic Pop Thrill* (Demon 1986)★★★, *Babble* (Polydor 1987)★★★★, *End Of The Millenium Psychosis Blues* (Virgin 1988)★★★, *Peel Sessions* (Strange Fruit 1989)★★★, *Chemicrazy* (Virgin 1990)★★★, *Fireproof* (Koogat 1993)★★★.

THEATRE OF HATE

Formed in September 1981, this UK post-punk group comprised Kirk Brandon (vocals, ex-Pack), John Lennard (saxophone), Stan Stammers (bass), Billy Duffy (guitar) and Nigel Preston (drums). This was in fact the band's second line-up, Brandon having ditched all his former Pack; Jonathan Werner (bass), Jim Walker (drums) and Simon Werner (guitar), following the release of the first of a series of live albums and three singles. After establishing a strong live reputation for their hard, uncompromising lyrics, and harrowing, martial rhythms, the group recorded their 1982 debut album, *Westworld*. Produced by Mick Jones of the Clash, the work proved commercial enough to infiltrate the UK Top 20. The attendant single, 'Do You Believe In The Westworld?', also gave the group their only Top 40 singles entry. Drummer Preston was replaced by Luke Rendle, while Duffy went on to form the Cult. Despite their promise and strong following, the group fell apart a year after their inception with Stammers and Brandon going on to form Spear Of Destiny.
●ALBUMS: *He Who Dares Wins Live At The Warehouse Leeds* (SS 1981)★★, *Live At The Lyceum* (Straight 1982)★★, *Westworld* (Burning Rome 1982)★★★★, *He Who Dares Wins Live in Berlin* (SS 1982)★, *Retribution* (Castle 1996)★.
●COMPILATIONS: *Revolution* (Burning Rome 1993)★★, *Ten Years After* (Burning Rome 1993)★★, *He Who Dares I & II* (Dojo 1996)★.

THEN JERICO

Titled, incorrectly, after the city whose walls fell to the trumpets of the Israelites in the Bible, UK group Then Jerico managed three Top 40 hits in 1989 before breaking up. Comprising Mark Shaw (b. 10 June 1961, Chesterfield, Derbyshire, England; vocals), Jasper Stainthorpe (b. 18 February 1958, Tonbridge, Kent, England), Robert Downes (b. 7 December 1961, Cheadle Hulme, Cheshire, England; guitar), Scott Taylor (b. 31 December 1961, Redhill, Surrey, England; guitar) and Steve Wren (b. 26 October 1962, Lambeth, London, England), the band formed when Shaw and Stainthorpe met in a north London studio, where the latter was working as an engineer. Stainthorpe recommended Wren though it transpired that he had already turned down an offer from Shaw two years earlier. Scott Taylor, former guitarist in Belouis Some's backing band, completed the line-up. The band always received more press for Shaw's good looks than their inoffensive

pop music. Their biggest hit was 'Big Area' which reached number 13. Shaw turned solo following the band's split, and released a poorly received solo album in 1991 on EMI Records.
●ALBUMS: *First (The Sound Of Music)* (London 1987)★★, *The Big Area* (London 1989)★★.

THIRD WORLD

Reggae band blending roots and soul, comprising Michael 'Ibo' Cooper (keyboards), Stephen 'Cat' Coore (guitar/cello), Richard Daley (bass), Willie 'Root' Stewart (drums), Irvin 'Carrot' Jarrett (percussion), William 'Bunny Rugs' Clarke (lead vocal/guitar) and Prilly Hamilton. Coore and Cooper first played together at the end of the 60s, and the early years of the band saw the line-up in a state of flux: Coore, Cooper and Daley, plus drummer Carl Barovier (later replaced by Cornell Marshall and Willie Stewart) had all played with Inner Circle, a band that pursued a similar 'uptown reggae' course. By 1975 the line-up had settled to the above, minus Bunny Rugs, who had been pursuing a soul-reggae direction in a series of solo projects, aided by a uniquely spirited voice. Their first album, *Third World*, found them signed to Island Records and supporting Bob Marley at his breakthrough concerts at London's Lyceum in the summer of 1975. It was a mellow, carefully crafted debut. *96 Degrees In The Shade* found the band and new singer Clarke in fine form, and delivered a huge international hit in the shape of a cover of the O'Jays/Gamble And Huff song, 'Now That We've Found Love'. The *Journey To Addis* album offered more of the same: a mix of roots and sweet soul. Further hits, 'Cool Meditation' (1979), 'Dancing On The Floor' (1981) and 'Try Jah Love' (1982), the latter two for a new label, CBS Records, kept their name in the public eye. A lone record for Winston 'Niney' Holness in Jamaica, pretty much summed up their attitude: 'Roots With Quality'. The late 80s saw the band increasingly lauded in America, drawing album contributions from Stevie Wonder, Stetsasonic's Daddy O, the Brecker Brothers and Jamal-Ski. Third World still gig regularly, have the wisdom to continue working with their original producer, Geoffrey Chung, from time to time, and remain a name always worth watching out for, even if they have not yet set alight the world on record.
●ALBUMS: *Third World* (Island 1976)★★★, *96 Degrees In The Shade* (Island 1977)★★★, *Journey To Addis* (Island 1978)★★★, *Prisoner In The Street* (Island 1980)★★★, *Rock The World* (Columbia 1985)★★★, *Sense Of Purpose* (Columbia

1985)★★★, *You've Got The Power* (Columbia 1987)★★★, *Hold On To Love* (Columbia 1987)★★★. ●COMPILATIONS: *Reggae Ambassadors* (Island 1985)★★★★.

THOMPSON TWINS

The origins of this UK synthesizer pop act were much less conventional than their chart material might suggest. Their name derived from the *Tin Tin* cartoon books of Hergé. Formed in 1977, the line-up featured Tom Bailey (b. 18 June 1957, Halifax, Yorkshire, England; vocals, keyboards, percussion), Peter Dodd (b. 27 October 1953; guitar) and John Roog (guitar, vocals, percussion), who were friends living in Chesterfield when they decided to experiment with music. Several gigs later they relocated to London where they picked up drummer Chris Bell (later Spear Of Destiny and Gene Loves Jezebel). After sporadic gigs 1981 saw their line-up extended to include Joe Leeway (b. 15 November 1957, Islington, London, England; percussion/vocals), Alannah Currie (b. 20 September, 1959, Auckland, New Zealand; percussion, saxophone), and Matthew Seligman (bass, ex-Soft Boys). This seven-piece became a cult attraction in the capital, where their favourite gimmick involved inviting their audience on stage to beat out a rhythmic backdrop to the songs. Their motivation was similar to that of the punk ethos: 'We were angry with the world in general - the deceit and the lies'. However, when *A Product Of ...* was released it showed a band struggling to make the transition from stage to studio. Producer Steve Lillywhite took them in hand for *Set*, and the Bailey-penned 'In The Name Of Love' saw them gain their first minor hit in the UK. It did much better in the USA, staying at the top of the *Billboard* disco charts for five weeks. Before this news filtered back, four of the band had been jettisoned, leaving just Bailey, Currie and Leeway. The cumbersome bohemian enterprise had evolved into a slick business machine, each member taking responsibility for either the music, visuals or production, in a manner not dissimilar to the original Public Image Limited concept. Reinventing their image as those of the Snap, Crackle and Pop characters of the Kelloggs' breakfast cereal, they set about a sustained assault on the upper regions of the UK charts. 1983's 'Love On Your Side' was their first major domestic hit, preceding *Quick Step And Side Kick*, their first album as a trio which rose to number 2 in 1983. Highly commercial singles, 'Hold Me Now', 'Doctor Doctor' and 'You Take Me Up', put them firmly in the first division of UK pop

acts. Further minor hits followed, most notably the anti-heroin 'Don't Mess With Doctor Dream'. However, when Leeway left at the end of 1986 the Thompson Twins became the duo their name had always implied. Bailey and Currie had been romantically involved since 1980, and had their first child eight years later. Unfortunately, success on the scale of their previous incarnation deserted them for the rest of the 80s, although their songwriting talents earned Deborah Harry a UK Top 20 hit in 1989 with 'I Want That Man'. Bailey and Currie formed Babble in 1994 following the demise of the trio of twins.

●ALBUMS: *A Product Of ...* (Arista 1981)★★, *Set* (Tee 1982)★★, *Quick Step And Side Kick* (Arista 1983)★★★, *Into The Gap* (Arista 1984)★★★, *Here's To The Future* (Arista 1986)★★, *Close To The Bone* (Arista 1987)★, *Big Trash* (Warners 1989)★★, *Queer* (Warners 1991)★★.

●COMPILATIONS: *Greatest Mixes* (Arista 1988)★★, *The Greatest Hits* (Stylus 1990)★★★, *The Singles Collection* (Camden 1997)★★★.

●FURTHER READING: *The Thompson Twins: An Odd Couple*, Rose Rouce.

THOMPSON, LINVAL

b. *c*.1959, Kingston, Jamaica. Thompson was raised in Queens, New York, and at the age of 16 recorded 'No Other Woman'. On returning to Jamaica he began recording with Phil Pratt, although little surfaced on vinyl from these sessions. Having declined the opportunity to record with Bunny Lee following an introduction by his long-time friend Johnny Clarke, he recorded a dub plate with Tippertone. Back in New York he resumed his studies in engineering but was soon drawn back towards the music business. Due to the increasing demand for reggae in the USA Linval had a fruitful business in supplying fresh rhythms to record buyers, and his success led him back to Jamaica. On his return he recorded 'Kung Fu Fighting' with manic producer Lee Perry, which announced the onset of a prolific career. Encouraged by the sales of 'Don't Cut Off Your Dreadlocks', produced by Bunny Lee, the album, including the title track, also appeared in the UK. Linval began to produce his own material and a contract with Trojan Records led to the release of *I Love Marijuana* and its dub version, *Negrea Love Dub*, both of which enjoyed healthy sales. Establishing his notoriety as a producer his services were enrolled by Cornell Campbell, the Wailing Souls, the Viceroys, Tapper Zukie, Barrington Levy, Trinity, Ranking Dread and Roman Stewart. Ranking Dread's set included

DJ versions of Linval's own 'I Love Marijuana' as 'Marijuana In My Soul', and 'Africa Is For Blackman' as 'Africa'. The DJ was to hit the UK headlines following suggestions that he was a member of the 'Yardies', supposedly a criminal West Indian organization, although Yardie simply refers to someone from Jamaica, i.e. 'Back A Yard'. Thompson was carving out quite a niche, with his productions appearing on a number of labels in the UK. His sessions with Trinity led to the release of *Rock In The Ghetto* through Trojan, while lifted from the same set, Greensleeves Records released 'Don't Try To Use Me'. In 1983 the release of *Baby Father* included the classic 'Shouldn't Lift Your Hand', a track that condemned violence against women with lyrics stating: 'You shouldn't lift your feet to kick the young lady, You shouldn't lift your hand to lick the young girlie'. Further illustrating his entrepreneurial skills a partnership in the UK was formed with Mikey Scott for the Strong Like Sampson and Thompson Koos record labels to distribute his output.

●ALBUMS: *Don't Cut Off Your Dreadlocks* (Third World 1976)★★★, *I Love Marijuana* (Trojan 1978)★★★, *I Love Jah* (Burning Sounds 1979)★★★, *If I Follow My Heart* (Burning Sounds 1980)★★, *Look How Me Sexy* (Greensleeves 1982), *Baby Father* (Greensleeves 1983)★★★, *Starlight* (Mango 1989)★★.

THOMPSON, RICHARD

b. 3 April 1949, Totteridge & Whetsone, London, England. The incredibly talented Thompson forged his reputation as guitarist, vocalist and composer with Fairport Convention which, although initially dubbed 'England's Jefferson Airplane', later evolved into the seminal folk rock act through such acclaimed releases as *What We Did On Our Holidays* (1968), *Unhalfbricking* (1968), *Liege And Leif* (1969) and *Full House* (1970). Thompson's sensitive compositions graced all of the above but none have been applauded more than 'Meet On the Ledge'. This simple lilting song oozes with restraint, class and emotion and is one of the most evocative songs to come out of the late 60's 'underground' music scene. Thompson's innovative guitar style brought a distinctive edge to their work as he harnessed such diverse influences as Django Reinhart, Charlie Christian, Otis Rush, James Burton and Mike Bloomfield. The guitarist left the group in 1971 and having contributed to two related projects, *The Bunch* and *Morris On*, completed an impressive solo debut, *Henry The Human Fly*. He then forged a professional partnership with

his wife, Linda Peters and, as Richard And Linda Thompson, recorded a series of excellent albums, notably *I Want To See The Bright Lights Tonight* (1974), and *Hokey Pokey* which established the artist's reputation for incisive, descriptive compositions. Thompson also collaborated with such disparate vocalists as Sandy Denny, John Martyn, Iain Matthews, Elvis Costello and Pere Ubu's David Thomas, which in turn enhanced his already considerable reputation.

The Thompsons separated in 1982, although the guitarist had completed his second solo album, *Strict Tempo*, a compendium of styles based on hornpipes, jigs and reels, the previous year. An in-concert set *Small Town Romance* followed, before the artist recorded the acclaimed *Hand Of Kindness* and *Across The Crowded Room*, the latter of which featured the embittered 'She Twists The Knife Again'. In 1986 Thompson undertook extensive US and UK tours to promote *Daring Adventures*, leading a group that included Clive Gregson and Christine Collister. He then completed the soundtrack to *The Marksman*, a BBC television series, before joining John French, Fred Frith and Henry Kaiser for the experimental *Live, Love, Larf And Loaf*. In 1988 Thompson switched outlets to Capitol Records, releasing *Amnesia* and the excellent *Rumor And Sigh* with little commercial success. Thompson recorded with the Golden Palominos in 1991 and the same year performed with David Byrne. *Watching The Dark* is a three-CD set covering Thompson's career and it puts into perspective what an important figure Thompson is. His own painful modesty underlies a masterful lyricist, an outstanding guitarist and a major songwriter. Quite what this man has to do to achieve commercial success remains a mystery.

●ALBUMS: see also Fairport Convention and Richard And Linda Thompson entries, *Henry The Human Fly* (Island 1972)★★★, *Strict Tempo* (Elixir 1981)★★★, *Hand Of Kindness* (Hannibal 1983)★★★★, *Small Town Romance* (Hannibal 1984)★★★★ *Across A Crowded Room* (Polydor 1985)★★★, *Daring Adventures* (Polydor 1986)★★★★ with French, Frith, Kaiser *Live Love Larf & Loaf* (Demon 1987)★★, with Peter Filleul *The Marksman* soundtrack (BBC 1987)★★, *Amnesia* (Capitol 1988)★★★, *Rumor And Sigh* (Capitol 1990)★★★★, with French, Frith, Kaiser *Invisible Means* (Demon 1990)★★, with the GP's *Saturday Rolling Around* (Woodworm 1991)★★, *Sweet Talker* soundtrack (Capitol 1991)★★, *Mirror Blue* (Capitol 1994)★★★★, with Danny Thompson *Live At Crawley 1993* (Whatdisc 1995)★★★, *You?*

Me? Us? (EMI 1996)★★★, as the Richard Thompson Band *Two Letter Words* (Hokey Pokey 1997)★★★, with Danny Thompson *Industry* (Parlophone 1997)★★★.

●COMPILATIONS: *Watching The Dark* 3-CD box set (Hannibal 1993)★★★★.

●VIDEOS: *Across A Crowded Room* (Sony 1983).

●FURTHER READING: *Meet On the Ledge*, Patrick Humphries. *Richard Thompson: 21 Years Of Doom & Gloom*, Clinton Heylin. *Gypsy Love Songs & Sad Refrains: The Recordings Of Richard Thompson & Sandy Denny*, Clinton Heylin. *Richard Thompson: Strange Affair, The Biography*, Patrick Humphries.

THOROGOOD, GEORGE

b. 31 December 1952, Wilmington, Delaware, USA. White blues guitarist George Thorogood first became interested in music, notably Chicago blues, when he saw John Paul Hammond performing in 1970. Three years later he formed the Destroyers in Delaware before moving them to Boston where they backed visiting blues stars. The Destroyers comprised Thorogood (guitar), Michael Lenn (bass), and Jeff Simon (drums). Schoolfriend Ron Smith played guitar on and off to make up the quartet. In 1974 they recorded some demos which were released later. They made their first album in 1975 after blues fanatic John Forward spotted them playing at Joe's Place in Cambridge, Massachusetts, and put them in touch with the folk label, Rounder Records. The album was not released immediately as Blough replaced Lenn and his bass parts had to be added. It was eventually released in 1978 (on Sonet Records in the UK) and the single 'Move It On Over' was Rounder's first release. Smith left in 1980 and was replaced by saxophonist Hank Carter. Thorogood, a former semiprofessional baseball player, took time away from music that season to play ball but by 1981 was back in the fold as the band opened for the Rolling Stones at several of their American gigs. The venues were unfamiliar to Thorogood as normally he shunned large arenas for smaller clubs, even going to the extent of playing under false names to prevent the smaller venues being overcrowded. After three albums with Rounder they signed to Capitol Records and continued to record throughout the 80s. In 1985 they appeared at Live Aid playing with blues legend Albert Collins.

●ALBUMS: *George Thorogood And The Destroyers* (Rounder 1978)★★★, *Move It On Over* (Rounder 1978)★★★, *Better Than The Rest* (Rounder 1979)★★, *More George Thorogood And The Destroyers* (Capitol 1980)★★, *Bad To The Bone* (Capitol 1982)★★★, *Maverick* (Capitol 1985)★★, *Live* (Capitol 1986)★★, *Born To Be Bad* (Capitol 1988)★★, *Killer's Bluze* (1993)★★, *Haircut* (1993)★★, *Let's Work Together* (EMI 1995)★★, *Rockin' My Life Away* (EMI 1997)★★.

3 MUSTAPHAS 3

This pseudo-Balkan group have often been included under the 'World Music' banner. Each group member has adopted 6 August as an official birthday in order to avoid confusion. Niaveti Mustapha III (flutes/German bagpipes), Hijaz Mustapha (violin/bouzouki), Houzam Mustapha (drums), Sabah Habas Mustapha (bass/percussion), Kemo 'Kem Kem' Mustapha (accordion/piano), and Daoudi Mustapha (clarinet) made their UK debut in August 1982. They hail from Szegerley, and their major breakthrough was going from Balkan Beat Bastard Bad Boys to Godfathers Of World Music, without changing their direction. The Mustaphas are occasionally joined by Expensive Mustapha (trumpet). The humorous ensemble was first brought to public attention by John Peel. The group have attracted a degree of criticism for not taking their music seriously, but the end product is still extremely popular with audiences both in Europe and the USA. As an indication of this, *Soup Of The Century* was number 1 in the *Billboard* World Music charts, and was voted the 'Best World Music/International' album for 1990 by NAIRD (National Association of Independent Record Distributors), in the USA. For *Heart Of Uncle*, on Globestyle Records, the group were joined by their sister Laura Tima Daviz Mustapha (vocals). They have backed a number of other artists, such as Ofra Haza where they sang 'Linda Linda' and managed to offend some people by singing half the lyrics in Hebrew and half in Arabic.

●ALBUMS: *Bam! Mustaphas Play Stereo* (Globestyle 1985)★★★, *From The Balkans To Your Heart-The Radio Years* (1985)★★★, *L'Orchestre Bam De Grand Mustapha International & Party Play "Local Music"* (Globestyle 1986)★★★, *Shopping* (Globestyle 1987)★★★, *Heart Of Uncle* (Globestyle 1989)★★★, *Soup Of The Century* (Fez-O-Phone 1990)★★★.

●COMPILATIONS: *Friends, Fiends & Fronds* (Globestyle 1991)★★★★.

THROBBING GRISTLE

Formed in London in September 1975, the group comprised Genesis P-Orridge (vocals), Cosey Fanni Tutti (guitar), Peter Christopherson (electronics) and Chris Carter (synthesizers). Essentially a performance art ensemble whose work often bordered on the obscene, they achieved a vague cult status in the wake of punk. Although boasting their own record company, early releases were limited to a few hundred copies. Some of their best-known compositions were characteristically tasteless with such titles as 'Hamburger Lady' and 'Five Knuckle Shuffle'. Their generally formless approach was sprinkled with arty in-jokes, such as speeding up a single to last a mere 16 seconds for inclusion on their second album. Other tricks involving misplaced grooves and misleading album titles were commonplace. Although derided or ignored by the music press they influenced a number of post-punk acts, not least Cabaret Voltaire. In May 1981 they broke up with the announcement: 'T.G. was a project not a life . . . we've exploited it completely - there's nothing else to say'. Except perhaps that their debut album *Second Annual Report* was reissued with the recording played backwards. Orridge and Christopherson soon resurfaced as Psychic TV while their erstwhile partners continued as Chris And Cosey.

● ALBUMS: *Second Annual Report* (Industrial 1977)★★★, *D.O.A. The Third And Final Report* (Industrial 1978)★★★, *20 Jazz Funk Greats* (Industrial 1979)★★, *Heathen Earth* (Industrial 1980)★★, *Second Annual Report* reissue (Fetish 1981)★★, *Funeral In Berlin* (Zensor 1981)★★, *Music From The Death Factory* (Death 1982)★★, *Journey Through A Body* (Walter Ulbricht 1982)★★, *Assume Power Focus* (Power Focus 1982)★★, *Live At The Death Factory, May '79* (TG 1982)★, *Live Box Set* (1993)★.

● COMPILATIONS: *Greatest Hits* (Rough Trade 1984)★★★.

● FURTHER READING: *Throbbing Gristle Scrapbook: First Annual Report*, Genesis P. Orridge.

THUNDERS, JOHNNY

b. John Anthony Genzale Jnr., 15 July 1952, New York City, New York, USA, d. 23 April 1991, New Orleans, Louisiana, USA. Johnny Thunders first gained recognition as a member of the New York Dolls, an aggregation that built a reputation for its hard R&B-influenced rock sound and glam/punk appearance in the early 70s. First calling himself Johnny Volume, the guitarist joined the high school band Johnny And The Jaywalkers, then a local band called Actress, which included in their line-up two other future Dolls members, Arthur Kane and Billy Murcia. Actress evolved into the New York Dolls in late 1971. Genzale, now renamed Johnny Thunders, recorded two albums

for Mercury Records with the Dolls. After leaving the band in 1975 along with drummer Jerry Nolan, the pair formed a new band alongside ex-Television guitarist Richard Hell called the Heartbreakers. This line-up was completed with the addition of guitarist Walter Lure. Hell left the group soon after to form the Voidoids with Billy Rath replacing him. Thunders and the Heartbreakers recorded prolifically for US and UK labels such as Track and Jungle Records. The group achieved greater popularity in the UK, where they were accepted as peers by early punk-rock bands that had idolized the Dolls. Thunders earned a reputation for his shambling stage performances owing to an excess of drugs and alcohol and he often made unscheduled guest appearances with other artists.

His first solo collection, *So Alone*, found him supported by many UK musicians, including Phil Lynott, Peter Perrett (Only Ones), Steve Jones and Paul Cook (Sex Pistols), Steve Marriott (Humble Pie/Small Faces) and Paul Gray (Eddie And The Hot Rods/Damned). Thunders later gigged with fellow junkie Sid Vicious, in the Living Dead. The Heartbreakers broke up and reformed numerous times, recording their last album together in 1984. Thunders then produced an album of 50s and 60s R&B/pop covers with singer Patti Palladin and an album with ex-MC5 guitarist Wayne Kramer. The latter featured a group called Gang War formed by Thunders and Kramer in the late 80s and early 90s. Despite the promise of all this activity, Thunders was found dead in a hotel room in New Orleans, Louisiana, in mysterious circumstances in 1991. He was 38. Despite Thunders' notorious drug dependency, the autopsy failed to reveal the cause of death although later reports cited a heroin overdose.

● ALBUMS: *So Alone* (Real 1978)★★★★, *In Cold Blood* (New Rose 1983)★★★, *Too Much Junkie Business* cassette only (ROIR 1983)★★★, *Hurt Me* (New Rose 1984)★★, *Que Sera Sera* (Jungle 1985)★★★, *Stations Of The Cross* cassette only (ROIR 1987)★★, with Patti Palladin *Copy Cats* (Restless 1988)★★★, *Gang War Featuring Johnny Thunders And Wayne Kramer* (Zodiac 1990)★, *Bootlegging The Bootleggers* (Jungle 1990)★★, *Live At Max's Kansas City '79* (ROIR 1996)★★★, *Have Faith* (Mutiny 1996)★★.

● COMPILATIONS: *Hurt Me* (Dojo 1995), *The Studio Bootlegs* (Dojo 1996)★★.

● FURTHER READING: *Johnny Thunders: In Cold Blood*, Nina Antonia.

TIFFANY

b. Tiffany Darwisch, 2 October 1971, Oklahoma, USA. Pop singer Tiffany, based in California, had immediate success with the release of the US number 1 singles 'I Think We're Alone Now' and 'Could've Been'. Both were included on the artist's 1987 debut album, recorded while she was still only 15 years old. So too was the number 7-peaking 'I Saw Him Standing There' (an utterly sexless version of the Beatles 'I Saw Her Standing There'), another bubblegum pop treatment of a well-loved standard. The album was helped by Tiffany's promotional tour of shopping malls - a gambit that pushed her ahead of the similarly gushing Debbie Gibson in US adolescent magazine circles The only hit on the follow-up collection, *Hold An Old Friend's Hand*, was 'All This Time' (number 6), indicating a lessening of her grip on the teen market. By the advent of *New Inside*, her 'mature' album, no-one was interested any more and her career effectively closed with it.
●ALBUMS: *Tiffany* (MCA 1987)★★, *Hold An Old Friend's Hand* (MCA 1988)★, *New Inside* (MCA 1990)★.

TIKARAM, TANITA

b. 12 August 1969, Munster, Germany. Tikaram's intense lyrics brought her instant commercial success at the age of 19. She spent her early years in Germany where her Fijian-born father was serving with the British army. In 1982 the family moved to England, settling in Basingstoke, Hampshire. Tikaram began writing songs and in November 1987 played her first gig at London's Mean Fiddler, after sending a cassette of her songs to the venue. By the time of her fourth gig she was supporting Warren Zevon at the Hammersmith Odeon. Following an appearance on a local London television show, she was signed to Warner Brothers Records and recorded *Ancient Heart* in 1988. The producers were Rod Argent (ex-Zombies) and experienced session musician Peter Van Hooke. 'Good Tradition' and 'Twist In My Sobriety' were immediate hits in the UK and across Europe. The album was a huge success and Tikaram became a late 80s role model of late 60s bedsitter singer-songwriters. She spent most of 1989 on tour before releasing her second album which included 'We Almost Got It Together' and 'Thursday's Child'. Although not as consistent as her debut it reached the same position in the UK album chart, number 3. *Everybody's Angel*, at Bearsville Studio in Woodstock, was co-produced with Van Hooke and Argent. Former Emerald Express violinist Helen O'Hara was among the backing musicians. 'Only The Ones We Love' with harmony vocals by Jennifer Warnes was issued in 1991, and in the same year she made her second world tour. In 1992 the self-produced *Eleven Kinds Of Loneliness* was released to a muted reaction and although her 1995 release had a much bigger publicity campaign it would seem that her highly commercial days are in the past.
●ALBUMS: *Ancient Heart* (Warners 1988)★★★★, *The Sweet Keeper* (East West 1990)★★, *Everybody's Angel* (East West 1991)★★, *Eleven Kinds Of Loneliness* (East West 1992)★★, *Lovers In The City* (East West 1995)★★★.

TIL TUESDAY

Boston, Massachusetts, USA-based band Til Tuesday are chiefly remembered for giving birth to the talents of singer-songwriter and bass player Aimee Mann. After an early hit single, 'Voices Carry' in 1985, the band failed to follow up on the promise of their debut album, though a rueful Mann places the blame for this squarely on the shoulders of record company intransigence and politicking. The group was formed around Mann, who had previously played with the Young Snakes, Michael Hausmann (drums), Robert Holmes (guitar) and Joey Pesce (keyboards). Their debut album, titled after the hit single, was produced by Mike Thorne and announced Mann's compositional skills and lyrical assurance. There remained those, however, not convinced by the strength of her vocal delivery. *Welcome Home* replaced Thorne with Rhett Davies as producer, but the record, though flawlessly constructed, lacked the sparkle of the debut. *Everything's Different Now* utilized a Jules Shear (then Mann's paramour) song as its title track. Expressing his happiness at falling for Mann, and sung by the subject of his affections, it offered an interesting insight into their relationship when compared to the same album's '(Believed You Were) Lucky', at which stage Mann had dumped Shear but still used his music to bear her own lyrics about their parting. 'The Other End (Of The Telescope)', meanwhile, was co-written and sung with Elvis Costello. However, the writing was on the wall for Til Tuesday, with Epic Records threatening to block any future release and not promoting the records in a satisfactory manner. The band broke up in 1988 allowing Mann to pursue a solo career, taking Hausmann with her.
●ALBUMS: *Voices Carry* (Epic 1985)★★★, *Welcome Home* (Epic 1986)★★★, *Everything's Different Now* (Epic 1988)★★★★.

TIMBUK 3

Formed in Madison, Wisconsin, USA, in 1978, Timbuk 3 was a duo consisting of husband and wife Pat MacDonald and Barbara Kooyman MacDonald. The pair met while attending the University of Madison and began writing and performing their songs. They went to New York City where they played on the street for tips before settling in Austin, Texas. While in Austin they became regulars at clubs such as the Hole In The Wall and the Austin Outhouse. They recorded a demo and made an appearance on MTV's *I.R.S. The Cutting Edge*, which led to a record contract with IRS Records. Using a boombox for their rhythm section, the duo (playing acoustic and electric guitars) began making appearances on other television programmes and recorded their debut, *Greetings From Timbuk 3*, in 1986. It reached number 50 in the US, largely on the strength of the sparkling first single, 'The Future's So Bright, I Gotta Wear Shades', a danceable novelty song which climbed to number 19 (21 in the UK). The album was a mixture of similarly light fare and darker, more serious themes, as was the 1988 follow-up, *Eden Alley*. Following the release of *Edge Of Allegiance*, the couple was joined by drummer Wally Ingram, and by *Big Shot In The Dark* they had evolved into a full band with the addition of bassist Courtney Audain.
●ALBUMS: *Greetings From Timbuk 3* (IRS 1986)★★★, *Eden Alley* (IRS 1988)★★★, *Edge Of Allegiance* (IRS 1989)★★★, *Big Shot In The Dark* (IRS 1991)★★★, *Espace Ornano* (Watermelon 1993)★★, mini-album *Looks Like Dark To Me* (High Street 1994)★★★, *One Hundred Lovers* (High Street 1995)★★★.
●COMPILATIONS: *Field Guide: Some Of The Best Of Timbuk 3* (IRS 1992)★★★.

TOM TOM CLUB

This US group was a spin-off of the Talking Heads featuring bassist Tina Weymouth (b. Martina Weymouth, 22 November 1950, Coronade, California, USA) and her husband, drummer Chris Frantz (b. Charlton Christopher Frantz, 8 May 1951, Fort Campbell, Kentucky, USA). The pair were on holiday in Nassau in the Bahamas (later buying a house there) when they met Stephen Stanley, the engineer at the studios and a keyboard player. They also met Monty Brown, the guitarist with T-Connection who were recording there. The four set about rehearsing and recording together and came up with 'Wordy Rappinghood' which was a UK hit in 1981 under the group name the Tom

Tom Club, taken from the name of a hall where they practised. The quartet stayed together on and off as a studio project utilizing various other people when necessary. These included Weymouth's two sisters on vocals, plus Steve Scales (percussion), Alex Weir (guitar) and Tyron Downie (keyboards). 'Genius Of Love' topped the US disco charts, and was followed by a cover of 'Under The Boardwalk'. It seemed as though they were in danger of overstating their separateness from Talking Heads: 'We've deliberately embraced all the types of music that Talking Heads hasn't. We like the accessibility and fun of dance music, but that's not all we do'. Frantz and Weymouth had produced Ziggy Marley early in 1988, and September saw the band playing a three-week stint at CBGB's with Lou Reed and Deborah Harry as guests. They began a UK tour with guitarist Mark Roule and keyboard player Gary Posner as the latest semi-permanent personnel. After the release of their third album, which this time included a cover of the Velvet Underground's 'Femme Fatale', they rejoined Byrne for Talking Heads' first live appearance since 1984 at the Ritz, New York.
●ALBUMS: *Tom Tom Club* (Sire 1981)★★★, *Close To The Bone* (Sire 1983)★★, *Boom Boom Chi Boom Boom* (Sire 1989)★★.

TOXIC EPHEX

Arguably the finest Scottish punk/folk crossover artists of the 80s, this Aberdeen six-piece comprised Dod (vocals), Carmen (fiddle), Fred (guitars), Mikey (bass), Chizel (drums) and Frankie (rhythm guitar). Local favourites for several years before their underground popularity spread throughout the rest of Scotland and England, their endeavours in this direction were helped by support slots to the politically and musically sympathetic New Model Army and Men They Couldn't Hang. Their vinyl debut had come on the early 80s Crass Records sampler, *Bullshit Detector 2*, after which they created their own, delightfully titled Green Vomit Records. From thence came a split album with fellow Scottish political punk outfit Oi Polloi, then the endearing *The Adventures Of Nobby Porthole - The Cock Of The North*. Staffed by mad fiddlers, snarling political vocals and diatribes against the Conservative government of the period, it also included an enchanting version of the Scottish folk standard, 'Bonnie Wee Jeanie McColl'. Alas, 1991 saw the demise of the fondly remembered sextet, although Carmen (dubbed by some sections of the press as 'a female Nigel Kennedy') reappeared both solo and with ceilidh specialists, Old Blind Dogs.

●ALBUMS: *Mad As Fuck (Don't You Think?)* split album with Oi Polloi (Green Vomit 1987)★★★, *The Adventures Of Nobby Porthole - The Cock Of The North* (Green Vomit 1990)★★★.

TOYAH

b. Toyah Ann Wilcox, 18 May 1958, Kings Heath, Birmingham, England. One of the more talented individuals to have risen under the banner of punk, Toyah roamed with the gangs of Birmingham before channelling her energy into Birmingham Old Rep Drama School. She later worked as a mime artist at the Ballet Rambert before getting her first professional acting role in the BBC television play *Glitter* with Noel Edmonds and Phil Daniels, in which she sang with the band Bilbo Baggins. Her next major role was as Emma in *Tales From The Vienna Wood*. Actor Ian Charleston then took her to tea with film maker Derek Jarman who offered her the part of Mad in *Jubilee*. It was here she met Adam Ant and for a time the pair, plus Eve Goddard, formed a band called the Man Eaters. However, the clash of egos ensured that the band was short-lived. While acting in Vienna they formed their first group with Peter Bush (keyboards), Steve Bray (drums, ex-Boyfriends) and Mark Henry (bass). Toyah then appeared in the film *The Corn Is Green* with Katharine Hepburn, and played Monkey in *Quadrophenia*. The band was signed to Safari in 1979 and released 'Victims Of The Riddle'. In August, Charlie Francis (ex-Patrick Fitzgerald group) replaced Henry. Toyah's extravagant vocal style and arresting lyrical subject matter were particularly evident on the powerful 'Bird In Flight'. While she was appearing in *Quatermass* the band started recording the *Sheep Farming In Barnet* mini-album. 1979 was one of Toyah's busiest years as she also hosted the *Look! Hear!* television series for BBC Midland, had a minor role in *Shoestring*, and made several other acting appearances. She was considered for the leading role in *Breaking Glass*, but it was eventually offered to Hazel O'Connor. Further singles followed the release of *Blue Meaning*, before Toyah was rewarded with the success of the *Four From Toyah* EP in 1981. Of the offerings, the repetitive lisp of 'Its A Mystery' carved out her identity with both public and press. Her first UK Top 10 hit, 'I Want To Be Free' came across as a petulant nursery anthem, but was attractive enough to appeal to a nation's teenagers. 1981 ended with Toyah's biggest hit, the exuberant 'Thunder In The Mountains', which peaked at number 4. The following year, she also charted with the startling, hypnotic 'Ieya' and the raucous 'Be Loud Be Proud (Be Heard)'. Bogan remained by her side musically but subsequent albums were recorded using session musicians instead of the band. Further acting roles came with the movie *The Tempest* and the stage play *Trafford Tanzi*. She became a Buddhist, married guitarist Robert Fripp and later recorded with him. She stayed with Safari until *Minx*, after which she went to Epic and then EG. Her last major hit was with a cover version of 'Echo Beach' in 1987. In Autumn 1991 she appeared with Tim Piggott-Smith in Peter Shaffer's *Amadeus Of Bradford*. She now pursues a successful career as a television presenter and stage actress.

●ALBUMS: *Sheep Farming In Barnet* (Safari 1980)★★, *The Blue Meaning* (Safari 1980)★★, *Toyah Toyah Toyah* (Safari 1981)★★★, *Anthem* (Safari 1981)★★★, *The Changeling* (Safari 1982)★★, *Warrior Rock (Toyah On Tour)* (Safari 1982)★★, *Love Is The Law* (Safari 1983)★★, *Minx* (Portrait 1985)★★, *Mayhem* (Epic 1985)★★, with Robert Fripp *The Lady And The Tiger* (Editions EG 1986)★★★, *Desire* (Editions EG 1987)★★★, *Prostitute* (Editions EG 1988)★★★, *Ophelia's Shadow* (Editions EG 1991)★★★, *Dreamchild* (Cryptic 1994)★★★.
●COMPILATIONS: *Best Of ...* (Connoisseur Collection 1994)★★★.
●FURTHER READING: *Toyah*, Mike West. *Toyah*, Gayna Evans.

TRANSVISION VAMP

Transvision Vamp was founded by the media-conscious Wendy James (b. 21 January 1966, London, England) and songwriter/guitarist Nick Christian Sayer (b. 1 August 1964). The group was completed by the arrival of Tex Axile (b. 30 July 1963; keyboards), Dave Parsons (b. 2 July 1962; bass) and Pol Burton (1 July 1964; drums). The band borrowed heavily, in terms of image and content, from a variety of sources such as T. Rex, the Clash and most notably, Blondie. James was frequently compared, usually unfavourably, to Blondie's former lead singer, the peroxide blonde Debbie Harry. Despite being an easy target for her detractors, James filled the space that had been long open for a British female teenage-rebel figure. On signing to MCA Records, Transvision Vamp made their initial foray on to the UK pop scene in 1987 with the single 'Revolution Baby', but it was not until the cover of Holly And The Italians' 'Tell That Girl To Shut Up' that they made any impact on the UK chart, while the follow-up, 'I Want Your Love' reached the UK Top 5. Their first album, *Pop Art* reached the UK Top 5. In 1989 further single chart hits with 'Baby Don't Care' (number 3), 'The Only One' and 'Landslide Of Love' (both Top 20) paved the way for the number 1 album, *Velveteen*. This run of success halted in 1991, with the result that MCA refused to release *The Little Magnets Versus The Bubble Of Babble* in the UK. The group's waning profile resulted in the inevitable break-up, with James going on to release an unsuccessful solo album written by Elvis Costello. James's sense of self-publicity and cheap outrage had given the group's name a consistently high profile, and it is likely that it will be her image and not the group's music that will have any lasting impression.

●ALBUMS: *Pop Art* (MCA 1988)★★, *Velveteen* (MCA 1989)★★, *The Little Magnets Versus The Bubble Of Babble* (MCA 1991)★.

TRAVELING WILBURYS

This group was formed in 1988 by accident as George Harrison attempted to make a new solo album, after enlisting the production talent of Jeff Lynne. At short notice only Bob Dylan's garage was available in which to rehearse, and over the next few days Tom Petty and Roy Orbison dropped by and dropped in. This wonderful pot-pourri of stars re-introduced 'having a good time' to their vocabulary and the result was not a Harrison solo but the superb debut from the Traveling Wilburys, *Handle With Care*. The outing proved to be a major success, bringing out the best of each artist; in particular this was a marvellous swansong for Roy Orbison who tragically died soon afterwards. The deliberately erroneously titled *Volume 3* was released in 1990 and received similar plaudits. The band were then under pressure to tour, but they were able to resist this, leaving open the possibility of future collaboration if this were mutually convenient at some point. This has to be the climate in which the last of the great supergroups can survive.

●ALBUMS: *Handle With Care* (Wilbury 1988)★★★★, *Volume 3* (Wilbury 1990)★★★.

TRIFFIDS

Hailing from the isolated Western Australian city of Perth, David McComb's group has, along with the Go-Betweens and Nick Cave, contributed greatly to increasing the northern hemisphere's respect for Antipodean rock, which for a long time was seldom taken seriously. The line-up was completed by McComb (b. 1962; lead vocals/guitar/keyboards), 'Evil' Graham Lee (pedal and lap steel guitar), Jill Birt (keyboards/vocals), Robert McComb

(violin/guitar/vocals), Martyn Casey (bass) and Alsy MacDonald (drums/vocals). The group's biggest success, providing the great breakthrough into the European market was 1986's *Born Sandy Devotional* on the Australian independent Hot label. This atmospheric set boasted a brooding, almost Bruce Springsteen-like 'Wide Open Road' and the desolate 'Sea Birds'. The follow-up found the Triffids returning to a simpler recording technique - an outback sheep-shearing shed and an eight-track recorder, producing a collection of Australian C&W/folk-blues songs. Departing from Hot, the Triffids secured a major contract with Island Records. McComb's lyrics, which are starkly evocative of the rural Australian townships and psyche, reached new peaks on *The Black Swan*, their most mature set to date. *Stockholm* was a live set released on the MNW label

●ALBUMS: *Treeless Plain* (Hot 1983)★★★, *Raining Pleasure* (Hot 1984)★★★, *Born Sandy Devotional* (Hot 1986)★★★★, *In The Pines* (Hot 1986)★★★, *Calenture* (Hot 1987)★★★, *The Black Swan* (Island 1989)★★★★, *Stockholm* (MNW 1990)★★★.

●COMPILATIONS: *Australian Melodrama* (1994)★★★.

TRIUMPH

A Canadian power-trio formed in Toronto during 1975. The band share many similarities to Rush other than geographical location, as they are all highly accomplished musicians who have experimented with many facets of high-tech melodic rock. Comprising Rik Emmet (guitar/vocals), Gil Moore (drums) and Mike Levine (bass/keyboards), they nevertheless followed a rockier road than their fellow countrymen. Interest built slowly, but the band finally made a breakthrough with *Progressions Of Power*, their fourth album, released in 1980. *Allied Forces* and *Never Surrender* saw the pinnacle of their success, with both albums attaining gold status in the USA. Their music is characterized by Emmet's high-pitched vocals and intricate guitar work, supplemented by keyboard fills and a thunderous rhythm section. *Thunder Seven*, a CD-only release, was a disjointed collection, while the live album that followed suffered from a wooden sound and flat production. In live settings the band frequently used Rick Santers as an extra guitarist to overcome the limitations of a three-man line-up. Again like Rush, their concerts were renowned for their sophisticated special effects rather than the actual music, and featured every conceivable pyrotechnic device available, plus the ultimate in computerized, laser-lighting rigs. *The Sport Of Kings* saw the band move in a blatantly commercial direction, but *Surveillance* marked a return to their roots: an aggressive and well-produced hard rock album. Emmett left the band in 1988 and was replaced by guitarist Phil Xenides. The vocals were taken over by Moore, but much of the group's character left with Emmett.

● ALBUMS: *Triumph* (Attic 1976)★★, *Rock 'N' Roll Machine* (RCA 1977)★★, *Just A Game* (RCA 1979)★★, *Progressions Of Power* (RCA 1980)★★★, *Allied Forces* (RCA 1981)★★★, *Never Surrender* (RCA 1982)★★★, *Thunder Seven* (RCA 1984)★★, *Stages* (MCA 1985)★★, *The Sport Of Kings* (MCA 1985)★★, *Surveillance* (MCA 1987)★★★, *Edge Of Excess* (1993)★★.

● COMPILATIONS: *Classics* (RCA 1989)★★★.

● VIDEOS: *Night Of Triumph Live* (1988), *Triumph At The US Festival* (1988).

TRUE BELIEVERS

Austin, Texas, USA band the True Believers burned brightly for a few years in the mid to late 80s but never achieved the audience they deserved. With a brand of guitar music that combined the rudiments of garage rock with glam rock (comparisons to the Faces, Mott The Hoople and New York Dolls featured in their press coverage), they nevertheless broke up after just one album, leaving a second set unreleased. The group's core members were Alejandro Escovedo (guitar/vocals) and brother Javier (guitar/vocals). The Escovedos' extended musical family also includes Pete and Coke Escovedo of Santana, and Sheila E. Javier had previously played with Los Angeles punk band the Zeros, while Alejandro joined the influential San Francisco band, the Nuns, before forming Rank And File in Austin, Texas. Alejandro left that band in 1983 before the recording of their second album, convincing Javier to relocate to Austin and join him in the True Believers, whose line-up was completed by bass player Denny DeGorgio. They became good friends and touring buddies with Los Lobos, earning a reputation as one of the hottest live acts in Texas. In the process they added third guitarist Jon Dee Graham, who also contributed to songwriting and vocals (many drummers passed through the ranks). They were signed by Rounder/EMI Records in 1985, entering the studio with producer Jim Dickinson (Replacements, Panther Burns) to record their debut album shortly thereafter. With glowing reviews, EMI asked them to repeat the process with a bigger budget for their projected second album, though they insisted the band use Georgia Satellites producer Jeff Glixman.

The result was barely concealed tension and hostility throughout the band, with DeGorgio and Kevin Foley, the then drummer, being fired. The ensuing album was never revealed to the public. Following a management rationalization at EMI the band was one of a clutch dropped from the roster. The True Believers continued to tour with the aid of Hector Munoz (drums) and J.D. Foster (bass/vocals, ex-Dwight Yoakam), but were unable to obtain the rights to their unreleased record. As a consequence the band disintegrated in late 1987. Alejandro Escovedo has gone on to record several acclaimed solo albums, while his brother worked with Will And The Kill, the Lost and Sacred Hearts. Graham has subsequently recorded with members of X. The True Believers' second album was finally made public in 1994 when Rykodisc issued the unreleased tracks alongside the contents of their debut album in one CD reissue.

● ALBUMS: *True Believers* (Rounder 1986)★★★.

● COMPILATIONS: *Hard Road* combines *True Believers* and the unreleased second album (Rykodisc 1994)★★★.

TUBE, THE

Though never a great ratings success, Channel 4's first music series, *The Tube*, is fondly recalled as one of British television's most exciting and pioneering music shows. It was produced by Malcolm Gerrie (formerly in charge of 'kiddie pop' show *Razzamatazz*) at Tyne Tees Television, with wife and husband team Andrea and Geoff Wonfor as executive producer and film director. Of fundamental importance to its success was the pairing of presenters Paula Yates and Jools Holland. The show ran from 1982-86, with the laconic duo (Yates' usual flirtatious persona contrasting with Holland's easy charm) introducing a series of bands and artists who had no previous television experience. The Fine Young Cannibals, Frankie Goes To Hollywood and Paul Young as a solo were all made famous by their appearances, as the show pursued an adventurous booking policy primarily directed by researcher Chris Phipps, Chris Cowie and Geoff Brown. This allowed space for acts as diverse as Rubella Ballet, Cameo, Public Image Limited (John Lydon famously returning to the Sex Pistols' 'Anarchy In The UK') and Iggy Pop to appear. Other presenters, including Muriel Gray, Leslie Ash and poet Mark Miwurdz also joined the team, though Yates and Holland remained the main pivots - despite the fact that the show's links were never as slick as conventional television demanded. While Yates continued to appear during the late stages of her pregnancy during the second series, Holland immortalized himself by swearing on air some weeks before the end of the *Tube*'s final series (he was 'suspended' for his errant behaviour). After the show's close, the various members of cast and crew have largely remained within the television industry - Holland presenting *Later With Jools Holland*, Yates hosting various shows, Gray joining *Frocks On The Box*, Mark Miwurdz returning to his real name, Mark Hurst, and pursuing a career as a stand-up comic and Ash returning to acting in *Men Behaving Badly*. In *The Tube*'s wake Channel 4 launched a number of new pop formats, including *Club X*, *Network 7*, *Big World Cafe*, *Friday Night At The Dome* and finally the lamentable *The Word*, without ever recapturing the shambolic magic of *The Tube* - an impression reinforced by the show's 90s repeats. After various freelance projects (notably with U2, whose appearance on *The Tube* is among the show's most memorable moments), Malcolm Gerrie, now of Initial Film And Television, launched Channel 4's *The White Room* in 1995.

TURNER, TINA

b. Annie Mae Bullock, 26 November 1939, Brownsville, Tennessee, USA. A singer while in her early teens, this enduring artist was a regular performer in St. Louis' nightclubs when she was discovered by guitarist Ike Turner in 1956. She joined his group as a backing singer, but quickly became the co-star and featured vocalist, a relationship sealed two years later with their marriage. Ike And Tina Turner were a highly successful act on the R&B circuit, before expanding their audience through a controversial liaison with producer Phil Spector. They emerged as a leading pop/soul act during the late 60s/early 70s with tours in support of the Rolling Stones and hits with 'Proud Mary' (1971) and 'Nutbush City Limits' (1973). However, the relationship between husband and wife grew increasingly strained as Ike's behaviour became irrational. Tina walked out of their professional and personal relationship during a 1975 tour, incurring the wrath of concert promoters who remained unsympathetic when the singer attempted a solo act. During this time the singer appeared in Ken Russell's film of the Who's rock-opera, *Tommy*, offering an outrageous portrayal of the Acid Queen; however, this acclaimed cameo failed to successfully launch Turner's solo career. Her career was rejuvenated in 1983 when British group Heaven 17 invited her to participate in an offshoot project dubbed BEF. She contributed a suitably rau-

cous version of the Temptations 'Ball Of Confusion' which in turn engendered a recording contract with Capitol Records. Turner's reading of Al Green's 'Let's Stay Together' reached the UK Top 10, while an attendant album, *Private Dancer*, hurriedly completed in its wake, spawned another major hit in 'What's Love Got To Do With It'. This melodramatic ballad topped the US chart, reached number 3 in Britain and won two Grammys as Record Of The Year and Best Pop Vocal Performance, Female. The title track, written by Mark Knopfler, was also a transatlantic hit. In 1984 Tina accepted a role in the film *Mad Max Beyond The Thunderdome*, the theme from which, 'We Don't Need Another Hero', was another international hit. The following year she duetted with Mick Jagger at the Live Aid concert and contributed to the US charity single, 'We Are The World'. Turner has since enhanced her popularity worldwide through a series of punishing tours, yet her energy has remained undiminished. Although commentators have criticized her one-dimensional approach, she enjoys massive popularity. She is truly happy with her present life and talks articulately about her difficult past. The voluptuous image is kept for the stage, while a quieter Tina offstage enjoys the fruits of her considerable success. Her 1985 autobiography was filmed in 1993 as *What's Love Got To Do With It?*, which also gave its title to a best-selling album and an extensive worldwide tour. Now allegedly retired from performing she released the title track from the James Bond movie *Goldeneye* in October 1995. The Bono/Edge composition had Turner sounding uncannily like Shirley Bassey (the vocalist on 'Goldfinger'). The Trevor Horn-produced *Wildest Dreams* was a further solid rock album, laying her strong R&B roots to history.

●ALBUMS: *The Country Of Tina Turner* reissued in 1991 as *Goes Country* (early 70s)★★★, *Acid Queen* (United Artists 1975)★★★, *Rough* (United Artists 1978)★★, *Love Explosion* (United Artists 1979)★★, *Private Dancer* (Capitol 1984)★★★★, *Break Every Rule* (Capitol 1986)★★★, *Live In Europe: Tina Turner* (Capitol 1988)★★, *Foreign Affair* (Capitol 1989)★★★, *What's Love Got To Do With It* film soundtrack (Parlophone 1993)★★★, *Wildest Dreams* (Parlophone/Virgin 1996)★★★.
●COMPILATIONS: *Simply The Best* (Capitol 1991)★★★★, *Tina Turner: The Collected Recordings, 60s To 90s* (Capitol 1994)★★★.
●VIDEOS: *Private Dancer Video EP* (1985), *Private Dancer Tour* (1985), *What You See Is What You Get* (1987), *Break Every Rule* (1987), *Rio 88* (1988), *Nice*

'n' Rough (1988), *Foreign Affair* (1990), *Do You Want Some Action* (1990), *Simply The Best* (1991), *Wild Lady Of Rock* (1992), *What's Love Live* (1994), *The Girl From Nutbush* (Strand 1995), *Wildest Dreams* (Feedback Fusion 1996), *Live In Amsterdam* (Castle Music Pictures 1997).

●FURTHER READING: *I, Tina*, Tina Turner with Kurt Loder. *The Tina Turner Experience*, Chris Welch.

TURTLE ISLAND STRING QUARTET

If one of the most interesting developments in popular music during the late 80s and early 90s has been the blurring of boundaries within genres, arguably the most extreme example of cross-fertilization has been the melding of rock, pop or jazz with classical music. Among the most popular and exciting musical ensembles to fall under this category are the Turtle Island String Quartet. Founded in 1985, the two sustained elements in the quartet since that time have been Darol Anger (violin/baritone violin) and Mark Summer (cello). Anger already had something of an illustrious past in 'new acoustic music'. He founded both the David Grisman Quintet and the Montreux band. He had also recorded as a solo artist (releasing an album, *Fiddlistics*), as well as collaborating with guitarist/mandolin player Mike Marshall. With fellow TISQ founder David Balakrishan and Matt Glaser he was part of an award-winning triple violin team, and has contributed to recordings by Suzanne Vega, Holly Near, Bela Fleck and John Gorka. His extensive *curriculum vitae* also includes performances with fellow Windham Hill artists Psychograss and Anger/Marshall And Hands On, and he has been pivotal in the development of synthesizer violin technology. Summer, meanwhile, is a graduate of the Cleveland Institute Of Music and has worked with the Winnipeg Symphony, the Oakland Symphony and the Chamber Symphony of San Francisco. He has also ventured outside of classical music into pop, rock and jazz. He has recorded with Will Ackerman and Toni Childs, and also works concurrently with San Francisco ensemble Trio Con Brio. His most enduring composition remains 'Julie-O' (from *Metropolis*), which has become a staple of the modern cello repertoire. This central duo were joined by Pittsburgh native Danny Seidenberg in January 1993, when he took over the viola role vacated by Katrina Wreede, who in turn had replaced founding member Irene Sazer. Schooled at Juilliard, and a member of Pittsburgh's Symphony Orchestra from the age of 16, Seidenburg has performed as principal violist for the Joffrey Ballet, Brooklyn Philharmonic, Soviet Emigre Orchestra and Juiliard Chamber Orchestra. His forays into rock and pop in the 70s included spells with rock band Spy and progressive fusion outfit Szobel. He has toured with a diverse array of artists ranging from Liza Minnelli and Steve Reich to Village People and James Brown. Founding violinist David Balakrishnan also retired from Turtle Island in 1993, though he chose to maintain his involvement as a composer and arranger. New York-born violinist Tracy Silverman replaced him. Silverman made his debut with the Chicago Symphony Orchestra at the age of 13, and has gone on to perform with Luciano Pavarotti as well as several ballets and acclaimed orchestras, and pop artists including Michael Bolton and Linda Ronstadt. Both New York band Stradivarius and Minneapolis trio Gutbucket allowed him to explore his rock instincts. The two new additions joined in time for Turtle Island's residency at the Stanford Jazz Workshop in the summer of 1993, collaborating with David Baker. The subsequent *Who Do We Think We Are?* featured guest appearances from drummer Scott Morris, guitarist Steve Erquiaga and vocalist Vicki Randle (the regular percussionist on US television's *The Tonight Show*). The material was largely drawn from the jazz tradition, with covers of Miles Davis's 'Seven Steps To Heaven', Charlie Parker's 'Moose The Mooch' and Thelonious Monk's 'Ruby My Dear'. Ample stylistic variation was offered in an adaptation of Jimi Hendrix's 'Gipsy Eyes'.

●ALBUMS: *Turtle Island String Quartet* (Windham Hill)★★★, *Skylife* (Windham Hill 1990)★★★, *On the Town* (Windham Hill 1991)★★★, *Spider Dreams* (Windham Hill 1991)★★★, *Metropolis* (Windham Hill 1992)★★★, soundtrack *A Shock To The System* (Windham Hill 1992)★★★, *Who Do We Think We Are?* (Windham Hill 1993)★★★, *By The Fireside* (Windham Hill 1995)★★★.

TV SMITH'S EXPLORERS

Formed from the punk debris of the Adverts, the Explorers saw TV Smith (b. Timothy Smith; vocals) and Tim Cross (guitar) combine with Erik Russell (guitar), Colin Stoner (bass) and John Towe (drums). After only one gig at the London Marquee in March 1980, Cross quit and, three performances later, Towe followed suit. With Mel Wesson and Dave Sinclair, respectively, stopping the musical gap, the new line-up signed to Chiswick Records. The aggressive 'Tomahawk Cruise' was voted Single Of The Week in *Sounds* music paper, but failed to chart. Over the next two years the group recorded several singles and an album for the Epic Records subsidiary Kaleidoscope, until Smith moved on to a solo career. After recording 'War Fever' and *Channel Five* (1983), he formed a new group, Cheap, though he remains best known for his work with the Adverts.

●ALBUMS: *Last Words Of The Great Explorer* (Kaleidoscope 1981)★★.

TWISTED SISTER

Formed in 1976, this New York quintet's original purpose was to provide the antidote to the disco music that was saturating the airwaves during the mid-70s. Featuring Dee Snider (vocals), Eddie Ojeda (guitar), Mark 'The Animal' Mendoza (bass; ex-Dictators), Jay Jay French (guitar) and Tony Petri (drums) they had a bizarre image that borrowed ideas from Kiss, Alice Cooper and the New York Dolls. Musically they combined sexually provocative lyrics and dumb choruses with heavy-duty, metallic rock 'n' roll. A.J. Pero (ex-Cities) took over on drums before the recording of their debut, *Under The Blade*. This was picked up from the independent Secret label by Atlantic Records, following a successful UK appearance at the Reading Festival and a controversial performance on *The Tube* television show in 1982. They never lived up to their initial promise, with successive albums simply regurgitating earlier ideas. Their greatest success was *Stay Hungry*, which reached the Top 20 album charts on both sides of the Atlantic. It also included the hit single, 'I Am, I'm Me', which peaked at number 18 in the UK. Their audience had become bored with them by the time *Come Out And Play* was released and the tour to support it was also a flop. Pero quit and returned to his former outfit, Cities; Joey 'Seven' Franco (ex-Good Rats) was drafted in as replacement. Snider steered the band in a more melodic direction on *Love Is For Suckers*. The album was stillborn, Atlantic terminated their contract, and the band imploded in 1987. Snider went on to form Desperado, with ex-Gillan guitarist Bernie Torme (subsequently evolving, more permanently, into Widowmaker). Looking back on his days dressing up with his old band, Snider would conclude: 'All that flash and shit wears thin. There's gotta be something beyond it. And there wasn't with Twisted Sister'.

●ALBUMS: *Under The Blade* (Secret 1982)★★, *You Can't Stop Rock 'N' Roll* (Atlantic 1983)★★, *Stay Hungry* (Atlantic 1984)★★★, *Come Out And Play* (Atlantic 1985)★★, *Love Is For Suckers* (Atlantic 1987)★★, *Live* (Music For Nations 1994)★★.

2 LIVE CREW

Rap headline-makers from Miami, Florida (via California), who formed in 1985 around central figure Luther Campbell. 2 Live Crew became unlikely figures in a media censorship debate when, in June 1990, *As Nasty As They Wanna Be* was passed sentence on by a judge in Broward County, Florida. In the process it became the first record in America to be deemed legally obscene (a federal appeal court overturned the decision in 1993). Their right to free speech saw them defended by sources as diverse as Sinead O'Connor, Bruce Springsteen and Mötley Crüe, but the overbearing impression remained that 2 Live Crew were a third-rate rap outfit earning first division kudos by little more than circumstance. Their debut set, recorded before Campbell became an actual member, marked out the band's territory. To this end, 2 Live Crew have several times expressed themselves to be an adult comedy troupe, 'The Eddie Murphys of Rap', in the best traditions of crude party records by Blowfly and others. Hence 'We Want Some Fussy' and other, inconsequential, mildly offensive tracks. Campbell was the founder of the band's record label, Luke Skyywalker Records (shortened to Luke Records when film-maker George Lucas, who created the Luke Skywalker character in the film *Star Wars*, filed suit), while Campbell's compatriots in 2 Live Crew numbered rappers Trinidad-born Chris Wong Won, New Yorker Mark Ross and California DJ David Hobbs (under the psuedonyms Brother Marquis and Fresh Kid Ice on the 'clean' version of *Move Somethin'*). Their music was underpinned by the familiar 'Miami Eass' sound, of synthesized, deep backbeats. *As Nasty As We Wanna Be*, replete with 87 references to oral sex alone, included the notorious 'Me So Horny', built around a sample from *Full Metal Jacket*. It is an unquestionably offensive lyric, but not any more so than that by the Geto Boys or others. There are probably worse examples within the 2 Live Crew's own songbook - 'The Fuck Shop', which samples Guns N'Roses guitar lines, or 'Head Booty And Cock' which became almost a battle cry, notably when repeated, Nuremburg-like, by chanting fans on the Phoenix, Arizona-recorded live album. Advocates of record stickering such as the Parents Music Resource Center (PMRC) and Florida attorney/evangelist Jack Thompson, argued strongly that the group's records should not be available for sale to minors. A retail record store owner arrested for selling a copy of their *Move Somethin'* - albeit to an adult - was later acquitted.

The group itself was then arrested for performing music from the *Nasty* album in an adults-only club, sparking charges by anti-censorship groups that the law enforcement officials were becoming over-zealous. There is not much doubt that this was true - Miami has one of the biggest pornography indus-tries in the country, and it was obvious the moguls behind it were not being pursued with equal vigour, if they were being pursued at all. Not that the band were going out of their way to help improve their public image (while doubtless real-ising the commercial advantages of such noto-riety). Luther Campbell claimed on CBS network TV show *A Current Affair* during 1992 that he had had oral sex on stage with female fans in Japan. Campbell had been acquitted a year earlier for giving an obscene performance in his home state, Florida. In 1993 they became legal ground-breakers again, this time over their 1989 parody of Roy Orbison's 'Pretty Woman'. For the first time, Acuff Rose Music Inc were suing an artist on the grounds that their version tarnishes the image of the orig-inal. On top of all the heat Campbell released a solo album, *Banned In The USA*. The scandal abated somewhat, and as 2 Live Crew's otherwise unre-markable career progressed, there was even an AIDS awareness ditty on *Nasty Weekend* - 'Who's Fuckin' Who'. They also promoted safe sex with their own brand of Homeboy Condoms, one of their more acceptable acts of mysoginist titilation.

●ALBUMS: *The 2 Live Crew Is What We Are* (Luke Skyywalker 1986)★★★, *Move Somethin'* (Luke Skyywalker 1988)★★, *As Nasty As They Wanna Be* (Luke Skyywalker 1989)★★, *As Clean As They Wanna Be* (Luke Skyywalker 1989)★, *Live In Concert* (Effect 1990)★★, *Sports Weekend (As Nasty As They Wanna Be Part II)* (Luke 1991)★★★, *Sports Weekend (As Clean As They Wanna Be Part II)* (Luke 1991)★★, *Shake A Lil' Somethin'* (Lil' Joe 1996)★★. Solo: Luther Campbell *Luke In The Nude* (Luke 1993)★★.

●COMPILATIONS: *Best Of* (Luke 1992)★★★, as Luther Campbell Featuring The 2 Live Crew *Banned In The USA* (Luke 1990)★★, as The New 2 Live Crew *Back At Your Ass For The Nine-4* (Luke 1994)★★.

●VIDEOS: *Banned In The USA* (1990).

TYGERS OF PAN TANG

This hard rock band was formed in Whitley Bay, Newcastle-upon-Tyne, England, in 1978, as part of the New Wave Of British Heavy Metal. The four-piece line-up comprised Jess Cox (vocals), Rob Weir (guitar), Rocky (bass) and Brian Dick (drums).

Their debut EP was the first rock release on Newcastle's Neat label, and it quickly topped all the metal charts. On the back of their first flush of success they moved to MCA Records. However, after one album Cox departed to be replaced by John Deverill (from Cardiff, Wales; vocals) and John Sykes (guitar). Sykes later left (to join Thin Lizzy and then Whitesnake) and was replaced by former Penetration guitarist Fred Purser. *The Cage* broke the band in the USA, before two years of dis-putes with MCA held up their career, and only compilation albums were released during this period. Steve Lamb joined as guitarist in 1985, and a year later former vocalist Cox formed Tyger Tyger in order to try and recapture past glories.

●ALBUMS: *Wild Cat* (MCA 1980)★★★, *Spellbound* (MCA 1981)★★, *Crazy Nights* (MCA 1981)★★, *The Cage* (MCA 1982)★★, *The Wreck-Age* (Music For Nations 1985)★★, *First Kill* (Neat 1986)★, *Burning In The Shade* (Zebra 1987)★. Solo: Jess Cox *Third Step* (Neat 1983)★.

●COMPILATIONS: *The Best Of The Tygers Of Pan Tang* (MCA 1983)★★.

TYLER, BONNIE

b. Gaynor Hopkins, 8 June 1951, Skewen, South Wales. Tyler's powerful, melodramatic voice was a perfect vehicle for the quasi-operatic imagination of producer Jim Steinman. After winning a talent contest in 1970, Tyler sang regularly in Welsh clubs and pubs, fronting a soul band called Mumbles. A throat operation in 1976 gave her voice an extra huskiness which attracted writer/producers Ronnie Scott and Steve Wolfe. Tyler successfully recorded their compositions 'Lost In France' and 'It's A Heartache', a million-seller in the USA. 'Married Men' (from the film *The World Is Full Of Married Men*) was only a minor hit and in 1981 Tyler changed labels to CBS Records and was teamed with Meat Loaf producer Steinman. He cre-ated 'Total Eclipse Of The Heart', a gigantic ballad which was probably Tyler's finest performance. The single reached number 1 on both sides of the Atlantic while 'Faster Than The Speed Of Night' also topped the UK charts. In 1984 Tyler duetted with fellow Welsh singer Shakin' Stevens on 'A Rockin' Good Way' and her dramatic delivery brought commissions to record the film themes 'Holding Out For A Hero' (a Steinman song from *Footloose* which reached the UK Top 10) and 'Here She Comes' from Giorgio Moroder's score for *Metropolis*. Next, Steinman paired Tyler with Todd Rundgren on 'Loving You's A Dirty Job But Someone's Got To Do It' (1986). Songwriter

Desmond Child was brought in to produce *Hide Your Heart* in 1988 and in the same year she took part in George Martin's recording of the Dylan Thomas verse drama *Under Milk Wood*. After a two-year absence from recording, Tyler signed to German label Hansa and *Bitterblue* was a big hit across northern Europe. Among those writing and producing for the album were Nik Kershaw, Harold Faltermeyer and Moroder. Her new contract with East West brought her together with Jim Steinman for *Free Spirit*, but even he could not rescue the production on an empty album of AOR vagaries.

●ALBUMS: *The World Starts Tonight* (RCA 1977)★★, *Natural Force* (*It's A Heartache* USA) (RCA 1978)★★★, *Diamond Cut* (RCA 1979)★★, *Goodbye To The Island* (RCA 1981)★★, *Faster Than The Speed Of Night* (Columbia 1983)★★, *Secret Dreams And Forbidden Fire* (Columbia 1986)★★, *Hide Your Heart* (Columbia 1988)★★, *Bitterblue* (Hansa 1991)★★, *Free Spirit* (East West 1996)★.

●COMPILATIONS: *The Very Best Of Bonnie Tyler* (RCA 1981)★★★, *Greatest Hits* (Telstar 1986)★★★, *The Best* (Columbia 1993)★★★, *Original Recordings* (1993)★★.

●FILMS: *Footloose* (1984).

U

U2

Indisputably the most popular group of the 80s in Britain, Irish unit U2 began their musical career at school in Dublin back in 1977. Bono (b. Paul Hewson, 10 May 1960, Dublin, Eire; vocals), The Edge (b. David Evans, 8 August 1961, Barking, Essex; guitar), Adam Clayton (b. 13 March 1960, Chinnor, Oxfordshire, England; bass) and Larry Mullen (b. Laurence Mullen, 1 October 1960, Dublin, Eire; drums) initially played Rolling Stones and Beach Boys cover versions in a group named Feedback. They then changed their name to the Hype before finally settling on U2 in 1978. After winning a talent contest in Limerick that year, they came under the wing of manager Paul McGuinness and were subsequently signed to CBS Records Ireland. Their debut EP *U2:3* featured 'Out Of Control' (1979), which propelled them to number 1 in the Irish charts. They repeated that feat with 'Another Day' (1980), but having been passed by CBS UK, they were free to sign a contract outside of Ireland with Island Records. Their UK debut, '11 O'Clock Tick Tock', produced by Martin Hannett, was well received but failed to chart. Two further singles, 'A Day Without Me' and 'I Will Follow', passed with little sales while the group prepared their first album, produced by Steve Lillywhite.

Boy, a moving and inspired document of adolescence, received critical approbation, which was reinforced by the live shows that U2 were undertaking throughout the country. Bono's impassioned vocals and the group's rhythmic tightness revealed them as the most promising live unit of 1981. After touring America, the group returned to Britain where 'Fire' was bubbling under the Top 30. Another minor hit with the impassioned 'Gloria' was followed by the strident *October*. The album had an anthemic thrust reinforced by a religious verve that was almost evangelical in its force. In February 1983 the group reached the UK Top 10 with 'New Year's Day', a song of hope inspired by the Polish Solidarity Movement. *War* followed soon after to critical plaudits. The album's theme covered both religious and political conflicts, especially in the key track 'Sunday Bloody Sunday', which had already emerged as one of the group's most startling and moving live songs. Given their power in concert, it was inevitable that U2 would attempt to capture their essence on a live album. *Under A Blood Red Sky* did not disappoint and as well as climbing to number 2 in the UK brought them their first significant chart placing in the US at number 28.

By the summer of 1984, U2 were about to enter the vanguard of the rock élite. Bono duetted with Bob Dylan at the latter's concert at Slane Castle and U2 established their own company Mother Records, with the intention of unearthing fresh musical talent in Eire. *The Unforgettable Fire*, produced by Brian Eno and Daniel Lanois, revealed a new maturity and improved their commercial and critical standing in the US charts. The attendant single, 'Pride (In The Name Of Love)', displayed the passion and humanity that were by now familiar ingredients in U2's music and lyrics. The group's commitment to their ideals was further underlined by their appearances at Live Aid, Ireland's Self Aid, and their involvement with Amnesty International and guest spot on Little Steven's anti-Apartheid single, 'Sun City'. During this same period, U2 embarked on a world tour and completed work on their next album. *The Joshua Tree* emerged in March 1987 and confirmed U2's standing, now as one of the most popular groups in the world. The album topped both the US and UK charts and revealed a new, more expansive sound, which complemented their soul-searching lyrics. The familiar themes of spiritual salvation permeated the work and the quest motif was particularly evident on both 'With Or Without You' and 'I Still Haven't Found What I'm Looking For', which both reached number 1 in the US charts. After such a milestone album, 1988 proved a relatively quiet year for the group. Bono and the Edge appeared on Roy Orbison's *Mystery Girl* and the year ended with the double-live album and film, *Rattle And Hum*. The group also belatedly enjoyed their first UK number 1 single with the R&B-influenced 'Desire'. The challenge to complete a suitable follow-up to *The Joshua Tree* took considerable time, with sessions completed in Germany with Lanois and Eno. Meanwhile, the group appeared on the Cole Porter tribute album *Red Hot + Blue*, performing a radical reading of 'Night And Day'. In late 1991, 'The Fly' entered the UK charts at number 1, emulating the success of 'Desire'. *Achtung Baby* was an impressive work, which captured the majesty of its predecessor yet also stripped down the sound to provide

a greater sense of spontaneity. The work emphasized U2's standing as an international group, whose achievements since the late 70s have been extraordinarily cohesive and consistent, and although the critics were less than generous with *Zooropa* and the house-orientated *Pop*, the band remain one of the most popular 'stadium' attractions of the 90s.

In the mid-90s Bono devoted much of his time to writing songs for others. With the Edge he wrote the theme 'Goldeneye' for Tina Turner and became involved in the Passengers project. His verbal lashing of the French president Jacques Chirac at the MTV awards in Paris created the biggest news, however. Obviously upset by the recent continuing nuclear tests Bono came onstage smiling to accept an award. The audience were brilliantly fooled by his perfectly delivered sarcasm; 'What a city' (cheers and applause), 'what a night' (cheers and applause), 'what a bomb' (confused laughter and applause), 'what a mistake' (mixed response), 'what a wanker you have for President' (sporadic boos).

●ALBUMS: *Boy* (Island 1980)★★★, *October* (Island 1981)★★★, *War* (Island 1983)★★★★, *U2 Live, Under A Blood Red Sky* (Island 1983)★★★, *The Unforgettable Fire* (Island 1984)★★★★, *Wide Awake In America* (Island 1985)★★★, *The Joshua Tree* (Island 1987)★★★★, *The Joshua Tree Singles* (Island 1988)★★★, *Rattle And Hum* (Island 1988)★★★, *Achtung Baby* (Island 1991)★★★★, *Zooropa* (Island 1993)★★★, *Pop* (Island 1997)★★★.

●VIDEOS: *Unforgettable Fire* (1985), *Under A Blood Red Sky (Live At Red Rocks)* (1988), *Under A Blood Red Sky* (1988), *Rattle And Hum* (1989), *Actung Baby* (1993), *Numb* (1993), *U2: Zoo TV Live From Sydney* (1994).

●FURTHER READING: *Unforgettable Fire: The Story Of U2*, Eamon Dunphy. *The U2 File: A Hot Press U2 History*, Niall Stokes (ed.). *U2: Three Chords And The Truth*, Niall Stokes (ed.). *Rattle And Hum*, Peter Williams and Steve Turner. *U2: Stories For Boys*, Dave Thomas. *U2: Touch The Flame. An Illustrated Documentary*, Geoff Parkyn. *U2 The Early Days: Another Time, Another Place*, Bill Graham. *U2: A Conspiracy Of Hope*, Dave Bowler and Brian Dray. *U2: The Story So Far*, Richard Seal. *U2: Burning Desire - The Complete Story*, Sam Goodman. *U2 Live*, Pimm Jal De La Perra. *Race Of Angels: The Genesis Of U2*, John Waters. *U2, The Rolling Stones File*, editors of *Rolling Stone*. *U2 At The End Of The World*, Bill Flanagan. *Wide Awake In America*, Alan Carter. *U2 Faraway So Close*, B.P. Fallon. *U2, The Rolling Stones File*, Editors of Rolling

Stone. *The Complete Guide To The Music Of ...*, Bill Graham. *The Making Of: U2's Joshua Tree*, Dave Thompson.

UB40

Named after the form issued to unemployed people in Britain to receive benefit, UB40 are the most long-lasting proponents of crossover reggae in the UK. The multiracial band was formed around the brothers Robin (b. 25 December 1954, Birmingham, England; lead guitar) and Ali Campbell (b. 15 February 1959, Birmingham, England; lead vocals/guitar), the sons of Birmingham folk club singers Lorna and Ian Campbell. Other founder-members included Earl Falconer (b. 23 January 1957, Birmingham, England; bass), Mickey Virtue (b. 19 January 1957, Birmingham, England; keyboards), Brian Travers (b. 7 February 1959; saxophone), Jim Brown (b. 21 November 1957; drums), and Norman Hassan (b. 26 January 1958, Birmingham, England; percussion). Reggae toaster Astro (b. Terence Wilson, 24 June 1957) joined UB40 to record 'Food For Thought' with local producer Bob Lamb (former drummer with Locomotive and the Steve Gibbons band). 'King' (coupled with 'Food For Thought') was a tribute to Martin Luther King. The debut *Signing Off*, boasted an album sleeve with a 12-inch square replica of the notorious, bright yellow unemployment card. This image attracted a large contingent of disaffected youth as well as proving popular with followers of the 2-Tone/ska scene. The following year the group formed their own label DEP International on which they released 'One In Ten', an impassioned protest about unemployment. *Labour Of Love*, a collection of cover versions, signalled a return to the reggae mainstream and it brought UB40's first number 1 in 'Red Red Wine' (1983). Originally written by Neil Diamond, it had been a big reggae hit for Tony Tribe in 1969. The album contained further hit singles in Jimmy Cliff's 'Many Rivers To Cross' (1983), Eric Donaldson's 'Cherry Oh Baby' (1984) and 'Don't Break My Heart' in 1985. The follow-up, *Geffrey Morgan*, a UK number 3 album, supplied the group with the Top 10 hit 'If It Happens Again'. 'I Got You Babe' (1986) was a different kind of cover version as Ali Campbell and Chrissie Hynde of the Pretenders duetted on the Sonny And Cher hit.

The same team had a further hit in 1988 with a revival of Lorna Bennett's 1969 reggae song 'Breakfast In Bed'. *Rat In Mi Kitchen* included the African liberation anthem 'Sing Our Own Song'

with Herb Alpert on trumpet. After performing 'Red Red Wine' at the 1988 Nelson Mandela, Wembley concert, re-promotion in the USA resulted in the single reaching the number 1 spot. The group had further single success with the Chi-lites' 'Homely Girl' (1989) and Lord Creator's 'Kingston Town' (1990), both of which would appear on a second volume of cover versions, *Labour Of Love II* (which has subsequently sold 5 million copies worldwide). In 1990, the group had separate Top 10 hits in the UK and USA as a Campbell/Robert Palmer duet on Bob Dylan's 'I'll Be Your Baby Tonight' charted in Britain and a revival of the Temptations' 'The Way You Do The Things You Do' was a hit in America. Throughout the 80s, the group toured frequently in Europe and North America and played in Russia in 1986, filming the tour for video release. Following a quiet period they returned in 1993 with a version of 'I Can't Help Falling In Love With You' which reached number 1 in the UK, also fostering the career of new pop-reggae star Bitty McClean. Litigation took place in 1995 when Debbie Banks, an amateur poet claimed that their major hit 'Don't Break My Heart' was based upon her lyrics. She won the case and was awarded a substantial amount in back royalties.

● ALBUMS: *Signing Off* (Graduate 1980)★★★, *Present Arms* (DEP 1981)★★★, *Present Arms In Dub* (DEP 1981)★★★, *UB44* (DEP 1982)★★★, *UB40 Live* (DEP 1983)★★★, *Labour Of Love* (DEP 1983)★★★★, *Geffrey Morgan* (DEP 1984)★★★★, *Baggariddim* (DEP 1985)★★★, *Rat In Mi Kitchen* (DEP 1986)★★★, *UB40* (DEP 1988)★★★★, *Labour Of Love II* (DEP 1989)★★★, *Promises And Lies* (DEP 1993)★★★, *Guns In The Ghetto* (DEP 1997)★★★. Solo: Ali Campbell *Big Love* (Virgin 1995)★★★.

● COMPILATIONS: *The Singles Album* (Graduate 1982)★★★, *The UB40 File* double album (Graduate 1985)★★★, *The Best Of UB40, Volume I* (DEP 1987)★★★★, *UB40 Box Set* (Virgin 1991)★★★, *The Best Of UB40 Vol. 2* (DEP 1995)★★.

● VIDEOS: *Labour Of Love* (1984), *Best Of* (1987), *Live* (1988), *Dance With The Devil* (1988), *Labour Of Love II* (1990), *CCCP* (1991), *A Family Affair Live In Concert* (1991), *Live In The New South Africa* (PMI 1995).

ULLMAN, TRACEY

b. 30 December 1959, Burnham, Buckinghamshire, England. A child actress, she later appeared in London stage productions of *Grease*, *The Rocky Horror Show* and *Elvis*, where she worked alongside Shakin' Stevens, and won the London Theatre

Critics Award for her performance in *Four In A Million*. She later starred in the BBC television comedy series, *Three Of A Kind,* with Lenny Henry and David Copperfield. Ullman secured a contract with Stiff Records and released an album in 1983 which climbed to number 14 in the UK chart. This collection comprised a set of cover versions from various eras of modern pop, spawning three Top 10 singles; 'Breakaway' (Jackie DeShannon), 'Move Over Darling' (Doris Day) and a version of Kirsty MacColl's 'They Don't Know', which earned Ullman a US Top 10 hit in April 1984. The accompanying videos generated interest in Britain owing to the cameo appearance of Labour Party leader, Neil Kinnock. The follow-up, *You Caught Me Out,* fared less well and her singing career was put on hold. More television comedy appearances in Independent television's *Girls On Top* with Dawn French, Jennifer Saunders and Ruby Wax was followed by a move to the USA, after her marriage to television producer, Allan McKeown. The couple relocated to Los Angeles, California, where Ullman acted alongside Meryl Streep in the film, *Plenty,* and starred in her own successful comedy series, *The Tracey Ullman Show.*

●ALBUMS: *You Broke My Heart In 17 Places* (Stiff 1983)★★, *You Caught Me Out* (Stiff 1984)★★.

●COMPILATIONS: *Forever* (Stiff 1985)★★.

●FILMS: *Give My Regards To Broad Street* (1985).

ULTRAVOX

The initial premise of Ultravox came from the 70s school of electro-rock from pioneers Kraftwerk and the glam rock of Brian Eno/Roxy Music. Formed in 1974, the early line-up comprised John Foxx (b. Dennis Leigh, Chorley, Lancashire, England; vocals), Steve Shears (guitar), Warren Cann (b. 20 May 1952, Victoria, British Columbia, Canada; drums), Chris Cross (b. Christopher Allen, 14 July 1952; bass) and Billy Currie (b. 1 April 1952, Huddersfield, Yorkshire, England; keyboards/synthesizer/violin). Their rise coincided with the ascendancy of the new wave although they were for the most part ignored by a rock press more concerned with the activities of the burgeoning punk scene and consequently live gigs were frequently met with indifference. Signed to Island Records in 1976, their albums made little impact on the record-buying public, despite the endorsement of Brian Eno who produced their first album. However, Ultravox's influence on a growing movement of British synthesizer music, in particular Gary Numan, was later acknowledged. Shears was replaced by Robin Simon in 1978, but after *Systems*

Of Romance had garnered disappointing sales, Island dropped the act, with both Simon and Foxx (who many felt was the main creative force behind the group) leaving to pursue solo careers. Ultravox were disbanded while the remaining members took stock. On a sojourn with Visage, Currie met Midge Ure (b. James Ure, 10 October 1953, Cambuslang, Strathclyde, Scotland; lead vocals/guitar) former member of Slik and the Rich Kids. The duo found a compatibility of ideas and decided to revive Ultravox as a quartet with Cross and Currie. Having departed from Island, the group signed to Chrysalis Records. Their new direction brought minor chart success with 'Sleepwalk' and 'Passing Strangers'. It was not until the magnificent 'Vienna' was released that Ultravox found the success that had eluded them for so long. Held at the UK number 2 spot in January and February of 1981 by Joe Dolce's inane 'Shaddap You Face' and hits from the recently murdered John Lennon, the song's moody and eerie atmosphere was enhanced by an enigmatic video. A string of Top 20 hits followed for the next three years, including 'All Stood Still' (1981), 'Reap The Wild Wind' (1982) and 'Dancing With Tears In My Eyes' (1984). Ure's anguished, melodramatic style blended well with the high-energy pop of their contemporaries, Duran Duran and Spandau Ballet, the UK's 'new romantics', finding success elsewhere in Europe, but never quite achieving the same level in the USA. While Ure's simultaneous solo career proved, for a short time, successful, group projects became less cohesive. *U-Vox* was released in 1986. Billy Currie had assumed control of the group, and, in 1993, with the aid of singer Tony Fennelle, a 'new' Ultravox released the poorly received *Revelation.* Ure has since continued his solo career with varying degrees of success. Curry assembled a further version of the band for *Ingenuity* with Sam Blue as the new vocalist and Vinny Burns (guitar).

●ALBUMS: *Ultravox!* (Island 1976)★★, *Ha! Ha! Ha!* (Island 1977)★★, *Systems Of Romance* (Island 1978)★★, *Vienna* (Chrysalis 1980)★★★, *Rage In Eden* (Chrysalis 1981)★★★, *Quartet* (Chrysalis 1982)★★, *Monument - The Soundtrack* (Chrysalis 1983)★★, *Lament* (Chrysalis 1984)★★, *U-Vox* (Chrysalis 1986)★★, *Revelation* (1993)★, *Ingenuity* (Resurgence 1995)★. Solo: Billy Currie *Stand Up And Walk* (Hot Food 1990)★★.

●COMPILATIONS: *Three Into One* Island recordings (Island 1980)★★, *The Collection* (Chrysalis 1984)★★★.

●FURTHER READING: *The Past, Present & Future Of Ultravox,* Drake and Gilbert.

UNDERTONES

Formed in Londonderry, Northern Ireland, in November 1975 this much-loved punk/pop quintet comprised Feargal Sharkey (b. 13 August 1958, Londonderry, Northern Ireland; vocals), John O'Neill (b. 26 August 1957, Londonderry, Northern Ireland: guitar), Damian O'Neill (guitar), Michael Bradley (bass) and Billy Doherty (drums). Playing on the local pub scene, the group were inspired by the punk movement to begin writing and playing their own songs. An early demo was rejected by Stiff, Chiswick and Radar Records, as the group continued to build a following with a series of local gigs. By 1978 the group were offered a one-off contract with the independent Belfast label Good Vibrations. Their debut EP, *Teenage Kicks*, was heavily promoted by the influential BBC disc jockey John Peel, who later nominated the lead track as his all-time favourite recording, saying that he cried when he first heard it. The group were still without a manager, so Sharkey took on the responsiblity for arranging a five-year contract with Sire Records (an early indication of the business acumen that would lead to an A&R position with Polydor Records in the 90s). The label then reissued *Teenage Kicks*, which eventually climbed to number 31 in the charts on the back of their first UK tour. By the spring of 1979, the group had entered the Top 20 with the infectious 'Jimmy Jimmy' and gained considerable acclaim for their debut album, which was one of the most refreshing pop records of its time. The group's genuinely felt songs of teenage angst and small romance struck a chord with young listeners and ingratiated them to an older public weaned on the great tradition of early/mid-60s pop. *Hypnotised* was a more accomplished work, which featured strongly melodic hit singles in 'My Perfect Cousin' and 'Wednesday Week'. The former was particularly notable for its acerbic humour, including the sardonic lines: 'His mother bought him a synthesizer/Got the Human League in to advise her'.

Despite a major tour of the USA, the group were unable to make an impact outside the UK and were released from their Sire contract, setting up their own label, Ardeck Records, licensed through EMI. The group then went to the Netherlands to record *Positive Touch* in 1981. Of the singles taken from the album the insistent 'It's Going To Happen' was a deserved success, but the romantic 'Julie Ocean' was not rewarded in chart terms. The Undertones' new-found maturity did not always work in their favour, with some critics longing for the innocence and naïvety of their initial recordings. With *The Sin Of Pride* and attendant 'The Love Parade', the group displayed a willingness to extend their appeal, both musically with the introduction of brass, and thematically with less obvious lyrics. With a growing need to explore new areas outside the restrictive Undertones banner the group ended their association in June 1983. The compilation, *All Wrapped Up*, complete with controversial sleeve, served as a fitting tribute to their passionate blend of punk and melodic pop. Sharkey went on to team up with Vince Clarke in the short-lived Assembly, before finding considerable success as a soloist. The O'Neill brothers subsequently formed the critically acclaimed That Petrol Emotion.

● ALBUMS: *The Undertones* (Sire 1979)★★★★, *Hypnotised* (Sire 1980)★★★★, *Positive Touch* (Ardeck/EMI 1981)★★★, *The Sin Of Pride* (Ardeck/EMI 1983)★★★, *The Peel Sessions Album* (Strange Fruit 1991)★★★.

● COMPILATIONS: *All Wrapped Up* (Ardeck/EMI 1983)★★★, *Cher O'Bowlies· Pick Of Undertones* (Ardeck/EMI 1986)★★★, *The Best Of: Teenage Kicks* (Castle 1993)★★★★.

URE, MIDGE

b. James Ure, 10 October 1953, Cambuslang, Strathclyde, Scotland. Midge Ure began his professional career as guitarist/vocalist with Salvation, a popular Glasgow-based act which evolved into Slik in 1974. Although accomplished musicians, Slik's recording contract bound them to ill-fitting, 'teenybop' material, reminiscent of fellow-Scots the Bay City Rollers. Frustrated at this artistic impasse, Ure opted to join the Rich Kids, a punk/pop act, centred on former Sex Pistols bassist Glen Matlock. However, despite strong support from EMI Records, the group's chemistry did not gel and they disbanded in November 1978, barely a year after inception. Ure subsequently joined the short-lived Misfits before founding Visage with Steve Strange (vocals) and Rusty Egan (drums). Ure's involvement with this informal 'new romantic' act ended when he replaced Gary Moore in Thin Lizzy midway through an extensive US tour. His position, however, was purely temporary as the artist had already agreed to join Ultravox, who rose from cult status to become one of the most popular acts of the early 80s. The ever-industrious Ure also produced sessions for Steve Harley and Modern Man, and in 1982 enjoyed a UK Top 10 solo hit with his version of 'No Regrets', penned by Tom Rush and previously a hit for the Walker Brothers.

Two years later he formed Band Aid with Bob Geldof. Their joint composition, the multi-million selling 'Do They Know It's Christmas?', was inspired by harrowing film footage of famine conditions in Ethiopia and featured an all-star cast of pop contemporaries. This commitment completed, and with Ultravox in suspension, Ure resumed his solo career with *The Gift*. The album spawned a number 1 single, 'If I Was', since which the singer enjoyed further success with 'That Certain Smile' (1985) and 'Call Of The Wild' (1986). However, a second set, *Answers To Nothing* proved less successful. This effort was not followed up until three years later when the singer, now signed to Arista Records, produced a new album in autumn 1991. He resurfaced with little fanfare in 1991 and immediately went back into the UK Top 20 singles charts with 'Cold, Cold Heart' which was closely followed by *Pure*. This clearly demonstrated that Ure had not lost his touch for melody, but although he still retains a following, his recent work (notably *Breathe*) has been undistinguished and the corresponding lack of chart success does not augur well for Ure's future as a solo artist.

●ALBUMS: *The Gift* (Chrysalis 1985)★★★, *Answers To Nothing* (Chrysalis 1988)★★, *Pure* (Arista 1991)★★, *Breathe* (Arista 1996)★★.
●COMPILATIONS: *If I Was: The Very Best Of ...* (Chrysalis 1993)★★★.

VAI, STEVE

b. 6 June 1960, Long Island, New York, USA. Vai began his musical career at the age of 13, forming his first rock band, Rayge, while still at school. At this time he was tutored by Joe Satriani, who was to have a profound effect on his style for years to come. He studied jazz and classical music at the Berklee College Of Music in Boston, Massachusetts, before relocating to Los Angeles, California, in 1979. He was recruited by Frank Zappa as the lead guitarist in his backing band, while he was still only 18 years old. By 1984 he had built his own recording studio and had begun experimenting with the fusion of jazz, rock and classical music. These pieces were eventually released as *Flex-able*, and were heavily influenced by Zappa's offbeat and unpredictable style. In 1985 Vai replaced Yngwie Malmsteen in Alcatrazz, then moved on to even greater success with Dave Lee Roth and later Whitesnake. *Passion And Warfare*, released in 1990, was the album that brought Vai international recognition as a solo performer. It welded together jazz, rock, funk, classical and metal nuances within a melodic instrumental framework. It climbed to number 18 on the *Billboard* album chart, earning a gold disc in the process. *Alien Love Secrets* further highlighted his extraordinary style with guitars sounding like horses on 'Bad Horsie' and a Venusian vocal on 'Kill The Guy With The Ball', created by utilizing massive EQ, his left foot and a digital whammy bar. Vai takes the instrument into new realms but still makes it sound like a guitar, most of the time. *Fire Garden* was half instrumental/half vocal. The former contained a bizarre mix of stunning guitar pyrotechnics together with one of his most evocative compositions, 'Hand On Heart'. His guitar is not to be argued with.

●ALBUMS: *Flex-able* (Relativity 1984)★★, *Flex-able Leftovers* (Relativity 1984)★★, *Passion And Warfare* (Relativity 1990)★★★; as Vai *Sex & Religion* (Relativity 1993)★★★, *Alien Love Secrets* (Relativity 1995)★★★, *Fire Garden* (Epic 1996)★★★.

VAN HALEN

The origins of this, one of America's most successful heavy metal bands, date back to Pasadena, California, in 1973. Edward (Eddie) Van Halen (b. 26 January 1957, Nijmegen, The Netherlands, guitar/keyboards), Alex Van Halen (b. 8 May 1955, Nijmegen, Netherlands; drums) and Michael Anthony (b. 20 June 1955, Chicago, Illinois, USA; bass) who were members of the Broken Combs, persuaded vocalist David Lee Roth (b. 10 October 1955, Bloomington, Indianapolis, USA) to leave the Real Ball Jets and become a member. After he consented they changed their name to Mammoth. Specializing in a mixture of 60s and 70s cover versions plus hard rock originals, they toured the bar and club circuit of Los Angeles virtually non-stop during the mid-70s. Their first break came when Gene Simmons (bassist of Kiss) saw one of their club gigs. He was amazed by the energy they generated and the flamboyance of their lead singer. Simmons produced a Mammoth demo, but surprisingly it was refused by many major labels in the USA. It was then discovered that the name Mammoth was already registered, so they would have to find an alternative. After considering Rat Salade, they opted for Roth's suggestion of simply Van Halen. On the strength of Simmons' recommendation, producer Ted Templeman saw the band, was duly impressed and convinced Warner Brothers Records to sign them. With Templeman at the production desk, Van Halen entered the studio and recorded their self-titled debut in 1978. The album was released to widespread critical acclaim and compared with Montrose's debut in 1973. It featured a unique fusion of energy, sophistication and virtuosity through Eddie Van Halen's extraordinary guitar lines and Roth's self-assured vocal style. Within 12 months it had sold two million units, peaking at number 19 in the *Billboard* chart; over the years this album has continued to sell and by 1996 had been certified in the USA alone at 9 million sales. Eddie Van Halen was named as Best New Guitarist Of The Year in 1978, by *Guitar Player* magazine. The follow-up, simply titled *Van Halen II*, kept to the same formula and was equally successful. Roth's stage antics became even more sensational - he was the supreme showman, combining theatrical stunts with a stunning voice to entertaining effect. *Women And Children First* saw the band start to explore more musical avenues and experiment with the use of synthesizers. This came to full fruition on *Fair Warning* which was a marked departure from earlier releases. *Diver Down* was the band's weakest album, with the cover versions of 60s standards being the strongest tracks. Nevertheless, the band could do no wrong in the eyes of their fans and the album, as had all their previous releases, went platinum. With *1984*, released on New Year's day of that year, the band returned to form. Nine original tracks reaffirmed their position as the leading exponents of heavy duty melodic metal infused with a pop sensibility. Spearheaded by 'Jump', a *Billboard* number 1 hit single, the album lodged at number 2 in the US chart for a full five weeks during its one-year residency. Eddie Van Halen was also a guest on Michael Jackson's 'Beat It' in the same year. This was easily his most high profile solo outing, though his other select engagements outside the band have included work with Private Life and former Toto member Steve Lukather. Roth upset the applecart by quitting in 1985 to concentrate on his solo career, and ex-Montrose vocalist Sammy Hagar (b. 13 October 1947, Monterey, California, USA) eventually filled the vacancy. Retaining the Van Halen name, against record company pressure to change it, the new line-up released *5150* in June 1986. The album name was derived from the police code for the criminally insane, as well as the name of Eddie Van Halen's recording studio. The lead-off single, 'Why Can't This Be Love', reached number 3 in the *Billboard* chart, while the album became their first number 1 and their biggest seller to date. *OU812* was a disappointment in creative terms. The songs were formularized and lacked real direction, but the album became the band's second consecutive number 1 in less than two years. *For Unlawful Carnal Knowledge*, written as the acronym F.U.C.K., stirred up some controversy at the time of release. However, the music on the album transcended the juvenile humour of the title, being an immaculate collection of gritty and uncompromising rockers. The band had defined their identity anew and rode into the 90s on a new creative wave - needless to say, platinum status was attained yet again. A live album prefigured the release of the next studio set, *Balance*, with Van Halen's popularity seemingly impervious to the ravages of time or fashion. It is unusual for a greatest hits compilation to debut at number 1 but the band achieved this on the *Billboard* chart in 1996 with *Best Of Volume 1*. Hagar departed in 1996 after rumours persisted that he was at loggerheads with the other members; fans immediately rejoiced when it was announced that the replacement would be David Lee Roth, although not on a full-time basis. A few months later Lee Roth issued a statement effectively ruling out any further involvement. The vacancy went to Gary Cherone soon after Extreme announced their formal disbanding in October 1996.

●ALBUMS: *Van Halen* (Warners 1978)★★★★, *Van Halen II* (Warners 1979)★★★★, *Women And Children First* (Warners 1980)★★★, *Fair Warning* (Warners 1981)★★★, *Diver Down* (Warners 1982)★★★, *1984 (MCMLXXXIV)* (Warners 1984)★★★★, *5150* (Warners 1986)★★★★, *OU812* (Warners 1988)★★★, *For Unlawful Carnal Knowledge* (Warners 1991)★★★, *Live: Right Here, Right Now* (Warners 1993)★★★, *Balance* (Warners 1995)★★★.
●COMPILATIONS: *Best Of Volume 1* (Warners 1996)★★★★.
●VIDEOS: *Live Without A Net* (1987), *Live; Right Here Right Now* (1993), *Video Hits Vol. 1* (Warner Music 1996).
●FURTHER READING: *Van Halen*, Michelle Craven. *Excess All Areas*, Malcolm Dome.

VAN ZANDT, STEVEN

b. 22 November 1950, Boston, Massachusetts, USA. From a professional beginning in Stell Mill (with Bruce Springsteen) and similar New Jersey bar bands, Van Zandt toured as backing guitarist to the Dovells before passing briefly through the ranks of Southside Johnny And The Asbury Jukes whose first three albums he supervised. He also contributed several compositions to these; some written with Springsteen whose E Street Band he served intermittently from 1975-81 when, without rancour, he was replaced by Nils Lofgren. Overcoming inhibitions about his singing, Van Zandt next led Little Steven And The Disciples Of Soul, a 12-piece that made its stage debut at London's Marquee Club with personnel that included the Asbury Jukes horn section and, on bass, ex-Plasmatics Jean Beauvior. Theirs was a body of recorded work that, lyrically, reflected Van Zandt's increasing preoccupation with world politics. This was exemplified by 'Solidarity' (from 1984's *Voice Of America*), which was covered by Black Uruhu. After a fact-finding expedition to South Africa, he masterminded Sun City, a post-Live Aid project that raised over $400,000 for anti-apartheid movements in Africa and the Americas via an album, single and concert spectacular featuring Bob Dylan, Lou Reed, Ringo Starr, Springsteen and other big names. To a less altruistic end, his reputation as a producer snowballed through his efforts on records by artists such as Gary U.S. Bonds (with Springsteen), Lone Justice and Ronnie Spector (with whom he had been

linked romantically), as well as his own gradually more infrequent offerings.
●ALBUMS: *Men Without Women* (EMI America 1982)★★★, *Voice Of America* (EMI America 1984)★★★, *Freedom - No Compromise* (Manhattan 1987)★★★, *Revolution* (RCA 1989)★★★, *Live Fast Diarrhea* (Nitro 1995)★★★, *The Quickening* (Nitro 1996)★★★.

VANDROSS, LUTHER

b. Luther Ronzoni Vandross, 20 April 1951, New York City, New York, USA. Born into a family immersed in gospel and soul singing, Vandross had already formed his own group while still at school and later worked with the musical theatre workshop, Listen My Brother. This enabled him to perform at Harlem's Apollo Theatre. After a brief hiatus from the music scene in the 70s, he was invited by an old schoolfriend and workshop colleague, Carlos Alomar, to join him in the studio with David Bowie for the recording of *Young Americans*. Vandross impressed Bowie enough to be invited to arrange the vocal parts and make a substantial contribution to the backing vocals for the album. By the time Bowie's US tour was underway Vandross had also secured the position as opening act. His vocal talent was soon in demand and his session credits with Chaka Khan, Ringo Starr, Barbra Streisand and Donna Summer generated sufficient interest from the Cotillion label to sign him as part of a specially assembled vocal group, Luther. *Luther* and *This Close To You* (both 1976) flopped, partly owing to the use of a disco backing in favour of allowing Vandross to express his more romantic, soul style.
The singer subsequently drifted back to session work putting in outstanding performances for Quincy Jones, Patti Austin, Gwen Guthrie, Chic and Sister Sledge. This work was subsidized by his composing advertising jingles. His performance as guest singer with the studio group Change on the 1980 *Glow Of Love* earned two UK Top 20 hits in 'Glow Of Love' and 'Searchin''. This led to the re-launch of a higher profile career, this time as solo artist with Epic/CBS Records. 'Never Too Much' earned him an R&B number 1 while the accompanying album reached the US Top 20. The single took a further eight years to reach the UK Top 20. Subsequent singles, including duets with Cheryl Lynn ('If This World Was Mine') and Dionne Warwick ('How Many Times Can We Say Goodbye'), saw him strengthen his popularity with the US R&B market and gave him two further R&B number 1 hits with 'Stop To Love' (1986) and a duet

with Gregory Hines, 'There's Nothing Better Than Love' (1987). All of his recent releases have become major hits, and Vandross has now risen to become one of the finest soul singers of the 80s and 90s. He has won countless awards and his reputation as a producer has been enhanced by his work with Dionne Warwick, Diana Ross and Whitney Houston.

●ALBUMS: *Never Too Much* (Epic 1981)★★★, *Forever, For Always, For Love* (Epic 1982)★★★, *Busy Body* (Epic 1983)★★★, *The Night I Fell In Love* (Epic 1985)★★★★, *Give Me The Reason* (Epic 1986)★★★, *Any Love* (Epic 1988)★★★, *Power Of Love* (Epic 1991)★★★★, *Never Let Me Go* (Epic 1993)★★★, *Songs* (Epic 1994)★★★, *Your Secret Love* (Epic 1996)★★★.

●COMPILATIONS: *The Best Of Luther Vandross ... The Best Of Love* (Epic 1989)★★★★, *Greatest Hits 1981-1995* (Epic 1995)★★★★.

●VIDEOS: *An Evening Of Songs* (1994), *Always And Forever* (1995).

VANGELIS

b Evangalos Odyssey Papathanassiou, 29 March 1943, Valos, Greece. A child prodigy, Vangelis gave his first public performance on the piano at the age of six. In the early 60s he joined the pop group Formynx, later forming Aphrodite's Child with vocalist Demis Roussos and Lucas Sideras (drums). The group moved to Paris in the late 60s, recording the international hit 'Rain And Tears'. After it disbanded in 1972, Vangelis concentrated on electronic music, composing classical works as well as film scores for wildlife documentaries by Frederic Rossif. He next built a studio in London where he further developed his fusion of electronic and acoustic sound. *Heaven And Hell* was a Top 40 hit in the UK while the concept album *Albedo 0.39* included the voices of astronauts landing on the moon, as well as the dramatic favourite 'Pulstar'. Returning to Greece in 1978, Vangelis collaborated with actress Irene Papas on settings of Byzantine and Greek traditional songs, before joining forces with Yes vocalist Jon Anderson who had previously sung on *Heaven And Hell*. As Jon And Vangelis they had enjoyed international success with 'I Hear You Now' (1980) and 'I'll Find My Way Home' (1982). The following year, Vangelis resumed his activities as a film music composer with the award-winning *Chariots Of Fire*. The title track was a worldwide hit and prompted scores of imitation 'themes'. This was followed by scores for Kuruhara's *Antarctica*, Ridley Scott's *Bladerunner* and Costas-Gavras' *Missing* and Donaldson's *The Bounty*. In 1988, he signed to Arista Records, releasing *Direct*, the first in a series of improvised albums which he composed, arranged and recorded simultaneously. His film credits in the early 90s included *Bitter Moon* and *1492: Conquest Of Paradise* (1993).

●ALBUMS: *Dragon* (1971)★★, *L'Apocalypse Des Animaux* (Polydor 1973)★★, *Earth* (Polydor 1974)★★, *Heaven And Hell* (RCA Victor 1975)★★★, *Albedo 0.39* (RCA 1976)★★, *Spiral* (RCA 1977)★★, *Beaubourg* (RCA 1978)★★, *Hypothesis* (Affinity 1978)★★, *Odes* (1978)★★, *Opera Sauvage* (Polydor 1979)★★, *China* (Polydor 1979)★★★, *See You Later* (Polydor 1980)★★, *Chariots Of Fire* film soundtrack (Polydor 1981)★★★, *To The Unknown Man* (RCA 1982)★★, *Soil Festivities* (Polydor 1984)★★, *Ignacio* soundtrack (Phonogram 1985)★★, *Invisible Connections* (Deutsche Grammophon 1985)★★, *The Mask* (Polydor 1985)★, *Direct* (Arista 1988)★★, *Antarctica* film soundtrack (Polydor 1988)★★, *The City* (East West 1990)★★★, *1492 - Conquest Of Paradise* film soundtrack (East West 1992)★★, *Entends - Tu Les Chiens* (1993)★★, *Voices* (Atlantic 1995)★★, *Oceanic* (Atlantic 1997)★★; as Jon And Vangelis *Short Stories* (Polydor 1980)★★, *The Friends Of Mr Cairo* (Polydor 1981)★★, *Private Collection* (Polydor 1983)★★, *Page Of Life* (Arista 1991)★★.

●COMPILATIONS: *The Best Of Vangelis* (RCA 1981)★★★, *Themes* (Polydor 1989)★★★.

VAPORS

This power pop quartet, based in Guildford, Surrey, England, came together officially in April 1979, although an earlier incarnation had existed a year earlier. The common thread was Dave Fenton, a graduate who dabbled in the legal profession before turning to music. His first band, the Little Jimmies, was formed while he studied at Nottingham University. To his rhythm guitar and vocals were added the lead guitar of Ed Bazalgette and the drums of Howard Smith, both former members of Ellery Bop. The line-up was completed by former Absolute drummer Steve Smith, who switched over to bass guitar. An early Vapors gig was watched by the Jam's Bruce Foxton who was impressed by their gutsy pop, not unlike the Jam's own style, and invited them to appear on the *Setting Sons* tour Foxton also became the band's manager in partnership with John Weller. After a promising but unsuccessful debut single, 'Prisoners' for United Artists, the follow-up 'Turning Japanese' catapulted them to number 3 in the UK charts. By May 1980 *New Clear Days* was released. The most notable track was the single, 'News At Ten', which underlined teenage insecurity with a power pop beat that recalled the Kinks. *Magnets* was more adventurous, with the lyrical focus moving from the Oriental to Americana. Unfortunately the band were receiving few plaudits for their ambitious efforts, with most critics unable to move away from the earlier Jam comparisons, which were no longer valid. The band disappeared from the scene quickly; the most recent sighting of Dave Fenton was as the landlord of a public house in Woking, Surrey. Steve Smith joined with ex-World Domination Enterprises bass player Steve Jameson to form Cut.

●ALBUMS: *New Clear Days* (United Artists 1980)★★, *Magnets* (United Artists 1981)★★.
●COMPILATIONS: *Turning Japanese: The Best Of The Vapours* (EMI 1996)★★★.

VAUGHAN, JIMMIE

b. 20 March 1951, Dallas, Texas, USA. Vaughan began playing rock music as an adolescent and worked with several local bands, moving nearer to the blues with each one, finally establishing a formidable reputation as a guitar player. In 1968 he saw Muddy Waters, and from then on concentrated almost exclusively on blues. He moved to Austin, Texas, in 1970 and formed the Fabulous Thunderbirds in 1975. The band were often cited as one of the prime movers in the blues revival in 80s America, with Vaughan's stylish, pared-down and economical guitar playing a major factor. He recorded on many sessions and left the Thunderbirds in 1990 to work with his brother Stevie Ray Vaughan, shortly before the latter's death.

●ALBUMS: with Stevie Ray Vaughan as the Vaughan Brothers *Family Style* (Epic 1990)★★★★, *Strange Pleasure* (Epic 1994)★★★.

VAUGHAN, MAURICE JOHN

b. 10 May 1952, Chicago, Illinois, USA. A self-taught blues musician, Vaughan began playing at the age of 12. Although he was primarily known as a guitarist and saxophonist, he also played piano and bass guitar. His influences include Howlin' Wolf, Elmore James and particularly Albert King. After appearing on several sessions (including Phil Guy's), he released his debut album on his own Reecy label in 1984. It was later picked up by Alligator; he also recorded for that label's *New Bluesblood* anthology in 1987, as well as for the French label Blue Phoenix. In 1988 *Guitar Player* magazine included him in its listing of the greatest working blues musicians.

●ALBUMS: *Generic Blues* (Reecy 1984)★★★, *Shadow Of The City* (1993)★★★.

VAUGHAN, STEVIE RAY

b. 3 October 1954, Dallas, Texas, USA, d. 27 August 1990, East Troy, Wisconsin, USA. This blues guitarist was influenced by his older brother Jimmie (of the Fabulous Thunderbirds), whose record collection included such key Vaughan motivators as Albert King, Otis Rush and Lonnie Mack. He honed his style on his brother's hand-me-down guitars in various high school bands, before moving to Austin in 1972. He joined the Nightcrawlers, then Paul Ray And The Cobras, with whom he recorded 'Texas Clover' in 1974. In 1977 he formed Triple Threat Revue with vocalist Lou Ann Barton. She later fronted Vaughan's most successful project, named Double Trouble after an Otis Rush standard, for a short period after its inception in 1979. The new band also featured drummer Chris Layton and ex-Johnny Winter bassist Tommy Shannon. Producer Jerry Wexler, an early fan, added them to the bill of the 1982 Montreux Jazz Festival, where Vaughan was spotted and hired by David Bowie for his forthcoming *Let's Dance* (1983). Vaughan turned down Bowie's subsequent world tour, however, to rejoin his own band and record *Texas Flood* with veteran producer John Hammond. *Couldn't Stand The Weather* showed the influence of Jimi Hendrix, and earned the band its first platinum disc; in February 1985, they picked up a Grammy for their contribution to the *Blues Explosion* anthology.

Soul To Soul saw the addition of keyboards player Reese Wynans; Vaughan, by this point a much sought after guitarist, could also be heard on records by James Brown, Johnny Copeland, and his mentor, Lonnie Mack. The period of extensive substance abuse that produced the lacklustre *Live Alive* led to Vaughan's admittance to a Georgia detoxification centre. His recovery was apparent on *In Step*, which won a second Grammy. In 1990 the Vaughan brothers worked together with Bob Dylan, on their own *Family Style*, and as guests on Eric Clapton's American tour. Vaughan died in 1990, at East Troy, Wisconsin, USA, when, anxious to return to Chicago after Clapton's Milwaukee show, he switched helicopter seats and boarded a vehicle which crashed, in dense fog, into a ski hill. Vaughan was a magnificent ambassador for the blues, whose posthumous reputation continues to increase. Plans to erect an 9-foot bronze statue to the guitarist in his hometown of Austin went ahead in October 1992.

●ALBUMS: *Texas Flood* (Epic 1983)★★★★, *Couldn't Stand The Weather* (Epic 1984)★★★★, *Soul To Soul* (Epic 1985)★★★★, *Live Alive* (Epic 1986)★★★, *In Step* (Epic 1989)★★★★, as the Vaughan Brothers *Family Style* (Epic 1990)★★★★, *The Sky Is Crying* (Epic 1991)★★★★, with Double Trouble *In The Beginning* rec. 1980 (Epic 1992)★★★.
●VIDEOS: *Live At The El Mocambo* (Epic 1992), *Live From Austin Texas* (Epic Music Video 1995).
●FURTHER READING: *Stevie Ray Vaughan: Caught In The Crossfire*, Joe Nick Patoski and Bill Crawford.

VEGA, SUZANNE

b. 12 August 1959, New York City, New York, USA. Vega is a highly literate singer-songwriter who found international success in the late 80s. She studied dance at the High School For the Performing Arts (as featured in the *Fame* television series) and at Barnard College, singing her own material in New York folk clubs. Signed by A&M Records in 1984, she recorded her first album with Lenny Kaye, former guitarist with Patti Smith. From this, 'Marlene On The Wall', a tale of bedsitter angst, became a hit. In 1987 'Luka' grabbed even more attention with its evocation of the pain of child abuse told from the victim's point of view. Vega's 'Left Of Center' appeared on the soundtrack of the film *Pretty In Pink* and she also contributed lyrics for two tracks on *Songs From Liquid Days* by Philip Glass. On her third album, Vega collaborated with keyboards player and co-producer Anton Sanko, who brought a new tightness to the sound. Meanwhile, Vega's lyrics took on a more surreal and precise character, notably on 'Book Of Dreams' and 'Men In A War', which dealt with the plight of amputees. In 1990 the serendipitous 'Tom's Diner' from *Solitude Standing* became a hit in Britain after it had been sampled by the group DNA. The track was remixed by Alan Coulthard for Vega's label A&M; its success led to the release of an album, *Tom's Album* (1991), devoted entirely to reworkings of the song by such artists as R.E.M. and rapper Nikki D. Vega was presumably bemused by the whole series of events. The promise that Vega gave has faded considerably in the 90s as little impression has been made since her first two albums. *Nine Objects Of Desire* was a move into a smoother sound, in her own words, 'sexier and less defiant'.
●ALBUMS: *Suzanne Vega* (A&M 1985)★★★★, *Solitude Standing* (A&M 1987)★★, *Days Of Open Hand* (A&M 1990)★★, *99.9°F* (A&M 1992)★★★, *Nine Objects Of Desire* (A&M 1996)★★★.

VELVET MONKEYS

Formed in Washington, DC, USA, the Velvet Monkeys made their recording debut in 1981 with *Everything Is Right*, a cassette-only collection issued on their own label. It revealed a love of pop culture from the 50s and 60s which was imbued with post-punk/hardcore love of noisy guitar patterns. This style was repeated on *Future*. In 1986 the Velvet Monkeys recorded the cassette-only *Big Big Sun*, a collaboration with Half Japanese, issued on Beat Happening's label, K. This collection accentuated the group's leanings towards pop's *avant garde*. The Velvet Monkeys split up in 1986 and their early incarnation is commemorated on the compilation, *Rotting Corpse Au Go-Go*. Group members Don Fleming (guitar/vocals) and Jay Spiegel (drums) moved to New York, USA, where they joined Mark Kramer in B.A.L.L. When B.A.L.L. disbanded Fleming revived the Velvet Monkeys for *Rake*, a 70s-influenced 'soundtrack' album. On this he was aided by Thurston Moore (Sonic Youth), J Mascis (Dinosaur Jr) and Julia Cafritz (ex-Pussy Galore). Fleming also enjoyed success as a producer, notably with Teenage Fanclub's *Bandwagonesque*.
●ALBUMS: *Everything Is Right* cassette only (Monkey Business 1981)★★, *Future* (Fountain Of Youth 1983)★★, *Rake* (Rough Trade 1990)★★.
●COMPILATIONS: *Rotting Corpse Au Go-Go* (Shimmy-Disc 1989)★★★.

VENOM

This influential English black metal band, who were a major influence on thrash pioneers Metallica, Slayer and Possessed, as well as the satanic fraternity, were formed in Newcastle Upon Tyne by Cronos (b. Conrad Lant; bass/vocals), Mantas (b. Geoff Dunn; guitar) and Abaddon (b. Tony Bray; drums). Their debut was the legendary *Welcome To Hell*, a raw collection of brutal songs filled with dark, satanic imagery. *Black Metal* was better in terms of playing and production, and remains Venom's best album, containing the atmospheric 'Buried Alive' amid the more customary speed bursts. *At War With Satan*, a semi-concept album, and numerous singles followed - BBC Radio One DJ Tommy Vance paid £100 to charity when Mike Read played 'Warhead' on his breakfast show for a bet - and Venom played numerous major shows worldwide (club dates were precluded by the nature of Venom's pyrotechnics, which tended to cause structural damage in enclosed spaces), proudly refusing to be anything but headliners. However, the poor *Possessed* and a spate of unofficial live and compilation releases hurt the band, and Mantas left as the *Eine Kleine Nachtmusik* live set emerged. Mike H and Jimi C were recruited for live commitments, and this line-up produced the commendable power metal of *Calm Before The Storm* before Cronos left, taking both guitarists for his Cronos band. Mantas, however, rejoined Abaddon, bringing rhythm guitarist Al Barnes, and the new Venom was completed by ex-Atomkraft bassist/vocalist Tony 'The Demolition Man' Dolan. *Prime Evil* harked back to the early Venom approach, albeit with rather more professionalism, and contained a good cover of Black Sabbath's 'Megalomania', but subsequent releases have yet to emulate these standards. Venom, already the subject of a tribute album, remain among the most important of all heavy metal acts, having originated a style which became a template for many of the music's modern practitioners.

●ALBUMS: *Welcome To Hell* (Neat 1981)★★★, *Black Metal* (Neat 1982)★★★, *At War With Satan* (Neat 1984)★★, *Possessed* (Neat 1985)★★, *Eine Kleine Nachtmusik* (Neat 1985)★★, *Calm Before The Storm* (Filmtrax 1987)★★, *Prime Evil* (Under One Flag 1989)★★★, *Tear Your Soul Apart* (Under One Flag 1990)★★, *Temples Of Ice* (Under One Flag 1991)★★, *The Waste Lands* (Under One Flag 1993)★★, *The Second Coming* (Nuclear Blast 1997)★★.

●COMPILATIONS: *The Singles '80 - '86* (Raw Power 1986)★★★.

VIOLENT FEMMES

From Milwaukee, Wisconsin, USA, the Violent Femmes comprise Gordon Gano (b. 7 June 1963, New York, USA; vocals/guitar), Brian Ritchie (b. 21 November 1960, Milwaukee, Wisconsin, USA; bass) and Victor De Lorenzo (b. 25 October 1954, Racine, Wisconsin, USA; drums). Gano and Ritchie first teamed up for an acoustic set at the Rufus King High School, Ritchie having formerly played with Plasticland (one single, 'Mushroom Hill'/'Color Appreciation'). Joined by De Lorenzo, they recorded a debut album (through Rough Trade Records in the UK). Its rough, acoustic style failed to hide the Femmes' intriguing variety of songs and lyrics; and although they have since mellowed, this formed the basis of what was to follow. Two acclaimed singles, 'Gone Daddy Gone' and 'It's Gonna Rain' (both 1984) were drawn from *Violent Femmes* before *Hallowed Ground* followed a year later, a more full-bodied work that lacked the

shambolic nature of their debut. *Hallowed Ground* contained, what is for many, the classic Violent Femmes composition, the macabre 'Country Death Song'. *The Blind Leading The Naked* nearly gave the group a hit single in their cover of T. Rex's 'Children Of The Revolution' early in 1986. There was then a long pause in the Femmes' activities while Gordon Gano appeared with his side-project, the gospel-influenced Mercy Seat, and Ritchie recorded two solo sets for the SST Records label, and one for Dali-Chameleon. De Lorenzo released 'Peter Corey Sent Me' in 1991 and played on Sigmund Snpek III's album, which also featured Ritchie. The release of the succinctly titled *3* re-introduced a more sophisticated Violent Femmes, although the grisly subject matter continued, while 1991's *Why Do Birds Sing?* included a savage version of the Culture Club hit, 'Do You Really Want To Hurt Me?'

●ALBUMS: *Violent Femmes* (Slash 1983)★★★, *Hallowed Ground* (Slash 1984)★★, *The Blind Leading The Naked* (Slash 1986)★★★, *3* (Slash 1989)★★, *Why Do Birds Sing?* (Slash 1991)★★, *New Times* (Elektra 1994)★★★.

●COMPILATIONS: *Add It Up (1981-1993)* (Slash 1993)★★★.

Solo: Gordon Gano in Mercy Seat *The Mercy Seat* (Slash 1988)★★. Brian Ritchie *The Blend* (SST 1987)★★, *Sonic Temple And The Court Of Babylon* (SST 1989)★★.

VIRGIN PRUNES

This Irish performance art/*avant garde* musical ensemble was originally formed in 1976. Fionan Hanvey, better known under his pseudonym Gavin Friday, was invited by Paul Hewson (later Bono of U2) to join a group of Dublin youths with artistic leanings who were inspired by the new wave explosion in the UK. A rough community had been formed under the title of the Village, a social club bound in secrecy. The Virgin Prunes became an official band, and an extension of the Village, by the end of 1977. Friday was joined by Guggi (Derek Rowen) and Dave-id (b. David Watson; vocals), Strongman (b. Trevor Rowen; bass), Dik Evans (brother of U2's The Edge; guitar) and Pod (b. Anthony Murphy; drums). Early gigs were very much performance events, with audiences bemused by the expectations placed on them. However, by the turn of the decade they had attracted strong cult support, and on the strength of the self-financed 'Twenty Tens', were signed to Rough Trade Records. Pod was the band's first casualty, opting out of their new disaffected religious stance. As a manifestation of their unconventional approach their first album was initially released as a set of 7, 10 and 12-inch singles, with component parts making up *New Forms Of Beauty*. After the brief tenure of Haa Lacka Binttii, Mary O'Nellon took over on drums. His instalment was in time for the band's second, and first complete album, *If I Die . . . I Die*. Less experimental and perverse than its predecessor, it continued nevertheless to explore the tenets of purity and beauty. At the same time a mixed studio/live album, *Heresie*, was released, which emphasized that the performance art aspect of the group had not been totally neglected. By 1984 Guggi had become disenchanted with the music industry and departed. When Dik Evans defected for similar reasons, O'Nellon switched to guitar and Pod rejoined as drummer. 1986's *The Moon Looked Down And Laughed* witnessed another change in direction. Produced by Soft Cell's Dave Ball, it consisted largely of ballads and melodic pop, with little hint of the band's usual confrontational approach. However, following the continued lack of response from the record-buying public, Friday called a halt to his involvement with the band. Subsequent solo endeavours from former members failed to sustain the Virgin Prunes' original spirit of adventure, although Gavin Friday's *Adam And Eve* set attracted music press acclaim.

●ALBUMS: *New Forms Of Beauty* (Rough Trade 1981)★★, *If I Die ... I Die* (Rough Trade 1982)★★★, *Heresie* (L'invitation Au Suicide 1982)★★, *The Moon Looked Down And Laughed* (Baby 1986)★★★, *Hidden Lie* (Baby 1986)★★.

VISAGE

A synthesizer 'jamming' band fronted by Steve Strange (b. Steve Harrington, 28 May 1959, Wales). Other members of the band included Midge Ure (b. James Ure, 10 October 1953, Cambuslang, Scotland; guitar), Rusty Egan (b. 19 September 1957), Billy Currie (b. 1 April 1952; violin), Dave Formula (keyboards), John McGeogh (guitar) and Barry Adamson (bass). The last three were all members of Magazine. Ure rose to fame with teenybopper stars Slik before joining the Rich Kids with whom Egan played drums. Both Egan and Ure also played in the short-lived Misfits during 1979 before Egan briefly joined the Skids and Ure linked with Thin Lizzy, then replaced John Foxx in Ultravox. Billy Currie was also in both Ultravox and Visage, not to mention Gary Numan's band at more or less the same time. The roots of Visage came about in late 1978 when Ure and Strange recorded a version of the old Zager And Evans' hit 'In The Year 2525' as a demo for EMI Records but had it turned down. The duo started recruiting instead, picking up the above-named musicians for rehearsals. The demo was hawked to Radar Records who signed them and released their first single, 'Tar', which concerned the joys of smoking. It was produced by Martin Rushent. Any hopes of releasing a follow-up on the label were dashed when Radar's parent company pulled the purse-strings tight and wound up the label. Polydor picked up on the band and were rewarded with a massive hit in 'Fade To Grey', which fitted in with the burgeoning synthesizer pop scene of the early 80s (New Romanticism). Although all of the band had other commitments Visage made a brief effort to continue their existence. The third single, 'Mind Of A Toy', with its memorable Godley And Creme-produced video (their first), was a Top 20 hit but subsequent singles were released at greater and greater intervals and did increasingly less well. The band fizzled out in the mid-80s, with Strange forming Strange Cruise with Wendy Wu (ex-Photos), and his collaborators returning to their main bands.

●ALBUMS: *Visage* (Polydor 1980)★★, *The Anvil* (Polydor 1982)★★, *Beat Boy* (Polydor 1994)★★.
●COMPILATIONS: *The Singles Collection* (Polydor 1983)★★★.

WAH!

Alongside the Teardrop Explodes and Echo And The Bunnymen, Wah!, led by the freewheeling Pete Wylie (guitar/vocals) through its various incarnations (Wah! Heat, Mighty Wah!, etc.), prompted a second beat boom in Liverpool, Merseyside, England, during the early 80s. Indeed, Wylie had originally been part of the historically brief but important Crucial 3 with Julian Cope and Ian McCulloch. Whereas those bands opted for a pristine guitar pop aesthetic, Wylie and Wah! were all pop melodrama and bluster. Occasionally they lacked the technical abilities to pull off some of their grand arrangements, especially when tackling the big soul ballads, but Wylie was always a supremely entertaining front man and amusing performer. His various collaborators included Colin Redmond (guitar), Oddball Washington (bass), Rob Jones (drums), Joe Musker (drums), Steven Johnson (guitar), John Maher (drums), Chris Joyce (drums), Charlie Griffiths (keyboards), Jay Naughton (piano) and many others, plus a brass section. Of these Washington enjoyed the longest tenure. The albums Wah! left behind are remarkably inconsistent, and a more informed purchase would be WEA Records 1984 compilation of the group's singles, *The Way We Wah!*. This included 'Come Back' and 'Hope', plus the group's major UK chart success, 'Story Of The Blues'. Afterwards Wylie became a solo artist with the release of 1987's *Sinful* for Virgin Records. Afterwards Wylie's reputation became that of 'expert ligger', partying throughout the north west and England as a 'face about town'. When fellow Liverpudlians the Farm broke through in the 90s the good-humoured Wylie was frequently to be seen accompanying them on record and stage.

●ALBUMS: *Nah = Poo - The Art Of Bluff* (Eternal 1981)★★, as Mighty Wah! *A Word To The Wise Guy* (Beggars Banquet 1984)★★.

●COMPILATIONS: *The Maverick Years '80 -'81* (Wonderful World 1982)★★, as Mighty Wah! *The Way We Wah!* (Warners 1984)★★★.

WAITE, JOHN

b. 4 July 1955, Lancaster, Lancashire, England. Waite is a singer, bassist and occasional harmonica player who has found greater fame and fortune in the USA than in his native land. A former art student, he began playing in bands in the late 60s and in 1976 formed the Babys with Mike Corby (b. 3 July 1955, England), Tony Brock (b. 31 March 1954, Bournemouth, Dorset, England) and Walter Stocker (b. 17 March 1954, London, England). They were signed to Chrysalis Records on the strength of a video demo directed by Mike Mansfield - a rather unique sales pitch at the time, but their brand of rock had become unfashionable in the UK and the Babys relocated to the USA where their career flourished. Corby was replaced by Ricky Phillips in 1977 and Jonathan Cain (later of Journey) joined the following year. The Babys split in 1981 after five albums and Waite embarked on a solo career. His debut single, 'Change', was not a chart hit and he had to wait until 'Missing You' was released from his second album for a breakthrough. In the UK the record made a respectable number 9 but in the US it went to the top. Waite formed the No Brakes band, joined by former David Bowie guitarist Earl Slick, to promote the new album, but Waite did not scale the same heights again. Instead, he formed the ill-fated Bad English in 1989, before resuming his solo career in the mid-90s. In 1995 he had his first hit for several years with the power ballad 'How Did I Get By Without You'. The album *Temple Bar* was more in the folk rock line and included covers of songs by Hank Williams and Bill Withers.

●ALBUMS: *Ignition* (Chrysalis 1982)★★, *No Brakes* (EMI America 1984)★★, *Mask Of Smiles* (Capitol 1985)★★, *Rovers Return* (EMI America 1987)★★, *Temple Bar* (Imago 1995)★★.

●COMPILATIONS: *The Essential* (EMI America 1992)★★★.

WAITRESSES

Formed in 1978 in Akron, Ohio, USA, the Waitresses were a new wave/pop band which achieved moderate popularity after relocating to the New York area in the early 80s. The group was led by Chris Butler (guitar, formerly of Tin Huey, an Akron, Ohio-based *avant garde* rock band), Patty Donahue (d. 1997; vocals), Dan Klayman (keyboards), Mars Williams (saxophone), Tracy Warmworth (bass), and Billy Ficca (drums, ex-Television). After releasing an independent single on the Clone label in 1978, the Waitresses signed to the PolyGram subsidiary Ze Records in 1982. Their single 'I Know What Boys Like', which cast Donahue as a tease who delighted in *not* giving boys what they liked, was a popular dance hit in clubs and received substantial college radio airplay, reaching number 62 in the USA. The debut, *Wasn't Tomorrow Wonderful?*, on Polydor Records, received critical acclaim and was their highest-charting record at number 41. The group's 1982 mini-album was issued in the USA under the title *I Could Rule The World If I Could Only Get The Parts*, and in the UK as *Make The Weather*; the US version featured 'Christmas Wrapping', which became a popular rap hit in clubs.

● ALBUMS: *Wasn't Tomorrow Wonderful?* (Polydor 1982)★★★, *I Could Rule The World If I Could Only Get The Parts* (Polydor 1982)★★, *Bruiseology* (Polydor 1983)★★.

● COMPILATIONS: *Best Of* (Polydor 1990)★★★.

WAITS, TOM

b. 7 December 1949, Pomona, California, USA. A gifted lyricist, composer and raconteur, Tom Waits began performing in the late 60s, inspired by a spell working as a doorman in a San Diego nightclub. Here he saw a miscellany of acts - string bands, comedians, C&W singers - and by absorbing portions of an attendant down-market patois, developed his nascent songwriting talent. Having appeared at the Los Angeles Troubador 'Amateur Hoot Nights', Waits was signed by manager Herb Cohen who in turn secured a recording contract with Asylum Records. *Tom Waits* revealed a still unfocused performer, as yet unable to draw together the folk, blues and singer-songwriter elements vying for prominence. It did contain 'Ol' 55', later covered by the Eagles, and 'Martha', a poignant melodrama of a now-middle-aged man telephoning his first love from 40 years previously. *The Heart Of Saturday Night* was an altogether more accomplished set in which the artist blended characterizations drawn from diners, truckers and waitresses, sung in a razor-edged, rasping voice, and infused with beatnik prepossessions. Waits' ability to paint blue-collar American life is encapsulated in its haunting, melodic title track. *Nighthawks At The Diner*, an in-concert set, and *Small Change*, closed the performer's first era, where the dividing line between life and art grew increasingly blurred as Waits inhabited the flophouse life about which he sang. *Foreign Affairs* unveiled a widening perspective and while the influence of 'Beat' writers Jack Kerouac and Allen Ginsberg still inhabited his work - as celebrated in

'Jack And Neal/California Here I Come' - a duet with Bette Midler, 'I Never Talk To Strangers', provided the impetus for his film soundtrack to *One From The Heart*. *Blue Valentine* was marked by its balance between lyrical ballads and up-front R&B, a contrast maintained on *Heartattack And Vine*. A tough combo prevailed on half of its content. Elsewhere, the composer's gift for emotive melody flourished on 'Jersey Girl', later covered by Bruce Springsteen. The album marked the end of Waits' term with both Cohen and Asylum; in 1983 he opted for Island Records and signalled a new musical direction with the radical *Swordfishtrombones*. Exotic instruments, sound textures and offbeat rhythms marked a content which owed more to Captain Beefheart and composer Harry Partch than dowdy motel rooms. Waits came close to having a hit single in 1983 with the evocative 'In The Neighbourhood', complete with a stunning sepia video. Waits also emphasized his interest in cinema with acting roles in *Rumble Fish*, *Down By Law* and *Ironweed*, in the process completing the exemplary *Rain Dogs*, which featured support from Keith Richard(s) on 'Big Black Mariah'. It also included 'Downtown Train', another in a series of romantic vignettes and later a hit for Rod Stewart. Waits' next release, *Frank's Wild Years*, comprised material drawn from a play written with his wife Kathleen Brennan and based on a song from *Swordfishtrombones*. *Big Time*, meanwhile, was the soundtrack to a concert film, since which the artist's recording career has been distinctly low-key. He continued his cinematic career with roles in *Candy Mountain* and *Cold Feet* and in 1989 Waits made his theatrical debut in *Demon Wine*. *Bone Machine* in 1992 was for many his finest album, although this perplexing genius still is only a cult figure. He entered into litigation in 1993 with his objection to the use of his 'Heartattack And Vine', with Screamin' Jay Hawkins' voice for a Levi's television advertisement. A grovelling public apology was made via the national music press from Levi's in 1995. Similarly he won his case against his previous music publisher for other songs licensed for television advertising, notably 'Ruby's Arms' and 'Opening Montage/Once Upon A Town'.

● ALBUMS: *Closing Time* (Asylum 1973)★★★, *The Heart Of Saturday Night* (Asylum 1974)★★★, *Nighthawks At The Diner* (Asylum 1975)★★★, *Small Change* (Asylum 1976)★★★★, *Foreign Affairs* (Asylum 1977)★★★, *Blue Valentine* (Asylum 1978)★★★★ *Heartattack And Vine* (Asylum 1980)★★★★, with Crystal Gayle *One From The*

Heart (Columbia 1982)★★★★, *Swordfishtrombones* (Island 1983)★★★★, *Rain Dogs* (Island 1985)★★★★, *Frank's Wild Years* (Island 1987)★★★, *Big Time* (Island 1988)★★★, *Night On Earth* film soundtrack (ISL 1992)★★★, *Bone Machine* (Island 1992)★★★★, *The Black Rider* (Island 1993)★★★.

●COMPILATIONS: *Bounced Checks* (Asylum 1981)★★★, *Asylum Years* (Asylum 1986)★★★★, *The Early Years Volume 1* (Bizarre/Straight 1991)★★★, *The Early Years Volume 2* (Bizarre/Straight 1993)★★.

●FURTHER READING: *Small Change: A Life Of Tom Waits*, Patrick Humphries.

WALKABOUTS

The Walkabouts are from Seattle, USA, and consist of Chris Eckman (vocals/guitar), a philosophy graduate, and Carla Torgerson (vocals/guitar). Two brothers, Curt (bass) and Grant Eckman (drums), were also in the band, but Curt left early on and was replaced by Michael Wells, while Glenn Slater (keyboards) joined in 1989. In 1992 Terri Moeller replaced Grant Eckman on drums and at the same time Bruce Wirth joined to provide pedal steel guitar and mandolin. The Walkabouts, who took their name from the Nicolas Roeg film, *Walkabout*, were formed on the understanding that 'twisting a take on punk didn't rule out a love for Appalachian mountain music'. Early on their energized folk rock was restricted by limited budget recordings, beginning with a self-titled cassette EP in 1984. It was *Cataract* in 1989 that truly announced their arrival, with its fine songs including the stinging lament, 'Hell's Soup Kitchen'. *Scavenger* had a bigger budget and helped the band become a major draw in America and Europe. *Satisfied Mind* was an album of cover versions, taking its material from blues, country and rock. Guests on the album included Peter Buck (R.E.M.), Mark Lanegan (Screaming Trees) and Ivan Kral (Patti Smith Group), while the songs covered included ones by Nick Cave, Neil Young and Charlie Rich. *Setting The Woods On Fire*, its title taken from the Hank Williams song, was a strong collection of original material accompanied by fiddle, pedal steel guitar, mandolin and the mysterious Tiny Hat Orchestra, and saw the band court comparisons to a 90s version of Neil Young And Crazy Horse. *Devil's Road* was their most commercial album and alienated them from some old fans in hoping to bring them many new ones. Even with the addition of the lush Warsaw Philharmonic Orchestra their new label Virgin must have been slightly disappointed at the reception it was given.

●ALBUMS: *The Walkabouts* tape-only EP (Necessity 1984)★★, *22 Disasters* mini-album (Necessity 1984)★★, *See Beautiful Rattlesnake Gardens* (PopLlama Products 1987)★★, *Cataract* (Sub Pop 1989)★★★, *Rag & Bone* mini-album (Sub Pop 1990)★★★, *Scavenger* (Sub Pop 1991)★★★, *New West Motel* double album (Sup Pop 1993)★★★, *Satisfied Mind* (Sub Pop 1993)★★★, *Setting The Woods On Fire* (Sub Pop 1994)★★★, *Devil's Road* (Virgin 1996)★★★.

WALKING SEEDS

Liverpool's premier psychedelic 'grunge' specialists arose early in 1986 out of the ashes of the Mel-O-Tones. In-between, John Neesam (drums), Frank Martin (vocals) and Bob Parker (bass/guitar) formed the Corinthians for three months, recording a seven-track demo that formed the basis of the Walking Seeds set. The group's first EP, *Know Too Much* (1986), set the pace, fronted by the strong 'Tantric Wipeout'. By the time of the follow-up, 'Mark Chapman' (1987), Neesam had been replaced by two former members of Marshmallow Overcoat, Tony Mogan (drums) and Baz Sutton (guitar). This was followed by the extreme but patchy *Skullfuck* (the title influenced by a Grateful Dead album cover) later that year. After lying low, the band signed to Glass Records, issuing *Upwind Of Disaster, Downwind Of Atonement* in 1989. Recorded in New York, the presence of Bongwater's Mark Kramer as producer helped create a more defined, but nevertheless uncompromising aura to the proceedings. Sutton left to join the La's and was briefly replaced by Andy Rowan for 1989's *Shaved Beatnik* EP (wherein the band admirably slaughtered Cream's 'Sunshine Of Your Love'). The mini-album, *Sensory Deprivation Chamber Quartet Dwarf*, was assisted by psychedelic wizard Nick 'Bevis Frond' Saloman and new bassist Lee Webster. When Glass folded, the Walking Seeds recorded 'Gates Of Freedom' (1990) which included a b-side cover of Pink Floyd's 'Astronomy Dominé'. This coincided with *Bad Orb ...Whirling Ball*, a more considered but still aggressively garage-like effort. The Seeds tore through Bevis Frond's 'Reflections In A Tall Mirror' (1990), backed by Bevis's interpretation of the band's 'Sexorcist'. But at this point, the band 'self-destructed', despondent about their lack of success, despite recruiting ex-Dinosaur Jr guitarist Don Fleming. A swan-song was offered in *Earth Is Hell* on the Snakeskin label, housing live material recorded in Germany earlier that year. Tony and Bob then set up the Del-Bloods, issuing 'Black

Rabbit' (1991). The pair also surfaced in White Bitch for 'Animal Woman' and teamed up with Martin for Batloaf's 'Meat Out Of Hell' soon afterwards. Webster, meanwhile, had joined Baz Sutton in Froth that same year.

●ALBUMS: *Skullfuck* (Probe 1987)★★, *Upwind Of Disaster, Downwind Of Atonement* (Communion 1989)★★★, *Sensory Deprivation Chamber Quartet Dwarf* (Glass 1989)★★, *Bad Orb ... Whirling Ball* (Shimmy-Disc 1990)★★★, *Earth Is Hell* (Snakeskin 1990)★★.

WALL OF VOODOO

Formed in Los Angeles, California, USA, in the immediate punk aftermath, Wall Of Voodoo was initially comprised of Stan Ridgway (vocals/keyboards), Bill Noland (guitar/vocals), Charles Gray (bass/keyboards/synthesizer) and Joe Nanini (drums). However, by the release of *Dark Continent*, Noland had been replaced by Marc Moreland while Bruce Moreland had been added on bass. The latter was then dropped for *Call Of The West*, arguably the unit's finest album, on which their sense of rhythm and wash of synthesizer lines underscored Ridgway's droning, offhand vocals. Any potential this offered was sadly sundered with the singer's departure in 1985. While Ridgway enjoyed a UK Top 5 single with 'Camouflage', Wall Of Voodoo pursued a less successful career led by new vocalist Andy Prieboy. Further personnel changes undermined the group's progress and subsequent albums, although of intermittent interest, lacked the adventure of their second set.

●ALBUMS: *Dark Continent* (IRS 1981)★★★, *Call Of The West* (IRS 1982)★★★, *Seven Days In Sammy's Town* (IRS 1985)★★, *Happy Planet* (IRS 1987)★★, *The Ugly Americans In Australia* (IRS 1988)★★.
●COMPILATIONS: *Grandma's House* (IRS 1984)★★★.

WANG CHUNG

This London-based new wave pop group was formed from the ashes of the Intellektuals and 57 Men. Originally called Huang Chung, they comprised Jack Hues (vocals/guitar), Nick Feldman (bass) and Darren Costin (drums). After four tracks featured on two 101 Records compilation albums, they released a 1980 single, 'Isn't It About Time We Were On Television?'. It was memorable enough to persuade Arista Records to sign the band in 1981. Despite an innovative first album which used prominent saxophone, they had pared back down to a trio by their second album. They went on to

achieve just one minor hit in the UK with 'Dance Hall Days' in 1984. However, they proved better suited to the US market where they enjoyed five Top 40 successes including the number 2 'Everybody Have Fun Tonight'. However, Costin left in 1985 when the band switched to A&M Records, then Geffen Records the following year. 'Hypnotise Me' was used in the 1987 feature film *Innerspace*.

●ALBUMS: *Huang Chung* (Arista 1982)★★★, *Points On A Curve* (Geffen 1984)★★, *Mosaic* (Geffen 1986)★★, *To Live And Die In LA* film soundtrack (Geffen 1986)★★, *The Warmer Side Of Cool* (Geffen 1989)★★.

WANGFORD, HANK

b Samuel Hutt, 15 November 1940, Wangford, Suffolk, England. Wangford's father, Allen Hutt, was chief sub-editor of the communist newspaper *The Daily Worker* and president of the National Union of Journalists. His mother taught English to Russian students. Wangford studied medicine at Cambridge University and later became a doctor. He was converted to country music by Gram Parsons who attended for treatment in 1971. After a period in the USA, Wangford became gradually more involved in country music and, despite the demands of his professional work, yearned to be a performer. When his girlfriend married his best friend, he consoled himself in a pub near the Wangford bypass in Suffolk. Here he devised the character of Hank Wangford, who would sing songs from the Wangford Hall of Pain. He says, 'Hank Wangford was a good name for the classic country star. He sings about pain, he sings about heartache, and that was good because Sam could go on living and being normal.' Starting in 1976, Wangford built a reputation on the London pub-rock circuit. His persona was both a glorification of country music and an affectionate parody of its excesses.

He formed Sincere Management (motto: 'It's in the post') and Sincere Products ('Brought to you with no regard to quality'). Wangford generated publicity as a gynaecologist-cum-country singer, often being photographed with a Harley Street sign. His media image, however, has proved more sustainable than the lightweight music which, in fairness, is highly successful in the pub/club environment. 'Chicken Rhythm' is derived from Ray Stevens' quirky 'In The Mood', and 'Cowboys Stay On Longer' is a close cousin to David Allan Coe's 'Divers Do It Deeper'. Wangford has always been able to surround himself with talented band members, notably Andy Roberts (Brad Breath) and

Melanie Harrold (Irma Cetas), who have more musical talent. His fiddler and co-singer, former member of the Fabulous Poodles and Clark Gable lookalike, Bobby Valentino, later embarked on a solo career. Wangford, with his ponytail, stubble and gap-toothed features is an engaging entertainer, creating a stage show 'Radio Wang' and presenting two country music series for Channel 4 television. He also works as the senior medical officer at a family planning clinic in London, and he says, 'I have had letters of referral from doctors which start 'Dear Dr. Wangford', so the transmogrification is complete.'

●ALBUMS: *Live: Hank Wangford* (Cow Pie 1982)★★, *Hank Wangford* (Cow Pie 1985)★★★, *Rodeo Radio* (Situation 2 1985)★★, *Stormy Horizons* (New Routes 1990)★★, *Hard Shoulder To Cry On* (1993)★★.

●FURTHER READING: *Hank Wangford, Vol.III The Middle Years*, Sam Hutt. *Lost Cowboys: From Patagonia To The Alamo*, Hank Wangford.

WARE, MARTYN

A founder-member of the Human League alongside Phil Oakey and Ian Craig Marsh, Ware departed after the albums *Reproduction* and *Travelogue* with Marsh to form Heaven 17. Heaven 17's career spanned several years, as did that of another Ware/Marsh offshoot, BEF (British Electronic Foundation). This 'collective' was announced with the release of *Music Of Quality And Distinction Vol. 1*, which also pointed the way to Ware's future career as a producer. Ware helped draw startling performances from some of soul and pop's foremost artists, including Chaka Khan, Mavis Staples, Billy MacKenzie (Associates), Lalah Hathaway, Paul Jones, Green Gartside (Scritti Politti), Gary Glitter and Sandie Shaw. Most important of all was Ware's treatment of Tina Turner on 'Let's Stay Together', an international hit which lifted that artist's career out of the mire (he would subsequently produce the huge seller, *Private Dancer*). Afterwards Ware produced Terence Trent D'Arby's spectacularly successful debut album. Other artists with whom he has worked in the 90s include Paul Weller (the *Council Collective* EP project), Dan Hartman (*Circle Of Light*), Jimmy Ruffin ('The Foolish Thing To Do'), Anabella LeWin (*Naked Experience*) and Hannah Jones (*What If*).

WARNES, JENNIFER

b. Seattle, Washington, USA. Warnes grew up in Orange County, California and first sang in public as a child. In 1967, her strong pop/MOR voice won a contract to appear (as Jennifer Warren) on the television series hosted by country group the Smothers Brothers. Her first recording session was a duet with Mason Williams and Warnes became part of the Los Angeles club scene. She also took a leading role in the west coast production of *Hair*. As a solo artist Warnes recorded unsuccessfully for Parrot and Reprise Records, where John Cale produced her 1972 album, before signing to Arista Records in 1975. There she had a Top 10 hit (and a country chart-topper) with 'Right Time Of The Night' in 1977 while 'I Know A Heartache When I See One' (1979) was also successful. During the 80s, Warnes gained a reputation as a singer of film themes after 'It Goes Like It Goes' from *Norma Rae* won an Oscar for Best Original Song in 1980. She performed Randy Newman's 'One More Hour' on the soundtrack of *Ragtime* before achieving her biggest hit in 1983 with 'Up Where We Belong'. A duet with Joe Cocker, the Oscar-winning song from *An Officer And A Gentleman* topped the US charts. Other film songs were 'Nights Are Forever' (from *The Twilight Zone: The Movie*) and 'All The Right Moves', sung with ex-Manfred Mann's Earthband vocalist Chris Thompson. Warnes again reached number 1 when she teamed up with Bill Medley for the *Dirty Dancing* theme, 'I've Had The Time Of My Life' in 1987. The previous year, she recorded a much-acclaimed selection of Leonard Cohen compositions, *Famous Blue Raincoat*. Warnes had first worked with Cohen on tour in 1973 and had created vocal arrangements for his *Recent Songs* (1979) as well as singing on his 1988 album *I'm Your Man*. Warnes co-produced her own 1992 album for Private Music as well as co-writing most of the songs. Among the musicians contributing were Richard Thompson, Van Dyke Parks and Donald Fagen.

●ALBUMS: *I Can Remember Everything* (Parrot 1968)★★, *See Me Feel Me, Touch Me Heal Me* (Parrot 1968)★★, *Jennifer* (Reprise 1972)★★★, *Jennifer Warnes* (Arista 1977)★★, *Shot Through the Heart* (Arista 1979)★★, *Famous Blue Raincoat* (RCA 1987)★★★★, *The Hunter* (Private 1992)★★★.

●COMPILATIONS: *The Best Of Jennifer Warnes* (Arista 1982)★★.

WARREN, DIANE

b. *c.*1956, Van Nuys, California, USA. With songs performed by Aretha Franklin, Cheap Trick, Cher, Chicago, Cyndi Lauper, Dusty Springfield, Elton John, Four Tops, Gladys Knight, Gloria Estefan, Joan Jett, John Waite, Joe Cocker, Heart, Roy Orbison, Celine Dion, the Jacksons, Tom Jones and Ziggy Marley, among well over one hundred others, 'Valley Girl' Warren is one of the most successful, gifted and prolific songwriters in the music industry. This, despite her guitar teacher having originally pronounced her tone deaf after her insurance salesman father brought home her first guitar, purchased in Tijuana, Mexico. Even as a child she maintained a constant output of compositions, until her family grew so weary of their constant repetition they erected a metal shed in the back yard in which she could practise. Having gleaned her interest in music from radio and her sisters' record collections, throughout she restrained any ambitions to perform her songs, electing instead to give them to a vast and grateful army of interpreters. Warren did struggle initially, however, only making songwriting a viable living by the time she was 24. She has less than fond memories of her initial attempts to enter the music industry: 'I got a lot of stupid advice. I remember one publisher looking at a verse of one of my songs and saying, "You have nine lines in this verse, you can only have eight lines. It has to be even."' However, always in place was the dedication which has hallmarked her career: 'I've written songs on Kotex, lyrics on the palm of my hand. If I don't have a tape recorder, I'll call home and sing into my answering machine'. She legendarily works over 12 hours a day, often seven days a week, ensconced in a tiny office-cum-studio. Before she became the hottest songwriting property in the contemporary US market she was also just as determined to see her work used - one anecdote concerns her falling on her knees to persuade Cher to sing 'If I Could Turn Back Time'. It became the artist's biggest hit for 15 years, and nowadays she has no need for such powers of persuasion. Her first major break had come when Laura Branigan recorded 'Solitaire', an MOR staple. By 1985 DeBarge had taken the altogether different 'Rhythm Of The Night' to number 3 in the *Billboard* charts and Warren was established as a major songwriting source to artists from almost every genre of popular music. She formed Realsongs in 1985 in response to contractual difficulties she experienced with former manager, and Laura Branigan producer, Jack White. Realsongs is administered by business colleague Doreen Dorion, who together with Ken Philips takes responsibility for placing Warren's songs with prospective artists. By now the hits were flowing freely, after the DeBarge hit had opened up a lucrative market to her. Some of her greatest compositions, such as 'Look Away' (Chicago), 'When I See You Smile' (Bad English),

'Blame It On The Rain' (Milli Vanilli), 'Love Will Lead You Back' (Taylor Dayne), 'Nothing's Gonna Stop Us Now' (Starship), 'I Get Weak' (Belinda Carlisle) and 'We're Not Making Love Anymore' (Barbra Streisand), were written between then and 1989. Her profile quickly earned her nicknames such as 'industry powerhouse' and 'hit machine'. Though she professes not to customize her material for such diverse artists, it is a source of considerable pleasure to her that critics have been unable to discern any 'house style', which is why she has been able to work with artists as diverse as Bette Midler and Bon Jovi. *Billboard* subsequently named Realsongs the top singles publisher of 1990. The flood of awards snowballed throughout the 90s. She has been voted Songwriter Of The Year by ASCAP in 1990, 1991 and 1993, Writer Of The Year in *Billboard* from 1990-93, and Songwriter Of The Year in the Los Angeles Music Awards in 1991. Realsongs has also remained in the Top 6 Publishing Corporations assessed by *Billboard* since 1990. By the mid-90s Warren had a staggering 100 million unit sales to her name, and 25 Top 10 US hits (including, at one point, holding the number 1 and 2 positions in the US singles chart via two separate artists). By now she had also moved heavily into film soundtracks, seeing her material aired on soundtracks including *Golden Child*, *Ghostbusters*, *License To Kill*, *White Men Can't Jump*, *Karate Kid III* and *Neverending Story III*. A *Billboard* special feature celebrated her achievements, interviewing several of the artists who had recorded her songs. One who regularly returns to her for his repertoire is Michael Bolton: 'She is destined to achieve her appropriate status as one of the greatest songwriters in the history of music.' Grace Slick offered a more personal tribute: 'I've never met anybody who is rolling around in that much fame and money who is that real, honest and funny.' One of the few writers qualified to assess her impact on the music scene as a genuine peer was Lamont Dozier: 'She's not only a gifted songwriter, but she seems to have a sixth sense about what music lovers want to hear.' Despite her multi-millionaire status and phenomenal success, Warren still maintains her stoic resistance to any interruption in her daunting work schedule.

WAS (NOT WAS)

An unlikely recording and production duo, childhood friends David Weiss (saxophone, flute, keyboards, vocals) and Don Fagenson (bass, keyboards, guitar) have used a variety of singers to front their records, including Sweat Pea Atkinson,

Leonard Cohen, Harry Bowens and Donny Ray Mitchell. Their debut album sought to imbue dance music with an intellectual credibility which it had previously lacked. While musicians were plucked from sources as varied as P-Funk and MC5, 'Tell Me That I'm Dreaming' incorporated a mutilated sample of a Ronald Reagan speech. 1983's *Born To Laugh At Tornadoes* included, bizarrely, Ozzy Osbourne rapping, and a snatch of Frank Sinatra. Geffen rewarded their eclecticism by dropping them. They moved on to Phonogram, managing to focus much more clearly on their prospective dance market in the process. Their biggest hit was the anthemic 'Walk The Dinosaur', which topped the US singles chart for six weeks, while 'Spy In The House Of Love' had similar crossover appeal. However, the music industry knows them better for their numerous production credits. These include the B-52's, Iggy Pop, Bonnie Raitt and Bob Dylan. The latter fulfilled an ambition for Weiss, who had long held Dylan as his personal idol. 1990's *Are You Okay?* was critically lauded, and they remain an enigmatic attraction on the periphery of the dance scene.
●ALBUMS: *Was (Not Was)* (Ze-Island 1981)★★★, *Born To Laugh At Tornadoes* (Ze-Island 1983)★★★, *What's Up, Dog?* (Chrysalis 1988)★★★, *Are You Okay?* (Chrysalis 1990)★★★.
●COMPILATIONS: *Hello Dad I'm In Jail* (Fontana 1992)★★★★.

WASHINGTON, GROVER, JNR.
b. 11 November 1943, Buffalo, New York, USA. Growing up in a musical family, Washington was playing tenor saxophone before he was a teenager. He studied formally and also paid his dues gigging locally on tenor and other instruments in the early 60s. After military service in the late 60s he returned to his career, recording a succession of albums under the aegis of producer Creed Taylor which effectively crossed over into the new market for jazz fusion. By the mid-70s, Washington's popular success had begun to direct the course of his music-making and he moved further away from jazz. Commercially, this brought continuing successes, among them 'The Two Of Us', with vocals by Bill Withers, which reached number 2 in the US pop charts in 1981, and the popular album *The Best Is Yet To Come* with Patti Labelle. Over the years Washington has had five gold albums. *Winelight* sold over a million copies, this achieving platinum status, and gained two Grammy awards. Washington's playing displays great technical mastery and early in his career his often blues-derived

saxophone styling sometimes gave his playing greater depths than the quality of the material warranted. The fact that much of his recorded output proved to be popular in the setting of discos tended to smooth out his playing as the years passed, depleting the characteristics that had attracted so much attention at the start of his career. By the late 80s Washington was still enjoying a degree of popular success, although not at the same high level as a few years earlier.
●ALBUMS: *Inner City Blues* (Motown 1971)★★, *All The King's Horses* (Motown 1972)★★, *Soul Box* (1973)★★, *Mister Magic* (Mister Magic 1975)★★★, *Feels So Good* (Motown 1975)★★★, *A Secret Place* (Motown 1976)★★★, *Live At The Bijou* (Motown 1977)★★★, with Locksmith *Reed Seed* (Motown 1978)★★, *Paradise* (Elektra 1979)★★★★, *Skylarkin'* (Motown 1980)★★★, *Winelight* (Elektra 1980)★★★★, *Come Morning* (Elektra 1981)★★★, *The Best Is Yet To Come* (Elektra 1982)★★★, *Inside Moves* (Elektra 1984)★★★, *Playboy Jazz Festival* (Elektra 1984)★★★, *Strawberry Moon* (CBS 1987)★★, *Then And Now* (CBS 1988)★★, *Time Out Of Mind* (Columbia 1989)★★, *Next Exit* (Columbia 1992)★★, *All My Tomorrows* (Columbia 1994)★★★, *Soulful Strut* (Columbia 1996)★★★.
●COMPILATIONS: *Baddest* (1980)★★★, *Anthology* (Motown 1981)★★★, *Greatest Performances* (Motown 1983)★★★, *At His Best* (Motown 1985)★★★, *Anthology* (Elektra 1985)★★★.

WATERBOYS
Formed by vocalist Mike Scott (b. 14 December 1958, Edinburgh, Scotland), a former fanzine writer, the Waterboys evolved from Another Pretty Face, which included John Caldwell (guitar) and a frequently changing line-up from 1979-81. A series of failed singles followed until Scott elected to form a new group. Borrowing the name Waterboys from a line in 'The Kids' from Lou Reed's *Berlin*, Scott began advertising in the music press for suitable personnel. Anthony Thistlethwaite (b. 31 August 1955, Leicester, England; saxophone) and Karl Wallinger (b. 19 October 1957, Prestatyn, Clwyd, Wales; keyboards/percussion/vocals) were recruited and work was completed on 'A Girl Called Johnny', a sterling tribute to Patti Smith that narrowly failed to become a big hit. The group's self-titled debut was also a solid work, emphasizing Scott's ability as a singer-songwriter. 'December', with its religious connotations, was an excellent Christmas single that again narrowly failed to chart. Augmented by musicians Kevin Wilkinson (drums), Roddy Lorimar (trumpet) and Tim

Blanthorn (violin), the Waterboys completed *A Pagan Place*, which confirmed their early promise. The key track for many was 'The Big Music', which became a handy simile for Scott's soul-searching mini-epics. For the following year's *This Is The Sea*, Scott brought in a new drummer, Chris Whitten, and added a folk flavour to the proceedings, courtesy of fiddler Steve Wickham. The attendant 'The Whole Of The Moon' only reached number 28 in the UK but later proved a spectacular Top 10 hit when reissued in 1990. It was a masterwork from a group seemingly at the height of its powers. Despite their promise, the Waterboys remained a vehicle for Scott's ideas and writing, a view reinforced when Karl Wallinger quit to form World Party. At this point Wickham, who had previously played with In Tua Nua, U2 and Sinead O'Connor, took on a more prominent role. He took Scott to Eire and a long sojourn in Galway followed. Three years passed before the Waterboys released their next album, the distinctively folk-flavoured *Fisherman's Blues*. Scott's assimilation of traditional Irish music, mingled with his own spiritual questing and rock background coalesced to produce a work of considerable charm and power.

Back in the ascendant, the group completed work on *Room To Roam*, which retained the folk sound, though to a lesser extent than its predecessor. Within days of the album's release, Wickham left the group, forcing Scott to reconstruct the Waterboys' sound once more. A revised line-up featuring Thistlethwaite, Hutchinson and new drummer Ken Blevins toured the UK playing a rocking set, minus the folk music that had permeated their recent work. After signing a US/Canadian contract with Geffen Records, the Waterboys line-up underwent further changes when, in February 1992, long-serving member Anthony Thistlethwaite left the group. During the rebuilding of the group, former Wendy And Lisa drummer Carla Azar took over the spot vacated by Ken Blevins, and Scott Thunes was recruited as the new bassist. Mercurial and uncompromising, Scott has continually steered the Waterboys through radically different musical phases, which have proven consistently fascinating.

●ALBUMS: *The Waterboys* (Ensign 1983)★★★, *A Pagan Place* (Ensign 1984)★★★, *This Is The Sea* (Ensign 1985)★★★★, *Fisherman's Blues* (Ensign 1988)★★★, *RoomTo Roam* (Ensign 1990)★★★, *Dream Harder* (Geffen 1993)★★.

●COMPILATIONS: *The Best Of 1981-90* (Ensign 1991)★★★, *The Secret Life Of The Waterboys: 1981-1985* (Ensign 1994)★★.

WEATHER GIRLS

Izora Rhodes and Martha Wash met in the San Francisco-based gospel group, NOW (News Of The World) prior to joining the backing group of rising disco star Sylvester. Dubbed 'Two Tons Of Fun' in deference to their rotund stature, the duo recorded for the Fantasy Records label before securing a measure of infamy for their tongue-in-cheek release, 'It's Raining Men'. First released in the USA in 1982, the single achieved a greater success in the UK where it later peaked at number 2 in 1984 after re-entering the chart. Subsequent releases however lacked the undeniable charm of their major hit, but admirably showcased the Weather Girls' powerful voices.

●ALBUMS: *Success* (Columbia 1983)★★★, *Big Girls Don't Cry* (Columbia 1985)★★★, *Weather Girls* (Columbia 1988)★★★.

WEBER, EBERHARD

b. 22 January 1940, Stuttgart, Germany. Weber's father taught him the cello from the age of six and he only turned to the bass in 1956. He liked the sound of Bill Haley's records, saw an old stand-up bass hanging on the wall in the school gym and tried it out. He played jazz in his spare time from making television commercials and working as a theatre director and only turned professional in 1972. With Wolfgang Dauner (keyboards) he had played in a trio inspired by the Bill Evans Trio and in Dauner's psychedelic jazz-rock band, Etcetera. He worked with the Dave Pike Set and then joined Volker Kriegel's Spectrum, but did not share Kriegel's fascination with rock rhythms and left in 1974. Weber had already recorded *The Colours Of Chloë* for ECM Records and had developed the five-string bass, which gives him his individual sound, from an old Italian bass with a long neck and a small rectangular soundbox he had seen in an antique shop. His composition style seemed to owe something to minimalist writing but had developed when he realized that he only liked bits and pieces of other people's music and he had concluded 'that when I came to compose I would only use chords and phrases I really liked - and use them over and over'. *The Colours Of Chloë* brought him international recognition and he then worked with guitarist Ralph Towner (1974) and Gary Burton (1974-76). Meanwhile, he formed his own band Colours with Rainer Brüninghaus, Charlie Mariano and first Jon Christensen and then John Marshall. He wanted a band that played in an absolutely European way with understated rhythm, spacey, impressionistic keyboard sounds and flowing melody. This European tradition provided 'the feeling for group empathy that I am drawn to' while the jazz tradition gave 'the whole feeling for improvisation . . . knowing when to stretch out or lay out'. He disbanded Colours when he could no longer hold these two traditions in balance and has since played with the United Jazz And Rock Ensemble and as a regular member of saxophonist Jan Garbarek's bands. Since 1985 he has also performed solo bass concerts, where his prodigious technique is evident. He is able to conjure from his electric instrument and a limited array of equipment, some glorious sounds.

●ALBUMS: *The Colours Of Chloë* (ECM 1974)★★★★, *Yellow Fields* (ECM 1975)★★★★, *The Following Morning* (ECM 1976)★★★★, *Silent Feet* (ECM 1977)★★★, *Fluid Rustle* (ECM 1979)★★★★, *Little Movements* (ECM 1980)★★★★, *Later That Evening* (ECM 1982)★★★★, *Chorus* (ECM 1984)★★★★, *Orchestra* (ECM 1988)★★★, *Pendulum* (ECM 1994)★★★.

●COMPILATIONS: *Works* (ECM 1989).

WEDDING PRESENT

Forthright and briefly fashionable indie band formed in Leeds, Yorkshire, England, in 1985 from the ashes of the Lost Pandas by David Gedge (b. 23 April 1960, Leeds, Yorkshire, England; guitar/vocals) with Keith Gregory (b. 2 January 1963, Co. Durham, England; bass), Peter Salowka (b. Middleton, Gt. Manchester, England; guitar) and Shaun Charman (b. Brighton, East Sussex, England; drums). The Wedding Present embodied the independent spirit of the mid-80s with a passion that few contemporaries could match. Furthermore, they staked their musical claim with a ferocious blend of implausibly fast guitars and lovelorn lyrics over a series of much-lauded singles on their own Reception Records label. As some cynics criticized the band's lack of imagination, *George Best* shared the merits of the flamboyant but flawed football star and reached number 47 in the UK chart. Similarly, as those same critics suggested the band were 'one-trick phonies', Pete Salowka's east European upbringing was brought to bear on the Wedding Present sound, resulting in the frenzied Ukrainian folk songs on *Ukrainski Vistupi V Johna Peel*, so called because it was a compilation of tracks from sessions they had made for John Peel's influential BBC Radio 1 show. Shaun Charman left the band as their debut was released, to join the Pop Guns, and was replaced by Simon Smith (b. 3 May 1965, Lincolnshire, England). Capitalizing on a still-burgeoning following, 'Kennedy' saw the band break into the Top 40 of the UK singles chart for the first time and revealed that, far from compromising on a major label, the Wedding Present were actually becoming more extreme. By their third album, *Seamonsters*, the band had forged a bizarre relationship with hardcore exponent Steve Albini (former member of the influential US outfit Big Black), whose harsh economic production technique encouraged the Wedding Present to juggle with broody lyrical mumblings and extraordinary slabs of guitar, killing the ghost of their 'jangly' beginnings. Before *Seamonsters* was released in 1991, Pete Salowka made way for Paul Dorrington, although he remained in the set-up on the business side of the band and formed the Ukrainians. In 1992 the Wedding Present undertook the ambitious project of releasing one single, every month, throughout the year. Each single charted in the UK Top 40 (admittedly in a depressed market), making the tactic a success, though the ever candid Gedge revealed that it had been done against a backdrop of record company opposition. Their relationship with RCA Records ended following the accompanying *Hit Parade* compilations, though Island Records were quick to pick up the out of contract band. Keith Gregory also left the fold before *Watusi* restored the band to their previous status (reviled by certain sections of the UK media, venerated by hardcore supporters). *Mini* enhanced their place as influential (although often overlooked) indie popsters and *Saturnalia* had the *New Musical Express* reviewer Mark Beaumont gasping that 'Gedge has been one of the most consistently brilliant and grossly underrated songwriters in Britain'. High praise indeed.

●ALBUMS: *George Best* (Reception 1987)★★★, *Bizarro* (RCA 1989)★★, *Seamonsters* (RCA 1991)★★★, *Watusi* (Island 1994)★★★, *Mini* (Cooking Vinyl 1996)★★, *Saturnalia* (Cooking Vinyl 1996)★★★.

●COMPILATIONS: *Tommy* (Reception 1988)★★★, *The BBC Sessions* (Strange Fruit 1988)★★, *Ukrainski Vistupi V Johna Peel* (RCA 1989)★★, *The Hit Parade Part One* (RCA 1992)★★★, *The Hit Parade Part Two* (RCA 1993)★★, *John Peel Sessions 1987-1990* (Strange Fruit 1993)★★★.

●FURTHER READING: *The Wedding Present: Thank Yer, Very Glad*, Mark Hodkinson.

WET WET WET

Formed in 1982, this Scottish pop group comprises Graeme Clark (b. 15 April 1966, Glasgow, Scotland; bass/vocals), Neil Mitchell (b. 8 June 1967,

Helensburgh, Scotland; keyboards), Marti Pellow (b. Mark McLoughlin, 23 March 1966, Clydebank, Scotland and Tom Cunningham (b. 22 June 1965, Drumchapel, Glasgow, Scotland; drums). The quartet took their name from a line in the Scritti Politti song 'Getting Having And Holding'. After frequent live performances, they recorded a promising demonstration tape, and were signed by Phonogram Records in 1985. Recordings in Memphis followed with veteran soul producer Willie Mitchell. In 1987, 'Wishing I Was Lucky' reached the UK Top 10, followed by the even more successful 'Sweet Little Mystery'. The group's agreeable blue-eyed soul was evident on their debut *Popped In Souled Out*, which climbed to number 2 in the UK album chart. Further hits followed with 'Angel Eyes (Home And Away)' and 'Temptation'. Unfortunately, the group suffered litigation at the hands of Van Morrison, who reached an out of court settlement over their use of his lyrics in part of 'Sweet Little Mystery' (also a John Martyn song title). In June 1988, the group's profile was increased when they reached number 1 in the UK with a track from the various artists compilation *Sgt Pepper Knew My Father*. Their innocuous reading of the Beatles' 'With A Little Help From My Friends' maintained their standing as 80s pin-up idols. Their reputation as one of the leading UK pop bands was enhanced in 1992 when 'Goodnight Girl' remained at the top of the charts for several weeks. Their broad appeal does not detract from the talent within, led by the confident vocals of Pellow. Their single, 'Lip Service' in Summer 1992 perhaps suggested a new interest in more dance-orientated music. Any suggestion that their commercial fortunes might be declining were blown apart by the staggering success of their cover of the Troggs' 'Love Is All Around', the theme song to the hit movie *Four Weddings And A Funeral*, which stayed at the top of the UK charts for 15 weeks, just one short of the record.

●ALBUMS: *Popped In Souled Out* (Precious 1987)★★★, *The Memphis Sessions* (Precious 1988)★★, *Holding Back The River* (Precious 1989)★★★, as Maggie Pie And The Imposters *Cloak And Dagger* (1990)★★★, *Live* cassette only (1991)★★, *High On The Happy Side* (Precious 1991)★★, *Live At The Royal Albert Hall* (Precious 1993)★★, *Picture This* (Mercury 1995)★★, *10* (Mercury 1997)★★.

●COMPILATIONS: *End Of Part One* (Precious 1993)★★★.

●FURTHER READING: *Wet Wet Wet Pictured*, Simon Fowler and Alan Jackson.

WHAM!

Generally acknowledged as the most commercially successful English pop group of the 80s, the Wham! duo first performed together in a ska-influenced school band the Executive. George Michael (b. Georgios (Yorgos) Kyriako Panayiotou, 25 June 1963, Finchley London, England) and Andrew Ridgeley (b. 26 January 1963, Windlesham, Surrey, England) streamlined the group and in 1982 began searching for a contract under their new name, Wham! Local boy Mark Dean was impressed with their demos and agreed to sign them to his recently formed label, Innervision. They next fell into the hands of music publishers Dick Leahy and Bryan Morrison; the former was to play a crucial part in guiding their career hereafter. After embarking on a series of 'personal appearances' at local clubs with backing singers Amanda Washbourn and Shirlie Holliman, they completed their debut single 'Wham! Rap', which had originally been intended as a disco parody. What emerged was an exhilarating dance number in its own right with intriguing double-edged lyrics. Wham! sang of soul on the dole and the need to rise above the stigma of unemployment. Although the song gained the boys some publicity, it initially failed to chart. However, the follow-up 'Young Guns' was a UK Top 10 hit in late 1982 and a remixed 'Wham Rap' belatedly repeated that feat.

A third hit, 'Bad Boys' indicated that the duo's macho, young rebel image was wearing thin, and Michael promised a change of direction in the future. In the meantime, they required an additional tentacle to hasten their mining of gold vinyl and, after consulting Morrison/Leahy, recruited two managers, Jazz Summers and Simon Napier-Bell. Their next hit, 'Club Tropicana', was a satire on élitist London clubland but for most listeners, the parodic elements were irrelevant. Fêted by teen magazines and increasingly photographed in exotic climes, the group soon found themselves a symbol of vainglorious beach-brain hedonism and *nouveau riche* vulgarity. A chart-topping album *Fantastic* was primarily a collection of singles with a pedestrian cover of the Miracles' 'Love Machine' to show their love of Motown Records.

An acrimonious dispute with Innervision culminated in a fascinating court case that freed the duo from their record company and they signed directly to Epic Records. They celebrated their release with their first UK number 1 'Wake Me Up Before You Go Go', quickly followed by 'Careless Whisper' (co-composed by Ridgeley, but credited to

George Michael as artist). *Make It Big* zoomed to number 1 and by the end of 1984 the group had two further major successes, 'Freedom' and 'Last Christmas'/'Everything She Wants'. The following year, the duo embarked on a much-publicized trip to China and enjoyed considerable success in America. Rumours of an impending split were confirmed the following year but not before Wham! fired their management team over the alleged sale of their company to the owner of Sun City. Wham's act of pop euthanasia was completed on 28 June 1986 when they played a farewell concert before 72,000 fans at London's Wembley Stadium which was captured on *The Final*. Since the split George Michael's solo career has blossomed, notably in the USA where he is taken more seriously as an AOR artist, while Ridgeley's career has found difficulty in taking off.
●ALBUMS: *Fantastic* (Inner Vision 1983)★★, *Make It Big* (Epic 1984)★★★, *The Final* (Epic 1986)★★★.
●VIDEOS: *Wham! The Video* (1987).
●FURTHER READING: *Wham! (Confidential) The Death Of A Supergroup*, Johnny Rogan. *Bare*, George Michael.

WHITE LION

This US group was formed in Brooklyn, New York, during 1983, by Mike Tramp (lead vocals, ex-Mabel) and Vito Bratta (guitar, ex-Dreamer). After a series of false starts, they signed to Elektra Records with Felix Robinson (bass, ex-Angel) and Dave Capozzi (drums) completing the line-up. However, the label were unhappy with the recording of *Fight To Survive* and after refusing to release the album, terminated their contract. RCA Victor Records picked up the release option and the album finally surfaced in Japan in 1984. By this stage, James Lomenzo and Gregg D'Angelo had taken over bass and drums, respectively, on a permanent basis. The album did in fact meet with favourable reviews, some critics comparing Mike Tramp to Dave Lee Roth and Vito Bratta to Eddie Van Halen, others likening the songs to those of Europe, Dokken or Journey. Signing to Atlantic Records, they released *Pride*, which developed their own identity, in particular Mike Tramp's characteristically watery falsetto style. The album catapulted them from obscurity to stardom, climbing to number 11 during its year-long stay on the *Billboard* album chart. It also spawned two US Top 10 hits with 'Wait' and 'When The Children Cry'. *Big Game* was a disappointing follow-up. Nevertheless, it still made the US charts, peaking at number 19. *Mane Attraction* released in 1991, saw

the band recapture lost ground over the course of a strong melodic rock collection. Lomenzo and D'Angelo quit due to 'musical differences' shortly after the album's release and were replaced by Tommy 'T-Bone' Caradonna (bass, ex-Alice Cooper) and Jimmy DeGrasso (drums, ex-Y&T).
●ALBUMS: *Fight To Survive* (Grand Slamm 1984)★★, *Pride* (Atlantic 1987)★★★, *Big Game* (Atlantic 1989)★★, *Mane Attraction* (Atlantic 1991)★★.
●COMPILATIONS: *The Best Of* (Atlantic 1992)★★★.

WIEDLIN, JANE

b. 20 May 1958, Oconomowoc, Wisconsin, USA. Wiedlin was originally the guitarist of the top US female band, the Go-Go's. When the split came in 1985, all five members embarked on solo careers. Wiedlin released a self-titled album which contained a minor hit, 'Blue Kiss'. However, her heart was also set on pursing an acting career and she made cameo appearances in *Clue* and *Star Trek 4: The Voyage Home*. A successful return to recording came in 1988 with the superb transatlantic hit, 'Rush Hour'. Much of Wiedlin's chart success however has largely been confined to the US charts. Her energies in the early 90s have been directed towards her involvement in the anti-fur trade movement. This resulted in the Go-Go's re-forming briefly in 1990 at a benefit for PETA (People for the Ethical Treatment of Animals), before a full reunion took place in 1994. Wiedlin currently heads FroSTed, who released their debut album *Cold* on the DGC label in 1996. The record was partly co-written with fellow ex-Go-Go's member Charlotte Coffey.
●ALBUMS: *Jane Wiedlin* (IRS 1986)★★★, *Fur* (Manhattan 1988)★★, *Tangled* (Manhattan 1990)★★.

WILDE, KIM

b. Kim Smith, 18 November 1960, Chiswick, London, England. The daughter of 50s pop idol Marty Wilde and Vernons Girls' vocalist Joyce Smith (née Baker), Wilde was signed to Mickie Most's Rak Records in 1980 after the producer heard a demo she recorded with her brother Ricky. Her first single, the exuberant 'Kids In America', composed by Ricky and co-produced by Marty, climbed to number 2 in the UK charts. A further Top 10 hit followed with 'Chequered Love', while her debut *Kim Wilde* fared extremely well in the album charts. A more adventurous sound with 'Cambodia' indicated an exciting talent. By 1982, she had already sold more records than her father had done in his entire career. While 'View From A Bridge' maintained her standing at home, 'Kids In America' became a Top 30 hit in the USA. A relatively quiet period followed, although she continued to enjoy minor hits with 'Love Blonde', 'The Second Time' and a more significant success with the Dave Edmunds-produced 'Rage To Love'. An energetic reworking of the Supremes' classic 'You Keep Me Hangin' On' took her back to UK number 2 at a time when her career seemed flagging. After appearing on the Ferry Aid charity single, 'Let It Be', Wilde was back in the Top 10 with 'Another Step (Closer To You)', a surprise duet with soul singer Junior Giscombe. Weary of her image as the girl-next-door, Wilde subsequently sought a sexier profile, which was used in the video to promote 'Say You Really Want Me'. Her more likely standing as an 'all-round entertainer' was underlined by the Christmas novelty hit 'Rockin' Around The Christmas Tree' in the company of comedian Mel Smith. In 1988, the dance-orientated 'You Came' reaffirmed her promise, and further Top 10 hits continued with 'Never Trust A Stranger' and 'Four Letter Word'. Her recent singles have gained only lowly positions in the charts and the subsequent *Love Is* was a pale shadow of *Close*. On *Now And Forever* Wilde abandoned pop for a slick soul groove.

●ALBUMS: *Kim Wilde* (RAK 1981)★★★, *Select* (RAK 1982)★★, *Catch As Catch Can* (RAK 1983)★★, *Teases And Dares* (MCA 1984)★★, *Another Step* (MCA 1986)★★, *Close* (MCA 1988)★★★★, *Love Moves* (MCA 1990)★★, *Love Is* (MCA 1992)★★★, *Now And Forever* (MCA 1995)★★.

●COMPILATIONS: *The Very Best Of Kim Wilde* (RAK 1985)★★★, *The Singles Collection 1981-1993* (MCA 1993)★★★, *The Gold Collection* (EMI 1996)★★★.

●VIDEOS: *Video EP: Kim Wilde* (1987), *Close* (1989), *Another Step (Closer To You)* (1990), *The Singles Collection 1981-1993* (1993).

WILLIS, BRUCE

b. 19 March 1955, Germany. Before beginning his acting career in the mid-70s, Willis played saxophone in the R&B band, Loose Goose. His musical ambitions were overshadowed by his growing success as an actor, which led to starring roles in the highly popular US television series *Moonlighting*, and the Hollywood film *Blind Date*. In 1987, Willis conceived and starred in the television special *The Return Of Bruno*, a biography (or rockumentary!) of a fictional rock star in which many real-life musicians testified to his influence on their careers. For the soundtrack, Willis revamped several classic soul songs, enjoying a surprise 1987 hit with the Staples Singers' 'Respect Yourself', and following up with the Drifters' 'Under The Boardwalk', on which he was supported by the Temptations.

●ALBUMS: *The Return Of Bruno* (Motown 1987)★★, *If It Don't Kill You It Just Makes You Stronger* (Motown 1989)★.

WILSON, CASSANDRA

b. 4 December 1955, Jackson, Mississippi, USA. Wilson started piano and guitar lessons at the age of nine. In 1975 she began singing professionally, primarily folk and blues, working in various R&B and Top 20 cover version bands. She emerged as a jazz singer while studying with drummer Alvin Fielder and singing with the Black Arts Music Society in her hometown. In 1981 she moved to New Orleans and studied with saxophonist Earl Turbinton. In 1982 she relocated to New York at the suggestion of trumpeter Woody Shaw and began working with David Holland and Abbey Lincoln. In 1985 she guested on Steve Coleman's *Motherland Pulse* and was asked by the JMT label to record her own album. Her debut was *Point Of View*, which featured Coleman and guitarist Jean-Paul Bourelly. New York's finest wanted to work with her. She sang with New Air Henry Threadgill's trio, and he returned the compliment by helping with arrangements on her second, more powerful album, *Days Aweigh*. Her mix of smoky, knowing vocals and expansive, lush music that travelled between psychedelia and swing was transfixing. The more conservative American audience was won over by her record of standards, *Blue Skies* (1988), which was named jazz album of the year by *Billboard* magazine. The follow-up, the innovative science-fiction epic *Jumpworld* (1990), showed that Cassandra Wilson was not to be easily categorized: it included raps and funk as well as jazz and blues. This stylistic diversity was maintained on 1991's *She Who Weeps*. In the meantime, Wilson has continued to record on Steve Coleman's albums and has also made guest appearances with other musicians associated with Coleman's M-Base organisation, such as Greg Osby and Robin Eubanks. Her latest recordings on Blue Note Records have exposed her to a much wider market. *New Moon Daughter* (a number 1 album in the USA jazz chart) featured songs by the Monkees, U2, Hank Williams, Son House and Neil Young.

●ALBUMS: *Point Of View* (JMT 1986)★★★, *Days*

Aweigh (JMT 1987)★★★, *Blue Skies* (JMT 1988)★★★★, *Jumpworld* (JMT 1990)★★★, *She Who Weeps* (JMT 1991)★★★, *Live* (JMT 1991), *Dance To The Drums Again* (DIW 1992)★★★, *After The Beginning Again* (JMT 1993)★★★, *Blue Light 'Til Dawn* (Blue Note 1993)★★★★, *New Moon Daughter* (Blue Note 1996)★★★★.

WILSON, MARI

b. Mari MacMillan Ramsey Wilson, 29 September 1957, London, England. In the mid-80s, Mari Wilson single-handedly led a revival of the world of 50s/early 60s English kitsch. Sporting a bee-hive hairdo, wearing a pencil skirt and fake mink stole, her publicity photos depicted a world of long-lost suburban curtain and furniture styles, tupperware, garish colours (often pink) and graphic designs from the period. The songs were treated in the same way, only affectionately and with genuine feeling. The whole image was the idea of Tot Taylor who, composing under the name of Teddy Johns and gifted with the ability to write pastiche songs from almost any era of popular music, also ran the Compact Organisation label. The label's sense of hype excelled itself as they immediately released a box-set of Compact Organisation artists, all of which, with the exception of Mari, failed to attract the public's attention. (Although 'model agent' Virna Lindt was a music press favourite.) Wilson was quickly adopted by press, television and radio as a curiosity, all aiding her early 1982 singles 'Beat The Beat' and 'Baby It's True' to have a minor effect on the chart. 'Just What I Always Wanted' a Top 10 hit, fully encapsulated the Wilson style. However, it was the following year's cover of the Julie London torch-song number, 'Cry Me A River', which, despite only reaching number 27, most people have come to associate with Wilson. The song also generated a revival of interest in London's recordings, resulting in many long-lost (and forgotten) albums being re-released. After touring the world with her backing vocal group, the Wilsations - which included Julia Fordham - the return home saw a slowing-down in activity. Although for the most part Wilson was out of the limelight, she provided the vocals to the sound-track to the Ruth Ellis bio-pic *Dance With A Stranger*. In 1985, she started playing small clubs with her jazz quartet performing standards, as well as writing her own material, which led to her appearance with Stan Getz at a London's Royal Festival Hall. Although still affectionately remembered for her beehive, she has been able to put that period behind her and is now taken more seriously as a jazz/pop singer and is able to fill Ronnie Scott's club for a season.

●ALBUMS: *Show People* (Compact 1983)★★★★, *Dance With A Stranger* film soundtrack (Compact 1987)★★, *The Rhythm Romance* (Dino 1991)★★★.

WINDHAM HILL RECORDS

New age record label Windham Hill Records was formed by husband and wife team Anne Robinson and William Ackerman in Menlo Park, California, USA, in 1976. Since that time the company has expanded to encompass one of the most important and commercially viable rosters in the new age/adult-orientated instrumental music genre. The label's best-selling artist is pianist George Winston, and a number of subsidiary labels have also been formed. These include Lost Lake Arts, High Street Records and Windham Hill Jazz. Among those to work with the label have been John Gorka, Jim Brickman, the Modern Mandolin Quartet, Ray Obiedo, Ray Lynch, the Turtle Island String Quartet and many others. The label also serves as distributor to George Winston's Dancing Cat label, and by the mid-90s had established satellite offices in Chicago, Atlanta, Beverly Hills and New York. Ackerman moved out of the day-to-day running and in 1995 Anne Robinson announced the sale of the company to BMG Entertainment North America. BMG already owned half the equity following a 50 per cent investment in May 1992, and had found the relationship to be mutually profitable. Other artists closely associated with the growth of Windham Hill have been Mark Isham, Michael Hedges, Alex De Grassi, Shadowfax and Liz Story.

WINSTON, GEORGE

b. 1949, Michigan, USA. Following many years of listening to music, his early heroes being Floyd Cramer, the Ventures and Booker T. And The MGs, Winston took up the piano at the age of 18. He switched to jazz after being influenced by the 'stride' piano of Fats Waller. The mysterious and enigmatic Winston stopped playing in 1977 until the music of Professor Longhair inspired him to return. Between 1980 and 1982 he recorded a trilogy of albums which have subsequently sold millions of copies. The sparse and delicate piano music of *Autumn*, *Winter Into Spring* and *December* gave a new dimension to solo piano recording, engineered to such perfection that the instrument truly becomes part of the room the listener is in. Not one note is wasted and he plays as if each were his last. Winston was part of the original Windham

Hill Record family of artists that pioneered the USA's west coast new age music of the early 80s. Winston kept a low profile for almost a decade until his return with *Summer* in 1991 continuing the tradition of his best solo work. *Forest*, released in 1994 won a Grammy at the 1996 awards. His tribute to pianist Vince Guaraldi (composer of 'Cast Your Fate To The Wind') became a major success in 1996.

●ALBUMS: *Ballads And Blues* (Takoma 1972)★★, *Autumn* (Windham Hill 1980)★★★★, *Winter Into Spring* (Windham Hill 1982)★★★★, *December* (Windham Hill 1982)★★★★, with Meryl Streep *Velveteen Rabbit* (Windham Hill 1982)★, *Summer* (Windham Hill 1991)★★★, *Forest* (Windham Hill 1994)★★★, *Linus And Lucy: The Music Of Vince Guaraldi* (Dancing Cat/Windham Hill 1996)★★.

●VIDEOS: *Seasons In Concert* (Dancing Cat Video 1997).

WINWOOD, STEVE

b. 12 May 1948, Birmingham, England. Steve and his older brother Muff Winwood were born into a family with parents who encouraged musical evenings at their home. Steve was playing guitar with Muff and their father in the Ron Atkinson Band at the age of eight, soon after he mastered drums and piano. The multi-talented Winwood first achieved 'star' status as a member of the pioneering 60s R&B band, the Spencer Davis Group. His strident voice and full-sounding Hammond organ emitted one of the mid-60s' most distinctive pop sounds. The group had a successful run of major hits in the UK and USA until their musical horizons became too limited for the musically ambitious Steve. In 1965, Winwood had previously recorded the UK turntable soul hit 'Incense' under the name of the Anglos, written by Stevie Anglo. This gave fuel to rumours of his imminent departure. It was not until 1967 that he left and went on to form Traffic, a seminal band in the development of progressive popular music. The short-lived 'supergroup' Blind Faith briefly interrupted Traffic's flow. Throughout this time his talents were sought as a session musician and he became the unofficial in-house keyboard player for Island Records. During 1972 he was seriously ill with peritonitis and this contributed to the sporadic activity of Traffic. When Traffic slowly ground to a halt in 1974, Winwood seemed poised to start the solo career he had been threatening for so long. Instead he maintained a low profile and became a musicians' musician contributing keyboards and backing vocals to many fine albums, including

John Martyn's *One World*, Sandy Denny's *Rendezvous*, George Harrison's *Dark Horse* and Toots And The Maytals *Reggae Got Soul*. His session work reads like a who's who: Jimi Hendrix, Joe Cocker, Leon Russell, Howlin' Wolf, Sutherland Brothers, Muddy Waters, Eric Clapton, Alvin Lee, Marianne Faithfull and many others. In 1976 he performed with Stomu Yamash'ta and Klaus Schulze, resulting in *Go* and *Go 2*. He also appeared on stage with the Fania All Stars playing percussion and guitar. The eagerly anticipated self-titled solo album did not appear until 1977, and was respectfully, rather than enthusiastically, welcomed. It displayed a relaxed Winwood performing only six numbers and using first class musicians like Willy Weeks and Andy Newmark. Following its release, Winwood retreated back to his 50-acre Oxfordshire farm and shunned interviews. He became preoccupied with rural life, and took up clay pigeon shooting, dog training and horse riding. It appeared to outsiders that his musical activity had all but ceased.

During the last week of 1980 the majestic *Arc Of A Diver* was released to an unsuspecting public. With his former songwriting partner Jim Capaldi now living in Brazil, Winwood had been working on lyrics supplied to him by Vivian Stanshall, George Fleming and Will Jennings. The album was an unqualified and unexpected triumph, particularly in the USA where it went platinum. The stirring single 'While You See A Chance' saw him back in the charts. He followed with the hastily put together (by Winwood standards) *Talking Back To The Night*, which became another success. Winwood, however, was not altogether happy with the record and seriously contemplated retiring to become a record producer. His brother, Muff, wisely dissuaded him. Winwood began to be seen more often, now looking groomed and well preserved. Island Records were able to reap rewards by projecting him towards a younger market. His European tour in 1983 was a revelation, a super-fit Winwood, looking 20 years younger, bounced on stage wearing a portable keyboard and ripped into Junior Walker's 'Roadrunner'. It was as if the 17-year-old 'Stevie' from the Spencer Davis Group had returned. His entire catalogue was performed with energy and confidence. It was hard to believe this was the same man who for years had hidden shyly behind banks of amplifiers and keyboards with Traffic.

Two years later, while working in New York on his forthcoming album, his life further improved when he met his future wife Eugenia, following a long and unhappy first marriage. His obvious elation overspilled into *Back In The High Life* (1986). Most of the tracks were co-written with Will Jennings and it became his most commercially successful record to date. The album spawned three hits including the superb disco/soul 'Higher Love', which reached number 1 in the USA. In 1987 his long association with Chris Blackwell and Island Records ended amid press reports that his new contract with Virgin Records guaranteed him $13 million. The reclusive 'Midland maniac' had now become one of the hottest properties in the music business, while the world eagerly awaited the next album to see if the star was worth his transfer fee. The single 'Roll With It' preceded the album of the same name. Both were enormous successes, being a double chart-topper in the USA. The album completed a full circle. Winwood was back singing his heart out with 60s-inspired soul/pop. His co-writer once again was the talented Will Jennings, although older aficionados were delighted to see one track written with Jim Capaldi.

In 1990, Winwood was involved in a music publishing dispute in which it was alleged that the melody of 'Roll With It' had been plagiarized from 'Roadrunner'. That year *Refugees Of The Heart* became his least successful album, although it contained another major US hit single with the Winwood/Capaldi composition 'One And Only Man'. Following the less than spectacular performance of that album rumours began to circulate that Traffic would be reborn and this was confirmed in early 1994. *Far From Home* sounded more like a Winwood solo album than any Traffic project, but those who love any conglomeration that has Winwood involved were not disappointed. Later that year he participated on Davey Spillane's album *A Place Among The Stones,* singing 'Forever Frozen', and also sang the theme song 'Reach For The Light' from the animated movie *Balto.* The long-awaited *Junction 7* was a major disappointment, and proved to be his least successful recording.

●ALBUMS: *Steve Winwood* (Island 1977)★★★★, *Arc Of A Diver* (Island 1980)★★★★, *Talking Back To The Night* (Island 1983)★★★, *Back In The High Life* (Island 1986)★★★★, *Roll With It* (Virgin 1988)★★★, *Refugees Of The Heart* (Virgin 1990)★★★, *Junction 7* (Virgin 1997)★★.
●COMPILATIONS: *Chronicles* (Island 1987)★★★★, *The Finer Things* 4-CD box set (Island 1995)★★★★.
●FURTHER READING: *Back In The High Life: A Biography Of Steve Winwood*, Alan Clayson. *Keep On Running: The Steve Winwood Story*, Chris Welch.

WOMACK AND WOMACK

One of modern soul's most successful duos, comprising husband and wife team Cecil Womack (b. 1947, Cleveland, Ohio, USA) and Linda Cooke Womack (b. 1953). Cecil had been the youngest of the Womack Brothers, who later evolved into the Valentinos. With them he signed to Sam Cooke's Star label, but Cooke's subsequent death left them homeless, and after a brief liaison with Chess Records, Bobby Womack left the group to go solo. Cecil later married singer Mary Wells, whom he managed until the couple separated. Linda, the daughter of Sam Cooke, had begun a songwriting career in 1964 at the age of 11, composing 'I Need A Woman'. She would also provide 'I'm In Love' for Wilson Pickett and 'A Woman's Gotta Have It' for James Taylor, but later forged a professional, and personal, partnership with Cecil. As she recalls: 'My father had the deepest regard for all the Womack brothers. He had talked about how talented Cecil was since I was four years old...We didn't actually meet until I was eight'. Together they worked extensively as a writing team for Philadelphia International, numbering the O'Jays and Patti Labelle among their clients. The couple achieved a notable success with 'Love TKO', a soul hit in 1980 for Teddy Pendergrass. This melodic ballad also provided the Womacks with their first US chart entry (and was also covered by Blondie), since when the duo's fortunes have prospered both in the USA and UK with several excellent singles, including the club favourite, 'Love Wars' (1984), and 'Teardrops' (1988), the latter reaching the UK Top 3. They continued to write for others also, contributing 'Hurting Inside' and 'Sexy' to Ruby Turner. In the early 90s the couple journeyed to Nigeria, where they discovered ancestral ties to the Zekkariyas tribe. They consequently adopted the names Zeriiya (Linda) and Zekkariyas (Cecil), in a nod to the Afrocentricity movement.

●ALBUMS: *The Composers/Love Wars* (Elektra 1983)★★★, *Radio M.U.S.I.C. Man* (Elektra 1985)★★★, *Starbright* (Manhattan/EMI 1986)★★★, *Conscience* (4th & Broadway 1988)★★, *Family Spirit* (Arista 1991)★★, *Transformed Into The House Of Zekkariyas* (1993)★★.

WONDER STUFF

Formed in Stourbridge, West Midlands, England, in April 1986, the Wonder Stuff featured Miles Hunt (vocals/guitar), Malcolm Treece (guitar), Rob Jones (b. 1964, d. 30 July 1993, New York, USA; bass, replacing original member Chris Fradgley) and former Mighty Lemon Drops drummer, Martin Gilks. The roots of the band lay in From Eden, a short-lived local group that featured Hunt on drums, Treece on guitar and Clint Mansell and Adam Mole, later of peers Pop Will Eat Itself, occupying the remaining roles. After amassing a sizeable local following the Wonder Stuff released their debut EP, It's A Wonderful Day, to favourable small press coverage in 1987. Along with the aforementioned PWEI and other Midlands hopefuls Crazyhead and Gaye Bykers On Acid, they were soon pigeonholed under the banner of 'grebo rock' by the national music press. Despite this ill-fitting description, the Wonder Stuff's strengths always lay in melodic pop songs braced against an urgent, power pop backdrop. After an ill-fated dalliance with EMI Records' ICA Rock Week, a second single, 'Unbearable', proved strong enough to secure a contract with Polydor Records at the end of 1987. 'Give Give Give Me More More More' offered a minor hit the following year, and was succeeded by arguably the band's best early song. Built on soaring harmonies, 'A Wish Away' was the perfect precursor to the Wonder Stuff's vital debut, The Eight Legged Groove Machine, which followed later that year and established them in the UK charts. 'It's Yer Money I'm After Baby', also from the album, continued to mine Hunt's cynical furrow (further evident on the confrontational b-side, 'Astley In The Noose' - referring to contemporary chart star, Rick Astley) and began a string of UK Top 40 hits. 'Who Wants To Be The Disco King?' and the more relaxed 'Don't Let Me Down Gently', both from 1989, hinted at the diversity of the group's second album, Hup. Aided by fiddle, banjo and keyboard player Martin Bell (ex-Hackney Five-O), the album contrasted a harder, hi-tech sound with a rootsy, folk feel on tracks such as 'Golden Green', a double a-side hit when combined with a cover of the Youngbloods' 'Get Together'.

The band's well-documented internal wrangles came to a head with the departure of Rob Jones at the end of the decade. He moved to New York to form his own band, the Bridge And Tunnel Crew, with his wife Jessie Ronson, but died of heart failure in 1993. 'Circlesquare' introduced new bass player Paul Clifford. A subsequent low profile was broken in April 1991 with 'Size Of A Cow'. A UK Top 10 hit, this was quickly followed by 'Caught In My Shadow' and Never Loved Elvis. Once again, this third album revealed the Wonder Stuff's remorseless progression. Gone were the brash, punk-inspired three-minute classics, replaced by a richer musical content, both in Hunt's song writing and musical performances.

The extent of their popularity was emphasized in late 1991 when, in conjunction with comedian Vic Reeves, they topped the UK charts with a revival of Tommy Roe's 'Dizzy'. The group made a swift return to the Top 10 in 1992 with the Welcome To The Cheap Seats EP, the title track's post-punk jig (with Kirsty MacColl on backing vocals) typifying the direction of the following year's Construction For The Modern Idiot. With songs now imbued with far more optimism due to Hunt's improved romantic prospects, singles such as 'Full Of Life' and 'Hot Love Now!' replaced previous uncertainties with unforced bonhomie. Thus, it came as something as a surprise when Hunt announced the band's dissolution to the press in July 1994 long before any grapes could sour - a decision allegedly given impetus by Polydor's insistence that the band should crack the USA (a factor in striking down the label's previous great singles band, the Jam). They bowed out at a final gig in Stratford-upon-Avon, Hunt leaving the stage with a pastiche of the Sex Pistols' epigram, 'Every Feel You've Been Treated?', ringing in fans' ears. Writer James Brown offered another tribute in his sleevenotes to the compulsory posthumous singles compilations: 'It was pointed out that if the writer Hunter S. Thompson had been the presiding influence over the Beatles, they they might have looked and sounded like the Wonder Stuff. Suitably abbreviated, it provided less accurate testimony than 'greatest hits', perhaps, but it was certainly more in keeping with the band's legacy. Former members of the band (Treece, Clifford and Gilks) regrouped in 1995 as Weknowwhereyoulive, with the addition of former Eat singer Ange Doolittle on vocals. Hunt also gave up his job as host of MTV's 120 Minutes to put together a new band known as Vent.

●ALBUMS: The Eight Legged Groove Machine (Polydor 1988)★★★, Hup (Polydor 1989)★★★, Never Loved Elvis (Polydor 1991)★★★, Construction For The Modern Idiot (Polydor 1993)★★, Live In Manchester (Strange Fruit 1995)★★.

●COMPILATIONS: If The Beatles Had Read Hunter ... The Singles (Polydor 1994)★★★★.

●VIDEOS: Welcome To The Cheap Seats (Polygram Video 1992), Greatest Hits Finally Live (1994).

WOODENTOPS

At one point, it seemed likely that the Woodentops from Northampton, England, would be commercially successful. After the offbeat 'Plenty', a one-off single for the Food Records label in 1984, songwriter Rolo McGinty (guitar/vocals), Simon

Mawby (guitar), Alice Thompson (keyboards), Frank de Freitas (bass) and Benny Staples (drums) joined Geoff Travis's Rough Trade Records and issued a string of catchy singles that fared increasingly well commercially. Released in 1985, the jolly 'Move Me' was followed by the menacing pace of 'Well Well Well' while 'It Will Come' seemed a likely hit. The band's critically acclaimed debut album, *Giant*, was an enticing mixture of frantic acoustic guitars and a warm yet offbeat clutch of songs. After 'Love Affair With Everyday Living' (1986), McGinty decided upon a change in direction, hardening up the Woodentops' sound and incorporating new technology within their live repertoire. The results were heard the following year on *Live Hypnobeat Live*, which relied on material from *Giant*, albeit performed live in a drastically revitalized way. *Wooden Foot Cops On The Highway* and the accompanying single, 'You Make Me Feel'/'Stop This Car', showed how far the Woodentops had progressed by early 1988. Although less uncompromising than their live project, the sound was more mature with an emphasis on detail previously lacking. What the band failed to achieve in commercial terms was more than compensated for by the level of critical and public respect they earned.

●ALBUMS: *Giant* (Rough Trade 1986)★★★★, *Live Hypnobeat Live* (Upside 1987)★★★, *Wooden Foot Cops On the Highway* (Rough Trade 1988)★★★★.

WORKING WEEK

The band was formed in 1983 around the nucleus of Simon Booth (guitar) and Larry Stabbins (saxophone) as an offshoot of the soft jazz-influenced group Weekend. Adopting a harder jazz/Latin direction, Working Week commanded much music press attention and, in particular, 'style' magazines (*Blitz* and *The Face*), who latched on to the band's connection with the London jazz dance teams. Their radical image was strengthened by Booth's and Stabbins' left-wing allegiances, borne out on their 1984 debut single on Paladin/Virgin Records, 'Venceremos (We Will Win)'. The song, dedicated to the Chilean protest singer Victor Jara, included guest vocals from Tracey Thorn, Robert Wyatt and Claudia Figueroa. The follow-up, 'Storm Of Light', featured Julie Tippetts on lead vocals. In time, the group recruited a permanent lead vocalist in Juliet Roberts. After her departure in 1988, Working Week reverted back to the system of guest vocalists until the addition of a new vocalist in Yvonne Waite for 1991's *Black And Gold*. Although Working Week has centred around Booth and Stabbins for recordings and live appearances they have employed a vast array of respected UK jazz musicians who, on various occasions, have included Harry Beckett (trumpet), Keith Tippett (piano), Kim Burton (piano), Cleveland Watkiss (vocals), Mike Carr (organ), Richard Edwards and Paul Spong (brass), Dave Bitelli (reeds), Annie Whitehead (trombone) and Nic France (drums). Since then, the group has continued to work, turning out high quality recordings, although that initial wave of interest and impetus in the mid-80s has somewhat subsided.

●ALBUMS: *Working Nights* (Virgin 1985)★★★, *Companeros* (Virgin 1986)★★★, *Knocking On Your Door* (Virgin 1987)★★★, *Fire In The Mountain* (Ten 1989)★★★, *Black And Gold* (Ten 1991)★★★.

●COMPILATIONS: *Payday* (Venture 1988)★★★.

WRATHCHILD

Formed in 1980 in Evesham, Worcestershire, England, as a Black Sabbath-influenced band, it was another two years before Wrathchild emerged at the forefront of the new glam rock scene. The original line-up comprised Rocky Shads (vocals) and Marc Angel (bass), who were joined by ex-Medusa personnel Lance Rocket (guitar) and Eddie Starr (drums). The group subsequently released an EP on Bullet Records and toured heavily to promote it. By 1983 they had developed a melodramatic live show and perfected their Kiss/Angel influences, while retaining a particular 'English' quality. A year later their hard work paid off when they secured a contract with Heavy Metal Records, but a bad choice of producer (Robin George) resulted in a slick but flat sound that was not at all representative of the group's sound. Soon afterwards they entered into a long-running legal battle with the company that almost killed off the group. During this time indie label Dojo released a compilation of early material that proved to be far superior to the official album - it also contained the definitive version of live favourite and title track, 'Trash Queen'. In 1988 they made their comeback with the aptly titled *The Bizz Suxx*. 'Nukklear Rokket', was also released as a single and was followed with a tour that lacked the early aggression and visual drama. The follow-up album in 1989 fared badly against the more established glam rock bands like Mötley Crüe. At this point the group once again became embroiled in a legal battle, this time to stop an American thrash metal band using their moniker. They won, and their namesakes appended America to their tag. None of this, however, did the band any favours, and they disappeared from view shortly thereafter.

●ALBUMS: *Stakk Attakk* (Heavy Metal 1984)★★, *Trash Queens* (Dojo 1985)★★★, *The Bizz Suxx* (FM Revolver 1988)★★★, *Delirium* (FM Revolver 1989)★★.
●VIDEOS: *War Machine* (1988).

WRECKLESS ERIC

b. Eric Goulden, Newhaven, Sussex, England. Launched by Stiff Records in the heyday of punk, Wreckless Eric, as his name suggested, specialized in chaotic pub rock and roots-influenced rock. His often tuneless vocals belied some excellent musical backing, most notably by producer Nick Lowe. Wreckless's eccentric single, 'Whole Wide World'/'Semaphore Signals' has often been acclaimed as one of the minor classics of the punk era. During 1977/8, he was promoted via the famous Stiff live revues where he gained notoriety offstage for his drinking. For his second album, *The Wonderful World Of Wreckless Eric*, the artist provided a more engaging work, but increasingly suffered from comparison with the other stars on his fashionable record label. Wreckless's commercial standing saw little improvement despite an attempt to produce a more commercial work, the ironically titled *Big Smash*. Effectively retiring from recording for the first half of the 80s, Wreckless returned with *A Roomful Of Monkeys*, credited to Eric Goulden, and featuring members of Ian Dury's Blockheads. He then formed the Len Bright Combo with ex-Milkshakes members Russ Wilkins (bass) and Bruce Brand (drums), who released two albums and found nothing more than a small cult following on the pub/club circuit. The eventual dissolution of that group led to the formation of Le Beat Group Electrique with Catfish Truton (drums) and André Barreau (bass). Now a resident in France, and a more sober personality, Eric has found an appreciative audience.
●ALBUMS: *Wreckless Eric* (Stiff 1978)★★, *The Wonderful World Of Wreckless Eric* (Stiff 1979)★★★, *The Whole Wide World* (Stiff 1979)★★, *Big Smash* (Stiff 1980)★★, as Eric Goulden *A Roomful Of Monkeys* (Go! Discs 1985)★★, as The Len Bright Combo *The Len Bright Combo Present The Len Bright Combo* (Empire 1986)★★, as The Len Bright Combo *Combo Time!* (Ambassador 1986)★★, *Le Beat Group Electrique* (New Rose 1989)★★, *At The Shop!* (New Rose 1990)★★, *The Donovan Of Trash* (Sympathy For The Record Industry 1991)★★★, as The Hitsville House Band *12 O'Clock Stereo* (Casino 1994)★★★.

WYATT, ROBERT

b. 28 January 1945, Bristol, Avon, England. As the drummer, vocalist and guiding spirit of the original Soft Machine, Robert Wyatt had established a style that merged the *avant garde* with English eccentricity. His first solo album, *The End Of An Ear*, presaged his departure from the above group, although its radical content resulted in a muted reception. Wyatt's next venture, the excellent Matching Mole, was bedevilled by internal dissent but a planned relaunch was forcibly abandoned following a tragic fall from a window, which left him paralyzed and confined to a wheelchair. *Rock Bottom*, the artist's next release, was composed while Wyatt lay in hospital. A heartfelt and deeply personal collection, the songs were marked by an aching vulnerability that successfully avoided any hint of self-pity. This exceptional album was succeeded by an unlikely hit single in the shape of an idiosyncratic reading of the Monkees hit, 'I'm A Believer'. *Ruth Is Stranger Than Richard*, released in 1975, was a more open collection, and balanced original pieces with outside material, including a spirited reading of jazz bassist Charlie Haden's 'Song For Che'. Although Wyatt, a committed Marxist, would make frequent guest appearances, his own career was shelved until 1980 when a single comprising two South American songs of liberation became the first in a series of politically motivated releases undertaken for Rough Trade Records. These performances were subsequently compiled on *Nothing Can Stop Us*, which was then enhanced by the addition of 'Shipbuilding', a haunting anti-Falkland War composition, specifically written for Wyatt by Elvis Costello, which was a minor chart entry in 1983. Wyatt's fluctuating health has undermined his recording ambitions, but his commitment remains undiminished. He issued singles in aid of Namibia and the British Miners' Hardship Fund, and contributed a compassionate soundtrack to the harrowing 1982 *Animals* film. Wyatt's works, *Old Rotten Hat* and *Dondestan*, are as compelling as the rest of his impressive catalogue.
●ALBUMS: *The End Of An Ear* (Columbia 1970)★★★, *Rock Bottom* (Virgin 1974)★★★★, *Ruth Is Stranger Than Richard* (Virgin 1975)★★★, *Nothing Can Stop Us* (Rough Trade 1982)★★★★, *Animals* film soundtrack (Rough Trade 1984)★★, *Old Rotten Hat* (Rough Trade 1985)★★★, *Dondestan* (Rough Trade 1991)★★★, *A Short Break* (Rough Trade 1992)★★★.
●COMPILATIONS: *Going Back A Bit: A Little*

History Of ...(Virgin Universal 1994)★★★★, *Flotsam Jetsam* (Rough Trade 1994)★★★.
●FURTHER READING: *Wrong Movements: A Robert Wyatt History*, Michael King.

WYNN, STEVE

Guitarist/vocalist Wynn is one of the pivotal figures in the Los Angeles 'paisley underground' rock scene of the early 80s. A former member of the Suspects, which included Gavin Blair and Russ Tolman, later of True West, he briefly joined the Long Ryders, before founding the Dream Syndicate in 1981. Starved of a suitable record label, Wynn established Down There Records, which issued important early sets by Green On Red and Naked Prey in addition to his own group's debut. Dream Syndicate have since pursued an erratic career, blighted by commercial indifference. During a long hiatus in its progress Wynn joined Gutterball and also worked with Dan Stuart from Green On Red in a ragged, bar-room influenced collection, *The Lost Weekend* (1985). Billed as by Danny And Dusty, the album featured support from friends and contemporaries and paradoxically outsold the musicians' more serious endeavours. *Melting In The Dark* was a collaboration with indie band Come.
●ALBUMS: *The Lost Weekend* (Down There 1985)★★★, *Kerosene Man* (World Service 1990)★★★★, *Dazzling Display* (RNA 1992)★★★, *Fluorescent* (Mute 1994)★★★, *Take Your Flunky And Dangle* (Return To Sender/Normal 1995)★★, with Come *Melting In The Dark* (Zero Hour 1996)★★★.

XENTRIX

Originally known as Sweet Vengeance, this UK rock band was formed in Preston, Lancashire, in 1986, and originally featured Chris Astley (vocals/guitar), Kristian Havard (guitar), Paul Mackenzie (bass) and Dennis Gasser (drums). The group had done little until signing to Roadrunner Records on the strength of their *Hunger For* demo tape in 1988. (They had already recorded one track, 'Blackmail', for inclusion on the Ebony Records compilation album, *Full Force*, under the Sweet Vengeance moniker.) It was their debut album, *Shattered Existence*, that bought them to the wider public's attention. Combining Metallica-style power riffs with Bay Area thrash pretensions, the band became popular on the UK club circuit and recorded a cover version of the Ray Parker Jnr. track 'Ghostbusters', a stage favourite, for their first single release. They had problems with the track, however, as they had used the *Ghostbusters* film logo for the cover without Columbia Pictures' permission. The resulting press did the band no harm and the single was released with a new cover in 1990. In the same year the band released their second album, *For Whose Advantage*. Musically similar to previous releases, it nevertheless did much to enhance their profile. With *Dilute To Taste* and *Kin* the band took a more traditional power metal approach which augured well without ever breaking them out into the mainstream. A full three year gap preceded the release of *Scourge* in 1996, by which time vocalist/guitarist Astley had been replaced by Simon Gordon (vocals) and Andy Rudd (guitar).
●ALBUMS: *Shattered Existence* (Roadrunner 1989)★★★, *For Whose Advantage* (Roadrunner 1990)★★★, *Dilute To Taste* (Roadrunner 1991)★★★, *Kin* (Roadrunner 1992)★★★, *Scourge* (Heavy Metal 1996)★★.

XMAL DEUTSCHLAND

This experimental and atmospheric band formed in the autumn of 1980 and were based in Hamburg, Germany. With no previous musical experience, the essential components were Anja Huwe (vocals), Manuela Rickers (guitar), and Fiona Sangster (keyboards). Original members Rita Simon and Caro May were replaced by Wolfgang Ellerbrock (bass) and Manuela Zwingmann (drums). Insisting on singing in their mother tongue and refusing to be visually promoted as a 'female' band (Ellerbrock is the 'token' male), they have continued to plough a singular, and largely lonely, furrow since their inception. They first came to England in 1982 to support the Cocteau Twins, joining 4AD Records soon afterwards. The debut *Fetisch* highlighted a sound that tied them firmly to both their Germanic ancestry and the hallmark spectral musicianship of their new label. Huwe's voice in particular, was used as a fifth instrument which made the cultural barrier redundant. After the release of two well-received singles, 'Qual' and 'Incubus Succubus II', they lost drummer Zwingmann who wished to remain in England. Her replacement was Peter Bellendir who joined in time for rehearsals for the second album.

● ALBUMS: *Festisch* (4AD 1982)★★, *Tocsin* (4AD 1984)★★.

XTC

Formed in Wiltshire, England, in 1972 as Star Park (Rats Krap backwards) this widely beloved UK pop unit became the Helium Kidz in 1973 with the addition of Colin Moulding (b. 17 August 1955, Swindon, Wiltshire, England), Terry Chambers (b. 16 July 1955, Swindon, Wiltshire, England) and a second guitarist Dave Cartner (b. c.1951, Swindon, Wiltshire, England), to the nucleus of Andy Partridge (b. 11 November 1953, Swindon, Wiltshire, England; guitar/vocals). The Kidz were then heavily influenced by the MC5 and Alice Cooper. In 1975 Partridge toyed with two new names for the band, the Dukes Of Stratosphear and XTC. At this time Steve Hutchins passed through the ranks and in 1976 Johnny Perkins (keyboards) joined Moulding, Partridge and Chambers. Following auditions with Pye, Decca and CBS Records they signed with Virgin Records - at which time they were joined by Barry Andrews (b. 12 September 1956, West Norwood, London, England). The band's sparkling debut, *White Music*, revealed a keener hearing for pop than the energetic new wave sound to which they were often aligned. The album reached number 38 in the UK charts and critics marked their name for further attention. Shortly after the release of *Go2*, Barry Andrews departed, eventually to resurface in Shriekback. Andrews and Partridge had clashed too

many times in the recording studio. With Andrews replaced by another Swindon musician Dave Gregory (b. 21 September 1952, Swindon, Wiltshire, England), both *Go2* and the following *Drums And Wires* were commercial successes. The latter album was a major step forward from the pure pop of the first two albums. The refreshingly hypnotic hit single 'Making Plans For Nigel' exposed them to a new and eager audience. Singles were regularly taken from their subsequent albums and they continued making the charts with quality pop songs, including Sgt Rock (Is Going To Help Me)' and the magnificently constructed 'Senses Working Overtime', which reached the UK Top 10. The main songwriter, Partridge, was able to put his sharp observations and nursery rhyme influences to paper in a way that made his compositions vital while eschewing any note of pretension. The excellent double set, *English Settlement*, reached number 5 on the UK album charts in 1982. Partridge subsequently fell ill through exhaustion and nervous breakdowns, and announced that XTC would continue only as recording artists, including promotional videos but avoiding the main source of his woes, the stage. Subsequent albums have found only limited success, though those of the Dukes Of Stratosphear, their *alter ego*, have reputedly sold more copies. *Mummer, The Big Express* and the highly underrated Todd Rundgren-produced *Skylarking* were all mature, enchanting works, but failed to set any charts alight. *Oranges And Lemons* captured the atmosphere of the late 60s perfectly, but this superb album also offered a further, perplexing commercial mystery. While it sold 500,000 copies in the USA, it barely made the UK Top 30. The highly commercial 'Mayor Of Simpleton' found similar fortunes, at a desultory number 46. The lyric from follow-up single 'Chalkhills And Children' states; 'Chalkhills and children anchor my feet/Chalkhills and children, bringing me back to earth eternally and ever Ermine Street.' In 1992 *Nonsuch* entered the UK album charts and two weeks later promptly disappeared. 'The Disappointed', taken from that album, was nominated for an Ivor Novello songwriters award in 1993, but could just as easily have acted as a personal epitaph. In 1995 the Crash Test Dummies recorded 'Ballad Of Peter Pumpkinhead' for the movie *Dumb And Dumber*, and in turn reminded the world of Partridge's talent. Quite what he and his colleagues in the band and Virgin Records feel they have to do remains uncertain. Partridge once joked that Virgin retain them only as a tax loss. It is debatable that if Partridge had not suffered from stage fright and a loathing of touring, XTC would have been one of the major bands of the 80s and would have sold millions of records. Those that are sensitive to the strengths of the band would rightly argue that this would have severely distracted Partridge and Moulding from their craft as songwriters. XTC remain one of the most original pop bands of the era and Partridge's lyrics place him alongside Ray Davies as one of the UK's most imaginative songwriters. After finally showing a profit the band decided to move from Virgin in 1996.

●ALBUMS: *White Music* (Virgin 1978)★★★, *Go2* (Virgin 1978)★★★, *Drums And Wires* (Virgin 1979)★★★★, *Black Sea* (Virgin 1980)★★★, *English Settlement* (Virgin 1982)★★★, *Mummer* (Virgin 1983)★★★, *The Big Express* (Virgin 1984)★★★, *Skylarking* (Virgin 1986)★★★★, *Oranges And Lemons* (Virgin 1989)★★★★, *Explode Together: The Dub Experiments 78-90* (Virgin 1990)★★★, *Rag And Bone Buffet* (Virgin 1990)★★★, *Nonsuch* (Virgin 1992)★★★★. Solo: Andy Partridge *Take Away (The Lure Of Salvage)* (Virgin 1980)★★★.

●COMPILATIONS: *Waxworks: Some Singles 1977-1982* originally released with free compilation, *Beeswax*, a collection of b-sides (Virgin 1982)★★★, *Beeswax* (Virgin 1983)★★, *The Compact XTC* (Virgin 1986)★★★★, *Live In Concert 1980* (Windsong 1992)★★★, *Drums And Wireless - BBC Radio Sessions 77-89* (Nighttracks 1995)★★★, *Fossil Fuel: The Singles 1977-92* (Virgin 1996)★★★★.

●FURTHER READING: *Chalkhills And Children*, Chris Twomey.

YACHTS

Another UK new wave act to emerge from the Liverpool art school student pool of the late 70s, the Yachts started life as the seven-piece Albert And The Cod Fish Warriors. Reduced to a five-piece of Henry Priestman (vocals/keyboards), J.J. Campbell (vocals), Martin Watson (guitar), Martin Dempsey (bass), and Bob Ellis (drums), they played their debut gig at Eric's in Liverpool supporting Elvis Costello. This led Stiff Records to sign them in October 1977 and they released one Will Birch-produced single before they departed (with Costello and Nick Lowe) for the newly formed Radar. Campbell left at this point but with Priestman in control they released several singles including the minor new wave classic 'Love To Love You'. They recorded their debut album in New York with Richard Gottehrer at the helm. Dempsey left in January 1980 to join Pink Military and when Radar was liquidated they switched to Demon for a further single. Inevitably they disintegrated and Priestman spent some time with It's Immaterial before forming the Christians, a group that would achieve far greater success. The Yachts' popularity was fleeting but they left behind several great three-minute slices of pop, including a cover of R. Dean Taylor's 'There's A Ghost In My House'.

●ALBUMS: *The Yachts* (Radar 1979)★★★, *Yachts Without Radar* (Radar 1980)★★★.

YANKOVIC, 'WEIRD AL'

b. 1959, USA. Yankovic achieved popularity during the 80s by creating parodies of popular songs and accompanying himself with an accordion. Yankovic first found renown in 1979 with a parody of the Knack's hit 'My Sharona', retitled 'My Bologna'. The song was recorded in a bathroom at a college he attended in San Luis Obispo, California, USA, and played on the syndicated Dr. Demento radio programme. It subsequently appeared on a Rhino Records sampler album, *Dementia Royale*, which led to further appearances on the Demento show. 'Another One Rides The Bus', Yankovic's version of Queen's 'Another One

Bites The Dust', became the most-requested song in the 10-year history of the radio programme and was issued as a single on TK Records.

In 1983 Yankovic signed to Rock 'n' Roll Records, a division of CBS Records, and released his self-titled debut album, produced by Rick Derringer. It included the Knack and Queen parodies as well as 'Ricky', a parody of the Toni Basil hit 'Mickey' which doubled as a salute to the *I Love Lucy* television programme. *Weird Al' Yankovic In 3-D*, also produced by Derringer (as were all of Yankovic's albums through the 80s) was released in 1984 and reached number 17 in the USA, with the single 'Eat It', a take-off of Michael Jackson's 'Beat It', reaching number 12. All of his record releases were accompanied by videos which received heavy play on MTV, furthering Yankovic's appeal. With his Hawaiian shirts and crazed appearance, Yankovic was a natural for the video age, as a postmodern version of early 60s parodist Allan Sherman, who was an inspiration to him. Although he included original material on his albums, all of it humorous in nature and much of it set to polka-like rhythms, Yankovic's biggest hits remained his song parodies. 'King Of Suede', a 1984 spoof of the Police's 'King Of Pain', was followed by 'I Lost On Jeopardy', a parody of Greg Kihn's 'Jeopardy' which changed the focus to that of the US television game show *Jeopardy*. In 1985, Yankovic took on Madonna, changing her 'Like A Virgin' into 'Like A Surgeon'. His final chart single of the 80s was 'Fat', which returned to Michael Jackson for inspiration, this time skewering his 'Bad'. The jacket of *Even Worse* was itself a parody of Jackson's *Bad*. Yankovic appeared in the 1989 film *UHF*. In 1996 further parodies contained on *Bad Hair Day* included 'Amish Paradise' (parody of Coolio and Stevie Wonder's song), and skits of TLC, Soul Asylum, Presidents Of The United States Of America and U2.

●ALBUMS: 'Weird Al' Yankovic (Rock 'n' R 1983)★★, 'Weird Al' Yankovic In 3-D (Rock 'n' R 1984)★★, *Dare To be Stupid* (Rock 'n' R 1985)★★, *Polka Party* (Rock 'n' R 1986)★★, *Even Worse* (Rock 'n' R 1988)★★, *UHF* soundtrack (Rock 'n' R 1989)★★, *Off The Deep End* (Scotti Bros 1992)★★, *Bad Hair Day* (Scotti Bros 1996)★★.

●COMPILATIONS: *Greatest Hits* (1989)★★★.

●VIDEOS: *Alapalooza: The Videos* (1994), *Bad Hair Day* (1996).

YARBROUGH AND PEOPLES

The duo of Calvin Yarbrough and Alisa Peoples was one of the most popular R&B pairs of the 80s, placing five singles in the R&B Top 10. The married couple had known each other since childhood, when they shared the same piano teacher in the Dallas, Texas, USA, area and sang together in their church choir. They lost track of each other during their college days and Yarbrough joined the R&B group Grand Theft. He was discovered by members of the Gap Band, who offered him work as a backing singer, after which Yarbrough returned to his own group. Peoples soon joined him onstage and they were taken on as a duo by the Gap band's manager and producer. Yarbrough And Peoples recorded their debut album for Mercury Records in 1980, which yielded the number 1 R&B single 'Don't Stop The Music', which later reached the pop Top 20. Yarbrough and Peoples switched over to the Total Experience label in 1982 and continued their hit streak for four more years with the singles 'Heartbeats' (number 10 R&B in 1983), 'Don't Waste Your Time' (number 1 R&B in 1984), 'Guilty' (number 2 R&B in 1986) and 'I Wouldn't Lie' (number 6 R&B in 1986).

●ALBUMS: *The Two Of Us* (Mercury 1980)★★★, *Heartbeats* (Total Experience 1983)★★★, *Be A Winner* (Total Experience 1985)★★★.

YAZOO

This promising UK pop group was formed at the beginning of 1982 by former Depeche Mode keyboardist Vince Clarke (b. 3 July 1961) and vocalist Alison Moyet (b. 18 June 1961, Billericay, Essex, England). Their debut single 'Only You' climbed to number 2 in the UK charts in May and its appeal was further indicated by the success of the Flying Pickets' *a cappella* cover which topped the UK chart the following year. Yazoo enjoyed an almost equally successful follow-up with 'Don't Go', which climbed to number 3. A tour of the USA saw the group change their name to Yaz in order not to conflict with an American record company of the same name. Meanwhile, their album *Upstairs At Eric's* was widely acclaimed for its strong melodies and Moyet's expressive vocals. Yazoo enjoyed further hits with 'The Other Side Of Love' and 'Nobody's Diary' before completing one more album, *You And Me Both*. Despite their continuing success, the duo parted in 1983. Moyet enjoyed success as a solo singer, while Clarke maintained his high profile with the Assembly and, particularly, Erasure.

●ALBUMS: *Upstairs At Eric's* (Mute 1982)★★★★, *You And Me Both* (Mute 1983)★★★.

YELLO

A Swiss dance duo led by Dieter Meier, a millionaire businessman, professional gambler, and member of the Switzerland national golf team. Meier provides the concepts whilst his partner Boris Blank writes the music. Previously Meier had released two solo singles and been a member of Periphery Perfume band Fresh Colour. Their first recording contract was with Ralph Records in San Francisco, a label supported by the enigmatic Residents. They opened their accounts there with 'Bimbo' and the album *Solid Pleasure*. In the UK they signed to the Do It label, launching their career with 'Bostisch', previously their second single for Ralph. They quickly proved popular with the Futurist and New Romantic crowds. Chart success in the UK began after a move to Stiff Records in 1983 where they released two singles and an EP. A brief sojourn with Elektra preceded a move to Mercury Records where they saw major success with 'The Race'. Accompanied by a stunning video - Meier saw visual entertainment as crucial to their work - 'The Race' easily transgressed the pop and dance markets in the wake of the Acid House phenomenon. On *One Second*, they worked closely with Shirley Bassey and Billy McKenzie (Associates), and have recently become more and more embroiled in cinema. Soundtracks include *Nuns On The Run*, and the Polish-filmed *Snowball*, a fairytale whose creative impetus is entirely down to Yello. Meier and Blank also run Solid Pleasure, the innovative Swiss dance label. In 1995 a 'tribute' album, *Hands On Yello*, was released by Polydor of Yello's music played by various artists including the Grid, Carl Craig, Orb and Moby. *Rocket Universe* gained them their best reviews since the mid-80s.

●ALBUMS: *Solid Pleasure* (Ralph 1980)★★★, *Claro Que Si* (Ralph 1981)★★★, *You Gotta Say Yes To Another Excess* (Elektra 1983)★★★★, *Stella* (Elektra 1985)★★★, *1980-1985 The New Mix In One Go* (Mercury 1986)★★★, *One Second* (Mercury 1987)★★, *Flag* (Mercury 1988)★★★, *Baby* (Mercury 1991)★★, *Zebra* (4th & Broadway 1994)★★★, *Pocket Universe* (Mercury 1997)★★★.
●COMPILATIONS: *Essential* (Smash 1992)★★, *Hands On Yello* various artists remix album (Polydor 1995)★★★.
●VIDEOS: *Video Race* (1988), *Live At The Roxy* (1991).

YELLOW MAGIC ORCHESTRA

Pioneers in electronic music, the influence of Yellow Magic Orchestra in this field is surpassed only by Kraftwerk. The band's massive commercial profile in their native country was the first example of the Orient grafting Western musical traditions into their own culture - and with Japan the birthplace of the world's technological boom in the late 70s, it was no surprise that the medium chosen was electronic. Session keyboardist Ryûichi Sakamoto met drummer Yukihiro Takahashi while recording his debut solo album. Takahashi had already released solo work, in addition to being a member of the Sadistic Mika Band (an art-rock conglomeration whose three progressive albums were released in the UK for Harvest Records). He had also played in a subsidiary outfit, the Sadistics. The final member of YMO was recruited when the pair met a further established musician, the bass player and producer Haruomi Hosono (as well as playing he would produce the group's first six albums). Having performed with two earlier recorded Japanese outfits, his was the most advanced solo career (he was on his fourth collection when he encountered Takahashi and Sakamoto).

Even though the trio's debut album together was inauspicious, consisting largely of unconnected electronic pulses and flashes, *Solid State Survivor* established a sound and pattern. With English lyrics by Chris Mosdell, the tracks now had evolved structures and a sense of purpose, and were occasionally deeply affecting. *X∞ Multiplies*, however, was a strange collection, comprising comedy skits and no less than two attempts at Archie Bell And The Drells' 'Tighten Up'. The UK issue of the same title added excerpts from the debut album (confusingly, a US version was also available, comprising tracks from *Solid State Survivor* in the main). There were elements of both on *BGM* and *Technodelic* which predicted the beautiful synth pop produced by later solo careers, but neither of the albums were cohesive or unduly attractive on their own account. More skits, again in Japanese, appeared on *Service*, masking the quality of several strong songs, leaving *Naughty Boys* to prove itself Yellow Magic Orchestra's second great album. As with its predecessor, *Naughty Boys* arrived with English lyrics now furnished by Peter Barakan (later a Takahashi solo collaborator). Accessible and less angular, the songs were no less enduring or ambitious. The band eventually sundered in the early 80s, with Ryûichi Sakamoto going on to solo and movie fame. His former collaborators also returned to their own pursuits, with Hosono enjoying success in production (Sandii And The Sunsetz, Sheena And The Rokkets, etc.) and Takahashi earning critical plaudits for his prolific and diverse solo output. News filtered through in 1993 that, on the back of interest generated by a number of techno artists name checking or simply sampling their wares, Yellow Magic Orchestra were to reform. The resultant *Technodon* was completed in March.

●ALBUMS: *Yellow Magic Orchestra* (Alfa 1978)★★, *Yellow Magic Orchestra* different mixes to debut (A&M 1979)★★, *Solid State Survivor* (Alfa 1979)★★★, *Public Pressure* (Alfa 1980)★★★, *X∞ Multiplies* (Alfa 1980)★★, *X∞ Multiplies* different track-listing (A&M 1980)★★, *BGM* (A&M 1981)★★★, *Technodelic* (Alfa 1981)★★★, *Service* (Alfa 1983)★★★, *After Service* (Alfa 1983), *Naughty Boys* (Alfa 1983)★★★★, *Naughty Boys Instrumental* (Pickup 1985)★★★, *Technodon* (Alfa 1993)★★★.

●COMPILATIONS: *Sealed* (Alfa 1985)★★★, *Characters - Kyoretsue Na Rhythm (Best Of)* (Restless 1992)★★★★, *Fakerholic* double CD (Restless 1992)★★★.

YELLOWJACKETS

Over two decades, the Yellowjackets have achieved a formidable reputation for their live performances and critical and commercial success with their recordings of electric pop jazz. The members of the band are accomplished musicians in their own right and perhaps this accounts for the Yellowjackets' two Grammys and six nominations. The band originally included: Robben Ford (guitar), Russell Ferrante (keyboards), Bob Mintzer (saxophone), Michael Franks (vocals), Ricky Lawson (drums). Their recording career began in 1980 with *The Inside Story*, when Ford heard Jimmy Haslip (bass) playing with veterans Airto Moreira and Flora Purim and decided to use them on his solo project. By the time of 1982's *Mirage à Trois*, Ford's presence was declining. New saxophonist Marc Russo featured prominently on *Samurai Samba* (1983) and *Shades* in 1986 rewarded the band's steady touring with a Grammy and six-figure sales. William Kennedy was the next addition to the line-up and this prompted the band to explore some new territory. *Politics* (1988) was another Grammy winner and the band took another radical change of direction. Their next project, *The Spin,* was recorded in Oslo, Norway, with well-known engineer Jan Erik Konshaug, and was a more acoustic, resolutely jazz album. *Live Wires*, the band's 1992 release, successfully demonstrated the multi-faceted approach the Yellowjackets like to adopt. Indeed, the simplicity of the band's sound belies the diversity of their influences: 'We spend hours experimenting, studying and listening to music from all over the world. You can't be afraid to take chances. That's what it takes to continue to grow!' The line-up in 1997 was Mintzer, William Kennedy, Haslip and Ferrante.

●ALBUMS: *The Inside Story* (1980)★★★, *Yellowjackets* (Warners 1981)★★★, *Mirage à Trois* (Warners 1982)★★★, *Samurai Samba* (Warners 1983)★★★, *Shades* (MCA 1986)★★★★, *Four Corners* (MCA 1987)★★★, *Politics* (MCA 1988)★★★★, *The Spin* (MCA 1990)★★★, *Greenhouse* (1991)★★★, *Live Wires* (GRP 1992)★★★, *Like A River* (GRP 1992)★★★, *Run For Your Life* (GRP 1994)★★★, *Dreamland* (Warners 1995)★★★, *Blue Hats* (Warners 1997)★★★.

●COMPILATIONS: *Collection* (GRP 1994)★★★★.

YELLOWMAN

b. Winston Foster, Jamaica, West Indies. Yellowman was the DJing sensation of the early 80s and he achieved this status with a fair amount of talent and inventive and amusing lyrics. He mainly built his early career around the fact that he was an albino and his success has to be seen within its initial Jamaican context. The albino or 'dundus' is virtually an outcast in Jamaican society and Foster's early years were more difficult than anyone outside of Jamaica could possibly imagine. Against the odds, he used this background to his advantage and, like King Stitt who had previously traded on his physical deformities, Foster paraded himself in the Kingston dance halls as 'Yellowman', the DJ with endless lyrics about how sexy, attractive and appealing he was to the opposite sex. Within a matter of months he went from social pariah to headlining act on Jamaican stage shows and his popularity rocketed. Obviously the irony of his act was not lost on his audiences. His records were both witty and relevant - 'Soldier Take Over' being a fine example - and he was the first to release a live album - not of a stage show but actually recorded live on a sound system - *Live At Aces*, which proved hugely successful and was widely imitated. It captured him at the height of his powers and in full control of his 'fans'. None of the excitement is lost in the transition from dancehall to record.

Yellowman's records sold well and he toured the USA and UK to ecstatic crowds - his first sell-out London shows caused traffic jams and road blocks around the venue. He could do no wrong and even his version of 'I'm Getting Married In The Morning' sold well. He was soon signed for a major contract to CBS Records and was 'King Yellow' to everyone in the reggae business. This did not last and by the mid-80s it had become difficult to sell his records to the fickle reggae market. By this time, however, he had been adopted by 'pop' audiences all over the world as a novelty act and while he has never become a major star he is still very popular and his records sell in vast quantities in many countries. He has released more records than a great many other reggae acts - no mean feat in a business dominated by excess. Made both rich and successful through his Djing work, it is mainly his ability to laugh at himself and encourage others to share the joke that has endeared him to so many. It should be immediately apparent to all who has had the last laugh.

● ALBUMS: *Them A Mad Over Me* (J&L 1981)★★★, *Bad Boy Skanking* (Greensleeves 1982)★★★, *Mr Yellowman* (Greensleeves 1982)★★★, *Live At Sunsplash* (Sunsplash 1982)★★★, *The Yellow, The Purple, And The Nancy* (Greensleeves 1983)★★, *Divorced* (Burning Sounds 1983)★★, *Zungguzungguguzunggueng* (Greensleeves 1983)★★, *King Yellowman* (Columbia 1984)★★, *Nobody Move, Nobody Get Hurt* (Greensleeves 1984)★★, with Josey Wales *Two Giants Clash* (Greensleeves 1984)★★★, *Galong Galong Galong* (Greensleeves 1985)★★, *Going To The Chapel* (Greensleeves 1986)★★, *Rambo* (Moving Target 1986)★★★, *Yellow Like Cheese* (RAS 1987)★★, *Don't Burn It Down* (Shanachie/Greensleeves 1987)★★, *Blueberry Hill* (Greensleeves/Rohit 1987)★★★, with General Trees *A Reggae Calypso Encounter* (Rohit 1987)★★, *King Of The Dancehall* (Rohit 1988)★★, with Charlie Chaplin *The Negril Chill* (ROIR 1988)★★★, *Sings The Blues* (Rohit 1988)★★, *Rides Again* (RAS 1988)★★★, *One In A Million* (Shanachie 1988)★★, *Badness* (La/Unicorn 1990)★★★, *Thief* (Mixing Lab 1990)★★, *Party* (RAS 1991)★★★, *Reggae On The Move* (RAS 1992)★★, *Live In England* (Greensleeves 1992)★★, *In Bed With Yellowman* (1993)★★.

● COMPILATIONS: *20 Super Hits* (Sonic Sounds 1990).

● VIDEOS: *Raw And Rough (Live At Dollars Lawn)* (1989).

YOAKAM, DWIGHT

b. 23 October 1956, Pikeville, Kentucky, USA. Yoakam, the eldest of three children, moved with his family to Columbus, Ohio, when he was two. A singer-songwriter with an early love of the honky-tonk country music of Buck Owens and Lefty Frizzell, he has always shown a distinct antipathy towards the Nashville pop/country scene. After an abortive spell studying philosophy and history at Ohio State University, he briefly sought Nashville success in the mid-70s, but his music was rated too country even for the *Grand Ole Opry*. He relocated to Los Angeles in 1978 and worked the clubs, playing with various bands including Los Lobos, but for several years he worked as a truck driver to sustain himself.

In 1984, the release of a self-financed mini-album on the Enigma label led to him signing for Warner/Reprise Records. Two years later following the release of his excellent debut *Guitars Cadillacs Etc* he registered Top 5 US country chart hits with Johnny Horton's 'Honky Tonk Man' and his own 'Guitars, Cadillacs'. His driving honky-tonk music made him a popular visitor to Britain and gave him some success in the USA, but his outspoken views denied him wider fame. In 1987 he scored with his version of the old Elvis Presley pop hit 'Little Sister'. He followed it in 1988 with a US country number 9 hit with his idol Lefty Frizzell's classic 'Always Late (With Your Kisses)', and a number 1 with his self-penned 'I Sang Dixie'. He also made the top of the country charts with 'The Streets Of Bakersfield', duetting with veteran 60s superstar Buck Owens. Yoakam played several concerts with Owens, after being instrumental in persuading him to come out of retirement and record again for Capitol Records. Like Don Williams and others he retains the traditional stetson hat. There seems little doubt that Yoakam's songwriting talents and singing style will ensure further major success and much of his hip honky-tonk music has paved the way for rock audiences accepting country music of the 90s, much in the way that Garth Brooks has done. His straight country style is his most effective, even though he attempted to cross over into the mainstream rock market with *La Croix D'Amour*. Alhough by nature shy of publicity, he earned notoriety by the bucketload when he arrived at the 1992 Academy Awards with Sharon Stone on his arm. She went public on the affair when their relationship ended, although Yoakam maintained a dignified silence. He has also recently turned his hand to acting, appearing in a Los Angeles stage production, *Southern Rapture*, directed by Peter Fonda.

He came back in 1993 with the hardcore country of *This Time*. The album included the number 1 country hit 'Ain't That Lonely Yet', which won a Grammy award for Best Country Vocal Performance, while 'A Thousand Miles From Nowhere' was accompanied by an excellent video. *Dwight Live*, recorded at San Francisco's Warfield Theatre, captured the fervour of his concert performances. He wrote all the tracks on *Gone* and to quote *Rolling Stone*, 'Neither safe nor tame, Yoakham has adopted Elvis' devastating hip swagger, Hank Williams' crazy-ass stare and Merle Haggard's brooding solitude into one lethal package. Yoakham is a cowgirl's secret darkest dream.' Quite brilliantly put and frighteningly true. After more than a decade of commercial success Yoakam has established beyond all doubts his staying power as one of the leading country artists of the new era of country music.

●ALBUMS: *Guitars, Cadillacs, Etc., Etc.* (Reprise 1986)★★★, *Hillbilly DeLuxe* (Reprise 1987)★★★, *Buenas Noches From A Lonely Room* (Reprise 1988)★★★★, *If There Was A Way* (Reprise 1991)★★★★, *La Croix D'Amour* (Reprise 1992)★★★, *This Time* (Reprise 1993)★★★★, *Dwight Live* (Reprise 1995)★★★, *Gone* (Reprise 1995)★★★★.

●COMPILATIONS: *Just Lookin' For A Hit* (Reprise 1989)★★★★.

●VIDEOS: *Dwight Yoakam, Just Lookin' For A Hit* (1989), *Fast As You* (1993), *Pieces Of Time* (1994).

YOUNG FRESH FELLOWS

Operating out of Seattle, USA, since the early 80s, the Young Fresh Fellows have released a body of rough hewn, understated pop gems. Their debut album was recorded in 1983 and released a year later. The band comprises Scott McCaughey (vocals), Chuck Carroll (guitar) and Tad Hutchinson (drums). *The Fabulous Sounds Of The North Pacific* picked up immediate plaudits, *Rolling Stone Record* going so far as to describe it as 'perfect'. Joined by Jim Sangster (Jimbo) (bass), they became a fully fledged offbeat new wave act, the dry humour and acute observations of their lyrics attracting a large college following. Their stylistic fraternity with the higher profile Replacements was confirmed by their joint tours, both bands sharing what *Billboard* magazine described as 'a certain deliberate crudity of execution'. After the mini-album *Refreshments* they moved to Frontier Records for 1988's *Totally Lost*. Despite being dogged by a 'joke band' reputation, brought about by an aptitude for satirizing high school traumas, the band's critical reaction was once more highly favourable. However, Carroll played his last gig for the band in winter 1989 in Washington. He was replaced by the Fastbacks guitarist Kurt Bloch (who continues with both bands). Their most polished album yet, *This One's For The Ladies*, highlighted McCaughey's successful adaptation of the spirit of the Kinks while Bloch's guitar melodies fitted in

seamlessly. Elsewhere, McCaughey released his first solo album and toured as second guitarist with R.E.M. in 1995.

●ALBUMS: *The Fabulous Sounds Of The Pacific Northwest* (PopLlama Products 1984)★★★, *Topsy Turvy* (PopLlama Products 1986)★★★, *The Men Who Loved Music* (PopLlama Products 1987)★★★★, *Refreshments* (PopLlama Products 1987)★★, *Totally Lost* (Frontier 1988)★★★, *Beans And Intolerance* (PopLlama Products 1989)★★, *This One's For The Ladies* (Frontier 1989)★★★, *Electric Bird Digest* (Frontier 1991)★★, *It's Low Beat Time* (Frontier 1992)★★★, *Gleich Jetzt* Japanese release (1+2 1992)★★, *Take It Like A Matador* Spanish release (Impossible 1993)★★, *Pop* Japanese release (PopLlama Products 1993)★★★.

●COMPILATIONS: *Includes A Helmet* UK sampler (Utility 1990)★★, *Somos Los Mejores!* Spanish release (Munster 1991)★★★.

YOUNG MARBLE GIANTS

Formed in 1978 as 'a desperate last-ditch attempt at doing something with my life' by Stuart Moxham (guitar/organ), this seminal, yet short-lived trio, from Cardiff, Wales, comprised the latter as the group's main songwriter, his brother Philip Moxham (bass) and Alison Statton (b. March 1958, Cardiff, Wales; vocals). Together they made their debut on *Is The War Over?*, a compilation of Cardiff groups, released in 1979. Their contribution reached the ears of Geoff Travis at Rough Trade Records who promptly invited them to record an album. Playing within minimalist musical landscapes the group utilized the superb, lyrical bass playing of Philip Moxham. The combination of Stuart's twangy/scratchy guitar and reedy organ with Alison's clear diction was evident on tracks such as 'Searching For Mr Right', 'Credit In The Straight World' and 'Wurlitzer Jukebox' from *Colossal Youth*. This highly acclaimed album was followed the next year by the impressive *Testcard* EP, which reached number 3 in the UK independent charts, by which time the group had amicably split. The brothers noted that recording separately would be the only way to maintain a healthy sibling relationship. Statton formed Weekend for two jazz-inspired albums, before joining Ian Devine (ex-Ludus) in Devine And Statton, releasing two albums, *The Prince Of Wales* and *Cardiffians*. Stuart Moxham established the Gist, recording *Embrace The Herd* (1983). This included the gorgeous 'Love At First Sight' which reached the UK independent Top 20. Stuart's producing talents where called upon to oversee the recording of the Marine Girls' second album, *Lazy Ways*. Other projects in the 90s included work with Beat Happening and a solo album, *Signal Path*, on Feel Good All Over Records, with Statton guesting on one track. In later years his other profession, that of animation painter, gave him a credit on the film *Who Killed Roger Rabbit?* Phil Moxham found work sessioning for both Weekend and the Gist. In 1987, the Young Marble Giants reformed briefly to record a French release, 'It Took You'.

●ALBUMS: *Colossal Youth* (Rough Trade 1980)★★★.

●COMPILATIONS: with Weekend and the Gist *Nipped In The Bud* (1984)★★★.

●VIDEOS: *Live At The Hurrah!* (Visionary 1994).

YOUNG, PAUL

b. 17 January 1956, Luton, Bedfordshire, England. Prior to his major success as a solo artist Young was a former member of Streetband, who made the UK charts with the novelty record 'Toast'. He was then part of the much-loved Q-Tips, a band that did much to preserve an interest in 60s soul and R&B. As Q Tips collapsed from exhaustion and lack of finance, Young signed as a solo artist with CBS Records. Following two flop singles, his smooth soul voice captured the public's imagination with a superb chart-topping version of Marvin Gaye's 'Wherever I Lay My Hat'. The following *No Parlez* was a phenomenally triumphant debut, reaching number 1 in the UK and staying in the charts for well over two years. Now, having sold several million copies, this album remains his finest work. It was a blend of carefully chosen and brilliantly interpreted cover versions including 'Love Will Tear Us Apart' (Joy Division) and 'Love Of The Common People' (Nicky Thomas), together with excellent originals like 'Come Back And Stay'. After touring to support the album, Young experienced a recurring problem with his voice, an ailment which continues to plague his career. It was two years before he was able to record *The Secret Of Association*, but the quality of material was intact. The album also topped the UK chart and produced three top 10 singles including 'Everything Must Change' and a cover of Daryl Hall's 'Every Time You Go Away'. He appeared at Live Aid, duetting with Alison Moyet, although it was obvious that his voice was once again troublesome. *Between Two Fires* was a below par album, although his fans still made it a hit.

Little was heard from Young for over a year, and while it was assumed that his voice was continuing to cause him problems, Young was merely reassessing his life. He made an encouraging return singing Crowded House's 'Don't Dream It's Over' at the Nelson Mandela Concert at Wembley in 1988 after which Young went into hibernation until 1990; this time by his own admission he was 'decorating his house'. In 1990 he returned with *Other Voices* and an accompanying tour. Once again his choice of material was tasteful and included versions of 'Don't Dream It's Over', Free's 'Little Bit Of Love' and Bobby Womack's 'Stop On By'. His was one of the better performances of the Freddie Mercury tribute concert at Wembley Stadium in May 1992. Voice permitting, Young seems destined for continuing success, having proved that with a sparse recorded output his sizeable following remains loyal and patient. Although Young's voice has lost the power and bite of old he is able to inject passion and warmth into his recent work. This was apparent on his excellent recording on soul classics. *Reflections* demonstrated the area of music with which he has the closest affinity and versions of 'Until You Come Back To Me', 'Ain't No Sunshine' and 'Reach Out I'll Be There' highlight a man who truly has soul even though his voice is leaving him. His first album of new material for over three years, *Paul Young*, was released in 1997.

●ALBUMS: *No Parlez* (Columbia 1983)★★★★, *The Secret Of Association* (Columbia 1985)★★★, *Between Two Fires* (Columbia 1986)★★, *Other Voices* (Columbia 1990)★★★, *The Crossing* (Columbia 1993)★★, *Reflections* (Vision 1994)★★★, *Acoustic Paul Young* mini-album (Columbia 1994)★★★★, *Paul Young* (East West 1997)★★★.

●COMPILATIONS: *From Time To Time* (Columbia 1991)★★★★, *Love Songs* (Columbia 1997)★★★.

●VIDEOS: *Paul Young: The Video Singles* (CBS-Fox 1986), *From Time To Time (The Singles Collection)* (Columbia 1991).

YOUTH BRIGADE

Formed in Los Angeles, California, USA, in the late 70s from the ashes of the Extremes, Youth Brigade initially comprised Shawn Stern (guitar/vocals), Adam Stern (bass/vocals), Mark Stern (drums, ex-No Crisis; Sado Nation) and Greg Louis Gutierrez (guitar). One of Los Angeles' finest hardcore bands of the period, they also formed the BYO label as a direct response to the Ellis Lodge riot of 1979 when bands including the Go-Go's played at a gig that was violently curtailed by riot police. BYO was housed at Skinhead Manor, an eight-bedroomed mansion in the heart of Hollywood rented by an assortment of mavericks intent on creating an alternative media base (including fanzines, pirate radio, live shows, etc.). It was named in honour of the visiting Sham 69. Youth Brigade had started out as part of the Skinhead Manor collective, originally as a six-piece group with two singers. They soon crystallized into a line-up consisting solely of the Stern brothers. Another band of the same name was born in Washington, DC at the same time (playing the same type of aggressive punk music), but luckily this group faded from view before too much confusion arose. Often compared to the Ruts because of their integration of reggae with punk pop, Youth Brigade's debut album was easily one of most accessible of the 'So-Cal Hardcore' scene. *Sound And Fury I* demonstrated the group's potential with a wide variety of music employed even at this early stage in their career. 'Men In Blue', for example, included a rap, and the group also tackled the doo-wop classic 'Duke Of Earl'. They embarked on a major tour playing at over one hundred venues in 1983 and 1984, covering much of the USA, Europe and Canada, but always using non-mainstream outlets to book the shows. Shawn's views were hardened by the experience. 'For me, time and time again the topic of ignorance comes up in interviews. That is the fundamental problem in the world and throughout history, and is the dominant subject of my lyrics and my whole life. Educate yourselves people!'

In 1986 they shortened their title to Brigade to accommodate 'a further progression in style'. The new line-up featured bass player Bob Gnarly, formerly of Plain Wrap (Gutierrez had long since joined Salvation Army and then the Three O'Clock). Their first album as the Brigade, *The Dividing Line*, featured a cameo appearance from Jane Wieldin on 'The Hardest Part' (in the character of a dizzy blonde actress called Candy). Stern's lyrics were evolving and taking in matters spiritual and emotional as well as social, but Brigade never took themselves too seriously, raps and breakdancing continuing to be features of their live shows. However, their previous audience remained unimpressed by what they saw as Brigade's conversion to conventional hard rock. The group disbanded, with Stern subsequently forming That's It with Tony Withers, formerly of UK punk band the Stupids. However, Youth Brigade, with the prefix back in place, re-formed again at the end of the 80s. Subsequent albums, such as 1996's *To Sell The Truth* (which featured the three brothers with guitarist Johnny Wickersham) returned the group to the primal punk sound of old, though much of the interest in them had by now dissipated.

◆ALBUMS: *Sound And Fury* (BYO 1982)★★★, *Sound And Fury II* (BYO 1983)★★★, as Brigade *The Lividing Line* (BYO 1986)★★★, *To Sell The Truth* (BYO 1996)★★★.
◆COMPILATIONS *Sink With Kalifornia* (BYO 1988)★★★.

ZAMFIR, GHEORGHE

b. Rumania. Zamfir is the best-known exponent of the pan-pipes or nei, an ancient instrument of southern Europe consisting of reed or wooden pipes graduated in size and bound together in a row. His recording career began when he linked up with Swiss record producer Marcel Cellier, who recorded traditional folk tunes by Zamfir in the early 70s for release on his own label. Already popular in France, Zamfir found a mainstream audience in the UK in 1976 when 'Doina De Jale', a traditional funeral tune was used as the theme for a BBC Television series, *The Light Of Experience*. Released as a single by Epic, it was a Top 10 hit. The record also sold well across Europe, and Zamfir was launched on a career in middle-of-the-road music, frequently recording pan-pipe versions of western tunes, pop, classical and religious. Thus, his 1985 album *Atlantis* included film music, pieces by Jacques Brel and Eric Satie, plus 'Stranger On The Shore', the 1962 Acker Bilk hit. In 1979 Zamfir and James Last had a Dutch hit with the theme from 'De Verlaten Mijn', and several of his 80s albums were recorded with Dutch orchestra leader Harry van Hoof.

●ALBUMS: *Roumanian Flutes, Vol 1* and *2* (Arion 1974)★★★, *Theme Light Of Experience* (Epic 1976)★★★, *Impressions* (Epic 1978)★★★, *L'Alouette* (Philips 1978)★★★, *Picnic At Hanging Rock* (Epic 1979)★★★, *Extraordinary Pan Pipe Vol 1-3* (Columbia 1981)★★★, *In Paris* (Columbia 1981)★★★, *Roumanian Folklore Instruments* (Columbia 1981)★★★, *In Paris 2* (Columbia 1981)★★, *Rocking Chair* (Philips 1981)★★★, *Zamfir* (Columbia 1981)★★★, *Lonely Shepherd* (Philips 1982)★★★, *Music For The Millions* (Philips 1983)★★★, *Christmas Album* (Philips 1984)★★, *Romance* (Philips 1984)★★★, *Atlantis* (Philips 1985)★★★, *Zamfir In Paris Live* (Delta 1986)★★, *Classics By Candlelight* (Philips 1986)★★, *Harmony* (Philips 1987)★★★, *Beautiful Dreams* (Philips 1988)★★★, *Easyriding* (Easyriding 1988)★★, *Golden Pan Flute* (Musique International 1988)★★★, *Images* (Images 1989)★★★.

●COMPILATIONS: *Great Successes Of* (Columbia 1981)★★★, *Best Of Gheorghe Zamfir* (Philips 1985)★★★, *King Of Pan Flute* (Timeless Treasures 1986)★★★, *Greatest Hits* (Delta 1987)★★★, *The Beautiful Sound Of The Pan Pipes* (Music Club 1995)★★★.

ZIMMER, HANS

b. 1957, Frankfurt, Germany. Apparently, from the age of six, Zimmer wanted to be a composer, although he had no formal musical education. When he was 16 he went to school in England, and, during the 70s, toured with bands in the UK. After spending some time at Air-Edel, writing jingles for television commercials, he collaborated with the established movie composer Stanley Myers, to write the score for Nicolas Roeg's *Eureka* (1981), and several other British films during the 80s, including *Moonlighting*, *Success Is The Best Revenge*, *Insignificance*, and *The Nature Of The Beast* (1988). His solo credits around that time included movies with such themes as apartheid (*A World Apart*), a psychological thriller (*Paperhouse*), eccentric comedies (*Twister* and *Driving Miss Daisy*), a tough Michael Douglas detective yarn (*Black Rain*), and a 'stiflingly old-fashioned' version of a Stefan Zweig short story, *Burning Secret* (1988). In that year Zimmer provided the music for 14 films, including the *Rain Man*, starring Dustin Hoffman and Tom Cruise. This earned Zimmer a nomination for an Academy Award ('When they found out that I was only 30, I didn't get it!'). He continued apace in the early 90s with scores for *Bird On A Wire*; *Chicago Joe And The Showgirl* (written with Shirley Walker), *Days Of Thunder*, *Green Card* (starring Gerard Depardieu in his English-language debut), *Pacific Heights*, *Backdraft*, *K2* (a crashing, electro-Mahlerian score), *Regarding Henry*, *Thelma And Louise* ('a twanging, shimmering score'), *Radio Flyer*, *Toys* (with Trevor Horn), *The Power Of One*, *A League Of Their Own*, *Point Of No Return*, *Where Sleeping Dogs Lie* (with Mark Mancina), *The Assassin*, *Cool Runnings*, *The House Of Spirits*, *Renaissance Man*, *Drop Zone*, and *The Lion King* (Academy Award, 1995). In 1992 Zimmer composed the music for 'one of the most bizarre television re-creations to date', the 10-hour series, *Millennium*. Other work for the small screen includes the popular *First Born* (1988) and *Space Rangers* (1992). He scored *Muppet Treasure Island* in 1996. Zimmer is most certainly a major figure in music; his accomplishments in the film world for a comparatively young man are already awesome.

ZORN, JOHN

b. 2 September 1953, New York City, New York, USA. Zorn trained in classical composition, initial inspirations being the American composer-inventors Charles Ives, John Cage and Harry Partch. He developed an interest in jazz when he attended a concert given by trumpeter Jacques Coursil, who was teaching him French at the time. His later jazz idols have included Anthony Braxton, Ornette Coleman, Jimmy Giuffre and Roscoe Mitchell. Since 1974 he has been active on New York's Lower East Side, a leading representative of the 'downtown' *avant garde*, applying 'game theory' to structure-free improvisation, a parallel technique to Butch Morris's 'conduction'. Zorn's keen study of bebop and his razor-sharp alto saxophone technique gained him respect from the jazz players: in 1977 he and guitarist Eugene Chadbourne were included in an 11-piece ensemble playing Frank Lowe's compositions (*Lowe & Behold*). A record collector, Zorn was inspired by Derek Bailey's Incus releases, and in 1983 recorded *Yankees* with him and trombonist George Lewis. The same year he wrote some music for Hal Willner's tribute-to-Thelonious Monk album, *That's The Way I Feel Now*. In 1985 he contributed to Willner's Kurt Weill album *Lost In The Stars* and made a commercial breakthrough with *The Big Gundown*, which interpreted Ennio Morricone's themes by deploying all kinds of unlikely musicians (including Big John Patton and Toots Thielemans). *News For Lulu* (1987), with Lewis and Bill Frisell, presented classic hard bop tunes from the 60s with Zorn's customary steely elegance: it was his second bebop venture, following *Voodoo* by the Sonny Clark Memorial Quartet (Zorn, Wayne Horvitz, Ray Drummond, Bobby Previte). Declaring that hardcore rock music had the same intensity as 60s free jazz, he championed Nottingham's Napalm Death and recorded hardcore versions of Ornette Coleman's tunes on the provocative *Spy Vs Spy* (1989). Naked City (Frisell - guitar, Fred Frith - bass, Joey Baron - bass) became his vehicle for skipping between sleaze-jazz, surf rock and hardcore: they made an impressive debut for Nonesuch/Elektra Records in 1990. In 1991 he formed Pain Killer with bassist/producer Bill Laswell and Mick Harris (the drummer from Napalm Death) and released *Guts Of A Virgin* on Earache, the Nottingham hardcore label. He played at Company Week 1991, proving by his commitment and enthusiasm that (relative) commercial success has not made him turn his back on free improvisation. Zorn's genre transgression seems set to become the commonsense of creative music in the 90s.

● ALBUMS: *School* (Parachute 1978)★★★, *Pool* (Parachute 1980)★★★, *Archery* (Parachute 1981)★★★, *The Classic Guide To Strategy Volume One* (Lumina 1983)★★★, *Locus Solus* (Eva/Wave 1983)★★★, with Derek Bailey, George Lewis *Yankees* (Celluloid 1983)★★★, with Jim Staley *OTB* (1984)★★★, with Michihiro Sato *Ganryu Island* (Yukon 1985)★★★, *The Big Gundown* (Elektra 1985)★★★★, *The Classic Guide To Strategy Volume Two* (Lumina 1986)★★★, with the Sonny Clark Memorial Quartet *Voodoo* (Black Saint 1986)★★★, *Cobra* rec. 1985-86 (Hat Art 1987)★★★, *News For Lulu* (Hat Art 1987)★★★★, *Spillane* (Elektra 1988)★★★★, *Spy Vs Spy: The Music Of Ornette Coleman* (Elektra 1989)★★★★, with Naked City *Naked City* (Elektra/Nonesuch 1990)★★★, with Naked City *Torture Garden* (Earache 1990)★★★, with Pain Killer *Guts Of A Virgin* (Earache 1991)★★★, with Naked City *Heretic - Jeux Des Dames Cruelles* (Avant 1992)★★★, *More News For Lulu* (Hat Art 1992)★★★★, *Filmworks 1986-1990* (Elektra 1992)★★★★, with Naked City *Grand Guignol* (Avant 1993)★★★, *Masada* (DIW 1994)★★★★, *Wav* (DIW 1996)★★★, *Hei* (DIW 1996)★★★, *Bar Kokhba* (Tzadik 1996)★★★.

ZZ TOP

Formed in Houston, Texas, USA, in 1970, ZZ Top evolved out of the city's psychedelic scene and consist of Billy Gibbons (b. 16 December 1949, Houston, Texas, USA; six-string guitar/vocals, ex-Moving Sidewalks), Dusty Hill (b. Joe Hill, 19 May 1949, Dallas, Texas, USA; bass/vocals, ex-American Blues) and Frank Beard (b. 11 June 1949, Houston, Texas, USA; drums), the last two both ex-American Blues. ZZ Top's original line-up; Gibbons, Lanier Greig (bass) and Dan Mitchell (drums), was also the final version of the Moving Sidewalks. This initial trio completed ZZ Top's debut single, 'Salt Lick', before Greig was fired. He was replaced by Bill Ethridge. Mitchell was then replaced by Frank Beard while Dusty Hill subsequently joined in place of Ethridge. Initially ZZ Top joined a growing swell of southern boogie bands and started a constant round of touring, building up a strong following. Their debut album, while betraying a healthy interest in blues, was firmly within this genre, but *Rio Grande Mud* indicated a greater flexibility. It included the rousing 'Francine' which, although indebted to the Rolling Stones, gave the trio their first hit and introduced them to a much wider audience. Their third album, *Tres Hombres,* was a powerful, exciting set which drew from delta music and high energy rock. It featured the band's first national hit with 'La Grange' and was their first platinum album. The group's natural ease was highly affecting and Gibbons' startling guitar work was rarely bettered during these times. In 1974, the band's first annual 'Texas-Size Rompin' Stompin' Barndance And Bar-B-Q' was held at the Memorial Stadium at the University Of Texas. 85,000 people attended; the size was so large that the University declined to hold any rock concerts, and it was another 20 years before they resumed. However, successive album releases failed to attain the same high standard and ZZ Top took an extended vacation following their expansive 1976/7 tour. After non-stop touring for a number of years the band needed a rest. Other reasons, however, were not solely artistic, as the group now wished to secure a more beneficial recording contract. They resumed their career in 1979 with the superb *Deguello*, by which time both Gibbons and Hill had grown lengthy beards (without each other knowing!) Revitalized by their break, the trio offered a series of pulsating original songs on *Deguello* as well as inspired recreations of Sam And Dave's 'I Thank You' and Elmore James' 'Dust My Broom'. The transitional *El Loco* followed in 1981 and although it lacked the punch of its predecessor, preferring the surreal to the celebratory, the set introduced the growing love of technology that marked the group's subsequent releases.

Eliminator deservedly became ZZ Top's best-selling album (10 million copies in the USA by 1996). Fuelled by a series of memorable, tongue-in-cheek videos, it provided several international hit singles, including the million-selling 'Gimme All Your Lovin'. 'Sharp Dressed Man' and 'Legs' were also gloriously simple yet enormously infectious songs. The group skilfully wedded computer-age technology to their barrelhouse R&B to create a truly memorable set which established them as one of the world's leading live attractions. The follow-up, *Afterburner*, was another strong album, although it could not match the sales of the former. It did feature some excellent individual moments in 'Sleeping Bag' and 'Rough Boy', and the cleverly titled 'Velcro Fly'. ZZ Top undertook another lengthy break before returning with the impressive *Recycler*. Other notable appearances in 1990 included a cameo, playing themselves, in *Back To The Future 3*. In 1991 a greatest hits compilation was issued and a new recording contract was signed the following year, with BMG Records.

Antenna was the first album with the new company. Over the years one of their greatest strengths has been their consistently high-standard live presentation and performance on numerous record-breaking (financially) tours in the USA. One of rock's maverick attractions, Gibbons, Hill and Beard have retained their eccentric, colourful image, dark glasses and stetson hats, complete with an almost casual musical dexterity which has won over hardened cynics and carping critics. In addition to having produced a fine (but sparse) canon of work they will also stay in the record books as having the longest beards in musical history (although one member, the inappropriately named Frank Beard, is clean-shaven). Whether it was by plan or chance, they are doomed to end every music encyclopedia.

●ALBUMS: *First Album* (London 1971)★★, *Rio Grande Mud* (London 1972)★★★, *Tres Hombres* (London 1973)★★★★, *Fandango!* (London 1975)★★, *Tejas* (London 1976)★★, *Deguello* (Warners 1979)★★★★, *El Loco* (Warners 1981)★★★, *Eliminator* (Warners 1983)★★★★, *Afterburner* (Warners 1985)★★★★, *Recycler* (Warners 1990)★★★★, *Antenna* (RCA 1994)★★★, *Rhythmeen* (RCA 1996)★★★★.

●COMPILATIONS: *The Best Of Z.Z. Top* (London 1977)★★★, *Greatest Hits* (Warners 1992)★★★★, *One Foot In The Blues* (Warners 1994)★★★.

●VIDEOS: *Greatest Hits Video Collection* (1992).

●FURTHER READING: *Elimination: The Z.Z. Top Story*, Dave Thomas.

INDEX